# REFERENCE

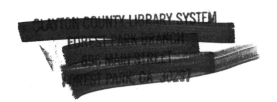

# Gale Encyclopedia of
# Everyday Law

# Gale Encyclopedia of
# Everyday Law

JEFFREY WILSON, EDITOR

VOLUME ONE, second edition

Americans with Disabilities Act
to
Family Law

GALE
CENGAGE Learning

Detroit • New York • San Francisco • New Haven, Conn • Waterville, Maine • London

**Gale Encyclopedia of Everyday Law**

**Project Editor**
Jeffrey Wilson

**Editorial**
Jeffrey Lehman

**Editorial Standards**
Laurie Andriot

**Product Design**
Jennifer Wahi

**Manufacturing**
Rhonda Williams

**LIBRARY OF CONGRESS CATALOGING-IN-PUBLICATION DATA**

Gale encyclopedia of everyday law / Jeffrey Wilson, editor.—2nd ed.
   p. cm.
   Includes bibliographical references and index.
   ISBN 1-4144-0353-4 (set : hardcover : alk.paper)—ISBN 1-4144-0401-8 (vol 1 : alk. paper)—ISBN 1-4144-0402-6 (vol 2 : alk. paper)
   1. Law—United States—Popular works.  I. Wilson, Jeffrey, 1971-  II. Title: Encyclopedia of everyday law.
   KF387.G27 2006
   349.73—dc22

2006010071

Printed in the United States of America
2 3 4 5 6 7 14 13 12 11 10 09 08

# TABLE OF CONTENTS

# INTRODUCTION

The *Gale Encyclopedia of Everyday Law* is a two-volume encyclopedia of practical information on laws and issues affecting people's everyday lives. Readers will turn to this work for help in answering questions such as, "What is involved in estate planning?" "Do I have any recourse to noisy neighbors?" and "What are the consequences of an expired visa?" This Encyclopedia aims to educate people about their rights under the law, although it is not intended as a self-help or 'do-it-yourself' legal resource. It seeks to fill the niche between legal texts focusing on the theory and history behind the law and shallower, more practical guides to dealing with the law.

This encyclopedia, written for the layperson, is arranged alphabetically by broad subject categories and presents in-depth treatments of topics such as consumer issues, education, family, immigration, real estate, and retirement. Individual entries are organized in alphabetical order within these broad subject categories, and include information on state and local laws, as well as federal laws. In entries where it is not possible to include state and local information, references direct the reader to resources for further research.

The work contains approximately 240 articles of 2,000-5,000 words each, organized within 26 broad subject categories, which are arranged alphabetically. Each article begins with a brief description of the issue's historical background, covering important statutes and cases. The body of the article is divided into subsections profiling the various U.S.

federal laws and regulations concerning the topic. A third section details variations of the laws and regulations from state to state. Each article closes with a comprehensive bibliography, covering print resources and web sites, and a list of relevant national and state organizations and agencies.

## How to Use This Book

This second edition of the *Gale Encyclopedia of Everyday Law* has been designed with ready reference in mind.

- **ENTRIES ARE ARRANGED ALPHABETICALLY WITHIN 24 BROAD CATEGORIES.** All entries are spelled-out in the Table of Contents.

- **BOLDFACED TERMS** direct readers to glossary terms, which can be found at the back of the book.

- A comprehensible **OVERVIEW OF THE AMERICAN LEGAL SYSTEM** details civil and criminal procedure; appeals; small claims court; in pro per representation; differences between local codes and state codes; and the difference between statutes and regulations.

- A list of **STATE AND FEDERAL AGENCY CONTACTS** gives web sites that lead the user to various state and federal agencies and organizations.

- A **GENERAL INDEX** at the back of the second volume, covers subject terms from throughout the encyclopedia, case and statute titles, personal names, and geographic locations.

# ACKNOWLEDGMENTS

## Advisory Board

In compiling this edition, we have been fortunate in being able to call upon the following people, our panel of advisors who contributed to the accuracy of the information in this second edition of the *Gale Encyclopedia of Everyday Law*. To them we would like to express sincere appreciation:

**Matthew C. Cordon**
Assistant Professor of Law & Reference Librarian
Baylor University Law School
Waco, TX

**Jim Heller**
Director of the Law Library and Professor of Law
College of William & Mary
Williamsburg, VA

**Matt Morrison**
Research Attorney and Lecturer in Law
Cornell University
Cornell Law School Library
Ithaca, NY

**Anna Teller**
Associate Director, Law Library
Texas Wesleyan University Law Library
Fort Worth, TX

## Contributors

Lauren Barrow, James Cahoy, Matthew C. Cordon, Richard Cretan, J. Alicia Elster, Mark D. Engsberg, Lauri Harding, Kristy Holtfreter, Sunwoo Kahng, Anne Kevlin, Frances Lynch, George A. Milite, Melodie Monahan, Joe Pascarella, Monica L. P. Robbers, Mary Hertz Scarbrough, Thomas W. Scholl, III, Scott Slick, Sherrie Voss Matthews, Eric L. Welsh

# OVERVIEW OF THE AMERICAN LEGAL SYSTEM

## FRAMEWORK OF GOVERNMENT IN THE UNITED STATES

### Basis of the American Legal System

The legal system of the United States is administered and carried on by the official branches of government and many other authorities acting within their official lawmaking capacity. The original basis of the law in this country is the United States Constitution, which lays the framework under which each of the different branches of government operates. The Constitution also guarantees the basic civil rights of the citizens of the United States. All authority of the federal government originates from the Constitution, and the Constitution serves as the supreme law of the land. The Constitution grants to the federal government certain enumerated powers, and grants to the states any power not specifically delegated to a branch of the federal government. Under this system, states retain significant authority and autonomy. The Constitutions in each of the fifty states contain many similar provisions to those in the U.S. Constitution in terms of the basic structure of government. Under the federal and state constitutions, the United States legal system consists of a system of powers separated among branches of government, with a system of checks and balances among these branches.

### Legislative Branches

The legislative branch is the primary law-making body among the three branches, although authority emanating from the other branches also constitutes law. The legislative branch consists of Congress, and is subdivided into two lower houses, the House of Representatives and the Senate. In addition to the powers granted to Congress, the Constitution sets forth specific duties of both the House and the Senate. Each Congress meets for two sessions, with each session lasting two years. For example, the 107th Congress met in its first session in 2001, and meets in its second session in 2002. State legislatures are structured similarly, with the vast majority of these legislatures consisting of two lower houses.

### Judicial Branches

The judicial branch in the federal system consists of three levels of courts, with the Supreme Court serving as the highest court in the land. The intermediate courts in the federal system are the thirteen Courts of Appeals. The United States is divided by circuits, with each circuit consisting of a number of states. The Fifth Circuit, for example, consists of Texas, Mississippi, and Louisiana. Each Court of Appeals has jurisdiction to decide federal cases in its respective circuit. The trial level in the federal judicial system consists of the District Courts. Each state contains at least one district, with larger states containing as many as four districts. Congress has also established a number of lower federal courts with specialized jurisdiction, such as the bankruptcy courts and the United States Tax Court.

Most state court systems are similar to that of the federal system, with a three-tiered system consisting of trial courts, appellate courts, and a highest court, which is also referred to as a "court of last resort." The names of the courts are similar from state to state, such as superior court, court of appeals, and supreme court. However, some states do not follow this structure. For example, in New York, the trial level court is the Supreme Court, while the court of last resort is the Court of Appeals. Texas, as another example, has two highest courts— the Supreme

Court and the Court of Criminal Appeals. In addition to the trial level courts, small claims courts or other county courts typically hear small claims, such as those seeking recovery of less than $1000.

### Executive Branches

The federal Constitution vests executive power in the President of the United States. The President also serves as the Commander in Chief of the Armed Forces and has the power to make treaties with other nations, with the advice and consent of the Senate. Besides those powers enumerated in Article II of the Constitution, much of the power of the executive branch stems from the executive departments, such as the Department of the Treasury and the Department of Justice. Congress has the constitutional authority to delegate power to administrative agencies, and many of these agencies fall under the executive branch and are known as executive agencies. Congress also has the authority to create agencies independent of the other branches of government, called independent agencies. Authority emanating from executive and independent agencies is law, and it is similar in many ways to legislation created by legislatures or opinions issued by courts. State executive branches and administrative agencies are similar to those of their federal counterparts.

## Constitutional Authority

### Interpretation of the Constitution

The federal Constitution is not a particularly lengthy document, and does not provide many answers to specific questions of law. It has, instead, been the subject of extensive interpretation since its original ratification. In the famous 1803 case of *Marbury v. Madison*, Chief Justice John Marshall wrote an opinion of the Supreme Court, which stated that the judicial branch was the appropriate body for interpreting the Constitution and determining the constitutionality of federal or state legislation. Accordingly, determining the extent of power among the three branches of government, or determining the rights of the citizens of the United States, almost always requires an evaluation of federal cases, in addition to a reading of the actual text of the Constitution.

### Powers of Congress

Most of the enumerated congressional powers are contained in section 8 of Article I of the Constitution. Many courts have been asked to review congressional statutes to determine whether Congress had the constitutional authority to enact such statutes. Among these powers, the power of Congress "to regulate [c]ommerce among the several [s]tates" has been the subject of the most litigation and outside debate. A number of cases during the New Deal era under President Franklin D. Roosevelt considered the breadth of this provision, which is referred to as the Commerce Clause. After the Supreme Court determined that many of these statutes were unconstitutional, Roosevelt, after a landslide election in 1936, threatened to add additional justices to the court, in order to provide more support for his position with respect to the pieces of legislation passed during the New Deal era (the reason he gave to Congress at the time was that many of the justices were over the age of seventy, and could no longer perform their job function, but the general understanding was that he wanted justices that would approve the New Deal legislation as constitutional). The threat of this so-called "Court-packing" plan succeeded, and the Commerce Clause has been construed very broadly since then. Other powers enumerated in Article I are generally construed broadly as well.

### Civil Rights Provisions in the Constitutions

The main text of the Constitution does not provide rights to the citizens of the United States. These rights are generally provided in the many amendments to the Constitution. The first ten amendments, all ratified in 1791, are called the "Bill of Rights," and confer many of the cherished and fundamental rights to the citizens of the United States. Among the rights included in the Bill of Rights are the freedoms of speech and religion (First Amendment); right to keep and bear arms (Second Amendment); right to be free from unreasonable searches and seizures (Fourth Amendment); right to be free from being compelled to testify against one's self in a criminal trial (Fifth Amendment); right to due process of law (Fifth Amendment); right to a jury trial (Sixth Amendment); and right to be free from cruel and unusual punishment (Eighth Amendment).

Between 1791 and 1865, no constitutional amendments were ratified that provided civil rights to citizens. However, at the conclusion of the Civil War and during the reconstruction period following the war, three major amendments were added to the Constitution. The first was the Thirteenth Amendment, ratified in 1865, which finally abolished slavery and involuntary servitude in the United States. The Fourteenth Amendment, ratified in 1868, provided some of the most significant rights to citizens, including the guarantee of equal protection of the laws and prohibited denial of life, liberty, or property without due process of law. The Fifteenth Amendment, ratified in 1870, provided that the right to vote could not be abridged on account of race, color, or previous condition of servitude. Fifty years later, women were guaranteed the right to vote with the ratification of the Nineteenth Amendment in 1920.

### Application of Constitutional Amendments

Like other constitutional provisions, the judicial branch is the appropriate body to interpret the Bill of Rights and other amendments to the Constitution. The plain language of the amendments can cause some confusion, since some, by their own terms, they apply specifically to Congress, while other apply specifically to states. For example, the First Amendment begins, "Congress shall make no law respecting an establishment of religion . . ." Similarly, the Fourteenth Amendment contains a provision that states, "No State shall make or enforce any law which shall abridge the privileges and immunities of the citizens of the United States . . ." Modern courts have resolved some of these questions by ruling that the Due Process Clauses of the Fifth and Fourteenth Amendments incorporate these provisions, so many provisions apply to both the federal and state governments, despite the language in the Constitution.

### State Constitutions

Many state constitutions are structured similarly to the federal Constitution, except that most are more detailed than the federal Constitution. Most citizens are guaranteed basic civil rights by both the federal Constitution and their relevant state constitutions. For example, it is common for state constitutions to include provisions guaranteeing freedom of speech or equal protection, and most are phrased similarly to the provisions in the First and Fourteenth Amendments. Since the federal Constitution is the supreme law of the land, any rights provided in it are guaranteed to all citizens and cannot be lost because a state constitution's provisions conflict with the corresponding provision in the federal Constitution. A state may provide greater rights to citizens than those provided in a federal counterpart, but may not remove rights guaranteed under the federal doctrine. Section 10 of Article I of the Constitution also prohibits states from making certain laws or conducting certain acts, such as passing an ex post facto law or coining money.

## International Treaties

### Authority of Treaties

Article VI of the Constitution provides, "This Constitution, and the Laws of the United States which shall be made in Pursuance thereof; and all Treaties made, or which shall be made, under the Authority of the Untied States, shall be the supreme Law of the Land." An international treaty is generally considered to be on the same footing as a piece of legislation. If a treaty and a federal statute conflict, the one enacted at a later date, or the one that more specifically governs a particular circumstance, will typically govern. State legislation may not contradict provisions contained in a treaty. Similarly, states are forbidden from entering into treaties under the provisions in Article I, Section 10.

### Creation of Treaties and Other International Agreements

The power to enter into treaties is vested in the President, though the executive must act with the advice and consent of the Senate, and receive the concurrence of two-thirds of the Senate before a treaty is ratified. The various Presidents have also entered into executive agreements with foreign nations when the President has not been able to receive approval from two-thirds of the Senate, or has not sought approval from the Senate. While nothing in the Constitution permits or forbids this practice, executives have entered into thousands of such agreements.

## Federal and State Legislation

### Federal Legislative Process

Members of Congress have the exclusive authority to introduce legislation to the floor of either the House of Representatives or Senate. Legislation is introduced to Congress in the form of bills. Most bills can originate either in the Senate or in the House, with the exception of bills to raise revenue, which must originate in the House under Article I of the Constitution. When a bill is introduced, it is designated with a bill number, and these bill numbers run sequentially through two sessions of Congress. For example, the fifty-sixth bill introduced in the House during the 108th Congress will be designated as "H.R. 56" ("H.R." is an abbreviation for House of Representatives). Likewise, the twelfth bill introduced in the Senate during the same Congress will be designated "S. 12." It is not uncommon that bills are introduced in both the House and the Senate simultaneously that address the same subject matter.

These bills are referred to as "companion bills," and the actual law that is passed often contains components from both the enacted bill and its companion bill. Thousands of bills are introduced in the House and Senate each session, and a relatively small proportion is actually passed into law.

After a bill has been introduced, it is sent to one or more appropriate committees in the House or Senate. The committee or committees analyze the provisions of the bill, including the reasoning for such legislation and the expected effect of the bill if it were enacted into law. A committee conducts hearings, where it hears testimony from experts and other parties that can provide information relevant to the subject matter covered by a bill. A committee may also order the preparation of an in-depth study (called a "committee print") that provides additional background information, often in the form of statistics and statistical analysis. A number of additional documents may also be produced during the committee stage, and practically every action is documented, including the production of written transcripts of committee hearings. A committee may amend or rewrite a bill before it approves it, which generally extends the length of time that a bill remains at the committee stage. The vast majority of bills, in fact, never leave the committee stage, and these bills are commonly said to have "died in committee."

When a committee completes its consideration of a bill, it reports the bill back to the floor of the House or Senate. A committee ordinarily accompanies the bill with a report that summarizes and analyzes each bill's provisions, and provides recommendations regarding the passage of the bill. Reports, as well as other documents, are designated with unique numbers and are made available to the public. An example of a report number is "H.R. Rep. No. 108-15," which indicates that it is the fifteenth report submitted to the House of Representatives in the 108th Congress.

Members of the houses of Congress debate the bills on the floor of the relevant house. These debates are transcribed, and the text of the transcription is routinely available to the public. During this period, the relevant chamber may amend the bill. Once the debates and other activities are completed, the chamber votes to pass the bill. If the chamber approves the bill, it is sent to the other chamber, and the entire process is repeated. The version of the bill sent to the other chamber of Congress is called the "engrossed" version of the bill. The other chamber must pass this version exactly as it appears in the engrossed version, or else the bill, assuming the second chamber passes it, is sent back to the original chamber for future consideration. If the House and Senate cannot agree to a single version of a bill, a conference, or joint, committee may be convened, where members of both chambers may compromise to complete a version of a bill acceptable to both chambers. If this conference committee is successful in doing so, the bill is returned to the House and Senate for another vote.

Once a bill passes both the House and the Senate, it is sent to the President as an "enrolled" bill. The President may sign the bill and make it law. If the President does not sign the bill, and Congress is still in session, the bill becomes law automatically after ten days. If the President does not sign the bill, and Congress adjourns within ten days, the bill does not become law. The President may also reject the bill by vetoing it. Congress may override this veto with a two-thirds majority vote in both chambers.

### Types of Laws Passed by Congress

Laws that apply to and are binding on the general citizenry are called public laws. Each public law is designated with a public law number, and the numbering system is similar to that of reports and other documents described above. For example, Public Law Number 108-1 represents that this is the first public law passed in the 108th Congress. Congress may also pass laws that apply only to individual citizens or small classes of individuals. These laws are called private laws, and are usually passed in the context of immigration and naturalization. Private laws are numbered identically to public laws, such as, for example, Private Law Number 108-2, which is the second private law passed in the 108th Congress.

Congress also passes various types of resolutions, some of which do not constitute law and do not contain binding provisions equivalent to public laws. A single chamber of Congress may pass simple resolutions, which relate to the operations of that chamber or express the opinion of that chamber on policy issues. Both chambers may pass a concurrent resolution, which relate to the entire operation of Congress, or the express opinion of the entire Congress. Neither simple nor concurrent resolutions constitute law, and are not submitted to the President for approval. Joint resolutions, on the other hand, have the same binding effect as bills, and must be submitted to the President for final approval. Appropriations and similar measures often enter Congress as joint resolutions. Some actions, particularly the introduction of a constitutional amendment, require the use of a joint resolution, and many of these actions do not require presidential approval.

### Publication of Federal Legislation

Practically all documents produced by Congress during the legislative process are published by the United States Government Printing Office and made available to the public. Most of items produced since 1995 are now also available on the Internet in electronic formats. Legislation first appears in the form of a slip law, named as such because the Government Printing Office prints these on unbound slips of paper. At the conclusion of a session of Congress, the laws passed during that session are compiled and appear in the form of session laws, organized in chronological order. The official source for federal session laws is the United States Statutes at Large.

Most legislation in force in the United States is organized into a subject matter arrangement and published in the United States Code. A statute contained in the United States Code is called a codified statute. The U.S. Code consists of fifty titles, with each title representing a certain area of law. For example, Title 17 contains the copyright laws of the United States; Title 26 contains the Internal Revenue Code; and Title 29 contains most of the labor laws of the United States.

### Relationship Between Federal and State Legislation

Federal legislation is superior to state legislation under the provisions of Article VI of the U.S. Constitution. Thus, the courts will resolve any potential conflicts between a state statute and a federal statute by enforcing the federal statute. Federal superiority, however, does not mean that states are forbidden from enacting legislation covering the same subject matter as a federal statute; it is common for both federal and state legislation to govern similar areas of law. This is true in such areas as securities regulation, consumer protection, and labor law. Federal labor relations laws, for example, apply specifically to private employers, but do not apply to public employers. Labor relations between public employers and their employees are governed generally by state labor relations laws.

If Congress wants an area of law to be governed solely by federal legislation, Congress may include a provision that such legislation preempts any state law related to the subject matter covered by the federal statute. Congress may preempt state regulation expressly through specific statutory language, or by implication based on the structure and purpose behind a federal statute. Examples of legislation that contain preemption provisions are the Employment Retirement Income Security Act of 1974, the Comprehensive Environmental Response, Compensation and Liability Act, and the Toxic Substance Control Act.

The Tenth Amendment to the federal Constitution reserves any power not delegated to the federal government to the states, or to the people. However, there have been questions among the courts and scholars regarding the extent of this amendment, and it has not generally been construed to grant any special powers to the states through its enactment. Rather, it is a clause that reserves power to the states where Congress has not acted, subject to some limitations.

### Legislative Process in State Legislatures

Most state legislatures follow similar processes as Congress. Each state legislature, with the exception of Nebraska, consists of two chambers. Most legislatures meet in regular session annually, though some meet biannually with special called sessions held periodically. In many states, the process of introducing a bill is streamlined, where only one chamber may introduce certain types of bills. Several states also permit citizens to initiate legislation, which is not possible in Congress. Some states allow citizens to vote directly on a proposed piece of legislation. Other states contain provisions that all citizens, once they have received a requisite number of signatures, may force the legislature to consider and vote on a particular issue.

### Publication of State Legislation

Most states publish enacted legislation in a similar manner as the publication of federal legislation. Laws passed during each session of a respective legislature are compiled as session laws, and laws currently in force are compiled in a subject matter arrangement. In most states, laws in force are compiled according to a numbering system similar to the United States Code, with title or chapter numbers representing the subject matter of the statute. Other states, most notably California and Texas, have created codes that are named to represent the subject matter of the statues contained in them. For example, the California Family Code contains the family law statutes of that state; similarly, the Texas Finance Code contains the statutes governing many of the financial operations in that state.

Bills introduced in every legislature during a current session are now available on the various legislatures' Internet sites, as are the current statutes. However, very little documentation from the legislative process is published in a fashion to make it readily available to interested members of the public. Legal researchers interested in such information must often travel to their respective state capitol to obtain this information.

### Interpretation of Legislation

The language of a statute may be somewhat ambiguous regarding their application, and the courts have the responsibility to interpret or construe the language to determine the proper application of the statute. Courts have developed "canons of construction" to aid in this interpretation. The most basic form of statutory construction is consideration of the text and plain meaning of a statute. This consideration includes the process of defining the terms and phrases used in statute, including the use of a dictionary to derive the common meaning of a term. Courts will also consider the application of the statute in the context of the broader statutory scheme, which can often indicate what the purpose of the statute was when the statute was enacted.

If the plain meaning of a statute cannot be derived from the statute or statutory scheme, courts may look to the history of the legislation to determine the intent of the legislature when it enacted the statute. It is possible that Congress or a state legislature specifically addressed a concern during the legislative process, and members of the legislature may have made statements indicating how the legislature intended for the statute to apply in a particular circumstance. Locating this information requires a legal researcher to locate documentation prepared during the legislative process, in a process called "compiling" a legislative history.

### Substantive vs. Procedural Laws

Many of the laws passed by legislatures are considered "substantive" laws, because they create, define, and regulate legal rights and obligations. If an individual has been harmed and wants to bring litigation against the person or group that harmed him or her, substantive statutes often provide the law that governs that situation, and also include provisions regarding the appropriate damages that can be awarded to the plaintiff should the plaintiff successfully prove his or her case.

By comparison, procedural laws are those that set forth the rules used to enforce substantive laws. These laws may dictate the steps that a litigant must take to bring a suit to court, or may dictate the appropriate courts where a case may be brought. Some statutes, called statutes of limitations, also limit the amount of time in which a particular case may be brought. Procedural laws are as important as substantive laws in many respects, because a party with a valid claim may nevertheless lose a case if the proper procedures are not followed, or if the claim is not filed in the time required under a statute of limitations.

### Criminal Law vs. Civil Law

Criminal laws are those designed to punish private parties for violating the provisions contained in these laws. Violations of these laws are crimes against society, and are brought as criminal actions against the alleged offenders by state or federal attorneys acting on behalf of the people. All citizens of the United States are guaranteed rights in criminal investigations and criminal trials, and law enforcement officers and prosecutors must follow certain procedures in order to protect these rights. For this reason, criminal procedure differs significantly from the procedures for bringing a civil case to court. Among the most fundamental rights is that all accused individuals are presumed innocent until the state proves them guilty beyond a reasonable doubt. This places the burden of proof in a criminal action on the state, rather than on the defendant. Title 18 of the U.S. Code contains most of the federal criminal laws, while state penal codes generally contain the state criminal laws.

The term "civil law" has different meanings in two distinct contexts. First, it refers to a system of law that differs from the common law system employed by the United States. This is discussed below. Second, it refers to a type of law that defines rights between private parties, and, as such, differs from criminal law. Civil laws are applicable in such situations as when two parties enter into a contract with one another, or when one party causes physical injury to another party. The procedures that must be followed in a civil court case are generally less stringent than those in a criminal case. Some civil laws include provisions designed to punish wrongdoers, usually in the form of punitive, or exemplary, damages that are paid to the other party.

### Municipal Ordinances and Other Local Laws

Local government entities are generally created by the various states, and are typically referred to as municipalities. The powers of a municipality are limited to those granted to it by the state, usually defined in the municipal charter that created the municipality. Charters are somewhat analogous to state constitutions, and usually were created by vote of the voters in the municipality. Local governing bodies may include a city council, county commission, board of supervisors, etc., and these bodies enact ordinances that apply specifically to the locality governed by these bodies. Ordinances are similar to state legislative acts in their function. In many municipalities, ordinances are organized into a subject matter arrangement and produced as municipal codes.

Local laws often govern everyday situations more so than many state or federal laws. These laws include many provisions for public safety, raise revenue through the creation and implementation of sales and other local taxes, and govern the zoning of the municipality. Decisions regarding education are also generally made through local boards of education, though these boards are entities distinct from the municipal government. Local laws cannot contradict federal or state law, including statutory or constitutional provisions.

## Cases and Case Law in the Judicial Systems of the United States

### Adversarial System

The judicial system in the United States is premised largely on the resolution of disputes between adversaries after evidence is presented on both sides to a judge or jury during a trial. Civil cases usually involve the resolution of disputes between private parties in such areas as personal injury, breach of contract, property disputes, or resolution of domestic relations disputes. Criminal cases involve the prosecution by the state or federal government of an individual accused of violating a criminal statute. The rules and procedures that parties must follow differ between criminal and civil trials, although similarities exist between the two types of rules. Some courts, such as probate courts and juvenile courts, have been developed to hear specific types of suits in a particular jurisdiction. Other tribunals, such as small claims courts and justice of the peace courts, have also been established to resolve minor disputes or try cases involving alleged infractions of minor crimes. The systems by which parties appeal decisions are also premised on an adversarial process.

### Civil Trials

A party commences a civil trial by filing a petition or complaint with an appropriate court. The party bringing the suit is usually referred to as the plaintiff, though in some cases the party is referred to as the petitioner. A petition or complaint must generally name the parties involved, the cause of action, the legal theories under which recovery may be appropriate, and the relief sought from the court. Once the petition or complaint is filed with the court, the plaintiff must serve the party or parties against whom the action was brought. The party against whom the case is brought is referred to as the defendant, though in some cases this party is referred to as the respondent. A defendant generally responds to a petition or complaint by filing an answer admitting or denying liability, though the filing of a pre-answer motion or motions may precede this.

A number of events occur between the time a petition or complaint is filed with a court and the time of trial. During the pretrial stage, the parties will usually file a series of motions with the court, requesting the addition or removal of a party, limits on evidence that may be presented at trial, or the complete dismissal of the case in its entirety. Parties also collect information in a process called discovery. During discovery, parties file interrogatories, which are written questions submitted to the other party or parties; seek admissions to certain facts from the other party or parties; and take depositions, which are oral questions asked of witnesses who are under oath. The pretrial stage is very important to the eventual resolution of a dispute, and many cases are settled by the parties outside of court or dismissed before the case actually goes to trial.

When a civil case goes to trial, a judge or a jury may try it. If a judge tries a case, he or she makes findings of facts and rulings of law, and the trial is usually referred to as a bench trial. If a jury tries a case, the jury makes findings of facts, such as whether a contract existed or whether one party assaulted another party. However, the judge makes rulings of law in a jury trial. A plaintiff who wants a jury to try his or her case must usually request it as a jury demand, or else the case will proceed as a bench trial. Some types of cases, such as family law cases, are never tried with juries. If a jury is requested, the case proceeds with the selection of jurors. During this time, a specified number of jurors are selected randomly from a pool of potential jurors. Both parties are permitted to question the jurors in a process called voir dire, and may ask that a certain number of jurors be removed from the final jury.

At the beginning of a trial, both sides give opening statements, providing an overview of the evidence that will be presented during the trial. After opening statements, both sides present evidence by questioning its own witnesses (called direct examination) and introducing physical items into evidence. Each party has the right to cross-examine witnesses produced by the opposing party. All jurisdictions have developed detailed rules of evidence that must be followed by both parties. Many of these rules govern the questions that may be asked on direct or cross-examination of witnesses. If one party enters something into evidence that violates the rules of evidence, the other party must raise an objection to the entry of this evidence, and the judge may sustain or overrule this objection. Some violations of the rules of evidence may result in a mistrial, in which the entire trial process must be repeated because it would be unfair to continue with the case. Even if the rule violation is not enough to cause a mistrial, a party who may wish to appeal an adverse ruling must raise objections during trial to "preserve error" for future consideration by appellate courts. Appellate courts will generally only consider points of possible error when the party seeking the appeal raised an objection and preserved error at the trial level.

A plaintiff generally has the burden to prove a case, and always introduces evidence before the defendant. Because a plaintiff has the burden of proof, a defendant is not required to introduce evidence, though the defendant will almost always do so. After the defendant concludes his or her presentation of evidence, the plaintiff may present evidence that rebuts evidence offered by the defense. Once all evidence has been introduced, both parties make closing arguments. Closing arguments are followed by jury deliberation, in which the jury determines whether the plaintiff or plaintiffs deserve to recover, and what amount of damages is appropriate. A jury relies on jury instructions (or court charges) given to them by the court, which describe the law and procedure that the jury must use to make its decision. The percentage of jurors that must be in agreement to render a decision ranges among different jurisdictions.

Once a jury renders a verdict, the parties may file post-trial motions that may still affect the outcome of the trial. These motions may include motion for new trial, which is usually awarded if something occurred during the trial that rendered the process unfair to one of the parties; or a motion for judgment notwithstanding the verdict (commonly referred to as "JNOV"), where the court renders judgment for one party, though the jury decided in favor of the other party, because the evidence presented at trial did not support the jury's decision. A party who wishes to appeal an adverse decision may also file a notice of appeal with the trial court, indicating that it wishes to appeal the ruling to an appellate court. Filing a notice of appeal within a certain time frame (30 days is common) is required in most jurisdictions in order to appeal a case to a higher court.

### Criminal Trials

State and federal prosecutors initiate criminal cases, which involve charges that an individual has violated a criminal law. In all criminal cases, the state or federal government serves as the plaintiff, while the person charged is the defendant. Criminal laws, which are promulgated by the various legislatures, consist of two major types of laws: felonies and misdemeanors. Felonies consist of the more serious crimes, and carry with them the most serious punishment. Both felonies and misdemeanors can result in jail or prison time, and both will usually result in a significant fine.

Citizens are guaranteed a number of rights in the context of criminal prosecution, and exercise of these rights is often the focus of criminal trials. The Fourth Amendment of the U.S. Constitution requires that law enforcement officials obtain a search warrant, upon showing of probable cause, before conducting searches or seizures of individuals or the property of individuals. The Fifth and Sixth Amendments contain a number of guarantees to all citizens that must be provided in a criminal trial. If a citizen's constitutional rights have been violated, the state may be required to proceed without the introduction of relevant evidence obtained illegally, or may be required to terminate the criminal action altogether.

When a person is arrested for violation of a criminal law, he or she must generally be brought before a judge within twenty-four hours of the arrest. The judge must inform the individual of the charges brought against him or her, and set bail or other condition of release. After other preliminary matters, the defendant is formally charged in one of two ways. First, the prosecutors may file a "trial information," which formally states the charges against the defendant. In more serious cases, such as murder trials, a panel of citizens will be convened as a grand jury to consider the evidence against the defendant. A grand jury, unlike a trial jury, only determines whether sufficient evidence to support the criminal charge exists, and will issue an indictment if evidence is sufficient. Either the filing of a trial information, or the return of an indictment, formally begins the trial process by charging the defendant. Once the defendant has been formally charged, he or she must appear for an arraignment, where the court reads the charge and permits the defendant to enter a plea. The defendant may enter a plea of guilty or not guilty at this time. Where it is permitted or required as a prerequisite to an insanity defense, the defendant may enter a plea of not guilty by reason of insanity. In some jurisdictions, including federal courts, the defendant may plead nolo contendere, or "no contest," which means that the defendant does not contest the charges. Its primary effect is the same as a plea of guilty, and its primary significance is that a plea of nolo contendere cannot be introduced into evidence in a subsequent civil action as proof of the defendant's guilt in the criminal action. Nolo contendere pleadings may usually only be entered with the permission of the court.

The Sixth Amendment guarantees the accused in a criminal prosecution a speedy and public trial. When a defendant enters a plea of not guilty, the trial is usually scheduled within ninety days of the filing of the trial information or indictment. The Sixth Amendment also guarantees citizens accused of crimes the right to a jury trial, though a defendant may waive this right and request a bench trial. During the pre-trial stage, the defendant may file motions with the court, such as those requesting exclusion of evidence from a trial because the evidence may have been obtained illegally. A defendant may also engage in pretrial discovery, including requests to view evidence in the possession of the prosecution. The prosecution and the defendant may engage in plea bargaining, whereby the prosecution may agree to reduce charges against the defendant in exchange for a plea of guilty or nolo contendere.

When a case proceeds to a jury trial, the parties have an opportunity to question prospective jurors, similar to the selection of jurors in a civil case, except that the final number of jurors in a criminal trial is usually larger than the number used in a civil case. Both the state and the defendant have the opportunity to strike jurors from the final jury. Once the final jury is selected and the trial begins, the prosecution reads the indictment or trial information, reads the defendant's plea, and makes an opening statement. The defendant may make an opening statement immediately after the prosecution, or may wait to do so until the time the defense introduces its evidence. Introduction of evidence in a criminal case is similar to that of a civil case, and the prosecution bears the

burden of proving that the defendant is guilty beyond a reasonable doubt. Until the state proves otherwise, the defendant is presumed innocent. The defendant is not required to introduce evidence since the prosecution bears the burden of proof, but if the defendant does produce evidence, the prosecution may present rebuttal evidence and cross-examine any witnesses. Once both sides have presented the evidence, each party may give a closing argument.

A jury in a criminal trial must return a unanimous verdict of "guilty" or "not guilty." If a jury fails to reach a unanimous verdict, it is referred to as a "hung" jury, and a mistrial is declared. In such a situation, a new jury must retry the entire case. If the jury returns a unanimous verdict of guilty, then the jury's duty is usually complete, since a jury in most jurisdictions is not involved in the sentencing of the defendant. A judge, when determining an appropriate sentence for a convicted defendant, considers testimony and reports from a number of different sources, such as probation officers and victims. The federal government and many state governments have established detailed sentencing guidelines that must be followed by judges in criminal cases. In addition to a sentence of imprisonment or of a fine, a court may place a convicted defendant on probation, meaning that the defendant is placed under the supervision of a local correctional program. A defendant must comply with specific terms and conditions of the probation in order to avoid time in prison or jail. Similar to probation, a judge may also give the defendant a deferred judgment, or may suspend the defendant's sentence. In either case, the defendant is given the opportunity to remove the crime from his or her criminal record by successfully completing a period of probation.

### Appeals

If a party in a case is not satisfied with the outcome of a trial decision, he or she may appeal the case to a higher court for review. Not all parties have the right to appeal, however, and parties must follow proper procedures for the higher court to agree to hear the appeal. During trial, parties must "preserve error" by making timely objections to violations of the rules of evidence and other procedural rules. After trial, the party seeking an appeal must file a notice of appeal with the trial court. The opposing party may file a notice of cross-appeal if that party is not satisfied with the final judgment from the lower court. The party bringing the appeal is usually referred to as the appellant (though in some cases this party is the petitioner), and the opposing party is referred to as the appellee (or respondent in some cases).

Once a party has filed a notice of appeal, both parties must comply with a series of rules of appellate procedure to continue with the appeal. The appellant usually requests that the transcript of the trial court proceeding from the trial court reporter be sent to the court of appeals. The appellant must also pay a docketing or similar fee with the court of appeals. Both parties then file briefs with the appellate court stating the facts from the case, stating the legal arguments and reasons for appeal, and requesting relief from the appellate court. Both parties have access to the other party's briefs submitted to the court. Parties also request an oral argument, where both sides are given the opportunity to make their legal arguments before the court, and answer questions from the appellate court justices. Appellate courts do not hear testimony from witnesses or consider evidence that was not introduced in the trial. Rather, a court of appeals reviews the trial court proceeding to determine whether the trial court applied substantive or procedural law to the facts of the case correctly. At the end of the appeal, the court will issue an opinion that states the conclusion of the court of appeals.

Almost all judicial systems in the United States consist of three tiers, and an intermediate appellate court hears the first level of appeals. If a party is dissatisfied with an intermediate court's opinion, the party may seek an appeal by its jurisdiction's court of last resort. In many cases, the decision of a court of last resort to hear an appeal is discretionary, and a party must petition the court to hear the appeal (intermediate appellate courts, by comparison, typically do not have this discretion). The United States Supreme Court is the court of last resort for all cases in the United States, including the intermediate federal courts of appeals and the highest state courts. The U.S. Supreme Court only hears cases involving the application of federal law, and in most cases, the decision to grant an appeal is completely discretionary on the part of the Supreme Court. A party seeking review from the Supreme Court must file a petition for writ of certiorari requesting that the Court review the lower court's decision, and if the Court grants the writ, the Court orders the submission of the lower court's case. The Supreme Court grants a writ of certiorari in a very small percentage of cases, usually when there is a controversial issue of federal law in question in the case.

Civil appeals and criminal appeals are similar, with two main exceptions. First, with very few exceptions, the state may not appeal an acquittal of a criminal in a trial court case. Second, in some criminal cases, especially murder cases where the defendant has received the death penalty, the right to appeal is guaranteed and automatic.

### Jurisdiction and Venue

When a party bring a lawsuit in a court in the United States, the party must determine which court has appropriate jurisdiction to hear the case, and which court is the proper venue for such a suit. Jurisdiction refers to the power of a court to hear a particular case, and may be subdivided into two components: subject matter jurisdiction and personal jurisdiction. Venue refers to the appropriateness of a court to hear a case, and applies differently than jurisdiction.

A court has proper subject matter jurisdiction if it has been given the power to hear a particular type of case or controversy under constitutional or statutory provisions. For example, a county court of law may have jurisdiction to hear cases and controversies where the amount in controversy of the claim is less than $5,000. If a claimant brings a case before the county court with an amount in controversy of $7,500, the court lacks jurisdiction to hear the case and will dismiss it. Subject matter jurisdiction is often a difficult issue with respect to the jurisdiction of federal courts, discussed below. Personal jurisdiction is based on the parties or property involved in the lawsuit. In personam jurisdiction refers to the power of a court over a particular person or persons, and usually applies when a party is a resident of a state or has established some minimum contact with that state. In rem jurisdiction, by comparison, refers to the power of a court over property located in a particular state.

Venue is often confused with jurisdiction because it applies when determining whether a particular court may hear a case. A court may have jurisdiction to hear a case, but may not be the proper venue for such a case. Statutes often provide that proper venue in a particular case is the county or location where the defendant or defendants reside. Even if a court in the county where the plaintiff resides has proper jurisdiction to hear the case, it may not be the proper venue because of a provision in a statute regarding venue.

### Jurisdiction of Federal Courts

Federal courts in the United States have limited jurisdiction to hear certain claims, based primarily on provisions in Article III of the U.S. Constitution. Federal courts can hear cases involving the application of the Constitution, federal statutes, or treaties. Federal courts may also hear cases where the amount in controversy is more than $75,000, and all of the parties are citizens of different states. State courts may also hear cases with federal questions or where parties reside in different states. If a party brings a case in state court and a federal court has jurisdiction to hear the case, the opposing party may remove the case to federal court. The federal court generally reviews each case to determine whether jurisdiction is appropriate. If federal jurisdiction is not appropriate, the court remands the case to state court.

Some suits may only be brought in federal court, such as those brought by or against the government of the United States. Other examples are those involving bankruptcy, patents, and admiralty.

### Legal vs. Equitable Remedies

Some remedies available from courts are considered "legal" remedies, while others are considered "equitable" remedies. Legal remedies are usually those involving an award of monetary damages. By comparison, a court through use of an equitable remedy may require or prohibit certain conduct from a party. The distinction between legal and equitable remedies relates to the historic distinction between "law" and "equity" courts that existed in England as far back as the fourteenth century. Law courts traditionally adhered to very rigid procedures and formalities in resolving the outcome of a legal conflict, while equity courts developed a more flexible system where judges could exercise more discretion. This system transferred to the United States, but today, most courts in the United States may hear cases in both law and equity, although the procedure and proof required to request an equitable remedy may differ from the requirements to request a legal remedy. Examples of equitable remedies are specific performance of a contract, reformation of a contract, injunctions, and restitution.

### Procedural Rules of the Courts

In addition to procedural laws promulgated by legislatures, judicial systems also adopt various rules of procedure that must be followed by the courts and parties to a case. Two main types of court rules exist. First, some rules have general applicability over all courts in a particular jurisdiction. Examples of such rules are rules of civil procedure, rules of appellate procedure, rules of criminal procedure, and rules of evidence. Second, some rules apply only to a particu-

lar court, and are referred to as local court rules. Many counties draft local court rules that apply to all courts in those particular counties. Local court rules are generally more specific than rules of general applicability, and both must be consulted in a given case.

### Pro Se Litigants and the Right to Representation

A litigant representing himself or herself, without the assistance of counsel, is called a pro se litigant. It is almost always advisable to seek counsel with respect to a legal claim, if possible. Defendants in criminal cases are entitled to legal representation, and a lawyer will be provided to a criminal if the criminal shows indigence. Such assistance in criminal cases is usually provided by a public defender's office. Claimants in civil cases, on the other hand, are not entitled to attorneys, though any of a number of legal aid societies may be willing to provide legal services free of charge. Many of these legal aid societies are subsidized by public agencies, and will accept a case only if a person meets certain criteria, usually focusing on the income of the party.

In a civil case, a court may appoint counsel after considering a number of factors, including the validity of the party's position, and the ability of the party to try the case. A party who is indigent must usually file a written motion with the court, explaining the party's indigence and need for counsel. An attorney who provides free legal assistance is said to provide a pro bono service. Attorneys are generally free to determine when they will provide pro bono services, and it is common in every jurisdiction for the number of litigants seeking the appointment of counsel to outweigh the number of attorneys willing to provide pro bono services.

If a party must continue pro se, the rules regarding sanctions of attorneys apply equally to this party. A party must verify the accuracy and reasonableness of any document submitted to the court. If any submission contains false, improper, or frivolous information, the party may be liable for monetary or other sanctions. Likewise, a pro se litigant may be held in contempt of court for failure to follow the directions of a court. Many courts provide handbooks that assist pro se litigants in following proper trial procedures.

### Small Claims Courts and Other Local Tribunals

Cases involving a relatively small amount in controversy may be brought before small claims court.

These courts exist only at the state court level. The maximum amount in controversy for a small claims court is usually $1,000 for a money judgment sought, or $5,000 for the recovery of personal property, though these amounts vary among jurisdictions. Witnesses are sworn, as they are in any trial, but the judge in a small claims court typically conducts the trial in a more informal fashion than in a trial at the district court level. Judges may permit the admission of evidence in a small claims action that may not be admissible under relevant rules of evidence or rules of procedure. One major exception is that privileged communication is usually not admissible in a small claims action. A small claims court usually only has the power to award monetary damages. If a party is unsatisfied with the judgment of the small claims court, the party may ordinarily appeal the case to a district court or other trial court.

### Alternative Dispute Resolution

A variety of procedures may be available to parties, which can serve as alternatives to litigation in the court system. Alternative dispute resolution, or ADR, has become rather common, because it is typically less costly and does not involve the formal proceedings associated with a trial. Parties usually enter into one of two types of ADR: arbitration or mediation. If a case is submitted to arbitration, a neutral arbitrator renders a decision that may be binding or non-binding, depending on the agreement of the parties. An arbitrator serves a function analogous to a judge, though the presentation of each party's evidence does not need to follow the formal rules that must be followed in a judicial decision. Though parties are generally not able to appeal an arbitrator's award, parties may seek judicial relief if the arbitrator acts in an arbitrary or capricious manner, shows bias towards one of the parties, or makes an obvious mistake. Arbitration may be ordered by a court, may be required under certain laws, or may be voluntary.

Mediation is similar to arbitration because it involves the use of a neutral third party to resolve a dispute. A mediator assists the parties to identify issues in a dispute, and makes proposals for the resolution of the dispute or disputes. However, unlike arbitrators, a mediator does not have the power to make a binding decision in a case. Also unlike arbitrators, a mediator typically meets with each of the interested parties in private to hold confidential discussions. Mediation may be court-ordered, may be required under certain laws, or may be voluntary. A number of organizations, including state bar associations, offer mediation services.

A number of other forms of ADR exist. For example, parties may employ the use of a fact finder, who resolves factual disputes between two parties. In some jurisdictions, parties may be required to submit a dispute to early neutral evaluation, where a neutral evaluator provides an assessment of the strengths and weaknesses of each party's position.

### Case Law in the Common Law System

Cases play a very important part in the legal system of the United States, not only because courts adjudicate the claims of parties before them, but also because courts establish precedent that must be followed in future cases. The United States adopted the common law tradition of England as the basis for its legal system. Under the common law system, legal principles were handed down from previous generations, first on an unwritten basis, then through the decisions of the courts. Though legislatures possess constitutional power to make law, in a common law system there is no presumption that legislation applies to every legal problem in the area addressed by the legislation. This differs from the legal systems based on the civil law tradition derived from Roman law (the use of the term civil law also refers to non-criminal laws, as discussed below, and the two uses of the term are distinct). In a civil law system, legislatures develop codes that are presumed to apply to all situations relevant to the code, and courts are employed only to adjudicate claims. The only state in the United States that does not consider itself a "common law state" is Louisiana, which adopted the civil law tradition based on its roots in French law. Accordingly, the codes (legislation) in that state are somewhat different than those in other states.

Courts in the United States follow the doctrine of precedent, which was also adopted from the English common law system. Under this doctrine, courts not only adjudicate the claims of the parties before them, but also establish a precedent that must be followed in future cases. The ruling of a court binds not only itself for future cases, but also any courts under which the court has appellate jurisdiction. Though trial level courts make rulings of law that are binding on future cases, the doctrine of precedent is most important in the legal system at the appellate levels.

### Publication of Case Law

Unlike statutes, cases are usually not available in a subject matter arrangement. When a case is first published, it is issued as a "slip opinion," named as such because these are printed on unbound sheets of paper. These opinions are compiled, and eventually published in bound case reporters. Cases from the U.S. Supreme Court and from courts in many jurisdictions are contained in reporters published by government bodies, and are called official reporters. These cases and other cases are also published in the National Reporter System, originally created by West Publishing Company (now West Group) in 1879. Case reporters in this system include state cases, federal cases, and cases from specialized tribunals, such as the bankruptcy courts. Cases may be readily located by finding their citation in the National Reporter System, or in another case reporter. An example of such a citation is "Roe v. Wade, 93 S. Ct. 705 (1973)." "Roe v. Wade" refers to the names of the parties of the case; "93" refers to the volume of the reporter; "S. Ct." is an abbreviation for Supreme Court Reporter; "705" refers to the page in the reporter where the case begins; and "(1973)" refers to year the case was decided.

Cases from all three levels of the federal judicial system are published. With few exceptions, only appellate court opinions from state courts are published. Unlike appellate courts, state trial judges seldom issue formal legal opinions about their cases, although rulings of law may be available in the record of the trial court. Most legal research in case law focuses on location of appellate court decisions.

### Reading a Judicial Opinion

Like other types of law, reading and understanding the meaning of a judicial opinion is more of an art than a science. The opinion of the case includes the court's reasoning in deciding a case, and is binding on future courts only if a majority of the court deciding the case joins the opinion (in which case the opinion is called the majority opinion). If an opinion is written in support of the court's judgment, but is not joined by a majority of justices, then the opinion is termed a plurality. Plurality opinions are not binding on future courts, but may be highly persuasive since they support the judgment of the court. Some justices may agree with the judgment, but may not agree with the majority opinion. These justices may write concurring opinions that state their reasons in support of the judgment. These opinions have no precedential value, but may be persuasive in future cases. Similarly, justices who disagree with the judgment, the opinion, or both, write dissenting opinions that argue against the judgment or majority opinion.

Some components of a majority opinion are binding on future courts, while others are not. The actual holding or reason for deciding (traditionally referred to as the ratio decidendi) provides the rule of law that is binding precedent in future cases. By comparison, dictum is the portion of an opinion that is not essential to a court's holding, and is not binding on future courts. Dicta may include background information about the holding, or may include the judge's personal comments about the reasoning for the holding. Dicta may be highly persuasive and may alter the holdings of future cases.

## Administrative Law and Procedure

### Creation and Empowerment of Government Agencies

Although the branches of government are primarily responsible for the development of law and resolution of disputes, much of the responsibility of the administration of government has been delegated to government agencies. While branches of government may not delegate essential government functions to agencies, agencies may administer government programs, and promulgate and enforce regulations. When a legislature creates a government agency, it does so through the passage of an enabling statute, which also describes the specific powers delegated to the agency. The Administrative Procedure Act (APA) governs agency action at the federal level, and state counterparts to the APA govern state agencies.

### Types of Government Agencies

Some government agencies are formed to carry out government programs, but do not promulgate regulations that carry the force of law. A number of these agencies have been established to administer such programs as highway construction, education, public housing, and similar functions. Other government agencies promulgate rules and regulations that govern a particular area of law. Examples of regulatory agencies include the Environmental Protection Agency and Nuclear Regulatory Commission, both of which promulgate regulations that are similar in function to legislation. Legislatures also create agencies that resolve dispute among parties, similar to the function of a judicial body. Agency decisions are usually referred to as agency adjudications. Examples of agencies that adjudicate claims are the National Labor Relations Board and Securities and Exchange Commission.

### Agency Rulemaking

Most agencies that have regulatory power promulgate regulations through a process called notice and comment rulemaking. Before a regulatory agency can promulgate a rule, it must provide notice to the public. Federal agencies provide notice in the Federal Register, a daily government publication that provides the text of proposed and final agency rules. After considering comments from the public and making additional considerations, the agency may issue a final, binding rule. The promulgation of a final rule can take months, or may take years, to complete. State agencies must follow similar procedures, including publication of proposed rules in a publication analogous to the Federal Register. Agency rules are functionally equivalent to statutes. Federal agency rules currently in force are published in a subject matter arrangement in the Code of Federal Regulations. Each state publishes its rules in force in a state administrative code.

Some agencies at the state and federal levels are required to follow more formal procedures. Agencies may not exceed the power delegated by a respective legislature, and may adopt rules without following the proper procedures provided in the enabling legislation or legislation governing administrative procedures.

### Agency Adjudications

Agencies with power to adjudicate claims operate similarly to a court. Such an agency considers evidence presented in a hearing, and makes a final, binding decision based on an application of the law to the facts in a case. An agency that adjudicates a claim must maintain a record of the hearing, and parties are generally able to seek judicial review of a decision, much like judicial review of a lower court decision. A court may overrule an agency decision if the agency acted in an arbitrary or capricious manner, made a decision unsupported by substantial evidence, or made a decision unsupported by the facts presented to the agency.

## Relationship Among Various Laws and Other Authority

Laws in the United States do not exist in a vacuum, and determining the appropriate outcome of a case may require consultation with several different types of laws. A single case may be governed by application of a statute, an administrative regulation, and cases interpreting the statute and regulation. Understanding the application of laws usually requires an understanding of the nature of legal authority.

Any authority emanating from an official government entity acting in its lawmaking capacity is referred to as primary authority, and this authority is what is binding on a particular case. Primary authority can be subdivided into two types: primary mandatory authority and primary persuasive authority. Primary mandatory authority is law that is binding in a particular jurisdiction. For example, a Fifth Circuit Court of Appeals decision is primary mandatory authority in Texas, Mississippi, and Louisiana, since the Fifth Circuit governs these states. By comparison, primary authority that is not binding in a particular jurisdiction is referred to as primary persuasive authority. It is considered persuasive because though such authority does not bind a decision-maker in a jurisdiction, the decision-maker may nevertheless be persuaded to act in a familiar fashion as the authority from outside the jurisdiction. In the example above, a Fifth Circuit decision in a court in California would be considered primary persuasive authority, and could influence the California tribunal in its decision-making.

A second type of authority—secondary authority—may also be helpful in determining the appropriate application of the law. Secondary authority includes a broad array of sources, including treatises (a term used for law book); law review articles, which are usually written by law professors, judges, or expert practitioners; legal encyclopedias, which provide an overview of the law; and several other items that provide commentary about the law. An individual who is not trained in the law (and in many cases those who are trained in the law) should ordinarily begin his or her legal research by consulting such authority to gain a basic understanding of the law that applies in a particular situation.

A final consideration that cannot be overlooked is that the law constantly changes. If a legal researcher comes across literature describing the law in a given area, he or she must always verify that the discussion in the literature reflects the current state of the law. Legislatures and agencies constantly add new laws, and revise and amend existing laws. Similarly, courts routinely overrule previous decisions and may rule that a statute or regulation is not valid under a relevant constitutional provision. Updating legal authority involves a process of consulting supplements and other resources, and is necessary to ensure that an individual knows the current state of the law.

# AMERICANS WITH DISABILITIES ACT

## EDUCATIONAL ACCOMMODATIONS

*Sections within this essay:*

- Background
- Defining Disability
- Accommodation of Disabilities
- Reasonable Accommodation
- Testing and Examinations
- Hidden Disabilities
- Private and Religious Schools
- Postsecondary Education
- Individuals with Disabilities Education Act
- State Laws Regarding Disabled Students
- Additional Resources

## Background

Congress enacted the **Americans with Disabilities Act** (ADA) to prohibit discrimination against those with disabilities. The statute, first enacted in 1990, applies in the areas of employment, public accommodations, transportation, services offered by governmental entities, and other areas. The act attempts to extend the types of rights provided under the **Civil Rights Act** of 1964 to those with disabilities. Included among the right in the ADA are provisions requiring educational institutions to provide accommodations to those with disabilities.

The first success the disability rights movement had was with Section 504 of the Rehabilitation Act of 1973. Based on the models of previous laws that prohibited discrimination based on race or gender, Section 504 prohibits **discrimination** in programs or activities receiving federal financial assistance. It provides: "No otherwise qualified individual with handicaps in the United States... shall, solely by reason of her or his handicap, be excluded from the participation in, be denied the benefits of, or be subjected to discrimination under any program or activity receiving Federal financial assistance." This provision marks the first time the disabled were viewed as a class of people, similar to a race or gender. The disabled used Section 504 to demand and enforce equal footing as a class under the law, one that could demand facilities to accommodate their disability.

Although this language offered some protection from educational discrimination for those with disabilities, Section 504 did not go far enough. It only applied in limited situations, where the program or building used federal financial aid in the form of grants. Those with disabilities still faced discrimination in the private sector, in private schools, and in those public facilities that did not use federal grant money. The disabled still faced a great many inaccessible schools; testing situations that did not offer alternatives for the deaf, the blind, or those with other types of disability; and other, similar barriers to equal education and access.

The Americans with Disabilities Act was passed on July 26, 1990, and signed into law by President George H.W. Bush. The intention of the Americans with Disabilities Act was to fill the gaps left behind by Section 504. The ADA builds upon the legal language within Section 504, so that applied together, both laws would cover almost any situation, public or private, that the disabled might encounter.

The ADA bars employment and educational discrimination against "qualified individuals with disabilities." Title II of the ADA applies specifically to educational institutions, requiring them to make educational opportunities, extracurricular activities, and facilities open and accessible to all students. The ADA applies equally to public and private sector institutions, although the requirements for private schools and institutions are slightly less stringent.

## Defining Disability

Section 504 of the Rehabilitation Act of 1973 defines individuals with disabilities as those who have a physical or mental impairment which substantially limits one or more major life activities; has a record of such impairment; or is regarded as having such an impairment. This category includes physiological disorders such as hearing impairment, vision impairment, or speech impairments; neurological disorders such as muscular dystrophy or multiple sclerosis; psychological disorders such as mental retardation, mental illness, or learning disabilities. The legislative definition does not spell out specific illnesses or impairments because of the difficulty of ensuring an all-inclusive list.

The deciding factor in determining whether or not a person suffers from a disability under Section 504 is whether the impairment limits one or more major life activities, such as walking, performing manual tasks, seeing, hearing, speaking, breathing, learning and/or working. The ADA defines a disability as a "physical or mental impairment that substantially limits one or more major life activity; a record of such impairment; or being regarded as having such impairment." The ADA covers obvious impairments such as difficulty in seeing, hearing, or learning, as well as less obvious impairments such as alcoholism, epilepsy, paralysis, mental retardation, and contagious and noncontagious diseases, specifically Acquired Immune Deficiency Syndrome (AIDS).

The difference between the two laws, as they apply to educational institutions, is that Section 504 applies to the recipients of grant monies from the federal government, while Title II of the ADA applies only to public entities, with some applications to private sector entities. These entities include nursery, elementary, secondary, undergraduate, or postgraduate schools, or other places of education, day care centers, and gymnasiums or other places of exercise or recreation.

## Accommodation of Disabilities

Section 504 of the Rehabilitation Act of 1973 and Title II of the ADA cover students in virtually any public school district, college, or university because they receive some form of federal assistance. Some private schools, colleges, and universities also receive such assistance, and students are protected under Section 504, but Title II does not apply to them. Both laws apply to all programs of a school or college, not simply academics. These include extracurricular activities such as band, clubs, or academic teams, as well as athletics and any activity that might occur off campus.

Neither law requires that all buildings be made fully accessible to students or teachers with disabilities. Those buildings constructed after the Section 504 regulation was issued in 1977 must be fully accessible. For older buildings, the law requires that the program or activity be made accessible. Often, classes or extracurricular activities are moved to another, more accessible, room to accommodate any disabled person who attends. An interpreter for the hearing-impaired or other types of assistance can be supplied.

## Reasonable Accommodation

One aim of the ADA was to make educational institutions more accessible for the disabled. This aim covers "reasonable accommodations" such as the following:

- Modification of application and testing
- Allowing students to tape-record or video-tape lectures and classes
- Modification of class schedules
- Extra time allotted between classes
- Notetakers
- Interpreters
- Readers
- Specialized computer equipment
- Special education

Accommodation also includes physical changes to an educational institution's buildings, including the following:

- Installing accessible doorknobs and hardware
- Installing grab bars in bathrooms

- Increasing maneuverability in bathrooms for wheelchairs

- Installing sinks and hand dryers within reach

- Creating handicapped parking spaces

- Installing accessible water fountains

- Installing ramps

- Having curb cuts, sidewalks, and entrances that are accessible

- Installing elevators

- Widening door openings

Public accommodation is not required if a particular aid or service would result in either fundamental alteration of the services offered or the facility if the accommodation would impose an undue burden. (See *Southeastern Community College v. Davis*, 442 U. S. 397 (1979)). Under the U.S. Supreme Court's interpretation, Congress intended that undue burden and hardship must be determined on a case-by-case basis.

### Testing and Examinations

Section 309 of the Americans with Disabilities Act fills the gap regarding testing and examination not defined by Section 504 of the Rehabilitation Act of 1973 or Title II of the ADA. Any educational facility that receives federal money or is a public facility because it is a function of the state or local government as defined under Title II of the ADA is required to make any examination accessible to persons with disabilities. This requirement includes physical access to the testing facility, as well as any modification of the way the test is administered to assist the disabled. Modifications may include offering extended time, written instructions, or the assistance of a reader.

Many licensing and testing authorities are not covered by Section 504 or Title II. In these cases, a provision in the ADA was included to assure that persons with disabilities are not prohibited from or disallowed in any educational, professional, or other **examination** opportunity because a test or course is conducted in an inaccessible location or is offered without the needed modifications to assist the disabled student. Modifications may include offering an examination with the assistance of a reader, in a braille or large print format, transcribers, or the proper computer equipment to help the disabled person.

Examiners may require proof of disability, but requests for documentation of the disability must be reasonable and must be limited to support for the modification or aid requested. The student or testing applicant may be required to bear the cost of providing such documentation for examination officials. Appropriate documentation would include:

- Letter from physician or psychiatrist or other qualified individual

- Evidence of prior diagnosis

- Evidence of prior accommodation

### Hidden Disabilities

Hidden disabilities are considered to be any physical or mental impairments that are not readily apparent to others. They include such conditions as learning disabilities, allergies, diabetes, epilepsy, as well as chronic illnesses such as heart, kidney, or liver disease. There are roughly four million American students with disabilities, many with impairments that are not immediately known without medical or diagnostic testing.

### Private and Religious Schools

The ADA covers private elementary and secondary schools as places of public accommodation; i.e., the schools must be physically accessible to those with disabilities. But these schools are not required to provide free appropriate education or develop an individualized educational program for students with disabilities. Any private school that receives federal grant monies or any type of federal assistance would then fall under the Department of Education's regulations regarding construction and alterations to the private school's structures and buildings, where it can be conveniently and economically incorporated.

### Postsecondary Education

Under Section 504, colleges and universities are not required to identify students with disabilities. They are required to inform all applicants of the availability of auxiliary aids, services, and academic adjustments. It is the student's responsibility to make his or her condition known and to seek out assistance.

## Individuals with Disabilities Education Act

In addition to the protections offered by the ADA and Section 504, another statute, the Individuals with Disabilities Education Act (IDEA), provides additional protection to those with disabilities in the context of education. The act was originally passed by Congress in 1975 but has been amended on several occasions since that time. The goals of IDEA are as follows:

- It ensures the disabled children are given a "free appropriate public education," emphasizing special education and related services that meet the specific needs of each disabled child

- It ensures the protection of the rights of disabled children and their parents

- It assists states, local governments, educational service agencies, and federal agencies to provide for the education of disabled children

- It assists states to implement a statewide system of early intervention services for disabled infants and toddlers; It ensures that educators and parents have the necessary tools to improve educational results for disabled children

- It assesses and ensures the effectiveness of efforts to educate disabled children

Unlike ADA and Section 504, which are nondiscrimination laws, IDEA is instead a grant program. It requires states that accept federal funds to provide free, appropriate public education to disabled children. Although the means by which IDEA operates differs from the ADA and Section 504, each of these statutes serve similar purposes for the most part.

## State Laws Regarding Disabled Students

Under IDEA, states that receive federal funding must conduct an approved plan for meeting guidelines in educating disabled students. Accordingly, each state has enacted a statute designed to assure compliance with guidelines. A brief summary of these statutes is as follows:

ALABAMA: The statute related to education for exceptional children is located in title 16 of the Alabama Code.

ALASKA: The statute related to education for exceptional children is located in title 14 of the Alaska Statutes.

ARIZONA: The statute related to special education for exceptional children is located in title 15 of the Arizona Revised Statutes.

ARKANSAS: The statute related to education for handicapped children is located in title 6 of the Arkansas Code.

CALIFORNIA: The statute related to special education programs is located in the California Education Code.

COLORADO: The Handicapped Children's Education Act is located in title 22 of the Colorado Revised Statutes.

CONNECTICUT: The Exceptional Children Act is located in title 10 of the Connecticut General Statutes.

DELAWARE: The statute related to education for exceptional and handicapped students is located in title 14 of the Delaware Code.

FLORIDA: The statute related to instruction of exceptional students is located in chapter 1003 of the Florida Statutes.

GEORGIA: The statute related to special education services is located in title 20 of the Georgia Code.

HAWAII: The statute related to education for exceptional children is located in chapter 301 of the Hawaii Revised Statutes.

IDAHO: The statute related to education of handicapped or others unable to attend school is located in title 33 of the Idaho Code.

ILLINOIS: The statute related to the education of disabled children is located in chapter 105 of the Illinois Compiled Statutes.

INDIANA: The statute related to special education programs is located in title 20 of the Indiana Code.

IOWA: The statute related to education of children requiring special education is contained in chapter 281 of the Iowa Code.

KANSAS: The Special Education for Exceptional Children Act is located in title 72 of the Kansas Statutes.

KENTUCKY: The statute related to special education programs is located in title 157 of the Kentucky Revised Statutes.

LOUISIANA: The statutes related to education opportunities for exceptional children is located in title 17 of the Louisiana Revised Statutes.

MAINE: The statute related to education for exceptional children is located in title 20-A of the Maine Revised Statutes.

MARYLAND: The statute related to compensatory education for disadvantaged and handicapped children is contained in the Maryland Education Code.

MASSACHUSETTS: The statute related to education of children with special needs is located in chapter 71B of the Massachusetts Laws.

MICHIGAN: The statute related to special education programs for the handicapped is located in chapter 380 of the Michigan Compiled Laws.

MINNESOTA: The statute related to special education for handicapped children is located in chapter 120 of the Minnesota Statutes.

MISSISSIPPI: The statute related to education for exceptional children is located in title 37 of the Mississippi Code.

MISSOURI: The statute related to special educational services for handicapped children is located in chapter 162 of the Missouri Revised Statutes.

MONTANA: The statute related to special education programs for handicapped children is located in title 20 of the Montana Code.

NEBRASKA: The statute related to special education is located in chapter 79 of the Nebraska Revised Statutes.

NEVADA: The statute related to education of handicapped minors is located in chapter 388 of the Nevada Revised Statutes.

NEW HAMPSHIRE: The statute related to programs of special education is located in chapter 186-C of the New Hampshire Revised Statutes.

NEW JERSEY: The statute related to classes and facilities for handicapped children is located in title 18A of the New Jersey Statutes.

NEW MEXICO: The statute related to special education for exceptional children is located in chapter 22 of the New Mexico Statutes.

NEW YORK: The statute related to children with handicapping conditions is located in sections 4401 *et seq.* of the New York Education Law.

NORTH CAROLINA: The statute related to special education programs is located in chapter 115C of the North Carolina General Statutes.

NORTH DAKOTA: The statute related to special education of exceptional children is located in title 15 of the North Dakota Century Code.

OHIO: The statute related to the education of handicapped children is located in chapter 3323 of the Ohio Revised Code.

OKLAHOMA: The statute related to special education for exceptional children is located in title 70 of the Oklahoma Statutes.

OREGON: The statute related to special education services is located in chapter 343 of the Oregon Revised Statutes.

PENNSYLVANIA: The statute related to education of exceptional children is located in title 24 of the Pennsylvania Statutes.

RHODE ISLAND: The statute related to education of handicapped children is located in title 16 of the Rhode Island General Laws.

SOUTH CAROLINA: The statute related to special education for handicapped children is located in title 59 of the South Carolina Code.

SOUTH DAKOTA: The statute related to special and prolonged educational assistance is located in title 13 of the South Dakota Codified Laws.

TENNESSEE: The statute related to special education programs is located in title 49 of the Tennessee Code.

TEXAS: The statute related to special education programs is located in the Texas Education Code.

UTAH: The statute related to the education of handicapped children is located in the Utah Code.

VERMONT: The statute related to education of handicapped children is located in title 16 of the Vermont Statutes.

VIRGINIA: The statute related to special education programs is located in title 22.1 of the Virginia Code.

WASHINGTON: The statute related to special education for handicapped children is located in title 28A of the Washington Revised Code.

WEST VIRGINIA: The statute related to education of exceptional children is located in title 18 of the West Virginia Code.

WISCONSIN: The statute related to children with exceptional needs is located in chapter 115 of the Wisconsin Statutes.

WYOMING: The statute related to programs for handicapped children is located in title 21 of the Wyoming Statutes.

## Additional Resources

*Americans with Disabilities Handbook* Equal Opportunity Commission and U.S. Department of Justice. October 1991.

*Auxiliary Aids and Services for Post–secondaryStudents with Disabilities: Higher Education's Obligations Under Section 504 and Title II of the ADA.* Office for Civil Rights, U. S. Department of Education. 1998.

*The Civil Rights of Students with Hidden Disabilities Under Section 504 of the Rehabilitation Act of 1973* Office for Civil Rights, U. S. Department of Education. 1995.

*Clearinghouse for information about federal government resources, pamphlets, and information regarding disabilities, maintained by the Presidential Task Force on Employment of Adults with Disabilities.* http://www.disAbility.gov.

*Education Law* James A. Rapp, LexisNexis/Matthew Bender, 2005.

*Student Placement in Elementary and Secondary Schools and Section 504 and Title II of the ADA.* Office for Civil Rights, U. S. Department of Education.1998.

## Organizations

### American Council on Rural Special Education (ACRES)

2323 Anderson Ave., Suite 226, Kansas State University
Manhattan, WA 66502
Phone: (785) 532-2737
Fax: (785) 532-7732

URL: http://www.ksu.edu/acres

### American Speech Language-Hearing Association (ASHA)

1801 Rockville Pike
Rockville, MD
Phone: (301) 897-5700
Phone: (800) 638-8255
URL: http://www.asha.org

### Children with Attention Deficit Disorders (CHADD)

8181 Professional Place, Suite 201
Landover, MD 20785
Phone: (301) 306-7070
Fax: (301) 306-7090
URL: http://www.chadd.org

### Clearinghouse of Disability Information Office of Special Education and Rehabilitative Services U. S. Department of Education

Switzer Building Room 3132 330 C Street SW
Washington, DC 20202
Phone: (202) 205-8241
Fax: (202) 401-2608

### Dyslexia Research Institute, Inc.

5746 Centerville Road
Tallahassee, FL 32308
Phone: (850) 893-2216
Fax: (850) 893-2440
URL: http://www.dyslexia-add.org

### Learning Disabilities Association of America (LDA)

4156 Library Road
Pittsburgh, PA 15234
Phone: (412) 341-1515
Fax: (412) 341-8077
URL: http://www.ldanatl.org

### National Center for Learning Disabilities (NCLD)

381 Park Avenue South, Suite 1401
New York City, NY 10016
Phone: (212) 545-7510
Fax: (212) 545-9665
URL: http://www.ncld.org

# AMERICANS WITH DISABILITIES ACT

## PUBLIC FACILITY ACCOMMODATIONS

*Sections within this essay:*

- Background

- Before ADA
    - Architectural Barriers Act
    - Rehabilitation Act of 1973
    - Uniform Federal Accessibility Standards (UFAS)

- ADA and Title III
    - Physical Accommodations
    - Auxiliary Accommodations
    - Other Accommodations

- Enforcing the Law

- Additional Resources

## Background

Many people think that the Americans with Disabilities Act (ADA) primarily covers workplace accommodations. The only public accommodations they associate with ADA are handicapped parking spaces and Braille numbers on elevator buttons. In fact, the ADA's public facilities rules, as outlined in Title III of the act, are far more comprehensive than that. All sorts of buildings and businesses fall under Title III: restaurants, schools, office buildings, banks, doctors' offices, and movie theaters, to name a few. Accommodation can include anything from adjusting store shelves to constructing special ramps and entryways.

Some people mistakenly believe that ADA requires businesses to make all sorts of prohibitively

expensive changes or else face stiff penalties. The truth is that ADA is designed to benefit the disabled, not to punish business owners. The key to understanding ADA is knowing what is and is not required, as well as what constitutes an acceptable accommodation.

## Before ADA

In years past, "disability" was not something people dealt with publicly; it was understood that those who were blind, deaf, paralyzed, or otherwise "handicapped" would not participate in ordinary life activities, such as school or work.

Attitudes changed slowly but steadily, and by the twentieth century such notable people as Helen Keller and Franklin D. Roosevelt helped break down stereotypes about disabilities. Accommodating the disabled was another matter. Only important public figures such as Roosevelt (who could not stand or walk unaided after his 1921 bout with polio) could expect that structural accommodations would be made for them, and even then those accommodations were limited in scope. There were simply some places that the disabled could not visit freely.

### Architectural Barriers Act

Although most people think that ADA was the first federal law regulating public facilities, in fact it was an earlier law that set the stage. The Architectural Barriers Act (ABA) was passed in 1968, and it mandated that any buildings designed, constructed, altered, or leased with federal funding had to be accessible to the disabled. This included post offices, national parks, some schools, some public housing, and mass transit systems. Because it dealt only with federally funded structures, it was (and still is) less well known than ADA, but it was an important early step.

### Rehabilitation Act of 1973

As important as ABA was, it was met with a certain degree of apathy that undermined its effectiveness. Congress, eager to improve ABA compliance and equally eager for the government to create new and more comprehensive design standards, passed the Rehabilitation Act in 1973. Perhaps the most important element of this law was Section 502, which established the Architectural and Transportation Barriers Compliance Board (later called simply the Access Board). Originally created to develop as well as enforce design requirements, its role later became more focused on ensuring compliance. Beginning in 1976, the Access Board started investigating ABA non-compliance complaints against a variety of public buildings. The law covers any facility that was designed, built, altered, or leased with federal funds after 1969.

### Uniform Federal Accessibility Standard (UFAS)

The design requirements that are supposed to be followed under ABA are spelled out by the Uniform Federal Accessibility Standard (UFAS), which was first published in 1984. These guidelines served as a precursor of sorts to guidelines later introduced under ADA. Today, some government agencies require compliance with both the ADA guidelines and UFAS.

## ADA and Title III

The Americans with Disabilities Act was signed into law on July 26, 1990. Title I of the law covers places of employment; Title II state and local governments. Title IV covers telecommunications for the deaf and hearing-impaired, and Title V covers miscellaneous items. The section of ADA that deals with public facilities, is Title III.

Public accommodations include any building or outdoor space through which any person can enter, with or without a fee. Essentially, that means all buildings except for "private" clubs (any club that requires members to vote to admit an individual) and religious facilities. Among the facilities covered as listed by ADA are the following:

- Lodgings (hotels, motels, inns)

- Establishments that serve food and drink (restaurants, bars, taverns)

- Establishments that offer entertainment (theaters, stadiums)

- Places where public gatherings may be held (auditoriums, convention halls)

- Sale or rental establishments (retail stores)

- Service establishments (medical offices, law offices, funeral parlors)

- Places of public display or collection (museums, galleries, public gardens)

- Social service centers (homeless shelters, day care centers)

- Recreation/exercise establishment (golf courses, gymnasiums)

It is important to understand not only which facilities are covered under ADA, but also who is considered disabled. Under ADA guidelines, anyone who possesses a physical or mental impairment that significantly limits at least one major life function—for example, the ability to feed oneself, the ability to walk, or the ability to breathe on one's own. Alcoholics and other substance abusers are also covered if they have been shown to have a history of such abuse.

A public accommodation is expected to follow three basic guidelines under Title III of ADA. First, it cannot deny goods or services to a disabled person covered under the legislation. Second, it cannot satisfy its commitment to the legislation by offering benefits that are separate or unequal. Finally, it must offer all services in as integrated a setting as possible.

This kind of wording frightens some owners of public facilities. Retail store owners, for example, sometimes fear that Title III compliance means having to make expensive structural changes to their stores or keep people on staff to accommodate all possible disabilities. Would a small company have to install an elevator in its building? Does a restaurant have to make Braille menus and sign-language interpreters available?

In fact, ADA's Title III guidelines do offer a certain degree of leeway for facilities, but that leeway is dependent on a number of factors including cost and a facility's special needs.

### Physical Accommodations

Under Title III, any new building first occupied after January 26, 1993 is required to meet full ADA standards (unless the building plans had been completed before January 26, 1992). The following are among the requirements that new buildings are expected to meet:

- Doorways must be wide enough to accommodate wheelchairs; doors must be easy to open.

- Restrooms must be equipped with adequately wide stalls, grab bars, and sinks and towel dispensers easily accessible for someone in a wheelchair.

- Pay phones must be provided at more than one height, and phones with amplifiers should also be available.

- Adequate parking spaces should be set aside to accommodate disabled patrons.

- Elevators must have Braille numbers and visual as well as audible operation signals.

- Alarm systems must be audible and visible.

Existing facilities that are being remodeled (and in some cases those that are not) must make sure that alterations are ADA-compliant, as long as such changes are deemed reasonable, or, in the words of the legislation, "readily achievable." An alteration is deemed readily achievable when it can be done relatively easily and without much expense. It might not be structurally or economically feasible for a public facility with no elevator to install one, for example, but it probably is feasible to install ramps, handrails, and grab bars. Shelving in stores, telephones mounted lower on the wall, soap dispensers in bathrooms, and brighter lights are all things that can be added with little difficulty or undue expense. In cases in which alterations are difficult or impossible, alternatives can be incorporated instead. Examples include providing taped lectures of inaccessible gallery exhibits or providing a water cooler or reachable paper cups instead of installing a new accessible drinking fountain

As for new buildings, the costs of incorporating ADA-compliant accessibility features has been estimated to be less than one percent of overall construction costs. Thus, it is unlikely that the owners of a building currently under construction would be able to make a case against accessibility. Nor should they want to; as more disabled people enter both the consumer market (as tourists, for example) and the workforce, it benefits building owners to make their structures ADA-compliant.

### Auxiliary Accommodations

A special accommodation category exists for those with visual and hearing impairments. The "auxiliary accommodations" are designed to make it easier to communicate with people who have difficulty seeing or hearing. Among the accommodations ADA can recommend are the following:

- Interpreters who speak sign language

- Special listening devices and headsets

- Texts in large print and Braille, or recorded on tape

- TDD/TTY text telephones for those with hearing impairments

As with physical alterations, auxiliary accommodations are not designed to create an undue burden on the building owner. Nor are they meant to alter the nature of goods or services offered by the public facility in question. For example, a museum whose art works are too delicate to be handled may implement a "no touch" policy, even though it means that certain blind people may not be able to enjoy the exhibit fully.

Stores are not required to have signs or price tags in Braille, nor do they need to have a sign language interpreter on staff. As long as an employee can read price tags and similar information to blind shoppers, and as long as store employees can communicate with deaf customers by writing out notes, there is no requirement for businesses to incur the expense of extra assistance.

Actually, many auxiliary accommodations can be made quite inexpensively. Most ordinary computer programs can be set to display and print in large type, for example. TDD/TTY telephone units equipped with printers cost about $500, which most fair-sized businesses could afford with little difficulty.

### Other Accommodations

There are a number of other accommodations that in general are cost-effective to implement. For example, restaurants that need to make more room for wheelchairs may be required to move their tables around; unless they had to remove a significant number of tables and thus lose business, this should not be a burden. (In fact, many restaurants add or remove tables for certain events as a matter of course.) Some stores may have to relocate display racks for the same reason. Outdoor cafes that crowd sidewalks may be required to reduce the number of tables or increase the space between them. Large plants, whether indoors or outdoors, may need to be moved to make room for disabled individuals.

## Enforcing the Law

In the 25-year period from 1976 to 2001, the Access Board investigated more than 3,300 complaints against public facilities, including post offices, military facilities, veterans hospitals federal courthouses, and prisons. In general, the Board works with the facility to find ways to bring it into compliance. One example is the Holocaust Memorial Museum in Washington, D.C. A group of children with varying degrees of hearing impairment were touring the museum when the fire alarm went off. Because the students actually thought the alarms were part of the exhibit, and because they could not hear the evacuation notices, there was potential for serious consequences. A complaint was filed with the Access Board, which worked with the museum to install new alarms that offered a more distinct and distinguishable signal.

Another example is a homeless shelter in Phoenix, Arizona. Although rest rooms in the shelter had been renovated twice using federal funds, they were still not ADA compliant. The Access Board worked successfully with the shelter to address the issue and make the rest rooms compliant.

Those who feel that a public facility is in violation of Title III may file their complaints with the U.S. Department of Justice. In cases of repeat violations, the Department has authorization to bring lawsuits against offenders, although the more desired outcome would be correction of the problem with the help of groups such as the Access Board. The Department of Justice web site that handles ADA issues is http://www.usdoj.gov/crt/ada/adahom1.htm.

## Additional Resources

*The ADA: A Review of Best Practices* Jones, Timothy L., American Management Association, Periodicals Division, 1993.

*Equality of Opportunity: The Making of ADA* Young, Jonathon M., National Council on Disability, 1997. Jordan I. Kosberg, ed., Wright-PSG, 1983.

*The New ADA: Compliance and Costs.* Kearney, Deboral S., R.S. Means, 1992.

## Organizations

### Access Board

1331 F Street NW, Suite 1000
Washington, DC 20004 USA
Phone: (202) 272-0080
Fax: (202) 272-0081
URL: http://www.access-board.gov
Primary Contact: Pamela Y. Holmes, Chair

### Council for Disability Rights

205 West Randolph Street, Suite 1645
Chicago, IL 60606 USA
Phone: (312) 444-9484
Fax: (312) 444-1977
URL: http://www.disabilityrights.org
Primary Contact: Jo Holzer, Executive Director

### U. S. Department of Justice, Civil Rights Division, Office of Disability Rights

950 Pennsylvania Avenue NW
Washington, DC 20530 USA
Phone: (202) 307-2227
Fax: (202) 307-1198
URL: http://www.usdoj.gov/crt/drs/drshome.htm
Primary Contact: John L. Wodatch, Chief

### U.S. Equal Employment Opportunity Commission (EEOC)

1801 L Street NW
Washington, DC 20507 USA
Phone: (202) 663-4900
Fax: (202) 663-4494 (TTY)
URL: http://www.eeoc.gov
Primary Contact: Cari M. Dominguez, Chair

# AMERICANS WITH DISABILITIES ACT

## WORK ACCOMMODATIONS

*Sections within this essay:*

- Background
- Rationale
- Reasonable Accommodations
- Procedure
- Types of Reasonable Accommodations
- Additional Resources

## Background

In the United States, approximately 43 million people have physical or mental disabilities or impairments that substantially limit major life activities. In an effort to avoid **discrimination** against disabled people in the workplace, Congress enacted in July of 1990 the Americans with Disabilities Act (ADA). One way that the ADA seeks to improve employment opportunities for disabled people is by requiring employers under certain circumstances to alter the workplace to accommodate disabilities. These alterations are known as workplace accommodations.

## Rationale

Just like individuals of different races, colors, religions, gender, or national origin, individuals with physical or mental disabilities historically have faced discrimination. Disabled people have been excluded from mainstream society, segregated, provided with inferior or unequal services, and denied benefits that non-disabled people enjoy. What is different about

the discrimination of disabled people as compared to other types of discrimination is that there is often a rational basis for treating disabled people differently from able-bodied people. Whereas there is usually no rational basis for treating, for example, a woman from South Africa differently from a woman from the United States, there may be a rational basis for treating a woman who is blind differently from a woman with good vision. The visually impaired woman may require the use of Braille, for example.

Another difference in **disability** discrimination is its intent. Many types of discrimination, such as racial discrimination, are rooted in hostility or hatred toward people who are different. But discrimination against disabled individuals more often is rooted in ignorance or apathy. Some people view disabilities with pity or discomfort, leading to behavior that may patronize people with disabilities. Other people simply fail to consider or understand the needs of disabled people, leading to benign neglect or misguided efforts to assist.

The U. S. Constitution does little to protect those with mental or physical disabilities from discrimination. Courts historically have not applied the Constitution's **Equal Protection** Clause to discrimination of **disabled persons** with the same level of scrutiny as discrimination of such protected classes as race, religion, and gender. People with disabilities, therefore, had little or no recourse when their disabilities unfairly prevented them from getting suitable jobs. Only two-thirds of employable disabled persons in the United States were employed in the late 1980s, and many of those employed were not working to their full capacity to earn given their disabilities. By 1990, more than 8 million disabled individuals were unemployed and forced to live on welfare and other forms of government assistance. Congress began enacting federal laws in the 1960s designed to protect disabled people, but these laws did not outlaw disability discrimination by employers. Such protections did not enter the workplace until the 1990 passage of the ADA.

The ADA prohibits private and state and local government employers, as well as employment agencies and labor unions, from discriminating on the basis of disability. It does not apply to private employers with fewer than 15 employees. The ADA prohibits several specific forms of disability discrimination. One example of an ADA violation occurs when an employer fails to make reasonable accommodations to allow disabled workers to work.

## Reasonable Accommodations

The ADA requires employers to make reasonable accommodations to qualified persons with disabilities unless such accommodations would cause an undue hardship to the employer. A disabled person under the ADA is someone who is substantially limited in the ability to perform a major life activity or who has a record of such an impairment or who is regarded as having such an impairment. To be qualified as a disabled person under the ADA, an individual must show an ability to perform all of the essential job functions either with or without a reasonable accommodation. Courts look at mitigating measures in determining whether an individual is disabled. For example, persons who need eyeglasses may be substantially limited in the ability to read, which is a major life activity, unless they wear eyeglasses. Because eyeglasses mitigate their bad vision and allow them to read normally, they are not considered to disabled under the ADA.

There are three general types of reasonable accommodations. The first type modifies the job application process to enable qualified job applicants with a disability to be considered for the job they want. The second type modifies the work environment or the manner in which the job is performed to allow disabled individuals to perform the job's essential functions. The third type modifies the workplace to allow disabled employees equal benefits and privileges as similarly situated employees without disabilities.

More specific types of reasonable accommodations may include making an office wheelchair acces-

sible; restructuring jobs; providing part-time or modified work schedules; modifying or purchasing special furniture or equipment; changing employment policies; providing readers or interpreters; and reassigning disabled individuals to vacant positions. An employer is not required to eliminate an essential job function or fundamental duty of the job to accommodate a disabled person. An employer is not required to lower production quotas or standards that apply to all employees, although an employer is required to provide reasonable accommodations to help a disabled individual meet production quotas or standards. An employer is not required to provide disabled employees with personal use items that are necessary both on and off the job, for example, hearing aids.

The ADA does not require that reasonable accommodations be made when the accommodations would cause employers an undue hardship. Undue hardship means significant difficulty or expense when compared with the employer's resources and circumstances. The employer's financial capabilities are one factor in defining undue hardship, but undue hardship also occurs when the reasonable accommodation would be unduly extensive or disruptive or would fundamentally alter the nature or operation of the business. Courts determine on a case-by-case basis whether a reasonable accommodation would be an undue hardship for the employer.

## Procedure

Individuals who want a reasonable accommodation must request it but need not mention the ADA or the phrase "reasonable accommodation." It is sufficient if employees simply ask for an accommodation for a medical reason. Once a request is made, employers are obligated to investigate the request and determine if the requesting employee is qualified as a disabled individual under the ADA. If that determination is positive, then the employer must begin an interactive process with that employee, determining that individual's needs and identifying the accommodation that should be made. Sometimes this is an easy process with both sides agreeing on the reasonable accommodation. Other times, the interactive process can be complicated and contentious.

Sometimes, employers do not know about or understand the disability enough to determine a reasonable accommodation. In these cases, employers are entitled to obtain documentation, such as medical records or a letter from a doctor, to learn about the disability, its functional limitations, and the sort of accommodation that needs to be made. Alternatively, employers may simply ask the requesting employee about the disability and limitations. Unless the disability is obvious, that employee must provide the employer with sufficient information about the disability to help the employer determine a reasonable accommodation.

As long as the reasonable accommodation is effective in allowing the disabled individuals to perform their job functions and receive the same benefits as other, non-disabled individuals, then employers have the right to choose among reasonable accommodation options. Employers may choose options that are cheaper or easier to provide, for example. If employers offer disabled employees reasonable accommodations that employees do not want, the employers may not force the employees to accept the accommodations. If, however, the employee's refusal of the reasonable accommodation results in the individual's inability to perform the essential functions of the job, the employee may be deemed unqualified for the job. The employer may then be justified in terminating the employee.

During the hiring process, employers are not permitted to ask whether job applicants require a reasonable accommodation unless an applicant's disability is obvious, such as an applicant who uses a wheelchair, or unless the applicant voluntarily informs the employer about the disability. If the employer offers the applicant a job, it is with the condition that the applicant is able to perform the essential job functions either with or without a reasonable accommodation. Once the applicant receives the job offer, the employer may inquire about the necessity of reasonable accommodations.

The ADA also mandates that employees with disabilities be permitted to enjoy the same benefits and privileges of employment as non-disabled employees enjoy. Therefore, employers must provide reasonable accommodations to allow the disabled worker to gain access to such privileges as workplace cafeterias or lounges, gyms or health clubs, training programs, credit unions, transportation, or any other perk offered to non-disabled employees. A blind employee, for example, would not be able to read employment related notices placed on bulletin boards. In that case, the employer would have to provide a reasonable accommodation, such as sending that employee telephone messages.

## Types of Reasonable Accommodations

An employer may restructure or modify a job as a reasonable accommodation for an employee with a disability. Job restructuring may include reallocating job functions or trading certain job functions that are difficult or impossible for the disabled worker with other job functions of a non-disabled worker. A disabled secretary who cannot climb stairs, for example, may be able to fulfill the essential functions of the job but cannot easily retrieve files from the upstairs storage room. In this case, an appropriate accommodation would be to assign the disabled worker additional filing duties and require an able-bodied co-worker to actually retrieve the files.

A disabled worker may be entitled to a paid or unpaid leave of absence from the job as a reasonable accommodation for such reasons as the worker's need for surgery or other medical treatment, the worker's recovery from illness related to the disability, or the worker's education or training related to the disability. An employer does not have to pay the disabled worker during a disability-related leave of absence beyond the employer's own policy regarding sick pay or vacation pay. The employer is required to hold open the disabled worker's job during the leave of absence, but the employer may demonstrate that holding open the position for an extended period would constitute an undue hardship. In the event of undue hardship, the employer can fill the disabled worker's position with another employee but then must try to identify an equivalent position for the disabled worker when the leave of absence ends.

Unless doing so would cause an undue hardship to the employer, the employer must allow a disabled worker the option of a modified or part-time work schedule if required by the disability. This may be necessary for individuals who need medical treatment periodically. Another type of job modification involves workplace policies. An employer who prohibits workers from eating or drinking at their workstations may amend that policy for a worker with a disability that requires this worker to eat or drink at specific times of the day. An employer who requires employees to work at the employer's office rather than at home may alter the policy if a disabled worker can perform the essential job functions from home but cannot perform them at the office.

An employer may claim that undue hardship prevents the provision of reasonable accommodations, but undue hardship is not easy to prove. The employer must demonstrate that the specific reasonable accommodation being considered would cause significant difficulty or expense. The determination of undue hardship is made on a case-by-case basis, and courts consider such factors as the type and cost of the accommodation, the financial resources of the employer, the number of employees, and the overall impact of the accommodation on the employer's operation. An employer cannot claim undue hardship resulting from fears or prejudices about an individual's disability or fears that an accommodation would result in a morale problem with co-workers. An employer may, however, demonstrate undue hardship if an accommodation would unduly disrupt the work of other employees.

## Additional Resources

*West's Encyclopedia of American Law.* West Group, 1998.

## Organizations

### U. S. Equal Employment Opportunity Commission

1801 L Street, NW

Washington, DC 20507 USA

Phone: 800-669-3362

URL: www.eeoc.gov

### Job Accommodation Network (JAN)

PO Box 6080

Morgantown, WV 26506-6080 USA

Phone: 800-232-9675

URL: http://janweb.icdi.wvu.edu/

### ADA Disability and Business Technical Assistance Centers USA

Toll-Free: 800-949-4232

# ATTORNEYS

## ATTORNEY FEES

*Sections within this essay:*

## Background

At the outset, it must be said that in the United States, the long-standing rule (derived from common law) is that each side to a legal controversy must pay for its own attorney. The prevailing litigant is generally not entitled to collect a reasonable attorney's fee from the loser. *Alyeska Pipeline Service Co. v. Wilderness Society,* 421 U.S. 240, 247 (1975). This is often referred to as the American rule (as distinguished from the English rule, which permits fee-shifting and derives from court-made law).

Of course, there are numerous common law exceptions and nearly two hundred statutory exceptions, some, if not most, having been enacted by Congress to encourage private litigants to implement public policy. For example, an award of attorney's fees is often statutorily designed to address the unequal bargaining and/or litigating power of big corporations or government against individual plaintiffs. Accordingly, provisions awarding attorneys' fees are most often found in consumer or citizen-oriented litigation, such as that found in civil rights, environmental protection, and consumer protection areas of law.

Under these exceptions, federal courts (and some federal agencies) may order the losing party in a lawsuit to pay the winning party's attorney's fees. In 1997, Congress enacted a statute that provided for the award of attorney's fees in some criminal defense cases. Additionally, the Equal Access to Justice Act (EAJA) provides for the United States to pay attorney fees in many court matters and some administrative proceedings in which the United States is a losing party and has failed to prove that its position was substantially justified.

All this having been said, in most matters of private litigation between private parties, the American rule still applies. Despite tort reform efforts by the

Bush Administration to adopt a "loser pays" rule, as well as the Common Sense Legal Reforms Act, which was part of the "Contract With America" legislation proposed by Republican House Members in 1994, the American rule continues.

### *Exceptions*

The American rule has two major common law exceptions, mostly affecting federal court litigation: the common benefit doctrine and the bad faith doctrine. The common benefit exception generally applies in cases where a particular plaintiff or number of plaintiffs have born the legal expenses for the benefit of a larger group of potential plaintiffs, as in shareholders' derivative suits or class actions. In these matters, district courts may equitably order that attorney fees for the plaintiffs be reimbursed from the total amount of the judgment.

The bad faith exception may be invoked under circumstances in which either an attorney or a party has acted in bad faith when filing or pursuing litigation, often evidenced by the frivolous nature of the particular claim. In this set of exceptions, the underlying rationale behind the award of attorney fees is not that of fee-shifting *per se,* but rather punitive in nature. [See, for example, *Hall v. Cole,* 412 U.S. 1, 5 (1973)].

## Types of Fee Arrangements

Attorneys charge for their services using a variety of fee structures and arrangements. Prospective clients who retain counsel to represent them should know in advance what such services will cost, commit the fee agreement to a writing, and understand their recourse if they believe there has been a deviation from the agreement. This does not imply dishonesty or misrepresentation on the part of counsel, but rather, the possibility of misunderstanding or miscomprehension between counsel and client.

Attorneys consider several factors when setting their fees. These include the area of law invoked, the experience of the lawyer, the simple or complicated nature of the issue, and the amount of time it will take to legally resolve the matter. The more aggressively an attorney wages a legal battle, the more expensive it becomes. Moreover, attorneys may not be able to offer a fair quote for their fee if a prospective client has waited until the last minute to obtain legal counsel, and matters must be acted upon very quickly. In such cases, the fees will typically be higher than otherwise.

Importantly, when dealing with a law firm instead of a sole practitioner, a legal client may be surprised to find that the attorney handling much of the case is not the one who initially met with the client. If a client wishes to retain a particular attorney within the firm to handle the case, this arrangement must be expressly articulated and agreed upon.

Finally, it should be noted that many of the routine legal services provided by law firms are performed by paralegals, and not attorneys. When this is the case, any fee arrangement should reflect a lowered hourly rate for these services, charged separately from attorney's rates.

### *Hourly Fees*

The most common form of charging legal clients is through an hourly rate. Most attorneys charge a rate between $100 and $300 per hour. Top legal counsel, with a reputation for success in complex or highly visible cases, may charge more. Rates tend to be higher in major urban areas, and in matters requiring special legal expertise (e.g., admiralty, tax, patent law).

The majority of attorneys charge in tenth-of-an-hour increments (every six minutes, expressed as 0.10 hours) for hourly fees. Since one-tenth of an hour (or six minutes) is the least billable amount, attorneys routinely bill for one-tenth of an hour even if only one or two minutes were physically spent on the case, e.g., a quick email or voice mail message; reviewing and signing correspondence, etc. This is neither improper nor illegal. In actuality, an attorney has dropped his or her other work to concentrate on the present case, thinking about what should be done or how it should be done; therefore, the final correspondence or voice mail does not truly reflect the actual amount of minutes spent on the matter.

Hourly charges tend to add up quickly, especially when every tenth of an hour is included. Clients may wish to discuss with their attorneys several money-saving measures, including discounted rates after a certain number of hours are worked in any month (the discounted rate applying to the excess hours). Clients may also wish to cap the total number of hours or fees charged. By the time most **discovery** is completed, both sides have a better idea of what the case is worth, and whether it is worth taking to trial. A client may request that the attorney try to settle the lawsuit once legal fees reach a certain amount. Even if the settlement amount is less than desired, it may be the wiser choice if additional legal fees and costs of trial would eat up the difference in dollar amount anyway.

Clients can also negotiate prior approval of major legal maneuvers, although deference to counsel's opinion should be exercised. For example, to save money, an attorney may serve written **interrogatories** upon a witness rather than take his **deposition** before a court reporter. However, if the attorney wishes to spring a question upon the witness by surprise (and to which the witness must answer immediately, without preparation), a deposition may be a smarter tactic, even though it costs more. Most conscientious attorneys discuss the pros and cons of various legal maneuvers with their clients as preparation for trial nears.

A final cost-cutting measure is to pay the top hourly rate for the best trial attorney, but ask for a less experienced attorney in the law firm, at a lower hourly rate, to handle the more routine matters. This is often the practice regardless, but either way, should be clarified in advance.

### Flat or Fixed Fees

Recognizing the runaway nature of hourly fees, many law firms and attorneys have established fixed or flat rates for routine legal matters, such as a simple will, a power of attorney, or a first DUIL (driving while under the influence of alcohol).

Typically, more complex legal matters are set up on a mixed fee basis. For example, a non-contested divorce may have a flat fee of $1500. But neither party to the divorce can guarantee that it will non-contested; an attorney's duty is to get the best advantage for his or her client. Therefore, an attorney may stipulate in a fee agreement that if some areas of the divorce settlement become contested, an hourly fee will be added to the $1500 flat fee for the resolution of the disputed matter.

Likewise, a prospective client may be quoted a flat fee of, e.g. $750 for a first-time charge of drunk driving. However, if it later turns out that the client had a previous drunk driving charge not communicated to the attorney, the fees will likely increase. Often, in matters involving a lawsuit, an attorney will charge a fixed or flat fee for all work performed up to the point of trial (or settlement), after which a separate fee will be added for each day at trial. This is because preparation for trial constitutes intense labor. Actually trying a case requires an entirely different set of skills and labor; hence, additional fees (usually by hour or day).

### Contingent Fees

In many litigation-oriented legal matters, the attorney representing the complaining party who suffered a loss (**plaintiff**) will take a percentage of the money received from either a settlement or a jury verdict (or judge's award) as the applicable fee. This type of fee arrangement is common in lawsuits involving money damages, such as for personal injury, medical malpractice, worker's compensation, employment discrimination or wrongful termination, etc. (Conversely, it is common for attorneys who represent the defendant in such matters to charge an hourly fee.)

Contingency fees are usually expressed as a percentage, and the payment of the fee is *contingent* upon success at trial or the client having prevailed in the legal matter. The fee may be based upon a percentage of the dollar amount or the value of property secured or won for the client, such as a contract. For this reason, attorneys carefully assess a potential lawsuit to determine the likelihood of success before they agree to represent a prospective client on a contingency fee basis.

Most contingency fee agreements quote a fee between 25 and 40 percent of the settlement, verdict or award. Importantly (see below), this percentage may be based on the gross settlement/verdict amount, or (less commonly) the net amount after deductions for costs and expenses.

Many contingent fee arrangements have a sliding-scale basis similar to the flat fee with add-on charges for complication. For example only, a contingency agreement may stipulate that if the legal controversy is negotiated to a settlement prior to the filing of a lawsuit, the fee will be 25 percent of the settlement amount. If the case continues and is settled in the interim between filing and trial, the fee will be 33.33 percent (the oft-quoted one-third attorney fee). But if the attorney must try the case, the fee will be 40 percent. Again, this sliding scale is meant to reflect the amount of work the attorney does at each stage of the litigation.

Contingency fees are not appropriate in all legal matters, and may in fact violate state ethics rules (see below). In divorce cases, for example, angry spouses may be determined to "bleed the other spouse dry" with hefty legal fees, and do so by challenging each and every settlement clause in court. Contingency fees are generally not permitted in criminal defense matters and most divorce cases. Likewise, it would be inappropriate for an attorney to charge a fee contingent upon whether or not the client is awarded custody of children (some states do allow contingency fees in property divisions based upon a percentage of the value of property secured for the client).

### Retainer Fees

For representation in a particular legal matter, a true retainer fee is not a separate or distinct fee, but rather an advancement of fees against what will ultimately be owed to the attorney, i.e., a "down payment" or credit toward what is owed. It is a guarantee that a client has "retained" a law firm or attorney for legal representation, and that, as such, the attorney or firm will be paid for work completed in behalf of the client's case.

A variation of this type of retainer fee is actually more like a flat fee paid in advance. Sometimes an attorney will estimate the amount needed to resolve a legal matter (see cautions mentioned above) and require the payment up front to "retain" his or her services.

In either of these retainer arrangements, a portion of the retainer fee may or may not be non-refundable. However, where the fee represents an advancement of fees for work actually done, attorneys and law firms must itemize the actual hours worked, or the work actually completed, in order to draw from the retained fee. Any excess fee will then be returned to the client (see remedies, discussed below).

An exception to the return of excess retainer funds involves still another classic form of retainer fee. This type of fee arrangement involves retaining a law firm or attorney to be at the service of, or on call and on demand for, (usually) a corporate client or wealthy individual with recurring legal problems. For a flat fee (generally on an annual basis), legal service and representation is on demand for the client, even to the extent that other clients or cases are turned down in order to serve the client. The retainer fee ensures that an attorney will always be available or "on call" to answer a client's legal questions, provide counsel and advice, or intervene/intercede on behalf of the client in a pending matter or dispute. This type of retainer fee is generally non-refundable, even if the client ultimately makes little use of the retained services over the subject period of retainer.

### Statutory Fees

For certain legal matters, the attorney fee is set by law. Whether by state law or federal statute, and as previously mentioned, the award or payment of attorney fees is generally invoked in cases involving matters of public concern (e.g., willful environmental pollution), or major violations of constitutional rights (e.g., civil rights violations under federal law).

At one time, the American Bar Association (ABA) favored a statutory scheme to standardize minimum fees or "recommended fee schedules" to circumvent fee-cutting competition and preserve the integrity of the legal profession. However, in 1975, the U.S. Supreme Court held that minimum fee schedules violated the Sherman Anti-Trust Act. Notwithstanding, many states and federal laws restrict maximum fees that may be charged for certain matters, as for probating a will or (with tort reform) in medical malpractice actions.

State laws awarding attorney fees, or providing for a fixed fee or percentage, or mandating court approval for a proposed fee are too varied to include herein. The following federal civil rights statutes provide for attorney fees to be paid:

- Civil Rights Act of 1964, Title II (Public Accommodations)
- Civil Rights Act of 1964, Title III (Public Facilities)
- Civil Rights Act of 1964, Title VII (Equal Employment Opportunities)
- Fair Housing Act
- Fair Labor Standards Act
- Age Discrimination in Employment Act of 1967
- Equal Credit Opportunity Act
- Voting Rights Act of 1965
- Civil Service Reform Act of 1978
- Age Discrimination Act of 1975
- Civil Rights of Institutionalized Persons Act
- Rehabilitation Act of 1973
- Individuals with Disabilities Education Act
- Americans with Disabilities Act of 1990
- Civil Rights Attorney's Fees Awards Act of 1976

### Prepaid Legal Plans

Usually associated with employers, unions, or credit union membership, prepaid legal plans operate like prepaid health organizations. Participants pay a monthly fee in exchange for access to legal advice and/or legal representation from one of the plan's member attorneys. However, most plans limit the number of services and/or number of hours of legal assistance each month. Also, types and costs for different services can vary from plan to plan. If, after consulting with legal counsel under the plan, it is determined that litigation or more intense legal work will be required, additional charges (established up front with plan membership) will apply. Additional information about prepaid legal plans can be obtained from American Prepaid Legal Services Institute (APLSI), 321 North Clark Street, Chicago IL 60601 (312) 988-5751, Web site at www.aplsi.org. APLSI is affiliated with the American Bar Association.

### Pro Bono Services

The Latin term "pro bono," being shortened in common usage from "pro bono publico," literally means for the good of the public. In cases involving social injustices (e.g., sexual harassment by an employer, freedom of speech or religion, spousal abuse, discrimination in housing or employment, whistle-blowing, environmental pollution), legal fees may be waived by attorneys or nonprofit legal organizations interested in the outcome of the case, especially if it raises new and important issues of law.

Some of the organizations that may offer legal resources or pro bono representation include the American Civil Liberties Union (ACLU), the National Association for the Advancement of Colored People (NAACP) Legal Defense Fund, the Natural Resources Defense Council, the National Women's Law Center, and the Lambda Legal Defense and Education Fund (for gay and lesbian rights).

## What is Covered by Fees

### Initial Consultation

Many attorneys do not charge for an initial private consultation. This is particularly true for plaintiff-oriented cases where the attorney will ultimately charge on a contingency fee basis. During the initial consultation, the attorney will assess the merits of success on the potential claim or lawsuit. However, if the purpose of consultation is for the rendering of a simple legal opinion, most attorneys will charge a relatively small fee, e.g., less than $100.

Since everything communicated during the initial consultation is protected by **attorney-client privilege,** it is important that clients are open and honest

with the attorney, providing all known information and (crucially) even the damaging facts. Even a low consultation fee is worthlessly spent if the attorney is not able to fairly assess the case because of withheld information.

During the initial consultation, the question of fees should be addressed and committed to writing. (This is also an appropriate time for the client to assess the experience, skills, and effectiveness of counsel.)

### Fees vs. Costs

Unfortunately, horror stories abound in which seriously injured plaintiffs who win their cases nonetheless take home less money than their attorneys. In all fairness, while it is true that an attorney or law firm may receive a large share of the settlement/verdict/award, the money does not all go to the attorneys. Costs and expenses often devour the largest chunk of the proceeds. In their minds, plaintiffs are thinking they will receive two-thirds of any settlement or award, based on e.g., a 33.33 percent contingency fee. But in reality, another third of the proceeds may be spent on costs and expenses associated with the case. In the end, the injured plaintiff may go home with one third, and the law firm will keep two-thirds of the proceeds (but earn considerably less once all costs and expenses are reimbursed). This, precisely, is what contributes to the perception that the "lion's share went to the lawyers."

Such a scenario is particularly true in personal injury/medical malpractice cases that require copious amounts of medical analyses and expert witness opinions. Trial expert witnesses charges thousands of dollars for reviewing files, rendering opinions (upon which reputations may be staked) and appearing to testify at trial.

But in reality, the attorneys only keep the agreed-upon fee. If they also receive monies for costs and expenses, it is merely to repay them for bills they have paid on behalf of the client. Costs are ultimately the responsibility of clients, even if initially paid by the law firm in order to move the case forward. Costs are itemized separately from the fee charged by attorneys for their legal work.

Costs include charges for all court filings (complaint, motions, discovery, etc.), process serving, investigations, mailing, photocopying, service of subpoenas for appearance of witnesses, as well as for records and document retrieval, court reporters and transcripts of depositions, motions, and other related proceedings, jury fees and mileage, expert witness fees and travel/lodging fees for both witnesses and attorneys.

Most often, costs are deducted from the gross amount of the settlement/verdict/award *after* the deduction of attorney fees. In other words, the attorney fee will be based on a percentage of the *gross* amount recovered, not the net amount after costs are deducted. Second in line will come such a deduction for costs and expenses paid or owing on behalf of the client. Finally, the remaining balance will represent the client's proceeds or share of the money.

### Fee Sharing and Fee Splitting

Generally, fee sharing or fee-splitting arrangements between attorneys do not increase the bottom-line fee paid by a client. However, there are ethical and professional rules addressing these subjects, and one recurring theme is that such arrangements must be communicated to a client in advance.

For example, ABA Model Rule 1.5(e) states that a division of fees between attorneys from different law firms may be made only if (1) the division is proportionate to the services performed by the respective attorneys, or a client agrees in writing that each attorney assumes joint responsibility for the representation; 2)the client is advised of and does not object to the participation of the additional attorneys; and (3)the total fee is reasonable.

## Ethical Considerations

### IOLTA Funds

The Interest on Lawyers' Trust Accounts (IOLTA) program has been adopted by all state bar associations and the District of Columbia as an innovative way to do a public good; simplify accounting on clients' accounts; and prevent the temptation of misuse/abuse of earned interest on those accounts. By authority of state supreme courts or legislative acts, attorneys can deposit client funds that are too small in amount, or are deposited for too short a time to earn interest, in a state-wide IOLTA account. These accounts represent pooled, interest-bearing trust accounts.(Larger amounts from clients are placed in client bank accounts where interest inures back to the benefit of the clients.)

Since the pooled funds generate interest where none had been previously paid, IOLTA provides a public benefit without cost to taxpayers. The funds are earmarked through a local grant process to not-for-profit organizations throughout each state. They are generally used to fund civil legal services for the poor, or for law-related public education or administration of justice.

### American Bar Association Code and Model Rules

State bar associations address ethical considerations of attorney fee-setting in their bar rules of professional conduct or professional responsibility. All states have similar rules, most often parallel to, or adopting *ver batim,* the ABA Model Rules or ABA Model Code of Professional Responsibility.

ABA Model Rule 1.5 states that a lawyer's fee must be reasonable. The rule lists the same criteria and factors to consider (in determining reasonableness) as those used when lawyers first assess a legal matter and then establish their fee arrangement with a client. These factors include the time and labor involved, the requisite legal skills needed, the fee customarily charged for such services, and the experience and reputation of the lawyer.

The ABA Model Code of Professional Responsibility, DR 2-106 prohibits clearly excessive fees. Factors to be considered as guidelines in determining the reasonableness or excessiveness of the fee again parallel the same considerations recommended when first establishing fees (see Rule 1.5, above).

More importantly, ABA Model Rule 1.5(d) prohibits fee arrangements that (1)are contingent upon the securing of a divorce, or the amount of alimony or support; or (2) are contingent fees for legal representation in a criminal defense matter.

## Recourse and Remedies

Attorneys cannot guarantee results. Clients must pay for the services rendered, whether they agree with the outcome or not. However, there are some measures that can be taken if an attorney has done something illegal or improper.

### Fees Owed to Attorneys Who Are Fired

If a client is unhappy with an attorney's representation, and hires another attorney, there are two caveats worthy of mention here. First, it is a violation of an attorney's code of ethics to work on a file or legal case while another attorney is still officially handling it. Therefore, a client should discharge the previous attorney in writing. Secondly, the terminated attorney is nonetheless entitled to compensation for the work completed thus far, and may place an attorney's lien on the file/case through the court. When the client is finally paid on the matter, the original attorney will receive whatever compensation he or she earned. If the original agreement was for a contingency fee, and the second attorney completed work on the case, the contingency fee will be split, with or without court intervention. Many jurisdictions permit the first (discharged) attorney to be paid a reasonable hourly fee for work completed, rather than a percentage of the contingency. The discharged attorney will need to itemize work done on the file prior to being discharged.

### Escrowed Funds and Retainers

Attorneys cannot spend retainer fees or funds advanced to them (fees, not costs) before earning them. State bar rules require attorneys to deposit all retainer and advance payment funds into interest-bearing accounts, which can only be withdrawn as the legal work is completed and billed against the account. Any interest earned on the account is usually donated to nonprofit legal clinics or (long-term) returned to the client.

If a client believes that an attorney has not returned excess retainer funds, or has not accounted for the entire amount in an itemized statement, the first step should be in the form of registered/certified correspondence to the attorney, requesting explanation. If such a step fails to satisfy the client, the next contact should be to the state bar association, which will have a forum for filing grievances against attorneys.

### Unreasonable Fees

Even though attorneys have quoted certain fees to a prospective client, they may be open to negotiating a lower fee, based upon the client's articulated reasons. Additionally, attorneys may allow installment payments or other payment plans to help clients meet their obligations.

However, if the fee paid is questionable, or the costs and expenses attached to the file seem unreasonable, the first step should be a registered/certified correspondence to the attorney, requesting explanation. If such a step fails to satisfy the client, the next contact should be the state bar association, which will have a forum for filing grievances against attorneys.

### Arbitration

For unresolved fee controversies between attorney and client, arbitration or mediation may offer an appropriate forum for resolution. This is particularly true if the reasonableness of a fee or the costs on a file case are questioned. The state bar association is the best place to start, and may be able to provide either an arbitration forum, or a list of private arbitrators and mediators skilled in this area. Finally, it should be noted that unhappiness with the costs or fees charged by the attorney does not necessarily mean that the charges were unreasonable. If the possibility of high costs was communicated to the client in advance, along with the amount and type of fee, the client's chance of prevailing at arbitration are slim.

Sometimes, as in personal injury cases, a client agrees to the fee and anticipated costs (e.g., for medical expert witnesses) and subsequently prevails at trial, but the verdict or award is less than anticipated. A good attorney may be willing to attempt to negotiate a reduced charge from the expert witnesses, along with some reduction in the attorney fee. However, the attorney is under no obligation to do either.

## Additional Resources

Cohen, Henry. "Awards of Attorneys' Fees by Federal Courts and Federal Agencies." CRS Report for Congress. Updated 24 January 2006. Washington: Library of Congress, Congressional Research Service.

"Fact Sheet on Interest on Lawyers' Trust Accounts (IOLTA)." American Bar Association Commission on IOLTA. Available at http://www.nlada.org/DMS/Documents/IOLTA

# ATTORNEYS

## ATTORNEY-CLIENT PRIVILEGE

*Sections within this essay:*

- Background

- The Elements, Scope, Application of the Attorney-Client Privilege
    - Elements of the Attorney-Client Privilege
    - Scope and Application of the Attorney-Client Privilege

- State Rules Governing Attorney-Client Privilege

## Background

The **attorney-client privilege** is an evidentiary rule that protects both attorneys and their clients from being compelled to disclose confidential communications between them made for the purpose of furnishing or obtaining legal advice or assistance. The privilege is designed to foster frank, open, and uninhibited discourse between attorney and client so that the client's legal needs are competently addressed by a fully prepared attorney who is cognizant of all the relevant information the client can provide. The attorney-client privilege may be raised during any type of legal proceeding, civil, criminal, or administrative, and at any time during those proceedings, pre-trial, during trial, or post-trial.

The privilege dates back to ancient Rome, where governors were forbidden from calling their advocates as witnesses out of concern that the governors would lose confidence in their own defenders. In 1577 the first evidentiary privilege recognized by the

English **common law** was the attorney-client privilege. The English common law protected the confidential nature of attorney-client communications, regardless of whether those communications took place in public or in private. The American colonies adopted this approach to the attorney-client privilege, and Delaware codified the privilege in its first constitution in 1776.

## The Elements, Scope, and Application of the Attorney-Client Privilege

### Elements of the Attorney-Client Privilege

Because the attorney-client privilege often prevents disclosure of information that would be relevant to a legal proceeding, courts are cautious when examining objections grounded in the privilege. Most courts generally require that certain elements be demonstrated before finding that the privilege applies. Although the elements vary from **jurisdiction** to jurisdiction, one often cited recitation of the elements was articulated in *U.S. v. United Shoe Machinery Corp.*, 89 F.Supp. 357 (D.Mass. 1950), where the court enumerated the following five-part test: (1) the person asserting the privilege must be a client or someone attempting to establish a relationship as a client; (2) the person with whom the client communicated must be an attorney and acting in the capacity as an attorney at the time of the communication; (3) the communication must be between the attorney and client exclusively; (4) the communication must be for the purpose of securing a legal opinion, legal services, or assistance in some legal proceeding, and not for the purpose of committing a crime or **fraud**; and (5) the privilege may be claimed or waived by the client only.

### Scope and Application of the Attorney-Client Privilege

The five-part test is typically the starting point in a court's analysis of a claim for privilege. Each element appears straight-forward on its face but can be tricky to apply, especially when the client is a corporation and not a natural person. **Corporate** clients raise questions as to who may speak for the corporation and assert the attorney-client privilege on behalf of the entity as a whole. Some courts have ruled that the attorney-client privilege may only be asserted by the upper management of a corporation. A vast majority of courts, however, have ruled that the privilege may be asserted not only by a corporation's officers, directors, and board members, but also by any employee who has communicated with an attorney at the request of a corporate superior for the purpose of obtaining legal advice. *Upjohn Co. v. U.S.*, 449 U.S. 383, 101 S.Ct. 677, 66 L.Ed.2d 584, (U.S. 1981).

Whether the client is a natural person or a corporation, the attorney-client privilege belongs only to the client and not to the attorney. As a result, clients can prevent attorneys from divulging their secrets, but attorneys have no power to prevent their clients from choosing to waive the privilege and testifying in court, talking to the police, or otherwise sharing confidential attorney-client information with third parties not privy to the confidential discussions. Clients may waive attorney-client privilege expressly by their words or implicitly by their conduct, but a court will only find that the privilege has been waived if there is a clear indication that the client did not take steps to keep the communications confidential. An attorney's or a client's inadvertent disclosure of confidential information to a third party will not normally suffice to constitute **waiver**. If a client decides against waiving the privilege, the attorney may then assert the privilege on behalf of the client to shield both the client and the attorney from having to divulge confidential information shared during their relationship.

In most situations, courts can easily determine whether the person with whom a given conversation took place was in fact an attorney. However, in a few cases courts are asked to decide whether the privilege should apply to a communication with an unlicensed or disbarred attorney. In such instances, courts will frequently find that the privilege applies if the client reasonably believes that he or she was communicating with a licensed attorney. *State v. Berberich*, 267 Kan. 215, 978 P.2d 902 (Kan. 1999). But courts in some jurisdictions have relaxed this standard, holding that the privilege applies to communications between clients and unlicensed lay persons who represent them in administrative proceedings. Woods on Behalf of *T.W. v. New Jersey Dept. of Educ.*, 858 F.Supp. 51 (D.N.J. 1993).

Although many courts emphasize that the attorney-client privilege should be strictly applied to communications between attorney and client, the attorney-client privilege does extend beyond the immediate attorney-client relationship to include an attorney's partners, associates, and office staff members (e.g., secretaries, file clerks, telephone operators, messengers, law clerks) who work with the attorney in the ordinary course of their normal duties. However, the presence of a third party who is not a member of the attorney's firm will sometimes defeat a claim for privilege, even if that third person is a member of the client's family.

Thus, one court ruled that in the absence of any suggestion that a criminal defendant's father was a confidential agent of the **defendant** or that the father's presence was reasonably necessary to aid or protect the defendant's interests, the presence of the defendant's father at a **pretrial conference** between the defendant and his attorney invalidated the attorney-client privilege with respect to the conference. *State v. Fingers*, 564 S.W.2d 579 (Mo.App. 1978). In the corporate setting, the presence of a client's sister defeated a claim for attorney-client privilege that involved a conversation between a client-company's president and the company's attorney, since the sister was neither an officer nor director of the company and did not possess an ownership interest in the company. *Cherryvale Grain Co. v. First State Bank of Edna*, 25 Kan.App.2d 825, 971 P.2d 1204 (Kan.App. 1999).

Many courts have described attorney-client confidences as "inviolate." *Wesp v. Everson*, — P.3d —, 2001 WL 1218767 (Colo. 2001). However, this description is misleading. The attorney-client privilege is subject to several exceptions. Federal Rule of **Evidence** 501 states that "the recognition of a privilege based on a confidential relationship... should be determined on a case-by-case basis." In examining claims for privilege against objections that an exception should be made in a particular case, courts will balance the benefits to be gained by protecting the sanctity of attorney-client confidences against the probable harms caused by denying the opposing party access to potentially valuable information.

The crime-fraud exception is one of the oldest exceptions to the attorney-client privilege. The attorney-client privilege does not extend to communications made in connection with a client seeking advice on how to commit a criminal or **fraudulent** act. Nor will a client's statement of intent to commit a crime be deemed privileged, even if the client was not seeking advice about how to commit it. The attorney-client privilege is ultimately designed to serve the interests of justice by insulating attorney-client communications made in furtherance of adversarial proceedings. But the interests of justice are not served by forcing attorneys to withhold information that might help prevent criminal or fraudulent acts. Consequently, in nearly all jurisdictions attorneys can be compelled to disclose such information to a court or other investigating authorities.

A party seeking **discovery** of privileged communications based upon the crime-fraud exception must make a threshold showing that the legal advice was obtained in furtherance of the fraudulent activity and was closely related to it. The party seeking disclosure does not satisfy this burden merely by alleging that a crime or fraud has occurred and then asserting that disclosure of privileged communications might help prove the crime or fraud. There must be a specific showing that a particular document or communication was made in furtherance of the client's alleged crime or fraud.

The fact that an attorney-client relationship exists between two persons is itself not typically privileged. *U.S. v. Leventhal*, 961 F.2d 936 (11th Cir. 1992). However, if disclosure of an attorney-client relationship could prove incriminating to the client, some courts will enforce the privilege. *In re Michaelson*, 511 F.2d 882 (9th Cir. 1975). Names of clients and the amounts paid in fees to their attorneys are not normally privileged. Nor will clients usually be successful in asserting the privilege against attorneys who are seeking to introduce confidential information in a lawsuit brought by a client accusing the attorney of wrongdoing. In such instances courts will not allow clients to use the attorney-client privilege as a weapon to silence the attorneys who have represented them. Courts will allow both parties to have their say in **malpractice** suits brought by clients against their former attorneys.

## State Rules Governing Attorney-Client Privilege

The body of law governing the attorney-client privilege is comprised of federal and state legislation, court rules, and **case law**. Below is a sampling of state court decisions decided at least in part based on their own state's court rules, case law, or legislation.

ARKANSAS: Attempts by both an attorney and his secretary to communicate with the client regarding his pending criminal case were protected by the attorney-client privilege. Rules of Evid., Rule 502(b). *Byrd v. State*, 326 Ark. 10, 929 S.W.2d 151 (Ark. 1996).

ALABAMA: Where a defendant asserted that his guilty pleas to robbery charges were the product of his defense counsel's **coercion**, the absence of the defense counsel's **testimony** to rebut the defendant's testimony could not be excused by any assertion of the attorney-client privilege. *Walker v. State*, 2001 WL 729190 (Ala.Crim.App., 2001).

ARIZONA: By asserting that its personnel understood the law on stacking coverage for under insured and uninsured motorist claims, the insurer affirmatively injected legal knowledge of its claims managers into the insureds' **bad faith** action and thus effectively waived the attorney-client privilege as to any communications between the insurer and its **counsel** regarding the propriety of the insurer's policy of denying coverage. *State Farm Mut. Auto. Inc. Co. v. Lee*, 199 Ariz. 52, 13 P.3d 1169 (Ariz. 2000).

CALIFORNIA: The attorney-client privilege is not limited to litigation-related communications, since the applicable provisions of the state Evidence Code do not use the terms "litigation" or "legal communications" in their description of privileged disclosures but instead specifically refer to "the accomplishment of the purpose" for which the lawyer was consulted. West's Ann.Cal.Evid.Code §§ 912, 952. *STI Outdoor v. Superior Court*, 91 Cal.App.4th 334, 109 Cal.Rptr.2d 865 (Cal.App. 2 Dist. 2001).

ILLINOIS: To prevail on an attorney-client privilege claim in a corporate context, a claimant must first show that a statement was made by someone in the corporate control group, meaning that group of employees whose advisory role to top management in a particular area is such that a decision would not normally be made without their advice or opinion and whose opinion, in fact, forms the basis of any final decision by those with actual authority. *Hayes v. Burlington Northern and Santa Fe Ry. Co.*, 323 Ill.App.3d 474, 752 N.E.2d 470, 256 Ill.Dec. 590 (Ill.App. 1 Dist. 2001).

MAINE: Counsel's inadvertent disclosure of a memorandum to opposing counsel, which summarized a telephone conference between counsel and his client, did not constitute a waiver of the attorney-client privilege, where the document was mistakenly placed in boxes of unprivileged documents that were available to opposing counsel to photocopy and the memorandum in question was labeled "confidential and legally privileged." *Corey v. Norman, Hanson & DeTroy*, 742 A.2d 933, 1999 ME 196 (Me. 1999).

MASSACHUSETTS: Hospital personnel were neither the defendant's nor his attorney's agents when they conducted a blood-alcohol test on the defendant at the attorney's request for sole purpose of gathering potentially exculpatory evidence, and thus the state's **grand jury subpoena** of the test results did not violate the attorney-client privilege. *Commonwealth v. Senior*, 433 Mass. 453, 744 N.E.2d 614 (Mass. 2001).

MICHIGAN: A Court of Appeals reviews de novo a decision regarding whether the attorney-client privilege may be asserted. *Koster v. June's Trucking, Inc.*, 244 Mich.App. 162, 625 N.W.2d 82 (Mich.App. 2000).

MINNESOTA: The presence of the defendant's wife at a joint meeting in which the defendant, his attorney, and his wife discussed financial aspects of a possible **divorce** prevented the attorney-client privilege from attaching. *State v. Rhodes*, 627 N.W.2d 74 (Minn. 2001).

NEW JERSEY: The person asserting the attorney-client privilege bears the burden to prove it applies to any given communication. *Horon Holding Corp. v. McKenzie*, 341 N.J.Super. 117, 775 A.2d 111 (N.J.Super.A.D. 2001)

NEW YORK: A client's intent to commit a crime is not a protected confidence or secret for the purposes of the attorney-client privilege. N.Y.Ct.Rules, § 1200.19. *People v. DePallo*, 96 N.Y.2d 437, 754 N.E.2d 751, 729 N.Y.S.2d 649 (N.Y. 2001).

NORTH DAKOTA: A communication is confidential, for the purposes of determining the applicability of attorney-client privilege, if it is not intended to be disclosed to persons other than those to whom the disclosure is made during the course of rendering

professional legal services or to those reasonably necessary for transmission of the communication during the course of rendering professional legal services. Rules of Evid., Rule 502(a)(5). *Farm Credit Bank of St. Paul v. Huether*, 454 N.W.2d 710 (N.D. 1990).

OHIO: The attorney-client privilege is not absolute, and thus the mere fact that an attorney-client relationship exists does not raise a presumption of confidentiality of all communications made between the attorney and client. *Radovanic v. Cossler*, 140 Ohio App.3d 208, 746 N.E.2d 1184 (Ohio App. 8 Dist. 2000).

TEXAS: Physicians who were defending against a malpractice action were not entitled to discover, under fraud exception to attorney-client privilege, material relating to a **settlement** between the plaintiffs and another defendant, although the physicians alleged that disparate distribution of the settlement proceeds was a sham intended to deprive the physicians of settlement credit, since there was no evidence that the plaintiffs made or intended to make hidden distributions. Vernon's Ann.Texas Rules Civ.Proc., Rule 192.5(a); Rules of Evid., Rule 503(d)(1). **In re** Lux, 52 S.W.3d 369 (Tex.App. 2001).

WASHINGTON: The federal constitutional foundation for the attorney-client privilege is found in the Fifth Amendment **privilege against self-incrimination**, the Sixth Amendment right to counsel, and the Due Process Clause of the Fourteenth Amendment, as these rights can be protected only if there is candor and free and open discussion between client and counsel. U.S.C.A. Const.Amends. 5, 6, 14. In re Recall of Lakewood City Council Members, 144 Wash.2d 583, 30 P.3d 474 (Wash. 2001).

## Additional Resources

*American Jurisprudence* West Group, 1998.

*http://cyber.lp.findlaw.com/privacy/attorney_client.html*FindLa w: CyberSpace Law Center: Privacy: Attorney-Client Privilege.

*West's Encyclopedia of American Law* West Group, 1998.

## Organizations

### *The American Bar Association*
740 15th Street, N.W.
Washington, DC 20005-1019 USA
Phone: (202) 662-1000
Fax: (816) 471-2995

URL: http://w ww.abanet.org
Primary Contact: Robert J. Saltzman, President

### National Lawyers Association
P.O. Box 26005 City Center Square
Kansas City, MO 64196 USA
Phone: (800) 471-2994
Fax: (202) 662-1777
URL: http://w ww.nla.org

Primary Contact: Mario Mandina, CEO

### National Organization of Bar Counsel
515 Fifth Street, N.W.
Washington, DC 64196 USA
Phone: (202) 638-1501
Fax: (202) 662-1777
URL: http://w ww.nobc.org
Primary Contact: Robert J. Saltzman, President

# ATTORNEYS

## HOW TO FIND AN ATTORNEY

*Sections within this essay:*

## Background

When the United States handed down its decision in Bates v. State Bar of Arizona which struck down state laws prohibiting lawyers from advertising as an unconstitutional interference with free speech, it was widely thought that it would then be easier to find an attorney. This belief was based on the premise that since lawyers were allowed to compete in the same way as other businesses do, it would be easier to meet one's needs for legal representation and that the costs would go down.

It is true that lawyer advertising has made it easier to find an attorney. However, there is still a problem in finding the right attorney for one's particular needs. If the selected lawyer is inexperienced, incompetent, or lacks the willingness or ability to communicate effectively with a client, the client will not be satisfied with the lawyer's service. Furthermore, the consequences for the client could be catastrophic, such as losing a business or being unable to recover for injuries the client sustained at the hands of a liable third party. In order to find the best attorney, one needs more than a list of names, even if these are specialists in the relevant legal area. Clients are best served by asking questions before they decide on an attorney to retain.

Consumer dissatisfaction with lawyers has become a major problem. A survey taken in 1995 by Consumer's Union revealed that out of 30,000 respondents, one–third were not well satisfied with the quality of their attorneys' services. The reasons for this dissatisfaction varied, ranging from attorneys failing to keep their clients informed on the progress of their cases, failing to protect clients' interests, failing to resolve cases in a timely manner, and continually charge unreasonable fees. The reason for this widespread dissatisfaction is linked to the lack of knowledge by consumers on how to find attorneys experienced with the kinds of problems they are facing as well as knowing what questions to ask a lawyer they are considering retaining. The results of a one thousand person survey reported in the Florida Bar Journal revealed that the average time spent in finding a lawyer was two hours or less. Nearly one half of those surveyed said it was hard to find a good lawyer, and over a quarter of them said they did not know how to find a lawyer. It is remarkable that 80 per cent of respondents said they wished there was a source for information on lawyers' credentials.

### Why It Is Difficult to Find an Attorney

One difficulty in finding the appropriate attorney is the ever expanding number of specialties practiced by lawyers. Specialization makes selection more complicated. Law has become more specialized because changes in technology have necessitated the development of new areas, such as Cyberlaw and Internet law. New areas of law have also been created by recently enacted laws and regulations from such federal administrative bodies as the Environmental Protection Agency. This could impact and complicate the problems of a person acquiring a business and trying to determine whether the seller or the buyer is liable for cleaning up a toxic waste site. The increasing number of laws and regulations have forced lawyers to become more specialized in order to keep up with new developments. Furthermore, many general areas of the law in which an attorney could become proficient, have now been split up into specialties. In business law, there are specialists for mergers and acquisitions because of the complexity involved in these transactions. Even criminal law is not immune to this trend since some lawyers now specialize in white collar crime.

### When Do I Need A Lawyer?

Potential clients should retain a lawyer for any of the following reasons:

- if they have been charged with a felony

- if they have been served with papers naming them as defendants in a lawsuit

- if their insurance coverage is less than the amount a third party is claiming due to their negligence

- if they are making a will or changing it

- if they wish to adopt a child

- if someone with whom they are involved in a business setting breaches his or her contract with the client

- if they are resulting in substantial harm, or if the person suing them has a lawyer.

If a person is a **defendant** in a civil lawsuit and fails to appear in court, a **default judgment** will be entered by the court against them, and for all practical purposes, they will be unable to overturn it.

### Avoiding the Dishonest or Unethical Lawyers

This situation is easy to fall into because with the exception or Oregon, at least some part of the disciplinary process is kept private. This means that potential clients have no way of knowing whether a complaint has been made against a lawyer if no action has been taken. Although some complaints against lawyers are frivolous, the consumer has no way of knowing whether the decision by the state bar not to take any action was made in **good faith**. Furthermore, the action taken may only amount to a private reprimand in the form of a letter sent to the attorney. According to a recent investigation by the Washington Times, lawyers guilty of serious ethical violations and felonies are at the most only suspended for a limited period of time and made to make **restitution** to the client. Even the most severe punishment, disbarment, is not permanent since in most states the attorney can apply for reinstatement in five years.

Not only are the actions taken against lawyers found guilty of ethical violations not published in many states, this information is unavailable even in publications and databases relied upon by consumers to avoid this problem. There are attorneys listed in the well–respected Martindale–Hubbell Lawyers Directory who may be under suspension, disbarred, or imprisoned. The database set up by the American **Bar Association** (ABA) to allow consumers to find out whether a lawyer has been sanctioned is a great deal less than helpful since no details are given as to the offense charged or the punishment given.

Out of all the complaints made against lawyers, only one half of one per cent result in disbarment, and a total of only one and one half percent result in any **sanction** at all including private reprimands.

## Methods of Finding an Attorney

### By Advertisement

In an advertisement, consumers cannot obtain the information you need in order to make a wise decision. There is nothing upon which to judge the legal skills of the attorney, whether his style would be conducive to achieving specific goals as to how to resolve specific problem, or whether there have been any complaints against the attorney resulting in a reprimand, suspension or disbarment. It also cannot determine from an advertisement whether the attorney will be accessible enough so that they can communicate effectively with their clients and willing to take the time necessary so that they understand the possible outcomes of handling the client's case in a given manner.

### By Personal Referral

Friends and business acquaintances whose judgment is trusted is a good source in finding an attorney, if they have used the attorney for the same kind of problem that a consumer is facing or at least practices in a specialty pertaining to the consumer's situation. An even better source is a friend or acquaintance who actually is an active or recently retired lawyer or judge. Such persons can inform potential clients as to attorneys' reputation in the legal community.

### By Published Directories

### Martindale Hubbell Law Directory

This annually published directory is the oldest and best known of those available today. It includes lawyers practicing in the United States as well as 159 other countries. This coverage of foreign countries will continue to become more important as laws in the United States are affected by foreign and international law.

Each individual lawyer entry will contain the date of birth, the year first admitted to a state bar, numeric codes indicating where all listed educational degrees were earned Specialized areas of law in which they practice, and a listing of representative clients, the firm where the lawyer practices, and contact information. If the entry has the bar registry designation (BR), it means that they are also listed in the Martindale Hubbell Directory for Pre–Eminent Lawyers.

Despite its enormous size, not all practicing attorneys are listed. In order for an attorney or firm to be included in this directory, they must send the appropriate information to the publisher.

Many, but not all of the attorneys and firms listed, are rated according to their degree of legal skill and whether they follow the highest ethical standards. The rating "AV" is the highest rating given. A "BV" rating is still above average in terms of legal skills and an indication the attorney subscribes to the same high ethical standards as those given the "AV" rating. The "CV" rating denotes an average rating in terms of legal skills and an indication the lawyer also follows the highest ethical standards. No attorney is given a rating without their consent. The ratings are based on confidential written evaluations by practitioners and judges in the position to know the given lawyer. There is no rating to indicate that a lawyer is below average in legal ability or that he does not follow the highest ethical standards.

### Martindale Hubbell Bar Register of Pre–Eminent Lawyers

Listings are restricted to those individual attorneys and firms that have earned the "AV" rating and who practice in the United States and Canada. Instead of being grouped by state and within each state by the locality in which the lawyer practices, the lawyers are first grouped according to the specialty in which they practice. Sixty specialties are included.

The primary value of these directories in your search for an attorney is that they tell you how long that lawyer has been in practice, whether he specializes in an area relevant to the problem you are facing, and whether there may be a **conflict of interest** if you retain that attorney based on the clients they represent.

### The Best Lawyers in America 1999–2000

Now in its eighth edition, the information is based on the polling of 11,000 lawyers who were asked which attorneys in practice for a minimum of ten years they consider to be the best in their specialty. In the 1995–1996 edition only one and one half percent of all lawyers practicing in the United States were listed.

### Lawyer's Register International by Specialties and Fields of Law. 16th ed. 1999

This directory gives a worldwide listing of attorneys who represent themselves as being certified or designated as practicing in one or more of 390 legal specialties. The designation as a specialist is given for one of three reasons. First, the attorney has successfully completed a certification program given for that specialty in the state in which they practice. Second, the state in which the lawyer practices has designated them on a defacto basis that they have sufficient experience to be qualified in a given specialty. Third, they have been certified by the National Board of Trial Advocacy. There is a separate designation given for each of these three reasons why a lawyer is designated as certified in a given specialty.

The directory is arranged alphabetically by specialty, and within each specialty alphabetically by where they practice. In order to assist the consumer, a separate table lists all states that have established certification programs in particular specialties. By using this table, you are able to more easily select attorneys that have been certified by a state program in a given specialty.

### Chambers Guide to the Legal Profession 2000–2001

### Chambers Global The World's Leading Lawyers

Published in London, England, by Chambers and Partners, this source is designed for those trying to find an attorney practicing in one of over sixty specialized areas of business and **corporate** law.

Evaluations are from leading practitioners in each specialty obtained through telephone interviews averaging thirty minutes. During these interviews, the person interviewed is asked who they consider to be the best attorney in their specialty and why they hold such a high opinion of them. This procedure, unlike the written questionnaires upon which other lawyer directories rely, allows for a more thorough investigation of the legal abilities of a given attorney. This is because a interview by telephone avoids the **bias** that is inherent in written questionnaires since the ones returned in such surveys are much more likely to be favorable. Conversely, attorneys who do not respect the abilities of another practitioner are less likely to send in their written responses.

### By the Internet

- America Online (AOL) Anywhere Lawyer Directory URL: http://aol.lawyers.com – Besides acting as an online aid to finding an attorney, this site also contains a link to answer questions that need to be asked by those seeking legal representation.

- Martindale Hubbell Lawyer Locator URL: www.martindale.com – This is the most frequently used lawyer directory on the internet.

- Lawyers.com URL: www.lawyers.com – This site also belongs to Martindale–Hubbell, but it differs from the preceding web site because it targets individuals and small business people. This site allows searches to be narrowed to those attorneys practicing a particular specialty in a given locality. It also has links to help a consumer determine whether they need a lawyer, how attorneys bill their clients and how much they charge as well as a list of questions to ask an attorney before you decide to retain them.

- Chambers and Partners URL: http://www.chambersandpartners.com – This organization's home page has links that enable you to find evaluations of lawyers and law firms as to their legal skill in various areas of business and corporate law.

### By Lawyer Referral Services of State Bar Associations

These sources are useful only to the extent they can give consumers the names of lawyers in a given locality who practice law in a given specialty and who have agreed to have their name put on the list maintained by the Bar Association. For a small fee, usually $25 – $30, each attorney on the list agrees to give a fifteen to thirty minute consultation. This can be helpful because consumers can get an opinion from a lawyer as to whether they have a case and whether it is worth pursuing. This can save consumers a great deal of time and effort as opposed to attempting to research the matter on their own. During the consultation, the lawyer should be able to inform the potential client whether the **statute of limitations** for filing their particular claim has expired or not. Although consumers could do research on their own, just reading the **statute** may be insufficient to determine whether the statute of limitations has run out; they may have to read the **case law** on this matter. Regardless of what the attorney tells the consumer regarding their case, they are under no obligation to retain the lawyer's services.

The following are a short list of directory services available:

- ABA Directory of Lawyer Referral Services – This directory lists state wide and local bar association referral services. The local referral services specify which counties they serve. Each referral service will indicate whether they give referrals for all specialties or exclude certain ones. Information is also given as to whether low fee or **pro bono** (no fee) programs are provided for low income clients.

- Law and Legal Information Directory by Steven & Jacqueline O'Brien Wasserman – This source has an alphabetical listing by state of referral services located in that **jurisdiction**. Included are entries for services provided by the state bar as well as local bar associations. Street and web site addresses, regular and toll–free telephone numbers Are provided. If you qualify by income, a listing of legal aid offices arranged alphabetically by state and cities within will include the same information the lawyer referral section provides.

- Web Services – If you do not have access to either of the above titles, you may obtain information on the legal referral services offered by your state bar by logging on to www.findlaw.com. From this cite you will be led to links for each state which in turn will include links to that state's bar association and the lawyer referral service it provides.

## Questions to Ask Before Retaining a Lawyer

There are four purposes to this process. First, it allows consumers to determine whether the attorney has sufficient experience not just in the specialty pertaining to their problem, but also whether the lawyer has had previously solved a similar problem for another client. Second, they can learn whether his style is suited to their goals in resolving the dispute they have with the other side. For example, if a potential client is hoping for a **settlement**, a hardball Rambo like style may backfire. Third, they will discover how well they and the attorney communicate with one another. Fourth, they can ask the attorney if they are able to devote sufficient time and resources, such as a support staff, to their case.

Consumer Reports suggests that the following questions be asked during an interview with any attorney a consumer is considering retaining:

- How many years of experience do you have in this specialty and how have you handled similar disputes in the past?

- What are the possible results from pursuing this matter?

- How long will you expect it to take to resolve this matter?

- How will you keep me informed of what is happening as the case proceeds?

- Will anyone else, such as one of your associates or paralegals, be working on my case?

- Do you charge a flat or an hourly rate and how much?

- What other expenses will there be besides your fee and how are they calculated?

- What's a reasonable approximate figure for a total bill?

- Can you give me a written estimate?

- Can some of the work be handled by members of your staff at a lower rate?

- Will unforeseen events increase the amount you charge me?

- If you charge on a contingency basis, what proportion of the amount I recover will be paid to you as your fee and can this figure be calculated after the expenses are deducted?

- How often will I be billed, and how are billing disputes resolved? If we cannot settle this, will you agree to mandatory arbitration?

- Do you need any further information from me?

- Can I do some of the work in exchange for a lower bill?

- Do you recommend that this matter be submitted to an arbitrator or mediator, and do you know anyone qualified to do this?

## Additional Resources

*Profile 2000: Characteristics of Lawyer Referral and Information Service.* ABA Committee on Lawyer Referral and Information Service, 1999.

*How to Find the Best Lawyers: And Save over 50% in Legal Fees.* John Roesler, Message Co., 1996.

*Lawyer Referral and Information Service Handbook.* ABA, 1980 - Published biannually.

*Guide to Consumer Services: Consumer Union's Advice on Credit, Income Tax, Choosing a Doctor or Dentist, Finding a Lawyer, Closing Costs, Auto Repair and Much More.* Consumer's Union, 1979.

*Do I Really Need a Lawyer?* Kahon, Stewart & Robert M. Cavello, Chilton Book Co., 1979.

*Using a Lawyer and What to Do if Things Go Wrong.* HALT.

*Finding the Right Lawyer.* Jay Foonberg, ABA Section of Law Practice and Management, 1995.

*Choosing a Matrimonial Lawyer: 10 Criteria for Finding the Right One for You.* David M. Wildstein, Wilentz, Goldman, & Spitzer, 1996.

*Consumer's Guide to Getting Legal Help.* ABA, 2001.

*Let's Talk Law: Selecting a Lawyer.* Crest Video Marketing.

## Organizations

### Help Abolish Legal Tyranny (HALT)
1612 K St., N.W. Suite 510
Washington, D.C. 20006 USA

Phone: (202) 887-8255
Phone: (888) FOR-HALT
URL: www.halt.org

**American Society for Divorced and Separated Men**
575 Keep St.
Elgin, IL 60120 USA
Phone: (847) 665-2200

**National Whistleblower Center**
3238 P St., N.W.
Washington, D.C. 20007 USA
Phone: (202) 342-1902

**Christian Legal Society**
4208 Evergreen Lane, Suite 222
Annandale, VA 22003 USA
Phone: (703) 642-1070

**Chicago Divorce Association**
One Pierce Center
Itasca, IL 60143 USA
Phone: (630) 860-2100

**Atlanta Lawyers for the Arts**
152 Nassau St.
Atlanta, GA 30303 USA
Phone: (404) 585-6110

**Military Law Task Force**
1168 Union, #200

San Diego, CA 92101 USA
Phone: (619) 233-1701

**National Counsel of Black Lawyers**
116 W. 111th St., 3rd Floor
New York, NY 10026 USA

**National Lawyers Guild**
126 University Place, 5th floor
New York, NY 10003-4538 USA

**American Divorce Association of Men International**
1519 S. Arlington Heights Rd.
Arlington Heights, IL 60005 USA
Phone: (847) 364-1555

**Find the Children**
3030 Nebraska Ave., Suite 207
Santa Monica, CA 90404-4111 USA
Phone: (310) 998-8444

**Families for Private Adoption**
P.O. Box 6375
Washington, D.C. 20015 USA
Phone: (202) 722-0338

**National Health Law Program**
2639 S. LaCienega Blvd.
Los Angeles, CA 90034 USA
Phone: (310) 204-0891

# ATTORNEYS

## LICENSING OF ATTORNEYS

*Sections within this essay:*

## Background

The terms lawyer and attorney are commonly used interchangeably; one refers to the other. In each of the 50 states and the District of Columbia, the practice of law is limited to attorneys/lawyers who have been formally registered and admitted to practice in that state or district. Being admitted to practice is generally a three-fold process: graduation from an accredited law school, obtaining a passing score on the multi-state and state bar examinations, and meeting all character and fitness criteria estab-

lished by a state administrative board responsible for overseeing the practice of law in that state. The unlicensed practice of law, by either a layman or a trained lawyer who has failed to obtain licensure, carries serious consequences, including administrative, civil, and/or criminal sanctions.

Technically speaking, successful graduation from an accredited law school, along with passing scores on multi-state and state bar examinations, objectively determine professional competency of an individual to practice law. However, because incompetency or unprofessional conduct can result in serious harm or damage to a client, licensure is mandated to ensure the overall and continued competence of each practitioner.

As with other licensed professions, the practice of law is primarily self-policed by the state administrative body that admits each person to practice. The state maintains a continued interest in the competency of attorneys after admission to practice, and has power to suspend or rescind licenses to practice within the state. Most states also mandate periodic continued legal education (CLE) after law school, to ensure that lawyers stay current on changing law and procedural practice.

## History

The framers of the U.S. Constitution clearly believed that the interpretation of constitutional rights should be entrusted to specialists. Article III provides for an independent judicial power equal in power to the executive and legislative branches, and one which has jurisdiction over both states and individuals. It also created a federal judiciary with the power to determine whether Congress had exceeded its powers, and the power to review state court decisions in certain cases.

Early colonial legislation was primarily reviewed by administrative authorities in the mother countries (e.g., England, Spain, France). As colonial industry and population increased (to approximately 300,000 in 1700), review of colonial legislation came under increasing scrutiny. As for colonists, the necessity of dealing in commercial matters with English merchants, and the reliance on English law to support colonists' grievances against the crown, enhanced the desire to create a native force of legal professionals who understood the nuances of legal terms and clauses.

Apprenticeships were completed in a manner similar to England's Inns of Court. There was no formal "admission" to practice law, but, following "book" study and apprenticeship, prospective lawyers were "accepted" into practice by local and experienced members of the profession. By the time of the American Revolution, each colony had a bar of legally trained and respected professionals.

Eventually and especially in colonial cities, the legal profession enjoyed both social status and economic success. With such status, colonial lawyers became increasingly involved in politics as well; 25 of the 56 signatories to the Declaration of Independence were lawyers.

### Formation of an Early American Legal System

With newly-gained American independence came a certain political antipathy toward English law, resulting in the creation of several early statutes prohibiting the citation of any English decision handed down after independence. Loyalist attorneys returned to England, and those that stayed to seize political or judicial posts under the new government found much of their talents and expertise no longer in demand. The opportunity to broaden the base of American law was considerable, with an expressed interest in Roman and French law for enlightenment and guidance. (The Code of Napoleon did not appear until the beginning of the 19th century.) However, few judges or lawyers were versed in foreign languages, and the lack of an adequate body of American case law to bridge the gap left the legal bar in splinters.

For the above reasons, the quality of lawyers in the states was palpably inferior to the systemically-trained professionals of England. Early American lawyers were generally self-taught and self-read. Respected laypersons were often elected or appointed as judges to fill the gap and keep up with the newly burgeoning nation. During the early 1800s, the state of Rhode Island had a farmer serving as its chief justice, as well as a blacksmith serving as a member of its highest court. Early judges grappled with jurisprudential conflicts to form new law that would fit the peculiar needs of a young growing country, and especially, the needs peculiar to their own jurisdictions. Eventually, judges "rode circuits," i.e., they traveled from county seat to county seat, hearing cases, and lawyers often traveled with them.

As the volume of new American case law grew, the uncertainty of earlier parochial court decisions gave way to more predictable and standard outcomes. Local judges increasingly strove to shape their own decisions so as to provide consistency with that of other regional (and eventually, state) jurisdictions.

By the end of the Civil War (1860s), the influence of English law upon America was negligible, although familiar procedures, vocabulary, and conceptual approaches to legal jurisprudence survived and were incorporated into American law. A few states originally paralleled the English system by distinguishing barristers from solicitors within the legal profession (Massachusetts, New Jersey, New York, Virginia). However, by the mid-1800s, such distinctions were dropped in favor of a single class of lawyers who dealt directly with both clients and courtrooms.

### Legal Education

Notwithstanding the splintered beginnings of American law, the accepted preparation for becoming a lawyer remained the completion of an apprenticeship under a trained lawyer, along with self-reading of such printed sources as the American edition of William Blackstone's "Commentaries on the Laws of England" (which first appeared in the 1760s) and James Kent's "Commentaries on American Law." Eventually, Blackstone's Commentaries sold as many copies in America as in England.

The earliest known formal legal education was at Oxford University, as early as the 1750s. William Blackstone began offering lectures on the English common law at that time (which became the source for his later Commentaries), and many smaller American universities later followed his example. In 1779, a chair of law was established at William and Mary College in Virginia. There followed a series of independent schools of law, not associated with universities or colleges, which functioned as offshoots of the apprenticeship system. The most notable of these (and credited as the first law school in the country) was the Litchfield Law School in Connecticut. Founded by Judge Tapping Reeve, the school looked much like a country schoolhouse, and operated solely on daily lectures. There were no prerequisites or entrance requirements and no final examinations. The school operated continuously from 1784 to 1833. After this time, schools like Litchfield died out or merged with instruction in a university setting.

It is important to note that from the latter 1700s to the second half of the 1800s, the legal profession in the United States was not considered academic or elite, but rather vocational and functional. The present day "law school" did not take shape until 1829, when Justice Joseph Story reorganized the separate law department at Harvard University. Prior to that time, legal studies were considered part of a broader liberal education at the universities, and non-university law schools were comparable to modern-day vocational schools.

Justice Story set up Harvard's law school curriculum as an exclusive legal education, premised on the assumption that its students had acquired a sufficient background in liberal arts prior to admission to law school. However, even the ambitious Harvard program had more intellectual pretension than substance. There were no entrance examinations, interim examinations, or final examination. The only requirement was the completion of two years at the school and the payment of fees.

By 1870, America had over 30 university law schools, mostly premised on Story's model. In reality, however, these schools had no academic admissions requirements, and no attempt was made to ensure that students had already achieved the antecedent liberal education contemplated by Story.

## Law School

Today, there are over 200 law schools in the United States, the great majority of which have been approved by the American Bar Association (ABA) and have met somewhat stricter standards of the Association of American Law Schools. In most schools, admission is premised on scores achieved on the Law School Admission Test (LSAT), undergraduate grade point average and course of study, and other personal criteria factored in, e.g., ethnic or cultural diversity, leadership or success in extra-curricular activities,

etc. Although not all law schools require a four-year undergraduate degree as a prerequisite for admission, an abundance of applicants creates a competitive edge that results in the great majority of vacancies being filled by college graduates. The formal three-year course of intensive professional training has replaced the apprenticeship form of training. (Law clerkships during law school are common in both the public and private sector, and again, create a competitive edge for job placement after graduation.)

## The Bar Examination

Each state prepares and administers its own written examination for applicants seeking licensure to practice law in that state. The vast majority of states incorporate the use of the Multi-state Bar Examination (MBE), a day-long multiple-choice test which challenges a candidate's basic understanding of general law and legal theories (e.g., torts, contracts, criminal procedure, constitutional rights, etc.). This is followed by another day-long written examination on particular state law, which tests candidates' knowledge of not only state statutes, but also state approach to common law issues. Finally, most states add a half-day written examination on ethics and professional responsibility.

## Character and Fitness Review

State bar associations conduct character and fitness reviews of prospective candidates seeking licensure to practice law in those states. This is generally conducted through a series of multi-page applications, reference-checking, employment history verifications, reviews of letters of recommendation, and criminal background investigations.

## The Role of the Organized Bar

The Association of the Bar of the City of New York was founded in 1870 by what one lawyer referred to as the "decent part of the profession." It was a group of 75 gentlemen from this state bar that ultimately met in 1878 to form the American Bar Association (ABA). Its goal was reform: fighting corruption, drafting better laws, and raising the prestige of the profession. From this group, the Association of American Law Schools was organized for the improvement of legal education.

By 1905, the ABA began to require (of its members, not of the profession as a whole) a minimum of three years of law study prior to practicing law. In fact, the ABA had become an elitist organization, representing the upper crust of the profession, with elitist values. Early on, it promoted codes of ethics for its members in an effort to define and uphold appropriate, professional conduct. Today, the ABA Model Rules of Professional Conduct have been adopted and/or incorporated by a majority of the states.

In 1952, the Association established three years of college as a prerequisite for admission to law school. By the 21st century, a majority of law schools either required or preferred the completion of course study for a four-year bachelor's degree prior to the study of law. After completion of an additional three years of law study, a law student is awarded the degree of juris doctorate (J.D.) and becomes a candidate for admission to the bar.

## Procedure for License to Practice Law

Today, the admission to, and regulation of, the legal profession is primarily the concern of state bar associations. Each state administers its own admissions requirements and procedures, although all states generally focus on law school completion, bar examination results, and background check.

While awaiting bar examination test results, prospective candidates for admission begin filing their applications with state bar organizations and forwarding law school and undergraduate transcripts. Bar admissions committees review the total submissions for each candidate and favorably select candidates considered qualified for practice.

Most selection decisions (or declinations) are communicated by correspondence to the applicants/candidates. The successful candidate is generally admitted to practice in a formal "swearing-in" ceremony or procedure before a court. Many states require the candidates to have "sponsors" who are attorneys already admitted to practice in that state. The newly-admitted attorneys receive personal identification numbers from the state bar, which are later generally added to their signatures on all court documents or legal proceedings handled in the practice of law.

## Scope of License

Few states actually issue a "license" to practice law *per se;* generally the attorney receives a formal frame-worthy certificate evidencing admission, the display of which is often required by several states.

Lawyers are only permitted to practice law in a state where they have been formally admitted. Obtaining license to practice accords each lawyer with all rights to perform all duties associated with the profession. These include counseling persons in legal matters; representing persons in a court of law, before an administrative tribunal, or in legal controversies; advocating persons' rights or legal positions in a legal controversy; preparing and drafting legal documents; and negotiating on behalf of other persons.

A license to practice law within a state refers to practice within the state courts. Federal trial courts generally premise their admissions on the policies of the state in which they are located. Other U.S. federal courts, particularly appellate courts, have open admissions policies, allowing attorneys to argue cases before them if they are licensed anywhere in the country.

## Suspension or Revocation of License

By virtue of state law, the highest court of each state generally delegates authority to state bar organizations to oversee, monitor, and discipline licensed attorneys within the state. This includes the vested authority to suspend or revoke licenses.

Generally, each state bar has an attorney grievance section that reviews and adjudicates complaints received. Procedural due process requires that the subject attorney receive notice of the substance of the complaint received. Additionally, the attorney must be granted sufficient time to prepare a response (usually first in writing, then finally, in a hearing). Because suspension or revocation of a license interferes with an attorney's ability to be gainfully employed, adverse decisions may be appealed in a court of law. Courts of law do not have the power to suspend or revoke an attorney's license. Their jurisdiction is limited to appellate review of a state bar's action.

However, outside of the bar association forum, an attorney may also be sued for legal malpractice in a court of law. If a judgment is entered against him or her, the damages are compensatory in nature (usually in the form of a monetary judgment) and payable to the complainant; the court cannot suspend or revoke the attorney's license as part of the award in the lawsuit. Notwithstanding, notice of the adverse judgment may then be forwarded to the state bar for review. It is the state bar organization that will decide whether the judgment against the attorney substantively represented a breach in the model rules, code of conduct, or code of ethics such that a suspension or revocation of the license to practice law is warranted.

## Reciprocity

Many states open the practice of law to out-of-state applicants who have already been admitted to the bar of another state. While each state establishes its own criteria for admission, reciprocal agreements between states are common. Depending on factors such as the number of graduating law students within the state, geographic desirability (high demand for "Sunbelt" states like California, Florida, and Arizona), or average earnings compared to other states, etc., state bars may lower or raise the threshold for admission of external candidates. Some may require prospective candidates to take the state's bar exam; others will accept a combination of passing results on the Multi-state bar examination and a minimum number of years' in practice in another state. For example, as of January 2005, the states of Maine, New Hampshire, and Vermont entered into a reciprocity agreement allowing attorneys to be admitted to one another's bars without taking the bar examination for that state. The geographic proximity of the states and the frequent representation by law firms of corporations who operate in all three states prompted the change.

ALABAMA: The state does not offer reciprocity.

ALASKA: The state has reciprocity agreements with the following other states: CO, CT, DC, GA, IL, IN, IA, KY, MA, MI, MN, MO, NE, NH, NY, ND, OH, OK, PA, TN, TX, UT, VT, VA, WA, WV, WY.

ARIZONA: The state does not offer reciprocity.

ARKANSAS: Admission by motion went into effect in October 2004.

CALIFORNIA: The state does not offer reciprocity, but offers a shorter bar examination for attorneys licensed in other states with good standing for at least four years prior to application.

COLORADO: Other states have to reciprocate for Colorado lawyers.

CONNECTICUT: Other states have to reciprocate for Connecticut lawyers.

DELAWARE: The state does not offer reciprocity.

DISTRICT OF COLUMBIA: Lawyers who have been admitted for five years in another jurisdiction immediately preceding application for admission in DC can be admitted without examination; other lawyers can be admitted without examination if they graduated from an ABA accredited law school and obtained certain minimum scores on the Multi-state Bar Examination and the Multi-state Professional Responsibility Examination.

FLORIDA: The state does not offer reciprocity.

GEORGIA: Georgia offers a shorter bar examination for lawyers admitted by examination and in good standing in another state for at least twelve months prior to taking its Attorneys' Examination. Also offers admission without examination for lawyers from reciprocal states who have practiced at least five years.

HAWAII: The state does not offer reciprocity.

IDAHO: Offers reciprocity only to certain lawyers licensed in Oregon, Utah, Washington, and Wyoming. However, lawyers who have actively practiced law for at least five of the last seven years immediately preceding their applications for admission do not have to take and pass the Multi-state Bar Examination, but must take and pass the remainder of the Idaho bar examination.

ILLINOIS: Has reciprocity agreements with the following states: AK, CO, CT, DC, GA, GU, IN, IA, KY, MA, MI, MN, MO, NE, NH, NMI, NY, NC, ND, OH, OK, PA, TN, TX, USVI, UT, VT, VA, WA, WV, WI, WY.

INDIANA: Has no formal reciprocity but provisionally admits lawyers who have practiced law for five years of the seven years immediately preceding their applications for admission without taking and passing the Indiana bar examination.

IOWA: Lawyers who have practiced law for five full years of the seven years immediately preceding their applications for admission to practice law in Iowa can be admitted to practice without taking and passing the Iowa bar examination.

KANSAS: Does not have reciprocity.

KENTUCKY: Kentucky has reciprocity agreements with the following states: AK, CO, CT, DC, GA, IL, IA, MA, MI, MN, MO, NE, NH, NY, NC, ND, OH, OK, PA, TN, TX, UT, WA, WV, WI, WY.

LOUISIANA: Has no express reciprocity agreements, but provisionally admits certain lawyers from other jurisdictions under special criteria.

MAINE: As of January 2005, the states of Maine, New Hampshire, and Vermont entered into a reciprocity agreement allowing attorneys to be admitted to one another's bars without taking the bar examination for that state. Shorter bar examination for lawyers in good standing in another state for at least three of the preceding five years prior to admission to practice law in Maine; shorter bar examination for lawyers in good standing in another state depending on passing score on MBE within sixty-one months of the current administration of the Maine bar examination.

MARYLAND: Has no formal reciprocity agreements, but offers shorter bar examination for lawyers in good standing in another state for at least five years of the ten years prior to application for admission in Maryland.

MASSACHUSETTS: To gain license in this state, an applicant must have been admitted to practice in another state, district or territory for at least five years prior to application for admission and be in good standing in each such state, district and territory. An applicant must be a graduate of a law school which at the time of graduation was approved by the American Bar Association or was authorized by a state statute to grant the degree of bachelor of laws or juris doctor.

MICHIGAN: Lawyers who have actively practiced law for three of the five years preceding their applications for admission can be admitted to practice in Michigan without taking and passing the Michigan bar examination.

MINNESOTA: Lawyers who have been, as their principal occupation, actively and lawfully engaged in the practice of law in another jurisdiction for at least five of the seven years immediately preceding application may be admitted without examination; other lawyers may be admitted based on a minimum passing score on the Multistate Bar Examination if they apply within two years of the date they passed that test in another jurisdiction

MISSISSIPPI: Mississippi has a very limited reciprocity admission rule with states who will offer similar reciprocity to Mississippi lawyers. Lawyers from other states who have practiced at least five years may be admitted after taking and passing an attorney's examination.

MISSOURI: Will admit lawyers from states that have similar reciprocity for Missouri lawyers.

MONTANA: The state does not offer reciprocity.

NEBRASKA: Lawyers who have graduated from an ABA accredited law school and who have passed a bar examination comparable to Nebraska's, including the Multi-state Professional Responsibility Examination, or who have graduated from an ABA accredited law school and who have actively and substantially practiced law for five of the last seven years prior to application for admission can be admitted to the practice of law in Nebraska without having to take and pass a written bar examination.

NEVADA: Does not have formal reciprocity agreements with any states.

NEW HAMPSHIRE: As of January 2005, the states of Maine, New Hampshire, and Vermont entered into a reciprocity agreement allowing attorneys to be admitted to one another's bars without taking the bar examination for that state. This state also has reciprocity with the following states: AK, CO, DC, GA, KY, MA, MN, MO, NB, NY, NC, ND, OK, PA, TX, UT, WA;

NEW JERSEY: The state does not offer reciprocity.

NEW MEXICO: The state does not offer reciprocity.

NEW YORK: Has reciprocity with the following states: AK, CO, DC, GA, IL, IN, IA, KY, MA, MI, MN, MO, NE, NH, NC, ND, OH, OK, PA, TN, TX, UT, VA, WA, WV, WI, WY.

NORTH CAROLINA: Has reciprocity agreements with the following states: AK, CO, CT, DC, GA, IL, IN, IA, KY, MA, MI, MN, MO, NE, NH, NY, ND, OH, OK, PA, TN, TX, UT, VT, WA, WV, WI, WY.

NORTH DAKOTA: Does not have formal reciprocity, but lawyers who have been admitted to the bar of another state or the District of Columbia for at least five years and who have been actively engaged in the practice of law for at least four of the last five years immediately preceding their applications for admission can be admitted on motion without examination. Applicants receiving particular scores on the Multi-state Bar Examination and Multi-state Professional Responsibility Examination may also be admitted on motion if their applications are received by the North Dakota Bar Board within two years of the date of the MBE examination if they were admitted in the jurisdiction in which they took that test.

OHIO: This state does not have formal reciprocity agreements with other states. However, it provisionally admits (without examination) applicants who have taken and passed a bar examination and been admitted as a lawyer in the highest court of another state or in the District of Columbia, and who have practiced law, as defined in the rule, subsequent to that admission for at least five full years of the ten years prior to filing an application. Applicants also must demonstrate that they intend to engage in the practice of law in Ohio actively on a continuing basis.

OKLAHOMA: This state has formal reciprocity agreements with the following states: AK, CO, CT, DC, GA, IL, IN, IA, KY, MA, MI, MN, MO, NE, NH, NY, NC, ND, OH, PA, TN, TX, UT, VT, VA, WA, WV, WI, WY.

OREGON: This state provisionally admits qualifying Idaho and Washington lawyers.

PENNSYLVANIA: This state has reciprocity with the following states: AK, CO, CT, DC, GA, IL, IN, IA, KY, MA, MI, MN, MO, NE, NH, NY, NC, ND, OH, OK, TN, TX, UT, VT, VA, WA, WV, WI, WY.

RHODE ISLAND: This state will provisionally admit persons admitted to the practice of law in another state, district or territory of the United States who have actively engaged in the practice law (including teaching law) there for at least five years of the last ten years immediately preceding application for admission to Rhode Island, and after taking and passing the essay portion of the Rhode Island bar examination.

SOUTH CAROLINA: : Does not have formal reciprocity agreements with any states.

SOUTH DAKOTA: This state has a reciprocity agreement that went into effect in 2004. Applicants must show five years prior practice in prescribed areas.

TENNESSEE: This state will provisionally admit applicants who meet the educational requirements applicable to Tennessee bar examination applicants and have actively engaged in the practice of law in another jurisdiction for at least five years immediately preceding their applications for admission in Tennessee.

TEXAS: This state has limited admission for certain lawyers to be admitted without examination and after passage of the full student examination.

UTAH: Has reciprocity agreements with the following states: AK, CO, CT, DC, GA, ID, IL, IN, IA, KY, MA, MI, MN, MO, NE, NH, NY, NC, ND, OH, OK, PA, TN, TX, VT, VA, WA, WY.

VERMONT: As of January 2005, the states of Maine, New Hampshire, and Vermont entered into a reciprocity agreement allowing attorneys to be admitted to one another's bars without taking the bar examination for that state. Otherwise, lawyers who have been admitted to the practice of law in another jurisdiction of the United States may be admitted upon motion and without examination provided that at the time of application they have been actively engaged in the practice of law for five of the preceding ten years in one or more jurisdictions of the United States, are currently licensed to practice in at least one such jurisdiction, and are not under suspension or revocation in any jurisdiction. Any or all of the five-year admission requirement may be waived in certain circumstances. Additionally, each applicant who at the time of application has been admitted in another state and has engaged in the practice of law for less than five of the preceding ten years, and who is currently licensed to practice in at least one such jurisdiction, and is not under suspension or revocation in any jurisdiction may be admitted after examination as described in Vermont Admission Rule 6(a)-(e).

VIRGINIA: Virginia will provisionally admit lawyers from other states who reciprocate for Virginia lawyers.

WASHINGTON: This state has formal reciprocity agreements with the following states: AK, CO, CT, DC, GA, ID, IL, IN, IA, KY, MA, MI, MN, MO, NE, NH, NY, NC, ND, OH, OK, OR, PA, TN, TX, UT, VT, VA, WV, WI, WY.

WEST VIRGINIA: This state has reciprocity agreements with the following states: CO, CT, DC, IL, IN, IA, KY, MA, MI, MN, MO, NE, NY, NC, ND, OK, PA, TX, VT, VA, WA, WI.

WISCONSIN: Wisconsin will offer provisional admission to practicing lawyers from states that reciprocate for Wisconsin lawyers.

WYOMING: Wisconsin will offer provisional admission to practicing lawyers from states that reciprocate for Wyoming lawyers.

## Additional Resources

Farnsworth, E. Allan. *An Introduction to the Legal System of the United States.* New York: Oceana Publications, Inc., 1999.

### *American Bar Association*
321 North Clark Street

Chicago, IL 60610
Phone: (312) 988-5000
URL: www.abanet.org

# ATTORNEYS

## MALPRACTICE

*Sections within this essay:*

## Background

**Malpractice** is professional **negligence** or (less frequently) professional misconduct. Attorney malpractice generally implies an unreasonable lack of skill, or failure to render professional services in a manner consistent with that degree of skill, care, and learning expected of a reasonably competent and prudent member of the legal profession. Claims against attorneys (lawyers) for legal malpractice are viable in all fifty states. There is no federal law governing attorney malpractice, and state statutes typically address only the appropriate **statute of limita-** **tions** (limiting the time period) for filing claims or lawsuits against attorneys. However, state **case law** will define and set the parameters for actionable cases of malpractice within the state.

For legal malpractice to be "actionable" (having all the components necessary to constitute a viable cause of action), there must be a duty owed to someone, a breach of that duty, and resulting harm or damage that is proximately caused by that breach. The simplest way to apply the concept of proximate cause to legal malpractice is to ask whether, "but for" the alleged negligence, the harm or injury would have occurred?

## Establishing the Attorney-Client Relationship

First and foremost, an attorney must owe a legal duty to a person before his or her competency in performing that duty can be judged. In American **jurisprudence**, a lawyer has no affirmative duty to assist someone—in the absence of a special relationship with that person (such as doctor-patient, attorney-client, guardian-ward, etc.). That "special relationship" between an attorney and his/her client is generally established by mutual assent/consent. This is most often confirmed by a written "retainer" agreement in which the client expressly and exclusively retains a lawyer and his/her law firm to represent the client in a specific legal matter.

Under rare and limited circumstances, a court may infer that an attorney-client relationship existed as a matter of law, even without a contract or agreement between the parties, and even without the attorney's **assent**. Such a legal conclusion may be drawn from the facts presented, such as reliance on the part of the client (who believed in **good faith** that an attorney-client relationship existed) or by the fact that the attorney provided more than just informal or anecdotal opinion or answer to a question. The paying of a fee or **retainer** is not dispositive in determining whether an attorney-client relationship existed, and courts generally defer to the "client" and base their conclusions on—or at least give substantial weight to—whether the client believed such a relationship existed, confided in the attorney, and relied upon the professional relationship to his or her detriment.

In any event, once the requisite attorney-client relationship is established, the attorney owes to the client the duty to render legal service and **counsel** or advice with that degree of skill, care, and diligence as possessed by or expected of a reasonably competent attorney under the same or similar circumstances. The "circumstances" may include the area of law in which the attorney practices (although all attorneys are deemed to have basic legal skill and knowledge in the general practice of law), the customary or accepted practices of other attorneys in the area, and the particular circumstances or facts surrounding the representation. The requisite degree of skill and expertise under the circumstances is established by "expert testimony" from other practicing attorneys who share the same or similar skill, training, certification, and experience as the allegedly negligent attorney.

## Conduct vs. Performance

The practice of law requires state licensure. All fifty states have criteria governing admission to practice within their states. Although requirements may vary slightly, almost all states require graduation from an accredited law school, passing the "bar exam" (referring to the professional **bar association** of that state), and submitting to a review and investigation of one's personal background for **assessment** of "character and fitness" to practice law. Accordingly, all new lawyers start their profession with an acceptable level of professional competency (as determined by graduation from law school and passage of a comprehensive bar exam which gauges their professional knowledge of the law), as well as an acceptable level of character and fitness to practice law (as determined by the state bar review board).

Each state also has adopted codes of conduct, disciplinary rules, and adjudicative boards to address issues of misconduct once attorneys are admitted to practice. The American Bar Association also promulgates and promotes its Model Rules of Professional Conduct (adopted by two-thirds of the states as of 2002).

Additionally, virtually all states now require periodic "updating" of technical and/or academic skills by the mandatory completion of a certain number of classroom or seminar hours each year. Attorneys may generally choose the topics in which these hours are completed, but there is usually a requirement that a minimum number of hours be completed in the area of "ethics." Attorneys who fail to complete these courses may not renew their license to practice for the upcoming year. Additional fines or penalties may apply.

That said, trained, licensed attorneys nonetheless may engage in questionable conduct, display a seeming lack of skill, or otherwise neglect or fail to properly render those duties owed to their clients, their adversaries, or to the judicial system as a whole, in their day-to-day practice of law. For those indiscretions and failures that have resulted in harm to a client, a lawsuit for legal malpractice may be an appropriate remedy.

## What Constitutes Actionable Malpractice

State laws govern the viability of causes of action for legal malpractice. The laws vary in terms of time limits to bring suit, qualifications of "expert" witnesses, cognizable theories of liability, and proper party defendants/proper party plaintiffs. Notwithstanding these differences, there are common themes for all cases, and general agreement from state to state on particular instances of nonfeasance or malfeasance of professional duties that may constitute legal malpractice.

Not all instances of malpractice involve an attorney's handling of a case for trial (although persons generally think of attorneys within the context of matters involving **litigation**). For example, an attorney may fail to file a request for variance in a county **zoning** matter involving a parcel of real property or may fail to catch an error on closing documents submitted to him/her. An attorney may erroneously advise a client about an area of law, e.g. foreign **adoption**. Or an attorney may otherwise act on behalf of a client, against that client's express authority or permission. Any of these may constitute examples of actionable legal malpractice.

### Omission or Failure to Do Something (Nonfeasance)

At the top of the list of dreaded mistakes for any attorney is the failure to file a claim, notice, or lawsuit within the time prescribed by law. Inevitably, the client loses his or her right of action, and the entire cause is lost. Such a failure is "black and white" in the eyes of jurors, and disastrous for the client. Similarly, the failure to answer a claim, notice, or lawsuit on behalf of a client may result in **forfeiture**, loss of defense, or **default judgment** entered against a client, often **fatal** failures. A failure to appear in time to set aside a **default** judgment is equally serious. Unfortunately, courts do not consider that the error was made by the attorney and not the client. The client must sue the attorney for malpractice to recoup his or her loss.

Probably second to the above, in terms of occurrence and viability, is the failure to provide required notice. Such failures may include the failure to notify potential heirs at law of a **probate** matter, failure to provide notice to creditors of a pending action, failure to post public notice regarding a real property action, failure to appear in court, or failure to notify a client of an offer to settle the case, received from the opposing party. These matters generally constitute actionable malpractice if the client has suffered harm or damage as a result of the alleged failures.

Third in line is that group of failures which are serious but not always fatal to a client's interest(s). These include such things as failure to file a certain motion in court, failure to name the right parties in a lawsuit (very serious if the time period for filing expires), failure to take or obtain certain **discovery** (e.g., documents or **evidence**), failure to object to the admission of certain evidence at trial (more serious), failure to raise certain issues or questions at depositions, public hearings, trials, arbitrations and mediations, etc.

Sometimes overlooked but nonetheless considered malpractice is the failure to communicate with a client and/or keep the client apprized of the status of the legal matter. However, such instances of malpractice are seldom "actionable" (because of impalpable damages) and are better addressed through a grievance process or letter of complaint.

The above instances of failures are not comprehensive and are intended only as representative by way of example. Not all occurrences of the above "failures" will result in actionable malpractice in all jurisdictions and under all factual scenarios.

### Failure to Perform or Do Something Competently (Malfeasance)

An attorney may be equally liable for malpractice if he or she performs the actions required by law, but does so in an incompetent or substandard manner. For example, an attorney may timely file a cause of action in court, but the complaint may fail to contain important details or averments (allegations), resulting in **dismissal** of the suit. An attorney may take the **deposition** of a witness but ask irrelevant questions or fail to ask the necessary questions needed to elicit needed **testimony**. An attorney may prepare a last will and **testament** for a client but accidentally leave out or miswrite a very important **bequest**. An attorney may appear in time for a criminal sentencing **hearing** but be wholly unprepared or unfamiliar with the case or the issues.

All of the above examples represent situations requiring levels of skill generally attributable to or expected of any competent attorney practicing law in any state. They do not require specialized knowledge in any particular area of law and do not require advanced levels of legal experience or expertise. They are considered examples of fundamental practice of law. Breaches or failures of this type are generally preventable, avoidable, and therefore, actionable in most cases.

Within the context of litigation, it should be mentioned that in most states, a client's retention of an attorney to represent an action at trial implies that the client has delegated to the attorney all decision-making regarding the manner in which the trial should be conducted or the case should be presented. Even if the attorney loses the case, and a judgment is entered against his or her client, it does not mean that any malpractice was committed; after all, in every trial, at least one competent attorney loses and one wins. Under a broad area of attorney discretion, commonly referred to as "trial tactics," errors in judgment at trial (e.g., whether or not to present a certain witness or introduce certain evidence) which are not patently substandard for the profession, do not generally give rise to a cause of action for malpractice.

### Acting Outside the Scope of Authority, Duty, or Area of Competence

In addition, there are clear instances when attorneys should decline representation because they are not skilled enough—or do not possess the requisite subject matter knowledge— to provide competent representation for a client. By way of example, such legal matters as **wrongful death** by **medical malpractice**, complex **corporate** mergers or buy-outs, or complex financial transactions, should not be handled by new attorneys without supervision. Often, mistakes in taking on a new client are made when new attorneys want to "impress" their colleagues or superiors, or when sole practitioners need money or more cases.

An attorney retained to represent a client in one matter may unilaterally and without authority decide to represent a client, or act on the client's behalf, in another unrelated matter. The client may subsequently ratify the representation, or, if harmed, may sue for malpractice. Likewise, an attorney retained for a specific matter may unilaterally and without authority decide to accept an offer of **settlement** for a certain amount of money, without the client's authority. This is a good example of malpractice but may not be "actionable" malpractice, if the client is unable to prove (by a preponderance) that he or she would have gotten more money had the matter gone to trial.

### Filing a Malpractice Lawsuit

There are two important factors to remember about a cause of action for malpractice. First, a client should realize that a poor, unfair, or unexpected result does not mean that any malpractice occurred. Second, in the event that malpractice has occurred, the client must prove that he or she has suffered harm or loss due to the alleged wrongs on the part of an attorney. This is not as easy to prove as one might think. For example, if the alleged malpractice involved a matter in litigation, the client must prove that he or she would have won the case, i.e., a jury would have ruled in his or her favor, "but for" the alleged malpractice. This means that, in proving a case for malpractice, the client will have to actually "try" the "underlying case" before a real jury, and win it, in order to prove the point. Consequently, many lawsuits for malpractice are settled out of court to avoid the time, expense, and uncertainty of such a burden.

### Alternatives for Addressing Malpractice

All states have attorney discipline boards or committees that accept informal or formal complaints from aggrieved clients. In matters that involve misconduct more than **incompetency**, this may be the forum of choice. Generally, disciplinary boards have authority to impose fines, order **restitution** to a client, and suspend or revoke a lawyer's license to practice law in that state. Clients also may wish to consider alternative dispute resolution, such as **arbitration** or **mediation**, to settle their claims of alleged malpractice.

Finally, it is worth noting that attorneys are generally required to advise their clients of known instances of actionable malpractice that have harmed the client or caused loss or damage. By far, the majority of attorneys are honest, competent, and committed to providing good service, and will so advise clients in the event of a known failure. However, what may appear to a layman as "malpractice" at first blush, may in reality constitute no more than a decision or tactic employed by the attorney that conflicts with a client's expectation of likely action or outcome. Persons who believe that their attorneys may have committed malpractice are encouraged to consult with legal counsel who specialize in the area of professional malpractice.

### Select State Laws on Limitations Period For Filing Malpractice Lawsuits

CALIFORNIA: Actions for legal malpractice must be brought within one year of discovery of a claim, with a maximum four years' limitation from the date of the alleged wrong. Proc: Section 340.6.

CONNECTICUT: Actions for legal malpractice must be brought within two years of discovery, with a maximum three years' limitation from the date of the alleged wrong. Section 52-584.

ILLINOIS: Actions for legal malpractice must be brought within a maximum of six years from discovery of the alleged wrong 735 ILCS 5/13/214/3.

KANSAS: Actions for legal malpractice must be brought within two years of discovery, with a maximum four years' limitation from the date of the alleged wrong. Section 60-513(a)(7), 60-513(c).

KENTUCKY: Actions for professional service malpractice must be brought within one year from discovery. Section 413-245.

MAINE: Actions for legal malpractice must be brought within two years, Section 753-A.

MISSISSIPPI: Actions for professional malpractice must be brought within two years. Section 15-1-36.

MONTANA: Actions for legal malpractice must be brought within three years from discovery, with a maximum ten years' limitation from the date of the alleged wrong. Section 27-2-206.

NEVADA: Actions for legal malpractice must be brought within four years. Section 11.207.

RHODE ISLAND: Actions for legal malpractice must be brought within three years. Section 9-1-14.1 and 9-1-14.3.

SOUTH DAKOTA: Actions for legal malpractice must be brought within three years. Section 15-2-14.2.

TENNESSEE: Actions for legal malpractice must be brought within one year Section 28-3-104.

## Additional Resources

*"American Bar Association Model Rules of Professional Conduct"* 2001. Available at http://www.abanet.org/crp/mrpc/mrpc_toc.html.

*"Attorney Malpractice"* 2001. Halt Legal Information Clearinghouse. Available at http://www.halt.org/ELS/ELScontrol.cfm?getELS=elsB1.

*"The Hierarchy of Attorney Malpractice"* 2001. Available at http://attorneymal-practice.com/heirarchy.htm.

*National Survey of State Laws* 3rd Edition. Richard A. Leiter, Ed. Gale Group, 1999.

# AUTOMOBILES

## ACCIDENT LIABILITY

*Sections within this essay:*

## Background

All fifty states and the District of Columbia provide "drivers' licenses" for their residents, permitting them to operate motor vehicles upon public roads. Once individuals have been licensed by a state, they are presumed qualified and competent to operate a motor vehicle for the period of time covered by the license. By far, the vast majority of automobile accidents are caused by persons well qualified to drive under state criteria but who are careless and/or reckless in their operation of motor vehicles at the time of an accident. Moreover, a high number of accidents are the result of intentional misconduct, such as alcohol consumption or excessive speeding.

## Concept of Fault or Liability

The determination of fault in an automobile accident may or may not establish the person or party liable for payment of the damages or injuries. This fact is wholly the result of legislative **lobbying** over the years by automobile liability insurance carriers, who have devised and promoted various alternative strategies to the **common law** concept that persons at fault pay for the damages. Under such legislative schemes, common law recovery for damages has been totally or partially abolished. In its place is a **statutory** reapportionment of liability for payment of damages. This arrangement does not mean that there is a statutory re-defining of actual "fault" **per se**. It simply means that many states have reapportioned the liability for fault, at least for purposes of automobile accident liability insurance. In all states, persons who fail to maintain liability insurance and who cause accidents may be personally sued, and their assets seized to satisfy any judgment against them.

### Common Law

In its purest form, "fault" for causing an accident is either created by **statute** or defined by common law. Common law recognizes four basic levels of fault: **negligence**, recklessness or wanton conduct, intentional misconduct, and strict liability (irrespective of fault).

Negligence generally means careless or inadvertent conduct that results in harm or damage. It is a recurring factor in an aggregate majority of automobile accidents. It encompasses both active and passive forms of fault. That is to say, failing or omitting to do something (e.g., yielding a right-of-way) may result in liability just as much as actively doing something wrong (e.g., running a red light). Reckless or wanton conduct generally refers to a willful disregard for whether harm may result and/or a disregard for the safety and welfare of others. Strict liability may be imposed, even in the absence of fault, for accidents involving certain defective products or extra hazardous activities (such as the transporting of explosive chemicals).

Under common law, individuals who have caused an automobile accident have committed a "tort," a private wrong against another, not founded in "contract," and generally not constituting a crime. Those who have committed torts are referred to as "tortfeasors" under the law. Many automobile insurance policies continue to use the word "tortfeasor" to refer to people who are at least partly "at fault" or responsible for an accident.

There is rarely a question of fault when the **tortfeasor** has engaged in intentional or reckless misconduct, such as drunk driving. But when it comes to something less than intentional misconduct, e.g., general negligence, establishing fault for an automobile accident becomes more complex. Moreover, it is often the case that more than one driver or person is negligent and/or has played a role (even inadvertently) in the resulting accident. When there are multiple tortfeasors involved in an accident, state law dictates who must pay for both damage to property and injuries to the occupants of vehicles.

### Motor Vehicle Statutory Violations

Every state has passed multiple laws which dictate the manner in which drivers must operate their vehicles upon public roads. Many of these statutes are actually codified versions of the common law, while others are the result of legislative initiative.

The important point to remember is that a violation of any of these statutes generally creates a presumption of negligence as a matter of law. Thus, "fault" in an accident may be established merely by citing a statute that has been violated. A tortfeasor who is presumed to have caused an accident by virtue of a statutory violation must bear the burden, in any legal dispute, of proving that he or she was not negligent, or (in the alternative) that his or her negligence was not a proximate cause in the accident. The simplest way to apply the concept of proximate cause to an automobile accident is to ask whether it would be true that, "but for" the violation, the accident would not have occurred.

## Automobile Accident Liability Insurance

The federal *McCarran-Ferguson Act,* 15 **USC** 1011, contains the basic provisions which give states the power to regulate the insurance industry. This power particularly applies to in the automobile insurance industry, where there is very little federal interest, excepting matters involving interstate commerce in general.

State law dictates not only what form of negligence law applies to automobile accidents but also what form of liability insurance individuals must maintain in order to lawfully operate a motor vehicle. The liability insurance that they purchase generally parallels the form of negligence law found in their particular state.

In general, liability for accidents can be affected by any of the following:

### Contributory Negligence Standards

Contributory Negligence: A minority of states have maintained the common law defense of contributory negligence. Its significance to automobile accident liability is that individuals cannot sue another for injuries or damages if they also contributed to the accident by his or their own negligence. For example, if they are making a left-hand turn in their vehicle and are struck by an oncoming vehicle that is traveling 10 mph over the speed limit, they cannot sue the motorist for damages if they failed to have their turn signal on and the speeding motorist did not know that they were going to turn in front of them. Under such a theory, their own negligence contributed to the accident, and, therefore, bars their right to recover from the other motorist. This situation is referred to as "pure contributory negligence." Some states have maintained a version referred to as "modified contributory negligence" in which individuals may file suit against another tortfeasor only if their own negligence contributed to the accident by less than 50 percent.

### Comparative Negligence Standards

Comparative Negligence: In states that utilize comparative negligence theories, individuals may sue another motorist whether or not their own negligence played any role in the accident. However, recovery for damages will be reduced by the percentage of fault attributable to them. This situation is often referred to as "apportionment of fault" or "allocation of fault." For example, in the above example, assume that the turning driver sues the speeding motorist for $100,000 in damages. At trial, a jury will be asked to determine what percentage of the accident was caused by the speeding and what percentage of the accident was caused by the turning driver's failure to operate the turn signal. Assume further that the jury finds that the turning driver's own negligence contributed to the accident by 30 percent and the negligence of the other motorist contributed to the accident by 70 percent. If the jury agrees that damages are worth $100,000 the turning driver would only be able to recover $70,000 in damages (or $100,000 reduced by 30 percent caused by that driver's own negligence). If, conversely, the negligence was found to have contributed 70 percent to the accident, the driver could only recover $30,000 for the 30 percent fault for which the other tortfeasor was responsible. Again, this is true in states that apply a "pure" theory of comparative negligence. Other states have modified comparative negligence principles to permit a lawsuit only if a person is were less than 50 percent negligent.

### No-Fault Liability Systems

No-Fault Systems: In states that have statutorily established a "no-fault" system of liability for negligence, each person's own insurance company pays for his or her injury or damage, regardless of who is at fault. No-fault insurance liability coverage does not apportion damages or fault. However, it usually does not cover damage to the automobile, and separate collision coverage is needed. In states with **no fault** systems, individuals may file suit only if certain threshold injuries have occurred or damages exceed insurance coverages.

### Components of an Automobile Insurance Policy

Depending on the state, automobile liability insurance policy may contain some or all of the following:

- Bodily Injury Liability: The insurer will pay damages when other persons are injured or killed in an accident for which the insured are at fault.

- **Personal Injury** Protection (PIP): The insurer will pay for the insured's injuries and other related damages to the insured and to passengers.

- Property Damage Liability: The insurer will pay damages when the property of other persons has been harmed or destroyed by the insured's vehicle and the insured is at fault.

- Collision Coverage: The insurer will pay for damages to the insured's own vehicle, when the insured is at fault. If the insured's vehicle is financed, the loaner may require the insured to maintain collision coverage on the vehicle.

- Comprehensive Coverage: The insurer will pay for damages to the insured's automobile caused by fire, theft, **vandalism**, acts of God, riots, and certain other perils. If the insured's vehicle is financed, the loaner may require the insured to maintain comprehensive coverage on the vehicle.

- Uninsured/Underinsured Motorist (UM/UIM) Coverage: The insurer will pay for injury or death to the insured and the insured's passengers if caused by an uninsured or underinsured tortfeasor or a hit-and-run motorist. In some states, the insurer will also pay for damage to the insured's vehicle. An uninsured at-fault tortfeasor may be sued and his or her personal assets attached to satisfy any judgment.

## When Accidents Occur

The following points may assist individuals in the event that they are involved in a motor vehicle accident:

### In a Rental or Leased Vehicle

In a Rental or Leased Vehicle: In most states, individuals' own insurance policy will protect them for any automobile that they are driving. There is no need to purchase additional insurance from the automobile rental or leasing company unless they wish to increase their coverage, e.g., add collision coverage.

### When a Pedestrian or Bicyclist is Hit

When a Pedestrian or Bicyclist is Hit: In some states, there is a presumption of fault if drivers strike a pedestrian or bicyclist, for want of care and defensive driving on the driver's part. However, the presumption can be overturned by **evidence** of fault or statutory violation on the part of the bicyclist or pedestrian, e.g., bicycling at night without a headlight, jaywalking, etc. In no-fault states, injured pedestrians are often covered by their own automobile policies, even though they were pedestrians at the time, and even if the driver was were at fault.

### When an Animal is Hit

When an Animal is Hit: When a domesticated animal is injured and/or damage occurs to the driver, there may be a presumption of fault on the part of the animal's owner for allowing the animal to run at large. If the accident was caused by driver negligence, the animal owner may file suit against the driver. Most states limit damages to the value of the animal or its medical care, and do not permit non-economic damages such as emotional damages associated with the loss of a pet. However, this is a rapidly developing area of law. Injury or damage to the driver's vehicle caused by collision with wild animals (e.g., deer) is generally covered without assignment of fault. The driver should render assistance to the animal only if the driver will not further endanger himself or other motorists.

### In One Vehicle Accidents

In One Vehicle Accidents: The insurance policy will generally cover injuries and damages, but the driver may still be found "at fault," which could affect the driver's insurance premiums.

### In Another State or Country

In Another State or Country: Generally, the laws of the state in which the accident occurs will govern the allocation of fault and liability.

### When One Causes Accident

When One Causes an Accident: Individuals should never leave the scene of the accident. They should avoid statements of apology or admissions of fault: there may be other factors involved that they are not aware of. They need to render assistance to any injured persons, but not to attempt to move them. They should not move their vehicle unless the accident is minor. They should attempt to secure the names and telephone numbers of witnesses, even though they believe they are at fault. They must always be truthful to their insurance company. Misrepresentations may result in cancellation of a policy for insurance and expose them to even more liability. Some states require that a police officer always be called to the scene; other states require police involvement only in circumstances of declared injury.

Generally, a police officer cannot issue a **citation** if he or she did not witness the accident, unless it is clear that the accident could only have been caused by one driver. Notwithstanding, others drivers may have contributed to the accident, even if they did not receive citations.

### When One is Injured in an Accident

When One is Injured in an Accident: People should never assume that they are not injured. They should remain in the vehicle and take a few moments to assess their physical condition and the situation. Some injuries, such as spinal vertebral displacements (e.g., narrowing of intervertebral disc spaces) do not manifest immediately. If you they are physically able, they should attempt to secure contact information of witnesses. If they are taken to a medical facility, their personal health care insurance provider may originally be billed, or the medical facility may request contact information for their automobile insurance provider. (Each state has its own law regarding the "priority" of insurers responsible for payment.) Individuals should remember that if they do not have either healthcare or automobile insurance, they are still entitled to emergency medical treatment until their condition is stabilized. This entitlement stands is true regardless of their ability to pay, and regardless of who caused the accident.

## Vicarious Liability and Negligent Entrustment

In most states, individuals may be liable for accidents caused by other persons who are driving their vehicle, with their direct or implied permission. In many states, both the owner and the driver of a vehicle may be named in a lawsuit under a theory of "vicarious liability." Even in the absence of "owner's liability" statutes, the common law theory of "negligent entrustment" of their vehicle to another person may result in liability exposure.

Likewise, under general negligence theories of vicarious liability and "respondeat superior" ("let the master answer"), employers may be liable (in addition to their employees) for accidents caused by their employees while operating company vehicles. Such vicarious liability is generally limited to automobile accidents caused during the course of employment and does not apply if the employee was using the vehicle beyond the scope of his or her authority.

In a roundabout way, the law permits two other circumstances for vicarious or remote liability. One involves an accident caused by a defective vehicle, in which a "product liability" lawsuit against the manufacturer may result in payment of damages. In the other, several state laws permit suits against state highway officers and departments in connection with the negligent construction or repair of highways, streets, bridges, and overpasses, that may have proximately caused an accident.

## Selected State Laws

ALABAMA: See Title 32 of the Alabama Code of 1975, (Motor Vehicles and Traffic), Chapter 7, Motor Vehicle Safety Responsibility Act. Available at http://www.legislature.state.al.us/CodeofAlabama/1975/coatoc.htm.

ALASKA: See Title 28 (Motor Vehicles) of the Alaska Statute, Chapter 28.20, "Motor Vehicle Safety Responsibility Act." Available at http://www.legis.state.ak.us/folhome.htm.

ARIZONA: See Title 28 (Transportation) of the Arizona Revised Statutes, Chapter 9, (Vehicle Insurance and Financial Responsibility). Available at http://www.azleg.state.az.us/ars/ars.htm#Listing.

ARKANSAS: See Title 23 (**Public Utilities** and Regulated Industries), Subtitle 3 (Insurance), Chapter 89 (**Casualty** Insurance), Subchapter 2 (Automobile Liability Insurance Generally) of the Arizona Revised Statutes, Chapter 9, "Vehicle Insurance and Financial Responsibility." Also see Title 27 (Transportation), Subtitle 2 (Motor Vehicle Registration and Licensing), Chapter 19, "Motor Vehicle Safety Responsibility Act," and Chapter 22, Motor Vehicle Liability Insurance. Available at http://www.azleg.state.az.us/ars/ars.htm#Listing.

CALIFORNIA: See California Insurance Code and California Vehicle Code, Division 7 (Financial Responsibility Laws), Chapter 3 (Proof of Financial Responsibility) Available at http://www.azleg.state.az.us/ars/ars.htm#Listing.

COLORADO: See Title 10, Chapter 40701 et seq., "Colorado Auto Accident Preparations Act," and Title 42, Chapter 7, "Motor Vehicle Financial Responsibility Act." Available at http://www.azleg.state.az.us/ars/ars.htm#Listing.

CONNECTICUT: See Title 38a (Insurance), Chapter 700, (Property and Casualty Insurance). Available at http://www.azleg.state.az.us/ars/ars.htm#Listing.

DELAWARE: See Title 21 (Motor Vehicles), part II (Registration, Titles, and Licenses), Chapter 21 (Reg-istration of Vehicles), Subchapter 1, Section 2118. Also see Chapter 29, Motor Vehicle Safety-Responsibility. Available at http://www.azleg.state.az.us/ars/ars.htm#Listing.

DISTRICT OF COLUMBIA: See DC Code, Title 35 (Insurance), Chapter 21 (Compulsory/No-Fault Motor Vehicle Insurance) and Title 40 (Motor Vehicles and Traffic), Chapter 4 (Motor Vehicle Safety Responsibility). Available at http://www.azleg.state.az.us/ars/ars.htm#Listing.

FLORIDA: See Florida Statutes Annotated, Title 37 (Insurance), Part 11 (Motor Vehicle and Casualty Insurance), and Title 23 (Motor Vehicles), Chapter 324 (Financial Responsibility) Available at http://www.azleg.state.az.us/ars/ars.htm#Listing.

GEORGIA: See Georgia Code, Section 40-9-1, "Motor Vehicle Safety Responsibility Act." Available at http://www.azleg.state.az.us/ars/ars.htm#Listing.

HAWAII: See Title 17 (Motor and Other Vehicles), Chapter 287, "Motor Vehicle Safety Responsibility Act." Available at http://www.azleg.state.az.us/ars/ars.htm#Listing.

IDAHO: See Titles 49 (Motor Vehicles), Chapter 12 (Motor Vehicle Financial Responsibility), Section 12-1229 (Required Motor Vehicle Insurance) Available at http://www.azleg.state.az.us/ars/ars.htm#Listing.

ILLINOIS: See Chapter 625 (Vehicles), 625 ILCS5/ (Illinois Vehicle Code), Chapter 7 (Illinois Safety and Family Financial Responsibility Law, Article II (Security Following Accident). Available at http://www.azleg.state.az.us/ars/ars.htm#Listing.

INDIANA: See Title 7 (Motor Vehicles), Article 25 (Financial Responsibility), Chapter 4 (Financial Responsibility). Available at http://www.azleg.state.az.us/ars/ars.htm#Listing.

IOWA: See Iowa Code, Chapter 321A (Motor Vehicle Financial Responsibility) Available at http://www.azleg.state.az.us/ars/ars.htm#Listing.

KANSAS: See Kansas Statutes, Title 40 (Insurance), Article 31, "Kansas Automobile Injury Reparations Act." Available at http://www.azleg.state.az.us/ars/ars.htm#Listing.

KENTUCKY: See KRS Title XXV (Business and Financial Institutions) Chapter 304, Subtitle 39 (Motor Vehicle Reparations Act). Available at http://www.azleg.state.az.us/ars/ars.htm#Listing.

LOUISIANA: See Louisiana Statutes Title 32, Sections 861 and 900. Available at http://www.azleg.state.az.us/ars/ars.htm#Listing.

MAINE: See Title 29A (Motor Vehicles), Ch. 13 (Financial Responsibility and Insurance), Subchapter II (General Financial Responsibility) Section 1605. Available at http://www.azleg.state.az.us/ars/ars.htm#Listing.

MARYLAND: See Statute Sections under Insurance (19-509) and Transportation (17-103). Available at http://www.azleg.state.az.us/ars/ars.htm#Listing.

MICHIGAN: See Chapter 500 (Insurance Code of 1956), Act 218, and MCL Chapter 31 (Motor Vehicle Personal and Property Protection). Available at http://michiganlegislature.org/law/ChapterIndex.asp.

MINNESOTA: See Minnesota Statutes Annotated, Chapter 65B (Automobile Insurance). Available at http://www.revisor.leg.state.mn.us/stats/.

MISSISSIPPI: See Title 63 (Motor Vehicles and Traffic Regulations), Chapter 15 (Motor Vehicle Safety-Responsibility. Available at http://www.lexislawpublishing.com/sdCGI-IN/om_isapi.dll?clientID=6125&infobase=ms code.NFO&softpage=doc_frame_pg.

MISSOURI: See Missouri Revised Statutes, Title XIX (Motor Vehicles, Watercraft and Aviation),Chapter 303 (Motor Vehicle Financial Responsibility). Available at http://www.moga.state.mo.us/STATUTES/STATUTES.HTM.

MONTANA: See Montana Code, Title 16 (Motor Vehicles), Chapter 6 (Responsibility of Vehicle Users and Owners), Part 1 (Financial Responsibility), Section 61-6-103, et seq. Available at http://statedocs.msl.state.mt.us/cgi-bin/om_isapi.dll?clientID=6928&infobase=MCA_97.NF O &softpage=Browse_Frame_Pg.

NEBRASKA: See Chapter 60 (Motor Vehicles), Section 501 et seq. (Motor Vehicle Safety Responsibility Act). Available at http://statutes.unicam.state.ne.us/

NEVADA: See Chapter 485 (Motor Vehicles: Insurance and Financial Responsibility Act). Available at http://www.leg.state.nv.us/NRS/SEARCH/NRSQuery.htm.

NEW HAMPSHIRE: See Title 21 (Motor Vehicles), Chapter 264 (Accidents and Financial Responsibility), Section 264.16 et seq. Available at http://199.92.250.14/rsa/.

NEW JERSEY: See Title 39 (Motor Vehicle and Traffic Regulation), Section 39:6A-1 (Maintenance of Motor Vehicle Liability Insurance Coverage. Available at http://www.njleg.state.nj.us/

NEW MEXICO: See Chapter 66 (Motor Vehicles), Article 5, Part 3 (Financial Responsibility), Mandatory Financial Responsibility Act, Section 66-5-201 to 239.

NEW YORK: See New York State Consolidated Laws, Chapter 28 (Insurance Law), Article 51 (Comprehensive Motor Vehicle Insurance Reparations). Available at http://www.findlaw.com/11statgov/ny/mycl.html.

NORTH CAROLINA: See Chapters 20 (Insurance) of the North Carolina General Statutes, Article 9A (Motor Vehicle Safety an Financial Responsibility Act of 1953), Section 20-279.1 et seq. Available at http://www.ncga.state.nc.us/Statutes/toc-1.html.

NORTH DAKOTA: See Title 26.1 (Insurance), Chapter 26.1-41 (Auto Accidents Reparations Act). Available at http://www.state.nd.us/lr/index.htm.

OHIO: See Title 29 (Insurance), Chapter 3937 (Casualty Insurance, Motor Vehicle Insurance), Section 3937.18 et seq; also Title 45 (Motor Vehicles-Aeronautics-Watercraft), Chapter 4509 (Financial Responsibility), Section 4509.20. Available at http://orc.avv.com/home.htm.

OKLAHOMA: See Section 47-7-101 et seq. Available at http://oklegal.onenet.net/statutes.basic.html.

OREGON: See Title 56 (Insurance), Chapters 731-752, including 742 (Insurance Policies Generally). Title 59 (Oregon Vehicle Code), Chapter 806 contains the Financial Responsibility Act. Available at http://www.leg.state.or.us/ors/.

PENNSYLVANIA: See Pennsylvania Statutes Annotated, Title 67 (Transportation), Part I (Department of Transportation), Subpart A (Vehicle Code Provisions), Article XIII (Administration and Enforcement), Chapter 219 (Proof of Financial Responsibility); Chapter 221 (Obligations of Insurers and Vehicle Owners); and Chapter 223 (Self-Insurance). Available at http://www.pacode.com/cgi-bin/pacode/ssecure/infosearch.pl

RHODE ISLAND: See Title 31 (Motor and Other Vehicles), Chapter 31-30 and 31-31 (Safety Responsibility Administration), and Chapter 31-47 (Motor Vehicle Reparations Act). Available at http://www.riiln.state.ri.us/Statutes/Statutes/html.

SOUTH CAROLINA: See Title 56 (Motor Vehicles), Chapter 9 (Motor Vehicle Financial Responsibility Act), Section 56-9-19 et seq. Available at http://www.lpitr.state.sc.us/code/statmast.htm.

SOUTH DAKOTA: See Title 58 (Insurance), Chapter 23 (Liability Insurance), and Title 32 (Motor Vehicles), Chapter 32-35 (Financial Responsibility of Vehicle Owners and Operators). Available at http://www.lixislawpublishing.com/sdCGI-IN/om_isapi.dll?clientID=1548&infobase=sdcode.NFO&softpage=browse_frame_pg.

TENNESSEE: See Tennessee Code, Title 56 (Insurance), Chapter 7 (Policies and Policyholders), Part 11 (General Provisions- Automobile Insurance) and Part 12 (Underinsured Motor Vehicle Coverage). Available at http://www.lixislawpublishing.com/sdCGI-BIN/om_isapi.dll?clientID=1548&infobase=sdcode.NFO&softpage=browse_frame_pg.

TEXAS: See Insurance Code, Chapter 5, Part I, Subchapter A, Article 5.06-3 (Personal Injury Protection Coverage); Transportation Code, Title 7 (Vehicles and Traffic), Subtitle D (Motor Vehicle Safety Responsibility), Chapter 601 (Motor Vehicle Safety Responsibility Act), Subchapter C (Financial Responsibility). Available at http://www.findlaw.com/11statgove/tx/txst.html

UTAH: See Title 41A (Motor Vehicles), Chapter 12a (Financial Responsibility of Motor Vehicle Owners and Operators Act). Available at http://www.le.satate.ut.us/-code/code.htm

VERMONT: See Title 23 (Motor Vehicles), Chapter 11 (Financial Responsibility and Insurance), Subchapter V (Insurance Against Uninsured, Underinsured or Unknown Motorists). Available at http://www.le.satate.ut.us/-code/code.htm.

VIRGINIA: See Title 38.2 (Insurance), Chapter 22 (Liability Insurance Policies), Title 46.2 (Motor Vehicles), Chapter 3 (Licensure of Drivers), Article 15 (Proof of Financial Responsibility). Available at http://www.le.satate.ut.us/-code/code.htm.

WASHINGTON: See RWC Title 46 (Motor Vehicles), Chapter 46.30 (Mandatory Liability Insurance). Available at http://search.leg.wa.gov/pub/textsearch/default.asp.

WEST VIRGINIA: See Chapter 17D (Motor Vehicle Safety Responsibility Act)/. Available at http://www.legis.state.wv.us/Code/toc.html.

WISCONSIN: See Chapter 632 (Insurance Contracts in Specific), Section 632.32 (Provisions of Motor Vehicle Insurance Policies) and Chapter 344 (Vehicles Financial Responsibility). Availability at http://ww.legis.state.wi.us/rsb/stats.html.

WYOMING: See Title 31 (Motor Vehicles), Chapter 9 (Motor Vehicle Safety Responsibility), Article 4 (Proof of Financial Responsibility). Available at http://legisweb.state.wy.us/titles/statutes.htm.

## Additional Resources

*Guide to Consumer Law* American Bar Association., Random House,1997.

"Introduction to Automobile Accident Liability." Available at http://www.claimrep.com/autoLiabRP1.asp.

*Law for Dummies.* Ventura., John, IDG Books Worldwide, Inc., 1996.

"The 6 Parts of an Auto Insurance Policy." Available at http://www.cwinsurance.com/auto/the6parts.xml?FromSource=lsl.

*"Websites for Motor Vehicle Laws of the 50 States."*Available at http://www.cousineaulaw.com/cma_links2.htm.

*"Who is Liable? Who Pays for Accident Injuries?"*Available at http://www.thenewway.com/personal-injury-guide/who_liable_who_pays.htm.

# AUTOMOBILES

## BUYING A CAR/REGISTRATION

*Sections within this essay:*

- Background
- Consumer Protections
    - Product Warranties
    - Lemon Laws for New and Used Vehicles
    - Right to Rescind Purchases
    - Credit Matters
- Title Transfers and Liens
- State Registration Requirements
- State Lemon Laws
- Additional Resources

## Background

Buying an automobile involves three essential components. First, there are the matters related to the vehicle itself, including product guarantees and warranties. Second, there are the matters relating to transferring ownership of the vehicle from the manufacturer or dealer to the buyer. Third, there are the matters required of the buyer to properly register and insure the vehicle before the buyer may operate it on a public road.

## Consumer Protections

Before individuals purchase a vehicle, there are already several federal laws at work that govern the quality and safety of products available for their purchase. Most of these are found under Title 15 (Commerce and Trade) of the U. S. Code.

- The federal Automobile Information Disclosure Act, 15 **USC** 1231 et seq., requires automobile manufacturers and importers of new cars to affix a sticker on the window of each vehicle, called the "Monroney label." The label must list the base price of the vehicle, each option installed by the manufacturer and its suggested retail price, the transportation charge, and the car's fuel economy (in miles per gallon). Only the ultimate user (the buyer) can remove the label.

- For used vehicles, the Federal Trade Commission (FTC) has passed its Used Car Rule under 15 USC 41, which applies in all states except Maine and Wisconsin. (These states have adopted their own rules governing used car sales.) Under the Used Car Rule, dealers must prominently post buyer's guides on used vehicles that advises whether the vehicles comes with a **warranty** and what type or are sold "as is." The buyer's guide must be given to the buyer if the buyer purchases a used vehicle, and it becomes part of the purchase contract, and its terms override any conflicting terms in the contract.

- The National Traffic and Motor Vehicle Safety Act of 1966, 15 USC 1381 et seq., has been broken down and re-codified over the years into many legal progeny. The following laws address such matters as motor vehicle or driver safety; minimum standards for motor vehicle emissions, fuel economy, bumper standards, or crash-worthiness; motor vehicle manufacturer recalls or advisories; manufacturer and dealer disclosures, etc.

- The Motor Vehicle Information and Cost Saving Act, 15 USC 1901 et seq., (much of which has been broken down into additional acts and laws, and recodified under Title 49, Transportation) contains numerous provisions for minimum quality and safety standards, disclosure, and reporting requirements.

- The federal Truth in Mileage Act of 1986, commonly referred to as the "Anti-Tampering Odometer Law," (PL 99-579) (49 CFR 580) criminalizes any act that falsifies actual odometer readings and mandates that each transferor of a motor vehicle furnish the transferee certain information concerning the vehicle's history.

- The Clean Air Act, 42 USC 7401 et seq., addresses minimum standards for exhaust emissions on motor vehicles.

- The Anti-Car Theft Act of 1992, 15 USC 2021 et seq., establishes, among other things, a national motor vehicle title information system to disrupt attempts to obtain legitimate vehicle ownership by auto thieves. It also provides for the inspection of exports for stolen vehicles.

### Product Warranties

The federal **Magnuson-Moss Warranty Act**, 42 USC 2301 et seq. (1984) is applicable to warranties for purchases of automobiles. Under the Act, any warranty accompanying a product must be designated as either "full" or "limited." Importantly, if a manufacturer has given a full or limited warranty on a new car, it cannot disclaim any implied warranties. However, some states have laws that effectively void any **implied warranty** for buyer's guide used vehicles that are checked "As Is-No Warranty."

Implied warranties are exactly that: implied. They follow the sale of certain consumer goods automatically, without any express writing or document. The implied warranty of merchantability basically guarantees that the product is what it is stated to be and is adequate for the purpose for which it is purchased. Under the **Uniform Commercial Code** (UCC), adopted in all 50 states, this implied warranty only applies to sellers in the business of selling the particular item and does not apply to incidental sales or cross-consumer sales.

However, the implied warranty of fitness for a particular purchase applies to all sellers, even non-

professionals. Under this warranty, the seller is presumed to guarantee that the car sold (e.g., a restored race car), is fit for the particular purpose for which it is being sold.

### Lemon Laws for New and Used Vehicles

All 50 states have enacted "lemon laws" to protect consumers from defective new automobiles. Some states have enacted separate **lemon laws** to cover used vehicles. While their application and protections vary from state to state, they generally protect consumers from having to keep defective new vehicles. Lemon laws entitle buyers to a replacement new vehicle or a full refund if a dealer cannot fix a vehicle to conform with a warranty after three or four repair attempts made within six months to a year (state variations). Some state laws also entitle buyers to such a remedy if the new vehicle is out of commission for more than 30 non-consecutive days during the warranty period or a **statutory** period, e.g., one year.

### Right to Rescind Purchases

Contrary to general assumption, there is no federal law giving buyers the right to cancel their new car purchase within three days of sale. The often-cited Federal Trade Commission (FTC) "Cooling Off" law is only effective for door-to-door sales or sales made at other than the seller's place of business. However, many states have enacted their own versions of the FTC law, affording broader protections than what the federal law does. Prior to purchase, prospective buyers should check with their state's attorney general's office to see if automobile purchases are covered under state law.

### Credit Matters

The federal **Consumer Credit Protection Act**, 15 USC 1601 et seq., also referred to as the Truth in Lending Act, assures that consumers receive specific information regarding the terms, conditions, and final cost of financing. It also requires disclosure of other information that will contribute to a meaningful choice and decision to finance the purchase.

If buyers finance their purchase of vehicles, they most likely will execute a document known as a security agreement, which gives their **creditor** a security interest in their vehicles. Under most state laws, if they seriously **default** on car payments, their creditor may repossess their vehicle, sometimes without advance notice. Although they generally have a right to "cure" the default and redeem the vehicle, they normally have to pay the entire balance on the car, not just the payments in **arrears**. Most financing agreements contain "acceleration clauses" which permit the termination of the **installment** payments once default occurs. Some states have laws that permit creditors to reinstate the contract terms once buyers pay the amount in arrears.

If buyers do not redeem the vehicle, the creditor may keep their vehicles to satisfy the debt, even if the vehicles are worth more than the debt owed. This is referred to as "strict foreclosure." However, if buyers have paid at least 60 percent of the purchase price, they generally are entitled to any excess money recouped from the vehicle's sale above and beyond the balance owed. Buyers are also entitled to take part in the bidding at the sale.

## Title Transfers and Liens

Under the UCC (Article 2), a new car contract which purports to transfer ownership to the purchaser must be in writing. It should include a description of the make and model of the vehicle, its full vehicle identification number (VIN), a statement as to whether the vehicle is new, used, a "demo," rental car, etc., the full price and any financing terms, a cancellation provision if certain conditions occur (such as the car not being delivered by a certain date), and a full statement of warranty terms.

Every transfer of title to a motor vehicle must include an odometer reading and statement of mileage from the transferor. For purposes of **taxation**, most states require an **affidavit** of purchase price as well.

Importantly, if the purchased vehicles are being financed, state law will dictate the form of title transfer. Some states will allow title to transfer to the buyers even though they have not yet fully paid for the vehicle, but the creditor/lender will encumber the title with a **lien**. Other states permit the creditor/lender to keep title in its name until they pay for the vehicle in total, then transfer title to them. In those states, the buyers maintain an "equitable lien" on the vehicle while it is being paid for but do not have legal title to it until their final payment has been made.

Under the UCC, after executing a purchase document, but prior to the delivery of the vehicle, the risk of loss or damage to the vehicle is allocated to the seller if the seller is a merchant (car dealer). If the seller is not a merchant under the UCC, the risk passes to the buyer upon tender of delivery, i.e., when the seller actually attempts delivery or makes the car available for pickup under the contract.

Generally, title to a vehicle cannot be transferred if there is any existing lien listed. Creditors will automatically file the necessary paperwork (buyers should receive a copy) to remove their liens against the title to their vehicles once buyers have paid them creditors in full. However, if buyers attempt to sell their vehicles while a lien is still recorded, the burden is on them to contact the necessary parties to effect a removal of the lien.

## State Registration Requirements

Registering a vehicle in the owner's name notifies the state of ownership of the vehicle, and provides the necessary documentation for the issuance of state license plates and tags to be affixed to the vehicle. Operating a motor vehicle that is not properly registered is usually an offense punishable by fine or **imprisonment**. Within most states, the Department of Motor Vehicles (DMV) or an office of the Secretary of State is the proper entity for registering vehicles.

The most common document requirements for registering a vehicle are the title and a certificate of automobile insurance coverage. Some states additionally require a copy of the contract or **bill of sale**, or in the alternative, an affidavit containing averments of purchase price, description of the vehicle, and the VIN number, names of seller and buyer, date of purchase, and odometer reading.

The title owner of the vehicle is generally, but not always, the party to whom the vehicle is registered. Even in states where creditors retain titles in their names until the buyer pays off the auto loan, registration of the vehicle will nonetheless be in the buyer's name. This means that the buyer will pay the sales taxes, use taxes, licensing plate fees, and (usually) fees associated with the transferring of the vehicle to the buyer's name.

If the buyer has a lien against the title to the buyer's vehicle, the state will most likely require the buyer to maintain full coverage insurance on the car, including, especially, collision coverage. Doing so protects the interests of the lienholder, who could stand to lose both payment and the vehicle if the buyer is involved in an accident and does not have the vehicle insured. Registration may be denied if the vehicle fails to pass auto emissions or operational testing, or if any taxes are pending. Additionally, registration may be denied to persons whose driving licenses have been suspended or revoked.

## State Lemon Laws

ALABAMA: See Article 8, Chapter 20A of the Alabama Code of 1975. Requires three repair attempts or 30 calendar days out of service.

ALASKA: See Title 45, Chapter 45, Sections 300 to 360 of the Alaska Statutes. Requires three repair attempts or 30 business days out of service.

ARIZONA: See Sections 44.1261 to 1265 of the Arizona Revised Statutes. Requires four repair attempts or 30 calendar days out of service.

ARKANSAS: See Title 4, Chapter 90, Sections 401 to 417 of Arkansas Statutes. Requires one repair attempt for defect that may cause death or serious injury or three repair attempts or 30 calendar days out of service.

CALIFORNIA: See California Civil Code 1793.22, the Tauner **Consumer Protection** Act. Requires two repair attempts for a defect which may cause death or serious injury or four repair attempts or 30 calendar days out of service.

COLORADO: See Colorado Statutes 42-10-101 to 107. Requires four repair attempts or 30 calendar days out of service.

CONNECTICUT: See Connecticut Statutes, Title 42, Chapter 743b for new vehicles, Chapter 743f for used vehicles. Requires two repair attempts if there is a serious safety hazard, otherwise four repair attempts or 30 calendar days out of service.

DELAWARE: See Title 6, Subtitle II, Chapter 50, Sections 5001 to 5009. Requires four repair attempts or 30 business days out of service.

DISTRICT OF COLUMBIA: See DC Code, Division VIII, Title 50, Subtitle II, Chapter 5. Requires four repair attempts or 30 calendar days out of service.

FLORIDA: See Florida Statutes Annotated, Chapter 681. Requires three repair attempts or 30 calendar days out of service.

GEORGIA: See Georgia Code, Section 10-1-780. Requires one attempt for a serious safety defect in braking or steering systems, otherwise three repair attempts or 30 calendar days out of service.

HAWAII: See Hawaii Revised Statutes, Chapter 481i. Requires one repair for defects which may cause death or serious injury, otherwise three repair attempts or 30 business days out of service.

IDAHO: See Titles 48, Chapter 9, Sections 901-903. Requires four repair attempts or 30 business days out of service.

ILLINOIS: See Chapter 815, 815 ILCS, Section 815.380. Requires four repair attempts or 30 business days out of service.

INDIANA: See Indiana Code Section 24-5-13. Requires four repair attempts or 30 business days out of service.

IOWA: See Iowa Code, Chapter 322G, Sections 1 to 15. Requires one repair attempt for defects that may cause death or serious injury, otherwise three repair attempts plus a final attempt or 30 calendar days out of service.

KANSAS: See Kansas Statutes, Chapter 50-645 to 646. Requires four repair attempts or ten repair attempts for different defects, otherwise 30 calendar days out of service.

KENTUCKY: See KRS 367.840 to 846, also KRS 860 to 870. Requires four repair attempts or 30 days out of service.

LOUISIANA: See Louisiana Revised Statutes Title 51, Sections 1941 to 1948. Requires four repair attempts or 30 calendar days out of service.

MAINE: See Title 10, Chapter 203A, Sections 1161 to 1169. Requires three repair attempts or 15 business days out of service.

MARYLAND: See Statutes under Commercial Law, 12-1504 and 14-501. Requires one unsuccessful repair for braking or steering system failures, otherwise four repair attempts or 30 calendar days out of service.

MICHIGAN: See MCL 257.1401 et seq. Requires four repair attempts or 30 business days out of service.

MINNESOTA: See Minnesota Statutes Annotated, 325F.665 for new cars, 325F.662 for used ones. Requires one unsuccessful repair for braking or steering system failures, otherwise four repair attempts or 30 business days out of service.

MISSISSIPPI: See **Statute** Sectiosnns 63-17-151 to 165. Requires three repair attempts or 15 working days out of service.

MISSOURI: See Missouri Revised Statutes 407.560 to 579. Requires four repair attempts or 30 business days out of service.

MONTANA: See Montana Code, Title 61, Chapter, Part 5, Section 61-4-501. Requires four repair attempts or 30 business days out of service.

NEBRASKA: See Chapter 60 (Motor Vehicles), Sections 60-2701 to 2709. Requires four repair attempts or 40 business days out of service.

NEVADA: See Nevada Revised Statutes, 597.600 to 680. Requires four repair attempts or 30 calendar days out of service.

NEW HAMPSHIRE: See Title 31, Chapter 3570. Requires three repair attempts or 30 business days out of service.

NEW JERSEY: See Title 56, Sections 56-12-29 to 49. Requires three repair attempts or 30 calendar days out of service.

NEW MEXICO: See Chapter 57, Article 16A. Requires four repair attempts or 30 business days out of service.

NEW YORK: See New York State General Business Laws (GBL), Section 198a for new vehicles, Section 198b for used vehicles. Requires four repair attempts or 30 calendar days out of service. Substantial defects must be repaired within 20 days of receipt of notice from the consumer using certified mail.

NORTH CAROLINA: See Chapters 20 of the North Carolina General Statutes, Article 15A. Requires four repair attempts or 20 calendar days out of service.

NORTH DAKOTA: See Title 51 of the Century Code, Sections 51-07-16 to 22. Requires three repair attempts or 30 business days out of service.

OHIO: See ORC 1345.71 to 78. Requires one repair attempt for condition likely to cause death or injury, three repair attempts for same defect, eight total repair attempts, or 30 calendar days out of service.

OKLAHOMA: See Section 15-901 of the Oklahoma Statutes. Requires four repair attempts or 45 calendar days out of service.

OREGON: See ORS 646.315 to 75. Requires four repair attempts or 30 business days out of service.

PENNSYLVANIA: See Pennsylvania Statutes Annotated, Title 73, Chapter 28, Sections 1951 to 63. Requires three repair attempts or 30 calendar days out of service.

RHODE ISLAND: See Rhode Island Code, Title 31 (Motor and Other Vehicles), Chapter 31-5.2. Requires four repair attempts or 30 calendar days out of service.

SOUTH CAROLINA: See Title 56 (Motor Vehicles), Chapter 28, Section 56.28-10. Requires three repair attempts or 30 calendar days out of service.

SOUTH DAKOTA: See Title 32, Chapter 32-6D.1 to 11. Requires four repair attempts plus a final attempt.

TENNESSEE: See Tennessee Code, Chapter 24, Sections 55-24-201. Requires four repair attempts or 30 calendar days out of service.

TEXAS: See Motor Vehicle Commission Code, Article 4413(36) of Vernon's Texas Civil Statutes. Requires two repair attempts for serious defects, otherwise four repair attempts or 30 days out of service.

UTAH: See Utah Administrative Code, Rule R152-20. Requires four repair attempts or 30 business days out of service.

VERMONT: See Chapter 115, Sections 4170 to 4181. Requires three repair attempts or 30 calendar days out of service.

VIRGINIA: See Title 59.1, Chapter 17.3, Sections 59.1-207.9 to 207.16. Requires one repair for serious safety defect, otherwise three repair attempts or 30 calendar days out of service.

WASHINGTON: See RCW Title 19, Chapter 118, Section 19.118.005. Requires two repair attempts for serious safety defect, otherwise four repair attempts or 30 calendar days out of service.

WEST VIRGINIA: See West Virginia Code 46A-6A, Sections 1 to 9. Requires three repair attempts or 30 calendar days out of service.

WISCONSIN: See Chapter 218.015. Requires four repair attempts or 30 days out of service.

WYOMING: See Title 40, Chapter 17, Section 101. Requires three repair attempts or 30 business days out of service.

## Additional Resources

"Buying a New/Used Car FAQ," Nolo Online Law. Available at http://www.nolo.com/lawcenter/faqs/detail.cfm.

*Guide to Consumer Law* American Bar Association. Random House,1997.

*Law for Dummies.* Ventura, John,. IDG Books Worldwide, Inc., 1996.

"State by State Lemon Law Summaries," Autopedia. Available at http://autopedia.com/html/HotLinks_Lemon2.html.

## Organizations

### The Automotive Consumer Action Program (AUTOCAP)

URL: http://www.autocap.com

# AUTOMOBILES

## DRIVER'S LICENSE

*Sections Within This Essay:*

## Background

In the United States, driver licenses are issued by the individual states for their residents. Protecting the **public interest** is the primary purpose of driver's licenses. They are required for operating all types of motor vehicles. Driver licenses are also used as an important form of photo identification in the United States, particularly in many non-driving situations where proof of identity or age is required. As identification, they are useful for boarding airline flights, cashing checks, and showing proof of age for activities such as purchasing alcoholic beverages.

The first driver's licenses were issued in Paris in 1893. To obtain one of these licenses, the driver was required to know how to repair his own car as well as drive it. In the United States, vehicle registration began in 1901. Licensing drivers began in 1916, and by the mid-1920s there were age requirements and other restrictions on who could be licensed to operate an automobile.

This authority is delegated to the states, although from the earliest years there have been challenges to particular aspects of state licensing laws, as well as outright challenges to the states' rights to license vehicles and drivers. With respect to the latter issue, the U. S. Supreme Court noted in 1915 in the case of *Hendrick v. Maryland* that "The movement of motor vehicles over the highways is attended by constant and serious dangers to the public and is also abnormally destructive to the [high]ways themselves . . . .[A] state may rightfully prescribe uniform regulations necessary for public safety and order in respect to the operation upon its highways of all motor vehicles—those moving in interstate commerce as well as others . . . .This is but an exercise of the police power uniformly recognized as belonging to the states and essential to the preservation of the health, safety, and comfort of their citizens" 235 US 610.

Driver's licenses perform several vital functions. When they were first issued in the United States, driver's licenses were meant to verify that the holder had complied with the regulations associated with operating a motor vehicle. In addition to verifying compliance with state laws, driver's licenses have become an almost essential form of identification for individuals, law enforcement authorities, and others who require validation of identity. Later, photographs were added to aid in positive identification and to help reduce instances of **fraud**. Other measures to prevent **counterfeiting** driver's licenses include using thumb print and hologram images on the license. Today, many states issues licenses with magnetic strips and bar codes to provide for the electronic recording of driver license information if a traffic **citation** is issued.

## Requirements

When individuals present themselves at a state's licensing facility as an applicants for a driver's licenses, there are several requirements they will be required to meet in order to obtain a valid driver's license. State statutes provide very specific information about the requirements for obtaining a driver's license. These requirements include:

- Residency requirements. For example, it is common for states to require individuals to apply for a driver's licenses within a certain time after moving to the state.

- Production of identification documents (there is a preference for photo identification) and disclosure of the individuals' Social Security numbers.

- Proof that the applicants meet the state's minimum age for possessing a driver's licenses.

- Three tests: a written exam, a vision test, and a driving test.

- If applicants are a foreign national, there may be additional requirements imposed by the state or by the INS.

- Payment of the appropriate application fees.

- Proof of insurance.

- Production of any other valid licenses and instructions permits from other states or foreign countries.

## Identification

Besides providing proof of an individual's' permission to drive, a driver's licenses are an important form of identification. Before licenses are awarded by a state, applicants will be asked to provide adequate proof of identity. Some of the common forms of identification accepted in many licensing facilities are:

- A military identification card

- A United States **Passport**

- A student driver permit

- A Social Security Card

- An identification card issued by a state

- An identification card issued by the U. S., a state, or an agency of either the U. S. or a state

- Immigration and Naturalization Service identification cards or forms

- The Alien Registration Card, I-151. Note that in some states, The Employment Authorization for Legalization Applicant's Card (I-688A and I-688B) may not be sufficient as an identification document.

In many states, individuals may present a combination of documents as proof of identity. These items may include:

- Birth certificate or registration cards. It is best to bring either the original or a **certified copy**

- The applicant's social security card

- A marriage certificate or **divorce decree**. Again, original or certified copies will be best.

- The applicant's voter registration card

- A government-issued business or professional licenses (e.g. cosmetology license, law license)

- The applicant's vehicle registration and/or title

- The applicant's original or a certified copy of his school transcripts

If applicants present documents written in a language other than English, there may be a delay. Most licensing facilities make **good faith** efforts to read and interpret these documents. Occasionally, they may need to FAX applicants' documents to another office for assistance. If an adequate translation cannot be obtained, they may be asked to provide an English translation along with the original document

## Age

States require applicants for drivers' licenses to be at least 16 years of age. In many states, if applicants are younger than 18, they must also provide a signed parental authorization form. This form states a person's relationship to the applicant for a license and gives permission for the person to acquire a driver's license.

Usually, states will require that the parental authorization form be notarized or signed in the presence of the proper authority at a licensing facility. Whenever individuals present themselves for a driver's **examination**, they must provide proof of their identification and age. This can be done with an official document such as a birth certificate or passport.

## Fees

When individuals apply for a driver's license, they are required to pay a fee based on the type of license for which they are applying and for any endorsement attached to the license. There are also fees assessed for license renewals and extensions. In most states, fees must be paid either in cash or by personal check. Few states accept credit cards or **debit** cards for payment of licensing fees. License fees are fairly moderate, but they do vary from state to state. Individuals can check with their state's department of motor vehicles for a fee schedule for driver's licenses, endorsements, or permits.

## Tests

### Written

As part of the driver's license application process, individuals will be required to take a written test. This exam tests their knowledge of the rules of the road and their ability to recognize and interpret road signs. Usually, they must successfully complete the written exam prior to scheduling the driving test.

### Vision

Good eyesight is of utmost importance for the safe operation of motor vehicles. Therefore, as part

of the driver's license application process, the department of motor vehicles in the state will administer a vision test. This is a brief test meant to evaluate the applicants' eyesight. The vision test evaluates three factors:

- Clarity of vision,

- How far individuals can see to either side while looking straight ahead (peripheral vision),

- Depth and color perception.

If individuals wear glasses or contact lenses, they will be asked to perform the exam with their corrective eyewear both on and off. The results of the test will determine whether there are restrictions placed on their driver's licenses (e.g. must wear corrective eyewear when operating a motor vehicle).

### Driving

The final portion of a driver's license application procedure is the driving test. Applicants will be required to provide a safe vehicle for the test. They will also need to provide proof of automobile insurance prior to the driving test. An unlicensed applicant may not use a rental car for the driving test. The driving test may be waived if an applicant has a valid driver license from another state and meets all other applicable requirements. The driving test will be required of applicants with licenses from foreign countries, including Mexico and Canada.

The driving test is an opportunity to demonstrate that the applicants are a safe drivers. There will be no passengers other than an examining official—a local or state police officer or authorized department of motor vehicles personnel—allowed on the drive test. The **examiner** in the front seat will give the applicants driving directions. The directions should be given in a clear manner and with enough time to allow the applicants to take appropriate action. Applicants will never be asked to do anything unsafe or illegal.

The exact procedure for driving tests will vary somewhat from state to state, although several features of these tests are fairly consistent throughout the United States. Before the test applicants will be asked to use their arms to signal for a right turn, left turn, slow, or stop. Along with noting their driving skills in normal traffic the examiner will also ask them to perform certain maneuvers such as parking on a hill, parallel parking, entering traffic from a parked position, and backing out of a driveway or around a corner.

A few of the most common test items the examiner will observe are:

- Backing up

- Controlling the vehicle

- Driving in traffic

- Driving through blind or crowded intersections

- Judging distance

- Leaving the curb

- Obeying traffic signals and signs

- Respecting the rights of pedestrians and other drivers

- Starting the vehicle

- Stopping

## Insurance

When individuals obtain a driver's licenses they will be required to provide proof that they have purchased adequate automobile insurance. Among other things, automobile insurance helps pay for medical bills and car repairs if drivers are in an automobile accidents. Every state requires drivers to purchase some auto insurance, and they specify the minimum amounts required. Individuals can purchase insurance from any company they choose, but should they be stopped by the police or should they be involved in a traffic accidents, they will most likely be required to supply proof of current insurance in their automobile or on their persons. There are several kinds of automobile insurance, including the following:

- Liability. There are two principal aspects to liability insurance, bodily injury coverage and property damage coverage. Bodily injury liability insurance covers costs up to certain limits if drivers kill or injure someone else in an accident. In these cases the drivers' insurance company pays for expenses like legal fees (if the insured is sued), medical bills, and lost wages of the other person if the insured is are at-fault. Property damage liability insurance covers the costs associated with damage to someone else's car or other property if the insured damaged that property while driving. Both bodily injury and property damage liability insurance can

be purchased in various amounts, but the state that licenses the individual to drive will set minimum amounts which that person must purchase.

- Uninsured motorist bodily injury coverage. This type of insurance covers individuals for their bodily injury caused by a hit-and-run driver or from injuries caused by a driver who has no auto liability insurance.

- Collision insurance. This type of insurance coverage reimburses drivers for damage to their cars if the car collides with another object. To figure out how much an insurance company will pay to fix the insured's car, a claims **adjuster** may look at the damage, or the insured may be asked to get estimates from body shops. If the insured's car is "totaled," the insured person gets what the car is worth (according to tables of vehicle values) at the time of the accident.

- Comprehensive insurance. Comprehensive insurance covers the cost of damage to the insured's car caused by most other causes such as fire, theft, hail, or other natural disasters. If the insured have a loan on the vehicle, the insured's lender may require the insured to carry this type of insurance.

The cost of automobile insurance varies according to a number of factors. For example, statistics show that drivers under the age of 25 are more likely to be involved in accidents; insurance companies charge them more for coverage. If drivers get a ticket for speeding or other traffic violation, their insurance costs may go up. Models of vehicles that are more dangerous to drive (e.g. convertibles) or cost more to repair if they're damaged will generally cost more to insure than safer cars or cars that cost less to repair. And if the insured lives in a city with greater chances that the car will be hit, stolen, or vandalized are higher—, the insurance costs will probably be higher as well.

There are some things individuals can do to help keep the cost of insurance down:

- Choose the vehicle carefully. Remember that some vehicles—like convertibles and sports cars—cost more to insure than others.

- Consider the age and condition of the vehicle. If the vehicle is an older model, it may not be cost-effective to pay for insurance that covers physical damage to the older car.

- Drive lawfully and defensively to avoid violations and accidents.

- Increase the **deductible** and thus lower the premium, however realize that by doing so, it will cause the owner to pay more out of pocket each time they have a claim.

- Students who get good grades may enjoy lower rates. For example, some companies give discounts to students with a B average or better.

## Kinds of Licenses

There are several kinds of driver's licenses. There are important distinctions among these types of licenses, as well as different requirements for obtaining them. The most common are:

- Instruction or learner's permit

- Commercial licenses

- International

- Motorcycle

### Instruction or Learner's Permit

In most states, individuals may apply for a driver instruction permit—often called a "learner's permit"—as early as the age of 15 on the condition that they are also enrolled in an approved traffic safety education course. Driving privileges under a learner's permit are restricted. The restrictions that apply to the learner's permit will vary from state to state. They may include restrictions on the age of the licensed driver accompanying the learner/driver, the hours in which the learner/driver may be able to drive, and even the types of highways that learners may drive on.

In some states, individuals may be able to apply for a learner's permit without being enrolled in a class, but they must take the written driving test to prove they are capable of understanding the fundamentals of driving and the rules of the road. Those with a learner's permit usually may drive a vehicle as long as a licensed driver is present in the vehicle at the time. There are additional requirements stating how long they must have a learner's permit before they may obtain a permanent license. Individuals can check with their state's department of transportation for the exact rules which will apply in their situation. As with a permanent driver's license, when they apply for a learner's permit, they will be required to supply proof of identification. Proof of age, documented parental consent, and other forms are also required, as well as a fee for the permit.

### Commercial

Since 1992 drivers of commercial motor vehicles (CMV) have been required to have a commercial driver's license (CDL). The Federal Highway Administration (FHWA) issues rules and standards for testing and licensing CMV drivers. These standards permit states to issue CDLs to drivers only after the drivers passes knowledge and skills tests related to the type of vehicle to be operated. CDLs fall into several categories depending on the weight of the vehicle and/or load being pulled and depending on the number of passengers in the vehicle. These categories are:

- Class A: The vehicle weighs 26,001 or more pounds and the vehicle(s) being towed is in excess of 10,000 pounds.

- Class B: The vehicle weighs 26,001 or more pounds, or any such vehicle towing a vehicle not in excess of 10,000 pounds.

- Class C: Any vehicle or combination of vehicles that is either designed to transport 16 or more passengers, including the driver or is marked as a carrier of hazardous materials.

Drivers who operate CMVs will be required to pass additional tests to obtain any of the following endorsements on their CDL:

- T: Double/Triple Trailers

- P: Passenger

- N: Tank Vehicle

- H: Hazardous Materials

- X: Combination of Tank Vehicle and Hazardous Materials

A state will determine the appropriate license fee, the rules for license renewals, and the age, medical and other driver qualifications of its intrastate commercial drivers. Drivers with CDLs who cross state lines must meet the Federal driver qualifications (49 CFR 391). All CDLs contain the following information:

- Color photograph or digital image of the driver

- Notation of the "air brake" restriction, if issued

- The class(es) of vehicle that the driver is authorized to driver

- The issue date and the expiration date of the license

- The driver's date of birth, sex, and height

- The driver's full name, signature, and address

- The driver's state license number

- The endorsement(s) for which the driver has qualified

- The name of the issuing state

- The words "Commercial Driver's License" or "CDL"

States may issue learner's permits for training on public highways as long as learner's permit holders are required to be accompanied by someone with a valid CDL appropriate for that vehicle. These learner's permits must be issued for limited time periods.

### International

If individuals are traveling to an English-speaking country, they may be able to get by with their U. S. driver's licenses. However, many other countries will ask that they also obtain an International Driver's Permit, which is a document that translates the information on the home driver's license into 11 different languages. More than 160 countries recognize the International Driver's Permit. If individuals plan to rent a car on their trip abroad, they will probably be asked to present one along with their valid state license. Some countries require special road permits, instead of tolls, to use on their major roads. They will fine those found driving without such a permit.

An International Driver's Permit must be issued in the home country. To obtain an International Driver's Permit, individuals will need to produce two passport photos and their valid state driver's licenses. Currently, an International Driver's Permit costs $10 for a one-year issue. Individuals must complete an application, which can be printed online or submitted by mail. Only two agencies in the United States are authorized to issue these licenses: the American Automobile Association and the American Automobile Touring Alliance. However, travelers should remember that an International Driver's Permit is not a license in and of itself, so drivers can not establish a separate driving record with one. If drivers get a traffic citation while driving with their international driver's permit, it will be reflected on their state licenses.

To apply for an international driving permit, individuals must:

- Be at least age 18

- Present two passport-size photographs

- Present their valid U. S. licenses

In most cases, U. S. auto insurance will not cover drivers abroad; however, their policy may apply when they drive to Mexico or Canada. Even if their U. S. policy is valid in one of these countries, it may not meet the minimum requirements in Canada or Mexico. Individuals may check with the embassy or consulate of the country they plan to visit for specific insurance requirements. Overseas car rental agencies usually offer auto insurance for an additional fee, but in some countries, the required coverage is minimal. If drivers rent a cars overseas, they ought to consider purchasing insurance coverage that is equivalent to the amount of automobile insurance coverage that they carry at home.

### Motorcycle

All states regulate the issuance of motorcycle permits and motorcycle endorsements. All states require that those wishing to operate motorcycles pass motorcycle knowledge and skill tests. These tests are separate from standard automobile driver license tests. Some states have mandatory motorcycle training in addition to the knowledge and skill tests. In most cases if individuals have successfully completed an approved motorcycle skills course, they may bring their completion cards to the vehicle licensing facility in their state (usually within a limited time) and if they pass the knowledge test, the skill test will be waived. As with other operator licenses, states assess a fee for issuing a motorcycle license, and individuals will also be required to provide proof that they are in compliance with the state's vehicular insurance laws.

## The Motor Voter Law

The National Voter Registration Act (commonly referred to as "motor voter," or, "NVRA") took effect in 1995. The NVRA requires states to offer voter registration to citizens when they apply for drivers' licenses. This tie between driver's licensing agencies or facilities and voter registration is the source of the term "motor voter." When individuals obtain drivers' licenses, states can also assess needs and benefits for other assistance programs such as food stamps, **Medicaid**, Aid to Families with Dependent Children, and Women, Infants, and Children. The Act also imposes on states a requirement to designate additional offices for voter registration services.

Additional provisions of the law require states to accept a national mail-in voter registration form and to establish guidelines for maintaining the accuracy of voter registration rolls—most notably prohibiting states from removing registrants from the rolls for not voting. Despite the mandatory provisions, states have some discretion in how they implement the act's provisions. The NVRA requires states to register voters in three specified ways in addition to any other procedures the state uses for voter registration:

- Simultaneous application for a driver's license and registration to vote

- Mail-in application for voter registration

- Application in person at designated government agencies

Election officials must send all applicants a notice informing them of their voter registration status.

## Organ Donation

Individuals can state on their driver's licenses their desire to donate their organs or bodily tissues upon their deaths. There is a brief questionnaire about organ donation that is part of the application for a driver's license. When individuals answer "yes" to the questions about organ and tissue donation on their license applications, then the department of motor vehicles will place a symbol (e.g. a red heart with a "Y" in the center) on the front of their licenses, permits, or ID cards. Individuals must also sign the back of the license and discuss their wish to donate their organs with their families. By indicating their wish to donate their organs, their names will most likely be entered in a computerized registry. For more information about organ and tissue donation, individuals can see "Organ Donation" in the *Gale Encyclopedia of Everyday Law*.

## Points

States use various methods to help enforce their traffic safety laws. All states use some variation of a point system as part of this effort. Depending on the state, individuals may begin with a certain number of points, have points deducted for traffic violations, or they may have points added for traffic violations. Points are assigned for only moving violations (violations that occur when the car is being driven); points are not assigned for parking, licensing, or other non-

moving violations. If a driver accumulates (or loses) a certain number of points within a prescribed amount of time, that driver's driving privileges may be suspended or revoked.

These point systems identify persistent or repeat violators. Several violations may indicate that a state should take action against the driver. Point systems may not be the only basis for suspending or revoking driver licenses. For example, several speeding violations in an 18-month period, or a single drunk driving violation, could result in the state's mandatory revocation of a license, regardless of the driver's number of points. While a **conviction** is required for the points to go on a record, the conviction date is not used to determine the point total. Points are reduced by not having any further violations over a period of time. The point systems differ in important ways from state to state. People can contact their state's department of motor vehicles for more details.

## License Suspension and Revocation

All licenses expire at some point, but there are ways to lose driving privileges before the license's expiration date. Early termination of the validity of a driver's license is known as suspension (where a license is temporarily rendered invalid), and revocation (where driving privileges granted by a license are fully terminated). In both cases, drivers would be are notified by the state and would have the right to a **hearing**. Examples of driver license suspensions and revocations are:

- Driving Under the Influence (DUI) of alcohol and other drugs.: If a breath, blood, or urine test reveals individuals are driving under the influence of alcohol or other drugs, or if individuals are convicted of DUI offenses, their licenses may be suspended or revoked.

- Failure to Appear: If individuals receive a traffic ticket and do not pay the fine on time or do not appear in court when required their licenses are subject to being suspended or revoked.

- Security Deposit: If individuals are in an accident and they do not have liability insurance, their driver licenses and their vehicle registration plates may be suspended.

- **Child Support Arrears**: If individuals are in arrears in court ordered child support payments the state may suspend or revoke licenses.

- Truancy: Juveniles can lose their driver's licenses, or their issuance may be delayed for **habitual** absence from school.

A driver's license suspension or revocation is usually handled as a separate action from any other court case in which individuals may be involved. A state does not automatically reinstate driving privileges if licenses were suspended or revoked. Individuals must follow reinstatement procedures to regain their driving privileges, even if the court case underlying the suspension or revocation was dismissed. Furthermore, all 50 states share license suspension and revocation information. If there is an active suspension or revocation in one state, no other state may issue a driver's license. Driving while suspended or revoked are serious criminal offenses. If individuals are apprehended driving a vehicle with a suspended or revoked license, they could pay hefty fines and even face a term of **imprisonment**.

## Renewing License

A driver's license expires within a statutorily set number of years after the driver first acquires it. The longevity of a license varies somewhat from state to state, with either three or five years being the normal term of a license. In some states, individuals may be able to renew their licenses by mail, but usually they will be required to appear in person and pass a vision test. Additionally, they may be required to take other exams if licensing officials in their state determine that it is necessary. States assess fee for a license renewals. Individuals should watch out for penalties if they fail to meet deadlines to renew their licenses after they has expired.

## Additional Resources

"A Citizen's Guide to the National Voter Registration Act of 1993" League of Women Voters, 1994. Available at http://www.nmia.com/lwvabc/TOC.html.

"State and Local Government on the Net" Piper Resources, 2002. Available at http://www.statelocalgov.net/index.cfm.

"*State Statutes on the Internet: Motor Vehicles.*" Cornell University, 2002. Available at http://www.law.cornell.edu/topics/state_statutes3.html#motor_vehicles,. Cornell University, 2002.

## Organizations

### *The International Council on Alcohol, Drugs & Traffic Safety (ICADTS)*

ICADTS Secretary, Mississippi State University
Mississippi State, MS 39762 USA
Phone: (601) 325-7959
Fax: (601) 325-7966
E-Mail: bwparke r@ssrc.msstate.edu

### *National Highway Traffic Safety Administration (NHTSA)*

400 7th St. SW
Washington, DC 20590 USA
Phone: (888) 327-4236
E-Mail: webmaster@nhtsa.dot.gov
URL: http://www.nhtsa.dot.gov/

### *U. S. Department of Transportation*

400 7th Street, S.W.
Washington, DC 20590 USA
Phone: (202) 366-4000
E-Mail: dot.comments@ost.dot.gov
URL: http://www.dot.gov

# AUTOMOBILES

## INSURANCE

*Sections within this essay:*

## Background

For anyone who has ever owned a car, auto insurance is something almost impossible to do without. Forty-six states and the District of Columbia now require automobile owners to carry some form of automobile insurance, and even if you are residents of one of the few states that does not require some sort of insurance policy on your car, it's a good idea probably if you to have insurance anyway.

Why? Because accidents do happen, they can be expensive, and auto insurance is often the only way for car owners to protect themselves from damages, liability, and possible a hefty court **settlement**. As with anything else so ubiquitous, there are different types of auto insurance designed to suit different types of drivers and cars. Auto insurance requirements vary from state-to-state, with some states re-

quiring more coverage than others. Some states also have **no fault** laws in place, which require insurers to pay for certain accidents no matter who is at fault. Whatever the case, it is good to know some of the basics of auto insurance before deciding on buying a specific policy for your car.

## Liability Insurance

Liability insurance is the most basic form of insurance. It pays if the insured is at fault in an accident. Generally speaking, it covers medical injuries and property damage to the other driver. It can also cover for pain and suffering and legal bills of the other driver as well. Owners are required to carry liability insurance in the vast majority of states. It is also required for rental cars and for drivers of third-party owned vehicles.

### What Is Covered

Liability insurance usually covers the named insured on the policy, the named insured's spouse and children, any blood relative of theirs by marriage, or **adoption**, including foster children, and anyone driving the car with the insured's permission. It covers named vehicles in the policy, as well as added vehicles that the named insured replaces the original named vehicle with in the policy. Most of the time (though not always), it also covers non-named vehicles if the named insured was driving, and any additional non-named vehicle the named insured acquires during the policy period, providing the named insured informs the insurance company during a specified period.

Temporary vehicles that substitute for an insured vehicle that is out of service because of repairs or because it has been totaled are usually covered as well, though again, this is not always the case and an insured individuals should check their policies to determine the exact limits of their coverage.

Drivers who use a named vehicle without the named insured's permission are not covered by a liability policy, although the vehicle itself may be. Also rental cars that are not being used to replace a named vehicle being repaired may not be covered unless the named insured pays a special premium.

### Liability Limits

In the 47 states and the District of Columbia that require liability insurance, a minimum amount of coverage is also required. Even the states that do not require liability insurance insist that when liability insurance is purchased in the state, it needs to meet a minimum requirement.

These minimum requirements are usually represented by a series of three numbers. The first number represents the amount of money (in thousands) an insurance company is required to pay for bodily injury for one person injured in an accident. The second number represents the amount an insurance company is required to pay in total for all the injuries in an accident. The final number represents the amount the insurance company must pay for property damage in an accident.

For example, the liability requirements of the state of Alabama are usually represented as 20/40/10. Thus, insured drivers in Alabama are required to carry a minimum of $20,000 of medical coverage for a single person injured in an accident, $40,000 of medical coverage for all people injured in an accident, and $10,000 of coverage for property damage.

Insurance companies are not allowed to sell policies that are under the liability limits. In Alabama, a motorist could not buy $10,000 worth of coverage for a single person injured in an accident or $5,000 of coverage for property damage. Insurance policies must at least meet the minimum requirements, although they can offer more coverage than the requirements. States that do not mandate liability insurance also have liability minimums—insurers cannot sell policies in those states below the minimums.

Not all states require medical liability insurance to be carried by drivers: - in Florida and New Jersey, only property damage liability is mandatory. California also allows lower minimums for eligible low-income drivers in the California Automobile Assigned Risk Plan. In New York, drivers are required to carry a higher amount of liability insurance designed to cover injury from the accident which results in death.

States have different laws as to when proof of insurance must be presented. Some states oblige such proof to be offered when a car is registered, others ask for such proof only when drivers are charged with a traffic violation or have an accident on their records.

## Collision and Comprehensive Coverage

Besides liability, drivers can get other coverage from auto insurance. Collision coverage insures drivers for the damage done to their own cars by an accident that was their fault. Collision insurance is the most expensive auto insurance coverage, and may come with a high **deductible**.

Comprehensive coverage pays for damage to a driver's car that was caused by events other than a car accident. Weather damage, theft damage, and fire damage are just some of the events covered by comprehensive. Many policies even cover damages from hitting a deer. Comprehensive coverage is not as expensive as collision, but it is still more expensive than liability and usually comes with a deductible.

### Determining Value of Car

With both collision and comprehensive, insurers will usually only cover the **Actual Cash Value** (ACV) of the cost of the car. ACV is determined by taking the replacement cost of the vehicle—what it would cost to repair damage to the vehicle without deducting for depreciation—and subtracting the **depreciation**. So, if a car is bought for $10,000, and is 10 years old, the ACV of the car would be substantially less than $10,000.

Drivers willing to pay a higher premium can get insurance policies that will cover the replacement costs of the car. Depending on the age and condition of the vehicle, these kinds of policies may be worth it, although they are usually not recommended for older vehicles.

## Uninsured/Underinsured Motorist Coverage

Uninsured motorist (UM) coverage provides coverage for the insured who is hit by a motorist who is uninsured or by a hit-and-run driver who remains unidentified. Since the injured party cannot get money for their injuries from the driver of the liable vehicle, uninsured motorist coverage picks up the bill. UM coverage is required in many states as part of a driver's liability coverage.

UM coverage pays for the driver or a relative who lives with the driver, or anyone else driving a named vehicle with a driver's permission, or anyone else riding with the driver in the named vehicle. UM coverage also covers the insured if they are passengers in someone else's car, although the passenger's UM insurance will not contribute until the driver's UM insurance is exhausted. For a hit-and-run, a driver is usually required to notify the police within 24-hours of the accident to receive the benefits of UM coverage.

Underinsured motorist (UIM) coverage operates in a similar fashion. With UIM coverage, the liability policy of the driver at fault is not enough to cover the injuries of the other driver or passengers. UIM coverage pays out the difference for the non-liable driver.

Generally speaking, UM or UIM coverage pays for only medical injury to the driver and passengers of the hit car. For a higher premium, it can cover property damage to the automobile as well. UM and UIM coverage is reduced by amounts the driver receives from other insurance coverage such as personal medical insurance or worker's compensation.

## No Fault Insurance

Since 1970, many states have passed a no-fault insurance law. This law requires drivers to buy insurance that covers their injuries in an auto accident no matter who is at fault. No-fault laws, which were first enacted in Canada in the 1940s and 1950s, are an attempt to rein in **litigation** by making the determination of fault irrelevant, thus allowing drivers to get reimbursed for their injuries faster and without court cost and delay.

Most no-fault insurance provides for very limited coverage—only providing for medical bills and lost income, and sometimes vehicle damage, though that is often paid outside no-fault by utilizing liability insurance. No fault does not pay for medical bills higher than the insured **Personal Injury** Protection (PIP) limits. If medical bills are higher, the insured must file a liability claim against the driver at fault. Some states put no restriction on an injured party's

right to sue under no-fault,; other states require the injured party to reach a certain threshold of injury, either monetary or physical, before the party can sue the other driver.

In addition, no-fault puts restriction on suing for pain-and-suffering damages. All states that have no-fault allow recovery for pain and suffering in the event of death; however, pain and suffering lawsuits may not be allowed for other injuries. Examples of injuries which no-fault states allow no or only limited recovery for pain and suffering include dismemberment, loss of bodily function, serious disfigurement, permanent injury or **disability**, serious fracture and temporary disability or loss of earning capacity.

Two states, Pennsylvania and New Jersey, allow policy holders to determine if their no-fault insurance gives them the right to sue for pain and suffering expenses. If the drivers are willing to pay a higher premium, they have an expanded right to sue for pain and suffering.

## State-By-State Insurance Requirements

The following is a list of state insurance liability requirements as of 2001, showing also whether the state is a no-fault state and whether uninsured motorist coverage is required. All liability minimums are in thousands of dollars, and the numbers are listed in the following order: coverage for injury per person, coverage for total injury, and coverage for property damage.

ALABAMA: Liability insurance required,; liability minimums 20/40/10

ALASKA: Liability insurance required,; liability minimums 50/100/25

ARIZONA: Liability insurance required,; liability minimums 15/30/10

ARKANSAS: Liability insurance required,; liability minimums 25/50/25

CALIFORNIA: Liability insurance required,; liability minimums 15/30/5

COLORADO: Liability insurance required,; liability minimums 25/50/15, no-fault state

CONNECTICUT: Liability insurance required,; liability minimums 20/40/10

DELAWARE: Liability insurance required,; liability minimums 15/30/5

DISTRICT OF COLUMBIA: Liability insurance required; liability minimums 25/50/10, uninsured motorist coverage required

FLORIDA: Liability insurance required for property damage only,; liability minimums 10/20/10, no fault state

GEORGIA: Liability insurance required,; liability minimums 25/50/25

HAWAII: Liability insurance required,; liability minimums 20/40/10, no fault state

IDAHO: Liability insurance required,; liability minimums 25/50/15

ILLINOIS: Liability insurance required,; liability minimums 20/40/15, uninsured motorist coverage required

INDIANA: Liability insurance required,; liability minimums 25/50/10

IOWA: Liability insurance required,; liability minimums 20/40/15

KANSAS: Liability insurance required,; liability minimums 25/50/10, no fault state, uninsured motorist coverage required

KENTUCKY: Liability insurance required,; liability minimums 25/50/10, no fault state

LOUISIANA: Liability insurance required,; liability minimums 10/20/10

MAINE: Liability insurance required,; liability minimums 50/100/25, uninsured motorist coverage required

MARYLAND: Liability insurance required,; liability minimums 20/40/15, uninsured motorist coverage required

MASSACHUSETTS: Liability insurance required,; liability minimums 20/40/5, no fault state, uninsured motorist coverage required

MICHIGAN: Liability insurance required,; liability minimums 20/40/10, no fault state

MINNESOTA: Liability insurance required,; liability minimums 30/60/10, no fault state, uninsured motorist coverage required

MISSISSIPPI: Liability insurance required,; liability minimums 10/20/5

MISSOURI: Liability insurance required,; liability minimums 25/50/10, uninsured motorist coverage required

MONTANA: Liability insurance required,; liability minimums 25/50/10

NEBRASKA: Liability insurance required,; liability minimums 25/50/10

NEVADA: Liability insurance required,; liability minimums 15/30/10

NEW HAMPSHIRE: Liability insurance not required,; liability minimums 25/50/25, uninsured motorist coverage required

NEW JERSEY: Liability insurance required -; drivers may choose standard or basic policy. For basic policy, minimums are 10/10/5 and only property damage is mandatory. For standard policy, minimums are 15/30/5 and all liability is mandatory. No fault state, uninsured motorist coverage required

NEW MEXICO: Liability insurance required,; liability minimums 25/50/10

NEW YORK: Liability insurance required,; liability minimums 25/50/10, liability must rise to 50/100/10 if injury results in death. No fault state, uninsured motorist coverage required

NORTH CAROLINA: Liability insurance required,; liability minimums 30/60/25

NORTH DAKOTA: Liability insurance required,; liability minimums 25/50/25, no fault state, uninsured motorist coverage required

OHIO: Liability insurance required,; liability minimums 12.5/25/7.5

OKLAHOMA: Liability insurance required,; liability minimums 10/20/10

OREGON: Liability insurance required,; liability minimums 25/50/10, uninsured motorist coverage required

PENNSYLVANIA: Liability insurance required,; liability minimums 15/30/5, no fault state

RHODE ISLAND: Liability insurance required,; liability minimums 25/50/25, uninsured motorist coverage required

SOUTH CAROLINA: Liability insurance required,; liability minimums 15/30/10, uninsured motorist coverage required

SOUTH DAKOTA: Liability insurance required,; liability minimums 25/50/25, uninsured motorist coverage required

TENNESSEE: Liability insurance not required,; liability minimums 25/50/10

TEXAS: Liability insurance required,; liability minimums 20/40/15

UTAH: Liability insurance required,; liability minimums 25/50/10, no fault state

VERMONT: Liability insurance required,; liability minimums 25/50/10, uninsured motorist coverage required

VIRGINIA: Liability insurance required,; liability minimums 25/50/20, uninsured motorist coverage required

WASHINGTON: Liability insurance required,; liability minimums 25/50/10 Washington D liability minimums 25/50/10, uninsured motorist coverage required

WEST VIRGINIA: Liability insurance required,; liability minimums 20/40/10, uninsured motorist coverage required

WISCONSIN: Liability insurance not required,; liability minimums 25/50/10, uninsured motorist coverage required

WYOMING: Liability insurance required,; liability minimums 25/50/20

## Additional Resources

*Digest of Motor Laws* Compiled by Butler, Charle A., Editor and Kay Hamada, Eedsitor., American Automobile Association, Heathrow, FL, 1996.

*http://www.iii.org* "Minimum Levels Of Required Auto Insurance", Insurance Information Institute, 2002.

*http://www.insure.com,* "Auto Insurance," Insure.com, 2002.

*http://www.nolo.com* "Auto Insurance FAQ's" Nolo Press, 2002.

*West's Encyclopedia of American Law* West Publishing Company, St. Paul, 1998.

## Organizations

### Insurance Information Institute
110 William Street
New York, NY 10038 USA
Phone: (212) 346-5500
E-Mail: carys@iii.org
URL: http://www.iii.org
Primary Contact: Gordon Stewart, President

## Organizations

### National Association of Insurance Commissioners
2301 McGee St, Suite 800
Kansas City, MO 64108-2660 USA
Phone: (816) 842-3600
URL: http://www.naic.org
Primary Contact: Therese Vaughan, President

### National Automobile Dealers Association
8400 Westpark Drive
McLean, VI 22102 USA
Phone: (800) 252-6232
E-Mail: nadainfo@nada.org
URL: http://www.nada.org
Primary Contact: H. Carter Myers, Chairman

# AUTOMOBILES

## LEASING A CAR

*Sections within this essay:*

- Background
- Federal Consumer Laws and Regulations
- Important Terms in Leasing Contracts and Negotiations
- Disclosures Required Under CLA and Regulation M
- Additional Disclosures Required under Certain State Laws
- Fraud and Overcharging
- Common Leasing Scams
- Should People Lease or Purchase?
- Additional Resources

## Background

Twenty-five percent of all new cars moved off dealers' lots are leased. The contract that defines this relationship between the consumers and the owner of these vehicles is complicated, subject to regulation, and often the site of misunderstanding and **fraudulent** activity. Leasing cars allows people to drive cars they believe they could not afford to buy. It appears to give people access to a better class of cars, while another party remains in charge of the car's mechanical problems. For many people, leasing a car feels like renting an apartment; it's a way to live without the responsibilities of personal ownership. For some people perhaps leasing is a good idea; it is certainly a good idea for the owners of leased vehicles who profit generally at a rate of about three times the list price of their vehicles.

A car **lease** is a contract between the party who owns the car (**lessor**) and the one who will use the car (leasee). A contract signed between these parties governs the terms, those conditions under which the car may be used and the obligation of each party. Consumers sign their lease agreements with automobile dealers. Shortly thereafter, the dealers sell the leased vehicles to a leasing company. The leasing company may be, in fact, the car dealer, or it may be a finance company subsidiary to a car manufacturer, or an independent leasing company. This leasing entity now owns the vehicles and is thus the lessor. Besides profiting from the sale of the car, the dealer enjoys financial incentives from the leasing company and manufacturer rebates.

The leasee acquires no equity in the vehicle. During the lease period, in fact, the leasee pays the leasing company for the car's **depreciation**, that is the difference between the list price of the car new and the value it has once it has been driven for the leased period. For this reason, consumers are better off leasing vehicles that hold their value.

## Federal Consumer Laws and Regulations

The Consumer Leasing Act (CLA) covers car leases of at least four months in duration in which the total amount of money a leasee owes does not exceed $25,000 for a vehicle limited to personal use. In 1998, regulations governing this act, referred to as Regulation M, were established by the Federal Reserve Board. Regulation M can be found in the **Code of Federal Regulations** (CFR), Title 12, Part 213.4. The CFR is available in many law libraries and on the Internet. Leasing law specifies the disclosures which must be contained in the lease document. For example, dealers must reveal the monthly and total cost of the lease, additional fees, and potential mileage and early termination penalties. Enforcement of these disclosures is handled through the Federal Trade Commission.

## Important Terms in Leasing Contracts and Negotiations

The lease contains terms which the consumer may not know but which are important to understand since they determine the nature of the contract the consumer is signing. The following are the important terms to know.

- Amortized Amounts: These consist of fees a lessor is required to collect, such as taxes and registration fees These expenses are paid off gradually as a part of each monthly payment. Expenses for insurance and maintenance, when provided by the dealer, are also amortized.

- Base Monthly Payment: This depreciation amount is the value the vehicle is calculated to lose each month, plus the amortized amounts and the interest leasees pay in financing charges over the lease term, divided by the number of months the vehicle is leased.

- Capitalized Cost: This is the total price of the car as agreed to by the lessor and the leasee over the life of the lease term, plus the registration fees, title fees, and taxes.

- Capitalized **Net** Cost: This is the amount the leasee will have paid for the car after all payments have been made. This is the same figure as the adjusted capitalized cost as it takes into account any **down payment** made.

- Depreciation plus Amortized Amounts: The difference between the value of the car at the beginning of the lease and at the end of the lease is the car's depreciation. If the leasee does not exercise the option to purchase the vehicle, the lessor will charge the leasee a fee averaging between $250 and $400 to cover the expenses the lessor incurs in preparing the car for sale.

- Open-End Lease: When this lease is terminated, the leasee is liable for the difference between a lesser **fair market value** and a comparable residual value given to the value in the lease. The residual value will be considered unreasonable if it exceeds the fair **market value** by more than triple that amount.

- Close-End Lease: When this lease is terminated, the leasee is not responsible for paying the difference between the residual value given to the vehicle in the lease and a lesser fair market value.

- Lease Rate: This figure is that percentage of the monthly payment which is rental charge. Some dealers will disclose to a lessor what this amount is. As of 2002, no federal standard governs how this amount is calculated, and dealers are not required to disclose how they arrive at the amount. However, if a lease rate is used in an advertisement, there must also be a disclaimer that the lease rate may not be an accurate reflection of the total cost leasee will pay for their leases. This figure is frequently used to deceive customers into believing they are paying less interest in financing the lease than they actually are.

- Money Factor: This is a decimal number used to determine the proportion of the monthly payment that consists of a rental charge. This figure is similar to an interest charge and is not required to be disclosed under federal law.

- Reasonable Standard: The Consumer Leasing Act stipulates that penalties for early termination and late payments or ceasing to make payments must be reasonable according to the amount of harm actually experienced or anticipated by the lessor.

## Disclosures Required Under CLA and Regulation M

When dealers and consumers discuss a potential lease, dealers are required by law to disclose certain factors. Disclosures include a description of the vehicle, the amount due at signing or delivery, the payment schedule, and other charges payable by the leasee. These charges need to be itemized. Dealers need to disclose the total dollar amount of the payments. Also the dealer needs to reveal the leasee's responsibility for compensating the owner for the car's depreciation. The payment calculation must disclose the following figures and explain how they were determined: gross capitalized cost, capitalized cost reduction, adjusted capitalized cost.

In addition, dealers need to explain the rules governing termination and the formula used in calculating the penalties. Leasees need to be warned that early termination may result in a **penalty** of several thousand dollars, the earlier the termination, the larger the penalty. Excessive wear and tear needs to be defined, along with all other possible additional fees. Liability, the right of the leasee to get an independent **appraisal** of damage and the vehicle's end value need to be explained. Responsibility for insuring the vehicle and for maintaining it need to be explained. Purchase options need to be spelled out as well.

Consumers need to know Regulation M does not cover all elements involved in the lease design. For example, it does not make clear that the leasee has the right to a written explanation of termination fees. Nor does Regulation M govern the fact that **taxation** can change over time. Tax rates may change and thus affect the costs leasees incur.

## Additional Disclosures Required under Certain State Laws

At least 20 states have chosen to adopt their own disclosure laws on car leases in order to provide more protection to consumers. These states are: Arkansas, California, Colorado, Florida, Illinois, Hawaii, Indiana, Iowa, Kansas, Louisiana, Maine, Maryland, Michigan, New Hampshire, New Jersey, New York, Oklahoma, Washington, West Virginia, and Wisconsin. Some laws are inconsistent with the CLA or Regulation M. Where these inconsistencies exist, state law is superseded by federal law. Moreover, some state laws give greater protection to the consumer. These laws require additional notices, warnings, disclosures regarding gap insurance and manufacturer warranties. Also, some newly enacted state laws have caused consumers confusion which is contrary to the intention of state reform.

California has enacted extensive reforms of leasing law. For example, the $25,000 maximum limit stipulated by the CLA and Regulation M does not apply to cars leased in California. Second, leasees are free to terminate at any time. Termination penalties are calculated according to a specified formula that sets a ceiling on the amount. Moreover, notice must be given at least ten days in advance by mail that a vehicle turned in by a leasee will be sold by the lessor. This disclosure allows those who terminated early to obtain an independent appraisal of the vehicle's worth. If the appraisal gives a value higher regarding the residual value, the leasee will owe less in termination fees.

## Fraud and Overcharging

In the 1990s, numerous instances of **fraud** occurred in car leasing transactions. ABC's Prime Time reported on an undercover investigation which puts car dealers under surveillance with hidden cameras. Half of the ten dealers surveyed attempted to cheat the undercover investigators. These dealers used various means, such as secretly raising the purchase price or capitalized cost of the vehicle or by quoting low-ball interest rates. In Florida, a probe by the state attorney general uncovered illegal business practices in 23.000 leases which overcharged leasees on an average of $1,450. The terms of the leasing contract are complicated, and fast talking dealers can all too easily mislead unsuspecting customers.

## Common Leasing Scams

There are a number of ways dealers can illegally increase the leasing fees they obtain for their vehicles. For example, they can use an undisclosed acquisition fee, concealed in the net capitalized cost of the car. This fee typically averages $450. Consumers should ask if the fee has been included in the cost of the vehicle and if it can be waived. Another way is for dealers to quote the money factor as an interest rate. Customers can be easily confused because both of these figures are quoted in decimal form. For example, a dealer may tell the customer that the interest rate is 2.6 percent. The use of a money factor of .00260 will be mistaken for the interest rate. When this money factor is used, the actual interest rate is 6.24 percent. If the customer is able to distinguish between these two figures and voices an objection, the dealer may say he said 6.2 instead of 2.6 percent.

Dealers may also "forget" to enter the value of the trade-in into the lease terms. Customers need to carefully examine the figures of the lease to make sure the value of their trade-in is listed. Then too dealers can secretly increase the cost of the vehicle. Customers need to insist the residual, money factor, applicable fees, taxes, and dealer incentives are fully disclosed. Then the customers can calculate the lease payment themselves. Moreover, termination penalty wording may be vague enough to allow some dealers to charge more than the leasee was expecting to pay. Finally, many customers may not know that so-called **Lemon Laws** pertain to leased vehicles as well, and dealers may not offer that information.

## Should People Lease or Purchase?

Leasing may be a good choice under certain circumstances. For example, if consumers use a vehicle in easy-wear situations only and for only the distance specified in the lease mileage terms. Also, it may pay to lease a car if the monthly payments for the lease are lower than those for a car loan to purchase that car. To calculate how to compare car loan payments with lease payments, follow these steps:

- Determine through negotiation the lowest possible price so that it is no more than $200 over the dealer invoice.

- Add **sales tax** and other up front costs applicable to purchasing and to leasing.

- Add the relevant figures in each case to arrive at the gross purchase price and the capitalized cost for the lease.

- Subtract from each of these figures the trade-in value if applicable.

- Subtract from each of these figures the amount of the down payment. Ideally, 20 percent of the figure calculated in the immediately preceding step should be put down for a purchase and nothing should be put down for a lease. This calculation gives the customer the net purchase price for buying and leasing.

- Next add the respective **finance charge** for leasing and purchasing. For a lease this amount will be listed as a rent charge. This will give the total cost in purchasing and leasing.

- Finally, divide each figure by the number of payments required.

After the comparative costs have been determined, customers need to remember that if they buy their cars, they will have a vehicle to sell the next time they enter the car market as consumers.

## Additional Resources

*Buying and Leasing Cars on the Internet* Raisglid, Ron et. al. St. Martin's Press, 1998.

*Car Buyers' and Car Leasers' Negotiating* Bible Bragg, W. James, Random House, 1999.

*Car Shopping Made Easy: Buying or Leasing, New or Used: How to Get the Car You Most Want at the Price You Want to Pay* Edgerton, Jerry, Warner Books, 2001.

*Complete Idiot's Guide to Buying or Leasing a Car* Nerad, Jack, Macmillan Spectra, 1996.

*Don't Get Taken Away Every Time: The Insider's Guide to Buying or Leasing Your New Car or Truck* Sutton, Remar, Penguin Books, 1997.

*How to Buy or Lease a Car Without Getting Ripped Off* Lyle, Pique, Adams Media Corp., 1999.

*Insider's Guide to Buying and Leasing* Wesley, John, Delmar-Thompson Learning, 2002.

*Keys to Leasing: A Consumer's Guide to Vehicle Leasing* Board of Governors Federal Reserve System, 1997.

*Leasing Lessons for Smart Shoppers* Eskeldson, Mark, Technews Pub., 1997.

*Smart Wheels, Hot Deals: A Layperson's Guide to Buying, Leasing, and Insuring the Best Car for the Least Money* Silver Lake Publishing, 2001.

*The Unofficial Guide to Buying or Leasing a Car* Howell, Donna, Macmillan 1998.

## Organizations

### American Council on Consumer Interests
240 Stanley Hall
Columbia, MO 65211 USA
Phone: (573) 882-3817
Phone: (573) 884-6571
URL: http://www.consumerinterests.org
Primary Contact: Carrie Paden

### Association of Consumer Vehicle Lessors
URL: http://www.acvl.com

### Auto Leasing Hot Line Service
Phone: (800) 418-8450

### Automotive Consumer Action Program
8400 Westpack Dr.
McLean, VA 22102 USA
Phone: (703) 821-7144

### Consumer Action
717 Market St.
San Francisco, CA 94103 USA
Phone: (415) 777-9635
Phone: (415) 777-5267
URL: ttp://www.consumeraction.org
Primary Contact: Ken McEldowney, Director

### Consumer Bankers Association

1000 Wilson Blvd.
Washington, DC 22209-3912 USA
Phone: (703) 276-1750
Phone: (703) 528-1290
URL: http://www.cbanet.org/
Primary Contact: Joe Belew, President

### Federal Trade Commission

6th and Pennsylvania Ave.
Washington, DC 20580 USA
Phone: (877) 382-4357
Phone: (202) 326-3676
URL: http://www.ftc.gov
Primary Contact: Robert Pitofsky, Chair

### National Vehicle Leasing Association

PO Box 281230
San Francisco, CA 94128 USA
Phone: (650) 548-9135
Phone: 650 548-9155
URL: http://www.nvla.org
Primary Contact: Rodney J. Couts, Executive
Director

# AUTOMOBILES

## LEMON LAWS

*Sections within this essay:*

- Background

- Magnuson-Moss Warranty Act

- State Lemon Laws

- Additional Resources

## Background

A "lemon law" is a consumer protection **statute** intended to provide a specific remedy for defects in the quality or function of motor vehicles. The term describes a defective vehicle as a "lemon." There is one main federal law covering such purchases, but it is state law that covers the vast majority of complaints. Although state laws vary in types of vehicles covered, they generally include all new vehicles and (with more limited application) used vehicles, trucks, motorcycles, and non-living areas of motor homes.

To qualify for protection under most state lemon laws, a purchaser must prove that (1) during the purchased car's **warranty** period, the purchaser reported a malfunction or defect to the manufacturer or authorized representative (e.g., the dealership); (2) the defect or malfunction was serious and substantially impaired the car's usefulness, functionality, and value; and (3) the manufacturer or dealer was unable to correct the defect/malfunction after a specified number of attempts (usually three or four) within a specified period of time.

## Magnuson-Moss Warranty Act

The federal Magnuson-Moss Warranty Act protects buyers of products that cost more than $25 and come with express written warranties. It covers all products that malfunction or do not perform as they should. The Act's purview includes vehicles, guaranteeing that certain minimum warranties are met and that the provisions of the vehicle warranties are disclosed prior to purchase. Under the Act, which includes vehicles that are "lemons," purchasers must be given the choice of either a refund or a replacement if the products are defective. State laws further modify this protection by providing conditions under which a manufacturer has the opportunity to repair the defect before being required to refund or replace it.

## State Lemon Laws

State laws differ greatly in the scope of covered "vehicles," but most allow only three or four unsuccessful attempts to repair the product (unless the defect could cause death or serious injury). Clearly, the intent of the various provisions is to limit the number of days a purchaser is deprived of use of the purchased product, and the number of times it must be returned for repair of the same defect.

In the interest of fairness, many states allow an offset for a consumer's use of a vehicle prior to making a lemon law claim, either by number of miles used or length of time the vehicle performed without defect. Finally, some states do permit the recovery of reasonable attorney's fees if the filing of a lemon law action is necessary.

ALABAMA: Covers vehicles for 12,000 miles or one year. Excludes motor homes or vehicles weighing more than 10,000 lbs. Must have been three repair attempts or 30 calendar days out of service.

ALASKA: Covers vehicles for their express warranty period or one year, whichever occurs first. Excludes tractors, farm vehicles, motorcycles, and off-road vehicles. Must have been three repair attempts or 30 calendar days out of service.

ARIZONA: Covers vehicles for their express warranty period or two years or 24,000 miles, whichever occurs first. Vehicles under 10,000 lbs. as well as self-propelled vehicles and a chassis of a motor home are all covered under the statute. Must have been four repair attempts or 30 calendar days out of service.

ARKANSAS: Covers vehicles two years or 24,000 miles, whichever occurs last. Covers leased as well as purchased vehicles. Excludes the living facilities of a mobile home or vehicles over 10,000 lbs. Excludes motorcycles and mopeds. Must have been one repair attempt for a defect that may cause death or serious injury; otherwise, three repair attempts or 30 calendar days out of service.

CALIFORNIA: Covers vehicles (including a dealer-owned vehicle used as a "demonstrator") for 18 months or 18,000 miles, whichever occurs first. Excludes the living facilities of a mobile home, motorcycles, off-road vehicles. Must have been two repair attempts for a defect that may cause death or serious injury; otherwise, four repair attempts or 30 calendar days out of service.

COLORADO: Covers vehicles sold within the state and used to carry not more than ten persons for the express warranty period or one year, whichever occurs first. Excludes motor homes and motorcycles. Must have been four repair attempts or 30 business days out of service.

CONNECTICUT: Covers sold and leased vehicles for two years or 18,000 miles, whichever occurs first. Excludes agricultural tractors. Must have been four repair attempts (two if involving serious hazard) or 30 calendar days out of service.

DELAWARE: Covers purchased, leased, or registered vehicles for their express warranty period or one year, whichever occurs first. Excludes motorcycles, and living facilities of motor homes. Must have been four repair attempts or 30 business days out of service.

DISTRICT OF COLUMBIA: Covers sold or registered vehicles for two years or 18,000 miles, whichever occurs first. Excludes buses, motorcycles, motor homes and recreation vehicles. Must have been four repair attempts or 30 days out of service.

FLORIDA: Covers vehicles leased, sold, or transferred in the state for 18 months or 24,000 miles, whichever occurs first. Excludes mopeds, motorcycles, living quarters of recreation vehicles, and off-road vehicles. Must have been three repair attempts or 30 calendar days out of service.

GEORGIA: Covers both leased and purchased vehicles for their 12,000 miles or one year, whichever occurs first. Excludes motorcycles, living quarters or office/commercial spaces of motor homes, and trucks weighing more than 10,000 lbs. Must have been one repair attempt for a serious safety defect in the braking or steering systems; otherwise, three repair attempts or 30 calendar days out of service.

HAWAII: Covers vehicles (including a dealer-owned vehicle used as a "demonstrator") for their express warranty period, two years, or 24,000 miles, whichever occurs first. Excludes mopeds, motorcycles, motor scooters, and dwelling quarters of mobile homes. Must have been one repair attempt for a serious safety defect in the braking or steering systems; otherwise, three repair attempts or 30 business days out of service.

IDAHO: Covers vehicles for their express warranty period or one year, whichever occurs first. Excludes tractors, house trailers, motorcycles, and vehicles weighing more than 12,000 lbs. Must have been four repair attempts or 30 business days out of service.

ILLINOIS: Covers vehicles under 8,000 lbs. and recreation vehicles for one year or 12,000 miles, whichever occurs first. Excludes camping and travel trailers and motorcycles. Must have been four repair attempts or 30 business days out of service.

INDIANA: Covers vehicles for 18 months or 18,000 miles, whichever occurs first. Excludes conversion vans, motor homes, all tractors, motorcycles, mopeds, snowmobiles, and off-road vehicles. Must have been four repair attempts or 30 business days out of service.

IOWA: Covers purchased or leased vehicles for two years or 24,000 miles, whichever occurs first. Excludes motorcycles, mopeds, motor homes or vehicles weighing more than 10,000 lbs. Must have been one repair attempt for a defect that may cause death or serious injury; otherwise, three repair attempts plus a final attempt, or 30 calendar days out of service.

KANSAS: Covers sold and registered vehicles under 12,000 lbs. for their express warranty period or one year, whichever occurs first. Must have been four repair attempts or 10 repair attempts for different defects; otherwise, 30 calendar days out of service.

KENTUCKY: Covers vehicles purchased or leased in the state and owned by Kentucky residents for one year or 12,000 miles, whichever occurs first. Excludes conversion vans, farm vehicles, motorcycles, mopeds, motor homes, and vehicles with more than two axles. Must have been four repair attempts or 30 days out of service.

LOUISIANA: Covers sold vehicles for their express warranty period or one year, whichever occurs first. Excludes motorcycles, motor homes, and commercial vehicles. Must have been four repair attempts or 30 calendar days out of service.

MAINE: Covers sold or leased vehicles for two years or 18,000 miles, whichever occurs first. Excludes commercial vehicles over 8,000 lbs. or business enterprises registering three or more motor vehicles. Must have been three repair attempts or 15 business days out of service.

MARYLAND: Covers purchased vehicles for 15 months or 15,000 miles; leased vehicles for 12 months or 12,000 miles, whichever occurs first. Excludes fleets of five or more vehicles, and certain motor homes. Must have been one repair attempt for a serious safety defect in the braking or steering systems; otherwise, four repair attempts or 30 calendar days out of service.

MASSACHUSETTS: Covers vehicles for oneyear or 15,000 miles, whichever occurs first. Excludes commercial vehicles, motorized bicycles, motor homes, and off-road vehicles. Must have been three repair attempts or 15 business days out of service.

MICHIGAN: Covers vehicles for their express warranty period or one year, whichever occurs first. Excludes fleets of ten or more vehicles, buses, trucks, motor homes, vans. Must have been four repair attempts or 30 business days out of service.

MINNESOTA: Covers sold or leased vehicles for their express warranty period or two years, whichever occurs first. Must have been one repair attempt for

a serious safety defect in the braking or steering systems; otherwise, four repair attempts or 30 business days out of service.

MISSISSIPPI: Covers vehicles for their express warranty period or one year, whichever occurs first. Excludes motorcycles, mopeds, customized portions of motor homes, and off-road vehicles. Must have been three repair attempts or 15 business days out of service.

MISSOURI: Covers vehicles for their express warranty period or one year, whichever occurs first. Excludes commercial vehicles, motorcycles, mopeds, and RVs, except for chassis, engine, or powertrain components. Must have been four repair attempts or 30 business days out of service.

MONTANA: Covers sold vehicles for two years or 18,000 miles, whichever occurs first. Excludes trucks weighing more than 10,000 lbs., motorcycles, and living quarters of motor homes. Must have been four repair attempts or 30 business days out of service.

NEBRASKA: Covers sold vehicles for their express warranty period or one year, whichever occurs first. Excludes self-propelled motor homes. Must have been four repair attempts or 40 days out of service.

NEVADA: Covers vehicles for their express warranty period or one year, whichever occurs first. Excludes motorjhomes or off-road vehicles. Must have been four repair attempts or 30 calendar days out of service

NEW HAMPSHIRE: Covers purchased or leased vehicles under 9,000 lbs. for one year beyond their express warranty period or final repair attempt. Excludes tractors, mopeds, and off-road vehicles. Must have been three repair attempts or 30 business days out of service.

NEW JERSEY: Covers purchased, leased, or registered vehicles for whichever occurs first. Excludes living quarters of motor homes. Must have been three repair attempts or 20 calendar days out of service.

NEW MEXICO: Covers sold and registered vehicles under 10,000 lbs. miles for express warranty period or one year, whichever occurs first. Must have been four repair attempts or 30 business days out of service.

NEW YORK: Covers purchased and leased passenger vehicles for two years or 18,000 miles, whichever occurs first. Must have been four repair attempts or 30 calendar days out of service. Substantial defects must be repaired within 20 days of notice by certified mail.

NORTH CAROLINA: Covers vehicles for two years or 24,000 miles, whichever occurs first. Excludes house trailers but includes motorcycles. Must have been four repair attempts or 20 calendar days out of service during any 12 month period.

NORTH DAKOTA: Covers vehicles under 10,000 lbs. miles for their express warranty period or one year, whichever occurs first. Excludes house cars and motocycles. Must have been three repair attempts or 30 business days out of service.

OHIO: Covers vehicles for 18,000 miles or one year, whichever occurs first. Excludes business or commercial fleets registering three or more vehicles and living quarters of motor homes. Must have been one repair attempt for defect likely to cause death or serious injury or three repair attempts for same defect or 8 total repairs or 30 calendar days out of service.

OKLAHOMA: Covers vehicles under 10,000 lbs. for their express warranty period or one year, whichever occurs first. Excludes living quarters of mobile homes. Must have been four repair attempts or 45 days out of service.

OREGON: Covers sold or purchased vehicles for 12,000 miles or one year, whichever occurs first. Must have been four repair attempts or 30 business days out of service.

PENNSYLVANIA: Covers purchased and registered vehicles for one year or 12,000 miles, whichever occurs first. Excludes motor homes, motorcycles, and off-road vehicles. Must have been three repair attempts or 30 calendar days out of service.

RHODE ISLAND: Covers sold or leasedvehicles under 10,000 lbs for one year or 15,000 miles, whichever occurs first. Excludes motorized campers. Must have been four repair attempts or 30 calendar days out of service.

SOUTH CAROLINA: Covers sold and registered non-commercial vehicles for 12,000 miles or one year, whichever occurs first. Excludes living quarters of recreational vehicles, trucks over 5,000 pounds, motorcycles, and off-road vehicles. Must have been three repair attempts or 30 calendar days out of service.

SOUTH DAKOTA: Covers vehicles for 12,000 miles or one year, whichever occurs first. Excludes tractors, farm vehicles, motorcycles, and off-road vehicles. Must have been four repair attempts plus a final attempt.

TENNESSEE: Covers Class "C" vehicles under 10,000 lbs. for their express warranty period or one year, whichever occurs first. Excludes motor and garden tractors, motor homes, motorcycles, and off-road vehicles. Must have been three repair attempts or 30 calendar days out of service.

TEXAS: Covers vehicles with two or more wheels, also covers engine transmissions and rear axles, for their express warranty period or one year, whichever occurs first. Must have been four repair attempts (two attempts for a serious hazard)or 30 days out of service.

UTAH: Covers new vehicles under 12,000 lbs. for their express warranty period or one year, whichever occurs first. Excludes truck and farm tractors, living quarters of motor homes, motorcycles, and off-road vehicles.Must have been four repair attempts or 30 calendar days out of service.

VERMONT: Covers purchased or registered vehicles for their express warranty period only. Excludes tractors, highway-building equipment and road-making appliances, motorcycles, mopeds, snowmobiles, and the living quarters of RVs. Must have been three repair attempts or 30 calendar days out of service.

VIRGINIA: Covers purchased and lease-purchased vehicles for 18 months. Must have been three repair attempts or 30 calendar days out of service, or one attempt for a serious defect.

WASHINGTON: Covers leased or purchased vehicles for two years or 24,000 miles, whichever occurs first. Excludes buses, vehicles in fleets of ten or more, living quarters of motor homes, and trucks weighing more than 19,000 lbs. Must have been two repair attempts for the same serious safety defect, one of which occurred during the manufacturer's warranty period; otherwise, four repair attempts or 30 calendar days out of service, 15 of which occurred during the manufacturer's warranty period.

WEST VIRGINIA: Covers vehicles for their express warranty period or one year, whichever occurs first. Must have been three repair attempts (or one attempt if it involved a condition likely to cause death or serious bodily injury) or 30 calendar days out of service.

WISCONSIN: Covers purchased, leased, or transferred vehicles for their express warranty period or one year, whichever occurs first. Excludes mopeds, semi-trailers, or trailers designed to be used with trucks or truck-tractors. Must have been four repair attempts or 30 days out of service.

WYOMING: Covers sold or registered vehicles under 10,000 lbs. for one year. Must have been three repair attempts or 30 business days out of service.

"State Lemon Law Summary." Available at http://www.autopedia.com.

### Consumer Federation of America

1424 16th St. NW, Suite 604
Washington, DC 20036 USA
Phone: (202) 387-6121
Fax: (202) 265-7989
URL: www.cfa.org

# AUTOMOBILES

## SAFETY

*Sections within this essay:*

## Background

Those who drive cars may not realize the amount of thought that goes into safety, both in terms of safety equipment in the vehicle and the requirements of safe driving. Safety is incorporated into the U.S. driving culture in many ways. From safety belts and air bags, to motorcycle helmet laws and driving while impaired laws, there is a delicate balance between the government's role of protecting the driving and pedestrian population through safety laws and regulations and the public's and the automobile industry's privacy interests.

For the most part, market forces determined how manufacturers addressed safety issues in their vehicles. There was a good deal of tension between obvious safety hazards and the public's unwillingness to pay for vehicle modifications or features that appeared to be "optional." But in the 1960s, a grassroots level movement, led by Ralph Nader and others, sought to inform the public, auto manufacturers, and the government about the serious safety risks in vehicles.

The late 1960s saw the first regulatory measures to make cars safer. For example, the threat of a federal mandate for auto manufacturers to install anchors for front safety belts prompted the industry to install them "voluntarily" as standard equipment. In hearings in 1965, **testimony** from many physicians resulted in a recommendation that all cars sold in the state of New York would have by 1968 the seventeen safety features already required in federally owned vehicles. Around that time Michigan, Iowa, Illinois, and Washington also conducted hearings on automobile safety.

As of 2002, there are large federal agencies that oversee an enormous array of federal laws and regulations that are intended to safeguard American drivers, passengers, and pedestrians. These are supplemented by many additional laws and regulations in all fifty states, the District of Columbia, and U.S. territories and possessions.

## Child Passenger Safety

Traffic crashes are one of the leading causes of death in the United States. All 50 states, the District of Columbia, Puerto Rico, and the U.S. territories have child passenger safety laws on the books. These do much to reduce the number of deaths and serious injuries from vehicle crashes. But the biggest problem with these laws remains the significant gaps and exemptions in coverage that diminish the protection that all children need in motor vehicles.

According to the September 1998 issue of the *Journal of Pediatrics*, the best predictor of child occupant restraint use is adult safety belt use. In other words, an adult driver who is buckled up is far more likely to restrain a child passenger than one who is not buckled.

### Proper Child Safety Seat Use

Perhaps the single most important rule about children in vehicles is that children should be seated in the back seat at all times.

The proper seating information for infants, birth to one year or up to twenty-two pounds is:

- If the car seat also converts to a carrier, the infant should face the rear

- Harness straps should be at or below the shoulders

- Infants should never be in the front seat, especially if the vehicle is equipped with passenger-side air bags.

The proper seating information for toddlers, twenty-two to forty pounds is:

- If the car seat also converts to a carrier, the child should face forward,

- Harness straps should be above shoulder level.

- Toddlers should never be in the front seat, especially if the vehicle is equipped with passenger-side air bags.

The proper seating information for preschool children, forty to eighty pounds is:

- They need a belt positioning booster seat,

- They should face forward,

- Their booster seat must be used with both lap and shoulder belts,

- The lap belt should fit low and tight.

There are child safety seat laws in every state plus the District of Columbia. Police and other law enforcement officers are allowed to issue a **citation**

when they see a violation of these laws. There are some 18 states that have gaps in their child passenger restraint laws; in these states, some children are not covered by either a child safety seat law or a safety belt law. Additionally, in states where children are protected under the safety belt law as opposed to specific child safety seat laws, police may enforce the law only if a driver violates an additional law.

Safety belt laws do protect children. For example, the NHTSA found that when Louisiana upgraded its safety belt law from secondary to standard enforcement, compliance with child restraint rules rose from 45 percent to 82 percent without any other change in the state's child passenger safety law.

### Booster Seat Safety

Automobile accidents are a leading cause of death and injury for American children. Approximately 500 of the nearly 19.5 million children in the five to nine year-old age group die in automobile accidents. About 100,000 more are injured in automobile crashes each year. Although the fatality rate has decreased for other age groups in the same time period, the fatality rate in automobile crashes for this age group has remained constant over the past twenty years. That is why this particular age group is sometimes known as "the forgotten child;" they have outgrown toddler-sized child safety seats but do not yet fit into adult safety belts properly. Despite this problem, neither government nor industry has made concerted efforts to address the safety needs of children ages five to nine.

Booster seats are one answer to this problem; they provide a proper safety belt fit. Booster seats lift children up off vehicle seats. This improves the fit of the adult safety belt on children. If used properly, boosters should also position the lap belt portion of the adult safety belt across the child's legs or pelvic area. An improper fit of an adult safety belt can expose a child to abdominal or neck injury because the lap belt rides up over the stomach and the shoulder belt cuts across the neck. When a child is restrained in an age-appropriate child safety seat, booster seat, or safety belt, his or her chance of being killed or seriously injured in a car crash is greatly reduced.

The facts about booster seat laws are sobering. For example, only seven states have booster seat laws: Arkansas, California, New Jersey, Oregon, Rhode Island, South Carolina, and Washington. Thirty-three states and the District of Columbia require all children up to age 16 to be restrained in every seating position. The other states require child restraint systems for children up to ages two, three, or four, with a few more requiring the use of safety belts after the age of four. According to some estimates, as many as 630 additional children's lives would be saved and 182,000 serious injuries prevented every year if the states closed all the gaps in their child occupant protection laws and all children—ages birth to fifteen years old—were properly restrained.

### Child Safety Law Exemptions

Several states have enacted laws which exempt children from passenger restraint laws in certain circumstances or under unique circumstances. These vary widely from state to state. The following is a list of some of the most common exemptions:

- Overcrowded vehicles. In nearly half of the states, children can ride unsecured if all safety belts are otherwise in use.

- "Attending to the personal needs of the child." This vague exemption may cover many activities.

- Medical waivers for children with special medical needs. These exemptions may disappear as advances in child restraint systems make it possible to accommodate children with most types of physical disabilities.

- Out-of-state vehicles, drivers, and children. Children in many states are frequently exempted if the vehicle or driver is from another state.

- Drivers who are not the vehicle owner or who are not related to the children being carried. Some states have laws that do not hold the driver responsible for unrestrained children.

## Safety Belt Laws

It is clear from the statistics that lives are saved when drivers and passengers in vehicles use safety belts. This is especially true when safety belt use is reinforced by meaningful safety belt laws. According to NHTSA, as of 2002, approximately 61 percent of passenger vehicle occupants killed in traffic crashes were not wearing safety belts. This figure is down from 65 percent in 1998.

### Standard Enforcement Information

Every state except New Hampshire has safety belt laws, but only 17 states and the District of Columbia have standard enforcement of their belt laws. Standard enforcement laws allow police officers to stop vehicles if the driver or front seat passenger is observed not wearing a safety belt; the law also applies to drivers who have not properly restrained a child. Secondary enforcement laws allow officers to issue a citation for failing to wear a safety belt only after stopping the vehicle for another traffic **infraction**.

Some have raised concerns that standard enforcement laws could lead to police harassment of minorities. However, according to a 1999 NHTSA report, surveys in California and Louisiana conducted shortly after these states upgraded to standard enforcement found that neither Hispanics (California) nor African Americans (Louisiana) reported receiving a greater number of safety belt citations than the public as a whole.

Currently, seventeen states, the District of Columbia and Puerto Rico have primary laws in effect. Another thirty-two states have secondary enforcement laws, and New Hampshire has no seat belt use law at all. Fines for not wearing a safety belt in the United States currently range from a low of $5 in Idaho to a high of $75 in Oregon. In twenty-seven states, the fine is just $20-25.

### Highway Safety Grant Programs for Occupant Protection Activities

Congress passed the Transportation Equity Act for the 21st Century (TEA-21) in May of 1998. There are several programs in TEA-21 that make a direct impact on seat belt use and occupant protection. The three most important programs funded by the Act are:

1. Section 157 Seat Belt Incentive Grant program. This program authorized half a billion dollars over five years to encourage states to increase seat belt use rates. States apply for grant money under this program and may use grant funds for any eligible Title 23 project (including approved construction projects). The TEA-21 Act also encourages innovative state-level projects that promote increased seat belt use rates and child passenger safety activities.

2. Section 405 (a) Occupant Protection Incentive Grant program. This program deploys $83 million over five years to target specific occupant protection laws and programs. States can receive grants under this program if they demonstrate that they have enacted certain occupant protection laws and programs, such as primary safety

belt use laws and special traffic enforcement programs.

3. Section 2003 (b) program. This portion of the TEA-21 established a two-year program for year 2000 and 2001. In the program, states received grants if they implemented child passenger protection education and training activities.

## Motorcycle Helmets

Motorcycle helmets are proven to save the lives of motorcyclists, and they help prevent serious brain injuries. Twenty states and the District of Columbia require motorcycle drivers and their passengers to use helmets. Twenty-seven other states have laws that apply to some riders only, particularly those younger than 18. Colorado, Illinois, and Iowa have no motorcycle helmet requirements at all.

Helmet laws increase motorcycle helmet use, thus saving lives and reducing serious injuries. The NHTSA reports that in 2000 there were 2,862 motorcycle riders killed on U.S. roads and highways. This number represents a 15 percent increase from 1999. There were 58,000 motorcycle-related injuries in 2000, a 16 percent increase from 1999.

## Speeding

Speeding is a factor in nearly one-third of all **fatal** crashes. Speeding entails exceeding the posted speed limit; it also means driving too fast for conditions (such as in fog, rain, or icy road conditions), regardless of the posted speed limit. Some 6.3 million vehicular crashes were reported in 2000.

When drivers speed, they cause the following:

- reduction in the amount of available time needed to avoid a crash,

- increase the likelihood of a crash

- increase the severity of a crash once it occurs

According to a report issued by the NHTSA in 2000, speed was a factor in 30 percent (12,628) of all traffic fatalities in 1999. It was second only to alcohol (39 percent) as a cause of fatal crashes.

Congress repealed the National Maximum Speed Limit in 1995. Accordingly, speeds increased on Interstate highways in the states that raised their speed limits. Twenty-four states raised their speed limits in late 1995 and in 1996. Twenty-nine states have currently raised speed limits to 70 MPH or higher on portions of their roads and highways.

## Blood Alcohol Content

Motor vehicle crashes are the number one cause of death for Americans ages six through thirty-three. Alcohol-related crashes are a big part of this problem. But alcohol-related accidents account for an inordinately large percentage of all deaths in automobile crashes. In fact, every 33 minutes someone is killed in an alcohol-related crash.

Individuals absorb alcohol at different rates. The main reason is body weight, but a number of other factors affect blood alcohol content (BAC):

- body type

- rate of metabolism, medications taken

- the strength of the drinks

- whether drinkers have eaten recently

Despite these factors, though, just one drink will degrade the physical and mental acuity of practically everyone. A person with a BAC in the range of .08 to .10 is considered legally intoxicated in every state. It takes just a few drinks to get there, even if drinkers do not "feel" the effects of the alcohol.

### Intoxicated Drivers Repeat Offender Laws

State law uses four general methods to deal with the problem of repeated offenses by intoxicated drivers. These are:

1. Addressing Alcohol Abuse: Some states require drivers with repeat violations to be assessed for their degrees of alcohol abuse; some also mandate appropriate treatment.

2. Licensing Sanctions: Suspending or revoking licenses of repeat intoxicated drivers for a greater period of time than they for first offenders is the law in most states.

3. Mandatory Sentencing: Some states have mandatory minimum sentences for repeat intoxicated drivers.

4. Vehicle Sanctions: Some states impound or immobilize the vehicles of repeat intoxicated drivers. This can involve installing an ignition interlock system, or other device on their vehicles that prevents a vehicle from starting if the driver's blood alcohol concentration is above a certain amount.

Programs that concentrate on an individual's alcohol-related behavior have also experienced success. For example, Milwaukee's Intensive Supervision **Probation** (MISP) program reduced recidivism by more than 50 percent. The MISP program includes a component of behavior monitoring. It seems that a variety of measures are needed to address this issue and that states are providing an array of sanctions to the problem of repeat offenders of impaired driving laws.

Revoking or suspending a driver's license is now a common **penalty** for violations related to impaired driving. Despite these penalties, many offenders continue to drive. Too many drivers with a suspended license receive additional traffic citations or become involved in crashes during the periods when their licenses are suspended. As a way to ameliorate this problem, many states have enacted legislation that directly affects the offender's vehicle or license plates as a penalty for the impaired driving offense and/or for driving with a suspended license.

Driver licensing sanctions have proven to help reduce the problem of impaired driving. Non-criminal licensing sanctions have resulted in reductions in alcohol-related fatalities of between 6 and 9 percent. According to a NHTSA study, the following states have seen significant reductions in alcohol-related fatal crashes following their implementation of administrative license revocation procedures: Colorado, Illinois, Maine, New Mexico, North Carolina, and Utah.

According to the NHTSA, these kinds of sanctions actually do prevent many repeat **DWI** offenders from driving. Those repeat offenders who continue to drive without a license tend to drive more infrequently or at least more carefully.

The NHTSA State Legislative Fact Sheet-Vehicle and License Plate Sanctions states that a variety of vehicle sanctions programs have been used successfully. For example, California's vehicle impoundment program substantially reduced subsequent offenses, convictions, and crashes for repeat offenders in the program. These penalties work by either separating repeat DUI/DWI offenders from their vehicles or by requiring them to be sober when they drive.

### Section 164 of 23 U.S.C.

Section 164 of 23 U.S.C. required states to enact certain laws regarding repeat intoxicated drivers. These were to be in place by October 1, 2000. States without these laws forfeited part of their Federal highway construction funds. These monies were redirected to the state's highway safety program to be used for alcohol-impaired driving countermeasures, or for enforcement of anti-drunk driving laws. Alternatively, states could also elect to use the funds for its hazard elimination program.

To be in compliance with Section 164, a state's laws related to subsequent convictions for driving while intoxicated or driving under the influence of alcohol must require the following:

- Behavior **Assessment**: States must mandate assessment of repeat intoxicated drivers' degree of alcohol abuse and refer them to treatment when appropriate

- Driver's License Suspension: suspension must be for a minimum of one year

- Mandatory Minimum Sentence: These should be not less than five days of **imprisonment** or 30 days of community service for the second offense. For the third or subsequent offense, the sentence should not be less than 10 days of imprisonment or 60 days of community service.

- Vehicle Seizure: all vehicles of repeat intoxicated drivers must be impounded or immobilized for some period of time during the license suspension period

The **statute** defines a repeat intoxicated driver as a driver convicted of driving while intoxicated or driving under the influence of alcohol more than once in any five-year period. This means that states need to maintain records on driving convictions for DWI/DUI for a minimum of five years. Additionally, states must certify that they are in compliance with all the provisions of the statute. The following states and the District of Columbia met the requirements of Section 164 by the end of 2000: Alabama, Arizona, Arkansas, Colorado, Florida, Hawaii, Indiana, Idaho, Iowa, Kentucky, Maine, Michigan, Mississippi, Nebraska, Nevada, New Hampshire, New Jersey, North Carolina, Oklahoma, Pennsylvania, Utah, Virginia, and Washington.

### Additional Resources

"Advocates for Auto and Highway Safety" Available at http://www.saferoads.org/. Advocates for Highway & Auto Safety, 2002.

"Buckle Up America." National Highway Traffic Safety Administration, 2002. Available at http://www.nhtsa.dot.gov/people/injury/airbags/buckleplan/.

*2001 Car and Vehicle Safety Data: National Highway Traffic Safety Administration (NHTSA) Documents and Reports* U.S. Government, Progressive Management, 2001.

*The Car Book: The Definitive Buyer's Guide to Car Safety, Fuel Economy, Maintenance, and Much More.* Gillis, Jack, Clarence M. Ditlow, Amy B. Curran, HarperPerennial, 1998.

*Drive to Survive!* Rich, Curt, Motorbooks International, 1999.

*Human Factors in Traffic Safety.* Olson, Paul L. and Robert E. Dewar, eds. Lawyers & Judges Publishing Company, 2001.

"NHTSA State Legislative Fact Sheet-Administrative License Revocation." http://www.nhtsa.dot.gov/people/outreach/stateleg/adminlicense.htm. National Highway Traffic Safety Administration, 2001.

"NHTSA State Legislative Fact Sheet-Vehicle and License Plate Sanctions." http://www.nhtsa.dot.gov/people/outreach/stateleg/veh_lic_sanctions.htm. National Highway Traffic Safety Administration, 2001.

"Transportation and Vehicle Safety." Safetyforum.com, 2002. Available at http://www.safetyforum.com/transportation/.

## Organizations

### AAA Foundation for Traffic Safety

1440 New York Ave., NW, Suite 201
Washington, DC 20005 USA
Phone: (202) 638-5944
Fax: (202) 638-5943
URL: http://www.aaafoundation.org/home/index.cfm

### Center for Auto Safety (CAS)

1825 Connecticut Ave., NW, Suite 330
Washington, DC 20009-5708 USA
Phone: (202) 328-7700
URL: http://www.autosafety.org/

### Kids 'N Cars

918 Glenn Avenue
Washington, MO 63090 USA
Fax: (636) 390-9412
E-Mail: Struttmann@kidsncars.org
URL: http://www.kidsncars.org/

### Mothers Against Drunk Driving (MADD)

P.O. Box 541688
Dallas, TX 75354-1688 USA
Phone: (800) 438-6233
URL: http://www.madd.org/home/

### Safetyforum.com

P.O. Box 470
Arlington, VA 22210-0470 USA
Phone: (703) 469-3700
Fax: (703) 469-3701
E-Mail: mail@safetyforum.com
URL: http://safetyforum.com

### National Highway Traffic Safety Administration (NHTSA)

400 7th St., SW
Washington, DC 20590 USA
Phone: (202) 366-0699
Fax: (202) 366-7882
E-Mail: webmaster@nhtsa.dot.gov
URL: http://www.nhtsa.dot.gov/

# AUTOMOBILES

## SEAT BELT USAGE

*Sections within this essay:*

## Background

More than 90 percent of Americans age 16 and above drive a motor vehicle; of those, nearly 80 percent claim to wear their seat belts at all times while driving. These figures come from the National Highway Traffic Safety Administration (NHTSA), which also estimates that seat belts saved more than 135,000 lives between 1975 and 2001. While many people wear their seat belts because they recognize the safety factor, others wear them because failure to do so can result in a fine. Regardless of the reason one wears a seat belt, the fact is that since the 1950s they have been proven to save lives.

However, many people refuse to wear seat belts. They say that the belts are too uncomfortable, or they say they are only driving a short distance. They may also say that they simply forget. With the grow-

ing prevalence of state "primary laws," in which police officers are allowed to stop cars at random to perform seat-belt checks, people are clearly more careful when they know they may be facing a fine.

The first seat belts were not installed in cars by auto manufacturers. Early automobiles did not go particularly fast, and there were relatively few cars on the road. As the number of motor vehicles increased, so did the amount of danger. In the 1930s, a number of physicians, seeing the results of traffic accidents, lobbied car makers to create some sort of restraining device to keep people from being thrown from a car in an accident. Several doctors actually designed their own lap belts and installed them in their autos.

It was not until the 1950s that seat belts began to appear with some regularity. In 1954 the Sports Car Club of America began to require drivers to wear lap belts as they raced. Soon afterward such groups as the National Safety Council (NSC), American College of Surgeons, and International Association of Chiefs of Police issued their own recommendations for the manufacture and installation of seat belts. The Swedish auto manufacturer Volvo began marketing lap belt in 1956; that same year both Ford and Chrysler decided to offer lap belts as well. Seat belts were not required by law, though, in the United States until 1968.

## Types of Seat Belts

The simple belt that was pulled across the lap (and that only came on the front seats) has long since been retired. That belt was known as *two-point* because of its simple A-to-B design. Today's seat belts are *three-point;* one strap goes across the lap while another goes over the shoulder and diagonally across the chest. In some automobiles, the two straps are connected and the occupant crosses it over the chest and the lap in one motion. In other cars, the occupant connects the lap belt while the shoulder belt slides into place automatically once the door is closed. A prototype for a *four-point* is being developed; it works more like a harness than a typical seat belt would.

Seat belts are made of lightweight but durable fabric that is designed to withstand impacts and hold the wearer in place. Of the roughly 40,000 automobile deaths that occur each year, safety experts say nearly half could have been prevented if a seat belt was being worn. In many cases, the person is killed as a result of being thrown from the vehicle upon crashing. In addition to being durable, seat belts are also designed to be much more comfortable than they were in the past. Most seat belts today employ a mechanism that allows the wearer to move fairly comfortably while driving; if the car comes to a sudden stop the belt locks and holds the wearer firmly in place.

## Legislation

### Federal

There is no federal seat belt law; such laws are left to the individual states. The U. S. Department of Transportation, through NHTSA, offers grant programs to states; in 2002, 48 states, the District of Columbia, and Puerto Rico shared a $44.4 million grant (Maine and Wyoming declined to take any grant money). Safety and public awareness campaigns are also conducted by NHTSA. Probably the best known is the series of print and broadcast advertisements that feature Vince and Larry, the crash test dummies.

In 1998, Congress passed the Transportation Equity Act for the 21st Century (TEA-21), which includes grant money for states to initiate new seat belt laws, traffic enforcement programs, and child passenger protection and training activities.

### State

Every state except New Hampshire has a seat belt requirement for adults. All 50 states and the District of Columbia have seat belt laws that cover children. These laws require children under a certain age (usually 3 or 4) to be placed in a child restraint (a baby seat, a booster seat, etc.); buckling these children up with adult belts is not permitted by law.

New York is one of the most active proponents of seat belt regulation. It was the first state to try to pass seat belt legislation when in 1959 it tried to mandate seat belts in all new cars sold in the state. In 1985, New York made seat belt use mandatory for back seat passengers aged 10 or older; in 1987 it became the first state to require seat belts on large school buses.

### Primary versus Secondary Laws

Primary seat belt laws are one of the most effective enforcement tools available. A primary law allows police to stop an automobile and ticket the driver for not wearing a seat belt. Seventeen states and the District of Columbia have primary laws.

Secondary laws allow the police to ticket a driver who is not wearing a seat belt, but the police must have already stopped the driver for some other reason. A person who is speeding or who goes through a red light or whose tail light is out can be stopped and ticketed; a person who is obeying all the laws but is not wearing a seat belt will not be pulled over in a state with no primary law.

Proponents of primary legislation point out the safety factor. More people will wear seat belts if they know they run the risk of being pulled over and ticketed. If the driver of a car is wearing a seat belt, chances are his or her passengers are too. Moreover, according to information from the National Safety Council (NSC), adults who buckle up are more likely to make sure their children are properly buckled up. In fact, according to NSC, overall seat belt usage can be as much as 15 percent higher in states with primary laws.

## Why People Ignore Seat Belts

Of the people who use seat belts, most say their reason for wearing them was to avoid injury. A study conducted in 1998 for NHTSA called the Motor Vehicle Occupant Safety Survey (MVOSS) revealed that 97 percent of frequent seat belt users and 77 percent of occasional users wear their seat belts as a safety measure. Other reasons cited included wanting to set a good example, being with other people who are wearing seat belts, and force of habit. More than 80 percent of the respondents admitted they use them because doing so is required by law.

Regarding people who do not wear seat belts, some wear seat belts occasionally and others admit never wear seat belts. According to the MVOSS study, the primary reason occasional seat belt users fail to buckle up is that they are only driving short distances (56 percent). More than half said that they simply forget on occasion. For those who never wear a seat belt, the most commonly cited reason (65 percent) is that seat belts are uncomfortable. Other reasons people gave for not wearing their seat belts include the following:

- Being in a hurry and not having time to buckle up

- Light traffic on the roads when respondent drives

- Not wanting to get clothing wrinkled

- Resentment at being told what to do

- Knowing someone who died in a crash while wearing a seat belt

- Resentment at government interference in personal behavior

- Never having gotten used to seat belts

- The belief that with air bags, seat belts are redundant

Safety experts point out that many of these reasons are based on faulty logic. For example, light traffic may have nothing to do with having to make a sudden stop. Air bags, while a valuable safety precaution, are limited in how much they can do. Some overweight people claim that they cannot wear seat belts because the seat belts do not fit them. Some, but not all, auto manufacturers offer seat belt extenders to deal with this problem; others offer customized longer seat belts. The fact remains, however, that there are people who simply will not wear seat belts; they are more comfortable risking being ticketed or potential injury or death.

### Seat Belts on School Buses

Smaller school buses are treated like passenger vehicles when it comes to seat belt requirements. Because of their small size they are more likely to eject passengers; as a result, they are equipped with seat belts as a matter of course. As for standard size school buses, the effectiveness of seat belts has been a source of debate for several years.

In 1992, five years after New York passed a law requiring seat belts on school buses, New Jersey passed a similar law. While New York's law makes use of the seat belts optional, New Jersey's law requires children to buckle up. In 1999, Florida, Louisiana, and California also enacted laws for what they called "improved occupant restraint systems" on large school buses, although they have not yet decided exactly what type of restraint they wish to require on their buses.

It may seem odd that in an atmosphere of increased emphasis on safety there would be any question about seat belts on large buses. Yet opponents, citing data from NHTSA, have said that seat belts on buses might do little to help children. Rather, they believe, the improved interior design of school buses (known as compartmentalization) is more effective. Since the 1970s, school bus seats have been mandated by law to be well-padded on both sides, with high backs and extra-sturdy anchoring, and no exposed rivets. The design of the modern school bus has been compared to that of an egg carton; the extra padding around the seats helps protect the passengers during sudden impacts and keeps them from being ejected from their seats. Moreover, say opponents of school bus seat belts, in the event of an accident, it would be much harder for someone to get children out of a bus if they are all wearing seat belts. This issue will not be resolved easily. What both sides can agree on, however, is that school buses are definitely safer today than they were in the early 1970s.

### Keeping Safe

The bottom line for drivers and automobile passengers is that in almost all cases it is wiser to buckle up. From a safety perspective, the **evidence** clearly points to the value of seat belts in saving lives. From a legal perspective, failure to wear a seat belt can mean being ticketed. Just as there are people who continue to smoke, no doubt there will be people who continue to avoid wearing seat belts. By getting into the habit of wearing them, say the safety experts, travelers will become more comfortable with seat belts, both as drivers and as passengers.

### Additional Resources

*Baby Seats, Safety Belts, and You* Breitenbach, Robert J., Janet B. Carnes, and Judy A. Hammond, U. S. Department of Transportation, 1995.

*SAE Vehicle Occupant Restraint Systems and Components Standards Manual* Society of Automotive Engineers, 1995.

*Standard Enforcement Saves Lives: The Case for Strong Seat Belt Laws* NHTSA, National Safety Council, 1999.

## Organizations

### Mothers Against Drunk Driving (MADD)
P. O. Box 541689
Dallas, TX 75354 USA
Phone: (800) 438-6233 (GET-MADD)
URL: http://www.madd.org
Primary Contact: Millie I. Webb, President

### National Association of Governors' Highway Safety Representatives (NAGHSR)
750 First Street NE, Suite 720
Washington, DC 20002 USA
Phone: (202) 789-0942
URL: http://www.statehighwaysafety.org
Primary Contact: Marsha M. Lembke, Chair

### National Safety Council
1121 Spring Lake Drive
Itasca, IL 60143 USA
Phone: (630) 285-1121
Fax: (630) 285-1315
URL: http://www.nsc.org
Primary Contact: Alan McMillan, President

### National Transportation Safety Board (NTSB)
490 L'Enfant Plaza SW
Washington, DC 20594 USA
Phone: (202) 314-6000
URL: http://www.ntsb.gov
Primary Contact: Marion C. Blakey, Chairman

### Society of Automotive Engineers (SAE)
400 Commonwealth Drive
Warrendale, PA 15096 USA
Phone: (724) 776-5760
URL: http://www.sae.org
Primary Contact: S. M. Shahed, Ph.D., 2002 President

### U. S. Department of Transportation, National Highway Traffic Safety Administration (NHTSA)
400 Seventh Street SW
Washington, DC 20590 USA
Phone: (888) 327-4236 (Auto Safety Hotline)
URL: http://www.nhtsa.dot.gov
Primary Contact: Jeffrey W. 0Runge, Administrator

# AUTOMOBILES

## TRAFFIC VIOLATIONS

*Sections within this essay:*

- Background

- Types of Traffic Violations

- Effect of Traffic Violations
    - Fines
    - Traffic School
    - Suspension of License
    - Insurance Premiums

- Drunk Driving
    - Drunk Driving Laws and Penalties

- Additional Resources

## Background

Traffic violations followed the invention of the automobile: the first traffic ticket in the United States was allegedly given to a New York City cab driver on May 20, 1899, for going at the breakneck speed of 12 miles per hour. Since that time, countless citations have been issued for traffic violations across the country, and states have reaped untold billions of dollars of revenue from violators.

Traffic violations can be loosely defined as any acts that violates a state or municipalities traffic laws. Most laws are local, though the federal government does regulate some traffic aspects, and it can deny federal money in order to coerce states to pass particular traffic laws. Today, motorists can find themselves faced with dozens of traffic laws, depending on where they are driving. These traffic laws vary by state, city, highway, and region

## Types of Traffic Violations

Traffic violations are generally divided into major and minor types of violations. The most minor type are parking violations, which are not counted against a driving record, though a person can be arrested for unpaid violations. Next are the minor driving violations, including speeding and other moving violations, which usually do not require a court appearance. Then there are more serious moving violations, such as reckless driving or leaving the scene of an accident. Finally there is drunk driving, also called Driving Under the Influence (DUI), which is a classification onto itself.

All but the most serious traffic violations are generally prosecuted as **misdemeanor** charges; however, repeat offenses can be prosecuted at the level of felonies. As misdemeanor charges, most traffic violations require payment of a fine but no jail time. State laws do not allow a judge to impose a jail sentence for speeding or failure to stop at a signal. However, more serious traffic violations, such as drunk or reckless driving, can result in jail time at the judge's discretion.

The most common type of traffic violation is a speed limit violation. Speed limits are defined by state. In 1973, Congress implemented a 55-miles-per-hour speed limit in order to save on energy costs, but these were abolished in 1995. Since then, most states have implemented 65-mph maximum speed limits. There are two types of speed limits: fixed maximum, which make it unlawful to exceed the speed limit anywhere at any time, and prima facie, which allow drivers to prove in certain cases that exceeding the speed limit was not unsafe and, therefore, was lawful.

Another common type of traffic violation is a seat belt violation. Most states now require adults to wear seatbelts when they drive or sit in the front seat, and all states require children to be restrained using seat belts. New York was the first state to make seat belts mandatory, in 1984.

## Effect of Traffic Violations

The effect of a traffic violation depends on the nature of the offense and on the record of the person receiving the traffic violation. Beyond the possibilities of fines and/or jail, other consequences of traffic violations can include traffic school, higher insurance premiums, and the suspension of driving privileges.

### Fines

Fines for traffic violations depend on the violation. Typically, states will have standard fines for a specific group of moving violations, with the fines increasing with the seriousness of the violation. Some states will also increase the fine if violators have other violations on their record. Courts will occasionally reduce fines on violations while still recording the violation as part of the violator's record.

### Traffic School

Virtually every state allows perpetrators of a traffic violation to attend some sort of traffic school in return for the violation being wiped off their records. Traffic school generally consists of a 6-8 hour class that describes the dangers of committing traffic violations. Different states have different procedures regarding their traffic schools. Some allow traffic schools in place of paying the fine; others require payment of the fine in addition to the traffic school cost of admission. Some allow traffic violators to go to traffic school once a year, whereas others require a longer waiting period between traffic school attendances. Also, the type of violation may affect whether the violator is allowed to go to traffic school: the more serious the violation, the less likely the violator will be allowed to go to traffic school to wipe it off their record.

Procedures for signing up for traffic school also differ from state to state: some states allow drivers to sign up with the school directly, others have them go through the clerk of court or judge in order to sign-up. Most states require drivers to go to a specific location for traffic school, although some, such as California, now offer an Internet option that allows a student to attend traffic school without leaving the comfort of home

### Suspension of Driving Privileges

A traffic violation not wiped out by traffic school will count against the suspension of driving privileges. In most states, suspension of driving privileges is calculated using a point system: the more points drivers have, the more likely it is their driving privileges could be suspended. Some states calculate the number of violations drivers have in a straightforward manner; if drivers reach the requisite number of violations within a certain time frame, their privileges are automatically suspended. Age can also be a factor in determining when a driver's license is suspended. Minor drivers typically see their licenses suspended with fewer violations than adults.

All states entitle persons facing suspended licenses to receive a **hearing**, typically in front of a hearing officer for that state's Department of Motor Vehicles. At that point, the person whose license is to be suspended may offer an explanation for why the violations in question occurred. The hearing officer usually has discretion in all but the most extreme cases (i.e. drunk driving) to reduce, defer the suspension, or cancel it entirely.

### Insurance Premiums

Beyond the suspension of driving privileges, traffic violators typically can face higher insurance. Insurance companies will raise insurance rates for **habitual** violators of traffic law. In many cases insurance rates will go up for as little as two violations within a three-year period. Different insurance companies follow different procedures. It is up to the discretion of the insurance company whether to raise rates as a result of a traffic violation.

## Drunk Driving

Among driving violations, drunk driving is usually considered a special case. Called by various names, including Driving Under the Influence (DUI), Driving While Intoxicated (**DWI**) and Operating While Intoxicated (OWI), drunk driving usually results in stronger fines and penalties than normal driving violations.

Drunk driving means that the persons driving have consumed enough alcohol to impair their driving abilities. This is usually determined either by a blood-alcohol test, some other sobriety test, or just the observations of the officer. The test is subjective: just because drivers do not feel drunk does not mean they cannot be arrested for drunk driving.

A blood alcohol test measures the amount of alcohol in a person's blood. This can be done directly, through drawing blood from the person, or it can be done with instruments measuring breath or urine. Some states allow a choice as to which test to take, others do not. If persons test above the level of **intoxication** for their state (.08 to.10 percent, depending on the state), they are considered drunk and a prima facie case of drunk driving has been shown.

A blood alcohol test can be refused, but the consequences can be severe. In most states, refusal to take a blood alcohol test is prima facie **evidence** of drunk driving. In some states refusal to take the test can result in the automatic revocation of a license for a year.

Whether a driver is drunk can also be measured using a sobriety test, such as requiring the driver to walk a straight line, stand on one leg, or recite a group of letters or numbers. A driver failing any of these tests can usually be arrested for drunk driving, though often the police officer requests a blood alcohol test as a follow up. The officer can also base the arrest on simple observation of the driver's behavior, although a request for a blood alcohol test is a standard follow-up in these instances as well.

Currently 31 states require a level of.08 or above in order for drivers to be considered intoxicated. They are: Alabama, Alaska, Arizona, Arkansas, California, Florida, Georgia, Hawaii, Idaho, Illinois, Indiana, Kansas, Kentucky, Louisiana, Maine, Maryland, Massachusetts, Missouri, Nebraska, New Hampshire, New Mexico, North Carolina, Oklahoma, Oregon, Rhode Island, Texas, Utah, Vermont, Virginia, Washington, and the District of Columbia. The other states all require.10 or above in order for a driver to be considered intoxicated. Currently all states have zero tolerance laws that make it illegal for drivers under the age of 21 to operate a motor vehicle with a blood alcohol level of.02 or less.

### Drunk Driving Laws and Penalties

Drunk driving has been considered a traffic violation since the turn of the century, but in recent years the penalties for drunk driving in most states have grown much harsher, as a result of the efforts of groups such as Mothers Against Drunk Driving (MADD), founded in 1980. In every state at a minimum, convicted drunk drivers automatically lose their licenses for a certain amount of time. Some states require short jail terms for first time offenders, and most states require drunk-driving offenders to go through some sort of treatment program.

In addition to the general penalties for drunk driving, many states have specific laws dealing with aspects of drunk driving. The following are some of the various state laws dealing with drunk driving, along with a list of the states that have them:

- Anti-Plea Bargaining: A policy that prohibits plea-bargaining or reducing an alcohol-related offense to a non-alcohol related offense. Arizona, Arkansas, California, Colorado, Florida, Kansas, Kentucky, Mississippi, Nevada, New Mexico, New York, Oregon, Pennsylvania, Wyoming

- Child Endangerment: Creates a separate offense or enhances existing DUI/DWI penalties for offenders who drive under the influence with a minor child in the vehicle. Alabama, Arizona, California, Colorado, Delaware, Florida, Georgia, Hawaii, Idaho, Illinois, Iowa, Kansas, Kentucky, Louisiana, Maine, Maryland, Michigan, Minnesota, Nevada, New Hampshire, New Jersey, North Carolina, North Dakota, Ohio, Rhode Island, South Carolina, Tennessee, Utah, Virginia West Virginia, Wisconsin

- Dram Shop: A law that makes liable establishments who sell alcohol to obviously intoxicated persons or minors who subsequently cause death or injury to third parties as a result of alcohol-related crashes. Alabama, Alaska, Arizona, Arkansas, California, Colorado, Connecticut, District of Columbia, District of Columbia, Florida, Georgia, Hawaii, Idaho, Illinois, Indiana, Iowa, Kentucky, Louisiana, Maine, Massachusetts, Michigan, Minnesota, Mississippi, Missouri, Montana, New Hampshire, New Jersey, New Mexico, New York, North Carolina, North Dakota, Ohio, Oklahoma, Oregon, Pennsylvania, Rhode Island, South Carolina, Tennessee, Texas, Utah, Vermont, Washington, West Virginia, Wisconsin, Wyoming

- **Felony** DUI: Makes drunk driving a felony offense based on the number of previous convictions. Alabama, Alaska, Arizona, Arkansas, California, Colorado, Connecticut, Delaware, District of Columbia, Florida, Georgia, Hawaii, Idaho, Illinois, Indiana, Iowa, Kansas, Kentucky, Louisiana, Maine, Massachusetts, Michigan, Mississippi, Missouri, Montana, Nebraska, Nevada, New Hampshire, New Jersey, New Mexico, New

York, North Carolina, North Dakota, Ohio, Oklahoma, Oregon, Rhode Island, South Dakota, South Carolina, Tennessee, Texas, Utah, Vermont, Virginia, Washington, West Virginia, Wisconsin, Wyoming

- High Blood Alcohol Content Laws: Result in increased penalties for driving with blood alcohol concentration of.15 or higher at time of arrest. Arizona, Arkansas, Colorado, Connecticut, Florida, Idaho, Illinois, Indiana, Iowa, Kentucky, Maine, Minnesota, Nevada, New Hampshire, New Mexico, Ohio, Oklahoma, Tennessee, Virginia, Washington, Wisconsin

- Hospital Blood Alcohol Content Reporting: Authorizes hospital personnel to report blood alcohol test results of drivers involved in crashes to local law enforcement where the results are available as a result of treatment. Florida, Hawaii, Illinois, Indiana, Oregon, Pennsylvania, Utah, Vermont

- Increased Penalties for Blood Alcohol Content Refusal: Provides for increased penalties for refusing to take a blood alcohol content test, higher than failing the test would bring. Arkansas, Georgia, Kansas, Virginia, Washington.

- Mandatory Alcohol Assessment/Treatment: Law that mandates that convicted drunk driving offenders undergo an **assessment** of alcohol abuse problems and participate in required treatment program. Alabama, Arizona, Arkansas, Colorado, Connecticut, Delaware, Florida, Georgia, Illinois, Kansas, Kentucky, Maine, Michigan, Mississippi, Missouri, Montana, Nevada, New Hampshire, New York, North Carolina, North Dakota, Ohio, Oklahoma, Oregon, Pennsylvania, Rhode Island, South Carolina, Tennessee, West Virginia, Wisconsin

- Mandatory Jail, Second Offense: Makes a jail term mandatory for a second drunk driving offense. Alabama, Alaska, Arizona, Arkansas, California, Colorado, Connecticut, Delaware, Florida, Georgia, Hawaii, Idaho, Illinois, Indiana, Iowa, Kansas, Kentucky, Louisiana, Maine, Maryland, Massachusetts, Michigan, Minnesota, Mississippi, Missouri, Montana, Nebraska, Nevada, New Hampshire, New Jersey, New Mexico, North Carolina, North Dakota, Ohio, Oklahoma, Oregon,

Pennsylvania, Rhode Island, South Carolina, Tennessee, Texas, Utah, Vermont, Virginia, Washington, West Virginia, Wisconsin, Wyoming

- Sobriety Checkpoints: Allows law enforcement officials to establish checkpoints to stop vehicles and examine their drivers for intoxication. Alabama, Arizona, Arkansas, California, Colorado, Connecticut, Delaware, District of Columbia, Florida, Georgia, Hawaii, Illinois, Iowa, Kansas, Kentucky, Louisiana, Maine, Maryland, Massachusetts, Mississippi, Missouri, Montana, Nebraska, Nevada, New Hampshire, New Jersey, New Mexico, New York, North Carolina, North Dakota, Ohio, Oklahoma, Pennsylvania, South Carolina, South Dakota, Tennessee, Utah, Vermont, Virginia, West Virginia, Wyoming

- Social Host: Imposes potential liability on social hosts as a result of their serving alcohol to obviously intoxicated persons or minors who subsequently are involved in crashes causing death or injury to third-parties. Alabama, Arizona, Colorado, Connecticut, Florida, Georgia, Idaho, Indiana, Iowa, Louisiana, Maine, Massachusetts, Michigan, Minnesota, Mississippi, Montana, New Hampshire, New Jersey, New Mexico, New York, North Carolina, North Dakota, Ohio, Oregon, Pennsylvania, Texas, Utah, Vermont, Wisconsin, Wyoming

## Additional Resources

*Digest of Motor Laws* Butler, Charles A. Editor and Kay Hamada, eds.Editor, American Automobile Association, Heathrow, FL, 1996.

*http://www.madd.org/home/* "Stats and Resources," Mothers Against Drunk Driving, 2002

*http://www.nolo.com* "Cars & Tickets," Nolo Press, 2002

*West's Encyclopedia of American Law* West Publishing Company, 1998.

## Organizations

### *Mothers Against Drunk Driving (MADD)*
P.O. Box 541688
Dallas, TX 75354-1688 USA
Phone: (1-800) 438-6233
URL: URL: http://www.madd.org

Primary Contact: Millie Webb, President

### National Highway Traffic Safety Administration (NHTSA)
400 Seventh Street, SW
Washington, DC, DC 20590 USA
Phone: (202) 366-9550
URL: http://www.nhtsa.dot.gov/
Primary Contact: Jeffrey Runge, Administrator

### U. S. Department of Transportation
400 Seventh Street, SW
Washington, DC, DC 20590 USA
Phone: (202) 366-4000
URL: http://www.dot.gov/
E-Mail: dot.comments@ost.dot.gov.
Primary Contact: Norman Mineta, Secretary of Transportation

# BANKING

## BANKING AND LENDING LAW

*Sections within this essay:*

- Background

- Bank Transactions
    - Checks and Other Negotiable Instruments
    - Checking Accounts
    - Funds Transfers
    - Letters of Credit
    - Secured Transactions

- Federal Reserve System

- Insurance of Deposits

- Interest Rates Charged by Banks

- Truth in Lending

- Usury Laws

- Crimes Related to Banks and Banking

- State Laws Governing Banks, Banking, and Lending

- Additional Resources

## Background

The law governing banks, bank accounts, and lending in the United States is a hybrid of federal and state **statutory** law. Consumers and businesses may establish bank accounts in banks and savings associations chartered under state or federal law. The law under which a bank is chartered regulates that particular bank. A mix of state and federal law, however, governs most operations and transactions by bank customers.

Article 3 of the **Uniform Commercial Code**, as adopted by the various states, governs transactions involving negotiable instruments, including checks. Article 4 of the Uniform **Commercial Code** governs bank deposits and collections, including the rights and responsibilities of **depository** banks, collecting banks, and banks responsible for the payment of a check. Other provisions of the Uniform Commercial Code are also relevant to banking and lending law, including Article 4A (related to funds transfers), Article 5 (related to letters of credit), Article 8 (related to **securities**), and Article 9 (related to secured transactions).

A number of regulations govern a check when it passes through the Federal Reserve System. These regulations govern the availability of funds available to a depositor in his or her bank account, the delay between the time a bank receives a deposit and the time the funds should be made available, and the process to follow when a check is dishonored for non-payment. Federal law also provides protection to bank customers. Prompted by banking crises in the 1930s, the federal government established the Federal Deposit Insurance Corporation, which insures bank accounts of individuals and institutions in amounts up to $100,000.

A number of laws have been passed affecting banks, banking, and lending. A brief summary of these is as follows:

- National Bank Act of 1864 established a national banking systems and chartering of national banks.

- Federal Reserve Act of 1913 established the Federal Reserve System. Banking Act of 1933

(**Glass-Steagall Act**) established the Federal Deposit Insurance Corporation (FDIC), originally intended to be temporary.

- Banking Act of 1935 established the FDIC as a permanent agency.

- Federal Deposit Insurance Act of 1950 revised and consolidated previous laws governing the FDIC.

- Bank **Holding Company** Act of 1956 set forth requirements for the establishment of bank holding companies.

- International Banking Act of 1978 required foreign banks to fit within the federal regulatory framework.

- Financial Institutions Regulatory and Interest Rate Control Act of 1978 created the Federal Financial Institutions **Examination** Council; it also established limits and reporting requirements for insider transactions involving banks and modified provisions governing transfers of electronic funds.

- Depository Institutions Deregulation and Monetary Control Act of 1980 began to eliminate ceilings on interest rates of savings and other accounts and raised the insurance ceiling of insured account holders to $100,000.

- Depository Institutions Act of 1982 (Gar-St. Germain Act) expanded the powers of the FDIC and further eliminated ceilings on interest rates. Competitive Equality Banking Act of 1987 established new standards for the availability of expedited funds and further expanded FDIC authority.

- Financial Institutions Reform, Recovery, and Enforcement Act of 1989 set forth a number of reforms and revisions, designed to ensure trust in the savings and loan industry.

- Crime Control Act of 1990 expanded the ability of federal regulators to combat **fraud** in financial institutions.

- Federal Deposit Insurance Corporation Act of 1991 expanded the power and authority of the FDIC considerably.

- Housing and Community Development Act of 1992 set forth provisions to combat **money laundering** and provided some regulatory relief to certain financial institutions.

- Riegle Community Development and Regulatory Improvement Act of 1994 established the Community Development Financial Institutions Fund to provide assistance to community development financial institutions.

- Riegle-Neal Interstate Banking and Branching Efficiency Act of 1994 permitted bank holding companies that were adequately capitalized and managed to acquire banks in any state.

- Economic Growth and Regulatory Paperwork Reduction Act of 1996 brought forth a number of changes, many of which related to the modification of regulation of financial institutions.

- Gramm-Leach Bliley Act of 1999 brought forth numerous changes, including the restriction of disclosure of nonpublic customer information by financial institutions. The Act provided penalties for anyone who obtains nonpublic customer information from a financial institution under false pretenses.

Numerous federal agencies promulgate regulations relevant to banks and banking, including the Federal Deposit Insurance Corporation, Federal Reserve Board, General Accounting Office, National **Credit Union** Administration, and Treasury Department.

The ability for bank customers to engage in electronic banking has had a significant effect on the laws of banking in the United States. Some laws that govern paper checks and other traditional instruments are difficult to apply to corresponding electronic transfers. As technology develops and affects the banking industry, banking law will likely change even more.

## Banking Transactions

### *Checks and Other Negotiable Instruments*

Article 3 of the Uniform Commercial Code, drafted by the National Conference of Commissioners on Uniform State Laws and adopted in every state except Louisiana, governs the creation and transfer of negotiable instruments. Since checks are negotiable instruments, the provisions in Article 3 apply. Because banks are lending institutions that create notes and other instruments, Article 3 will also apply in other circumstances that do not involve checks.

A person who establishes an account at a bank may make a written order on that account in the form of a check. The account holder is called the drawer, while the person named on the check is called the payee. When the drawer orders the bank to pay the person named in the check, the bank is obligated to do so and reduce the drawer's account by the amount on the check. A bank ordinarily has no obligation to honor a check from a person other than a depositor. However, both the drawer's and payee's banks generally must honor these checks if there are sufficient funds to cover the amount of the check. The payee's bank must generally honor a check written to the order of the payee if the payee has sufficient funds to cover the amount of the check, in case the drawer of the check does not have sufficient funds. A drawer may request from the bank a **certified check**, which means the check is guaranteed. Certified checks must be honored by any bank, and, as such, are considered the same as cash.

A customer's bank has a duty to know each customer's signature. If another party forges the signature of the customer, the customer is generally not liable for the amount of the check. Banks may recover from the forger but may not generally recover from the innocent customer or a third person who in **good faith** and without notice of the **forgery** gave cash or other items of value in exchange for the check. Drawers have the right to inspect all checks charged against their accounts to ensure that no forgeries have occurred. Drawers also have rights to stop payment on checks that have been neither paid nor certified by their banks. This is done through a **stop payment order** issued by the customer to the bank. If a bank pays a check notwithstanding the stop payment order, the bank is liable to the customer for the value of the check.

Many of the rules applying the checks apply to all negotiable instruments. Banks that serve as lending institutions routinely exchange loans for promissory notes, which are most likely negotiable instruments. These instruments are considered property and may be bought and sold by other entities.

### Checking Accounts

Article 4 of the Uniform Commercial Code governs the operation of checking accounts, though several federal laws supplement the provisions of Article 4. The provisions of this uniform law define rights regarding bank deposits and collections. It governs such relationships as those between a depository bank and a collecting bank and those between a payor bank and it customers.

### Funds Transfers

Article 4A of the Uniform Commercial Code governs methods of payment whereby a person making a payment (called the "originator") transmits directly an instruction to a bank to make a payment to a third person (called the "beneficiary"). Article 4A covers the issuance and acceptance of a payment order from a customer to a bank, the **execution** of a payment order by a receiving bank and the actual payment of the payment order.

### Letters of Credit

Article 5 of the Uniform Commercial Code governs transactions involving the issuance of letters of credit. Such letters of credit are generally issued when a party (the "applicant") applies for credit in a transaction of some sort with a third party (the "beneficiary"). The bank will issue a letter of credit to the **beneficiary** prior to the transaction. This letter is a definite undertaking by the bank to honor the letter of credit at the time the beneficiary presents this letter. Article 5 governs issuance, amendments, cancellation, duration, transfer, and assignment of letters of credit. It also defines the rights and obligations of the parties involved in the issuance of a letter of credit.

### Secured Transactions

When a bank agrees to enter into a loan with a bank customer, the bank will most likely acquire a security interest in property owned or purchased by the customer. This transaction, called a secured transaction, governed by Article 9 of the Uniform Commercial Code. Article 9 was substantially revised in 2000, and the vast majority of states have now adopted the revised version. The security interest provides protection for the bank in case the customer fails to pay a debt owed to the bank, even if the customer enters into **bankruptcy**. A number of steps must be followed for the bank to "perfect" the security interest, including the filing of documents with the secretary of state or other appropriate officer in the state where the customer resides.

## Federal Reserve System

The Federal Reserve Board has been delegated significant responsibility related to the implementation of laws governing banks and banking. The Board has issued more than thirty major regulations on a variety of issues affecting the banking industry. When a check passes through the Federal Reserve System, Regulation J applies. This regulation governs the collection of checks and other items by Federal Reserve

Banks, as well as many funds transfers. This regulation also establishes procedures, responsibilities, and duties among Federal Reserve banks, the payors, and other senders of checks through the Federal Reserve System, and the senders of wire transmissions. Regulation J is contained in Title 12 of the **Code of Federal Regulations**, Part 210.

A second significant regulation promulgated by the Federal Reserve Board is Regulation CC, which governs the availability of funds in a bank customer's account. This regulation also governs the collection of checks. Under this regulation, cash deposits made by a customer into a bank account must be available to the customer no later than the end of the business day after the day the funds were deposited. The next-day rule also applies to several check deposits, as defined by the regulation, although banks are not required to make funds available for as long as five days after deposit for many other types of checks. Regulation CC also governs the payment of interest, the responsibilities of various banks regarding the return of checks. Liabilities to the bank for failure to adhere to these rules are defined by the regulation. Regulation CC is contained in Title 12 of the Code of Federal Regulations, Part 229.

Other Federal Reserve Board regulations cover a variety of transactions under a myriad of statutes. These include such provisions as those requiring equal credit opportunity; transfer of electronic funds; consumer leasing; privacy of consumer financial information; and truth in lending.

## Insurance of Deposits

Congress in 1933 established the Federal Deposit Insurance Corporation, which is funded by premiums paid by member institutions. If a customer holds an account at a bank that is a member institution of the FDIC, the customer's accounts are insured for an aggregate total of $100,000. Banks that are member institutions are required to display prominently signs indicating that the bank is a member of the FDIC or a sign that states "Deposits Federally Insured to $100,000—Backed by the Full Faith and Credit of the United States Government." This applies to many banks that are chartered either federally or by way of state **statute**.

## Interest Rates Charged by Banks

The federal government until the early 1980s regulated interest rates charged on bank accounts. Interest rates on savings accounts were generally limited, while interest rates on other types of accounts were generally prohibited. The Depository Institutions Deregulation Act of 1980 and Garn-St. Germain Depository Institutions Act eliminated restrictions and prohibitions on interest rates on savings, checking, money market and other types of accounts.

## Truth in Lending

The Truth in Lending Act, which was part of the **Consumer Credit Protection Act**, provides protection to consumers by requiring lenders to disclose costs and terms related to a loan. Most of these disclosures are contained in a loan application. Lenders must include several of the following items:

- Terms and costs of loan plans, including annual percentage rates, fees, and points

- The total amount of principal being financed

- Payment due dates, including provisions for late payment fees

- Details of variable-interest loans

- Total amount of finance charges

- Details about whether a loan is assumable

- Application fees

- Pre-payment penalties

The Truth in Lending Act also requires lenders to make certain disclosures regarding advertisements for loan rates and terms. Specific terms of the credit must be disclosed, and if the advertisement indicates a rate, it must be stated in terms of an **annual percentage rate**, which takes into account additional costs incurred relating to the loan. Other restrictions on advertising loan rates also apply. If a bank or other lending institution fails to adhere to the provision of the Truth in Lending Act, severe penalties apply.

The Federal Reserve Board has been delegated authority to prescribe regulations to enforce the provisions of the Truth in Lending Act. These regulations are contained in Regulation Z of the Board.

## Usury Laws

Every state establishes a ceiling interest rate that can be charged by creditors. If a **creditor** charges an interest rate higher than the rate established by the state, the penalties to the creditor can be severe.

Such penalties may include the **forfeiture** of the principal debt owed to the creditor by the **debtor**. Debtors that are subjected to high interest rates should consult the **usury** laws in that state to determine whether these laws may apply.

## Crimes Related to Banks and Banking

Congress has promulgated a number of criminal statutes applicable to crimes against banks and banking institutions. Some crimes are related to more violent acts, such as robbery, while others focus on nonviolent crimes, such as money laundering. Each of the crimes listed below is contained in Title 18 of the United States Code.

- Bank **bribery** is prohibited under Title 18, sections 212 through 215.

- Theft by a bank officer or employee is prohibited under Title 18, section 656.

- False bank entry is prohibited under Title 18, section 1005.

- False statements to the FDIC are prohibited under Title 18, section 1007.

- Bank fraud is prohibited under Title 18, section 1344.

- Obstruction of an examination of a financial institution is prohibited under Title 18, section 1517.

- Money laundering is prohibited under Title 18, sections 1956 through 1960.

- Bank robbery is prohibited under Title 18, section 2113.

- Crimes involving coins and currency are prohibited under provisions in Title 18, Chapter 17.

## State Laws Governing Banks, Banking, and Lending

All U. S. states have adopted at least a portion of the Uniform Commercial Code, including Articles 3 (1990 version), 4 (1990 version), 4A (1989 version), and 5 (1995 version). Article 9 was last revised in 2000, with the previous major revision occurring in 1972. Most state laws governing banks, banking, and lending are consistent from one state to the next. Moreover, due to federal regulation of banks and banking, states are rather limited in their ability to enact laws that differ from the majority of states.

ALABAMA: Adopted Articles 3 and 4 in 1995; Article 4A in 1992; and Article 5 in 1997. The state has adopted the Revised Article 9 (2000).

ALASKA: Adopted Articles 3 and 4 in 1993; Article 4A in 1993; and Article 5 in 1999. The state adopted the majority of the provisions in the Revised Article 9 (2000) in 2000.

ARIZONA: Adopted Articles 3 and 4 in 1993; Article 4A in 1991; and Article 5 in 1996. The state has adopted the Revised Article 9 (2000).

ARKANSAS: Adopted Articles 3 and 4 in 1991; Article 4A in 1991; and Article 5 in 1997. The state has adopted the Revised Article 9 (2000).

CALIFORNIA: Adopted Articles 3 and 4 in 1992; Article 4A in 1990; and Article 5 in 1996. The state has adopted the Revised Article 9 (2000).

COLORADO: Adopted Articles 3 and 4 in 1994; Article 4A in 1990; and Article 5 in 1996. The state has adopted the Revised Article 9 (2000).

CONNECTICUT: Adopted Articles 3 and 4 in 1991; Article 4A in 1990; and Article 5 in 1996. The state has adopted the Revised Article 9 (2000).

DELAWARE: Adopted Articles 3 and 4 in 1995; Article 4A in 1992; and Article 5 in 1998. The state adopted the majority of the provisions in the Revised Article 9 (2000) in 2000.

FLORIDA: Adopted Articles 3 and 4 in 1992; Article 4A in 1991; and Article 5 in 1999. The state has adopted the Revised Article 9 (2000).

GEORGIA: Adopted Articles 3 and 4 in 1996; Article 4A in 1993. The state has adopted the Revised Article 9 (2000).

HAWAII: Adopted Articles 3 and 4 in 1991; Article 4A in 1991; and Article 5 in 1996. The state adopted the majority of the provisions in the Revised Article 9 (2000) in 2000.

IDAHO: Adopted Articles 3 and 4 in 1993; Article 4A in 1991; and Article 5 in 1996. The state has adopted the Revised Article 9 (2000).

ILLINOIS: Adopted Articles 3 and 4 in 1991; Article 4A in 1990; and Article 5 in 1996. The state adopted the majority of the provisions in the Revised Article 9 (2000) in 2000.

INDIANA: Adopted Articles 3 and 4 in 1991; Article 4A in 1991; and Article 5 in 1996. The state adopted the majority of the provisions in the Revised Article 9 (2000) in 2000.

IOWA: Adopted Articles 3 and 4 in 1994; Article 4A in 1992; and Article 5 in 1996. The state adopted the majority of the provisions in the Revised Article 9 (2000) in 2000.

KANSAS: Adopted Articles 3 and 4 in 1991; Article 4A in 1990; and Article 5 in 1996. The state adopted the majority of the provisions in the Revised Article 9 (2000) in 2000.

KENTUCKY: Adopted Articles 3 and 4 in 1996; Article 4A in 1992; and Article 5 in 2000. The state adopted the majority of the provisions in the Revised Article 9 (2000) in 2000.

LOUISIANA: Adopted Articles 3 and 4 in 1992; Article 4A in 1990; and Article 5 in 1999. The state has adopted the Revised Article 9 (2000).

MAINE: Adopted Articles 3 and 4 in 1993; Article 4A in 1992; and Article 5 in 1997. The state adopted the majority of the provisions in the Revised Article 9 (2000) in 2000.

MARYLAND: Adopted Articles 3 and 4 in 1996; Article 4A in 1992; and Article 5 in 1997. The state has adopted the Revised Article 9 (2000).

MASSACHUSETTS: Adopted Articles 3 and 4 in 1998; Article 4A in 1992; and Article 5 in 1998. The state has adopted the Revised Article 9 (2000).

MICHIGAN: Adopted Articles 3 and 4 in 1993; Article 4A in 1992; and Article 5 in 1992. The state adopted the majority of the provisions in the Revised Article 9 (2000) in 2000.

MINNESOTA: Adopted Articles 3 and 4 in 1992; Article 4A in 1990; and Article 5 in 1997. The state adopted the majority of the provisions in the Revised Article 9 (2000) in 2000.

MISSISSIPPI: Adopted Articles 3 and 4 in 1995; Article 4A in 1992; and Article 5 in 1997. The state has adopted the Revised Article 9 (2000).

MISSOURI: Adopted Articles 3 and 4 in 1992; Article 4A in 1992; and Article 5 in 1997. The state has adopted the Revised Article 9 (2000).

MONTANA: Adopted Articles 3 and 4 in 1991; Article 4A in 1991; and Article 5 in 1997. The state has adopted the Revised Article 9 (2000).

NEBRASKA: Adopted Articles 3 and 4 in 1991; Article 4A in 1991; and Article 5 in 1996. The state has adopted the Revised Article 9 (2000).

NEVADA: Adopted Articles 3 and 4 in 1993; Article 4A in 1991; and Article 5 in 1997. The state has adopted the Revised Article 9 (2000).

NEW HAMPSHIRE: Adopted Articles 3 and 4 in 1993; Article 4A in 1993; and Article 5 in 1998. The state has adopted the Revised Article 9 (2000).

NEW JERSEY: Adopted Articles 3 and 4 in 1995; Article 4A in 1995; and Article 5 in 1998. The state has adopted the Revised Article 9 (2000).

NEW MEXICO: Adopted Articles 3 and 4 in 1992; Article 4A in 1992; and Article 5 in 1997. The state has adopted the Revised Article 9 (2000).

NEW YORK: Adopted older uniform law on negotiable instruments in 1897; Article 4A in 1990; and Article 5 in 2000. The state has adopted the Revised Article 9 (2000).

NORTH CAROLINA: Adopted Articles 3 and 4 in 1995; Article 4A in 1993; and Article 5 in 1999. The state adopted the majority of the provisions in the Revised Article 9 (2000) in 2000.

NORTH DAKOTA: Adopted Articles 3 and 4 in 1991; Article 4A in 1991; and Article 5 in 1997. The state has adopted the Revised Article 9 (2000).

OHIO: Adopted Articles 3 and 4 in 1994; Article 4A in 1991; and Article 5 in 1997. The state has adopted the Revised Article 9 (2000).

OKLAHOMA: Adopted Articles 3 and 4 in 1991; Article 4A in 1990; and Article 5 in 1996. The state adopted the majority of the provisions in the Revised Article 9 (2000) in 2000.

OREGON: Adopted Articles 3 and 4 in 1995; Article 4A in 1992; and Article 5 in 1997. The state has adopted the Revised Article 9 (2000).

PENNSYLVANIA: Adopted Articles 3 and 4 in 1992; Article 4A in 1992; and Article 5 in 2001. The state has adopted the Revised Article 9 (2000).

RHODE ISLAND: Adopted Articles 3 and 4 in 2000; Article 4A in 1991; and Article 5 in 2000. The state adopted the majority of the provisions in the Revised Article 9 (2000) in 2000.

SOUTH CAROLINA: Adopted older uniform law on negotiable instruments in 1914; Article 4A in 1996; and Article 5 in 2001. The state has adopted the Revised Article 9 (2000).

SOUTH DAKOTA: Adopted Articles 3 and 4 in 1994; Article 4A in 1991; and Article 5 in 1998. The state adopted the majority of the provisions in the Revised Article 9 (2000) in 2000.

TENNESSEE: Adopted Articles 3 and 4 in 1994; Article 4A in 1991; and Article 5 in 1998. The state adopted the majority of the provisions in the Revised Article 9 (2000) in 2000.

TEXAS: Adopted Articles 3 and 4 in 1994; Article 4A in 1991; and Article 5 in 1998. The state has adopted the Revised Article 9 (2000).

UTAH: Adopted Articles 3 and 4 in 1993; Article 4A in 1990; and Article 5 in 1997. The state adopted the majority of the provisions in the Revised Article 9 (2000) in 2000.

VERMONT: Adopted Articles 3 and 4 in 1994; Article 4A in 1994; and Article 5 in 1998. The state adopted the majority of the provisions in the Revised Article 9 (2000) in 2000.

VIRGINIA: Adopted Articles 3 and 4 in 1992; Article 4A in 1990; and Article 5 in 1997. The state adopted the majority of the provisions in the Revised Article 9 (2000) in 2000.

WASHINGTON: Adopted Articles 3 and 4 in 1994; Article 4A in 1991; and Article 5 in 1998. The state adopted the majority of the provisions in the Revised Article 9 (2000) in 2000.

WEST VIRGINIA: Adopted Articles 3 and 4 in 1993; Article 4A in 1990; and Article 5 in 1996. The state adopted the majority of the provisions in the Revised Article 9 (2000) in 2000.

WISCONSIN: Adopted Articles 3 and 4 in 1996; and Article 4A in 1992. The state has adopted the Revised Article 9 (2000).

WYOMING: Adopted Articles 3 and 4 in 1991; Article 4A in 1991; and Article 5 in 1997. The state has adopted the Revised Article 9 (2000).

## Additional Resources

*Banking Law* Matthew Bender & Co., 1981.

*Code of Federal Regulations, Title 12: Banks and Banking.* Government Printing Office, 2002. Available at http://www.access.gpo.gov/nara/cfr/cfr-table-search.html.

*Consumer Banking and Payments Law.* Budnitz, Mark, National Consumer Law Center, 2001.

*Lender Liability and Banking Litigation.* Mannimo, Edward F., and Richard E. Kaye, Law Journal Press, 2001.

*Truth in Lending, Fourth Edition.* 4th ed., Renuart, Elizabeth, and Kathleen E. Keest, National Consumer Law Center, 1999.

*U. S. Code, Title 12: Banks and Banking.* U. S. House of Representatives, 1999. Available at http://uscode.house.gov/title_12.htm.

## Organizations

### Board of Governors of the Federal Reserve System, Division of Consumer and Community Affairs

20th and C Streets, NW, MS 804
Washington, DC 20551 USA
Phone: (202) 452-3667
URL: http://www.federalreserve.gov/

### Federal Deposit Insurance Corporation (FDIC)

550 17th Street, NW
Washington, DC 20429-9990 USA
Phone: (877) ASK-FDIC
URL: http://www.fdic.gov

### National Conference of Commissioners on Uniform State Laws (NCCUSL)

211 E. Ontario Street, Suite 1300
Chicago, IL 60611 USA
Phone: (312) 915-0195
Fax: (312) 915-0187
E-Mail: nccusl@ nccusl.org
URL: http://www.nccusl.org/

### Office of the Comptroller of the Currency, Customer Assistance Group

1301 McKinney, Suite 3710
Houston, TX 77010 USA
Phone: (800) 613-6743
URL: http://www.occ.treas.gov/

### Office of Thrift Supervision, Consumer Program Division

1700 G Street, NW
Washington, DC 20552 USA
Phone: (800) 842-6929
URL: http://www.ots.treas.gov

# BANKING

## BANKS, SAVINGS & LOANS, CREDIT UNIONS

*Sections Within This Essay:*

- Background

- Types of Financial Institutions
  - Banks
  - Savings and Loans
  - Credit Unions

- Automated Teller Machines (ATMs)

- Federal Laws

- Additional Resources

- Organizations

## Background

Banks are only one of several kinds of financial institutions that offer financial services to their patrons. The term "bank" is often used as a collective term to describe any one of the numerous forms of financial institutions. Banks, like most other bank-like financial institutions, are established by charters. A charter is official permission from a regulating authority (like a state) to accept deposits and/or to provide financial services. Charters provide the specifics of a bank's powers and obligations. State and federal governments closely regulate banks and bank accounts. Accounts for customers may be established by national and state financial institutions, all of which are regulated by the law under which they are established.

The federal government regulated and controlled interest rates on bank accounts for many decades.

There was a cap on interest rates for savings accounts, and most interest bearing payments–on–demand deposit accounts (e.g. checking accounts) were prohibited. Banks were also prevented from offering money market accounts. But sweeping changes in banking law in the early 1980s transformed the way banks and other financial institutions do business. For example, interest rate controls on savings accounts were eliminated by the **Depository** Institutions Deregulation Act of 1980 (DIDRA), and the Garn-St Germain Depository Institutions Act and the DIDRA lifted restrictions on checking and money market accounts.

One common and important service offered by banking institutions is the checking accounts. Federal and state laws govern the operation of checking accounts. Article 4 of the **Uniform Commercial Code**, which has been adopted at least in part by every state, enumerates the rights and obligations between financial institutions and their customers with respect to bank deposits and collections. The five principal sections of Article 4 cover the following:

1. general provisions and definitions.

2. the actions of one bank in accepting the check of another and those of other banks that handle the check but are not responsible for its final payment

3. the actions of the bank responsible for payment of the check

4. the relationship between the bank responsible for payment of the check and its customers

5. the handling of documentary drafts, which are checks or other types of drafts that will only be honored if certain papers are first presented to the institution responsible for payment of the draft.

Checks are commercial documents called "negotiable instruments." Negotiable instruments are mainly governed by Article 3 of the Uniform **Commercial Code**. All states have adopted Article 3 of the Uniform Commercial Code (UCC), with some modifications, as the law governing negotiable instruments. Other types of negotiable instruments include drafts and notes. Drafts are documents ordering some type of payment to be made to a person or an institution. Checks are one kind of draft. Notes are documents promising payment will be made. A **mortgage** is a kind of note. Money, investment **securities**, and some forms of payment orders are not considered negotiable instruments under Article 3.

In the Great Depression, banks that could not meet their financial obligations to their customers or their creditors failed (became bankrupt). Because the deposits were not insured, individuals and businesses with money on deposit at the time a bank failed lost whatever was in the account at the time the bank failed. The depression and the banking crisis of the 1930's gave rise to the development of federal insurance for deposits administered by the Federal Deposit Insurance Corporation (FDIC). The program is funded from premiums paid by member institutions. Under the FDIC, individual bank accounts at insured institutions are protected up to $100,000. Multiple accounts in a single financial institution and belonging to the same customer are combined for purposes of the FDIC limits.

Banks are strictly regulated by three federal agencies. Banks are also subject to regulation by state bank regulators.

The federal agencies are given below:

- **Comptroller** of the Currency (for national banks)
- Federal Deposit Insurance Corporation
- Federal Reserve Board

States regulate banks through their banking commission or department of banking and finance. An official called the Commissioner or Director or Superintendent of Banks manages the state's banking commission or department of banking and finance. These state banking authorities may regulate only banks that have been chartered by the state.

The Gramm-Leach-Bliley Act, signed into law on November 12, 1999, is one of the most significant pieces of banking legislation in over fifty years. This law is the result of decades of effort to restructure the U. S. financial system. The Gramm-Leach-Bliley Act is complex and far-reaching, and contains a host of banking and financial services issues. Perhaps the most important feature of the Act is that it permits formal affiliations among banks, securities firms, and insurance companies. With the passage and implementation of these laws, the entire U. S. banking industry has been transformed. The U. S. banking system is innovative, yet it remains one of the safest, most secure systems in the world. It is also one of the most complex.

## Types of Financial Institutions

### Banks

In common parlance the term "bank" refers to many types of financial institutions. In addition to a bank, the term can refer to a **trust company**, a savings bank, savings and loan institution, **credit union**, thrift, thrift and loan, or trust company

There is a wide variety of banking institutions. The differences among these financial institutions is the result of both history and politics. Some banks may be regulated and supervised by different federal and/or state agencies. While these institutions may appear quite similar, they actually have different rights, powers, and obligations; they may even have different tax obligations. Savings and loan associations must invest more of their assets in home mortgages than traditional banks. Trust companies manage and administer trust funds of individuals and **pension** plans but may not take deposits into checking or savings accounts. Credit unions enjoy certain tax advantages. Some banking institutions have special deposit insurance arrangements. Some financial institutions can sell other financial services or products—like insurance—and other financial institutions may not. And some financial institutions must put significant cash reserves on deposit with the federal government, whereas others do not.

Banks that are chartered by the Comptroller of the Currency are called "National banks." National banks usually bear the words "national" or "national association" in their titles; sometimes they carry the letters N. A. or N. S. & T. in their titles.

### Savings and Loan Institutions

The primary function of savings and loan associations is the financing of long-term residential mortgages. Savings and loan associations accept deposits in savings accounts, pay interest on these accounts, and make loans to residential home buyers. They do not make business loans of any kind, nor do they provide many of the other business services one finds in commercial banks. A privately managed home financing institution, a savings and loan accepts savings accounts from individuals and other sources. This money is then principally invested in loans for the construction, purchase, or improvement of homes.

Savings and loan associations are primarily involved in making residential loans. Consequently, they may be good sources of indirect business financing for homeowners who own substantial equity in their homes. For example, if homeowners need money for their businesses, they can refinance their homes or take out a second mortgage on the equity through a **savings and loan association**. The home equity loan application process at a savings and loan association is generally simpler than it is for a commercial bank because it is made on the equity of the home up to a maximum percentage of the equity, usually between 75 percent to 80 percent. The savings and loan association bears little risk if the home is located in a stable or appreciating **market value** area. If the borrower defaults on the loan, the savings and loan association can foreclose the mortgage and, sell the property to retire the loan, doing so often for a profit.

### Credit Unions

The first credit union in the United States was formed in Manchester, New Hampshire, in 1909. As of 2002, there are over 10,000 credit unions in the United States. They control assets of nearly one–half a trillion dollars and serve about one–quarter of the population. Credit unions are members–only institutions. Individuals must join a credit union to take advantage of its services. But they cannot join just any credit union— they must first be eligible for membership. Most credit unions are organized to serve members of a particular community, group or groups of employees, or members of an organization or association. Large **corporations**, unions, or educational institutions are some of the groups who commonly form credit unions for their members or employees.

Federal credit unions are nonprofit, cooperative financial institutions owned and operated by their members. Credit unions are democratically controlled with members given the opportunity to vote on important issues that affect the running of the credit union. For example, the board that runs a credit union is elected by its members. Credit unions provide an alternative to banks and savings and loan associations as safe places in which to place savings and borrow at reasonable rates. Credit unions pool their members' funds to make loans to one another.

In addition to typical credit unions that serve members and provide banking and lending services, there are a few special types of credit unions:

* Community development credit unions: The NCUA established the Office of Community Development Credit Unions in early 1994. These credit unions serve mostly low-income members in economically distressed and/or financially deprived areas. Part of their function is to educate their members in fundamental money management concepts. At the same time, they provide an economic base in order to stimulate economic development and renewal to their communities.

* **Corporate** credit unions: These institutions do not provide services to individuals, but they serve as a sort of credit union for credit unions. Nationwide, there are over thirty federally insured corporate credit unions; they provide investment, liquidity, and payment services for their member credit unions.

## Automated Teller Machines (ATMs)

Not all banks or financial institutions have ATMs. Before ATMs, banks employed tellers to help their customers conduct all their banking business. Because ATMs can inexpensively perform many of the functions formerly done by tellers, ATMs have replaced many tellers in the banking institution. There are no laws requiring banks or other financial institutions to have ATMs. Instead, having one is a business decision for each bank. ATMs offer distinct advantages over traditional teller operations in terms of their locations and hours of operation. ATMs are relatively small and can be placed where banks would not ordinarily open a branch (gas stations, hotel lobbies, airports). Furthermore, ATMs are open when banks are closed; ATMs can function for twenty-four hours a day, seven days a week.

There has been a process of homogenization in the banking and financial industries. Services appear to be similar in many types of institutions. Nevertheless, some important differences among institutions remain. These differences may exist among banking institutions within a single state, and among the same type of institution from state to state. For example, a Missouri state chartered bank may have authority to conduct certain forms of business that are very different from those of a Missouri savings bank. Likewise, a Missouri savings and loan may have different powers from a Missouri national bank. These various rules and powers result in a difference in services among the spectrum of financial institutions. These differences can affect factors like interest rates, issuance of credit cards, ATM services, and so forth.

ATMs can be cost effective to operate when compared to the cost of hiring and training bank tellers. Even so, there are costs associated with owning and operating ATMs, including the costs for the following:

- buying the machine

- renting space for the ATM

- maintaining the ATM's mechanical parts

- paying personnel to load it with money and remove deposits (if any)

Banks or other financial institutions may charge patrons for using their bank's ATM as long as the bank or financial institution informs patrons of the terms and conditions of their accounts, and all applicable charges. This information is often contained in the monthly statements. On the other hand, if individuals use an ATM that does not belong to their own bank, the ATM's owner can charge them for using it. This is true even though they are gaining access to their own money kept in their own bank. Likewise, a bank can also charge its patrons for using someone else's ATM machine. In this way, individuals may incur two charges for using an ATM that does not belong to the bank or financial institution at which they are customers.

## Federal Laws

There are many laws that apply to financial institutions. Most of these are found in Title 12 of the United States Code. Some of the most important laws are:

- 12 U.S.C. §§ 1461-1470: Laws regulating Federal Savings and Loan Associations

- 12 U.S.C. §§ 4001-4010: The Expedited Funds Availability Act

- 12 U.S.C. § 371a: Garn-St. Germain Depository Institutions Act

- 12 **USC** §§ 1811-1832: Federal Deposit Insurance Corporation

- 12 U.S.C.: Banks and Banking

- 28 U.S.C. § 1348: Banking Associations as Parties to Civil Litigation

In addition to statutes, there are administrative rules that govern financial institutions. These rules have the same force and effect as actual laws passed by Congress. Title 12 of the **Code of Federal Regulations** is the site of most federal agency regulations that deal with banks and banking.

## Additional Resources

*"Bank and Thrift Rating Services for Consumers."* http://www.fdic.gov/bank/individual/bank/index.html. FDIC, 2002.

*Banking Law* Graham, Ann, ed., Matthew Bender, Inc., 1981.

*"Consumer Rights: Federal Laws."* http://www.fdic.gov/consumers/consumer/rights/index.html. FDIC, 2002.

*"Federal Financial Institutions Examination Council."* http://www.ffiec.gov/.

## Organizations

### American Bankers Association (ABA)
1120 Connecticut Avenue, N.W.
Washington, DC 20036 USA
Phone: (800) 226-5377
E-Mail: custserv@aba.com
URL: http://www.aba.com/default.htm

### Conference on State Bank Supervisors (CSBS)
1015 18th Street NW, Suite 1100
Washington, DC 20036 USA
Phone: (202) 296-2840
Fax: (202) 296-1928
URL: http://www.csbs.org/

### Office of Thrift Supervision (OTS)
1700 G Street, NW
Washington, DC 20552 USA
Phone: (800) 842-6929
E-Mail: consumer.complaint@ots.treas.gov
URL: www.ots.treas.gov

**National Credit Union Administration (NCUA)**
1775 Duke Street
Alexandria, VA 22314 USA
Phone: (703) 518-6300
URL: http://www.ncua.gov/

**Federal Depository Insurance Corporation (FDIC)**
550 Seventeenth Street, NW

Washington, DC 20429 USA
URL: http://www.fdic.gov/

**Office of the Comptroller of the Currency (OCC)**
1301 McKinney Street, Suite 3710
Houston, TX 77010 USA
URL: http://www.occ.treas.gov/

# BANKING

## FDIC

*Sections within this essay:*

- Background

- History

- How the FDIC Works

- Definitions

- Additional Resources

## Background

Congress created the Federal Deposit Insurance Corporation (FDIC) in 1933 to protect consumers who hold their money in banks from bank failures. Depositors—persons who hold money in savings accounts, checking accounts, certificates of deposit, money market accounts, Individual Retirement Accounts (IRAs), or Keogh accounts—have FDIC protection of up to $100,000 in the event of a bank failure. The FDIC regulates all banks that are members of the Federal Reserve System and certain banks that are not members of the Federal Reserve System. It is the FDIC's mission to monitor and regulate the banking industry, making certain that banks operate safely and legally, and to prevent bank failures while encouraging healthy competition within the industry. When a bank does fail by not having sufficient assets, the FDIC uses its money to reimburse the bank's depositors. It then sells the failed bank's assets and uses the profits to assist when other banks fail.

The FDIC employs approximately 8,000 people throughout the country. The headquarters are in Washington, D.C., but regional offices exist in Atlanta, Boston, Chicago, Dallas, Kansas City, Memphis, New York City, and San Francisco. In addition, field examiners, whose job is to conduct on-site inspections of banks, have field offices in 80 more locations throughout the country.

The FDIC has **jurisdiction** over banks in the 50 states, the District of Columbia, Guam, Puerto Rico, and the Virgin Islands. It regulates banks, enforcing rules such as the Equal Credit Opportunity Act that prohibits certain forms of **discrimination** in lending, and inspects banks to be sure they are operating profitably and legally. Banks that are insured by the FDIC pay an **assessment** four times per year to the FDIC. The amount of assessment paid by the bank depends in part on the amount of funds deposited with the bank.

## History

Banking history in the United States changed forever with the Great Depression. The Great Depression began when the stock market crashed in October 1929, causing numerous banks to fail, which in turn caused bank depositors in many cases to lose most or all of their money. U. S. President Franklin Delano Roosevelt and Congress responded by creating the FDIC to guarantee the safety of bank deposits and regain the public's confidence in the banking industry. The history of the FDIC, however, may be traced back even before the Great Depression.

When the United States was formed in 1776, the thirteen original colonies each had their own banking systems, with no uniform currency and little government involvement in the banking systems. In

1791, Congress created the First Bank of the United States, a bank in Philadelphia that closed in 1811. As the country grew, banking remained largely unregulated and inconsistent. Following the Civil War, the economy in the North prospered while the economy in the South floundered. To encourage economic stability and consistency throughout the country, the National Banking Act of 1864 created national banks as well as the Office of the **Comptroller** of the Currency (OCC), and the dollar became the national currency. Bank failures in the early twentieth century led the creation of the Federal Reserve System, a central bank that continues to oversee and regulate national banks throughout the country.

The economy grew rapidly in the 1920s until the stock market crash in 1929. Stocks quickly lost their value, and as a result, banks lost money, farm prices fell, unemployment soared, and consumers began taking their money out of banks. Many banks failed and closed, lacking sufficient funds to pay their lenders and depositors. Finally, in 1933, President Roosevelt closed all banks temporarily and enacted the Banking Act. The Banking Act of 1933 established the FDIC, giving it authority to regulate and oversee banks and to provide insurance to bank depositors.

In early 1934, the maximum amount of insurance offered by the FDIC was $2,500, but by the end of the year the maximum amount increased to $5,000. Also in 1934, Congress created an entity similar to the FDIC to protect depositors from failures of federal savings and loan institutions. This entity was known as the Federal Savings and Loan Insurance Corporation (FSLIC).

The Banking Act of 1935 made the FDIC a permanent and independent corporation. Banks continued to fail throughout the 1930s, and the FDIC honored its promise to depositors by reimbursing them up to $5,000 for money lost in bank failures. Gradually, the number of bank failures declined, and by the late 1930s banks were becoming more profitable. In 1950, the FDIC maximum amount of insurance rose from $5,000 to $10,000.

In 1960, only four banks insured by the FDIC failed. The FDIC at that time employed approximately 2,500 bank examiners, and by 1962, no banks insured by the FDIC failed. In 1966, the FDIC maximum amount of insurance rose to $15,000, and in 1969, it rose again to $20,000. In 1980, the maximum amount of insurance was $100,000. It remained at that amount as of 2002.

Inflation skyrocketed to 14 percent by 1981, and the interest rates for home mortgages were extremely high at 21 percent. In 1983, the FDIC continued to collect more in premiums from member banks than it paid out for bank failures, but that same year, 48 banks insured by the FDIC failed. By 1984, the FDIC was paying more on bank failures than it collected in bank assessments, with 79 banks failing. In 1985, 125 banks failed, and in 1986, 138 banks, with assets totaling $7 billion, failed. What was worse, savings and loans were failing at an unprecedented rate, prompting Congress to act in 1989 with the Financial Institutions Reform, Recovery, and Enforcement Act (FIRREA). This act created the Resolution Trust Corporation (RTC) as a temporary agency charged with administering and cleaning up the savings and loan failures. The act also established the Savings Association Insurance Fund (SAIF), which insures deposits in savings and loan associations and charged the FDIC with administering the SAIF. The SAIF replaced the FSLIC.

In 1990, the FDIC began to increase its premium rate for the first time in its history, charging banks more to remain FDIC insured. The Federal Deposit Insurance Corporation Improvement Act of 1991 allowed the FDIC to borrow additional funds from the U. S. Treasury to rebuild its coffers. It also instructed the FDIC to set premiums for banks based upon each bank's level of risk and to close failing banks in more cost-effective ways. No longer was the FDIC permitted to repay all deposits to encourage consumer confidence; rather, Congress strictly limited the FDIC to reimburse only insured depositors and only to the maximum amount allowed by law. Congress also mandated that the Federal Reserve System not lend money to banks in financial trouble. By 1993, bank failure rates were down to their lowest number in twelve years. Congress dissolved the RTC and transferred its duties back to the FDIC that same year.

## How the FDIC Works

Provided a financial institution is insured by the FDIC, the FDIC protects any depositor—individual or entity—regardless of whether the depositor is a U. S. citizen or resident. Federally chartered banks, as well as some state chartered banks, are protected by the FDIC. If a banking institution is FDIC-insured, it must display an official FDIC sign at each teller station. The FDIC insures deposits that are payable in the United States; deposits that are only payable overseas do not receive FDIC protection. Investments such as stocks or mutual funds are not FDIC protected. Deposits into accounts such as savings, checking, Christmas Club, certificates of deposit (CDs) are FDIC insured, as are cashiers' checks, expense checks, loan disbursement checks, interest checks, money orders, and other negotiable instruments.

A depositor who has more than $100,000 in deposits is protected only to the extent of $100,000 per FDIC insured institution. This means that consumers who have assets exceeding $100,000 are best served by keeping no more than $100,000 in any one FDIC insured bank. A bank with more than one branch is considered to be one institution, so merely keeping funds in different branch locations may not be safe. For purposes of determining deposit insurance coverage, the FDIC will add all deposits from all branch offices of the same bank for each depositor. Deposits of more than $100,000 maintained in a single banking institution are protected so long as they are maintained in different categories of legal ownership. Examples of different categories of legal ownership include single ownership versus joint accounts, or individual retirement accounts (IRAs), Keogh accounts, or **pension** or profit-sharing accounts. Different types of accounts, however—checking, savings, certificates of deposit—are not categories of legal ownership. Money contained in separate types of accounts is added together for purposes of determining FDIC insurance coverage.

The FDIC determines legal ownership of bank deposits by examining the bank deposit account records. Assuming those records are unambiguous, the FDIC insurance goes to the individual or entity named. FDIC protection continues for up to six months following the death of a depositor as though the depositor were alive. This protection is important in cases in which the funds of the deceased are left to a survivor whose own bank deposits, combined with those of the deceased, exceed $100,000. Without this protection, the survivor would only receive $100,000 in FDIC insurance; with this protection, the survivor may receive the insurance afforded the deceased depositor as well.

Some states have **community property** laws, meaning that the property of one spouse may legally be considered as the property of the other spouse as well. Community property laws, however, do not affect the coverage afforded by the FDIC. Even in states that have community property laws, an account held solely in the name of one spouse will not be considered by the FDIC as also belonging to the other spouse. Accounts held in the name of both spouses will be insured by the FDIC as joint accounts. With joint accounts, the interests of each individual are added together and insured by the FDIC to the extent of $100,000. This means that if Mary and Bill have a joint savings account totaling $200,000, the FDIC would completely insure Mary's portion of $100,000 and would also completely insure Bill's portion of $100,000.

In the case of retirement funds, such as IRAs and Keogh accounts, the FDIC considers the accounts to be insured separately from other non-retirement funds held by the depositor at the same financial institution. If a depositor has both IRA and Keogh accounts at the same institution, however, those funds will be added together and insured only to the extend of $100,000. Roth IRAs are treated in the same manner as traditional IRAs.

In the case of business accounts, funds deposited in the name of a corporation or other business entity receive the same FDIC protection—up to $100,000—as do individual accounts. A business entity must not exist merely to increase the FDIC protection afforded an individual depositor; the business entity must exist to perform an "independent activity" to receive FDIC protection. When a business entity owns more than one account, even when each account is designated for different purposes, the FDIC will add the total amounts of all accounts and insure the business entity to a maximum of $100,000. This rule also applies if a corporation has separate units or divisions that are not separately incorporated. If a business entity is a **sole proprietorship**, the FDIC treats deposits of the sole proprietorship as the funds of the individual who is the sole proprietor. Those funds will be added to any other insured accounts held by the individual, and the FDIC will insure no more than $100,000.

In addition to its powers of insuring bank and savings and loan deposits, the FDIC regulates the banking industry and may, after proper notice and a **hearing**, discontinue its insurance coverage if a bank engages in overly risky banking practices. When this happens, the FDIC requires the bank to provide timely notice to its depositors of the termination of FDIC coverage.

## Definitions

Bank: a financial institution, chartered by the state or federal government, that exists to keep and protect the money of depositors, disburse funds for payment on checks, issue loans to businesses and consumers, and perform other money-related functions.

Savings and loan: a financial institution, similar to a bank, whose primary purpose it to make loans to customers, most often for the purchase of homes or other real estate.

## Additional Resources

*FDIC: Your Insured Deposit* www.fdic.gov, 2002.

*West's Encyclopedia of American Law.* West Group, 1998.

## Organizations

### Board of Governors of the Federal Reserve System Division of Consumer and Community Affairs

20th and C Streets, NW MS 804

Washington, DC 20551 USA

Phone: (202) 452-3667

URL: www.federalreserve.gov

### Federal Deposit Insurance Corporation (FDIC)

550 Seventeenth Street, NW

Washington, DC 20409 USA

Phone: (877) ASK-FDIC

URL: www.fdic.gov

### Office of the Comptroller of the Currency

1301 McKinney Suite 3710

Houston, TX 77010 USA

Phone: (800) 613-6743

URL: www.occ.treas.gov

### Office of Thrift Supervision Consumer Program Division

1700 G Street, NW

Washington, DC 20552 USA

Phone: (800) 842-6929

URL: www.ots.treas.gov

# BANKING

## INTEREST RATES

*Sections within this essay:*

- Background
- History
- Interest and Inflation
- State Usury Laws
- Additional Resources

## Background

In the world of banking and finance, interest is money that is paid by a borrower to a lender in exchange for the use of the credit. Money held in an account, such as a bank savings or checking account, may earn interest also because the bank has use of the money while it is held in the account and the interest constitutes payment to the account holder for the temporary use of the money.

Typically, interest is computed as a percentage of the amount borrowed, which is known as the principal. Interest may be computed on a yearly basis, which is known as simple interest. For example, if a borrower borrows $1,000 at a simple interest rate of 12 percent, with the loan due to be repaid in one year, the total interest owed on the loan is $120. Alternatively, interest may be compounded. With compounded interest, the calculation of interest occurs periodically and unpaid interest is added to the premium. For example, assuming a loan of $1,000 with a 12 percent interest rate compounded monthly, the interest that accrues during the first month of the loan is $120. That amount is added to the principal,

making the total amount $1,120. The interest accruing during the second month of the loan—12 percent of $1,120—is $134.40. With compounded interest, the interest rate stays the same but the amount of interest may increase periodically.

## History

Interest on borrowed funds has existed since ancient times, but interest was not always an acceptable means of conducting business. Religious groups in the Middle Ages—Jewish, Christian, and Islamic—forbade the use of interest, considering it reprehensible. Romans in ancient times also outlawed the practice of charging interest, as did the English government until the thirteenth century. In time, and with increasing demands for credit to support the growth of commerce and trade, a distinction was made between moderate interest rates and excessive interest rates. Chinese and Hindu laws prohibited excessive interest rates, known as **usury**, and in 1545, England set a maximum rate of interest. Other countries followed England's practice. In the United States as of 2002, the payment of interest for loans is a widely accepted business practice, with illegal usury reserved for interest rates exceeding the maximums set by law.

## Interest and Inflation

Interest rates fluctuate constantly. They are controlled by supply and demand and other economic indicators. Other factors that help determine an interest rate include the length of the loan and any **collateral** used to secure the loan in the event the borrower cannot repay the loan. Low interest rates can stimulate the economy; consumers are attracted to low interest rates on consumer goods, cars, and houses and may spend more when interest rates are low. High interest rates usually have the opposite effect. Consumers are reluctant or unable to spend money, or spend as much money, when interest rates climb.

The Federal Reserve Board of Governors, part of the Federal Reserve System, sets a benchmark interest rate known as the prime rate. The Federal Reserve, the central bank of the United States, was founded in 1913 to help regulate the country's money supply. The goals of the Federal Reserve Board are to control inflation, maintain stable prices, and promote maximum employment and output of products for a favorable economy. This is done, in part, by raising and lowering interest rates. Low interest rates spur the economy but may lead to inflation, which harms the economy in the long term. The Federal Reserve Board looks at a range of economic indicators to help it determine what its policies should be and whether to raise, lower, or maintain the prime interest rate.

Any national bank must be a member of the Federal Reserve System and is governed by its **fiscal** policies. State banks may belong to the Federal Reserve System but are not required to; state agencies regulate state banks. Savings and loans, which are similar to banks in many ways, are regulated at the federal level by the Federal Home Loan Banks System. However, regardless of the Federal Reserve's **jurisdiction** over any financial entity, the prime interest rate is often the **arbiter** of interest rates.

Interest rates have a profound effect on the national and worldwide economies and are affected by economic changes as well. Economists like Adam Smith and David Ricardo theorized that interest rates are the key in balancing investments with savings. Marxist economists believe that interest benefits only capitalists, leaving other classes exploited, since no service is rendered to those who pay interest. Other economic theorists have deemed interest as a sort of reward for those who save, rather than spend, their money, since bank accounts and other investment vehicles typically pay interest to account holders.

## State Usury Laws

ALABAMA: Legal rate of interest is 6 percent. Usury limit is 8 percent. Judgment rate is 12 percent.

ALASKA: Legal rate of interest is 10.5 percent. Usury limit is 5 percent above the Federal Reserve interest rate as of the date of the loan.

ARIZONA: Legal rate of interest is 10 percent.

ARKANSAS: Legal rate of interest is 6 percent. For consumers, the usury limit is 17 percent; for non-consumers, the usury limit is 5 percent above the Federal Reserve interest rate. Judgment rate is 10 percent per annum or the lawful agreed upon rate, whichever is higher.

CALIFORNIA: Legal rate of interest is 10 percent for consumers. Usury limit is 5 percent above the Federal Reserve Bank of San Francisco rate.

COLORADO: Legal rate of interest is 8 percent. Usury limit is 45 percent. Maximum rates to consumers is 12 percent per annum.

CONNECTICUT: Legal rate of interest is 8 percent. Usury rate is 12 percent. Interest allowed in civil suits is 10 percent.

DELAWARE: Legal rate of interest is 5 percent over the Federal Reserve Rate.

DISTRICT OF COLUMBIA: Legal rate of interest is 6 percent. General usury limit is 24 percent.

FLORIDA: Legal rate of interest is 12 percent. General usury limit is 18 percent. For loans exceeding $500,000, the maximum rate is 25 percent.

GEORGIA: Legal rate of interest is 7 percent. Usury limit for loans less than $3,000 is 16 percent; otherwise 5 percent. For loans below $250,000, interest rate must be specified in writing and in simple interest.

HAWAII: Legal rate of interest is 10 percent. Usury limit for consumers is 12 percent.

IDAHO: Legal rate of interest is 12 percent. Judgment interest is 5 percent above U. S. Treasury **Securities** rate.

ILLINOIS: Legal rate of interest is 5 percent. General usury limit is 9 percent. Judgment rate is 9 percent.

INDIANA: Legal rate of interest is 10 percent. Judgment rate is 10 percent.

IOWA: Legal rate of interest is 10 percent. Maximum rate for consumer transactions is 12 percent.

KANSAS: Legal rate of interest is 10 percent. Usury limit is 15 percent. Judgment rate is 4 percent above federal discount rate. For consumer transactions, maximum rate of interest for first $1,000 is 18 percent; otherwise 14.45 percent.

KENTUCKY: Legal rate of interest is 8 percent. Usury limit is 4 percent above Federal Reserve rate or 19 percent, whichever is less. No limit for loans exceeding $15,000. Judgment rate is 12 percent compounded annually or at a rate set by the court.

LOUISIANA: Legal rate of interest 1 percent above average prime rate, not exceeding 14 percent or less than 7 percent. Usury limit is 12 percent.

MAINE: Legal rate of interest is 6 percent. Judgment rate is 15 percent for judgments below $30,000; otherwise the 52 week average discount rate for T-Bills plus 4 percent.

MARYLAND: Legal rate of interest is 6 percent. Usury limit is 24 percent. Judgment rate is 10 percent.

MASSACHUSETTS: Legal rate of interest is 6 percent. Usury limit is 20 percent. Judgment rate is 12 percent of 18 percent if the court finds a frivolous defense.

MICHIGAN: Legal rate of interest is 5 percent. Usury limit is 7 percent. Judgment rate is 1 percent above the five year T-note rate.

MINNESOTA: Legal rate of interest is 6 percent. Usury limit is 8 percent. Judgment rate is secondary market yield for one year T-Bills.

MISSISSIPPI: Legal rate of interest is 9 percent. Usury limit is 10 percent or 5 percent above the federal reserve rate. No usury limit on commercial loans exceeding $5,000. Judgment rate is 9 percent or legally agreed upon rate.

MISSOURI: Legal rate of interest is 9 percent. Judgment rate is 9 percent.

MONTANA: Legal rate of interest is 10 percent. General usury limit is 6 percent above New York City bank's prime rate. Judgment rate is 10 percent.

NEBRASKA: Legal rate of interest is 6 percent. Usury limit is 16 percent. Judgment rate is 1 percent above bond yield equivalent to T-Bill auction price.

NEVADA: Legal rate of interest is 12 percent. No usury limit.

NEW HAMPSHIRE: Legal rate of interest is 10 percent. No general usury limit.

NEW JERSEY: Legal rate of interest is 6 percent. Usury limit generally is 30 percent for individuals and 50 percent for **corporations**.

NEW MEXICO: Legal rate of interest is 15 percent. Judgment rate is determined by the court.

NEW YORK: Legal rate of interest is 9 percent. General usury limit is 16 percent.

NORTH CAROLINA: Legal rate of interest is 8 percent. General usury limit is 8 percent.

NORTH DAKOTA: Legal rate of interest is 6 percent. General usury limit is 5.5 percent above six-month treasury bill interest rate. Judgment rate is 12 percent.

OKLAHOMA: Legal rate of interest is 6 percent. Consumer loans may not exceed 10 percent unless lender is licensed; usury limit on non-consumer loans is 45 percent. Judgment rate is 4 percent above T-Bill rate.

OREGON: Legal rate of interest is 9 percent. Judgment rate is 9 percent or agreed upon rate, whichever is higher. Usury limit is 12 percent for loans less than $50,000.

PENNSYLVANIA: Legal rate of interest is 6 percent. General usury limit is 6 percent for loans less than $50,000. Criminal usury limit is 25 percent. Judgment rate is 6 percent.

PUERTO RICO: Legal rate of interest is 6 percent.

RHODE ISLAND: Legal rate of interest is 12 percent. Judgment rate is 12 percent. Usury limit is 21 percent or 9 percent above the interest rate charged for T-Bills.

SOUTH CAROLINA: Legal rate of interest is 8.75 percent. Judgment rate is 14 percent.

SOUTH DAKOTA: Legal rate of interest is 15 percent. Judgment rate is 12 percent.

TENNESSEE: Legal rate of interest is 10 percent. Judgment rate is 10 percent. General usury limit is 24 percent, or 4 percent above average prime rate, whichever is less.

TEXAS: Legal rate of interest is 6 percent. Judgment rate is 18 percent or contracted rate, whichever is less.

UTAH: Legal rate of interest is 10 percent. Judgment rate is 12 percent or contracted rate.

VERMONT: Legal rate of interest is 12 percent. Judgment rate is 12 percent. General usury limit is 12 percent.

VIRGINIA: Legal rate of interest is 8 percent. Judgment rate is 8 percent or contracted rate. No usury limit for corporation or business loans.

WASHINGTON: Legal rate of interest is 12 percent. General usury limit is 12 percent or 4 percent above average T-Bill rate, whichever is greater. Judgment rate is 12 percent or contracted rate, whichever is higher.

WEST VIRGINIA: Legal rate of interest is 6 percent.

WISCONSIN: Legal rate of interest is 5 percent. Judgment rate is 12 percent.

WYOMING: Legal rate of interest is 10 percent. Judgment rate is 10 percent or contracted rate, whichever is less.

## Additional Resources

*Lectric Law Library* Lectric Law Library, 2002. Available at www.lectlaw.com.

*West's Encyclopedia of American Law.* West Group, 1998.

## Organizations

### American Bankers Association
1120 Connecticut Avenue, NW
Washington, DC 20036 USA
Phone: (800) 226-5377
URL: www.aba.com

### bankrate.com
11811 U.S. Highway 1
North Palm Beach, FL 33408 USA
Phone: (561) 630-2400
URL: www.bankrate.com

### United States Federal Reserve
20th Street and Constitution Avenue, NW
Washington, DC 20551 USA
Phone: (202) 452-3819
URL: www.federalreserve.gov

### American Bankers Association
1120 Connecticut Avenue NW
Washington, DC 20036 USA
Phone: (800) 226-5377
URL: www.aba.com

### bankrate.com
11811 U.S. Highway 1
North Palm Beach, FL 33408 USA
Phone: (561) 630-2400
URL: www.bankrate.com

# BUSINESS LAW

## ACCOUNTING REQUIREMENTS

*Sections within this essay:*

## Background

The field of accounting embodies a set of concepts and techniques that are used to measure and report financial information about a particular economic entity (or smaller unit of an entity). An economic entity may be an individual, a for-profit or non-profit business or organization, or a unit of government.

Accounting information is useful not only to owners of entities or their creditors, but also to business planners and forecasters, government administrators, financial analysts, and even individual employees of a company. Investors are hoping to learn as much as possible about a business enterprise before purchasing an interest; creditors are interested in the enterprise's ability to repay obligations. Business enterprise managers need financial information to make sound business decisions. Governmental units need accurate financial profiles in order to tax and regulate. Analysts use this information to form opinions and forecast local or national economic profiles. Individual employees often have bonuses or options tied to enterprise performance.

### Financial vs. Managerial Accounting

Accounting practices can be divided into two broad areas of function: financial accounting and managerial accounting. Both areas are dependent upon a strong information system that can reliably capture and summarize personal and business transactional data. At the heart of all accounting practices and procedures is a basic understanding of assets and liabilities (debts). However, with the advent of computers and sophisticated software capability, tedious bookkeeping tasks largely have been relegated to the annals of history, and replaced with software programs with dynamic, proactive decision-making capability in the field of financial and managerial accounting.

Financial accounting concerns itself with external reporting of information to parties outside of the subject business or entity. To ensure consistency and structure in reporting, financial accounting is managed by many rules or standards, such as those developed by the private sector group called the Financial Accounting Standards Board (FASB) (see below). Financial reports prepared under these standards have a general-purpose orientation with which all intended user groups are familiar, thus rendering the reports ostensibly neutral and free from bias. Most earnings reports are based on these established measurement and reporting rules, known as generally accepted accounting principles (GAAP)(see below).

In contrast, managerial accounting benefits internal management of an entity by providing information that will assist in planning, controlling, and decision-making. In contrast to financial accounting, internal management accounting dictates its own information needs and specifies the way that data is accumulated and presented. It need not follow any particular rules or guidelines, as its intended purpose is for internal decision-making.

## The Accounting Profession

Like law or medicine, the field of accounting involves specialized study and experience in a variety of disciplines. The simplest of accounting tasks is no more than detailed bookkeeping; on the other end of the spectrum is analysis of complex data and economic predictions at the global level.

Auditing services involve the examination of transactions and systems that constitute an organization's financial reports. The objective of an audit is to provide an independent review and report on the appropriateness and correctness of financial statements.

Tax services relate to providing help in the preparation and filing of tax returns to governmental entities, and the rendering of advice on the tax consequences of alternative filing or income-classifying actions.

Consulting services include such diverse activities as evaluating production methods or developing information systems capable of multi- data-processing tasks.

Accountants may work in areas of product costing and pricing, budgeting, or diversifying investments. They may focus on internal auditing of controls and procedures used by their employers, to safeguard company resources and develop reliable and accurate accounting information and systems. They may specialize as tax accountants, auditors, or financial managers. Their expertise is widely used in governmental agencies such as the Internal Revenue Service, General Accounting Office, or Securities and Exchange Commission.

### Accountants, PAs, and CPAs

Referring to oneself as an accountant *implies,* but does not require, a college education or license. It does require, at a minimum, a mastery of specialized expertise in the understanding and presentation of complex financial data. Many smaller business entities retain accountants/bookkeepers internally as employees, to handle the internal financial matters of the business.

Engaging in the practice of "public accounting" involves auditing, taxing, and consulting services to the general public. The term "PA" has become somewhat obsolete (or at least subsumed within the broader category of CPA) in that most, but not all, public accountants are licensed as Certified Public Accountants (CPAs) and hold themselves out as certified to engage in the practice of public accounting. CPAs have received a public accountant registration or license from an accountancy board within the jurisdiction in which they practice, after having met all requirements for such license.

### Qualification and Licensure

The federal government plays no role in establishing minimum criteria for the profession, and instead defers to states. Qualification to practice accounting in each state is controlled by that state's board of accountancy (see below).

Generally speaking, modern references to the term "accountant" imply a profession dictated by the fulfillment of minimum education requirements and experience. Certainly this is true for the CPA subcategory. Most colleges offer bachelors' degrees in accounting, which is almost universally a minimum requirement for employment in the field. While experience was often substituted for education in earlier job vacancies, the technical nature of liability exposure for accounting errors now dictates a more comprehensive minimum educational requirement that ensures uniformity in the learning of various accounting practices and procedures.

### CPA Requirements

The objective of most prospective accounting professionals is the attainment of a CPA license. All CPA candidates in all 50 state jurisdictions (and DC) must meet minimum educational criteria, successfully pass the Uniform Certified Public Accountant (CPA) Examination, and undergo background investigation to qualify for the CPA license/certificate permitting them to practice.

All states now require (New York is the last to implement, in 2009) a minimum 150-hour education requirements. This essentially equates to the completion of a standard 120-semester-hour bachelor's (baccalaureate) degree plus 30 hours of specialized course study in accounting, as found in typical master's degree programs. All states have a minimum number of core semester hours in accounting that must be completed as part of the educational requirement.

The Uniform CPA Examination was adopted by all 50 states and the DC as a way to protect the public interest in helping to ensure that only qualified individuals become licensed as CPAs. A revised examination was implemented in 2004, and new simulations on the exam were upgraded in 2006. Subjects covered in the examination include auditing and attestation; financial accounting and reporting; regulation; and business environments and concepts.

Each state accountancy board has additional criteria that must be met in order to obtain a license to practice within that state's jurisdiction. They include minimum age, residency, and experience requirements.

## Professional Ethics

The Code of Professional Conduct promulgated by the American Institute of Certified Public Accountants (AICPA)(the premier association of certified professionals) contains both (1) Principles and (2) Rules governing the profession. The accounting Principles provide the framework for the Rules, which, in turn, govern the performance of professional services by members. Compliance with the Code depends primarily on members' understanding and voluntary actions, as tempered by peer reviews and public opinion, and ultimately disciplinary proceedings when necessary.

Membership in the AICPA is limited to those practitioners who are practicing in firms enrolled in an AICPA-approved practice-monitoring program (peer review). Firms that are required to register with, and be inspected by the Public Company Accounting Oversight Board (PCAOB) must have a peer review program developed and administered by the AICPA's Center for Public Company Audit Firms (Center PRP).

State boards of accountancy also regulate the type of fees that accountants may charge for their services. The majority of states do permit CPAs to accept commission-based fees, with full disclosure to cli-

ents, except in situations where CPAs perform "attest services". Generally, a CPA is prohibited from charging or accepting contingency fees for preparation of tax returns or tax refund claims, unless the CPA could reasonably expect that the claim would undergo substantive review by the taxing authority.

## Accounting's Watchdog

In 1997, the American Institute of Certified Public Accountants (AICPA) and the National Association of State Boards of Accountancy (NASBA) jointly approved and published significant changes to their Uniform Accountancy Act (UAA) and Uniform Accountancy Act Rules. The UAA model bill and rules were designed to provide a uniform approach to regulation of the accounting profession, which had been largely self-regulated and self-policed, as are several other professions. The changes to the UAA reflected major recommendations by a joint committee of the two organizations that studied the issue of regulation for at least one year before issuing its report. The report focused on a number of contemporary issues facing the profession, including:

- globalization of business
- demographic shifts in the profession
- expansion of services
- dynamic information and electronic technology
- legal challenges to the current regulatory system

### Controlling Interstate Practice

One of the most significant changes in the UAA concerns the portability of a CPA license, and mobility across state lines for CPAs engaged in interstate practice, both personally and electronically. The approach taken was to establish, under Section 23 of the UAA, a "substantial equivalency" concept. The NASBA's National Qualification Appraisal Service (NQAS) first determined which states' CPA licensure requirements were substantially equivalent to that of the UAA (Section 23). CPAs who are licensed to practice in substantially equivalent states and who plan to practice in other states that have adopted Section 23 may lawfully practice in those states by simple notification of intent. A majority of states and jurisdictions were found to have CPA licensure requirements that were substantially equivalent to that of the UAA. As of 2005, five states were found to have non-substantially equivalent requirements: Colorado, Delaware, Florida, New Hampshire, and Vermont (as well as Puerto Rico and the Virgin Islands).

At the same time, even though the vast majority of states met the equivalency criteria, only a few were expressly serviced by NASBA to accept documentation for the reciprocal licensing and notification process. They were: Arkansas, California, Kansas, New Mexico, New York, North Dakota, Oregon, and Tennessee.

### Regulation of Accounting Firms

The UAA requires that all individuals referring to themselves as CPAs must hold a valid license obtained only after demonstrating a jurisdiction's licensing requirements [UAA Sections 3(c),5, and 14(c)]. This license must be periodically renewed by demonstrated compliance with continuing education (CPE) requirements (UAA Section 6). All licenses must comply with the accountancy law and regulations (UAA Section 10). Importantly, any individual holding a CPA license is subject to the state board of accountancy, regardless of how that individual earns his/her living or whether he or she uses the CPA title.

Under the UAA, CPAs who offer or render "attest services" (audits, reviews, and examinations of financial statements or information) for the public must do so in a CPA firm that is duly licensed by the state board of accountancy (UAA Section 7). These firms undergo peer review every three years to assure that those CPAs within the firm who supervise, sign, or authorize someone to sign "attest" engagements or reports on financial statements have met an appropriate competency requirement that is spelled out in professional standards.

However, CPAs are not required to offer general services through a CPA firm, and may offer other services through any type entity they choose; these entities are not licensed by the state board. Conversely, CPA firms using the term "CPAs" in association with the entity name are subject to regulation and discipline by the state board [UAA Section 7(a)].

### Generally Accepted Accounting Principles (GAAP)

Generally Accepted Accounting Principles (GAAP) refer to a combination of authoritative standards (set by policy boards) and a common set of accounting principles, standards and procedures that most companies use to compile their financial statements. The reason that GAAP are imposed on company reporting is to ensure that investors have an ascertained level of consistency when analyzing companies for investment purposes. Companies are expected to use GAAP when reporting their financial data via financial statements. The GAAP is not written into law, but the U.S. Securities and Exchange Commission (SEC) requires that it be adhered to in the financial reporting of all publicly-traded companies.

Three organizations developed, or influenced the development of, the GAAP in the United States: the SEC, the AICPA, and the FASB. A separate but similar set of rules and principles govern state and local government reporting, as determined by the Governmental Accounting Standards Board (GASB).

Accountants generally apply GAAP through the use of FASB pronouncements referred to as Financial Accounting Standards (FASs), which are periodically published in industry bulletins. There are more than 100 FASs that have been issued over the years. They are supplemented by formal opinions and generally accepted assumptions in a particular sub-segment of the industry. For example, there exists a general assumption that financial statements must be based on the premise that a company will continue in existence unless there is substantial evidence to the contrary. Accountants are guided by these formal standards, rules, and principles, but must also incorporate their own professional judgment into their practices.

In 2005, the U.S. Supreme Court overturned the conviction of accounting firm Arthur Andersen, previously indicted and convicted of obstructing justice for shredding documents of its work done for Enron, the energy services giant under investigation for financial wrongdoing. *U.S. v. Arthur Andersen,* No. 04-0368 (2005). The government had cited various provisions of the GAAP as evidence of wrongdoing. (However, the conviction was overturned on a technicality, involving the wording of a principal jury instruction that, according to the Supreme Court, was vague and failed to convey the required consciousness of wrongdoing in order to convict.)

### Sarbanes-Oxley Act

Following the Enron and WorldCom scandals, President George W. Bush signed into law the Sarbanes-Oxley Act of 2002 (P.L. 107-104, 116 Stat 745), which applies to publicly-traded companies and their audit firms (or CPAs actively working as auditors of, or for, publicly traded companies). There are some basic implications for accountants, including:

- The Establishment of a Public Company Accounting Oversight Board (PCAOB): Appointed and overseen by the SEC, its function is to oversee and investigate the audits and auditors of public companies, and it has sanctioning power over both firms and individuals for violations of laws, regulations, and rules.

- The Creation of Criminal Penalties and Protections for Whistleblowers: Tough penalties are now available for those who destroy records, commit securities fraud, or fail to report fraud. The SEC established new rules covering the retention of "audit or review work papers." Other standards compel auditors to keep documentation for seven years. It is now a felony punishable by up to 20 years' imprisonment for destruction of documents in a federal or bankruptcy investigation.

- Other checks and balances prohibit firms from providing audit services to any public company if any of that company's top officials was employed by the firm and worked on the company's audit during the previous year. Further, auditors now report to and are overseen by a company's audit committee and not by its management.

### Peer Review

As previously mentioned, membership in the AICPA is limited to those practitioners who are practicing in firms enrolled in an AICPA-approved practice-monitoring program (peer review). Firms that are required to register with, and be inspected by the PCAOB (see above) must have a peer review program developed and administered by the AICPA's Center for Public Company Audit Firms (Center PRP).

Accounting firms that are members of the Center for Public Company Audit Firms that are not required to be registered with and inspected by the PCAOB may enroll in either the Center PRP or the AICPA PRP. Those firms that are not members of the Center for Public Company Audit Firms but want or are required to be enrolled in the Center PRP must submit an enrollment form and the Center Peer Review Committee will consider the request. All other firms have a peer review under the AICPA PRP. The AICPA's PRP was developed by and is overseen by the AICPA and administered by 41 state CPA societies across the country.

## Who's Watching the Watchdog?

Ever since the PCAOB was created in 2002, business executives and free-market groups have argued that, as an accounting industry regulator, the Board has wielded too much unchecked power. In early 2006, the Free Enterprise Fund joined a Nevada accounting firm in filing suit in U.S. district court in Washington, challenging the constitutionality of the PCAOB. The suit alleged that the process for selecting PCAOB members violated the U.S. Constitution's separation of powers. Under Sarbanes-Oxley (which created the PCAOB), the SEC appoints them, rather than the president (confirmed by the Senate). Although the PCAOB considers its members lower-level officials (not subject to Constitutional provisions), it sets its own budget and pays its members upward of $450,000 a year, without Congressional oversight. Notwithstanding, when Sarbanes-Oxley was first being drafted, these arguments had been previously considered by constitutional scholars in Congress and several universities, and the provisions passed muster under these reviews.

Also in early 2006, the tax return-preparation giant, H&R Block Inc. revealed that it had miscalculated and understated its own state income tax liability for 2004 and 2005, amounting to approximately $32 million in arrears. The company had just settled four state class-action lawsuits related to "refund anticipation loans," where customers were advanced their tax refunds in return for a percentage of the refund being paid to H&R Block. However, the Center for Responsible Lending had alleged that the annual interest rates on these types of loans often turned out to be as high as 40 to 700 percent annualized. The settlement affected more than eight million customers.

In 2005, the General Accounting Office (GAO) performed its first audit of the SEC and released a mixed report. It found that the Commission had inadequate controls over its financial statement preparation process. This included a lack of sufficiently documented internal policies and procedures, raising questions of whether the balances presented in SEC's own financial statements were supported by SEC's underlying accounting records.

## Finding a Good Accountant

Word-of-mouth recommendations remain the most preferred method to find high-quality accountants. Checking with other business owners in the area, as well as industry trade associations, often results in recommendations of good accountants familiar with issues specific to a particular business or industry.

Users of accounting services should always check with the local Better Business Bureau and local or state professional accountancy boards to ensure that accountants' credentials are good and licenses are current.

It is now possible for public accounting services to be purchased and provided over the Internet. Despite its ostensible convenience, consumers are reminded that since there is no face-to-face contact, unqualified persons may masquerade as fully-licensed accountants. Internet accountants may be physically located anywhere in the world. Therefore, any problems encountered with the purchased services may not be resolved if the provider of the service is not licensed in the consumer's state or jurisdiction. It is recommended that investigative e-mails and telephone conversations precede any commitment for services.

## Accounting Discipline and Malpractice

Substantiated complaints and grievances against accountants are best addressed by state accountancy boards, most of which provide a forum and specific procedures for resolution. However, state boards are limited, for the most part, to suspensions or revocations of licenses to practice, and cannot award money damages for harm or loss.

Clients should also be sure, before any work is done, that a CPA provides an engagement letter outlining the work that will be performed, who will specifically perform the work, and what it will cost. In a majority of complaints received by accountancy boards that allege poor or incorrect services, no engagement letter had been provided that clearly described the agreement between client and CPA. In such cases, both CPA and client can only provide verbal recollections of the services, and discipline for substandard work is limited.

If substandard work performed by an accountant has caused financial loss or harm to a client, a civil lawsuit for professional malpractice is the most appropriate remedy (in addition to filing a complaint with the state board of accountancy). Some jurisdictions offer alternative dispute resolution (arbitration, mediation), which is particularly helpful if privacy is a consideration.

Unlike complaints filed with a state board, lawsuits carry a heavy burden of proof before a complaining party may recover monetary damages for substandard accounting work. As in other professional malpractice cases, expert witnesses from the same accounting discipline must testify that the defendant accountant (or accounting firm) breached its duty of care (such as those considered as GAAP) by providing services that violated GAAP or other established practices and procedures. However, and more importantly, the complaining party has the burden of showing that, but for the substandard work, the complaining party would not have suffered the financial loss, or would have gained more financial benefit. By the time that costs and expenses of expert witnesses and litigation are taken into account, accountant malpractice suits should be considered a last resort.

Accountant malpractice lawsuits sometimes involve alleged violations of state and federal statutes relating to the sale of securities. If the attested financial statements contain errors and lead to negative market impact, investors may try to recoup damages by asserting securities claims against the accountants who prepared the statements. The statutes most commonly cited to bring such claims are the Securities Act of 1933, the Securities Act of 1934, and the Racketeer Influenced and Corrupt Organizations Act (RICO).

## State Boards of Accountancy

ALABAMA STATE BOARD OF PUBLIC ACCOUNTANCY: Suite 226, 770 Washington Ave., P.O. Box 300375, Montgomery, AL 36130 (334) 242-5700; fax (334) 242-2711

ALASKA STATE BOARD OF PUBLIC ACCOUNTANCY: Division of Occupational Licensing, Box 110806, Juneau, AK 99811-0806 (907) 465-3811; fax (907) 465-2974

ARIZONA STATE BOARD OF ACCOUNTANCY: 100 N. 15th Ave., Suite 165, Phoenix, AZ 85007 (602) 364-0804; fax (602) 364-0903

ARKANSAS STATE BOARD OF ACCOUNTANCY: 101 East Capitol, Suite 450, Little Rock, AR 72201 (501) 682-1520; fax (501) 682-5538

CALIFORNIA BOARD OF ACCOUNTANCY: 2000 Evergreen Street, Suite. 250, Sacramento, CA 95815 (916) 263-3680; fax (916) 263-3675

COLORADO STATE BOARD OF ACCOUNTANCY: 1560 Broadway, Suite 1340, Denver, CO 80202 (303) 894-7800; fax (303) 894-7692

CONNECTICUT STATE BOARD OF ACCOUNTAN-CY: 30 Trinity St., Hartford, CT 06106 (860) 509-6179; fax (860) 509-6247

DELAWARE STATE BOARD OF ACCOUNTANCY: Cannon Bldg., Suite. 203, 861 Silver Lake Blvd, Dover, DE 19904 (302) 744-4511; fax (302) 739-2711

DISTRICT OF COLUMBIA BOARD OF ACCOUN-TANCY: Occupational & Professional Licensing, Room 7200, 941 North Capitol St., NE, Washington, D.C. 20002 (202) 442-4461; fax (202) 442-4528

FLORIDA BOARD OF ACCOUNTANCY: 240 NW 76 Drive., Ste A, Gainesville, FL 32607 850-487-1395; fax: 352-333-2508

GEORGIA STATE BOARD OF ACCOUNTANCY: 237 Coliseum Dr., Macon, GA 31217-3858 (478) 207-1300; fax (478) 207-1363

HAWAII BOARD OF ACCOUNTANCY: P.O. Box 3469, Honolulu, HI 96801 (808) 586-3000; fax (808) 586-2689

IDAHO STATE BOARD OF ACCOUNTANCY: P.O. Box 83720, Boise, ID 83720 (208) 334-2490; fax (208) 334-2615

ILLINOIS BOARD OF EXAMINERS: 100 Trade Centre Drive, Suite 403, Champaign, IL 61820 (217) 531-0950; fax (217) 531-0960

INDIANA STATE BOARD OF PUBLIC ACCOUN-TANCY: Professional Licensing Agency, 302 West Washington St., Room W 072, Indianapolis, IN 46204 (317) 234-3040; fax (317) 232-2312

IOWA ACCOUNTANCY EXAMINING BOARD: 1920 SE Hulsizer Road, Ankeny, IA 50021-3941 515-281-5910, FAX: 515-281-7411

KANSAS BOARD OF ACCOUNTANCY: 900 S.W. Jackson St., Suite 556, Topeka, KS 66612-1239 (785) 296-2162; fax (785) 291-3501

KENTUCKY STATE BOARD OF ACCOUNTANCY: 332 West Broadway, Suite 310, Louisville, KY 40202 (502) 595-3037; fax (502) 595-4281

STATE BOARD OF CPAs OF LOUISIANA: 601 Poydras Street, Suite 1770, New Orleans, LA 70130 (504) 566-1244; fax (504) 566-1252

MAINE BOARD OF ACCOUNTANCY: #35 State House Station, Augusta, ME 04333-0035 (207) 624-8603; fax (207) 624-8637

MARYLAND STATE BOARD OF PUBLIC ACCOUN-TANCY: 500 N. Calvert Street, Room 308, Baltimore, MD 21202 (410) 230-6258; fax (410) 333-6314

MASSACHUSETTS BOARD OF PUBLIC ACCOUN-TANCY: 239 Causeway Street, Boston, Massachusetts 02114 (617) 727-1806 Fax: (617) 727-2197

MICHIGAN BOARD OF ACCOUNTANCY: P.O. Box 30018, Lansing, MI 48909 (517) 241-9249; fax (517) 241-9280

MINNESOTA STATE BOARD OF ACCOUNTANCY: 85 E. 7th Place., Suite 125, St. Paul, MN 55101 (651) 296-7937; fax (651) 282-2644

MISSISSIPPI STATE BOARD OF PUBLIC ACCOUN-TANCY: 5 Old River Place, Suite 104, Jackson, MS 39202 (601) 354-7320; fax (601) 354-7290

MISSOURI STATE BOARD OF ACCOUNTANCY: P.O. Box 1335, Jefferson City, MO 65102 (573) 526-1555; fax (573) 751-0735

MONTANA STATE BOARD OF PUBLIC ACCOUN-TANCY: P.O. Box 200513, Helena, MT 59620 (406) 841-2300; fax (406) 841-2309

NEBRASKA STATE BOARD OF PUBLIC ACCOUN-TANCY: P.O. Box 94725, Lincoln, NE 68509 (402) 471-3595; fax (402) 471-4484

NEVADA STATE BOARD OF ACCOUNTANCY: 1325 Airmotive Way, Suite #220, Reno, NV 89502 (775) 786-0231; fax (775) 786-0234

NEW HAMPSHIRE BOARD OF ACCOUNTANCY: 78 Regional Dr., Building 2, Concord, NH 03301 (603) 271-3286; fax (603) 271-8702

NEW JERSEY STATE BOARD OF ACCOUNTANCY: P.O. Box 45000, Newark, NJ 07101 (973) 504-6380; fax (973) 648-2855

NEW MEXICO STATE BOARD OF PUBLIC AC-COUNTANCY: 5200 Oakland NE, Suite D, Albuquerque, NM 87113 (505) 222-9850; Fax (505)222-9855

NEW YORK STATE BOARD FOR PUBLIC AC-COUNTANCY: 89 Washington Ave., Albany, NY 12234 (518) 474-3817 ext. 270; fax (518) 402-5354

NORTH CAROLINA STATE BOARD OF CPA EX-AMINERS: P.O. Box 12827, Raleigh, NC 27605-2827 (919) 733-4222; fax (919) 733-4209

NORTH DAKOTA BOARD OF ACCOUNTANCY: 2701 S. Columbia Rd., Grand Forks, ND 58201 (800) 532-5904; fax (701) 775-7430

ACCOUNTANCY BOARD OF OHIO: 77 S. High St., 18th Floor, Columbus, OH 43215-6128 (614) 466-4135; fax (614) 466-2628

OKLAHOMA STATE BOARD OF PUBLIC ACCOUNTANCY: 4545 N Lincoln Blvd., Suite 165, Oklahoma City, OK 73105 (405) 521-2397; fax (405) 521-3118

OREGON STATE BOARD OF ACCOUNTANCY: 3218 Pringle Rd. S.E., Suite #110, Salem, OR 97302-6307 (503) 378-4181; fax (503) 378-3575

PENNSYLVANIA BOARD OF ACCOUNTANCY: P.O. Box 2649, Harrisburg, PA 17105-2649 (717) 783-1404; Fax (717) 705-5540

RHODE ISLAND BOARD OF ACCOUNTANCY: 233 Richmond St., Providence, RI 02903 (401) 222-2246; fax (401) 222-6098

SOUTH CAROLINA BOARD OF ACCOUNTANCY: Street Address: 110 Centerview Dr., Columbia, SC Mailing Address: PO Box 11329, Columbia, S.C. 29211 803-896-4770; Fax: 803-896-4554

SOUTH DAKOTA BOARD OF ACCOUNTANCY: 301 E. 14th St., Suite 200, Sioux Falls, SD 57104-5022 (605) 367-5770; fax (605) 367-5773

TENNESSEE STATE BOARD OF ACCOUNTANCY: 500 James Robertson Parkway, 2nd Floor, Nashville, TN 37243-1141 (615) 741-2550; fax (615) 532-8800

TEXAS STATE BOARD OF PUBLIC ACCOUNTANCY: 333 Guadalupe Tower III, Suite 900, Austin, TX 78701-3900 (512) 305-7851; fax (512) 305-7875

UTAH BOARD OF ACCOUNTANCY: 160 East 300 South, Salt Lake City, UT 84111-2316 (801) 530-6628; fax (801) 530-65111

VERMONT BOARD OF ACCOUNTANCY: 26 Terrace St., Montpelier, VT 05609-110 (802) 828-2837; fax (802) 828-2465

VIRGINIA BOARD FOR ACCOUNTANCY: 3600 W. Broad St., Suite 378, Richmond, VA 23230 (804) 367-8505; fax (804) 367-2174

WASHINGTON STATE BOARD OF ACCOUNTANCY: P.O. Box 9131, Olympia, WA 98507-9131 (360) 753-2586; fax (360) 664-9190

WEST VIRGINIA BOARD OF ACCOUNTANCY: 122 Capitol Street, Suite 100, Charleston, WV 25301 (304) 558-3557; fax (304) 558-1325

WISCONSIN ACCOUNTING EXAMINING BOARD: 1400 East Washington Ave., P.O. Box 8935, Madison, WI 53708-8935 (608) 266-5511; fax (608) 267-3816

WYOMING BOARD OF CPAs: 2020 Carey, Cheyenne, WY 82002 (307) 777-7551; fax (307) 777-3796

## Additional Resources

"Background on AICPA/NASBA Uniform Accountancy Act-Third Editon (UAA)." American Institute of Certified Public Accountants, 2005. Available at "http://www.aicpa.org/states/uaa/briefs/newuaa.htm"

Barr, Alistair. "H&R; Block Gets Its Own Taxes Wrong." *AOL News,* 23 February 2006. Available at "http://aolsvc.news.aol.com/business/article.adp?id-20060223195309900248"

Borrus, Amy. "Who Watches Accounting's Watchdog?" *Business Week,* 8 February 2006. Available at cl "http://www.businessweek.com/investor/content/feb2006/pi20060208_072238.htm"

Dharan, Bala G., et al.(contributors). *Enron: Corporate Fiascos and Their Implications.* Foundation Press, 2004.

Walther, Larry, PhD., CPA, CMA. "Principles of Accounting." Online publication available at "http://www.principlesofaccounting.com"

## Organizations

### American Institute of Certified Public Accountants
1211 Avenue of the Americas
New York, NY 10036-8775 USA
Phone: (212) 596-6200
Fax: (212) 596-6213

### National Association of State Boards of Accountancy
150 Fourth Avenue North, Suite 700
Nashville, TN 37219-2417 USA
Phone: (615) 880-4200
Fax: (615) 880-4292

# BUSINESS LAW

## CONFLICTS OF INTEREST

*Sections within this essay:*

- Background

- Handling Conflicts of Interest

- Law
    - Lawyers
    - Judges

- Accounting

- Stock Analysis

- Business

- Medical and Scientific Research

- Federal Employment

- State Law Applying to Elected Officials

- Additional Resources

## Background

Conflicts of interest arise in several different environments. A conflict may arise when the personal interests of someone in a position of trust clashes with the person's professional interests. A conflict may also arise when a person has different professional responsibilities and those responsibilities collide. A person who has these types of competing interests may have difficulty in fulfilling professional obligations.

Examples of professionals that may face conflicts of interest are numerous, although such conflicts generally arise in some professions more than others. For instance, judge may have personal interests

that could be affected by the outcome of a case. Likewise, an attorney or law firm may have interests that conflict with the interests of a client. Similar problems may arise in the fields of accounting, stock analysis, education, and business, as well as federal employment. Elected officials also face conflicts of interest in fulfilling their duties and are subject to rules of ethics that regulate how the officials must handle these conflicts.

## Handling Conflicts of Interest

A person who faces a conflict of interest may not be able to avoid the conflict. In such an instance, the person may be required to take certain steps by law or may need to follow certain practices in order to avoid any appearance of impropriety. The following are some of the means by which conflicts of interest may be handled, either by law or as good professional practice:

- Duty of Loyalty: In partnership law, for example, a partner is bound by a duty of loyalty, which forbids the partner from personally engaging in a business transaction to the detriment of the partnership.

- Fairness: Some laws, such as those governing conflicts of interest within corporations, require that transactions involving such conflicts are fair.

- Full Disclosure: Many professionals, such as lawyers and government officials, are required by law to give full, written disclosure of any conflicts of interest.

- Recusal: Decision-makers, such as judges or members of government agencies, may choose to recuse themselves in situations where the subject of a decision involves a conflict of interest.

- Third-Party Evaluations: In some situations, such as where majority shareholders in a corporation decide to buy out minority shareholders, a neutral third party may be used to determine a fair market price for the minority shares.

## Field of Law

### Lawyers

A lawyer's relationship with a client is based largely on trust and confidence, such that the lawyer can provide the best possible representation of the client. Because of the nature of this relationship, a lawyer may frequently encounter a conflict of interest with the client. One instance may occur when one of the lawyer's clients has an interest that clashes with an interest of another client.

The American Bar Association's (ABA) Model Rules of Professional Conduct, which have been adopted by the majority of states, forbid or restrict lawyers from representing a client if a conflict exists. Under the Model Rules, a "concurrent conflict of interest" exists when: (1) the lawyer's representation of one client will be directly adverse to another client; or (2) the lawyer's representation of one or more clients runs a significant risk of being materially limited by the attorney's representation of another client, a former client, or a third person.

The Model Rules allow a lawyer to represent a client notwithstanding a conflict of interest when each of the following four criteria are met: the lawyer reasonably believes that he or she can still provide competent and diligent representation in spite of the conflict; the lawyer's representation of the client is not prohibited by law; the representation does not involve an instance where a claim by one of the lawyer's clients is brought against another of the lawyer's clients in the same litigation or other proceeding before a tribunal; and each affected client provides consent in writing after being informed of the conflict.

Under the Model Rules, a lawyer may neither engage in a business practice with a client nor acquire an ownership, possessory, security, or other pecuniary interest that is adverse to the client. The exception to this rule applies when the terms of the transaction are reasonable and fair to the client and are fully disclosed in writing; the client is advised in writing that he or she should seek the advice of independent legal counsel regarding the transaction; and "the client gives informed consent, in a writing signed by the client, to the essential terms of the transaction and the lawyer's role in the transaction, including whether the lawyer is representing the client in the transaction."

Lawyers are also limited from engaging in specified conduct that would involve conflicts of interest. These types of conduct include the following:

- Using information relating to the representation of a client to the disadvantage of the client unless the client gives informed consent.

- Soliciting any substantial gift from a client, including a testamentary gift, unless the client is related to the lawyer.

- Negotiating an agreement that gives the lawyer literary or media right to a portrayal or accounted based on information relating to the representation.

- Providing financial assistance to a client in connection with pending or contemplated litigation, except that a lawyer may advance court costs on behalf of a client or pay the court costs and expenses of an indigent client.

- Accepting compensation for representing a client from someone other than the client, unless the client gives informed consent, the payment of compensation does not interfere with the lawyer's independence of professional judgment or with the lawyer-client relationship, and the information pertaining to the client remains confidential.

- Acquiring a proprietary interest in a client's cause of action or the subject matter of a client's case, except in certain situations.

- Having sexual relations with a client unless a consensual sexual relationship existed between the lawyer and client when the lawyer-client relationship began.

The Model Rules also restrict lawyers from representing a client where a conflict of interest may exist between the prospective client and another member of the firm. The Model Rules likewise limit lawyers from representing someone who has interests that are adverse to one of the lawyer's former clients.

## Judges

Perhaps even more so than in the case of attorneys, conflicts of interest can prevent judges from carrying out their responsibilities. The Model Code of Judicial Conduct, which was drafted by the ABA and has been adopted by the majority of states, strictly forbids a judge from taking part in a case where the judge's interest may conflict with his or her professional responsibilities. According to Canon 2 of the Model Code, "[a] judge shall avoid impropriety and the appearance of impropriety in all of the judge's activities." In a more specific provision, the Model Code states, "A judge shall not allow family, social, political or other relationships to influence the judge's judicial conduct or judgment. A judge shall not lend the prestige of judicial office to advance the private interests of the judge or others; nor shall a judge convey or permit others to convey the impression that they are in a special position to influence the judge. A judge shall not testify voluntarily as a character witness."

A judge who faces a conflict of interest in a case is expected to recuse himself or herself from the case. A judge who presides over a case where the judge has a conflict of interest could face impeachment from the bench.

## Accounting

The accounting industry faced a great deal of criticism in 2001 and 2002 following a scandal involving Enron Corporation and its auditors. During the fall of 2001, Enron was the seventh-largest company in the United States. Over the period of a few months, however, the company collapsed due to accounting fraud and other instances of wrongdoing. In the aftermath of the scandal, Arthur Andersen, an accounting firm hired by Enron as an outside auditor, shredded hundreds of documents related to Enron. The firm was later convicted of obstruction of justice.

Prior to these scandals, accountants and accounting firms often engaged in consulting work, earning considerable fees in the process. Critics charged that accountants were reluctant to challenge clients about questionable financial activities because the accountants earned such large fees from these clients. The Enron scandal and other events that followed led to the enactment of the Sarbanes-Oxley Act of 2002, Pub. L. No. 107-204, 116 Stat. 745, which addressed these concerns.

The Sarbanes-Oxley Act restricts accounting firms from engaging in consulting work that could result

in a conflict of interest. The statute also forbids a public accounting firm from performing an audit on a company where the accounting firm previously employed an officer of that company and the officer participated in an audit of the same company.

## Stock Analysis

In addition to conflicts of interest in the accounting industry, critics during the early 2000s became concerned about conflicts that occurred with respect to stock analysts in securities firms. These concerns arose because analysts made recommendations regarding the potential value of securities in public communications. A conflict could occur in several situations, such as where a stock analyst firm had a financial relationship with a company that issued securities.

In 2002, the U.S. Securities and Exchange Commission approved rule changes that addressed conflicts of interest that may arise with respect to stock analysts. These rules include provisions relating to the following:

- Analysts are prohibited from offering or threatening to withhold a favorable rating or price target with respect to stock in order to induce companies to employ the analyst for investment banking purposes.

- Research analysts may not be supervised by a company's investment banking department. Rules also restrict communications between investment banking personnel and research analysts.

- Securities firms may not tie in an analyst's compensation with a specific investment banking transaction.

- A securities firm must disclose in a research report that it received compensation for investment banking services from a company that is the subject of the report.

- A stock analyst may not personally invest in a company's securities prior to the company's initial public offering if the company is in the same business sector that the analyst covers.

- Stock analysts are required to disclose whether they own shares in companies that they recommend.

## Business

Owners and managers of businesses may encounter conflicts during the course of the business. Laws governing these businesses handle conflicts by several different means. For instance, partners in a partnership are bound by a duty of loyalty that prevents the partner from competing in a business to the detriment of the partnership.

A conflicts of interest is often the result of a transaction between a business, such as a corporation, and a manager of the business. The manager may take advantage of this relationship and complete a transaction that benefits himself or herself and not the corporation. In the majority of U.S. jurisdictions, the resolution of a conflict of interest for a controlling shareholder, director, or officer of a corporation focuses on the fairness of the transaction. The person who is involved in the transaction must prove that the transaction is the result of fair dealing and demonstrates a fair price.

## Medical and Scientific Research

Because the publication of research is so important in the medical and scientific communities, conflicts of interest may interfere with the dissemination of accurate information. For example, a pharmaceutical company that is producing a drug may fund research that is the subject of an article that is published in a reputable journal. Due to the possibility that the company's funding causes a conflict of interest with the person or entity conducting the research, most medical journals require researchers to disclose the sources of funding for their research.

## Federal Employment

Under a federal criminal statute at 18 U.S.C. § 208, federal employees are forbidden from participating "personally and substantially in his official, governmental capacity in a matter" where the employee "knew that he, his spouse, or another statutorily-listed person had a financial interest" in a particular matter. The Office of Government Ethics (OGE) has promulgated regulations that have clarified to some extent the terms of this statute.

In order to participate "personally and substantially" in an action, a federal employee must have done more than participated in a ministerial or procedural role. Prosecutors may prove that the defendant had requisite knowledge by proving that the de-

fendant knew about the forbidden financial interest, even if the employee did not intend to violate the statute. Courts and the OGE have further established that the statute applies only where there is a "real possibility" of gain or loss as a result of the matter.

## State Law Applying to Elected Officials

Members of state legislatures are subject to a number of rules pertaining to conflicts of interest, most of which relate to disclosure of specified types of information. According to the National Conference of State Legislatures, every state except for Idaho, Michigan, and Vermont requires members of the legislative body to file personal financial disclosures. The majority of states also require disclosure of other types of information, such as the names of clients or the names of certain debtors or creditors. The following is a summary of some of these requirements.

ALABAMA: State law does not require the disclosure of the names of individual clients. Legislators must reveal any indebtedness to banks, savings and loan associations, insurance companies, mortgage firms, stockbrokers, bond firms, or other specified organizations.

ALASKA: State law requires disclosure of names of clients who have an interest in legislation or in other specified instances. Legislators must reveal the names and addresses of the sources of loans or loan guarantees. Certain gifts must also be disclosed.

ARIZONA: State law does not require the disclosure of the names of individual clients. Legislators must reveal the names and addresses of certain debtors and creditors. The names of the sources of gifts of more than $500 must also be disclosed.

ARKANSAS: State law does not require the disclosure of the names of individual clients. Legislators must reveal the names and addresses of certain debtors and creditors. The sources and amount of gifts of more than $100 must be disclosed.

CALIFORNIA: State law requires disclosure of the names of certain clients. Legislators must reveal the names and addresses of certain creditors. The name of the source of any gift of more than $50 must be disclosed.

COLORADO: State law does not require the disclosure of the names of individual clients. Legislators must reveal the names and addresses of certain creditors. The name of the source of certain gifts of more than $25 must be disclosed.

CONNECTICUT: State law does not require the disclosure of the names of individual clients. Legislators must reveal the names and addresses of certain creditors.

DELAWARE: State law does not require the disclosure of the names of individual clients. Legislators must reveal the names and addresses of certain creditors. The name of the source of any gift of more than $250 must be disclosed.

FLORIDA: State law requires disclosure of the names of certain clients. Legislators must reveal every liability that is greater than the legislator's net worth. The name of the source of any gift of more than $100 must be disclosed.

GEORGIA: State law does not require the disclosure of the names of individual clients. The sources and actual amounts of honoraria must be disclosed.

HAWAII: State law requires disclosure of the names of certain clients. Legislators must reveal the names and addresses of certain creditors. The name of the source of certain gifts of more than $200 must be disclosed.

IDAHO: State law does not require a personal financial disclosure.

ILLINOIS: State law does not require the disclosure of the names of individual clients. The name of the source of any gift of more than $500 must be disclosed.

INDIANA: State law requires disclosure of the names of clients who the legislator has represented before a state agency for a fee. The name of the source of certain gifts of more than $100 must be disclosed.

IOWA: State law does not require the disclosure of the names of individual clients.

KANSAS: State law requires disclosure of the names of certain clients. The name of the source of any gift of more than $500 must be disclosed.

KENTUCKY: State law does not require the disclosure of the names of individual clients. Legislators must reveal the names and addresses of certain creditors. The name of the source of any gift of more than $200 must be disclosed.

LOUISIANA: State law does not require the disclosure of the names of individual clients.

MAINE: State law requires disclosure of the names of certain clients. Legislators must reveal the source of any unsecured loan of $3000 or more. The name of the source of any gift or honoraria must be disclosed.

MARYLAND: State law does not require the disclosure of the names of individual clients. Legislators must reveal the names and addresses of certain creditors. The name of the source of certain gifts of more than $100 must be disclosed.

MASSACHUSETTS: State law does not require the disclosure of the names of individual clients. Legislators must reveal the names and addresses of certain creditors. The name of the source of certain gifts of more than $100 must be disclosed.

MICHIGAN: State law does not require a personal financial disclosure.

MINNESOTA: State law does not require the disclosure of the names of individual clients. Officials may not accept gifts from lobbyists.

MISSISSIPPI: State law does not require the disclosure of the names of individual clients.

MISSOURI: State law does not require the disclosure of the names of individual clients. The name of the source of any gift of more than $200 must be disclosed.

MONTANA: State law does not require the disclosure of the names of individual clients.

NEBRASKA: State law does not require the disclosure of the names of individual clients. Legislators must reveal the names and addresses of certain creditors. The name of the source of any gift of more than $100 must be disclosed.

NEVADA: State law does not require the disclosure of the names of individual clients. Legislators must reveal the names and addresses of certain creditors. The name of the source of any gift of more than $200 must be disclosed.

NEW HAMPSHIRE: State law does not require the disclosure of the names of individual clients. The name of the source of any gift or honorarium of more than $50 must be disclosed.

NEW JERSEY: State law does not require the disclosure of the names of individual clients. The sources of any fees, honoraria, travel expenses, or other prepaid expenses must be disclosed.

NEW MEXICO: State law does not require the disclosure of the names of individual clients.

NEW YORK: State law does not require the disclosure of the names of individual clients. The name of the source of any gift of more than $1000 must be disclosed.

NORTH CAROLINA: State law does not require the disclosure of the names of individual clients. Legislators must reveal the names and addresses of certain creditors.

NORTH DAKOTA: State law does not require the disclosure of the names of individual clients.

OHIO: State law requires disclosure of the names of certain clients. Legislators must reveal the names and addresses of certain creditors. The name of the source of any gift of more than $75 must be disclosed.

OKLAHOMA: State law requires disclosure of the names of clients who the legislator has represented before a state agency for a fee. The name of the source of any gift of more than $200 must be disclosed.

OREGON: State law requires disclosure of the names of certain clients. Legislators must reveal the names and addresses of certain creditors. The name of the source of any gift of more than $100 must be disclosed.

PENNSYLVANIA: State law requires disclosure of the names of certain clients. Legislators must reveal the names and addresses of certain creditors. The name of the source of any gift of more than $250 must be disclosed, as well as the source of any travel reimbursement of more than $650 for a single trip.

RHODE ISLAND: State law does not require the disclosure of the names of individual clients. Legislators must reveal the names and addresses of certain creditors. The name of the source of any gift of more than $100 must be disclosed.

SOUTH CAROLINA: State law requires disclosure of the names of certain clients. Legislators must reveal the names and addresses of certain creditors. The name of the source of certain gifts of more than $200 per year must be disclosed.

SOUTH DAKOTA: State law does not require the disclosure of the names of individual clients.

TENNESSEE: State law does not require the disclosure of the names of individual clients. The name of the source of certain gifts must be disclosed.

TEXAS: State law requires, in some instances, disclosure of the names of legislator's clients who are also lobbyists. Legislators must reveal the names and addresses of certain creditors. The name of the source of any gift of more than $250 must be disclosed.

UTAH: State law does not require the disclosure of the names of individual clients.

VERMONT: State law does not require a personal financial disclosure.

VIRGINIA: State law requires disclosure of the names of certain clients, including lobbyists. The name of the source of certain gifts and travel expenses must be disclosed.

WASHINGTON: State law does not require the disclosure of the names of individual clients. Legislators must reveal the names and addresses of certain creditors. The name of the source of any gift of more than $50 must be disclosed.

WEST VIRGINIA: State law does not require the disclosure of the names of individual clients. Legislators must reveal the names and addresses of certain creditors. The name of the source of any gift of more than $100 must be disclosed.

WISCONSIN: State law requires disclosure of the names of certain clients. Legislators must reveal the names and addresses of certain creditors. The name of the source of any gift of more than $50 must be disclosed.

WYOMING: State law does not require the disclosure of the names of individual clients.

## Additional Resources

*Alleged Conflicts of Interest Because of the "Appearance of Impropriety."* Rotunda, Ronald, Hofstra Law Review, Summer 2005, 1141.

*Financial Conflicts of Interest: The Impact on Contractors and Federal Employees.* Soller, Mary Lou and Brian A. Hill, Procurement Lawyer, Spring 2005, 1.

*How to Deal with Conflicts of Interest.* Kerns, Peggy, State Legislatures, July/August 2004, 36.

*Senators to Battle Over Accounting.* Hirsch, Jerry, Los Angeles Times, May 20, 2002.

## Organizations

### American Bar Association
740 15th Street, N.W.
Washington, DC 20005-1019 USA
Phone: (202) 662-1000
Fax: (202) 662-1506
URL: http://www.abanet.org

### National Conference of State Legislatures
444 North Capitol Street, N.W., Suite 515
Washington, DC 20001 USA
Phone: (202) 624-5400
Fax: (202) 737-1069
URL: http://www.ncsl.org

# BUSINESS LAW

## CORPORATIONS

*Sections within this essay:*

- Background
- History
- Laws Governing Corporations
- Forming a Corporation
- Shareholders, Directors, and Officers
- State Corporation Laws

### Background

A corporation is a distinct legal entity created by **statute**. **Corporations** have many of the same legal rights and obligations as do individuals. They can own and sell property, they can hold profits or acquire debts, they can enter into contracts and sue or be sued, and governments can tax them. Corporations are advantageous primarily because they become legal entities that are separate and distinct from the individuals who own and control them. This separation is important because in most cases these individuals have limited or no legal liability for the corporation's wrongdoings.

### History

Roman law first developed the concept of corporations, and England adopted the concept long before the founding of the United States. As the states became independent from England in 1776, they too adopted corporations as distinct legal entities and assumed **jurisdiction** over them. Today, the federal government continues to leave the control of corporations primarily to the states.

Corporations did not become commonplace in the United States until the Industrial Revolution at the turn of the nineteenth century. They then quickly developed as an efficient manner in which to conduct a large enterprise while at the same time offering a degree of protection to investors and owners from legal liability. Investors and owners increasingly were drawn to the idea of the corporation, and today, corporations are a mainstay in domestic and international business.

There are several types of corporations. Private corporations exist to make money for their investors and owners. Non-profit corporations, such as charities, exist to help a certain group of citizens or the general public. Municipal corporations are cities. Quasi-public corporations are entities such as telephone or electric companies that exist to make a profit as well as provide a service to the general public. A public corporation exists to make a profit, but it is distinguishable because it has a large number of investors known as shareholders. Shareholders own portions, known as shares, of the public corporations and may buy, sell, or trade their shares. Closely-held corporations have shareholders also but usually a much smaller group of shareholders. Often, closely-held corporations are owned by members of a family. Shareholders in closely-held corporations usually run the business, whereas shareholders in public corporations usually do not.

### Laws Governing Corporations

Many states based their laws governing corporations on the Model Business Corporations Act, which was first approved by the American Bar Association (ABA) in 1950. This act was significantly revised by the ABA in 1969 and again in 1984. A second popular source for corporation laws is the Delaware General Corporation Law. Delaware has a history of legislation that is particularly friendly to corporations, and so many corporations historically have chosen to incorporate there (see below). Lastly, the American Law Institute has produced **Principles of Corporate Governance: Analysis and Recommendations**, which courts often rely upon when ruling on matters related to the conduct of a business corporation.

## Forming a Corporation

An individual who wishes to start a corporation is known as a promoter. The promoter must find the money to start a corporation. This financing is known as capital and can be the promoter's own money, a loan from a bank or other financial institution, or money from an investor or group of investors who lend money to the promoter typically in exchange for future **corporate** profits. Before legally forming the corporation, or incorporating, the promoter often locates office or building space to house the corporation, identifies the people who will run the corporation, and then prepares the documents to make the corporation a legal entity. The work accomplished by the promoter prior to incorporation often necessitates contractual arrangements such as leases and loans. Because the corporation does not officially exist yet, the promoter must be the entity that enters into contracts. Later, when the corporation is legally formed, the corporation is considered as having assented to those contracts that were formed to benefit it prior to its official birth.

Corporation laws vary from state to state, but most states have the same basic requirements for forming a corporation. Promoters must file a document called the **articles of incorporation** with the secretary of state. These articles must include the corporation's name, whether the corporation will exist for a limited period of time or perpetually, the lawful business purpose of the corporation, the number of shares that the corporation will issue to shareholders as well as the types and preferences of the shares, the corporation's registered agent and address for the purpose of accepting service of process in the event that the corporation is sued, and the names and addresses of the corporation's directors and incorporators.

A corporation must also have **bylaws**, although states generally do not require that corporations file the bylaws with the secretary of state. Bylaws are rules that dictate how the corporation is going to be run. Bylaws are fairly easy to amend. They may include rules regarding the conduct of corporate officers, directors, and shareholders, and typically they designate times, locations, and voting requirements for corporate meetings.

Small corporations frequently incorporate in the state in which they operate. However, promoters can incorporate in any state they wish. Delaware is the most popular state for corporations because the Delaware General Corporation Law has been considered to be so favorable to corporate bodies. With other states recently adopting laws modeled after Delaware's, however, Delaware has lost some of its competitive edge in recent years. Still, Delaware continues to lead the nation in incorporations largely because corporate attorneys throughout the country are familiar with the laws in that state, because Delaware infrequently changes its corporate laws, and because Delaware courts specialize in legal issues regarding corporations.

## Shareholders, Directors, and Officers

Shareholders are the individuals or groups that invest in the corporations. Each portion of ownership of a corporation is known as a share of stock. An individual may own one share of stock or several shares. Shareholders have certain rights when it comes to the corporation. The most important one is the right to vote, for example, to elect the corporation's board of directors or change the corporation's bylaws. Shareholders vote on only a very limited number of corporate issues, but they nevertheless have the right to exert some control over the corporation's dealings. Shareholder voting typically takes place at an annual meeting, which states usually require of corporations. Corporations or shareholders may also request special meetings when a shareholder voting issue arises. It is not always practical for shareholders, who may live in various parts of the country or the world, to attend corporate meetings. For this reason, states permit shareholders to vote by authorizing, in writing, that another person may vote on behalf of the shareholder. This manner of voting is known as proxy.

Shareholders also have the right to investigate the corporation's books. So long as the shareholder seeking to investigate the corporation's records is doing so for a proper purpose or a purpose that reasonably relates to the shareholder's financial interests, the corporation must allow the inspection. In some cases, a corporation may require that the shareholder hold a minimum number of shares or that the shares be held for a certain period of time before allowing a shareholder to inspect the corporation's books and records.

A corporation is governed by a board of individuals known as directors who are elected by the shareholders. Directors may directly manage the corporation's affairs when the corporation is small, but when the corporation is large, directors primarily oversee the corporation's affairs and delegate the management activities to corporate officers. Directors usually receive a salary for their work on the corporate board, and directors have a **fiduciary** duty to act in the best interests of the corporation. These fiduciary duties require the directors to act with care toward the corporation, to act with loyalty toward the corporation, and to act within the confines of the law. A director who breaches this fiduciary duty may be sued by the shareholders and held personally liable for damages to the corporation.

The articles of incorporation or the corporate bylaws determine how many directors will serve on the board of directors and how long the directors' terms will be. Directors hold meetings at regular intervals as defined in the corporate bylaws and, in addition, may also call special board meetings when needed. At board meetings, directors discuss issues affecting the corporation and make decisions about the corporation. Before the board can make a decision affecting the corporation, however, there must be a quorum, or certain minimum number of directors, present at the meeting. The precise number constituting a quorum may be determined by the bylaws or by statute.

The fiduciary duty held by directors requires them to act with due care, which means that the director must act reasonably to protect the corporation's best interests. Courts will find a breach of the fiduciary duty when a director engages in self-dealing or **negligence**. Self-dealing occurs when the director makes a decision on behalf of the corporation that simultaneously benefits the director's personal interests. For example, assume a director for a wholesale foods corporation also owns separately a grocery store. At a corporate board meeting, the director votes to reduce by fifty percent the cost of wholesale apples sold by the corporation to independent grocery stores. Such an act would likely benefit the director's grocery store and could hurt the corpora-

tion's profitability. A court would likely determine such an act to be a breach of the director's fiduciary duty toward the corporation.

Directors are not in breach of their fiduciary duty merely because a decision they make on behalf of the corporation results in trouble for the corporation. Directors who base their decisions on reasonable information and who act rationally in making their decisions may not be held personally liable even if those decisions turn out to be poor ones. This legal emphasis on protecting a director's decision-making process is known as the business judgment rule.

The roles of corporate officers—typically the corporation's president, vice presidents, treasurer, and secretary—are defined by the corporate by-laws, articles of incorporation, and statutes. The president acts as the primary officer and sometimes is called the chief executive officer or CEO. The vice president is second in command and makes decisions in the president's absence. The secretary keeps track of the corporate records and takes minutes at corporate meetings. The treasurer keeps track of corporate finances. Corporate officers act as agents of the corporation and have the responsibility of negotiating contracts to which the corporation is a party. When a corporate officer signs a contract on behalf of the corporation, the corporation is legally bound to the terms of the contract. Officers, like directors, also have a fiduciary duty toward the corporation and may be held personally liable for acts taken on behalf of the corporation.

When a corporation engages in wrongdoing, such as **fraud**, fails to pay taxes correctly, or fails to pay debts, the people behind the corporation generally are protected from liability. This protection results from the fact that the corporation takes on a legal identity of its own and becomes liable for its acts. However, courts will in some cases ignore this separate corporate identity and render the shareholders, officers, or directors personally liable for acts they have taken on the corporation's behalf. This assignment of liability is known as piercing the corporate veil. Courts will pierce the corporate veil if a shareholder, officer, or director has engaged in fraud, illegality, or misrepresentation. Courts also will pierce the corporate veil when the corporation has not followed the **statutory** requirements for incorporation or when corporate funds are commingled with the **personal property** of an individual or when a corporation is undercapitalized or lacks sufficient funding to operate.

## Shares and Dividends

The articles of incorporation define how many shares, or ownership portions, the corporation will issue as well as what types of stock the corporation will issue. A corporation that issues only one type of stock issues common shares, or **common stock**. Common shareholders have the right to vote and also the right to the corporation's **net** assets, also known as dividends. A corporation may designate different classes of common stock, with different voting and **dividend** rights for those shareholders. **Preferred stock** is a type of stock issued by corporations that in most cases do not grant the shareholder the right to vote. However, owners of preferred stock usually have greater rights to receive dividends than do owners of common stock.

## State Corporation Laws

The majority of states have adopted the Model Business Corporation Act (MBCA) as the basis of their own state laws, though each of these states has modified the provisions of the MBCA. The following lists the laws that govern corporations and indicates which government body provides general supervision over corporations.

ALABAMA: The state corporation statute is based on the MBCA. The Secretary of State provides general supervision over corporations.

ALASKA: The current Alaska Corporations Code was adopted in 1989.

ARIZONA: The state corporation statute is based on the MBCA. The Arizona Corporation Commission provides general supervision over corporations.

ARKANSAS: The state corporation statute is based on the MBCA. The Secretary of State provides general supervision over corporations.

CALIFORNIA: The General Corporation Law has been in effect since 1977. The Secretary of State provides general supervision over corporations.

COLORADO: The state corporation statute is based on the MBCA. The Secretary of State provides general supervision over corporations.

CONNECTICUT: The current version of the Connecticut Business Corporation Act was completed in 1997.

DELAWARE: The Delaware General Corporation Law applies to corporations. The Division of Corporations of the Secretary of State governs corporations.

DISTRICT OF COLUMBIA: The District of Columbia Business Corporation Act was adopted in 1954 and was based on the MBCA. In addition to the provision allowing for the general formation of corporations, Congress may form a corporation through the enactment of a special act.

FLORIDA: The state corporation statute is based on the MBCA. The Secretary of State provides general supervision over corporations.

GEORGIA: The state corporation statute is based on the MBCA. The Corporations Division of the Secretary of State provides general supervision over corporations.

HAWAII: The state corporation statute is based on the MBCA. The Director of the Department of Commerce and Consumer Affairs provides general supervision over corporations.

IDAHO: The state corporation statute is based on the MBCA.

ILLINOIS: The Illinois Business Corporation Act became effective on July 1984. The Secretary of State provides general supervision over corporations.

INDIANA: The state corporation statute is based on the MBCA.

IOWA: The Iowa Business Corporation Act became effective in 1989.

KANSAS: The state corporation statute is based on the Delaware General Corporation Law. The Secretary of State provides general supervision over corporations.

KENTUCKY: The state corporation statute is based on the MBCA. The Secretary of State provides general supervision over corporations.

LOUISIANA: The Business Corporations Law was enacted in 1968. No government office provides general supervision, except that documents submitted by corporations are filed with the Secretary of State.

MAINE: The state corporation statute is based on the MBCA. The Secretary of State provides general supervision over corporations.

MARYLAND: The state corporation statute is based on the MBCA. The State Department of Assessments and Taxation provides general supervision over corporations.

# BUSINESS LAW

## INDEPENDENT CONTRACTORS

*Sections within this essay:*

- Background
- Significance
- Treatment of Independent Contractors Under Various Laws
-
  - Title VII Claims and the Economic Realities Test
  - Equal Pay Act and FLSA
  - Section 1981 Claims
  - Age Discrimination in Employment Act (ADEA)
  - Veterans' Reemployment Rights Act
  - Family and Medical Leave Act (FMLA)
  - Leased or Temporary Workers
- Consequences for Improper Classification
- Summary of Significant Factors in Classification
- Additional Resources

### Background

An independent contractor is a person who performs work or services for another person or company, for pay, but who is not employed by that person or company. The term itself is intended to convey the status of the individual as an *independent* worker who is a party to a *contract for specific work* (rather than a contract for employment), the performance of which is *not* controlled or supervised by the party requesting the service or work. As in any contract, there is no control of the physical conduct of the worker; only the end result (i.e., the fruit of the worker's labor) is accepted or rejected. For example, persons who hold themselves out as "consultants" are often retained by companies "independent contractors" who will provide expertise and assistance without actually being employed by the company requesting their expertise.

### Significance

The distinction between employee and independent contractor is crucial in determining the application of several important federal and state laws, including those involving wages and withholding taxes, as well as such entitlements as eligibility for **workers' compensation**. Generally, when disputed, there is no single, dispositive test for government agencies to determine whether workers are independent contractors to a company, or employees thereof. Moreover, different criteria and legal tests are used for determining worker status, because each government agency is concerned with worker classification for a different reason. Accordingly, agencies may use their own independent worker classification criteria, without regard to what other agencies have done. By analogy, this is similar in application to that of a person who might be considered "disabled" for purposes of workers' compensation, but not for social security benefits. Also possible (but not common) is the result that a worker may be deemed an independent contractor in one state, but an employee in another.

## Treatment of Independent Contractors Under Various Laws

### *Title VII Claims and the Economic Realities Test*

Title VII [42 USC § 2000(e)] defines an "employer" as a person or entity who employs 15 or more employees in 20 or more calendar weeks in the current or preceding calendar year. The term "employee" is only loosely defined as "an individual employed by an employer." Importantly, Title VII prohibits discrimination by an employer against any individual "with respect to terms, conditions, and privileges of employment." Once a company or person reaches the status of "employer" under the statute, there may be liability exposure for claims that independent contractors were essentially functioning as employees and therefore entitled to the same privileges and conditions as employees.

Why is the distinction important if Title VII protects any individual, whether an employee or independent contractor? What is meant by the statutory provision is that an employer cannot choose to speciously label one worker as an employee and another as an independent contractor, for the purpose of paying one less than the other or providing less benefit coverage for one than the other, or otherwise illegally discriminate between them. If two workers are substantially performing the same work, for purposes of Title VII claims of discrimination, both will be deemed employees and the employer will be required to treat them equally in "terms, conditions, and privileges of employment."

In adjudicating such claims and controversies, courts often refer to what is known as the "economic realities" of the employment relationship to make a determination of status as applied to the facts presented. In applying an "economics reality test" to the situation before it, a court will review the employment relationship of the parties to see if the worker in question is actually functioning as an employee, because the worker performs most of his work for the employer and derives most of his income from the employer. Conversely, if the worker held himself and his services out to several companies, and derived his overall income from several of them, he might be more appropriately deemed an independent contractor.

Still, other courts find the economic realities test too superficial, and instead look to the common law for guidance. Under the common law standard, the primary emphasis is on a review of the degree of control and autonomy the worker has over his hours, methods used to complete the work, and materials used for the work. If the employer only looks to the end result, the worker is more likely an independent contractor. A milestone court decision on this matter was the case of *Viscaino v. Microsoft Corp*, (9th Circuit, 1997). Microsoft had routinely brought in outside "independent contractors" to work on various software programs. Microsoft needed their expertise, but made them sign contract agreements, in which they understood that they were not employees of Microsoft. Many of them worked several years in this capacity for Microsoft, and ultimately, a group of them filed suit under ERISA, hoping to recover lost pension and other benefits. Microsoft defended that these individuals were "independent contractors" and had accepted the work with that knowledge and understanding. The Court thought otherwise. It found that the workers had assigned desks, assigned phone numbers, and were otherwise treated essentially as Microsoft employees. In fact, the only difference was that they did not receive company-paid benefits. Microsoft lost the case.

### *Equal Pay Act and FLSA*

Likewise, claims also may be brought under the Equal Pay Act [29 USC § 206(d)], which amends the **Fair Labor Standards Act (FLSA)**. Generally, for wage/hour claims, the "economic realities test" in used in determining the true status of the worker. An example of this type of claim might involve an independent contractor who is to be paid a contract amount when the work is completed, but in reality, that amount is less than the **minimum wage** or does not account for applicable overtime pay. If the worker is deemed to be actually functioning as an employee, the employer may be liable for monetary damages.

### *Section 1981 Claims*

The old **Civil Rights** law, passed during the post-Civil War era [42 USC § 1981] prohibits discrimination upon the basis of race in making and enforcing contracts. This has provided a cognizable cause of action for independent contractors involving their contractual relations with employers. (See *Danco v. Wal-Mart Stores*, 1st Circuit, 1999.)

### *Age Discrimination in Employment Act (ADEA)*

Definitions found in the ADEA [29 USC § 621] are similar to those in Title VII, except that an "employer," for purposes of the ADEA, must employ 20 or more employees for each working day in 20 or more calendar weeks in the current or preceding calendar year. Likewise, protection against age discrimination by employers covers both employees and independent contractors.

### Veterans' Reemployment Rights Act

Unlike Title VII and the ADEA, the Veterans' Reemployment Rights Act [38 USC § 4301] defines an employer as any person or entity "that pays salary or wages for work performed or that has control over employment opportunities." Under this Act, discrimination is prohibited against applicants as well as employees, due to their absence for service-related reasons.

### Family and Medical Leave Act (FMLA)

Under the FMLA, an employer is defined as any person or entity that employs 50 or more employees for each working day in 20 or more calendar weeks in the current or preceding year. Eligibility for family leave is premised upon the completion of 1250 hours of service and a work status for at least 12 months. Because the FMLA incorporates FLSA definitions, the same rules would apply in determining worker status (the economic realities test).

### Leased or Temporary Workers

Companies ("employers") also may be liable to temporary workers who are employed through third parties (such as personnel agencies). Case law holds that the personnel agency is generally deemed to be a nominal employer and the end-user company is the true employer. In the alternative, some jurisdictions have found that both are joint employers of the worker.

However, where an agency is merely leasing back employees to the company and has no meaningful contact with them, only the end-user will be found to be the employer.

## Consequences for Improper Classifications

Employers are not required to withhold taxes from independent contractor earnings. Instead, they file information returns to the Internal Revenue Service and state authorities, indicating the amount paid in wages to the independent contractor. This information is also provided to the contractor on IRS Form 1099-MISC.

The Internal Revenue Code and various state laws impose substantial penalties on employers for improper classification of employees as independent contractors. Likewise, the Code imposes penalties

and fines upon independent contractors who either fail to report income or who do not file self-employment quarterly returns. Additionally, the independent contractor will have to back-pay all taxes and social security deductions accrued during the misclassified period, in addition to those currently due.

Penalties to employers for failure to withhold income taxes are generally equal to 1.5 percent of the wages, plus 20 percent of the social security and medicare taxes that should have been paid by the employee. There is also a liability for the unpaid portion of the *employer's* portion of the social security and medicare taxes.

## Summary of Significant Factors in Classification

In summary, the following factors are key in determining whether a worker is more correctly classified as an employee:

- The worker can be terminated at will;

- A manager (or designated person) assigns, reviews, and supervises the worker's work product.

- The worker performs services that are a part of the regular operation of the business.

## Additional Resources

"Employer's Supplemental Tax Guide" (Publication 15-A) Internal Revenue Service. Washington: GPO, 2005.

Matthies Law Firm, P.C. "Treatment of Independent Contractors under Discrimination Laws." Undated. Available at http://members.aol.com/mattlawfrm/indcont.html

## Organizations

### Alabama Labor Department
64 North Union Street, Room 651
Montgomery, AL 36130
Phone: (205) 242-3460

### Alaska Labor Department
P.O. Box 1149
Juneau, AK 99802
Phone: (907) 465-2700

### Arizona Labor Division
800 West Washington Street

Phoenix, AZ 85007
Phone: (602) 542-4515

**Arkansas Labor Department**
10421 West Markham Street
Little Rock, AR 72205
Phone: (501) 682-4500

**California Industrial Relations Department**
P.O. Box 603
San Francisco, CA 94101
Phone: (415) 737-2600

**Colorado Labor and Employment Department**
600 Grant Street
Denver, CO 80203-3528
Phone: (303) 837-3801

**Connecticut Labor Department**
200 Folly Brook Boulevard
Wethersfield, CT 06109
Phone: (203) 566-4384

**Delaware Labor Department**
820 North French Street
Wilmington, DE 19801
Phone: (302) 571-2710

**District of Columbia Human Rights Office**
2000-14th Street NW
Washington, DC 20009
Phone: (202) 939-8740

**Florida Labor and Employment Security Department**
2590 Executive Circle East
Tallahassee, FL 32399
Phone: (904) 488-4398

**Georgia Labor Department**
148 International Boulevard
Atlanta, GA 30303
Phone: (404) 656-3011

**Hawaii Labor and Industrial Relations Department**
830 Punchbowl Street
Honolulu, HI 96813
Phone: (808) 548-3150

**Idaho Labor and Industrial Services Department**
Stateouse Mail
Boise, ID 83720
Phone: (208) 334-3950

**Illinois Labor Department**
310 South Michigan, 10th Floor
Chicago, IL 60604
Phone: (312) 793-2800

**Indiana Labor Department**
100 North Senate Avenue, Room 1013
Indianapolis, IN 46204
Phone: (317) 232-2378

**Iowa Human Rights Department**
Lucas State Office Building
Des Moines, IA 50319
Phone: (515) 281-5960

**Kansas Civil Rights Commission**
Landon State Office Building, No. 851, South
Topeka, KS 66612-1258
Phone: (913) 296-3206

**Kentucky Labor Cabinet**
127 Building, U.S. Highway 27 South
Frankfort, KY 40601
Phone: (502) 564-3070

**Louisiana Labor Department**
P.O. Box 94094
Baton Rouge, LA 70804
Phone: (225) 342-3011

**Maine Labor Department**
20 Union Street, P.O. Box 309
Augusta, ME 04333-0309
Phone: (207) 289-3788

**Maryland Licensing and Regulation Department, Labor and Industry Division**
501 St. Paul Place
Baltimore, MD 21202
Phone: (410) 333-4179

**Massachusetts Labor Executive Office**
1 Ashburton Place, Room 2112
Boston, MA 02108
Phone: (617) 727-6573

**Michigan Labor Department**
611 West Ottawa Street
Lansing, MI 48909
Phone: (517) 373-9600

**Minnesota Labor and Industry Department**
443 Lafayette Road
St. Paul, MN 55155
Phone: (651) 296-2342

**Mississippi Employment Security Division**
P.O. Box 1699

Jackson, MS 39215-1699
Phone: (601) 359-1031

**Missouri Labor and Industrial Relations Department**
421 Dunklin Street
Jefferson City, MO 65101
Phone: (573) 751-4091

**Montana Labor and Industry Department**
P.O. Box 1728
Helena, MT 59624
Phone: (406) 444-3555

**Nebraska Labor Department**
P.O. Box 94600
Lincoln, NE 68509
Phone: (402) 475-8451

**Nevada Labor Commission**
505 East King Street, Room 602
Carson City, NV 89710
Phone: (775) 885-4850

**New Hampshire Labor Department**
19 Pillsbury Street
Concord, NH 03301
Phone: (603) 271-3171

**New Jersey Labor Department**
John Fitch Plaza, CN110
Trenton, NJ 08625
Phone: (609) 292-2323

**New Mexico Labor Department**
1596 Pacheco Street
Santa Fe, NM 87501
Phone: (505) 827-6838

**New York Labor Department**
State Campus. Building 12
Albany, NY 12240
Phone: (518) 457-2741

**North Carolina Labor Department**
4 West Edenton Street
Raleigh, NC 27601
Phone: (919) 733-7166

**North Dakota Labor Department**
600 East Boulevard Avenue
Bismarck, ND 58505
Phone: (701) 224-2661

**Ohio Civil Rights Commission**
220 Parsons Avenue
Columbus, OH 43266-0543
Phone: (614) 466-2785

**Oklahoma Labor Department**
4001 Lincoln Boulevard
Oklahoma City, OK 73105
Phone: (405) 528-1500

**Oregon Labor and Industries Bureau**
1400 S.W. 5thAvenue, Suite 409
Portland, OR 97201
Phone: (503) 229-5737

**Pennsylvania Labor and Industry Department**
Labor and Industry Building
Harrisburg, PA 17120
Phone: (717) 787-3756

**Rhode Island Labor Department**
220 Elmwood Avenue
Providence, RI 02907
Phone: (401) 457-1800

**South Carolina Labor Department**
P.O. Box 11329
Columbia, SC 29211-1329
Phone: (803) 734-9594

**South Dakota Labor Department**
700 Governors Drive
Pierre, SD 57501
Phone: (605) 773-3101

**Tennessee Labor Department**
501 Union Building
Nashville, TN 37219
Phone: (615) 741-2582

**Texas Employment Commission**
101 East 15th Street
Austin, TX 78778
Phone: (512) 463-2800

**Utah Commerce Department**
P.O. Box 45802
Salt Lake City, UT 84145-0801
Phone: (801) 530-6701

**Vermont Labor and Industry Department**
State Office Building, 120 State Street
Montpelier, VT 05602
Phone: (802) 828-2286

**Virginia Office of Economic Development**
205 North 4th Street, Box 12064
Richmond, VA 23241
Phone: (804) 786-2377

### Washington Labor and Industries Department

General Adminstration Building, HC-101
Olympia, WA 05602
Phone: (206) 753-6307

### West Virginia Commerce, Labor, and Environment Department

1800 Washington Street East
Charleston, WV 25305
Phone: (304) 348-7890

### Wisconsin Industry Labor and Human Relations Department

P.O. Box 7946
Madison, WI 53707
Phone: (608) 266-7552

### Wyoming Labor and Statistics Department

122 West 25th Street, 2nd Floor East
Cheyenne, WY 82002
Phone: (307) 777-7261

# BUSINESS LAW

## LIMITED LIABILITY ENTITIES

*Sections within this essay:*

## Background

Since the 1990s, individuals who wish to form businesses have seen a significant increase in the types of business entities that may be formed. Laws governing these newer forms of businesses limit the liability that business owners may face. In general, a person who invests in a limited liability entity is only liable for an amount equivalent to the investment made by the investor.

Some limited liability entities resemble general partnerships, except for the limitations in liability. Other entities, especially limited liability companies, are more similar to **corporations** in their structure.

Although some entities are taxed in a manner similar to partnerships, other forms of limited liability entities may be taxed similar to corporations.

## Entities Without Limited Liability

Owners of three types of businesses are not protected by the limited liability that other business forms offer. An owner of such a business is personally liable for the debts incurred by the business. These businesses include general partnerships, joint ventures, and sole proprietorships. General partnerships are formed when two or more agree to engage in a business for profit. A joint venture is similar to a general partnership, except that two or more people form a venture for a particular business project. A sole proprietorship is a business that is carried on by an individual.

The law traditionally has not treated these types of business as independent and distinct from the owners. Owners of these types of business also do not need to follow the formalities that owners of other forms of businesses, such as corporations, must follow. Moreover, these business entities generally are not governed as heavily by state and federal regulations. Thus, although limitations on liability provide considerable incentive to form a limited liability entity, other factors may lead business owners to form an entity that does not enjoy limited liability.

## Corporations

The corporation is the most common form of business entity in the United States. A corporation is formed when individuals complete certain formalities, including the filing of documents known as articles of incorporation and the payment of fees to the proper authority. The secretary of state in most states is the official responsible for receiving the documents and filing fees from the corporations.

Traditionally, the corporate form of business was the preferred limited liability entity because the corporation exists separate from its owners and investors. The corporation, although an artificial entity, is treated like an individual in most respects. It may enter into contracts, it may sue or be sued, and it may own property. A corporation may also exist perpetually because it may continue to exist even when owners and investors change.

As an entity separate from its owners and investors, a corporation is liable for its own **contracts**. Owners and investors generally are only liable to the extent of the amount that these individuals invested in the corporation.

Many states base their laws governing corporations on the Model Business Corporation Act (MBCA), which was prepared by the Section of Business Law of the American Bar Association. However, most of these states have deviated from the MBCA with respect to some of the provisions. Other states have chosen not to follow the MBCA and have instead drafted their own statutes.

## Limited Partnerships

Parties form a limited partnership in a manner similar to a general partnership. The most significant difference between these two types of businesses is that some of the owners of the limited partnership, known as limited partners, do not participate in the management and control of the partnership's business. Instead, limited partners provide capital contributions to the partnership and are liable only to the extent of those capital contributions.

Like a general partnership, owners of a limited partnership enter into a partnership agreement. A limited partnership must file a certificate with an appropriate state authority, usually the secretary of state. The certificate provides the limited partnership's name and character of business, along with the names and addresses of the general and limited partners. A limited partnership's name must include "L.P.," "Ltd," or "Limited Partnership" to identify the form of the business entity. The purpose for this requirement is to warn those who deal with the part-

nership that some of the partners are not personally liable for the partnership's debts.

Nearly every state adopted the Uniform Limited Partnership Act, which was approved in 1916 and again in 1976 by the National Conference of Commissioners on Uniform State Laws (NCCUSL). The NCCUSL significantly revised this uniform law in 2001, though as of 2005 only a small number of states had adopted the revised version.

## Limited Liability Partnerships

The limited liability partnership (LLP) emerged as a business form during the 1990s. This type of business entity is similar to a general partnership in that each partner may share in the management of the business and that each partner shares in the profits. However, unlike a general partnership, partners in an LLP do not incur personal liability for claims that are brought related to the actions of a copartner. Moreover, this form of business shields a partner from liability for the acts of the partnership's employees or agents. On the other hand, a partner in an LLP is liable for his or her own negligence or malfeasance and the negligence and malfeasance of anyone under the supervision and control of the partner.

Owners of an LLP register the business by filing a registration with the appropriate state authority, usually the secretary of state. Owners of an LLP may be required to prove that the entity has adequate liability insurance or assets to satisfy claims that may be brought against the business. This type of partnership must include the word "Registered Limited Liability Partnership" or the initials "LLP" in its name.

Every state now allows businesses to form as LLPs. The NCCUSL in 1996 amended the Uniform Partnership Act (UPA) to include sections governing limited liability partnerships. The majority of states have adopted the revised UPA.

## Limited Liability Limited Partnerships

A small minority of states recognize a form of business called the limited liability limited partnership (LLLP). An LLLP is formed when a limited partnership registers as a limited liability partnership, thus allowing partners to benefit from different limitations in liability. In other words, limited partners in an LLLP are still only liable for the partnership's debts to the extent of the limited partner's contributions, while a general partner is not personally liable for the negligence or malfeasance of another general partner.

The NCCUSL modified the Uniform Limited Partnership Act in 2001 to allow limited partnerships to register as limited liability limited partnerships. Although only a small number of states had enacted the revised uniform act by 2005, several states had considered bills that would have adopted this act.

## Limited Liability Companies

The limited liability company (LLC) first appeared as a business form in Wyoming during the 1970s and became more prevalent during the 1990s. This type of business entity combines aspects of a partnership with aspects of a corporation. Those who form an LLC may choose to have the owners of the company (called "members") manage the company. This type of management structure is more similar to a partnership. Alternatively, an LLC may choose to have managers run the company in a structure that is more similar to a corporation. The Internal Revenue Service allows an LLC to elect whether it wants to be taxed as a partnership or as a corporation, and so this form of business offers flexibility in both management and taxation.

In order to form an LLC, the owners must file articles of organization with an appropriate state authority, usually the secretary of state. Articles of organization are similar to articles of incorporation, which must be filed in order to form a corporation. Owners of an LLC must also pay a filing fee at the time of registration.

Members of an LLC enjoy similar protections against liability as shareholders in a corporation, limited partners in a limited partnership, or partners in a limited liability partnership or limited liability limited partnership. These members are generally not personally liable for the debts and obligations of the LLC, except in certain circumstances.

Although every state now provides for the LLC as a business entity, state laws vary from one to the next. The NCCUSL completed the Uniform Limited Liability Company Act in 1996, but only eight states and one territory has adopted this act as of 2005.

## Issues Regarding Limited Liability Entities

### Taxation

Corporations are taxed on one of two ways, depending on the type of corporation that has been structured. A "C Corporation," also known as a standard business corporation, is an entity that is taxed separately from its owners. Dividends that are passed on to shareholders of the corporation are also taxable, thus meaning that income received by a corporation may be taxed twice. Another type of corporation, known as an "S Corporation" is considered to be a "pass-through" entity with respect to taxation. That is, the corporation itself is not taxed, and profits and losses are passed down as income or losses to the owners of the corporation. An S Corporation is taxed in a manner similar to a partnership, which is also treated as a pass-through entity.

When new forms of business entities began to emerge in the 1990s, taxation of the entity was a major consideration. Limited partnerships and limited liability partnerships were easily classified as pass-through entities. However, the Internal Revenue Service (IRS) had some difficulty in determining how an LLC should be taxed. Under regulations that existed prior to 1997, if an LLC was operated in a manner more similar to a C Corporation, then the LLC was taxed as a corporation. However, the IRS changed its regulations in 1997 to allow an LLC to select how it should be taxed. Since the passage of those regulations, LLCs have been free to operate in a manner similar to corporations, but these LLCs may elect to be taxed like partnerships.

### "Piercing the Veil"

Under the law governing corporations, where an owner or owners of a corporation use the corporate form of business to engage in fraud while hiding behind the shield of limited liability, a court may hold the owners of the corporation personally liable to a third party. This is referred to as piercing the corporate veil. Since partners in a general partnership are personally liable for the debts of the partnership, this theory of liability did not apply to entities other than corporations.

Because these new limited liability entities shield owners of businesses from personal liability, commentators have suggested that the piercing-the-veil theory can apply to LLCs and LLPs. This theory would apply only in narrow circumstances, such as where owners of an LLC or LLP fail to follow proper formalities in forming or running the business, or where the business entity is being used to perpetuate fraud.

### Liability for Torts and Other Obligations

Owners and managers of limited liability entities are never completely shielded from personal liability. For instance, laws that govern these types of entities do not generally shield owners or managers from liability for torts that are committed while the person is acting on behalf of the business. Whether a business owner or manager is shielded from liability with respect to his or her involvement in the business depends on the type of limited liability entity and the individual state law that governs that type of entity.

## State Laws Governing Limited Liability Entities

ALABAMA: The state has adopted provisions of the Model Business Corporation Act. The state adopted the 1997 version of the Uniform Partnership Act, including provisions governing limited liability partnerships. The state also adopted the Uniform Limited Liability Company Act.

ALASKA: The state adopted the 1997 version of the Uniform Partnership Act, including provisions governing limited liability partnerships.

ARIZONA: The state has adopted provisions of the Model Business Corporation Act. The state adopted the 1997 version of the Uniform Partnership Act, including provisions governing limited liability partnerships.

ARKANSAS: The state has adopted provisions of the Model Business Corporation Act. The state adopted the 1997 version of the Uniform Partnership Act, including provisions governing limited liability partnerships.

CALIFORNIA: The state adopted the 1997 version of the Uniform Partnership Act, including provisions governing limited liability partnerships.

COLORADO: The state has adopted provisions of the Model Business Corporation Act. The state adopted the 1997 version of the Uniform Partnership Act, including provisions governing limited liability partnerships.

CONNECTICUT: The state adopted the 1994 version of the Uniform Partnership Act.

DELAWARE: The state adopted the 1997 version of the Uniform Partnership Act, including provisions governing limited liability partnerships.

DISTRICT OF COLUMBIA: The state has adopted provisions of the Model Business Corporation Act. The state adopted the 1997 version of the Uniform Partnership Act, including provisions governing limited liability partnerships.

FLORIDA: The state has adopted provisions of the Model Business Corporation Act. The state adopted the 1997 version of the Uniform Partnership Act, including provisions governing limited liability partnerships. The state also adopted the 2001 revisions to the Uniform Limited Partnership Act.

GEORGIA: The state has adopted provisions of the Model Business Corporation Act.

HAWAII: The state has adopted provisions of the Model Business Corporation Act. The state adopted the 1997 version of the Uniform Partnership Act, including provisions governing limited liability partnerships. The state also adopted the Uniform Limited Liability Company Act and the 2001 revision to the Uniform Limited Partnership Act.

IDAHO: The state has adopted provisions of the Model Business Corporation Act. The state adopted the 1997 version of the Uniform Partnership Act, including provisions governing limited liability partnerships.

ILLINOIS: The state adopted the 1997 version of the Uniform Partnership Act, including provisions governing limited liability partnerships. The state also adopted the Uniform Limited Liability Company Act and the 2001 revision to the Uniform Limited Partnership Act.

INDIANA: The state has adopted provisions of the Model Business Corporation Act.

IOWA: The state adopted the 1997 version of the Uniform Partnership Act, including provisions governing limited liability partnerships. The state also adopted the 2001 revisions to the Uniform Limited Partnership Act.

KANSAS: The state adopted the 1997 version of the Uniform Partnership Act, including provisions governing limited liability partnerships.

KENTUCKY: The state has adopted provisions of the Model Business Corporation Act.

MAINE: The state has adopted provisions of the Model Business Corporation Act.

MARYLAND: The state has adopted provisions of the Model Business Corporation Act. The state adopted the 1997 version of the Uniform Partnership Act, including provisions governing limited liability partnerships.

MASSACHUSETTS: The state has adopted provisions of the Model Business Corporation Act.

MINNESOTA: The state adopted the 1997 version of the Uniform Partnership Act, including provisions governing limited liability partnerships. The state also adopted the 2001 revisions to the Uniform Limited Partnership Act.

MISSISSIPPI: The state has adopted provisions of the Model Business Corporation Act. The state adopted the 1997 version of the Uniform Partnership Act, including provisions governing limited liability partnerships.

MISSOURI: The state has adopted provisions of the Model Business Corporation Act.

MONTANA: The state has adopted provisions of the Model Business Corporation Act. The state adopted the 1997 version of the Uniform Partnership Act, including provisions governing limited liability partnerships. The state also adopted the Uniform Limited Liability Company Act.

NEBRASKA: The state has adopted provisions of the Model Business Corporation Act. The state adopted the 1997 version of the Uniform Partnership Act, including provisions governing limited liability partnerships.

NEVADA: The state adopted the 1997 version of the Uniform Partnership Act, including provisions governing limited liability partnerships.

NEW HAMPSHIRE: The state has adopted provisions of the Model Business Corporation Act.

NEW JERSEY: The state adopted the 1997 version of the Uniform Partnership Act, including provisions governing limited liability partnerships.

NEW MEXICO: The state has adopted provisions of the Model Business Corporation Act. The state adopted the 1997 version of the Uniform Partnership Act, including provisions governing limited liability partnerships.

NORTH CAROLINA: The state has adopted provisions of the Model Business Corporation Act.

NORTH DAKOTA: The state has adopted provisions of the Model Business Corporation Act. The state adopted the 1997 version of the Uniform Partnership Act, including provisions governing limited liability partnerships. The state also adopted the 2001 revisions to the Uniform Limited Partnership Act.

OKLAHOMA: The state adopted the 1997 version of the Uniform Partnership Act, including provisions governing limited liability partnerships.

OREGON: The state has adopted provisions of the Model Business Corporation Act. The state adopted the 1997 version of the Uniform Partnership Act, including provisions governing limited liability partnerships.

RHODE ISLAND: The state has adopted provisions of the Model Business Corporation Act.

SOUTH CAROLINA: The state has adopted provisions of the Model Business Corporation Act. The state also adopted the Uniform Limited Liability Company Act.

SOUTH DAKOTA: The state has adopted provisions of the Model Business Corporation Act. Provisions of the state's partnership statute are similar to 1997 version of the Uniform Partnership Act, including provisions governing limited liability partnerships. The state also adopted the Uniform Limited Liability Company Act.

TENNESSEE: The state adopted the 1997 version of the Uniform Partnership Act, including provisions governing limited liability partnerships.

TEXAS: The state has adopted provisions of the Model Business Corporation Act. The state adopted the 1997 version of the Uniform Partnership Act, including provisions governing limited liability partnerships.

UTAH: The state has adopted provisions of the Model Business Corporation Act.

VERMONT: The state adopted the 1997 version of the Uniform Partnership Act, including provisions governing limited liability partnerships. The state also adopted the Uniform Limited Liability Company Act.

VIRGINIA: The state has adopted provisions of the Model Business Corporation Act. The state adopted the 1997 version of the Uniform Partnership Act, including provisions governing limited liability partnerships.

WASHINGTON: The state has adopted provisions of the Model Business Corporation Act. The state adopted the 1997 version of the Uniform Partnership Act, including provisions governing limited liability partnerships.

WEST VIRGINIA: The state adopted the 1994 version of the Uniform Partnership Act. The state also adopted the Uniform Limited Liability Company Act.

WISCONSIN: The state has adopted provisions of the Model Business Corporation Act.

WYOMING: The state has adopted provisions of the Model Business Corporation Act. The state adopted the 1994 version of the Uniform Partnership Act.

## Additional Resources

*Agency, Partnership, and the LLC in a Nutshell, 3rd Edition.* Hayes, J. Dennis and Mark J. Loewenstein, Thomson/West, 2005.

*Limited Liability Companies: A State by State Guide to Law and Practice.* Callison, J. William, and Maureen A. Sullivan, Thomson/West, 2005.

*Macey on Corporation Laws.* Johnathan R. Macey, Aspen Publishers, 2005.

*West's Encyclopedia of American Law, 2nd Edition.* West Group, 2004.

## Organizations

### Council of Better Business Bureaus

4200 Wilson Blvd., Suite 800
Arlington, VA 22203-1838 USA
Phone: (703) 525-8277
URL: http://www.bbb.org

### Small Business Advancement National Center

UCA Box 5018, 201 Donaghey Avenue
Conway, AR 72053-0001 USA
Phone: (501) 450-5300
Fax: (501) 450-5360
URL: http://www.sbaer.uca.edu

### United States Chamber of Commerce

1615 H Street, NW
Washington, DC 20062-2000 USA
Phone: (202) 659-6000
URL: http://www.uschamber.com/default

# BUSINESS LAW

## NONPROFIT ORGANIZATIONS

*Sections within this essay:*

## Background

Nonprofit organizations exist in the United States for a number of reasons. Many of these organizations are formed for the purpose of fulfilling needs in society by providing an organization that handles what the government would handle otherwise. Nonprofit organizations exist along with two other types of entities: for-profit businesses and government agencies. Each of these serves different purposes in society.

Many people associate nonprofit organizations and tax exemption, though not all nonprofit entities are exempt from **taxation**. Moreover, a nonprofit organization is not prohibited from earning a profit, for many of these organizations generate profits. To the contrary, the law governing nonprofit entities sets forth requirements as to what each entity must do with the profits it earns. More specifically, the law expects nonprofit organizations to devote any profits to the goal of furthering the purposes and activities of the organization.

Additionally, not all nonprofit organizations are charitable in nature. Although contributions to charitable organizations generally qualify for a charitable contribution deduction, some nonprofit entities that are not charitable in nature are also tax exempt.

## Purpose of a Nonprofit Organization

One of the first steps in forming a nonprofit entity is to define the purpose of the entity. This statement of purpose, which must be made in writing, will define the type of tax exemption for which that organization is qualified. The following list provides examples of the types of tax-exempt nonprofit organizations:

- Organizations formed for charitable purposes
- Organizations that advocate for social welfare
- Professional associations
- Labor organizations
- Chambers of commerce and business leagues

- Social clubs
- Homeowners associations
- Employee benefit funds
- Fraternal societies
- Political organizations

The purpose driving a for-profit business is to benefit the owners of the business. By comparison, the activities of a nonprofit entity must be conducted for the benefit of the organization and not the owners. In order to qualify for tax exempt status, the organization must benefit the public.

## Location of the Organization

Once a person or group decides to form a nonprofit organization, one of the first issues that must be addressed is where this entity will be formed. Some states may be more attractive than others due to several factors. For instance, states such as New York and California are more intense in terms of regulating nonprofit entities than other states. Moreover, state laws may differ about the requirements the entity must satisfy in order to qualify for tax-exempt status.

A nonprofit organization may form under the laws in one state but operate in a different state. This option may be advantageous when the laws of one state allow those who form the nonprofit entity to fulfill the purpose of the entity better than the laws of another state. On the other hand, this option is usually more costly because both the state in which the entity is formed and the state where the entity operates will charge fees.

## Choice of Organizational Form

Another complicated decision that those who form nonprofit entities must make is what organization form the entity will take. In general, nonprofit entities appear in four organizational forms, including the following: **corporations**, charitable trusts, **limited liability companies**, and unincorporated associations. Each of these forms has some benefits and some disadvantages that must be considered when the organization is formed.

### Corporations
The most common form of nonprofit organization is the corporation. A corporation is a creation of the law. Those who create a corporation must file a document known as articles of incorporation, which sets forth important information about the corporation itself. Once a corporation is formed, it becomes its own "person" under the law, separate from its directors, officers, or owners. The corporation itself may sue others or be sued.

A nonprofit entity benefits from forming as a corporation for two primary reasons. First, the laws governing corporations provides considerable protection to officers, directors, members, employees, and volunteers against personal liability. This means that if the corporation itself incurs liability (e.g., a third person successfully sues the corporation), those who act on the corporations behalf usually do not incur liability. Second, the law governing corporations is generally well-settled, meaning that the rules that govern the operation of the corporation are more clearly defined.

Several states have adopted the Model Nonprofit Corporation Act, which was first drafted by the Business Law Section of the American Bar Association in 1964. It was subsequently revised in 1987.

### Unincorporated Associations
Unlike a corporation, which must be created and structured according to the directives of state law, two or more people may form an unincorporated association without following those formalities. Those who form an unincorporated association may choose how the association should be governed, which is one of the benefits of this form of entity. Such an entity may be formed as a nonprofit entity.

However, whether those associated with the entity are liable for the entity's debts is not clear. In several states, including those that have adopted the Uniform Nonprofit Unincorporated Association Act, an unincorporated association is treated as an entity separate from its members. Where a state recognizes the association as a separate entity, then the members of the entity are probably shielded from personal liability for the association debts. On the other hand, some states may not recognize the association as separate, meaning that the members could incur personal liability.

### Limited Liability Companies
The limited liability company (LLC) is a newer form of business entity. The organizational structure of an LLC borrows from the structures of both unincorporated entities and corporations. The benefit in forming an LLC is its flexibility, since someone who

creates an LLC may form the entity to appear more like a partnership or more like a corporation, depending on the needs and preferences of the person who is forming it. An LLC may elect to be taxed as a corporation or as a partnership.

Although the LLC form of organizational structure may provide some benefits, the use of the LLC for nonprofit entities is not well settled. Questions about the taxation of a nonprofit LLC have yet to be answered, and in some states, state law is not clear whether an LLC may be formed for nonprofit purposes. On the other hand, this form of entity provides flexibility in terms of structure and may be preferable to some nonprofit entities.

### Charitable Trusts

A person who wishes to set aside property for the benefit of another may form a trust. Unlike a corporation or LLC, a person may form a trust without filing anything with the government. Instead, the trust is formed when a person transfers property to a person or an entity, known as a trustee, and directs the trustee to use the transferred assets for the benefit of a third person, known as a beneficiary. State law dictates how a trustee must handle the property that is being used for the benefit of the beneficiary.

Some nonprofit entities are formed as charitable trusts, where the beneficiaries are not specific individuals. Instead, the trustee of a charitable trust uses the property for the benefit of a specified purpose, such as education of disadvantaged youth. The laws that apply to trusts in general also apply to charitable trusts. Because modern corporations are generally easy to form, those who wish to form a charitable nonprofit entity are more likely to form a corporation than they are to create a charitable trust.

## Meaning of Tax Exemption

Although some people associate nonprofit organizations with tax-exempt organizations, certainly not all nonprofit entities are exempted from taxes. Moreover, even though a tax-exempt organization may be free from paying federal income taxes, such an organization may still be liable for other types of taxes. For instance, a tax-exempt organization may be liable for taxes on net investment income as well as income derived from business activities that do not relate to the organization's exempt functions (known as unrelated business activities, discussed below).

## Determining Tax-Exempt Status

Statutory law generally determines whether an organization is exempt from taxes. Section 501 of the Internal Revenue Code (IRC) provides the basic rules for tax-exempt status at the federal level. The Internal Revenue Service (IRS) is the federal body responsible for recognizing that an organization qualifies for tax-exempt status. An entity that wants to seek recognition for this status must file a form entitled "Application for Recognition of Exemption."

State laws regarding tax exemptions vary. Those who form nonprofit entities should consult the laws of relevant states to determine which organizations are eligible for tax-exempt status and which steps, if any, the organization must take in order for the state to recognize that status.

## Categories of Tax-Exempt Organizations

The IRC contains a laundry list of organizations that qualify as tax-exempt organizations. The most common of these are charitable organizations, though the IRC also includes educational, scientific, and religious organizations. Moreover, the Code includes several other types of entities, such as labor organizations, social clubs, credit unions, employee benefit trusts, and farmers' cooperatives.

## Charitable Organizations

Federal law recognizes several different forms of charitable organizations. Charitable organizations are often referred to as Section 501(c)(3) organizations, named after the section of the IRC section under which these organizations are formed. The definition of charitable has been developed through the promulgation of tax regulations and tax rulings, as well as through federal and state judicial cases. The following list includes the purposes that are generally recognized as charitable:

- Relief of poverty
- Relief of the distressed
- Advancement of religion
- Advancement of education
- Advancement of science
- Lessening the burdens of government (e.g., erecting a public building)
- Community beautification and maintenance
- Promotion of health

- Promotion of social welfare
- Promote environmental conservation
- Promotion of patriotism
- Promotion of the arts

## Taxation of Unrelated Business Activities

Federal tax law distinguishes between activities that relate to the exempt functions of a nonprofit and those activities that are unrelated. Gross revenues that are gained on unrelated business activities are subject to taxation. Because most nonprofit organizations conduct some sort of business, most of these organizations must determine whether any aspect of their businesses may be characterized as an unrelated business activity.

In order for income of a tax-exempt organization to be taxable, the income must be produced from a trade or business that the organization carries on regularly. An organization carries on a trade or business regularly if it does so frequently and continually, as opposed to sporadically or infrequently. The income must also be unrelated to the purpose for which the organization has been formed and which forms the basis for the tax exemption. Income from activities that bear a substantial relationship to the purpose of the nonprofit entity are not subject to tax, while income from activities that do not bear a substantial relationship to the purpose of the entity are subject to taxation.

Revenue that a tax-exempt organization gains on an unrelated business activity is subject to the federal corporate income tax that applies to non-exempt entities. An exempt organization is entitled to certain deductions related to the business that earned this income, much like a for-profit entity may be entitled to deductions for certain activities.

## Public Charities and Private Foundations

The Internal Revenue Code distinguishes between nonprofit entities that are public charities and those that are private foundations. A public charity is one that has involvement from the public in general, earns financial support from the public in general, or has an operating relationship with a public organization. By comparison, a private foundation usually derives its financial support from one source; earns money through investment assets, rather than through contributions from the public; and makes grants to other charitable organizations instead of operating its own activities.

Private foundations are subject to certain restrictive rules and taxes for which public charities are not subject. Thus, those who form nonprofit organizations often would like to avoid the status of a private foundation. Several types of institutions are exempted from the rules governing private foundations. These institutions include certain churches, educational institutions, health care providers, and governmental units.

## Reporting Requirements

Those organizations that are exempt from federal taxes must file what is known as an information return with the IRS. Most organizations that are entitled to tax exemptions must file a Form 990 with the IRS. This form, which is about 20 pages long including schedules, requires an exempt entity to report on items of revenue, including a balance sheet. The form also asks the organization questions about the organization's operation, mostly relating to issues dealing with the organizations tax-exempt status. The public is entitled to inspect this form.

## Disclosure Requirements

In addition to annual information returns, nonprofit organizations are required to disclose information about their operations. The reason behind these requirements is to ensure that each nonprofit organization is acting in a transparent manner. Those items that are subject to disclosure requirements include the following:

- Substantiation of charitable gifts
- Quid pro quo contributions (i.e., where a donor pays an amount in excess of the value of goods or services received by the nonprofit entity)
- Gifts of property
- Dispositions of contributed property
- Appraisals
- Tax shelters

## Legal Protections for Officers, Directors, Employees, and Volunteers

State laws generally provide some protection for directors, employees, and volunteers against liability.

One type of law includes volunteer protection statutes, which limit liability that may be incurred by volunteers of a nonprofit entity. Congress also enacted the Volunteer Protection Act of 1997 to provide additional protection. However, several commentators have noted that these statutes have largely failed in their purpose because the statutes generally do not prohibit lawsuits against volunteers but rather merely limit liability in some circumstances.

Other state laws limit liability for directors and officers of nonprofit organizations. These laws restrict the amount that someone can recover for damages stemming from the activities of an officer or director of a nonprofit entity. Much like volunteer protection acts, however, commentators often note that these statutes that limit liability are fairly weak.

## State Laws Governing Nonprofit Corporations

Several states have modeled their state laws after the Model Nonprofit Corporation Act, which was approved by the Business Law Section of the American Bar Association in 1964 and revised in 1987. Other states have not explicitly adopted either version of the model act but may borrow provisions from the model legislation. Another source of law governing nonprofit entities appears in the form of the Uniform Unincorporated Nonprofit Association Act, which was approved by the National Conference of Commissioners on Uniform State Laws in 1996. Eleven states have adopted this uniform law, which serves as a complement to the model act.

ALABAMA: Alabama has adopted both the Model Nonprofit Corporation Act and the Uniform Unincorporated Nonprofit Association Act.

ARKANSAS: Arkansas has adopted both the Model Nonprofit Corporation Act and the Uniform Unincorporated Nonprofit Association Act.

COLORADO: Colorado has adopted the Uniform Unincorporated Nonprofit Association Act.

DELAWARE: Delaware has adopted the Uniform Unincorporated Nonprofit Association Act.

DISTRICT OF COLUMBIA: The District of Columbia has adopted the Uniform Unincorporated Nonprofit Association Act.

HAWAII: Hawaii has adopted the Uniform Unincorporated Nonprofit Association Act.

IDAHO: Idaho has adopted the Uniform Unincorporated Nonprofit Association Act.

INDIANA: Indiana has adopted the Model Nonprofit Corporation Act.

MISSISSIPPI: Mississippi has adopted the Model Nonprofit Corporation Act.

MONTANA: Montana has adopted the Model Nonprofit Corporation Act.

NORTH CAROLINA: North Carolina has adopted the Model Nonprofit Corporation Act.

SOUTH CAROLINA: South Carolina has adopted the Model Nonprofit Corporation Act.

TEXAS: Texas has adopted the Uniform Unincorporated Nonprofit Association Act.

WASHINGTON: Washington has adopted the Model Nonprofit Corporation Act.

WEST VIRGINIA: West Virginia has adopted the Uniform Unincorporated Nonprofit Association Act.

WISCONSIN: Wisconsin has adopted the Uniform Unincorporated Nonprofit Association Act.

WYOMING: Wyoming has adopted both the Model Nonprofit Corporation Act and the Uniform Unincorporated Nonprofit Association Act.

## Additional Resources

*The ABCs of Nonprofits.* Runquist, Lisa A., American Bar Association, 2005.

*Nonprofit Law Made Easy.* Hopkins, Bruce R., John Wiley & Sons, Inc., 2005.

*Starting and Managing a Nonprofit Organization: A Legal Guide, 4th Edition.* Hopkins, Bruce R., John Wiley & Sons, Inc., 2005.

## Organizations

### *Action Without Borders*
360 West 31st Street
New York, NY 10001 USA
Phone: (212) 843-3973
Fax: (212) 564-3377
URL: http://www.nonprofits.org

### *Society for Nonprofit Organizations*
5820 Canton Center Rd., Ste. #165
Canton, MI 48187 USA
Phone: (734) 451-3582
URL: http://www.snpo.org/index.php

# BUSINESS LAW

## OFFICER AND DIRECTOR LIABILITY

*Sections within this essay:*

- Background
- Functions of Officers and Directors
    - Rights and Powers of Officers
    - Rights and Powers of Directors
- Responsibilities of Officers and Directors
    - Decision-making Responsibilities
    - Fiduciary Duties
    - Duty of Care
    - Duty of Loyalty
- Business Judgment Rule
- Securities Regulations
- Rights and Duties of Shareholders
- Insurance and Indemnification
- State Laws Governing Officer and Director Liability
- Additional Resources

## Background

Decisions made by officers and directors of **corporations** typically have not subjected these individuals to personal liability. Even if an officer or director makes what turns out to be a bad business decision, the law does not render the person liable unless that decision violates a specific duty imposed on the officer or director.

On the other hand, the law governing corporations has expanded liability in many instances. This is especially applicable when a director or officer makes a decision that causes financial harm to a corporation, acts in their own interests in making decisions to the detriment of the corporation, or commits a wrongful act or crime.

High-profile cases involving wrongdoing by corporate executives in the early 2000s intensified the exposure on how decisions made by those executives can impact a large number of people. For example, Enron Corporation, an energy company based in Houston, Texas, suffered a major collapse in 2001 that led to the largest **bankruptcy** in U.S. history. Acts of **fraud** on the part of corporate officers and others caused many of the problems. Employees of the company lost most of their retirement investments as a result of the company's collapse. Other companies, such as WorldCom, Tyco International, and Global Crossing, suffered similar fates.

Both officers and directors of those corporations faced civil and criminal liability. Members of boards of directors for Enron and WorldCom agreed to pay millions of dollars out of their own pockets as part of settlement agreements. The U.S. Securities and Exchange Commission brought charges against top company officers, seeking to recover large fines in addition to criminal convictions. These incidents also led to major changes in federal securities laws regarding the potential liability for officers and directors.

## Officers' and Directors' Roles in Corporate Governance

Officer and directors share in the responsibility of governing a corporation. Shareholders in the corporation elect a board of directors to be in charge of the business. The board of directors is primarily responsible for making decisions, but not for carrying out those decisions. The task of carrying out the decisions made by the board falls on the officers, such as the chief executive officer and the chief financial officer.

State law prescribes the basic powers of officers and directors. Many states have adopted provisions of the American Bar Association's Model Business Corporation Act (MBCA) or Delaware's corporation laws. Other states have adopted their own unique laws. In general, if a state law does not provide a requirement pertaining to officers or directors, then the corporation's articles of incorporation and/or bylaws usually establish these requirements.

### Officers

The MBCA and the Delaware corporation statute allow a corporation's bylaws or board of directors to specify which officers the corporation must have. In many jurisdictions, though, state law requires each corporation to have certain officers, such as a president, secretary, and treasurer. Smaller corporations generally have only a few officers, such as a president who serves as the executive officer and a treasurer who serves as the financial officer. Larger corporations have many more officers and subordinates.

In some instances, a state's corporation statute may dictate the functions of corporate officers. Some states allow the corporation's articles of incorporation or bylaws to dictate the officers' functions. The MBCA provides, "Each officer has the authority and shall perform the functions set forth in the bylaws or, to the extent consistent with the bylaws, the functions prescribed by the board of directors or by direction of an officer authorized by the board of directors to prescribe the functions of other officers."

The issue of the authority that is delegated to an officer usually pertains to whether the officer has bound the corporation to another party. If the officer had express authority or implied authority to enter into a transaction on behalf of a corporation, then the officer's actions could lead to liability on the part of the corporation. Typically, however, an officer of a corporation, even if the officer is the president of the corporation, has less power than the board of directors.

### Directors

The vast majority of states and the MBCA require corporations to have one or more directors, as specified in the corporation's articles of incorporation or bylaws. This number may be increased or decreased as needed by amending the articles or bylaws. In many states, the board of directors itself may increase or decrease its size. Most modern **statutes** allow corporations to compensate directors for their services. A board may take an official action if it has a quorum present at its meeting, meaning that at least half of the board members are in attendance.

A director of a corporation is well-advised to stay abreast of the activities of the board. A director has the legal right to have access to information that allows the director to perform his or her job. To perform properly, a director should be diligent in studying the information that is available. This may include the following:

- Review board meeting agendas.

- Review minutes of corporation board meetings.

- Inspect books and records of the corporation, as well as any other data that the director may reasonably request.

- Inspect corporate facilities as appropriate

Directors may take steps to negate the possibility of becoming personally liable if the board of directors approves a questionable transaction. Under the MBCA, a board member who is present at a meeting assents to a board action unless the board member takes one of three steps. These include the following:

- Objecting at the beginning of a meeting to holding the meeting or transacting business at the meeting;

- Dissenting or abstaining from the action and having the dissent or abstention recorded in the minutes of the meeting; or

- Delivering written notice of the dissent or abstention to the presiding officer of the meeting before or immediately after the adjournment of the meeting.

A director who is not present at a meeting is not deemed to have assented to any action of the board in the director's absence. However, a director who votes in favor of a corporation's actions cannot later submit a dissent or abstention.

## Responsibilities of Officers and Directors

Whereas the powers of a director or an officer usually do not give rise to liability, the responsibilities of these positions may give rise to litigation. Directors and officers both owe certain duties to the corporation, and breach of these duties can give rise to liability.

### Decision-making Responsibilities

Most duties that apply to corporate governance relate to decision-making responsibilities. Duties most clearly apply to the directors of a corporation since the directors are the decision-makers in the business. Officers owe similar duties as directors, especially officers that exercise judgment or discretion. In a closely held corporation, the same individual may serve as an officer and as a director, and so the same duties would apply to the person's title in either position.

### Fiduciary Duties

Directors and officers owe what are termed **fiduciary** duties to the corporation due to the positions of trust that these individuals have within the corporation. The MBCA prescribes several aspects of this type of fiduciary relationship, including the following:

- Act in good faith: this is carried out by acting honestly and dealing fairly.

- Reasonably believe that the director is acting in the corporation's best interests: reviewed objectively, the director has acted with the corporation's interests in mind, rather than his or her own.

- Exercise duties with a level of care that a person in a like position would under similar circumstances.

### Duty of Care

The duty of care that an officer or director must exercise relates to the diligence that the person uses to make decisions. In order to fulfill this duty, an officer or director should follow several practices, including the following:

- Regularly attend board and committee meetings.

- Remain informed about the business and affairs of the corporation.

- Rely on information provided by others, such as reports, financial statements, and opinions.

- Make inquiries about problems that may arise with respect to the corporation.

### Duty of Loyalty

The duty of loyalty requires an officer or director to act in the best interests of the corporation and not in the person's own best interest. Several instances may give rise to issues that implicate the duty of loyalty, and an officer or director should be aware of how to handle each of these instances should they arise.

- An officer's or director's **conflict of interest** may or may not cause the person to breach the duty of loyalty, but the officer or director should always disclose conflicts with other directors. The disinterested directors may elect to allow the corporation complete a transaction where a conflict exists, but the interested director should not take part in this vote.

- If an officer or director identifies a business opportunity that could benefit the corporation, the officer or director must first allow the corporation to pursue the opportunity before pursuing the opportunity himself or herself.

- Any transaction that involves a conflict of interest or self-dealing on the part of an officer or director must be fair to the corporation.

- Any conflict of interest and subsequent actions taken by the board with respect to the conflict must be documented.

- Corporations should adopt written policies governing conflicts of interest.

- A corporation should seek independent advice regarding transactions that involve conflicts of interest.

## Business Judgment Rule

The business judgment rule is a doctrine developed by courts in reviewing the actions of directors. Generally, courts do not hold directors personally liable for a business decision, even when a decision turns out to be a bad one, so long as the director has not breached a duty to the corporation. A director who acts in good faith, remains informed about the corporation's business, and does not engage in self-dealing or transactions involving conflicts of interest will not be subject to personal liability.

## Securities Regulations

The Enron and WorldCom fiascos, along with others referred to in the discussion above, gave rise to the Sarbanes-Oxley Act of 2002, a federal statute that placed greater controls on how publicly traded corporations must conduct business. Under this statute, officer and directors who commit fraud or other crimes face greater penalties than they did in the past. The statute also gave greater power to the Securities and Exchange Commission in investigating and prosecuting acts of wrongdoing by corporate officers and directors.

## Rights and Duties of Shareholders

Shareholders in publicly-traded corporations generally are not involved in decisions made by the corporation, other than their act of electing members of the board of directors. In a closely-held corporation, however, it is common that a shareholder or group of shareholders control the corporation. Most courts require that the controlling shareholders uphold a duty of fairness in dealing with the non-controlling shareholders. Minority shareholders in some instances may also demand an appraisal of the fair value of their shares or may demand that the corporation dissolve due to one of several occurrences.

## Insurance and Indemnification

Liability **insurance** and indemnification by the corporation provide protection to an officer or director of a corporation from having to pay out-of-pocket for expenses that arise due to litigation. Indemnification refers to an agreement by the corporation to pay legal fees and other expenses when an officer or director faces a civil claim or criminal prosecution. An indemnification agreement also requires the corporation to pay a settlement or judgment against an officer or director. In some instances, public policy may limit when a corporation may indemnify an officer or director, such as when litigation is based on intentional wrongdoing.

Liability insurance for directors and officers, also referred to as D & O insurance, is provided by third party insurers to provide protection for the corporation and the directors and officers for expenses that arise due to litigation. Most state statutes expressly permit corporations to purchase D & O insurance, although policies are very expensive, potentially costing hundreds of thousands of dollars for larger corporations.

## State Laws Governing Officer and Director Liability

Most state statutes governing corporations contain provisions that prescribe the situations in which an officer or director may be liable. Below is a sampling of some of these state statutes.

ALABAMA: The statute imposes a duty of good faith on directors and officers. A director or an officer may not act with intent to depreciate stocks or bonds with the further intent to buy the depreciated stocks or bonds.

ARKANSAS: The statute does not allow a corporation to limit or eliminate liability for any of the following: breach of the duty of loyalty; acts that are not carried out in good faith or that involve intentional misconduct; unlawful distributions; transactions that involve an improper personal benefit; or any breach of duty that creates third party liability.

CALIFORNIA: The director's standard of care is to serve the corporation in good faith and in the best interests of the corporation. The director must exercise such care, including reasonable inquiry, as an ordinarily prudent person in a like position would use in similar circumstances.

CONNECTICUT: A director may be liable for the willful nonpayment of certain taxes. A director must perform duties in good faith, with care an ordinarily prudent person in a like position would exercise in a similar circumstance, and in a manner that the director reasonably believes is in the best interests of the corporation.

DELAWARE: A director may be liable for the payment of an unlawful dividend or from an unlawful stock purchase or redemption, unless the director's dissent or absence is noted in the corporation's minutes. Liability for breach of fiduciary duty may be limited or eliminated in some circumstances.

FLORIDA: A director who acts in good faith, in a manner that the director reasonably believes is in the best interests of the corporation, and with the degree of diligence, care, and skill that an ordinarily prudent person would exercise under similar circumstances will not be subject to personal liability.

HAWAII: A corporation may not limit or eliminate the personal liability of a director in the following instances: the director receives an a financial benefit for which the director is not entitled; the director intentionally inflicts harm on the corporation or the shareholders; or the director intentionally violates criminal law.

ILLINOIS: A director faces penalties for improperly paying dividends or distributing assets, for failing to take reasonable steps to cause notice of dissolution to be mailed to known creditors, or for actively carrying on a business after filing articles of dissolution. A corporate director who commits an act of commercial bride or who receives a commercial bribe is liable to the corporation for three times the aggregate amount given or received in the bribe, plus attorneys' fees.

KENTUCKY: A director is not liable for monetary damages unless the director has breached a fiduciary duty in a manner that constitutes willful misconduct or wanton or reckless disregard for the best interests of the corporation.

LOUISIANA: A director or an officer of a corporation may be liable if the corporation transacts business before capital is received or the director or officer consent to the issuance of shares in violation of the law.

MARYLAND: A corporation's charter may expand or limit the liability of a director for money damages unless: the director received an improper benefit or profit; the director is adjudicated to have been guilty of active and deliberate dishonesty that was material to the cause of action; or the director was also a director of certain banking and/or financial institutions.

NEVADA: A director may be liable for the following: breach of fiduciary duty where breach involved intentional misconduct, fraud, or knowing violation of the law; wrongful declaration of distributions; or debts or liabilities where the director acts as the alter ego of the corporation.

NEW YORK: A director who votes for or concurs in the following actions may be liable to the corporation for the benefit of creditors and shareholders: improper declaration of a dividend; improper purchase or redemption of the corporation's shares; improper distribution of assets after dissolution; or improper loans made to the director.

TENNESSEE: A director may not participate in a transaction involving a known conflict of interest without the approval of the shareholders or other directors unless the transaction was fair; make loans to officers or directors without shareholder approval;

or vote for or assent to distribution in violation of the law or the corporation's charter.

TEXAS: A director or an officer may demonstrate that he or she exercised ordinary care by relying on certain statements, opinions, reports, and other documents. An officer may be personally liable for tortious acts when the officer participates in the wrongdoing.

## Additional Resources

*Corporation Law.* Gevurtz, Franklin A., West Group, 2000.

*Folk on the Delaware General Corporation Law.* Rodman Ward, Jr., Edward P. Welch, and Andrew J. Turezyn, Aspen Law and Business, 1999.

*The Law of Corporations in a Nutshell.* Hamilton, Robert W., Thomson/West, 2000.

*Macey on Corporation Laws.* Johnathan R. Macey, Aspen Publishers, 2005.

*Managing Closely Held Corporations: A Legal Guidebook.* Committee on Corporate Laws, American Bar Association, 2003.

*West's Encyclopedia of American Law, 2nd Edition.* West Group, 2004.

## Organizations

### Association of Corporate Counsel
1025 Connecticut Avenue, NW, Suite 200
Washington, D.C. 20036 USA
Phone: (202) 293-4103
URL: http:\\www.state.de.us.corp

### Business Law Section, American Bar Association
321 North Clark Street
Chicago, Illinois 60610 USA
Phone: (800) 285-2221
URL: http://www.abanet.org/buslaw/home.shtml

### Council of Better Business Bureaus
4200 Wilson Blvd, Suite 800
Arlington, Virginia 22203 USA
Phone: (703) 276-0100
URL: http://www.bbb.org

### Delaware Division of Corporations
401 Federal Street, Suite 4
Dover, Delaware 19901 USA
Phone: (302) 739-3073
URL: http:\\www.state.de.us.corp

# BUSINESS LAW

## PARTNERSHIPS

*Sections within this essay*

## Background

When two or more people carry on a business for profit, the law recognizes the existence of a general partnership. Unlike **corporations**, limited liability companies, limited partnerships, and limited liability partnerships, owners of a business do not need to follow specific formalities to form a general partnership. At the same time, however, partners are not protected from liability for the business' debts. Sole proprietorships and general partnerships are considered the "default" forms of business when an individual or more than one individual establish a business, since one form of business entity or the other is generally established if the parties do not choose an alternate form.

Partnerships are governed in the vast majority of states by one of the versions of the Uniform Partnership Act (UPA), which was originally drafted by the Uniform Law Commissioners in 1914. Prior to 1994, every state, with the exception of Louisiana, adopted the UPA. The National Conference of Commissioners on Uniform State Laws significantly revised the UPA in 1994, with subsequent modifications in 1995, 1996, and 1997. The majority of states have adopted the 1997 version of the act, which is generally referred to as the Revised Uniform Partnership Act (RUPA). The RUPA revised the UPA in several key areas, though many of the basic rules governing partnerships did not change from the older law to the new law.

The UPA and RUPA, in many ways, provide "default" rules that govern general partnerships. That is, the rules in the UPA and RUPA govern the partnership, unless the partners agree otherwise. Thus, each partner generally has a right to manage the partnership that is equal to the rights of other partners. Similarly, partners can agree how they will share profits, how they will contribute to pay for losses, how they will divide the labor, and how the partnership will

**dissolve** when the partnership ends. Parties cannot, however, agree to shield personal liability from one or more of the partners. If a partner or partners want to avoid personal liability for the debts of the partnership, they will need to form one of the business entities that provide limited liability.

## Forming and Managing a General Partnership

Several of the rules related to general partnerships vary between the UPA and the RUPA. Individuals who are forming a general partnership or are concerned about management issues should consult their state statutes to determine which law is in effect in that state.

### Characteristics of a General Partnership

A general partnership must consist of two or more individuals or entities, including another partnership or corporation. Thus, it is possible that two very large corporations could form a partnership between the two entities, though in the modern business world, when large entities agree to form a new business entity between them, they most often form some kind of limited liability entity. In order to form a general partnership, the business must be unincorporated and intended to make a profit. The "unincorporated" requirement is obvious; an entity that has complied with the formalities to form a corporation cannot be a partnership. Partnership law is limited to entities organized to make a profit, since partnership law is a subcategory of commercial law. Other business entities, such as corporations, do not need to be formed to seek a profit. Agreeing to share a profit creates a rebuttable presumption under the RUPA that a partnership exists.

Generally, each partner in a partnership has something to offer the business, including labor, ideas, money, and/or property. Each of the partners in a general partnership co-owns the business and has a right to manage the business with other partners. This right, however, can be modified by agreement of the partners. Similarly, partners have a general right to share profits and contribute to pay for losses, though either of these can be modified by agreement of the parties.

Many partnerships are formed when one or more partners agree to provide money, property, and other types of capital to the business ("capital partners"), while one or more of the other partners agree to provide work and other labor expertise

("labor partners"). For example, assume that two people agree to form a business to build custom furniture. One partner agrees to provide the work facility and office and also agrees to supply $100,000 to finance the business. The other partner, who is an expert in building furniture, agrees to build all of the furniture and manage the business. The first partner is the capital partner, while the latter is the labor partner. This general partnership can be beneficial to both parties if the business is successful but can cause significant problems if the business fails. Many of these problems are cause for disputes over which party should bear the burden of the losses suffered by the partnership.

Partnerships are generally categorized in three types, which are defined by the agreement of the partners. In a partnership at will, every partner has the right to end the partnership, subject to some restrictions. In a partnership for a term, the partners' agreement determines the time when a partnership will end. In a partnership for a particular undertaking, the partners' agreement indicates that completion of a particular task or goal will cause the partnership to end.

### Consent and the Partnership Agreement

As noted above, forming a partnership requires few specific formalities, such as a written agreement or registration with a state agency. Nevertheless, all parties that are considered partners must consent to be such. The consent may be express, such as signing a written partnership agreement or implied by the conduct of the parties. Parties do not need to agree specifically to form a "partnership;" rather, their agreement or conduct must be such that they agree to run a business for profit. Even if the parties agree that their business will not be labeled a partnership, the business may be found to be one if it meets the definition of a partnership.

If two or more individuals enter a partnership without a partnership agreement, problems are likely to arise. The **default** rules found in the UPA and the RUPA may not be sufficient for the parties based on their wants and needs when they formed the business. Similarly, the rules in the UPA and RUPA may not reflect the understanding of the parties when they entered into the business. Since all partners are liable for the debts of the partnership, if a partnership is formed inadvertently, it may cause significant problems for the partner who was not aware of the legal consequences of his or her decision. Should an individual wish to enter into a business that has not been registered as a limited liability entity, he or she should be sure to demand the drafting of a written partnership agreement so that the understanding and agreement of the parties can be reflected more clearly in a document.

### Profit Sharing

Agreeing to share profits is a precondition for the formation of a partnership. Sharing profits is not the same as sharing revenues. Revenues refer to all of the money received by a business, including income, receipts, or proceeds. Profits are the amount remaining of the revenue after expenses incurred by the business are subtracted. If one party agrees to share revenues with another party, but the agreement makes not stipulation for profits, then a partnership has not been formed. The focus on profits requires the partners to pay attention to the management of the entire business, not only the amount of money taken in by the business. By comparison, a person who receives revenues, but not profits, is much more likely to focus on the sales of a business but not the costs in doing business.

Partners do not need to share profits equally. Under both the UPA and the RUPA, partners can agree to the division of profits made by a business. In a situation where there is a capital partner and a labor partner, the partnership agreement will most likely include a salary for the labor partner, with the capital partner receiving the profits.

### Loss Sharing

An agreement to share losses in all jurisdictions is strong **evidence** that a partnership exists. Though neither the UPA nor the RUPA expressly requires an agreement to share losses to find that a partnership exists, some jurisdictions require a finding of such an agreement as a prerequisite for a finding that a partnership has been formed. Under both the UPA and the RUPA, the definition of partnership does not include sharing losses but rather requires that losses be shared in the same proportion as profits. Like many other rules in the UPA and the RUPA, the parties can agree otherwise.

### Ownership and Management

All partners in a general partnership are considered co-owners. By default, partners also have equal rights to manage the partnership. If an agreement contemplates joint ownership of a business for profit, as well as joint decision-making regarding the partnership's business, then the likelihood increases that a partnership exists. More difficult questions are raised when co-ownership and co-management are

considered in the context of control of the partnership. For example, under the default rules in the UPA and RUPA, both a capital partner and a labor partner have equal rights to manage the partnership, even if the labor partner is much more qualified to manage the business. Similarly, all partners have the authority to bind a partnership by transacting partnership business. In almost all situations, it is beneficial to include management and control provisions in a partnership agreement to avoid conflicts.

## Liability and Duties of Partners in a General Partnership

### Partner as an Agent of a Partnership

Under both the UPA and the RUPA, all partners serve as general agents of the partnership. Accordingly, partners may bind the partnership through their actions. They often have the actual authority to conduct partnership business, though the extent of this authority often focuses on the language included in a partnership agreement. Authority may be implied through the action or inaction of other partners in the management of the business. For example, if one partner has entered into contracts on behalf of the partnership in the past, and none of the partners has objected (assuming they have knowledge of the transaction), the partner most likely has implied authority to enter into the contract.

### Tort Liability to Third Parties

Since partners are considered agents of the partnership, a partner's wrongful act or omission can bind the partnership if the wrongdoing partner has acted within the ordinary course of the partnership's business. Such liability is referred to as vicarious liability, a term that is also used when a business is liable for the acts of an employee acting within the scope of his or her employment. Moreover, partners in a partnership generally are jointly and severally liable for torts charged against the partnership. Thus, any or all of the partners in a partnership can be sued individually for the entire amount of the injury caused by the partner. For example, if two lawyers form a general partnership, and one lawyer is liable for **malpractice**, then the person injured by the malpractice may sue the partnership, the lawyer who committed malpractice, and/or the other lawyer in the partnership. In this situation, the person who is injured could chose to sue only the lawyer who did not commit malpractice, since that lawyer is jointly and severally liable for the torts of the other partner acting in the partnership's business.

Well-planned businesses will usually avoid the seemingly harsh consequences caused by joint and several liability. One of the more obvious solutions is for the partnership to form a limited liability entity, such as a **limited liability partnership**. Other solutions may be provided in a partnership agreement, such as the inclusion of a provision requiring the wrongdoing partner to indemnify the other partners if the other partners are vicariously liable for the torts of the wrongdoing partner.

### Contract Liability to Third Parties

Under the UPA, partners are jointly liable for contractual liability of the partnership. The RUPA modifies this provision so that partners are jointly and severally liable for the contractual liability of the partnership. The difference between the two types of liability is really procedural. If partners are jointly liable, all of the partners must be sued at the same time, and omission of a partner means that the suit must be dropped. By comparison, if partners are jointly and severally liable, suits may proceed against individual partners even if some partners are omitted from the suit.

### Tax Liability of Partners and Partnerships

One of the most practical benefits of forming a partnership, as opposed to a corporation, is the tax treatment of partnerships by the federal government in the Internal Revenue Code. Owners of a corporation, in effect, pay double taxes. The corporation itself must pay taxes on business income. The money, which has already been taxed, is eventually distributed to pay salaries, dividends, and other forms of income to those involved in the corporation. These individuals must pay tax on the money received, even though the corporation was initially taxed. Partnerships, by comparison, are treated as so-called "pass-through" entities. The partnership itself does not pay taxes. The partnership's income "passes through" the partnership and is distributed to the partners. When the partners pay taxes on their income, this money has not yet been taxed.

### Ownership of Property

Since partners often contribute property for the use of the partnership, the question of ownership of this property is sometimes difficult. For example, if a partner purchases **personal property** with his own money, but the property is used exclusively by the partnership, then it could be questionable whether this property is the partner's separate property or whether it is the partnership's property. The UPA creates a presumption that property acquired

with partnership funds is partnership property, unless the partners intend otherwise. The RUPA extends this presumption and adds a presumption that if one or more partners purchase property in their own name and without use of partnership funds, the property is considered the separate property of the partner or partners. This is true even if the property is used for partnership purposes.

Both the partnership and individual partners can hold legal title to real property, and both the UPA and the RUPA contain provisions prescribing the conveyance of real property by partners or the partnership. Under the RUPA, partners and partnerships have the option of filing and recording a statement indicating the authority of the partners to transfer real property in the name of the partnership.

## Duties of the Partners

Partners in a partnership owe each other certain **fiduciary** duties. One of the more significant changes between the UPA and the RUPA was the clarification of fiduciary duties in the RUPA. Under the revised act, partners owe each other the duty of loyalty and the duty of care. The RUPA restricts the ability of partners to waive these fiduciary duties.

### Duty of Loyalty

The duty of loyalty refers to the duty of a partner to refrain from competing with the partnership in another endeavor or profiting individually from a transaction related to the partnership. This duty does not mean that a partner cannot further his or her own interests; a partner may not further his or her own interests to the detriment of the partnership. Application of this duty may arise when one of the partners owns several businesses, and the potential for competition between a separate business and the partnership arises. Another situation occurs when one the partners wants to leave the partnership. It is not uncommon that the partner may take steps to set up a separate business, and establishing the new business may conflict with the interests of the partnership.

### Duty of Care

The duty of care does not refer to acts of mere **negligence** by a partner. For example, if a partner unintentionally makes a bad business decision, his or her negligence will not necessarily violate the duty of care. On the other hand, the duty of care proscribes **gross negligence**, recklessness, intentional misconduct, or knowing violation of the law on the part of each of the partners. Though partners cannot waive the duty of care under the RUPA, partners can hold themselves to a higher standard of care, including ordinary negligence.

## Dissociation and Dissolution

The RUPA made other significant changes with respect to the **dissolution** of a partnership and winding up of partnership affairs. Under the UPA, if a partner withdraws from the partnership, an event occurs that ends the partnership, the partners agree to end the partnership, or any of a number of situations occurs, the partnership dissolves. When dissolution occurs, the partnership's business generally ends, the affairs of the business wind up, and partnership property is sold. Partnership agreements, even before the enactment of the RUPA, often provide a method whereby the withdrawing partner's interests are purchased and the partnership continued. In the absence of such an agreement, the remaining partners may continue the partnership's business, but the resulting business is considered a completely new partnership.

The RUPA altered this situation, providing that when certain events occur, such as a partner's withdrawal from the partnership, the partnership is not necessarily dissolved. The RUPA introduced dissociation, whereby a partner can be dissociated from a partnership without the partnership ending. If a partner dissociates from a partnership, the partnership will not necessarily dissolve. The remaining partners can instead purchase the interests of the dissociating partner and continue partnership business.

When a partnership is dissolved, it enters into a stage called winding up. Both the UPA and the RUPA provide rather detailed provisions for winding up the affairs of the partnership. One restriction is that partners who have wrongfully caused the dissolution of the partnership or have wrongfully dissociated from the partnership cannot participate in the winding up process. The most significant part of the winding up process is the **liquidation** of partnership assets and payment of partnership creditors. When the assets are liquidated, creditors who are not also partners are generally paid first. If a partner is also a **creditor** of the partnership, he or she is then reimbursed. Once each of the creditors is reimbursed, partners may recover their capital contributions. Finally, if assets remain, the partners will receive their share, in accordance with a partnership agreement or according to the provisions of the UPA or the RUPA.

## State Laws Governing Partnerships

The majority of states have adopted the Revised Uniform Partnership Act, though some have retained the Uniform Partnership Act. Some states have modified certain provisions of their versions of the **uniform acts**, so researchers should be sure to check their states' versions of the act to determine which provisions may differ from the uniform law. The only state that has not adopted the uniform law is Louisiana.

ALABAMA: Adopted the Revised Uniform Partnership Act in 1998. Previously adopted the Uniform Partnership Act in 1972.

ALASKA: Adopted the Uniform Partnership Act in 1917.

ARIZONA: Adopted the Revised Uniform Partnership Act in 1996. Previously adopted the Uniform Partnership Act in 1954.

CALIFORNIA: Adopted the Revised Uniform Partnership Act in 1996. Previously adopted the Uniform Partnership Act.

COLORADO: Adopted the Revised Uniform Partnership Act in 1997. Previously adopted the Uniform Partnership Act in 1931.

CONNECTICUT: Adopted the Revised Uniform Partnership Act in 1995. Previously adopted the Uniform Partnership Act in 1961.

DELAWARE: Adopted the Revised Uniform Partnership Act in 1999. Previously adopted the Uniform Partnership Act in 1947.

DISTRICT OF COLUMBIA: Adopted the Revised Uniform Partnership Act in 1997. Previously adopted the Uniform Partnership Act in 1962.

FLORIDA: Adopted the Revised Uniform Partnership Act in 1995. Previously adopted the Uniform Partnership Act in 1973.

GEORGIA: Adopted the Uniform Partnership Act.

HAWAII: Adopted the Revised Uniform Partnership Act in 1999. Previously adopted the Uniform Partnership Act in 1972.

IDAHO: Adopted the Revised Uniform Partnership Act in 1998. Previously adopted the Uniform Partnership Act in 1919.

ILLINOIS: Adopted the Uniform Partnership Act in 1917.

INDIANA: Adopted the Uniform Partnership Act in 1949.

IOWA: Adopted the Revised Uniform Partnership Act in 1998. Previously adopted the Uniform Partnership Act in 1971.

KANSAS: Adopted the Revised Uniform Partnership Act in 1998. Previously adopted the Uniform Partnership Act in 1972.

LOUISIANA: Louisiana is the only state that has adopted neither the Uniform Partnership Act nor the Revised Uniform Partnership Act. Though many of the provisions of the Louisiana law governing partnership are similar to the UPA and RUPA, individuals in Louisiana should consult the Louisiana Civil Code to determine the law of Louisiana with respect to partnerships.

MAINE: Adopted the Uniform Partnership Act in 1973.

MARYLAND: Adopted the Revised Uniform Partnership Act in 1997. Previously adopted the Uniform Partnership Act in 1916.

MASSACHUSETTES: Adopted the Uniform Partnership Act in 1922.

MICHIGAN: Adopted the Uniform Partnership Act in 1917.

MINNESOTA: Adopted the Revised Uniform Partnership Act in 1997. Previously adopted the Uniform Partnership Act in 1921.

MISSISSIPPI: Adopted the Uniform Partnership Act in 1976.

MISSOURI: Adopted the Uniform Partnership Act in 1949.

MONTANA: Adopted the Revised Uniform Partnership Act in 1997. Previously adopted the Uniform Partnership Act in 1947.

NEBRASKA: Adopted the Revised Uniform Partnership Act in 1997. Previously adopted the Uniform Partnership Act in 1943.

NEVADA: Adopted the Uniform Partnership Act in 1931.

NEW HAMPSHIRE: Adopted the Uniform Partnership Act in 1973.

NEW JERSEY: Adopted the Revised Uniform Partnership Act in 2001. Previously adopted the Uniform Partnership Act in 1919.

NEW MEXICO: Adopted the Revised Uniform Partnership Act in 1997. Previously adopted the Uniform Partnership Act in 1947.

NEW YORK: Adopted the Uniform Partnership Act in 1919.

NORTH CAROLINA: Adopted the Uniform Partnership Act in 1941.

NORTH DAKOTA: Adopted the Revised Uniform Partnership Act in 1997. Previously adopted the Uniform Partnership Act in 1959.

OHIO: Adopted the Uniform Partnership Act in 1949.

OKLAHOMA: Adopted the Revised Uniform Partnership Act in 1997. Previously adopted the Uniform Partnership Act in 1959.

OREGON: Adopted the Revised Uniform Partnership Act in 1997. Previously adopted the Uniform Partnership Act in 1939.

PENNSYLVANIA: Adopted the Uniform Partnership Act in 1915.

RHODE ISLAND: Adopted the Uniform Partnership Act in 1957.

SOUTH CAROLINA: Adopted the Uniform Partnership Act in 1950.

SOUTH DAKOTA: Adopted the Revised Uniform Partnership Act in 2001. Previously adopted the Uniform Partnership Act in 1923.

TENNESSEE: Adopted the Revised Uniform Partnership Act in 2001. Previously adopted the Uniform Partnership Act in 1917.

TEXAS: Adopted the Revised Uniform Partnership Act in 1998. Previously adopted the Uniform Partnership Act in 1961.

UTAH: Adopted the Uniform Partnership Act in 1921.

VERMONT: Adopted the Revised Uniform Partnership Act in 1998. Previously adopted the Uniform Partnership Act in 1941.

VIRGINIA: Adopted the Revised Uniform Partnership Act in 1996. Previously adopted the Uniform Partnership Act in 1918.

WASHINGTON: Adopted the Revised Uniform Partnership Act in 1998. Previously adopted the Uniform Partnership Act in 1945.

WEST VIRGINIA: Adopted the Revised Uniform Partnership Act in 1995. Previously adopted the Uniform Partnership Act in 1953.

WISCONSIN: Adopted the Uniform Partnership Act in 1915.

WYOMING: Adopted the Revised Uniform Partnership Act in 1993. Previously adopted the Uniform Partnership Act in 1917.

## Additional Resources

*Agency and Partnerships: Examples and Explanations* Kleinberger, Daniel S., Aspen Law and Business, 1995.

*Agency, Partnership, and the LLC in a Nutshell.* Hayes, J. Dennis, West Group, 2001.

*Partnerships: Laws of the United States.* Sitarz, Daniel, Nova Publishing Company, 1999.

*Partnership Laws of the United States: Introduction and List of Articles.* USLaw.com, 1999. Available at http://www.uslaw.com/library/article/noparIntro.html

*Uniform Partnership Act.* National Conference of Commissioners on Uniform State Laws, 1997. Available at http://www.law.upenn.edu/bll/ulc/upa/upa1200.htm

## Organizations

### Council of Better Business Bureaus (CBBB)
4200 Wilson Blvd., Suite 800

Arlington, VA, VA 22203-1838 USA
Phone: (703) 276-0100
Fax: (703) 525-8277
URL: http://www.bbb.org/

### National Conference of Commissioners on Uniform State Laws (NCCUSL)
211 E. Ontario Street, Suite 1300
Chicago, IL, IL 60611 USA
Phone: (312) 915-0195
Fax: (312) 915-0187
E-Mail: nccusl@nccusl.org
URL: http://www.nccusl.org/

### Small Business Advancement National Center (SBANC)
University of Central Arkansas
College of Business Administration
UCA Box 5018
201 Donaghey Avenue
Conway, AR, AR 72053-0001 USA
Phone: (501) 450-5300
Fax: (501) 450-5360
URL: http://www.saber.uca.edu/

### United States Chamber of Commerce
1615 H Street, NW
Washington, DC, DC 20062-2000 USA
Phone: (202) 659-6000
E-Mail: custsvc@uschamber.com
URL: http://www.uschamber.com

# BUSINESS LAW

## SHAREHOLDER RIGHTS

*Sections within this essay:*

## Background

Investors who purchase **corporate** stock enjoy a number of rights pertaining to their ownership. Unlike partnership law, where the owners of businesses are also the primary managers of the businesses, owners of a corporation generally do not run the company. Shareholders in a corporation are shielded from personal liability for the debts and obligations of the corporation. However, shareholders can lose their investments should the corporation fail.

Laws governing **corporations** in the United States are fairly standard from one state to the next. The commissioners on uniform state laws drafted the Uniform Business Corporations Act in 1928, though only three states adopted this act. The American **Bar Association** in 1950 drafted the Model Business Corporation Act, which subsequently has been modified numerous times. The last major redrafting occurred in 1984, but there were substantive revisions in 2002 and 2005. A large majority of states have adopted all or a significant portion of the Model Act. Other states have modified their own state corporation statutes to contain sections similar to the Model Act. Delaware's corporation **statute** is also significant, since most large, public corporations are incorporated in that state.

The rights of shareholders depend largely on provisions in a corporation's charter and by-laws. These are the first documents which a shareholder should consult when determining his or her rights in a corporation. Shareholders also generally enjoy the following types of rights:

- Voting rights on issues that affect the corporation as a whole

- Rights related to the assets of the corporation

- Rights related to the transfer of stock

- Rights to receive dividends as declared by the board of directors of the corporation

- Rights to inspect the records and books of the corporation

- Rights to bring suit against the corporation for wrongful acts by the directors and officers of the corporation

- Rights to share in the proceeds recovered when the corporation liquidates its assets

## Ownership of Stock

The two broad types of financing available to a corporation include equity financing and debt financing. Equity financing involves the issuance of stock, which investors purchase and which represent a share in the ownership of the corporation. The two basic types of stock are **common stock** and **preferred stock**. Debt financing involves a loan of money from an investor to the corporation in exchange for debt **securities**, such as a bond. Holders of debt securities generally do not enjoy the same rights as shareholders in terms of voting rights, participating rights, or other rights related to the ownership of stock.

### Common Stock

The lowest level of stock in a corporation is common stock. The rights related to common stock depend largely on the **articles of incorporation** and by-laws of the corporation. In general, owners of common stock have voting rights in a corporation as well as rights to receive distributions of money from the corporation (dividends). In a successful corporation, common stock ownership can be very lucrative. However, if a corporation is unsuccessful, common stock owners are usually the last in line to receive a distribution of the corporation's assets when the corporation's assets are liquidated.

State statutes often vary with respect to the **default** rights of common stock owners. The corporation may also issue multiple classes of common stock, such as nonvoting common stock or common stock with special **dividend** rights.

### Preferred Stock

Unlike common stock, holders of preferred stock are entitled to fixed dividends and fixed rights to receive a percentage of a corporation's assets are liquidated. With respect to the dividend rights, an example of such stock would include a name such as "$20 preferred," which means the shareholder has a right to receive $20 in dividends per share before dividends are paid to common stock owners.

It is noteworthy that the board of directors in a corporation usually has the discretion to decide whether dividends are issued in a given year. If dividends are not distributed during one year, whether preferred stock owners receive dividends in a subse-

quent year depends on whether the preferred stock is cumulative or noncumulative. If the rights are cumulative, the corporation must be dividends during some subsequent year. If the rights are noncumulative, the rights to receive dividends are lost if the corporation does not issue dividends in a given year.

Preferred stock owners generally do not have the same rights to vote as common stock owners. However, a corporation may grant voting rights and additional rights in its articles of incorporation or other provisions. State statutes also provide some rights to preferred stock owners by default.

### Bonds and Debentures

Corporations may seek to borrow money in addition to (or in lieu of) issuing stock. One method for borrowing money is to exchange the loan for a debt security that can be traded on a public market. **Bonds** are long-term debt securities that are secured by corporate assets. Debentures are unsecured debt securities. Owners of debt securities generally do not enjoy the same types of rights are owners of stock. However, a corporation may grant voting rights to the owners of debt securities. These owners may also have the right to redeem debt securities in exchange for stock.

## Shareholder Meetings and Voting Rights

Shareholders hold general meetings on an annual basis or at fixed times according to the by-laws of the corporation. The primary purpose of these meetings is for shareholders to elect the directors of the corporation, though shareholders may also vote on a number of additional issues. Persons with authority to do so may also call special meetings on matters that require immediate attention, though only those issues set forth in the notice of the special meeting may be the subject of the vote.

A quorum must be present at the shareholder meeting for a decision to be binding. The typical quorum consists of more than half of the outstanding shares of the corporation. This percentage may be increased or decreased in the by-laws of the corporation. Prior to each shareholder meeting, a list of shareholders eligible to vote must be prepared. Shareholders have the right to inspect the voting list at any time.

Shareholders may appoint proxies to vote their shares, which is common in publicly-held corporations. Most states prescribe few specific rules with respect to the proxy appointment, other than the issue of whether this appointment may be revoked. Proxy appointments must be in writing, and the proxy does not need to be a fellow shareholder. Since the relationship between the shareholder and the proxy is one of principal and agent, the proxy must abide by the instructions of the shareholder.

Shareholders by unanimous consent may conduct business without holding a shareholder meeting. Such actions are more common in closely held corporations, where shareholder actions are typically unanimous. In a larger, publicly held corporation, such actions are much less practical, especially because decisions of the shareholders affect a larger number of people.

Matters upon which shareholders vote, in addition to the election of the directors, depend on the issues affecting the corporation. The following are the most significant of these matters.

- Approval or disapproval of changes in the articles of incorporation

- Approval or disapproval of a merger with another corporation

- Approval or disapproval of the sale of substantially all of the corporation's assets that is not in the ordinary course of the corporation's business

- Approval or disapproval of the voluntary **dissolution** of the corporation

- Approval or disapproval of corporate transactions where some directors have a conflict of interest

- Approval or disapproval of amendments to **bylaws** or articles of incorporation

- Make nonbinding recommendations about the governance and management of the corporation to the board of directors

## Shareholder Rights, Actions, and Liabilities

As noted above, many of the rights afforded to shareholders are contained in each corporation's articles of incorporation or bylaws. It is also noteworthy that shareholders generally do not have the right to vote on management issues that occur in the ordinary course of the corporation's business. Many decisions of the corporation must be made by the board

of directors or officers of the corporation, and in most cases, shareholders may not compel the board or officers to take or refrain from taking any action.

### Shareholder Direct Litigation

Shareholders can protect their ownership rights in their shares by bringing a direct action against a corporation. Such cases may involve contract rights related to the shares; rights granted to the shareholder in a statute; rights related to the recovery of dividends; and rights to examine the books and records of a corporation. Some cases are not appropriate for direct actions by a shareholder against a corporation, however. For example, a shareholder may not bring a direct action against a corporation by alleging that an officer has breached a **fiduciary** duty owed to the corporation. Such a case involves all shareholders and is more appropriate as a derivative action. By comparison, a shareholder may bring a direct action if he or she has been prevented from voting his or her shares in a vote.

### Shareholder Derivative Litigation

Shareholders may bring suit as representatives of the corporation in a derivative action. Such an action is designed to prevent wrongdoing by the officers or directors of the corporation or to seek a remedy for such wrongdoing. These suits are generally brought when the corporation itself (through its officers and directors) refuses to bring suit itself. A party bringing a derivative suit acts as a representative of an appropriate class of shareholders, and in the action the shareholders enforce claims that would be appropriate between the corporation and the officers and directors of the corporation. For example, if the officers of the corporation have breached a fiduciary duty owed to the corporation, shareholders may bring a derivative action to protect the interests of the corporation on behalf of the corporation. While these actions in many cases protect the rights of the corporation and shareholders of the corporation, these actions are often controversial. Shareholders should study the procedural and substantive provisions of state statutes to determine whether the action is appropriate and determine which formalities should be followed with respect to these actions.

### Shareholder Preemptive Rights

Corporations retain the right to issue new shares of stock, which could dilute the ownership of existing stockholders. Existing shareholders often hold preemptive rights, which allow the shareholders to purchase these new shares of stock before they are made available to the public. Thus, if a shareholder owns 10 percent of a corporation, and the corporation issues new stock, the shareholder would own less than 10 percent if he or she did not purchase new stock. If the shareholder exercises preemptive rights, he or she may purchase as many new shares as necessary to retain that 10 percent interest.

### Shareholder Liabilities

As the owners of a limited liability entity, shareholders are generally shielded from personal liability for claims against the corporation. Thus, if a corporation incurs a debt or obligation against it, creditors cannot recover the personal assets of the shareholders. However, the average life of a corporation in the United States is only seven years, and more than half fail before seven years have elapsed. A shareholder can lose his or her entire investment if the corporation fails.

## Transfer of Stock Ownership

### Securities Laws

Federal and state securities laws govern the distribution and exchange of stock in a corporation. Many of these laws are designed to avoid **fraud** by the corporation to the detriment of prospective or existing shareholders, so shareholders should consult relevant securities laws if they believe they have been defrauded in the sale or exchange of stock. The sale and exchange of stock through electronic media have provided new methods for defrauding investors, and new securities laws have been enacted in the past ten years to address these issues.

### Conversion Rights

Owners of one type of stock may want, at some point, to convert their stock to a different type of stock in the same corporation, rather than sell the stock outright. For example, an owner of preferred nonvoting stock may want to own common stock that has voting rights. If the shareholder has conversion rights, he or she may convert the preferred stock for the common stock. These rights can, and often are, limited by the corporation.

### Redemption Rights

Shareholders may also possess redemption rights, which permit the shareholders to redeem their stock to the corporation for a value specified in the articles of incorporation or set by the board. In other words, the shareholder can demand that the corporation repurchase the shareholder's stock. This right may be limited by the corporation.

## Sharing Proceeds Upon Liquidation of Corporate Assets

When a corporation dissolves, one of its first actions is the **liquidation** of corporate assets. Creditors of the corporation are the first to be paid with the funds received from the liquidation. Owners of debt securities are also paid before shareholders. Once these debts are paid, the remainder is paid to the stockowners. Preferred stock is paid before common stock. Some preferred stock includes a liquidation preference that fixes a price per share of preferred stock. If preferred stock includes this preference, it must be paid before the corporation pays any amount to the common stock. Common stock owners do not have any special liquidation rights and will receive assets on dissolution only after senior claims have been paid.

## State Laws Governing Shareholder Rights

Since the majority of states have adopted the Model Business Corporation Act, shareholder rights are generally consistent from one state to the next. State statutes should be consulted to determine whether an individual state has granted any specific rights to shareholders of businesses incorporated in that state.

ALABAMA: Alabama statute is based on the Model Business Corporation Act. Shareholders are granted preemptive rights in the statute. Shareholders may bring derivative actions for fraud, dishonesty, or gross abuse on the part of the directors. Holders of 10 percent of the votes may call a special meeting.

ALASKA: A shareholder may bring a derivative action on behalf of the corporation. Each record shareholder is entitled to written notice of meetings.

ARIZONA: Arizona statute is based on the Model Business Corporation Act. Corporations must provide shareholders with a stock certificate upon request. Shareholders may petition for a special meeting.

ARKANSAS: Arkansas statute is based on the Model Business Corporation Act. Shareholders are entitled to notice of annual and special shareholder meetings. The statute grants preemptive rights to shareholders.

CALIFORNIA: The statute provides special rights to shareholders who dissent to corporate reorganization or merger.

COLORADO: Colorado statute is based on the Model Business Corporation Act. Statute provides special rules regarding entitlement to voting with respect to fractional shares. The statute provides specific rules regarding derivative actions.

CONNECTICUT: The articles of incorporation of a corporation must provide preemptive rights. The statute governs derivative suits brought by shareholders.

DELAWARE: The statute provides specific rules regarding derivative actions. The statute prescribes specific rules shareholder meetings and voting, including voting agreements and voting by proxy.

DISTRICT OF COLUMBIA: The statute is based on the Model Business Corporation Act. The statute permits derivative actions brought by shareholders, and prescribes specific rules for such actions.

FLORIDA: Florida statute is based on the Model Business Corporation Act. The statute permits derivative actions and prescribes specific rules for such actions. The statute prescribes specific rules for voting by shareholders, including voting trusts and voting agreements.

GEORGIA: Georgia statute is based on the Model Business Corporation Act. The statute does not provide preemptive rights to shareholders, except those in close corporations or in those corporations in existence prior to July 1, 1989. The statute permits derivative actions by shareholders.

HAWAII: Hawaii statute is based on the Model Business Corporation Act. The statute provides preemptive rights to shareholders. The statute permits derivative actions by shareholders and prescribes specific rules for such.

IDAHO: Idaho statute is based on the Model Business Corporation Act.

ILLINOIS: The statute permits derivative actions by shareholders. The statute requires vote of shareholders to approve mergers, acquisitions, and other significant and fundamental changes in the corporate structure.

INDIANA: Indiana statute is based on the Model Business Corporation Act. The statute restricts preemptive rights, except those provided under prior law. Shareholder derivative action is permitted, subject to some restrictions. The statute permits the creation of a disinterested committee of the corporation to consider a derivative action.

IOWA: The statute does not provide preemptive rights, which may only be granted by the articles of incorporation. The statute provides specific rules regarding shareholder meetings and shareholder voting.

KANSAS: The statute provides specific rules regarding derivative actions. The statute prescribes specific rules shareholder meetings and voting, including voting agreements and voting by proxy.

KENTUCKY: Kentucky statute is based on the Model Business Corporation Act. The statute permits derivative actions by shareholders and provides specific rules regarding representation of the corporation's rights.

LOUISIANA: The statute does not provide preemptive rights, which may only be granted in the articles of incorporation. The statute provides specific rules regarding shareholder meetings and voting, including the creation of voting trusts.

MAINE: Maine statute is based on the 1960 version of the Model Business Corporation Act. The statute grants limited preemptive rights in some circumstances. The statute permits derivative actions and prescribes specific rules regarding such actions.

MARYLAND: Maryland statute is based on the Model Business Corporation Act. The statute prescribes specific rules regarding shareholder meeting and voting, including voting by proxy.

MASSACHUSETTS: The statute does not provide preemptive rights to shareholders. The statute permits derivative suits by shareholders under appropriate circumstances.

MICHIGAN: Shareholders are permitted to bring an action to establish that the acts of directors or other managers are illegal, **fraudulent**, or willfully unfair or oppressive to the shareholders or corporation. The statute sets forth detailed rules regarding shareholder meetings and voting, including voting without a meeting and voting trusts.

MINNESOTA: The statute sets forth detailed rules regarding shareholder meetings and voting and the rights of shareholders to inspect the books and records of the corporation.

MISSISSIPPI: Mississippi statute is based on the Model Business Corporation Act.

MISSOURI: The statute permits shareholders to bring suit to enjoin ultra vires acts. The statute provides detailed rules regarding shareholder meetings and voting, including voting trusts.

MONTANA: Montana statute is based on the Model Business Corporation Act. The statute provides specific rules regarding shareholder meetings and voting, including a provision that permits shareholders to participate by telephone if the corporation consists of 50 or fewer shareholders.

NEBRASKA: Nebraska's statute is based on the Model Business Corporation Act.

NEVADA: The statute provides specific rules regarding shareholder meetings and voting, including voting trusts.

NEW HAMPSHIRE: New Hampshire statute is based on the Model Business Corporation Act.

NEW JERSEY: Statute does not provide preemptive rights for shareholders. The statute permits derivative suits subject to some restrictions, and provides specific rules regarding shareholder meetings and voting, including voting trusts and voting by proxy.

NEW MEXICO: New Mexico statute is based on the Model Business Corporation Act. The statute permits shareholder derivative suits, subject to some restrictions.

NEW YORK: In some limited circumstances, majority shareholders may incur personal liability for corporation's debts. The statute provides detailed rules regarding shareholder meetings and voting, including voting trusts.

NORTH CAROLINA: North Carolina statute is based on the Model Business Corporation Act. Shareholders under current statute do not have preemptive rights. The statute provides detailed rules regarding shareholder meetings and voting, including voting trusts and voting by proxy.

NORTH DAKOTA: Shareholder meetings are held on an annual or other periodic basis, but do not need to be held unless required by the articles of incorporation or the by-laws. A shareholder with more than 5 percent of voting power may demand a meeting.

OHIO: The statute permits derivative actions brought by shareholders. Shareholders provide detailed rules regarding shareholder meetings and voting, including voting trusts.

OKLAHOMA: The statute permits derivative actions brought by shareholders. Statute and provides

detailed rules regarding shareholder meetings and voting, including voting trusts.

OREGON: Oregon statute is based on the Model Business Corporation Act. The statute provides detailed rules regarding shareholder meetings and voting, including voting trusts.

PENNSYLVANIA: The statute permits derivative actions brought by shareholder and provides detailed rules regarding these actions. The statute provides detailed rules regarding shareholder meetings and voting, including voting trusts.

RHODE ISLAND: Rhode Island statute is based on Model Business Corporation Act. The statute permits derivative actions brought by shareholders and provides some limitation for voting trusts and shareholder agreements.

SOUTH CAROLINA: South Carolina statute is based on the Model Business Corporation Act. The statute provides detailed rules on shareholder meetings and voting, including voting trusts and voting by proxy.

SOUTH DAKOTA: South Dakota statute is based on the Model Business Corporation Act.

TENNESSEE: The statute contains special rules regarding derivative actions brought by shareholders.

TEXAS: The statute permits shareholder agreements, subject to a number of restrictions and provides detailed rules regarding shareholder meetings and voting, including voting trusts.

UTAH: Utah statute is based on the Model Business Corporation Act. The statute provides detailed rules regarding shareholder meetings and voting, including voting entitlement, voting trusts, voting agreements, and other shareholder agreements.

VERMONT: The statute does not provide preemptive rights to shareholders. The statute provides specific rules regarding voting trusts and voting by proxy and permits derivative actions brought by shareholders.

VIRGINIA: Virginia statute is based partially on the Model Business Corporations Act. The statute provides preemptive rights to shareholder by default. Statute and permits derivative actions brought by shareholders.

WASHINGTON: Washington statute is based on the Model Business Corporations Act. The statute provides preemptive rights to shareholders by default.

WEST VIRGINIA: The West Virginia statute is based primarily on the Model Business Corporation Act. The statute provides detailed rules regarding shareholder meetings and voting, including voting trusts.

WISCONSIN: The statute does not provide pre-emptive rights to shareholders. Statute and provides detailed rules regarding shareholder meetings and voting, including voting by proxy and voting trusts.

WYOMING: Wyoming's statute is based on the Model Business Corporations Act.

## Additional Resources

*The Active Shareholder: Exercising Your Rights, Increasing Your Profits, and Minimizing Your Risks.* Mahoney, William F., Wiley, 1993.

*Corporate Governance.* Monks, Robert A.G., and Nell Minow, Blackwell Publishers, 2001.

*Corporations: Examples and Explanations,* 3rd ed., Soloman, Lewis D., and Alan R. Palmiter, Aspen Law & Business, 1999.

*Law of Corporations in a Nutshell.* Hamilton, Robert W., West Group, 2000.

*Model Business Corporation Act Annotated,* 3rd ed., American Bar Association, 1998/1999.

## Organizations

### American Bar Association, Section of Business Law
740 15th Street, NW
Washington, DC 20005-1019 USA
Phone: (312) 988-5522
URL: http://www.abanet.org/buslaw/home.html
E-Mail: businesslaw@abanet.org

### Center for Corporate Law, University of Cincinnati College of Law
P.O. Box 210040
Cincinnati, OH 45221-0040 USA
Phone: (513) 556-6805
Fax: (513) 556-2391
URL: http://www.law.uc.edu/CCL/
Primary Contact: Peter Letsou, Director

### Council of Better Business Bureaus (CBBB)
4200 Wilson Blvd., Suite 800
Arlington, VA 22203-1838 USA
Phone: (703) 276-0100
Fax: (703) 525-8277
URL: http://www.bbb.org/

### United States Chamber of Commerce
1615 H Street, NW
Washington, DC 20062-2000 USA
Phone: (202) 659-6000
E-Mail: custsvc@uschamber.com
URL: http://www.uschamber.com

# CIVIL RIGHTS

## AFFIRMATIVE ACTION

*Sections within this essay:*

- Background

- Affirmative Action Defined

- History of Affirmative Action

- Supreme Court Decisions on Affirmative Action
  - *Griggs v. Duke Power Co.*
  - *Regents of the University of California v. Bakke*
  - *United Steel Workers of America v. Weber* and *Fullilove v. Klutznick*
  - *Johnson v. Santa Clara County Transportation Agency*
  - *City of Richmond v. J.A. Croson*
  - *Adarand Constructors v. Pena*
  - *Gratz v. Bollinger* and *Grutter v. Bollinger*

- Forms of Affirmative Action
  - Required Affirmative Action For Federal Contractors
  - Voluntary Implementation of Affirmative Action
  - What An Affirmative Action Plan Should Include

- Abolishing Affirmative Action

- Additional Resources

## Background

**Affirmative action** has been the most contentious area of **civil rights** law during the past 30 years. Despite several Supreme Court decisions, numerous **executive orders**, and laws passed by legislators at the state and federal level, it is still considered an unsettled area of law. Because of this current lack of resolution, any article written about affirmative action may soon become outdated with the latest law or court decision. Nevertheless, the broad outlines of what affirmative action has been and presumably will be in the future can be established.

## Affirmative Action Defined

Although the term "affirmative action" can be used in a variety of contexts, the most popular definition currently is within the arena of civil rights. There, affirmative action has been held to provide a special boost to qualified minorities, women, and disabled individuals in order to make up either for past **discrimination** or for their under representation in a specific area of the work force or academia. Though these categories of individuals have historically benefited most, affirmative action programs can also apply to other areas of discrimination, such as age, nationality, and religion.

Affirmative action can be administered in several ways. One way is through "quotas," defined as a strict requirement for a proportion or share of jobs, funding, or other placement to go to a specific group, e.g., 50 percent of all new hires must be women. Another is "goals," which require agencies and institutions to exert a good-faith effort toward reaching the assigned proportion or share goal but do not require that the proportion be reached. Affirmative action can also take the form of intangible "boosts" for the respective beneficiaries of the program; for example, all men shorter than 5'8" will be given ten extra points on the physical fitness exam.

The reasons for affirmative action are myriad and tend to overlap, but generally two justifications have stood out. One is that the group has been discriminated against in the past, for example black Americans, and needs affirmative action in order to "catch up" to the majority that has not suffered discrimination. The other is that the group is under represented in whatever area is being scrutinized, say women in construction jobs, and needs to be helped to achieve some sort of representation in the area. Even in this situation, however, there is the tacit admission that discrimination might be the underlying cause of the under representation.

## History of Affirmative Action

Affirmative action has its origins in the civil rights movement of the late 1950s and early 1960s. The movement brought a dramatic change to U. S. social life through protests, court decisions, and legislative action, culminating in the passage of the 1964 Civil Rights Act, popularly known as Title VII.

But Title VII mentioned affirmative action in a positive sense only in the context of the American Indian. It allowed preferential treatment to be given "to individuals because they are Indians living on or near a reservation." Otherwise, Title VII outlawed discrimination in a "color blind" fashion. The relevant part of Title VII states: "Nothing contained in this [law] shall be interpreted to require any employer, employment agency, labor organization, or joint labor-management committee subject to this [law] to grant preferential treatment to any individual or to any group because of the race, color, religion, sex, or national origin of such individual or group on account of an imbalance which may exist with respect to the total number or percentage of persons of any race, color, religion, sex, or national origin employed . . . in comparison with the total number or percentage of persons of such race, color, religion, sex, or national origin in any community, State, section, or other area, or in the available work force in any community, State, section, or other area."

This part of Title VII was passed to assuage the concerns of moderate members of Congress that the Civil Rights Act would become a quota bill, requiring reverse discrimination against whites. Civil rights leaders, who for the most part felt distinctly ambivalent about affirmative action, did not object to the in-

clusion of this passage. Many saw affirmative action as a way of dividing working class whites from blacks and the civil rights movement from its natural allies in the labor movement.

But the riots of the mid and late-1960s convinced more and more civil rights leaders that a color-blind policy of enforcing civil rights was not enough and that there had to be steps taken to ensure blacks could complete equally with whites. President Lyndon Johnson endorsed this view in a speech before Howard University in 1965 in which he stated: "You do not take a person who for years has been hobbled by chains and liberate him, bring him to the starting line and say you are free to compete with all the others."

That same year, Johnson issued Executive Order 11246, requiring firms under contract with the federal government not to discriminate, and to "take affirmative action to ensure that applicants are employed and that employees are treated during employment, without regard to their race, creed, color, or national origin." Although not specifying what would constitute affirmative action and not applying to any firms outside the federal government, this order is considered the first attempt at positive affirmative action by a governmental entity. The order also created the Office of Federal Contract Compliance (OFCC) to enforce this policy.

Because the term, affirmative action, was left intentionally vague by the executive order, however, the OFCC was unsure how to enforce it. The OFCC formulated plans in several cities, such as Cleveland and Philadelphia, to facilitate the hiring of minorities for federal government work, but for various reasons these plans were determined to be illegal or never seriously enforced. Johnson left office without any definite affirmative action plan put forth on his watch.

It was left to the Nixon administration, ironically considered an administration not particularly friendly to civil rights interests, to pick up the issue and promote the first serious affirmative action plan that required government-determined, numerically specific percentages of minorities to be hired.

In 1969, the Nixon administration picked up a plan that the Johnson administration had put forth for the construction industry in the city of Philadelphia, referred to as the Philadelphia Plan. The Johnson administration plan was faulted for not having definite minimum standards for the required affirmative action programs. The Nixon plan did issue minimum standards—specific targets for minority employees in several trades. It did not require these minimum standards be met, simply that contractors submitting bids make a "good faith" effort to achieve these targets. This allowed the administration to argue it was not setting quotas, though critics of the plan suggested the administration was in fact doing so.

The Philadelphia Plan survived several challenges, both legal and Congressional, before being accepted as legitimate. The Plan set the tone for affirmative actions plans that followed. Soon, the standards put forth in the Philadelphia Plan were incorporated into Executive Order 11246 which affected all federal government contractors, who were required for the first time to put forth written affirmative action plans with numerical targets.

After the implementation of the Philadelphia Plan, legislation was passed at the federal, state, and municipal level implementing affirmative action plans using the Philadelphia Plan as a model. Today, almost all government affirmative action plans are offshoots of the Philadelphia Plan. Its mixture of numerical targets and requirements of "good faith" effort was a milestone in the history of affirmative action.

## Supreme Court Decisions on Affirmative Action

The Supreme Court has given its opinion on affirmative action on numerous occasions since the Philadelphia Plan was put into effect in 1970. By–and–large, these Supreme Court decisions were more open to the idea of affirmative action during the 1970s and early 1980s and then gradually tightened the requirements for affirmative action plans. Generally, the question before the Supreme Court regarding affirmative action plans asked what kind of scrutiny to give the plans.

### Griggs v. Duke Power Co.

Decided in 1971, this decision is generally held to have laid the foundation for affirmative action programs based on the rationale of under representation. The case involved black workers at a power plant in North Carolina who sued, arguing that the plant's requirements of a high school education or passing a standardized intelligence test in order to fill certain jobs was discriminatory. The plaintiffs argued that the requirements operated to disqualify blacks at a substantially higher rate than white applicants.

The plant argued that the requirements served a legitimate business purpose.

A unanimous Supreme Court disagreed with the employer, ruling that the tests did not serve any job-related requirement. The Court pointed out that the plant had practiced discrimination in the past and that the effect of these requirements was to prevent black workers from overcoming the effects of such discrimination. "Practices, procedures, or tests neutral on their face, and even neutral in terms of intent, cannot be maintained if they operate to 'freeze' the status quo of prior discriminatory employment practices," said the court.

The effect of *Griggs v. Duke Power* was to legitimize the so-called disparate impact theory—the idea that if a qualification had a disparate impact on a specific group, an organization could justify that qualification only if it could prove a business related purpose for such a requirement. This point opened the door to forcing employers (including the government) to taking a hard look at the effect of their employment practices and their relation to race.

### Regents of the University of California v. Bakke

This was the first instance of the court taking a case specifically involving affirmative action. The case involved a white man, Allan Bakke, who had applied for a seat at the medical school at the University of California at Davis. Bakke was rejected, and then he sued, arguing that less qualified minorities were being allowed into the school under a quota system reserving a specific number of seats for minorities.

In a 5-4 ruling, a divided Supreme Court in 1978 ruled that the specific quota system used by the University of California at Davis was illegal but that race could be taken into consideration in determining admission slots at the school. The result was the first time the Court had held that reverse discrimination could be justified under certain circumstances.

### United Steel Workers of America v. Weber and Fullilove v. Klutznick

These two cases, decided a year apart, further legitimized the use of affirmative action as a tool for increasing minority employment. In the *Weber* case, the Supreme Court in 1979 ruled that an affirmative action plan for on-the-job training that mandated a one-for-one quota for minority workers admitted to the program was legal, since the plan was a temporary measure designed to correct an imbalance in the workforce.

In *Fullilove,* the Supreme Court upheld the "minority business enterprise" provision of Public Works Employment Act of 1977, which requires that at least 10 percent of federal funds granted for local public works projects must be used by the state or local grantee to procure services or supplies from businesses owned by minority group members.

### Johnson v. Santa Clara County Transportation Agency

This 1987 decision expanded the Court's protection of affirmative action programs to ones benefiting women. The Court ruled that the county agency did not violate civil rights laws by taking the female employee's sex into account and promoting her over male employee with a higher test score. By doing so, the court upheld the county's affirmative action plan directing that sex or race be considered for purpose of remedying under representation of women and minorities in traditionally segregated job categories.

### City of Richmond v. J.A. Croson

Beginning with this case in 1989, the Supreme Court began to cut back on the leeway it had given affirmative action programs. The Court struck down a set-aside program mandated by the city of Richmond, Virginia, which required prime contractors awarded city construction contracts to subcontract at least 30 percent of the dollar amount of each contract to one or more "Minority Business Enterprises." The Court ruled that the city failed to demonstrate compelling governmental interest justifying the plan, and the plan was not narrowly tailored to remedy effects of prior discrimination.

In handing down this ruling, the Court determined that any **judicial review** of municipal affirmative action plans would be reviewed with "strict scrutiny." Under the strict scrutiny test, defendants are required to establish they have a compelling interest in justifying the measure or that the affirmative action program advances some important governmental or societal purpose. For all practical purposes, this ruling makes it very hard to justify an affirmative action plan unless past discrimination can be shown, and the under representation of minorities is a product of that discrimination.

### Adarand Constructors v. Pena

In this Supreme Court case, the Court applied the standards propagated in *City of Richmond v. Croson* to the federal government, ruling that all racial classifications imposed by whatever federal, state, or local governmental actor must be analyzed by the reviewing court under strict scrutiny. The Court overturned a decision dismissing a suit brought by a contractor challenging the constitutionality of a federal program designed to provide highway contracts to minority business enterprises.

The results in *Adarand* confirmed the conservative direction in which the Supreme Court moved with respect to affirmative action plans. It seemed clear after this decision that affirmative action plans would only survive court challenges by being narrowly tailored to rectify past discrimination.

### Gratz v. Bollinger and Grutter v. Bollinger

These two cases further illustrate the complexity of the issue. Jennifer Gratz was denied admission to the University of Michigan's undergraduate program in 1995, while in 1997 Barbara Grutter was denied admission to the university's law school. Both women were white, and they claimed that the university's admissions program discriminated against white students. The university used a point system for undergraduate admissions, assigning extra points to what it considered "under-represented" racial and ethnic minorities. Since it also assigned extra points to athletes, children of alumni, and men enrolling in the nursing school, the university argued, there was nothing out of the ordinary about adding points for race as well. As for the law school, there was no point system, but race was used as a determining factor because, the university maintained, it helped promote cross-racial understanding. Civil rights organizations, academicians, political leaders, and many others took sides. Former U.S. president Gerald R. Ford (a University of Michigan alumnus) spoke out in support of the university's system in an op-ed piece in *The New York Times* in 1999.

The court voted 6-3 to strike down the undergraduate point system, but it upheld the law school's less rigid program in a 5-4 vote. While the dual votes were not a total victory for affirmative action, they clearly showed what the courts would consider valid and what they would consider too broad a reach. More importantly, they showed that the U.S. Supreme Court, however conservative, was not ready to abolish affirmative action arbitrarily.

## Forms of Affirmative Action

Affirmative actions can take different forms. Often affirmative actions are written into federal or state law. They can also take the form of voluntary plans or consent decrees. Occasionally, although rarely these days, a court will impose an affirmative action plan to remedy the effects of past discrimination.

Although affirmative action has been employed in the private sector, its use has been most pronounced in the public sector, in regard to both hiring and contract requirements. Affirmative action has been broadly used across a wide spectrum of federal, state, and municipal governments.

Samples of Affirmative Action at the Federal Level are as follows:

Department of Defense: Strives to award five percent of Department of Defense procurement, research and development, construction, operation and maintenance contracts to minority businesses and institutions.

Federal Home Loan Banks: Provides for preservation and expansion of minority owned banks.

Department of State: Mandates at least 10 percent of amount of funds appropriated for Department of State and foreign affairs diplomatic construction projects be allocated to American minority contractors.

NASA: Requires NASA administrator to establish annual goal of at least eight percent of total value of prime contracts and subcontracts awarded to be made to small disadvantaged businesses and minority educational institutions.

FCC: Must ensure that minority- and women-owned businesses have opportunity to participate in providing spectrum-based services.

Department of Energy: Works to achieve five percent of combined total funds of Department of Energy used to carry out national security programs be allocated to minority businesses and institutions.

Department of Energy: Strives for five percent of combined total funds of Department of Energy used to carry out national security programs be allocated to minority businesses and institutions.

Department of Transportation: Requires that not less than 10 percent of funds appropriated under the Intermodal Surface Transportation Efficiency Act of 1991 be expended on small and minority businesses.

Environmental Protection Agency: Must allocate no less than 10 percent of federal funding to minority businesses for research relating to requirements of Clean Air Act Amendments of 1990.

Samples of Affirmative Action at the State Level are as follows:

ARKANSAS: Requires Division of Minority Business Enterprise to develop plans and participation goals for minority businesses.

CONNECTICUT: Mandates that contractors on state public works contracts make **good faith** efforts to employ minority businesses as subcontractors and suppliers, allows municipalities to set aside up to 25 percent of dollar amount of construction and supply contracts to award to minority businesses.

DISTRICT OF COLUMBIA: Requires District of Columbia agencies to allocate 35 percent of dollar amount of public construction contracts to minority businesses.

FLORIDA: Allows municipalities to set aside up to 10 percent of dollar amount of contracts for procurement of **personal property** and services to award to minority businesses.

ILLINOIS: Requires Metropolitan Pier and Exposition Authority to establish goals of awarding not less than 25 percent of dollar amount of contracts to minority contractors and not less than five percent to women contractors.

INDIANA: Requires that state agencies establish goal that five percent of all contracts awarded be given to minority businesses.

KANSAS: Allows Secretary of Transportation to designate certain state highway construction contracts, or portions of contracts, to be set aside for bidding by disadvantaged businesses only.

LOUISIANA: Requires establishment of annual participation goals for awarding contracts for goods and services and public works projects to minority- and women-owned businesses.

MARYLAND: Requires that Maryland award 14 percent of dollar amount of procurement contracts to minority businesses.

MICHIGAN: Establishes participation goals for awarding of government contracts to minority- and women-owned businesses.

NEW JERSEY: Allows municipalities to set aside certain percentage of dollar value of contracts to award to minority businesses.

NEW YORK: Allows municipalities to set aside certain percentage of dollar value of contracts to award to minority businesses.

OHIO: Provides that a prime contractor on a state contract must award subcontracts totaling no less than five percent of the total value of the contract to Minority Business Enterprises (MBE) and that the total value of both the materials purchased from MBE's and of the subcontracts awarded will equal at least seven percent of the total value of the contract.

TENNESSEE: Requires all state agencies to actively solicit bids from small businesses and minority-owned businesses whenever possible. Local education agencies and state colleges and universities may set aside up to 10 percent of their funds allocated for procurement of personal property and services for the purpose of entering into contracts with small businesses and minority-owned businesses.

### Required Affirmative Action For Federal Contractors

Contractors with the federal government are required to have affirmative action plans under various federal laws. These laws include:

Executive Order 11246: This 30-year-old order, signed by President Johnson and amended by President Nixon, applies to all nonexempt government contractors and subcontractors and federally assisted construction contracts and subcontracts in excess of $10,000. Under the Executive Order, contractors and subcontractors with a federal contract of $50,000 or more and 50 or more employees are required to develop a written affirmative action program that sets forth specific and result-oriented procedures to which contractors commit themselves to apply every good faith effort.

Section 503 of the Rehabilitation Act of 1973: Requires affirmative action plans in all personnel practices for qualified individuals with disabilities. It applies to all firms that have a nonexempt government contact or subcontract in excess of $10,000.

The Vietnam Era Veterans' Readjustment Assistance Act of 1974 (VEVRAA): Requires affirmative action programs in all personnel practices for special disabled veterans, Vietnam Era veterans, and veterans who served on active duty during a war or in a campaign or expedition for which a campaign badge has been authorized. It applies to all firms that have a nonexempt government contract or subcontract of $25,000 or more.

### What An Affirmative Action Plan Should Include

The Office of Federal Contract Compliance Programs (OFCCP) suggests that non-construction contractors' written affirmative action plans include the following affirmative action as part of an action-oriented program:

- Contact with specified schools, colleges, religious organizations, and other institutions that are prepared to refer women and minorities for employment;

- Identification of community leaders as recruiting sources;

- Holding of formal briefing sessions, preferably on company premises, with representatives from recruiting sources;

- Conduct of plant tours, including presentation by minority and female employees of clear and concise explanations of current and future job openings, position descriptions, worker specifications, explanations of the company's selection process, and recruitment literature;

- Encouragement of minority and female employees to refer applicants;

- With special efforts the inclusion of minorities and women in personnel department staffs;

- The availability of minority and female employees for participation in career days, youth motivation programs, and related community activities;

- Recruitment at secondary schools, junior colleges, and colleges with predominantly minority or female enrollments;

- With special efforts the contact with minorities and women when recruiting at all schools;

- Special employment programs undertaken whenever possible, such as technical and non-technical co-op programs with predominantly black and women's colleges, summer jobs for underprivileged youth, and motivation programs for the hardcore unemployed;

- Inclusion of minority and female employees in recruiting brochures pictorially presenting work situations;

- Expansion of help-wanted advertising to regularly include the minority news media and women's interest media.

### Voluntary Implementation of Affirmative Action

Both private and public employers use voluntary affirmative action. However, both private and public employers must satisfy certain criteria in order to comply with Title VII. The employer must have a legitimate reason for adopting a plan. Also, the plan cannot unduly interfere with the employment opportunities of non-minority or male workers or job applicants to the extent that their interests are "unnecessarily trammeled." The **EEOC** has promulgated Guidelines on Affirmative Action that explain how to develop a lawful affirmative action plan under Title VII.

Often, affirmative action remedies are agreed upon to settle a discrimination case. These remedies are implemented by a consent **decree**. A court must approve provisions in consent decrees that provide for the employer's **adoption** of an affirmative action program. Affirmative action contained in the decree is viewed as voluntary. The action may benefit individuals who were not the victims of the discriminatory practice at issue.

## Abolishing Affirmative Action

In the 1990s, several states moved to abolish affirmative action programs. California voted in 1996 to abolish affirmative action, and Washington State voted similarly in 1998. The California ban asserts: "the state shall not discriminate against, or grant preferential treatment to, any individual or group on the basis of race, sex, color, ethnicity, or national origin in the operation of public employment, public education, or public contracting." The wording of the Washington law is identical. Both laws were passed in voter referenda.

There is no question that affirmative action remains a controversial issue in the eyes of many—and that many people would like to abolish it. But it seems reasonable to say that society in general is mindful that affirmative action in some form is acceptable and in fact worthwhile. Those who either favor or oppose it strongly will likely have to accept some sort of middle ground in the future.

## Additional Resources

*Affirmative Action.* A.E. Sadler, Ed., Greenhaven Press, 1996.

*Affirmative Action Fact Sheet.* Office of Federal Contract Compliance Programs, 2000. Available at http://www.dol.gov/dol/esa/public/ofcp_org.htm.

*Alice in Preference Land: A Review of Affirmative Action in Public Contracts.* Denise Farris, Construction Lawyer, Fall, 1991.

*American Jurisprudence.* Second Edition, Job Discrimination §§ 600-678 (2000).

*Equality Transformed: A Quarter-Century of Affirmative Action.* Herman Belz, Transaction Publishers, 1991.

*Federal Law of Employment Discrimination.* Mack Player, West Group, 1989.

*Has Affirmative Action Been Negated? A Closer Look at Public Employment.* Honorable H. Lee Sarokin, et al; San Diego Law Review, Summer, 2000.

*The Ironies of Affirmative Action.* John David Skrentny, University of Chicago Press, 1996.

*Setting Aside Set Asides: The New Standards for Affirmative Action Programs in the Construction Industry.* Steven K. DiLiberto, Villanova Law Review, 1997.

*U.S. Code, Title 42: United States Code Annotated Title 42: The Public Health And Welfare Chapter 21: Civil Rights.* U. S. House of Representatives, 1999. Available at http://uscode.house.gov/title_42.htm.

## Organizations

### *Office of Federal Contract Compliance Programs (OFCCP)*

200 Constitution Ave., NW
Washington, DC 20210 USA
Phone: (202) 693-0101
URL: http://www.dol.gov/esa/ofccp/name
Primary Contact: Charles E. James, Sr., Deputy Assistant Secretary

### *U. S. Equal Employment Opportunity Commission*

1801 L Street, N.W.
Washington, DC 20507 USA
Phone: (202) 663-4900
URL: http://www.eeoc.gov/
Primary Contact: Cari M. Dominguez, Chair

# CIVIL RIGHTS

## AGE DISCRIMINATION

*Sections within this essay:*

- Background
- Discrimination in the Twentieth Century
  - Changing Attitudes
  - Retirement Plans
- Subtle Discrimination
- Legal Protection
  - Bona Fide Occupational Qualifications
- Finding Answers
- Additional Resources

## Background

Age **discrimination** occurs when an older person is pressured in the workplace to leave. Under the law a person's career cannot be jeopardized solely because of age. Unfortunately, many employers resort to subtler but equally damaging tactics to thin the ranks of older workers. Today, "older worker" can mean anyone over the age of 40. Employees who fall into this group need to understand their rights under the law; this way, if they suspect discrimination, they can take appropriate action.

Until the early twentieth century discrimination based on age was not a clear-cut issue in most professions, Most people worked until they reached an age at which they were no longer able to be productive. For the remainder of their lives they would be taken care of by their families.

With the rise in industrialization and in unions, specific guidelines were set in place for how long people should stay on the job. The introduction of **pension** programs allowed workers the opportunity to stop working when they reached old age, secure in the knowledge that they would be able to take care of themselves financially. Later, government initiatives such as Social Security made it still easier for people to retire.

Beginning after World War II, dramatic changes in the workplace created a shift in policies and attitudes. Technology had made many jobs obsolete, and employees had to learn more and learn faster. As the postwar "baby boom" generation came of age, a growing emphasis on youth pervaded an increasingly crowded workplace. People who had reached old or even middle age began to face increasing pressure to leave the workforce. Sometimes they were simply forced out. Older workers who happen to be women or members of a minority group have to be particularly diligent, since they could be subject to discrimination on additional factors.

Discrimination of any kind is determined by either direct or indirect **evidence** under the law. Direct evidence can include outright statements an employer makes about a particular job candidate that shows intent to exclude. Indirect evidence can be when an employer makes job qualifications vague enough to exclude certain people even though everything looks legal and ethical. In age discrimination cases, direct evidence would be an employer telling an older worker, "You're doing that job much more slowly than the others," or "I don't think you'll be able to learn our new computer system." Indirect evidence would be when a potential employer turns down a qualified older job applicant in favor of someone younger. Of course, if the younger employee is demonstrably better qualified, it may not be a case of discrimination. But if, for example, a qualified older worker is passed over for a job and the employer continues to interview other candidates, the employer may be deliberately excluding the older candidate.

## Discrimination in the Twentieth Century

### Changing Attitudes

The "baby boom" that began at the end of World War II in 1945 and lasted until the early 1960s generated an enormous number of new employees in the 1970s and 1980s. Interestingly, many companies saw the baby boomers as detrimental to productivity. To be sure, the youthful boomers lacked the experience of mature workers. But they were also the victims of stereotypes. Companies believed that these young people, born in the heady days of the postwar economy, would be less willing to work their way up from the bottom, as their parents had done. The younger workers would probably be spoiled and arrogant, and, consequently, less productive.

At the same time, rapid advances in technology meant that workers needed to be able to adapt to new ways of doing their jobs. Many companies that had prided themselves on a policy of "lifetime employment" began to see their longtime workforce as a drain on productivity. The reasoning had less to do with any belief that older workers would be unable to master new skills than it did with the fear that the older workers had grown complacent in their jobs. Moreover, older workers commanded the highest salaries and were the most likely to incur high health care costs. As the number of baby boomers in the market increased, companies began to shift their commitment from experience to a younger, less expensive workforce that could be trained (and whose jobs were made easier by technology).

### Retirement Plans

While there are many older workers who want to continue in the jobs because they enjoy their work, many others continue to work because they cannot afford to retire. Thanks in large part to unions, many employees are guaranteed a good pension from their company after a set number of years, regardless of their age at retirement. Known as "30-and-Out" programs (based on a United Auto Workers deal with Chrysler in 1973), they allow workers to put in their 30 or however many years and retire with full pen-

sion benefits instead of having to wait until age 65 (when people can collect their full Social Security benefits).

Many companies offer some sort of early retirement package for employees, in part to make room for younger workers but also in part to cut down on the number of top-salaried people on the payroll. Such offers are not illegal and in fact can be beneficial to both the company and the employee. The issue takes a different turn when the employee is being pressured to accept an early retirement plan.

Setting a mandatory retirement age is illegal in most professions, although there are exceptions. Federal law recognizes ADEA exemptions in the case of such employees as air traffic controllers, federal police officers, airline pilots, and firefighters. In 1996 Congress passed legislation that allowed state and local governments to set retirement ages for these and similar employees to as young as 55. State and local judges are often required to step down at a certain age as well. In addition to mandatory retirement ages, many public safety jobs also have mandatory hiring ages, thus closing the door to potentially otherwise qualified people. The argument against mandatory retirement claims that it would be fairer to all employees to rely on periodic fitness testing, since some older workers may be just as able (or perhaps more so) to carry out their duties as younger ones.

## Subtle Discrimination

Blatant discrimination is deplorable, but it is easy to spot and usually easy to determine accountability. More ambiguous, and thus more dangerous to older workers, is subtle discrimination. This can take many forms, and by its nature it is probably more pervasive than most people realize. Some examples are as follows:

- A longtime employee's supervisor makes comments in his or her presence about the benefits of retirement
- An employee whose company "restructures," and who subsequently ends up with a smaller office down a little-used corridor
- An employee who gets passed over for promotions, always in favor of younger staffers
- A worker who is reassigned to a job with fewer responsibilities, even if the assignment is considered a lateral move
- An employee who is no longer sent on business trips, provided membership in profes-

sional associations, or encouraged to take job-related courses

What makes subtle discrimination so much more dangerous than blatant discrimination in the minds of many experts is that it is harder to prove. Perhaps the supervisor is making comments about retirement because he or she is looking forward to being retired. Maybe the employee who was passed over for promotions has never asked to be promoted and thus is considered to be lacking in leadership initiative. Subtle forms of age discrimination may make older workers uncomfortable or unhappy enough that they will retire, even though they may not be able to pinpoint actual discrimination as their reason for leaving. The bottom line, however, is that subtle discrimination is no more acceptable in the workplace than blatant actions directed at older workers. Determining the difference between innocent remarks or coincidence and true discrimination may be difficult, but an older worker who suspects discrimination should know that taking action is a viable option.

## Legal Protection

Older workers have legal protection from age discrimination. The Age Discrimination in Employment Act (ADEA) was passed by Congress in 1967. The ADEA extends the law as spelled out in the **Civil Rights** Act of 1964, which prohibits discrimination based on race, sex, creed, color, religion, or ethnic origin. (Title VII of the Civil Rights Act is important to older workers who could suffer discrimination based on any of those factors as well.) Under the ADEA, workers age 40 and above are protected from discrimination in recruitment, hiring, training, promotions, pay and benefits, **dismissal** and layoffs, and retirement. The Older Workers Benefit Protection Act (OWBPA), passed in 1990, guarantees protection against discrimination in benefits packages. For example, OWPBA sets strict guidelines prohibiting companies from converting their pension plans in a way that would provide fewer pension dollars to older workers.

While the ADEA has been a critical factor in guarding against age discrimination, certain decisions by the U. S. Supreme Court have made it somewhat less effective. Part of the reason is that the Civil Rights Act of 1991, which amended Title VII of the 1964 Civil Rights Act, did not similarly amend the ADEA. Thus, although Title VII allows victims to recover compensatory and **punitive damages** since the 1991

amendment, the ADEA does not. Recent Supreme Court actions have suggested that using pension eligibility or high salaries as a basis for layoff decisions (a practice that generally has the greatest impact on older workers) may not be discriminatory.

In 2000, the Supreme Court ruled in *Kimel v. Florida Board of Regents* that states are protected from ADEA suits by individuals. Legislation was introduced in the U.S. Senate in 2001 that would require states agencies to waive their **immunity** from ADEA suits or else **forfeit** federal funding.

Most ADEA suits are based on charges brought before the Equal Employment Opportunity Commission (**EEOC**). The EEOC is responsible for investigating charges of age discrimination and seeking remedies. Rarely does it file actual lawsuits (in fact EEOC **litigation** across the board dropped through the 1990s and into the twenty-first century), but individuals are allowed to sue on their own.

In 1995 the EEOC conducted a comprehensive review of its procedures and developed new National and Local Enforcement Plans. These plans provide guidelines for dealing with discrimination issues against older workers.

The EEOC has long suffered from inadequate funding, which limits its ability to investigate charges as quickly as it would like. As a result, EEOC chooses its lawsuits carefully to ensure maximum impact.

### Bona Fide Occupational Qualifications

Under the law, not all age-related job exclusions are discriminatory. In fact, both Title VII and the ADEA recognize exclusions known as bona fide occupational qualifications (BFOQs) as legitimate. For example, a kosher meat market can legitimately require that it can hire only Jewish butchers. An employer seeking an BFOQ exclusion must be able to prove that those from within an excluded group would not be able to perform the job effectively. Thus, a moving company might be able to exclude a 75-year-old as a mover because moving requires heavy lifting and driving long distances. An accounting firm would be unable to make a similar claim in trying to force a 75-year-old bookkeeper to retire solely based on age.

### Finding Answers

Age discrimination has a twofold negative effect on older workers. The **tangible** effect is loss of a job or limited employment opportunities. Not only is it harder for an older worker to keep a job, it becomes harder for an older worker to find a new job. (Economic realities often dictate that early retirees may have to supplement their pensions before they turn 65 and collect their full Social Security benefits.) The psychological effect is that older workers become frustrated by their situation. If they are working, this could affect their productivity, which could feed the stereotypes about older workers. If they are looking for work, they may simply give up, believing that they are unemployable.

Individuals who think they are victims of age discrimination can turn to the local office of the EEOC for assistance. The EEOC will provide information about how to file charges at the state and federal levels. It is also useful to contact the state office of civil rights.

Older workers have a strong ally and resource in the form of AARP (formerly known as the American Association of Retired Persons). Founded in 1958, AARP had 35 million members across the country in 2001. AARP acts as an information clearinghouse for legislation and other materials, and it also serves as a powerful **lobbying** force at the federal and state level. Through its lobbying network, AARP seeks to get Congress to enact new laws, enforce existing laws, and revise flawed legislation. AARP is headquartered in Washington, D.C., but it has regional offices to serve at the local level. Its leadership works actively to combat all discrimination.

## Additional Resources

*Aging and Competition: Rebuilding the U. S. Workforce.* Auerbach, James A., and Joyce C. Welsh, editors, National Planning Association, 1994.

*The Aging of the American Work Force.* Bluestone, Irving, Rhonda J. V. Montgomery, and John D. Owen, editors, Wayne State University Press, 1990.

*American Bar Association Guide to Workplace Law.* White, Charles, Series Editor, Times Books, 1997.

## Organizations

### AARP
601 E Street NW
Washington, DC 20049 USA
Phone: (202) 434-2257
Fax: (202) 434-2588
URL: http://w ww.aarp.org
Primary Contact: William Novelli, CEO

### Equal Employment Opportunity Council (EEOC)
1801 L Street NW
Washington, DC 20507 USA
Phone: (202) 663-4900
Fax: (202) 376-6219
URL: http://w ww.eeoc.gov
Primary Contact: Cari M. Dominguez, Chairperson

### National Council on the Aging
409 Third Street, Suite 200
Washington, DC 20024 USA
Phone: (202) 479-1200
Fax: (202) 479-0735
URL: http://w ww.ncoa.org
Primary Contact: James P. Firman, President and CEO

### U. S. Department of Health and Human Services, Administration on Aging
330 Independence Avenue SW
Washington, DC 20201 USA
Phone: (202) 619-0724
Fax: (202) 260-1012
URL: http://w ww.aoa.gov
Primary Contact: Josefina G. Carbonell, Assistant Secretary for Aging

# CIVIL RIGHTS

## ASSEMBLY

*Sections within this essay:*

## Background

The First Amendment of the **Bill of Rights** provides that "Congress shall make no law . . . abridging . . . the right of the people peaceably to assemble."

This provision applies to state government entities through the Due Process Clause of the Fourteenth Amendment. Though neither the federal Constitution nor any state constitution specifically protects rights of association, the United States Supreme Court and other courts have extended assembly rights to include rights of association.

Rights to free speech and assembly are not absolute under the relevant **jurisprudence**. Government entities may restrict many types of speech without violating First Amendment protections. Many of the Supreme Court's First Amendment cases focus on two main questions: first, whether the restriction on speech was based on the content of the speech; and second, whether the speech was given in a traditional public forum or elsewhere. Some questions focus exclusively on the actual speech, rather than on aspects of the right to assembly. Other questions contain aspects of both the right to free speech and the right to assemble peacefully. Cases addressing free speech plus some conduct in the exercise of assembly rights often pose complex questions, since either the speech rights or the assembly rights may not protect the parties in these types of cases.

Since the courts take into consideration such a variety of factors when determining whether a particular speech or whether a particular assemblage is protected by the First Amendment, it is difficult to provide a concise definition of rights of assembly. Even in areas where a government entity may restrict speech or assembly rights, courts are more likely to find a violation of the First Amendment if speech or assembly is banned completely. Some restrictions merely involve the application for a permit or license to assemble, such as obtaining a license to hold a parade in a public street. Other time, place, and/or manner restrictions may also apply.

## Content-Based vs. Content-Neutral Restrictions on Free Speech

The outcome of a First Amendment case may very well hinge on whether the restriction of speech is based on the content of the speech. If the restriction is content-based, courts scrutinize the restriction under a heightened standard compared with restrictions that are content-neutral. When courts apply this heightened scrutiny, they are more likely to find a First Amendment violation. Courts also recognize that content-neutral restrictions may cause as much or more harm than content-based restrictions. For example, a ban on all parades on public streets is much more intrusive than a ban on only some parades. If a restriction is content-neutral, a court will employ an intermediate standard of scrutiny.

Determining whether a restriction is content-neutral or content-based may be more difficult in the context of assembly rights than in the context of speech rights. For example, if a city requires that all groups obtain a permit to hold a parade, the restriction is more likely, at least on its face, to be content-neutral. However, if the city, through official or unofficial action, only issues permits to certain groups and restricts issuing permits to other groups, the restriction in its application is content-based, not content neutral.

## Public vs. Private Speech

In addition to determining whether a restriction is content-based or content-neutral, courts also consider whether the speech or assembly is given or held in a public or private forum. Government property that has traditionally been used by the public for the purpose of assembly and to disseminate ideas is considered a traditional public forum. Content-based regulations in a traditional public forum are the most likely forms of speech to be found in violation of the First Amendment. Some content-neutral restrictions on the time, place, and manner of the speech are permitted, however, even in the traditional public forum.

Public-owned facilities that have never been designated for the general use of the public to express ideas are considered nonforums. Government may reasonably restrict speech, including some content-based speech, in these nonforums. This does not mean that all speech may be restricted on such property, but it does mean that speech can be restricted to achieve a reasonable government purpose if is not intended to suppress the viewpoint of a particular speaker.

Some public property that is not a traditional public forum may become a designated or limited public forum if it is opened to the use of the general public to express ideas. Examples include a senior center that has been opened for the general public to express ideas or a state-operated television station used for political debates. Courts will strictly scrutinize content-based restrictions in a designated or limited public forum when the restriction on speech is related to the designated public use of the property.

## Reasonable Time, Place, and Manner Restrictions

Government entities may make reasonable content-neutral restrictions on the time, place, and manner of a speech or assemblage, even in a traditional public forum. This action directly affects the rights of assembly, since a government entity may restrict the time and place where an assembly may take place, as well as the manner in which the assembly occurs. The restrictions must be reasonable and narrowly tailored to meet a significant government purpose. The government entity must also leave open ample channels for interested parties that wish to communicate.

## Overbreadth and Vagueness

Statutes and ordinances are often found to infringe on First Amendment rights because they are unconstitutionally vague or the breadth of the **statute** or **ordinance** extends so far that it infringes on protected speech. For example, some statutes and ordinances prohibiting loitering on public property have been found to be unconstitutional on the grounds of overbreadth since some people could be prosecuted for exercising their protected First Amendment rights. Similarly, statutes and ordinances restricting speech may be so vague that a person of ordinary intelligence could not determine what speech was restricted based on a reading of the law.

For example, in *Virginia v. Hicks* (2003), the City of Richmond, Virginia was challenged for restricting access to a street by non-residents, in an attempt to stop suspected drug dealers from frequenting the area. Loitering notices were served on outsiders, including Hicks, who told the police that he was delivering diapers. As a non-resident, he had previously been served notice, and this time, was arrested. He challenged the law as overbroad, alleging interference with his First Amendment rights. However, the Supreme Court upheld the law, finding First Amendment restrictions too speculative or insignificant to outweigh the government's interest in controlling known crime in the area.

## Permissible and Impermissible Restrictions on Rights of Assembly

It is difficult to make general statements about when assembly rights are guaranteed and when they are not. Whether assembly is or is not guaranteed depends largely on where and when the assembly takes place, as well as the specific restrictions that were placed on this right by government entities.

### Speech and Assembly in Public Streets and Parks

Public streets, sidewalks, and parks are generally considered public forums, and content-based restrictions on these will be strictly scrutinized by the courts. However, reasonable time, place, and manner restrictions are permitted if they are neutral regarding the content of the speech.

The use of public streets, sidewalks, and parks may not always be considered use of public forums, which often causes confusion in this area. For example, in the 1990 case of *United States v. Kokinda*, the Supreme Court held that a regulation restricting use of a sidewalk in front of a post office was valid because, in part, that particular sidewalk was not a public forum. Similar results have been reached with respect to some public parks.

### Parade Permits and Other Restrictions

The right to assemble and hold parades on public streets is one of the more important rights of assembly. However, these rights must be balanced with the interests of government entities to maintain peace and order. The Supreme Court in the 1992 case of *Forsyth County v. Nationalist Movement*, held that a government entity may require permits for those wishing to hold a parade, march, or rally on public streets or other public forums. Local officials may not be given overly broad discretion to issue such permits.

### Speech and Assembly in Libraries and Theaters

The Supreme Court has held that a publicly-owned theatre is a public forum. Thus, government may not make content-based restrictions on speech or assembly in these theaters. However, government entities may make reasonable time, place, and manner restrictions in publicly-owned theaters. Libraries, on the other hand, are not considered public forums and may be regulated "in a reasonable and nondiscriminatory manner, equally applicable to all and administered with equality to all."

### Speech and Assembly in Airports and Other Public Transportation Centers

The Supreme Court has held that airports are not traditional public forums, so government may make certain reasonable restrictions on assembly and speech rights in these areas. Courts have reached different conclusions with respect to other centers of public transportation, such as bus terminals, railway stations, and ports.

### Picketing and Other Demonstrations

The act of picketing is unquestionably intertwined with the First Amendment right to peaceful assembly. Courts have often recognized the right to picket and hold other peaceful demonstrations particularly in public forums. The right to picket, however, is limited and depends on the specific activities of the participants and the location of the demonstration. For example, if a demonstration breaches the peace or involves other criminal activity, law enforcement may ordinarily end the demonstration in a reasonable manner. Similarly, a government entity may reasonably restrict demonstrations on public streets in residential areas.

### Loitering and Vagrancy Statutes

State and local governments have often sought to eliminate undesirable behavior by enacting statutes and ordinances that make loitering a crime. Many of these statutes have been held to be constitutional, even those that prohibit being in a public place and hindering or obstructing the free passage of people. Such rulings have a significant effect on the rights of assembly, since these crimes involve a person's presence in a certain place, in addition to suspicious behavior.

A number of courts have held that specific antiloitering statutes and ordinances have been unconstitutional. Some of these decisions are hinged on First Amendment rights, while others hinge on other rights, such as Fourth Amendment protections against unreasonable searches and seizures. Several of these statutes have been struck down on grounds of vagueness or overbreadth. Similarly, courts have struck down statutes and ordinances outlawing **vagrancy** on the grounds of vagueness or overbreadth.

### Speech and Assembly on Private Property

The general rule is that owners of private property can restrict speech in a manner that the owner deems appropriate. Some older cases have held that private property, such a privately owned shopping center, could be treated as the equivalent of public property. However, modern cases have held otherwise, finding that private property was not subject to the same analysis regarding First Amendment rights as public property.

## State Laws Affecting Rights of Assembly

Some municipalities in every state require interested individuals to file for a permit to hold a parade or other gathering on public property. These ordinances are often the subject of **litigation** regarding alleged **infringement** on First Amendment rights of peaceful assembly. Antiloitering statutes are also commonplace, though several of these have been challenged on First Amendment grounds as well. Whether a specific ordinance, statute, or official action constitutes a violation of the First Amendment depends largely on the specific facts of the case or the specific language of the statute or ordinance.

ALABAMA: Several municipalities require that interested parties file for a permit to hold a parade in public streets. A number of these ordinances have been attacked on First Amendment grounds, and some ordinances have been found to be in violation of First Amendment rights. The state's criminal laws prohibit loitering, including begging and criminal **solicitation**.

ARIZONA: Several municipalities require that interested parties file for a permit to hold a parade in public streets. The state's criminal laws prohibit loitering, including begging and criminal solicitation.

ARKANSAS: Several municipalities require that interested parties file for a permit to hold a parade in public streets. Some of these ordinances have been attacked on First Amendment grounds, and some ordinances have been found to be in violation of First Amendment rights. The state's criminal laws prohibit loitering.

CALIFORNIA: Several municipalities require that interested parties file for a permit to hold a parade

in public streets. A number of these ordinances have been attacked on First Amendment grounds, and some ordinances have been found to be in violation of First Amendment rights. The state's criminal laws prohibit loitering, and these laws have generally been upheld in First Amendment challenges.

COLORADO: Several municipalities require that interested parties file for a permit to hold a parade in public streets. A number of these ordinances have been attacked on First Amendment grounds, and some ordinances have been found to be in violation of First Amendment rights. The state requires a permit for parties to use the state capitol building grounds. The state's criminal laws prohibit loitering, including begging and criminal solicitation. The Colorado Supreme Court held that the state's loitering statute was unconstitutional; this statute was subsequently modified.

DELAWARE: Several municipalities require that interested parties file for a permit to hold a parade in public streets. The state's criminal laws prohibit loitering, including begging, criminal solicitation, and loitering on public school grounds.

FLORIDA: Several municipalities require that interested parties file for a permit to hold a parade in public streets. The state's criminal laws regarding loitering have been the subject of several lawsuits. These laws make it a crime to loiter or prowl in a place, at a time or in a manner not usual for a law-abiding individual.

GEORGIA: Several municipalities require that interested parties file for a permit to hold a parade in public streets. A number of these ordinances have been attacked on First Amendment grounds, and some ordinances have been found to be in violation of First Amendment rights. The state's criminal laws regarding loitering have been the subject of several lawsuits. These laws make it a crime to loiter or prowl in a place, at a time, or in a manner not usual for a law-abiding individual.

HAWAII: Several municipalities require that interested parties file for a permit to hold a parade in public streets. The state's criminal laws prohibit loitering for solicitation of prostitution.

IDAHO: Several municipalities require that interested parties file for a permit to hold a parade in public streets.

ILLINOIS: Several municipalities require that interested parties file for a permit to hold a parade in public streets or public assembly. A number of these ordinances have been attacked on First Amendment grounds, and some ordinances have been found to be in violation of First Amendment rights. The state statutes permit municipalities to prohibit vagrancy, and loitering is prohibited in the state by criminal statute.

INDIANA: Several municipalities require that interested parties file for a permit to hold a parade in public streets. Criminal gang activity is a separate offense under state criminal laws.

IOWA: Several municipalities require that interested parties file for a permit to hold a parade in public streets. The state provides specific laws prohibiting loitering and other congregation on election days near polling places.

KANSAS: Several municipalities require that interested parties file for a permit to hold a parade in public streets.

KENTUCKY: Several municipalities require that interested parties file for a permit to hold a parade in public streets. The state's criminal laws prohibit loitering for the purpose of engaging in criminal activity.

LOUISIANA: Several municipalities require that interested parties file for a permit to hold a parade in public streets. The state's criminal laws prohibit vagrancy and loitering, though these statutes have been attacked on First Amendment grounds several times.

MAINE: Several municipalities require that interested parties file for a permit to hold a parade in public streets.

MARYLAND: Several municipalities require that interested parties file for a permit to hold a parade or other public assembly in public streets or areas. The state's criminal laws prohibits loitering or loafing around a business establishment licensed to sell alcohol.

MASSACHUSETTS: Several municipalities require that interested parties file for a permit to hold a parade in public streets, though a number of these ordinances have been the subject to challenges on First Amendment grounds. The state's criminal laws prohibit loitering in some specific venues, such as railway centers.

MICHIGAN: Several municipalities require that interested parties file for a permit to hold a parade in

public streets. A number of these ordinances have been attacked on First Amendment grounds, and some ordinances have been found to be in violation of First Amendment rights.

MINNESOTA: Several municipalities require that interested parties file for a permit to hold a parade, march, or other form of procession on public streets and other areas. The state's criminal laws prohibit vagrancy, including some instances of loitering.

MISSISSIPPI: Several municipalities require that interested parties file for a permit to hold a parade in public streets. A number of these ordinances have been attacked on First Amendment grounds, and some ordinances have been found to be in violation of First Amendment rights.

MISSOURI: Several municipalities require that interested parties file for a permit to hold a parade in public streets. The state's criminal laws prohibit vagrancy, including some instances of loitering.

MONTANA: Several municipalities require that interested parties file for a permit to hold a parade in public streets. The state's criminal laws prohibit vagrancy and loitering around public markets.

NEBRASKA: Several municipalities require that interested parties file for a permit to hold a parade in public streets. The state's criminal laws prohibit loitering in specified venues.

NEVADA: Several municipalities require that interested parties file for a permit to hold a parade in public streets. The state's criminal laws prohibit loitering around schools and other areas where children congregate. The state permits municipalities to enact ordinances to prohibit loitering.

NEW HAMPSHIRE: Several municipalities require that interested parties file for a permit to hold a parade in public streets. The state's criminal laws prohibit loitering and prowling in specified circumstances.

NEW JERSEY: Several municipalities require that interested parties file for a permit to hold a parade in public streets. A number of these ordinances have been attacked on First Amendment grounds, and some ordinances have been found to be in violation of First Amendment rights. The state's criminal laws prohibit loitering for the purpose of soliciting criminal activity or in public transportation terminals.

NEW YORK: Several municipalities require that interested parties file for a permit to hold a parade in public streets. A number of these ordinances have been attacked on First Amendment grounds, and some ordinances have been found to be in violation of First Amendment rights. The state has enacted a number of laws prohibiting loitering, including loitering for the purpose of soliciting passengers for transportation, loitering for the purpose of criminal solicitation, and loitering in public transportation centers. The statute permits municipalities to enact ordinances prohibiting loitering. Several of the antiloitering laws have been the subject of litigation attacking the laws on First Amendment grounds.

NORTH DAKOTA: Several municipalities require that interested parties file for a permit to hold a parade or other processions in public streets.

OHIO: Several municipalities require that interested parties file for a permit to hold a parade or engage in the solicitation of business. The state's criminal laws prohibit loitering in public transportation centers and in polling centers during elections.

OKLAHOMA: Several municipalities require that interested parties file for a permit to hold a parade in public streets. The state's criminal laws prohibit loitering for the purpose of engaging in specified criminal acts.

OREGON: Several municipalities require that interested parties file for a permit to hold a parade in public streets. Some municipalities also require a noise permit when playing amplified noise in a public place.

PENNSYLVANIA: Several municipalities require that interested parties file for a permit to hold a parade in public streets. A number of these ordinances have been attacked on First Amendment grounds, and some ordinances have been found to be in violation of First Amendment rights. The state's criminal laws prohibit loitering for the purpose of engaging in specified criminal acts.

RHODE ISLAND: Several municipalities require that interested parties file for a permit to hold a parade in public streets. The state's criminal laws prohibit loitering for indecent purposes, loitering in public transportation centers, and loitering at or near schools.

SOUTH CAROLINA: Several municipalities require that interested parties file for a permit to hold a parade in public streets. The state's laws prohibit loitering in public transportation centers.

TENNESSEE: Several municipalities require that interested parties file for a permit to hold a parade on public streets. The state's criminal laws prohibit loitering for the purpose of engaging in specified criminal acts.

TEXAS: Several municipalities require that interested parties file for a permit to hold a parade on public streets. The state's laws prohibit loitering in polling centers during elections.

UTAH: Several municipalities require that interested parties file for a permit to hold a parade on public streets.

VERMONT: The state's laws prohibit loitering in public transportation centers and other public property.

WASHINGTON: Several municipalities require that interested parties file for a permit to hold a parade or march on public streets. The state's laws prohibit loitering in public transportation centers.

WEST VIRGINIA: Several municipalities require that interested parties file for a permit to hold a parade on public streets. The state's laws prohibit loitering at or near school property.

WISCONSIN: Several municipalities require that interested parties file for a permit to hold a parade on public streets. The state's laws prohibit loitering in public transportation centers.

## Additional Resources

*The Constitutional Right of Association.* Fellman, David, University of Chicago Press, 1963.

*The First Amendment: A Reader.* Garvey, John H., and Frederick Schaver, West Publishing Co., 1992.

*Freedom of Association.* Gutman, Amy, Princeton University Press, 1998.

*Law and the Company We Keep.* Soifer, Aviam, Harvard University Press, 1995.

*The Right of Assembly and Association, Second Revised Edition.* 2nd rev. ed., Abernathy, M. Glenn, University of South Carolina Press, 1981.

## Organizations

***American Civil Liberties Union (ACLU)***
125 Broad Street, 18th Floor
New York, NY 10004 USA
Phone: (212) 344-3005

URL: http://www.aclu.org/

### National Coalition Against Censorship (NCAC)

275 Seventh Avenue
New York, NY 10001 USA
Phone: (212) 807-6222
Fax: (212) 807- 6245
E-Mail: ncac@n cac.org
URL: http://www.ncac.org/

### National Freedom of Information Center (NFOIC)

400 S. Record Street, Suite 240
Dallas, TX 75202 USA

Phone: (214) 977-6658
Fax: (214) 977- 6666
E-Mail: nfoic@r eporters.net
URL: http://www.nfoic.org/

### The Thomas Jefferson Center for the Protection of Free Expression

400 Peter Jefferson Place
Charlottesville, VA 22911-8691 USA
Phone: (804) 295-4784
Fax: (804) 296- 3621
E-Mail: ch@tjcenter.org
URL: http://www.tjcenter.org
Primary Contact: Robert M. O'Neill, Director

# CIVIL RIGHTS

## CHILDREN'S RIGHTS

*Sections within this essay:*

- Background
- Before the Twentieth Century
    - Fair Labor Standards Act (FLSA)
- Children's Rights Violations in the United States
    - Child Labor Violations
    - Benefits of Joint Custody
    - Children as Detainees
- Convention on the Rights of the Child
- Additional Resources

## Background

When people in the United States think of **children's rights** they usually think of children in third world countries who are victims of abusive child labor practices or insurmountable poverty. They may not realize that the rights of children are violated in the United States as well. Even though **child labor laws** were passed decades ago prohibiting employment of underage youngsters, pockets of oppressive child labor exist, literally, on American soil; child farm laborers work long hours in squalid conditions and often receive half the standard **minimum wage**. And although numerous studies show that children do better when two parents are involved their upbringing, many **custody** laws make it extremely difficult for non-custodial parents to spend quality time with their children.

To be sure, the United States is still better than most countries when it comes to how children are treated. Yet children's rights is a topic that few people know much about. In fact, although many people know that the United Nations Convention on the Rights of the Child was formulated in 1989, they are probably unaware that the United States is one of two countries (the other is Somalia) that have not ratified the Convention. The U.S. government has given what it believes are sound reasons for not having ratified the Convention and repeatedly has affirmed its commitment to children's rights in the United States and abroad. Yet there is no question that some children do fall into the cracks, and others' problems are unwisely minimized.

## Before the Twentieth Century

It was not uncommon for children to be exploited before the 1930s. Children routinely worked in hazardous conditions in mills, factories, and sweatshops, and on farms. They might begin working before they had reached their tenth birthday, and they received little in the way of wages. Labor laws did not exist to protect children or adults, but children were often subject to more exploitative conditions because they were easier to manipulate.

The plight of small children did lead to the enactment of some laws, and the federal government tried in 1918 and agin in 1922, to enact national child labor laws. Both times, the effort was struck down by the U.S. Supreme Court, which ruled that it was up to the individual states to enact child labor legislation.

### The Fair Labor Standards Act (FLSA)

In 1938, partly in response to the Great Depression, Congress passed the **Fair Labor Standards Act** (FLSA). This law protected workers from long hours and unfair pay by establishing a 40-hour work week and a minimum wage. It also protected children from exploitation by establishing that they would have to be at least 16 to work in most non-agricultural industries. Younger children could still work certain jobs provided the hours and wages were fair. (It was still possible, in other words, for children to get a newspaper route.) FLSA was challenged in the courts soon after its passage but its constitutionality was upheld by the U.S. Supreme Court in 1941.

## Children's Rights Violations in the United States

Although the United States does not have the gruesome record of children's rights violations that other countries have, it is not free of violations. Some are more subtle than others, but they do exist. **Human rights** groups monitor alleged instances of violations and work to educate the public and the government with the goal of correcting the problem.

### Child Labor Violations

FLSA protects, among other groups, child laborers. When it was enacted, farming was primarily a family activity, and it was understood that children would help on the family farm. Thus, the restrictions on agricultural work are much less stringent. By the end of the twentieth century, the number of family farms had dwindled, and most farming was done on large commercial establishments. But the lax restrictions remained, and farm conglomerates took advantage of this.

Under FLSA, no child under the age of 13 can work in a nonagricultural setting, and children of 14 and 15 can work but only for a set number of hours each day. For children working on a farm, the situation is quite different. Children can go to work in the fields as young as nine years old in some states, as long as they have signed parental consent.

Even with the relaxed standards for agricultural work, children are often overworked, are expected to work during what would be school hours, and are paid far less than what is legally required. A report issued in 2000 by Human Rights Watch noted that children under the age of 16 are often required to put in several hours before the school day begins; during the summer months they may work 12-hour days.

The dangers of agricultural work are surprisingly many, and for minors these dangers are even more troubling. Agricultural workers can be exposed to pesticides and other chemicals. They may be sent to work in oppressive heat but without adequate water to keep from becoming dehydrated. Often, they work with heavy or dangerous equipment—equipment that children often have little experience with. Because they work long hours, often having to rise before dawn to begin their work, lack of sleep is a major problem. For children, this is not only more dangerous, it also curtails their ability to succeed in school. Injury is common; children can fall or have accidents with heavy equipment or sharp objects.

It is important to remember that many adult farm workers are also exploited, forced to work long hours for little pay. Often, families are so poor and desperate that they feel compelled to give their young children permission to work on the farm, thus bringing in a small but needed amount of extra money.

Organizations such as Human Rights Watch have urged the U.S. government to revise FLSA to offer additional protection to minor children working on farms, and to ensure that farms are more careful about whom they hire and also more diligent about improving working conditions and wages.

### Benefits of Joint Custody

**Divorce** was less common before 1970 than it was by the end of the twentieth century, but children whose parents divorced were likely to be placed in the custody of one parent. The other parent might get visitation rights, but these were usually limited. For children whose parents are both loving and responsible but no longer married to each other, this can be emotionally devastating.

The concept of *joint custody* was developed in the early 1970s to **redress** this imbalance. In 1973, Indiana passed the first state joint custody **statute** in the United States. As of 2002, all states have a joint custody statute on the books. There are two types of joint custody. In *Joint legal custody* both parents share decision-making responsibility. In *Joint physical custody* children spend almost an equal amount of time with each parent. Unfortunately, joint custody is still not particularly common. In some cases, of course, there are **mitigating circumstances**. One parent may have abandoned the family or may have verbally, physically, or even sexually abused the children in question. But for the average parent, who wants what is best for the child but is no longer able to see the child except for brief visits, the issue is one of fairness to that parent as well as the child. The majority of non-custodial parents are fathers.

According to statistics released by the U.S. Department of Health and Human Services in 1999, children who do not live with both parents are twice as likely to drop out of school, twice as likely to end up in jail, and four times as likely to need help for behavioral or emotional problems. Organizations such as the Children's Rights Council (CRC) raised the level of awareness on this issue to the point that joint custody, both legal and physical, became more common.

### Children as Detainees

Illegal **aliens** who try to enter the United States may be detained and deported. This is true whether the aliens are adults or children. In 2000, nearly 4,700 children were detained by the U.S. **Immigration** and Naturalization Service (INS). Children are detained by INS after being picked up at U.S. borders without a parent or **guardian** and without proper documentation. The issue with these children is not that they are stopped from entering the United States illegally, but that they are held in such facilities as juvenile and county jails. Moreover, they face **deportation**, often to countries where they may be persecuted. They have no right to paid legal **counsel**. Reports that some who are detained in jails are mistreated has led human rights organizations to call for investigations.

In 2001 U.S. Senator Dianne Feinstein introduced the Unaccompanied Alien Child Protection Act, which would establish an Office of Children's Service at the U.S. Department of Justice. This office would be in charge of ensuring that children are treated humanely while in custody and that decisions on their future would be made based on their short- and long-term needs. It would also provide for legal counsel and guardians, as necessary, to be appointed to represent the children's interests.

## Convention on the Rights of the Child

In an effort to create a universally accepted set of children's rights, the United Nations General Assembly adopted the Convention on the Rights of the Child in November 1989. This document promises children the basic human rights of life and liberty, as well as access to education and health care. It also calls for protection against **discrimination** and abuse, protection from economic exploitation, and protection against torture.

While children's rights have become more visible since then, there are still many instances around the world of children's rights violations.

The United States did sign the Convention in 1995 but it was never submitted to the Senate for **ratification**. Although the government has stated that it has no intention of ratifying the Convention, it has consistently reaffirmed its commitment to children's rights.

Among the reason the United States has failed to ratify the Convention is the fact that the Convention clearly states that anyone under the age of 18 is a child. The U.S. government has reservations about how that would affect matters when a 16- or 17-year old commits a crime; currently, in certain instances that child can be tried as an adult. Also, the United States Government says that many of the declarations included in the document are not issues for which the federal government is in charge. For example, education in the United States is controlled by the states, not the federal government.

Whether the United States eventually ratifies the Convention, it still does maintain an enviable record of honoring most children's rights. Human rights groups are convinced that the United States can and should do more, and they continue to make their points of view known in the United States and abroad.

## Additional Resources

*The Child Advocacy Handbook* Fernandez, Happy Craven, Pilgrim Press, 1980.

*Children's Rights: A Reference Handbook* Edmonds, Beverly C., and William R. Fernekes, ABC-CLIO, 1996.

*Children's Rights in the United States: In Search of a National Policy* Walker, Nancy E., Catherine M. Brooks, and Lawrence S. Wrightsman, Sage Publications, 1999.

*The Children's Rights Movement: A History of Advocacy and Protection* Hawes, Joseph M., Twayne Publishers, 1991.

*What Are My Rights? Ninety-Five Questions and Answers about Teens and the Law* Jacobs, Thomas A., Free Spirit Publications, 1997.

## Organizations

### Amnesty International USA
322 Eighth Avenue
New York, NY 10001 USA

Phone: (212) 807-8400
Fax: (212) 627-1451
URL: http://www.aiusa.org
Primary Contact: Bill Schulz, Executive Director

### Children's Rights Council

6200 Editors Park Drive, Suite 103 Avenue
Hyattsville, MD 20782 USA
Phone: (301) 559-3120
Fax: (301) 559-3124
URL: http://www.gocrc.com
Primary Contact: David L. Levy, President

### Human Rights Watch

350 Fifth Avenue
New York, NY 10118 USA
Phone: (212) 490-4700
Fax: (212) 736-1300
URL: http://www.hrw.org
Primary Contact: Kenneth Roth, Executive Director

### United Nations Children's Fund (UNICEF)

3 United Nations Plaza
New York, NY 10017 USA
Phone: (212) 326-7000
Fax: (212) 887-7465
URL: http://www.unicef.org
Primary Contact: Carol Bellamy, Executive Director

### United States Department of Justice, Civil Rights Division

950 Pennsylvania Avenue NW
Washington, DC 20530 USA
Phone: (202) 514-2648
Phone: (800) 375-5283
Fax: (202) 514-1776
URL: http://www.usdoj.gov
Primary Contact: Ralph L. Boyd, Jr., Assistant
Attorney General

# CIVIL RIGHTS

## CIVIL LIBERTIES

*Sections within this essay:*

## Overview

The Declaration of Independence states that all individuals have a right to "life, liberty, and the pursuit of happiness." When the United States Constitution was signed on September 17, 1787, it further established those rights for Americans. Anyone born or living in the United States would have the right to speak or write freely on any topic, the right to choose any religion, the right to assemble peacefully for any purpose, and the right to a trial by jury. More that two centuries later, the Constitution still guarantees those rights.

The Constitution was hardly a perfect reflection of true civil liberties; it would be nearly a hundred years before slaves were freed and more than fifty years after that before women could vote in national elections. What has made the Constitution work is its ability to accommodate social justice and the fact that there have always been people willing to fight for civil liberties.

There have been times when people questioned whether Americans needed as many civil liberties as they have. In times of war, for example, debates over whether certain liberties must be curtailed always take place. During World War II, the federal government placed 110,000 Japanese Americans, two thirds of whom were U.S. citizens, in internment camps. The measure was deemed necessary on account of the possible danger of espionage and infiltration of enemy forces. In hindsight, the government realized that this was an egregiously mistaken action (many Japanese American' in fact, had served bravely during the war in the U.S. armed forces), and Congress issued an official apology in 1993. After the war ended, fear of Communism caused state and federal governments to pass legislation requiring certain government employees to take "loyalty oaths" assuring that they were not Communists or members of like-minded groups. The issue reached the boiling point when Senator Joe McCarthy of Wisconsin claimed that there were Communists working in the federal government. McCarthy launched a series of Senate hearings, and people who were accused of being Communists often lost their jobs. The Communist scare burned itself out, but not before destroying many lives.

Those who feel that civil liberties can be curtailed under special circumstances will explain that special circumstances call for special measures. Civil libertarians will remind them that there is always a danger that once the special circumstances end, there is no guarantee that the self-imposed restrictions will also end.

Many people mistakenly believe that civil libertarianism is the same as political liberalism. Civil libertarians can be liberal, conservative, or anywhere within the political spectrum. Gun control is a good example. Most people do not think of groups such as the National Rifle Association (NRA) as a politically liberal entity. Yet the NRA, which was founded in 1871, has long been a vocal supporter of the Second Amendment, which gives citizens the right to keep firearms. The NRA's commitment to civil liberties, as it sees them in this regard, is hardly in question even by its opponents.

## The Bill of Rights

The first ten amendments to the U.S. Constitution are commonly known as the Bill of Rights. They set the groundwork for what we today consider our basic civil liberties. These amendments guarantee the following rights:

- Right to free speech. The First Amendment guarantees the right to freedom of speech, freedom of the press, and freedom to assemble peaceably.

- Right to bear arms. The Second Amendment guarantees each state's right to keep a militia, and arguably the right of individuals to keep firearms.

- No unauthorized quartering of soldiers. The Third Amendment prohibits soldiers from being quartered in private residences during peacetime without permission, nor during war time except under special circumstances.

- Freedom from search and seizure. The Fourth Amendment guarantees the right against search and seizure of personal property or private papers.

- Freedom from self-incrimination. The Fifth Amendment protects against self-incrimination and double jeopardy, and it guarantees due process.

- Trial by jury. Under the Sixth Amendment, individuals have a right to be tried by a jury of their peers in criminal cases. The Seventh Amendment guarantees trial by jury in civil cases involving certain set sums of money.

- Protection from excessive bail. The Eighth Amendment protects against excessive bail and also against cruel and unusual punishment.

- Unlisted rights and powers. The Ninth Amendment states that any rights not listed

are retained by the people, and the Tenth Amendment states that powers not delegated to the federal government are retained by either the states or the people.

Other key amendments guaranteeing civil rights and liberties include the Thirteenth Amendment (which prohibits slavery), the Fourteenth Amendment (which granted citizenship to former slaves), the Fifteenth Amendment (which guaranteed that the right to vote could not be denied on account of race), and the Nineteenth Amendment (which granted women the right to vote).The Twenty-Fourth Amendment, ratified in 1962, prohibited the imposition of a voters' poll tax on any individual

The Constitution was designed so that it could be amended, but the amendment process is by design not easy. Both houses of Congress must approve a proposed amendment by a two-thirds majority, and the amendment must then be ratified by three quarters of the states within a specific time frame (typically seven years). This procedure keeps the Constitution from becoming bogged down with scores of frivolous or narrow-issue amendments. This can work for or against the interests of civil libertarians. The proposed "Equal Rights Amendment" was passed by Congress in 1972 but failed to get ratified even after the ratification period was extended by three years. A proposed amendment in 2004 that would have imposed a constitutional prohibition on same-sex marriage did not receive enough Congressional support to be voted into existence.

## The ACLU

The best known civil liberties organization in the United States is the American Civil Liberties Union (ACLU). Founded in 1920, the ACLU works at the national, state, and local level through the courts, legislatures, and communities to ensure individual rights and liberties are not abridged. The ACLU has branches across the United States and maintains an active network of professionals and volunteers. The ACLU challenges legislation and any government action that it feels endanger civil rights.

The list of issues the ACLU handles is quite comprehensive: discrimination, religious freedom, privacy, free speech, prisoners' rights, immigrants' rights, rights of the poor, the death penalty—to name a few. The ACLU initiates lawsuits and often offers to defend those whose civil liberties have been challenged. In addition, the ACLU also issues "friend of the court" briefs for cases that go before the courts.

One of the ACLU's earliest battles was the Scopes trial in Dayton, Tennessee in 1925. Tennessee had enacted legislation prohibiting the teaching of evolution and the ACLU decided to seek out a test case to argue for free speech. John T. Scopes volunteered to be the test case, and the ACLU agreed to provide legal counsel. The lead attorney was the noted defense lawyer Clarence Darrow, who argued vigorously in defense of Scopes' right to teach evolution. Although Scopes was convicted and fined $100, the case brought the issue, and the ACLU, to national prominence.

A more recent case, one that was a victory for the ACLU, was *ACLU v. Reno.* The ACLU challenged the constitutionality of the Communications Decency Act of 1996, which prohibited "indecent" speech over the Internet. The act was too broad and sweeping, claimed the ACLU, and threatened to endanger the free exchange of ideas online. The U.S. Supreme Court agreed and voted unanimously that the act was unconstitutional.

Many people think of the ACLU as a liberal organization aimed promoting a leftist agenda. In fact, the ACLU has defended people and institutions of all political beliefs. For example, the organization has opposed the creation of "hate speech" regulations on college and university campuses. The argument is that even hateful speech is protected under the Constitution (unlike hate-based actions), and a better way to deal with hate speech is to find its root causes instead of merely banning it.

## Other Organizations

Although the ACLU is the best known and most prominent civil liberties organization, other national and local groups also challenge what they see as the erosion of civil liberties. The New York Civil Liberties Union (NYCLU), for example, does much of the same legal and advocacy group that the ACLU does. (The NYCLU was actually founded in 1951 as the New York affiliate of the ACLU.) The NYCLU focuses on civil liberties issues in New York, including issues surrounding security measures put in place since the September 11 attacks. A typical example is a federal suit filed in January 2006 by the NYCLU and the New York University Civil Rights Clinic on behalf of a filmmaker who was detained in May 2005 for filming on a Manhattan street. He was warned that he needed a permit, but when he applied for one some months later his application was denied without explanation. The

lawsuit filed by the NYCLU claimed that the film-permit requirement is unconstitutional.

People for the American Way, founded in 1980 by television and film producer Norman Lear, works to protect civil liberties by advocating with government agencies, providing statistics and information on civil rights activities across the country, and educating the public on civil liberties issues.

The American Library Association (ALA), which has more than 64,000 members across the country, works to ensure high quality information in libraries, and public access to that information. The ALA, through its Office for Intellectual Freedom, provides information on legislation and government activity that can affect how libraries disseminate information. Its opposition to Section 215 of the USA PATRIOT ACT (see below) is one example. ALA also created guidelines for librarians on how to comply with the Children' Internet Protection Act (CIPA), which requires libraries to use filters to keep minors from accessing adult material.

## Civil Liberties Issues

Although civil liberties groups have actively advocated on behalf of civil rights over the decades, and although they have had many successes, they are quick to point out that vigilance is the key to ensuring civil liberties are not allowed to slide. Below are some typical issues from the late twentieth and early twenty-first centuries.

### *Banning Books in Schools*

School boards regularly attempt to ban books, with classics such as *The Adventures of Huckleberry Finn* and *Of Mice and Men* among the most frequently challenged, according to ALA. In the early years of the twenty-first century, the Harry Potter series of books, which tell the story of a young aspiring wizard and his adventures in wizard school, have become a focal point for many who oppose the focus on wizardry and magic.

School boards do not have an absolute right to remove books from school library shelves. In the case of *Board of Education v. Pico.*, decided in 1982 by a 5-4 majority, the U.S. Supreme Court case ruled against the school board of Island Trees, New York, which had removed several books from the school library shelves. Included among these books were *The Fixer* by Bernard Malamud, *Slaughterhouse Five* by Kurt Vonnegut, *Best Short Stories of Negro Writers* (edited by Langston Hughes), *A Hero Ain't Nothin' But A Sandwich* by Alice Childress, and *A Reader for Writers* (edited by Jerome Archer).

The court noted that school boards do have discretion in what books to acquire for the school, and it could reject any works deemed to be "pervasively vulgar." But Justice William Brennan wrote that "the special characteristics of the school library make that environment especially appropriate for the recognition of First Amendment rights of students."

### DNA and Exoneration

DNA evidence can be used to convict criminals, and it has successfully been used to exonerate individuals, some of whom were wrongly imprisoned for more than two decades. Often, when a person who has been convicted of a crime tries to get DNA evidence admitted as evidence, the courts are reluctant, despite the fact that such evidence could exonerate an innocent person.

Often, the person who is wrongly convicted of a serious crime such as murder or rape has a criminal record for petty crimes, which means a record already exists. Civil libertarians have argued that many of these individuals were arrested and convicted more as a matter of expediency than of true suspicion.

The Innocence Project, created in 1992 by Peter Neufeld and Barry Scheck at the Benjamin Cardozo School of Law in New York, works to exonerate people by use of postconviction DNA, in which DNA from the crime scene is tested against the accused's DNA. Often, physical evidence from a crime is kept for many years. If the evidence includes samples of blood, hair, skin, or other evidence that can include DNA, and if that evidence has not been contaminated or corrupted, it can often be used to prove a person's innocence. Between 1992 and 2005, the Innocence Project helped exonerate 173 prisoners.

### The USA PATRIOT Act

On October 26, 2001, less than two months after the September 11 attacks, Congress passed the USA PATRIOT Act (Uniting and Strengthening America by Providing Appropriate Tools Required to Intercept and Obstruct Terrorism). This act gave the government greater ability to seek out and combat terrorist activity in the United States. The PATRIOT Act grants the Secretary of the Treasury with new regulatory powers to fight money laundering from foreign countries in U.S. banks; secures national borders against foreign nationals who are terrorists or who support terrorism; eases restrictions on interception and surveillance of correspondence and communication that may link to terrorist activity; stiffens penalties against money laundering, counterfeiting, charity fraud, and similar crimes; and creates new crimes and penalties for such acts as harboring terrorists and giving terrorists material support.

Civil liberties groups complained that the PATRIOT Act, hastily passed in a national atmosphere of grief, anger, and fear, granted the federal government too much power over innocent people or to track private records. One of the most controversial provisions was Section 215 of the Act, which gives the FBI permission to examine business records for foreign intelligence and international terrorism investigations. Called the "library provision" because some have read it to mean that libraries will be required to turn over lists of who has checked out which books, it has been criticized as overly broad by groups such as the ACLU and the American Library Association, but also by political leaders from both parties.

Another point of contention is the existence of National Security Letters, which give federal law enforcement agencies the authority to access an individual's personal records without first seeking a warrant. Opponents of this procedure said that such letters should only be issued when a reasonable connection can be made between the subject and terrorist activity. They also said that targets of these letters should have the right to challenge them in court.

As of the end of 2005 certain provisions of the PATRIOT Act were slated to sunset by February 2006, although members of Congress were planning to seek renewal or compromise on certain sections that were controversial.

### Monitoring Domestic Phone Calls

In December 2005 *The New York Times* published a story claiming that President George W. Bush had authorized the National Security Agency to monitor domestic telephone calls without first obtaining a warrant, as required under the Federal Intelligence Surveillance Act of 1978 (FISA). The Bush Administration confirmed that the wiretaps had been authorized, but he also claimed that as president, he had the right to make such an authorization, citing a joint resolution by Congress shortly after the September 11 attacks. That resolution, President Bush said, authorized him to take whatever steps were necessary to pursue individual terrorists and terrorist groups. He insisted that his actions were legal and necessary.

Civil libertarians, however, did not see the issue the way the Bush Administration did. Groups such as the ACLU claimed that Bush had circumvented the law by failing to get the proper warrants from a special FISA court set up to serve exactly that purpose. The problem, they maintained, was not so much that the president felt compelled to conduct the wiretaps, but that he did not even inform the relevant agencies about what he was planning to do.

The rationale behind this is what makes civil liberties such a complex issue. On the one hand, the libertarians make a valid point: There was no reason for the president to bypass the FISA court, and by omitting this step he may have compromised individual freedom more than he realizes. On the other hand, the president's supporters make an equally valid observation: If just one overheard telephone conversation gives the nation a piece of valuable information (such as the location for a terrorist attack) that saves lives and destruction, the benefit is well worth the trade-off of not obtaining a warrant first.

As of January 2006 it was unclear whether Congress would declare the Bush Administration's actions illegal under existing legislation.

## Additional Resources

*At War with Civil Rights and Liberties,* Thomas E. Baker and John F. Stack, Jr., eds. Rowman and Littlefield Publishers, 2006.

*Banned in the USA: A Reference Guide to Book Censorship in Schools and Public Libraries,* Herbert N. Foerstel, Greenwood Press, 2002.

*In Defense of American Liberties: A History of the ACLU,* Samuel Walker, Southern Illinois University Press, 1999.

## Organizations

### American Civil Liberties Union (ACLU)
125 Broad Street, 18th Floor
New York, NY 10004 USA
Phone: (212) 344-3005
URL: http://www.aclu.org/
Primary Contact: Anthony D. Romero, Executive Director

### American Library Association
50 East Huron Street
Chicago, IL 60611 USA
Phone: (800) 545-2433
URL: http://www.ala.org
Primary Contact: Keith Michael Fiels, Executive Director

### Fairness and Accuracy in Reporting (FAIR)
112 West 27th Street
New York, NY 10001 USA
Phone: (212) 633-6700
Fax: (212) 727-7668
URL: http://www.fair.org

### People for the American Way
2000 M Street, NW
Washington, DC 20036 USA
Phone: (202) 467-4999
URL: http://www.pfaw.org
Primary Contact: Ralph G. Neas, President

# CIVIL RIGHTS

## DUE PROCESS

*Sections within this essay:*

## Background

Under both the Fifth and Fourteenth Amendments to the U.S. Constitution, neither the federal government nor state governments may deprive any person "of life, liberty, or property without due process of law." A similar due process provision was found in the Magna Charta, as well as early state constitutions. Chief Justice William Howard Taft explained the purpose behind the clauses in *Truax v. Corrigan* (1921) as follows: "The due process clause requires that every man shall have the protection of his day in court, and the benefit of the general law, a law which hears before it condemns, which proceeds not arbitrarily or capriciously, but upon inquiry, and renders judgment only after trial, so that every citizen shall hold his life, liberty, property and immunities under the protection of the general rules which govern society. It, of course, tends to secure equality of law in the sense that it makes a required minimum of protection for every one's right of life, liberty, and property, which the Congress or the Legislature may not withhold."

Courts have interpreted the due process clauses as providing two distinct limitations on government. First, the clauses provide for procedural due process, which requires the government to follow certain procedures before it deprives a person of life, liberty, or property. Cases that address procedural due process usually focus on the type of notice that is required of the government or the type of hearing that must be held when the government takes a particular action. Second, the clauses establish substantive due process, under which courts determine whether the government has sufficient justification for its actions. Because courts use substantive due process to protect certain fundamental rights of U.S. citizens, issues related to substantive due process have been the subject of extensive debate.

## Procedural Due Process

Procedural due process focuses primarily on a person's right to be heard, rather than a person's right to prevail in a dispute. Courts usually consider two broad questions in cases involving procedural due process. First, courts consider whether the government's action involves an interest in life, liberty, or property. Second, courts consider whether the procedures that the government has employed assure that a person receives fair treatment.

### Deprivation of Life

The term "life" in the due process clauses is not often the subject of dispute. Even where the government deprives a person of life (e.g., through enforcement of the death penalty), the government seldom does so without following proper procedures. Where the government has allegedly taken a life in an impermissible manner, challenges to the action are usually based on another constitutional provision. For instance, challenges to the death penalty have typically been based on the Eighth Amendment's proscription against cruel and unusual punishment. Similarly, arguments related to whether life begins at conception or birth, especially in abortion cases, focus on the liberty interests of the mother rather than the definition of "life" in the due process clauses.

### Deprivation of Liberty

The U.S. Supreme Court has sought on a few occasions to clarify the meaning of the term "liberty," though the term has never had a precise definition. In *Meyer v. Nebraska* (1923), the Court stated that liberty "denotes not merely freedom from bodily restraint but also the right of the individual to contract, to engage in any of the common occupations of life, to acquire useful knowledge, to marry, establish a home and bring up children, to worship God according to the dictates of his own conscience and generally to enjoy those privileges long recognized as essential to the orderly pursuit of happiness of free men." This statement has been quoted by several subsequent Supreme Court cases.

Liberty interests are most clearly involved when the government's action results in physical restraint, especially in cases involving prisoners. In the examples below, the Supreme Court determined that the government was required to provide due process because of the deprivation of liberty interests:

- Revocation of parole (*Morrissey v. Brewer* [1972])

- Revocation of probation (*Gagnon v. Scarpelli* [1973])

- Revocation of "good time credits" awarded to prisoners under state law (*Wolff v. McDonnell* [1974])

- Involuntary civil commitment to a mental institution (*Addington v. Texas [1979]*)

- Transfer of inmates to a strict ("supermax") prison facility (*Wilkinson v. Austin* [2005])

- Transfer of a prisoner to a mental hospital (*Vitek v. Jones* [1980])

- Involuntary administration of antipsychotic medications (*Washington v. Harper* [1990])

By comparison, the Court has refused to recognize other forms of liberty interests related to prisoners, including the following examples:

- Remaining in a minimum security prison, as opposed to a maximum security prison (*Meachum v. Fano* [1976])

- A review of a prisoner's request to commute his life sentence (*Connecticut Board of Pardons v. Dumschat* [1981])

- Visitation, including visits from family members (*Kentucky Department of Corrections v. Thompson* [1989])

- Rescission of discretionary **parole** prior to a prisoner's release (*Jago v. Van Curen* [1981])

In addition to restrictions on physical freedom, liberty interests include all of the rights that are granted to the people either expressly in the Constitution, such as freedom of speech or freedom from unreasonable searches and seizures. Liberty also includes rights that are implied from the Constitution by the courts, such as the fundamental right for parents to raise their children.

### Deprivation of Property

The Constitution clearly requires that the government must provide due process before it deprives a person of real or personal property. The issue that is most often in dispute in this context is whether a person has a property interest in a government benefit. The Supreme Court, in *Roth v. Board of Regents* (1970), noted that, "[t]o have a property interest in a benefit, a person clearly must have more than an abstract need or desire for it. He must have more than a unilateral expectation of it. He must, instead, have a legitimate claim or entitlement to it." Hence, the key to whether a person has a property interest in a benefit is whether that person is entitled to the benefit.

In order to determine whether a person is entitled to a benefit, courts generally consider the terms under which the government has offered the benefit. If a government employee has a reasonable expectation that he or she will continue to receive a benefit, then the person may successfully assert that he or she has a recognized property interest in the benefit. For instance, a public employee who holds a position that is terminable at the will of either party does not generally have a property interest in that position. *Bishop v. Wood* (1976). However, where a state statute allows public servants to retain the positions in the absence of "misfeasance, malfeasance, or nonfeasance in office," the person could have a property interest in continued employment. *Cleveland Board of Education v. Loudermill* (1985). The Supreme Court has recognized property interests protected by the due process clauses in the following instances:

- A state **statute** allowing the government to aid in the collection of debts through wage garnishment without notice or a hearing violated due process rights of the person whose wages were garnished (*Sniadach v. Family Finance Corp. of Bay View* [1969])

- Welfare recipients were entitled to notice and a hearing prior to the termination of public assistance payments (*Goldberg v. Kelly* [1970])

- Suspension of a driver's license by a state department of public safety required notice and a hearing (*Bell v. Burson* [1971])

- A teacher who was employed by a junior college under a series of one-year contracts could prove entitlement to continued employment based on a provision of an employee handbook (*Perry v. Sinderman* [1972])

### *Procedural Requirements*

In some instances, the government may have deprived a person of life, liberty, or property without following any form of procedure. Other instances, where a governmental unit has followed some sort of a procedure, present more difficult questions for courts, which must consider whether the procedures were adequate for the protection of the rights involved. In this context, due process is concerned only that the governmental actor followed a fair decision-making process and not that the government reached a fair result.

Due process basically requires that a person who is deprived of a recognized right must be given some sort of notice and an opportunity for a hearing on the government's action. Where individual rights are affected by legislation, the publication of a statute is

sufficient to provide notice to all individuals. On the other hand, an action by an agency or a court requires notice that will ensure that interested parties will, in fact, become aware of a proposed action.

At a minimum, a person who will be deprived of a right is entitled to a fair decision-making process by an impartial decision-maker. However, rather than establish a single rule that all governmental bodies must follow in terms of the specific procedures that are employed during a hearing, courts instead balance various interests when determining what procedures that a governmental entity must use. The Supreme Court in *Mathews v. Eldridge* (1976) explained these factors as follows: "First, the private interest that will be affected by the official action; second, the risk of an erroneous deprivation of such interest through the procedures used, and the probative value, if any, of additional or substitute procedural safeguards; and finally, the Government's interest, including the function involved and the fiscal and administrative burdens that the additional or substitute procedural requirement would entail."

The Supreme Court has continued to adhere to the balancing test announced in *Mathews*, although this test does not require the government to provide a formal adversarial proceeding when it deprives a person of a right. In *Wilkinson v. Austin* (2005), the U.S. Supreme Court reviewed a case where prisoners were transferred from a state penitentiary to a so-called "supermax" facility, which was reserved for the most dangerous criminals. The state adopted an informal, nonadversarial procedure for determining which inmates would be transferred. Inmates received notice of their transfer as well as the factual basis for their transfer. Moreover, inmates had an opportunity to rebut accusations, and multiple levels of review were available for an appeal. After stating that the *Mathews* test still constituted good law, the Court determined that these procedures were adequate to provide due process.

## Substantive Due Process

### *History*

The Fourteenth Amendment, ratified by the states in 1866, included among is provisions the Privileges and Immunities Clause. This clause provides that no state "shall abridge the privileges and immunities of the citizens of the United States." Many commentators have long argued that this provision, rather than the Due Process Clause of the Fourteenth Amendment, should protect substantive rights of citizens. The Supreme Court, however, limited the application of the Privileges and Immunities Clause in the *Slaughterhouse Cases* (1872) by stating that the amendment did not create any new federal rights. The Court has rarely applied the Privileges and Immunities Clause since that time.

Although some cases during the nineteenth century suggested that the due process should protect substantive rights, the Supreme Court generally avoided this question. In *Lochner v. New York* (1905), however, the Court reversed its position, ruling that a state statute limiting the number of hours that employees could work violated due process because it interfered with the workers' right to contract. After this decision, the Court engaged in a practice where it effectively substituted its own judgment for the judgment of a legislative body.

Several pieces of legislation enacted under President Franklin Roosevelt's New Deal program were challenged on due process grounds. The Court at that time continued to strike down legislation based on the due process clause under *Lochner*, and the economic beliefs of the justices conflicted with the goals of Roosevelt's legislation. In a direct clash between two of the branches of government, Roosevelt threatened to add Supreme Court justices who were more likely to uphold the statutes. Although Congress later rejected the court-packing plan, the Court nevertheless reversed its position. By 1937, the Court no longer subjected legislation to the same type of scrutiny that it did under *Lochner*.

### Modern Protection of Fundamental Rights

Beginning with *United States v. Carolene Products Co.* (1938), the Court significantly revised its approach to the review of legislation. The Court presumes that legislation is constitutional and places the burden on the person challenging the law to prove that the law is not rationally related to a permissible government interest. Under this rational basis test, the Court strikes down very few pieces of legislation.

The Court's review of legislation changes when the law affects a fundamental constitutional right. A fundamental right may arise explicitly from the Constitution or may be implied from the Constitution by the courts. The application of the due process clauses in the context of the protection of fundamental rights overlaps with the application of the Equal Protection Clause. If a law classifies certain people based on their exercise of a fundamental right, then the Court applies the Equal Protection Clause to the

analysis. However, if the law restricts the fundamental rights of all persons, the Court engages in a due process analysis.

Under either the Equal Protection Clause or the due process clauses, where a law infringes upon a fundamental right, the Court subjects the law to close scrutiny. Unlike laws that are reviewed under the rational basis test, the Court presumes that a law that restricts a fundamental right is unconstitutional, and the state may only prove that the law is constitutional by showing that the law is "narrowly tailored" to further a compelling governmental interest. This standard is very difficult for the government to overcome.

One of the more controversial aspects of both due process and equal protection jurisprudence is the recognition of the fundamental rights that the Court has determined are implied in the Constitution. Few tend to question that citizens of the United States have a fundamental right to freedom of religion, since the Constitution explicitly provides this right. However, it is less clear that citizens have a general right to privacy since the Constitution says nothing about these types of rights. Nevertheless, the Court has recognized a number of these implied rights, which are often identified more generally as privacy rights.

### Right to Procreate

The Court has long recognized that the right to procreate is a fundamental right protected by the Constitution. In *Skinner v. Oklahoma* (1942), the Court invalidated a state statute that provided for the mandatory sterilization of certain habitual criminals. Noting that the right to procreate was a "basic right of man," the Court strictly limited the power of a state to impose involuntary sterilization.

### Use of Contraceptives

Much of the modern focus on the protection of privacy rights began with the case of *Griswold v. Connecticut* (1965), which involved a challenge of a criminal law that proscribed the use of contraceptives, even in private. According to the lead opinion written by Justice William Douglas, even though the Constitution was silent about the right to privacy, the Constitution nevertheless contained a "penumbra" of rights within the Bill of Rights that included the right to privacy. Since the criminal law in this case infringed upon the privacy rights of those who wished to use contraceptives, the Court ruled that it violated the Due Process Clause of the Fourteenth Amendment. Although other justices disagreed with the underlying rationale for recognizing privacy rights, the decision led to the recognition other fundamental rights in later cases.

### Abortion

Probably the most debated right that the Court has recognized relates to whether a woman has a right to terminate her pregnancy. In *Roe v. Wade* (1973), the Court found that a woman's right to make this decision was indeed a fundamental right protected by the Constitution. Competing with this right of the woman is the state's interest in maternal health. The Court in *Roe* established the time during which the state could not prevent a woman from having an abortion (i.e., during the first trimester of the pregnancy) and the time during which the state could place restrictions on abortions (i.e., after the first trimester).

Critics have attacked *Roe* since the decision was handed down, often on the grounds that it represents judicial activism at its worst. On the other hand, supporters have defended the decision with equal vigor on the basis that it represents one of the more important rights of women. Subsequent cases, especially *Planned Parenthood of Southeastern Pennsylvania v. Casey* (1992), have diluted *Roe* to a large extent, even though the basic holding of *Roe* has remained intact.

### Sodomy

Most states outlawed homosexual acts for many years through the application of sodomy laws. The repeal of these sodomy laws as they applied to homosexual acts became a focal point for gay and lesbian rights groups, much like the right to an abortion has been a focal point for women's rights groups. In the case of *Bowers v. Hardwick* (1986), however, the Court explicitly refused to recognize that the Constitution "would extend a fundamental right to homosexuals to engage in acts of consensual sodomy."

Critics argued that the Court misconstrued the basic rights at issue in *Bowers*, saying that the case was really about the right to be left alone rather than the right to engage in homosexual conduct (the case arose after police arrested a man engaged in a sex act in his own house). Seventeen years after the decision in *Bowers*, the Court reconsidered its position, and in *Lawrence v. Texas* (2003), it declared that sodomy laws were indeed unconstitutional. According to Justice Anthony Kennedy, "*Bowers* was not correct when it was decided, and it is not correct today. It

ought not to remain binding precedent. *Bowers v. Hardwick* should be and now is overruled."

### Marital Rights

The Court in *Loving v. Virginia* (1967), recognizing a fundamental right to marriage, invalidated a state statute that forbid interracial marriage. Chief Justice Earl Warren wrote that "[t]he freedom to marry has long been recognized as one of the vital personal rights essential to the orderly pursuit of happiness by free men. Marriage is one of the 'basic civil rights of man,' fundamental to our very existence and survival."

### Parental Rights

In addition to marital rights, the Court has recognized several other family-related rights, including the rights of parents to raise their children as they see fit. In *Santosky v. Kramer* (1982), the Court noted that "freedom of personal choice in matters of family life is a fundamental liberty interest protected by the Fourteenth Amendment." Further, the Court recognized a "fundamental liberty interest of natural parents in the care, custody, and management of their child."

Custody of one's children is considered to be a fundamental right, though the Court in several cases has refused to protect the rights of unmarried fathers. Parents also have a fundamental right to keep their family together, as well as to control the upbringing of their children. This includes the rights of parents to raise their children without interference from others, including grandparents. In *Troxel v. Granville* (2000), the Court in a plurality opinion struck down a Washington statute that allowed any person to petition a court for visitation rights if visitation was in the best interests of the child. Under this case, even though a state statute may still allow courts to grant visitation right to grandparents (and perhaps others), such a law may not do so in a manner than infringes upon a parent's right to make decisions regarding the "care, custody, and control" of his or her children.

### Other Fundamental Rights

In addition to privacy rights, the Supreme Court has recognized several other fundamental rights. Among these rights are the following:

- Freedom of association
- Right to vote and participate in the electoral process
- Right to interstate travel
- Right to fairness in the criminal process

## Additional Resources

*Constitutional Law in a Nutshell*, 5th Edition. Barron, Jerome A. and C. Thomas Dienes, Thomson/West, 2003.

*Constitutional Law: Principles and Policies*, 2d Edition. Chemerinsky, Erwin, Aspen Publishers, 2002.

*Constitutional Law*, 7th Edition. Nowak, John E. and Ronald D. Rotunda, Thomson/West, 2004.

## Organizations

### American Civil Liberties Union (ACLU)
1400 20th Street, NW, Suite 119
Washington, DC 20036 USA
Phone: (202) 457-0800
URL: http://www.aclu.org

### Human Rights Watch
350 Fifth Avenue
New York, NY 10118 USA
Phone: (212) 490-4700
Fax: (212) 736-1300
URL: http://www.hrw.org

### United States Department of Justice, Civil Rights Division
950 Pennsylvania Avenue NW
Washington, DC 20530 USA
Phone: (202) 514-2648
Fax: (202) 514-1776
URL: http://www.usdoj.gov

# CIVIL RIGHTS

## ESTABLISHMENT CLAUSE

*Sections within this essay:*

- Background

- Tests Used to Determine Constitutional Violations

- Religious Education in Public Schools
    - School Prayer
    - Creationism, Evolution, and Intelligent Design
    - School Vouchers

- Religious Displays on Government Property
    - Happy Holidays
    - Ten Commandments

- Governmental Assistance or Benefits

- National Symbols

- Blue Laws and Sunday Closings

- Additional Resources

## Background

The First Amendment to the U.S. Constitution states, in part, that "Congress shall make no law respecting an establishment of religion, or prohibiting the exercise thereof." This two-part protection guarantees not only religious liberty, but also freedom from governmental action that purports to establish or support religious causes. The Establishment Clause, or "establishment of religion" clause, is most often invoked in constitutional challenges regarding separation of church and state, whereas the "free exercise" clause is invoked when challenging governmental interference with personal and fundamental religious freedom. The Fourteenth Amendment makes these protections applicable to the states and subdivisions thereof.

In its purest form, the Establishment clause prohibits the state or federal government from establishing or setting up a church or religion as the official state or federal religion; it is said to provide "a wall of separation between church and state," in the words of Thomas Jefferson. Several U.S. Supreme Court justices, including prior long-term Chief Justice William Rehnquist, believed that the literal translation of the term meant that it only intended to prohibit the establishment of a single national church or the preference of one religion over another. This interpretation was premised on the historical context of the Constitution being drawn up by colonists fleeing oppression under the national Church of England. But other justices interpret a broader application of the term, to include prohibiting the government from promoting religion in general. This broader interpretation prohibits the government from passing laws that tend to favor or show preference for one or all religions, or tend to force belief or disbelief in any particular religion.

Accordingly, over the years, courts have eked out parameters of what government can or cannot do with respect to religion. For example, courts of law cannot adjudicate religious/ecclesiastical questions, nor can a religious test be used for election to public office. Likewise, providing testimony under oath need not be done by using a Bible and swearing before God; persons may substitute with an "affirmation," a solemn declaration that does not invoke or mention God.

However, in reality, constitutional challenges invoking the Establishment clause tend to be more complicated and/or subtle. Judicial interpretation of the Establishment clause is an ever-evolving area of law, made more so in the 20th and 21st centuries because of the increasing cultural and ethnic diversity of the American population, as well as advancement in scientific technology that speaks to creationism and evolution.

## Tests Used to Determine Constitutional Violations

To pass muster under the Establishment clause, governmental actions are scrutinized by courts, using a few key tests. One of the most often used and quoted is that outlined in the U.S. Supreme Court case of *Lemon v. Kurtzman,* (1971). In that case, the Court struck down a Pennsylvania state program providing aid to religious elementary and secondary schools, in the form of reimbursement for salaries, textbooks, and instructional materials. However, payment was premised upon the condition, among others, that the courses taught be secular in nature, similar to those presented in the public schools. Notwithstanding, the high court was presented with the issue of whether payment of salary supplements was unconstitutional under the Establishment clause.

The *Lemon* Court, under Chief Justice Warren Burger, outlined a three-prong test to be used in such challenges. To pass constitutional muster, a government action: (1) must have a secular legislative purpose; (2) its principal or primary effect must neither advance nor inhibit religion; and (3) it must not foster an excessive governmental entanglement with religion. The Court found the Pennsylvania school aid passed the first two prongs, but also found there was excessive entanglement with religion in its cumulative effect. While religion and government must co-exist in society and normally will interact at some points, they should not so overlap and intertwine as to cause persons to have difficulty differentiating between the two.

In 1997, the Supreme Court modified the *Lemon* test in its *Agostini v. Felton* decision. It combined the last two prongs (effect and entanglement), now using only the "purpose" and "effects" prongs. It still used the "excessive entanglement" criterion, but within the context of determining whether a governmental action had a primary effect of advancing religion.

In other Establishment clause cases, courts also look to a test first advanced by Justice Anthony Kennedy, known as the "coercion" test. Under this test, government actions would be deemed constitutional unless they (1) provided direct aid to religion in a way that tended to establish a state church; or (2) coerced people to support or participate in religion against their will.

Still another, the "endorsement test" advanced by Justice Sandra Day O'Connor, asks whether the government action amounts to an endorsement of religion. Her primary focus was whether a government action conveyed "a message to non-adherents [of religion] that they are outsiders, not full members of the political community, and an accompanying message to adherents that they are insiders, favored members of the political community," (from her dissenting opinion in the 1984 case of *Lynch v. Donnelly*). The endorsement test has been somewhat subsumed into the remaining *Lemon* prongs. The endorsement test is often used to consider cases in which the government is engaged in expressive activities such as graduation prayers, religious signs on government property, etc.

## Religious Education in Public Schools

Religious instruction in public schools is prohibited under the Establishment clause. But seldom is the constitutional challenge so well defined. Instead, questions arise about the nature of the instruction (whether it is truly "religious") or what constitutes instruction or teaching.

In 1948, the U.S. Supreme Court struck down "released time" programs in public schools, which allowed early release from classes in order to receive religious instruction. However, the religious instruction was conducted elsewhere in the same public school buildings. The Court found that, in essence, the government was allowing publicly funded facilities to be used for the teaching of specific religious doctrine.

### School Prayer

For almost one hundred and fifty years, courts permitted schools to require student prayer. Finally, in 1963, the U.S. Supreme Court held that requiring prayer or Bible study in public schools, even if generalized and nondenominational, violated the Establishment clause of the First Amendment (*Abington School District v. Schempp*). Since then, various school systems have attempted to comply with this holding, but still allow some freedom. In the latter part of the 20th century and the early 2000s, the high court has increasingly been petitioned to refine and clarify the parameters of separation of church and state as it relates to prayer. While early cases prohibited praying out loud, later decisions also forbade compelled moments of silence or meditation. In *Wallace v. Jaffe* (1985), the Court banned a compelled "daily moment of silence" during which students were "encouraged" to use the time for silent prayer. In *Lee v. Weisman* (1992), the Court struck down invocations at public school graduation ceremonies, on the grounds that they had the effect of advancing religion and promoting excessive entanglement between church and state.

In the 1990s, the Supreme Court issued some decisions that seemed to suggest the need or desire to carve some exceptions out of the stricter separation of church and state decisions. In *Westside Community Board Of Educ. v. Mergens* (1990), the Court held that if a school provided its facilities to some groups during off-hours, it must also make those facilities available to religious groups as well. In another case, the Court held that allowing a public employee to serve as a sign-language interpreter for a deaf child attending a religious school was permissible, even though the public employee would be spending at least part of his time interpreting religious beliefs and translating religious teachings.

### Creationism, Evolution, and Intelligent Design

Despite the 1925 Scopes "Monkey Trial," it was not until much later that a formal approach to teaching evolution was outlined. The general rule, set down in the 1987 U.S. Supreme Court case of *Edwards v. Aguillard* is that evolution must only be taught as scientific fact. Creationism may not be taught as a science. Moreover, the Court struck down a law requiring both theories to be taught side by side in public schools. In *Freiler v. Tangipahoa Parish Board Of Educ.* (cert. denied 2000), the appellate court struck down a Louisiana school board rule mandating that teachers read a disclaimer to students stating that the teaching of evolution was "not intended to influence or dissuade the Biblical version of Creation or any other concept."

In the *Aguillard* case (above), the high court offered some guidance, by stating that "teaching a variety of scientific theories about the origins of humankind to school children might be validly done with the clear secular intent of enhancing the effectiveness of science instruction." In the 1990s, some

teachers and school boards began telling students (by presenting only *scientific* evidence that supported it) about the scientific theory of "Intelligent Design." This theory, vouched for by many world-renowned scientists, does not displace Darwinism's focus on evolution, but rather adds to it the scientific theory of an organized, planned, and designed evolution far too complex for coincidence or happenstance. Critics have belittled Intelligent Design as merely a veiled teaching of creationism, but legal scholars believe its scientific basis and arguments actually fulfill the Supreme Court's mandate. As of 2005, the constitutionality of teaching a scientific theory of Intelligent Design had not come before the high court.

### School Vouchers

As mentioned, in matters of government expression, courts often look to the endorsement test, but when involving the use of government funds, courts are most interested in determining the *neutrality* of the financial aid. By determining whether the governmental action is neutral in treatment, the Supreme Court has allowed religious schools to participate in generally-available state voucher programs. It also has allowed states to provide computers to both public and religious schools, as well as provide remedial teachers to low-achieving students, whether attending religious or public schools. *Mitchell v. Helms* (2000), *Zelman v. Simmons-Harris* (2002), Under this analysis, the faith-based initiatives of the Bush administration, when structured appropriately, appeared to conform to constitutional standards.

## Religious Displays on Governmental Property

### Happy Holidays

Nativity scenes and other religious displays are generally permitted on public property if used in conjunction with the secular celebration of holidays. A publicly-sponsored Nativity scene standing alone is unconstitutional. The same holds true for publicly sponsored Christmas pageants with religious music, unless other secular holiday songs are included. Interestingly, *privately-sponsored* nativity scenes displayed on public property are constitutional, even in the absence of other secular symbols. However, equal access must be provided to competing interests/symbols, and to avoid confusion or challenge, public acknowledgment of the private sponsorship should be posted conspicuously.

The first big legal case resolving nativity scenes was *Lynch v. Donnely* (1984), a 5-4 decision allowing the display of a city-sponsored creche scene in a public park, alongside other secular symbols of the holiday (Christmas tree, Santa Claus, and cut-out figures of a clown, teddy bear, and dancing elephant). In 1989, the Court ruled against a different nativity display (in another narrow 5-4 decision), striking the privately-owned nativity scene displayed in a public county courthouse because the scene stood alone, without the display of other secular holiday symbols, —making this one indisputably religious in nature. *Allegheny County v. ACLU* (1984)

### *Ten Commandments*

As early as 1980, the Supreme Court had banned the posting of the Ten Commandments on public school walls. *Stone v. Graham* But the Court continued to be pressed into making determinations about displays in other settings. Proponents for display argued that the Ten Commandments were non-denominational and were part of the historical underpinnings of America: a moral reminder of right and wrong applicable to all citizens. Opponents argued that it was an impermissible endorsement of Judeo-Christian religion.

The issue was revisited in 2005, with two highly-publicized cases before the Supreme Court. Both decisions evidenced a split court; both decisions were 5-4 rulings. In *Van Orden v. Perry,* the high court narrowly ruled in favor of allowing the Ten Commandments to be displayed at the Texas state capitol. But in *McCreary County, Kentucky v. ACLU,* the Court, again narrowly, ruled that they could not be displayed (in framed copies) at two Kentucky court houses. In the Texas case, the six-foot high granite monument of the Ten Commandments was one among several national and historical markers spread across 22 acres of the state capitol grounds. The Court noted that 40 years had passed, without challenge, since the monument was first erected in the 1960s. The Court concluded that the Texas display represented a mixed but primarily non-religious purpose.

Conversely, the framed copies of the Ten Commandments displayed inside Kentucky courthouses stemmed from a governmental effort "substantially to promote religion," concluded the Court. (In an image that hangs above the courtroom in the Supreme Court, Moses is seen carrying the Ten Commandments. However, the tablets' text is not shown, and he is one of many historical figures depicted, including Mohammed and Confucius.)

## Governmental Assistance or Benefits

Financial aid given indiscriminately to all parents of school children (whether in public or religious schools) has tended to pass muster when challenged in court. If the aid is limited or directed to only parochial schools, it will generally fail for inability to show that the aid or assistance was limited to a non-religious purpose.

Paying bus fares and lending secular text books to parochial and private schools do not violate the Establishment clause. However, direct grants, including the supplementing of salaries is prohibited.

## National Symbols

Legal scholars have continued to dissect Supreme Court decisions to reach some palpable and instructive guidance in matters relating to the separation of church and state when it involves national symbols created by colonial Americans and steeped in historical symbolism. U.S. currency carries the motto "In God We Trust," and most school students (at least in the elementary grades) begin each day reciting the Pledge of Allegiance to "one nation, under God." Each meeting of the U.S. Congress begins with an invocation, which the Supreme Court found quite permissible, since the very first Congress paid a chaplain to provide an opening prayer.

Most legal authorities distinguish a general acknowledgement of God from the acknowledgement of a particular religious belief. They also make the distinction between invocations at the commencement of a congressional session, attended by adults, and school prayer, which may involve teachers and other students exerting influence over children more vulnerable to external suggestion or example.

In *West Virginia Board Of Educ. v. Barnette* (1943), the parents of Jehovah's Witnesses school children brought suit after their children were expelled from West Virginia public schools. A tenet of that faith is the commandment against bowing down to "graven images," which practitioners believe forbids them to recite the Pledge of Allegiance to one nation, under God. The West Virginia Board of Education defended that the children who refused to recite the Pledge disrupted the order and discipline of the classroom, which the board had a responsibility to maintain. The U.S. Supreme Court, reversing an earlier decision that resulted in gross harassment toward Witnesses, ruled that the expulsion of the children was an unjustified intrusion upon their religious freedom and was tantamount to a governmental censure of their religious beliefs.

In 2004, the issue again came before the Court in *Elk Grove Unified School District v. Newdow*. However, the Court dismissed this case on the issue of standing, without ever reaching the substantive issue. Nevertheless, its decision served to reverse a trial court decision that teacher-led recitation of the Pledge was unconstitutional. The case had been brought by an atheist who objected to his daughter having to listen to "one nation under God" in the Pledge. Since the divorced plaintiff did not have custody of his daughter, the Court ruled he had no standing and could not speak for his daughter in court.

## Blue Laws and Sunday Closings

Generally, Sunday closing laws (blue laws) have been upheld, because they were deemed to have been created to provide a day of rest and not a day of religious observation.

DeWolf, David K., Stephen C. Meyer, and Mark E. DeForrest. "Intelligent Design in Public School Science Curricula: A Legal Guidebook." 1999. Richardson, TX: Foundation for Thought and Ethics.

Larson, Edward. "Summer for the Gods: The Scopes Trial and America's Continuing Debate Over Science and Religion." 1997, published by Basic Books.

"Religious Liberty in Public Life: the Establishment clause." Published by the First Amendment Center. Undated. Available at http://www.firstamendmentcenter.org/rel_liberty/establishment/topic

*First Amendment Center*
1101 Wilson Blvd.
Arlington, VA 22209
Phone: (703) 528-0800
Fax: (703) 284-3519
URL: firstamendmentcenter.org

*First Amendment Center at Vanderbilt University*
1207 18th Ave.S.
Nashville, TN 37212
Phone: (615) 727-1600
Fax: (615) 727-1319
URL: firstamendmentcenter.org

# CIVIL RIGHTS

## FIREARM LAWS

*Sections within this essay:*

- Background

- Acquisition and Possession of Firearms
    - Eligibility to Purchase or Own a Firearm
    - Acquiring Firearms
    - Antique Firearms
    - Prohibited Firearms
    - Shipping Firearms
    - Transporting Firearms in Automobiles
    - Transporting Firearms on Aircraft
    - Transporting Firearms on Other Commercial Carriers
    - Ammunition
    - Firearms in National and State Parks
    - Hunters

- State and Local Restrictions on the Transportation of Firearms

- Special Rules Governing Traveling with Firearms in Other Countries

- Additional Resources

## Background

The Second Amendment of the **Bill of Rights** provides: "A well regulated **Militia**, being necessary to the security of the free State, the right of the people to keep and bear Arms, shall not be infringed." The Supreme Court has historically defined the Second Amendment as giving states the right to maintain a militia separate from a federally controlled army. Courts have consistently held that the state and federal governments may lawfully regulate the sale, transfer, receipt, possession, and use of certain categories of firearms, as well as mandate who may and may not own a gun. As a result, there are numerous federal, state, and local laws in existence today, through which a person must navigate in order to lawfully possess a firearm.

There were relatively few laws passed regarding **gun control** prior to the twentieth century. In fact, most legislation has been passed in the last fifty years.

- The National Firearms Act of 1934 was passed to hinder machine guns and sawed-off shotguns.

- The Firearms Act of 1938 provided for federal licensing of firearms dealers, regulated firearms transportation across state lines by dealers, outlawed the transportation of stolen guns with the manufacturer's mark eradicated or changed, and outlawed firearms from being carried by fugitives, indicted defendants or convicted felons.

- The National Firearms Act was later amended significantly by the Gun Control Act of 1968, putting more stringent control on licensed sales, buyer requirements, and the importation of sporting guns.

- Prompted by the fear of hijacking, the Undetectable Firearms Act of 1988 banned plastic and other undetectable guns.

- The Crime Act of 1994 banned the sale and possession of 19 assault-type firearms and certain high-capacity ammunition magazines.

- The Gun-Free School Zone Act of 1990 outlawed the knowing possession of firearms in school zones, and made it a crime to carry unloaded firearms within 1,000 feet of the grounds of any public or private school. The law was later held unconstitutional in 1995, in United States vs. Lopez.

- The 1982 assassination attempt on President Ronald Reagan resulted in the Brady Handgun Violence Prevention Act of 1993. The Brady Bill imposed a five-day waiting period before a handgun could be taken home by a buyer. Though the law also mandated that local law enforcement officers conduct background checks on prospective handgun purchasers buying from federally licensed dealers, this part of the law was struck down by the Supreme Court in 1997 in Printz vs. United States as unconstitutional.

Depending on where one lives, a person may only be forbidden to carry a concealed weapon, or may be forbidden to own a handgun at all. People who disobey or are not aware of the laws pertaining to firearms in their local areas and in areas to which they travel may be subject to tough criminal prosecution. It is therefore best to be familiar with the local and national laws before owning a firearm.

## Acquisition and Possession of Firearms

### Eligibility to Purchase or Own a Firearm

In general, persons who are twenty-one years of age or older can purchase a firearm from a federally licensed dealer licensed to sell within the state. Purchasers of rifles or shotguns must be eighteen years or older and may purchase in any state.

However, the following classes of people are ineligible to possess, receive, ship, or transport firearms or ammunition:

- Those convicted of crimes punishable by **imprisonment** for over one year, except state misdemeanors punishable by two years or less.

- Fugitives from justice.

- Unlawful users of certain depressant, narcotic, or stimulant drugs.

- Those deemed legally incompetent and those committed to mental institutions.

- Illegal aliens.

- Citizens who have renounced their citizenship.

- Those persons dishonorably discharged from the armed services.

- Persons less than eighteen years of age for the purchase of a shotgun or rifle.

- Persons less than twenty-one years of age for the purchase of a firearm that is other than a shotgun or rifle.

- Persons subject to a court order that restrains such persons from harassing, **stalking**, or threatening an intimate partner.

- Persons convicted in any court of a **misdemeanor** crime of domestic violence.

Under limited conditions, exceptions may be granted by the U.S. Secretary of the Treasury, or through a **pardon**, restoration of rights, or setting aside of a **conviction**.

### Acquiring Firearms

Once a person has made the decision to purchase a gun, a federally licensed dealer will fill out a federal form 4473, which requires identifying and other information about the buyer, and record the make, model, and serial number of the firearm. The licensee initiates a background check on the buyer through the National Instant Criminal Background Check System (NCIS) to determine whether the buyer is not qualified to own a firearm. This NCIS background check may be immediate, or may take up to three business days. Prior to November 30, 1998, a five-day waiting period was required.

It is unlawful for an individual to purchase a firearm through mail-order from another state. Only licensed dealers are allowed to purchase firearms across state lines from other licensed dealers.

Provided that all other laws are complied with, a person may temporarily borrow or rent a firearm for lawful sporting purposes throughout the United States.

### Antique Firearms

Antique firearms and replicas are exempted from the above restrictions. Antique firearms are any firearms manufactured in or before 1898 (including any firearms with a matchlock, flintlock, percussion cap, or similar type of ignition system). Also, any replica of an antique firearm qualifies if the replica is not designed or redesigned for using rimfire or conventional centerfire ammunition; if the replica uses fixed ammunition which is no longer manufactured in the United States and which is not readily available; if the replica is of any muzzle loading rifle, shotgun, or pistol, which is designed to use black powder or a black powder substitute and which cannot use fixed ammunition. (Note: Antiques exemptions vary considerably under state laws).

### Prohibited Firearms

The 1994 Omnibus Crime Bill included a provision that prohibited the manufacture and sale to non-military and police, after September 13, 1994, of semi-automatic rifles equipped with detachable magazines and two or more of the following: bayonet lugs, flash suppressors, protruding pistol grips, folding stocks or threaded muzzles. There are similar guidelines on handguns and shotguns. Additionally, the manufacture and sale to non-military or police of "large-capacity" ammunition magazines (holding more than 10 rounds) were also outlawed. "Assault weapons" and "large" magazines manufactured before September 13, 1994, are exempt from the law.

### Shipping Firearms

Personally owned rifles and shotguns may be mailed or shipped only to dealers or manufacturers for any lawful purpose, including sale, repair, or customizing. A person may not ship a firearm to another private individual across state lines. Handguns may not be mailed but may be otherwise shipped to dealers or manufacturers for any lawful purpose. Shipping companies must be notified in writing of the contents of any shipments containing firearms or ammunition.

### Transporting Firearms in Automobiles

Under federal law, a person is allowed to transport a firearm across state lines from one place where it is legal to possess firearms to another place where it is legal to possess firearms. The firearm must be unloaded and in the trunk of a vehicle. If the vehicle has no trunk the firearm must be unloaded and in a locked container (not the glove compartment or console). This federal law overrides state or local laws.

Many states have laws governing the transportation of firearms. Also, many cities and localities have ordinances restricting their transportation. Travelers must be aware of these laws and comply with the legal requirements in each **jurisdiction**. There is no uniform state transportation procedure for firearms. Upon reaching one's destination, the state law—or,

in some areas, municipal law—will control the ownership, possession, and transportation of the firearms.

It must be stressed that as soon as any firearm—handgun, rifle, or shotgun—is carried on or about the person, or placed in a vehicle where it is readily accessible, state and local firearms laws dealing with carrying come into play. If a person wishes to transport firearms in such a manner, it is advisable to contact the Attorney General's office in each state through which the person may travel; reviewing an *NRA State Firearms Law Digest* is also recommended to determine whether a permit is needed and how to obtain one. While many states require a permit for this type of carrying, most will not issue such permits to non-residents, and other prohibit such carrying altogether.

### Transporting Firearms on Aircraft

Federal law prohibits the carrying of any firearm, concealed or unconcealed, on or about the person or in carry-on baggage while aboard an aircraft. Unloaded firearms not accessible to the passenger while aboard the aircraft are permitted when:

1. The passenger has notified the airline when checking the baggage that the firearm is in the baggage and that it is unloaded.

2. The firearm is carried in a hard-sided container.

3. The baggage in which the firearm is carried is locked and only the passenger checking the baggage retains a key. Moreover, the passenger should remain present during airport screening to provide the key, if necessary, and to lock the case afterward.

4. Ammunition must be securely packed in fiber (such as cardboard), wood or metal boxes or other packaging specifically designed for small amounts of ammunition.

Violations of transportation regulations may result in criminal prosecution and civil penalties up to $10,000 per violation. Because air carriers may impose additional requirements on the transportation of firearms and ammunition, the Transportation Security Administration advises travelers to check with specific air carriers to find out any additional transportation policies.

### Transporting Firearms in Other Commercial Carriers

Any passenger who owns or legally possesses a firearm being transported aboard any common or contract carrier in interstate or foreign commerce must deliver the unloaded firearm into the **custody** of the pilot, captain, conductor, or operator of such common or contract carrier for the duration of the trip. Check with each carrier before your trip to avoid problems.

Bus companies usually refuse to transport firearms. Trains usually allow the transportation of encased long guns if they are disassembled or the bolts removed.

### Ammunition

Ammunition may be bought or sold without regard for state **boundaries**. Ammunition shipments across state lines by commercial carriers are subject to strict explosives regulations. As with firearms, shipments of ammunition must be accompanied by a written notice of the shipment's contents.

It is illegal to manufacture or sell armor-piercing handgun ammunition.

### Firearms in National and State Parks

Generally, firearms are prohibited in national parks. Individuals in possession of an operable firearm in a national park are subject to arrest. Rules in state park systems vary, so inquiry should be made concerning the manner of legal firearms possession in a particular park system.

### Hunters

In many states, game wardens strictly enforce regulations dealing with the transportation of firearms during hunting season. Some states prohibit the carrying of uncased long guns in the passenger compartment of a vehicle after dark. For up-to-date information on these regulations, it is advisable to contact applicable fish and game authorities.

## State and Local Restrictions on the Possession and Transportation of Firearms

Most states permit the carrying of a concealed weapon by a resident who has been granted a permit to do so. Two states, Alaska and Vermont, allow residents to carry a concealed weapon without obtaining a permit. According to the Brady Campaign to Prevent Gun Violence Report Card for 2004, Illinois, Kansas, Nebraska, and Wisconsin completely prohib-

it the carrying of concealed weapons. Nonresident travelers should check with appropriate governmental departments before traveling to another jurisidiction with a concealed weapon; concealed weapons laws are often different for nonresidents than they are for residents.

States that permit the carrying of concealed weapons are classified as either "shall issue" or "may issue." In a "shall issue" jurisdiction, authorities are required to issue a permit to carry a concealed weapon to anyone who meets statutory requirements. In a "may issue" jurisdiction, authorities are granted discretion and may require that an applicant show a demonstrable need to carry a concealed weapon.

It is important to check with local authorities a complete listing of restrictions on carrying concealed weapons in a particular state. Many states restrict carrying in bars, restaurants (where alcohol is served), establishments where packaged alcohol is sold, schools, colleges, universities, churches, parks, sporting events, correctional facilities, courthouses, federal and state government offices/buildings, banks, airport terminals, police stations, polling places, any posted private property restricting the carrying of concealed firearms, etc. In addition to state restrictions, federal law prohibits carrying on military bases, in national parks and in the sterile area of airports. National forests usually follow laws of the states in which they are located.

## Special Rules Governing Traveling with Firearms in Other Countries

Most countries have special laws governing the possession and transportation of firearms by nonresidents, and in many countries individual possession of firearms is illegal. Travelers should contact the appropriate government departments to learn about the laws prior to traveling. All firearms must be declared and registered with United States Customs on form 4457. This registration must be done at a U.S. Customs and Border Protection office before leaving the U.S.

The following are summaries for Canada and Mexico:

CANADA: Visitors who wish to bring firearms into Canada must declare the firearms in writing with a "Non-Resident Firearms Declaration" form. Multiple firearms may be declared on the same form. Three copies of the unsigned declaration must be presented to a Canadian customs officer at the border. The declaration costs $50 (Canadian) and serves as a temporary license and registration certificate for up to 60 days. Visitors who plan to borrow a weapon in Canada must obtain in advance a "Temporary Firearms Borrowing license" for $30 (Canadian).

Canadian authorities recommend that visitors fill out the declaration form and make copies before arrival at the port-of-entry. Requests for photocopies at the border may be denied. The applicant is required to sign the form in front of a Customs officer at the point of entry.

Canada has three classes of firearms: non-restricted (most ordinary rifles and shotguns); restricted (mainly handguns); and prohibited (full automatics, converted automatics, handguns with a barrel length of 4 inches or less, and .25 or .32 caliber handguns among others). Prohibited firearms are not allowed in the country, but restricted firearms are allowed if an "Authorization to Transport" (ATT) has been obtained from a provincial or territorial Chief Firearms Officer before arrival at the point of entry into Canada. An ATT will not be authorized for restricted firearms intended for hunting or self-protection.

More information can be obtained from the Canadian Firearms Centre via the Internet at www.cfc-ccaf.gc.ca, under the heading "Visitors to Canada" or by calling the Canadian Firearms Centre information line.

MEXICO: According to the U.S. Department of State, Bureau of Consular Affairs, U.S. travelers to Mexico should leave their weapons at home, unless they have obtained written permission from Mexican government authorities in advance of their visit. Many U.S. residents are arrested or fined every year for firearms violations in Mexico. Many of these offenders are licensed to carry the firearms in the U.S. and only inadvertently transported a firearm to Mexico, without any intention of violating the Mexican law.

## Additional Resources

*Encyclopedia of Gun Control and Gun Rights.* Glen H. Utter, Oryx Press, 1999.

*Gun Laws of America: Everyday Federal Gun Law on the Books, with Plain English Summaries,* Third Edition. Michael P. Anthony and Alan Korwin, Bloomfield Press, 1999.

*http://www.nraila.org.* "Firearm Laws" National Rifle Association Institute for Legislative Action, 2006.

*U.S. Code, Title 18: Crimes and Criminal Procedure, Part I: Crimes, Chapter 44: Firearms.* U.S. House of Representatives, 1999. Available at http://uscode.house.gov/download/pls/18C44.txt.

## Organizations

### Center to Prevent Handgun Violence (CPHV)
1225 Eye St. NW, Ste, 1100
Washington, DC 20005 USA
Phone: (202) 289-7319
Fax: (202) 408-1851
URL: http://www.cphv.org
Primary Contact: Sarah Brady, Chair

### Citizens Committee for the Right to Keep and Bear Arms (CCRKBA)
Liberty Park
12500 NE 10th Pl.
Bellevue, WA 98005 USA
Phone: (425) 454-4911
Fax: (425) 451-3959
E-Mail: info @ccrkba.org
URL: http://www.ccrkba.org
Primary Contact: Joe Waldron, Executive Director

### National Rifle Association of America (NRA)
11250 Waples Mill Rd.
Fairfax, VA 22030 USA
Phone: (703) 267-1000
Fax: (703) 267-3989
Toll-Free: 800-672-3888
E-Mail: comm@nrahq.org
URL: http://www.nra.org
Primary Contact: Wayne R. LaPierre, Jr., Executive Vice President

# CIVIL RIGHTS

## FREE SPEECH/FREEDOM OF EXPRESSION

*Sections within this essay:*

- Background

- Protection of Core Political Speech

- Permissible Restrictions on Freedom of Expression
    - Speech that Incites Illegal or Subversive Activity
    - Fighting Words
    - Symbolic Expression
    - Commercial Speech
    - Freedom of Expression in Public Schools
    - Obscenity and Pornography
    - Regulation of the Internet

- State Law Protecting Free Expression

- Additional Resources

## Background

The First **Amendment** to the U.S. Constitution provides that "Congress shall make no law... abridging the freedom of speech." The rights protected under the First Amendment are among the freedoms most cherished by Americans. Democratic societies by definition are participatory and deliberative. They are designed to work best when their representative assemblies conduct informed deliberation after voters voice their opinions about particular issues or controversies. But neither elected representatives nor their constituents can fully discharge their democratic responsibilities if they are prevented from freely exchanging their thoughts, theories, suspicions, beliefs, and ideas, or are hindered from gaining access to relevant facts, data, or other kinds of useful information upon which to form their opinions.

The theory underlying the Free Speech Clause of the First Amendment is that truthful and accurate information can only be revealed through robust and uninhibited discourse and that the best way to combat false, deceptive, misleading, inaccurate, or hateful speech is with countervailing speech that ultimately carries the day with a majority of the populace and its elected representatives. Of course, the majority is not always persuaded by countervailing truthful and accurate speech, especially in capitalistic democracies where factions that spend the most money tend to have the loudest and most prevalent voices through radio and television advertisements. Supreme Court Justice Oliver Wendell Holmes articulated an extreme view of the risks underlying freedom of speech when he wrote "that a law should be called good if it reflects the will of the dominant forces of the community, even if it will take us to hell." (Levinson). Similarly, Holmes wrote that freedom of speech does not protect "free thought for those who agree with us, but freedom for the thought that we hate." *U.S. v. Schwimmer*, 279 U.S. 644, 49 S. Ct. 448, 73 L. Ed. 889 (1929).

The Supreme Court has never literally interpreted the Free Speech Clause as an absolute prohibition against all restrictions on individual speech and expression. Instead, the Supreme Court has identified several kinds of expression that the government may regulate to varying degrees without running afoul of the Constitution, including the following: speech that incites illegal or subversive activity; fighting words; symbolic speech; commercial speech; student speech; and obscenity and **pornography**. The degree to which the government may regulate a particular kind of expression depends on the nature of the speech, the context in which the speech is made, and its likely impact upon any listeners. However, both state and federal courts will apply the same level of scrutiny to government regulation of free speech under the First Amendment, since the Free Speech Clause has been made applicable to the states via the Fourteenth Amendment's **Equal Protection** and **Due Process** Clauses. *Gitlow v. New York*, 268 U.S. 652, 45 S. Ct. 625, 69 L. Ed. 2d 1138 (1925).

## Protection of Core Political Speech

Core political speech consists of conduct and words that are intended to directly rally public support for a particular issue, position, or candidate. In one prominent case, the U.S. Supreme Court suggested that core political speech involves any "interactive communication concerning political change." *Meyer v. Grant*, 486 U.S. 414, 108 S. Ct. 1886, 100 L. Ed. 2d 425 (1988). Discussion of public issues and debate on the qualifications of candidates, the Supreme Court concluded, are forms of political expression integral to the system of government established by the federal Constitution. *Buckley v. Valeo*, 424 U.S. 1, 96 S. Ct. 612, 46 L. Ed. 2d 659 (1976). Thus, circulating handbooks and petitions, posting signs and placards, and making speeches and orations are all forms of core political speech, so long as they in some way address social issues, political positions, political parties, political candidates, government officials, or governmental activities.

The First Amendment elevates core political speech above all other forms of individual expression by prohibiting laws that regulate it unless the laws are narrowly tailored to serve a compelling state interest. Known as "strict scrutiny" analysis, the application of this analysis by a court usually sounds the death knell for the law that is being challenged. This application is especially true when the core political speech is expressed in traditional public forums, such as streets, sidewalks, parks, and other venues that have been traditionally devoted to public assembly and social debate. Strict scrutiny is also applied to laws that regulate core political speech in "designated public forums," which are areas created by the government specifically for the purpose of fostering political discussion. For example, state fair grounds may be considered designated public forums under

appropriate circumstances. *Heffron v. International Society for Krishna Consciousness, Inc.*, 452 U.S. 640, 101 S. Ct. 2559, 69 L. Ed. 2d 298 (1981). In nonpublic forums, however, courts apply a lower level of scrutiny, allowing the government to limit core political speech if the limitation is reasonable and not aimed at silencing the speaker's viewpoint. Examples of nonpublic forums include household mail boxes, military bases, airport terminals, indoor shopping malls, and most private commercial and residential property.

## Permissible Restrictions on Freedom of Expression

### Speech that Incites Illegal or Subversive Activity

Some speakers intend to arouse their listeners to take constructive steps to alter the political landscape. Every day in the United States people hand out leaflets imploring neighbors to write Congress, vote on a referendum, or contribute financially to political campaigns or civic organizations. For other speakers, existing political channels provide insufficient means to effectuate the type of change desired. These speakers may encourage others to take illegal and subversive measures to change the status quo. Such measures have included draft resistance during wartime, threatening public officials, and joining political organizations aimed at overthrowing the U.S. government.

The Supreme Court has held that government may not prohibit speech that advocates illegal or subversive activity unless that "advocacy is directed to inciting or producing imminent lawless action and is likely to incite or produce such action." *Brandenburg v. Ohio*, 395 U.S. 444, 89 S. Ct. 1827, 23 L. Ed. 2d 430 (1969). Applying the *Brandenburg* test, the Supreme Court has ruled that the government may not punish an antiwar protestor who yells "we'll take the f——— street later" because such speech "amounted to nothing more than advocacy of illegal action at some indefinite future time." *Hess v. Indiana*, 414 U.S. 105, 94 S. Ct. 326, 38 L. Ed. 2d 303 (1973). Nor could the government punish someone who, in opposition to the draft during the Vietnam War, proclaimed "if they ever make me carry a rifle, the first man I want in my sights is [the President of the United States] L.B.J." *Watts v. U.S.*, 394 U.S. 705, 89 S. Ct. 1399, 22 L. Ed. 2d 664 (1969). Such politically charged rhetoric, the Supreme Court held, was more hyperbole and not a threat intended to be acted on at a definite point in time.

### Fighting Words

"Fighting words" are another form of speech receiving less First Amendment protection than core political speech. Fighting words are those words that "by their very utterance inflict injury or tend to incite an immediate breach of the peace" or have a "direct tendency to cause acts of violence by the person to whom, individually, the remark is addressed." *Chaplinski v. New Hampshire*, 315 U.S. 568, 62 S. Ct. 766, 86 L. Ed. 2d 1031 (1942). Where subversive advocacy exhorts large numbers of people to engage in lawless activity, fighting words are aimed at provoking a specific individual. For example, calling someone a derogatory epithet such as "fascist," "kike," or "faggot" may result in a street brawl, but cannot be accurately described as subversive speech.

Fighting words should also be distinguished from speech that is merely offensive. Unkind and insensitive language is heard everyday at work, on television, and sometimes even at home. But the Supreme Court has ruled that the First Amendment protects speech that merely hurts the feelings of another person. The Court has also underscored the responsibility of listeners to ignore offensive speech. Television channels can be changed, radios can be turned off, and movies can be left unattended. Other situations may require viewers of offensive expressions simply to avert their eyes. In one noteworthy case, the Court ruled that a young man had the right to wear a jacket in a state courthouse with the aphorism "F— the Draft" emblazoned across the back because persons in attendance could look away if they were offended. *Cohen v. California*, 403 U.S. 15, 91 S. Ct. 1780, 29 L. Ed. 2d 284 (1971). "One man's vulgarity," the Court said, "is another's lyric," and the words chosen in this case conveyed a stronger message than would a subdued variation such as "Resist the Draft."

### Symbolic Expression

Not all forms of self-expression involve words. The nod of a head, the wave of a hand, and the wink of an eye each communicate something without resort to language. Other forms of non-verbal expression communicate powerful symbolic messages. The television image of the defenseless Chinese student who faced down a line of tanks during the 1989 democracy protests near Tiananmen Square in China is one example of symbolic expression that will be forever seared into the memories of viewers. The picture of three New York City firefighters raising the American flag amid the rubble and ruins at the World Trade Center following the terrorist attacks of September 11, 2001, is another powerful example of symbolic expression.

The First Amendment does not protect all symbolic expression. If an individual intends to communicate a specific message by symbolic expression under circumstances in which the audience is likely to understand its meaning, the government may not regulate that expression unless the regulation serves a significant societal interest unrelated to suppressing the speaker's message. *Spence v. Washington*, 418 U.S. 405, 94 S. Ct. 2727, 41 L. Ed. 2d 842 (1974). Applying this standard, the U.S. Supreme Court reversed the conviction of a person who burned the American flag in protest over the policies of President Ronald Reagan (*Texas v. Johnson*, 491 U.S. 397, 109 S. Ct. 2533, 105 L. Ed. 2d 342 (1989)), and invalidated the suspension of a high school student who wore a black arm-band in protest of the Vietnam War (*Tinker v. Des Moines Independent Community School District*, 393 U.S. 503, 89 S. Ct. 733, 21 L. Ed. 2d 731 (1969)). To the contrary, however, the Court has upheld federal legislation that prohibited the burning of draft cards. *United States v. O'Brien*, 391 U.S. 367, 88 S. Ct. 1673, 20 L. Ed. 2d 672 (1968). Of the governmental interests asserted in these three cases, maintaining the integrity of the selective service system was the only interest of sufficient weight to overcome the First Amendment right to engage in evocative symbolic expression.

### Commercial Speech

Commercial speech, such as advertising, receives more First Amendment protection than subversive advocacy, fighting words, and obscenity, but less protection than core political speech. Advertising is afforded more protection than these other categories of expression because of consumers' interest in the free flow of market information. *Virginia State Board of Pharmacy v. Virginia Citizens Consumer Council, Inc.*, 425 U.S. 748, 96 S. Ct. 1817, 48 L. Ed. 2d 346 (1976). In a free enterprise system, consumers depend on information regarding the quality, quantity, and price of various goods and services. Society is not similarly served, for instance, by the free exchange of obscenity.

At the same time, commercial speech deserves less protection than core political speech because society has a greater interest in receiving accurate commercial information and may be less savvy in flushing out false and deceptive ads. The average citizen is more conditioned, the Supreme Court has suggested, to discount the words of a politician than the words of a Fortune 500 company. The average citizen may also be more vulnerable to misleading commercial advertising. Even during an election year, most people view more commercial advertisements than political and rely on those advertisements when purchasing the clothes they wear, the food they eat, and the automobiles they drive. Thus, the First Amendment permits governmental regulation of commercial speech so long as the government's interest in doing so is substantial (e.g., the prohibition of false, deceptive, and misleading advertisements), the regulations directly advance the government's asserted interest, and the regulations are no more extensive than necessary to serve that interest.

### Freedom of Expression in Public Schools

In 1969 the Supreme Court articulated one of its most cited First Amendment pronouncements when it said that "[n]either students [n]or teachers shed their constitutional rights to freedom of speech or expression at the schoolhouse gate." *Tinker v. Des Moines School District,* 393 U.S. 503, 89 S. Ct. 733, 21 L. Ed. 2d 731 (1969). Despite the frequency in which other courts have quoted this passage in addressing the free speech rights of public school students, as a principle of First Amendment law the passage represents somewhat of an overstatement. The First Amendment does not afford public school student the same liberty to express themselves as they would otherwise enjoy if they were adults speaking their minds off school grounds. In fact, the Supreme Court has since qualified this principle by stating that a public school student's right to free speech is "not automatically co-extensive with the rights of adults in other settings." *Hazelwood School District v. Kuhlmeier,* 484 U.S. 260, 266, 308 S. Ct. 562, 98 L. Ed. 2d 592 (1988). In *Hazelwood,* the Court held that educators may control the style and content of school-sponsored publications, theatrical productions, and other expressive conduct, so long as the educator's actions are reasonably related to legitimate pedagogical concerns. In short, student speech that is not consistent with a school's educational mission can be censored.

Applying the standard set forth in *Hazelwood,* the U.S. Court of Appeals for the Sixth Circuit upheld the disqualification of a candidate for student council president after he made discourteous remarks about an assistant principal during a campaign speech at a school-sponsored assembly. *Poling v. Murphy,* 872 F.2d 757 (6th Cir. 1989). "Civility is a legitimate pedagogical concern," the court declared. Even state universities may adopt and enforce reasonable, nondis-

criminatory regulations as to the time, place, and manner of student expressions. *Bayless v. Martine,* 430 F.2d 873 (5th Cir. 1970). However, a state university's refusal to recognize a gay student services organization violated the First Amendment because it denied the students' right to freely associate with political organizations of their choosing. *Gay Student Services v. Texas A&M University,* 737 F.2d 1317 (5th Cir. 1984).

### Obscenity and Pornography

Artful depictions of human sexuality highlight the tensions between lust and love, desire and commitment, fantasy and reality. Vulgar depictions can degrade sexuality and dehumanize the participants, replacing stories about love with stories about deviance, abuse, molestation, and pedophilia. State and federal laws attempt to enforce societal norms by encouraging acceptable depictions of human sexuality and discouraging unacceptable depictions. Libidinous books such as *Lady Chatterley's Lover* and pornographic movies such as *Deep Throat* have rankled communities struggling to determine whether such materials should be censored as immoral or protected as works of art.

The Supreme Court has always had difficulty distinguishing obscene material, which is not protected by the First Amendment, from material that is merely salacious or titillating, which is protected. Justice Potter Stewart once admitted that he could not define obscenity, but he quipped, "I know it when I see it." *Jacobellis v. Ohio,* 378 U.S. 184, 197, 84 S. Ct. 1676, 1683, 12 L. Ed. 2d 793 (1964). Nonetheless, the Supreme Court has articulated a three-part test to determine when sexually oriented material is obscene. Material will not be declared obscene unless (1) the average person, applying contemporary community standards, would find that the material's predominant theme appeals to a "prurient" interest; (2) the material depicts or describes sexual activity in a "patently offensive" manner; and (3) the material, when taken as a whole, lacks serious literary, artistic, political, or scientific value. *Miller v. California,* 413 U.S. 15, 93 S. Ct. 2607, 37 L. Ed. 2d 419 (1973).

Although the Supreme Court has failed to clearly define words and phrases such as "prurient," "patently offensive," and "serious artistic value," literary works that deal with sexually related material are protected by the First Amendment, as are magazines like *Playboy* and *Penthouse.* More difficult questions are presented in the area of adult cinema. Courts generally distinguish hard-core pornography that graphically depicts copulation and oral sex from soft-core pornography that displays nudity and human sexuality short of these "ultimate sex acts." In close cases falling somewhere in the grey areas of pornography, outcomes may turn on the "community standards" applied by the jury in a particular locale. Thus, pornography that could be prohibited as obscene in a small rural community may receive First Amendment protection in Times Square.

### Regulation of the Internet

Although the Internet has increased the amount of information available to the average person by many times, it has also become the medium for the transmission of information that some deem harmful. This is particularly true in the case of child pornography. Congress and several state legislatures have attempted to enact legislation that would ban the transmission of this type of pornography. For instance, the Child Pornography Prevention Act of 1996, Pub. L. No. 104-208, 110 Stat. 3009, banned the electronic transmission of depictions of pornographic images of children, including computer-generated images.

Groups have successfully opposed these laws on the grounds that they are overly broad and infringe upon First Amendment rights to free speech. In *Ashcroft v. Free Speech Coalition*, 535 U.S. 234, 122 S. Ct. 1389, 152 L. Ed. 2d 403 (2002), the U.S. Supreme Court struck down the Child Pornography Prevention Act. Although the statute banned pictures of actual children engaged in sexual acts, it is also applied to images that appeared to be of a minor engaged in such an act. Because the statute prohibited protected speech (i.e., images that did not involve children) in addition to unprotected speech (i.e., pictures of actual children), the Court found that the statute was unconstitutional.

Other statutes related to the use of the Internet have withstood constitutional challenges. In *United States v. American Library Association, Inc.,* 539 U.S. 194, 123 S. Ct. 2297, 156 L. Ed. 2d 221 (2003), the Court reviewed the Children's Internet Protection Act, Pub. L. No. 106-554, 114 Stat. 2763 (2000), which requires libraries that receive public funds to install filters on their computers so that neither adults nor children can access inappropriate materials. Despite arguments that the filtering software could effectively block access to constitutionally protected speech, the Court held that the statute was a valid exercise of Congress' spending power. The Court noted that the use of filtering software was no different in a library setting than was the selection of books and other physical items and that patrons could request that the filtering software be disabled.

## State Law Protecting Free Expression

The federal Constitution establishes the minimum amount of freedom that must be afforded to individuals under the First Amendment. State constitutions may offer their residents more freedom of speech than is offered under the federal Constitution, but not less. Below is a sampling of state court cases decided at least in part based on their own state's constitutional provisions governing freedom of speech and expression.

ARKANSAS: A state statute penalizing night-riding did not abridge the freedom of speech guaranteed by the state or federal constitutions. *Johnson v. State*, 126 S.W.2d 289 (Ark. 1939).

ALABAMA: A city's ordinance forbidding a business from permitting consumption of alcoholic beverages and nude dancing at the same time regulated conduct and not individual expression; thus, the ordinance did not violate the state's constitutional right to freedom of speech. *Ranch House, Inc. v. City of Anniston*, 678 So. 2d 745 (Ala. 1996).

ARIZONA: The state's statutory ban on targeted residential picketing was a valid accommodation for the right to freedom of speech explicitly protected by the state constitution. *State v. Baldwin*, 908 P.2d 483 (Ariz. App. 1995).

CALIFORNIA: The free speech clause in the state constitution contains a state action limitation and, thus, that clause only protects against government regulation of free speech and not private regulation thereof. *Golden Gateway Center v. Golden Gateway Tenants Ass'n*, 29 P.3d 797 (Cal. 2001).

ILLINOIS: The defendants' arrest for protesting on the premises of an abortion clinic did not violate the defendants' state constitutional right of free speech, since the clinic's policy required removal of all demonstrators from the clinic's premises regardless of their beliefs, and there was no indication that the clinic's policy of excluding demonstrators was ever applied in a discriminatory manner. *People v. Yutt*, 597 N.E.2d 208 (Ill. App. 1992).

MAINE: The state's statute allowing the State Employees Association to pay 80% of the collective bargaining unit dues for association members, while contributing nothing toward the dues of non-members, violated neither the state nor federal guarantees to freedom of speech. *Opinion of the Justices*, 401 A.2d 135 (Me. 1979).

MARYLAND: A county zoning ordinance for adult entertainment businesses violated the federal and state constitutions because the ordinance failed to leave open adequate alternative channels of communication. The land in the county that was available for adult businesses was less than one-tenth of one percent of the land available for commercial enterprises in the county. *Pack Shack, Inc. v. Howard County*, 832 A.2d 170 (Md. 2003).

MASSACHUSETTS: A conviction for threatening to commit a crime does not violate a defendant's free speech rights under the federal or state constitution if the evidence is sufficient to satisfy each element of the crime, since those elements are defined in a way that prevents a conviction based on protected speech. *Commonwealth v. Sholley*, 739 N.E.2d 236 (Mass. 2000).

MICHIGAN: A state administrative rule prohibiting simulated sexual conduct in licensed liquor establishments did not violate the state's constitutional provision guaranteeing free speech. *Kotmar, Ltd. v. Liquor Control Comm'n*, 525 N.W.2d 921 (Mich. App. 1994).

MINNESOTA: Differences in terminology between the free speech protection in the federal Constitution and the free speech protection under the state constitution did not support a conclusion that the state constitutional protection should be more broadly applied than the federal. *State v. Wicklund*, 589 N.W.2d 793 (Minn. 1999).

NEW JERSEY: Although the right to free speech under the state constitution is broader than the corresponding right under the federal Constitution, nothing in the state constitution gives a person the right to videotape public proceedings. *Tarus v. Borough of Pine Hill*, 886 A.2d 1056 (N.J. Super. 2005).

NEW YORK: A state statute banning the televising of any court proceeding in which the testimony of a witness by subpoena is or may be taken denies free speech guarantee by the state and federal constitutions. *Coleman v. O'Shea*, 707 N.Y.S. 308 (N.Y. Sup. Ct. 2000).

OHIO: The state constitution's separate and independent guarantee of free speech applies to defamatory statements only if those statements are matters of opinion, and citizens who abuse their constitutional rights to freely express their sentiments by uttering defamatory statements of fact will remain liable for the abuse of that right. *Wampler v. Higgins*, 752 N.E.2d 962 (Ohio 2001).

OREGON: A statute prohibiting a "live public show" during which participants engage in "sexual conduct" violated rights to freedom of expression under the state constitution. However, a statute prohibiting the promotion of prostitution was not unconstitutional. *State v. Ciancanelli*, 121 P.3d 613 (Ore. 2005).

PENNSYLVANIA: Regulations that barred nude dancing in public places violated both the federal and state constitutions. *Pap's A.M. v. City of Erie*, 812 A.2d 591 (Pa. 2002).

TEXAS: The state constitution offers greater free speech protection than the federal Constitution for political speech, but this greater protection does not extend to exotic dancing businesses. Society has a lesser interest in protecting material on the borderline between pornography and artistic expression than it does in protecting the free dissemination of ideas of social and political significance. *Kaczmarek v. State*, 986 S.W.2d 287 (Tex. App. 1999).

WASHINGTON: Nude dancing receives constitutional protection under the free speech guarantees of the First Amendment and the state constitution, although nudity itself is subject to the police powers of the state. *DCR, Inc. v. Pierce County*, 964 P.2d 380 (Wash. App. 1998).

## Additional Resources

## Additional Resources

*American Jurisprudence.* Thomson/West 2005.

*Fan Letters: The Correspondence of Holmes and Frankfurter.* Levinson, Sanford, 75 Tex. L. Rev. 1471, 1997.

*First Amendment Law in a Nutshell.* Barron, Jerome A. and C. Thomas Dienes, Thomson/West, 2004.

*West's Encyclopedia of American Law, 2nd Edition.* Thomson/Gale, 2004.

## Organizations

### American Bar Association

740 15th Street NW

Washington, DC 20002 USA
Phone: (202) 544-2114
Fax: (202) 544-2114
URL: www.abanet.org

### American Civil Liberties Union (ACLU)
1400 20th Street, NW, Suite 119
Washington, DC 20036 USA
Phone: (202) 457-0800

URL: http://www.aclu.org

### Free Speech Coalition
904 Massachusetts Ave NE
Washington, DC 20002 USA
Phone: (202) 638-1501
Fax: (202) 662-1777
URL: http://www.freespeechcoalition.com

# CIVIL RIGHTS

## RACIAL DISCRIMINATION

*Sections within this essay*

## Background

Citizens of the United States are protected against racial **discrimination** by many laws, including Constitutional protections, **civil rights** statutes, and civil rights regulations. The Fourteenth Amendment, which provides all citizens with **equal protection** of the laws, was ratified in 1868; however, the most significant changes in the law with respect to racial discrimination have occurred in the last fifty years. In this time, a number of landmark events have occurred and a number of landmark laws have been passed that prevent discrimination on the basis of race in many circumstances.

- In 1954, the United States Supreme Court ruled in *Brown v. Board of Education* that the Equal Protection Clause of the Fourteenth Amendment to the United States Constitution prohibited **segregation** in public schools on the basis of race. The Court then required public school districts to begin the process of integration "with all deliberate speed."

- The Civil Rights Act of 1964 brought about the most significant changes in civil rights protection in the history of the country. It prohibited racial and other discrimination in employment, education, and use of public accommodations and facilities.

- The **Voting Rights Act of 1965** prevented racial and other forms of discrimination with respect to access to the ballots.

- The Fair Housing Act, part of the Civil Rights Act of 1968, prohibited discrimination in the sale and renting of housing. It also extended these prohibitions to lending and other financial institutions.

- The Civil Rights Act of 1991 was designed to strengthen and improve previous civil rights legislation.

Civil rights laws do not render every form of racial discrimination unlawful. For example, laws do not proscribe general notions of racial prejudice by private individuals in most circumstances. However, when racial prejudices or preferences interfere with the rights of others, then the law is more likely to provide protection. This distinction applies to government entities or business entities engaged in interstate commerce.

## Constitutional Protection Against Racial Discrimination

### Supreme Court's Involvement in Protections Against Racial Discrimination

The U. S. Supreme Court has been called upon on numerous occasions to address the constitutionality of state actions that may involve racial discrimination. Prior to the enactment of the Thirteenth, Fourteenth, and Fifteenth Amendments to the U. S. Constitution, the Court rendered several decisions on the issue of slavery, many of which affected the future of the United States regarding the Civil War. The most significant of these decisions occurred in 1857, when the Court in *Scott v. Sanford* decided that slaves were not "citizens" as the term was used in the Constitution. The Court also determined Congress could not constitutionally prohibit slavery in the territories.

After the enactment of the Constitutional Amendments during the reconstruction period after the Civil War, the Court was called upon to decide a number of issues related to these amendments and civil rights legislation passed during this period. The most significant of these cases was called the **Civil Rights Cases**, in which the court restricted considerably the power of Congress to proscribe discrimination by operators of public accommodations. In 1896, the Court ruled in *Plessy v. Ferguson* that the Constitution did not prohibit states from enacting laws that distinguished people of different races. In the fifty years after *Plessy v. Ferguson*, states could constitutionally segregate members of different races under the "separate-but-equal" doctrine. The Court reversed its position in 1954 with the decision in *Brown v. Board of Education*, which also led to the enactment of the civil rights legislation by Congress.

### State Action

The Supreme Court has long held that the Constitution applies only to the actions of government, not to the actions of private individuals or entities. This restriction traditionally enabled private individuals to circumvent the rights provided in the Constitution. The first **casualty** was the civil rights statutes passed during Reconstruction after the Civil War. Subsequent cases involved such efforts as those by private individuals to prevent blacks from voting. Since these actions were not officially considered "state actions," the Court held that the Constitution did not apply.

The Court in more modern times has taken a more liberal view of which actions constitute state actions. In some circumstances, a state's approval of private action may constitute state action. Even if an action is not considered a state action, however, modern civil rights legislation may provide protection against private actions that is equivalent to constitutional protection.

### Thirteenth Amendment Protections

The United States abolished slavery in the United States when it ratified the Thirteenth Amendment in 1865. Under this amendment, slavery and involuntary servitude, except as punishment for crimes, were outlawed. The amendment also permitted Congress to enact legislation to enforce this amendment. The Supreme Court restricted Congressional power to enforce the act in the Civil Rights Cases in 1883, and relatively little **litigation** occurred over the next eighty years. However, the Court held in the 1968 case of *Jones v. Alfred H. Mayer Co.* that Congressional authority to proscribe private discrimination was granted by the Thirteenth Amendment. Since that time, the Thirteenth Amendment has served as part of the basis of authority under which Congress may enact civil rights legislation.

### Fourteenth Amendment Protections

One of the more controversial laws in the history of the United States is the Fourteenth Amendment to the United States. This amendment prohibits government from denying equal protection of the laws or **due process of law** to the citizens of the United States. Defining "equal protection" and "due process," however, has perplexed the U. S. Supreme Court, lower federal courts, and state courts since the **ratification** of the amendment in 1868. Though ironically the Equal Protection Clause was the basis for such historic doctrines as "separate-but-equal" in Plessy v. Ferguson, it has also served as the basic constitutional protection against racial discrimination by government entities in modern civil rights **jurisprudence**.

Laws designed to give preferences to whites to the detriment of members of the minority races are clearly unconstitutional. More difficult questions are raised with respect to **affirmative action** programs designed to give minorities opportunities they may lack due to a history of discrimination. Since the late 1980's, the Supreme Court has struck down several of these programs as unconstitutional. Similar problems have been raised with respect to efforts to **gerrymander** voting districts in order to ensure that minority (or nonminority) political candidates have a better chance to win seats. Unless such efforts have been designed to remedy specific instances of discrimination, they are most likely in violation of the Equal Protection Clause.

### Fifteenth Amendment Protection

All citizens are guaranteed the right to vote through the Fifteenth Amendment. This amendment, ratified in 1870, was designed to eradicate efforts to disenfranchise blacks during Reconstruction following the Civil War. The Supreme Court limited the application of this amendment in several cases decided between 1876 and 1903, and the Court has traditionally placed much more weight on the Fourteenth Amendment than the Fifteenth Amendment with respect to racial discrimination. This tendency applies even in cases involving allegations of **infringement** on the right to vote. The most significant exception was the case of *Smith v. Allwright* in 1944, in which the Supreme Court invalidated an election on the basis of Fifteenth Amendment protections.

### State Protections Against Racial Discrimination

The Thirteenth, Fourteenth, and Fifteenth Amendments, by their own terms, apply to the state governments. The Fourteenth Amendment, for example, states, "No State shall . . . deny to any person within its **jurisdiction** the equal protection of the laws." State constitutions and state laws can provide greater protection to prevent racial discrimination than federal constitution guarantees. Since the U. S. Constitution is the supreme law of the land, no state constitution or **statute** can restrict the rights granted to all citizens of the United States. In other words, the federal Constitution provides the minimum level of rights to citizens in this country, and states may only raise this level rather than reduce it.

### Judicial Review of Constitutional Violations

Supreme Court jurisprudence in the area of racial discrimination is often very confusing due to the terminology used when the Court reviews these cases.

When the government classifies people differently, courts will employ various levels of scrutiny to determine whether that classification is constitutionally permissible. Many classifications are generally permissible, such as those classifications that differentiate on the basis of income for tax purposes. These classifications are presumed constitutional and will be upheld unless a party can prove that the government has no rational basis for its decision.

If a government entity makes a classification based on race, courts employ a heightened standard of review. These classifications are presumed to be unconstitutional and will be upheld only if the government can prove that the program is narrowly tailored to address a compelling government interest. Very few government programs that make racial classifications can satisfy strict scrutiny, including many affirmative action programs. The Court's position in this area can shift as new justices join the Court.

## Civil Rights Acts and Their Applications

### History of Civil Rights Acts

Congress attempted to provide a number of rights to members of minority races in the Civil Rights Act of 1875. However, the Supreme Court in the Civil Rights Cases in 1883 significantly curtailed this effort by ruling that Congress did not have the authority to restrict segregation in public accommodations and public conveyances. Only state governments had the power to address racial discrimination by private actors. After the decision in *Plessy v. Ferguson,* states were able to enact legislation segregating the different races, and Congress was powerless to restrict these laws.

Beginning primarily with the Supreme Court's decision in *Brown v. Board of Education* in 1954, the Court established a more expansive view of congressional authority in the area of racial discrimination. Congress enacted a number of statutes between 1957 and 1968 that granted equal rights to all races in education, employment, voting, and many other areas relevant to interstate commerce.

### Employment

Employers are prohibited from discriminating on the basis of race, sex, religion, or national origin by the provisions of Title VII of the Civil Rights Act of 1964. To enforce this Act, which neither defines discrimination nor sets forth mechanisms for enforcement, Congress established the Equal Employment Opportunity Commission (**EEOC**). The EEOC views discrimination on a broad level, considering "discrimination" to include not only blatant acts of **bias** but also programs that have a disparate impact on minorities. The EEOC has enacted numerous regulations that give guidance to employers regarding employment discrimination.

### Voting

Despite the enactment of the Fifteenth Amendment, governments and private individuals used a variety of tactics to prevent blacks from exercising their right to vote. Such tactics included poll taxes, property requirements, intimidation, and other mechanisms designed to discourage blacks from voting. To address these inequities, Congress in 1965 passed the Voting Rights Act. Among other provisions, this Act prohibited requirements that voters take literacy tests or pay poll taxes prior to receiving the right to vote. Provisions in other statutes further enhanced voting rights. The Equal Protection Clause of the Fourteenth Amendment provides additional protection against discrimination in voting.

### Education

School segregation and desegregation were among the most controversial topics in the civil rights movement in the 1950s and 1960s. The Supreme Court's decision in *Brown v. Board of Education* outlawed segregation of blacks and whites in public schools, though studies have shown that the educational levels of white students and minority students remains unequal. The Civil Rights Act of 1964 prohibits discrimination in education on the basis of race but does not contain mechanisms to ensure that education of all students, minority or nonminority, remains entirely equal.

Initial efforts to ensure educational equality focused on forced integration of students of different races. This effort involved the process of busing students from areas with a largely black population to schools in traditionally white areas. Many of these efforts have been found to be unconstitutional. Schools in higher education sought to provide some level of equality by mandating that a certain number of minorities fill positions in entering classes. However, the Supreme Court in *Bakke v. Board of Regents* ruled that such a requirement violated the Equal Protection Clause. Though some schools continue to consider race as a factor in college admissions, the legality of such considerations are progressively becoming more questionable. For example, in 1996, the Fifth Circuit Court of Appeals ruled in the 1996 case of *Hopwood v. Texas* that the University of

Texas School of Law could not consider race as a factor in the admission of law students, even though the law school traditionally did not admit many minorities. In the cases of *Gratz v. Bollinger* and *Grutter v. Bollinger*, the issue of race was considered acceptable in one scenario but not in another. Jennifer Gratz was denied admission to the University of Michigan's undergraduate program in 1995, and in 1997 Barbara Grutter was denied admission to the university's law school. Both women were white, and they claimed that the university's admissions program discriminated against white students. The university was using a point system for undergraduate admissions, assigning extra points to what it considered "under-represented" racial and ethnic minorities. Since it also assigned extra points to athletes, children of alumni, and men enrolling in the nursing school, the university felt there was nothing problematic with assigning points for race as well. The law school did not have a point system, but it did use race used as a determining factor because, the university maintained, it helped promote cross-racial understanding. In 2003 the U.S. Supreme Court voted 6-3 to strike down the undergraduate point system, but it upheld the law school's less rigid program in a 5-4 vote. In so doing, the courts acknowledged that race could be a factor in admissions, but only one of several of equal weight.

### Housing

Many studies have shown a relationship between school segregation and residential segregation. If whites and minorities are segregated in the areas in which they live, the schools in these areas are more likely to be segregated as well. As noted above, some efforts to desegregate schools focused on busing students from proportionately black areas to proportionately white areas. Even these efforts, however, do not address the problem with segregation in housing. Congress passed the Fair Housing Act in 1968 to prohibit real estate sellers, landlords, and others from discriminating on the basis of race. However, this Act was not enforced or applied routinely for several years, and proving discrimination in housing can be difficult. Though the legal mechanisms to prevent discrimination are in place, societal changes are likely to be necessary to eradicate discrimination in this area.

### Remedies for Civil Rights Violations

The Civil Rights Act of 1991 and other federal statutes permit civil actions for a deprivation of civil rights, including violations of constitutional protections, violations of civil rights legislation, or any other antidiscrimination law. Victims of racial discrimination may recover monetary damages, including **punitive damages** and attorney's fees in appropriate circumstances. Victims may also seek an injunction or other equitable remedy.

## State Provisions Regarding Racial Discrimination

Many states have established their own rights related to protection of civil rights, including racial discrimination. Several of these states have established agencies or delegated authority to existing agencies to handle civil rights claims. In some states, civil rights law preempts other ordinary tort actions and in many cases limits the amount of recovery available to litigants with complaints related to violations of civil rights.

ALABAMA: Alabama has not enacted legislation dealing specifically with civil rights.

ALASKA: Complaints for relevant civil rights violations are submitted to the Commission for **Human Rights**. Private actions are permitted, and causes of action are not preempted by administrative action. The **statute of limitations** for a civil rights action is one year.

ARIZONA: Complaints for relevant civil rights violations are submitted to the Civil Rights Advisory Board. Private actions are permitted, and causes of action are not preempted by administrative action. The statute of limitations for a civil rights action is generally two years.

ARKANSAS: Private actions are permitted, except for those related to discrimination in public employment. Causes of action are not preempted by administrative action.

CALIFORNIA: Complaints for relevant civil rights violations are submitted to the Department of Employment and Housing. Private actions are permitted, and causes of action are not preempted by administrative action. The statute of limitations for a civil rights action is three years.

COLORADO: Complaints for relevant civil rights violations are submitted to the Civil Rights Commission. Private actions are permitted for some causes of action, but causes of action are preempted by administrative action. The statute of limitations for a civil rights action is sixty days.

CONNECTICUT: Complaints for relevant civil rights violations are submitted to the Commission on Human Rights and Opportunities. Private actions are permitted, and only certain causes of action are preempted by administrative action.

DELAWARE: Complaints for relevant civil rights violations are submitted to the Human Relations Commission or Department of Labor. Some private actions are permitted, but causes of action are preempted by administrative action. The statutes of limitations vary depending on the complaint.

DISTRICT OF COLUMBIA.: Complaints for relevant civil rights violations are submitted to the Commission on Human Rights. Private actions are permitted, and causes of action are not preempted by administrative action. The statute of limitations for a civil rights action is one year.

FLORIDA: Complaints for relevant civil rights violations are submitted to the Commission for Human Relations. Private actions are not permitted, and causes of action are preempted by administrative action. The statute of limitations for a civil rights action is eighty days.

GEORGIA: Some private causes of action are permitted, but none is preempted by administrative action.

HAWAII: Complaints for relevant civil rights violations are submitted to the Civil Rights Commission or Department of Commerce and Consumer Affairs. Private actions are not permitted, and causes of action are preempted by administrative action. The statute of limitations for a civil rights action is ninety days.

IDAHO: Complaints for relevant civil rights violations are submitted to the Commission on Human Rights. Private actions are permitted, and causes of action are not preempted by administrative action. The statute of limitations for a civil rights action is two years.

ILLINOIS: Complaints for relevant civil rights violations are submitted to the Human Rights Commission and Department of Human Rights. Some private actions are permitted, but causes of action are preempted by administrative action. The statute of limitations for a civil rights action is 180 days.

INDIANA: Complaints for relevant civil rights violations are submitted to the Civil Rights Commission. Private actions are permitted, and causes of action are not preempted by administrative action.

IOWA: Complaints for relevant civil rights violations are submitted to the Civil Rights Commission.

Private actions are permitted, but causes of action are preempted by administrative action. The statute of limitations for a civil rights action is 180 days.

KANSAS: Complaints for relevant civil rights violations are submitted to the Commission on Human Rights. Some private actions are permitted, but causes of action are preempted by administrative action. The statutes of limitations for civil rights actions vary depending on the complaint.

KENTUCKY: Complaints for relevant civil rights violations are submitted to the Commission on Human Rights. Private actions are permitted, but causes of action are preempted by administrative action. The statute of limitations for a civil rights action is 180 days.

LOUISIANA: Louisiana civil rights statutes are limited to those regarding the handicapped.

MAINE: Complaints for relevant civil rights violations are submitted to the Human Rights Commission. Private actions are permitted, but causes of action are preempted by administrative action. The statute of limitations for a civil rights action is six months.

MARYLAND: Complaints for relevant civil rights violations are submitted to the Commission on Human Relations. Private actions are not permitted, and causes of action are preempted by administrative action. The statute of limitations for a civil rights action is six months.

MASSACHUSETTS: Complaints for relevant civil rights violations are submitted to the Commission Against Discrimination. Some private actions are permitted, and some causes of action are preempted by administrative action. The statutes of limitations vary depending on the complaint.

MICHIGAN: Complaints for relevant civil rights violations are submitted to the Civil Rights Commission. Private actions are permitted, and causes of action are not preempted by administrative action.

MINNESOTA: Complaints for relevant civil rights violations are submitted to the Department of Human Rights. Private actions are permitted, and causes of action are not preempted by administrative action. The statute of limitations for a civil rights action is one year.

MISSISSIPPI: Complaints for relevant civil rights violations are submitted to the Home Corporation Oversight Committee. Private actions are not permitted, and causes of action are preempted by administrative action.

MISSOURI: Complaints for relevant civil rights violations are submitted to the Commission on Human Rights. Some private actions are permitted, and some causes of action are preempted by administrative action. The statutes of limitations vary depending on the complaint.

MONTANA: Complaints for relevant civil rights violations are submitted to the Commission for Human Rights. Some private actions are permitted, and some causes of action are preempted by administrative action. The statutes of limitations vary depending on the complaint.

NEBRASKA: Complaints for relevant civil rights violations are submitted to the Equal Opportunity Commission. Private actions are permitted, but some causes of action are preempted by administrative action. The statute of limitations for a civil rights action is 180 days.

NEVADA: Complaints for relevant civil rights violations are submitted to the Equal Rights Commission, Labor Commission, or Banking Division. Private actions are permitted, but some causes of action are preempted by administrative action. The statutes of limitations vary depending on the complaint.

NEW HAMPSHIRE: Complaints for relevant civil rights violations are submitted to the Commission for Human Rights. Private actions are permitted, and causes of action are not preempted by administrative action. The statute of limitations for a civil rights action is 180 days.

NEW JERSEY: Complaints for relevant civil rights violations are submitted to the Division on Human Rights. Private actions are permitted, and causes of action are not preempted by administrative action. The statute of limitations for a civil rights action is 180 days.

NEW MEXICO: Complaints for relevant civil rights violations are submitted to the Human Rights Commission. Private actions are permitted, but causes of action are preempted by administrative action. The statute of limitations for a civil rights action is 180 days.

NEW YORK: Complaints for relevant civil rights violations are submitted to the Division of Human Rights, Banking Department, or State Human Rights

Appeal Board. Private actions are permitted, and causes of action are not preempted by administrative action. The statute of limitations for a civil rights action is usually one year.

NORTH CAROLINA: Complaints for relevant civil rights violations are submitted to the Human Relations Commission. Private actions are not permitted, and causes of action are not preempted by administrative action.

NORTH DAKOTA: Complaints for relevant civil rights violations are submitted to the Department of Labor. Private actions are permitted, and causes of action are not preempted by administrative action. The statutes of limitations vary depending on the complaint.

OHIO: Complaints for relevant civil rights violations are submitted to the Civil Rights Commission. Some private actions are permitted, and causes of action are preempted by administrative action. The statutes of limitations vary depending on the complaint.

OKLAHOMA: Complaints for relevant civil rights violations are submitted to the Human Rights Commission. Private actions are not permitted, and causes of action are preempted by administrative action. The statute of limitations for a civil rights action is 180 days.

OREGON: Complaints for relevant civil rights violations are submitted to the Bureau of Labor and Industries. Private actions are permitted, and causes of action are not preempted by administrative action. The statute of limitations for a civil rights action is one year.

PENNSYLVANIA: Complaints for relevant civil rights violations are submitted to the Human Rights Commission. Private actions are permitted, and causes of action are not preempted by administrative action. The statute of limitations for a civil rights action is 180 days.

RHODE ISLAND: Complaints for relevant civil rights violations are submitted to the Commission for Human Rights or the Department of Labor. Some private actions are permitted, and some causes of action are preempted by administrative action. The statutes of limitations vary depending on the complaint.

SOUTH CAROLINA: Complaints for relevant civil rights violations are submitted to the Human Affairs Commission. Private actions are permitted, and causes of action are not preempted by administrative action. The statute of limitations for a civil rights action is 180 days.

SOUTH DAKOTA: Complaints for relevant civil rights violations are submitted to the Commission of Humanities. Private actions are permitted, and causes of action are not preempted by administrative action. The statutes of limitations vary depending on the complaint.

TENNESSEE: Complaints for relevant civil rights violations are submitted to the Human Rights Commission. Private actions are permitted, and causes of action are not preempted by administrative action. The statutes of limitations vary depending on the complaint.

TEXAS: Complaints for relevant civil rights violations are submitted to the Department of Human Resources. Private actions are permitted, and causes of action are not preempted by administrative action.

UTAH: Complaints for relevant civil rights violations are submitted to the Antidiscrimination Division. Some private actions are permitted, and some causes of action are preempted by administrative action. The statutes of limitations vary depending on the complaint.

VERMONT: Complaints for relevant civil rights violations are submitted to the Human Rights Commission. Private actions are permitted, and causes of action are not preempted by administrative action. The statutes of limitations vary depending on the complaint.

VIRGINIA: Private actions are permitted, and causes of action are not preempted by administrative action. The statutes of limitations vary depending on the complaint.

WASHINGTON: Complaints for relevant civil rights violations are submitted to the Washington State Human Rights Commission. Private actions are permitted, and causes of action are not preempted by administrative action. The statute of limitations for a civil rights action is six months

WEST VIRGINIA: Complaints for relevant civil rights violations are submitted to the Human Rights Commission. Private actions are permitted, and causes of action are not preempted by administrative action. The statute of limitations for a civil rights action is 180 days.

WISCONSIN: Complaints for relevant civil rights violations are submitted to the Department of Industry, Labor, and Human Relations. Some private actions are permitted, and some causes of action are preempted by administrative action. The statutes of limitations vary depending on the complaint.

WYOMING: Complaints for relevant civil rights violations are submitted to the Fair Employment Commission. Private actions are permitted, and causes of action are not preempted by administrative action. The statute of limitations for a civil rights action is two years.

## Additional Resources

*The Civil Rights Era: Origins and Development of National Policy.* Graham, Hugh Davis, Oxford University Press, 1990.

*Constitutional Civil Rights in a Nutshell.* Vieira, Norman, West Group, 1998.

*Oxford Companion to the Supreme Court of the United States.* Hall, Kermit L., Oxford University Press, 1992.

*Race Law: Cases, Commentary, and Questions.* Higginbotham, F. Michael, Carolina Academic Press, 2001.

*A Reader on Race, Civil Rights, and American Law: A Multiracial Approach.* Davis, Timothy, Kevin R. Johnson, and George A. Martinez, Carolina Academic Press, 2001.

*U. S. Code, Title 42: The Public Health and Welfare.* U. S. House of Representatives, 1999. Available at http://uscode.house.gov/title_42.htm.

## Organizations

### American Civil Liberties Union (ACLU)
125 Broad Street, 18th Floor
New York, NY 10004 USA
Phone: (212) 344-3005
URL: http://www.aclu.org/
Primary Contact: Anthony D. Romero, Executive Director

### Center for Equal Opportunity (CEO)
14 Pidegon Hill Drive, Suite 500
Sterling, VA 20165 USA
Phone: (703) 421-5443
Fax: (703) 421-6401
E-Mail: comment@ceousa.org
URL: http://www.ceousa.org/
Primary Contact: Linda Chavez, President

### National Association for the Advancement of Colored People (NAACP)
4805 Mt. Hope Drive
Baltimore, MD 21215
Phone: (410) 521-4939
URL: http://www.naacp.org/
E-Mail: members@naacp.org
Primary Contact: Bruce S. Gordon, President

### U.S. Equal Employment Opportunity Commission (EEOC)
1801 L Street, N.W.
Washington, DC 20507
Phone: (202) 663-4900
URL: http://www.eeoc.gov/
Primary Contact: Cari M. Dominguez, Chair

# CIVIL RIGHTS

## RELIGIOUS FREEDOM

*Sections within this essay:*

## Background

The First Amendment to the U. S. Constitution provides that "Congress shall make no law respecting an establishment of religion or prohibiting the free exercise thereof." The U. S. Supreme Court has interpreted this provision as guaranteeing two separate rights: (1) the right to live in a society where the government does not sponsor an official religion that dictates what God citizens must worship or what church they must attend; and (2) the right to exercise one's own religious faith in accordance with his or her conscience free from governmental intrusion. The first right is protected by the Establishment Clause of the First Amendment, while the second right is protected by the Free Exercise Clause of the First Amendment. Both clauses have their origins in American colonial history, and that history sheds light on the subsequent development of the First Amendment by state and federal courts.

## The Establishment Clause

### *History Behind the Establishment Clause*

Prior to the American Revolution, the English parliament designated the Anglican Church as the official church of the England and the American colonies. The church was supported by **taxation**, and English citizens were required to attend services. No marriage or baptism was sanctioned outside the church. Religious minorities who failed to abide by the strictures of the church were forced to endure civil and criminal penalties, including banishment and death. Some American colonies were also ruled by theocrats, such as the Puritans in Massachusetts.

The English and colonial experiences influenced the Founding Fathers, including Thomas Jefferson and James Madison. Jefferson supported a high "wall of separation" between church and state and opposed religious interference with the affairs of government. Madison, conversely, opposed governmental interference with matters of religion. For Madison, the establishment of a national church differed from the Spanish Inquisition only in degree, and he vociferously attacked any legislation that would have led in this direction. For example, Madison fought against a Virginia bill that would have levied taxes to subsidize Christianity.

The Founding Fathers' concerns about the relationship between church and state found expression in the First Amendment. Despite the unequivocal nature of its language, the Supreme Court has never interpreted the First Amendment as an absolute prohibition against all laws concerning religious institutions, religious symbols, or the exercise of religious faith. Instead, the Court has turned for guidance to the thoughts and intentions of the Founding

Fathers when interpreting the First Amendment, in particular the thoughts and intentions of its primary architect, James Madison.

But Madison's views have not produced a uniform understanding of religious freedom among the Supreme Court's justices. Some justices, for example, have cited Madison's opposition to the Virginia bill subsidizing Christianity as **evidence** that he opposed only discriminatory governmental assistance to particular religious denominations but favored non-preferential aid to cultivate a diversity in faiths. Thus, the Framers of the First Amendment left posterity with three considerations regarding religious establishments: (1) a wall of separation that protects government from religion and religion from government; (2) a separation of church and state that permits non-discriminatory governmental assistance to religious groups; and (3) governmental assistance that preserves and promotes a diversity of religious beliefs.

### Case Law Interpreting the Establishment Clause

The Supreme Court attempted to incorporate these three considerations under a single test in Lemon v. Kurtzman, 403 U.S. 602, 91 S.Ct. 2105, 29 L.Ed.2d 745 (1971). In Lemon the Court held that state and federal governments may enact legislation that concerns religion or religious organizations so long as the legislation has a secular purpose, does not have the primary effect of advancing or inhibiting religion, and does not otherwise foster excessive entanglement between church and state. Under this test, the Supreme Court held that the First Amendment prohibits schools from beginning each day with a 22-word, non-denominational prayer. Engel v. Vitale, 370 U.S. 421, 82 S.Ct. 1261, 8 L.Ed.2d 601 (1962). Such a prayer would be tantamount to the government sanctioning religion at the expense of agnosticism or atheism, the Court said, something not permitted by the Establishment Clause.

Similarly, the Supreme Court struck down a clergy-led prayer at a public school graduation ceremony as violative of the First Amendment. Lee v. Weisman, 505 U.S. 577, 112 S.Ct. 2649, 120 L.Ed.2d 467 (1992). By contrast, lower federal courts are split over the issue of whether a student-led, non-denominational prayer at a graduation ceremony violates the Establishment Clause, with some cases finding the prayers unconstitutional because they are initiated on school grounds at a school-sponsored activities and other cases finding no constitutional violation because the prayers are initiated by students and not public em-

ployees. However, the Supreme Court has ruled that the First Amendment does permit state legislatures to open their sessions with a short prayer each day. Marsh v. Chambers, 463 U.S. 783, 103 S.Ct. 3330, 77 L.Ed.2d 1019 (1983). The Supreme Court concluded that history and tradition have secularized this otherwise religious act.

The Court has produced seemingly inconsistent results in other areas of First Amendment law as well. In one case the Court permitted a municipality to include a nativity scene in its annual Christmas display, Lynch v. Donnelly, 465 U.S. 668, 104 S.Ct. 1355, 79 L.Ed.2d 604 (1984), while in another case it prohibited a county courthouse from placing a cross on its staircase during the holiday season. County of Allegheny v. American Civil Liberties Union Greater Pittsburgh Chapter, 492 U.S. 573, 109 S.Ct. 3086, 106 L.Ed.2d 472 (1989). In Allegheny the Court said that there was nothing in the county courthouse to indicate that the cross was anything other than a religious display, while in Lynch the Court said that the nativity scene was part of a wider celebration of the winter holidays.

The desire to avoid excessive entanglement between church and state has also produced a body of law that often turns on subtle distinctions. On the one hand, the Supreme Court ruled that public school programs violate the Establishment Clause when they allow public school students to leave class early for religious training in classrooms located on taxpayer-supported school property. McCollum v. Board of Education, 333 U.S. 203, 68 S.Ct. 461, 92 L.Ed. 649 (1948). On the other hand, such programs pass constitutional muster if the students leave class early for religious training off school grounds, where all of the program's costs are paid by the religious organizations. Zorach v. Clauson, 343 U.S. 306, 72 S.Ct. 679, 96 L.Ed. 954 (1952).

## The Free Exercise Clause

### History Behind the Free Exercise Clause

The Establishment Clause and the Free Exercise Clause represent opposite sides of the same issue. Where the Establishment Clause focuses on governmental action that would create, support, or endorse an official national religion, the Free Exercise Clause focuses on the pernicious effects that governmental action may have on an individual's religious beliefs or practices. Like the Establishment Clause, the Free Exercise Clause was drafted in response to the

Founding Fathers' desire to protect religious minorities from persecution.

The Founding Fathers' understanding of the Free Exercise Clause is illustrated in part by the New York Constitution of 1777, which provided that "the free exercise and enjoyment of religious . . . worship, without **discrimination** or preference, shall forever . . . be allowed . . . to all mankind." (WEAL, v. 5, p. 37) However, the same constitution cautioned that "the liberty of conscience, hereby granted, shall not be so construed as to excuse acts of licentiousness, or justify practices inconsistent with the peace or safety of this State." The New Hampshire Constitution of 1784 similarly provided that "[e]very individual has a natural and unalienable right to worship God according to the dictates of his own conscience, and reason; and no subject shall be hurt . . . in his person, liberty or estate for worshipping God" in a manner "most agreeable" to those dictates, "provided he doth not disturb the public peace." (WEAL, v. 5, p.37).

### Case Law Interpreting the Free Exercise Clause

These eighteenth-century state constitutional provisions not only provide insight into the Founding Fathers' original understanding of the Free Exercise Clause, they embody the fundamental tenants of modern First Amendment **jurisprudence**. The Supreme Court has identified three principles underlying the Free Exercise Clause. First, no individual may be compelled by law to accept a particular religion or form of worship. Second, all individuals are constitutionally permitted to freely choose a religion and worship in accordance with their conscience and spirituality without interference from the government. Third, the government may enforce its criminal laws by prosecuting persons whose religious practices would thwart a compelling societal interest.

Only in rare instances is a law that infringes upon someone's religious beliefs or practices supported by a compelling state interest. The Supreme Court has held that no compelling societal interest would be served in offending someone's deeply held religious beliefs with a law coercing members of the Jehovah's Witnesses to salute the American flag in public schools (West Virginia State Board of Education v. Barnette, 319 U.S. 624, 63 S.Ct. 1178, 87 L.Ed. 1628 (1943), a law denying unemployment benefits to Seventh Day Adventists who refuse to work on Saturdays (Sherbert v. Verner, 374 U.S. 398, 83 S.Ct. 1790, 10 L.Ed.2d 965 (1963)), or a law requiring Amish families to keep their children in state schools until the age of sixteen (Wisconsin v. Yoder, 406 U.S. 205, 92 S.Ct. 1526, 32 L.Ed.2d 15 (1972)). However, a compelling governmental interest is served by the Internal Revenue System (**IRS**), such that no member of any religious sect can claim exemption from paying taxes. U. S. v. Lee, 455 U.S. 252, 102 S.Ct. 1051, 71 L.Ed.2d 127 (1982).

A different question is presented when the government disputes whether a particular belief or practice is actually religious in nature. In some instances the Supreme Court is required to determine what constitutes a "religion" for the purposes of the First Amendment. For example, this determination occurs when conscientious objectors resist the government's attempt to conscript them into military service during wartime. Some draft resisters object to war on moral or ethical grounds unrelated to orthodox or doctrinal religions. If a conscientious objector admits that he is atheistic or agnostic, the government asks, how can he or she rely on the First Amendment to avoid conscription when it protects the free exercise of religion?

In effort to answer this question, the Supreme Court has explained that the government cannot "aid all religions against non-believers" any more than it can aid one religion over another. Torcaso v. Watkins, 367 U.S. 488, 81 S.Ct. 1680, 6 L.Ed.2d 982 (1961). So long as a non-believer holds a sincere and meaningful belief that occupies a place in that person's life parallel to the place held by God in a believer's life, then it qualifies as a religious belief under the First Amendment. As to conscientious objectors, the Court has ruled that the First Amendment will insulate them from criminal prosecution if they resist the draft based on "deeply and sincerely" held beliefs that "are purely ethical or moral in source and content but that nevertheless impose . . . a duty of conscience to refrain from participating in any war at any time." Welsh v. U. S., 398 U.S. 333, 90 S.Ct. 1792, 26 L.Ed.2d 308 (1970). However, a religious, moral, or ethical belief that manifests itself in a person's selective opposition to only certain wars or military conflicts is not protected by the Free Exercise Clause. The same holds true for a religious, moral, or ethical beliefs that are insincere.

In 1993 Congress attempted to add to the body of law protecting the free exercise of religion by enacting the Religious Freedom Restoration Act (RFRA), which provided that the "[g]overnment shall not substantially burden a person's exercise of religion," unless in doing so it furthers "a compelling governmental interest" and "is the least restrictive means of furthering that . . . interest." 42 U.S.C. § 2000bb-1(a). Congress enacted RFRA in response to Employment Division v. Smith, 494 U.S. 872, 110 S.Ct. 1595, 108 L.Ed.2d 876, (1990), a Supreme Court decision that upheld the denial of **unemployment compensation** claims made by two employees who had been fired for ingesting an illegal drug during a religious ceremony. In passing the law Congress made a specific finding that the Supreme Court in Smith "virtually eliminated" any requirement that the government provide a compelling justification for the burdens it places on the exercise of religion. 42 USCA § 2000bb. Congress hoped that RFRA would restore that requirement.

The constitutionality of RFRA was immediately challenged in a flurry of cases, one of which eventually made its way to the Supreme Court in City of Boerne v. Flores, 521 U.S. 507, 117 S.Ct. 2157, 138 L.Ed.2d 624 (1997). Acknowledging that section 5 of the Fourteenth Amendment grants Congress the authority to enforce the First Amendment through measures that "remedy" or "deter" constitutional violations, the Supreme Court said that this authority did not include the power to define "what constitutes a constitutional violation." Yet this is exactly what Congress attempted to do by enacting RFRA, the Court said. Congress cannot effectively overrule Supreme Court precedent, the Court continued, without violating the separation of powers and other constitutional principles vital to maintaining the balance of power between the state and federal governments. The powers of the legislative branch are "defined and limited," the Court concluded, and only the judicial branch of government is constitutionally endowed with the authority to interpret and apply the First Amendment or any other provision of the federal Constitution. Thus, RFRA was declared unconstitutional and the precedential value of Smith was restored.

## State Laws Protecting Religious Freedom

The Free Exercise and Establishment Clauses of the First Amendment have been made applicable to the states through the Fourteenth Amendment. In a series of cases the Supreme Court has ruled that the rights guaranteed by the First Amendment establish the minimum amount of religious freedom that must be afforded to individuals in state or federal court. States may provide more religious freedom under their own constitutions, but not less. Below is a sam-

pling of state court decisions decided at least in part based on their own state constitution's guarantee of religious freedom.

ALABAMA: The state's constitutional provision guaranteeing freedom of religion did not bar the court from resolving a dispute between congregational factions over the title to church property, even though spiritual issues arguably prompted the congregation's dispute, since the case involved civil conflicts of trusteeship and property ownership and required the court to review church records and incorporation documents without delving into spiritual matters. U.S.C.A. Const.Amend. 1; Const. Art. 1, § 3. Murphy v. Green, 794 So.2d 325 (Ala. 2000).

ARIZONA: A residential picketing **statute** did not facially infringe upon the religious freedom guaranteed by the state and federal constitutions as they were applied to an **abortion** protestor who was convicted for protesting abortion in a residential neighborhood. Even though her protest was motivated by a deeply held religious belief, the statute did not single out religious picketing or religious demonstrations for prohibition. U.S.C.A. Const.Amend. 1; A.R.S. Const. Art. 20, par. 1; A.R.S. § 13-2909. State v. Baldwin,184 Ariz. 267, 908 P.2d 483 (Ariz.App. Div. 1 1995)

CALIFORNIA: In guaranteeing the free exercise of religion "without discrimination or preference," the plain language of the state constitution ensures that the state neither favor nor discriminate against religion. West's Ann.Cal. Const. Art. 1, § 4. East Bay Asian Local Development Corp. v. California, 24 Cal.4th 693, 13 P.3d 1122, 102 Cal.Rptr.2d 280 (Cal. 2000).

FLORIDA: Inherent in parents' authority over their unemancipated children living in their parents' household is the parents' right to require their children to attend church with them as part of the children's religious training, and neither the state nor federal constitutions entitle unemancipated minors to prevent such parent-mandated religious training on grounds that it violates the minors' religious freedom. U.S.C.A. Const.Amend. 1; West's F.S.A. Const. Art. 1, § 3. L.M. v. State, 610 So.2d 1314 (Fla.App. 1 Dist. 1992).

ILLINOIS: A state statute permitting certain burials on Sundays and legal holidays did not abridge the union members' freedom to contract. Nor did it violate the federal and state constitutional prohibitions against impairment of contractual obligations, since the statute's provisions were narrowly drawn to permit free exercise of religious rights guaranteed by the state constitution while allowing labor to restrict its working schedules accordingly. S.H.A. ch. 21, ¶ 101 et seq. Heckmann v. Cemeteries Ass'n of Greater Chicago, 127 Ill.App.3d 451, 468 N.E.2d 1354, 82 Ill.Dec. 574 (Ill.App. 1 Dist. 1984).

MICHIGAN: The Michigan **Civil Rights** Act's prohibition on housing discrimination based on marital status did not violate the state constitution's guarantee of religious freedom, and thus the act was violated when two landlords refused to rent their apartments to unmarried couples, even though their refusal was based on religious grounds. M.C.L.A. Const. Art. 1, § 4; M.C.L.A. § 37.2502(1). McCready v. Hoffius, 459 Mich. 131, 586 N.W.2d 723 (Mich. 1998).

MISSOURI: State and federal constitutions guarantee of religious freedom entitled a taxpayer to delete every reference to God on the state's tax form before taking the oath or affirmation required by the form. U.S.C.A. Const.Amend. 1; V.A.M.S. Const. Art. 1, §§ 5, 7; V.A.M.S. § 137.155. Oliver v. State Tax Commissioner of Missouri, 37 S.W.3d 243 (Mo. 2001).

MONTANA: The freedom of religion provisions set forth in the state constitution protect the freedom to accept or reject any religious doctrine, including religious doctrines relating to abortion, and the right to express one's faith in all lawful ways and forums. Const. Art. 2, §§ 5, 7. Armstrong v. State, 296 Mont. 361, 989 P.2d 364 (Mont. 1999).

NEBRASKA: Ex parte communications in which a trial judge during a capital murder case asked the jurors to join hands, bow their heads, and say words to the effect of "God be with us" did not infringe on the defendant's religious rights under the state or federal constitutions, since the defendant's rights to freedom of religion and to worship as he pleased did not suffer in any way. U.S.C.A. Const.Amend. 1; Const. Art. 1, § 4. State v. Bjorklund, 258 Neb. 432, 604 N.W.2d 169 (Neb. 2000).

NEW HAMPSHIRE: The state's constitutional provision guaranteeing freedom of religion prohibited the state from revoking a psychologist's license for his religious views but did not prohibit revocation for acts that otherwise constituted unprofessional conduct, regardless of their religious character. Thus, the court upheld the state's revocation of the psychologist's license on the grounds that he had provided incompetent therapy to a patient, even though part of the therapy involved reading the Bible. Const.

Pt. 1, Art. 5. Appeal of Trotzer, 143 N.H. 64, 719 A.2d 584 (N.H. 1998).

NEW YORK: The state constitution's guarantee of religious freedom entitled a state correctional facility inmate to participate in all Jewish religious observances open and available to any other inmate, even though the inmate was not recognized as Jewish by the Jewish chaplain at the facility. McKinney's Const. Art. 1, § 3; McKinney's Correction Law § 610. Thomas v. Lord, 174 Misc.2d 461, 664 N.Y.S.2d 973, 1997 N.Y. Slip Op. 97576 (N.Y.Sup., 1997).

OHIO: A court order requiring that a noncustodial parent pay 40 percent of his child's tuition at a private Catholic school did not violate the Establishment Clause of the First Amendment or the religious freedom provision of the state constitution. U.S.C.A. Const.Amend. 1; Const. Art. 1, § 7. Smith v. Null, — Ohio App.3d —, — N.E.2d —, 2001 WL 243419 (Ohio App. 4 Dist. 2001).

TEXAS: A state court could not hear a lawsuit alleging that a church minister and his wife negligently or intentionally misapplied the church's doctrine in attempting to drive out demons from plaintiff's minor daughter, since the lawsuit would involve a searching inquiry into the church's beliefs and the validity of those beliefs, an inquiry that would infringe up the defendants' religious freedom. **In re** Pleasant Glade Assembly of God, 991 S.W.2d 85 (Tex.App.-Fort Worth 1998).

VERMONT: The state's constitution expresses two related, but different, concepts about the nature of religious liberty: no governmental power may interfere with or control an individual's free exercise of religious worship, and no person can be compelled to attend or support religious worship against that person's conscience. Const. C. 1, Art. 3. Chittenden Town School Dist. v. Department of Educ., 169 Vt. 310, 738 A.2d 539 (Vt. 1999).

WASHINGTON: Requiring a church to apply for a conditional use permit in a rural estate **zoning** district, while requiring a county to reduce or waive the application fee following a showing of the church's inability to pay, was not an impermissible burden on the free exercise of religion guaranteed by the state and federal constitutions. Open Door Baptist Church v. Clark County, 140 Wash.2d 143, 995 P.2d 33 (Wash. 2000). U.S.C.A. Const.Amend. 1; West's RCWA Const. Art. 1, § 11.

## Additional Resources

*American Jurisprudence* West Group, 1998.

*West's Encyclopedia of American Law* West Group, 1998.

*U.S. Constitution: First Amendment* Available at: http://caselaw.lp.findlaw.com/data/constitution/amendment01

## Organizations

### The American Bar Association

740 15th Street, N.W.
Washington, DC 20002 USA
Phone: (202) 544-1114
Fax: (202) 544-2114
URL: http://w ww.abanet.org
Primary Contact: Robert J. Saltzman, President

### American Civil Liberties Union(ACLU)

1400 20th St., NW, Suite 119
Washington, DC 20036 USA
Phone: (202) 457-0800
E-Mail: info@aclu.org
URL: http://www.aclu.org/
Primary Contact: Anthony D. Romero, Executive Director

### Association for Religion

50 Pintard Ave
New Rochelle, NY 10801-7148 USA
Phone: (914) 235-1439
Fax: (914) 235-1622
URL: http://w ww.ats.edu/faculty/spons/A0000020.HTM
Primary Contact: John Crocker, Principal

# CIVIL RIGHTS

## SEXUAL DISCRIMINATION AND ORIENTATION

*Sections within this essay:*

- Background

- Gender Discrimination
    - Equal Pay Act
    - Title VII of the Civil Rights Act
    - Title VII: Sexual Harassment
    - Civil Rights Act of 1991
    - Title IX
    - Pregnancy Discrimination Act and Family and Medical Leave Act
    - Supreme Court Standards for Sexual Discrimination

- Sexual Orientation Discrimination
    - The Supreme Court and Gay Rights
    - *Bowers v. Hardwick*
    - *Romer v. Evans*
    - *Boy Scouts of America v. Dale*
    - *Lawrence v. Texas*
    - Other Supreme Court Decisions

- State And Municipal Sexual Orientation Anti-Discrimination Laws

- Additional Resources

## Background

"Remember the ladies," stated Abigail Adams to her husband John in 1776 while he was helping to draft the Declaration of Independence. Unfortunately, throughout most of American history, the ladies were not remembered when it came to laws, as women were treated at best as second-class citizens and at worst as the virtual property of their husbands. U. S. law has witnessed a gender revolution, starting with the passage of the Equal Pay Act in 1963. In the process, areas of the law that had never existed before, such as **sexual harassment litigation**, were articulated and applied.

Six years after the Equal Pay Act was passed, riots at the Stonewall Inn in New York City began the gay rights movement. Legally, homosexuals were barely recognized by the law except in anti-sodomy rules virtually every state possessed. Today, gay rights are at the cutting edge of sexual **discrimination** law, an area both unsettled and controversial. Sexual discrimination law advanced a long way in the latter half of the twentieth century. How much more it will advance remains an interesting question.

## Gender Discrimination

Discrimination on the basis of sex was first addressed in federal law in the Equal Pay Act of 1963. Since that act was passed, several other laws affecting the rights of women have been enacted. They include:

- Title VII of the **Civil Rights** Act of 1964
- The Civil Rights Act of 1991, which expanded some of the protections granted by Title VII
- Title IX of the Education Amendments of 1972 (Title IX)
- The Pregnancy Discrimination Act of 1978
- The Family and Medical Leave Act of 1993

### The Equal Pay Act

The Equal Pay Act, passed in 1963, was the first law to address gender inequality in the workplace and one of the first laws to benefit women explicitly since they gained the right to vote earlier in the century. The Equal Pay Act guaranteed equal pay for equal work for men and women. For the act to take effect, men and women must be employed under similar working conditions, and equal is defined as "equal skill, effort and responsibility." Overtime and travel are included among the provisions of the act.

The Equal Pay Act is part of the **Fair Labor Standards Act**, although it is unlike the other parts of the act in that there are no exceptions for executive, administrative, professional employees, or outside salespeople. But the Equal Pay Act contains the same business exceptions as the Fair Labor Standards Act and covers only employees "engaged in commerce." In practice, this law applies to vast majority of businesses in the country.

There are four affirmative defenses to the Equal Pay Act: merit, production, seniority, and "factor other than sex." The most litigated of these defenses is the "factor other than sex" because of the ambiguous nature of the clause. For example, prior wages, profitability of the company, and evaluation of a personal interview have all been held to be a factor other than sex justifying pay discrepancies between men and women under the Equal Pay Act.

### Title VII of the Civil Rights Act

Title VII, passed in 1964, is arguably the most important legislation protecting the equality of women in the workplace. Title VII, which was originally proposed as an anti-racial discrimination bill, included sex as a protected class largely as an afterthought. The amendment adding the term sex was proposed by a conservative legislator from Virginia, probably as a way of scuttling the whole bill. Despite this, Title VII passed with its protections against sexual discrimination intact.

Title VII prohibits discrimination by employers, employment agencies, and labor organizations with 15 or more full-time employees on the basis of race, color, religion, sex, or national origin. It applies to pre-interview advertising, interviewing, hiring, discharge, compensation, promotion, classification, training, apprenticeships, referrals for employment, union membership, terms, working conditions, working atmosphere, seniority, reassignment, and all other "privileges of employment."

The operative question in a Title VII **sex discrimination** case is whether the litigant has suffered unequal treatment because of his or her sex. Courts look at whether the disparate treatment of the employee was sex-related. If it was, it is actionable under Title VII unless the employer uses an affirmative defense; if not, it is not actionable.

Affirmative defenses under Title VII include all of the affirmative defenses under the Equal Pay Act. In addition, defenses include situations in which sex is a bona fide occupational requirement (BFOQ) for the job; when sex discrimination occurs as a result of adhering to a bona fide seniority system (unless the system perpetuates past effects of sex discrimination); or when sex discrimination is justified by "business necessity."

When employers assert a mixed motive under Title VII, that is, the action taken against the employee has both an discriminatory and non-discriminatory reason, the employer must prove by a preponderance of the **evidence** the employment decision would have been made absent the discriminatory factors.

Plaintiffs can also sue under Title VII using a theory of "disparate impact" that is, showing that while an employment decision or policy is not discriminatory on its face, it has resulted in discrimination on the basis of sex. The intent of discrimination can be inferred by the impact of the policy.

**Affirmative action** for women is allowed under Title VII. In the decision of *Johnson v. Transportation Agency, Santa Clara County,* the Supreme Court determined an affirmative action program that promoted a woman over a more qualified man was legal under Title VII as long as her sex was just one factor in the decision, and the affirmative action plan was carefully drafted to remedy the effects of past discrimination.

### Title VII: Sexual Harassment

Title VII prohibits acts of sexual harassment when such harassment becomes a "term or condition" of employment, when rejection of the harassment could be used as the basis for an employment decision or when such conduct creates an intimidating "hostile" work environment. The types of sexual harassment prohibited by Title VII are grouped into two categories: **quid pro quo** sexual harassment, when the harassment is directly linked to the grant or denial of an employee's economic benefits, and hostile environment harassment, when the harassment creates a difficult working environment for an employee. Because the first type of harassment is relatively straightforward, the second type has been the subject of more litigation.

The Supreme Court has ruled that a hostile working environment is created when a workplace is permeated with "discriminatory intimidation, ridicule, and insult" which is widespread enough to change the conditions of employment for the person being harassed. Hostile work environments have been held by courts to be created when female employees are subjected to pornographic pictures, to unsolicited love letters and request for dates, and sexual innuendos and crude remarks where those remarks were pervasive.

Employees can sue for sexual harassment even when they have suffered no **tangible** financial problems as a result of such harassment. They can sue even though they have not experienced concrete psychological injury because of the harassment. However, such conduct must do more than offend the employee. Moreover, the harassment does not have to be cross-gender in nature. The Supreme Court in 1998 held that same-sex harassment, e.g. male sexual harassment of another male, is actionable under Title VII.

### The Civil Rights Act of 1991

The Civil Rights Act of 1991 enhanced the protections granted in Title VII. It added compensatory (i.e., pain and suffering) damages and **punitive damages**, sometimes known as exemplary damages, for all victims of intentional discrimination. (Previously these had only been available for victims of racial discrimination.) These damages are capped from $50,000 for employers with 100 or fewer employees to $300,000 for employers with more than 500 employees. It also added a right to a jury trial. Previously, sex discrimination plaintiffs had to file an Equal Pay Act or **common law fraud** claim to get a jury trial.

The Act also made it easier to file disparate impact cases by reversing a 1989 Supreme Court decision and establishing that to disprove a disparate impact charge, employers must show that the practice is job related for the position in question and consistent with business necessity. In addition, the Act allows employees to file a discrimination charge at the time they are affected by the discrimination, rather than when they are first notified of the discriminatory act and the Act applies Title VII to American citizens living overseas.

### Title IX

Title IX addresses sexual discrimination in the area of education. It applies to all federally funded educational institutions, including any college or university "any part of which is extended federal financial assistance." It provides that no person shall be excluded from participation in or be subjected to discrimination on the basis of sex in any educational activity. Title IX has wrought an enormous change on American schools and universities since its enactment in 1972. It has forced schools to equalize sports programs between men and women, resulting in a boom for women's athletics. It has caused the Supreme Court to hold single sex public colleges to be unconstitutional, most famously in the case of the Virginia Military Institute. Many hold Title IX responsible for the tremendous increase in women in postsecondary graduate schools since 1970, to the point where women now make up half of all law and medical students in the country.

### The Pregnancy Discrimination Act and Family and Medical Leave Act

The Pregnancy Discrimination Act of 1978 protects pregnant women by stating that employers must treat pregnancy as a temporary **disability**, and they may not refuse to hire a woman or fire her because she is pregnant or compel her to take maternity leave.

The Family and Medical Leave Act of 1993 built upon the rights granted under the Pregnancy Discrimination Act. This act applies to employers of 50 or more employees, and permits up to 12 weeks of unpaid leave for the birth, **adoption**, or foster care placement of a child; the serious medical condition of a parent, spouse, or child; and the worker's own serious medical condition that prevents the worker from performing the essential functions of his or her job.

Except for highly paid positions, individuals must be given back their former positions or one fully equivalent. Employees are eligible for family or medical leave after working for 12 months or at least 1,250 hours. Part-time employees are eligible for such leaves as these numbers average 24 hours a week.

### Supreme Court Standards for Gender Discrimination

The Supreme Court has dealt with a variety of gender discrimination cases over the years. Until 1976, it used a rational basis test to determine whether the discrimination it was reviewing was constitutional. Since 1976, beginning with the case of *Craig v. Boren,* the court has used what is referred to as "intermediate" scrutiny in regard to gender discrimination cases. This standard states that a classification based on gender must be reasonable, not arbitrary, and must serve important governmental objectives and be substantially related to the achievement of those objectives.

This scrutiny is less of standard than the court uses in racial discrimination cases, which are subject to strict scrutiny. A classification based on race must serve a compelling government interest and be strictly tailored to the achievement of the purpose. This standard makes courts more willing to uphold a classification based on sex than to uphold one based on racial classification.

## Sexual Orientation Discrimination

In contrast to women over the last 40 years, homosexuals have seen slow progress in their attempts for equal rights. In areas ranging from marriage and family to job discrimination to organizations such as the military and boy scouts, discrimination against homosexuals is still sanctioned in a variety of ways. The military, for example, currently has a policy of "don't ask, don't tell" implemented in 1993, which allows a serviceman or woman to be discharged if he or she publicly admits to being homosexual. This policy was upheld in 1998 by Second Circuit Court of Appeals in the case of *Able v. U.S.A.* in which the court found that "don't ask, don't tell" did not violate the First Amendment or the Equal Protection Clause of the U.S. Constitution.

One of the biggest ways sexual orientation differs from other suspect classifications such as race or sex is there is no nationwide law dealing with discrimination against homosexuals. For example, Title VII has been consistently held not to apply to discrimination against homosexuals. Nevertheless, many states and municipalities have adopted sexual orientation anti-discrimination laws. The twenty-first century has witnessed a clear movement toward gay rights in the United States, at least in some regions and areas.

### The Supreme Court and Gay Rights

In the absence of any national law on sexual orientation discrimination, the Supreme Court decisions on these issues have assumed a great importance. The Supreme Court's record on gay rights issues has been mixed. The Court has issued four comparatively landmark decisions on gay rights since it first tackled the issue in 1985, and several other less important holdings.

### Bowers v. Hardwick

In this 1986 case, the Court reviewed an anti-sodomy **statute** in Georgia. The plaintiff was arrested in his bedroom for having sex with another man. The court ruled on a 5-4 vote that the constitutional right to privacy did not apply to conduct between members of the same sex. In handing down this ruling, the court made a distinction between homosexual behavior and actions such as **birth control**, **abortion**, and interracial marriage. While the court had previously found that all of these were covered by the right to privacy in the due process clause of the Fourteenth Amendment, homosexual acts were not covered by this clause, according to the Court.

### Romer v. Evans

In contrast to *Bowers v. Hardwick, Romer v. Evans* was considered a big victory for gay rights. In 1992, Colorado voters had approved Amendment 2, which prohibited or preempted any law or policy "whereby homosexual, lesbian or bisexual orientation, conduct, practices or relationships shall constitute or otherwise be the basis of or entitled any person or class of persons to have or claim any minority status, quota preference, protected status or claim of discrimination" In other words, the law banned any Colorado municipality from passing an sexual orientation anti-discrimination law.

The Supreme Court ruled in a 6-3 decision in 1996 that Amendment 2 violated homosexuals **equal protection** rights in Colorado. Applying the rational basis test, which requires that a policy or law discriminating against a specific non-protected class have a rational relationship to a legitimate **public interest**, the court determined that a "desire to harm a politically unpopular group cannot constitute a legitimate government interest." The Court noted that Amendment 2 identified homosexuals by name and denied them equal protection across the board. "[It's] shear breadth is so discontinuous with the reasons offered for it that the amendment seems inexplicable by anything but animus toward the class it affects," said the Court. The Court's decision in Evans seemed to indicate the Court would accept some equal protection rights for homosexuals, though it certainly did not offer the same protection to sexual orientation discrimination as it would to race or sex.

### Boy Scouts of America v. Dale

The Supreme Court did another reversal in 2000 and ruled in the case of *Boy Scouts of America v. Dale* that a private organization had a right not allow in homosexuals under the theory of freedom of association. In this case, the Boy Scouts of America had dismissed a scout leader who was openly homosexual. The court determined that a New Jersey public accommodation law, which required organizations using public facilities in the state not to discriminate on the basis of sexual orientation, violated the scouts First Amendment rights. "Forcing a group to accept certain members may impair the ability of the group to express those views, and only those views, that it intends to express," said the Court, which added that "the presence of Dale as an assistant scoutmaster would... interfere with the Boy Scouts' choice not to propound a point of view contrary to its beliefs." This decision was differentiated from the way the court had refused to apply freedom of association rights in the past when dealing with gender and racial discrimination. "Until today," Justice John Paul Stevens pointed out in a dissent, "we have never once found a claimed right to associate in the selection of members to prevail in the face of a State's anti-discrimination law."

### Lawrence v. Texas

In 2003, the Supreme Court reconsidered its position regarding the constitutionality of sodomy laws as they applied to homosexual acts. In *Lawrence v. Texas,* two men were arrested and charged with sodomy when police caught them engaging in consensual sexual activity in one of the men's homes. The state courts upheld the conviction, relying on *Bowers v. Hardwick.* The Supreme Court, in a 6-3 decision, determined that the sodomy law violated the Due Process Clause, thus overruling *Bowers.* According to the lead opinion by Justice Anthony Kennedy, "The petitioners are entitled to respect for their private lives. The State cannot demean their existence or control their destiny by making their private sexual conduct a crime. Their right to liberty under the Due Process Clause gives them the full right to engage in their conduct without intervention of the government." Gay rights activists celebrated the decision as a major victory.

### Other Supreme Court Decisions

Several other Supreme Court rulings were handed down in the 1990s on the issue of homosexual rights. These rulings did not have the impact of the above three, although they also yielded a mixed position on gay rights. *Onacle v. Sundowner Offshore Services* in 1998 found the Court unanimously ruling that same sex harassment was actionable under Title VII. The Court found even though same sex harassment was not contemplated by the statute, "statutory prohibitions often go beyond the principal evil to cover reasonably comparable evil." The 1998 case of *Bragdon v. Abbott* found a divided Supreme Court allowing persons with HIV to be considered disabled

under the Americans With Disabilities Act, even when the disease had not progressed to a symptomatic stage. This action was considered a major gay rights victory.

## State And Municipal Sexual Orientation Anti-Discrimination Laws

While the Supreme Court has failed to set a consistent national policy regarding sexual orientation discrimination, many states and municipalities have taken the lead in passing protections for homosexuals in areas such as employment and public accommodations. The first of these were passed in the early 1970s, subsequently hundreds of municipalities and many states have adopted anti-sexual orientation protections.

Probably the most famous anti-discrimination sexual orientation law was when the state of Massachusetts legalized same-sex marriage in 2004. Vermont's Civil Union Law, passed in 2000, and a similar law passed in Connecticut in 2005, permit same-sex couples to enter into "civil union" relationships. These laws, while not using the language of marriage, gives same-sex couples virtually all of the 300 or so rights available to married couples. The issue of civil union has been raised in a number of states' the issue of same-sex marriage has been raised, but in fewer venues.

No other state gives same-sex couples this sort of protection, but several other states currently have anti-discrimination laws and protection for homosexuals:

CALIFORNIA: Protections against discrimination in employment and public accommodations

CONNECTICUT: Protections against discrimination in employment, public accommodation, housing, and credit

DISTRICT OF COLUMBIA: Protections against discrimination in employment, public accommodation, housing, and credit, although religious educational institutions are exempt from protections

HAWAII: Protections against discrimination in employment

ILLINOIS: Protections against discrimination in public employment

MARYLAND: Protections against discrimination in employment

MASSACHUSETTS: Protections against discrimination in employment, public accommodation, housing, and credit

MINNESOTA: Protections against discrimination in employment, public accommodation, housing, and credit

NEVADA: Protections against discrimination in employment

NEW HAMPSHIRE: Protections against discrimination in employment, public accommodation, and housing

NEW JERSEY: Protections against discrimination in employment, public accommodation, housing, and credit

NEW YORK: Protections against discrimination in public employment

PENNSYLVANIA: Protections against discrimination in public employment

RHODE ISLAND: Protections against discrimination in employment, public accommodation, housing, and credit

VERMONT: Protections against discrimination in employment, public accommodation, housing, and credit, civil union law

WASHINGTON: Protections against discrimination in public employment

WISCONSIN: Protections against discrimination in employment, public accommodation, housing, and credit

## Additional Resources

*An Analysis of the U. S. Supreme Court's Decision Making In Gay Rights Cases* Johnson, Scott Patrick, Ohio Northern University Law Review, 2001.

*Gaylaw: Challenging the Apartheid of the Closet* Eskridge, William N., Jr., Harvard University Press, 1999.

*Fighting Gender and Sexual Orientation Harassment: The Sex Discrimination Argument in Gay Rights Cases* Hunter, Nan, Journal of Law and Policy, 2001.

*Recent Decisions: Harris v. Forklift Systems, Inc.* Gleeson, Kathleen, Duquesne Law Review, Fall 1994.

*Sex Discrimination* Motto, Patricia, Illinois Institute for Continuing Legal Education, July 2000.

*Sex Discrimination* Thomas, Claire Sherman, West Group, 1991.

*U. S. Code, Title 20: Education, Chapter 38: Discrimination Based on Sex or Blindness.* U. S. House of Representatives, 1999. Available at: http://uscode.house.gov/title_20.htm

*U. S. Code, Title 42: The Public Health and Welfare, Chapter 21: Civil Rights, Subchapter VI: Equal Employment Opportunities* U. S. House of Representatives, 1999. Available at http://uscode.house.gov/title_42.htm

## Organizations

***Concerned Women for America (CWA)***
1015 Fifteenth St. NW, Suite 1100
Washington, DC 20005 USA
Phone: (202) 488-7000
Fax: (202) 488-0806
URL: http://www.cwfa.org/
Primary Contact: Beverly LaHaye, President

***Lambda Legal Defense and Education Fund***
120 Wall Street, Suite 1500
New York, NY 10005-3904 USA
Phone: (212) 809-8585
Fax: (212) 809-0055
URL: www.lambdalegal.org
Primary Contact: Kevin Cathcart, Executive Director

***National Organization For Women (NOW)***
1100 H Street, NW, Third Floor
Washington, DC 20005 USA
Phone: (202) 628-8NOW (8669)
Fax: (202) 785-8576
URL: http://www.now.org/
Primary Contact: Kim Gandy, President

# CIVIL RIGHTS

## USA PATRIOT ACT

*Sections within this essay:*

- Background
- Provisions of the Patriot Act
    - Title I: Enhancing Domestic Security Against Terrorism
    - Title II: Enhanced Surveillance Procedures
    - Title III: Money Laundering
    - Title IV: Border Protection
    - Titles V, VI, and VII
    - Title VIII: Criminal Law Changes
    - Title IX: Improved Intelligence
- Additional Resources

## Background

In the aftermath of the terrorist attacks of September 11, 2001, President George Bush and his administration devised legislation now known as the Patriot Act (or USA Patriot Act). The Patriot Act was intended to thwart future terrorist attacks, through identification and punishment of its perpetrators. "USA Patriot Act" is an acronym for "Uniting and Strengthening America by Providing Appropriate Tools Required to Intercept and Obstruct Terrorism Act of 2001."

The proposed legislation was submitted to Congress just one week after the attacks, and quickly gained approval in both houses. It passed in the Senate without debate; Russell Feingold (D-WI) was the lone vote against the measure. Feingold said, "Preserving our freedom is one of the main reasons that we are now engaged in this new war on terrorism. We will lose that war without firing a shot if we sacrifice the liberties of the American people." In the House of Representatives, the legislation passed 357 to 66, after receiving minor modifications. The president signed the 342-page bill into law on October 26, 2001. When he signed it, he said, "We're dealing with terrorists who operate by highly sophisticated methods and technologies, some of which were not even available when our existing laws were written. The bill before me takes account of the new realities and dangers posed by modern terrorists."

Congress declared its commitment to protecting Americans' civil rights and civil liberties in the "quest to identify, locate, and bring to justice the perpetrators and sponsors of the terrorist attacks," but the Patriot Act has sparked fierce debate. Proponents say the act enhances national security. Opponents, including the ACLU, contend the Patriot Act severely undercuts basic civil liberties. The ACLU has charged that the Patriot Act "vastly expand[s] the government's authority to spy on its own citizens, while simultaneously reducing checks and balances on those powers like judicial oversight, public accountability, and the ability to challenge government searches in court." Many other groups have criticized the act as well. For example, according to the National League of Cities, by mid-2005 more than 2,000 communities had passed resolutions expressing concern with civil liberties issues in the Patriot Act.

The Patriot Act's stated purpose is "to deter and punish terrorist acts in the United States and around the world, to enhance law enforcement investigatory tools, and for other purposes." The act is comprised of the ten categories, called titles:

- Title I: Enhancing domestic security against terrorism
- Title II: Enhancing surveillance procedures
- Title III: Abatement of international money laundering
- Title IV: Protecting the borders
- Title V: Removal of obstacles to investigate terrorism
- Title VI: Providing for victims of terrorism, public safety officers, and their families
- Title VII: Increased information sharing
- Title VIII: Strengthening criminal laws against terrorism
- Title IX: Improved intelligence
- Title X: Miscellaneous provisions

According to the Department of Justice's website devoted to the Patriot Act, the following successes can be attributed, wholly or in part, to the Patriot Act:

- Intelligence and law enforcement communities, both in the U.S. and abroad, have identified and disrupted over 150 terrorist threats and cells

- Nearly two-thirds of al Qaida's known senior leadership has been captured or killed

- Worldwide, more than 3,000 operatives have been incapacitated

- Five terrorist cells in Buffalo, Detroit, Seattle, Portland (Oregon), and Northern Virginia were broken up

- Terrorism-related investigations has resulted in criminal charges against 401 individuals

- 212 individuals have been convicted or have pleaded guilty in the United States, including shoe-bomber Richard Reid and John Walker Lindh

- More than 515 individuals linked to the September 11th investigation have been removed from the United States

## Provisions of the Patriot Act

### Title I: Enhancing Domestic Security Against Terrorism

Provisions in Title I set up a Counterterrorism Fund in the U.S. Treasury, and appropriated $200 million for each fiscal year from 2002 through 2004. Section 106 of the title increases presidential authority to seize the property of foreign persons, organizations, or countries that the president determines "has planned, authorized, aided, or engaged in such hostilities or attacks against the United States." Title I also orders the U.S. Secret Service to develop a national network of electronic crime task forces to "purpose of preventing, detecting, and investigating various forms of electronic crimes, including potential terrorist attacks against critical infrastructure and financial payment systems."

### Title II: Enhanced Surveillance Procedures

This title contains the act's most controversial provisions. Title II extends the government's authority to use wiretaps under the Foreign Intelligence Survey Act of 1978 (FISA). FISA authorized the government to conduct wiretap surveillance in foreign intelligence investigations, without having to show probable cause to obtain a warrant. Typically, the Fourth Amendment requires a showing of probable cause before a warrant will be issued in a criminal case. Before the Patriot Act, the government could conduct such wiretaps only where the primary purpose was to obtain foreign intelligence. The Patriot Act expanded the Fourth Amendment exception. Now, pursuant to section 218, FISA may be used where a "significant" purpose of the investigation is foreign intelligence gathering.

In 2001, laws did not exist regarding Internet surveillance. As the Internet grew, authorities relied on pre-Internet era wiretap laws to gather information. Essentially, whenever law enforcement personnel wanted access to Internet addresses (URLs), they sought authorization through the "pen register" and "trap and trace" laws of telephone surveillance. Pen registers capture the phone numbers of outgoing telephone calls. Trap and trace devices capture incoming phone numbers. Neither method captures the actual content of a telephone call, so investigators could obtain a search warrant without establishing probable cause that a crime was being committed. When faced with Internet surveillance requests, some judges applied the telephone surveillance rules, but others refused. In Section 216, the Patriot Act specifically applies pen register and trap-and-trace law to the Internet. Moreover, pen registers and trap and trace wiretaps are valid nationwide, not just in the jurisdiction of the court that approved it. The section does not permit examination of the content of a communication. Nevertheless, critics argue that web addresses are different than telephone numbers. According to the ACLU, "When we 'visit' a Web page what we are really doing is downloading that page from the Internet onto our computer....That is much richer information than a single list of the people we have communicated with; it is intimate information that reveals who we are and what we are thinking about - much more like the content of a phone call than the number dialed."

Section 214 deals with wiretapping authority under FISA and makes it easier for authorities to obtain approval for pen register and trap and trace wiretap devices. Investigators must certify that information obtained will be relevant to an investigation, rather than the previous, stricter standard that permitted wiretaps when a line was used for communications with someone involved in terrorism.

Section 209 permits seizure of voice mail messages with a search warrant. Previously, authorities needed a wiretap order.

Title II also gives the government broad authority to share "electronic, wire, and oral interception information" gleaned from an investigation with other federal agencies. Pursuant to FISA, it also allows authorities to compel Internet service providers to disclose information about a user's e-mail activity, and to compel businesses to turn over personal information related to a criminal investigation. Moreover, section 213 provides that authorities executing a search warrant may delay notice of the search under certain circumstances. Critics allege this delay impinges upon a person's right to challenge the constitutionality of the search.

Pursuant to the act, the federal government may examine the library records of patrons without their knowledge. The American Library Association (ALA) has condemned this authorization, arguing that it violates user privacy and thereby threatens the free access to knowledge and information. The 64,000-member ALA passed the resolution in early 2003.

Section 224 is a sunset provision, intended to allay concern over the controversy in some of its sections. Accordingly, a number of the act's surveillance and intelligence- gathering provisions, if not re-approved, were set to expire on December 31, 2005. The House of Representatives voted on December 14, 2005, by a vote of 251 to 174, to extend the law for another four years. The House voted to renew sections that permit roving wiretaps. Roving wiretaps are wiretaps placed on every telephone a suspect uses. It also approved extension of provisions that

permit the FBI to use secret warrants to obtain medical, business, and library records. In the Senate, however, the re-approval process was much more uncertain. Finally, the Senate and House compromised and approved a renewal of the act in March 2006.

Provisions in Title II have been successfully employed in non-terrorist cases. In an address to Congress on July 13, 2004, Attorney General John Ashcroft noted several instances where provisions in Title II were used in domestic criminal investigations. The cases cited involved sexual predators and electronic surveillance under sections 210 and 212 of the act. Ashcroft told Congress, "When it comes to saving lives and protecting freedom, we must use the Patriot Act and every legal means available to us."

### Title III: Money Laundering

The official name of Title III is the "International Money Laundering Abatement and Financial Anti-Terrorism Act of 2001." In passing these provisions, Congress cited International Monetary Fund figures which estimate that between two and five percent of the global gross domestic product comes from money laundering with money from illegal drug and smuggling activities. The law called these gains from money laundering the "financial fuel" of terrorist operations. According to the Justice Department, money laundering provisions have been used to:

- Freeze $136 million in assets world-wide

- Charge 113 individuals with crimes related to terrorist financing, resulting in 57 convictions or guilty pleas to date

- Establish an FBI Terrorist Financing Operations Section (TFOS)

- "Identify, investigate, prosecute, disrupt, and dismantle terrorist-related financial and fundraising activities" through TFOS and the Joint Terrorism Task Forces

### Title IV: Border Protection

Provisions in this title authorized appropriations to triple the number of U.S. Border Patrol, Customs Service, and Immigration and Naturalization Service (INS) personnel posted at the border with Canada. (In other legislation related to the September 11, 2001, attacks, in March 2003, Customs, INS, and Border Patrol became part of the newly formed Department of Homeland Security.) Provisions in this title also enhance immigration provisions. For example, the Secretary of State now has the authority to designate domestic terrorist organizations. A domestic terrorist organization is defined as any organization that has ever used a weapon or dangerous device to cause substantial damage to property. The law also makes any non-citizen members of the group inadmissible to the U.S.; payment of dues is a deportable offense. Moreover, aliens are inadmissible to the U.S. if they belong to a group "whose public endorsement of acts of terrorist activity the Secretary of State has determined undermines United States efforts to reduce or eliminate terrorist activities."

Section 416 addresses the foreign student monitoring program. It compels schools to turn over information on foreign students for analysis and investigation.

Section 412 of Title IV is another controversial section of the Patriot Act. It permits up to seven days of detention for aliens suspected of terrorism, before they must be charged with a crime or removal proceedings are commenced. Moreover, an immigrant who has been charged with a violation may be held for up to six months if the immigrant's release would threaten national security.

The first Secretary of the Department of Homeland Security, Tom Ridge, stated in 2004, "We share nearly 7,500 miles of land border with Canada and Mexico, across which more than 400 million people, 130 million motor vehicles and 2.5 million rail cars pass every year. We patrol almost 95,000 miles of shoreline and navigable waters... We have to get it right millions of times a week. But the terrorists only have to get it right once."

### Titles V, VI, and VII

These titles have not been the source of controversy. The purpose of Title V is to enhance the federal government's ability to offer rewards for information offered for terrorism investigations. Title VI is concerned with providing funds and assistance to the victims of terrorism and to public safety officers and their families, where the officers are killed or suffer catastrophic injury due to terrorism. Title VII amends the Omnibus Crime Control and Safe Streets Act of 1968 to facilitate communication among federal, state, and local authorities in the event of a terrorist attack.

### Title VIII: Criminal Law Changes

Title VIII's numerous sections are intended strengthen criminal laws against terrorism. This title adds offenses for terrorism against mass transportation. It also addresses domestic terrorism, defining it as involving "acts dangerous to human life that are

a violation of the criminal laws of the United States or of any State" that "appear to be intended to intimidate or coerce a civilian population; to influence the policy of a government by intimidation or coercion; or to affect the conduct of a government by mass destruction, assassination, or kidnapping; and occur primarily within the territorial jurisdiction of the United States." Section 803 makes it illegal to harbor or conceal terrorists or suspected terrorists. Moreover, section 809 extends certain criminal statutes of limitations. Where the commission of certain terrorism offenses "resulted in, or created a forseeable risk of, death or serious bodily injury to another person," the statute of limitations is eliminated. Section 814 is intended to deter and prevent cyber-terrorism by increasing criminal penalties for Computer Fraud and Abuse Act violations. It amends the statutory definition of "protected computers" so that computers located outside the United States are included.

### Title IX: Improved Intelligence

This title addresses various intelligence concerns, within the federal government, including the Central Intelligence Agency (CIA). Congress directed the CIA to set up a "National Virtual Translation Center" to provide "timely and accurate translations of foreign intelligence for all other elements of the intelligence community."

## Additional Resources

*USA PATRIOT Act of 2001.* Available at http://frwebgate.access.gpo.gov/cgi-bin/getdoc.cgi?dbname=107_cong_public_laws&docid=f:publ056.107

*http://www.lifeandliberty.gov* Department of Justice's Patriot Act website, 2006.

*The Patriot Act: Opposing Viewpoints* Greenhaven Press, 2005.

*The USA PATRIOT Act,* Online Newshour, The website of The Newshour with Jim Lehrer. Available at http://www.pbs.org/newshour/bb/terrorism/homeland/patriotact.html

## Organizations

### American Civil Liberties Union

125 Broad Street, 18th Floor
New York, NY 10004 USA
Phone: (212) 549-2500
URL: http://www.aclu.org
Primary Contact: Nadine Strossen, President

**Department of Justice**

950 Pennsylvania Ave., NW
Washington, DC 20530-0001 USA
Phone: (202) 514-2000
URL: http://www.doj.gov

**American Library Association**

50 East Huron Street
Chicago, IL 60611 USA
Phone: (800) 545-2433
Primary Contact: Keith Michael Fiels, Executive
Director

# CIVIL RIGHTS

## VOTING RIGHTS

*Sections within this essay:*

- Background
- The Nineteenth Amendment
- Black Suffrage
- Grandfather Clauses, Literacy Tests, and the White Primary
- The Fifteenth Amendment
- The Voting Rights Act
  - Section Two and Section Five
  - Malapportioned Districts
- Minority Majority Districts
- Additional Resources

## Background

During colonial times, the right to vote (also known as being enfranchised) was severely limited. Mostly, adult white males who owned property were the only people with the right to vote. Women could not vote, though some progressive colonies allowed widows who owned property to vote. After the United States gained its independence from Great Britain, the Constitution gave the states the right to decide who could vote. Individually, the states began to abolish property requirements and, by 1830, adult white males could vote. Suffrage (the right to vote) has been gradually extended to include many people, and the U.S. Constitution has been amended several times for this purpose. A time line of major developments in U.S. voting rights contains at least the following seventeen events:

- 1789: The first presidential election is held, electing George Washington by unanimous vote of the country's "electors," a group of mostly white male landowners.

- 1868: The Fourteenth Amendment declares that any eligible twenty-one year old male has the right to vote.

- 1870: The Fifteenth Amendment says that the right to vote cannot be denied "on account of race, color, or previous condition of servitude," thus extending the right to vote to former (male) slaves.

- 1876: Wyoming becomes a state, and is the first state to give voting rights to women.

- 1884: The U.S. Supreme Court rules "grandfather clauses" unconstitutional.

- 1890: Southern states pass laws designed to limit the voting rights of African Americans. Some of the laws require voters to pay a poll tax or to prove that they can read and write.

- 1920: The U.S. Supreme Court rules that since Native Americans who live on reservations pay no state taxes, they cannot vote.

- 1920: Women gain the vote when the Nineteenth Amendment declares that the right to vote cannot be denied "on account of sex."

- 1947: A court ruling grants Native Americans the right to vote in every state.

- 1961: The Twenty-third Amendment establishes that the citizens of the District of Columbia have the right to vote in presidential elections. D.C. is given 3 electoral votes.

- 1964: The Twenty-fourth Amendment declares that the states cannot require citizens to pay a poll tax in order to vote in federal elections.

- 1965: Voting Rights Act bans literacy tests as a voting requirement and bars all racist voting practices in all states.

- 1971: The Twenty-Sixth Amendment lowers the voting age to 18 and gives all Americans the right to vote.

- 1975: Additions to the Voting Rights Act require translations of all election materials to be made available for non-English speaking citizens.

As this list illustrates, suffrage has been expanded to include a greater number of people belonging to diverse demographic groups based on age, sex, and race. Without a doubt, the most dramatic and controversial developments in the history of U.S. voting rights expansion involves the movement to grant suffrage to women and African Americans. For African Americans, this includes a long history of ensuring unimpeded access to the polls in order to exercise their constitutional right to vote. For women, gaining suffrage was a very long struggle as well.

## The Nineteenth Amendment

The Nineteenth amendment to the United States Constitution guarantees U.S. women the right to vote. But this right was not easily won for women. It took many decades of political agitation and protest before such a right became part of U.S. law. The struggle for women's right to vote began in the middle of the nineteenth century. A movement arose that included several generations of woman suffrage supporters, who became known as suffragettes. These women lectured, wrote articles, marched, lobbied, and engaged in acts of civil disobedience to achieve what many Americans then considered to be an enormous change in the Constitution. Few of the movement's early supporters lived to see the amendment ratified in 1920.

The amendment was first introduced in Congress in 1878, but it was ratified on August 18, 1920. Those who supported voting rights for women used a variety of strategies to achieve their goal. Some worked to pass suffrage acts in each state; their efforts resulted in nine western states adopting female suffrage legislation by 1912. Others used the courts to challenge male-only voting laws. Some of the more militant suffragettes organized parades, vigils, and even hunger strikes. Suffragettes frequently met resistance and even open hostility. They were heckled, jailed, and sometimes even attacked physically.

By 1916, however, almost all of the major female suffrage organizations had agreed that the best strategy was to pursue the goal of a **constitutional amendment**. The following year, New York granted suffrage to women. This was quickly followed in 1918 by President Woodrow Wilson's change in his position to support an amendment in 1918. These important events helped shift the political balance in favor of the vote for women. Then, on May 21, 1919, the U.S. House of Representatives passed the amendment, followed in two weeks by the Senate. With Tennessee becoming the 36th state to ratify the amendment on August 18, 1920, the amendment had thus been ratified by three-fourths of the states. The U.S. Secretary of State, Bainbridge Colby, certified the **ratification** on August 26, 1920, and women had gained the constitutional right to vote. Women's collective experience in pursuit of this goal differed significantly from that of Black Americans, who had actually gained the right much earlier but who had to struggle against sustained efforts to curtail their exercise of this right.

## Black Suffrage

Prior to the Civil War, free blacks were denied the right to vote everywhere but in New York and several New England states. By the close of the Civil War, suffrage for African Americans had become a possibility throughout the country. The Reconstruction Act of 1867 imposed conditions on former states of the Confederacy for re-admission to the Union. Some of these conditions touched on black suffrage. For example, former Confederate states were required to call conventions to which blacks could be elected as delegates and devise new state constitutions guaranteeing voting rights to black men. By the end of registration for 1867, more than 700,000 southern black men had been added to the rolls. By 1872 there were 342 black officials elected to state legislatures and to the U.S. Congress. Despite such progressive legislation, not all black **civil rights** or suffrage measures succeeded. Constitutional amendments that would have prohibited states from imposing birth requirements, property ownership, or literacy tests, as well as giving the federal government complete control over voting rights were rejected.

Unfortunately, the progress of black voting rights can be characterized as a stumbling trajectory of success. There were gains, often followed by severe setbacks. For example, in 1870 and 1871 three Enforcement Acts were passed that strengthened the constitutional guarantee of black voting rights. Moreover, the year 1870 also witnessed the ratification of the Fifteenth Amendment. However, just a few years later, two Supreme Court decisions, *United States v. Reese* (1876) and *United States v. Cruikshank* (1876), weakened the Fourteenth and Fifteenth Amendments. By 1877, the Union was withdrawing federal troops from the South as a compromise with Democrats to allow the election of Rutherford B. Hayes as president of the United States. This move gave the largely racist Southern Democrats control over the lives of blacks including black suffrage. Accordingly, this and other like-minded groups launched a wave of repressive measures to curtail the freedoms of blacks in the South.

## Grandfather Clauses, Literacy Tests, and the White Primary

After the Civil War and Reconstruction, southern states employed a range of tactics to prevent blacks from exercising their right to vote. They used violence, vote **fraud**, gerrymandering, literacy tests, white primaries, among others. These tactics caused registration by blacks to drop significantly. Such measures as the poll tax, literacy tests, grandfather clauses, and the white primary proved especially effective in disfranchising blacks.

The poll tax, as it applied to primary elections leading to general elections for federal office, was abolished in the Twenty-fourth Amendment, ratified in 1964. Qualifications to vote based on some element of property ownership have a history that extends to colonial days. However, the poll tax was instituted in seven southern states following Reconstruction. The poll tax was a flat fee required before voting; it was often levied as high as $200 per person. The voting rights of poor blacks were disproportionately discriminated against in this method.

The U.S. Congress eventually came to view the financial qualification as an impediment to individuals' suffrage rights. Despite Congressional sentiment, though, a constitutional amendment was necessary to abolish poll taxes, as the poll tax had previously withstood constitutional challenges in the courts. Even with the ratification of the Twenty-fourth Amendment, some states continued to look for ways

to use poll taxes as an impediment to blacks' exercising their right to vote. Finally, in the 1965 opinion in the case of *Harman v. Forssenius*, the Supreme Court struck down a Virginia law which had partially eliminated the poll tax as an absolute qualification for voting in federal elections. The Virginia law had given voters in federal elections the choice of either paying the tax or of filing a certificate of residence six months before the election. The Court found the latter requirement to be an unfair procedural requirement for voters in federal elections, particularly because the law was not imposed on those who otherwise agreed to pay the poll tax. The Court unanimously held the law to conflict with the Twenty-fourth Amendment as it penalized those who chose to exercise a right guaranteed them by the amendment.

There were many uneducated African Americans in the post-Civil War era. Literacy tests were used to help exclude them from the polls. However, whites found that literacy tests also would exclude large numbers of whites from becoming eligible voters since many whites could not read or write either. As a remedy, some jurisdictions adopted a "reasonable interpretation" clause; these laws gave voting registrars discretion to evaluate applicants' performance on literacy tests. The effect was predictable: most whites passed and most blacks did not. By the beginning of the twentieth century, almost every black had been disfranchised in the South.

Grandfather clauses, a peculiarly irksome impediment to achieving voting rights for African Americans, were enacted by seven Southern states between 1895 and 1910. These laws provided that those who had enjoyed the right to vote prior to 1866 or 1867 or their lineal descendants would be exempt from educational, property, or tax requirements for voting. Because former slaves had not been granted the right to vote until the Fifteenth Amendment was ratified in 1870, these clauses effectively excluded blacks from the vote. At the same time, grandfather clauses assured the right to vote to many impoverished, ignorant, and illiterate whites. In 1915, the U.S. Supreme Court finally declared the **grandfather clause** unconstitutional because it violated equal voting rights guaranteed by the Fifteenth Amendment.

The so-called white primary was a tactic Southern whites used in which the Democratic Party was declared a private organization that could exclude whomever it pleased. State party rules or state laws that excluded blacks from the Democratic primary virtually disenfranchised all blacks (and only blacks) by keeping them out of the election that generally determined who would hold office in a state that was dominated by the Democratic Party. In 1944, the white primary was ruled unconstitutional in the U.S. Supreme Court case of *Smith v. Allwright*.

## The Fifteenth Amendment

The Fifteenth Amendment to the United States Constitution was ratified in 1870, just a few years after the end of the Civil War. This Amendment prohibits both federal and state governments from infringing on a citizen's right to vote "on account of race, color, or previous condition of servitude." The Fifteenth Amendment is the third of three "Reconstruction Amendments" ratified in the aftermath of the Civil War. The other two are the Thirteenth Amendment that abolished slavery, and the 14th Amendment granted citizenship to all persons, "born or naturalized in the United States."

Prior to the Fifteenth Amendment, the states were empowered to set the qualifications for the right to vote. The Fifteenth Amendment essentially transferred this power to the federal government. Its ratification, however, had little effect for nearly a century. It had practically no effect in southern states, which devised numerous ways such as poll taxes and grandfather clauses to keep blacks from voting. Over time, federal laws and Supreme Court judicial opinions eventually struck down voting restrictions for blacks. Eventually, Congress passed the Civil Rights Act of 1957 which established a commission to investigate voting **discrimination**. And in 1965 the Voting Rights Act was passed to increase black voter registration by empowering the **Justice Department** to closely monitor voting qualifications.

## The Voting Rights Act

The **Voting Rights Act of 1965** (VRA) is arguably the most significant piece of federal legislation aimed at enforcing and protecting the voting rights of minorities. While the Fifteenth Amendment enfranchises African Americans, it does not necessarily clear the way to the polls for them. After nearly a century of countenancing various forms of intimidation and legalistic obstructions to black voters, the federal government passed sweeping legislation that fills important gaps in African Americans' constitutional right to vote. The VRA essentially mandates access to the polls for minority groups. The VRA prevents states from enforcing a range of discriminatory practices legislated to prevent African Americans from participating in the voting process. As a result of the VRA, the federal government intervened directly in areas where African Americans had been denied the right to vote.

### Section Two and Section Five

Sections Two and Five of the VRA are especially important. Section 2 prohibits attempts to dilute the votes of minorities. Dilution occurs when the full effect of a block of voters is deliberately and unfairly negated. Vote dilution can occur through legislation or other situations that weaken the voting strength of minorities. Section Two prohibits cities and towns from establishing practices designed to prevent minorities a fair chance to elect candidates of their choice. Section Two is enforceable nationwide.

Section Five of the VRA requires certain designated areas of the country to obtain "pre-clearance" from the U.S. attorney general or the U.S. District Court for the District of Columbia for any changes that impact voting. These special areas are called "covered jurisdictions." Accordingly, covered jurisdictions must obtain approval before they can administer any new electoral practices. All areas in the following states are subject to Section Five pre-clearance.

- Alabama
- Alaska
- Arizona
- Georgia
- Louisiana
- Mississippi
- South Carolina
- Texas
- Virginia

Parts of the following states are also subject to pre-clearance:

- California
- Florida
- Michigan
- New Hampshire
- New York
- North Carolina

- South Dakota

Section Five was necessary because of the purpose or intent in some areas to dilute or weaken the strength of minority voters. They did this by changing electoral rules such that minorities had decreased opportunities to elect someone of their choice. Additionally, Section 5 considers the effect of a proposed change. The U.S. attorney general or the U.S. District Court for the District of Columbia considers whether the proposed change will lead to a worsening of the position of minority voters, an effect known as "retrogression."

In 1975 an important amendment was added to the VRA to include rights for language minorities. These amendments required jurisdictions to provide bilingual ballots and even translation services to those who speak any of the following languages:

- Spanish

- Chinese

- Japanese

- Korean

- Native American languages

- Eskimo languages

### *Malapportioned Districts*

The first version of the VRA was insufficient to prevent efforts to continue vote dilution. Many areas had a winner-take-all, at-large electoral system, as well as severely malapportioned districts. Malapportioning, also known as "gerrymandering," is the deliberate rearrangement of the **boundaries** of congressional districts with the intent to influence the outcome of elections. Gerrymandering either concentrates opposition votes in a few districts to gain more seats for the majority in surrounding districts (a process called packing) or diffuses minority votes across many districts (called dilution). The term came about in 1812 when Massachusetts's governor Elbridge Gerry created a district for political purposes that resembled a salamander.

The at-large electoral system where representatives are chosen area-wide dilutes minority voting strength because whites so frequently outnumber blacks. In 1973 the U.S. Supreme Court in the case of *White v. Register* ruled that at-large elections were unconstitutional if they diluted or minimized minority votes.

In terms of malapportionment, there were problems of state legislatures adhering to outmoded rural

interests. For example, in the 1962 case *Baker v. Carr*, malapportionment claims from some of Tennessee's big cities were found justifiable under the Fourteenth Amendment. *Baker v. Carr* involved **apportionment** schemes whereby less populated rural counties had obtained disproportionate political strength as opposed to the densely populated cities.

Such malapportionment procedures became tinged with racism as redistricting practices maximized the political advantage or votes of one group and minimized the political advantage or votes of another. In *Gomillion v. Lightfoot*, the board of supervisors in Tuskegee, Alabama, annexed territory to increase the size of the city, but excluded all the blacks around the city. The Supreme Court found that such racial gerrymandering violated constitutional guarantees. A related case, *Reynolds v. Sims* put a stop to a gerrymandering scheme that discriminated heavily against populated urban areas in favor of rural areas and small towns. Through such cases, the U.S. Supreme Court advanced toward the goal of full and effective participation by all citizens in state government.

## Minority Majority Districts

Through the VRA, the federal government moved to guarantee access for all citizens to the ballot. Even so, the right to vote did not necessarily translate into electing representatives for voters who were in the minority. In jurisdictions, particularly in the South, voters who historically had faced racial discrimination (African-Americans, Latinos, Asian-Pacific Americans and Native Americans) had been unable to elect candidates of their choice unless they constituted a majority of voters in a given electoral district. In 1982, Congress amended the VRA to include requirements that certain jurisdictions provide minority voters opportunities to elect candidates of their choice.

Initially, these jurisdictions turned minority populations into a majority through re-drawing legislative districts. This created an overall racial majority from a formerly minority population in a particular district. But this approach has serious drawbacks, especially when a minority group is not centralized, but is dispersed geographically or interspersed with other groups of voters. Consequently, these race-conscious districts encountered setbacks at the Supreme Court, which outlawed explicit "racial gerrymanders."

As a result of many legal disputes and public controversies concerning effective minority representation, courts have ordered ward-based systems (single-member districts) as remedies in vote dilution cases. This supports the notion that the best determinant of a black candidate's electoral success is the racial composition of the electoral jurisdictions. But in the 1993 Supreme Court decision of *Shaw v. Reno*, the Court declared that a North Carolina reapportionment scheme constituted racial gerrymandering under the **Equal Protection** Clause of the Fourteenth Amendment. This ruling allows white voters to object to what they perceive as racially motivated districting. Cases similar to *Shaw*, and cases resulting from the *Shaw* decision filled the courts. Voting rights attorneys, civil rights groups, and community activists defended majority minority voting districts and to protect them in light of the *Shaw* decision.

Many would agree that the VRA is perhaps the most significant piece of legislation designed to secure minority electoral rights. However, the VRA is vulnerable to attack on the grounds that it may overextend its original mandate. Some have argued that proponents of the VRA have confused the "right to vote" with the "right to be elected." Many people of color have won federal, state, and local elections. Their success may not have been possible without such aggressive policy measures as the VRA. Yet despite the protections of the VRA, courts continue to address controversies surrounding new methods to dilute the collective strength of black voters.

The creation of majority-black districts has been the overarching federal policy regarding minority representation after the VRA was enacted. Even so, there are many views about the need and effectiveness of majority-black districts. Likewise, the case of *Shaw v. Reno* places majority-black districting in a somewhat tenuous position as more and more groups of whites begin to assert that redistricting plans have resulted in a new kind of "political apartheid," preventing them from full and effective use of the ballot. Efforts continue to work out a solution that passes constitutional muster and it remains to be seen what that solution will be.

## Additional Resources

*Along Racial Lines: Consequences of the 1965 Voting Rights Act*. David M. Hudson, Peter Lang Publishing, 1998.

*The Appearance of Equality: Racial Gerrymandering, Redistricting, and the Supreme Court*. Christopher Matthew Burke, Greenwood Publishing Group, 1999.

*A Free Ballot and a Fair Count: The Department of Justice and the Enforcement of Voting Rights in the South, 1877-1893*. Robert Michael Goldman, Fordham University Press, 2001.

*Feminism and Suffrage: The Emergence of an Independent Women's Movement in America, 1848-1869*. Ellen Carol Dubois, Cornell University Press, 1999.

*Struggle for Mastery: Disfranchisement in the South, 1888-1908*. Michael Perman, University of North Carolina Press, 2001.

*Voting Rights and Redistricting in the United States*. Edited by Mark E. Rush, Greenwood Publishing Group, 1998.

*Voting Rights on Trial: A Handbook with Cases, Laws, and Documents*. Charles L. Zelden, ABC-CLIO, 2002.

## Organizations

### The Center for Voting and Democracy (CVD)
6930 Carroll Ave. Suite 610
Takoma Park, MD 20912 USA
Phone: (301) 270-4616
Fax: (301) 270-4133
E-Mail: info@fairvote.org
URL: http://www.fairvote.org/index.html

### Federal Election Commission (FEC)
999 E Street, NW
Washington, DC 20463 USA
Phone: (202) 694-1100
E-Mail: Webmaster@fec.gov
URL: http://www.fec.gov/

### Joint Center for Political and Economic Studies (JCPES)
1090 Vermont Ave., NW, Suite 1100
Washington, DC 20005-4928 USA
Phone: (202) 789-3500
Fax: (202) 789-6390
E-Mail: athompson@jointcenter.org
URL: http://www.jointctr.org/index.html

### League of Women Voters (LWV)
1730 M Street NW, Suite 1000
Washington, DC 20036-4508 USA
Phone: (202) 429-1965
Fax: (202) 429-0854
E-Mail: lwv@lwv.org
URL: http://www.lwv.org/

### National Voting Rights Institute (NVRI)
One Bromfield Street, 3rd Floor
Boston, MA 02108 USA
Phone: (617) 368-9100
Fax: (617) 368-9101
E-Mail: nvri@nvri.org
URL: http://www.nvri.org/

# CONSUMER ISSUES

## ADVERTISING

*Sections within this essay:*

## Background

The Federal Trade Commission (FTC) works to ensure that the nation's markets are efficient and free of practices which might harm consumers. To ensure the smooth operation of our free market system, the FTC enforces federal **consumer protection** laws that prevent **fraud**, deception, and unfair business practices. The Federal Trade Commission Act allows the FTC to act in the interest of all consumers to prevent deceptive and unfair acts or practices. In interpreting the Act, the Commission has determined that, with respect to advertising, a representation, omission, or practice is deceptive if it is likely to mislead consumers and affect consumers' behavior or decisions about the product or service. In addition, an act or practice is unfair if the injury it causes, or is likely to cause, is substantial, not outweighed by other benefits, and not reasonably avoidable.

The FTC Act's prohibition on unfair or deceptive acts or practices broadly covers advertising claims, marketing and promotional activities, and sales practices in general. The Act is not limited to any particular medium. Accordingly, the Commission's role in protecting consumers from unfair or deceptive acts or practices encompasses advertising, marketing, and sales online, as well as the same activities in print, television, telephone and radio. For certain industries or subject areas, the Commission issues rules and guides. Rules prohibit specific acts or practices that the Commission has found to be unfair or deceptive. Guides help businesses in their efforts to comply with the law by providing examples or direction on how to avoid unfair or deceptive acts or practices. Many rules and guides address claims about products or services or advertising in general and is not limited to any particular medium used to disseminate those claims or advertising. Therefore, the plain language of many rules and guides applies to claims made on the Internet. Solicitations made in print, on the telephone, radio, TV, or online naturally fall within the Rule's scope.

## Bureau of Consumer Protection

The FTC's Bureau of Consumer Protection protects consumers against unfair, deceptive, or **fraudulent** practices. The Bureau enforces a variety of consumer protection laws enacted by Congress, as well as trade regulation rules issued by the Commission. Its actions include individual company and industry-wide investigations, administrative and federal court **litigation**, rule-making proceedings, and consumer and business education. In addition, the Bureau contributes to the Commission's on-going efforts to inform Congress and other government entities of the impact that proposed actions could have on consumers. The Bureau of Consumer Protection is divided into six divisions and programs, each with its own areas of expertise. One of the divisions is the Division of Advertising Practices.

Within the Bureau of Consumer Protection is the Division of Advertising Practices and the Division of Enforcement. These entities are the nation's enforcers of federal truth-in-advertising laws. The FTC Act prohibits unfair or deceptive advertising in any medium. That is, advertising must tell the truth and not mislead consumers. A claim can be misleading if relevant information is left out or if the claim implies something that is not true. In addition, claims must be substantiated especially when they concern health, safety, or performance. The type of **evidence** may depend on the product, the claims, and what experts believe necessary. Sellers are responsible for claims they make about their products and services. Third parties such as advertising agencies or website designers and catalog marketers also may be liable for making or disseminating deceptive representations if they participate in the preparation or distribution of the advertising or know about the deceptive claims.

The Division of Advertising Practices focuses its enforcement activities on claims for foods, drugs, dietary supplements, and other products promising health benefits; health fraud on the Internet; weight-loss advertising and marketing directed to children; performance claims for computers, ISPs and other high-tech products and services; tobacco and alcohol advertising; protecting children's privacy online; claims about product performance made in national or regional newspapers and magazines; in radio and TV commercials, including infomercials; through direct mail to consumers; or on the Internet.

### Advertising Agency Obligations

Advertising agencies (and more recently, website designers) are responsible for reviewing the information used to **substantiate** ad claims. These agencies may not simply rely on an advertiser's assurance that the claims are substantiated. In determining whether an ad agency should be held liable, the FTC looks at the extent of the agency's participation in the preparation of the challenged ad and whether the agency knew or should have known that the ad included false or deceptive claims.

### Publisher Obligations

Like advertising agencies, catalog and magazine publishers can be held responsible for material distributed. Publications may be required to provide documentation to back up assertions made in the advertisement. Repeating what the manufacturer claims about the product is not necessarily sufficient. The Division of Enforcement conducts a wide variety of law enforcement activities to protect consumers, including deceptive marketing practices. This division monitors compliance with Commission cease and desist orders and federal court injunctive orders, investigates violations of consumer protection laws, and enforces a number of trade laws, rules, and guides.

### Franchises and Businesses

The Franchise and Business Opportunity Rule requires franchise and business opportunity sellers to give consumers a detailed disclosure document at least 10 days before the consumer pays any money or legally commits to a purchase. The document must include:

- the names, addresses, and telephone numbers of other purchasers

- a fully-audited **financial statement** of the seller

- the background and experience of the business's key executives

- the cost of starting and maintaining the business

- the responsibilities of the seller and purchaser once the purchase is made

In addition, companies that make earnings representations must give consumers the written basis for their claims, including the number and percentage of owners who have done at least as well as claimed.

Multi-level marketing (MLM), sometimes known as network or matrix marketing, is a way of selling goods and services through distributors. These plans typically promise that people who sign up as distributors will get commissions two ways: On their own sales and on the sales their recruits have made.

Pyramid schemes are a form of multi-level marketing which involves paying commissions to distributors only for recruiting new distributors. Pyramid schemes are illegal in most states because the plans inevitably collapse when no new distributors can be recruited. When a plan collapses, most people except those at the top of the pyramid lose money. Lawful MLMs should pay commissions for the retail sales of goods or services, not for recruiting new distributors. MLMs that involve the sale of business opportunities or franchises, as defined by the Franchise Rule, must comply with the Rule's requirements about disclosing the number and percentage of existing franchisees who have achieved the claimed results, as well as cautionary language.

### Telemarketing Sales

The FTC's Telemarketing Sales Rule requires certain disclosures and prohibits misrepresentations. The Rule covers most types of telemarketing calls to consumers, including calls to pitch goods, services, sweepstakes, and prize promotion and investment opportunities. It also applies to calls consumers make in response to postcards or other materials received in the mail. Calling times are restricted to the hours between 8 a.m. and 9 p.m. Telemarketers must disclose that it is a sales call, and for which company. It is illegal for telemarketers to misrepresent any information, including facts about goods or services, earnings potential, profitability, risk or liquidity of an investment, or the nature of a prize in a prize-promotion scheme. Telemarketers must disclose the total cost of the products or services offered and all restrictions on getting or using them, or that a sale is final or non-refundable. Although most types of telemarketing calls are covered by the Rule, the Rule does not cover calls placed by consumers in response to general media advertising (except calls responding to ads for investment opportunities, credit repair services, recovery room services, or advance-fee loans). It also does not cover calls placed by consumers in response to direct mail advertising that discloses all the material information required by the Rule (except calls responding to ads for investment opportunities, prize promotions, credit repair services, recovery room services, or advance-fee loans). The Mail or Telephone Order Merchandise Rule requires companies to ship purchases when promised (or within 30 days if no time is specified) or to give consumers the option to cancel their orders for a refund.

### Environmental Marketing Practices

Guidelines for using environmental marketing claims have been established by the Federal Trade Commission. The guides themselves are not enforceable regulations, nor do they have the force and effect of law. These guides specifically address the application of Section 5 of the Federal Trade Commission Act that makes deceptive acts and practices in or affecting commerce unlawful to environmental advertising and marketing practices. Guides for the Use of Environmental Marketing Claims provide the basis for voluntary compliance with such laws by members of industry and are available from the EPA and the FTC. The guides apply to advertising, labeling, and other forms of marketing to consumers and do not preempt state or local laws or regulations. Generally, environmental claims must specify application to the product, the package, or a component of either. Environmental claims should not overstate the environmental attributes or benefit. Every express and material implied claim conveyed to consumers about an objective quality should be substantiated and other broad environmental claims should be avoided or qualified.

A product which purports to offer an environmental benefit must be backed with factual information. Green Guides govern claims that consumer products are environmentally safe, recycled, recyclable, ozone-friendly, or biodegradable. These guides apply to environmental claims included in labeling, advertising, promotional materials, and all other forms of marketing. The guides apply to any claim about the environmental attributes of a product, package, or service in connection with the sale, offering for sale, or marketing of such product, package, or service for personal, family, or household use, or for commercial, institutional, or industrial use.

According to the guidelines, a product or package should not be marketed as recyclable unless it can be collected, separated, or otherwise recovered from the solid waste stream for reuse or in the manufacture or assembly of another package or product through an established recycling program. Products or packages that are made of both recyclable and non-recyclable components must have any recyclable claim adequately qualified to avoid consumer deception about which portions or components of the product or package are recyclable. Claims of recyclability should be qualified to the extent necessary to avoid consumer deception about any limited availability of recycling programs and collection sites. If an incidental component significantly limits the ability to recycle a product or package, a claim of recyclability would be deceptive. A product or package that is made from recyclable material, but, because of its shape, size, or some other attribute, is not accepted in recycling programs for such material, should not be marketed as recyclable.

Likewise, claims that a product or package is degradable, biodegradable, or photodegradable should be substantiated by competent and reliable scientific evidence that the entire product or package will completely break down and return to nature, i.e., decompose into elements found in nature within a reasonably short time after customary disposal. Claims of degradability, biodegradability, or photodegradability should be qualified to the extent necessary to avoid consumer deception about the product or package's ability to degrade in the environment where it is customarily disposed and the rate and extent of degradation.

A recycled content claim may be made only for materials that have been recovered or otherwise diverted from the solid waste stream, either during the manufacturing process (pre-consumer) or after consumer use (post-consumer). To the extent the source of recycled content includes pre-consumer material, the manufacturer or advertiser must have substantiation for concluding that the pre-consumer material would otherwise have entered the solid waste stream. In asserting a recycled content claim, distinctions may be made between pre-consumer and post-consumer materials. Where such distinctions are asserted, any express or implied claim about the specific pre-consumer or post-consumer content of a product or package must be substantiated. For products or packages that are only partially made of recycled material, a recycled claim should be adequately qualified to avoid consumer deception about the amount, by weight, of recycled content in the finished product or package. Additionally, for products that contain used, reconditioned, or remanufactured components, a recycled claim should be adequately qualified to avoid consumer deception about the nature of such components. No such qualification would be necessary in cases where it would be clear to consumers from the context that a product's recycled content consists of used, reconditioned, or remanufactured components.

### Labeling Rules

The Textile, Wool, Fur, and Care Labeling Rules require proper origin and fiber content labeling of textile, wool and fur products, and care label instructions attached to clothing and fabrics.

For a product to bear the label "Made in USA," the product must be "all or virtually all" made in the United States. The term "United States," as referred to in the Enforcement Policy Statement, includes the 50 states, the District of Columbia, and the U.S. territories and possessions. "All or virtually all" means that all significant parts and processing that go into

the product must be of U.S. origin. That is, the product should contain no, or negligible, foreign content. The product's final assembly or processing must take place in the United States. The Commission then considers other factors, including how much of the product's total manufacturing costs can be assigned to U.S. parts and processing and how far removed any foreign content is from the finished product. In some instances, only a small portion of the total manufacturing costs is attributable to foreign processing, but that processing represents a significant amount of the product's overall processing. Claims that a particular manufacturing or other process was performed in the United States or that a particular part was manufactured in the United States must be truthful, substantiated, and clearly refer to the specific process or part, not to the general manufacture of the product, to avoid implying more U.S. content than exists.

A product that includes foreign components may be called "Assembled in USA" without qualification when its principal assembly takes place in the United States and the assembly is substantial. For the assembly claim to be valid, the product's last substantial transformation should have occurred in the United States.

## Comparative Advertising

It is completely legal for a company to compare its product or service to another company's in an ad provided the comparison is truthful and accurate. However, it is illegal to mislead through an implied comparison. A statement in an ad that a product is more reliable than another because it does something that the other product may also do, can manipulatively imply a falsehood.

## FTC Litigation

Typically, FTC investigations are non-public to protect both the investigation and the companies involved. If the FTC believes that a person or company has violated the law, the agency may attempt to obtain voluntary compliance by entering into a consent order with the company. A company that signs a consent order need not admit that it violated the law, but it must agree to stop the disputed practices outlined in an accompanying complaint. If a consent agreement cannot be reached, the FTC may issue an administrative complaint or seek injunctive relief in the federal courts. The FTC's administrative complaints initiate a formal proceeding that is much like a federal court trial but before an administrative law judge; evidence is submitted, **testimony** is heard, and witnesses are examined and cross-examined. If a law violation is found, a **cease and desist order** may be issued. Initial decisions by administrative law judges may be appealed to the full Commission. Final decisions issued by the Commission may be appealed to the U.S. Court of Appeals and, ultimately, to the U.S. Supreme Court.

In some circumstances, the FTC can go directly to court to obtain an injunction, civil penalties, or consumer **redress**. The injunction preserves the market's competitive status quo. The FTC seeks federal court injunctions in consumer protection matters typically in cases of ongoing consumer fraud.

## Additional Resources

*Advertising: Principles And Practice* Wells, William, Prentice Hall, 1999.

*Copywriting for the Electronic Media: A Practical Guide* Meeske, Milan, Wadsworth Publishing Company, 1999.

*Trust Us, We're Experts: How Industry Manipulates Science and Gambles with Your Future* Rampton, Sheldon and John Stauber, Putnam, 2000.

## Organizations

### *The Council of Better Business Bureaus*

4200 Wilson Blvd., Suite 800
Arlington, VA 22203-1838 USA
Phone: (703) 276-0100
Fax: (703) 525-8277
URL: http://www.bbb.org

### *Federal Trade Commission*

600 Pennsylvania Avenue, NW
Washington, DC 20580 USA
Phone: (877) FTC-HELP
URL: http://www.ftc.gov

# CONSUMER ISSUES

## BANKRUPTCY

*Sections within this essay:*

- Background
- History
- Types of Bankruptcies
- Jurisdiction and Procedure
- Exemptions from the Bankruptcy Estate
- Additional Resources

## Background

**Bankruptcy** is a procedure, authorized under federal law, that relieves an individual or corporation of debts. With bankruptcy, debtors rarely escape completely from liability for their debts; instead, they partially or completely repay creditors under an arrangement that is court approved and authorized and in exchange, any remaining debt is forgiven.

Once considered shameful, bankruptcy still is a method of last resort for relieving financial obligations, but in recent decades bankruptcy in the United States has become more common and more acceptable. Individuals can seek the protection of the bankruptcy courts for personal debts such as credit cards, home mortgages, and medical bills, among others. **Corporations**, farms, and even local governments also can find themselves lacking enough financial resources to pay their debts and can turn to the bankruptcy law for help.

Bankruptcy exists to allow debtors to have a "fresh start," so that they can settle their debts and

return to being productive members of society. The goal is to prevent individual debtors from becoming destitute and to prevent **corporate** debtors and other entities from becoming non-existent. At the same time, it is the goal of bankruptcy to repay creditors, at least partially. This is done by having the bankruptcy court **liquidate**, or sell, the assets of the **debtor** or restructure the debtor's finances so that creditors are paid at least part of what is owed. The bankruptcy court protects the debtor from further debt-collecting actions by the **creditor** so long as the debtor complies with the court's **liquidation** or restructuring plan. Bankruptcy thereby allows the debtor to emerge from the debt and move forward. This is why bankruptcy is sometimes referred to as "bankruptcy protection" or "bankruptcy relief." A significant deterrent to bankruptcy is the damaged credit rating that results. An individual who files for bankruptcy may have a difficult time obtaining credit for up to seven years or more.

Although federal law generally governs bankruptcies in the United States, states still govern issues and disputes over financial obligations such as rental leases, utility bills, and other contracts involving finances. Federal law concerning these issues overrides state law once a debtor files for bankruptcy protection. This is warranted by the Constitution and ensures economic stability and uniformity among the states.

## History

The evolution of bankruptcy laws in the United States began in England in the sixteenth century. At that time, debtors who would not, or could not, pay their debts unhappily found themselves in debtors prison. By the eighteenth century, public sentiment was shifting with the realization that imprisoning debtors was not only cruel, it also prevented creditors from ever getting paid. New laws developed that allowed debts to be reduced or forgiven in exchange for the debtor's efforts to repay them.

Before the signing of the Declaration of Independence, colonies in the United States followed the earlier, punitive English laws that imprisoned debtors. States developed their own laws regarding debtors after 1776, but these laws lacked uniformity. The U.S. Constitution in 1789 charged Congress with enacting laws concerning bankruptcy and the Bankruptcy Act of 1800 became the country's first uniform bankruptcy law.

But three years after its enactment, Congress repealed the 1800 law over public sentiment that disfavored its emphasis on creditor rights. Congress struggled during the next century to strike the delicate balance between protecting debtors and repaying creditors. In 1841, Congress for the first time permitted debtors to choose whether to obtain bankruptcy relief rather than being forced to do so. Other bankruptcy laws came and went, but the Bankruptcy Act of 1898 and its many amendments lasted for eighty years and became the model for current bankruptcy laws in the United States. The 1898 act established special bankruptcy courts and bankruptcy trustees, charged with the duty of overseeing bankruptcy liquidations and financial restructuring. The Bankruptcy Reform Act of 1978 replaced the 1898 act and, along with amendments passed in 1984, 1986, 1994, and 2005, this act is known as the bankruptcy code. The 2005 changes, which fall under the Bankruptcy Abuse Prevention and Consumer Protection Act (BAPCPA), introduced what many experts consider to be among the most sweeping changes to personal bankruptcy law, particularly for those who seek to liquidate their debts.

## Types of Bankruptcies

There are generally two types of bankruptcy relief. Liquidation, governed by chapter seven of the bankruptcy code and commonly referred to as chapter seven bankruptcy, involves converting the debtor's assets into cash and using the cash to pay the creditors. The bankruptcy code defines how bankruptcy courts and trustees are to prioritize creditors. Some creditors receive only partial satisfaction, or in some cases no satisfaction, of the debt. Once the liquidation and distribution of assets to the creditors is com-

plete, in the case of an individual debtor, the court will forgive any remaining debt. In the case of a corporation, the corporation is rendered defunct upon liquidation and distribution. There is no need to forgive remaining debts of a corporation since the corporation is no longer a legal entity for creditors to pursue.

The second type of bankruptcy relief is called rehabilitation or reorganization. This type of bankruptcy usually gives creditors a better chance of being repaid, although the duration of repayment may be extended. In a reorganization bankruptcy, the debtor may keep assets but must strictly abide by a reorganization plan that the bankruptcy court authorizes. The reorganization plan defines when and how much each creditor will be repaid, but allows the debtor to continue to function as normally as possible. While the reorganization plan is in place the court prevents creditors from pursuing additional payments from the debtor. Over time and with diligence, the debtor repays the creditors according to the reorganization plan. Once the plan is completed, remaining debts are discharged, or forgiven. If the debtor does not comply with the reorganization plan, the court may order that the debtor's assets be liquidated to pay the debts.

The most common forms of reorganization bankruptcies are chapter eleven bankruptcy, which normally applies to individuals and corporations with large and complex debts, and chapter thirteen bankruptcy, which normally applies to individual consumers. The bankruptcy code has a special chapter for family farmers, chapter twelve, but family farmers may opt to file under chapters eleven or thirteen instead. Municipalities seeking bankruptcy protection do so under chapter nine, which mandates reorganization.

## Sweeping Changes in 2005

The Bankruptcy Abuse Prevention and Consumer Protection Act (BAPCPA) was signed into law in April 2005 and went into effect on October 17, 2005. This act, designed to curb instances of bankruptcy fraud, had a direct impact on chapter seven bankruptcies. The most significant change was a requirement for chapter seven filers to pass a means test to determine whether they might be able to file chapter thirteen and pay back their debts over a five-year period. Debtors whose income was above the state median (variable based on the number of people in the debtor's household) would be required to file chapter thirteen. Even those deemed eligible to file for chapter seven would still face stricter requirements. Mandatory debt counseling must be completed within 180 days prior to filing for bankruptcy and the debtor must provide a certificate of counseling. The debtor must also supply additional proof of assets, including the most recent year's tax return, evidence of payment from employers made 60 days before filing, and other forms and documents (including a photo ID). The amount of time before a debtor can file again for chapter seven bankruptcy has risen from six years to eight years.

Banks and credit card agencies hailed the new act as a much-needed check on an easy way out of paying legitimate debts (in 2003 there were 1.6 million filings for personal bankruptcy). Consumer advocates claimed that the new act punished those who were legitimately seeking relief and who now would have a harder time trying to get a fresh start. One development that could have an impact on this issue was a change in regulations regarding minimum monthly payments on credit card accounts. The federal government compelled banks and other credit card issuers to raise the minimum monthly payments, in some cases to double what they had been. While such a change could be a hardship on borrowers who may have trouble making higher payments, ultimately it could help lower outstanding debt by getting people to pay their credit card bills down more quickly.

In October 2005, the U.S. Department of Justice announced that it would grant temporary waivers to chapter seven filers who were affected by Hurricane Katrina, which devastated Louisiana and Mississippi. Victims of the hurricane were given additional time to get the necessary paperwork and debt counseling requirements completed before filing for bankruptcy.

## Jurisdiction and Procedure

Federal **statute** requires that federal district courts maintain **jurisdiction** over bankruptcy matters. District court judges do not preside over bankruptcy cases, however. Instead, units within the district courts manage bankruptcy cases. Federal **appellate court** judges appoint bankruptcy judges to these units, and these judges, with their specialized knowledge of the bankruptcy laws and rules, preside over bankruptcy cases. Thus, the federal district courts technically have jurisdiction over bank-

ruptcy filings but in practice refer the matters to the bankruptcy judges.

Most bankruptcy cases require that the bankruptcy court appoint a **trustee**. The bankruptcy trustee's job is to impartially administer the bankruptcy estate, which includes the assets of the debtor. Once a debtor files for bankruptcy protection, the debtor's assets—savings, houses, cars, jewelry, stocks, and **bonds** are examples of assets—become the bankruptcy estate, and the bankruptcy estate becomes a distinct legal entity separate from the debtor. The trustee represents the bankruptcy estate and at the direction of the bankruptcy judge may sell assets, or otherwise oversees if, when, and how the assets will be distributed to pay the debts.

In 1986, Congress permanently established a central office to oversee the work of bankruptcy trustees throughout the country. The office of the U.S. trustee has trustees, appointed by the U.S. attorney general, in each region of the United States. These appointed U.S. trustees, in turn, appoint and supervise additional trustees, ensuring that trustees do their jobs competently and honestly. U.S. trustees also have the responsibility to monitor and report **fraud** by debtors and abuse by creditors.

One important aspect of the bankruptcy laws is the "automatic stay." As soon as a debtor files the proper legal documents requesting bankruptcy protection, the automatic stay takes effect. This means that all efforts by creditors to collect from the debtor are, by law, frozen, and a creditor who ignores the automatic stay faces severe penalties. The automatic stay gives the debtor, the trustee, and the court time to determine the proper course of action in getting the debts repaid. A party who has a claim against the bankruptcy estate and shows good cause for not being included in the requirements of the automatic stay may ask the bankruptcy judge for "relief from the automatic stay."

When the debtor complies with the bankruptcy liquidation or reorganization plan and the plan is completed, the bankruptcy judge may discharge any remaining debt and terminate the bankruptcy case. This action also terminates the automatic stay and ends the bankruptcy court's involvement with the debtor. Typically, the debtor is left without any debts since the bankruptcy plan has repaid them or the bankruptcy court has discharged them. Also typically, the debtor is left with a poor credit rating and has difficulty borrowing money, obtaining credit cards, and financing things like homes, cars, and business ventures. Credit bureaus can report a bankruptcy for ten years after the date of filing.

Sometimes creditors offer debtors the opportunity to "reaffirm" a debt—in other words, to keep the debt and agree to pay it off even if it is eligible for liquidation. Debtors often do this when they feel it would be to their advantage to maintain a good relationship with certain creditors. Reaffirming a debt does not improve the debtor's credit rating, and leaves the debtor with an undischargable debt, thus defeating the purpose of bankruptcy as a form of financial relief. Many lending institutions do allow debtors to obtain credit in the form of a "secured" credit card, in which the debtor deposits money into a bank account as collateral against the use of the card. This can be useful for people who wish to gradually rebuild their credit ratings.

## Exemptions from the Bankruptcy Estate

In keeping with the goal of bankruptcy laws to rehabilitate rather than punish the debtor, the individual debtor is permitted to keep some property that otherwise would be included in the bankruptcy estate and liquidated. These are called exemptions. Exemptions ensure that the debtor is able to survive the bankruptcy process without becoming destitute and having to rely on additional government assistance once the process is complete. Property that is commonly deemed exempt from the bankruptcy estate usually includes a home, a personal car, and personal items such as clothing.

The federal bankruptcy statute lists allowable exemptions, and these are followed in some states. But the federal law also permits states to legislate their own list of bankruptcy exemptions (in fact, 35 states do not allow debtors to take the federal exemptions). This results in widely varying types and amounts of exemptions that depend on the debtor's state of residence.

## State Bankruptcy Exemptions

Below are some examples of typical state exemptions. Some of the exempt items listed (sewing machines, farm tools) are a holdover from earlier days when such items would have been essential to the debtor's ability to rebuild a life.

ALABAMA: Residents may not elect federal exemptions. State exemptions include up to $5,000 in homestead equity and up to $3,000 in **personal property**. Personal items such as family books and photos are exempt.

ARIZONA: Residents may not elect federal exemptions. Residents may exempt up to $100,000 in homestead property and up to $4,000 in household furnishings and appliances, food and provisions for use of individual or family for six months, life insurance proceeds, retirement fund, tools or equipment used in a trade or profession.

CALIFORNIA: Residents can elect federal exemptions or California exemptions. California homestead exemptions include up to $50,000 in home equity for individuals, up to $75,000 in home equity for heads of households, and up to $100,000 for seniors or disabled individuals. Ordinarily and reasonably necessary household furnishings and clothing used by the debtor and spouse are completely exempt. Other exemptions include jewelry, heirlooms, and works of art up to $5,000, tools of trade up to $5,000 per spouse, cemetery plots.

FLORIDA: Residents may not elect federal exemptions. Homestead is completely exempt. Personal property worth up to $1,000 is exempt. Personal vehicle up to $1,000 is exempt. Professionally prescribed health aids are exempt.

IDAHO: Residents may not elect federal exemptions. Homestead equity of up to $50,000 is exempt. Personal property valued up to $500 per item or an aggregate of $4,000 for all items is exempt; jewelry of aggregate value up to $250 is exempt; personal vehicle up to $1,500 is exempt; professional books and tools of the trade up to aggregate value of $1,000 is exempt.

KENTUCKY: Residents may not elect federal exemptions. Real or personal property valued up to $5,000 used by the debtor as a residence is exempt. Personal property valued up to $3,000; equipment and livestock valued up to $3,000 and personal vehicle valued up to $2,500 are exempt.

MICHIGAN: Homestead exemption of up to 40 acres of land and dwelling house not exceeding $3,500 in value are exempt. Family pictures and clothing are exempt. Household goods not exceeding $1,000 are exempt. Seat or pew used by debtor in public house of worship is exempt. **Individual Retirement Account** is exempt.

NEVADA: Residents may not elect federal exemptions. Homestead equity up to $125,000 is exempt.

Private libraries up to $1,500 in value and personal belongings up to $3,000 in value are exempt. Farm trucks, stock, and equipment not to exceed $4,500 are exempt; tools of the profession not to exceed $4,500 are exempt. Qualified retirement plans not exceeding $500,000 in present-day value are exempt.

NEW YORK: Homestead equity of up to $10,000 is exempt. Personal belongings such as family bible, pictures, school books, one sewing machine, pets and pet food, all clothing and household furniture, one television set, one refrigerator, one radio, one wedding ring, one watch up to $35 in value are exempt.

OKLAHOMA: Homestead is exempt. Exempt personal property may include all household furniture; cemetery plots; family books, portraits, and pictures; clothing valued up to $4,000; five milk cows and their calves up to six months old; 100 chickens; two horses and two bridles and two saddles; one gun; one vehicle valued up to $3,000; ten hogs; twenty sheep; and one year's supply of provisions for stock.

RHODE ISLAND: There is no exemption for homestead. Exempt personal property includes clothing up to $500; furniture up to $1,000; bibles, school books, and family books valued up to $300; cemetery plot.

UTAH: Residents may not elect federal exemptions. Homestead equity up to $10,000 is exempt. Personal property such as burial plots; necessary health aids; clothing not including jewelry and furs; one washing machine; one dryer; one microwave oven; one refrigerator; one freezer; one stove; one sewing machine; beds and bedding are exempt. Personal vehicle up to $2,500 is exempt. Household furnishings up to $1,000 in value are exempt. Heirlooms up to $500 are exempt. Animals, books, and musical instruments up to $500 are exempt. Tools of trade up to $3,500 are exempt.

WASHINGTON: Resident may elect state exemptions, federal exemptions, or both. Homestead equity up to $30,000 is exempt. Personal property that is exempt includes clothing; jewelry, and furs valued up to $1,000; private libraries valued up to $1,500 per individual; household furnishings up to $2,700; two cars; $100 in cash; and tools of the trade not to exceed $5,000 in value.

## Federal Bankruptcy Exemptions

Federal bankruptcy exemptions include the following: Residence of debtor up to $17,450 in value is exempt. Personal vehicle up to $2,775 in value is exempt. Household furnishings, books, clothing, pets, and other personal items not to exceed $425 per item or $9,300 in aggregate value are exempt. Jewelry not to exceed $1,150 in value is exempt. Tools of the trade valued up to $1,750 are exempt. Benefits such as social security, **disability**, unemployment, **alimony**, and certain pensions are exempt. A "wild card" exemption of up to $925, plus up to $8,725 of unused homestead exemption funds, can be applied to any property.

Some states allow debtors to combine state and slected federal exemption items.

## Additional Resources

*West's Encyclopedia of American Law.* West Group, 1998.

## Organizations

### American Bankruptcy Institute
44 Canal Center Plaza, Suite 404
Alexandria, VA 22314 USA
Phone: ((703)) 739-0800
URL: www.abiworld.org
Primary Contact: Sam Gerdano, Executive Director

# CONSUMER ISSUES

## CONSUMER DEBT COLLECTION AND GARNISHMENT

*Sections within this essay:*

- Background
    - General and Secured Creditors

- Sequence of Events

- Internal Efforts by Original Creditor

- Collection Agencies

- Offers of Settlement

- Attorneys for the Creditor

- Formal Proceedings

- Satisfaction of Judgment

- Property Seizure and Garnishment

- The Fair Debt Collections Practices Act

- State Laws

- Additional Resources

## Background

In a robust economy (such as that of the economic boom during the 1990s and early 2000s), credit comes easy and consumers often respond by over-indulging in purchases and loans. Many consumers ultimately find themselves overextended in both available credit and outstanding debt. However, when credit tightens, or personal circumstances in the life of a consumer-debtor change, there can be a domino effect spreading from individual debtors all the way to the national economy.

During rough financial times, there is often nothing as difficult as picking up the telephone and in-forming a creditor that a payment will be late or not coming at all. However, this is precisely what needs to be done. Creditors often have as much at stake in a defaulting account as the debtor. Therefore, it is to the benefit of both parties to attempt a solution short of formal proceedings.

In order to fairly accomplish this, debtors should be acquainted with their rights and the various laws, remedies, and procedures available to both them and their creditors.

### General and Secured Creditors

At the outset, it is important to distinguish between two main classes of creditors, to whom debts may be in default. The distinction directly affects the outcome of a debt collection matter.

A secured loan is one that requires the debtor to pledge something of value as collateral for the loan. Home mortgages and auto loans are common examples affecting most consumers. In each of these two examples, the purchased house or the purchased automobile becomes the collateral for the loan, and the lender has a "security interest" in the collateral/property that secures the debt. When a debtor defaults in payments, the "secured creditor" can simply repossess the car or house. (A foreclosure on a house is a form of repossession by the lender, but federal and state laws impose additional notice requirements upon defaulting debtors. However, in the classic "land contract" sale of property at common law, debtors who defaulted in payments generally lost the property and all equity therein.)

On the other hand, most credit card debts, revolving credit at retail stores, student loans, etc., are unsecured debts. The "general" (unsecured) creditors must file suit and win a judgment against the debtor before they can seize or sell any assets or belongings of a debtor to satisfy the debt. Once the general creditor has obtained a judgment against a defaulting debtor, the general creditor stands as a secured creditor who may then move on to levy liens or writs of execution against a debtor's assets and personal property. (See "Formal Proceedings" below.)

## Sequence of Events

Once a debtor has defaulted on making a payment as originally agreed to between the debtor and creditor, the creditor has several choices. It may contact the debtor directly, turn the matter over to an internal collections department, or turn the matter over to external collection agencies.

### Internal Efforts by Original Creditor

It is clearly within the best interests of both creditor and debtor to resolve the matter "internally." Depending on whether the creditor is a general or secured one, the options available are broad. Generally, however, most consumer debt (other than for houses and automobiles) is unsecured, and creditors are general creditors whose collection activities are more limited prior to obtaining an actual judgment against a debtor.

Depending upon the debtor's prior payment history with a particular creditor, no action may be taken at all, other than a friendly "reminder" letter, if a monthly payment is missed on an installment agreement, revolving credit account, or credit card account. Creditors are happy to charge late fees, add accrued interest to the new balance, and double the amount owed for the following month. However, after a certain number of days without payment (again, depending on the debtor's prior history), creditors will contact the debtor, usually by correspondence and telephone. If there is no satisfactory payment or arrangement made, most major creditors will turn the account over to an internal collections department.

Typically, letters from the internal collections department of a creditor will ask the debtor to send payment or contact the creditor immediately. The creditor will attempt to collect at least the past due payment prior to the end of the month (irrespective of the original payment due date) in order to avoid reporting the late payment to a credit reporting bureau or agency. The creditor will also attempt to secure a payment over the telephone, and preferable

secure staggered payments, using postdated checks, for the next three payments. At this point, it behooves the creditor to work with a debtor, because if it must turn the account over to a collection agency, it will only be paid a percentage of the amount collected from the debtor after the collection agency has been paid its share.

### Collection Agencies

If a creditor is unsuccessful in collecting a debt payment, it may retain an outside service, or collection agency, to continue efforts to collect on the debt. A collection agency receives a percentage of the amount recovered, usually between 10 and 50 percent, in return for its efforts. Because its chief concern is to maximize its own potential earnings on the account, a collection agency's tactics are regulated by both federal and state law (see below).

Within five days of its first telephone call to a debtor, a collection agency must send a notice in writing that states the total amount owed, and the name of the original creditor for whom the agency is attempting to collect. The written notice must also inform the debtor that he or she has 30 days from receipt of notice to dispute the debt in writing, and/or request a written verification of it.

Debtors are usually authorized at this point to make payments directly to the collections agency, which will forward the net balance (after deducting its percentage of the recovered amount) to the original creditor. It is imperative, prior to making any payment, that the debtor verify that the collection agency indeed represents, and is the agent for, the principal creditor. A debtor may reasonably rely on correspondence from the collection agency, stating the name of its creditor client, as evidence of this.

### Offers of Settlement

At all stages up to this point, creditors may be open to negotiating a settlement in lieu of the entire amount owed. The more it will cost a creditor to pursue collection activity against a debtor, the more it may be interested in a lump sum settlement offer. However, because the creditor has incurred additional costs and expenses in pursuing collection, a proffered settlement amount may not be palpably less than the amount of the original debt. For example, a defaulted debt of $10,000 may result in the addition of late fees, accrued interest, and attorney or collection fees, such that the debtor now owes $14,000. If the creditor agrees to accept $10,000 in full settlement of the outstanding debt, the debtor is no further along than he was before he defaulted in the first place.

### Attorneys for the Creditor

If a collection agency is unable to secure payment or contact with a debtor, the next step in usually litigation. Once the debtor's account file has been turned over to an attorney for litigation, the debtor's chances of negotiating payment or settlement with the creditor are slim to none. Moreover, once the matter has gone this far, the debtor will most likely be responsible for the payment of all attorney fees and costs associated with collection efforts, in addition to the original debt owed. Importantly, attorneys or law firms that regularly engage in the collection of debts are subject to the provisions of the Fair Debt Collection Practices Act (FDCPA) as are collection agencies.

At this stage (even though it can legally be done at an earlier stage), the creditor, or attorney acting on its behalf, will invoke any "acceleration clause" that may be in the original loan or credit agreement. These clauses are common, but usually not acted upon until a debtor fails to pay the delinquent amounts or falls seriously behind in payments. If a debtor defaults on payments, an acceleration clause, to which the debtor has agreed in the original paperwork for the credit or loan, "accelerates" all future payments so that the entire loan balance (not just the payments in arrears) is immediately due and payable in full. If a debtor has not already received notice that the creditor is demanding the entire loan balance, an attorney will be certain to do this prior to filing suit against the debtor.

Of course, if the debtor was able to pay off the entire loan in question, he or she would not be in default in the first place. Even if the attorney makes one last settlement offer of a percentage of the entire balance, the likelihood of the debtor being able to pay is nil. This, then, is a very serious stage of default that will most likely result in a lawsuit being filed against the debtor.

### Formal Proceedings

If the above measures have all failed to resolve a debtor's default, creditors may file suit in local state or federal court. This makes the debt collection a matter of public record. There are very few available defenses, except those permitted by the **Uniform Commercial Code** (UCC) for defective products

Creditors' lawsuits are generally grounded in contract. Damages are limited to the face amount of the loan balance, accrued interest, (sometimes) attorney fees, and court costs. Creditors will sue for the entire balance owed on the account, not just the payments in arrears. They seldom ask other creditors to join them in a suit, even if those other creditors also have defaulted loans. This is because there seldom is sufficient assets to cover the entire judgment immediately, and the creditor that filed suit wants to be first in line. If a defendant-debtor fails to appear in response to the lawsuit, a default judgment will likely be entered against him or her.

### Satisfaction of Judgment

After a judgment is entered against a debtor, the prevailing creditor (now a "judgment creditor") will employ various tactics to collect on the judgment. State laws dictate the number of years a creditor may pursue collection on an outstanding judgment; typically, they are 10 to 20 years. Debtors whose attitude had been, "Go ahead and sue me, I don't have any money" are surprised to learn that any assets they acquire for the next several years can be seized or forfeited in satisfaction of an outstanding judgment.

### Property Seizure and Garnishment

Following successful judgment against a defaulting debtor, creditors will usually ask a court for a creditor's hearing, in which the debtor must make a sworn declaration of all assets and property. This may be done in writing or by oral deposition. Exempted property (that which cannot be seized in satisfaction of a judgment) includes a primary residence up to a certain value, vehicles not used for employment, tools used for employment, some personal effects and household goods, and life insurance/retirement proceeds. However, funds in bank accounts, extra vehicles, boats, campers, and other items of value (musical instruments, stocks and bonds) are subject.

Judgment creditors generally do not come upon a debtor's property and seize items. Instead, they present a copy of their court judgment, along with a "writ of execution" form, to local law enforcement officials (sheriff, marshal, constable) who will "execute" the writ and seize property.

A judgment creditors may also request that the court issue of writ for garnishment of the debtor's wages. If granted, the court order for garnishment is served directly upon the debtor's employer, who must comply with its terms. Generally, up to 25 percent of wages can be garnished from a judgment debtor's wages. The garnished amount is paid directly to the judgment creditor by the debtor's employer.

Seized property may be sold at public auction, with proceeds returned to the judgment creditor. Most states permit "redemption" (repurchase by the debtor) of real property (real estate) sold at auction, within a specified time, e.g., one year. Money received at auction which is in excess of the debt owed is returned to the debtor.

## Fair Debt Collection Practices Act

The Fair Debt Collection Practices Act of 1977 (FDCPA) (15 USC 1601) protects consumers from illegal or improper practices in debt collecting. Its mandates apply only to consumer debts and not to business debts. Further, they do not apply to collection efforts made directly by the creditor to whom the debt is owed. The law is enforced by the Federal Trade Commission (FTC).

What may be perceived as improper conduct or harassment by a stressed debtor may not in fact be illegal or improper at all under the Act. What is prohibited of a collection agency includes the following:

- Communicating with the debtor's employer, neighbors, or anyone else for any reason except to ask where the debtor lives

- Informing any person that an attempt is being made to collect a debt from the debtor

- Sending postcards or mail that reveal the sender as a collection agency

- Contacting a debtor at a place of employment, if the debtor or the employer objects

- Telephoning a debtor before 8:00 a.m. or after 9:00 p.m.

- Using obscene, profane, or threatening language

- Make the debtor's name public as a person who fails to pay debts

- Failing to identify himself/herself as a collector; pretending to be a lawyer, law enforcement officer, or other government official

- Obtaining information from the debtor under false pretenses, e.g., taking a survey or suggesting that the debtor has committed a crime

- Contacting a debtor who has informed the collector that he or she is represented by an attorney

- Communicate in any way with a debtor who has informed the collector in writing that no more contact with the debtor is to be made

### State Laws

Creditors that violate the rights of debtors should be reported to the Federal Trade Commission (see below) or the National Consumer Law Center (see below), which will refer the debtor to a consumer law attorney practicing in the area. The following states permit debtors to secretly tape telephone calls from collection agencies:

- Alabama
- Alaska
- Arizona
- Arkansas
- Colorado
- District of Columbia
- Georgia
- Hawaii
- Idaho
- Indiana
- Iowa
- Kansas
- Kentucky
- Louisiana
- Maine
- Minnesota
- Mississippi
- Missouri
- Nebraska
- Nevada
- New Jersey
- New Mexico
- New York
- North Carolina
- North Dakota
- Ohio
- Oklahoma
- Rhode Island
- South Carolina

- Tennessee

- Texas

- Utah

- Virginia

- West Virginia

- Wisconsin

- Wyoming

In the remaining 15 states, a debtor must secure permission from the collector. While failure to secure permission may prevent the recording of illegal or improper collection agency tactics, it does have a chilling effect on a collector who has been asked if the conversation can be recorded. He or she will most likely not engage in improper tactics, for fear that the debtor is recording the communication, even without permission.

## Additional Resources

Baird, Douglas G., et al.(compilers). *Commercial and Debtor-Creditor Law: Selected Statutes.* Foundation Press, 2005.

## Organizations

### Federal Trade Commission (FTC) Consumer Response Center

600 Pennsylvania Avenue NW
Washington, DC 20580 USA
Phone: (877) 382-4357
URL: www.ftc.gov

### National Association of Consumer Advocates (NACA) USA

Phone: (202) 452-1989
URL: www.naca.net

### National Consumer Law Center (NCLC) USA

Phone: (617) 542-8010
URL: www.consumerlaw.org

### National Foundation for Consumer Credit USA

Phone: (800) 388-2227
URL: www.nfcc.org

# CONSUMER ISSUES

## CONSUMER RIGHTS AND PROTECTION

*Sections within this essay:*

## Background

**Consumer protection** encompasses a broad range of consumer issues including, credit, utilities, services and goods. Many consumer complaints arise from simple disputes that may be resolved through communication between the consumer and the business. Others, however, may accuse a manufacturer or seller of engaging in **fraudulent** transactions. Consumers are protected under both state and federal laws. Some states have laws regarding major purchases that allow for a "cooling off" period in which the consumer can return the item or cancel the contract with no **penalty**. Each state Attorney General's office has some type of public protection division responsible for enforcing the rights of consumers in business and service transactions and to protect the **civil rights** of citizens. Federal standards are enforced by the Federal Trade Commission, which oversees a number of federal antitrust and consumer protection laws. The Commission seeks to ensure that the nation's markets function competitively and are vigorous, efficient, and free of undue restrictions. The Commission also works to enhance the smooth operation of the marketplace by eliminating acts or practices that are unfair or deceptive. In general, the Commission's efforts are directed toward stopping actions that threaten consumers' opportunities to exercise informed choice.

## Warranties

A **warranty** is the promise made by a manufacturer or seller to resolve problems the product may have. Warranties can cover the retail sale of consumer goods. Consumer goods include new products or parts which are used, bought, or leased for use primarily for personal, family, or household purposes. There are two kinds of warranties: implied warranties and express warranties.

### Implied Warranties

Implied warranties are unspoken, unwritten promises that are created by state law. In consumer product transactions, there are two types of implied warranties: the **implied warranty** of merchantability and the implied warranty of fitness for a particular purpose. The implied warranty of merchantability is a merchant's basic promise that the goods sold will function and have nothing significantly wrong with them. The implied warranty of fitness for a particular purpose is a promise that the seller's product can be used for some specific purpose. Implied warranties are promises about the condition of products at the time they are sold, but they do not assure that a product will last for a specific length of time. Implied warranties do not cover problems caused by misuse, ordinary wear, failure to follow directions, or improper maintenance. Generally, there is no specified duration for implied warranties under state laws. However, the state statutes of limitations for breach of either an express or an implied warranty are generally four years from date of purchase. This means that buyers have four years in which to discover and seek a remedy for problems that were present in the product at the time it was sold. It does not mean that the product must last for four years. Implied warranties apply only when the seller is a merchant who deals in such goods, not when a sale is made by a private individual.

### Express Warranties

Express warranties are explicit warranties. Express warranties can take a variety of forms, ranging from advertising claims to formal certificates. An express warranty can be made either orally or in writing; however, only written warranties on consumer products are covered by the **Magnuson-Moss Warranty Act**.

### Extended Warranties

Extended warranties are actually service contracts. Like warranties, service contracts provide repair and/or maintenance for a specific period of time; however, service contracts cost extra and are sold separately. Warranties are included in the price of the product; service contracts are not.

## Federal Acts

### Food Quality Protection Act

The Food Quality Protection Act (FQPA) of 1996 amended the Federal Insecticide, Fungicide, and Rodenticide Act (FIFRA) and the Federal Food Drug, and Cosmetic Act (FFDCA). These amendments fundamentally changed the way EPA regulates pesticides. The requirements included a new safety standard—reasonable certainty of no harm—that must be applied to all pesticides used on food.

### Safe Drinking Water Act

The Safe Drinking Water Act was promulgated in 1974 to protect the quality of drinking water in the United States. This law focuses on all waters actually or potentially designed for drinking use, whether from above ground or underground sources. The Act authorizes EPA to establish safe standards of purity and required all owners or operators of public water systems to comply with primary (health-related) standards. State governments, which assume this power from EPA, also encourage attainment of secondary standards (nuisance-related).

### Federal Insecticide, Fungicide, and Rodenticide Act

The primary focus of the Federal Insecticide, Fungicide, and Rodenticide Act (FIFRA), enacted in 1972, was to provide federal control of pesticide distribution, sale, and use. EPA was given authority under FIFRA not only to study the consequences of pesticide usage but also to require users (farmers, utility companies, and others) to register when purchasing pesticides. Through later amendments to the law, users were required to take exams for certification as applicators of pesticides. All pesticides used in the United States must be registered (licensed) by EPA. Registration assures that pesticides will be properly labeled and that if when used in accordance with specifications will not cause unreasonable harm to the environment.

## Consumer Vehicle Purchases

The Federal Anti-Tampering Odometer Law prohibits anyone from falsifying mileage readings in a new or used vehicle. The Federal Used Car Law requires used car dealers to post Buyers Guides on used cars. The Federal Automobile Information Disclosure Act requires new car dealerships to put a sticker on the windshield or side window of the car. This sticker must list the base price of the car, the options added and their costs, as well as the dealer's cost for transportation and the number of miles per gallon the car uses.

Dealers are not required by law to give used car buyers a three-day right to cancel. The right to return the car in a few days for a refund exists only if the dealer grants this privilege to buyers. The Federal Trade Commission's Used Car Rule requires dealers to post a Buyers Guide in every used vehicle they offer for sale. This includes light-duty vans, light-duty trucks, demonstrators, and program cars. Demonstrators are new cars that have not been owned, leased, or used as rentals, but have been driven by dealer staff. Program cars are low-mileage, current-model-year vehicles returned from short-term leases or rentals. Buyers Guides do not have to be posted on motorcycles and most recreational vehicles, nor by any seller that sells less than six vehicles a year. The Buyers Guide becomes part of the sales contract and overrides all contrary provisions. Dealers who offer a written warranty must complete the warranty section of the Buyers Guide. Dealers may offer a full or limited warranty on all or some of a vehicle's systems or components. Most used car warranties are limited and their coverage varies. A full or limited warranty is not required to cover the entire vehicle. The dealer may specify that only certain systems are covered. Some parts or systems may be covered by a full warranty; others by a limited warranty. The dealer must check the appropriate box on the Buyers Guide if a service contract is offered, except in states where service contracts are regulated by insurance laws.

### Lemon Laws

So-called **Lemon Laws** vary from state to state. Typically, a defect covered by the Lemon Law must be a major defect which substantially impairs the use, value, or safety of the vehicle. Lemon laws generally impose time or mileage limitations regarding when the defect must be presented to the manufacturer or dealer in order to be covered under the Lemon Law. The manufacturer must repair the defect within a reasonable number of repair attempts. If the manufacturer fails to repair the defect or defects in the vehicle within a reasonable number of repair attempts, the consumer is entitled to a repurchase or replacement of the vehicle. In some states if the defect is of such a character that there is a substantial risk of death or serious bodily injury if the vehicle is driven, the vehicle is presumed to be a lemon if the defect continues to exist after even one repair attempt. If the defect does not fall into this category, additional repair attempts are normally required. In some states, three repair attempts for a defect is enough to **warrant** a buy back or replacement. Other states require four repair attempts or more.

## Federal Agencies

While many states have enacted comprehensive products liability statutes, there is no federal products liability law. There are, however, a number of federal entities responsible for maintaining and enforcing regulation of consumer products.

### Consumer Product Safety Commission

The U.S. Consumer Product Safety Commission (CPSC) is an independent federal regulatory agency created to protect the public from unreasonable risks of injuries and deaths associated with some 15,000 types of consumer products. Defective product law, commonly known as products liability, refers to the liability of parties along the chain of manufacture of any product for damage caused by that product. A defective product is one that causes some injury or damage to person because of some defect in the product or its labeling or the way the product was used. Those responsible for the defect can include the manufacturers of component parts, assembling manufacturers, wholesalers, and retail stores. The CPSC uses various means to inform the public about potential risks. These include local and national media coverage, publication of numerous booklets and product alerts, a web site, a telephone Hotline, the National Injury Information Clearinghouse, CPSC's Public Information Center and responses to **Freedom of Information Act** (FOIA) requests. For nearly 30 years the U.S. Consumer Product Safety Commission (CPSC) has operated a statistically valid injury surveillance and follow-back system known as the National Electronic Injury Surveillance System (NEISS). The primary purpose of NEISS has been to provide timely data on consumer product-related injuries occurring in the United States. NEISS injury data are gathered from the emergency departments of 100 hospitals selected as a probability sample of all U.S. hospitals with emergency departments. The system's foundation rests on emergency department surveillance data, but the system also has the flexibility to gather additional data at either the surveillance or the investigation level. Surveillance data enable CPSC analysts to make timely national estimates of the number of injuries associated with (not necessarily caused by) specific consumer products. These data also provide **evidence** of the need for further study of particular products. Subsequent follow-back studies yield important clues to the cause and likely prevention of injuries.

### Office of Consumer Litigation

When a client agency refers a case to the Department of Justice, the Office of Consumer **Litigation**

(OCL) generally receives the referral and will either retain it or ask a United States Attorney's Office (USAO) to handle the case. Frequently, OCL and the USAO work jointly on these matters. Established in 1971, the OCL enforces and defends the consumer protection programs of the Food and Drug Administration (FDA), the Federal Trade Commission (FTC), the Consumer Product Safety Commission (CPSC), and the Department of Transportation's National Highway Traffic Safety Administration (NHTSA). OCL has responsibility for litigation under federal consumer protection laws. These include the Federal Food, Drug, and Cosmetic Act; the odometer tampering prohibitions of the Motor Vehicle Information and Cost Savings Act; the Consumer Product Safety Act; and a variety of laws administered by the Federal Trade Commission, such as the Fair Debt Collection Practices Act.

### Internet Fraud Complaint Center

The mission of the Internet **Fraud** Complaint Center is to combat fraud committed over the Internet. The IFCC Web site allows consumers nationwide to report Internet fraud; enables the development of educational programs aimed at preventing Internet fraud; offers local, state, and federal law enforcement agencies training in Internet fraud; and allows for the sharing of fraud data by all law enforcement and regulatory authorities.

### U.S. Food and Drug Administration

The U.S. Food and Drug Administration (FDA) monitors food, cosmetics, medicines and medical devices, and ensures the safety of radiation-emitting consumer products such as microwave ovens. FDA also oversees feed and drugs for pets and farm animals. Authorized by Congress to enforce the Federal Food, Drug, and Cosmetic Act and several other public health laws, the agency monitors the manufacture, import, transport, storage, and sale of $1 trillion worth of goods annually.

### Center for Biologics Evaluation and Research

A biological product subject to licensure under the Public Health Service Act is any virus, therapeutic serum, toxin, antitoxin, vaccine, blood, blood component or derivative, allergenic product, or analogous product, applicable to the prevention, treatment, or cure of diseases or injuries to humans. Biological products include, but are not limited to, bacterial and viral vaccines, human blood and plasma and their derivatives, and certain products produced by biotechnology, such as interferons and erythropoietins. The Center for Biologics Evaluation and Re-

search (CBER) is responsible for ensuring the safety and efficacy of blood and blood products, vaccines, allergenics, and biological therapeutics. CBER's regulation of biological products has expanded in recent years to include a wide variety of new products such as biotechnology products, somatic cell therapy and gene therapy, and banked human tissues.

### Federal Trade Commission

The Federal Trade Commission (FTC) works to ensure that the nation's markets are efficient and free of practices which might harm consumers. To ensure the smooth operation of our free market system, the FTC enforces federal consumer protection laws that prevent fraud, deception and unfair business practices. The Commission also enforces federal antitrust laws that prohibit anticompetitive mergers and other business practices that restrict competition and harm consumers.

### National Highway Traffic Safety Administration

The National Highway Traffic Safety Administration (NHTSA), within the U.S. Department of Transportation, was established by the Highway Safety Act of 1970, to carry out safety programs under the National Traffic and Motor Vehicle Safety Act of 1966 and the Highway Safety Act of 1966. NHTSA also carries out consumer programs established by the Motor Vehicle Information and Cost Savings Act of 1972. NHTSA has consumer information on motor vehicle safety, crash worthiness, and recalls among other areas. OCL works with NHTSA to enforce the provisions of the federal odometer tampering **statute**.

State Laws

ALABAMA: State law forbids false advertising and automobile odometer tampering. A law suit may be brought by a consumer, the state attorney general, or a district attorney.

ALASKA: State law forbids false advertising and automobile odometer tampering. A law suit may be brought by a consumer or the state attorney general.

ARIZONA: State law forbids false advertising and automobile odometer tampering, the latter of which constitutes a misdemeanor offense. A law suit may be brought by the state attorney general.

ARKANSAS: State law forbids false advertising and automobile odometer tampering. A law suit may be brought by the state attorney general.

CALIFORNIA: State law forbids false advertising and automobile odometer tampering. A law suit may be brought by a consumer, the state attorney general, or a district or prosecuting attorney.

COLORADO: State law forbids false advertising and automobile odometer tampering. A law suit may be brought by a consumer, the state attorney general, or a district attorney.

CONNECTICUT: State law forbids automobile odometer tampering, which is defined as a misdemeanor offense. A law suit may be brought by a consumer, the state attorney general, the Commissioner of Consumer Protection.

DELAWARE: State law forbids false advertising and automobile odometer tampering. A law suit may be brought by a consumer or the state attorney general.

DISTRICT OF COLUMBIA: The law of the district forbids false advertising. A law suit may be brought by a consumer or the director of the Department of Consumer and Regulatory Affairs.

FLORIDA: State law forbids false advertising and automobile odometer tampering, the latter of which is a felony offense. A law suit may be brought by a consumer or certain state officials.

GEORGIA: State law forbids false advertising and automobile odometer tampering. A law suit may be brought by a consumer.

HAWAII: State law forbids false advertising and automobile odometer tampering. A law suit may be brought by a consumer or the Consumer Protection Agency.

IDAHO: State law forbids false advertising and automobile odometer tampering. A law suit may be brought by a consumer or by the state.

ILLINOIS: State law forbids false advertising and automobile odometer tampering, the latter of which is a misdemeanor offense. A law suit may be brought by a consumer, the state attorney general, or a state attorney.

INDIANA: State law forbids false advertising and automobile odometer tampering, the latter of which is a felony offense. A law suit may be brought by a consumer and the state attorney general.

IOWA: State law forbids false advertising and automobile odometer tampering. A law suit may be brought by a consumer or the state attorney general.

KANSAS: State law forbids false advertising and automobile odometer tampering. A law suit may be

brought by a consumer, the state attorney general, or a district attorney.

KENTUCKY: State law forbids false advertising and automobile odometer tampering. A law suit may be brought by a consumer or the state attorney general.

LOUISIANA: State law forbids false advertising and automobile odometer tampering, the latter of which is a misdemeanor offense. A law suit may be brought by a consumer or the state attorney general.

MAINE: State law forbids false advertising and automobile odometer tampering, the latter of which is class D offense. A law suit may be brought by a consumer or the state attorney general.

MARYLAND: State law forbids false advertising and automobile odometer tampering. A law suit may be brought by a consumer, the state attorney general, or the Consumer Protection Division.

MASSACHUSETTS: State law forbids false advertising and automobile odometer tampering. A law suit may be brought by a consumer or the state attorney general.

MICHIGAN: State law forbids false advertising and automobile odometer tampering. A law suit may be brought by a consumer, the state attorney general, or a prosecuting attorney.

MINNESOTA: State law forbids false advertising and automobile odometer tampering, the latter of which is a misdemeanor offense. A law suit may be brought by a consumer, the state attorney general, or a county attorney.

MISSISSIPPI: State law forbids false advertising and automobile odometer tampering, the latter of which is a misdemeanor offense. A law suit may be brought by a consumer, the state attorney general, or a district or county attorney.

MISSOURI: State law forbids false advertising and automobile odometer tampering, the latter of which can be a criminal offense. A law suit may be brought by a consumer or the state attorney general.

MONTANA: State law forbids false advertising and automobile odometer tampering. A law suit may be brought by a consumer, the state attorney general, a county attorney, or the Department of Commerce.

NEBRASKA: State law forbids false advertising and automobile odometer tampering. A law suit may be brought by a consumer or the state attorney general.

NEVADA: State law forbids false advertising and automobile odometer tampering, the latter of which is a misdemeanor offense. A law suit may be brought by a consumer, the state attorney general, or a district attorney.

NEW HAMPSHIRE: State law forbids false advertising and automobile odometer tampering, the latter of which is a misdemeanor offense. A law suit may be brought by a consumer or the state attorney general.

NEW JERSEY: State law forbids false advertising and automobile odometer tampering. A law suit may be brought by a consumer or the state attorney general.

NEW MEXICO: State law forbids false advertising and automobile odometer tampering, the latter of which is a misdemeanor offense. A law suit may be brought by a consumer, the state attorney general, or a district attorney.

NEW YORK: State law forbids false advertising and automobile odometer tampering, the latter of which is a misdemeanor offense. A law suit may be brought by a consumer or the state attorney general.

NORTH CAROLINA: State law forbids false advertising and automobile odometer tampering. A law suit may be brought by a consumer or the state attorney general.

NORTH DAKOTA: State law forbids false advertising and automobile odometer tampering, the latter of which is a misdemeanor offense (or a felony offense when the defendant has a prior conviction). A law suit may be brought by a consumer, the state attorney general, or a state's attorney.

OHIO: State law forbids false advertising and automobile odometer tampering. A law suit may be brought by a consumer, the state attorney general, or a district attorney. A law suit may be brought by a consumer or the state attorney general.

OKLAHOMA: State law forbids false advertising and automobile odometer tampering, the latter of which is a misdemeanor offense. A law suit may be brought by a consumer, the state attorney general, or a district attorney.

OREGON: State law forbids false advertising and automobile odometer tampering. A law suit may be brought by a consumer or by the state.

PENNSYLVANIA: State law forbids false advertising and automobile odometer tampering. A law suit may

be brought by a consumer, the state attorney general, or a district attorney.

RHODE ISLAND: State law forbids false advertising and automobile odometer tampering. A law suit may be brought by a consumer or the state attorney general.

SOUTH CAROLINA: State law forbids false advertising. A law suit may be brought by a consumer, the state attorney general, a solicitor, a county attorney, or city attorney.

SOUTH DAKOTA: State law forbids false advertising and automobile odometer tampering, the latter of which is a misdemeanor offense (subsequent offenses are felony offenses). A law suit may be brought by a consumer or the state attorney general.

TENNESSEE: State law forbids false advertising and automobile odometer tampering, the latter of which is a misdemeanor offense. A law suit may be brought by a consumer, the state attorney general, or the Division of Consumer Affairs of the Department of Commerce and Insurance.

TEXAS: State law forbids false advertising and automobile odometer tampering. A law suit may be brought by a consumer, the state attorney general, a district attorney, or the state consumer protection division.

UTAH: State law forbids false advertising and automobile odometer tampering, the latter of which is a felony offense. A law suit may be brought by a consumer or by the state.

VERMONT: State law forbids false advertising and automobile odometer tampering. A law suit may be brought by a consumer, the state attorney general, or a state attorney.

VIRGINIA: State law forbids false advertising and automobile odometer tampering. A law suit may be brought by a consumer, the state attorney general, or a commonwealth attorney.

WASHINGTON: State law forbids false advertising and automobile odometer tampering. A law suit may be brought by a consumer or the state attorney general.

WEST VIRGINIA: State law forbids false advertising. A law suit may be brought by an injured consumer.

WISCONSIN: State law forbids false advertising and automobile odometer tampering. A law suit may be brought by an injured consumer.

WYOMING: State law forbids false advertising and automobile odometer tampering. A law suit may be brought by a consumer or the state attorney general.

## Additional Resources

*Consumer Protection Law in a Nutshell, Third Edition* Marsh, Gene A., West Group, 1999.

*Product Liability Entering the 21st Century: The U.S. Perspective* Moore, Michael J., Brookings Institution Press, 2001.

*Why Lawsuits Are Good for America: Disciplined Democracy, Big Business, and the Common Law* Bogus, Carl, NYU Press, 2001.

## Organizations

### Consumer Action

717 Market Street, Suite 310
San Francisco, CA 94103 USA
Phone: (415) 777-9635

Fax: (415) 777-5267
URL: http://www.consumer-action.org

### Federal Trade Commission

600 Pennsylvania Avenue, NW
Washington, DC 20580 USA
Phone: (877) FTC-HELP
URL: http://www.ftc.gov

### National Consumers League

1701 K Street, NW, Suite 1200
Washington, DC 20006 USA
Phone: (202) 835-3323
Fax: (202) 835-0747
URL: http://www.nclnet.org

### U.S. Consumer Product Safety Commission

4330 East-West Highway
Bethesda, MD 20814-4408 USA
Phone: (301) 504-0990
Fax: (301) 504-0124
URL: http://www.cpsc.gov

# CONSUMER ISSUES

## CONTRACTS

## Background

A contract is an agreement between two parties that creates an obligation to do or refrain from doing a particular thing. The purpose of a contract is to establish the terms of the agreement by which the parties have fixed their rights and duties. Courts must enforce valid contracts, unless one party has legal grounds to bar enforcement.

Consumers and commercial entities both depend on the enforceability of contracts when conducting business relations. When consumers or commercial entities enter a contract to buy goods or services at a particular price, in a particular amount, or of a particular quality, they expect the seller to deliver goods and services that conform to the contract. Manufacturers, wholesalers, and retailers similarly expect that their goods and services will be bought in accordance with the terms of the contract.

A legal action for breach of contract arises when at least one party's performance does not live up to the terms of the contract and causes the other party to suffer economic damage or other types of measurable injury. The injury may include any loss suffered by the plaintiff in having to buy replacement goods or services at a higher price or of a lower quality from someone else in the market. It may also include the costs and expenses incurred by the plaintiff in having to locate replacement goods or services in the first place.

Contract disputes may be governed by the common law, statutory law, or both. Each state has developed its own common law of contracts, which consists of a body of jurisprudence developed over time by trial and appellate courts on a case-by-case basis. Many states have been influenced by the Restatement (Second) of Contracts, which was approved by the American Law Institute (ALI) in 1979.

For contracts involving commercial transactions, all fifty states have enacted, at least partially, a body of statutory law called the Uniform Commercial Code (UCC), which governs a variety of commercial relations involving consumers and merchants, among others. Article 2 of the U.C.C. governs the sale of goods, which are defined by the code as items that are "movable" at the time of the contract. The National Conference of Commissioners on Uniform States Laws, along with the ALI and the American Bar Association, approved a revised version of Article 2 in 2003. However, as of February 2006, no state had adopted the revised version.

State legislatures have also enacted a host of other statutes governing contracts that affect the public interest. For example, most states have passed legislation governing the terms of insurance contracts to guarantee that sufficient financial resources will be available for residents who are injured by accident. Congress has passed a number of laws governing contracts as well, ranging from laws that regulate the terms of collective bargaining agreements between labor and management to laws that regulate false advertising and promote fair trade.

## Elements of a Contract

The requisite elements that must be established to demonstrate the formation of a legally binding contract are (1) offer; (2) acceptance; (3) consideration; (4) mutuality of obligation; (5) competency and capacity; and, in certain circumstances, (6) a written instrument.

### Offer

An offer is a promise to act or refrain from acting, which is made in exchange for a return promise to do the same. Some offers anticipate not another promise being returned in exchange but the performance of an act or forbearance from taking action. For example, a painter's offer to paint someone's house for $100 is probably conditioned on the homeowner's promise to pay upon completion, while a homeowner's offer to pay someone $100 to have his or her house painted is probably conditioned upon the painter's successfully performing the job. In either case, an offeree's power of acceptance is created when the offeror conveys a present intent to enter a contract in certain and definite terms that are communicated to the offeree.

Courts distinguish preliminary negotiations from formal legal offers in that parties to preliminary negotiations lack a present intent to form a contract. Accordingly, no contract is formed when parties to pre-

liminary negotiations respond to each other's invitations, requests, and intimations. Advertisements and catalogues, for example, are treated as forms of preliminary negotiations. Otherwise, the seller of the goods or services would be liable for countless contracts with consumers who view the ad or read the catalogue, even though the quantity of the merchandise may be limited.

However, sellers must be careful to avoid couching their advertisements in clear and definite terms that create the power of acceptance in consumers. For example, sellers have been found liable to consumers for advertising a definite quantity of goods for sale at a certain price on a "first come, first serve" basis, after consumers showed up and offered to pay the advertised price before the goods sold out. In such situations, the seller may not withdraw the offer on grounds that market factors no longer justify selling the goods at the advertised price. Instead, courts will compel them to sell the goods as advertised.

The rejection of an offer terminates the offeree's power of acceptance and ends the offeror's liability for the offer. Rejection might come in the form of an express refusal to accept the offer or by implication when the offeree makes a counteroffer that is materially different from the offeror's original proposal. Most jurisdictions also recognize an offeror's right to withdraw or revoke an offer as a legitimate means of terminating the offer.

Offers that are not rejected, withdrawn, or revoked generally continue until the expiration of the time period specified by the offer, or, if there is no time limit specified, until a reasonable time has elapsed. A reasonable time is determined according to what a reasonable person would consider sufficient time to accept the offer under the circumstances. Regardless of how much time has elapsed following an offer, the death or insanity of either party before acceptance is communicated normally terminates an offer, as does the destruction of the subject matter of the proposed contract and any intervening conditions that would make acceptance illegal.

Sometimes offerees are concerned that an offer may be terminated before they have had a full opportunity to evaluate it. In this case, they may purchase an "option" to keep the offer open for a designated time. During that time the offer is deemed irrevocable, though some jurisdictions allow the offeror to revoke the offer by paying the offeree an agreed upon sum to do so.

### Acceptance

Acceptance of an offer is the expression of assent to its terms. Acceptance must generally be made in the manner specified by the offer. If no manner of acceptance is specified by the offer, then acceptance may be made in a manner that is reasonable under the circumstances. An acceptance is only valid, however, if the offeree knows of the offer, the offeree manifests an intention to accept, and the acceptance is expressed as an unequivocal and unconditional agreement to the terms of the offer.

Many offers specify the method of acceptance, whether it be oral or written, by phone or in person, by handshake or by ceremony. Other offers leave open the method of acceptance, allowing the offeree to accept in a reasonable manner. Most consumer transactions fall into this category, as when a shopper "accepts" a merchant's offer by taking possession of a particular good and paying for it at the cash register. But what constitutes a "reasonable" acceptance will vary according to the contract.

Some offers may only be accepted by the performance or non-performance of a particular act. Once formed, these types of agreements are called unilateral contracts, and they are discussed more fully later in this essay. Other offers may only be accepted by a return promise of performance from the offeree. Once formed, these agreements are called bilateral contracts, and they are also discussed more fully later in this essay.

Problems can arise when it is not clear whether an offer anticipates the method of acceptance to come in the form of performance or a return promise. Section 32 of the Restatement (Second) of Contracts attempts to address this issue by providing that "in case of doubt an offer is interpreted as inviting the offeree to accept either by promising to perform what the offer requests or by rendering performance, as the offeree chooses." A growing number of jurisdictions are adopting this approach.

Jurisdictions are split as to the time when an air-mailed acceptance becomes effective. Under the majority approach, known as "the mailbox rule," an acceptance is effective upon dispatch in a properly addressed envelope with prepaid postage, even if the acceptance is lost or destroyed in transit. Under the minority approach, acceptance is effective only upon actual receipt by the offeror, no matter what precautions the offeree took to ensure that the acceptance was properly mailed.

In certain cases acceptance can be implied from a party's conduct. Suppose a consumer orders a personal computer (PC) with exact specifications for its central processing unit (CPU), hard drive, and memory. Upon receipt, the consumer determines that the PC does not match the specs. If the consumer nonetheless pays the full amount on the invoice accompanying the PC without protest, the consumer has effectively communicated a legally binding acceptance of the non-conforming good.

Acceptance cannot generally be inferred from a party's silence or inaction. An exception to this rule occurs when two parties have a prior course of dealings in which the offeree has led the offeror to believe that the offeree will accept all goods shipped by the offeror unless the offeree sends notice to the contrary. In such instances, the offeree's silence or inaction constitutes a legally binding acceptance upon which the offeror can rely.

### Consideration

Each party to a contract must provide something of value that induces the other to enter the agreement. The law calls this exchange of values "consideration." The value exchanged need not consist of currency. Instead, it may consist of a promise to perform an act that one is not legally required to do or a promise to refrain from an act that one is legally entitled to do. For example, if a rich uncle promises to give his nephew a new sports car if he refrains from smoking cigarettes and drinking alcohol for five years, the law deems both the uncle's promise and the nephew's forbearance lawful consideration.

A court's analysis as to whether a contract is supported by sufficient consideration typically focuses more on the promise or performance of the offeree than the promise or performance of the offeror. Courts often say that no consideration will be found unless the offeree suffers a "legal detriment" in making the return promise or in performing the act requested by the offeror. As a general rule, legal detriment is found if the offeree relinquishes a legal right in fulfilling his or her contractual duties. Thus, promises to give love and affection or make a gift or donation are not sufficient consideration to support a contract because no one is under a legal duty to give or refrain from giving these things to others. Similarly a promise to perform an act that has already been completed in the past fails to offer consideration to support a new agreement.

## Mutuality of Obligation

Closely related to the concept of consideration is the mutuality of obligation doctrine. Under this doctrine, both parties must be bound to perform their obligations or the law will treat the agreement as if neither party is bound to perform. When an offeree and offeror exchange promises to perform, one party may not be given the absolute and unlimited right to cancel the contract. Such arrangements attempt to allow one party to perform at her leisure, while ostensibly not relieving the other party of his obligations to perform. Most courts declare these one-side arrangements null for lack of mutuality of obligation. Some courts simply invalidate such contracts for lack of consideration, reasoning that a party who is given absolute power to cancel a contract suffers no legal detriment.

To avoid having a contract subsequently invalidated by a court, the parties must be careful to limit their discretion to cancel the contract or otherwise not perform. As long as the right to avoid performance is dependent on some condition or event outside the control of the party seeking to cancel the contract, courts will find that mutuality of obligation exists. Thus, a farmer might lawfully be given the right to cancel a crop-watering service if the right to cancel were conditioned upon the amount of rain that fell during a given season, something outside the farmer's control. But a court would find mutuality lacking if the farmer were given the right to terminate the service short of full performance simply by giving notice of his or her intention to cancel.

## Competency and Capacity

A natural person who enters a contract possesses complete legal capacity to be held liable for the duties he or she agrees to undertake, unless the person is a minor, mentally incapacitated, or intoxicated. A minor is defined as a person under the age of 18 or 21, depending on the jurisdiction. A contract made by a minor is voidable at the minor's discretion, meaning that the contract is valid and enforceable until the minor takes some affirmative act to disavow the contract. Minors who choose to disavow their contracts entered may not be held liable for breach. The law assumes that minors are too immature, naïve, or inexperienced to negotiate on equal terms with adults, and thus courts protect them from being held accountable for unwisely entering contracts of any kind.

When a party does not understand the nature and consequences of an agreement that he or she has entered, the law treats that party as lacking mental capacity to form a binding contract. However, a party will not be relieved from any contractual duties until a court has formally adjudicated the issue after taking evidence concerning the party's mental capacity, unless there is an existing court order declaring the party to be incompetent or insane. Like agreements with minors, agreements with mentally incapacitated persons are voidable at that person's discretion. However, a guardian or personal representative may ratify an agreement for an incapacitated person and thereby convert the agreement into a legally binding contract.

Contracts entered into by persons under the influence of alcohol and drugs are also voidable at that person's discretion, but only if the other party knew or had reason to know the degree of impairment. As a practical matter, courts rarely show sympathy for defendants who try to avoid contractual duties on grounds that they were intoxicated. However, if the evidence shows that the sober party was trying to take advantage of the intoxicated party, courts will typically intervene to void the contract. Persons who are intoxicated from prescription medication are treated the same as persons who are mentally incompetent or insane and are generally relieved from their contractual responsibilities more readily than are persons intoxicated from non-prescription drugs or alcohol.

## Writing Requirement

Not every contract need be in writing to be valid and binding on both parties. But nearly every state legislature has enacted a body of law that identifies certain types of contracts that must be in writing to be enforceable. In legal parlance this body of law is called the statute of frauds.

Named after a seventeenth-century English statute, the statute of frauds is designed to prevent a plaintiff from bringing an action for breach of contract based on a nonexistent agreement for which the only proof of the agreement is the plaintiff's perjured testimony. The statue of frauds attempts to accomplish this objective by prohibiting the enforcement of particular contracts, unless the terms of the contract are expressly reflected by written note, memorandum, or agreement that is signed by the parties or their personal representatives.

As originally conceived, the statute of frauds applied to four types of contracts: (1) promises to pay a debt owed by another person; (2) promises to marry; (3) promises to perform an act that cannot possibly be performed within a year from that date of the promise; and (4) agreements involving real estate. However, most states have since expanded the class of contracts that must be in writing to be enforceable. For example, in many jurisdictions long term leases, insurance contracts, agreements for the sale of securities, and contracts for the sale of goods above a specified amount are unenforceable unless the terms of the parties' agreement are memorialized in writing.

### Contract Formation Under the U.C.C.

The U.C.C. does not require a specific manner of expression in order for two parties to enter into an agreement. Under § 2-204, "A contract for the sale of goods may be made in any manner sufficient to show agreement, including offer and acceptance, conduct by both parties which recognizes the existence of a contract" and other means. The revised version of the U.C.C., as approved in 2003, also allows a contract to be formed through the interaction of "electronic agents," which include computer programs that may initiate a transaction without human review.

## Types of Contracts

### Contracts under Seal

Early English common law required all contracts to be stamped with a seal before a party could enforce them in court. The seal memorialized the parties' intention to honor the terms of the contract. No consideration was required, since the seal symbolized a solemn promise undertaken by all parties to the contract.

With the onset of the industrial era during the eighteenth century, however, sealed contracts were increasingly seen as an impractical and inefficient impediment to fast paced commercial relations. Sealed contracts were gradually replaced by other types of agreements, including express and implied contracts. In fact, nearly all jurisdictions have eliminated the legal effect of sealed contracts. Thus, contracts under seal will not generally be enforced unless they are supported by independent consideration.

### Express and Implied Contracts

Express contracts consist of agreements in which the terms are stated by the parties. The terms may be stated orally or in writing. But the contract as a whole must reflect the intention of the parties. As a general rule, if an express contract between the parties is established, a contract embracing the identical subject cannot be implied in fact, as the law will not normally imply a substitute promise or contract for an express contract of the parties.

Contracts implied in fact are inferred from the facts and circumstances of the case or the conduct of the parties. However, such contracts are not formally or explicitly stated in words. The law makes no distinction between contracts created by words and those created by conduct. Thus, a contract implied in fact is just as binding as an express contracts that arises from the parties' declared intentions, with the only difference being that for contracts implied in fact courts will infer the parties' intentions from their business relations and course of dealings.

Whereas courts apply the same legal principles to express contracts and contracts implied in fact, a different body of principles is applied to contracts implied in law. Also known as quasi-contracts, contracts implied in law are agreements imposed by courts despite the absence of at least one element essential to the formation of a binding agreement. The law creates these types of fictitious agreements to prevent one party from being unjustly enriched at the expense of another.

For example, suppose that a husband and wife ask a third party to hold a sum of money in trust for their children. But instead of holding the money in trust, the third party absconds with it. The law will not allow the third party to keep the money simply because all the requisite elements of a formal contract have not been proven by the husband and wife. Although the law is generally wary of imposing contracts on parties who did not agree to their terms, courts will find that a contract implied in law exists when (1) the defendant has been enriched at the expense of the plaintiff; (2) the enrichment was unjust (3) the plaintiff's own conduct has not been inequitable; and (4) it is otherwise reasonable for the court to do so in light of the relationship between the parties and the circumstances of the case.

### Bilateral and Unilateral Contracts

A bilateral contract arises from the exchange of mutual, reciprocal promises between two persons that requires the performance or non-performance of some act by both parties. The promise made by one party constitutes sufficient consideration for the promise made by the other party. A unilateral contract involves a promise made by only one party in exchange for the performance or non-performance of an act by the other party. Stated differently, acceptance of an offer to form a unilateral contract cannot be achieved by making a return promise, but only by performance or non-performance of some particular act. Accordingly, acceptance of an offer to enter a unilateral contract can be revoked until performance is complete or until the date has passed for non-performance.

It should be remembered, however, that courts are asked to interpret contracts long after they have been formed. As a result, courts will often take into account how the parties actually acted on the terms of a particular contract. Not surprisingly, courts will avoid interpreting a contract as unilateral or bilateral when such an interpretation would leave one party in the lurch or the opposite interpretation would yield a more commercially reasonable result. This is not to say that courts do not enforce one-sided agreements, but only that the evidence of the parties' understanding must be clear before a court will do so.

## Breach of Contract: Definition

An unjustifiable failure to perform all or some part of a contractual duty is a breach of contract. A breach may occur when one party fails to perform in the manner specified by the contract or by the time specified in the contract. A breach may also occur if one party only partially performs his or her duties or fully performs them in a defective manner.

Courts distinguish total breaches from partial breaches. A total breach of contract is the failure to perform a material part of the contract, while a partial breach results from merely a slight deviation. In determining whether a breach is total or partial, courts typically examine the following factors: (1) the extent to which the non-breaching party obtained the substantial benefit of the contract despite the breach; (2) the extent to which the non-breaching party can be adequately compensated for the breach with money damages; (3) the extent to which the breaching party has already performed or made preparations for performance; (4) the extent to which the breaching party mitigated the hardship on both parties by not fully performing; (5) the willful, negligent, or innocent behavior of the breaching party; and (6) the likelihood that the breaching party will perform the remainder of the contract if allowed.

## Breach of Contract: Defenses

A number of defenses are available to defendants who are sued for breach of contract. For example, a

defendant might assert that no breach was committed because the parties never actually formed a contract due to the lack of an offer, an acceptance, consideration, mutuality of obligation, or a writing. Alternatively, a defendant might assert that he or she lacked capacity to enter the contract, arguing that the contract should be declared void on the grounds that the defendant was incompetent, insane or intoxicated at the time it was entered.

The law also affords defendants several other defenses in breach of contract actions. They include: (1) unconscionability; (2) mistake; (3) fraud; (4) undue influence; and (5) duress. Each of these are discussed below.

### Unconscionability

Unconscionable contracts are those that violate public policy by being so unjust as to offend the court's sense of fairness. Sometimes called "contracts against public policy," unconscionable contracts usually result from a gross disparity in the parties' bargaining power, as can happen when one party is a savvy business person and the other party is elderly, illiterate, or not fluent in English. But a mere disparity in bargaining power will not suffice to overturn an otherwise valid contract, unless a court finds that the resulting contract is one that no mentally competent person would enter and that no fair and honest person would accept.

### Mistake

Ordinarily, to constitute a valid defense in an action for breach of contract the mistake must be a mutual one made by all of the parties to the contract. However, when the mistake is obvious from the face of the contract, knowledge of the mistake will be imputed to each party. Thus, a contract that by its terms designates a horse as the subject matter will be enforced unless both parties agree that a different subject matter was intended. On the other hand, if the same contract designates a pig as the subject matter in 99 paragraphs of the agreement, but mentions a horse in only one paragraph, a court will not force the defendant to sell his horse if it is obvious that the one paragraph contains an error.

### Fraud

Fraud occurs when one party intentionally deceives another party as to the nature and consequences of a contract, and the deceived party is injured as a result. In most cases, fraud requires an affirmative act, such as a willful misrepresentation or concealment of a material fact. In a few cases where a special relationship exists between the parties, such as between attorney and client, simple nondisclosure of a material fact may amount to fraud. Regardless of the underlying relationship between the parties, however, a court will not void a contract due to fraud unless the defendant demonstrates that he or she was induced to enter the contract by fraudulent conduct and not merely that the plaintiff made a false statement at some point in time.

### Undue Influence

Undue influence occurs when one party exercises such control over a second party as to overcome the independent judgment and free will of the second party. In reviewing claims of undue influence, courts look to see whether the plaintiff preyed on and exploited a known psychological or physical weakness when securing the defendant's assent to a contract. However, evidence that the plaintiff merely used aggressive and unsavory tactics in securing the defendant's asset will not suffice to overturn a contract on grounds of undue influence, unless those tactics had the effect of substituting the plaintiff's will and judgment for the defendant's.

### Duress

Duress consists of any wrongful act that coerces another person to enter a contract that he or she would not have entered voluntarily. Blackmail, physical violence, a show of force, and threats to institute legal proceedings in an abusive manner may all constitute sufficient duress to void a contract. However, a defendant claiming duress must demonstrate that sufficient harm was threatened or inflicted to justify finding that the defendant had no reasonable choice but to enter the contract on the terms dictated by the plaintiff.

## Breach of Contract: Remedies

The five basic remedies for breach of contract include the following: money damages, restitution, rescission, reformation, and specific performance. A money damage award includes a sum of money that is given as compensation for financial losses caused by a breach of contract. Parties injured by a breach are entitled to the benefit of the bargain they entered, or the net gain that would have accrued but for the breach. The type of breach governs the extent of damages that may be recovered.

If the breach is a total breach, a plaintiff can recover damages in an amount equal to the sum or value the plaintiff would have received had the contract been fully performed by the defendant, including

lost profits. If the breach is only partial, the plaintiff may normally seek damages in an amount equal to the cost of hiring someone else to complete the performance contemplated by the contract. However, if the cost of completion is prohibitive and the portion of the unperformed contract is small, many courts will only award damages in an amount equal to the difference between the diminished value of the contract as performed and the full value contemplated by the contract.

For example, if the plaintiff agreed to pay the defendant $200,000 to build a house, but the defendant only completed 90 percent of the work contemplated by the contract, a court might be inclined to award $20,000 in damages if it would cost the plaintiff twice as much to hire someone else to finish the last 10 percent. The same principles apply to damages sought for contracts that are fully performed, but in a defective manner. If the defect is significant, the plaintiff can recover the cost of repair. But if the defect is minor, the plaintiff may be limited to recovering the difference between the value of the good or service actually received and the value of the good or service contemplated by the contract.

Restitution is a remedy designed to restore the injured party to the position occupied prior to the formation of the contract. Parties seeking restitution may not request to be compensated for lost profits or other earnings caused by a breach. Instead, restitution aims at returning to the plaintiff any money or property given to the defendant under the contract. Plaintiffs typically seek restitution when contracts they have entered are voided by courts due to a defendant's incompetence or incapacity. The law allows incompetent and incapacitated persons to disavow their contractual duties but generally only if the plaintiff is not made worse off by their disavowal.

Parties that are induced to enter into contracts by mistake, fraud, undue influence, or duress may seek to have the contract set aside or have the terms of the contract rewritten to do justice in the case. Rescission is the name for the remedy that terminates the contractual duties of both parties, while reformation is the name for the remedy that allows courts to change the substance of a contract to correct inequities that were suffered. Like contracts implied in law, however, courts are reluctant to rewrite contracts to reflect the parties' actual agreement, especially when the contract as written contains a mistake that could have been rectified through pre-contract investigation. Thus, one court would not reform a contract that stipulated an incorrect amount of acreage being purchased, since the buyer could have ascertained the correct amount by obtaining a land survey before entering the contract. *Little Stillwater Holding Corp. v. Cold Brook Sand & Gravel Corp.,* 151 Misc. 2d 457, 573 N.Y.S.2d 382 (N.Y. Co. Ct. 1991).

Specific performance is an equitable remedy that compels one party to perform, as nearly as practicable, his or her duties specified by the contract. Specific performance is available only when money damages are inadequate to compensate the plaintiff for the breach. This ruling often happens when the subject matter of a contract is in dispute.

Every parcel of land by definition is unique, if for no other reason than its location. However, rare articles that are not necessarily one of a kind are still treated by the law as unique if it would be impossible for a judge or jury to accurately calculate the appropriate amount of damages to award the plaintiff in lieu of awarding him or her the unique article contemplated by the contract. Heirlooms and antiques are examples of such rare items for which specific performance is usually available as a remedy. However, specific performance may never be invoked to compel the performance of a personal service, since doing so would constitute slavery in violation of the Thirteenth Amendment to the U.S. Constitution.

## Additional Resources

*American Jurisprudence.* 2d Edition. Thomson/West, 2005.

*Contracts.* 4th Edition. Calamari, John D. and Joseph M. Perillo, Thomson/West, 2004.

*Restatement (Second) of Contracts.* American Law Institute, 1979.

*West's Encyclopedia of American Law.* 2d Edition. Thomson/West, 2004.

## Organizations

### Consumer Contact Services, Inc.
6125 Black Oak Blvd.
Fort Wayne, IN 46835-2654 USA
Phone: (219) 486-2453

### National Organization of Bar Counsel
515 Fifth Street, NW
Washington, DC 64196 USA
Phone: (202) 638-1501
Fax: (202) 662-1777
URL: http://www.nobc.org

### Office of Consumer Protection, Federal Trade Commission
600 Pennsylvania Ave NW
Washington, DC 20580 USA
Phone: (877) 382-4357
Fax: (202) 326-3529
URL: http://www.ftc.gov/ftc/consumer.htm

# CONSUMER ISSUES

**CREDIT/TRUTH-IN-LENDING**

*Sections within this essay:*

## Background

Credit is money granted by a **creditor** or lender to a **debtor** or borrower, who defers payment of the debt. In exchange for the credit, the lender gets back the money, usually paid on a monthly basis, plus finance charges or interest. Entities within the credit industry, including banks, mortgage lenders, and credit card companies, earn billions of dollars per year from these charges and the interest received from outstanding balances.

The government regulates the credit industry due the potential for abuse by those who issue credit.

Without government regulation, creditors could attempt to confuse debtors regarding the terms of credit or could deny credit on improper grounds, such as the race or gender of the potential debtor. Identity theft, which occurs when one person uses another's personal identification to commit **fraud** or other crimes, has become a major problem in the United States due to the continually increasing use of the Internet. Legislatures, including Congress, have enacted **statutes** in recent years that are designed to protect the credit histories of those who may be the victims of identity theft.

## Types of Credit

### Same-as-Cash Credit

Same-as-cash, or noninstallment, credit is the simplest form of credit. Same as cash credit is usually due after a very short term, such as a 30-day period. Same-as-cash credit enables consumers to take possession of property today and pay for it within a set amount of time. Many department stores offer noninstallment credit; however, many same-as-cash plans can convert to high interest credit if the customer does not pay in full on the due date.

### Installment Credit

With installment, closed-end credit, a creditor loans a particular amount of money, usually the amount of the purchase price of the goods. The full amount of the principal and interest must be paid within a pre-determined time period. Failure on the part of the debtor to pay within this time period may mean that the debtor must return the goods to the creditor.

### Revolving Credit

Revolving, open-end credit is found with most credit cards. Under agreement with the lender, an amount of credit is extended to the consumer. An outside limit is established, depending upon the consumer's credit history and ability to handle the debt repayment. The financial institution gives the consumer a credit card with a credit limit, and the consumer can choose how much of the available credit to use at any given time. Usually the consumer makes monthly payments. Revolving credit requires active management by the consumer. The consumer can decide to pay off the entire outstanding debt when the statement is present, pay off more than the required minimum payment, or simply make the minimum required payment.

## Interest

Interest is the compensation paid by a debtor to a creditor for the use of the creditor's money. Over time, due to inflation, the value of money decreases. Interest on credit can be either simple or compound. Simple interest is interest charged only on the principal amount borrowed. Simple interest does not add the interest charge back to the outstanding loan during the length of the loan. Thus, simple interest charges are less than compound interest charges. Compound interest is interest charged not only on the principal, but on the interest accrued during the length of the loan. Compound interest is more expensive to the consumer because interest is charged on top of interest.

The amount of interest that can be charged is limited and regulated by state laws. The percentage interest rate allowed varies from state to state, depending on the type of credit being extended. A fixed interest rate does not change throughout the duration of the extension of credit. Under a variable rate loan, the finance charge is determined by an index, such as the "prime rate" published nationally each quarter for short-term loans charged by banks. This allows the lender to charge an interest rate that reflects current market conditions. Regardless of whether the interest rate charged is fixed or variable, the rate may not exceed the permissible rate set by state usury laws.

## Truth In Lending Act

The Truth in Lending Act is a federal law which sets minimum standards for the information which a creditor must provide in an installment credit contract. The amount being financed, the amount of the required minimum monthly payment, the total number of monthly payments, and the annual percentage rate (APR) must all be provided to the consumer prior to entering into a credit contract. In addition, the Truth in Lending Act regulates the advertising of credit. The Federal Trade Commission (FTC) works to ensure that the nation's markets are efficient and free of practices that might harm consumers. To ensure the smooth operation of the free market system, the FTC enforces federal consumer protection laws that prevent fraud, deception, and unfair business practices. The Federal Trade Commission Act allows the FTC to act in the interest of all consumers to prevent deceptive and unfair acts or practices. In interpreting the Act, the Commission has determined that, with respect to advertising, a representation, omission or practice is deceptive if it is likely to mislead consumers and affect consumers' behavior or decisions about the product or service. In addition, an act or practice is unfair if the injury it causes, or is likely to cause, is substantial, not outweighed by other benefits, and not reasonably avoidable.

The FTC's Bureau of Consumer Protection protects consumers against unfair, deceptive, or fraudulent practices. The Bureau enforces a variety of consumer protection laws enacted by Congress, as well as trade regulation rules issued by the Commission. Its actions include individual company and industry-wide investigations, administrative and federal court litigation, rule-making proceedings, and consumer and business education. In addition, the Bureau contributes to the Commission's on-going efforts to inform Congress and other government entities of the impact that proposed actions could have on consumers. The Bureau of Consumer Protection is divided into six divisions and programs, each with its own areas of expertise.

Within the Bureau of Consumer Protection are the Division of Advertising Practices and the Division of Enforcement. These entities are the nation's enforcers of federal truth-in-advertising laws. The FTC Act prohibits unfair or deceptive advertising in any medium. That is, advertising must tell the truth and not mislead consumers. A claim can be misleading if relevant information is left out or if the claim implies something that is not true. In addition, claims must be substantiated especially when they concern health, safety, or performance. The type of **evidence** may depend on the product, the claims, and what experts believe necessary. Sellers are responsible for claims they make about their products and services. Third parties such as advertising agencies or website designers and catalog marketers also may be liable for making or disseminating deceptive representations if they participate in the preparation or distribution of the advertising, or know about the deceptive claims.

## FTC Litigation

Typically, FTC investigations are not revealed to the public in order to protect both the investigation and the companies involved. If the FTC believes that a person or company has violated the law, the agency may attempt to obtain voluntary compliance by entering into a consent order with the company. A company that signs a consent order need not admit that it violated the law, but it must agree to stop the disputed practices outlined in an accompanying complaint. If a consent agreement cannot be reached, the FTC may issue an administrative complaint or seek injunctive relief in the federal courts. The FTC's administrative complaints initiate a formal proceeding that is much like a federal court trial but before an administrative law judge: Evidence is submitted, testimony is heard, and witnesses are examined and cross-examined. If a violation of the law is found, a judge may issue a cease and desist order. Initial decisions by administrative law judges may be appealed to the full Commission. Final decisions issued by the Commission may be appealed to the U.S. Court of Appeals for the District of Columbia and, ultimately, to the U.S. Supreme Court.

In some circumstances, the FTC can go directly to court to obtain an injunction, civil penalties, or consumer redress. The injunction preserves the market's competitive status quo. The FTC seeks federal court injunctions in consumer protection matters typically in cases of ongoing consumer fraud.

## Equal Credit Opportunity Act

The Equal Credit Opportunity Act (ECOA) ensures that all consumers are given an equal chance to obtain credit. Factors such as income, expenses, debt, and credit history are always valid considerations for creditworthiness; however, there are certain areas about which it unlawful for a potential creditor to inquire. These include sex, race, national origin, or religion. A creditor may ask for to voluntarily disclosure of this information if the loan is a real estate loan. This information helps federal agencies

enforce anti-discrimination laws. When permitted to ask marital status, a creditor may only use the terms: married, unmarried, or separated. A creditor may ask for such information in community property states. A creditor in any state may ask for this information if the account is joint and spouses apply together. A potential creditor many not inquire about plans a consumer may have for having or raising children, except that a creditor many inquire about court-ordered alimony, child support, or separate maintenance payments a potential debtor may to obligated to make.

As creditors decide whether to grant credit, they may not base their decision on sex, marital status, race, national origin, religion, or age (unless the applicant is a minor and without capacity to contract) or if age is used to determine the meaning of other factors important to creditworthiness. A potential creditor must consider public assistance income, part-time employment or pension, annuity, or retirement income as well as any reported alimony, child support, or separate maintenance payments.

Creditors are required to notify applicants within 30 days whether the application has been approved or denied. Creditors who reject potential consumers must provide a notice explaining either the specific reasons for rejection or the procedure for discovering the reason within 60 days.

## Fair Credit Reporting Act

The Fair Credit Reporting Act (FCRA) is a federal law which regulates the activities of credit reporting bureaus. The FCRA is designed to protect the privacy of credit report information and to guarantee that information supplied by consumer reporting agencies (CRAs) is as accurate as possible. Private credit reporting bureaus, such as TransUnion, Equifax Information Services, and Experian, maintain records of financial payment histories, public record data, along with personal identification information. The FCRA punishes unauthorized persons who obtain credit reports, as well as employees of credit reporting bureaus who furnish credit reports to unauthorized persons. The FTC also places responsibilities on those who supply the reporting bureaus with the initial information.

## Credit Reports

A credit report is a type of consumer report which contains information about where a consumer lives and how that consumers pays bills. It also may show whether an individual has been sued, arrested, or has filed for bankruptcy. Companies called consumer reporting agencies (CRAs) or credit bureaus compile and sell consumer credit reports to businesses. Businesses use this information to evaluate applications for credit, insurance, employment, and other purposes allowed by the (FCRA).

Due to concerns about the effect of identity theft on consumer credit reports, Congress amended the FCRA in 2003 with the enactment of the Fair and Accurate Credit Transactions Act. This statute allows every consumer to receive a free copy of his or her credit report. This legislation does not allow consumers to obtain a free credit report directly from a credit bureau. A consumer must instead obtain this report through one of the following: via phone at 1-877-322-8228; online at http://www.annualcreditreport.com; or by submitting a form to Annual Credit Report Request Service, P.O. Box 105281, Atlanta, Georgia, 30348-5281.

A person may be entitled to a free report in some other instances as well. Any consumer who is denied credit insurance or employment because of information supplied by a CRA is entitled to receive the CRA's name, address, and telephone number. If the consumer contacts the agency for a copy of the report within 60 days of receiving a denial notice, the report is free. In most other instances, however, credit bureaus may charge a fee of up to $9.95 for one of these reports.

### Credit Report Errors

Under the FCRA, both the CRA and the organization that provided the information to the CRA, such as a bank or credit card company, have responsibilities for correcting inaccurate or incomplete information in consumer credit reports. If a consumer disputes an item on the credit report in writing, the CRAs must reinvestigate the items in question within 30 days. After the information provider receives notice of a dispute from the CRA, it must investigate, review all relevant information provided by the CRA, and report the results to the CRA. If the information provider finds the disputed information to be inaccurate, it must notify all nationwide CRAs. Disputed information that cannot be verified must be deleted from a consumer credit report. When the reinvestigation is complete, the CRA must give the consumer written results and a free copy of the report if the dispute results in a change. If an item is changed or removed, the CRA cannot put the disputed informa-

tion back into a consumer file unless the information provider verifies its accuracy and completeness, and the CRA gives the consumer a written notice that includes the name, address, and phone number of the provider. Upon a consumer request, the CRA must send a notice of a correction to anyone who received a report in the previous six months. Job applicants can have a corrected copy of their report sent to anyone who received a copy during the past two years for employment purposes. If a reinvestigation does not resolve a dispute, consumers have a right to ask the CRA to include a statement of the dispute in the file and in future reports.

### Accurate Negative Information

When negative information in a consumer report is accurate, only the passage of time can assure its removal. Accurate negative information can generally stay on a consumer report for seven years. However, **bankruptcy** information may be reported for 10 years. Information about a lawsuit or an unpaid judgment can be reported for seven years or until the statute of limitations runs out, whichever is longer.

Credit counseling services can assist consumers. Some of these services contact creditors and attempt to consolidate debts, putting together repayment plans. Most of these businesses are non-profit agencies that charge small or even no fees to provide credit counseling. Other for-profit organizations sometimes advise consumers to apply for new employee ID numbers, and then use them instead of their Social Security numbers to apply for more credit. Using an identification number in order to defraud creditors, however, may constitute criminal activity.

## Fair Debt Collection Practices Act

The Fair Debt Collection Practices Act is a federal law which regulates the activities of those who regularly collect debts from others. Many states have adopted similar laws regulating the practices of debt collectors. Under this law, debt collectors may contact debtors by mail, in person, by telephone, or by telegram during "convenient hours" (commonly between 8 AM and 9 PM). Debt collectors are prohibited from contacting the debtor at work if the collector knows or has reason to know that the employer forbids employees from being contacted by debt collectors at the workplace. Finally, debt collectors may not contact individuals who are represented by an attorney.

Additional provisions specify that debt collectors may not threaten violence, use obscene or profane language, repeatedly telephone to annoy or harass, make collect telephone calls, or use false or misleading information in an effort to collect the debt. Consumers who believe this law has been violated may contact the regulating body, which is the Federal Trade Commission. Consumers also have the option of filing a lawsuit against the debt collector for violation of the law.

## Additional Resources

*Credit after Bankruptcy: A Step-by-Step Action Plan to Quick and Lasting Recovery after Personal Bankruptcy.* Snyder, Stephen, Bellwether, 2000.

*How to Fix Your Credit Report Yourself.* Lamet, Jerome, Jerome Limited, 1998.

*The Insider's Guide to Managing Your Credit: How to Establish, Maintain, Repair, and Protect Your Credit.* McNaughton, Deborah, Berkley Publishing Group, 1999.

## Organizations

### Council of Better Business Bureaus (CBBB)
4200 Wilson Blvd., Suite 800
Arlington, VA 22203-1838 USA
Phone: (703) 276-0100
Fax: (703) 525-8277
URL: htt://www.bbb.org

### Equifax Information Services, LLC
P.O. Box 740241
Atlanta, GA 30374 USA
Phone: (800) 685-1111
URL: http://www.equifax.com

### Experian
P.O. Box 2002
Allen, TX 75013 USA
Phone: (888) 397-3742
URL: http://www.experian.com

### Federal Trade Commission
600 Pennsylvania Avenue, N.W.
Washington, DC 20580 USA
URL: http://www.ftc.gov

### National Conference of State Legislatures
444 North Capitol Street, N.W., Suite 515
Washington, DC 20001 USA
Phone: (202) 624-5400
Fax: (202) 737-1069
URL: http://www.ncsl.org

### TransUnion
P.O. Box 1000
Chester, PA 19022 USA
Phone: (800) 888-4213
URL: http://www.transunion.com/index.jsp

# CONSUMER ISSUES

## DECEPTIVE TRADE PRACTICES

*Sections Within This Essay:*

## Background

Federal legislation and statutes in every state prohibit employment of unfair or deceptive trade practices and **unfair competition** in business. The Federal Trade Commission regulates federal laws designed to prohibit a series of specific practices prohibited in interstate commerce. Several states have established **consumer protection** offices as part of the state attorney general offices.

The Federal Trade Commission Act (FTCA), originally passed in 1914 and amended several times thereafter, was the original **statute** in the United States prohibiting "unfair or deceptive trade acts or practices." Development of the federal law was related to federal antitrust and trademark **infringement** legislation. Prior to the enactment in the 1960s of state statutes prohibiting deceptive trade practices, the main focus of state law in this area was "unfair competition," which refers to the tort action for practices employed by businesses to confuse consumers as to the source of a product. The tort action for a business "passing off" its goods as those of another was based largely on the **common law** tort action for trademark infringement.

Because the law governing deceptive trade practices was undefined and unclear, the National Conference of Commissioners on Uniform State Laws in 1964 drafted the Uniform Deceptive Trade Practices Act. The NCCUSL revised this uniform law in 1966. The law was originally "designed to bring state law up to date by removing undue restrictions on the common law action for deceptive trade practices." Only eleven states have adopted this act, but it has had a significant effect on other states. Most state deceptive or unfair trade practices statutes were originally enacted between the mid-1960s and mid-1970s.

## Applicability of Deceptive Trade Practices Statutes

Deceptive trade practices statutes do not govern all situations where one party has deceived another party. Most states limit the scope of these statutes to commercial transactions involving a consumer purchasing or leasing goods or services for personal, household, or family purposes. The terms used in each statute to set forth the scope of the statute are often the subject of **litigation**. The majority of states requires a liberal interpretation of the terms of the deceptive trade practices statutes, including those describing the applicability of the statutes.

### Trade or Commerce

Several states limit the applicability of deceptive trade practices to transactions in trade or commerce. This requirement usually incorporates a broad range of profit-oriented transactions. But it generally excludes trade between non-merchants and similar transactions.

### Consumer Transactions

The appropriate plaintiff under most deceptive trade practices acts is a consumer, commonly defined as a person who will use a good or service for personal, family, or household purposes. The determination of whether a plaintiff is a consumer often requires use of one of two types of analysis, a subjective test and an objective test. The subjective analysis typically considers the intended use of the good or service at the time of the transaction. Thus, if a buyer of a good intends at the time of a purchase to use to good for a personal, family, or household purpose, the buyer will likely be considered a consumer under the relevant statute. The objective analysis considers whether the type of good or service involved in the transaction is ordinarily used for a personal, family, or household purpose.

### Goods or Services

Goods are defined under the **Uniform Commercial Code** as those items movable at the time of a purchase. Many deceptive trade practices statutes apply this definition to the requirement that goods are involved in a transaction for a deceptive trade practices statute to apply. Livestock are also usually included in the definition of a good. Statutes and courts usually define services broadly, including in the definition most activities conducted on behalf of another. Some states require that consumers seek to purchase merchandise, which incorporates goods, services, real property, commodities, and some intangibles.

### Prohibited Acts and Practices

Most state deceptive trade practices statutes include broad restrictions on "deceptive" or "unfair" trade practices. These states often include prohibitions against **fraudulent** practices and unconscionable practices. The Federal Trade Commission, when interpreting the FTCA, does not require that the person committing an act of deception have the intent to deceive. Moreover, the FTC does not require that

actual deception occur. The FTC merely requires that a party have the capacity to deceive or commit an unfair trade practice. If a business or individual has this capacity or tendency to deceive, the FTC under the FTCA may order the company to cease and desist the deceptive or unfair practice. State statutes similarly do not require that a company specifically intends to deceive, nor must a company always have knowledge that a statement is false to be liable for misrepresentations made to a consumer.

A consumer who has been victimized by a potential deceptive or unfair trade practice should consult the deceptive trade practice statute in that state, plus consult **case law** applying this statute, to determine whether he or she has a cause of action. In addition to the broad prohibition against deception, most state statutes also include a list of practices that are defined as deceptive. Under the Uniform Deceptive Trade Practices Act, if a business or person engages in the following, the action constitutes a deceptive trade practice:

- Passes off goods or services as those of another

- Causes likelihood of confusion or of misunderstanding as to the source, sponsorship, approval, or certification of goods or services

- Causes likelihood of confusion or of misunderstanding as to affiliation, connection, or association with, or certification by, another

- Uses deceptive representations or designations of geographic origin in connection with goods or services

- Represents that goods or services have sponsorship, approval, characteristics, ingredients, uses, benefits, or qualities that they do not have or that a person has a sponsorship, approval, status, affiliation, or connection that he does not have

- Represents that goods are original or new if they are deteriorated, altered, reconditioned, reclaimed, used, or second-hand

- Represents that goods or services are of particular standard, quality, or grade, or that goods are of particular style or model, if they are of another

- Disparages the goods, services, or business of another by false or misleading misrepresentation of fact

- Advertises goods or services with intent not to sell them as advertised

- Advertises goods or services with intent not to supply reasonably expected public demand, unless advertisement discloses a limitation of quantity

- Makes false or misleading statements of fact concerning the reasons for, existence of, or amounts of price reductions

- Engages in any other conduct which similarly creates the likelihood of confusion or of misunderstanding

Most states include similar items in their lists of deceptive trade practices violations, even if those states have not adopted the uniform act. In addition, the FTC and many states prohibit other unfair practices, including the following:

- Unfair provisions in contracts of adhesion

- Coercive or high-pressure tactics in sales and collection efforts

- Illegal conduct

- Taking advantage of bargaining power of vulnerable groups

- Taking advantage of emergency situations

- Unconscionable activities, including outrageous and offensive conduct by a business in the sale of goods or services

## Other Practices Deemed Deceptive or Unfair

### Debt Collection

The Federal Fair Debt Collection Practices Act and state debt collection statutes govern most abuses by debt collectors in debt collection activities. Deceptive trade practices statutes may provide remedies in situations that are not covered by these debt collection statutes. For example, most debt collection statutes do not cover some forms of debt collection, such as foreclosures, repossessions, and evictions, but a deceptive trade practices statute may apply. Moreover, deceptive trade practices statutes may also permit a consumer to bring a cause of action against a **creditor** for debt collection practices of an independent agency hired by the creditor. Several cases have dealt with issues regarding misrepresentations made by debt collectors or deceptive agreements proposed by debt collectors.

### Breach of Warranties

Consumers have several means of enforcing a **warranty** provided in a sales or service contract. If a business employs deceptive practices with respect to the advertisement or negotiation of a warranty, a deceptive trade practices statute may provide a consumer a remedy in addition to a breach of warranty claim.

### Insurance

Most states have enacted legislation regarding deceptive practices of insurance companies, including those practices related to the sale of policies and the payment of claims. In some states, employment of a deceptive practice in insurance is also a deceptive trade practice. A deceptive trade practices statute may also provide a remedy in insurance cases where state insurance laws do not apply.

### Pyramid Schemes and Similar Practices

Several states prohibit certain illegal business schemes through deceptive trace practices statutes. One such scheme is a "pyramid scheme," where investors make money by recruiting others to join and invest in a company rather than selling a product as claimed by the company. Other schemes include deceptive employment opportunity claims and misleading or deceptive game or contest promotions. Some states do not specifically include these schemes in the statute, but courts in those states may have applied provisions of the relevant deceptive trade practices statute in cases involving these schemes.

## Remedies for Violations of Deceptive Trade Practices Statutes

A consumer who has been the victim of a deceptive trade practice has a variety of remedies. State deceptive trade practices statutes have been particularly successful due to the damages provisions included in the statutes. About half of the states provide minimum **statutory** damages to a litigant who has proven a deceptive trade practice, even if the litigant has not proven actual damages. Many states also permit courts to award treble damages, which means the actual damages to a party injured by a deceptive trade practice are tripled. Several states also permit courts to impose **punitive damages** and/or attorney's fees for these practices.

In addition to monetary damages, several other options may exist for a person injured by a deceptive trade practice. When the FTC has **jurisdiction** over a case, it may enjoin a deceptive trade practice of a company under the FTCA. Statutes in each of the states also permit government enforcement officials to seek cease and desist orders to prevent businesses from engaging in deceptive trade practices. These remedies may be available in addition to civil remedies sought by private litigants.

## State and Local Provisions Prohibiting Deceptive Trade Practices

Although many state deceptive trade practices statutes include similar provisions, application of these statutes often differs from state to state. Consumers who have been victimized by a deceptive trade practice should be sure to consult their relevant state statutes to determine the appropriate procedures to follow, the appropriate office to contact, and special requirements that must be met to bring a suit in that state. Each state has adopted some version of a deceptive trade practices statute. The following are brief summaries of these statutes.

ALABAMA: The state statute prohibits 22 specific practices, plus any other deceptive or unconscionable acts or practices. The transaction must be conducted in trade or commerce for the statute to apply. The attorney general's office or a district attorney's office may enforce the statute for violations by a business.

ALASKA: The state statute prohibits 41 specific practices, plus other unfair methods of competition and unfair or deceptive acts or practices. The transaction must be conducted in trade or commerce for the statute to apply. The attorney general's office may enforce the statute for violations by a business.

ARIZONA: The state statute prohibits deception or an omission of a material fact by one party to a transaction with the intent to deceive the other party. The transaction must involve the sale, offer for sale, or **lease** of goods, real property, services, or intangibles for the statute to apply. The attorney general's office or a county attorney's office may enforce the statute for violations by a business.

ARKANSAS: The state statute prohibits 10 specific practices, plus any other deceptive or unconscionable acts or practices. The transaction must involve the sale or advertisement of goods or services for the statute to apply.

CALIFORNIA: The state statute prohibits 23 specific practices, plus any other unfair methods of competition and unfair or deceptive practices. Parties must intend for the transaction to result in the sale or lease of goods or services to a consumer for the statute to apply.

COLORADO: The state legislature adopted the Uniform Deceptive Trade Practices Act which prohibits 43 specific practices. Transactions must be in the course of a person's business, vocation, or occupation, and involve the sale of goods, services, or real property for the statute to apply. The attorney general's office or a district attorney's office may enforce the statute for violations by a business.

CONNECTICUT: The state statute prohibits unfair methods of competition and unfair or deceptive acts or practices. The transaction must be conducted in trade or commerce for the statute to apply. The Commission of Consumer Protection or the attorney general's office may enforce the statute for violations by a business.

DELAWARE: The state legislature adopted the Uniform Deceptive Trade Practices Act which prohibits 12 specific practices, plus other conduct that creates the likelihood of a misunderstanding on the part of a consumer. The transaction must be conducted in the course of business, vocation, or occupation for the statute to apply. The attorney general's office may enforce the statute for violations by a business.

DISTRICT OF COLUMBIA: The state statute prohibits 31 specific practices, plus other unfair, deceptive, or unlawful trade practices. The transaction must involve trade practices involving consumer goods or services. The Office of Consumer Protection may enforce the statute for violations by a business.

FLORIDA: The state statute prohibits unfair methods of competition, unconscionable acts or practices, and deceptive or unfair acts or practices. A finding of a violation may be based on rules promulgated by the Federal Trade Commission. The transaction must be conducted in trade or commerce for the statute to apply. The Department of Legal Affairs or the state attorney's office may enforce the statute for violations by a business.

GEORGIA: The state legislature adopted the Uniform Deceptive Trade Practices Act which prohibits deceptive or unfair acts or practices in a consumer transaction or an office supply transaction. A number of specific examples are included in the statute. The statute applies to consumer transactions in trade or commerce. Georgia Office of Consumer Affairs may enforce the statute for violations by a business.

HAWAII: The state legislature adopted the Uniform Deceptive Trade Practices Act which prohibits 12 specific practices, plus any other conduct that creates a misunderstanding on the part of a consumer. The transaction must be conducted in the course of a business, vocation, or occupation for the statute to apply.

IDAHO: The state statute prohibits 18 specific practices, plus any misleading consumer practices or unconscionable practices. The transaction must be conducted in trade or commerce for the statute to apply. The attorney general's office may enforce the statute for violations by a business.

ILLINOIS: The state legislature adopted the Uniform Deceptive Trade Practices Act which prohibits 26 specific practices, plus other unfair methods of competition and unfair or deceptive acts or practices. Proscribed practices include concealment or omission by a business of any material fact with an intent to cause reliance by a consumer. The transaction must be conducted in trade or commerce for the statute to apply. The attorney general's office may enforce the statute for violations by a business.

INDIANA: The state statute prohibits a number of specific practices, including transactions involving contracts with unconscionable provisions. The transaction must be a consumer transaction as defined by the statute for the statute to apply. The attorney general's office may enforce the statute for violations by a business.

IOWA: The state statute prohibits four specific practices, plus any other unfair or deceptive acts, or concealment or omission of a material fact by a business with the intent to cause reliance on the part of the consumer. The transaction must involve the sale, offer of sale, or advertisement of goods, real property, or several intangible items described in the statue for the statute to apply. The attorney general's office may enforce the statute for violations by a business.

KANSAS: The state statute prohibits 11 specific practices, plus any unconscionable practices as defined by the statute. The transaction must involve the sale or lease of property or services intended for personal, family, household, business, or agricultural purposes. The attorney general's office or local prosecuting attorney's office may enforce the statute for violations by a business.

KENTUCKY: The state statute prohibits unfair or deceptive acts or practices, including unconscionable practices. The transaction must be conducted in trade or commerce for the statute to apply. The attorney general's office or county attorney's office may enforce the statute for violations by a business.

LOUISIANA: The state statute prohibits unfair methods of competition and unfair or deceptive acts or practices. The transaction must be conducted in trade or commerce for the statute to apply. The Governor's Consumer Protection Division may enforce the statute for violations by a business.

MAINE: The state legislature adopted the Uniform Deceptive Trade Practices Act. The state statute prohibits 12 specific practices, plus conduct likely to create confusion or misunderstanding to a consumer, unfair methods of competition, and unfair or deceptive acts or practices. The transaction must be conducted in trade or commerce for the statute to apply. The attorney general's office may enforce the statute for violations by a business.

MARYLAND: The state statute prohibits unfair or deceptive trade practices, including a number of practices specified in the statute. The transaction must involve the sale, offer for sale, or lease of consumer goods, real property, or services. Consumer debt collection and extension of consumer credit are also within the scope of the statute. The Division of Consumer Protection of the Attorney General's office may enforce the statute for violations by a business.

MASSACHUSETTS: The state statute prohibits unfair methods of competition and unfair or deceptive acts or practices. The transaction must be conducted in trade or commerce for the statute to apply. The attorney general's office may enforce the statute for violations by a business.

MICHIGAN: The state statute prohibits 31 specific practices, plus any other deceptive, unfair, or unconscionable acts or practices. The transaction must be conducted in trade or commerce for the statute to apply. The attorney general's office or a district attorney's office may enforce the statute for violations by a business.

MINNESOTA: The state legislature adopted the Uniform Deceptive Trade Practices Act which prohibits 13 specific practices, plus any other deceptive or unconscionable acts or practices. The transaction must be conducted in the course of business, vocation, or occupation for the statute to apply. The attorney general's office may enforce the statute for violations by a business.

MISSISSIPPI: The state statute prohibits 22 specific practices, plus any other deceptive or unconscionable acts or practices. The transaction must be conducted in trade or commerce for the statute to apply. The Attorney General's Office of Consumer Protection may enforce the statute for violations by a business.

MISSOURI: The state statute prohibits deceptive or unfair acts or concealment or omission of a material fact from a consumer. The transaction may involve the sale, offer for sale, or advertisement of any merchandise for the statute to apply. The attorney general's office may enforce the statute for violations by a business.

MONTANA: The state statute prohibits unfair methods of competition and unfair or deceptive acts or practices. The transaction must involve the sale, offer for sale, or advertisement of any real or **personal property**, services, intangibles, or anything of value. The attorney general's office may enforce the statute for violations by a business.

NEBRASKA: The state legislature adopted the Uniform Deceptive Trade Practices Act which prohibits 14 specific practices, plus unfair methods of competition, other unfair or deceptive acts or practices, and all unconscionable acts by a supplier in a consumer transaction. The transaction must be conducted in trade or commerce for the statute to apply. The attorney general's office may enforce the statute for violations by a business.

NEVADA: The state statute prohibits a number of deceptive trade practices set forth in the statute. The transaction must be conducted in the course of a business or occupation. The Commissioner of Consumer Affairs, Director of the Department of Commerce, attorney general's office, or a district attorney's office may enforce the statute for violations by a business.

NEW HAMPSHIRE: The state statute prohibits 12 specific practices, plus any unfair methods of competition or any other unfair of deceptive act or practice. The transaction must be conducted in trade or commerce for the statute to apply. The attorney general's office may enforce the statute for violations by a business.

NEW JERSEY: The state statute prohibits unconscionable commercial practices, deception, **fraud**,

or the knowing concealment or omission of a material fact with the intent to cause reliance on the part of a consumer. The statute includes numerous specific prohibitions. The transaction may be conducted in conjunction with the sale or advertisement of any merchandise or real property for the statute to apply. The attorney general's office or the director of a county or municipal office of consumer affairs may enforce the statute for violations by a business.

NEW MEXICO: The state legislature adopted the Uniform Deceptive Trade Practices Act which prohibits 17 specific deceptive practices, two specific unconscionable practices, and other unfair or deceptive trade practices. The transaction must be conducted in trade or commerce for the statute to apply. The attorney general's office may enforce the statute for violations by a business.

NEW YORK: The state statute prohibits deceptive acts or practices and **false advertising**. The transaction must be conducted in business, trade, or commerce, or in the furnishing of a service in the state, for the statute to apply. The attorney general's office may enforce the statute for violations by a business.

NORTH CAROLINA: The state statute prohibits unfair methods of competition and unfair or deceptive acts or practices. The transaction must be conducted in or affect commerce, including all business activities. The attorney general's office may enforce the statute for violations by a business.

NORTH DAKOTA: The state statute prohibits deceptive acts or practices, fraud, or misrepresentation with the intent for consumer to rely on the representation. The transaction may involve a sale or advertisement of any merchandise for the statute to apply. The attorney general's office may enforce the statute for violations by a business.

OHIO: The state legislature adopted the Uniform Deceptive Trade Practices Act. The state statute prohibits 11 specific practices, plus any other deceptive or unconscionable acts or practices. The transaction must be a consumer transaction for the statute to apply. The attorney general's office may enforce the statute for violations by a business.

OKLAHOMA: The state legislature adopted the Uniform Deceptive Trade Practices Act which prohibits 11 specific deceptive trade practices. The transaction must be conducted in a course of a business, vocation, or occupation for the statute to apply. The attorney general's office or a district attorney's office may enforce the statute for violations by a business.

OREGON: The state statute prohibits 20 specific unfair or deceptive acts or practices, plus two unconscionable tactics. The transaction must be conducted in trade or commerce for the statute to apply. The attorney general's office or a district attorney's office may enforce the statute for violations by a business.

PENNSYLVANIA: The state statute prohibits 21 practices, plus other unfair methods of competition, deceptive acts or practices, or any fraudulent or deceptive conduct that is likely to create confusion to a consumer. The transaction must be conducted in trade or commerce for the statute to apply. The attorney general's office may enforce the statute for violations by a business.

RHODE ISLAND: The state statute prohibits 19 specific unfair methods of competition or unfair or deceptive practices. The transaction must be conducted in trade or commerce for the statute to apply. The attorney general's office may enforce the statute for violations by a business.

SOUTH CAROLINA: The state statute prohibits unfair methods of competition and unfair or deceptive acts or practices. The transaction must be conducted in trade or commerce for the statute to apply. The attorney general's office may enforce the statute for violations by a business.

SOUTH DAKOTA: The state statute prohibits knowing and intentional deceptive practices, plus practices involving an omission of a material fact in connection with a sale of merchandise to a consumer. The transaction must be conducted in business for the statute to apply. The attorney general's office or the state's attorney with attorney general approval may enforce the statute for violations by a business.

TENNESSEE: The state statute prohibits 30 specific practices, plus any other deceptive or unfair acts or practices. The transaction must be conducted in trade or commerce for the statute to apply. The attorney general's office may enforce the statute for violations by a business.

TEXAS: The state statute prohibits 25 specific practices, plus additional actions for breach of warranty, insurance violations, or unconscionable acts or practices. The transaction must be conducted in trade or commerce for the statute to apply. The Consumer Protection Division of the attorney general's office or a district attorney's office may enforce the statute for violations by a business.

UTAH: The state statute prohibits 15 specific unconscionable practices by a supplier in a consumer transaction, plus other deceptive acts or practices. The transaction must be a consumer transaction for the statute to apply. The Division of Consumer Protection or other state officials or agencies with authority over suppliers may enforce the statute for violations by a business.

VERMONT: The state statute prohibits unfair methods of competition and unfair or deceptive acts or practices. The transaction must be conducted in commerce for the statute to apply. The attorney general's office may enforce the statute for violations by a business.

VIRGINIA: The state statute prohibits 32 specific practices, plus any other fraudulent acts or practices. A supplier must conduct a consumer transaction for the statute to apply. The attorney general's office may enforce the statute for violations by a business.

WASHINGTON: The state statute prohibits unfair methods of competition and unfair or deceptive acts or practices. The transaction must be conducted in trade or commerce for the statute to apply. The attorney general's office may enforce the statute for violations by a business.

WEST VIRGINIA: The state statute prohibits 16 specific practices, plus other unfair methods of competition and unfair or deceptive practices. The transaction must be conducted in trade or commerce for the statute to apply. The attorney general's office may enforce the statute for violations by a business.

WISCONSIN: The state statute prohibits 14 specific practices, plus other untrue, deceptive, or misleading representations; unfair methods of competition; and unfair trade practices. The statute applies to virtually any transaction due to the broad scope of the statutory language. The Department of Agriculture, Trade, and Consumer Protection may enforce the statute for violations by a business.

WYOMING: The state statute prohibits several specific practices, plus other unfair or deceptive acts or practices. The transaction must be conducted in the scope of a business and in a consumer transaction for the statute to apply. The attorney general's office may enforce the statute for violations by a business.

## Additional Resources

*Revised Uniform Deceptive Trade Practices Act.* National Conference of Commissioners on Uniform State Laws, 1966. Available at http://www.law.upenn.edu/bll/ulc/fnact99/1920_69/rudtpa66.htm.

*State Unfair Trade Practices Law: In One Volume.* Commerce Clearing House, Inc., 2000.

*Unfair and Deceptive Acts and Practices, Fourth Edition.* Sheldon, Jonathan, and Carolyn L. Carter, National Consumer Law Center, 1997.

*Unfair Trade Practices Laws: Resource Book.* Alliance of American Insurers, 1986.

*U.S. Code, Title 15: Commerce and Trade, Chapter 2: Federal Trade Commission; Promotion of Export Trade and Prevention of Unfair Methods of Competition.* U. S. House of Representatives, 1999. Available at http://uscode.house.gov/title_15.htm

## Organizations

### American Council on Consumer Interests (ACCI)

240 Stanley Hall
University of Missouri
Columbia, MO 65211 USA
Phone: (573) 882-3817
Fax: (573) 884-6571
URL: http://www.consumerinterests.org/
Primary Contact: Carrie Paden, Executive Director

### Call for Action (CFA)

5272 River Road, Suite 300
Bethesda, MD 20816 USA
Phone: (301) 657-8260
Fax: (301) 657-2914
URL: http://www.callforaction.org

### Consumer Action (CA)

717 Market Street, Suite 310
San Francisco, CA 94103 USA
Phone: (415) 777-9635
Fax: (415) 777-5269
URL: http://www.consumer-action.org
Primary Contact: Ken McEldowney, Executive Director

### Council of Better Business Bureaus, Inc.

4200 Wilson Blvd.
Arlington, VA 22203 USA>
Phone: (703) 276-0100
Fax: (703) 525-8277
URL: http://www.bbb.org/

### National Consumer Law Center (NCLC)

18 Tremont Street
Boston, MA 02108 USA>
Phone: (617) 523-8089
Fax: (617) 523-7398
URL: http://www.consumerlaw.org/
Primary Contact: Willard P. Ogburn, Executive Director

### National Consumers League (NCL)

1701 K Street, NW, Suite 1201
Washington, DC 20006 USA>
Phone: (202) 835-3323
Fax: (202) 835-0747
URL: http://www.nclnet.org/

### National Fraud Information Center (NFIC)

P.O. Box 65868
Washington, DC 20035 USA>
Phone: (800) 876-7060
Fax: (202) 835-0767
URL: http://www.fraud.org/

# CONSUMER ISSUES

## DEFECTIVE PRODUCTS

*Sections within this essay:*

## Background

Defective product law, commonly known as products liability, refers to the liability of parties along the chain of manufacture of any product for damage caused by that product. A defective product is one that causes some injury or damage to person as a result of some defect in the product or its labeling or the way the product was used. Those responsible for the defect can include the manufacturers of component parts, assembling manufacturers, wholesalers, and retail stores. Many states have enacted comprehensive products liability statutes. There is no federal products liability law.

## Theories of Product Liability

Some consumer advocates believe that a products liability lawsuit is a consumer's most effective weapon against dangerous products. While the government regulates products, regulations may not require the offending company to suffer much of a penalty. A products liability lawsuit allows the individual citizen to **prosecute** a case against reckless, incompetent, or negligent manufacturers. Typically, product defect cases are based on strict liability, rather than **negligence**. It is irrelevant whether the manufacturer or supplier exercised great care. If there is a defect in the product that causes harm, that entity will be liable for it. This means that it is not necessary to prove "fault" on the part of the **defendant**. To win the case, the plaintiff must prove that the product was unreasonably dangerous or defective; that injury resulted from use of the defective product; and that the injury was caused by the defect in the product. A repairer, seller, or manufacturer of a defective product is liable for injuries sustained by persons using the defective product. Liability may also extend to persons who did not purchase the product but were using the product in a foreseeable manner. Also, people injured as a result of someone else using a defective product may be able to recover if their injuries were caused by the product's defect. All jurisdictions require a connection between the product defect and the injury. Many **product liability** cases turn on experts' **testimony**, where both plaintiff and defendant use expert testimony to establish or deny a link between an alleged defect and an injury. Although strict liability is most common, products liability lawsuits also include negligence theories, and breach of **warranty** theories.

## Negligence

A negligence theory requires the plaintiff to prove that the defendant owed a duty to the consumer. Manufacturers do, in fact, owe a duty to the users of its products and to bystanders likely to be injured. The manufacturer also has a duty in making its product to guard against injuries likely to result from reasonably foreseeable misuse of the product. The plaintiff must also show that the manufacturer breached its duty. The plaintiff should be able to prove that a reasonable manufacturer, with knowledge or constructive knowledge of the product's defect, would not have produced the product. The plaintiff also must prove injury and that the defendant's breach caused the injury.

## Strict Liability

Strict liability does not require that the injured plaintiff show knowledge or fault on the manufacturer's part. The plaintiff must show only that the product was sold or distributed by a defendant and that the product was unreasonably dangerous at the time it left the defendant's possession. The behavior or knowledge (or lack thereof) of a products liability defendant regarding the dangerous nature of a product is not an issue for consideration under a strict liability theory. Strict liability concerns only the condition of the product itself while a negligence theory concerns not only the product, but also the manufacturer's knowledge and conduct.

## Breach of Warranty

Every product comes with an **implied warranty** that it is safe for its intended use. A defective product that causes injury was not safe for its intended use and thus can constitute a breach of warranty.

# Types of Product Defects

There are three types of product defects: design defects, manufacturing defects, and defects in marketing, sometimes known a failure to warn. Design defects exist before the product is manufactured. Manufacturing defects result from the actual construction or production of the item. Defects in marketing deal with improper instructions and failures to warn consumers of potential dangers with the product.

## Design Defects

In these cases injury results from a poor design, even though there may be no defect in the manufacture of the individual product. A product can be unreasonably dangerous for various reasons. The design of the product could be unreasonably dangerous resulting in the entire line of products being defective. Generally, in order to prove a design defect case, the plaintiff is obligated to offer a reasonable alternative design that the manufacturer could have employed, which would have prevented the injury and which would not have substantially diminished the product's effectiveness. If the jury finds that the plaintiff's proposed alternative is reasonable and would have eliminated the product's risk, the product is determined defective.

The manufacturer in a design defect case cannot escape liability by relying on industry standard as a defense or alleging that because the other manufacturers used the same design, the product was not defective. Theoretically, the entire industry could be producing products with design defects. However, the industry standard defense is not the same as the state of the art defense, which may be a valid defense if the defendant can show that at the time the product was built, no safer, alternative design existed. The state of the art defense protects a manufacturer from liability for a product, which was reasonably safe years earlier but by current standards might be deemed defective.

## Manufacturing Defects

A manufacturing defect occurs when a particular product is somehow manufactured incorrectly and in its condition is unreasonably dangerous. The plaintiff must show that the product was in its defective condition when it left the manufacturer's possession and that it was unaltered at the time it caused the injury. In short, the consumer must prove that the manufacturer caused the defect. If the defective part was a component in a larger product (for example, a defective tire on an automobile), the component producer may be liable, as well as the manufacturer of the larger product.

## Marketing Defects

A product can also be unreasonably dangerous absent appropriate warnings. If a product could reasonably have been designed with a higher degree of safety, a proper warning will not necessarily convert the unreasonably dangerous product into a safe, nondefective one. An appropriate warning however, can transform certain dangerous products, which would be defective without the warning, into reasonably safe ones. The warning must be thorough and conspicuous, and it must evaluate the magnitude of the risk involved in failing to abide by the manufacturer's instructions. Failure to warn, or "inadequate warning" cases refer to injuries caused as a result of a product already known to be potentially dangerous which was sold without a proper warning to the consumer. Every product has a potential to be unsafe if it is used incorrectly. Whether a warning is adequate requires weighing all the possible circumstances. Juries are typically left with the task of determining whether a given warning is adequate, appropriate, suitable, or sufficient under the specific facts of a particular case.

## Used Merchandise

Sellers of used merchandise may be liable depending on the factual situation. If the product was warranted or guaranteed, there may be a basis of liability. **Corporate** takeovers, purchases, and break-ups of companies may create additional potentially responsible parties who are liable for injuries caused by defective products created initially by others.

## Exported Goods

Many products manufactured outside the United States are sold in the United States. Additionally, U.S. companies frequently outsource the production of certain components to companies in foreign countries. While it is possible to sue a foreign corporation for a defective product, the requirements of proper legal procedure are sometimes extensive.

Because the number of exports to the United States has increased significantly in the last decade, the U.S. government has entered into agreements with several countries to help ensure the safety of exported products. In 2005 the U.S. Consumer Product Safety Commission (CPSC) signed agreements with the governments of Canada and Mexico to improve the safety of products imported to and from both countries. These agreements were designed to build on the North American Security and Prosperity Partnership (SPP), signed earlier that year by the United States, Canada, and Mexico. (The SPP is a more broadly based agreement that calls for improved security to keep borders free from terrorism but open to trade.) In 2006 the CPSC signed a Memorandum of Understanding with the government of India to improve the safety of consumer exports to the U.S. This agreement includes exchanging product safety information and providing training programs that focus on safety issues. (In 2004, India imported $8.3 billion worth of consumer goods to the United States.)

## Comparative Fault

While under a products liability theory a manufacturer may be strictly liable for defects, the law recognizes that certain products are inherently dangerous and that consumers should know that the product is dangerous when they purchase it. If a consumer uses a defective product in a manner that an ordinary consumer would and is injured as a result, then a valid case may exist. Conversely, if a consumer uses a product in a manner other than that intended by the manufacturer, the consumer may be partially at fault, despite the fact that the product may have been defective.

## Statute of Limitations

All states have some form of **statute of limitations**, which limits the time allowed for filing a lawsuit. The time frame in which the **statute** of limitations runs usually begins from the time of the injury as a result of the defect. However, most states have some form of a delayed **discovery** rule, which states that the statute does not begin to run until the injury is discovered. This may be important when the injury is not obvious, perhaps until years later. There is a related statute in some jurisdictions called a statute of repose. It essentially provides that no claim can be made based upon a defective product beyond a specified number of years after the date of manufacture.

## Damages

**Compensatory damages** awardable in products liability cases include medical bills, reimbursement for lost wages, and property damaged as a result of the defective product. Pain and suffering experienced as a result of injury and general damages are also recoupable. And if the conduct of the defendant was egregious, the plaintiff may be entitled to **punitive damages**.

## Consumer Product Safety Commission

The U.S. Consumer Product Safety Commission (CPSC) is an independent federal regulatory agency created to protect the public from unreasonable risks of injuries and deaths associated with some 15,000 types of consumer products. CPSC uses various means to inform the public. These include local and national media coverage, publication of numerous booklets and product alerts, a website, a telephone Hotline, the National Injury Information Clearinghouse, CPSC's Public Information Center and responses to **Freedom of Information Act** (FOIA) requests. CPSC staff participates in voluntary standards activities for a variety of products ranging from children's products to heating units to bicycles to paper shredders.

For more than 30 years CPSC has operated a statistically valid injury surveillance and follow-back system known as the National Electronic Injury Surveillance System (NEISS). The primary purpose of NEISS has been to provide timely data on consumer product-related injuries occurring in the U.S. NEISS injury data are gathered from the emergency departments of 100 hospitals selected as a probability sample of all U.S. hospitals with emergency departments. The system's foundation rests on emergency department surveillance data, but the system also has the flexibility to gather additional data at either the surveillance or the investigation level. Surveillance data enable CPSC analysts to make timely national estimates of the number of injuries associated with (not necessarily caused by) specific consumer products. These data also provide **evidence** of the need for further study of particular products. Subsequent follow-back studies yield important clues to the cause and likely prevention of injuries.

## Additional Resources

*Product Liability Entering the 21st Century: The U.S. Perspective* Moore, Michael J., Brookings Institution Press, 2001.

*Why Lawsuits Are Good for America: Disciplined Democracy, Big Business, and the Common Law* Bogus, Carl, NYU Press, 2001.

## Organizations

### *Consumer Action*
221 Main Street, Suite 480
San Francisco, CA 94105 USA
Phone: (415) 777-9635
Fax: (415) 777-5267
URL: http://www.consumer-action.org
Primary Contact: Ken McEldowney, Executive Director

### *National Consumers League*
1701 K Street, NW, Suite 1200
Washington, DC 20006 USA
Phone: (202) 835-3323
Fax: (202) 835-0747
URL: http://www.nclnet.org
Primary Contact: Linda Golodner, President and CEO

### *U.S. Consumer Product Safety Commission*
4330 East-West Highway
Bethesda, MD 20814-4408
Phone: (301) 504-7923
URL: http://www.cpsc.gov
Primary Contact: Hal Stratton, Chairman

# CONSUMER ISSUES

## FEDERAL TRADE COMMISSION/ REGULATION

*Sections within this essay:*

- Background
- Bureau of Consumer Protection
    - The Division of Advertising Practices
    - The Division of Enforcement
    - The Division of Financial Practices
    - The Division of Marketing Practices
    - The Division of Planning and Information
- Bureau of Economics
- Bureau of Competition
    - Antitrust Laws
    - Mergers
- FTC Litigation
- Additional Resources

## Background

The Federal Trade Commission (FTC) works to ensure that the nation's markets are efficient and free of practices which might harm consumers. To ensure the smooth operation of our free market system, the FTC enforces federal **consumer protection** laws that prevent **fraud**, deception, and unfair business practices. The Commission also enforces federal antitrust laws that prohibit anticompetitive mergers and other business practices that restrict competition and harm consumers.

The FTC was created in 1914 to prevent unfair methods of competition in commerce. In 1938, Con-

gress passed the Wheeler-Lea Amendment, which included a broad prohibition against "unfair and deceptive acts or practices." After that, the FTC was directed to administer a wide variety of other consumer protection laws, including the Telemarketing Sales Rule, the Pay-Per-Call Rule and the Equal Credit Opportunity Act. In 1975, Congress passed the Magnuson-Moss Act which gave the FTC the authority to adopt trade regulation rules which define unfair or deceptive acts in particular industries. Trade regulation rules have the force of law.

Today, the FTC is an independent agency which reports directly to Congress. The commission is headed by five commissioners, nominated by the president and confirmed by the Senate, each serving a seven-year term. The president chooses one commissioner to act as chairman. No more than three commissioners can be of the same political party. The commission is further divided into bureaus and divisions, which are responsible for various aspects of FTC operations.

## Bureau of Consumer Protection

Bureau of Consumer Protection's mandate is to protect consumers against unfair, deceptive, or **fraudulent** practices. The bureau enforces a variety of consumer protection laws enacted by Congress, as well as trade regulation rules issued by the commission. Its actions include individual company and industry-wide investigations, administrative and federal court **litigation**, rulemaking proceedings, and consumer and business education. In addition, the Bureau contributes to the commission's on-going efforts to inform Congress and other government entities of the impact that proposed actions could have on consumers. The Bureau of Consumer Protection is divided into six divisions and programs, each with its own areas of expertise.

### The Division of Advertising Practices

The Division of Advertising Practices is the nation's enforcer of federal truth-in-advertising laws. Its law enforcement activities focus on claims for foods, drugs, dietary supplements, and other products promising health benefits, health fraud on the Internet, weight-loss advertising and marketing directed to children, performance claims for computers, ISPs and other high-tech products and services, tobacco and alcohol advertising, children's privacy online, claims about product performance made in national or regional newspapers and magazines; in radio and TV commercials, including infomercials, through direct mail to consumers, or on the Internet.

### The Division of Enforcement

The Division of Enforcement conducts a wide variety of law enforcement activities to protect consumers, including ensuring compliance with administrative and federal court orders entered in consumer protection cases, conducting investigations and prosecuting civil actions to stop fraudulent, unfair or deceptive marketing and advertising practices, and enforcing consumer protection laws, rules and guidelines. This division monitors compliance with commission cease and desist orders and federal court injunctive orders, investigates violations of consumer protection laws, and enforces a number of trade laws, rules and guides, including:

The Mail or Telephone Order Merchandise Rule, which requires companies to ship purchases when promised (or within 30 days if no time is specified) or to give consumers the option to cancel their orders for a refund.

The Textile, Wool, Fur and Care Labeling Rules, which require proper origin and fiber content labeling of textile, wool, and fur products, and care label instructions attached to clothing and fabrics.

Energy Rules, which require the disclosure of energy costs of home appliances (the Appliance Labeling Rule), octane ratings of gasoline (the Fuel Rating Rule), and the efficiency rating of home insulation (the R-Value Rule).

Green Guides, which govern claims that consumer products are environmentally safe, recycled, recyclable, ozone-friendly, or biodegradable.

### The Division of Financial Practices

The Division of Financial Practices is responsible for developing policy and enforcing laws related to financial and lending practices affecting consumers. It also is responsible for most of the agency's consumer privacy program. Its duties include enforcement of the **Fair Credit Reporting Act** (FCRA) which ensures the accuracy and privacy of information kept by credit bureaus and other consumer reporting agencies and gives consumers the right to know what information these entities are distributing about them to creditors, insurance companies, and employers. This division also enforces the Gramm-Leach-Bliley Act (GLBA). The GLBA requires financial institutions to provide notice to consumers about their information practices and to give consumers an opportunity to direct that their personal information not be shared with non-affiliated third parties.

The Division of Financial Practices monitors the Truth in Lending Act, which requires creditors to disclose in writing certain cost information, such as the **annual percentage rate** (APR), before consumers enter into credit transactions, the Consumer Leasing Act, which requires lessors to give consumers information on **lease** costs and terms, and the Fair Debt Collection Practices Act, which prohibits debt collectors from engaging in unfair, deceptive, or abusive practices, including over-charging, harassment, and disclosing consumers' debt to third parties.

### The Division of Marketing Practices

The Division of Marketing Practices enforces federal consumer protection laws by filing actions in federal district court on behalf of the commission to stop scams, prevent scam artists from repeating their fraudulent schemes in the future, freeze assets, and obtain compensation for scam victims. The division also is responsible for enforcement of the Telemarketing Sales Rule, which prohibits deceptive sales pitches and protects consumers from abusive, unwanted, and late-night sales calls, the 900 Number Rule, which requires sellers of pay-per-call (900 numbers) to clearly disclose the price of services, and the Funeral Rule, which requires funeral directors to disclose price and other information about their services to consumers.

### The Division of Planning and Information

The Division of Planning and Information helps consumers get information. This Division runs the Consumer Response Center, with counselors who respond to consumer complaints and requests for information. It also supervises the Identity Theft Data Clearinghouse, with staff who tell consumers how to protect themselves from identity theft and what to do if their identity has been stolen. Additionally, this division manages the Consumer Sentinel, a secure, online database and cyber tool available to hundreds of civil and criminal law enforcement agencies in the United States and abroad.

## Bureau of Economics

The Bureau of Economics helps the FTC evaluate the economic impact of its actions. To do so, the Bureau provides economic analysis and support to antitrust and consumer protection investigations and rulemakings. It also analyzes the impact of government regulation on competition and consumers and provides Congress, the **Executive Branch** and the public with economic analysis of market processes as they relate to antitrust, consumer protection, and regulation.

This Bureau provides guidance and support to the agency's antitrust and consumer protection enforcement activities. In the antitrust area, the Bureau participates in the investigation of alleged anticompetitive acts or practices and provides advice on the economic merits of alternative antitrust actions. If an enforcement action is initiated, the Bureau integrates economic analysis into the proceeding (sometimes providing the expert witness at trial) and works with the Bureau of Competition to devise appropriate remedies. In the consumer protection area, this bureau provides economic support and analysis of potential commission actions in both cases and rulemakings handled by the Bureau of Consumer Protection. Bureau economists also provide analysis of appropriate **penalty** levels to deter activity that harms consumers.

The Bureau of Economics also conducts economic analysis of various markets and industries. This work focuses on the economic effects of regulation and on issues important to antitrust and consumer protection policy. Many of these analyses are published as staff reports.

## Bureau Of Competition

The Bureau of Competition prevents anticompetitive mergers and other anticompetitive business practices in the marketplace. The bureau fulfills this role by reviewing proposed mergers and other busi-

ness practices for possible anticompetitive effects, and, when appropriate, recommending that the commission take formal law enforcement action to protect consumers. The bureau also serves as a research and policy resource on competition topics and provides guidance to business on complying with the antitrust laws.

### Antitrust Laws

The bureau protects competition through enforcement of the antitrust laws. These laws include: Section 5 of the Federal Trade Commission Act, which prohibits unfair methods of competition, Section 1 of the Sherman Act, which outlaws every contract, combination, or **conspiracy**, in restraint of trade, Section 2 of the Sherman Act, which makes it unlawful for a company to monopolize, or attempt to monopolize, trade or commerce, Section 7 of the **Clayton Act**, which prohibits mergers and acquisitions the effect of which may be substantially to lessen competition or to tend to create a **monopoly**, and Section 7A of the Clayton Act (added in 1976 by the Hart-Scott-Rodino Antitrust Improvements Act), which requires companies to notify antitrust agencies before certain planned mergers.

### Mergers

Most mergers actually benefit competition and consumers by allowing firms to operate more efficiently. In a competitive market, firms pass on these lower costs to consumers. But some mergers, by reducing competition, can cost consumers many millions of dollars every year in the form of higher prices and reduced product quality, consumer choice, and innovation. The Bureau of Competition reviews mergers to determine which ones have the potential to harm consumers; thoroughly investigates those that may be troublesome; and recommends enforcement action to the commission when necessary to protect competition and consumers. The FTC challenges only a small percentage of mergers each year. Various remedies may be suitable for transactions that pose antitrust concerns. These include **settlement**, litigation, or **abandonment** of the transaction by the parties.

## FTC Litigation

Typically, FTC investigations are non-public to protect both the investigation and the companies involved. If the FTC believes that a person or company has violated the law or that a proposed merger may violate the law, the agency may attempt to obtain voluntary compliance by entering into a consent order with the company. A company that signs a consent order need not admit that it violated the law, but it must agree to stop the disputed practices outlined in an accompanying complaint or undertake certain obligations to resolve the anticompetitive aspects of its proposed merger. If a consent agreement cannot be reached, the FTC may issue an administrative complaint or seek injunctive relief in the federal courts. The FTC's administrative complaints initiate a formal proceeding that is much like a federal court trial but before an administrative law judge. **Evidence** is submitted, **testimony** is heard, and witnesses are examined and cross-examined. If a law violation is found, a **cease and desist order** may be issued. Initial decisions by administrative law judges may be appealed to the full commission. Final decisions issued by the commission may be appealed to the U.S. Court of Appeals and, ultimately, to the U.S. Supreme Court.

In some circumstances, the FTC can go directly to court to obtain an injunction, civil penalties, or consumer **redress**. In the merger enforcement arena, the FTC may seek a **preliminary injunction** to block a proposed merger pending a full **examination** of the proposed transaction in an administrative proceeding. The injunction preserves the market's competitive status quo. The FTC seeks federal court injunctions in consumer protection matters typically in cases of ongoing consumer fraud.

## Additional Resources

*Antitrust Enforcement Agencies: The Antitrust Division of the Department of Justice and the Bureau of Competition of the Federal Trade Commission: Congressional Hearing* Hyde, Henry, DIANE Publishing, 2000.

## Organizations

### American Antitrust Institute

2919 Ellicott Street, NW, Suite 1000
Washington, DC 20008-1022 USA
Phone: (202) 244-9800
URL: http://www.antitrustinstitute.org

### Federal Trade Commission

600 Pennsylvania Avenue, NW
Washington, DC 20580 USA
Phone: (877) FTC-HELP (382-4357)
URL: http://www.ftc.gov

# CONSUMER ISSUES

## IDENTITY THEFT

*Sections within this essay:*

- Background
- How Identity Theft Occurs
- Self-Help Measures
    - Determine Whether Identity Theft Has Occurred
    - Obtain a Credit Report
    - File Fraud Alerts
    - Submit an ID Theft Affidavit
    - Report to Local Police
    - File a Complaint with the Federal Trade Commission
    - Protect Against Identity Theft
- Federal Statutes
    - Identity Theft and Assumption Deterrence Act
    - Identity Theft Penalty Enhancement Act
    - Fair and Accurate Credit Transactions Act
    - Other Statutes
- State Statutes
    - Credit Card Numbers on Receipts
    - Credit Card Skimming
    - Breach of Information
    - Consumer Report Security Freeze
- State Identity Theft Laws
- Additional Resources

## Background

The person becomes the victim of identity theft when someone else uses the person's personal infor-mation to commit **fraud** or other crimes. An individ-ual who commits identity theft may appropriate a name, bank account number, credit card number, social security number, or other personal informa-tion. With the increase in the amount of personal in-formation that is exchanged on the Internet, identity theft has developed into a major concern in the Unit-ed States and abroad.

Both state government and the federal govern-ment have enacted a series of **statutes** that are de-signed to deter identity theft. Many of these statutes increase penalties or expand the roles that law en-forcement officials play in the investigation of identi-ty theft. Other statutes assist victims after their iden-tities have been stolen.

## How Identity Theft Occurs

The Federal Trade Commission (FTC), which serves as a clearinghouse for complaints about iden-tity theft, has identified several means by which an identity thief may perpetrate the crime. These in-clude the following:

- Obtaining personal information of others while on the job
- Hacking personal records
- Bribing or conning an employee who has ac-cess to personal records
- Stealing a victim's wallet or purse
- Stealing personal information through email, phone, or other means, in a practice known as "phishing"

- Stealing credit or debt card numbers by capturing information in a data storage device, in a practice known as "skimming"

- Obtaining a person's credit report

- Rummaging through a person's trash can or the trash can of a business, in a practice known as "dumpster diving"

- Stealing personal information found in a victim's home

- Stealing mail, including bank and credit card statements, offers for new credit cards, new checks, and tax information

- Completing a change of address form so that the victim's mail is sent to another location

Once an identity thief has obtained the personal information of a victim, the perpetrator may engage in a number of activities. Some of these illegal activities include the following:

- Establishing a phone or wireless service in the name of the victim

- Opening new credit card accounts in the victim's name

- Calling credit card companies to change the billing address of the victim's account (so that the victim will not receive statements)

- Creating counterfeit checks, credit cards, or debit cards

- Authorizing electronic transfers in the victim's name

- Draining bank accounts

- Buying a car or taking out a automobile loan in the victim's name

- Getting a job or filing a fraudulent tax return in the victim's name

- Giving the victim's name to the police during an arrest

## Self-Help Measures

Those who have become the victims of identity theft may take certain actions in order to protect themselves. In some situations, a person may not be aware that he has become a victim; in others, a person may suspect that she has been victimized, but needs to determine whether this is so. The information below summarizes the some of the steps that victims or potential victims of identity theft may take.

### *Determine Whether Identity Theft Has Occurred*

In some instances, identity theft will be obvious to the victim. A victim may receive a telephone call from a creditor after an identity thief has opened an account in the victim's name. In other circumstances, the victim may notice unusual charges on his or her credit card statement or unauthorized withdrawals from a checking or savings account.

Even where identity theft is not immediately obvious, a victim may experience other signs that this theft has taken place. For example, the victim may stop receiving bills or other mail, indicating that an identity thief has submitted a change of address form for the victim. Similarly, a victim may be denied credit for no apparent reason or may receive credit cards for which the victim did not apply.

### *Obtain a Credit Report*

Three nationwide consumer credit reporting companies, also referred to as credit bureaus, maintain credit reports about each consumer. These companies maintain such information as how many accounts a consumer has and whether the consumer has paid his or her bills on time. The three companies include the following: Equifax, Experian, and TransUnion. Contact information for these companies is available under "Organizations" at the conclusion of this essay.

Under amendments to the federal Fair Credit Reporting Act, passed in November 2003, each of these credit bureaus must provide every consumer with a free copy of the consumer's credit report. The credit report cannot be obtained directly from the credit bureaus, however. Instead, these reports must be obtained through one of the following: online at www.annualcreditreport.com; via phone at 1-877-322-8228; or by submitting a form to Annual Credit Report Request Service, P.O. Box 105281, Atlanta, Georgia, 30348-5281.

In some instances under federal law, a consumer is entitled to additional free reports, such as when a company denies credit to a consumer. Moreover, some states provide for free access to credit reports. Otherwise, consumers may pay up to $9.95 to order a credit report from one of the reporting services.

### *File a Fraud Alert*

Each of the three major credit bureaus maintains a fraud department. A consumer who is the victim of identity theft should contact the fraud department of one of the credit bureaus and ask that the company place a fraud alert on the consumer's account. Once a consumer has contacted one of these bureaus, this bureau is required to contact the other two.

This fraud alert indicates to a creditor that the creditor must contact the consumer before opening a new account or changing an existing account. If the consumer requests, the credit bureaus may only display the last four digits of the consumer's social security number on the credit reports.

### Submit an ID Theft Affidavit

When an identity thief opens a new unauthorized account, the victim may dispute the opening of the account. The Federal Trade Commission has prepared an ID Theft Affidavit that may be used when a consumer reports fraudulent activity and disputes an account. The ID Theft Affidavit is available at http://www.consumer.gov/idtheft/pdf/affidavit.pdf.

### Report to Local Police

A victim of identity theft should file a report with the victim's local police or the police in the community where the theft took place. The victim should submit a copy of the police report, or at least the number of the report, to creditors and anyone else who might require proof that the crime has occurred.

### File a Complaint with the Federal Trade Commission

A victim should submit a complaint with the FTC, which maintains a database of information regarding identity theft cases. Law enforcement agencies use this database during investigations. The FTC also uses this information in order to gather more data about identity theft in an effort to address the problem as a whole.

### Manage Personal Information

The FTC and others warn consumers that they should take active steps to protect their personal information. For credit card, bank, and phone accounts, consumers should create a password that a thief cannot guess. Similarly, a consumer should not give out personal information, via computer or otherwise, to anyone unless the consumer knows with whom he or she is dealing.

## Federal Statutes

Congress has enacted a number of statutes that address identity theft. Some of these statutes focus on criminal sanctions for identity theft, while others focus more on protecting the victims of identity theft crimes.

### Identity Theft and Assumption Deterrence Act

The Identity Theft and Assumption Deterrence Act was promulgated in 1998 to establish identity theft as a federal crime. Under this law, a person who commits identity theft faces a maximum of 15 years in prison and/or a fine. The maximum term of imprisonment increases under some circumstances, such as when identity theft occurs in connection with drug trafficking or as a means to facilitate international terrorism. The statute also requires the FTC to receive complaints from individuals who have been victims of identity theft (discussed above).

Prior to the enactment of this statute, federal law only applied to the theft of identification documents and not identifying information. The 1998 law extends its application to the theft of "means of identification," which may include any of the following:

* Name

* Social security number

* Date of birth

* Official state or government issued driver's license or identification number

* Alien registration number

* Government passport number

* Employer or taxpayer identification number

* Unique biometric data, including a fingerprint, a voice print, a retina or iris image, or another unique physical representation

* A unique electronic identification number, address, or routing code

* Telecommunication identifying information or access device.

### Identity Theft Penalty Enhancement Act

In 2004, President George W. Bush signed the Identity Theft Penalty Enhancement Act. The statute strengthens penalties for those who possess someone else's personal information with the intent to use the information to commit a crime. Penalties are further enhanced when the identity theft is done to commit an act of terrorism.

### Fair and Accurate Credit Transactions Act

Congress passed the Fair and Accurate Credit Transactions Act in 2003 in an effort to prevent identity theft, among other purposes. The statute provides that consumers may request that the credit bureaus place fraud alerts on their accounts. The act also specifies that only the last five digits of a credit card number may appear on an electronically printed receipt. Moreover, this statute directs the FTC to prepare a model summary of the rights of consumers with respect to procedures to remedy fraud or identity theft.

### Other Statutes

Several other federal statutes have been enacted in an effort to combat identity theft. Some of these statutes limit the financial liability of identity theft victims. Others prohibit the release of personal information, including social security numbers.

## State Statutes

The various states have enacted several types of statutes that apply to identity theft cases. The following are some of the more common types of identity theft statutes.

### Credit Card Numbers on Receipts

As of 2005, the majority of states have enacted pieces of legislation that restrict the number of digits that may be printed on electronic receipts. Most states prohibit merchants from printing more than four or five digits, and several prohibit merchants from printing the card's expiration date. Some statutes limit the type of information that may be displayed in a receipt, restricting such data as a consumer's name or telephone number.

### Credit Card Skimming

About half of the states have approved legislation that criminalizes the unauthorized use of encoded credit card information. In some states, such as Texas, the statute requires restaurants and bars to post signs warning employees against fraudulent use of or possession of identifying information.

### Breach of Information

Approximately 17 states as of 2005 have enacted statutes that require state agencies and companies to disclose security breaches that involve the potential release of personal information of consumers. In some instances, these breaches have compromised personal information of hundreds of thousands of individuals. These statutes provide notification to those who potentially could be the victims of identity theft as a result of such a breach.

### Consumer Report Security Freeze

Some states allow victims of identity theft to demand that credit reporting services freeze the vic-

tims' credit reports. The provisions of these statues are similar to those found in the federal Fair and Accurate Credit Transactions Act.

### Anti-Phishing

California in 2005 became the first state to enact legislation that addresses phishing, which is a practice of duping Internet users into divulging personal information. Congressional attempts to enact similar legislation failed in Congress in 2004 and 2005.

## State Identity Theft Laws

ALABAMA: The Consumer Identity Protection Act makes identity theft either a felony or a misdemeanor, depending on whether the defendant has had a prior conviction and the amount of financial loss involved with the theft.

ALASKA: The state's statute addressing theft by deception makes identity theft either a felony or a misdemeanor, depending on the circumstances.

ARIZONA: The state has enacted legislation addressing credit card numbers on receipts and credit card skimming. The state's statute addressing theft by deception makes identity theft a felony.

ARKANSAS: The state has enacted legislation addressing credit card skimming and breach of information. The state's statute addressing financial identity fraud makes identity theft a felony.

CALIFORNIA: The state has enacted legislation addressing credit card numbers on receipts, credit card skimming and breach of information. The state's statute addressing identity theft provides for both a fine and a jail term.

COLORADO: The state has enacted legislation addressing credit card numbers on receipts.

CONNECTICUT: The state has enacted legislation addressing breach of information. The state's statute addressing identity theft makes identity theft a felony.

DELAWARE: The state has enacted legislation addressing credit card numbers on receipts, credit card skimming, and breach of information. The state's statute addressing identity theft makes identity theft a felony.

FLORIDA: The state has enacted legislation addressing credit card numbers on receipts, credit card skimming, and breach of information. The state's statute addressing criminal use of personal identification information makes identity theft either a felony or a misdemeanor, depending on the circumstances.

GEORGIA: The state has enacted legislation addressing credit card numbers on receipts and breach of information. The state's statute addressing financial identity fraud makes identity theft a crime punishable by either a fine or a term of imprisonment.

HAWAII: The state's statute addressing identity theft makes identity theft a felony.

IDAHO: The state has enacted legislation addressing credit card numbers on receipts and credit card skimming. The state's statute addressing misappropriation of personal identifying information makes identity theft a misdemeanor or a felony, depending on the circumstances.

ILLINOIS: The state has enacted legislation addressing credit card numbers on receipts, credit card skimming and breach of information. The state's statute addressing identity theft makes identity theft a misdemeanor or a felony, depending on the circumstances.

INDIANA: The state has enacted legislation addressing breach of information. The state's statute addressing identity theft makes identity theft a felony.

IOWA: The state has enacted legislation addressing credit card skimming. The state's statute addressing identity theft makes identity theft a misdemeanor or a felony, depending on the circumstances.

KANSAS: The state has enacted legislation addressing credit card numbers on receipts. The state's statute addressing identity theft makes identity theft a felony.

KENTUCKY: The state has enacted legislation addressing credit card numbers on receipts and credit card skimming. The state's statute addressing identity theft makes identity theft a crime subject to a fine or term of imprisonment.

LOUISIANA: The state has enacted legislation addressing credit card numbers on receipts, credit card skimming, and breach of information. The state's statute addressing identity theft makes identity theft a felony.

MAINE: The state has enacted legislation addressing credit card numbers on receipts, credit card skimming, and breach of information. The state's

statute addressing misuse of identification makes identity theft a class D crime.

MARYLAND: The state has enacted legislation addressing credit card numbers on receipts. The state's statute addressing identity theft makes identity fraud a misdemeanor or a felony, depending on the circumstances.

MASSACHUSETTS: The state's statute addressing identity theft makes identity theft a felony.

MICHIGAN: The state has enacted legislation addressing credit card skimming. The state's statute addressing identity theft makes identity theft a felony.

MINNESOTA: The state has enacted legislation addressing breach of information. The state's statute addressing identity theft makes identity theft a crime punishable by a fine or jail term.

MISSISSIPPI: The state has enacted legislation addressing credit card skimming. The state's statute addressing fraudulent use of identity makes identity theft a crime punishable by a fine or jail term.

MISSOURI: The state has enacted legislation addressing credit card numbers on receipts and credit card skimming. The state's statute addressing identity theft makes identity theft either a felony or a misdemeanor depending on the circumstances.

MONTANA: The state has enacted legislation addressing breach of information. The state's statute addressing identity theft makes identity theft a crime punishable by a fine or a jail term.

NEBRASKA: The state has enacted legislation addressing credit card numbers on receipts. The state's statute addressing criminal impersonation makes identity theft either a misdemeanor or a felony depending on the circumstances.

NEVADA: The state has enacted legislation addressing credit card numbers on receipts, credit card skimming and breach of information. The state's statute addressing identity theft makes identity theft a felony.

NEW HAMPSHIRE: The state has enacted legislation addressing credit card skimming. The state's statute addressing identity theft makes identity theft a felony.

NEW JERSEY: The state has enacted legislation addressing credit card numbers on receipts, credit card skimming, and breach of information. The state's statute addressing identity theft makes identity theft a crime punishable by fine or jail term.

NEW MEXICO: The state has enacted legislation addressing credit card numbers on receipts. The state's statute addressing identity theft makes identity theft a misdemeanor.

NEW YORK: The state has enacted legislation addressing credit card numbers on receipts and breach of information. The state's statute addressing identity theft makes identity theft either a felony or a misdemeanor, depending on the circumstances.

NORTH CAROLINA: The state has enacted legislation addressing credit card numbers on receipts and breach of information. The state's statute addressing fraudulent identity fraud makes identity theft a felony.

NORTH DAKOTA: The state has enacted legislation addressing credit card numbers on receipts and breach of information. The state's statute addressing identity theft makes identity theft a felony.

OHIO: The state's statute addressing identity theft makes identity theft either a felony or a misdemeanor depending on the circumstances.

OKLAHOMA: The state has enacted legislation addressing credit card numbers on receipts. The state's statute addressing identity theft makes identity theft a felony.

OREGON: The state has enacted legislation addressing credit card numbers on receipts and credit card skimming. The state's statute addressing identity theft makes identity theft a felony.

PENNSYLVANIA: The state's statute addressing identity theft makes identity theft either a felony or a misdemeanor depending on the circumstances.

RHODE ISLAND: The state has enacted legislation addressing credit card numbers on receipts and breach of information. The state's Impersonation and Identity Fraud Act makes identity theft a crime punishable by fine or jail term.

SOUTH CAROLINA: The state's Personal Financial Security Act makes identity theft a felony.

SOUTH DAKOTA: The state has enacted legislation addressing credit card skimming. The state's statute addressing identity theft makes identity theft a misdemeanor.

TENNESSEE: The state has enacted legislation addressing credit card numbers on receipts and breach of information. The state's statute addressing identity theft makes identity theft either a felony or a misdemeanor depending on the circumstances.

TEXAS: The state has enacted legislation addressing credit card numbers on receipts, credit card skimming, and breach of information. The state's statute addressing identity theft makes identity theft a felony.

UTAH: The state has enacted legislation addressing credit card skimming. The state's statute addressing identity theft makes identity theft either a felony or a misdemeanor depending on the circumstances.

VERMONT: The state's statute addressing identity theft makes identity theft either a felony or a misdemeanor depending on the circumstances.

VIRGINIA: The state has enacted legislation addressing credit card numbers on receipts and credit card skimming. The state's statute addressing identity theft makes identity theft either a felony or a misdemeanor depending on the circumstances.

WASHINGTON: The state has enacted legislation addressing credit card numbers on receipts, credit card skimming, and breach of information. The state's statute addressing identity theft makes identity theft a felony.

WEST VIRGINIA: The state has enacted legislation addressing credit card skimming. The state's statute addressing identity theft makes identity theft a felony.

WISCONSIN: The state's statute addressing misappropriation of personal identifying information makes identity theft a felony.

WYOMING: The state has enacted legislation addressing credit card skimming. The state's statute addressing identity theft makes identity theft either a felony or a misdemeanor depending on the circumstances.

## Additional Resources

*Identity Theft: A Legal Research Guide.* Best, Reba A., William S. Hein & Co., Inc., 2004.

"Take Charge: Fighting Back Against Identity Theft." Federal Trade Commission, 2004. Available at http://www.ftc.gov/bcp/conline/pubs/credit/idtheft.htm.

## Organizations

### *Equifax Information Services, LLC*
P.O. Box 740241
Atlanta, GA 30374 USA

Phone: (800) 685-1111
URL: http://www.equifax.com

### Experian

P.O. Box 2002
Allen, TX 75013 USA
Phone: (888) 397-3742
URL: http://www.experian.com

### Federal Trade Commission

600 Pennsylvania Avenue, N.W.
Washington, DC 20580 USA
URL: http://www.ftc.gov

### National Conference of State Legislatures

444 North Capitol Street, N.W., Suite 515
Washington, DC 20001 USA
Phone: (202) 624-5400
Fax: (202) 737-1069
URL: http://www.ncsl.org

### TransUnion

P.O. Box 1000
Chester, PA 19022 USA
Phone: (800) 888-4213
URL: http://www.transunion.com/index.jsp

# CONSUMER ISSUES

## MAIL-ORDER PURCHASES/ TELEMARKETING

*Sections within this essay:*

- Background

- Direct Mail
  - Deceptive Mail Prevention and Enforcement Act
  - 900 Telephone Number Solicitations
  - Solicitations Disguised As Invoices
  - Sexually Oriented Mail Solicitations

- Telephone Solicitation
  - The Telephone Consumer Protection Act
  - Automatic Telephone Dialing Systems
  - Do Not Call Lists

- The Federal Trade Commission
  - Mail or Telephone Order Rule
  - Bureau of Consumer Protection
  - Obligations of Publishers and Agencies

- FTC Litigation

- Additional Resources

## Background

Mail order advertising has its roots in the 1800s, when Richard Sears, a railroad clerk in Minnesota, found himself with an abandoned case of pocket watches. Using his list of other railroad clerks throughout the Midwest, he marketed these watches and quickly sold them. Sears recognized immediately

that an entrepreneur with a list of accurate names and addresses and a stock of quality merchandise no longer needed a store. He only needed a good message delivery vehicle and first-rate customer service. And so began the company that would later become known as Sears Roebuck. With the advent of the telephone, telemarketing followed suit. Along with direct mail and telemarketing came governmental regulation.

## Direct Mail

The U.S. Postal Inspection Service is the law enforcement branch of the U.S. Postal Service, empowered by federal laws and regulations to investigate and enforce over 200 federal statutes related to crimes against the U.S. Mail, the Postal Service, and its employees. Postal inspectors investigate any crime in which the U.S. Mail is used to further a scheme, whether it originated in the mail, by telephone or on the Internet. The illegal use of the U.S. Mail determines a **mail fraud**. If **evidence** of a postal-related violation exists, postal inspectors may seek prosecutive or administrative action against a violator. Postal inspectors base their investigations of mail **fraud** on the number, pattern and substance of complaints received from the public.

### *Deceptive Mail Prevention and Enforcement Act*

The Deceptive Mail Prevention and Enforcement Act of 1999 requires mailings to clearly display on rules and order forms, that no purchase is necessary to enter contest and state that a purchase does not improve the chance of winning. They must state the terms and conditions of the sweepstakes promotion, including rules and entry procedures; the sponsor or mailer of the promotion and principal place of business, or other contact address of sponsor or mailer; estimated odds of winning each prize; the quantity, estimated retail value, and nature of each prize; and the schedule of any payments made over time. The act imposes requirements for mail related to skill contests mailings, which must disclose the number of rounds, cost to enter each round, whether subsequent rounds will be more difficult, and the maximum cost to enter all rounds; the percentage of entrants who may solve correctly the skill contest; the identity of the judges and the method used in judging; the date the winner will be determined, as well as quantity and estimated value of each prize. The law imposes new federal standards on facsimile checks sent in any mailing. The checks must include a statement on the check itself that it is non-negotiable and has no cash value. The law prohibits mailings that imply a connection to, approval of, or endorsement by the federal government through the misleading use of a seal, insignia, reference to the postmaster general, **citation** to a federal statue, trade or brand name, or any other term or symbol, unless the mailings carry two disclaimers. The law requires companies sending sweepstakes or skill contests to establish a system and include in their mailings a telephone number or address, which consumers could use to have themselves removed from the mailing lists of such companies. The U.S. Postal Inspection Service is responsible for investigating cases of fraud when the U.S. Mail is used as part of the scheme.

### 900 Telephone Number Solicitations

The 900 telephone numbers, in which the caller pays a fee per minute, have been used by legitimate entities; however, some mailings attempt to lure consumers into calling a 900 number claiming the consumer has won a sweepstakes or prize. Other 900 number solicitations offer products or services, such as credit repair or a travel package. People with bad credit who hope to receive a credit card by calling a 900 number might receive a list of banks to which they can apply for such a card. Those who are told to call because they're winners in a sweepstakes may receive nothing but a charge on a phone bill. Sometimes, a call to a 900 number requires the consumer to listen to a long recorded sales pitch, resulting in a high phone charge.

### Solicitations Disguised as Invoices

Title 39, United States Code, Section 3001, makes it illegal to mail a **solicitation** in the form of an invoice, bill, or statement of account due unless it con-

spicuously bears a notice on its face that it is, in fact, merely a solicitation. This disclaimer must be in very large (at least 30-point) type and must be in boldface capital letters in a color that contrasts prominently with the background against which it appears. The disclaimer must not be modified, qualified, or explained, such as with the phrase "Legal notice required by law." It must be the one prescribed in the **statute**, or alternatively, the following notice prescribed by the U.S. Postal Service: THIS IS NOT A BILL. THIS IS A SOLICITATION. YOU ARE UNDER NO OBLIGATION TO PAY THE AMOUNT STATED ABOVE UNLESS YOU ACCEPT THIS OFFER. Some solicitations disguise their true nature. Others identify themselves as solicitations, but only in the "fine print." A solicitation whose appearance does not conform to the requirements of Title 39, United States Code, Section 3001, constitutes prima facie evidence of violation of the federal False Representation Statute. Therefore, solicitations in the form of invoices, bills, or statements of account due which do not contain the large and conspicuous disclaimer required by the law will not be carried or delivered by mail if they come to the attention of the Postal Service, and will be disposed of as the Postal Service shall direct.

### Sexually Oriented Mail Solicitations

Consumers can have their names and the names of their minor children placed on a United States Postal Department list of persons who do not want to receive unsolicited sexually oriented advertisements through the mail. Form 1500, Application for Listing and/or Prohibitory Order, is available at any local post office. Thirty days after protection begins, any mailer who sends the consumer sexually oriented advertisements may be subject to civil and criminal sanctions. Name will remain on the list for five years.

## Telephone Solicitation

A telephone solicitation is a telephone call that acts as an advertisement. In some cases unlisted or non-listed numbers can be obtained from a directory assistance operator. They, along with non-published numbers, may be sold to other organizations. Some sales organizations call all numbers in numerical order for a neighborhood or area. The FCC's rules prohibit telephone solicitation calls to homes before 8 am or after 9 p.m. A person placing a telephone solicitation call must provide his or her name, the name of the person or entity on whose behalf the call is being made, and a telephone number or address at which that person or entity may be contacted. The term telephone solicitation does not include calls or messages placed with the receiver's prior consent, regarding a tax-exempt non-profit organization, or from a person or organization with which the receiver has an established business relationship. An established business relationship exists if the consumer has made an inquiry, application, purchase, or transaction regarding products or services offered by the person or entity involved.

### The Telephone Consumer Protection Act

The Telephone **Consumer Protection** Act of 1991 (TCPA) was enacted by Congress to reduce the nuisance and invasion of privacy caused by telemarketing and prerecorded calls. Congress ordered the FCC to make and clarify certain regulations. The TCPA imposes restrictions on the use of automatic telephone dialing systems, of artificial or prerecorded voice messages, and of telephone facsimile machines to send unsolicited advertisements. Specifically, the TCPA prohibits autodialed and prerecorded voice message calls to emergency lines, health care facilities or similar establishments, and numbers assigned to radio common carrier services or any service for which the called party is charged for the call. The TCPA also prohibits artificial or prerecorded voice message calls to residences made without prior express consent. Telephone facsimile machines may not transmit unsolicited advertisements. Those using telephone facsimile machines or transmitting artificial or prerecorded voice messages are subject to certain identification requirements. Finally, the TCPA requires that the Commission consider several methods to accommodate telephone subscribers who do not wish to receive unsolicited advertisements, including live voice solicitations. The statute also outlines various remedies for violations of the TCPA.

### Automatic Telephone Dialing Systems

Automatic telephone dialing systems, also known as autodialers, generate a lot of consumer complaints. Autodialers produce, store, and dial telephone numbers using a random or sequential number generator. Autodialers are usually used to place artificial (computerized) or prerecorded voice calls. Autodialers and any artificial or prerecorded voice messages may not be used to contact numbers assigned to any emergency telephone line, the telephone line of any guest or patient room at a hospital, health care facility, cellular telephone service, or other radio common carrier service. Calls using au-

todialers or artificial or prerecorded voice messages may be placed to businesses, although the FCC's rules prohibit the use of autodialers in a way that ties up two or more lines of a multi-line business at the same time.

If an autodialer is used to deliver an artificial or prerecorded voice message, that message must state, at the beginning, the identity of the business, individual, or other entity initiating the call. During or after the message, the caller must give the telephone number (other than that of the autodialer or prerecorded message player that placed the call) or address of the business, other entity, or individual that made the call. It may not be a 900 number or any other number for which charges exceed local or long distance transmission charges. Autodialers that deliver a recorded message must release the called party's telephone line within 5 seconds of the time that the calling system receives notification that the called party's line has hung up.

### Do Not Call Lists

The FCC requires a person or entity placing live telephone solicitations to maintain a record of any consumer request not to receive future telephone solicitations from that person or entity. A record of a do-not-call request must be maintained for ten years. This request should also stop calls from affiliated entities if individuals would reasonably expect them to be included, given the identification of the caller and the product being advertised. Tax-exempt non-profit organizations are not required to keep do-not-call lists. The Direct Marketing Association (DMA) sponsors the Telephone Preference Service (TPS) which maintains a do-no-call list. DMA members are required to use this list. Registration is free and the request remains on file for 5 years. Finally, as of 2002, many states had statewide no-call lists for residents in that state.

Some states permit consumers to file law suits against violators who continue to call despite the consumer being on a no-call list. Consumers can sometimes seek **punitive damages** if the caller willfully and knowingly violated do-not-call requirements. States themselves may initiate a civil suit in federal district court against any person or entity that engages in a pattern or practice of violations of the TCPA or FCC rules. While the FCC may not award monetary or other damages, it can give citations or fines to those violating the TCPA or other FCC rules regarding unsolicited telephone marketing calls. Consumers who file complaints with the FCC retain their private right of action.

## The Federal Trade Commission

One of the most important enforcement agencies for direct marketers is the Federal Trade Commission (FTC), which enforces federal consumer protection laws passed by Congress and which has the authority to adopt regulations and rules interpreting and implementing those laws. There are rules on marketing to children online, on regulations for distance selling delivery requirements, for telemarketing, and many other subjects. Each of the states has similar powers and authority, usually under the office of the state's attorney general, the chief law enforcement officer of the state. The Federal Trade Commission (FTC) Telemarketing Sales Rule requires certain disclosures and prohibits misrepresentations. The Rule covers most types of telemarketing calls to consumers, including calls to pitch goods, services, sweepstakes, prize promotions, and investment opportunities. It also applies to calls consumers make in response to postcards or other materials received in the mail. Calling times are restricted to the hours between 8 a.m. and 9 p.m. Telemarketers must disclose that it is a sales call and for which company. It is illegal for telemarketers to misrepresent any information, including facts about goods or services, earnings potential, profitability, risk or liquidity of an investment, or the nature of a prize in a prize-promotion scheme. Telemarketers must disclose the total cost of the products or services offered and all restrictions on getting or using them, and that a sale is final or non-refundable.

The FTC works to ensure that the nation's markets are efficient and free of practices which might harm consumers. To ensure the smooth operation of a free market system, the FTC enforces federal consumer protection laws that make illegal fraud, deception, and unfair business practices. The Federal Trade Commission Act allows the FTC to act in the interest of all consumers to prevent deceptive and unfair acts or practices. In interpreting the Act, the Commission has determined that, with respect to advertising, a representation, omission, or practice is deceptive if it is likely to mislead consumers and affect consumers' behavior or decisions about the product or service. In addition, an act or practice is unfair if the injury it causes, or is likely to cause, is substantial, not outweighed by other benefits, and not reasonably avoidable.

The FTC Act's prohibition on unfair or deceptive acts or practices broadly covers advertising claims, marketing and promotional activities, and sales practices in general. The Act is not limited to any particular medium. Accordingly, the Commission's role in protecting consumers from unfair or deceptive acts or practices encompasses advertising, marketing, and sales online, as well as the same activities in print, television, telephone, and radio. For certain industries or subject areas, the Commission issues rules and guides. Rules prohibit specific acts or practices that the Commission has found to be unfair or deceptive. Guides help businesses in their efforts to comply with the law by providing examples or direction on how to avoid unfair or deceptive acts or practices. Many rules and guides address claims about products or services or advertising in general and are not limited to any particular medium used to disseminate those claims or advertising. Therefore, the plain language of many rules and guides applies to claims made on the Internet. Solicitations made in print, on the telephone, radio, TV or online fall within the rule's scope.

### Mail or Telephone Order Rule

Shopping by phone or mail is a convenient alternative to shopping at a store. By law, a company must ship a consumer's order within the time stated in its ads. If no time is promised, the company should ship the order within 30 days after receiving it. If the company is unable to ship within the promised time, it must provide the consumer with an option notice. This notice gives the consumer the choice of agreeing to the delay or canceling the order and receiving a prompt refund. If a company does not promise a shipping time and the consumer is applying for credit, the company has 50 days to ship after receiving the order.

### Bureau of Consumer Protection

The FTC's Bureau of Consumer Protection protects consumers against unfair, deceptive, or **fraudulent** practices. The Bureau enforces a variety of consumer protection laws enacted by Congress, as well as trade regulation rules issued by the Commission. Its actions include individual company and industry-wide investigations, administrative and federal court **litigation**, rulemaking proceedings, and consumer and business education. In addition, the Bureau contributes to the Commission's on-going efforts to inform Congress and other government entities of the impact that proposed actions could have on consumers. The Bureau of Consumer Protection is divided into six divisions and programs, each with its own areas of expertise. One of the divisions is the Division of Advertising Practices.

Within the Bureau of Consumer Protection is the Division of Advertising Practices and the Division of

Enforcement. These entities are the nation's enforcers of federal truth-in-advertising laws. The FTC Act prohibits unfair or deceptive advertising in any medium. That is, advertising must tell the truth and not mislead consumers. A claim can be misleading if relevant information is left out or if the claim implies something that is not true. In addition, claims must be substantiated especially when they concern health, safety, or performance. The type of evidence may depend on the product, the claims, and what experts believe necessary. Sellers are responsible for claims they make about their products and services. Third parties such as advertising agencies or website designers and catalog marketers also may be liable for making or disseminating deceptive representations if they participate in the preparation or distribution of the advertising, or know about the deceptive claims.

### Obligations of Publishers and Agencies

Advertising agencies (and more recently, website designers) are responsible for reviewing the information used to **substantiate** ad claims. These agencies may not simply rely on an advertiser's assurance that the claims are substantiated. In determining whether an ad agency should be held liable, the FTC looks at the extent of the agency's participation in the preparation of the challenged ad, and whether the agency knew or should have known that the ad included false or deceptive claims. Likewise, catalog and magazine publishers can be held responsible for material distributed. Publications may be required to provide documentation to back up assertions made in the advertisement. Repeating what the manufacturer claims about the product is not necessarily sufficient. The Division of Enforcement conducts a wide variety of law enforcement activities to protect consumers, including deceptive marketing practices. This division monitors compliance with Commission cease and desist orders and federal court injunctive orders, investigates violations of consumer protection laws, and enforces a number of trade laws, rules and guides.

## FTC Litigation

Typically, FTC investigations are non-public to protect both the investigation and the companies involved. If the FTC believes that a person or company has violated the law, the agency may attempt to obtain voluntary compliance by entering into a consent order with the company. A company that signs a consent order need not admit that it violated the law, but it must agree to stop the disputed practices outlined in an accompanying complaint. If a consent agreement cannot be reached, the FTC may issue an administrative complaint or seek injunctive relief in the federal courts. The FTC's administrative complaints initiate a formal proceeding that is much like a federal court trial but before an administrative law judge: Evidence is submitted, **testimony** is heard, and witnesses are examined and cross-examined. If a law violation is found, a **cease and desist order** may be issued. Initial decisions by administrative law judges may be appealed to the full Commission. Final decisions issued by the Commission may be appealed to the U.S. Court of Appeals and, ultimately, to the U.S. Supreme Court. In some circumstances, the FTC can go directly to court to obtain an injunction, civil penalties or consumer **redress**. The injunction preserves the market's competitive status quo. The FTC seeks federal court injunctions in consumer protection matters typically in cases of ongoing consumer fraud.

## Additional Resources

*Advertising: Principles and Practice* Wells, William, Prentice Hall, 1999.

*Copywriting for the Electronic Media: A Practical Guide* Meeske, Milan, Wadsworth Publishing Company, 1999.

*Trust Us, We're Experts: How Industry Manipulates Science and Gambles with Your Future* Rampton, Sheldon and John Stauber, Putnam, 2000.

## Organizations

### The Council of Better Business Bureaus
4200 Wilson Blvd., Suite 800
Arlington, VA 22203-1838 USA
Phone: (703) 276-0100
Fax: (703) 525-8277
URL: http://www.bbb.org

### Direct Marketing Association
P.O. Box 9014
Farmingdale, NY 11735 USA
URL: www.the-dma.org

### Federal Communications Commission
445 12th Street SW
Washington, DC 20554 USA
Phone: (888) CALL-FCC
Fax: (202) 418-0232
URL: http://www.fcc.gov

**Federal Trade Commission**
600 Pennsylvania Avenue, NW
Washington, DC 20580 USA
Phone: (877) FTC-HELP
URL: http://www.ftc.gov

# CONSUMER ISSUES

## OMBUDSMAN PROGRAMS

*Sections within this essay:*

- Background
- Three Basic Types of Ombuds
- Ombudsmen Programs as Impetus for Change
- Attributes and Traits of Ombuds
- Public Sector Programs
    - United States Ombudsman Association (USOA)
- Special Interests
    - Elder Rights
    - Child Welfare
    - Juvenile Corrections
    - Adult Corrections
    - Workers' Compensation
    - Small Business
    - Students
    - Environmental Protection
    - Consumer Affairs
    - Insurance and Banking
- Private Sector Programs and Organizations
    - International Ombudsman Association
    - National Credit Union Administration
- Additional Resources

## Background

The term "ombudsman" is derived from the Swedish word meaning agent or representative. For as long as governments have existed, there has always been a parallel concern for the fair and equitable treatment of citizens and a guarantee that their rights are protected. The first public sector ombudsman was appointed by the Parliament of Sweden in 1809 with the express charter to protect individual citizen's rights against the excesses of government bureaucracy. The ombudsman was to receive and investigate citizen complaints against administrative acts of the government. The ombudsman concept spread across Europe and then to the United States in the 1960s. This was partly in response to the civil rights movement and citizen efforts for more openness in politics and government activities.

Typically, an ombudsman is a non-partisan, neutral, fact-finding person or office that takes no side in a dispute, but rather recommends solution. However, in broader usage, the term has come to mean more than just an agent or representative, but can also refer to an advocate or trustee who looks after the interests of a particular group or class of persons, and therefore serves as an agent of justice.

Within the United States, the term has taken on broader meaning that represents departure from the original Swedish model. While denoting an intermediary serving between citizens and the government, the term is now also used to describe any machinery adopted by private organizations (e.g., educational institutions of higher learning, large business corporations) or government to investigate complaints of administrative abuses. They may be been vested with general or special jurisdiction over specific governmental functions (e.g., corrections), and may exercise advocacy in their recommendations, if granted such authority.

Throughout federal and state governments today, public ombudsmen offices have been specially created (by legislative, executive, or judicial authority) to act as independent agencies monitoring the delivery of government services to certain populations (e.g., the elderly, disabled, juveniles, incarcerated adults, government employees, etc.) An ombudsman is generally independent (although a government employee), impartial, universally accessible, and empowered only to assess and make recommendations. The American Bar Association (ABA) defines an ombudsman as "a government official who hears and investigates complaints by private citizens against government agencies."

## Three Basic Types of Ombuds

Traditional ombuds (the gender-neutral and simpler term used for "ombudspersons") operate in the public sector, and many are public employees. They typically address issues raised by members of the general public (or within their organization), usually concerning the actions or policies of a branch of government or of public officials.

Organizational ombuds are found in both public and private sectors. They typically address the concerns presented by members, employees, or contractors of a particular organization or entity concerning its policies or practices.

Advocate ombuds are also found in both public and private sectors, and also evaluate claims or complaints objectively. However, they typically are authorized or even required to advocate on behalf of individuals or groups found to be aggrieved. Importantly, and unique from other ombuds, an advocate ombud may have additional vested powers to represent an aggrieved party and litigate a problem on behalf of that party.

## Ombudsmen Programs as Impetus for Change

One of the key roles of an ombudsman is to consider how issues and problems in individual cases may require system-wide change in order to impact organizational culture. The independence of an ombudsman's office gives it the credibility, respect, and ability to aggregate individual grievances and cases, and use them to promote systemic change at the top administrative levels. A systems change approach emphasizes monitoring performance, assessing outcome, and ensuring public accountability. It also promotes cross-agency collaboration and partnership to provide coordinated and comprehensive service throughout the system.

Typically, ombuds are intermediaries who assess problems and recommend solutions or change. Even though they have limited authority to directly act on a problem, they nonetheless hold powerful positions, because resolution and solution is the quintessential objective of their profession. Without ombuds, an aggrieved individual must travel up the chain of command, management, or supervision to find a sympathetic ear or even an answer. However, since resolving complaints is not the primary function of management within an organization, a response to a complaint is often delegated to administrative staff, and the complaining party may get no further than a "thank you and we'll look into it and get back with you." response.

Conversely, the principal and full-time duty of an ombudsman is to provide a forum for the registering of a complaint or issue, then investigate and assess its merits, and offer recommendations or solutions to the respective parties. Advocate ombuds have additional authority to advocate the complaining party's position. Ultimately, the likelihood of more timely resolution is enhanced by the direct involvement of the ombudsman, whose duties and resources exist for the very purpose of such problem-solving.

Ombudsman programs serve a variety of functions, including educating the community; investigating allegations; monitoring programs, offices and facilities; conducting research; providing recommendations for change or improvement; and, if necessary and so authorized, bringing litigation.

## Attributes and Traits of Ombuds

Probably the most important attribute of the office/position of ombudsman is that of objectivity. This implies and includes:

- the exercise of discretion and confidentiality
- the ability to provide objective leadership
- accessibility
- an absence of any conflicts of interest
- a perseverance to cut through "red tape" and follow through with complaints without getting "stonewalled"

- an ability to dissect fact from hyperbole and get to the bottom line

- an ability to mobilize political power, even if acting "behind the scenes"

Additionally, ombuds should have:

- sufficient statutory authority to carry out investigations and mandate improvement

- ready access to documents, records, witnesses, and subpoena power

- full independence from the agency in which the ombudsman operates

- no interference by officials or administrators of the agency or service provider that is the subject of a complaint

- assurance that the complaining party will suffer no retaliation

- good-faith immunity from civil liability for investigations, recommendations, and mandates

- sufficient funding and resources

- qualified staff, including legal experts to investigate and substantiate violations and subject matter experts.

## Public Sector Programs

There are a few key areas involving the general welfare of the public, for which Congress has created federal ombudsman programs. They generally address the concerns of citizens whose status or condition may warrant extra protection or monitoring of rights. They include the elderly, those requiring long-term care in nursing facilities, juvenile offenders, and children in general. Other specialty ombudsman programs, such as for environmental protection or small business organizations, also have been established at the federal level.

Through special or earmarked funds and grants, federal monies assist many state ombudsman programs in several of the above areas of concern, as well as additional ones (such as workers' compensation or public transportation). In large jurisdictions, the monies may trickle down to local government. New York City holds the unique distinction of being the only geographic entity in the world to have an elected ombudsman.

Where there is no ombudsman office at the state level, inspectors general (including offices of an at-

torney general) and internal affairs programs provide much of the same function. Every state has an inspector general or attorney general, although such positions are more often concerned with systemic problems than individual grievances. However, when state inspectors general receive complaints from more than one individual, they may investigate for more systemic waste or fraud, or they may initiate class action suits on behalf of individuals with similar complaints. These organizations are parallel with ombuds in that they are intended to function independent of an agency's administration or influence.

### United States Ombudsman Association (USOA)

Probably the largest and most important of the public sector ombudsman organizations is the United States Ombudsman Association (USOA). Founded in 1977, it is also the oldest in North America. It serves governmental ombudsman offices across the country as well as member offices in Canada and other global sites. It publishes a legislative model of characteristic official offices, in an effort to promote and establish ombudsman offices at the international, national, state, and local levels.

## Special Interests

### Elder Rights

Under Title 42 of the United States Code (Public Health and Welfare), Congress created, among other things, several programs for older Americans. One of them was a provision for state Long-Term Care Ombudsman programs (42 USC § 3058g). Accordingly, even though federally- established and mandated, the program has been delegated to, and actually managed by, the states through block grants, special appropriations, foundation grants, etc.

Ombuds in this sector act as advocates for residents of nursing homes, board and care facilities, and assisted living residential setups. They not only investigate complaints, but also provide information to help persons find an appropriate facility for care, and help them get quality care.

Under the federal Older Americans Act, every state is required to have an ombudsman program to address concerns within long term care (LTC) system. These ombuds not only investigate complaints, but also are authorized to advocate for improvement in the system. The best way to find a particular state's LTC ombudsman is to go to the online Web site of the National Long Term Care Ombudsman Resource

Center (www.ltcombudsman.org) and click on any individual state. Another resource, Memberofthe-Family.Net (www.memberofthefamily.net), provides information for approximately 16,000 Medicare/Medicaid-certified nursing homes. It also maintains a National Watch List of homes recently cited for violations or substantiated complaints. Finally, it has an Honor Roll of facilities found to be deficiency-free.

### Child Welfare

As of 2005, there were more than 25 child welfare ombudsman programs in the United States. They generally address "out-of-home" situations involving minors, such as residential care facilities (public orphanages), public agencies providing health and dental care services, public foster care and placement agencies, and family social services agencies. Several states also extend ombudsman services to juvenile offender concerns (juvenile detention programs and juvenile corrections) under the broader umbrella of child welfare ombudsman programs.

Because children cannot legally speak for themselves, ombudsman programs involving them are generally advocacy-based, and are referred to as such, e.g., Connecticut's Office of the Child Advocate, or Tennessee's Ombudsman for Children and Families. Ombudsman advocates for children are mostly concerned with complaints or issues involving:

- overcrowded foster homes

- abuse

- neglect

- inappropriate placements

- dangerous environment placements

- services not being provided

- state agency visitation schedules not being followed

- lack of contact with caseworkers

- death or physical injury to a child

- education and training not available or insufficient

### Juvenile Corrections

Starting in 1995, the Office of Juvenile Justice and Delinquency Prevention (OJJDP) within the U.S. Department of Justice began offering "challenge grant" money to states for use in ten specifically-earmarked activities. One of those ten priorities was the estab-lishment of state ombudsman offices to investigate and resolve complaints relating to providers of "out-of-home" care to children and youths, including juvenile detention and correctional facilities. Tennessee and Maryland were the first two states to be awarded this funding specifically for ombudsman programs overseeing juvenile detention and correctional facilities.

Some key issues facing juvenile corrections ombuds include:

- expansion and accessibility of support and services for special- needs, especially mental health needs

- access to mental health services for families of juvenile offenders, to prevent youth from being placed in detention or other alternative

- preventing the juvenile justice system from becoming a "safety net" for at-risk youth

- expanding prevention and detention programs

- moving confined females into facilities where they can receive gender-responsive services

- intervention to prevent court involvement for at-risk youths.

### Adult Corrections

Likewise, a majority of adult correction facilities include some form of spokesperson representing the concerns of incarcerated persons, and this is often an ombudsman. By monitoring the relationship between inmates and prison officials, such programs have been successful at improving conditions within correctional institutions to ensure safe and humane treatment of incarcerated persons.

However, the success of an adult correctional ombudsman program has more risk and often depends on the authority of the ombudsman to pursue remedies and manage the competing interests of prisoners and officials. If inmates do not trust an ombudsman's ability to fairly address their complaints, or if prison officials feel that the ombudsman's recommendations are unreasonable, serious obstacles to harmonious relations may undermine the program. An ombudsman's statutory authority must be exercised with care to maintain balanced relationships among correctional administrators, staff, and inmates. However, when created and administered correctly, a correctional ombudsman program that remains independent of a department of corrections can palpably reduce tension within a prison facility and achieve many positive results in the overall running of the facility.

### Workers' Compensation

The International Association of Industrial Accident Boards and Commissions (IAIABC) (http://www.iaiabc.org/) maintains a detailed list of workers' compensation agencies, including ombuds. However, the most accessible, up-to-date, and probably the most complete of its kind is a Web site for the North Carolina Industrial Commission's list of U.S. workers' compensation agencies. Online Web browsers can go to http://www.comp.state.nc.us/pages/all50.htm and have instant access to all 50 states' and D.C.'s home pages for workers' compensation agencies, as well as contact information for state workers' compensation ombudsman offices.

### Small Businesses

The U.S. Small Business Administration (SBA) maintains an Office of the National Ombudsman to assist small businesses burdened with unfair or excessive federal regulatory enforcement, such as repetitive audits or investigations, excessive fines and penalties, retaliation, arbitrary or discriminatory regulatory enforcements, or other unfair actions by federal agencies. Working from a central office in Washington, DC, the SBA National Ombudsman covers only federal regulatory enforcement and compliance actions. Moreover, it can only assist small businesses, small government entities, and non-profit organizations. The Environmental Protection Agency (EPA) Small Business Ombudsman Clearinghouse and Hotline serves private individuals, small communities, small business enterprises, and trade associations representing the small business sector. The office provides public mailings to update recent regulatory actions. Special attention is directed toward answering technical questions and apprising the trade associations that represent small business interests of current regulatory developments.

### Students

Many major colleges and universities throughout the United States and Canada have a student ombudsman on campus. The ombudsman is generally responsible for assisting students with problems involving school rules, policies, and procedures. Most often, the ombudsman is another student, preferably a graduate student who knows and understands the functions of various offices and organizations on campus. Students are able to discuss matters confidentially, knowing that a student ombudsman will consider all sides in an impartial and objective way.

### Environmental Protection

In 2002, the Senate Environment and Public Works Committee reauthorized an ombudsman post within the Environmental Protection Abency (EPA). Congress originally established the EPA ombudsman in 1984 to receive complaints about hazardous waste. When the authorization expired in 1988, the EPA retained the ombudsman, but transferred the office to the Office of Solid Waste and Emergency Response. The 2002 bill (S. 606) established an independent Office of the Ombudsman within the EPA. Under the Solid Waste Disposal Act, the ombudsman is authorized to render assistance, conduct investigations, make findings of fact, and forward non-binding recommendations to the EPA administrator.

Many individual states have separate offices for environmental affairs in which an ombudsman is available to investigate complaints of toxic waste or illegal hazardous material handling. However, a minority of states have independent offices dedicated for this function; most fall under the purview of other functions such as inspectors general.

### Consumer Affairs

To help investigate and enforce consumer protection laws, many states have established consumer affairs ombuds to provide the first forum for complaint and/or investigation. Arizona, California, Texas, and Virginia are examples of states maintaining such offices.

### Insurance and Banking

The Federal Deposit Insurance Corporation (FDIC)Office of the Ombudsman handles inquiries involving problems or complaints related to the FDIC. Although FDIC insures almost all banks and savings associations in the United States, it may not be the primary regulator of a particular institution. Consumers should initially attempt to resolve a matter with the institution or the institution's primary regulator.

Recurring issues before the FDIC Ombudsman include those regarding bank application processes, the Bank Secrecy Act, and Regulation B and the Equal Credit Opportunity Act (ECOA), particularly relating to laws governing spousal signatures and the propriety of requesting information about an applicant's life insurance.

## Private Sector Programs and Organizations

### International Ombudsman Association

The International Ombudsman Association (IOA) was officially formed in 2005, following the merger of the University and College Ombuds Association (UCOA) and the Ombudsman Association (TOA). It is the largest international association of professional organizational ombuds, with over 500 members globally. The IOA offers professional training and education programs for practicing ombuds, and works to support and promote the profession through strategic partnerships with government agencies and other professional organizations.

### National Credit Union Administration

The Ombudsman for the National Credit Union Administration investigates complaints and recommends solutions relating to regulatory issues that cannot be resolved at a regional level. The NCUA Ombudsman assists complainants with defining options and recommending appropriate actions. This ombud does not advocate for any party, but does insure confidentiality of all interviews and records, used exclusively for internal investigation and recommendation. The NCUA Ombudsman will not handle any matter that involves a conservatorship or liquidation; that is in litigation; that involves an enforcement action where a notice of charges has been filed; or one that is within the jurisdiction of the Inspector General.

### State Organizations

In 1969, Hawaii became the first state to appoint an ombudsman. There are only five states in which the ombudsman office is a legislative agency:

### Alaska Office of the Ombudsman

P.O. Box 102636
Anchorage, AK 99510-2636 USA
Phone: (907) 269-5290
URL: ombudsman@legis.state.ak.us

### Arizona Office of the Ombudsman

740 15th Street NW
Washington, DC 20005 USA
Phone: (202) 992-1000
URL: www.azleg.state.az.us/ombudsman

### Hawaii Office of the Ombudsman

465 South King Street, 4th Floor
Honolulu, HI 96813 USA
Phone: (808) 587-0770
URL: complaints@ombudsman.Hawaii.gov

### Iowa Office of Citizens' Aid Ombudsman

Ola Babcock Bldg, 1112 East Grand
Des Moines, IA 50319 USA
Phone: (888) 426-5065
URL: www.legis.state.ia.us.ombudsman

### Nebraska Office of the Ombudsman

Room 807 State Capitol, P.O. Box 94604
Lincoln, DC 20005 USA
Phone: (402) 471-2035
URL: www.unicam.state.ne.us/offices/ombud.htm

"Citizen Representatives: Statewide Ombudsman." *SLGN Notes,* 25 August 2004. Available at http://www.statelocalgov.net

Jones, Judith and Alvin W. Cohn. "State Ombudsman Programs." *Juvenile Justice Bulletin,* February 2005. U.S. Department of Justice, Office of Juvenile Justice and Prevention.

Sharn, Lori. "Ombudsman Post." *Congress Daily,* 27 September 2002. Available at http://www.GovExec.com

## Organizations

### The American Bar Association (Commission on Legal Problems of the Elderly

740 15th Street NW
Washington, DC 20005 USA
Phone: (202) 992-1000
URL:

### Asbestos Abatement/Management Ombudsman

Washington, DC USA
Phone: (800) 368-5888
Fax: (202) 566-2848

### Federal Deposit Insurance Corporation Ombudsman

E-2022, 3501 Fairfax Drive
Arlington, VA 2226 USA
Phone: (202) 942-3040
URL:

### National Credit Union Association Ombudsman

1775 Duke Street
Alexandria, VA 22314-3428 USA
Phone: (703) 518-6510
URL:

***National Long Term Care Ombudsman Resource Center***

1828 L Street NW, Suite 801
Washington, DC 20036 USA
Phone: (202) 332-2275
URL: www.ltcombudsman.org

## Organizations

### SBA Ombudsman Hotline

Washington, DC USA
Phone: (800) 368-5888

Fax: (202) 566-0954

***The Ombudsman Association***

203 Towne Center Drive
Hillsborough, NJ 08844-4693 USA
Phone: (908) 359-1184
Fax: (908) 359-7619
URL: www.ombuds-toa.org

***United States Ombudsman Association***

P.O.Box 8096
Madison, WI 53708-8096 USA
Phone: (608) 661-0402
URL: www.usombudsman.org

# CONSUMER ISSUES

## PHISHING

*Sections within this essay:*

## Background

Phishing (analogous to fishing, and hence the term) refers to a practice where a perpetrator attempts to lure a victim into visiting an authentic-looking Web site and entering personal information. The purpose of a phishing scheme is to steal personal information from the victim in the form of account numbers, social security numbers, passwords, and so forth. Although these schemes are blatantly illegal forms of identity theft, those individuals who are responsible are difficult to catch and prosecute because they are often located overseas.

Statistics have shown that phishing has continually escalated as a problem in the United States. According to one estimate, about 1.2 million people between May 2004 and May 2005 suffered losses due to phishing schemes. One prominent computer security company, Symantec, determined that one of out every 125 emails sent in 2005 was part of a phishing scheme. Although legislative efforts to combat this problem have proven ineffective, consumers can take a number of steps to protect themselves from being victimized by this form of fraud.

## Phishing and Related Schemes

### *Typical Phishing Scams*

A phishing scam begins with the distribution of an email that appears to be from a legitimate company, usually a bank or Internet shopping site. The email, which is typically addressed to a generic customer (e.g., "Dear Valued eBay Customer"), often contains authentic-looking logos from a legitimate company. Messages in these emails vary, but most indicate either that the company is undergoing a process of updating its records or that the customer's account information has been compromised through fraud. The email directs the user to click on a link that takes the user to a Web site that also looks authentic. Once on the site, the page directs the user to enter personal information, including the user's password.

Many victims of phishing schemes are unaware of what happened to them because they have been led to believe that the email and Web site were authentic. The person responsible for the phishing attack creates deception by producing a URL that looks like it belongs to an actual company. A victim often sees words in the hyperlink that are associated with the company, such as "eBay" or "CitiBank," and have no idea that the URL is fake. The Web site that the victim visits is likewise designed to deceive the victim because it usually looks identical to a company's actual site.

### Spear Phishing

A more recent variation of phishing involves emails that are targeted towards employees of specific companies. Emails that are sent as part of this scheme appear to be from an employee's actual company and ask for the user to update personal information. However, like other phishing schemes, a link contained in the email message sends the user to a site that is completely unrelated to the company. This type of targeted phishing scheme has become known as "spear phishing."

Spear phishing has become prevalent. The *Wall Street Journal* reported that between January and June 2005, an estimated 35 million targeted messages were sent in the United States. This form of phishing has also proven to be effective. In one mock attack designed to study users' responses, 500 cadets from West Point received a targeted email asking for personal information. More than 80% of these cadets responded to the email and provided the requested information.

### Pharming

The term pharming refers to a practice where perpetrators redirect users from legitimate Web sites to fraudulent Web sites. This is done by exploiting weaknesses in Domain Name Service (DNS) software, which is used to resolve Internet names with the corresponding Internet Protocol (IP) address. For example, when a user enters http://www.mybank.com, DNS software resolves that name with an IP address that consists of a series of numbers, such as 201.26.156.98. When pharming has occurred with respect to that Internet name, the DNS software sends users to another IP address that does not belong to the actual business.

### Evil Twins

Another recent scam that is similar to phishing schemes employ the use of wireless devices. In these schemes, known as evil twin scams, attackers lure users into connecting their laptops or PDA devices into what appear to be legitimate wireless hotspots.

An example of such a hotspot would be an airport lounge. Once a person has connected the wireless device, the attacker can steal information from the user.

### Spyware and Keyloggers

More sophisticated Internet attacks can be carried out through the use of spyware and keyloggers. Spyware that is installed unknowingly on a victim's computer can be used to track the victim's Internet usage and steal personal information. Similarly, a keylogger that is installed on a computer can record anything that is typed on a computer, such as user names and passwords, and send that information to a perpetrator who installed the keylogger.

## Difficulty in Controlling Phishing Scams

Several factors make it difficult for law enforcement to catch those who run phishing scams. The Web sites that are used in these scams are often only active for a few days, so even if law enforcement discovers a scam, the site may be removed long before it is investigated. Moreover, many of the servers that house these sites are located in foreign countries, making enforcement of domestic laws very difficult.

## Federal Laws Related to Phishing Activities

Although some members of Congress have introduced pieces of legislation focusing specifically on phishing, none of these bills have been enacted. Nevertheless, several federal laws prohibit phishing as well as other forms of fraud.

### Credit Card Fraud Act

Originally enacted in 1984, the Credit Card Fraud Act prohibits the purchase of goods with an "access device." Access devices include credit cards, account numbers, personal identification numbers, and similar items "that can be used, alone or in conjunction with another access device, to obtain money, goods, services, or any other thing of value, or that can be used to initiate a transfer of funds... ." A violation of the statute can result in a prison term of 15 years and a fine.

### Identity Theft and Assumption Deterrence Act

The Identity Theft and Assumption Deterrence Act applies to the unauthorized transfer or use of a means of identification. A means of identification includes personal information, such as a social security number or date of birth, as well as biometric data, such as a fingerprint. Although the two statutes are similar, the Identity Theft and Assumption Deterrence Act differs from the Credit Card Fraud Act in that the former defines "victim" as the person whose identity is stolen. By comparison, the Credit Card Fraud Act defines victim as the bank, credit issuer, or merchant, since one of those entities is financially responsible for any fraudulent purchases.

### *Fair and Accurate Credit Transaction Act*

Congress enacted the Fair and Accurate Credit Transaction Act in 2003 to allow consumers to check their credit reports and correct mistakes on those reports. The statute amended the Fair Credit Reporting Act, which is designed to protect the privacy of consumer information in credit reports as well as to promote accuracy in those reports.

## California's Anti-Phishing Law

California in 2005 became the first state to enact legislation designed specifically to deter phishing. Under the Anti-Phishing Act of 2005, it is unlawful in the state "for any person, by means of a Web page, electronic mail message, or otherwise through use of the Internet, to solicit, request, or take any action to induce another person to provide identifying information by representing itself to be a business without the authority or approval of the business."

Unlike federal statutes, the California law provides for civil liability as opposed to criminal penalties. Some victims of phishing, including those who provide Internet access service to the public, own a Web page, or own a trademark, may recover up to $500,000 for each proven violation of the statute. Other victims may recover up to $5000 for each violation of the statute. The statute also allows the state's attorney general or a district attorney in the state to bring an action to enjoin further violations.

California is also among a few states that allow consumers to place freezes on their credit reports. This option is similar to provisions in the federal Fair and Accurate Transactions Act, although the state's option is stronger than the federal counterpart. Nevertheless, few consumers in those states take advantage of this option, primarily because it is not well advertised and it is costly.

## Self-Help Measures

Without effective state or federal legislation, most experts recommend that consumers employ one of several self-help measures. These measures include increased education and awareness of the threat of phishing scams, review of credit records, placing freezes on credit reports, and using one of several different types of insurance.

### *Education and Awareness*

In 2003, the Federal Trade Commission (FTC) released the Identity Theft Survey Report, which indicated that many victims expressed that they would have benefited a great deal if they had better awareness of the potential for identity theft. Although phishing remains prevalent, many consumers have become sophisticated enough to identify fraudulent emails. Nevertheless, more advanced scams, such as spear phishing and pharming schemes, may still lure a consumer to provide personal information.

Banks, credit issuers, and other businesses have made efforts to educate their customers about the potential for phishing schemes and other fraudulent scams. Most businesses do not request personal information from their customers through email messages, and so almost all emails that request this information are illicit. Consumers who receive any suspicious correspondence requesting personal information should contact the business that apparently sent the request.

Several businesses and law enforcement agencies have joined the Anti-Phishing Working Group (APWG), which has been formed to eliminate the threat of phishing scams. Both the APWG and the FTC offer several suggestions in addition to those summarized above.

- Use anti-virus software and a firewall, and keep both up-to-date.

- Do not use email to send personal or account information.

- Review credit card and bank accounts as soon as they are received.

- Regularly log on to online accounts.

- Be cautious about opening any attachment or downloading any files from emails.

- Forward phishing emails to the appropriate authorities, including the following email addresses: spam@uce.gov (FTC); reportphishing@antiphishing.com (APWG).

- File a complaint with the FTC. More information is available online at http://www.consumer.gov/idtheft/.

### Review of Credit Records

Consumers should take advantage of federal laws that allow consumers to review their credit reports. At the least, this allows consumers to identify suspicious activity that may have occurred with respect to their personal information. However, the effectiveness of this option may be limited because personal information stolen through a phishing scheme may have occurred months before the consumer checks the credit report.

### Anti-Identity Theft Freeze

A freeze on a credit account can prevent identity theft attackers from using a consumer's personal information for fraudulent purposes. If a phisher obtains personal information, a freeze would prevent the attacker from using the information for fraudulent purposes. On the other hand, if a consumer provides bank or credit card information to a phisher, such a freeze would not protect the consumer.

### Insurance

Several companies offer different types of insurance to protect consumers against instances of fraud. Some of these plans monitor a consumer's credit activity, while others reimburse victims after identity theft has occurred.

## Additional Resources

*Federal Trade Commission— Identity Theft Survey Report.* Synovate, 2003. Available at http://www.ftc.gov/os/2003/09/synovatereport.pdf.

*Identity Theft: A Legal Research Guide.* Best, Reba A., William S. Hein & Co., Inc., 2004.

*Identity Theft in Cyberspace: Crime Control Methods and Their Effectiveness in Combating Phishing Attacks.* Jennfier Lynch, Berkeley Technology Law Journal, 2005.

*Take Charge: Fighting Back Against Identity Theft.* Federal Trade Commission, 2004. Available at http://www.ftc.gov/bcp/conline/pubs/credit/idtheft.htm.

## Organizations

### Anti-Phishing Working Group
URL: http://www.antiphishing.org
E-Mail: info@antiphishing.org

### Council of Better Business Bureaus (CBBB)
4200 Wilson Blvd., Suite 800
Arlington, VA 22203-1838 USA
Phone: (703) 276-0100
Fax: (703) 525-8277
URL: htt://www.bbb.org

### Federal Trade Commission
600 Pennsylvania Avenue, N.W.
Washington, D.C. 20580 USA
URL: http://www.ftc.gov

# CONSUMER ISSUES

## PURCHASES AND RETURNS

*Sections Within This Essay*

## Background

Just about everyone has purchased something that looked like a bargain but proved to be an unfortunate mistake. Nearly all of these poor purchasing decisions do have a remedy. It is not necessary that the purchase involves a great deal of money, but there must be a genuine, serious, and material error. In these cases, the reason is clear: the parties somehow made a mistake as to what was being purchased. This general principle applies any time a merchant sells a **tangible** piece of property to an amateur consumer, even if the dealer claims the product is offered ''as is.''

What are the consumers' options? First, they should consider whether the merchant has any of the following policies:

- Returns:. These are policies that allow buyers to bring the product back to the mer-

chant and get their money back for the product.

- Exchanges.: These policies allow buyers to bring back a product to the merchant and exchange it for a different product.

- Refunds.: This kind of policy allows buyers to get their money back from an unsatisfactory product; these almost always accompany return policies.

If the product itself is somehow defective, buyers should try to discover the warranties or guarantees that cover the product (if any). The product's manufacturer rather than the seller usually offer warranties, except of course in cases where the manufacturer is also the seller of the product.

But before buyers try to return their products or make a claim under its **warranty**, there are preventive measures they can take to protect their rights as consumers.

- Particularly for more expensive items, consumers should insist on a signed, written, or printed receipt describing the product and the price that they are paying for it. The seller's business name, address, and the date of purchase should appear on the receipt. Most store cash register receipts contain this information.

- In some cases, it is reasonable to request the right to submit the product to a third party for an independent evaluation. For example, if customers are buying a car, they can ask the dealer to permit a mechanic look at it. They can ask for a refund from the seller if the item is not as described. They can add this provision to the invoice. It will contain words similar to this: "Buyer has the right to submit this item to **examination** by a third party within five business days and to return to seller for a full refund if not as described."

Ultimately, it can be expensive, time-consuming, and a hassle to take a merchant to court, even small claims court. In many cases, a simple complaint letter may do the trick.

## Warranties

In most cases, any item purchased is covered by some kind of warranty. A warranty (also known as a guarantee) is a type of assurance from the manufacturer or merchant about the quality of goods or services purchased. A warranty gives consumers recourse if something they buy fails to live up to what they were promised.

Warranties take two forms: implied or expressed. A seller may also sell a product "as is," meaning that the product comes with no warrantee at all. Implied warranties are just that; they are not written or stated, but exist nonetheless. Almost everything customers buy comes with two implied warranties:

1. The **implied warranty** of merchantability: The implied warranty of merchantability warrants or guarantees that a new product will work correctly as long as customers use it for a reasonably expected purpose. For used products, the warranty of merchantability warrants or guarantees that the product will work as expected, considering its age and condition.

2. The implied warranty of fitness: The implied warranty applies when customers buy a product with a specific purpose in mind. If they explained their specific needs to the merchant, the implied warranty of fitness guarantees them that the product will meet their need.

In contrast to implied warranties, expressed warranties are usually written and included with the product. An expressed warranty may be part of an advertisement or included on a sign or display in a store (e.g. "genuine full lead crystal"), or it may even be an oral description of a product's features. Most typical expressed warranties contain words to the effect that "this product is warranted against defects in materials or workmanship" for a certain time. Expressed warranties are not automatic. Most expressed warranties come directly from the product's manufacturer, although some are included in the merchant's sales contract.

In most states, implied warranties last indefinitely. In a few states, however, implied warranties last only as long as any expressed warranty that comes with a product. In these states, if there are no expressed warranties, the implied warranties last forever.

### Enforcing a Warranty

If a product is defective, the defect will show up immediately in most cases. When it does, customers can request that the seller or manufacturer fix or replace the defective merchandise. If the seller or manufacturer refuses, or if any repair work fails to fix the defect in the product, customers may have to take additional steps in order to resolve the problem.

If the product has not been completely paid for (e.g. something purchased on an **installment** plan), customers may choose to withhold payment. If they made the purchase with their credit card, they can call the credit company and instruct them to refuse payment for the purchase. Customers should use this strategy with care because not every problem or defect is serious enough to permit them to stop payment. It may be best to try to work out a compromise with the seller. If the seller refuses to cooperate, it may be helpful to seek assistance or mediation services through the local Better Business Bureau mediation program.

If informal means do not work, customers may have to resort to **litigation**. In most states, there is a **statute of limitations** on breach of warranty lawsuits. Typically, the **statute** tolls within four years of when customers discovered the defect.

### Remedies After the Warranty Expires

If an item fails to perform or otherwise gives customers trouble while it is under warranty, and they have it repaired by someone authorized by the manufacturer to make repairs, the manufacturer must extend the original warranty for the time the item was in the repair shop. This rule applies in most states. In addition, customers can call the manufacturer and speak to the department that handles warranties. If the product was trouble-free during the warranty period, the manufacturer may offer to repair for a problem for free if the problem arose after the warranty expired. This may happen if the problem is a common one. Many manufacturers have fix-it lists —

items with defects that do not cause a safety hazard and do not require a recall. Sometimes the manufacturer will repair these types of defects for free. Customers will not know of this remedy, though, unless they call and ask.

### Extended Warranties

When customers purchase a vehicle, appliance, or an electronic item the merchant may try to encourage them to buy an extended warranty (also known as "service contracts"). These are legitimate contracts. They are intended to extend the period of warranty coverage in the other manufacturer warranties that come with the product. These contracts can be a source of significant profit for stores, which get to keep up to 50% of the amount customers pay for the warranty.

Rarely will customers need to exercise their rights under an extended warranty or service contract. Quality vehicles, electronic equipment, and appliances do not usually experience problems during the first few years of their use. If they do experience problems during this time, they are usually covered by the original warranty. Besides, such merchandise often has a useful life well beyond the length of the extended warranty.

## Returning Consumer Purchases

It is not true that consumers have a right to return almost anything they buy in a store. Although there are laws to protect consumers who buy defective products or who are led to make purchases based on misleading advertising, there is generally no rule or law that absolutely requires merchants to offer refunds, exchanges or credits on the items they sell.

There are four basic principles customers should know about returning goods they purchase in a store:

1. Merchants can set their own policies on refunds and exchanges. Generally, consumers are not entitled to either a refund or an exchange.

2. Although merchants are not required to do it, many of them will exchange non-sale items whether customers paid for them with cash, check, or credit.

3. Sale items are commonly exempt from merchants' refund and exchange policies.

4. If customers exchange a product for another one that costs less, the store can re-

quire the customers to spend the difference in cost in their store.

Because it makes their stores more attractive to customers, most retailers do offer refunds, exchanges, or credits voluntarily, although they usually impose a "reasonable time" condition for these refunds, exchanges, or credits. These kinds of policies have become so common that people have come to expect them. When retail sellers fail to post notices to the contrary, consumers often wrongly assume that the return, refund, or exchange policy exists. Therefore, before customers make a purchase at a store, try to determine the store's refund policy because these exchange privileges vary from merchant to merchant. A copy of a store's return policy should be posted near cash registers; they are also frequently printed on sales receipts.

Before making a retail purchase, it is a good idea to find out the following:

- The store's return policy

- The store's exchange policy

- Whether the store will refund customers' money if they return a product

- Whether sales are final (this is especially important for goods that have been marked down)

- How the store's normal return policy is affected if customers have to sign a contract to buy the product,

- If customers are prevented from returning a damaged product if the product came with a separate written warranty.

Most stores that have a refund and/or exchange policy require that the item be returned within a specific time. These periods vary considerably from one merchant to the next, but most will be in the range of about seven to 90 days. The product usually must be in new condition, with the original packaging, and with the original sales receipts. There are a few retailers that will accept goods returned in any condition, at any time, and with no questions asked, but liberal return policies like these are very rare.

### Mandatory policy posting

In the past, some retailers did not post their policies reflecting imposed conditions or limits on accepting returned merchandise, and some did not accept returns at all. Naturally, this policy caused a great deal of frustration for consumers. Consequently, some states have enacted laws that require merchants or retailers to post their refund policies if they do not meet certain common expectations, such as the following:

- The store gives a full refund, an equal exchange, or some combination of these

- The customer may return the merchandise within seven days of the purchase, as long as it is returned with proof of purchase

Basically, if a merchant does not follow a typical return policy, the merchant must post the alternate return policy so that its customers are aware of the return policy.

## Responses to Dishonest or Unfair Merchants

If a dishonest or unfair merchant has victimized buyers, but they do not relish going to court for a remedy, they have several alternatives. If the merchant is clearly the party at fault, there are many assistants whose aid buyers can enlist. Before taking action, however, they must be sure that they are completely truthful and accurate in their claims. Here are some suggestions to alternative measures to litigation:

- Try to learn whether the offending merchant is a member of a trade organization (most belong to at least one trade group); buyers can complain to the organization.

- If customers paid for the item or service with a credit card, they can refuse to pay the bill when they get their statement from the credit card company. When they dispute a bill, their credit card company will usually give them an immediate credit for the amount in question and then reverse the credit it gave the merchant for their purchase. It will then ask for an explanation from the merchant. In some cases, a merchant will give up rather than take the time to write letters and participate in a credit dispute. If they claim they never received the merchandise for which they were charged, or that it was damaged or defective and they sent it back, the credit card company may refuse payment completely, regardless of what the merchant claims.

- Customers can contact the local Better Business Bureau or the Federal Trade Commission.

- Customers can contact their state, county, or municipal consumer affairs department. A telephone call followed by a letter to these organizations can be very effective at getting action from a recalcitrant merchant.

Most merchants just want to do business. They do not want to lose business. They want to make money on sales, not by cheating customers. Likewise, most merchants will not stand to be taken advantage of, so customers need to be sure they have their facts straight and that the disagreement is not merely a misunderstanding. But a merchant who refuses to adjust the matter or even to be reasonable about it may have an ulterior motive.

Before customers take these steps, it is a good idea for them to inform the merchant about what he intends to do. Sometimes, just informing the merchant of his intentions to pursue the matter is enough. But sometimes it is not, in which case the customer should be ready to follow through on the plan of action. Before the customer sends a complaint letter to a consumer or regulatory authority, the customer might want to consider sending a copy of the letter to the merchant, in advance. They can advise the merchant that the letter will be sent in five business days if the matter is not resolved. Sometimes, the mere threat of action can bring about resolution.

## The Cooling-Off Rule

If customers buy a product at a store and later change their minds, they may not be able to return the merchandise. However, federal and state laws provide certain protections for consumers who purchase items sold outside the vendor's usual place of business. For example, under the Federal Trade Commission's (FTC's) "Cooling Off Rule," consumers have until midnight of the third business day after signing a contract to cancel the contract. This rule applies when a consumer has entered the following deals:

- A door-to-door contract involving a sale over $25

- A contract for more than $25 made at a place other than the seller's regular place of business. There are similar laws in every state

The fact is the FTC's Cooling-Off Rule only applies to purchases made at a place that is not the seller's permanent place of business. For example, the law would apply to goods customers buy in their own homes, their workplaces, in a student's dormitory, or at spaces temporarily rented by the seller, like hotel or motel rooms, convention centers, fairgrounds, and community centers.

The Cooling-Off Rule guarantees the customer's right to cancel a sale and to receive a full refund. This right extends only until midnight of the third business day after the sale. If the customer notifies the seller of the intent to cancel the purchase within the **cooling-off period**, the customer is entitled to a full refund, and any contract that the customer signed must be rescinded without further obligation.

Under the FTC's Cooling-Off Rule the seller must inform customers about their cancellation rights; this should happen at the time of the sale. Additionally, the seller is obligated to provide customers with two copies of a cancellation form. One the customer can keep for his records and one to send with the returned merchandise. The seller must also provide the customer with a copy of the contract or receipt. The contract or receipt must be in the same language that was used in the sales presentation. For example, if the presentation was made in Chinese, the contract or receipt must also be in Chinese.

The contract or receipt must contain the following information:

- date of the sale
- the seller's name and address
- an explanation of right to cancel the sale

### Exceptions to the Cooling-Off Rule

Some types of sales cannot be canceled even if they do occur in locations normally covered by the rule. The cooling off rule does not cover sales that have the following conditions:

- the goods or services are intended for commercial purposes
- the goods cost less than $25
- the goods are needed for an emergency
- part of the buyer's request is that the seller perform maintenance or repairs on the buyer's personal property
- the purchase results from negotiations whereat the site where the seller's goods are regularly sold.

Many states have similar **consumer protection** statutes that contain similar exceptions to the federal cooling-off rule.

## Other Kinds of Contracts

In addition to the consumer protections outlined above for typical consumer products, there are also protections for other kinds of purchases. The Truth in Lending Act is a federal law that permits individuals to cancel a home improvement loan, a second **mortgage**, or other loan when the home has been pledged as security for the loan. This law does not apply to first mortgages. The law allows borrowers to cancel one of these contracts until midnight of the third business day after signing the contract. In some cases, the three-day period may be extended for up to three years. The Act requires the lender to inform borrowers about their right to cancel such contracts. Additionally, the borrower must provide a cancellation form when the borrower signs the loan documents.

Many states have enacted laws that allow consumers to cancel written contracts covering the purchase of certain goods or services within a few days of signing. Some of these include contracts for the following:

- dance or martial arts lessons
- memberships in health clubs
- dating services
- weight loss programs
- time share properties
- hearing aids

State consumer protection agencies have a complete listing of the kinds of contracts covered in their state.

## Additional Resources

*Consumer Rights Law (Oceana's Legal Almanac Series. Law for the Layperson)* Jasper, Margaret C. Oceana Publishers, 1997.

*http://www.abanet.org/lawinfo/home.html* "LawInfo.org" American Bar Association, 2002.

*http://www.safeshopping.org/* "Safeshopping.org" American Bar Association, 2002.

*http://www.consumer.gov/* "FirstGov for Consumers," Consumer.gov, 2002.

*http://www.bbbonline.org/* "Better Business Bureau Online" Council of Better Business Bureaus, Inc., 2002.

*Your Rights as a Consumer: Legal Tips for Savvy Purchasing of Goods, Services and Credit.* Lieberman, Marc R., Career Press, 1994.

*Understanding Consumer Rights (Essential Finance).* Parisi, Nicolette, and Marc Robinson, DK Publishers, 2001.

*Law and Changing Society: Administration, Human Rights, Women and Children, Consumer Protection, Education, Commercial Contract.* Eds. Saxena, Manju, and Harish Chandra, eds. Deep & Deep Publishers, 1999.

*Consumer Rights Law (Oceana's Legal Almanac Series. Law for the Layperson).* Margaret C. Jasper. Oceana Publishers, 1997.

## Organizations

### The Council of Better Business Bureaus (BBB)
4200 Wilson Blvd., Suite 800
Arlington, VA 22203-1838 USA
Phone: (703) 276-0100
Fax: (703) 525-8277
URL: http://www.bbb.org/

### Federal Trade Commission (FTC)
600 Pennsylvania Avenue, N.W.
Washington, D.C., DC 20580 USA
Phone: (877) 382-4357
URL: http://www.ftc.gov/index.html

### The Council of Better Business Bureaus (BBB)
4200 Wilson Blvd., Suite 800
Arlington, VA 22203-1838 USA
Phone: (703) 276-0100
Fax: (703) 525-8277
URL: http://www.bbb.org/

### The National Association of Attorneys General (NAAG)
750 First Street, NE, Suite 1100
Washington, DC, DC 20002 USA
Phone: (202) 326-6000
Fax: (202) 408-7014
URL: http://www.naag.org/

# CONSUMER ISSUES

## RECALLS BY MANUFACTURERS

*Sections Within This Essay:*

- Background
- Consumer Product Recalls
- Food, Drug, and Cosmetics Recalls
- Meat, Poultry, and Egg Safety
- Automobile Recalls
- Lemon Laws
- Additional Resources

## Background

Sometimes certain defects in a product become apparent after the product has entered the marketplace and been sold. These defects can be related to safety, such as when a certain model of automobile has problems with its braking system, where small pieces from a toy pose a choking hazard to young children, or where a medication poses a previously undiscovered, serious adverse health risk to users. Sometimes the problem is another kind of defect, as when a certain model of vacuum cleaner consistently fails to work properly. A recall may be necessary to remedy problems with a product. Recalls are procedures taken by a manufacturer to remove a product from the market. Recalls allow a manufacturer the opportunity to repair or replace the defective product. Recalls can be costly procedures for manufacturers, but are often less costly than multiple lawsuits or the loss of goodwill among consumers. Recalls may be voluntary on the part of a manufacturer, or they may be mandated by the government.

Six agencies within the U.S. government have jurisdiction over recalls:

- The Consumer Product Safety Commission (CPSC) has jurisdiction over thousands of products used in homes, schools, and for sports and recreation
- The Food and Drug Administration (FDA) has oversight over food, drugs, medical devices, animal feed, cosmetics, and radiation-emitting products such as lasers, microwaves, and cell phones
- The Food Safety and Inspection Service (FSIS) of the Department of Agriculture (USDA) inspects and regulates meat, poultry products, and eggs and egg products
- The National Highway Traffic Safety Administration (NHTSA) is responsible for recalls of motor vehicles and related equipment, child safety seats, and tires
- The Coast Guard covers recreational boats and related equipment
- The Environmental Protection Agency (EPA) has recall jurisdiction over insecticides, rodenticides, fungicides, and vehicle emission testing

## Consumer Product Recalls

Manufacturers recall many of their own products every year when defects and/or safety risks are discovered in their products. Most recalls occur for safety-related reasons. Sometimes, a manufacturer will voluntarily recall products, and sometimes they are compelled to issue recalls.

The Consumer Product Safety Commission has jurisdiction over more than 15,000 consumer products. According to the agency, deaths, injury, and property damage from consumer product incidents costs the U.S. more than $700 billion a year. CPSC contends that its advocacy since 1972 has resulted in a 30 percent reduction in death and injury from consumer products. CPSC announces recalls of products that present risks to consumers because the products are either defective or violate mandatory safety standards issued by CPSC.

When a consumer discovers that a product that she owns is recalled, she should stop using it. The consumer should also follow the specific guidance in CPSC's recall announcement on that product. A product recall usually lasts indefinitely. Even if more than a year has passed since CPSC issued a recall notice, product owners should read and follow the instructions in the recall notice.

The remedies for recalled products are specific to each product; no single remedy applies to all products. Each recall announcement is as specific as possible and details the remedy for the product. An announcement typically includes information on where the product was sold, the type and number of injuries or damage caused by the product, and contact information needed to obtain the remedy. The announcement frequently limits recalls to products manufactured during a specific time period. For example, CPSC may announce a recall on toy X, manufactured between June 17, 2005 and August 23, 2006. Owners may or may not get a refund of their recalled product.

## Food, Drug, and Cosmetics Recalls

The Food and Drug Administration is charged with overseeing the safety and effectiveness of food, drugs, and many cosmetics products. As with other consumer goods and motor vehicles, recalls may be necessary when it is determined that a consumable product may pose considerable risk of harm to individuals. In terms of food, drugs, or cosmetics, recalls may proceed under a manufacturer's own initiative, by FDA request, or by FDA order. There are three classes of recalls in descending order of urgency:

1. Class I recalls are cases in which there is a reasonable chance that the use of or exposure to a product will cause serious adverse health consequences or even death.

2. Class II recalls are cases in which exposure to a product may cause temporary or re-

versible adverse health consequences, or where the odds of serious adverse health consequences are not great.

3. Class III recalls are situations in which use of or exposure to a product is unlikely to cause adverse health consequences.

Examples of Class I recalls are foods found to contain botulinal toxin, foods with undeclared allergens, or mislabeling a life-saving drug. A drug that is under-strength but not used to treat life-threatening situations is one example of a Class II recall; another is where two units of blood are collected from a donor who has traveled to a country where malaria is endemic. Class III recalls might include container defects such as a lid that does not seal, a product that is off-taste or color, or a retail food that does not have a label in English.

Recalls may happen in three ways. First, a manufacturer or distributor may decide on its own initiative to issue a recall to remove a product from the market. Second, FDA may request a recall. Finally, two things can happen in the rare instances where a firm does not comply with FDA request. In certain circumstances the FDA has statutory authority to order a recall; in other cases the FDA must seek legal action under the Food, Drug, and Cosmetic Act. The FDA can prescribe a recall only when a medical device, human tissue products, or infant formula pose a risk to human health. Legal remedies available to FDA include seizure of the available product, an injunction against the manufacturer, and/or a court request for recall of the product.

A market withdrawal is a less drastic step than a recall. A market withdrawal is voluntary on the part of a manufacturer, and occurs when a product has a minor violation that would not otherwise be subject to FDA legal action. In these cases, a firm will remove its product from the market or otherwise correct the problem. For example, a product will be removed from the market if there is **evidence** that its packaging has been compromised. This can happen without any manufacturing or distribution problems.

A medical device safety alert is issued in situations involving a medical device that presents an unreasonable risk of substantial harm. These are primarily intended to inform potential users of possible hazards. In some cases, these alerts also are considered recalls.

## Meat, Poultry, and Egg Safety

The Department of Agriculture's Food Safety and Inspection Service is responsible for meat, egg products, and poultry products inspections. The Federal Meat Inspection Act provides FSIS with inspection duties for meat products sold in interstate commerce. FSIS also reinspects imported meat products to ensure they meet U.S. food safety standards. The Poultry Products Inspection Act and the Egg Products Inspection Act provides similar jurisdiction over those products. For example, in an egg processing plant, an inspector would examine eggs before and after breaking, that are intended for further processing and for use as food. FSIS works with manufacturers and distributors to uncover problems, set the parameters for recall, and monitor its implementation.

## Automobile Recalls

The Department of Transportation's National Highway Traffic Safety Administration (NHTSA) is the federal agency authorized to issue vehicle safety standards and to require manufacturers to recall vehicles with safety-related defects (49 **USC** §301). Since NHTSA's inception in 1966, more than 299 million vehicles of all types, 43 million tires, and 84 million pieces of motor vehicle equipment (including child seats) have been recalled to correct safety defects. Vehicle manufacturers initiated some of these recalls. Others have come about after NHTSA investigation or through court action, instigated by the agency.

A safety defect is defined as a problem with a motor vehicle or motor vehicle equipment that poses a risk to motor vehicle safety. Moreover, it must be common to a group of vehicles of the same manufacture or design, or to items of equipment of the same type and manufacture. If a manufacturer identifies a safety defect, the manufacturer notifies NHTSA, as well as vehicle or equipment owners, dealers, and distributors. The manufacturer must then fix the problem, typically without charge to vehicle owners. NHTSA assesses the adequacy of the manufacturers' corrective action and makes sure manufacturers comply with all **statutory** requirements.

Vehicle owners should report possible auto safety issues to NHTSA. The combined effect of a number of similar complaints can trigger an investigation into the alleged safety defect and ultimately lead to a recall. However, there is no set number of complaints

an agency must receive before launching an investigation; NHTSA reviews every report of an alleged safety issue. A report to NHTSA can be made three ways: through the agency's toll-free telephone hotline, by mail, or via the Internet. Consumers are asked to supply specific information necessary for NHTSA staff to evaluate the problem. The information is entered into NHTSA's database and a copy is forwarded to agency staff for evaluation. The agency assesses the information individually, as well as in combination with other information in its database. The information is organized according to vehicle make, model, model year, manufacturer, and the affected part, assembly or system. NHTSA staff monitor such complaints to determine whether a pattern emerges that may indicate potential safety-related problems on any specific vehicle, tires, or equipment.

The Office of Defects Investigation (ODI) within NHTSA is responsible for investigating potential safety defects. The investigative process consists of four parts:

- Screening. ODI determines whether to open an investigation. During this phase, ODI will conduct a preliminary review of consumer complaints and other information related to the alleged defect.

- Petition Analysis. ODI processes petitions for defect investigations during petition analysis.

- Investigation. ODI conducts an investigation of the alleged defect(s).

- Recall Management. Assuming the investigation leads to a recall, ODI will monitor the overall adequacy of safety recalls and the safety-relatedness of service bulletins.

In most cases, manufacturers discover safety defects through their own testing procedures, and make voluntary recalls to remedy the defects without NHTSA involvement. Federal law requires manufacturers to report the findings that safety defects exist in their product, and to take appropriate action to fix the defects. As some vehicles age, however, certain design and performance problems may occur. These problems often lead to complaints to NHTSA by vehicle owners. These consumer complaints can form the basis for a defect investigation, possibly leading to a recall.

After the NHTSA determines a safety defect or other noncompliance issue exists, manufacturers are given a reasonable time to notify, by first-class mail, all registered owners and purchasers of the affected vehicles. (State motor vehicle offices provide the names of vehicle owners.) Manufacturers must inform vehicle owners of the safety problem and provide an evaluation of its risk to the vehicle's safety. The letter must also instruct consumers on the following details:

- How to get the problem corrected

- That corrections are to be made at no charge

- When the remedy will be available

- How long the remedy will take to perform

- Who to contact if there are difficulties in obtaining the free recall work

Once NHTSA has made a defect determination, the manufacturer has three options to correct the defect: repair, replace, or refund the product. The circumstances of the defect and the overall cost of remedying the problem will determine the manufacturer's course of action. In the case of tires and equipment, the manufacturer can either repair or replace, but need not refund the tires or equipment. If a vehicle owner makes repairs before a recall is announced, manufacturers typically must still provide reimbursement to owners for costs incurred to remedy the defect.

A consumer's right to take advantage of a recall is limited by the age of the vehicle. In order to be eligible for free repairs, refund, or replacement, the vehicle must be less than 10 years old on the date the defect or noncompliance is determined. The age of the vehicle is based on the date it was sold to the first purchaser.

If a manufacturer challenges NHTSA's recall in court; the manufacturer is not required to perform any repairs while the case is pending. Owners who take a vehicle in for repairs after NHTSA's decision to order a recall, but before the case is finally decided, will not be reimbursed if the court finds in favor of the manufacturer. If the court rules against the manufacturer, owners may be entitled to reimbursement upon proof that the repairs were made.

Recall remedies do not foreclose other legal remedies; recalls are an additional layer of consumer protection. Persons who have been injured due to a safety-related defect may still bring suit against the manufacturer.

## Lemon Laws

Lemon laws, found in every state, provide another layer of protection for vehicle owners. Lemon Laws entitle aggrieved consumers to a replacement vehicle, or a full refund, where the vehicle is so defective that the dealer cannot satisfactorily repair it. Before a lemon law can be invoked, the dealer must be given a reasonable opportunity to repair the defect.

Lemon laws usually apply to purchases or leases of new cars, trucks, motorcycles or motor homes. Additionally, lemon laws cover "demonstrator" or "executive" vehicles that are less than a year old and still under original warranties. Generally, the laws do not apply to purchases of mopeds or trailers.

Lemon laws vary from state to state. Basically, a mechanical defect must be one which substantially impairs the use, value, or safety of a vehicle. Lemon laws usually have time or mileage limits. A defect must be presented to the manufacturer or authorized dealer within these limits in order to be covered under the lemon law.

Once notified of a problem with a vehicle, the manufacturer must be allowed to repair the defect within a reasonable number of repair attempts. If the manufacturer cannot repair the defect in the vehicle within a reasonable number of repair attempts, the vehicle owner will be entitled to a refund or replacement. How many repair attempts constitutes a "reasonable number" varies from state-to-state, but a typical number is four repairs for the same problem within six months or a year. A lemon law may also be invoked where a vehicle with substantial defects is out of service for a certain number of days during a specified time period.

The nature of the defect also bears on the number of repair attempts permitted. If the defect could cause death or serious bodily injury, only one repair attempt will be allowed before the vehicle is presumed to be a lemon. If the defect is not so serious or potentially dangerous, then the manufacturer will be permitted additional repair attempts to correct the defect.

If an owner believes he has purchased a lemon, he should write the manufacturer and request a replacement vehicle or a refund. In some states the dealer must also be notified. Assuming the request is granted, the owner will not be allowed to keep the defective vehicle. If the defective vehicle is replaced, the manufacturer should refund repair costs and charge the owner nothing for mileage. If a refund is given instead of a replacement vehicle, the refund should include:

- The entire purchase price
- Any **sales tax** paid on the vehicle
- Finance charges
- The cost of repairs to the defective vehicle
- A **deduction** for mileage

If a manufacturer refuses to give a refund or provide a replacement of a defective vehicle, an owner may be able to get relief by submitting her complaint to an **arbitration** forum. This is often quicker and less expensive than **litigation**. In some states, if the manufacturer of the vehicle has a state certified arbitration program, the owner must use it before suing the manufacturer in court for a refund or replacement vehicle.

In some cases, a court may need to decide if a vehicle is a lemon and what remedy to provide. If an owner prevails in a lawsuit against the manufacturer, some jurisdictions allow damages worth double the vehicle's purchase price and repair costs, in addition to other costs and attorney fees.

An owner needs to provide **documentary evidence** to demonstrate that a car is a lemon. This includes all records of any repairs done, including dates of service and descriptions of the exact repairs made. This information is particularly critical when the car is repaired at some place other than the dealership where the car was purchased. In addition to repair records, an owner should retain the purchase contract, any written warranties, and should note on a calendar when the vehicle is at a dealership or other shop for **warranty** repairs. If a vehicle is operable, it may be driven while the appropriate authorities determine whether it is a lemon. If the vehicle is indeed a lemon, the dealership is often allowed to deduct a certain amount for mileage from the refund.

In many states consumers who purchase a used car are also covered under the lemon laws. For example, an owner who has recently purchased a used car may be entitled to cancel the purchase and receive a refund, where the vehicle fails a safety inspection. Vehicle safety inspections are mandatory in most states. Generally, the safety inspection must occur within a certain period of time after the purchase of the car, and the repairs must exceed a stated percentage of the purchase price of the car. In some

states, a vehicle that has passed its inspection may still qualify as a lemon. Moreover, some jurisdictions apply lemon laws to both dealers and private sellers.

## Additional Resources

*Consumer Product Safety* Howells, Geraint G., Dartmouth Publishing Co., 1999.

*Product Warnings, Defects, and Hazards, Second Edition.* O'Reilly, James T., Aspen Publishers, Inc., 1998.

*Safer by Design: A Guide to the Management and Law of Designing for Product Safety, Second Edition* Abbott, Howard and Mark Tyler, Gower Publishing Co., 1997.

*Safety Recall Compendium: A Guide for the Reporting, Notification, and Remedy of Motor Vehicle and Motor Vehicle Equipment in Accordance with Title 49 of the United States Code, Chapter 301 and Supporting Federal Regulations.* NHTSA, 2001.

## Organizations

### American Bar Association
321 North Clark Street
Chicago, IL 60610 USA
Phone: (312) 988-5000
URL: http://www.abanet.org/publiced/practical/car_lemon.html

### Consumer Reports
101 Truman Avenue
Yonkers, NY 10703 USA
URL: http://www.consumerreports.org/Recalls/

### U.S. Department of Agriculture (USDA)
1400 Independence Avenue, S.W.
Washington, D.C.20250 USA
Phone: (800) 535-4555
URL: http://www.fsis.usda.gov
URL: http://www.recalls.gov/

### U.S. Food and Drug Administration (FDA)
5600 Fishers Lane
Rockville, MD 20857-0001 USA
Phone: (888) 463-6332
URL: http://www.fda.gov
URL: http://www.recalls.gov/

### National Highway Transportation Safety Administration (NHTSA)
400 Seventh Street, S.W.
Washington, D.C.20590 USA
Phone: (888) 327-4236
URL: http://www.nhtsa.dot.gov
URL: http://www.recalls.gov/

**Federal Consumer Information Center (FCIC)**

1800 F Street, NW, Room G-142, (XC)
Washington, DC 20405 USA
Phone: (800) 326-2996
URL: http://www.pueblo.gsa.gov/

**U.S. Consumer Product Safety Commission (CPSC)**

4330 East-West Highway
Bethesda, MD 20814-4408 USA
Phone: (301) 504-0990
Fax: (301) 504-0124
E-Mail: info@cpsc.gov
URL: http://www.cpsc.gov/
URL: http://www.recalls.gov/

# CONSUMER ISSUES

## WARRANTIES

*Sections within this essay:*

- Background
- Types of Warranties
    - Implied Warranties
    - Express Warranties
    - Used and "As Is" Goods
    - Extended Warranties
    - Extension of Warranties to Remote Purchasers
- Magnuson-Moss Warranty Act
- Self-Help Measures
- Additional Resources

## Background

In simplest terms, a warranty (also called a guarantee) is an agreement between a seller and a buyer to ensure that a product will work properly. While the concept is simple, the actual application of a warranty can be quite complex. There is no law requiring a company to offer a written warranty on a product it manufactures or sells. The absence of a written warranty, however, does not mean that a product is not warranted to perform according to expectation. When a written warranty does exist, it binds the company under state and federal law into assuming responsibility in the event that a product malfunctions.

Warranties promise that a product will perform properly. When a product fails to perform, it will be replaced or repaired, or the consumer will be given a refund or a credit toward another product. The re-

tail pioneer John Wanamaker, who introduced the concept of the "department store" in Philadelphia in 1876, is also credited with introducing the money-back guarantee. Wanamaker was a progressive businessman who was among the first to offer benefits such as paid vacations to his employees. He was also a deeply ethical man who believed that his customers should be satisfied with their purchases. The money-back guarantee earned the trust and the loyalty of Wanamaker's customers.

Trust and loyalty represent sound business practice for most companies. In fact, it is not uncommon for companies to use warranties as a selling point. By offering a better warranty than their competitors, companies are saying in effect that they believe more strongly in the quality of their products.

Warranty problems occur when the company has misstated its policy, or when the language included in the warranty is confusing. The concept of the "lifetime warranty" provides a good illustration of how this sort of confusion can develop. The Federal Trade Commission (FTC) offers the example of an automobile muffler with a so-called "lifetime" guarantee. "Lifetime" can mean the life of the automobile in which the new muffler was installed. Alternatively, it can mean the duration of the buyer's ownership of the car, or it can mean the buyer's actual lifetime. It is an unfortunate fact that some companies are unscrupulous and try to renege on their warranty agreements. But as the seemingly straightforward example of the muffler shows, sometimes the problem is misinterpretation. That said, it is the seller's responsibility to make sure that the warranty's language and intent is clear.

## Types of Warranties

Under the law, there are two types of warranties: implied and express. Implied warranties exist under state law, as outlined in Article 2 of the **Uniform Commercial Code** (UCC). The UCC, which covers all 50 States and the District of Columbia, is a means of consolidating laws regarding commerce as a means of streamlining interstate legal issues. This allows each state to adopt the same definitions of, in this case, implied warranties. In 2003, a substantially revised version of Article 2 of the UCC was approved by the National Conference of Commissioners on Uniform State Laws and American Law Institute, but as of early 2006 no state had adopted the revised Article 2.

### Implied Warranties

Implied warranties are exactly what the term says they are: unspoken and unwritten promises made by a seller to a buyer that the product being sold works. These warranties are created through the application of the law, rather than through statements that are made by a seller. The concept that encompasses the implied warranty comes from common law, specifically, the principle of "fair value for money spent." Actually, there are two types of implied warranties, both outlined under Article 2 of the UCC.

The *implied warranty of merchantability* is simply the promise that the product sold is in good working order and will do what it is supposed to do. For instance, a vacuum cleaner is expected to pick up dirt and dust from carpets and floors. A refrigerator is expected to keep food cold. A toaster is expected to toast bread. If the consumer buys a product and the product does not work, then this constitutes a breach of the implied warranty. The seller is required to remedy the problem, whether by repairing or replacing the product. (It should be noted that the section of the UCC covering this type of implied warranty, Section 2-314, is law in every state except Louisiana.)

The *implied warranty of fitness for a particular purpose* is the promise that the seller's advice on how to use the product will be correct. For example, it a consumer asks an appliance dealer whether a particular air conditioner can cool a 600 square-foot room and the dealer says yes, that dealer has effectively created a warranty of fitness. In other words, the dealer has impliedly guaranteed that the air conditioner is fit for the purpose for which the consumer needs to use it as expressed to the seller. If the air conditioner can only cool a 400 square-foot room ef-

fectively, the dealer has breached the warranty. The idea behind this is that the dealer is expected to know which product will be best for which use.

### Express Warranties

An express warranty is an explicit offer made voluntarily by the seller that a product will perform according to particular expectations. The typical express warranty offers specific remedies in the event that the product is defective. Express warranties can be oral or written. Written warranties are covered under the federal Magnuson-Moss Act, which is explained in detail below. If a seller offers an express warranty, the product in question is still covered under implied warranty.

The length of a warranty may be specified, but if it is not, the general rule is that consumers have four years from the date of purchase to enforce a warranty claim. This does not mean that the product must last four years. Rather, it means that if there was a defect in the product at the time of purchase that manifests itself later, the consumer is entitled to some sort of remedy.

### Used and "As Is" Goods

Used goods are covered under implied warranties if the seller is a merchant who is in the business of selling similar products. A private individual who chooses to sell a toaster at a flea market is not expected to take responsibility for the product's performance.

In most states, goods can be sold "as is." These goods do not require the seller to offer even an implied warranty. What the seller is required to do for these products is make clear to consumers that the product is being sold in less than prime condition and that the consumer assumes all responsibility for any faults and flaws. Some states prohibit this practice, including the following: Alabama, Connecticut, Kansas, Maine, Maryland, Massachusetts, Minnesota, Mississippi, New Hampshire, Vermont, Washington, West Virginia, and the District of Columbia. If a product is sold as is and it turns out to have a defect that results in personal injury, the seller is liable even in the absence of any warranty.

### Extended Warranties

Anyone who has purchased appliances, stereos, computers, or similar items knows that many stores will try to sell an "extended warranty" along with the standard one. These warranties, also known as service **contracts**, are often unnecessary because they duplicate current warranty coverage. The reason merchants are so eager to sell service contracts in general is that they make a handsome profit off those agreements. Service contracts are not illegal and in some cases they may be useful, but consumers are well advised to read the existing warranty before spending unnecessary money on redundant coverage.

Another important point that consumers should know is that if they do wish to purchase a service contract, they are allowed by law to do so up until 30 days from the regular warranty's expiration date. Stores that claim a "now or never" policy are being deceptive.

### Extension of Warranties to Remote Purchasers

Situations often arise where someone who purchases goods from the original buyer bring an action for breach of warranty against the original seller. The general rule under the UCC is that a buyer must have privity of contract with the original seller in order to recover for breach of either an express or an implied warranty. In other words, the person who actually purchased the goods from the buyer is the only person who can sue for breach of a warranty.

Some exceptions to this general rule may apply. For example, a third-party beneficiary to a seller's promise may recover from the seller even in the absence of privity of contract between the seller and the eventual buyer. The revised Article 2 of the UCC includes two new provisions that extend warranties to remote purchasers in some other circumstances, but as noted above, no state has adopted the revised Article 2.

## Magnuson-Moss Warranty Act

In 1975, Congress passed the Magnuson-Moss Warranty Act as a means of providing comprehensive information to consumers about their rights under product warranties. It is important to note once again that companies are not required to provide written warranties on their products. If they do, however, they are subject to the regulations spelled out under Magnuson-Moss.

Oral warranties are not covered by Magnuson-Moss, nor are warranties on services or commercial products. Only written warranties on consumer goods are covered. The company issuing the warranty (the warrantor) or the seller must meet three basic requirements under the Act:

- The warranty must be designated as either full or limited.

- The warranty must be written in a single document that is clearly written and easy to understand.

- The warranty must be readily available for inspection where the product covered is being sold.

Anyone who offers a written warranty is prohibited from disclaiming or modifying implied warranties. In other words, consumers are protected under the implied warranty of merchantability no matter how broad or narrow the scope of the written warranty. The only exception is that the company can restrict the duration of an implied warranty to match that stated in a written limited warranty. If a company offers a three-year limited warranty on a product, for instance, it is permissible to limit the implied warranty to three years as well.

Magnuson-Moss prohibits companies from including tie-in sales provisions in its warranties. In other words, the company cannot state that owners of product X must use only product X accessories or have the product serviced at specific locations. However, companies can void a warranty if the consumer has it serviced or repaired inappropriately or incorrectly. Moreover, if the company can prove to the FTC that its products must be serviced or maintained through tie-in services, the FTC may waive this requirement.

No deceptive or misleading terms are permitted in a written warranty under Magnuson-Moss. A common example is a warranty covering moving parts in an item that has no moving parts. Moreover, the company cannot claim to offer services that it either cannot or will not provide.

Magnuson-Moss makes breach of warranty a violation of federal law and allows plaintiffs to recover court costs and reasonable attorney's fees. In general, most warranty-related lawsuits are brought in state courts, but class action suits can be brought in federal court. This is not to say that Magnuson-Moss has litigation as its goal. Rather, the goal is to make companies think carefully before they breach a warranty.

Under Magnuson-Moss, companies can include a provision in their warranties that requires customers to attempt to resolve warranty disputes through informal means (informal in the sense that they do not require the same rules of evidence and procedure as found in a courtroom). These informal means are known as dispute resolution mechanisms. For a company to be able to require this option, it has to meet certain requirements as stated in the FTC's Rule on Informal Dispute Settlement Procedures. The "rule" is actually a set of guidelines that requires the company to provide a means of resolution that is adequately funded and staffed to resolve disputes quickly, free of charge to customers, able to gather all necessary facts and make decisions independently, and audited annually to ensure compliance. This function can be performed by a third party (such as the Better Business Bureau) or by employees specifically on staff to handle warranty disputes objectively. Among the means of settling the dispute can be conciliation, mediation, and arbitration; if either party is still dissatisfied, the matter can still be brought to court.

While having an informal dispute procedure in place eliminates the necessity of going to court, it is clearly still enough of a burden on a company that it makes more sense to offer clear-cut warranties and honor them.

## Self-Help Measures

The FTC recommends that consumers take several steps in order to minimize problems that they may have with respect to warranties. These steps include the following:

- Read the Warranty Before Buying an Item: Consumers should read a seller's full warranty and understand exactly what protection the warrant offers.

- Consider a Company's Reputation: Consumers who are unfamiliar with a company should consult with a local or state consumer protection office or Better Business Bureau.

- Save Receipts Along with the Warranty: The receipt may be necessary to document that the a consumer is the original owner.

- Perform Maintenance and Inspections That Are Required by the Warranty.

- Use the Product According to Instructions Provided by the Manufacturer: Some forms of abuse or misuse of a product could void a warranty.

- Attempt to Resolve a Problem Directly with the Seller.

- Consider Filing a Claim in Small Claims Court: A dispute that involves less than a relatively small amount of money, such as $750, may be resolved in small claims court. Costs in small claims court are usually low, procedures are relatively simple, and lawyers are not necessary.

The FTC provides additional information at http://www.ftc.gov/ftc/consumer.htm.

## Additional Resources

*The Consumer Movement: Guardians of the Marketplace.* Mayer, Robert N., Twayne Publishers, 1989.

*Consumer Warranty Law.* 2d Edition. Sheldon, Jonathan and Carolyn L. Carter, National Consumer Law Center, 2001.

*Extraordinary Guarantees: A New Way to Build Quality Throughout Your Company and Ensure Satisfaction for Your Customers.* L. Hart, Christopher W. L., AMACOM, 1993.

*Return to Sender: Getting A Refund or Replacement for Your Lemon Car.* Barron, Nancy, National Consumer Law Center, 2000.

*Sales and Leases: Examples and Explanations.* Brook, James, Aspen Publishers, 2003.

*Understanding Consumer Rights.* Parisi, Nicolette, Dorling Kindersley, 2000.

## Organizations

### Better Business Bureau
4200 Wilson Blvd, Suite 800
Arlington, VA 22203-1838 USA
Phone: (703) 276-0100
Fax: (703) 525-8277
URL: http://www.bbb.org

### Consumers Union
101 Truman Avenue
Yonkers, NY 10703 USA
Phone: (914) 378-2000
Fax: (914) 378-2928
URL: http://www.consumersunion.org

### Federal Trade Commission
600 Pennsylvania Avenue, NW
Washington, DC 20580
Phone: (877) 382-4357
URL: http://www.ftc.gov

# COURTS AND PROCEDURES

## BURDEN OF PROOF

*Sections within this essay:*

## Background

A burden of proof refers to the responsibility each party to a controversy bears in proving its claim, defense (see below), or objection. It refers to that body of law dealing with evidence presented in a formal adjudication of a controversy which tends to prove or disprove a disputed fact. In civil cases, a general rule is that the burden of proof rests with the party advancing the matter to be proved. Courts apply three different standards in determining whether a party has met its burden of proof, discussed below.

In application, a party to a controversy must convince the adjudicative entity (court, jury, arbitrator, administrative law judge) to rule in its favor. It does this by presenting evidence that it believes supports its position. The party typically presents evidence to support each **element** of the claim or defense it proffers. How much weight and credibility to afford each item of evidence is up to the adjudicative entity before which the evidence is presented.

### *Preponderance of the Evidence*

In most civil cases/lawsuits as well as administrative hearings, a party must prove its claim or position by a preponderance, defined as a superiority in weight, force, importance, etc. In legal terms, a preponderance of evidence means that a party has shown that its version of facts, causes, damages, or fault is *more likely than not* the correct version, as in personal injury and breach of contract suits. This standard is the easiest to meet and applies to all civil cases unless otherwise provided by law.

The concept of "preponderance of the evidence" can be visualized as a scale representing the burden of proof, with the totality of evidence presented by each side resting on the respective trays on either side of the scale. If the scale tips ever so slightly to one side or the other, the weightier side will prevail. If the scale does not tip toward the side of the party bearing the burden of proof, that party cannot prevail.

Trial lawyers will often instruct juries that their clients must prevail at trial if they have proved their positions by as little as 51 percent likelihood of probability (anything from 51 to 100 percent constitutes a preponderance of evidence). In other words, if a jury believes there is a 51-49 percent likelihood that a defendant (in a civil case) was negligent or liable, the plaintiff/complainant has met its burden of a preponderance of evidence, and will prevail. This is particularly helpful when juries are torn between the testimony of two expert witnesses presenting opposite opinions or views. Whether it is an issue of credibility or of expertise, the jury will decide which is the more likely version that warrants more evidentiary weight.

### *Clear and Convincing Evidence*

Certain civil suits require a stronger burden of proof, in terms of percentage of weight of the presented evidence. A burden to show "clear and convincing evidence" refers to more than a mere preponderance but something just short of conclusive (which would be more tantamount to the "beyond a reasonable doubt" burden used in criminal cases). However, in reality, "clear and convincing" burden of proof generally requires proof which leaves no reasonable doubt concerning the truth of the matters at issue.

This higher burden is generally employed when the alleged offense has special elements to establish, such as in a claim for fraud, for a lost will of inheritance, or when family members wish to withdraw life support from a loved one. In these and other cases, the stakes at risk are high and the defending party serves to lose a substantial benefit, property, (or especially) personal or fundamental liberty such as those protected under the First Amendment.

### Beyond a Reasonable Doubt

This standard of proof is used exclusively in criminal cases, and a person cannot be convicted of a crime unless a judge or jury is convinced of the defendant's guilt beyond a reasonable doubt. Precisely, if there is any reasonable uncertainty of guilt, based on the evidence presented, a defendant cannot be convicted.

Ostensibly, this burden requires that a trier of fact (judge, jury, arbiter) is fully satisfied and entirely convinced to a moral certainty that the evidence presented proves the guilt of the defendant. There is essentially no room for wavering or uncertainty; the trier of fact believes the evidence to be precise, indubitable, and leaves one with an inescapable conclusion of certainty. Whereas, in a civil trial, a party may prevail with as little as 51 percent probability (a preponderance), those legal authorities who venture to assign a numerical value to "beyond a reasonable doubt" place it in the certainty range of 98 or 99 percent.

In a criminal trial, the state must prove that the defendant is guilty, and the burden of proof is always with the state for the **case in chief.** The defendant, carrying a presumption of innocence, has no burden of proof, and need prove nothing. A defendant may sit mute at a criminal trial, because the state has the burden of proof to show that the defendant satisfied each element of the statutory definition of a crime by his or her action/participation or failure to act. Any evidence offered by the defense is generally directed toward discrediting or undermining the state's evidence, and does not contribute to any evidentiary burden.

However, if a defendant initiates to offer a defense to the jury, such as a defense of insanity, the burden technically shifts to the defendant to prove insanity and avoid a verdict of guilt. Likewise, a defendant claiming self-defense or duress carries the burden of proof to establish all elements of those defenses to either avoid or mitigate a guilty verdict.

### Shifting Burden of Proof

In contrast to the rare circumstances where a burden of proof may shift in a criminal trial, there are several applications of such a concept in civil matters.

Generally speaking, the party that filed the action (be it a criminal complaint by the state's attorney, or a civil law suit by a private party), has the burden of proof to establish, through evidence, all the requisite elements of a *prima facie case.* For example, in a case for the offense of tortious battery, the complainant has the burden of proof to establish (1) that there was a specific intent to make contact with the person of another (2) in a harmful or offensive manner, (3) without consent, and (4) a harmful or offensive contact occurred.

If that burden is met, the burden of proof then shifts to the defendant in the case, who now has to plead and prove any defense, by a **preponderance** of evidence. Often, the defendant raises an **affirmative defense,** which will have its own elements of proof that must be met by the defendant. Of course, if the defendant raises a **counterclaim** against the plaintiff, the entire burden of proof shifts to the defendant on the matter of the counterclaim (or **third party claim**).

Another example of a shifting burden is that in employment discrimination cases. Once the plaintiff has met his or her burden of proof by establishing a prima facie case, the burden of proof shifts to the defendant to show some non-discriminatory reason for its action. If the defendant essentially meets that burden of proof by presenting legitimate reasons for the alleged action, the burden again shifts back to the plaintiff to show that the proffered "legitimate" reasons were **pretextual.**

A burden of proof generally attaches at the trial or adjudicatory stage. A plaintiff (in a civil case) or a petitioner (in an administrative case), or the state (in a criminal case) need only allege the existence of facts needed to prove each requisite element of the alleged wrong, offense, or crime. The **averments** or **allegations** contained therein are presumed to be true during this initial stage. However, at the actual trial, the party then bears the burden of proof to present evidence tending to support or prove the facts alleged in the complaint or petition. Following this presentation of the case in chief, an opposing party may then petition the court to dismiss the case (before it reaches a jury), for failure in meeting a required burden of proof.

## Administrative Tribunals

In matters coming before an administrative tribunal, such as workers' compensation boards, social security benefits hearings, or Internal Revenue Service audits or hearings, the burden of proof generally lies with the party claiming the benefit or beneficial treatment. The agency or board need only articulate a reasonable basis for denial of a claim or benefit. Of course, its decision can generally be appealed, but only in limited context (e.g., **abuse of discretion**). However, in cases involving the suspension, revocation, or forfeiture of some benefit *already being received* by a party, the burden typically rests with the agency, as it is the agency that initiates the action.

## Additional Resources

*Criminal Procedure.* Wayne R. LaFave, Jerold h. Israel, and Nancy J. King. West Group, 2001.

# COURTS AND PROCEDURES

## CIVIL PROCEDURE

*Sections within this essay:*

- Background
- Authority
- Jurisdiction
    - Subject Matter Jurisdiction
    - Jurisdiction over the Parties
    - Jurisdictional Amounts
- Venue
- Federal Rules of Civil Procedure (FRCP)
    - Parties
    - Commencement of an Action
    - Pleadings
    - Pre-trial Procedure
    - Trial
    - Judgment
    - Appeal
- State Rules of Civil Procedure
- Additional Resources

## Background

**Civil procedure** refers to that body of law (usually in the form of collective and published rules) that concerns itself with the methods, procedures, and practices used in civil proceedings. Civil proceedings are distinguished from criminal or administrative proceedings, which are governed by their own respective rules of procedure. Most (but not all) civil proceedings involve "litigation" or lawsuits between private parties or entities (such as business **corporations**) and the focus herein generally relates to key procedures in the **litigation** process.

**Procedural law** is intended to safeguard those vested rights in life, liberty, and property that are guaranteed by the U.S. Constitution. The Fifth Amendment to the Constitution provides that "No person shall be . . . deprived of life, liberty, or property without **due process of law** [the "due process clause"]; nor shall private property be taken for public use, without just compensation." The Fourteenth Amendment to the Constitution makes those provisions applicable to the states.

In almost every civil lawsuit, there will be a prevailing (winning) party and a defeated (losing) party. Judgment against the losing party (whether it is the person who filed the claim or the person against whom the claim was made) generally means he or she will be adversely affected. The constitutional guarantee of "due process of law" ensures that persons whose rights may be adversely affected by litigation have the opportunity for their "day in court,"—to be heard and to present proof(s) in support of their claim or defense. Accordingly, before any judgment can be made for or against a party, certain procedural safeguards **warrant** that a just and **fair hearing** on the matter has been conducted and that all parties whose interests may be affected by the controversy have been notified of their right to be heard.

Civil procedure, then, helps provide the "structure" needed to guarantee a fair and just determination of the controversy, while also serving to move the matter through the legal system in an orderly and consistent manner. It governs such actions as the way in which service of process is made upon a **defendant**, the number of days and manner in which parties may "discover" one another's **evidence**, and the manner in which parties may present their controversies or objections to the court. Additional rules of procedure may have more simple purposes, such as uniformity or judicial economy. In any event, courts have the power and authority of law (in the absence of abuse of discretion) to dismiss lawsuits and/or deny remedies if procedural rules are not followed.

## Authority

Article III of the U.S. Constitution expressly creates a federal court system, and Section 2 of that Article further declares that **jurisdiction** (See Jurisdiction, below) of the U.S. Supreme Court and courts within the federal system shall be subject to "such Regulations as the Congress shall make." Those regulations are contained in Section 1251 of Title 28 of the United States Code (U.S.C. or U.S.C.A.—designating the annotated version). Section 2072 of 28 U.S.C. 131 (The Rules Enabling Act) authorizes the Supreme Court to "prescribe general rules of practice and procedure and rules of evidence for cases in the U.S. district courts (including proceedings before magistrates thereof) and courts of appeals." Similarly, state constitutions and statutes empower the states' highest courts (usually) to regulate civil procedures in state courts.

## Jurisdiction

An important and early determination to be made in each pending action is whether to file a civil lawsuit in the "forum" of a federal court or state court. A court's general authority to hear and/or "adjudicate" a legal matter is referred to as its "jurisdiction." In the United States, jurisdiction is granted to a court or court system by **statute** or by constitution. A legal decision made by a court that does not have proper jurisdiction is deemed void and non-binding upon the litigants.

Jurisdiction may be referred to as "exclusive," "original," concurrent, general, or limited. Article III, Section 2 of the U.S. Constitution limits the types of cases that federal courts may hear. Generally speaking, federal courts may hear only those cases involving federal laws, federal or sovereign parties (including states), or disputes between citizens from different states. Thus, federal courts have "limited" jurisdiction, which may be "exclusive" over a matter or party (to the exclusion of any other forum), or may be "concurrent" and shared with state courts.

In matters where both federal and state courts have concurrent jurisdiction, state courts may hear federal law claims (e.g., violations of **civil rights**), and parties bringing suit may choose the forum. However, when a plaintiff raises both state and federal claims in a state court, the defendant may be able to "remove" the case to a federal court.

### Subject Matter Jurisdiction

A court is competent to hear and decide only those cases whose subject matter fits within the court's scope of authority. Courts of "limited" jurisdiction may be competent to hear only certain matters, such as those involving **probate** or juvenile cases. Even courts of broad or general jurisdiction may have certain matters removed from their jurisdiction (by statute or state constitution), such as **divorce** or **custody** matters, to be handled by other courts. If the controversy involves a parcel of real estate instead of a person, the property must be located within the territorial jurisdiction of the court.

### Jurisdiction over the Parties

A court must have jurisdiction not only over the subject matter of the controversy, but also the parties to the litigation. There is seldom a question of jurisdiction over the plaintiff, since by bringing the action into the court, the plaintiff consents to the court's jurisdiction over him or her. But the plaintiff must also show that the court has jurisdiction over the defendant. In general, this may be established by the defendant's consent, by the defendant's general appearance in court, or by proving a defendant's domicile within the geographic area of the court's jurisdiction (in combination with serving process upon the defendant). A fourth way of acquiring jurisdiction over a defendant relies on "long-arm statutes," which permit a court to "reach" absent defendants or defendants residing in other states by establishing their relationship with the state in which the action was filed (the "forum" state). It may be that they committed the wrongful act within the forum state or transact business within that state or own property in that state, etc.

### Jurisdictional Amounts

Finally, many courts limit their jurisdiction to cases in which the amount in controversy exceeds a certain minimum amount. For example, no complaint may be filed in a federal court unless the amount in controversy exceeds the sum or value of $75,000. Many state circuit courts have minimum "jurisdictional amounts" of $10,000, $15,000, or $25,000. Conversely, many local or district courts within state court systems have maximum jurisdictional amounts; if the amount in controversy exceeds the jurisdictional maximum, either the case must be re-filed in the next level court or the complaining party must waive his or her right to any judgment that exceeds the maximum.

## Venue

Venue refers to the geographic location of the court in which to bring an action. Most court systems (federal and state) have statutes that dictate the particular district, county or city in which a court with jurisdiction may hear a case. Usually, venue is premised on where a defendant resides or does business, where the wrongful act occurred, or alternatively, where a plaintiff resides. The general venue statute governing federal cases is 28 U.S.C.A. Section 1391. Venue provisions for state courts are generally found in statutes rather than rules of civil procedure; the rules of procedure may address the way in which one motions a court for a "change of venue."

## Federal Rules of Civil Procedure (FRCP)

A major step toward establishing uniform federal procedures was undertaken in 1934, when the U.S. Supreme Court promulgated the Federal Rules of Civil Procedure (FRCP). The bible for practicing attorneys, the Rules govern all civil actions in federal courts nationwide, including federal **bankruptcy** court. The Rules are frequently amended and updated and contain Supplemental Rules sections for cases in admiralty and maritime actions, as well as "local rules" pertaining to specific courts within the federal system.

Although the Rules were intended to apply to U.S. district courts within the federal system, nearly all state courts have since replaced their own procedural rules with new rules modeled after the FRCP. At a minimum, it can be said that the FRCP represents the dominant style of American civil procedure, whether in federal or state court. Although there is not uniformity **per se**, there is general consistency of approach to matters common in most causes of action.

### Parties

In civil procedure, the prosecuting party (the one filing a complaint or lawsuit or petition) is referred to as a "plaintiff" or "petitioner" or "complainant" (depending upon the court and the nature of the matter), while the opposing party is referred to as a "defendant" or "respondent." (For purposes of simplicity, the terms "plaintiff" and "defendant" are used exclusively herein, but imply any or all of the above, respectively.)

Any person may file a lawsuit under his or her own name, but the person must have "legal capacity" to sue (the legal competency to stand before the court). This requirement implies, among other factors, minimum **legal age** and mental competency. FRCP 17(c) provides that a **guardian** or conservator may sue or defend on behalf of an infant or legally incompetent person; or, if none exists, the court will appoint a "next friend" or "guardian ad litem" to represent the interest of the child or incompetent person. A deceased person may be represented in an action by the personal representative (executor or administrator) of the deceased's estate. FRCP 17(b) also provides that in federal court, the legal capacity of a business corporation to sue or be sued is determined by the law under which it was organized.

Several parties may be joined in an action, as co-plaintiffs or co-defendants. Under FRCP 23 and most state rules, multiple plaintiffs who have suffered harm as a result of the actions of a common defendant may be joined together in one lawsuit called a "class action." Under such a suit, only a few plaintiffs will be named in the action, but they will represent all plaintiffs within the certified "class," and their claims must be fairly representative of the interests of all the persons within the class.

A lawsuit may become fairly complicated when the original parties (and sometimes the court) bring in third or additional parties not initially named in the suit. Parties joined on the same side are referred to as "co-parties." If co-parties raise claims against one another (e.g., a defendant blames another defendant), they are "cross-parties" as to each other. But if a "counter-claim" is raised against an opposing party, they become "counter-parties" as to the **counterclaim**. In the "caption," or heading of the original action, the parties may be referred to as co-plaintiffs, co-defendants, cross-plaintiffs, cross-defendants, counter-plaintiffs, counter-defendants, or "interested parties," depending upon the claims or defenses raised.

### Commencement of an Action

A lawsuit must be commenced within the limitation period provided by law (the applicable "statute of limitations"). Lawsuits not filed within the period of the applicable **statute of limitations** will be dismissed. Under the U.S. Supreme Court decision in *Erie v. Tompkins*, federal courts will apply the statute of limitations of the state in which the federal court lies. Statutes of limitations generally begin to run when the cause of action arises. Many states have exceptions that allow for "tolling" of their statutes of limitations (temporarily "stopping the clock") during periods of absence from the forum state, war, legal **incompetency**, etc. There are also special rules that apply if death occurs prior to the expiration of the limitations period.

Under FRCP 3 and many state jurisdictions, an action commences when a complaint is filed. However, many states do not consider the action to have commenced until service of process has been made upon the defendant. Service of process may be made by personal service of the complaint and **summons** upon the defendant (many states permit registered mail service); constructive service by notice or publication; or substituted service on a registered agent of the defendant (as for business corporations). There are strict rules that limit the use of constructive or substituted service on defendants.

### Pleadings

Pleadings are written formal allegations in support of either a claim or a defense, presented for the court's consideration and judgment. Under FRPC 7, pleadings are limited to a complaint and an answer, a reply (to a counterclaim), an answer to a cross-claim, a third-party complaint, and a third-party answer.

The first pleading in an action is called a "complaint." (In a minority of jurisdictions, the pleading may still be referred to as a "bill of complaint" or "declaration.") FRCP 10(a) requires that a complaint contain, at a minimum the following:

- a caption that contains the name of the court, the title of the action, the file number (provided by the court), and the names of all the parties

- a short and plain statement of facts which tend to show that the pleader is entitled to relief

- a demand for judgment for the relief to which plaintiff deems himself or herself entitled

- a signature of an attorney of record and the attorney's business address (or the party's signature and address, if not represented by an attorney)

- a short and plain statement of the grounds upon which the court's jurisdiction depends

FRCP 7 provides that the responsive pleading to a complaint is called an answer. It generally contains denials of the allegations in the complaint and/or new matters asserted as counterclaims or affirmative defenses. However, under FRCP12 and most states' rules, an interim responsive pleading may be in the form of a motion to dismiss or a motion for **summary judgment**, for such reasons as failure to state a claim, lack of jurisdiction, insufficiency of process, etc. These generally constitute "affirmative defenses" that do not speak to the specific facts alleged in the complaint but rather challenge the validity of the complaint on some other grounds.

Under FRCP 8, allegations in a pleading to which a responsive pleading is required are admitted unless they are specifically denied in the answer. Moreover, under the federal rules, the defendant is required to assert all defenses in the responsive pleading or they will be waived. As part of the responsive pleading, FRCP 13 permits the raising of a counterclaim against the plaintiff, or a cross-claim against a co-party or a third party claim against a non-party (who will be served and joined as a party). There must be a reply to a counterclaim or cross-claim. Amendments to pleadings are permitted in the furtherance of justice and on the terms deemed proper by the court (FRCP 15).

### Pre-trial Procedure

Following the filing of all initial pleadings, there begins a period of "discovery" which enables each party to learn of evidence held by opposing or other parties to the action. Generally speaking, the scope of allowable **discovery** is broad: FRCP 26 provides that parties may obtain discovery on any matter, not privileged, which is relevant to the subject matter involved in the pending action. Discovery is accomplished by means of subpoenas; requests for inspection of documents, photographs, recordings, or other items of evidence; the taking of **testimony** of witnesses (usually by **deposition**); review and copying of relevant records; written interrogatories (questions that must be answered under oath); written requests for admissions (requiring admission or denial of the facts posed); requests for physical or mental **examination** of a party; and often, visitation to sites, premises, or geographic locations relevant to the case.

Also during the pre-trial period (and continuing through the trial process), various "motions" may be filed with the court, requesting that the court grant an order on some matter related to the progress of the case. A motion may request immediate relief for an interim dispute (such as a motion to compel the release of evidence) or it may request "dispositive" relief (such as a motion to dismiss the case for lack of evidence or failure to state a cause of action).

### Trial

At the close of discovery, parties are encouraged to review the sum total of evidence and attempt to settle the case. In many state jurisdictions, there is compulsory (but non-binding) "mediation" of the case, in which an independent panel reviews the pleadings and evidence and makes a **settlement** recommendation. If no viable settlement results, the case will move on to the trial stage. Prior to trial, attorneys for the parties will provide written requests for jury instructions they wish to include in the charge to the jury (FRCP 51). Attorneys will also have the opportunity to examine and rule out prospective jurors ("voir dire") for such disqualifying factors as **bias**, personal familiarity with the parties or witnesses, **felony conviction**, legal relationship with any party or witness (such as **landlord**, employer, partner), etc. (FRCP 47). These are referred to as "challenges for cause." Most jurisdictions also permit a certain number of "peremptory challenges," wherein trial attorneys may rule out prospective jurors without stating their reason for doing so. After a final jury is agreed upon and all last-minute motions have been heard, trial begins.

In general, the order of proceedings at trial are: opening statements (first plaintiff, then defendant); introduction of evidence (first plaintiff, then defendant, then rebuttal evidence); closing arguments (first plaintiff, then defendant); instructions to the jury ("jury charge") by the court; return of verdict and poll of jury; and entry of a judgment.

The normal order for the presentation of proofs (evidence) is: the plaintiff introduces all the evidence for his or her "case in chief"; the defendant then introduces his or her evidence in chief; the plaintiff then offers rebuttal evidence; and finally, the defendant may be permitted to present evidence in rebuttal of any new matter brought out in the plaintiff's rebuttal evidence (called surrebuttal). Objections to any proffered evidence must be timely made or they are waived; proper and/or permissible objections are covered in the Federal Rules of Evidence (FRE) rather than the FRCP.

Closing arguments are then made (plaintiff first, followed by defendant, then followed with plaintiff's final rebuttal), and the jury is charged and sequestered for deliberations. The jury normally renders it verdict through its foreman, and the entire jury must be present when the verdict is delivered in court. Barring any defects in form or challenges to the verdict, a judgment is declared for the prevailing party.

Prior to the delivery of a verdict, either party may motion the court for a judgment on the evidence (e.g., a motion for summary judgment) or for **mistrial** (based upon an objection made during trial). Following delivery of a verdict, a party may motion for a new trial or partial retrial (FRCP 59).

### Judgment

A judgment on the verdict is not the only way to prevail in a **civil action**. In fact, at the conclusion of trial, either party may motion a court for a "judgment notwithstanding the verdict," (following the party's earlier motion for a **directed verdict**), even though there has been a jury verdict for the other party.

Rather than defend a civil complaint, a party may merely consent to judgment, as in claims of debt, and such "consent judgments" are entered on the record and are as binding as a full jury verdict.

A "default judgment" may be rendered against a party if it is the result of a party's failure to take a necessary step in the action within the proper time; this generally means a failure to plead or otherwise defend within the time allowed. Since, under rules of procedure, allegations not specifically denied are deemed admitted, failure to file a responsive pleading will generally result in the entry of a **default judgment** against the defendant.

Finally, under FRCP 57 and most state rules and/or statutes, courts are authorized to grant "declaratory judgments" in cases where the requested relief is in the form of a court's declaration of certain rights, status, or legal relations between parties or entities. Some examples include actions to "quiet title" to real property, actions regarding ownership, or use of intellectual property rights (such as copyrights or **patents**), etc. In order to invoke the court's jurisdiction in a declaratory matter, there must be an actual controversy and not a mere desire for an advisory opinion from the court.

### Appeal

In both federal and state courts, a party may appeal only final orders, decisions, or judgments. After the entry of a final order, decision, or judgment, there are strict procedural deadlines as to the number of days within which an appeal must be filed. Grounds for appeal are extremely limited. An order of a court will not be reversed unless the **appellant** can show that either the order was clearly contrary to law or that the judge abused his or her discretion.

Likewise, there is limited review of trial judgments. It is not generally sufficient to show error in the conduct of trial; the appellant must show harm or prejudice that was caused by the error (for example, the introduction of evidence which the appellant argued was improper and without which the appellant most likely would have prevailed). **Appellate** courts disregard harmless errors or defects that do not affect the substantial rights of the parties in determining whether a particular case should be reversed. (FRCP 61)

## State Rules of Civil Procedure

The first state to establish uniform rules of civil procedure was New York, which in 1848 enacted the Field Code, named after its principal author, David Dudley Field. Over the next several decades, nearly all states had either adopted the Code outright or had made other considerable changes to their procedures. As of 2002, the Code has been replaced with modified versions of the FRCP in nearly all states. Notwithstanding, there are procedural differences from state to state, and it is imperative that litigants are familiar with state rules before proceeding in court. Copies of state rules may often be found at public libraries, college libraries, and/or on states' official Internet websites.

ALABAMA: See Title 6 of the Alabama Code of 1975, also available at http:// www.legislatures.state.al.us/codeofAlabama/1975.

ALASKA: See Title 9 of Alaska Statutes, "Code of Civil Procedure."

ARIZONA: See Title 12 of the Arizona Revised Statutes, available at http://www.azleg.state.ar.us/

ARKANSAS: See Title 16, Subtitle 5 of the Arkansas Code, available at http://www.arkleg.state.ar.us/dcode.

CALIFORNIA: See the "California Code of Civil Procedure."

COLORADO: See Title 13 of the Colorado Constitution, "Colorado Rules of Civil Procedure."

CONNECTICUT: See Title 52 of the General Statutes of Connecticut, available at http:// www.cga.state.ct.us/2001/pub/Title52.

DELAWARE: See Title 10, Part 3 of the Delaware Code, "Courts and Judicial Procedure."

DISTRICT OF COLUMBIA: See Titles 13-17.

FLORIDA: See "Florida Rules of Civil Procedure," from the Florida Lawyers World Wide Web Resource Center at http://phonl.com/fl_law/rules/frcp/

GEORGIA: See Title 9, Chapter 10 of the Georgia Code.

IDAHO: See Titles 1-13 of the Idaho Code.

ILLINOIS: See Code of Civil Procedure, 735 IL CS 5.

INDIANA: See Title 34 of the Indiana Code, Articles 1-57, available at www.state.in.us/legislature/ic/code/title34.

IOWA: See Title X, Subtitle 3 of the Iowa Code, available at www.legis.state.ia.us/IACODE.

KANSAS: See Chapters 60 and 61of the Kansas Statutes, available at http://www.kslegislature.org/cgi-bin/statutes/index.cgi.

KENTUCKY: See Kentucky Rules of Court, authority found in Kentucky Constitution, Articles 109-116.

LOUISIANA: See the Louisiana Code of Civil Procedure, available at http://www.legis.state.la.us.

MAINE: See Maine Rules of Civil Procedure, available at http://www.cleaves.org/sc-rules.htm.

MARYLAND: See "Courts and Judicial Procedures," Section 1-101, et seq., available at http://mlis.state.md.us/cgi-win/web_statutes.exe.

MASSACHUSETTS: See Chapters 211-262 of the General Laws of Massachusetts, "Courts, Judicial Officers and Proceedings in Civil Cases."

MICHIGAN: See "Michigan Rules of Court," available at http://www.michiganlegislature.org/law/MCLSearch.asp.

MINNESOTA: See Chapters 540-552.

MISSISSIPPI: See Title 11of Mississippi Code of 1972, available at http://www.mscode.com/free/statutes.

MISSOURI: See Missouri Revised Statutes, Title XXXV, Chapters 506-517, available at http://www.moga.state.mo.us/STATUTES.

MONTANA: See Title 25 of state statute.

NEBRASKA: See Chapters 25 and 26 of Nebraska statutes, available at http://statutes.unicam.state.ne.us/

NEVADA: See Titles 3-6 of the Nevada Revised Statutes.

NEW HAMPSHIRE: See Title LIII, Chapters 514-526 of the New Hampshire Revised Statutes, "Proceedings in Court," available at http://sudoc.nhsl.lib.nh.us/rsa/LIII.htm.

NEW JERSEY: See Chapter 2A of the New Jersey Permanent Statutes, available at http://www.njleg.state.nj.us/

NEW YORK: See Chapter 8 of the New York State Consolidated Laws, available at http://assembly.state.ny.us/leg/

NORTH CAROLINA: See Chapters 1 and 1A of the North Carolina General Statutes.

NORTH DAKOTA: See Chapter 28 of the Century Code. "Judicial Procedure, Civil."

OKLAHOMA: See Title 12 of the Oklahoma Statutes.

OREGON: See Chapters 12-36 of the Oregon Revised Statutes.

PENNSYLVANIA: See Pennsylvania Constitution of 1968, Article V, Section 10C, 42 PA CS 1722, available at http://member.aol./com/RulesPA/civil.hyml.

RHODE ISLAND: See Title 9, available at http://www.rilin.state.ri.us/statutes/Title9/INDEX.

SOUTH CAROLINA: See Title 15 of the Code of Laws, available at http://www.lpitr.state.sc.us/code/tit15.htm.

SOUTH DAKOTA: See Title 15.

TENNESSEE: See Titles 19 and 20.

TEXAS: See "Civil Practice and Remedies Code," available at http://www.capitol.state.tx.us/statutes/cvtoc.html.

UTAH: See Future Title 28-"Judicial Code" of the Utah Code, available at http://www.le.state.ut.us/FTITL78.

VERMONT: See Title 12 of the Vermont Statutes.

VIRGINIA: See Virginia Code Section 915a, available at http://www.leg1.state.va.us/000/cod/code915a.htm#751573.

WASHINGTON: See Title 4, "Civil Procedure," of the Revised Code of Washington, available at http://www.leg.wa.gov/wsladm/rcw.cfm.

WEST VIRGINIA: See Chapters 55-58.

WISCONSIN: See Chapters 801-847 of the Wisconsin Statutes.

WYOMING: See Title 1 of the Wyoming Statutes, available at http://legisweb.state.wy.us/title/97titles/title1.htm.

## Additional Resources

"Civil Procedure: an Overview" Available at http://www.law.cornell.edu/topics/civil_procedure.html.

*The Court TV Cradle-to-grave Legal Survival Guide* Little, Brown and Company, 1995.

*Federal Rules of Civil Procedure* Available at http://www.law.cornell.edu/topics/civil_procedure.html.

*The Law of the Land* Rembar, Charles, Simon & Schuster, 1993.

*West's Encyclopedia of American Law* West, 1998.

# COURTS AND PROCEDURES

## FEDERAL COURTS AND JURISDICTIONS

*Sections within this essay:*

## Background

Article III of the United States Constitution establishes the judicial power of the federal government. Under the Constitution, the authority of the federal judiciary extends only to certain "cases" and "controversies," which are identified by either the nature of the suit or the parties involved. The Constitution establishes the Supreme Court of the United States and permits Congress to establish "inferior" federal courts. The federal judiciary currently consists of the Supreme Court, courts of appeals in 12 regional judicial circuits, two intermediate **appellate** courts with special power to hear cases originating nationwide, a total of 94 judicial districts throughout the 50 states

that contain at least one federal district court and one **bankruptcy** court, territorial courts that function as district courts in several territories, and specialized tribunals that have been established by Congress pursuant to power provided in Article I of the Constitution. The district courts serve as the trial courts in the federal system, while the courts of appeals serve as intermediate appellate courts.

The power or authority of a court to hear and decide a case or controversy is called the **jurisdiction** of the court. Jurisdiction may be divided into two broad categories: subject-matter jurisdiction and personal jurisdiction. Subject-matter jurisdiction refers to the authority of a court to hear a certain type of case, while personal jurisdiction refers to the power with which a court may bind an individual party. Most cases and controversies that can be heard by the federal judiciary consist of the following:

- Cases governed by federal law, such as the federal Constitution, federal **statutory** provisions, or federal regulations (federal question jurisdiction)

- Suits between citizens of different states (diversity jurisdiction)

- Suits between a citizen of a state and a citizen of a foreign country

- Admiralty and maritime cases

- Suits in which the United States is a party

- Suits between two states

The United States operates with a dual system of courts: the federal judiciary and the judicial systems of the states. If a party brings an action in a state court, but a federal court has jurisdiction to hear the case, the **defendant** may choose to "remove" the case to the federal court, subject to several limitations set forth in Title 28 of the United States Code. The defendant is not obligated to remove such a case, and questions about whether removal is proper in a particular case are often subjects of controversy in federal courts. In a case where a federal court permits a state court case to be removed but later determines that removal was improper, the federal court will remand the case to the state court.

## Structure and Power of the Federal Courts

Pursuant to its Constitutional power, Congress has established inferior courts in the federal judiciary at the intermediate appellate and trial court levels. Courts that have been established under Article III of the Constitution, including the Supreme Court of the United States, United States Courts of Appeals, and United States District Courts, are called constitutional, or Article III, courts. Congress, pursuant to powers granted in Article I, may also establish legislative, or Article I, courts. These courts are designed to carry out specific legislative directives. Examples of such courts are the United States Court of Federal Claims and the United States Tax Court.

### Supreme Court of the United States

The Supreme Court of the United States consists of the **chief justice** of the United States and, since 1869, eight associate justices. The number of justices varied during the first 80 years of the country's history, beginning with five justices in 1798 and growing to as many as ten in 1863. Congress retains authority under the Constitution to establish the number of associate justices. The president of the United States nominates Supreme Court justice candidates, and appointments are made "with the advice and consent of the Senate." Under Article III of the Constitution, United States Supreme Court justices have lifetime tenure in their positions "during time of good Behaviour." Lifetime tenure is also true of the judges in the lower constitutional courts of the federal system. The chief justice presides over the Supreme Court and also holds leadership roles on the Judicial Conference of the United States, the Administrative Office of the United States, and the Federal Judicial Center.

In the vast majority of Supreme Court decisions, the Court exercises its appellate jurisdiction. The Court may assert original jurisdiction (that is, decide

a case from beginning to end) if the case involves states or a state and the federal government. These types of cases are seldom filed with the Court. In exercising its appellate jurisdiction, the Court can hear cases appealed from both lower federal courts and state supreme courts if a case involves an issue of federal law. With respect to cases originating in state court, parties must exhaust their possibilities in the state court system before the Supreme Court will consider **hearing** a case.

The Supreme Court is not required to hear most requests for appeals. The decision of the Supreme Court to hear an appeal is discretionary in almost all cases today. Unless an appeal is mandatory, which is very rare, a party who wishes for the Supreme Court to hear an appeal must file a **writ** of **certiorari**, which requests that the Court review the decision of a lower court. The Court denies writs of certiorari in the vast majority of cases. The Court today grants appeals in only about one percent of the cases filed before it each year. If the Court refuses an appeal, it permits the lower court's decision to stand but does not have any other significant meaning (for example, it is not an affirmance of the lower court's opinion).

Many of the Supreme Court's decisions involve interpretation of the Constitution. The Court established itself as the primary authority to interpret the Constitution in the famous case of Marbury v. Madison in 1803. As the primary interpreter, the Court may invalidate an act of Congress if the act violates a right granted under the Constitution or Congress has misused powers granted to it under the Constitution. The Court does not decide ldquo;political questions," meaning those questions that another branch of government is better suited to answer. The Court also refuses to provide advice to the other branches of government. This restriction stems from the famous refusal of Chief Justice John Jay to provide advice to President George Washington about the implications under the new Constitution of a foreign policy decision.

### Federal Courts of Appeals

Congress through the Judiciary Act of 1891 originally established the intermediate appellate courts in the federal judiciary to relieve the caseload on the Supreme Court justices. Prior to 1891, cases were appealed routinely to the Supreme Court, which was required in most cases to hear the appeal. The courts of appeals now have jurisdiction to hear appeals from the federal district courts in virtually all cases. Unlike the Supreme Court, courts of appeals do not have discretionary jurisdiction to decide whether to grant an appeal. Other Acts of Congress have expanded the jurisdiction of the courts of appeals to hear appeals of decisions of federal administrative agencies. Courts of appeals also have a number of additional administrative functions that have been directed by Congress.

The federal court system currently consists of 12 regional circuits, each with one court of appeals. Eleven of these circuits are numbered (for example, the Fifth Circuit governs Texas, Mississippi, and Louisiana). The twelfth circuit, the Court of Appeals of the District of Columbia, governs only Washington, D. C., but hears a number of cases involving federal agencies. Congress in 1982 created the United States Court of Appeals for the Federal Circuit, which combined the functions of the United States Court of Customs and **Patent** Appeals and the United States **Court of Claims**. The Federal Circuit's jurisdiction, unlike the regional circuits, is nationwide, though it only applies to areas of law that are dictated by Congress.

### Federal District Courts

The federal court system includes 94 district courts in the 50 states, Washington, D. C., Puerto Rico, Guam, U. S. Virgin Islands, and Northern Marinara Islands. Most states have only one judicial district. Larger states can have between two and four districts. The district courts serve as the general trial courts of the federal system. Each district also has a bankruptcy unit, as district courts have exclusive jurisdiction over bankruptcy cases.

District courts generally have jurisdiction to hear cases involving federal law and those involving citizens of different states. If a party in a state case can prove that a federal district court has jurisdiction to hear a case, the party may remove the case to the federal court. However, the federal court may abstain from hearing a case that involves questions of both federal law and state law. A situation may also arise where a federal district court may no longer have jurisdiction to hear a case because of changes in the parties to the suit. If a case has been removed to federal district court and the federal district court lacks jurisdiction, the court on motion of one of the parties will remand the case to the appropriate state court.

### Specialized Federal Courts

Congress has created a number of courts in the federal system that have specialized jurisdiction. Unlike constitutional courts, judges appointed to legis-

lative courts do not enjoy lifetime tenure, unless Congress specifically authorized a life term. Moreover, judges in legislative courts do not enjoy the Constitutional prohibition against salary reductions of judges. A summary of these courts is as follows:

- The United States Court of Appeals for the Armed Forces reviews court martial convictions from the armed forces. Only the Supreme Court of the United States can review its cases. Judges sitting on this court enjoy neither life tenure nor protection against salary reduction.

- The United States Court of Federal Claims has jurisdiction to hear a broad range of claims brought against the United States. The court was called the United States Claims Court from 1982 to 1992. Many cases brought before this **tribunal** are tax cases, though the court also hears cases involving litigants who were federal employees and other parties with monetary claims against the United States. Judges sitting on this court enjoy neither life tenure nor protection against salary reduction. An adverse decision in this court is appealed to the United States Court of Appeals for the Federal Circuit.

- The United States Court of International Trade has jurisdiction to hear cases involving customs, unfair import practices, and other issues regarding international trade. This court is a constitutional court, so its judges have lifetime tenure and protection against salary reduction.

- The United States Court of Appeals for Veterans Claims reviews decisions of the Board of Veteran Appeals. Appointments of judges last 15 years. An adverse decision in this court is appealed to the United States Court of Appeals for the Federal Circuit.

- The United States Tax Court is a legislative court that resolves disputes between citizens and the Internal Revenue Service. Appointments of judges last 15 years. Adverse decisions are appealed to a court of appeals in an appropriate regional circuit.

## Jurisdiction of Federal Courts

No federal court has general jurisdiction, meaning that the court could hear any type of case brought before it in a particular location. The authority of a federal court to hear a case must be based on a federal law, whether it is the United States Constitution or a federal **statute**. Courts created by Congress with specialized jurisdiction are, of course, the most limited to hear a particular case because Congress permits these courts only to hear certain prescribed cases. The jurisdiction of constitutional courts is usually limited to one of two types of cases: cases involving a federal question and cases with parties with diversity of citizenship.

### Diversity Jurisdiction

Article III of the Constitution provides that a federal court may hear a controversy between citizens of different states or citizens of the United States and citizens of foreign nations. Congress in Title 28 of the United States Code limits this power by requiring that the amount in controversy exceed $75,000. The broad purpose behind diversity jurisdiction is that a state court may show **bias** towards its own citizen to the detriment of the citizen from another state. Diversity jurisdiction, to say the least, has long been a source of controversy.

One initial question in a diversity case is whether each of the parties does, in fact, reside in different states. For individuals, the question focuses on the individual's domicile rather than mere residence in a state. Thus, for example, if a party has a residence in both Texas and California, but his true domicile is Texas, then the party will be considered a citizen of Texas rather than a citizen of both states. Diversity jurisdiction requires complete diversity by all plaintiffs and all defendants in the suit, though there are limitations to this rule in the United States Code. For example, federal courts may have diversity jurisdiction to hear a case because all parties have diverse citizenship, but the court will not have supplemental jurisdiction over parties that are joined as plaintiffs in the case or over parties that intervene as plaintiffs in the case.

More difficult questions often arise when a corporation or association is a party to the suit. The right of a corporation is, in many respects, no different than the rights of an individual, since a corporation can sue or be sued. However, a corporation does not have a "domicile" that is similar to an individual. For diversity jurisdiction purposes, Congress provides that a corporation is a citizen in the state in which it is incorporated and in the state where it has its principal place of business. For smaller **corporations**, this question is usually not difficult, especially

if the corporation has most of its offices and business in a single state. However, large national corporations may have offices in every state, so the question is much more complex. For these types of corporations, courts look to the so-called "nerve center" of the corporation, meaning the state in which most of the corporation's business is conducted.

### Federal-Question Jurisdiction

The Constitution provides that federal courts have the power to hear cases that arise under the Constitution, laws, or treaties of the United States. Congress has granted this jurisdiction to federal district courts in Title 28 of the United States Code. The question of whether a case arises under a federal law is often clouded when a case involves issues with the application of both state and federal law. If a case primarily involves an issue of state law, but it also involves a remote federal issue, then the federal court is not the proper forum, and the case will be dismissed or remanded to state court. However, if a case involves important issues of both state and federal law, Congress permits a federal court, with some exceptions, to invoke supplemental jurisdiction to hear both the state claim and the federal claim in the same case.

Federal question jurisdiction must be based on the complaint of the plaintiff, not on the possibility of a federal defense. This limitation stems from the famous 1908 case of *Louisville & Nashville Railroad v. Mottley,* where the plaintiff anticipated a federal defense to a state law contract case. The Supreme Court held that the plaintiff's cause of action stated in the complaint must be based on federal law. This limitation is called the well-pleaded complaint rule. Since nothing prohibits state courts from hearing cases involving federal laws, federal courts are not required to hear all cases that involve federal laws.

### Admiralty and Maritime Cases

Since the development of the Constitution, federal courts have had jurisdiction to hear admiralty and maritime cases. In contract cases, the question to determine jurisdiction is whether a contract relates to maritime commerce, not the place where a contract was made or was to be performed. However, a contract to build or sell a ship does not give rise to admiralty jurisdiction. Admiralty jurisdiction arises in tort cases if the tort occurred in navigable waters or if a vessel has caused injuries on land.

### Bankruptcy

Federal courts have exclusive jurisdiction over bankruptcy cases. Each federal district court has a bankruptcy unit. Bankruptcy actions arise under Title 17 of the United States Code and generally incorporate all claims brought by a **creditor** against the **debtor** in the bankruptcy action. The federal bankruptcy laws differ from other state laws that govern the relationship between debtor and creditor, so certainly not all debtor-creditor cases are heard in federal court.

### Other Areas of Federal Jurisdiction

The Constitution and federal statutes provide federal jurisdiction in a number of areas in addition to those discussed above. Such areas include, for example, prize cases (those determining the rights to cargo and ships captured at sea), and **copyright**, patent, and trademark cases.

## Jurisdictions of Federal Courts in the U. S. States and Territories

Each state, the District of Columbia, and Puerto Rico contain between one and four federal districts, with the number of authorized judgeships in each district varying. Other territories, including Guam, the Virgin Islands, and the Northern Mariana Island, contain district courts as well. Each state also falls within one of the twelve circuits.

ALABAMA: Located in the 11th Circuit, the state is divided into three federal districts: Northern (Birmingham), Middle (Montgomery), and Southern (Mobile).

ALASKA: Located in the 9th Circuit, the state has one federal judicial district, based in Anchorage.

ARKANSAS: Located in the 8th Circuit, the state is divided into two federal districts: Eastern (Little Rock) and Western (Fort Smith).

CALIFORNIA: Located in the 9th Circuit, the state is divided into four districts: Northern (San Francisco), Eastern (Sacramento), Central (Los Angeles), and Southern (San Diego).

COLORADO: Located in the 10th Circuit, the state has one federal judicial district, based in Denver.

CONNECTICUT: Located in the 2nd Circuit, the state has one federal judicial district, based in New Haven.

DELAWARE: Located in the 3rd Circuit, the state has one federal judicial district, based in Wilmington.

FLORIDA: Located in the 11th Circuit, the state has three federal judicial districts: Northern (Talla-hassee), Middle (Jacksonville), and Southern (Miami).

GEORGIA: Located in the 11th Circuit, the state has three federal judicial districts: Northern (Atlanta), Middle (Macon), and Southern (Savannah).

GUAM: The territory contains a federal district, based in Agana.

HAWAII: Located in the 9th Circuit, the state has one federal district, based in Honolulu.

IDAHO: Located in the 9th Circuit, the state has one federal district, based in Boise.

ILLINOIS: Located in the 7th Circuit, the state has three federal districts: Northern (Chicago), Southern (East Saint Louis), and Central (Springfield).

INDIANA: Located in the 7th Circuit, the state has two federal districts: Northern (South Bend) and Southern (Indianapolis).

IOWA: Located in the 8th Circuit, the state has two federal districts: Northern (Cedar Rapids) and Southern (Des Moines).

KANSAS: Located in the 10th Circuit, the state has one federal district, based in Wichita.

KENTUCKY: Located in the 6th Circuit, the state has two federal districts: Eastern (Lexington) and Western (Louisville).

LOUISIANA: Located in the 5th Circuit, the state has three federal districts: Eastern (New Orleans), Middle (Baton Rouge), and Western (Shreveport).

MAINE: Located in the 1st Circuit, the state has one federal district, based in Portland.

MARYLAND: Located in the 4th Circuit, the state has one federal district, based in Baltimore.

MASSACHUSETTS: Located in the 1st Circuit, the state has one federal district, based in Boston.

MICHIGAN: Located in the 6th Circuit, the state has two federal districts: Eastern (Detroit) and Western (Grand Rapids).

MINNESOTA: Located in the 8th Circuit, the state has one federal district, based in St. Paul.

MISSISSIPPI: Located in the 5th Circuit, the state has two federal districts: Northern (Oxford) and Southern (Jackson).

MISSOURI: Located in the 8th Circuit, the state has two federal districts: Eastern (Saint Louis) and Western (Kansas City).

MONTANA: Located in the 9th Circuit, the state has one federal district, based in Billings.

NEBRASKA: Located in the 8th Circuit, the state has one federal district, based in Omaha.

NEVADA: Located in the 9th Circuit, the state has one federal district, based in Las Vegas.

NEW HAMPSHIRE: Located in the 1st Circuit, the state has one federal district, based in Concord.

NEW JERSEY: Located in the 3rd Circuit, the state has one federal district, based in Newark.

NEW MEXICO: Located in the 10th Circuit, the state has one federal district, based in Albuquerque.

NEW YORK: Located in the 2nd Circuit, the state has four federal districts: Northern (Syracuse), Eastern (Brooklyn), Southern (New York City), and Western (Buffalo).

NORTH CAROLINA: Located in the 4th Circuit, the state has three federal districts: Eastern (Raleigh), Middle (Greensboro), and Western (Asheville).

NORTH DAKOTA: Located in the 8th Circuit, the state has one federal district, based in Bismarck.

NORTH MARINA ISLANDS: The territory contains a federal district, based in Saipan.

OHIO: Located in the 6th Circuit, the state has two federal districts: Northern (Cleveland) and Southern (Columbus).

OKLAHOMA: Located in the 10th Circuit, the state has three federal districts: Northern (Tulsa), Eastern (Muskogee), and Western (Oklahoma City).

OREGON: Located in the 9th Circuit, the state has one federal district, based in Portland.

PENNSYLVANIA: Located in the 3rd Circuit, the state has three federal districts: Eastern (Philadelphia), Middle (Scranton), and Western (Pittsburgh).

PUERTO RICO: The territory contains a federal district, based in Hato Rey.

RHODE ISLAND: Located in the 1st Circuit, the state has one federal district, located in Providence.

SOUTH CAROLINA: Located in the 4th Circuit, the state contains one federal district, located in Columbia.

SOUTH DAKOTA: Located in the 8th Circuit, the state contains one federal district, based in Sioux Falls.

TENNESSEE: Located in the 6th Circuit, the state contains three federal districts: Eastern (Knoxville), Middle (Nashville), and Western (Memphis).

TEXAS: Located in the 5th Circuit, the state contains four federal districts: Northern (Dallas), Southern (Houston), Eastern (Tyler), and Western (San Antonio).

UTAH: Located in the 10th Circuit, the state contains one federal district, based in Salt Lake City.

VERMONT: Located in the 2nd Circuit, the state contains one federal district, based in Burlington.

VIRGIN ISLANDS: The territory contains a federal district, based in Saint Thomas.

VIRGINIA: Located in the 4th Circuit, the state contains two federal districts: Eastern (Alexandria) and Western (Roanoke).

WASHINGTON: Located in the 9th Circuit, the state contains two federal districts: Eastern (Spokane) and Western (Seattle).

WASHINGTON, D.C.: Located in the D. C. Circuit, Washington, D. C., has its own federal district.

WEST VIRGINIA: Located in the 4th Circuit, the state contains two federal districts: Northern (Elkins) and Southern (Charleston).

WISCONSIN: Located in the 7th Circuit, the state contains two federal districts: Eastern (Milwaukee) and Western (Madison).

WYOMING: Located in the 10th Circuit, the state contains one federal district, based in Cheyenne.

## Additional Resources

*Desk Reference on American Courts.* Barnes, Patricia G., CQ Press, 2000.

*The Federal Courts,* Carp, Robert A., and Ronald Stidham, CQ Press, 2001.

*Federal Jurisdiction in a Nutshell,* Currie, David P., West Group, 1999.

*Understanding Federal Courts and Jurisdiction* Mulleniz, Linda, Martin Redish, and Georgene Vairo, Matthew Bender, 1998.

*U. S. Code, Title 28: Judiciary and Judicial Procedure.* U. S. House of Representatives, 1999. Available at http://uscode.house.gov/title_28.htm.

## Organizations

### Administrative Offices of the Courts

Thurgood Marshall Federal Judiciary Building,
Office of Public Affairs
Washington, DC 20544 USA
Phone: (202) 502-2600
URL: http://www.uscourts.gov/

### Federal Judicial Center (FJC)

Thurgood Marshall Federal Judiciary Building
One Columbus Cir. NE
Washington, DC 20002 USA
Phone: (202) 502-4000
URL: http://www.fjc.gov/

### Supreme Court of the United States

U. S. Supreme Court Building
One First Street, N.E.
Washington, DC 20543
Phone: (202) 479-3000
URL: http://www.supremecourtus.gov/

### United States Sentencing Commission (USSC)

Office of Public Affairs
One Columbus Circle, NE
Washington, DC 20002-8002
Phone: (202) 502-4500
URL: http://www.ussc.gov/

# COURTS AND PROCEDURES

## JURIES

*Sections within this essay:*

- Background
    - Historical Roots in England
    - Development in America from Colonial Times
    - Grand Juries as Distinct from Civil and Criminal Juries
    - Constitutional Right to a Jury Trial

- How People are Chosen for a Jury Pool
    - Diversity and Cross Section of Community Requirement

- Selection Process at the Courthouse
    - Disqualification Grounds for Jury Service
    - Exemptions from Jury Service
    - PeremptoryPreemptory Challenges
    - Use of Jury Consultants

- The Function of the Jury at the Trial
    - Role as a Factfinder
    - How Juries Weigh the Evidence
    - Standards of Proof Used

- Jury Instructions and Their Purpose
    - Special Kinds of Instructions Limiting the Discretion of the Jury
    - Jury Nullification

- Issues Pertaining to the Jury's Performance of Its Duties
    - The Hung Jury and the Unanimous Requirement
    - Judge's Discretion to Set Aside Verdicts
    - Jury Sequestration
    - Juror Misconduct

    - Notetaking by Jurors
    - Questioning of Witnesses by Jurors

- Future Prospects of the Jury System
    - Decline in the Use of Jury Trials
    - Prospects for Reform

- Additional Resources

## Background

### *Historical Roots in England*

The idea for disputes to be resolved by a jury began out of necessity. In medieval England, it had been increasingly difficult to have a peaceful society when the only way of resolving disputes was by force. The first time the idea of a right to a trial by jury was mentioned was in the Magna Carta signed by King John in 1215. However, this new right to a jury trial did not apply to everyone in England at that time. Only knights and landowners were entitled to the right not to have their lives or property taken without a **hearing** before a jury of their peers.

### *Development in America from Colonial Times*

The most famous incident in America that gave a tremendous boost to the idea of the right to have a jury trial occurred in New York in 1734. At that time New York was one of thirteen British colonies administered by a royal governor appointed by the king of England. Peter Zenger, a journalist, had written an article ridiculing this official. The British authorities in response charged Zenger with seditious libel. Zenger's lawyer, Andrew Hamilton, put on a defense stating that his client was not guilty because the statements in Zenger's article were true.

However, there were two problems with Hamilton's trial strategy. First, he was unable to bring in witnesses who could **testify** as to the truth of Zenger's article. More important, as the judge pointed out, this defense could not be used for the crime with which Zenger was charged. As an alternative, Hamilton said that the question of whether Zenger had committed seditious libel should not be decided by the judge but should be left to the jury to decide. The judge capitulated to Hamilton's request and permitted the jury to return a not guilty verdict. The jury in this case took this action based on the principle that a trial cannot be fair if the **accused** is prevented by the court from putting on a defense.

From colonial times until well into the twentieth century, not all citizens of the various states were universally allowed to serve on a jury. At first, only white men owning property were permitted to be on a jury. After the United States became a nation, states were allowed to enact their own restrictions on jury service based on race, gender, and ownership of property. Some of those denied the right to serve on a jury did not see these restrictions removed until well after they were given the right to vote.

Because in America's early history there were so few lawyers who were specifically trained in the law, juries exercised the power to decide not only factual questions concerning a case but also questions as to how the law should be interpreted in applying it to the facts of the case. Judges on their part were allowed to make comments regarding the **evidence** presented at trial. Today juries in all states can only decide questions of fact, such as whether a car ran a red light prior to an accident. They can no longer decide questions of law which consist of what the law is on a particular issue of the trial and how it is to be interpreted so it can be correctly applied to the facts of the case. Judges can no longer comment on the evidence because this is seen as preventing the jury from being **impartial**.

In criminal trials, it is always required that jury verdicts of guilty or innocent must be unanimous. Beginning in California in 1879, this requirement was phased out for civil trials, proceedings that do not involve criminal accusations, such as whether a driver was not careful enough in backing out of his driveway and injured a pedestrian.

### Grand Juries as Distinct from Civil and Criminal Juries

A **grand jury** is formed only in criminal cases. The purpose of the grand jury is not to determine whether a **defendant** is guilty or not. This group of usually 23 people meets to determine whether persons suspected by police as responsible for a crime should be indicted, allowing them to be brought to trial before a regular jury consisting of six to twelve persons. Grand juries are required by the Fifth Amendment of the U. S. Constitution which says a person suspected of a crime must be indicted before he is tried. This action is considered a safegurard against prosecuting a person without any legitimate reason.

### Constitutional Right to a Jury Trial

Three separate provisions of the U. S. Constitution provide for the right to a trial by jury. Article III, Sec. 2 provides: "The trial of all crimes shall be by jury and such trial shall be held in the state where the said crimes have been committed." The Sixth Amendment says: "In all criminal prosecutions, the accused shall enjoy the right to a speedy and public trial by an impartial jury of the state where the said crimes shall have been committed." Finally, for civil matters, the Seventh Amendment provides: "In all suits at **common law**, where the value in controversy shall exceed twenty dollars, the right of trial by jury shall be preserved and no fact tried by a jury shall be otherwise reexamined by an court of the United States."

The first two above provisions as to criminal trials greatly overlap. The Sixth Amendment was added as part of the **Bill of Rights** that would be guaranteed by the Constitution. However, it has only been relatively recently has this right been mandatory in both federal and state courts. As to the Seventh Amendment which covers civil trials, this provision only applies to federal courts which deal only with laws passed by Congress and signed into law by the president. According to the U. S. Supreme Court in a 1999 decision, the Seventh Amendment does not apply in state courts.

## How People are Chosen for a Jury Pool

### Diversity and Cross Section of Community Requirement

The U. S. Supreme Court has repeatedly ruled it is necessary for a jury to be comprised of a "fair cross section of the community" in order to satisfy the trial right guaranteed by the Sixth Amendment of impartiality. The Federal Jury Selection and Service Act of 1968 was written for this same purpose. Thus, a jury pool of persons eligible to serve reflects the spectrum of society.

In order to comply with the U. S. Supreme Court rulings and the above federal **statute**, all the states have had to change their laws to insure that a broad cross section will make up the jury pool. Typically names appearing on voter registration lists for each locality are drawn. Many people who are otherwise eligible are not included because they have moved to another locality or state. In order to help solve this problem, names for juror pools are drawn from the list of licensed drivers for that state. Over half the states have made this change, and some have gone even further and have drawn names from lists of customers for utilities and even welfare recipients. This initial list is referred to as a source list.

From the source list, a locality randomly draws a second list referred to as "master wheel" or "qualified wheel" depending upon the statute for that state. These lists are replenished at intervals as required by the law for that state. Questionnaires are sent to those on the "wheel" lists in order to determine whether a particular individual is qualified to serve on a jury. Because between one–quarter to one–half of these forms are not returned, some jurisdictions will send a notice requiring such persons to explain why they have not responded.

## Selection Process at the Courthouse

### Disqualification Grounds for Jury Service

Each state by law lists what reasons disqualify someone from jury service. Many of these reasons are included because they may prevent explain why a person cannot listen to **testimony** and other evidence with an open mind. Prior contact with one of the parties or lawyers connected with the case as well as knowledge obtained prior to the trial is sufficient reason to excuse a person from serving on the jury for a particular case. Statements made by jurors while they are being questioned by the attorneys for both sides which indicate they are biased in favor of or against one of the parties have the same result as **discovery** that a potential juror has a prior **felony conviction**. In criminal trials it is common for an individual to be excused because of a relationship with a witness in the case.

### Exemptions from Jury Service

Formerly it was common for people otherwise qualified to serve on a jury to be exempt based on their occupation. Prior to a recent change in the law, New York had recognized more than a dozen such exemptions to include lawyers, doctors, clergy, den-

tists, pharmacists, optometrists, psychologists, podiatrists, nurses, embalmers, police officers, and firefighters. The reason given for these exemptions were that each of these groups performs functions necessary to the **public interest**. As of 2002, 26 states have eliminated occupational exemptions while an additional nine have placed strict limitations on them.

Exemptions are also granted for business or financial hardship according to the circumstances of that individual. A judge may grant a business hardship exemption if they are convinced that jury service would result in the business closing permanently. Financial exemptions are also given to employees of private businesses since in most states the employer is not required to pay them for the time spent on a jury. Other exemptions also granted on a case by case basis at the discretion of the judge or court officials include incapacitating physical or mental illnesses, and extreme inconvenience such as having to travel a much greater distance to the courthouse.

### Preemptory Challenges

When selecting a jury, attorneys for both sides ask questions of each person sent to that courtroom to be considered for service on that case. The questions asked are designed to reveal if a particular potential juror has either a conscious or unconscious **bias** affecting their ability to be impartial. Because these questions may be intrusive, and include such areas as reading habits, favorite television shows, amount of income, and feelings towards different racial, ethnic, or other groups, it is not uncommon for individuals required to answer such inquiries to be less than truthful or to give general answers that may conceal a biased attitude. A good trial lawyer senses bias without needing it stated explicitly.

States give each side a designated number of persons they can have excused without having to give reason. When a person is excused in this way, the attorney is said to have exercised a preemptory challenge. Because personal bias is often difficult to detect, the **peremptory challenge** allows lawyers to act on their instincts in order to obtain impartial juries.

Sometimes a judge will grant one side more preemptory challenges than is allowed by state law. The attorney who objects to this action and then loses his case will not be able to have the trial judge reversed by a higher court unless that lawyer has exhausted all preemptory challenges and can show to that because they were not granted the same number of preemptory challenges, one or more persons they would have found to be objectionable was able to serve on that jury.

In recent years, two decisions by the U. S. Supreme Court have placed limits on the use of preemptory challenges if the complaining side or party is able to prove that the use of preemptory challenges by the opposing lawyer were designed to exclude persons from a jury based on their race and gender. In the first of these cases, an African-American criminal defendant named Batson was convicted of **burglary**. On appeal to the U. S. Supreme Court, his lawyer argued the prosecution used his preemptory challenges so that no black person in the jury pool served on the jury. The Supreme Court ruled in Batson's favor for three reasons. First, excluding jurors on the basis of race denies a defendant the right to an impartial trial since it works against the cross section of the community requirement for jury membership. Second, the excluded jurors are denied the right to take part in the judicial process. Third, this use of peremptory challenges is harmful to the local community because it encourages its citizens to believe that a fair trial cannot be obtained there.

However, the Supreme Court made clear that future defendants in seeking to have trial verdicts against them overturned on appeal to a higher court would have to prove to that court all of the following: first, the defendant is a member of an identifiable racial group. Second, the prosecution used preemptory challenges to prevent those of the defendant's race from serving on the jury. Third, the lawyer for the defendant must show that the facts and circumstances of the case imply the prosecution did this intentionally.

Even though the defense attorney is faced with having to prove all of the above, the **prosecutor** must show the peremptory challenges were applied neutrally. Non-African American defendants have not been successful in challenging their convictions because U. S. Supreme Court decisions have declined to apply *Batson v. Kentucky* to their racial group. The principles in Batson have since been made applicable in civil as well as criminal trials.

In 1994, eight years after *Batson* was decided, the U. S. Supreme Court said preemptory challenges could not be used to exclude members of a particular gender from jury service. In *J. E. B. v. Alabama*, the state agency regulating the welfare of children filed a **paternity** action against J. E. B. for failing to pay

the **child support** he owed to the mother. Alabama used its preemptory strikes to prevent nine men from serving on the jury eventually resulting in a panel consisting entirely of women. The jury found J. E. B. guilty of the charge, and he successfully argued for the application of *Batson* to his case on grounds that the use of preemptory challenges based on gender violated the constitutional principle that persons should not be discriminated against or treated unequally on the basis of sex.

However, it is now questionable how useful *Batson* and *J. E. B.* will be in future cases for defendants. In 1995, in *Puckett v. Elam*, the Supreme Court said that a prosecutor's reason for excluding a juror on a preemptory challenge does not have to make any sense so long as it is applied neutrally as to the race and gender of the defendant. Justice John Paul Stevens in disagreeing with other justices on the Supreme Court, complained that the Court had made its decisions in *Batson* and *J. E. B.* meaningless.

Some state and federal courts lower than the U. S. Supreme Court have said preemptory challenges cannot be used to exclude persons of particular religious groups. Other courts on these levels have ruled in the opposite way. The U. S. Supreme Court has not yet resolved the difference of opinion among the courts on this issue.

### Use of Jury Consultants

There are two scenarios in which attorneys may consider using a jury consultant to further assist them in selecting jurors. First, if their client is a celebrity, there may be very strongly divided opinions among potential jurors on whether they like or dislike that client. This would be a great obstacle to finding at least an impartial jury. Second, even if their client does not provoke any strong sentiment, if he has a great deal to lose, they may still want to improve the probability of a favorable outcome. In either instance, to use a jury consultant constitutes an additional expense. The average cost is $250 per hour, and it could total anywhere from $10,000 to $250,000.

Most jury consultants have backgrounds in law, psychology, or sociology. In spite of the expertise a jury consultant may have, the profession is largely unregulated. Although jury consultants claim to be accurate in their appraising potential jurors, many scholars are skeptical. Another criticism is that using a jury consultant gives the general public the impression that a favorable verdict can be purchased if the right jury is selected. In light of this criticism, some judges have taken the initiative to have consultants appointed for indigent defendants.

The primary purpose of hiring a jury consultant is to help uncover hidden bias of potential jurors. Because preemptory challenges are limited, lawyers may be unsure about some of those questioned. The job of jury consultants is to give attorneys the criteria necessary for the ideal jury for their clients and to assist in determining what biases do not fit that criteria.

A good illustration of this principle is the trial of Daniel and Philip Berrigan in 1972, the first known use of jury consultants. The Berrigan brothers were accused of conspiring to plan violent demonstrations against the Vietnam War. The defense attorneys decided that in order to have the best jury possible they should poll those persons likely to qualify as jurors in Harrisburg, Pennsylvania, the site of the trial. The purpose of this polling was to determine which demographic groups would be most sympathetic to their clients. The results led the defense attorneys to conclude that Episcopalians, Presbyterians, and other Protestant denominations with a fundamentalist outlook would favor the prosecution, as would college graduates because of their support for the position of the U. S. Government on the Vietnam conflict. Accordingly, the defense was successful in having a jury selected that consisted of entirely blue collar workers who would likely not have graduated from college and who were also of a different denomination from those listed above. This jury deadlocked at 10-2 in favor of **acquittal**. The government afterwards declined to retry the case.

There are two kinds of techniques jury consultants use. The first category is pretrial research. The easiest research in this category is attitude surveys conducted in phone or in person as was done in the *Berrigan* trial. A second technique is to form a trial simulation with a group of people representative of what the jury picked will most resemble. At the end of this mock trial, the participants are surveyed as to how persuasive each side was in general and in its use of the evidence. Also, a focus group may be formed and the facts of the case and the position of each side will be explained to it. Those in the focus group will be asked how they would decide the case and their opinion on which side had the best arguments supporting their position. A third method is personal background research made through credit checks, hand writing analysis, and an **examination** of property and tax records.

A second category relates to what they do when the trial takes place. One commonly used method is for the consultant to prepare a questionnaire for the attorney designed to uncover juror biases. Another is for the consultant to observe the facial expressions and posture of those being considered for the jury; these unconscious reactions may indicate whether the response to the questions of the lawyer are sincere or misleading. A third technique is to observe the jury during breaks for lunch; if certain persons on the jury always eat together this may indicate that alliances have formed that could impact how the juries will deliberate once the case is given to them to decide and could help determine the verdict they reach. In some cases, consultants will recruit a shadow jury resembling by various demographic factors the one actually deciding the case. This shadow jury will be interviewed during the trial for the purpose of determining how the real jury is perceiving their side.

Moreover, some jury consultants believe that people in general fall into one of two groups: Those who conclude that what happens to a person is determined by the person's reaction to those events, and the rest who believe what happens to an individual is dictated by circumstances and context.

## The Function of the Jury at the Trial

### Role as a Factfinder

In every case there are allegations made. In a civil case, they are made by the party known as the plaintiff while in a case involving criminal law, the party making the charges or allegations is the prosecutor who is employed by the state **jurisdiction** in which he practices. If the case involves federal law, the prosecutor is the U. S. **Justice Department**, a federal agency.

In order to win the case, the plaintiff, or whoever is making the allegations, must make his case by showing the allegations are true according to a given standard of proof to the satisfaction of a jury. For example, Smith alleges that Jones negligently backed his car into Smith, breaking his leg. In order to prove the allegations to be true, Smith must present evidence based on facts and testimony.

The facts that Smith is able to prove are true are then applied to see if the four elements necessary for Smith to win are proven. These elements in this **negligence** claim are the issues that the judge will submit to the jury. The issues are: did Jones owe a duty to be reasonably careful to Smith, did Jones breach or violate that duty, was this violation by Jones of his duty to Smith the cause of Smith's broken leg, and did Smith actually have his leg broken.

In its role as a fact finder, a jury decides, based on the evidence presented, what is the truth in regard to the facts of the case. The jury will decide on the above four issues based on the facts they have found to be true, and if their answer is yes to all four of these issues, Smith wins. In determining what their conclusion is to each of these issues, the jury is given considerable discretion even when evidence regarding the same fact conflicts to the extent that opposite inferences could be drawn. This discretion even extends to cases in which the facts are undisputed; different inferences could still be found by a rational jury.

However, the judge still has discretion to withhold from the jury the right to decide a particular issue if he believes the evidence is insufficient for the jury to come to a reasonable conclusion. Because each of the issues that Smith must prove in his favor to the jury are essential to his case, a decision by the judge that the evidence presented is not enough to support only one of the four issues would result in Smith losing the case.

### How Juries Weigh the Evidence

Allowing evidence in the form of facts, such as testimony, to be admitted at trial by the judge depends on whether it is pertinent or relates to the issue the jury is asked to decide and whether it has probative value, meaning it helps to determine whether a fact is true or false. Once the evidence is actually admitted and the jury tries to reach a verdict they must evaluate this evidence as to its **credibility**. For example, if a witness saw Smith being struck by Jone's car, the jury will determine whether the facts **warrant** their accepting his testimony as being a true account of what occurred, issues such as whether the witness was close enough to see what had occurred.

### Standards of Proof Used

In a civil court case such as one of Smith, the plaintiff, versus Jones, the defendant, the burden is on the plaintiff to show or prove by the facts presented into evidence he has been injured by the defendant. In other kinds of civil lawsuits, such as those involving contracts between the plaintiff and defendant, the plaintiff still has the burden. The standard of proof that the plaintiff must meet is the preponderance of the evidence. This means that a fact put into evidence in supporting Smith's contention

Jones was negligent is more likely to be true than false. The degree to which the jury must believe a fact is more likely to be true than not true in order to meet this standard of proof need only be by the smallest degree; 51 percent would be sufficient.

Sometimes the rules of evidence in a given case will have a standard of proof known as clear and convincing evidence. In order to show that a fact presented into evidence is true according to this standard, the plaintiff Smith must show there is a high probability that a given fact is true or that a juror according to the evidence presented would come to firmly believe the fact alleged by Smith was true. This is a greater degree of proof than preponderance of the evidence, but it is not as high as the **beyond a reasonable doubt** standard required in criminal cases.

In a criminal trial, the plaintiff is not a person or corporation, but the state or federal government as represented by the prosecutor. The prosecutor, regardless of his title, has the responsibility of enforcing the criminal laws of his jurisdiction. The elements of the allegations a prosecutor must prove will vary with the offense charged, but in any event, it must be proven the defendant committed the offense he is accused of and that he intentionally did so willingly. Because the consequences of a criminal conviction are more severe than in a civil lawsuit, the highest standard of proof, beyond a **reasonable doubt**, is required. This burden of proof is always on the prosecution because a criminal defendant can remain silent if he chooses. This standard means the prosecutor must convince the jury to the point where they firmly believe the defendant is guilty as charged.

## Jury Instructions and Their Purpose

A jury instruction is a guideline given by the judge to the jury about the law they will have to apply to the facts they have found to be true. The purpose of the instructions is to help the jury arrive at a verdict that follows the law of that jurisdiction. In his instructions a judge may explain the legal principles pertaining to the subject matter of the case, make it clear to the jury the legal issues they must decide in order to arrive at a verdict, point out what each side must prove in order to win, and summarize the evidence he sees as relevant and explain how it relates to the issues they must decide. For example, do the facts admitted as evidence and found credible by the jury according to the preponderance of the evidence combined with the application of the legal principles of negligence law warrant a finding by the jury that Smith owed a duty to Jones to be reasonably careful in operating his car?

In giving these instructions, the judge binds the jury. The judge makes clear to the jurors that they are to apply the law to the facts as he gives it to them; they are not to substitute their own judgment as to whether a different law should be applied or whether the law as has been explained to them is unjust. The instructions are to be given in terms a layperson can easily understand. In order to help the jury understand the instructions, the judge may give pre-instructions prior to the time immediately following the presentation of both sides of the case. However, the judge is forbidden to comment on the evidence presented in the case. It is the jury's responsibility to independently evaluate the evidence.

### Special Kinds of Instructions Limiting the Discretion of the Jury

The judge has a number of devices by which he can limit the discretion of the jury in applying the instructions to their deliberations. Through an additional instruction, the judge may supplement instructions he has already given. These instructions are usually given at the request of the jury to clarify some point regarding the law given in a previous instruction they do not understand. If a judge gives a mandatory instruction, this requires the jury to reach a verdict in favor of a particular party if the evidence indicates that a particular set of facts is true. Through a peremptory instruction, a jury is directed to find in favor of a particular party regardless of how credible they regard the evidence to be. The judge is taking the case away from the jury because he believes a reasonable juror could not rule in favor of the other party.

### Jury Nullification

Jury nullification is the right of a jury in a criminal case to disregard the evidence admitted at trial and the law as explained to them by the judge and to give a verdict of not guilty for reasons having nothing to do with the case. There may be several reasons for ignoring the evidence and the instructions of the judge. First, they may wish to use a not guilty verdict to communicate to the community their views on a social issue outside the scope of the trial. Second, having to convict a defendant may offend the jurors' sense of justice and fair play or jurors may believe the law itself is immoral.

A judge is powerless to **sanction** the jury in any way. The jury is not required to give any reason at all

for its decision which cannot be appealed by the prosecution to a higher court because of the **Double Jeopardy** Clause of the Constitution that says a defendant is prohibited from being tried more than once for the same crime.

The right of jury nullification originated in what is referred to as Bushell's Case, an English court decision from 1670. William Penn, the eventual founder of Pennsylvania, was accused of holding an illegal meeting. The jury, based on inconclusive evidence, acquitted Penn and his co-defendant Bushell. The judge retaliated against the jury by fining and imprisoning them. After several weeks, Bushell asked for an appeal of the trial judge's action against the jurors. The judge for a higher court set the jury free and said that because reasonable people can look at the same evidence and come to a different conclusion, juries are free to decide as they see fit regardless of whether the judge believes they had an legally adequate reason.

Although this case is English and would not normally be binding in the United States, U. S. courts over a long period of time consistently upheld the right of juries to use the right of nullification. However, the use of this device by juries seems at least on the surface to apply only to criminal cases. Some scholars contend that it takes place in secret because the jury proceedings are confidential but have been unable to document any case that expressly endorse nullification in a civil trial.

## Issues Pertaining to the Jury's Performance of Its Duties

### The Hung Jury and the Unanimous Requirement

It is required that in order for a jury to reach a verdict, everyone must agree to the decision made. Unanimity is required in all federal court civil and criminal trials, in all state court criminal trials, and in most civil trials in those courts. Sometimes the entire jury is not able to agree on the verdict, resulting in a deadlocked or **hung jury**.

When judges are informed this situation has occurred, they tell the jury to continue the deliberations because the alternative is to have the entire case tried over again with a new jury. In order to push the jury into arriving at a verdict, judges urge those in the minority to reconsider their positions by reexamining the evidence carefully and to ask themselves whether their disagreement with the majority is still correct from their viewpoint. Although this device was popular among judges, many courts have abandoned it because it seems coercive.

Many courts now use another instruction drafted by the American **Bar Association** which asks jurors in the minority to reconsider their position and the evidence; jurors should change their stand only if they are convinced based on the evidence but not because they feel pressed to conform to the majority view.

### Judge's Discretion to Set Aside Verdicts

In a civil trial, a judge may set aside the verdict regarding how much money should be awarded by the jury to the plaintiff in **punitive damages**. These damages consist of a dollar figure the jury awards the plaintiff in order to punish the defendant. This amount is totally distinct from **compensatory damages**, which are meant to reimburse the plaintiff for lost wages as well as pain and suffering. Given the purpose of punitive damages, juries can award verdicts that in punitive damages alone amount to millions of dollars.

The Seventh Amendment to the U. S. Constitution precludes review by any court of a judgment over $20. In light of this provision, courts will not overturn an award made by a jury just because of its large size or because the judge, if he had been standing in their shoes, would have awarded a smaller sum. However, a judge may reduce the amount of the award if it is far in excess of any rational calculation. Because compensatory damages such as lost wages have formulas by which juries can arrive at an acceptable figure, the reduction of an award is usually applied to punitive damages. The specific ground judges use to justify this action is that the award was made out of "passion and prejudice".

In criminal cases, judges may disregard a jury's guilty verdict and **acquit** or grant a new trial if they believe the evidence was insufficient to support the decision made by the jurors. Judges may also set aside a verdict if they believe the verdict was reached on a basis that violates the U. S. or respective State constitution or if the legal theory on which the jury based their decision does not conform to the law.

### Jury Sequestration

Judges will have members of a jury sequestered or kept together in order to protect juries from outside influences This includes any communication with persons not allowed to be in contact with the jurors as well as the content of news reports concerning the case. Courts view sequestration as a great burden on the personal lives of the jurors as well as the cost involved, and it is used, therefore, only if the lawyer for the defense is able to show the judge there is prejudice in the surrounding community against the defendant, or that news reports would prevent members of the jury from being impartial. While even criminal defendants do not have the right to have the jury sequestered, it may be required under state law where a defendant could be sentenced to death.

Sequestration is more common in criminal than in civil trials and is likely to be imposed once the jury has been selected. In a civil trial, jurors are not sequestered until the jury has heard all of the evidence and has received their instructions from the judge.

Once a jury is sequestered, strict measures are imposed to insure their objectivity. For example, jurors are not allowed to use a public restroom without a court **bailiff** or marshal being present. Receiving and making telephone calls is forbidden but will not result in a trial verdict being reversed by a higher court so long as the court officer can hear the conversation and nothing pertaining to the case is mentioned. Jurors must also be transported as a group, eat together, and sleep at the same lodging.

### Juror Misconduct

Even if they are not sequestered, jurors are instructed not to discuss any subject pertaining to the trial prior to the time the jury begins their deliberations. This includes fellow jurors.

Each juror has a duty to report as soon as possible any incident where any person attempted to influence any member of the jury outside of the room where the jurors deliberate. A Jurors must report to the court any violation they see committed by other jurors against warnings given by the judge not to discuss the case outside the jury room or against listening, reading or viewing news reports about the case. In regard to jurors' avoidance of any contact with news reports, the judge in many jurisdictions is required to explain to the jury his reason for warning them to do so.

There are a number of documented examples of juror misconduct that illustrate the above principles. The first kind of example is jurors bringing in outside information not given to them at trial. In an automobile accident case, a juror on his own visited the accident site and drew a diagram of the intersection. The next day when the jury deliberated, he showed the jury the diagram and brought into the room a copy of a book on state traffic laws, the contents of which they discussed. In a second instance communication was said to have taken place between members of the jury and a customer in a restaurant who approached their table and urged them to impose the death penalty. In these instances, what occurred was clearly prejudicial and resulted in the trial verdict being overturned.

There are some instances in which the rules about outside communication were not followed, but were not considered egregious enough to warrant the verdict being overturned. In one case, the jury did not understand what was meant by the term proximate cause. Instead of asking the judge for clarification, they brought in a dictionary to help them. Because the dictionary definition did not conflict with what the judge had told them earlier as to what that word mean, it was not considered to be prejudicial.

There have been a large number of cases where jurors have gone to the judge or other court officials after the trial is over to complain they were intimidated by other jurors into voting with the majority. Courts will not take any action at this point for these reasons. First, before deliberations have concluded, a juror can report intimidation to court officials. Second, the jury can be polled individually in **open court** to see if each person voluntarily agrees with the verdict. Third, courts are unwilling to meddle in or speculate about how the jury reached its decision; a jury's deliberations are meant to be secret in order for non-jurors not to have any influence. Outbursts of emotion, such as throwing chairs or cursing, are looked upon by courts as consequences that should not be unexpected and will not in themselves be sufficient to have intimidated jurors into not voting according to their own evaluation of the evidence. Finally, allowing inquiries after a verdict would jeopardize the finality of a jury's decision and might result in endless additional time wasted.

### Notetaking by Jurors

As trials have become more complex, and the information given more difficult to remember and place in perspective, a number of states have made express permission for jurors to take notes during the trial. These states include Arizona, Arkansas, Connecticut, Missouri, New Jersey, New York, North Dakota, Ohio, Washington, Wisconsin, and Wyoming. Although only one state expressly prohibits this practice, in most jurisdictions whether members of a jury are allowed to take notes will depend upon the discretion of the judge. One survey indicated that

37 percent of the judges in state courts indicate they do not allow jurors to take notes during a trial. In federal courts, this matter is also left up to the judge.

Many judges oppose juror notetaking because in their view jurors cannot make the distinction between important and trivial evidence. As a result, the more vital evidence may not be recorded and the less important may be, making it impossible for a jury to reach a rational verdict. However, studies performed in Wisconsin and Arizona indicate that notetaking did not influenced the verdict, or distract the jurors; notes taken were accurate and did not result in the notetakers dominating non-notetakers in the jury deliberations.

### Questioning of Witnesses by Jurors

A small number of states have changed their laws and court rules to allow jurors to ask witnesses questions, either orally or in writing through the judge. Written questions submitted in advanced allow attorneys for both sides to make objections based either on the ground they would violate the rules governing the admission of evidence or would result in prejudice against their clients.

The states that expressly encourage judges to allow jurors to question witnesses are Arizona, Arkansas, Florida, Indiana, Iowa, Kentucky, Nevada and North Carolina. Out of these jurisdictions, Arizona, Florida, and Kentucky require that judges allow jurors to ask written questions. The respective highest state courts of Indiana and Kentucky have ruled jurors have a right to ask questions of witnesses.

Other jurisdictions give a more restricted endorsement of this practice. In Pennsylvania and Michigan, the respective state supreme courts have said it is permissible at the discretion of the trial judge. Texas does not permit jurors to question witnesses in criminal trials and Georgia law requires all questions to be written and submitted to the judge. Only Mississippi law expressly forbids jurors from questioning witnesses.

Plaintiffs of civil trials and prosecutors in criminal proceedings favor this practice because it assists them in sustaining the burden of proof required in order for them to win their case. When jurors ask questions, they are able to gain a better understanding of the facts brought into evidence, especially when it is highly technical, such as DNA analysis. Bias in members of the jury that was undetected during the selection process can be exposed through questions they ask, enabling the judge to give an instruction against this bias or removing and replacing jurors with alternates.

Defense attorneys in civil and criminal trials are against jurors questioning witnesses at least partly because it may lead to information being disclosed that could be detrimental to their case. If oral questions are permitted, it could put the defense attorney in an uncomfortable position if a truthful answer would prejudice the jury as a whole against their client. One example would be if a juror were to ask if the defendant had a prior criminal record. If the defense attorney objects to the question, the attorney runs the risk of antagonizing the jury. If the attorney chooses not to object, his client may have waived any right on appeal to a higher court that his verdict should be overturned because of the prejudicial nature of the question. Even if the questions are submitted to the judge first in writing, defense attorneys say jurors will inevitably put more weight than they should on their own questions and makes it more likely jurors will rush to judgment without taking into account all the evidence admitted at trial.

## Future Prospects of the Jury System

### Decline in the Use of Jury Trials
Only two percent of civil cases and a similar proportion of criminal cases that are not dismissed are settled by **plea bargaining** are decided by a jury.

The low percentage of criminal prosecutions being resolved by a jury trial is the result of their being settled by **plea** bargaining which helps manage the heavy caseloads in most jurisdictions. The reason for the low use of trials in civil cases is more complex. Various studies have indicated that compared to a bench trial where a case is heard only by a judge, a jury trial costs much more and lasts from twice to three times as long. The increasing complexity of what a jury has to decide in a civil trial makes such alternatives as **mediation**, negotiation, **arbitration**, and mini-trials attractive because individuals involved in the proceedings are already knowledgeable in the subject matter of the case. The increased complexity of modern civil cases makes jurors less likely to understand the judges' instructions. Finally, the jury selection process itself tends to weed out the more well informed jurors who are able to handle complex case subject matter.

### Prospects for Reform
Jury reform is needed because less than half of those summoned to the courthouse bother to show up, and out of this group between 85 to 95 percent do not serve since they are either exempt, disqualified, or not chosen. Because of the increased importance placed on the ideal jury as conceived by jury consultants, less informed and qualified persons are more likely to be on a jury.

Arizona has made the following reforms: allowing jurors to take notes during a trial, allowing them to question witnesses, and permitting jurors to discuss the case among themselves prior to the time all evidence has been presented. These reforms are needed because the present laws and court rules on juries were put in place many years ago and do not reflect the advances scientists have made regarding how people retain and process new information.

In Arizona, a committee including former jurors made further recommendations such as increasing public awareness of jury service, having short opening statements prior to attorneys selecting juries, giving jurors copies of jury instructions, encouraging jurors to ask questions about these instructions, offering assistance by the judge and attorneys for both sides to a deadlocked jury, and obtaining jurors' reaction to their experience after the verdict is rendered.

## Additional Resources

*Civil Wrongs and the Anatomy of a Jury Trial,* Sigman, Robert S., Legovac Publishing, 1991.

*Commonsense Justice: Juror's Notions of Law,* J. Finkel, Norman J., Harvard University Press, 1995.

*Enhancing the Jury System: A Guidebook for Legal Reform,* American Judicature Society, 1999.

*The Historical Development of the Jury System,* Lesser, Maximus, Gordon Press, 1976.

*Inquiry into the Powers of Juries to Decide Incidentally on Questions of Law,* Worthington, George, W. S. Hein, 1995.

*Inside the Jury: The Psychology of Juror Decision Making,* Hastie, Reid, Cambridge University Press, 1994.

*Judging the Jury,* Vidmar, J. Hass & N., Perseus Publishing, 1986.

*Jury Duty What You Need to Know Before You Are Called for Jury Duty Find Out What Its All About,* Jones, Alfred, Graduate Group, 1999.

*Jury Manual: A Guide for Prospective Jurors,* Pabst, William R., Metro Publishing, 1985.

*Jury Research: A Review and Bibliography,* Abbott, Walter F., American Law Institute, 1993.

*Juries in Colonial America: Two Accounts., 1680-1722,* Hawles, John, Arno Press, 1972.

*Juror's Rights,* Stanley, Jacqueline D., Sphinx Publishing, 1998.

*Mind of the Juror as Judge of the Facts: or the Layman's View of the Law,* Osborn, Albert S., W. S. Hein, 1982.

*Race and the Jury: Racial Disenfranchisement and the Search for Justice,* Fukurai, H., et. al., Perseus Publishing, 1992.

*Suggestions for Improving Juror Utilization in the United States, Final Report,* Stoever, William A., Institute of Judicial Administration, 1971.

*Trends in Civil Trial Verdicts Since 1985,* Moller, Erik T., Rand Corporation, 1996.

*What Makes Juries Listen,* Sonya Hamilton, Sonya, Aspen Law, 1984.

## Organizations

### Association of Trial Lawyers of America (ATLA)
1050 31st St.
Washington, DC 20007 USA
Phone: (202) 965-3500
Fax: (202) 625-7312
URL: http://www.atlanet.org
Primary Contact: Thomas H. Henderson, Exec. Dir.

### Council for Court Excellence
1717 K St., N.W.
Washington, DC 20036 USA
Phone: (202) 785-5917
Fax: (202) 785-5922
URL: http:www.courtexcellence.org/
Primary Contact: Samuel F. Harahan, Exec. Dir

### Fully Informed Jury Association
P.O. Box 59
Helena, MT 59843 USA
Phone: (406) 793-5500
Fax: (406) 793-5500
URL: http:www.fija.org/
Primary Contact: Larry Dodge, Ed.

### National Center for State Courts
300 Newport Ave.
Willamsburg, VA 23185 USA
Phone: (757) 253-2000
Fax: (757) 220-0449
URL: http://www.ncsonline.org/
Primary Contact: Roger K. Warren, Pres.

### Roscoe Pound Institute
1050 31st St., NW
Washington, DC 20007 USA
Phone: (202) 965-3500
Fax: (202) 965-0335
URL: http://www.atlanet.org/foundations/pound/rpfmenu.htm
Primary Contact: Meghan Donohoe, Exec. Dir.

# COURTS AND PROCEDURES

## SELECTION OF JUDGES

*Sections within this essay:*

- Background and History

- Formal and Informal Requirements of Judges

- Selection of Federal Judges
    - Supreme Court, Courts of Appeals, District Courts
    - Chief Justice of the Supreme Court
    - Chief Judges
    - Senior Judges
    - Bankruptcy Judges
    - Federal Magistrate Judges

- State Methods of Judicial Selection
    - Election
    - Appointment and Merit Selection
    - Reelection and Retention

- State-by-State Summary of Judicial Selection

- Additional Resources

## Background and History

The method by which judges are selected in the United States has been the subject of debate that predates the Revolutionary War. The king of Great Britain selected colonial judges but retained considerable power over them. The colonists so resented this power that the Declaration of Independence includes the following statement in reference to injuries that the colonists endured: "He has made Judges dependent on his Will alone, for the tenure of their offices, and the amount and payment of their salaries."

The states initially adopted the appointment method for selecting judges. In the early 1800s, the states of Georgia and Indiana modified their laws so that judges of lower courts were selected by popular election. Other states, including Michigan and Mississippi, also provided for selection by popular election by the 1830s. By the time the Civil War began, 24 of the 34 states elected their judges.

Election of judges lost some of its support after the Civil War. Critics charged that political machines had become responsible for the selection of judges like any other type of politician. Judges earned the reputation of being corrupt and incompetent. To combat this perception, a few states chose to elect judges based on nonpartisan elections where judges were not associated with political parties. The idea behind this option was that the parties could not control the judges, but in reality, the electorate had difficulty making decisions without the party labels attached to the judges.

The methods of judicial selection continued to be debated into the 20th century. Some organizations and individuals began to advocate for a method of selecting judges based on merit. Plans for merit selection of judges included provisions that would ensure that candidates would not be limited to friends of politicians, and that the merit of the prospective judge would be the primary factor in determining who could be a judge. Organizations such as the American Judicature Society and the American Bar Association endorsed such plans.

The method judicial selection varies considerably now from state to state. Methods for retaining judges after their initial term has expired likewise vary among the states.

## Formal and Informal Requirements of Judges

Formal requirements vary among the states, although many states do not have strict minimum requirements. Neither the U.S. Constitution nor any federal statute set forth formal qualifications for federal judges. However, other factors may determine who will earn a seat on a federal bench. Although federal law does not require a federal judge to be an attorney, the vast majority of judges have distinguished themselves professionally as lawyers. This becomes even more important at the intermediate appellate court and Supreme Court levels.

Moreover, though certainly not a requirement, judges generally need some record of political activity for two main reasons. First, the prospective judge's service in politics may be rewarded through an appointment to the federal bench. Second, a judge generally needs to have some level of political activity to become noticed by those who select judges in the federal system.

## Selection of Federal Judges

### Supreme Court, Courts of Appeals, District Courts

Potential judges for positions on the benches of the U.S. Supreme Court, the courts of appeals and the district courts are nominated by the president and confirmed by the Senate. The president makes nominations after consultation with staff members in the White House and the attorney general's office. Individual members of the Senate and other political operatives may also have a say in the selection of these judges.

Once a judge is nominated, the Federal Bureau of Investigation conducts a routine security check on the nominee. The Senate Judiciary Committee is the body primarily responsible for screening judicial nominees. After conducting hearings on each candidate, the committee forwards its recommendations to the Senate as a whole. The Senate either approves or rejects a recommendation of the Senate Judiciary Committee by a simple majority vote. The decision to approve the judge is a permanent one, for under the Constitution, federal judges serve life terms.

### Chief Justice of the United States

The process by which the chief justice of the Supreme Court is selected is the same as the initial selection of a judge or justice. The president nominates a person to serve as chief justice, the Senate Judiciary Committee reviews the nomination and makes a recommendation, and the Senate as a whole votes whether to accept the recommendation of the Judiciary Committee.

Although most chief justices have previously been associate justices of the Supreme Court, this is not always the case. In 2005, President George W. Bush nominated John Roberts to be chief justice after Roberts previously served on the D.C. Circuit Court of Appeals. Similarly, Warren Berger, a nominee of President Richard Nixon in 1969, elevated to the position of chief justice directly from a position on the D.C. Court of Appeals.

### Chief Judges

Unlike the chief justice of the Supreme Court, a chief judge of a federal court assumes that position through seniority. In order to become a chief judge, a judge must satisfy the following conditions: (1) the judge must be 64 years of age or younger; (2) the judge must have served for at least one year on the bench; and (3) the judge must not have served previously as a chief judge.

### Bankruptcy Judges

A bankruptcy judge serves as a judicial officer of a U.S. district court. Judges of the various courts of appeals appoint bankruptcy judges to serve in the bankruptcy courts within the various circuits. Unlike district court judges, bankruptcy judges do not serve life terms but are rather appointed to serve 14-year terms.

### Federal Magistrate Judges

Magistrate judges are appointed by a vote of the active judges of a particular district court. These magistrate judges fulfill duties prescribed by statute and also as directed by the district court judges. Full-time magistrate judges serve terms of eight years.

## State Methods of Judicial Selection

States vary in their methods of selecting judges, with judges elected in some states and appointed in others. Moreover, some states employ a hybrid system, where judges at one level of court are selected differently than those at another level of court. States also vary in their methods for retaining or reelecting judges.

## Election

More than half of the states choose judges for at least some of their judges through popular election. Nonpartisan elections are slightly more prevalent than partisan elections. The initial terms of office vary widely from state to state

## Appointment and Merit Selection

Many states employ nomination commissions to assist the respective governors or legislatures to select their judges. Most of these states use these commissions for initial appointments, though a few states only use them for interim appointments (i.e., appointments to fill vacancies). In a few states, the governor or legislature makes selections without the aid of nominating commissions.

## Reelection and Retention

States likewise vary in their approaches when a judge's term expires. States generally follow one of three methods. First, some judges are reelected by popular election. Second, some judges are subject to a retention election, where the judge is the only person listed on a ballot. The question posed in a retention election asks voters whether a judge should be retained. Third, some judges are reappointed to additional terms.

## State-by-State Summary of Judicial Selection

ALABAMA: All judges are selected by partisan elections. The initial term of office is six years. Judges are subsequently reelected to six-year terms.

ALASKA: All judges are chosen through a merit selection process involving a nominating commission. The initial term of office is three years. All judges are subject to retention elections, though subsequent terms vary depending on the level of court.

ARIZONA: Most judges are chosen through a merit selection process involving a nominating commission. The initial term of office is two years. Judges are subject to retention elections, though subsequent terms vary depending on the level of court. Judges for superior courts in counties with populations of less than 250,000 are elected by way of nonpartisan elections to four-year terms. These judges are reelected to four-year terms.

ARKANSAS: All judges are selected by nonpartisan elections. The initial term of office is eight years, except for circuit court judges, who are elected to six-year terms. Judges are subject to reelection.

CALIFORNIA: The governor appoints nominees to the supreme court and courts of appeals to 12-year terms. These judges are subject to retention elections for additional 12-year terms. Superior court judges are elected in nonpartisan elections for six-year terms and may be reelected to additional six-year terms.

COLORADO: All judges are chosen through a merit selection process involving a nominating commission. The initial term of office is two years. All judges are subject to retention elections, though subsequent terms vary depending on the level of court.

CONNECTICUT: All judges are chosen through a merit selection process involving a nominating commission. The initial term of office is eight years. After a commission reviews a judge's performance, the governor nominates the judge for retention, and the state legislature confirms.

DELAWARE: All judges are chosen through a merit selection process involving a nominating commission. The initial term of office is 12 years. An incumbent subsequently reapplies to a nominating commission and competes with other applicants to be renominated by the governor. The state senate confirms the governor's appointment.

DISTRICT OF COLUMBIA: All judges are chosen through a merit selection process involving a nominating commission. The initial term of office is 15 years. A judicial tenure commission reviews each judge's performance six months prior to the expiration of the judge's term of office.

FLORIDA: Judges for the supreme court and district courts of appeal are chosen through a merit selection involving a nominating commission. The initial term of office is one years. Judges are subject to retention elections for six-year terms. Judges for circuit courts are elected by way of nonpartisan elections to six-year terms. These judges are reelected to additional terms.

GEORGIA: All judges are selected by nonpartisan elections. The initial term of office is six years for appellate judges and four years for superior court judges. Judges are subsequently reelected to additional terms.

HAWAII: All judges are chosen through a merit selection process involving a nominating commission. The initial term of office is 10 years. A judicial selection commission reappoints judges to additional 10-year terms.

IDAHO: All judges are selected by nonpartisan elections. The initial term of office is six years for appellate judges and four years for district court judges. Judges are subsequently reelected to additional terms.

ILLINOIS: All judges are selected by partisan elections. The initial term of office is 10 years for appellate judges and six years for superior court judges. Judges are subject to retention elections for additional terms.

INDIANA: Appellate judges are chosen through a merit selection process involving a nominating commission for two-year terms. Appellate judges are subject to retention elections for 10-year terms. Circuit and superior court judges are generally selected through partisan election for six-year terms. Judges in some counties, however, are elected in nonpartisan elections.

IOWA: All judges are chosen through a merit selection process involving a nominating commission. The initial term of office is one year. All judges are subject to retention elections, though subsequent terms vary depending on the level of court.

KANSAS: Most judges are chosen through a merit selection process involving a nominating commission. The initial term of office is one year. These judges are subject to retention elections, though subsequent terms vary depending on the level of court. Judges in courts of 14 districts are elected in partisan elections.

KENTUCKY: All judges are elected in nonpartisan elections to eight-year terms. Judges are subsequently reelected to additional terms.

LOUISIANA: All judges are elected in partisan elections. Appellate judges are elected to 10-year terms, while district court judges are elected to six-year terms. Judges are subsequently reelected to additional terms.

MAINE: Judges are appointed by the governor for seven-year terms. Judges are reappointed by the governor, subject to confirmation by the legislature.

MARYLAND: All judges are chosen through a merit selection process involving a nominating com-

mission to one-year terms. Appellate judges are subject to retention elections for subsequent 10-year terms. Circuit court judges are selected in nonpartisan elections.

MASSACHUSETTS: All judges are chosen through a merit selection process involving a nominating commission. Judges serve until they reach the age of 70.

MICHIGAN: Supreme court judges are elected in partisan elections to eight-year terms. Intermediate appellate court judges and circuit court judges are elected in nonpartisan elections to six-year terms. All judges are subsequently reelected to additional terms.

MINNESOTA: All judges are appointed by nonpartisan elections. The initial term of office is six years. Judges are subsequently reelected to additional terms.

MISSISSIPPI: All judges are appointed by nonpartisan elections. The initial term of office is eight years, except for chancery court and circuit court judges, who are elected to four-year terms. Judges are subject to reelection for additional terms.

MISSOURI: Appellate court judges are chosen through a merit selection process involving a nominating commission to one-year terms. These judges are subject to retention elections for 12-year terms. Circuit court judges are elected to six-year terms and are subject to reelection for additional terms.

MONTANA: Judges are elected by nonpartisan elections. Judges are subject to reelection, except that unopposed judges are subject to retention elections.

NEBRASKA: All judges are chosen through a merit selection process involving a nominating commission to three-year terms. Judges are subject to retention elections for six-year terms.

NEVADA: All judges are appointed by nonpartisan elections to six-year terms. Judges are subject to reelection for additional terms.

NEW HAMPSHIRE: All judges are appointed by the governor. Judges serve until they reach the age of 70.

NEW JERSEY: All judges are appointed by the governor to seven-year terms. Judges are reappointed by the governor with the advice and consent of the senate.

NEW MEXICO: All judges are chosen through a merit selection process involving a nominating commission.

NEW YORK: Appellate court judges are chosen through a merit selection involving a nominating commission. Judges on the Court of Appeals serve 14 years, while judges in the Appellate Division of the Supreme Court serve five-year terms. Supreme Court and county court judges are elected in partisan elections.

NORTH CAROLINA: All judges are selected in nonpartisan elections. The initial term of office is eight years, and judges are subject to reelection.

NORTH DAKOTA: All judges are selected in nonpartisan elections. The initial term of office for the supreme court is ten years, while district court judges are elected to six-year terms. Judges are reelected to additional terms.

OHIO: All judges are selected in partisan elections for six-year terms. Judges are reelected to additional terms.

OKLAHOMA: Appellate court judges are chosen through a merit selection process involving a nominating commission to one-year terms. These judges are subject to retention elections for additional six-year terms. District court judges are selected in nonpartisan elections for four-year terms and are reelected for additional terms.

OREGON: All judges are selected in nonpartisan elections for six year terms. Judges are reelected for additional terms.

PENNSYLVANIA: All judges are selected in partisan elections for ten-year terms. Judges are subject to retention elections for additional ten-year terms.

RHODE ISLAND: All judges are chosen through a merit selection process involving a nominating commission. Judges serve life tenure.

SOUTH CAROLINA: The state employs a 10-member Judicial Merit Selection Commission to screen judicial candidates. This committee recommends candidates to the General Assembly, which appoints judges. Judges are subject to reappointment by the legislature.

SOUTH DAKOTA: Supreme court judges are chosen through a merit selection process involving a nominating commission for a three-year term. These judges are subject to retention elections for eight-

year terms. Circuit court judges are selected in nonpartisan elections for eight year terms and are reelected for additional terms.

TENNESSEE: Appellate court judges are chosen through a merit selection process involving a nominating commission. These judges are subject to retention elections for additional eight-year terms. Judges in the chancery courts, criminal courts, and circuit courts are selected in partisan elections for eight-year terms and are reelected for additional terms.

TEXAS: All judges are selected in partisan elections. Appellate judges are elected to six-year terms, while district court judges are elected to four-year terms. Judges are subsequently reelected to additional terms.

UTAH: All judges are chosen through a merit selection process by a nominating committee. Judges are subject to retention elections for additional terms.

VERMONT: All judges are chosen through a merit selection process by a nominating committee for six-year terms. Judges are retained by a vote of the General Assembly for additional six-year terms.

VIRGINIA: All judges are appointed by the legislature. Supreme court justices are selected for 12 years, while lower court judges are selected for eight year terms. The legislature reappoints judges for additional terms.

WASHINGTON: All judges are selected in nonpartisan elections. Appellate court judges are elected to six-year terms, while superior court judges are elected to four-year terms. Judges are reelected for additional terms.

WEST VIRGINIA: All judges are selected through partisan election. Supreme court justices are elected for 12 years, while circuit court judges are selected for eight-year terms. Judges are reelected for additional terms.

WISCONSIN: All judges are selected through nonpartisan election. Supreme court justices are elected to ten-year terms, while lower court judges are elected to six-year terms. Judges are reelected for additional terms.

WYOMING: All judges are chosen through a merit selection process by a nominating committee for one-year terms. Judges are subject to retention elections for additional terms.

## Additional Resources

*Advice and Consent: The Politics of Judicial Appointments.* Epstein, Lee and Jeffrey A. Segal, Oxford University Press, 2005.

*Choosing Justice: The Recruitment of State and Federal Judges.* Sheldon, Charles H. and Linda S. Maule, WSU Press, 1997.

*Judicial Selection in the States: Appellate and General Jurisdiction Courts.* American Judicature Society, 2004. Available at: http://www.ajs.org/js/JudicialSelectionCharts.pdf.

*The Relationship Between Judicial Performance Evaluations and Judicial Elections.* Brody, David C., Judicature, Jan. 2004. Available at: http://www.kcba.org/judicial_selection/pdf/brody.pdf.

## Organizations

### Alliance for Justice
11 Dupont Circle NW, 2d Floor
Washington, DC 20036 USA
Phone: (510) 444-6070
Fax: (510) 444-6078
URL: http://www.allianceforjustice.org

### American Judicature Society
2700 University Avenue
Des Moines, IA 50311 USA
Phone: (515) 271-2281
Fax: (515) 279-3090
URL: http://www.ajs.org

### Center for Judicial Accountability
Box 69, Gedney Station
White Plains, NY 10605-0069 USA
Phone: (914) 421-1200
Fax: (914) 428-4994
URL: http://www.judgewatch.org

# COURTS AND PROCEDURES

## SMALL CLAIMS COURTS

*Sections within this essay:*

## Background

Small claims courts are intended to resolve civil disputes involving small amounts of money, without formal rules of **evidence** and long delays. The parties involved may present their own claims or defenses or may be represented by **counsel**; however, in a handful of states, attorneys are prohibited. The cases move quickly through the court dockets, the judges often render their opinions in the same day, and the parties are generally satisfied with the quick resolution of the controversy. However, there is a downside. All small claims courts have "limited jurisdiction" (authority to hear and adjudge a matter) involving not only the dollar amount but also the sub-

ject matter of the controversy. Secondly, if parties do not understand what they are doing in presenting their claim or defense, they could stand to lose, badly, and there is no going back.

## Anatomy of a Small Claim Action

Resolving a dispute in small claims court is very much like conducting a mini-trial, although generally less formal. There is a claim and a defense, the presentation of evidence, and a judgment. Rules of procedure vary from state to state, but the overall process is remarkably similar.

### *Maximum Dollar Value of Case*
The maximum dollar value of the dispute or claim varies greatly from state to state. Typically, the maximum amount plaintiffs may be awarded in a judgment ranges from $3,000 in New York to $7,500 in Minnesota. If the amount they are asking for in damages is more than the allowable amount in their state's small claims court system, they have two choices: either to either waive their right to any amount above and beyond the maximum allowable, or file their case in the next level of court.

### *Nature of Dispute or Controversy*
Small claims courts are mostly intended to resolve minor monetary disputes. A limited number of state small claims courts permit other forms of remedy besides money, for example, evictions or requests for the return of **personal property**. However, individuals generally cannot use small claims courts to file for **divorce**, guardianship, **bankruptcy**, name changes, **child custody**, or "injunctive relief" (emergency relief, usually to stop someone from doing something). In many states, they cannot sue

for **defamation** (slander or libel) or **false arrest** in small claims court. Finally, they cannot sue the federal government or any of its branches, agencies, or employees in their official capacities in small claims court.

### Time Limitations

Each state has its own rules regarding how long individuals have to file suit, once they have been harmed or an event occurs that gives rise to a claim. The same time limits ("statutes of limitation") apply to small claims courts as to other courts. Generally, they have at least one year from the injury or event (or its **discovery**, in some cases) to file their suit.

### Procedure

To start the process, individuals should check with their local court clerk to find out where their small claims complaint should be filed: most states require that they file suit in a small claims court in the county wherein which the party being sued actually resides (or has business headquarters), rather than the one in which the plaintiff resides. Alternatively, some courts allow the suit to be filed in the district where the injury or event occurred (where "the cause of action arises").

Generally, the complaint itself may be handwritten or prepared on a special form available from the court itself, with "fill in the blanks" ease-of-completion. If individuals are composing their own complaints, they need to make sure that it contains, at a minimum, the following:

- The plaintiff's complete name and address

- The complete name and address of the party being sued

- The date of the injury or event which gives rise to the plaintiff's claim

- A brief statement of facts relating to the injury or the event, and the role that the party being sued played in it

- The type of harm that was suffered by the plaintiff as a result of it

- The amount of damages or other remedy the plaintiff seeks are asking

Individuals must also check local law to ensure that the party being sued is properly served with the complaint. In many small claims courts, a court clerk will take care of "service of process," but in many states, plaintiffs are responsible.

The court will notify plaintiffs of the date for their trials. Plaintiffs should request from the court clerk any available information that may help them with procedure (unless they have retained an attorney). Generally, plaintiffs are allowed to bring witnesses to **testify** in support of their claims. Some courts may accept affidavits (sworn statements) from persons who cannot appear in person; however, since the other side has no opportunity to "cross-examine" an absent witness, most courts will give only minor consideration to affidavits. Plaintiffs' most important witnesses are themselves. Be prepared, be professional, and be brief (but to the point). They need to have extra copies of all documents, not only for the judge, but also for the opposing party. Remember that they will most likely be cross-examined not only on their **testimony**, but also and on the substance of any evidence they present.

Generally, there are no juries, and a judge or **magistrate** will decide the case. Often, the judgment is rendered immediately, and placed on the record. In other cases, individuals may receive written word of a decision and judgment within a few days. In some states, they may appeal a judgment, but not in all cases. The court is not responsible for collecting any judgment they have been awarded, but they can generally return to court for "post-judgment" proceedings if the other party fails to pay.

## Special Considerations

### When Individuals Are Sued in Small Claims Court

If individuals have been served with a complaint, it is imperative that they respond to the court within the time indicated. Not only do they have the right to "tell their side of the story" in their defense, but they may also, in some small claims courts, be permitted to "counter-claim." The counter-claim may be related to the original complaint (tending to diminish the complaint's value or truth), or it may be wholly unrelated but still properly raised against the person who has sued them. Defendants must check local procedure for details on the permissibility of counter-claims.

Defendants may raise the defense that they were not properly "served" with court papers according to local rules. They may raise the defense that the time for filing suit against them has expired. They may raise the defense that the person suing them has not stated a viable claim or cause of action. They may raise any other defense that they believe diminishes the value or the existence of the complaint against them.

Finally, individuals being sued need to study carefully the charges against them very carefully. First and foremost, they need to develop any facts that tend to show that they are not liable. Secondly, they need to develop any facts that tend to diminish or reduce the amount of damages the person claims they have caused. Third, they need to develop any evidence that will support their defense (or counterclaim) and/or that will corroborate their own testimony. Finally, they should practice their presentation: they will want their side of the dispute to be logical, to-the-point, and damaging to the claims against them.

### Collecting on a Judgment

Before individuals sue, they should ask themselves whether it may cost them more than they may gain. Do the people they want to sue have steady employment, valuable real estate, or other **tangible** assets? In many states, judgments are collectible (with accrued interest) for ten years or more, so individuals may wish to wait, and attach assets of the judgment **debtor** down the road in the future. If individuals want to are suing a small business contractor, their state may permit them to file a copy of the judgment with the state licensing board. If the contractor does not post bond or pay it off, the license may be suspended or revoked. Finally, there is a danger that the judgment debtor may file for bankruptcy. Even if plaintiffs are listed as a **creditor**, they may only get pennies on every dollar of their judgment.

### Small Claims for Small Business Owners

If individuals own a small business, small claims court may be helpful for collecting unpaid bills because owners do not need to go through bill collectors or lawyers, which could substantially reduce their **net** profit. Often the debtor fails to appear in court, and creditors may be entitled to a **default judgment**. But again, creditors need to be wary of collecting in the future, especially if the judgment debtor is another small business that may not be around in a few years.

### Small Claims in U. S. Tax Court

If individuals are faced with a dispute involving the U. S. Internal Revenue Service (**IRS**), the federal Tax Court maintains a special division for small cases. Their case will qualify for the small case division if the disputed amount that the IRS claims they owe for any one tax year is $50,000 or less, including taxes and penalties. A case that qualifies for small claims handling is given an "S" designation. Most tax court cases are settled without a trial.

## State Provisions

ALABAMA: In Alabama, the Small Claims Division of the District Court hears claims limited to $3,000 or less.

ALASKA: In Alaska, the District Court Civil Division processes small claims that do not exceed $7,500. Each county has a District Court.

ARKANSAS: In Arkansas, the Claims Court is a special civil division of the Municipal Court. Claims are limited to $5,000 or less.

ARIZONA: In Arizona, every **Justice of the Peace** Court has a small claims division. Disputes must not exceed $2,500. All cases are heard by judges or **hearing** officers. No attorneys are allowed to represent clients in these cases. Justice Courts share **jurisdiction** with the Superior Court in cases of landlord/tenant disputes where damages are between $5,000 and $10,000. They can hear matters regarding possession of, but not title to, real property.

CALIFORNIA: In California, individuals can file as many claims as they wish for up to $2,500 in the Small Claims Court. However, individuals may only file two (2) claims in any calendar year for up to $5,000. However, they cannot sue a guarantor for more than $4,000. A guarantor is one who promises to be responsible for the debt or **default** of another.

COLORADO: In Colorado, the County Court Civil Division processes small claims that do not exceed $5,000. Each county has a District Court. No plaintiff may file more than two claims per month or 18 claims per year in small claims courts.

CONNECTICUT: In Connecticut, the Small Claims Court is a division of the Superior Court and has a maximum jurisdictional amount of $3500. Attorneys are permitted. There are no rights of appeal. The official court form is "JD-CV-40." Individuals should call the Secretary of State at 860-509-6002 to find out if a **defendant** is a corporation and to get the address. There is a $30 filing fee.

DELAWARE: In Delaware, the Justice of the Peace Court handles both civil and criminal cases. Civil cases handled in the Justice of the Peace Court are those involving money debts, property damages, or return of personal property. The amount of damages that may be sought in the Justice of the Peace Court is limited to $15,000.

DISTRICT OF. COLUMBIA.: In Washington, D.C the District of Columbia., the Small Claims Division of the Superior Court of D.C. hears cases that are only for the recovery of money up to $5,000. The Small Claims Division of the Superior Court of D.C. hears cases that are only for the recovery of money up to $5,000.00, not including interest, attorneys fees, and court costs. If both parties to an action agree, a Superior Court judge may settle a case by **arbitration**, regardless of the amount of the claim. DC Code 11-1321,1322; McCray v. McGee, 504 A.2d 1128 (App D.C. 1986.)

FLORIDA: In Florida, a County Court civil division handles small claims under $5,000.

GEORGIA: In Georgia, a County Magistrate Small Claims Court handles money claims under $15,000. Individuals may file a claim in Magistrate Court with or without an attorney. They may have an attorney represent them if they choose; this would be at their own expense. The court does not appoint attorneys for civil cases.

HAWAII: In Hawaii, the Small Claims Division of the District Courts may only handle cases for the recovery of money where the amount claimed is no more than $3,500. The Small Claims Division publishes its own procedural rules.

ILLINOIS: In Illinois, the County Circuit Court processes small claims of $5,000 or less. The parties are not required to have lawyers but may choose to have one.

INDIANA: In Indiana, the Small Claims Division of the Superior Court hears claims limited to $3,000 or less ($6,000 in Marion and Allen Counties).

IOWA: In Iowa, the Small Claims Division of the Superior Court hears claims limited to $4,000 or less.

KANSAS: In Kansas, the District Court hears small claims actions. Amounts at issue are limited to $1,800. Lawyers are not allowed to represent parties in small claims proceedings prior to the entry of judgment. There is a $19.50 filing fee for claims up to $500, and a $39.50 filing fee for claims from $500 to $1,800. The hearing is conducted informally before a judge. The judgment debtor has ten days after the judgment is entered to file an appeal. The judgment debtor has 30 days to either pay the judgment or file a "Judgment Debtor's Statement of Assets" with the court, which will forward it to parties.

KENTUCKY: In Kentucky, the Small Claims Division of the District Court hears cases involving small claims under $1,500.

LOUISIANA: In Louisiana, the City Court hears small claims actions. Some **eviction** cases are heard in small claims court, if the rent at issue is sufficiently small. Amounts at issue are limited to $3,000 ($2,000 for movable property).

MAINE: In Maine, the Small Claims Court is a special civil division of the District Court. Claims are limited to $4,500 or less.).

MARYLAND: Maryland does not have a specific small claims court, but the District Court has exclusive jurisdiction for claims involving less than $25,000. No formal pleadings are required for claims under $2,500. Unfortunately, the trials in these courts are much more formal than in typical small claims courts. Therefore, individuals may wish to consider obtaining the services of an attorney before going into court. MD CJ 4-401, 405.

MASSACHUSETTS: In Massachusetts, small claims are heard in every District Court, in every Housing Court, and at the Boston Municipal Court. Small claim actions are limited to disputes under $2,000.

MICHIGAN: In Michigan, individuals can sue for up to $3,000 in the Small Claims Division of the District Court. Michigan does not allow attorneys in small claims court. Decisions are final and cannot be appealed. Filing fees are $17.00 for claims up to $600, and $32.00 for claims from $600 to $3,000.

MINNESOTA: In Minnesota, the Small Claims Court is part of the District Court. Claims may not exceed $7,500.

MISSISSIPPI: In Mississippi, individuals may sue in small claims court for up to $2,500. There are no Internet resources for Mississippi small claims courts as of 2002.

MISSOURI: In Missouri, civil claims for $3,000 or less may be filed in Small Claims Court. This court has very simple rules that allow parties to resolve disputes with or without a lawyer. Rules 140 through 152 govern all civil actions pending in the small claims division of the circuit court.

MONTANA: In Montana, the Justice Court hears small claims actions of $3,000 or less.

NEBRASKA: In Nebraska, small claims court is limited to civil (non-criminal) actions involving disputes over amounts of money owed, damage to property, or seeking the return of personal property. Judgments in small claims court may not exceed $2,400.

NEVADA: In Nevada, the Small Claims Division of the County Court hears small claims actions of $5,500 or less.

NEW HAMPSHIRE: In New Hampshire, Small Claims Courts are divisions of District Courts. Small claims are regulated by RSA 503. A small claim action may not exceed $5,000. Attorneys are permitted.

NEW JERSEY: In New Jersey, small claim cases are heard in the Special Civil Part of the Civil Division of the Superior Court. These cases are for less than $2,000. The Special Civil Part also hears cases between $2,000 and $10,000.

NEW MEXICO: In New Mexico, the County Magistrate Court is authorized to hear cases that do not exceed $5,000.

NEW YORK:

New York City: In New York, the City, District, and Justice Courts in the state have Small Claims Parts that are authorized to hear cases that do not exceed $3,000.

NORTH CAROLINA: In North Carolina, the County District Court is authorized to hear cases that do not exceed $4,000.

NORTH DAKOTA: In North Dakota, the District Court is authorized to hear small claims cases that do not exceed $5,000.

OHIO: In Ohio, civil claims for $3,000 or less may be filed in Small Claims Court. This court has very simple rules that allow parties to resolve disputes without hiring an attorney. However, attorneys are permitted to represent parties if desired.

OKLAHOMA: In Oklahoma, the District Court small claims division handles cases that do not exceed $4,500.

OREGON: In Oregon, the Small Claims Department of the Justice Court processes small claim actions involving disputes under $5,000.

PENNSYLVANIA: In Pennsylvania, District Justice Courts hear claims that do not exceed $8,000. The Municipal Court of Philadelphia may hear claims of $10,000 or less. It also may hear rent only disputes in **Landlord** Tenant cases of an unlimited amount.

RHODE ISLAND: In Rhode Island, the small claims courts handle cases that do not exceed $1,500.

SOUTH CAROLINA: In South Carolina, the Magistrate Court processes small claim actions involving

disputes under $5,000. This amount was raised to $7,500 on January 1, 2001.

SOUTH DAKOTA: In South Dakota, the small claims court is authorized to hear cases for $8,000 or less.

TENNESSEE: In Tennessee, the Court of General Sessions hears small claims actions involving disputes for $15,000 or less. In counties of 700,000 or more people, the Court hears small claims disputes for up to $25,000. However, there is no dollar limit for cases involving **unlawful detainer** and the recovery of personal property.

TEXAS: In Texas, a Justice Court handles small claims under $5,000.

UTAH: In Utah, the District Court processes small claim actions involving disputes under $5,000. Each county has a District Court. Small Claims rules and fees are covered under Title 78, Chapter 06 of the Utah Code.

VERMONT: In Vermont, the small claims courts handle cases that do not exceed $3,500.

VIRGINIA: In Virginia, the small claims divisions of the general district courts hear disputes of $1,000 or less. The general district courts, themselves, hear disputes of $3,000 or less. Cases involving amounts between $3,000 and $15,000 may be heard by either the general district court or the circuit court. VA Code 16.1-122.1.

WASHINGTON: In Washington State, the District Court Civil Division processes small claims in amounts not exceeding $2,500. Each county has a District Court. Note that small claims are not handled in municipal court. Procedural guidelines for small claims actions are found in the Revised Code of Washington (RCW) Chapters 3.66, 4.28, 12.40, and applicable provisions in the Civil Rules for Courts of Limited Jurisdiction, Rule 5 (CRLJ5).

WEST VIRGINIA: In West Virginia, the Magistrates Courts handle small claims with $5,000 or less in dispute.

WISCONSIN: In Wisconsin, the District Courts handle small claims of $5,000 or less. For landlords seeking eviction, the $5,000 limit does not apply.

WYOMING: In Wyoming, the Justice of the Peace Courts hear small claims of up to $3,000. Circuit courts hear cases of up to $7,000.

## Additional Resources

*The Court TV Cradle-to-grave Legal Survival Guide* Little, Brown and Company, 1995.

*Everybody's Guide to Small Claims Court.* Warner., Ralph, Nolo Press, 1991.

*Law for Dummies.* Ventura., John, IDG Books Worldwide, Inc., 1996.

*"Small Claims Court."* Nolo Press, 2002. Available at http://www.nolo.com/lawcenter/ency/article.cf.

# COURTS AND PROCEDURES

## STATE COURTS AND PROCEDURES

*Sections within this essay:*

- Background

- Function and Scope of State Courts

- The Concept of Jurisdiction

- General Structure of State Court Systems

- Judges and Administrative Staff

- State Provisions

- Additional Resources

## Background

The judicial powers of individual states are generally vested in various courts created by state constitution or (less frequently) state **statute**. Within the **boundaries** of each state and coexisting with state courts are numerous federal district and/or **appellate** courts that function independently. Also coexisting within state boundaries are various administrative tribunals that also hear and decide legal matters, such as worker's compensation boards, professional licensing boards, and state administrative tribunals. Yet, there are often local, district, and/or municipal courts within the community. At first blush, it may appear overwhelming and confusing to consider what legal matter may be decided in which forum. But for the most part, each of the above courts has its own separate function and role in applying the laws to the controversies brought before it and administering justice to all.

## Function and Scope of State Courts

To understand the function and scope of state courts, it is necessary to consider them in relation to the federal court system expressly created in Article III of the U. S. Constitution. Article III also establishes the type of cases that federal courts may hear and decide (federal "jurisdiction").

Article VII of the Constitution declares that "This Constitution, and the Laws of the United States . . . and all Treaties made . . . under the Authority of the United States, shall be the supreme Law of the Land; and the Judges in every State shall be bound thereby, any Thing in the Constitution or Laws of any State to the Contrary notwithstanding." Later in the Constitution, the Tenth Amendment provides that "powers not delegated to the United States by the Constitution, nor prohibited by it to the States, are reserved to the States respectively, or to the people."

The ultimate effect these provisions have upon state courts is to reserve to them the right to hear and decide any legal matter not expressly reserved for the exclusive **jurisdiction** of federal courts (such as lawsuits between states). This matter mostly involves the "adjudication" of controversies concerning state laws, which impact the daily lives of citizens in a much greater manner than federal laws. State courts may also rule upon certain issues concerning federal law and the federal Constitution.

State legislatures are therefore free to create—and state courts are free to enforce—any law, regulation, or rule that does not conflict with or abridge the guarantees of the federal Constitution (or the state's own constitution). The wide variance, from state to state, of both structure and procedure within the court systems is precisely due to the preservation of those independent powers to the states by the U. S. Constitution.

## The Concept of Jurisdiction

A court's general authority to hear and/or "adjudicate" a legal matter is referred to as its "jurisdiction." In the United States, jurisdiction is granted to a court or court system by statute or by constitution. A court is competent to hear and decide only those cases whose subject matter fits within the court's jurisdiction. A legal decision made by a court that did not have proper jurisdiction is deemed void and non-binding upon the litigants.

Jurisdiction may be referred to as "exclusive," "original," concurrent, general, or limited. Federal court jurisdiction may be "exclusive" over certain matters or parties (to the exclusion of any other forum) or may be "concurrent" and shared with state courts. In matters where both federal and state courts have concurrent jurisdiction, state courts may hear federal law claims (e.g., violations of **civil rights**), and parties bringing suit may choose the forum. However, when a plaintiff raises both state and federal claims in a state court, the **defendant** may be able to "remove" the case to a federal court.

## General Structure of State Court Systems

The general workhorse of a state court system is the trial court. This is the lowest level of court and is usually the forum in which a case or lawsuit originates. It may be a court of general jurisdiction, such as a circuit or superior court, or it may be a court of special or limited jurisdiction, such as a **probate**, juvenile, traffic, or family court. Some states handle "small claims" in separate courts, while others handle such claims in special divisions of the general trial courts. This is also true for probate and juvenile matters. Although someone may broadly refer to "juvenile court" or "small claims court," he or she may actually be referring to the juvenile or small claims "division" of the general circuit court.

- Probate courts primarily handle the administration of estates and the probating of wills. In many states, probate courts also handle such matters as competency hearings, applications for guardianships, adoptions, etc. In a minority of jurisdictions, probate courts may be referred to as surrogate's courts.

- Family courts hear cases involving (mostly) **custody** and **child support**, neglect and abuse cases, and, sometimes, juvenile crime or truancy. Most family courts do not handle divorces, which are generally handled by the courts of general jurisdiction.

- Traffic courts handle civil infractions and violations involving motor vehicles, petitions for reinstatement of driving privileges, and related matters. Some may handle minor (**misdemeanor**) criminal offenses related to motor vehicle-related violations. Most traffic courts do not handle automobile accident cases (as between the parties involved in an accident).

- Housing courts, or landlord-tenant courts, handle exactly that. In many jurisdictions, landlords must choose to file their cases in one of two courts, depending upon whether they seek **eviction**, injunction, etc. (landlord-tenant court), or seek money damages (small claims court). Other jurisdictions handle all landlord-tenant related matters in a single court.

- Small-claims courts handle all civil matters in which the dollar amount in controversy does not exceed a certain amount. If a party seeks damages in an amount greater than the jurisdictional limit of the small claims court, the party must either waive his or her right to the exceeding amount or re-file the case in a court with greater jurisdiction. The maximum jurisdictional limit of small claims courts varies greatly from state to state but mostly falls in the range of $3000 to $7500.

- Juvenile courts handle truancy and criminal offenses of minors. The maximum age of the minor varies from state to state but generally is either 16 or 18 years. Older juveniles who have committed serious crimes may be "bound over" to a court of general jurisdiction for determination of whether they should be tried as adults.

Importantly, states may have separate courts for criminal and civil matters. Most often, a trial court of general jurisdiction will handle both, but often on separate dockets. Many local or district courts will have limited jurisdiction for criminal matters (e.g. misdemeanors only). In such circumstances, a person charged with a **felony** may be arraigned in the district court and then "bound over" to the next level court (having proper jurisdiction) for criminal trial. Again, this varies greatly from state to state.

Every state has its own system to handle appeals from the trial courts. Most states have a three-tiered court system in which there are intermediate "appellate" courts that review jury verdicts or the opinions of trial court judges (on a limited basis and under strict criteria). These appellate courts may or may not be distinguished by separate buildings or courthouses. Often, what is referred to as a "court of appeals" is in reality a panel of justices who merely convene to hear and decide cases at the appellate level.

In a minority of states, trial court decisions receive only one appellate review at the level of the state's highest court or the court "of last resort" (generally referred to as the state's "supreme court"). Once a state's highest court has decided a matter, the only available appeal is to the U. S. Supreme Court. However, the Supreme Court is generally deferential to state supreme courts, and only reviews matters in very limited circumstances (e.g, where a state's highest court has ruled that a federal statute or treaty is invalid or unconstitutional, or where the highest courts of two or more states have ruled differently on federal issues). When a state's highest court has decided a matter that involves both federal and state issues, the U. S. Supreme Court will nonetheless refuse to review the matter if the non-federal question is decisive in the case.

## Judges and Administrative Staff

Whereas most federal judges are appointed to their positions, the majority of state trial court judges are elected to their positions by the general populace. Appellate (especially supreme court) justices are often appointed by state governors or legislatures but may also be elected by voters.

What does vary greatly from state to state is whether judicial elections involve partisan politics. In some states, party politics play a direct role in judgeships; in other states, a judicial candidate's party affiliation is treated as private data (such as religious affiliation) not disclosed in campaign profiles. States also vary greatly in the extent to which they permit judicial candidates to "advertise" their candidacy and/or raise campaign funds.

State courts employ a large number of support staff, who are usually public employees paid by taxpayer funds. Generally, a judge's staff may include

one or more private assistants, law clerks, court reporters, bailiffs and other court officers, and court clerks. The most important administrative office of the courthouse is that of the court clerk. This is the office that stamps and dates all lawsuits filed, serves process (or verifies the parties' service of process), posts legal notices, subpoenas witnesses, **summons** and prepares juries, and sends sheriffs or other court officials out to serve writs of **execution** to collect on unpaid judgments.

## State Provisions

ALABAMA: See Title 12 of the Alabama Code of 1975, also available at http://www.legislatures.state.al.us/codeofAlabama/1975. Alabama's courts of limited jurisdiction are probate, county, justice, and recorder's courts. Its trial court of general jurisdiction is the "circuit court." Alabama has separate appellate courts for criminal and civil appeals and one supreme court.

ALASKA: Alaska has **magistrate** and district courts of limited jurisdiction. Its general trial courts are called "superior courts." Its court of last resort is its state supreme court.

ARIZONA: Courts of limited jurisdiction include "justice courts," municipal courts, and magistrate offices. The superior courts are the trial courts of general jurisdiction. Arizona has a court of appeals and a supreme court.

ARKANSAS: See Title 16, Subtitle 2 of the Arkansas Code establishes the state court system, available at http://www.arkleg.state.ar.us/dcode. Arkansas operates county, municipal, common pleas, justice, and police courts of limited jurisdiction. It maintains the **common law** general jurisdiction courts of Chancery and Probate and has a single supreme court of last resort.

CALIFORNIA: California's circuit courts are the courts of general jurisdiction. It also maintains municipal and justice courts of limited jurisdiction. California has both a court of appeals and a supreme court.

COLORADO: See Title 13 of the Colorado Constitution. Colorado maintains limited jurisdiction courts, including superior, juvenile, probate, county, and municipal courts. The superior court is the court of general jurisdiction. Colorado has both a court of appeals and a supreme court.

CONNECTICUT: Connecticut has juvenile, common pleas, and probate courts of limited jurisdiction. The district court is the court of general jurisdiction. Appeals go directly to the state supreme court.

DELAWARE: Delaware maintains limited jurisdictions courts for family, municipal, and justice. Its general jurisdiction court is the superior court, and appeals are made directly to the state supreme court. See Title 10 of the Delaware Code.

DISTRICT OF COLUMBIA: See Title 11 of the statutes.

FLORIDA: Florida's court of general jurisdiction is its circuit court. It also maintains county courts of limited jurisdiction. It has a district court of appeals and a state supreme court. See Title V of Florida's statutes.

GEORGIA: See Title 15 of the Georgia Code. Georgia has probate, civil justice, criminal justice, and small claims courts of limited jurisdiction. Its superior courts are the courts of general jurisdiction. The state maintains both an appeals court and a supreme court.

HAWAII: Division 4 of the state laws discuss the state's court system. Hawaii utilizes district courts of limited jurisdiction and circuit courts of general jurisdiction. Appeals go directly to the Hawaii Supreme Court.

IDAHO: The district court is the court of general jurisdiction, but within that court is the magistrate's court of limited jurisdiction. Idaho's appeals go directly to the state supreme court.

ILLINOIS: Illinois circuit courts are the courts of general jurisdiction. The state maintains both a court of appeals and a state supreme court.

INDIANA: The Indiana Code establishes county, municipal, magistrate, probate, juvenile, and **justice of the peace** courts of limited jurisdiction. Indiana has circuit civil and criminal courts of general jurisdiction, and has both a court of appeals and a state supreme court.

IOWA: See Title XV, Subtitle 2 of the Iowa Code establishes the court system, which includes the district court as the court of general jurisdiction and appeals go directly to the state supreme court.

KANSAS: See Chapters 20 of the Kansas Statutes, available at http://www.kslegislature.org/cgi-bin/statutes/index.cgi. Kansas has probate, municipal, county, and juvenile courts of limited jurisdiction. Its district courts are courts of general jurisdiction, and appeals are made to the state supreme court.

KENTUCKY: Kentucky has county, justice, and police courts of limited jurisdiction. It has a claims court for claims against the state or its agencies. Kentucky's courts of general jurisdiction are its district and circuit courts, and the state maintains both a court of appeals and a state supreme court.

LOUISIANA: Louisiana has city, juvenile, mayor's justice, traffic, family, municipal, and parish courts of limited jurisdiction. It maintains both a court of appeals and a supreme court. http://www.legis.state.la.us.

MAINE: See Maine Statutes, Titles 14, 15, and 16. Maine has limited jurisdiction probate and district courts. Its superior courts are courts of general jurisdiction, and the court of last resort is called the "supreme judicial court."

MARYLAND: See "Courts and Judicial Proceedings," available at http://mlis.state.md.us/cgi-win/web_statutes.exe. Maryland has orphans and district courts of limited jurisdiction. Its "circuit of counties" courts are the courts of general jurisdiction, and its court of appeals and court of special appeals are the courts of last resort.

MASSACHUSETTS: See Chapters 211-222 of the General Laws of Massachusetts, "Courts, Judicial Officers and Proceedings." The state's courts of general jurisdiction are its superior courts. The state has land, probate, municipal, district, juvenile, and housing courts of limited jurisdiction. The court of last resort is the state's supreme judicial court, but the state also has a court of appeals.

MICHIGAN: Michigan's Constitution creates its courts, which include a court of appeals and a state supreme court. Michigan's courts of general jurisdiction are its circuit courts, generally at the county level. It maintains a few "recorder's courts" for criminal cases. Limited jurisdiction courts include those for common pleas, municipal, district, and probate.

MINNESOTA: See Chapters 480-494 for court systems. Minnesota has county, municipal, and probate courts of limited jurisdiction. Its district courts have general jurisdiction, and it has a supreme court and court of appeals.

MISSISSIPPI: See Title 9 of Mississippi Code of 1972, available at http://www.mscode.com/free/

statutes. The state maintains family, county, city police, and justice courts of limited jurisdiction, has chancery and circuit courts of general jurisdiction, and a state supreme court.

MISSOURI: The state has probate, courts of criminal correction, magistrate, and municipal courts of limited jurisdiction. Its circuit courts are courts of general jurisdiction, and the state has both a court of appeals and a state supreme court.

MONTANA: See Title 3 of state statutes. The state maintains municipal, justice, city, and workman's compensation courts of special or limited jurisdiction. The district court is the state's court of general jurisdiction, and maintains a state supreme court.

NEBRASKA: See Chapters 24 to 27 of the Nebraska statutes at http://statutes.unicam.state.ne.us/ Nebraska has county, municipal, juvenile, and workman's compensation courts of limited jurisdiction. Its district court is the state's court of general jurisdiction, and it maintains a state supreme court.

NEVADA: See Title 1 of the Nevada Revised Statutes for a general discussion of the state's court system. Nevada has municipal and justice courts of limited jurisdiction. Its district court is the state's court of general jurisdiction, and it maintains a state supreme court.

NEW HAMPSHIRE: New Hampshire has probate, district, and municipal courts of limited jurisdiction. Its superior court is the state's court of general jurisdiction, and it maintains a state supreme court.

NEW JERSEY: New Jersey maintains municipal, county district, juvenile and domestic relations courts of limited jurisdiction. Its superior court is the state's court of general jurisdiction, and it maintains a state supreme court.

NEW MEXICO: Chapters 34 and 35 of the state statutes address the court system. New Mexico maintains probate, municipal, small claims, and magistrate courts of limited jurisdiction, as well as a court of appeals and a state supreme court.

NEW YORK: See Chapter 30 of the New York State Consolidated Laws, available at http://assembly.state.ny.us/leg/ New York refers to its highest **appellate court** as its "superior court," and its courts of general jurisdiction as "supreme courts," mostly at the county level. New York City maintains several courts of limited jurisdiction for civil and criminal dockets, and the state also maintains a court of appeals.

NORTH CAROLINA: See Chapters 7 of the North Carolina General Statutes. The state maintains its superior courts as courts of general jurisdiction. It has a court of appeals and a state supreme court.

NORTH DAKOTA: See Chapter 27-33 of the Century Code. Its district court is the court of general jurisdiction. The county courts are courts of limited jurisdiction. North Dakota has a state supreme court.

OHIO: Ohio's Courts of Common Pleas are the courts of general jurisdiction. It also maintains municipal, county, and courts of claims are courts of limited jurisdiction. It maintains a court of appeals and the court of last resort is the state supreme court.

OKLAHOMA: See Title 20 of the Oklahoma Statutes. The district court is the court of general jurisdiction. The state maintains municipal courts of limited jurisdiction. It has separate courts of appeal for criminal and civil cases and has a supreme court of last resort.

OREGON: See Chapters 1 to 10 of the Oregon Revised Statutes. Oregon maintains district, county, justice, and municipal courts of limited jurisdiction. Its court of general jurisdiction is the circuit court. Oregon maintains a court of appeals and a state supreme court.

PENNSYLVANIA: Pennsylvania's Courts of Common Pleas are the courts of general jurisdiction. It also maintains municipal, traffic, and justice of the peace courts of limited jurisdiction. Its appellate courts are the superior court and the commonwealth court, and the court of last resort is the state supreme court.

RHODE ISLAND: The state maintains district, probate, family and police courts of limited jurisdiction. The court of general jurisdiction is the superior court, and the state has a supreme court.

SOUTH CAROLINA: The circuit court is the court of general jurisdiction. South Carolina maintains county, probate, magistrate, city recorder's, and family courts of limited jurisdiction. The state's court of last resort is the state supreme court.

TENNESSEE: See Titles 16. The courts of general jurisdiction include chancery court, circuit court, criminal court, and law equity court. There are limited jurisdiction courts for municipal, juvenile, domestic relations cases. Tennessee has separate courts of appeals for criminal and civil cases, and a state supreme court.

TEXAS: Texas maintains criminal district, domestic relations, juvenile, probate, and county courts of limited jurisdiction. Its court of general jurisdiction is the district court. There are separate courts of appeal for civil and criminal cases, and the state has a supreme court.

UTAH: The state has juvenile, city, and justice courts of limited jurisdiction. The district court is the court of general jurisdiction, and the state has a supreme court.

VERMONT: Vermont maintains district and probate courts of limited jurisdiction, while its superior courts are the courts of general jurisdiction. Vermont has a state supreme court.

VIRGINIA: Virginia has general district, juvenile, and domestic relations courts of limited jurisdiction. Its circuit courts are the courts of general jurisdiction, and the state supreme court is the court of last resort.

WASHINGTON: See Titles 2 and 3 of the Revised Code of Washington, and the superior court is the court of general jurisdiction. It maintains district and municipal courts of limited jurisdiction. The state has a court of appeals and a state supreme court.

WEST VIRGINIA: See Chapters 50 and 51. Police courts of limited jurisdiction, circuit courts of general jurisdiction. The court of last resort is the supreme court of appeals.

WISCONSIN: See Chapters 750 to 758 of the Wisconsin Statutes. The state maintains municipal courts of limited jurisdiction. The county circuit courts are the courts of general jurisdiction. The state supreme court is the court of last resort.

WYOMING: Wyoming maintains justice and municipal courts of limited jurisdiction. Its court of general jurisdiction is the state district court, and it has a state supreme court.

## Additional Resources

*The Court TV Cradle-to-grave Legal Survival Guide* Little, Brown and Company: 1995.

*How and When to Be Your Own Lawyer* Schachner, Robert W., Avery Publishing Group, Inc. 1993.

# CRIMINAL LAW

## APPEALS

*Sections Within This Essay*

- What is an Appeal?

- The Basis for an Appeal

- Where are Appeals Filed?

- The Number of Appeals

- Reversing a Conviction

- Writs

- Writs of Habeas Corpus

- The U.S. Supreme Court

- Costs

- Additional Resources

- Organizations

## What is an Appeal?

An appeal is a request from a party in a lower court proceeding to a higher (**appellate**) court asking the **appellate court** to review and change the decision of the lower court. If a **defendant** in a criminal case is found guilty of a charge or charges, the defendant has the right to appeal that **conviction** or the punishment or sentencing. It is common for convicted defendants to appeal their convictions.

The defendant in a criminal trial may appeal after she or he is convicted at trial. In fact, it is very common for convicted defendants to appeal their convictions and/or sentencing. Usually only the defendant in a criminal trial may appeal. The **prosecutor** may

not appeal if the defendant is acquitted (found "not guilty") at trial. The prosecutor may not put the same defendant on trial for the same charge with the same **evidence**. This kind of retrial is known as "double jeopardy." **Double jeopardy** is expressly prohibited under the Fifth Amendment of the United States Constitution. However, prior to or during a criminal trial, a prosecutor may be able to appeal certain rulings, such as when a judge has ordered that some evidence be "suppressed" Appeals that take place in the midst of a trial are called interlocutory appeals. In most cases, appeals can be very complicated; the appellate court tends to enforce technical rules for proceeding with an appeal.

In criminal cases, a federal court may review a conviction after all of the usual appeals have been exhausted. A convicted defendant may request one of these reviews in a petition for a **writ** of habeas corpus—Latin for "you have the body." Only a very small percentage of these petitions are granted. In death penalty cases, these proceedings have become highly controversial. Since a judicial or prosecutor's error in a death penalty case has such extreme consequences, courts review petitions for writs of **habeas corpus** very carefully.

The procedures of appellate courts consist of the rules and practices by which appellate courts review trial court judgments. Federal appellate courts follow the Federal Rules of Appellate Procedure. State appellate courts follow their own state rules of appellate procedure. In both state and federal jurisdictions, appeals are commonly limited to "final judgments." There are exceptions to the "final judgment rule," including instances of plain or fundamental error by the trial court, questions of subject-matter **jurisdiction** of the trial court, or constitutional questions.

The issues under review in appellate court centers on written briefs prepared by the parties. These complex documents list the questions for the appellate court and enumerate the legal authorities and arguments in support of each party's position. Most appellate courts do not hear oral arguments unless there is a specific request by the parties. Few jurisdictions allow for oral argument as a matter of course. Where it is allowed, oral argument is intended to clarify legal issues presented in the briefs and lawyers are constrained to keep their oral presentations strictly to the issues on appeal. Ordinarily, oral arguments are subjected to a strictly enforced time limit. This time limit can be extended only upon the discretion of the court.

## The Basis for an Appeal

There is an institutional preference for a trial court's rulings and findings in the U. S. judicial system. Thus, for an appellate court to hear an appeal from a lower court the aggrieved party must demonstrate to the appellate court that an error was made at the trial level. The error must have been substantial. "Harmless errors," or those unlikely to make a substantial impact on the result at trial, are not grounds for reversing the judgment of a lower court. Any error, defect, irregularity, or variance, which does not affect substantial rights, shall be disregarded.

Assuming that there was no harmless error, there are two basic grounds for appeal:

1. the lower court made a serious error of law (plain error),

2. the weight of the evidence does not support the verdict.

Plain error is an error or defect that affects the defendant's substantial rights, even though the parties did not bring this error or defect to the judge's attention during trial. Of course, some plain errors or defects affecting substantial rights may be noticed although they were not brought to the attention of the court. In any event, plain error will form a basis for an appeal of a criminal conviction.

It is much more difficult to prevail in an appeal based on the alleged insufficient **weight of evidence**. Although appellate courts review the transcripts of trials, they almost never hear actual **testimony** of witnesses, view the presentation of evidence, or hear the parties' opening and closing arguments. Consequently, they are not in the best position to assess the weight of evidence in many cases. For this reason they place much confidence in trial courts' decisions on issues of facts. In an appeal based on an alleged insufficient weight of evidence to support a verdict, the error or misjudgment of evidence must truly be egregious for a defendant to expect to prevail on appeal.

## Where are Appeals Filed?

Usually, individuals may only file an appeal with the next higher court in the same system in which the case originated. For example, if persons want to file an appeal from a decision in a state trial court, normally they may file their appeals only to the state intermediate appellate court. The party who loses on appeal may next appeal to the next higher court in the system, usually the state supreme court. The state's highest court is almost always the final word on matters of that state's law.

## The Number of Appeals

Generally, the final judgment of a lower court can be appealed to the next higher court one time only. Thus, the total number of appeals depends on how many courts are "superior" to the court that made the contested decision, and sometimes what the next higher court decides the appeal's basis. In states with large populations, it is common to find three or even four levels of courts, while in less populous states there may be only two. There are important differences in the rules, time limits, costs, and procedures depending on whether the case is in Federal court or state court. Also, each state has different rules. Finally, even within a single state one may find that there are different rules for appeals depend on the court in which the case originated.

Filing a Notice of Appeal is the first step in the appeal process. An appellate court cannot adjudicate a case if the notice is not properly filed in a timely manner. The notice must be filed within a definite time, usually 30 days in civil appeals and 10 days in criminal appeals. The period within which to file usually starts on the date a final judgment in the lower court is filed.

## Reversing a Conviction

As noted above, appeals judges generally defer to trial court findings, particularly findings of fact (as opposed to findings of law). Appellate courts resist overruling trial court judgments and provide trial courts with wide discretion in the conduct of trials. "Prefect trials" are not guaranteed. In most cases, an appellate court will overturn a guilty verdict only if the trial court made an error of law that patently or significantly contributed to the trial's outcome. In other words, a trial judge's error will not lead to a reversal of a conviction as long as the error can reasonably be considered harmless. Most errors are deemed "harmless," and there are consequently few reversals of convictions. There are, of course, some types of errors that are so egregious that they are presumed harmful, such as the use of a coerced **confession**.

Sentencing is a different matter. When a trial court exercises its discretion in sentencing, an appellate court will rarely interfere. In some cases, however, the law specifies a particular sentence; if the judge gets it wrong, the appellate court will usually send the case back for resentencing.

## Writs

A writ is a document or an order from a higher court that directs a lower court or a government official to take some kind of action. In any given trial, a defendant may appeal a case to the next higher appellate body only once, but the defendant may file multiple writs in that same trial. Defendants may seek several types of writs from appellate judges directed at the trial court or at a lower appellate court. Most writs require advanced legal knowledge and involve detailed procedures. Defendants contemplating making an application for a writ are wise to consult **counsel**.

Courts view writs as extraordinary remedies. This means that is, courts permit them only when a criminal defendant has no other adequate remedy, such as an appeal. In other words, a defendant may seek a writ to contest an issue that the defendant could not raise in a regular appeal. This action generally applies when the alleged error or mistake is not apparent in the record of the case. Generally, courts will adjudicate writs more quickly than regular appeals. If a defendant feels wronged by actions of the trial judge, he or she may need to take a writ to obtain an early review by a higher court. Some of the most common grounds for seeking a writ include:

- The defense failed to make a timely objection at the time of the alleged error or injustice

- A final judgment has not yet been entered in the trial court, but the party seeking the writ requires immediate relief to prevent further injustice or unnecessary expense

- Urgency

- The defendant has already lodged an unsuccessful appeal. Merely filing a writ that repeats the same unsuccessful grounds or arguments of an appeal is a frivolous writ and an appellate court will dismiss those writs immediately

- when an attorney has failed to investigate a possible defense

## Writ of habeas corpus

In many countries, authorities may take citizens and incarcerate them for months or years without charging them. Those imprisoned have no legal means by which they can protest or challenge the **imprisonment**. The framers of the U. S. Constitution wanted to prohibit this kind of occurrence in the new United States. Therefore, they included a clause in the Constitution that allows courts to issue writs of habeas corpus.

Defendants who are considering challenging the legal basis of their imprisonment—or the conditions in which they are being imprisoned—may seek relief from a court by filing an application for a "writ of habeas corpus." A writ of habeas corpus (which literally means to "produce the body") is a court order to a person or agency holding someone in **custody** to deliver the imprisoned individual to the court issuing the order. Many states recognize writs of habeas corpus, as does the U. S. Constitution. The U. S. Constitution specifically prohibits the government from suspending proceedings for writs of habeas corpus except under extraordinary circumstances—such as during times of war.

Convicted defendants have a number of options for challenging guilty verdicts and/or for seeking remedy for violations of constitutional rights, including motions, appeals, and writs. Note that convicted defendants must first have sought relief through the available state courts before they are permitted to seek relief in federal courts. Thus, defendants should consult lawyers to determine which remedies are available to them.

## The U. S. Supreme Court

The United States Supreme Court is the "highest" court in the land. It has authority to hear appeals in nearly all cases decided in the Federal court system. It can also hear appeals that involve a "federal question", such as an issue involving a federal **statute** or an issue arising under the U. S. Constitution. The Supreme Court will generally hear cases that originate in state court only after a decision by that state's highest court. Despite the great number of criminal cases that are appealed, very few criminal cases are ever heard by the Supreme Court. Fewer than 100 cases are actually heard and decided by the Supreme Court in any given year, and of these only a few are criminal cases.

## Costs

Surprisingly, many appeals can be very inexpensive. If the appeal is focused on only one clearly defined issue of law, and all sides have prepared good briefs, it may cost very little to appeal. On the other hand, appeals—such as claims that the verdict was against the weight of the evidence—typically require both the printing of the entire trial record and extensive analysis and briefing. Such appeals are relatively expensive as they can require large amounts of lawyers' time. Additionally, they often turn out to be less successful.

## Additional Resources

*Briefing and arguing federal appeals: a new edition of "effective appellate advocacy"* Frederick Bernays Wiener, Lawbook Exchange, 2001.

*Criminal procedure, constitutional limitations in a nutshell* fifth ed., Israel, Jerold H. and Wayne R. LaFave. West Publishing Co., 1993.

*Federal Court of Appeals manual: a manual on practice in the United States Court of Appeals* third ed., Knibb, David G., West Publishing Co., 1997.

*http://www.appellate-counsellor.com/* "Appellate Counsellor Home Page" Calvin House, 2002.

*http://www.currentlegal.com/uscourtrules/frap/* "Federal Rules of Appellate Procedure" Legal Content Inc., 2001.

*http://www.kentlaw.edu/7circuit/map.html* "U.S. Federal Appellate Courts" Center for Law and Computers at Chicago-Kent College of Law, Illinois Institute of Technology, 2002.

*http://vls.law.vill.edu/Locator/statecourt/* "State Court Locator" Villanova University School of Law, 2000.

## Organizations

### American Bar Association, Criminal Justice Section

740 15th Street, NW, 10th Floor
Washington, DC 20005-1009 USA
Phone: (202) 662-1500
Fax: (202) 662-1501
URL: http://www.abanet.org/crimjust/contact.html

### National Association of Criminal Defense Lawyers (NACDL)

1025 Connecticut Avenue, NW, Suite 901
Washington, DC 20036 USA
Phone: (202) 872-8600
Fax: (202) 872-8690
E-Mail: assist@nacdl.org
URL: http://www.criminaljustice.org/public.nsf/
FreeForm/PublicWelcome?OpenDocument

# CRIMINAL LAW

## BAIL AND BAIL BOND AGENTS

*Sections within this essay:*

## Background

Bail is an amount of money that a criminal defendant may be ordered to pay before being released from custody pending trial. Its purpose is to ensure a defendant's return at subsequent trial proceedings. Bail is typically determined during a defendant's first appearance in court. A judge or other court officer sets the amount and conditions of bail. At a bail hearing, a judge has three options:

- Release the defendant on his or her own **recognizance** or upon an unsecured appearance bond

- Deny bail to the accused

- Set terms of bail, including the amount of bail and any special conditions for release

In common usage, bail typically refers to criminal proceedings. However, in rare instances bail may be imposed in civil cases. Civil bail is used to directly or indirectly secure payment of a debt or to secure a performance of a civil duty. For example, bail may be employed in a civil case to arrest someone to prevent them from fleeing to avoid litigation, or it may be used to prevent an unlawful concealment or disposal of assets. The amount of bail set will be based on the probable amount of damages the plaintiff could collect. Sometimes the deposit may be used to pay the judgment to a plaintiff.

Bail law came to the U.S. through English tradition and laws. Even before the adoption of the U.S. Constitution and Bill of Rights, a judiciary act in 1789 guaranteed a right to bail in all noncapital cases. For a person charged with a capital offense (where death is a possible punishment), bail was discretionary, depending upon the seriousness of the offense. The Eighth Amendment to the U.S. Constitution provides, "excessive bail shall not be required." The U.S. Supreme Court has ruled that the constitution permits holding a defendant without bail pending a criminal trial. No absolute right to bail exists.

Bail is not meant to act as pre-trial punishment, or as a fine. Modern bail laws reflect an intentional emphasis on non-monetary methods to ensure a defendant's appearance at trial. This is meant to avoid discrimination against poor defendants.

Bail may or may not be required in **misdemeanor** cases, depending upon the circumstances and seriousness of the offense. More serious misdemeanor cases and **felonies** often require a bail determination. Bail may come into play at three stages of a criminal proceeding:

- During the pretrial period

- Pending imposition or execution of sentence

• Pending appeal of a conviction or sentence

If bail is not required, a defendant may be released on his or her own recognizance. Releasing someone on personal recognizance means that the person has promised to show up for trial or other court proceedings, without posting a bond. Release on personal recognizance may be appropriate when a person has ties to the community and has lawful and steady employment. Family status is also taken into account. Before release, a defendant must sign a document promising to appear. Failure to abide by the terms of release on personal recognizance may result in revocation of the privilege, or further criminal charges, including immediate arrest. A defendant released on personal recognizance may be required to abide by certain rules. For example, the defendant may be forbidden from traveling outside of the court's jurisdiction, or may be forbidden from contacting the victim or the victim's family.

A court may also impose an unsecured appearance bond on a criminal defendant. A bond amount is set, but the defendant is not required to post any money. If the defendant fails to appear at subsequent proceedings, or violates any terms of the bond, he or she will be required to pay the full amount of the bond.

According to the Department of Justice's Bureau of Justice statistics, for all defendants charged with state felonies in May 2000 in the 75 most populous counties in the country:

• 62 percent were released prior to the disposition of their case

• 38 percent were detained, including 7 percent who were denied bail

• Of those released, 26 percent were released on their own recognizance

• 37 percent were released on a commercial surety bond

• About a third of those released failed to appear for a scheduled appearance, were rearrested for a new offense, or committed a violation that resulted in revocation of the pretrial release

## The Bail Reform Act of 1984

The Bail Reform Act of 1984, found in Title 18 of the United States Code, replaced the Bail Reform Act of 1964. The 1964 act did not allow judges in noncapital cases to consider the danger a defendant posed to the community. In some cases, this resulted in defendants who committed further violent crimes after being released on personal recognizance. The 1984 law closed this loophole, and allowed for detention where necessary for the safety of the community. In addition to the federal statutes governing bail in federal criminal cases, every state has its own bail laws.

Pursuant to federal statute, a detention hearing is required in cases involving violence, including any offense where the maximum sentence is life imprisonment or death, or for certain drug offenses where a maximum sentence of ten years or more is prescribed. Moreover, a hearing is required for certain defendants who have multiple convictions. A hearing will also be held if it appears to involve a serious risk that the defendant will flee, or where it appears that the defendant will obstruct or attempt to obstruct justice or tamper with prospective witnesses or jurors. The detention hearing must be held promptly, preferably at the time of the defendant's first appearance in court. If bail is denied, the court must issue a written order with findings of fact and a statement of the reasons for the detention.

### Detention Hearing Procedures

To determine what is necessary to ensure a defendant's appearance at trial, a judge or magistrate examines the nature and circumstances of the charges, with particular attention to whether the offense involves violence or narcotic drugs. The court may inquire into the nature and value of any property that might be offered as collateral. The court also examines the weight of the evidence against the defendant, whether the person was on parole or probation at the time of the present arrest, the nature and seriousness of danger to others in the community, and evidence of the defendant's character. When examining the history and character of a person, the court may look at:

• Physical and mental condition

• Financial resources

• Family ties

• History relating to drug and alcohol abuse

• Criminal history

• Record concerning appearance at court proceedings

• Length of residence in the community

Where a defendant poses a threat to the safety of the community, he or she may be held without bail. In other situations, federal law typically requires that a defendant in a federal criminal case be released on personal recognizance or upon execution of an unsecured appearance bond. Released defendants must not commit any crimes during the period of release. However, if a court determines that personal recognizance or an unsecured appearance bond will not reasonably assure the defendant's appearance, or determines that the safety of a person or the community is endangered, a defendant may be released upon conditions. Federal law delineates a number of conditions that may be imposed. Defendants may be required to:

- Limit travel

- Maintain or seek employment

- Undergo drug and alcohol testing

- Undergo medical, psychiatric, or psychological treatment

- Maintain or commence an educational program

- Comply with a curfew

- Refrain from excessive use of alcohol or any use of narcotic drugs

- Remain in the custody of a designated person

- Comply with periodic check-ins with authorities

- Refrain from possession of a firearm

- Refrain from contact with crime victim or others designated by the court

- Execute a bond agreement with the court or a solvent surety in an amount as is reasonably necessary to ensure the defendant's appearance

- Agree to other reasonable conditions the court may impose to ensure a defendant's appearance

Both the defendant and the government may appeal an adverse bail decision. The scope of review is limited, however. The only question for an appellate court is whether the trial court abused its discretion.

### Material Witnesses, Bonds on Appeal or Pending Sentencing

In rare instances, persons not charged with a crime may be detained, or ordered to post bond. A material witness is subject to arrest and federal release and detention laws it is shown that a subpoena is not sufficient to secure the person's presence in court.

A defendant who was released prior to trial on his or her own recognizance may, if convicted, be required to post a bond during the appeal process or pending sentencing. A court may also determine detention is required. Release is generally appropriate in cases where no sentence of imprisonment is likely, if acquittal or a motion for a new trial is likely, or where the court finds by clear and convincing evidence that a person is not likely to flee or pose a danger.

### Posting Bail

Once a court has set the amount of bail, that amount, or a specified percentage, is paid to the court. Payment may be made in cash or in an approved cash substitute, such as a money order or cashier's check. A defendant may post his or her own bail, or may find another person to do so. Once bail has been posted, whether by the defendant or someone else, the court will issue a document or a court order that shows the defendant may be released.

If another person posts bond on the behalf of a defendant, the bail bond becomes a three-party contract between the defendant, the court, and the **surety**. The surety is the party who, at the request of a defendant, becomes responsible for securing the defendant's appearance in court. People who may act as a surety for a criminal bond include licensed bond agents and friends and relatives of the defendant. As part of the contract, the defendant promises to appear at future proceedings. The surety promises to forfeit to the court the amount of the bond if the defendant fails to appear as required.

The penalty for failure to appear as required after release is a fine, imprisonment, or both. Federal law provides that any term of imprisonment for failure to appear must run consecutively to any other criminal sentence. However, if uncontrollable circumstances caused the failure to appear, and if the person immediately appeared once it was possible to do so, the person will have a valid defense to the failure to appear charge.

Once a case is over and all obligations have been fulfilled, the bond money is typically returned. Sometimes administrative costs are deducted.

## Bail Bond Agents

Many defendants lack the financial means to post their own bail. To secure release, they may contract a commercial bond agent to act as surety for the bond. The agent posts bail after collecting a nonrefundable fee (typically 10 to 20 percent) from the defendant or family or friends. Assuming the defendant does not have money to give the agent as security, an agent will obtain other collateral, such as jewelry, securities, or electronics. In return, the bail bond agent agrees to pay the remaining amount to the court if the defendant fails to appear.

There are approximately 14,000 bond agents in the U.S. Most states require a bond agent to be licensed. However, the license typically is not specifically for bonding purpose, but for property and casualty insurance. To obtain the license, the applicant must meet certain educational requirements. This allows a potential bail bond agent to be appointed by an insurance company to write bail bonds. The defendant pays the agent for writing the bond. In turn, the agent pays the insurance company a premium. The bail agent is responsible for bond payment in the event a defendant fails to appear and cannot be located.

To ensure a defendant's appearance in court, a bail bond agent may require a defendant to check in by telephone or in person, or may require the defendant to be monitored in some other way. In extreme cases, a bail bondsperson may place a guard on the defendant. A bail bond agent is not obligated to post bail if the agent concludes a defendant is not likely to fulfill the obligations of the bond.

Illinois, Kentucky, Oregon and Wisconsin have outlawed the practice of posting bond for profit. In those jurisdictions, a defendant may be allowed to satisfy the requirements of the bond by posting 10 percent of the bail amount with the court. Some other jurisdictions, such as Maine and Nebraska, allow commercial bail on a limited basis.

## Additional Resources

*"How Courts Work,"* Division for Public Education, American Bar Association. Available at http://www.abanet.org/publiced/courts/bail.html, The American Bar Association, 2006.

## Organizations

***Professional Bail Agents of the United States***
1301 Pennsylvania Ave., N.W., Suite 925
Washington, DC 20004 USA
Phone: (202) 783-4120
URL: http://www.pbus.com/
Primary Contact: Linda Braswell, President

# CRIMINAL LAW

## CRIMES

*Sections within this essay:*

## Background

Criminal offenses are classified according to their seriousness. For crimes against property, the gravity of a crime is generally commensurate with the value of the property taken or damaged: the greater the property value, the more serious the crime. For crimes against persons, the same proportionality principle applies to bodily injury inflicted upon individuals: the greater the injury, the more serious the crime. However, a host of other factors can influence the seriousness of a criminal offense. These factors include whether the **defendant** had a prior criminal record; whether the defendant committed the crime with cruelty, **malice**, intent, or in reckless disregard of another person's safety; and whether the victim was a member of a protected class (i.e., minors, minorities, senior citizens, the handicapped, etc.). Thus, a less serious crime can be made more serious by the presence of these additional factors, and a more serious crime can be made less serious by their absence.

Three categories of criminal offenses were known at **common law**, **treason**, **felony**, and **misdemeanor**, with treason being the most serious type of crime and misdemeanor being the least serious. The common law distinction between treason and felony was particularly important in England because a traitor's lands were forfeited to the Crown. Under a doctrine known as "corruption of the blood," the traitor also lost the right to **inherit** property from relatives, while the relatives lost the right to inherit from the traitor. U. S. law has never endorsed corruption of the blood as a criminal **penalty**, and so treason was dropped as a separate classification of crime in the colonies.

Today every U. S. **jurisdiction** retains the distinction between felony level criminal offenses and misdemeanor level offenses. However, most jurisdictions have added a third-tier of criminal offense, typically called an **infraction** or a petty offense. Although the definitions of all three classes differ from one jurisdiction to the next, they do share some common characteristics.

## Felonies, Misdemeanors, and Infractions

The power to define a crime and classify it as a felony, misdemeanor, or infraction rests solely with the legislature at the federal level (see *U. S. v. Hudson*, 7 Cranch 32, 11 U.S. 32, 3 L.Ed. 259 [U. S. 1812]). Federal courts do not have the power to punish any act that is not forbidden by federal **statute**. Most crimes made punishable by federal law are set forth in Title 18 U.S.C. sections 1 et seq.

In the eighteenth century U. S. courts possessed the power to define crimes and establish classifications for criminal offenses. These judicially-created offenses were known as common law crimes. By the early nineteenth century, federal common law crimes were under increasing attack as violating the mandate of the separation of powers established by the U. S. Constitution. Article I of the Constitution gives Congress the power to make law, while Article III gives the judiciary the power to interpret and apply it. Thus, the constitutionally limited role of federal courts precludes them from defining crimes or creating classifications for criminal offenses.

Most states have also abolished common law crimes. In these states the legislature is given the primary and often sole responsibility for defining illegal behavior (the **executive branch** in a few states plays a limited lawmaking function via **executive orders** and administrative agency rules and regulations). In the minority of states that still recognize common law crimes, judges generally are not permitted to create new common law crimes from the bench. Instead, all 50 states and the District of Columbia rely on their penal code to shape the nature and scope of their jurisdiction's criminal laws, and when a penal code designates an offense as a felony, misdemeanor, or infraction, that designation is normally deemed conclusive by the courts.

### Felonies

Felonies are deemed the most serious class of offense throughout the United States. Many jurisdictions separate felonies into their own distinct classes so that a repeat offender convicted of committing a felony in a heinous fashion receives a more severe punishment than a first-time offender convicted of committing a felony in a comparatively less hateful, cruel, or injurious fashion. Depending on the circumstances surrounding the crime, felonies are generally punishable by a fine, **imprisonment** for more than a year, or both. At common law felonies were crimes that typically involved moral turpitude, or offenses that violated the moral standards of the community. Today many crimes classified as felonies are still considered offensive to the moral standards in most American communities. They include **terrorism**, treason, **arson**, murder, rape, robbery, **burglary**, and **kidnapping**, among others.

In many state penal codes a felony is defined not only by the length of **incarceration** but also by the place of incarceration. For example, crimes that are punishable by incarceration in a state prison are deemed felonies in a number of states, while crimes that are punishable only by incarceration in a local

jail are deemed misdemeanors. For crimes that may be punishable by incarceration in either a local jail or a state prison, the crime will normally be classified according to where the defendant actually serves the sentence.

### Misdemeanors

A misdemeanor, a criminal offense that is less serious than a felony and more serious than an infraction, is generally punishable by a fine or incarceration in a local jail, or both. Many jurisdictions separate misdemeanors into three classes, high or gross misdemeanors, ordinary misdemeanors, and petty misdemeanors. Petty misdemeanors usually contemplate a jail sentence of less than six months and a fine of $500 or less. The punishment prescribed for gross misdemeanors is greater than that prescribed for ordinary misdemeanors and less than that prescribed for felonies, and some states even define a gross misdemeanor as "any crime that is not a felony or a misdemeanor" (see MN ST § 609.02). Legislatures sometimes use such broad definitions to provide prosecutors and judges with flexibility in charging and sentencing for criminal conduct that calls for a punishment combining a fine normally assessed for a misdemeanor and an incarceration period normally given for a felony.

### Infractions

An infraction, sometimes called a petty offense, is the violation of an administrative regulation, an **ordinance**, a municipal code, and, in some jurisdictions, a state or local traffic rule. In many states an infraction is not considered a criminal offense and thus not punishable by incarceration. Instead, such jurisdictions treat infractions as civil offenses. Even in jurisdictions that treat infractions as criminal offenses, incarceration is not usually contemplated as punishment, and when it is, confinement is limited to serving time in a local jail. Like misdemeanors, infractions are often defined in very broad language. For example, one state provides that any offense that is defined "without either designation as a felony or a misdemeanor or specification of the class or penalty is a petty offense" (see AZ ST § 13-602).

### Substantive and Procedural Implications of a Crime's Classification

The category under which a crime is classified can make a difference in both substantive and procedural criminal law. Substantive criminal law defines the elements of many crimes in reference to whether they were committed in furtherance of a felony. Burglary, for example, requires proof that the defendant broke into another person's dwelling with the intent to commit a felony. If a defendant convinces a jury that he only had the intent to steal a misdemeanor's worth of property after breaking into the victim's home, the jury cannot return a **conviction** for burglary.

The substantive consequences for being convicted of a felony are also more far reaching than the consequences for other types of crimes. One convicted of a felony is disqualified from holding public office in many jurisdictions. Felons may also lose their right to vote or serve on a jury. In several states attorneys convicted of a felony lose their right to practice law. Misdemeanants with no felony record rarely face such serious consequences.

**Criminal procedure** sets forth different rules that govern courts, defendants, and law enforcement agents depending on the level of offense charged. The Fourth Amendment to the U. S Constitution allows police officers to make warrantless arrests of suspected felons in public areas so long as the arresting officer possesses **probable cause** that the suspect committed the crime. Officers may make warrantless arrests of suspected misdemeanants only if the crime is committed in the officer's presence. Police officers do not have the authority to shoot an alleged misdemeanant while attempting to make an arrest, unless the shots are fired in self–defense. Officers generally have more authority to use deadly force when effectuating the arrest of a **felon**.

Most criminal courts have limited jurisdiction over the kinds of cases they can hear. A court with jurisdiction over only misdemeanors has no power to try a defendant charged with a felony. Defendants may be charged by information (i.e., a formal written instrument setting forth the criminal accusations against a defendant) when they are **accused** of a misdemeanor, whereas many jurisdictions require that defendants be charged by a **grand jury** when they are accused of a felony.

Defendants charged with capital felony offenses (i.e., offenses for which the death penalty might be imposed as a sentence) are entitled to have their cases heard by a jury of twelve persons who must unanimously agree as to the issue of guilt before returning a conviction. Defendants charged with noncapital felonies and misdemeanors may have their cases heard by as few as six jurors who, depending on the jurisdiction and the size of the jury actually impaneled, may return a conviction on a less than unanimous vote. The right to trial by jury is generally not afforded to defendants charged only with infrac-

tions or petty offenses. Defendants charged with felonies or misdemeanors that actually result in confinement to a jail or prison are entitled to the advice and representation of a court appointed **counsel** (see USCA.Const.Amend.6). Defendants charged with infractions or misdemeanors that do not result in incarceration are not entitled to court appointed counsel.

Accused felons must generally be present during their trials, while accused misdemeanants may agree to waive their right to be present. The **testimony** of defendants and witnesses may be impeached on the ground of a former felony conviction. But a misdemeanor is not considered sufficiently serious to be grounds for **impeachment** in most jurisdictions. Because of all the additional procedural safeguards afforded to defendants charged with more serious criminal offenses, defendants must usually consent to any prosecution effort to downgrade a criminal offense to a lower level at which fewer safeguards are offered.

## State Laws Governing the Classification of Crimes

ALABAMA: The state criminal code defines the term, crime, as either a felony or a misdemeanor, providing that a misdemeanor is an offense for which the term of imprisonment does not exceed one year, while a felony is an offense for which the term of imprisonment is in excess of one year (see AL ST § 13A-1-2).

ARKANSAS: The state criminal procedure code permits police officers to make warrantless arrests for any crime committed in their presence, for situations where the officer possesses probable cause to believe the suspect committed a felony, and for misdemeanors that the officer has probable cause to believe that the suspect committed battery upon another person, so long as there is **evidence** of bodily harm and the officer reasonably believes that there is danger of further violence unless the suspect is arrested without delay (see AR ST § 16-81-106).

ALASKA: Any person prosecuted for an infraction of the state's Motor Vehicle Code is not entitled to a court-appointed person or the right to a jury trial (see AK ST § 28.40.050).

ARIZONA: State law governing the city of Tucson defines "civil parking infraction" as "any violation of the city code or city ordinances that regulate the time, place, or method of parking." (see AZ ST TUC-SON CITY CT Rule 2).

CALIFORNIA: State law makes it an infraction punishable by a fine of up to $200.00 for any person to violate the Election Code provisions governing voter registration cards (see CA ELEC § 18107).

FLORIDA: Where a defendant commits only a misdemeanor in the presence of a police officer prior to a collision of the squad car with the defendant's bicycle, the officer has no authority to use deadly force except in **self-defense** or if the defendant committed a new felony (see F.S.A. § 776.05[1, 3]).

GEORGIA: While the value of stolen property is not an element of the offense of theft by receiving stolen property, it is relevant for the purpose of distinguishing between a misdemeanor and a felony for sentencing (see O.C.G.A. § 16-8-12[a]).

HAWAII: A court may sentence a person who has been convicted of certain felonies to life imprisonment without **parole** if the court finds that the felony was committed in an especially "heinous," "atrocious," or "cruel" manner that manifests "exceptional depravity" (see HI ST § 706-6570.

ILLINOIS: A motorist's minor traffic offenses, including speeding and improper lane usage, are petty offenses, and thus are not subject to the expungement procedures set forth in the state statute allowing expungement of convictions for municipal ordinance violations, misdemeanors, and felonies (see S.H.A. 20 ILCS 2630/5[a]).

INDIANA: A sentencing court may enhance a sentence for felony murder by declaring the crime "heinous" and articulating specific facts that suggest heinousness (see A.I.C. 35-42-1-1[2]).

MASSACHUSETTS: For crimes against property, the value of the property destroyed is what distinguishes a felony that is punishable by a prison sentence of up to ten years from a misdemeanor that is punishable by a prison sentence of not more than two and one-half months (see MA ST 266 § 127).

MICHIGAN: A misdemeanor that results in two years' imprisonment may be deemed a felony for purposes of the **habitual** offender provisions in the state Code of Criminal Procedure (see M.C.L.A. §§ 750.7, 750.8, 750.9, 760.1 et seq).

MINNESOTA: The Rule of Criminal Procedure allowing the state to appeal a felony sentence does not give the state the right to appeal from a trial court's order involving a gross-misdemeanor sentence (see MN ST RCRP Rule 28.04; *State v. Loyd,* 627 N.W.2d 653 [Minn.App. 2001]).

MISSOURI: The state Court of Appeals ruled that private citizens may arrest a suspected felon upon a showing of reasonable grounds to do so or to prevent an affray or breach of the peace, while they may only arrest a suspected misdemeanant if authorized by statute (see *State v. Cross,* 34 S.W.3d 175 [Mo.App. 2000]).

NEW JERSEY: The state insurance statute denies coverage for **personal injury** protection (PIP) benefits if the insured suffers personal injuries while committing a high misdemeanor or felony (see NJ ST 39:6A-7).

NEW YORK: Any violation of the Vehicle and Traffic Code must be charged by way of a formal information, unlike mere traffic infractions that may be charged via a simplified traffic information (see *People v. Smith,* 163 Misc.2d 353, 621 N.Y.S.2d 449 (N.Y.Just.Ct. 1994); NY CRIM PRO § 100.10).

NORTH DAKOTA: Because punishment is irrelevant to a jury's consideration of guilt or innocence, a jury instruction should not inform the jurors about the penalty to be imposed, and thus jury instructions should not disclose whether the defendant stands to be convicted of a felony or misdemeanor (see *State v. Mounts,* 484 N.W.2d 843 [N.D. 1992]).

TEXAS: The state Court of Criminal Appeals ruled that an act authorizing a jury of 6 in a trial for misdemeanors is contrary to the constitutional requirement that the jury in a district court shall be composed of 12 men. *Rochelle v. State,* 89 Tex.Crim. 592, 232 S.W. 838 (Tex.Crim.App. 1921); TX CONST Art. 5, § 13.

UTAH: The state supreme court held that law enforcement officers may not use lethal force to stop one who has committed a misdemeanor. *Day v. State ex rel. Utah Dept. of Public Safety,* 980 P.2d 1171 (Utah 1999).

VIRGINIA: The State Court of Appeals ruled that defendants have a duty as well as the right to be present at their trials. Even when there is a statute authorizing trial of misdemeanor cases in the absence of the accused, the defendant has no right to be absent at trial and to appear only by counsel (see *Durant v. Commissioner,* 35 Va.App. 459, 546 S.E.2d 216 [Va.App. 2001]).

## Additional Resources

*American Jurisprudence.* Lawyers Co-operative Publishing Company, 2001.

*Black's Law Dictionary* 6th ed. West Group, 2000.

*Criminal Procedure.* Wayne R. LaFave, Jerold H. Israel, and Nancy J. King, West Group, 2001.

*Oxford Companion to the Supreme Court.* Kermit Hall, ed., Oxford University Press, 1992.

*West's Encyclopedia of American Law.* West Group, 1998.

## Organizations

### American Civil Liberties Union (ACLU)

1400 20th St., NW, Suite 119
Washington, DC 20036 USA
Phone: (202) 457-0800
E-Mail: info@aclu.org
URL: http://www.aclu.org/
Primary Contact: Anthony D. Romero, Executive Director

### Center for Human Rights and Constitutional Law

256 S. Occidental Blvd.
Los Angeles, CA 90057 USA
Phone: (213) 388-8693
Fax: (213) 386-9484
E-Mail: mail@centerforhumanrights.org
URL: http://www.centerforhumanrights.org
Primary Contact: Peter A. Schey, Executive Director

### National District Attorneys Association (NDAA)

99 Canal Center Plaza
Alexandria, VA 22314 USA
Phone: (703) 549-9222
Fax: (703) 836-3195
URL: http://www.ndaa.org
Primary Contact: Thomas J. Charron, Director

### Association of Federal Defense Attorneys

8530 Wilshire Blvd, Suite 404
Beverly Hills, CA 90211 USA
Phone: (714) 836-6031
Fax: (310) 397-1001
E-Mail: AFDA2@AOL.com
URL: http://www.afda.org
Primary Contact: Gregory Nicolaysen, Director

# CRIMINAL LAW

## CRIMINAL PROCEDURE

*Sections within this essay:*

- Background
- The Fourth Amendment and Criminal Procedures Governing Police Investigations, Arrests, Searches, and Seizures
    - The Text of the Fourth Amendment
    - Case Law Interpreting the Fourth Amendment
- The Fifth Amendment and Criminal Procedures Governing Post-Arrest and Pre-Arraignment Proceedings
    - The Text of the Fifth Amendment
    - Case Law Interpreting the Fifth Amendment
- The Sixth Amendment and Criminal Procedures Governing Post-Arraignment and Pre-Sentencing Proceedings
    - The Text of the Sixth Amendment
    - Case Law Interpreting the Sixth Amendment
- The Eighth Amendment's Limitations on Sentencing
    - The Text of the Eighth Amendment
    - Case Law Interpreting the Eighth Amendment
- Appeal and other Post-Conviction Proceedings
- Additional Resources

## Background

**Criminal procedure** is the body of state and federal constitutional provisions, statutes, court rules, and other laws governing the administration of justice in criminal cases. The term encompasses procedures that the government must follow during the entire course of a criminal case, ranging from the initial investigation of an individual suspected of criminal activity, through arrest, arraignment, **plea** negotiations, pre-trial hearings, trial, post-trial motions, pre-sentence interviews, sentencing, appeals, and **probation** and **parole** proceedings. The rules of criminal procedure may also apply after a **defendant** has been unconditionally released following an **acquittal**. For example, the **Double Jeopardy** Clause of the Fifth Amendment to the U. S. Constitution may be invoked by individuals who are facing prosecution on charges for which they have already been found not guilty.

Criminal procedures are designed to safeguard both the innocent and the guilty from indiscriminate application of substantive criminal laws (i.e., laws prohibiting rape, murder, **arson**, and theft, etc.) and from arbitrary or abusive treatment at the hands of law enforcement, the courts, or other members of the justice system. At the federal level these safeguards are primarily set forth in three places: the Federal Rules of Criminal Procedure, Title 18 of the United States Code sections 3001 et seq., and Amendments IV, V, VI, and VIII to the U. S. Constitution. The rules and statutes reference each other, and both are designed to enforce and delineate in greater detail the rights established by the federal Constitution.

The Fourth Amendment prohibits the government from conducting unreasonable searches and seizures while investigating criminal activity and building a case against a particular suspect. The Fifth

Amendment prohibits the government from compelling individuals to **incriminate** themselves, from denying individuals **due process of law**, from subjecting individuals to multiple punishments or prosecutions for a single offense, and from being prosecuted in federal court without first being indicted by a **grand jury**. The Sixth Amendment guarantees defendants the right to a speedy and public trial by an **impartial** jury, the right to be informed of all charges against them, the right to confront adverse witnesses, the right to **subpoena** favorable witnesses, and the right to an attorney. The Eighth Amendment prohibits the government from requiring excessive **bail** to be posted for pre-trial release, from imposing excessive fines, and from inflicting cruel and unusual punishments.

The freedoms safeguarded by the Fourth, Fifth, Sixth, and Eighth Amendments have two lives, one static and the other organic. Their static life exists in the original language of the amendments as they were ratified by the states in 1791, while their organic life exists in the growing body of state and federal **case law** interpreting their text, applying it, and defining its scope as different factual situations come before the courts. All of the rights protected by these four amendments, except the right to **indictment** by a grand jury, have been made applicable to state criminal proceedings via the doctrine of incorporation. Under this doctrine U. S. Supreme Court has said that no state may deny any citizen a fundamental liberty without violating the Fourteenth Amendment's **Equal Protection** and Due Process Clauses. The fundamental liberties guaranteed to criminal defendants by the Fourth, Fifth, Sixth, and Eighth Amendments are best understood in the context of the criminal proceeding during which they are normally triggered.

## The Fourth Amendment and Criminal Procedures Governing Investigation, Arrest, and Search and Seizure

### The Text of the Fourth Amendment

The right of the people to be secure in their persons, houses, papers, and effects, against unreasonable searches and seizures, shall not be violated, and no Warrants shall issue, but upon **probable cause**, supported by Oath or affirmation, and particularly describing the place to be searched, and the persons or things to be seized.

### Case law interpreting the Fourth Amendment

Law enforcement officers are entrusted with the power to conduct investigations, make arrests, perform searches and seizures of persons and their belongings, and occasionally use lethal force in the line of duty. But this power must be exercised within the **boundaries** of the law, and when police officers exceed those boundaries they jeopardize the admissibility of any **evidence** collected for prosecution. By and large, the Fourth Amendment and the case law interpreting it establish these boundaries.

The safeguards enumerated by the Fourth Amendment only apply against governmental action, namely action taken by a governmental official or at the direction of a governmental official. Thus, actions taken by state or federal law enforcement officials or private persons working with law enforcement officials will be subject to the strictures of the Fourth Amendment. Bugging, **wiretapping**, and other related surveillance activity performed by purely private citizens, such as private investigators, will not receive Fourth Amendment protection.

Nor will individuals receive Fourth Amendment protection unless they can demonstrate that they have a reasonable expectation of privacy in the place to be searched or the thing to be seized. The U. S. Supreme Court explained that what "a person knowingly exposes to the public, even in his own home or office, is not a subject of Fourth Amendment protection.... But what he seeks to preserve as private, even in an area accessible to the public, may be constitutionally protected" (see *Katz v. United States*, 389 U.S. 347, 88 S. Ct. 507, 19 L. Ed. 576 [1976]). In general the Court has said that individuals enjoy a reasonable expectation of privacy in their own bodies, **personal property**, homes, and business offices. Individuals also enjoy a qualified expectation of privacy in their automobiles.

Once it has been established that an individual possesses a reasonable expectation of privacy in a place to be searched or a thing to be seized, the Fourth Amendment's protections take hold, and the question then becomes what are the nature of those protections. Searches and seizures performed without a **warrant** (a court order approving a search, a seizure, or an arrest) based on probable cause are presumptively invalid. However, in certain situations the Supreme Court has ruled that warrantless searches may be reasonable under the circumstances and thus pass constitutional muster.

Police officers need no justification to stop someone on a public street and ask questions, and individuals are completely entitled to refuse to answer any such questions and go about their business. However, the Fourth Amendment prohibits police officers from detaining pedestrians and conducting any kind of search of their clothing without first possessing a reasonable and articulable suspicion that the pedestrians are engaged in criminal activity (see *Terry v. Ohio*, 392 U.S. 1, 88 S. Ct. 1868, 21 L. Ed. 889 [1968]). Police may not even request that a pedestrian produce identification without first meeting this standard. Similarly, police may not stop motorists without first having a reasonable and articulable suspicion that the driver has violated a traffic law. If a police officer has satisfied this standard in stopping a motorist, the officer may conduct a search of the vehicle's interior, including the glove compartment, but not the trunk unless the officer has probable cause to believe that it contains **contraband** or the instrumentalities of criminal activity.

The Fourth Amendment also expresses a preference for arrests to be based on a warrant. But warrantless arrests can be made when the circumstances make it reasonable to do so. For example, no warrant is required for a **felony** arrest in a public place, even if the arresting officer had ample time to procure a warrant, so long as the officer possessed probable cause that the suspect committed the crime. Felony arrests in places not open to the public generally do require a warrant, unless the officer is in "hot pursuit" of a fleeing **felon** (see *Warden v. Hayden*, 387 U.S. 294, 87 S.Ct. 1642, 18 L.Ed.2d 782 [1967]). The Fourth Amendment also allows warrantless arrests for misdemeanors committed in an officer's presence.

The exceptions to the Fourth Amendment's warrant requirement are based on the court's reluctance to unduly impede the job of law enforcement officials. Courts attempt to strike a balance between the practical realities of daily police work and the privacy and freedom interests of the public. Requiring police officers to take the time to obtain an arrest or **search warrant** could result in the destruction of evidence, the disappearance of suspects, or both.

When an officer does seek a search or **arrest warrant**, the officer must present evidence to a neutral judge or **magistrate** sufficient to establish probable cause that a crime has been committed. The Supreme Court has said that probable cause exists when the facts within an officer's knowledge provide a reasonably trustworthy basis for a man of reasonable caution to believe that an offense has been committed or is about to be committed. Courts will deny requests when the warrant fails to describe in particularized detail the person to be arrested or the place to be searched. The evidence upon which a warrant is based need not be ultimately **admissible** at trial, but it cannot be based on knowingly or intentionally false statements or statements made in reckless disregard of the truth. Courts will usually invalidate searches, seizures, and arrests made pursuant to a defective warrant. Inaccuracies found in a warrant due to ordinary **negligence** will not typically jeopardize a warrant's validity.

## The Fifth Amendment and Criminal Procedures Governing Post-Arrest and Pre-Arraignment Proceedings

### The Text of the Fifth Amendment

No person shall be held to answer for a capital, or otherwise infamous crime, unless on a presentment or indictment of a Grand Jury, except in cases arising in the land or naval forces, or in the **Militia**, when in actual service in time of War or public danger; nor shall any person be subject for the same offence to be twice put in **jeopardy** of **life or limb**; nor shall be compelled in any criminal case to be a witness against himself, nor be deprived of life, liberty, or property, without due process of law; nor shall private property be taken for public use, without just compensation.

### Case Law Interpreting the Fifth Amendment

Once a suspect has been arrested or taken into **custody**, the rights guaranteed by the Fifth Amendment are triggered. In *Miranda v. Arizona*, 384 U.S. 436, 86 S. Ct. 1602, 16 L. Ed.2d 694 (1966), the Supreme Court held that under the Fifth Amendment's **Self-Incrimination** Clause, statements made to the police during custodial interrogation will later be deemed **inadmissible** at trial unless the suspect is first told that he or she has: (1) the right to remain silent; (2) the right to consult an attorney before being questioned by the police; (3) the right to have an attorney present during police questioning; (4) the right to a court appointed attorney if the defendant cannot afford to hire a private attorney; and (5) the right to be informed that any statements they do make can and will be used against them at trial.

If a suspect makes a request to consult with an attorney, the interrogation must immediately cease or any subsequent statements made without the attorney present will be ruled inadmissible. However, a suspect's request for an attorney will not prevent law enforcement from compelling the suspect to participate in a **lineup** of persons for the victim to review or from having the suspect's picture taken and shown to the victim in a photo array. Nor may a suspect raise the Self-Incrimination Clause as an objection to giving a writing sample, providing a voice exemplar, or taking a blood test. Applying a Fourth Amendment analysis, the Supreme Court has said that the Self-Incrimination Clause does not apply to these situations because individuals have no privacy interest in their physical characteristics.

The purpose of the right against self-incrimination is to deter the government from compelling a **confession** through force, **coercion**, or deception. Confessions produced by these methods are not only considered uncivilized by modern standards, but they are also considered unreliable, since they are often involuntary or unwitting or the result of the accused's desire to avoid further browbeating, instead of being the product of candor or a desire to confess.

The Fifth Amendment guarantees three other rights that relate to criminal procedure. First, every defendant has the right to be indicted by a grand jury before standing trial in federal court. As noted above, the Grand Jury Clause has not been made applicable to the states, and many states allow prosecutions based on information or complaint, which are written instruments prepared by the **prosecutor**. In federal criminal proceedings and in states that use the grand jury system, grand juries are normally comprised of between 16 and 23 persons from the district in which the crime occurred, and they can return an indictment against the defendant by majority vote.

Second, the Fifth Amendment prohibits the government from subjecting individuals to multiple prosecutions or multiple punishments for a single offense. This prohibition is called the right against double jeopardy. Defendants may bring motions pursuant to the Double Jeopardy Clause either before a trial to prevent a subsequent prosecution or punishment or after trial to overturn a subsequent prosecution or punishment.

Third, the Fifth Amendment guarantees every defendant the right to due process. The Due Process Clause requires that all criminal proceedings be conducted in a fair manner by an impartial judge who

will allow **accused** individuals to fully present their defense, and proceedings that produce arbitrary or capricious results will be overturned as unconstitutional. The right to due process applies to every phase of criminal proceedings from pre-trial questioning to post-trial hearings and appeals, and its application to some of these proceedings will be discussed below.

## The Sixth Amendment and Criminal Procedures Governing Post-Arraignment and Pre-Sentencing Proceedings

### The Text of the Sixth Amendment

In all criminal prosecutions, the accused shall enjoy the right to a speedy and public trial, by an impartial jury of the State and district wherein the crime shall have been committed, which district shall have been previously ascertained by law, and to be informed of the nature and cause of the **accusation**; to be confronted with the witnesses against him; to have compulsory process for obtaining witnesses in his favor, and to have the Assistance of **Counsel** for his defense.

### Case Law Interpreting the Sixth Amendment

Once a suspect has been arrested, the rights created by the Sixth Amendment take hold. The Sixth Amendment right to a speedy trial arises after a defendant has been arrested, indicted, or otherwise formally accused. Title 18 USCA sections 3161 et seq explain the nature of this right. Prior to the point of formal accusation, the government is under no constitutional or **statutory** obligation to discover or investigate criminal activity or accuse or **prosecute** suspected criminals within a particular amount of time. Nor is the Speedy Trial Clause implicated after the government has dropped criminal charges, even if the government refiles those charges at a much later date.

The Supreme Court has declined to draw a bright line separating permissible pre-trial delays from delays that are impermissibly excessive. Instead, the Court has developed a balancing test that weighs the reasons for delay against the prejudice suffered by the defendant in having to endure the delay. A delay of at least one year in bringing a defendant to trial following arrest will create a presumption that the Speedy Trial Clause has been violated. However, defendants whose own actions lengthen the pretrial phase or who fail to assert this right early in a criminal proceeding hurt their chances of prevailing on a speedy trial claim.

The point at which defendants are formally charged also triggers the Sixth Amendment right to be informed of the nature and cause of every accusation against them. Courts have interpreted this provision to have two elements. First, defendants must receive notice of any criminal accusations that the government has formally lodged against them through an indictment, information, or complaint. Second, defendants may not be tried, convicted, or sentenced for a crime that materially varies from the crime set forth in the formal charge. If either element is not satisfied and the defendant is convicted, the court will set aside the verdict and sentence.

Once a defendant has been formally charged by the prosecution in writing, the defendant will be arraigned before a court. At the arraignment the court generally reads the written charges to the defendant and attempts to determine if the defendant understands the charges or needs further explanation. Defendants are also provided with the opportunity to enter a plea of guilty or not guilty at the arraignment.

The arraignment is important for Sixth Amendment purposes because it gives rise to defendants' right to counsel, after which defendants are entitled to have counsel present at every "critical stage" of the proceedings. A critical stage is every stage of a criminal proceeding at which the advice of counsel is necessary to ensure defendants' right to a fair trial or every stage at which the absence of counsel might impair the preparation or presentation of a defense. Critical stages include important pre-trial hearings, such as a **hearing** upon a motion to suppress evidence, jury selection, trial, and sentencing. Non-critical stages include pre-trial procurement of defendants' **fingerprints**, blood, DNA, clothing, hair, and handwriting or voice samples. Denial of counsel to a defendant during a critical stage is considered tantamount to an unfair trial warranting the reversal of a **conviction**.

Defendants are not required to be represented by counsel but may instead choose to represent themselves throughout the course of a criminal prosecution, which is called appearing **pro se**. However, the **waiver** of the right to counsel must be done in a knowing and intelligent fashion by a defendant who is aware of the advantages to being represented by counsel. Before accepting a defendant's waiver of counsel, courts will normally explain many of these advantages to the defendant. For example, attorneys can advise their clients whether it is in their self-interest to make any statements to the police. Attor-

neys can also determine the propriety of bringing any pre-trial motions, including motions to dismiss the case, compel the production of exculpatory evidence, limit **testimony** of adverse witnesses, and suppress evidence seized in violation of the Constitution. Under case law interpreting the Fourth Amendment, not only is unconstitutionally obtained evidence rendered inadmissible at trial under the **exclusionary rule**, but any evidence derived from the constitutional violation is also subject to suppression via the "fruit of the poisonous tree" doctrine. Pro se defendants are not likely to understand these nuances of criminal procedure.

Attorneys can also influence the amount of bail that is set by a court following arrest. The Eighth Amendment prohibits courts from setting bail in an excessive amount. Criminal defense attorneys are accustomed to making arguments in favor of setting bail at a level proportionate to the severity of the crime so that gainfully employed defendants accused of less serious offenses can continue earning a living while awaiting trial. In certain instances when defendants have strong ties to a community, attorneys can convince courts to waive bail and release the defendants on their own recognizance, which means that defendants will not be incarcerated prior to trial but are obligated to appear for scheduled court appointments in a timely fashion or risk losing this privilege.

Once the trial begins, the Sixth Amendment guarantees that the defendant be tried in a court open to the public before an impartial jury. The right to a jury trial only applies to charges for which the defendant will be incarcerated upon conviction. If a defendant is tried by the court without a jury, the Sixth Amendment precludes **imprisonment** as a punishment. The right to a public trial is personal to the defendant and may not be asserted by either the media or the public in general. However, both the media and members of the public have a qualified First Amendment right to attend criminal proceedings.

The right to an impartial jury entitles the defendant to a jury pool that represents a fair cross section of the community. From the pool a panel of jurors is chosen to hear the case through a process called **voir dire**. During voir dire the presiding judge, the prosecution, and attorneys for the defense are allowed to ask members of the jury pool a variety of questions intended to reveal biases, prejudices, or other influences that might affect their impartiality.

Jurors may be excluded from service for a specific reason, called a challenge for cause, or for strategic purposes, called a peremptory strike. Attorneys for both sides may exercise an infinite number of challenges for cause, while all jurisdictions limit the number of peremptory strikes. For example, in New York state courts both the prosecution and defense receive three peremptory strikes plus one extra for each alternate juror (see NY CPLR ¤4109). The Equal Protection Clause of the Fourteenth Amendment also limits attorneys' use of peremptory strikes, making it unlawful to exclude jurors on account of their race (see *Batson v. Kentucky*, 476 U.S. 79, 90 L.Ed.2d 69, 106 S.Ct. 1712 [1986]). The jurors who are ultimately impaneled for trial need not represent a cross section of the community as long as they maintain their impartiality throughout the proceedings. The presence of even one biased juror impaneled to hear the case is not permitted under the Sixth Amendment.

The constitutional parameters governing the size of a jury in criminal cases are not established by the Sixth Amendment but by the Due Process Clauses of the Fifth and Fourteenth Amendments. The Supreme Court has ruled that in capital cases (i.e., cases in which the death penalty may be imposed) a defendant's right to a fair trial requires that the jury be comprised of twelve members who must unanimously agree on the issue of guilt before the defendant may be convicted and sentenced to death. For non-capital cases, the Supreme Court has ruled that the Constitution permits a verdict to be rendered by a majority vote of as few as nine jurors when the panel consists of twelve. The Court has also said that the Constitution permits trial by as few as six jurors in non-capital cases but that if a six-person jury is impaneled to decide a criminal case, all six must agree on the defendant's guilt before a conviction can be returned.

After the jury has been selected, the prosecution presents its case in chief. The Sixth Amendment guarantees defendants the right to confront witnesses who **testify** against them. In all but exceptional circumstances, the type of confrontation contemplated by the Sixth Amendment is face-to-face confrontation, allowing defendants to hear evidence against them, consult with their attorneys, and participate in **cross-examination** to test the **credibility** and reliability of the victim or other prosecution witnesses.

Once the prosecution finishes presenting its case in chief, the defendant must be allowed the opportunity to put on a defense. The Sixth Amendment gives defendants the right to subpoena witnesses and compel the production of evidence favorable to their case. The Sixth Amendment guarantees this right even if an indigent defendant cannot afford to pay the expenses that accompany the use of judicial resources to subpoena evidence. Defendants are under no obligation to testify themselves, as the Fifth Amendment right to remain silent applies during trial just as fully as it does during pre-trial questioning by the police. In fact, the defense need not call any witnesses or offer any evidence at all. The prosecutor has the burden of proving the defendant's guilt **beyond a reasonable doubt**, and the defendant may decide that the prosecution's case is sufficiently weak that the jury will vote to **acquit** without hearing from the defense.

If the court hears from the defense, each side is then allowed to present rebuttal testimony after which both sides will normally rest. The Sixth Amendment right to an impartial jury prohibits jury members from deliberating before all of the evidence has been submitted, the attorneys have made their closing arguments, and the judge has read the instructions. Once deliberations begin, jurors may ask the court for clarification of the instructions and for portions of the testimony transcribed for their review. If the jurors cannot reach a verdict after discussing the evidence amongst themselves, the judge will try to determine if they are hopelessly deadlocked. However, the judge cannot force a jury to reach a verdict, but the judge may encourage the jurors to make every reasonable effort to resolve their differences. If the jurors remain deadlocked for a reasonable period of time after meeting with the judge, the court will declare a **mistrial** and dismiss the panel from further service.

If the jurors return a verdict of not guilty, the court will enter a judgment of acquittal, and the defendant is free to leave the courthouse without limitation or condition. If the jurors return a verdict of guilty, the case will proceed to sentencing. For lesser offenses, such as simple or petty misdemeanors, sentencing may immediately follow the verdict. For all other offenses, sentencing is usually conducted by the court in a separate hearing held several days or weeks after the verdict. Both the prosecution and defense are permitted to make arguments as to the appropriate sentence, and courts are generally given wide latitude in crafting individualized punishments within the statutory guidelines. Sometimes this discretion is curtailed by guidelines that require mandatory minimum sentences. Punishments may include any combination of community service, **forfeiture** of property, fines, probation, or **incarceration**. In 38 states and in federal court, defendants may be sentenced to death for first-degree murder, felony murder, and other similarly serious crimes.

## The Eighth Amendment Limitations on Sentencing

### The Text of the Eighth Amendment

Excessive bail shall not be required, nor excessive fines imposed, nor **cruel and unusual punishment** inflicted.

### Case Law Interpreting the Eighth Amendment

A court's discretion in sentencing a defendant is also limited by the Eighth Amendment, which prohibits the imposition of excessive fines and the infliction of cruel and unusual punishment. The Excessive Fines Clause has proven to have little effect over the course of the last two centuries. Trial judges are afforded extremely wide discretion in assessing fines on criminal defendants, and they are rarely overturned on appeal. For a fine to be overturned there must be proof that it was arbitrary, capricious, or so grossly excessive as to amount to a deprivation of property without due process of law. As a practical matter, the cost of appealing a fine often exceeds the amount of the fine itself, thereby reducing the incentive to appeal.

On the other hand, the Cruel and Unusual Punishment Clause has been the subject of much **litigation**. This clause requires every punishment imposed by the government to be commensurate with the offense committed by the defendant. Punishments that are disproportionately harsh will be overturned on appeal. Examples of punishments that have been overturned on Eighth Amendment grounds include two Georgia statutes that prescribed the death penalty for rape and **kidnapping** (see *Coker v. Georgia*, 433 U. S. 584, 97 S. Ct. 2861, 53 L. Ed.2d 982 (1977); *Eberheart v. Georgia*, 433 U.S. 917, 97 L. Ed.2d 2994, 53 L. Ed. 2d 1104 [1977]). The Supreme Court has also ruled that criminal sentences that are inhumane, outrageous, barbarous, or shock the social consciousness also violate the Eighth Amendment.

In 1972 the U. S. Supreme Court placed a moratorium on **capital punishment** throughout the United States, declaring that the statutes authorizing the death penalty were too broad and allowed for arbi-

trary and discriminatory application by judges and juries (see *Furman v. Georgia*, 408 U.S. 238, 92 S.Ct. 2726, 33 L.Ed.2d 346 [1972]). But four years later the Supreme Court upheld three new state statutes that were enacted to cure those flaws (see *Gregg v. Georgia*, 428 U.S. 153, 96 S.Ct. 2909, 49 L.Ed.2d 859 [1976]). Thirty-five states and the federal government soon followed suit by revising their death penalty statutes to comply with the Eighth Amendment, and the nation's high court has since shown reluctance to closely scrutinize these statutes.

However, in 2001 the Georgia Supreme Court surprised many legal observers when it banned use of the electric chair in executing death row inmates (see *Dawson v. State*, — S.E.2d ——, 2001 WL 1180615 [GA.2001]). The court said that death by electrocution violated the state constitution's prohibition against cruel and unusual punishment because it inflicted purposeless violence and needless mutilation on the prisoner, and as such made no measurable contribution to the accepted goals of punishment (see GA Const. Art. 1, ¤ 1, par. 17). At the same time, the court stressed that it was not calling into question Georgia's entire system of capital punishment. On the contrary, the court said that death by lethal injection raised no constitutional questions because it was minimally intrusive and involved no mutilation.

## Appeal and other Post-Conviction Proceedings

The federal Constitution does not guarantee the right to appeal a criminal conviction. However, every state affords defendants the right to have at least one **appellate court** review the record for trial court errors. Many of these states restrict the subject matter of what may be appealed, curtail the time in which an appeal may be taken, or permit **appellate** courts to issue decisions upon the record and briefs submitted by the parties without holding a hearing or entertaining oral arguments. Federal statutes grant criminal defendants in federal court the right to appeal. Only one review is granted as a matter of right, and this is to the U. S. Court of Appeals. Review of state and federal convictions by the U. S. Supreme Court is discretionary.

After incarcerated defendants have exhausted all appeals without success, they may file a **writ** of **habeas corpus**. This is a civil suit against the warden of the prison, challenging the constitutionality of the incarceration. A habeas corpus petition is not another appeal. The only basis for granting relief to a habeas corpus petitioner is the deprivation of a constitutional right. For example, an inmate might claim that he or she was denied the assistance of counsel guaranteed by the Sixth Amendment on grounds that their attorney was incompetent. Violations of the Fourth Amendment's prohibition against unreasonable searches and seizures are not grounds for granting a writ of habeas corpus.

If a defendant loses on appeal and is denied a writ of habeas corpus, most jurisdictions offer a few last-ditch remedies. If the sentence includes parole, an inmate may petition the parole board to move up the date for parole. Inmates of state prisons may ask the governor of the state in which they are imprisoned for **clemency**. If granted, clemency normally includes the restoration of a released inmate's **civil rights**, such as the right to vote and own a gun. A commutation of sentence is a lesser form of clemency, since it does not restore the legal rights of the inmate but only releases him or her from incarceration. Federal inmates may ask the president of the United States for a **pardon**, which, like clemency, releases the inmate from custody and restores his or her legal rights and privileges.

## Additional Resources

*American Jurisprudence.* Lawyers Co-operative Publishing Company, 2001.

*Criminal Procedure.* Wayne R. LaFave, Jerold H. Israel, and Nancy J. King, West Group, 2001.

*http://sol.lp.findlaw.com* Criminal Law and Procedure Decisions of the October 2000-2001 Supreme Court Term

*Oxford Companion to the Supreme Court.* Kermit Hall, ed., Oxford University Press, 1992.

*West's Encyclopedia of American Law.* West Group, 1998.

## Organizations

### American Civil Liberties Union (ACLU)
1400 20th St., NW, Suite 119
Washington, DC 20036 USA
Phone: (202) 457-0800
E-Mail: info@aclu.org
URL: http://www.aclu.org/
Primary Contact: Anthony D. Romero, Executive Director

### Association of Federal Defense Attorneys
8530 Wilshire Blvd, Suite 404
Beverly Hills, CA 90211 USA
Phone: (714) 836-6031
Fax: (310) 397-1001
E-Mail: AFDA2@AOL.com
URL: http://www.afda.org
Primary Contact: Gregory Nicolaysen, Dir.

### Center for Human Rights and Constitutional Law
256 S. Occidental Blvd.
Los Angeles, CA 90057 USA
Phone: (213) 388-8693
Fax: (213) 386-9484
E-Mail: mail@centerforhumanrights.org
URL: http://www.centerforhumanrights.org
Primary Contact: Peter A. Schey, Executive Director

### National District Attorneys Association (NDAA)
99 Canal Center Plaza
Alexandria, VA 22314 USA
Phone: (703) 549-9222
Fax: (703) 836-3195
URL: http://www.ndaa.org
Primary Contact: Thomas J. Charron, Dir.

# CRIMINAL LAW

## DEATH PENALTY

*Sections within this essay:*

## Background

### History of Death Penalty Laws

The first recognized death penalty laws date back to eighteenth century B.C. and can be found in the Code of King Hammaurabi of Babylon. The Hammurabi Code prescribed the death penalty for over twenty different offenses. The death penalty was also part of the Hittite Code in the fourteenth century B.C. The Draconian Code of Athens, in seventh century B.C., made death the lone punishment for all crimes. In the fifth century B.C., the Roman Law of the Twelve Tablets also contained the death penalty. Death sentences were carried out by such means as beheading, boiling in oil, burying alive, burning, crucifixion, disembowelment, drowning, flaying alive, hanging, impalement, stoning, strangling, being thrown to wild animals, and quartering (being torn apart).

In Britain, hanging became the usual method of **execution** in the tenth century A.D. In the eleventh century, William the Conqueror would not allow persons to be hanged or otherwise executed for any crime, except in times of war. However, this trend did not last long. As many as 72,000 people were executed in the sixteenth century during the reign of Henry VIII. Common execution methods used during this time included boiling, burning at the stake, hanging, beheading, and drawing and quartering. Various capital offenses included marrying a Jew, not confessing to a crime, and **treason**.

The number of capital crimes in Britain increased throughout the next two centuries. By the 1700s, over two hundred crimes were punishable by death in Britain, including stealing, cutting down a tree, and robbing a rabbit warren. However, due to the severity of the death penalty, many juries would not convict defendants if offenses were not serious. Such practices led to early reform of Britain's death penalty. From 1823 to 1837, the death sentence was eliminated for over half of the crimes previously punishable by death.

## The United States and the Death Penalty

In colonial North America, use of the death penalty was strongly influenced by European practices. When European settlers came to the new world, they brought along their practice of **capital punishment**. In the territory now recognized as the United States, the first known execution was that of Captain George Kendall in the Jamestown colony of Virginia in 1608. Kendall was executed for being a spy for Spain. In 1612, Virginia governor Sir Thomas Dale enacted the Divine, Moral and Martial Laws, which provided the death penalty for even minor offenses such as stealing grapes, killing chickens, and trading with Indians.

Death penalty laws varied considerably from colony to colony. The Massachusetts Bay Colony held its first execution in 1630, although the Capital Laws of New England did not go into effect until many years later. The New York Colony instituted the Duke's Laws of 1665. Under these laws, offenses such as striking one's mother or father or denying the "true God," were punishable by death.

## The Abolitionist Movement

### The Colonial Period

The abolitionist movement is rooted in the writings of European social theorists Montesquieu, Voltaire, and Bentham, and English Quakers John Bellers and John Howard. However, it was a 1767 essay, *On Crimes and Punishment,* written by Cesare Beccaria, which principally influenced thinking about punishment throughout the world. Beccaria wrote that there was no justification for the state's taking of a life. The essay gave abolitionists an authoritative voice and renewed energy, one result of which was the **abolition** of the death penalty in Austria and Tuscany. Scholars in the United States were also affected by Beccaria's work. The first known attempted reforms of the death penalty in the United States occurred when Thomas Jefferson introduced a bill to revise Virginia's capital punishment laws, recommending that the death penalty be used only in the case of murder and treason offenses. Jefferson's bill was defeated by one vote.

Other challenges to early capital punishment laws were based on the idea that the death penalty was not a true deterrent. Dr. Benjamin Rush, founder of the Pennsylvania Prison Society, believed in the brutalization effect and argued that having a death penalty actually increased criminal behavior. Benjamin

Franklin and Philadelphia attorney general William Bradford supported Rush. Bradford, who would later become the U. S. attorney general, led Pennsylvania to become the first state to consider degrees of murder based on culpability. In 1794, Pennsylvania repealed the death penalty for all offenses except premeditated murder.

### The Nineteenth Century

In the early to mid-nineteenth century United States, the abolitionist movement gained support in the northeast. In the early part of the century, many states reduced the number of capital crimes and built state penitentiaries. In 1834, Pennsylvania became the first state to move executions away from the public by carrying them out in correctional facilities. In 1846, Michigan was the first state to abolish the death penalty for all crimes except treason. Later, Rhode Island and Wisconsin abolished the death penalty for all crimes. By the end of the century, the countries of Venezuela, Portugal, Netherlands, Costa Rica, Brazil, and Ecuador followed suit. While some states began abolishing the death penalty, most held onto it. Some states even made more crimes punishable by death, especially those committed by slaves. In 1838, in an effort to make the death penalty more acceptable to the public, some states began passing laws against mandatory death sentencing, instead enacting discretionary death penalty statutes. The 1838 enactment of discretionary death penalty statutes in Tennessee and later in Alabama were seen as a great reform. This introduction of sentencing discretion in the capital process was perceived as a victory for abolitionists because prior to the enactment of these statutes, all states mandated the death penalty for anyone convicted of a capital crime, regardless of circumstances. With the exception of a small number of rarely committed crimes in a few jurisdictions, all mandatory capital punishment laws were abolished by 1863.

During the Civil War, opposition to the death penalty diminished, as more attention was given to the anti-slavery movement. After the war, new developments in the means of executions emerged. In 1888, the electric chair was introduced in the state of New York. In 1890 William Kemmler became the first man executed by electrocution. Other states followed New York and used the electric chair as the primary method of execution.

### The Progressive Period

While some states eliminated the death penalty in the mid-nineteenth century, it was the first half of the twentieth century that marked the beginning of the Progressive Period of reform in the United States. From 1907 to 1917, six states completely outlawed the death penalty, and three limited it to the rarely committed crimes of treason and first-degree murder of a law enforcement official. These reforms did not last long. There was a frenzied atmosphere in the United States, as citizens began to panic about the threat of revolution in the wake of the Russian Revolution. In addition, the United States had recently entered World War I, and there were intense class conflicts as socialists mounted the first serious challenge to capitalism. By 1920, these circumstances led five of the six abolitionist states to return to capital punishment.

In 1924, the use of cyanide gas was introduced in the state of Nevada as a more humane way of execution. Gee Jon was the first person executed by lethal gas. The state tried to pump cyanide gas into Jon's cell while he slept, but this proved impossible, and the gas chamber was constructed.

From the 1920s to the 1940s, there was a revival in the use of the death penalty, due, in part, to the writings of criminologists, who argued that the death penalty was a necessary social measure. In the United States, people were suffering through Prohibition and the Great Depression. There were more executions in the 1930s than in any other decade in U. S. history, an average of 167 per year.

In the 1950s, however, public sentiment began to turn against capital punishment. Many allied nations either abolished or limited the death penalty, and in the U. S., the number of executions dropped dramatically. Whereas there were 1,289 executions in the 1940s, there were 715 in the 1950s, and the number fell even further, to only 191, from 1960 to 1976. In 1966, support for capital punishment reached an all-time low. A Gallup poll showed support for the death penalty at only 42 percent.

## The United States Constitution and the Death Penalty

### Death Penalty Challenges

The 1960s brought challenges to the presumed legality of the death penalty. Before then, the Fifth, Eighth, and Fourteenth Amendments were interpreted as permitting the death penalty. However, in the early 1960s, it was suggested that the death penalty was a "cruel and unusual" punishment and, therefore, unconstitutional under the Eighth Amendment.

In 1958, the Supreme Court decided in *Trop v. Dulles* (356 U. S. 86), that the Eighth Amendment contained an "evolving standard of decency that marked the progress of a maturing society." Although *Trop* was not a death penalty case, abolitionists applied the Court's logic to executions and maintained that the United States did indeed progress to a point that its "standard of decency" should no longer tolerate the death penalty. In the late 1960s, the Supreme Court began to reconsider the way the death penalty was administered. In 1968, the Court heard two cases which dealt with prosecutorial and jury discretion in capital cases. In *U. S. v. Jackson* (390 U.S. 570), the Supreme Court heard arguments regarding a provision of the federal **kidnapping statute** requiring that the death penalty be imposed only upon recommendation of a jury. The Court held that this practice was unconstitutional because it encouraged defendants to waive their right to a jury trial to ensure they would not receive a death sentence.

In *Witherspoon v. Illinois* (391 U. S. 510), the Supreme Court maintained that a potential juror's reservations about the death penalty were insufficient grounds to prevent that person from serving on the jury in a death penalty case. Jurors could be disqualified only if prosecutors could show that their attitudes toward capital punishment would prevent them from making an **impartial** decision about the punishment.

In 1971, the Supreme Court twice addressed the problems associated with the role of jurors and their discretion in capital cases, in *Crampton v. Ohio* and *McGautha v. California* (consolidated under 402 U. S. 183). The defendants argued it was a violation of their Fourteenth Amendment right to due process for jurors to have unrestricted discretion in deciding whether the defendants should live or die, and such discretion resulted in arbitrary and capricious sentencing. Crampton also argued that it was unconstitutional to have his guilt and sentence determined in one set of deliberations, as the jurors in his case were instructed that a first-degree murder **conviction** would result in a death sentence. The Court rejected these claims, thereby approving of unfettered jury discretion and a single proceeding to determine guilt and sentence. The Court stated that guiding capital sentencing discretion was "beyond present human ability."

### Temporary Abolition of the Death Penalty

The issue of arbitrariness of the death penalty was again brought before the Supreme Court in 1972 in

*Furman v. Georgia, Jackson v. Georgia,* and *Branch v. Texas* (known collectively as the landmark case *Furman v. Georgia* (408 U. S. 238)). Furman, like McGautha, argued that capital cases resulted in arbitrary and capricious sentencing. Furman, however, was a challenge brought under the Eighth Amendment, unlike McGautha, which was a Fourteenth Amendment due process claim. With the *Furman* decision the Supreme Court set the standard that a punishment would be "cruel and unusual" if it were too severe for the crime, if it were arbitrary, if it offended society's sense of justice, or it if were not more effective than a less severe penalty.

In nine separate opinions, and by a vote of 5-4, the Court held that Georgia's death penalty statute, which gave the jury full discretion in sentencing, could result in arbitrary sentencing. The Court maintained that the scheme of punishment under the statute was thus "cruel and unusual" and violated the Eighth Amendment. As a result, the Supreme Court voided forty death penalty statutes on June 29, 1972, thereby commuting the sentences of 629 death row inmates in the United States and suspending the death penalty because existing statutes were no longer valid.

### Reinstatement of the Death Penalty

Although the separate opinions by Justices Brennan and Marshall stated that the death penalty itself was unconstitutional, the overall conclusion in *Furman* was that the specific death penalty statutes were unconstitutional. That decision by the Court opened the door for states to revise death penalty statutes to eliminate the problems cited in *Furman.* Advocates of capital punishment began proposing new statutes that they believed would end arbitrariness of capital sentences. The states were led by Florida, which rewrote its death penalty statute only five months after *Furman.* Shortly after, 34 other states enacted new death penalty statutes. To address the unconstitutionality of unguided jury discretion, some states removed all discretion by mandating capital punishment for those convicted of capital crimes. This practice was ultimately found unconstitutional by the Supreme Court in *Woodson v. North Carolina* (428 U.S. 280 [1976]).

Other states began to limit discretion by providing sentencing guidelines for judges and juries considering death sentences. Such guidelines allowed for the introduction of aggravating and mitigating factors in sentencing. In 1976, the Supreme Court approved these discretionary guidelines in *Gregg v. Georgia*

(428 U. S. 153), *Jurek v. Texas* (428 U. S. 262), and *Proffitt v. Florida* (428 U. S. 242), collectively referred to as the *Gregg* decision. This landmark decision held that the new death penalty statutes in Florida, Georgia, and Texas were constitutional, thus reinstating the death penalty in those states. Additionally, the Court maintained that the death penalty itself was constitutional under the Eighth Amendment.

In addition to sentencing guidelines, the Court approved three additional reforms in the *Gregg* decision. The first was bifurcated trials, in which there are separate deliberations for the guilt and penalty phases of the trial. Only after the jury determines that the **defendant** is guilty of capital murder does it decide in a second trial whether the defendant should be sentenced to death or given a lesser sentence of prison time. Another reform was the practice of automatic **appellate** review of convictions and sentence. The final procedural reform was proportionality review, a practice that assists states in identifying and eliminating disparities in sentencing. The state **appellate court** can use this process to compare the sentence in a case being reviewed with other cases within the state, to see if it is disproportionate. Because the reforms were acknowledged by the Supreme Court, some states wishing to reinstate their death penalty sentences included them in revised statutes. However, inclusion was not required by the Court. Therefore, some of the resulting new statutes include variations on the procedural reforms found in *Gregg.*

The ten-year moratorium on executions that began with the *Jackson* and *Witherspoon* decisions ended on January 17, 1977, with the execution of Gary Gilmore by firing squad in Utah. Gilmore did not challenge his death sentence. That same year, Oklahoma became the first state to adopt lethal injection as a means of execution, though it would be five more years until Charles Brooks became the first person executed by lethal injection in Texas on December 2, 1982.

## Recent Developments in the Death Penalty

In June 2003 Governor George Ryan of Illinois stirred controversy when he commuted the death sentences of 167 inmates to life imprisonment. Ryan said he had concluded the state's capital punishment system was "haunted by the demon of error." His action came three years after he ordered a moratorium on executions after evidence proved that 13 inmates on death row had been wrongly convicted. Ryan, a Republican, had sought office with a platform that supported capital punishment.

In a 1989 case, the U.S. Supreme Court upheld the execution of mentally retarded inmates. In the years following, however, many states enacted legislation to prohibit such executions. In 2002, in *Atkins v. Virginia*, the Supreme Court voted 6-3 that the execution of mentally retarded persons is prohibited under the Eighth Amendment as cruel and unusual punishment.

Despite his role in a landmark court decision, Daryl Atkins currently resides on Virginia's death row. When the Supreme Court reversed the lower court ruling, it also **remanded** Atkins' case so that he could be resentenced. After the decision in *Atkins*, the Virginia legislature passed legislation to define mental retardation. A jury then heard evidence only on the issue of his mental ability. After deliberating 13 hours, and weighing conflicting testimony, the jury concluded that Atkins was not mentally retarded and could, therefore, be sentenced to death. Attorneys for Atkins filed an appeal in October 2005.

In 2005, in another historic decision, the U.S. Supreme Court barred the execution of persons who are under the age of 18 when they commit capital crimes. The ruling in *Roper v. Simmons* followed the same reasoning used by the court in *Atkins* In a 5-4 decision, the majority found that "evolving standards of decency" and the Eighth Amendment's prohibition of cruel and unusual punishment required the banning of juvenile executions. In its reasoning, the court gave credence to the fact that few nations in the world allow the execution of juveniles.

### Capital Punishment at the Federal Level

In addition to the death penalty laws in many states, the federal government has also employed capital punishment for certain federal offenses, such as murder of a government official, kidnapping resulting in death, running a large-scale drug enterprise, and treason. When the Supreme Court struck down state death penalty statutes in *Furman,* the federal death penalty statutes suffered from the same problems that the state statutes did. As a result, death sentences under the old federal death penalty statutes have not been upheld.

In 1988, a new federal death penalty statute was enacted for murder in the course of a drug-kingpin **conspiracy**. The statute was modeled on the post-

*Gregg* statutes that the Supreme Court had approved. Since its enactment, six people have been sentenced to death for violating this law, though none has been executed.

In 1994, President Clinton signed the Violent Crime Control and Law Enforcement Act that expanded the federal death penalty to sixty crimes, three of which do not involve murder. The exceptions are **espionage**, treason, and drug trafficking in large amounts.

Two years later, in response to the Oklahoma City bombing of a federal building, President Clinton signed the Anti-Terrorism and Effective Death Penalty Act of 1996. The Act, which affects both state and federal prisoners, restricts review in federal courts by establishing stricter filing deadlines, limiting the opportunity for evidentiary hearings, and ordinarily allowing only a single **habeas corpus** filing in federal court. Proponents of the death penalty argue that this streamlining will speed up the death penalty process and significantly reduce its cost, although others fear that quicker, more limited federal review may increase the risk of executing innocent defendants.

When he was executed on June 11, 2001, Timothy McVeigh became the first federal prisoner executed in 38 years. McVeigh was executed by lethal injection at the U.S. Penitentiary in Terre Haute, Indiana, for the April 19, 1995 Oklahoma City bombing.

## Worldwide Abolition

In the 1980s the international abolition movement gained momentum, and treaties proclaiming abolition were drafted and ratified. Protocol No. 6 to the European Convention on **Human Rights** and its successors, the Inter-American Additional Protocol to the American Convention on Human Rights to Abolish the Death Penalty, and the United Nations' Second Optional Protocol to the International Covenant on Civil and Political Rights Aiming at the Abolition of the Death Penalty, were created with the goal of making abolition of the death penalty an international norm.

Today, the Council of Europe requires new members to undertake and ratify Protocol No. 6. This requirement has, in effect, led to the abolition of the death penalty in Eastern Europe. For example, the Ukraine, formerly one of the world's leaders in executions, halted the death penalty and was admitted to the Council. In addition, in June 1999, Russian president Boris Yeltsin signed a **decree** commuting the death sentence for all of the convicts on Russia's death row. In 2005, Mexico and Liberia abolished the death penalty for all crimes.

In April 1999, the United Nations Human Rights Commission passed the Resolution Supporting Worldwide Moratorium on Executions. The resolution calls on countries which have not abolished the death penalty to restrict the use of the death penalty, including not imposing it on juvenile offenders and limiting the number of offenses for which it can be imposed. Ten countries, including the United States, China, Pakistan, Rwanda, and Sudan voted against the resolution.

### Capital Punishment Today

Currently, more than half of the countries in the international community have abolished the death penalty by law or by practice. However, according to Amnesty International, 72 countries retain the death penalty, including China, Iran, and the United States. In 2004 at least 3,797 people were executed in 25 countries, although the actual number may be significantly greater, according to reports of Amnesty International.

### Recent Death Penalty Statistics

Since the reinstatement of the death penalty in *Gregg v. Georgia,* the majority of inmates under sentence of death have been white. In 2004, the most recent year for which Bureau of Justice Statistics data were available, there were 3,315 inmates on federal and state death rows. More than half were white, while African American inmates made up the next largest group, with 1,390. Hispanics accounted for 13 percent of inmates with a known ethnicity. In 2004, 59 persons were executed in 12 states; the number of executions was six less than in 2003. The number of executions hit a post-1976 high of 98 in 1999. All the executions in 2004 were men. One person was executed by electrocution; lethal injection accounted for the rest. The data available indicate that almost two-thirds of those sentenced to death had previous **felony** convictions, and slightly less than ten percent had prior convictions for **homicide**. Ages of inmates sentenced to death ranged from 18 to 89. Additionally, 52 women were under sentence of death at the end of 2004. In 2004, 38 of the fifty states in the United States allowed the death penalty.

## Additional Resources

*Amnesty International, List of Abolitionist and Retentionist Countries.* Available at http://web.amnesty.org/pages/deathpenalty-countries-eng

*Capital Punishment Statistics.* Available at http://www.ojp.usdoj.gov/bjs/cp.htm

*Corrections in America.* Harry E. Allen and Clifford E. Simonsen, Prentice Hall, 1995.

*Deathquest: An Introduction to the Theory and Practice of Capital Punishment in the United States.* Robert Bohm, Anderson Publishing, 1999.

*Death Work: A Study of the Modern Execution Process.* Robert Johnson, Wadsworth Press, 1998.

*Discipline and Punish: The Birth of the Prison.* Michel Focault, Vintage Books, 1977.

*The Abolition of the Death Penalty in International Law.* William Schabas, Cambridge University Press, 1997.

*The Dilemmas of Corrections: Contemporary Readings, 4th Edition.* Kenneth C. Haas and Geoffrey P. Alpert, Waveland Press, Inc., 1999.

## Organizations

### Federal Bureau of Prisons

320 First Street NW
Washington, DC 20534 USA
Phone: (202) 307-3198
URL: http://www.bop.gov/

### National Institute of Corrections

1860 Industrial Circle, Suite A
Longmont, CO 80501 USA
Fax: (303) 682-0213
Toll-Free: 800-877-1461
URL: http://www.nicic.org/

### Death Penalty Information Center

1320 Eighteenth Street NW
Washington, D.C. 20036 USA
Phone: (202) 293-6970
Fax: (202) 822-4787
URL: http://www.deathpenaltyinfo.org/

# CRIMINAL LAW

## DNA TESTING, FINGERPRINTS, AND POLYGRAPHS

*Sections within this essay:*

- Background
- Comparing the Techniques
    - Fingerprints: The First ID
    - "Lie Detectors"
    - DNA: Greater Accuracy
- DNA As An Exoneration Tool
- Additional Resources

## Background

Viewers who watch police investigation shows on television often see intrepid experts solve crimes with the aid of a fingerprint on a doorknob or a strand of DNA from a hair miles from the crime scene. While the ease with which criminals are identified is exaggerated, the general picture is correct: Both DNA and fingerprints can help identify individuals through their unique markers—which means they can be useful tools both in identifying criminals and in clearing those who have been wrongly accused.

Polygraph machines, better known as "lie detectors," are also seen on television, but usually they can be found on older programs. The polygraph does not actually measure whether a person has made a true or false statement; in fact, it measures changes in breathing, blood pressure, and perspiration. A person who is lying, claim polygraph proponents, will breathe more rapidly, have a faster heartbeat, and sweat more profusely than one who is telling the truth.

## Comparing the Techniques

All three of these tools have an established place in the criminal justice system, as well as other areas of society. When determining a person's culpability in committing a crime, law enforcement experts agree, the more corroborating evidence, the stronger the case. Even if a person confesses and witnesses to the crime come forward, having indisputable physical evidence helps guarantee that the right person will be called to account for the crime.

### Fingerprints: The First ID

Fingerprints are the oldest and most accurate method of identifying individuals. No two people (not even identical twins) have the same fingerprints, and it is extremely easy for even the most accomplished criminals to leave incriminating fingerprints at the scene of a crime.

Each fingerprint has a unique set of ridges and points that can be seen and identified by trained experts. If two fingerprints are compared and one has a point not seen on the other, those fingerprints are considered different. If there are only mathing points and no differences, the fingerprints can be deemed identical. (There is no set number of points required, but the more points, the stronger the identification. Fingerprints can be visible or latent; latent fingerprints can often be seen with special ultraviolet lights, although on some surfaces a simple flashlight will identify the print. Experts use fingerprint powder or chemicals to set a print; they then "lift" the print using special adhesives.

The use of fingerprints for identification goes back to ancient times. In ancient Babylonia and China, thumbprints and fingerprints were used on clay tablets and seals as signatures. The idea that fingerprints might be unique to individuals dates from the fourteenth century. In 1686 the physiologist Marcello Malpighi examined fingerprints under a microscope and noted a series of ridges and loops. In 1823, another physiologist, Jan Purkinje, noted at least nine different fingerprint patterns.

The pioneer in fingerprint identification was Sir Francis Galton, an anthropologist by training, who was the first to show scientifically how fingerprints could be used to identify individuals. Beginning in the 1880s, Galton (a cousin of Charles Darwin) studied fingerprints to seek out hereditary traits. He determined through his studies not only that no two fingerprints are exactly alike, but also that fingerprints remain constant throughout an individual's lifetime. Galton published a book on his findings in 1892 in which he listed the three most common fingerprint types: loop, whorl, and arch. These classifications are still used today.

It did not take long for law enforcement officials to recognize the potential value of fingerprint evidence. Sir Edward Richard Henry, a British official stationed in India, began to develop a system of fingerprint identification for Indian criminals. (Henry created 1,024 primary fingerprint classifications.) In Argentina, Juan Vucetich, a police official, also used Galton's findings to create a fingerprint system. (He used Galton's research to make a fingerprint identification of a murderer in 1892.) By the beginning of the twentieth century, Scotland Yard had begun to compile fingerprint information, using a classification system based on Henry's work and creating a Central Fingerprint Bureau. In the United States, the New York Police Department, the New York State Prison System, and the Federal Bureau of Prisons instituted a fingerprint system in 1903, and in 1905 the U.S. Army began using fingerprint identification.

The first murder case in the United States in which fingerprint evidence was used successfully was in Illinois in 1910, when Thomas Jennings was accused of murdering Clarence Hiller after his fingerprints were found at Hiller's house. Jennings appealed his conviction, but the Supreme Court of Illinois upheld the evidence in 1911 and Jennings was executed in February 1912. *People v. Jennings* thus established fingerprint evidence as a reliable standard.

The Federal Bureau of Investigation (FBI) established a fingerprint repository through its Identification Division beginning in 1924. This repository held fingerprint cards in a central location. Over the next 50 years the FBI processed more than 200 million fingerprint cards. To eliminate duplicate fingerprints and make it easier to store and share fingerprints among law enforcement agencies, the FBI developed the Automated Fingerprint Identification System (AFIS) in 1991, which computerized the card system. The Integrated AFIS system (IAFIS) was introduced in 1999; a law enforcement official can request a set of criminal prints from IAFIS and get a response within two hours.

Fingerprints are kept for criminals, but civil fingerprints are also kept. People who apply for government jobs, jobs that handle confidential information, banking jobs, teaching jobs, law enforcement jobs, and any job that involves security issues can be fingerprinted. IAFIS stores civil prints as well as criminal prints.

### "Lie Detectors"

The word polygraph comes form the Greek for "many writings." The polygraph machine measures physiological information from the body: breathing, blood pressure, and perspiration. The faster the breathing, the higher the blood pressure, and the greater the amount of sweat, the more likelihood the person being tested is nervous.

Although it had been suggested in the nineteenth and early twentieth centuries that physiological changes could help determine whether a person was telling the truth, the first serious effort to apply this information came in 1920 when John Larson, a police officer in Berkeley, California, developed a device (which he called a polygraph) that could measure breathing and blood pressure. Larson believed that his invention could help determine whether a suspect was telling the truth. When the results of a polygraph test were included as evidence in a criminal case in 1923, they were challenged, and the D.C. District Circuit Court ruled in *U.S. v. Frye* that polygraph evidence needed to meet three criteria to be accepted: (1) that the general scientific community must acknowledge the test's reliability, (2) that the person conducting the test must be qualified to do so, and (3) that it can be proven that correct procedures were followed. Known as the "Frye test," it remained the judicial standard for 70 years.

During that time, scientists worked at refining Larson's invention. Leonarde Keeler, who had worked with Larson, began developing more sensitive polygraph machines in the 1930s, even starting a polygraph school in 1948.

Through the years, polygraphs were used by law enforcement agencies, but they were not considered definitive. To begin with, the person who is hooked up to the polygraph would already be quite nervous, and to have tubes placed on the chest, a blood pressure cuff on the arm, and metal plates on the fingers would not relax most people. Moreover, there is a difference of opinion on the accuracy of polygraph tests. The American Polygraph Association has stated that *inconclusive* polygraph results are not the same as *incorrect* results. Yet typically inconclusive readings are figured in with incorrect ones when establishing a percentage of accuracy.

Polygraph experts continued to fine-tune the machines, and also developed a questioning technique that was intended to produce fewer incorrect readings (the subject is asked to respond "yes" or "no" to questions, and unrelated questions are mixed in with relevant ones; this is meant to eliminate nervous affect).

In 1975, federal judges were given more discretion about the admissibility of evidence under new "Federal Rules of Evidence." Thus, a judge could allow a jury to consider polygraph results even if they did not pass the Frye Test. In 1993, the U.S. Supreme Court issued an opinion on *Daubert v. Merrell Dow Phramaceuticals* that definitively replaced the Frye standard. The court said that judges could admit certain scientific evidence as long as the theory behind it could be been tested, it had been subject to peer review and publication, the potential error was known, and the scientific community in general accepted the theory. In the 1998 case of *U.S. v. Scheffer*, the U.S. Supreme Court ruled that polygraph tests did not have to be admitted as evidence in military trials. (President George H.W. Bush had banned the admission of polygraph evidence from military trials in 1991, citing their unreliability.) But it did not ban polygraph evidence outright. *Daubert* grants judges the right to determine whether polygraph evidence can be used or ignored, so it is generally up to the judge.

The polygraph has also been used to pre-screen job applicants or to test employees to measure their truthfulness about such issues as drug use or theft. In 1988 Congress passed the Employee Polygraph Protection Act (EPPA), which prohibited business from using polygraph evidence to pre-screen employees or to test current employees, and which prohibited companies from disciplining or firing employees solely for failing a polygraph test.

(Polygraphs can be used if an employer can show other evidence against an employee, but the employee still has the right to refuse.) EPPA does not apply to government workers.

### DNA: Greater Accuracy

The use of DNA (deoxyribonucleic acid) as a method of identification is relatively new, but it has proven an effective means of identifying criminals—and perhaps more important, eliminating people as crime suspects. A fingerprint is the only unique identification source (identical twins have the same DNA). But if a criminal leaves no prints behind, law enforcement officials must rely on minute DNA samples from blood, saliva and other bodily fluids, hair, or skin. DNA testing is also used in paternity disputes to determine the identity of the actual father in custody, inheritance, or child support suits.

DNA testing can be done by standard techniques such as restrictive fragment length polymorphisms (RFLP), polymerase chain reaction (PCR), short tandem repeat (STR), and mitochondrial analysis. In RFLP testing, a DNA sample is mixed with a chemical substance that helps examiners isolate and identify specific key fragments of the sample that can be used in comparison analysis. A drawback of RFLP is that it requires a fairly large DNA sample. With PCR, a series of chemical reactions helps generate copies of a minute DNA sample, thus amplifying a small or degraded piece of information. In STR, various DNA regions in a sample are compared with other samples for similarities. The FBI uses STR using special software that can identity thirteen of these regions in a DNA sample. Mitochondrial DNA analysis is often used for extracting samples from bones and teeth, for which the other methods are not effective.

The FBI keeps a computerized databank of DNA samples called CODIS (Combined DNA Index System), which contained about 1.7 million DNA profiles as of 2003. The profiles stored in CODIS can be used to convict criminals, and also to exonerate innocent people. There are numerous examples of criminals whose DNA matched a profile from an earlier crime and who were then charged with the crime; likewise, there are examples of individuals whose innocence was confirmed when DNA found at a crime scene turned out to belong to another person identified through the profiles.

## DNA As An Exoneration Tool

Not oly can DNA be used to convict criminals, it has successfully been used to exonerate individuals, some of whom were wrongly imprisoned for more than two decades.

Often, the person who is wrongly convicted of a serious crime such as murder or rape has a criminal record for petty crimes, which means a record already exists. These individuals are frequently convicted on eyewitness testimony, but without any physical evidence tying them to the crime.

The Innocence Project, created in 1992 by Peter Neufeld and Barry Scheck at the Benjamin Cardozo School of Law in New York, works to exonerate people by use of postconviction DNA, in which DNA from the crime scene is tested against the accused's DNA. Often, physical evidence from a crime is kept for many years. If the evidence includes samples of blood, hair, skin, or other evidence that can include DNA, it can often be used to prove that the person accused could not have committed the crime. Morover, if it turns out that the DNA matches a profile in a database such as CODIS, the real criminal can be located and tried. From 1992 to the beginning of 2006, the Innocence Project helped exonerate 173 prisoners.

Opponents of capital punishment have pushed for DNA testing to be used more regularly, and many of those who favor capital punishment agree that those convicted for a capital offense should be allowed to make use of all evidence. One of the fears that come with capital punishment is that the wrong person could be executed for a crime. A case involving a many who was executed in 1992 gained national attention in 2005 when Governor Mark Warner of Virginia ordered DNA testing on a 24-year-old DNA sample to determine whether Roger Keith Coleman had murdered his sister-in-law in 1981. Coleman had proclaimed his innocence, and although his DNA had been tested before his execution, lawyers said the examiner might have misinterpreted the results. Using more advanced technology, Coleman's DNA was tested in January 2006, and the results confirmed that he was in fact the killer. Although supporters of capital punishment said that claims of the death penalty's fallibility were unfounded, but opponents noted that the danger of a wrongful execution still existed, and called for increased use of DNA as an identification tool.

## Additional Resources

*Advances in Fingerprint Technology,* Henry C. Lee and R.E. Gaensslen, eds., CRC Press, 2001.

*DNA: Forensic and Legal Applications,* Lawrence Kobilinsky, Thomas F. Liotti, and Jamel-Oesel-Sweat, Wiley-Interscience, 2005.

*Fingerprints: TheOrigins of Crime Detection and the Murder Case That Launched Forensic Science,* Colin Beaven, Hyperion, 2001.

"The Unrealized Potential of DNA Testing," Victor Walter Weedn and John W. Hicks, National Institute of Justice, 1998.

*Lie Detectors: A Social History,* Kerry Segrave, McFarland, 2004.

### American Polygraph Association

P. O. Box 8037
Chattanooga, TN 37414 USA
Phone: (423) 892-3993
Fax: (423) 894-5435
URL: http://www.polygraph.org
Primary Contact: Milton O. Webb, Jr., Executive Director

### Federal Bureau of Investigation

J. Edgar Hoover Building, 935 Pennsylvania Avenue NW
Washington, DC 20535 USA
Phone: (202) 324-3000
URL: http://www.fbi.gov
Primary Contact: Robert Mueller, Director

### The Innocence Project

100 Fifth Avenue, Third Floor
New York, NY 10011 USA
Phone: (212) 364-5340
Fax: (212) 364-5341
URL: http://www.innocenceproject.org
Primary Contact: Peter J. Neufeld and Barry C. Scheck, Co-Directors

### National Institute of Justice (U.S. Department of Justice)

810 Seventh Street, NW
Washington, DC 20531 USA
Phone: (202) 307-2942
URL: http://www.ojp.usdoj.gov/nij/
Primary Contact: Glenn R. Schmitt, Acting Director

# CRIMINAL LAW

## DOUBLE JEOPARDY

*Sections within this essay:*

## Background

The **double jeopardy** clause in the Fifth Amendment to the U. S. Constitution prohibits the government from prosecuting individuals more than one time for a single offense and from imposing more than one punishment for a single offense. It provides that "No person shall . . . be subject for the same offence to be twice put in **jeopardy** of life or limb." Most state constitutions also guarantee this right to defendants appearing in state court. Even in states that do not expressly guarantee this right in their laws, the protection against double jeopardy must still be afforded to criminal defendants because the Fifth Amendment's Double Jeopardy Clause has been made applicable to state proceedings via the doctrine of incorporation.

Under this doctrine, the Supreme Court has ruled in a series of cases that the Due Process and **Equal Protection** Clauses of the Fourteenth Amendment guarantee to the citizens of every state the right to exercise certain fundamental liberties. These liberties include, but are not limited to, every liberty set forth in the **Bill of Rights**, except the Second Amendment right to bear arms, the Third Amendment right against quartering soldiers, the Seventh Amendment right to trial by jury in civil cases, and the Fifth Amendment right to **indictment** by **grand jury**.

The concept of double jeopardy is one of the oldest in Western civilization. In 355 B. C. Athenian statesmen Demosthenes said that the "law forbids the same man to be tried twice on the same issue." The Romans codified this principle in the Digest of Justinian in 533 A. D. The principle also survived the Dark Ages (400-1066 A.D.) through the **canon law** and the teachings of early Christian writers, notwithstanding the deterioration of other Greco-Roman legal traditions.

In England the protection against double jeopardy was considered a universal maxim of the **common law** and was embraced by eminent jurists Henry de Bracton (1250), Sir Edward Coke (1628), Sir Matthew Hale (1736), and Sir William Blackstone (1769). However, the English double jeopardy doctrine was extremely narrow. It afforded protection only to defendants **accused** of capital felonies and applied only after **conviction** or **acquittal**. It did not apply to cases dismissed prior to final judgment and was not immune to flagrant abuse by the British Crown.

The American colonists were intimately familiar with the writings of Bracton, Coke, and Hale. Copies of Blackstone's Commentaries on English law were available in most of the colonies, and Blackstone's teachings were often quoted by the colonists in support of their claims that Parliament was exceeding its lawful authority.

The colonists were also familiar with how narrowly the right against double jeopardy had been defined in England. During the constitutional convention James Madison sought to enlarge the definition by making the right against double jeopardy applicable to all crimes not just capital felonies. Yet Madison's original draft of the Double Jeopardy Clause was perceived by some as too restrictive. It provided that "No person shall be subject . . . to more than one punishment or one trial for the same offense" (*United States v. Halper*, 490 U.S. 435, 109 S. Ct. 1892, 104 L. Ed. 2d 487 [1989]). Several House members objected to this wording, arguing that it could be misconstrued to prevent defendants from seeking a second trial on appeal following conviction. Although the language of the Fifth Amendment was modified to address this concern, the final version ratified by the states left other questions for judicial interpretation.

## Policy Considerations Underlying the Right Against Double Jeopardy

Five policy considerations underpin the right against double jeopardy, sometimes known as the right against former jeopardy: (1) preventing the government from employing its superior resources to wear down and erroneously convict innocent persons; (2) protecting individuals from the financial, emotional, and social consequences of successive prosecutions; (3) preserving the finality and integrity of criminal proceedings, which would be compromised were the government allowed to arbitrarily ignore unsatisfactory outcomes; (4) restricting prosecutorial discretion over the charging process; and (5) eliminating judicial discretion to impose cumulative punishments that are otherwise not clearly prohibited by law.

## The Common Law Development of the Right Against Double Jeopardy

Double jeopardy **litigation** revolves around four central questions: In what type of legal proceeding does double jeopardy protection apply? When does

jeopardy begin, or, in legal parlance, attach? When does jeopardy terminate? What constitutes successive prosecutions or punishments for the same offense? Although courts have answered the second and third questions with some clarity, they continue struggling over the first and last questions.

### Where Jeopardy Applies

Only certain types of **legal proceedings** invoke double jeopardy protection. If a particular proceeding does not place an individual in jeopardy, then subsequent proceedings against that individual for the same conduct are not prohibited. The text of the Fifth Amendment suggests that the protection against double jeopardy extends only to proceedings threatening "life or limb." Nevertheless, the Supreme Court has established that the right against double jeopardy is not limited to capital crimes or corporeal punishment but extends to all felonies, misdemeanors, and juvenile delinquency adjudications, regardless of the punishments they prescribe.

In *Benton v. Maryland*, 39 U.S. 784, 89 S. Ct. 2056, 23 L. Ed.2d 707 (1969), the U. S. Supreme Court ruled that the Fifth Amendment's Double Jeopardy Clause is applicable to both state and federal proceedings. Prior to this ruling, an individual accused of violating state law could rely only on that particular state's protection against double jeopardy. Some states offered greater protection against double jeopardy than did others, and frequently the level of protection offered was less than that offered under the federal Constitution. The Supreme Court said this was impermissible.

Relying on the doctrine of incorporation described above, the Court held that the right against double jeopardy is so important that each state must afford criminal defendants at least the same amount of protection from multiple prosecutions and punishments that is afforded by the federal government under the Fifth Amendment. Consequently, state courts cannot provide their residents with less protection against double jeopardy than is offered by federal courts, though variations in the level of protection offered can still arise when states offer their residents more protection under their state constitutional provisions than is provided under the federal Constitution.

The Supreme Court has also ruled that the right against double jeopardy precludes only subsequent criminal proceedings. It does not preclude subsequent civil proceedings or administrative proceedings (e.g., a license revocation **hearing**) against a person who has already been prosecuted for the same act or omission, even if that person is fined in the later civil or administrative proceeding. Nor is prosecution barred by double jeopardy if it is preceded by a final civil or administrative determination on the same issue.

Courts have drawn a distinction between criminal proceedings on the one hand and civil or administrative proceedings on the other, based on the different purposes served by each. Criminal proceedings are punitive in nature and serve the purposes of deterrence and retribution. Civil and administrative proceedings are more remedial in nature. Civil proceedings, for example, seek to compensate injured persons for any losses they have suffered, while administrative proceedings can serve various remedial functions (e.g., license revocation) unrelated to deterrence or retribution. Because civil, administrative, and criminal proceedings serve different objectives, a single course of conduct can give rise to multiple trials in different types of courtrooms.

The multiple legal proceedings brought against O. J. (Orenthal James) Simpson over the death of Nicole Brown Simpson and Ronald Lyle Goldman illustrate these various objectives. The state of California prosecuted Simpson for the murders of his former wife and her friend. Despite Simpson's acquittal in criminal court, the families of the two victims filed three civil suits against him. The criminal proceedings had been instituted to punish Simpson, incarcerate him, and deter others from similar behavior. The civil suits were designed in part to make the victims' families whole by compensating them with money damages for the losses they suffered.

### When Jeopardy Attaches

While the differences between civil, criminal, and administrative proceedings are not always perfectly clear, courts have done a much better job of explaining when jeopardy begins, or attaches. This question is crucial because any action taken by the government before jeopardy attaches, such as dismissing the indictment, will not prevent later proceedings against the same person for the same offense. Once jeopardy has attached, the full array of Fifth Amendment protections against multiple prosecutions and multiple punishments takes hold.

The U. S. Supreme Court has held that jeopardy attaches during a jury trial when the jury is sworn. In criminal cases tried by a judge without a jury, also called a bench trial, jeopardy attaches when the first witness is sworn. Jeopardy begins in juvenile delin-

quency adjudications when the court first hears **evidence**. If the **defendant** or juvenile enters a **plea** agreement with the prosecution, jeopardy does not attach until the plea is accepted by the court.

### When Jeopardy Terminates

Determining when jeopardy terminates is no less important than determining when it begins, but it is a little more complicated. Once jeopardy has terminated, the government cannot detain someone for additional court proceedings on the same matter without raising double jeopardy questions. If jeopardy does not terminate at the conclusion of one proceeding, jeopardy is said to be "continuing," and further criminal proceedings are permitted. Jeopardy can terminate in four instances: 1) after acquittal; 2) after **dismissal**; 3) after a **mistrial**; and 4) on appeal after conviction.

A jury's verdict of acquittal terminates jeopardy, and verdicts of acquittal cannot be overturned on appeal even if there is overwhelming proof of a defendant's guilt or even if the trial judge committed reversible error in ruling on an issue at some point during the proceedings. This fundamental maxim of double jeopardy **jurisprudence** entrusts the jury with the power to nullify criminal prosecutions tainted by egregious misconduct on the part of the police, the **prosecutor**, or the court, a tremendous bulwark against tyranny in a democratic society.

A jury can also implicitly **acquit** a defendant. If a jury has been instructed by the judge on the elements of a particular crime and a lesser-included offense, and the jury returns a guilty verdict as to the lesser offense but is silent as to the greater offense, re-prosecution for the greater offense is barred by the Double Jeopardy Clause. For example, a jury that has been instructed as to the crimes of first- and second-degree murder will implicitly acquit the defendant of first-degree murder by returning a guilty verdict only as to murder in the second degree. A not guilty verdict as to the greater offense is inferred from the jury's silence.

Dismissals are granted by the trial court for miscellaneous procedural errors and defects that operate as an absolute barrier to prosecution. For example, the prosecution must establish that a court has **jurisdiction** over a defendant before prosecution may commence. Failure to establish jurisdiction will normally result in a dismissal upon an objection raised by the defendant. Dismissals may be entered before a jury has been impaneled, during trial, or after conviction. But jeopardy must attach before a dismissal implicates double jeopardy protection.

Once jeopardy attaches, a dismissal granted by the court for insufficient evidence terminates jeopardy and bars further prosecution with one exception. The prosecution may appeal a dismissal entered after the jury has returned a guilty verdict. If the **appellate court** reverses the dismissal, the guilty verdict can be reinstated without necessitating a second trial. A dismissal granted for lack of evidence after a case has been submitted to a jury, but before a verdict has been reached, may not be appealed by the state.

Re-prosecution is permitted and jeopardy continues against the defendant when a case is dismissed by the court at the defendant's request for reasons other than sufficiency of the evidence. For example, courts may dismiss a case when the defendant's right to a speedy trial has been denied by prosecutorial pretrial delay. The Supreme Court has held that no double jeopardy interest is triggered when defendants obtain a dismissal for reasons unrelated to their guilt or innocence (see *United States v. Scott*, 437 U.S. 82, 98 S.Ct. 2187, 57 L.Ed.2d 65 [1978]).

Mistrials are granted when it has become impracticable or impossible to finish a case. Courts typically declare mistrials when jurors fail to unanimously reach a verdict. Like dismissals, mistrials declared at the defendant's behest will not terminate jeopardy or bar re-prosecution. Nor will a mistrial preclude re-prosecution when it is declared with the defendant's consent. Courts disagree whether a defendant's mere silence is tantamount to consent.

A different situation is presented when a mistrial is declared over the defendant's objection. Re-prosecution will be allowed only if the mistrial resulted from "manifest necessity," a standard more rigorous than "reasonably necessary" and less exacting than "absolutely necessary." A mistrial that could have been reasonably avoided will terminate jeopardy, but jeopardy will continue if the mistrial was unavoidable.

The manifest necessity standard has been satisfied where mistrials have resulted from defective indictments, disqualified or deadlocked jurors, and procedural irregularities willfully occasioned by the defendant. Manifest necessity is not present when mistrials result from prosecutorial or judicial manipulation. In each of these cases, courts balance the defendant's interests in finality against society's interest in a fair and just legal system.

Every defendant has the right to at least one appeal after conviction. If the conviction is reversed on appeal for insufficient evidence, it is treated as an acquittal, and further prosecution is not permitted. However, a defendant may be re-prosecuted when the reversal is not based on lack of evidence. The grounds for such reversals include defective search warrants, unlawful seizure of evidence, and other so-called "technicalities." Retrials in these instances are justified by society's interest in punishing the guilty. Defendants' countervailing interests are subordinated when a conviction rendered by 12 jurors is overturned for reasons unrelated to guilt or innocence.

The interests of the accused are also subordinated when courts permit prosecutors to seek a more severe sentence during the retrial of a defendant whose original conviction was thrown out on appeal. Defendants who appeal their conviction assume the risk that a harsher sentence will be imposed during re-prosecution. However, in most circumstances, courts are not permitted to impose a death sentence on a defendant during a second trial when the jury recommended life in prison during the first. The recommendation of life **imprisonment** is construed as an acquittal on the issue of **capital punishment**.

### What Constitutes the Same Offense

The final question courts must resolve in double jeopardy litigation is determining whether successive prosecutions or punishments are for the "same offense." Jeopardy may have already attached and terminated in a prior criminal proceeding, but the state may bring further criminal action against a person so long as it is not for the same offense. Courts have analyzed this question in several ways, depending on whether the state is attempting to re-prosecute a defendant or impose multiple punishments.

At common law a single episode of criminal behavior produced only one prosecution, no matter how many wrongful acts may have been committed during that episode. But over the last fifty years the proliferation of overlapping and related offenses has made it possible for the government to **prosecute** someone for several different crimes stemming from the same set of circumstances. For example, an individual who has stolen a car to facilitate an abduction resulting in attempted rape could be separately prosecuted and punished for auto theft, **kidnapping**, and molestation. This development has significantly enlarged prosecutors' discretion over the charging process.

The Supreme Court curbed this discretion in *Blockburger v. United States*, 284 U.S. 299, 52 S.Ct. 180, 76 L.Ed. 306 (1932). The Court said that the government may prosecute an individual for more than one offense stemming from a single course of conduct only when each offense requires proof of a fact the other does not. Blockburger requires courts to examine the elements of each offense as they are delineated by **statute**, without regard to the actual evidence that will be introduced at trial. The prosecution has the burden of demonstrating that each offense has at least one mutually exclusive element. If any one offense is completely subsumed by another, such as a lesser included offense, the two offenses are deemed the same, and punishment is allowed only for one.

Blockburger is the exclusive means by which courts determine whether cumulative punishments pass muster under the Double Jeopardy Clause. But several other methods have been used by courts to determine whether successive prosecutions are for the same offense. **Collateral estoppel**, which prevents the same parties from relitigating ultimate factual issues previously determined by a valid and final judgment, is one such method. In *Ashe v. Swenson*, 397 U.S. 436, 90 S.Ct. 1189, 25 L.Ed.2d 469 (1970), the Supreme Court collaterally estopped the government from prosecuting an individual for robbing one of six men at a poker game when a jury had already acquitted him of robbing another one of the six. Although the second prosecution would have been permitted under Blockburger because two different victims were involved, the government here was not allowed to rehearse its case and secure a conviction against a person already declared not guilty of essentially the same crime.

The "same transaction" analysis is another means by which courts determine whether successive prosecutions will survive constitutional scrutiny. It requires the prosecution to join all offenses committed during a continuous interval that share a common factual basis and display a single goal or intent. The same transaction test is used by many state courts to bar successive prosecutions for the same offense. However, no federal court has ever adopted it.

Both state and federal courts have employed the "actual evidence" test to preclude successive prosecutions for a single offense. Unlike Blockburger, which examines the **statutory** elements of proof, the "actual evidence" test requires courts to compare the evidence "actually" introduced during the first trial with the evidence sought to be introduced by the prosecution at the second trial. Criminal offenses are characterized as the same when the evidence necessary to support a conviction for one offense would be sufficient to support a conviction for the other.

Under the "same conduct" analysis the government is forbidden from twice prosecuting an individual for the same criminal behavior, regardless of the actual evidence introduced during trial and regardless of the statutory elements of the offense. For example, this analysis has been applied to prevent prosecuting someone for vehicular **homicide** resulting from drunk driving, when the defendant had been earlier convicted for driving while under the influence of alcohol. The second prosecution would have been permitted had the state been able to prove the driver's **negligence** without proof of his **intoxication**. The U. S. Supreme Court applied this analysis for three years before abandoning it in 1993. However, the "same conduct" analysis is still utilized by some state courts interpreting their own constitutions and statutes.

## State Court Decisions Interpreting State Constitutional Provisions Governing Double Jeopardy

The U. S. Constitution and the Supreme Court cases interpreting it establish the minimum amount of protection that a state court must provide when it is interpreting a section of the Bill of Rights that has been made applicable to the states via the doctrine of incorporation, including instances that require a state court to interpret and apply the Double Jeopardy Clause of the Fifth Amendment. A state court interpreting the double jeopardy clause of its own constitution may provide more protection than is afforded by the federal constitution but not less. Below is a sampling of cases decided in part based on a state court's interpretation of its own state constitutional provision governing double jeopardy.

ALABAMA: Reintroduction of two prior convictions at re-sentencing of the defendant for the purpose of enhancement under the **Habitual Felony** Offender Act did not violate the Double Jeopardy Clauses of the federal or state constitutions, even though the convictions were not certified at original sentencing hearing, where the defendant was put on notice at the original sentencing hearing of the state's intention to offer evidence of his prior felony convictions (see Ex parte Randle, 554 So.2d 1138

(Ala. 1989); AL Const. Art. I, § 9; Alabama Code 1975, §§ 13A-5-9, 13A-5-9(b)(2), (c)(2); U.S.C.A. Const.Amend. 5; Const. § 9).

ARKANSAS: Although both the United States and Arkansas constitutions provide that no person shall be subjected to two punishments based on same offense, remedial civil sanctions may be properly imposed without placing the person in jeopardy (see *Cothren v. State*, 344 Ark. 697, 42 S.W.3d 543 (Ark. 2001); Const.Amend. 5; AR CONST Art. 2, § 8).

ARIZONA: If a mistrial is granted as result of conduct that the prosecutor knew or should have known would prejudice the defendant and that could not be cured short of a mistrial, the double jeopardy clause of the Arizona Constitution bars a retrial (see *Beijer v. Adams ex rel. County of Coconino*, 196 Ariz. 79, 993 P.2d 1043, (Ariz.App. Div. 1 1999); AZ CONST Art. 2 § 10).

CALIFORNIA: A court-ordered victim **restitution** imposed for the first time at re-sentencing following appeal and partial reversal of the defendant's murder convictions was not considered a "punishment" and was therefore not barred under California's constitutional double jeopardy provisions (see *People v. Harvest*, 84 Cal.App.4th 641, 101 Cal.Rptr.2d 135, (Cal.App. 1 Dist., Oct 31, 2000); West's Ann.Cal. Const. Art. 1, § 15; West's Ann.Cal.Penal Code § 1202.4).

FLORIDA: The state's constitutional double jeopardy provision does not prohibit a defendant's retrial when a prior trial has been concluded by mistrial because of a **hung jury** (see *Lebron v. State*, 2001 WL 987233, 26 Fla. L. Weekly S553 (Fla. 30, 2001); West's F.S.A. Const. Art. 1, § 9).

GEORGIA: The double jeopardy clause of state constitution does not prohibit additional punishment for a separate offense that the legislature has deemed to **warrant** a separate **sanction** (see *Mathis v. State*, 273 Ga. 508, 543 S.E.2d 712 (Ga. 2001); GA Const. Art. 1, § 1, Par. 18).

ILLINOIS: The protection against double jeopardy afforded by the Illinois Constitution is no greater than that provided by the U. S. Constitution (see *People v. Ortiz*, 196 Ill.2d 236, 752 N.E.2d 410, 256 Ill.Dec. 530 (Ill. 2001); U.S.C.A. Const.Amend. 5; S.H.A. Const. Art. 1, § 10).

MASSACHUSETTS: The double jeopardy provision of the state constitution was not implicated by reuse of evidence of drunk driving at the defendant's trial on the charge of vehicular homicide by negligent operation, even though the defendant was acquitted in the first-tier trial on drunk driving charges, since in the state's two-tier trial system the defendant remained in continuing jeopardy with regard to other offenses for which he was originally convicted (see *Commissioner v. Woods*, 414 Mass. 343, 607 N.E.2d 1024 (Mass. 1993); M.G.L.A. c. 218, § 26A).

MICHIGAN: Convictions and punishments for **involuntary manslaughter** and operating a motor vehicle while under the influence of intoxicating liquor (OUIL) causing death do not violate the Double Jeopardy Clauses of the federal or state constitutions, since the offenses protect distinct societal norms, and the statute defining each offense requires proof of an element that the other does not (see *People v. Kulpinski*, 243 Mich.App. 8, 620 N.W.2d 537 (Mich.App. 2000); U.S.C.A. Const.Amend. 5; M.C.L.A. Const. Art. 1, § 15; M.C.L.A. §§ 257.625(4), 750.321).

MINNESOTA: **Forfeiture** of a motorist's vehicle after he had been convicted and sentenced for **misdemeanor** driving while intoxicated (**DWI**) was not double punishment in violation of the state constitution's double jeopardy clause, since the motorist provided no basis for reading the state double jeopardy clause more broadly than its federal counterpart in the context of DWI-related vehicle forfeitures (see *Johnson v. 1996 GMC Sierra*, 606 N.W.2d 455 (Minn.App. 2000); M.S.A. Const. Art. 1, § 7; M.S.A. § 169.1217).

NEW YORK: Defendant's re-prosecution for first-degree criminal **contempt** after being found guilty on the lesser charge of second-degree criminal contempt violated the Double Jeopardy Clauses of both the federal and state constitutions, where the defendant's trial was originally on both charges and the defendant was convicted on the second-degree charge only after a partial mistrial was declared as to the first-degree charge (*People v. Campbell*, 269 A.D.2d 460, 703 N.Y.S.2d 498 (N.Y.A.D. 2 Dept. 2000); U.S.C.A. Const.Amends. 5, 14; McKinney's Const. Art. 1, § 6).

TEXAS: A defendant's conviction for **assault** of a public servant did not violate the double jeopardy provisions of either the federal or state constitutions, even though the defendant had already received prison discipline for the same incident, since prison sanctions are not considered "punishment" for the purposes of double jeopardy analysis (see *Rogers v. State*, 44 S.W.3d 244 (Tex.App. 2001); U.S.C.A.

Const.Amend. 5; Vernon's Ann.Texas Const. Art. 1, § 14).

## Additional Resources

*American Jurisprudence.* Lawyers Co-operative Publishing Company, 2001.

*Criminal Procedure.*Wayne R. LaFave, Jerold H. Israel, and Nancy J. King, West Group, 2001.

*http://supreme.lp.findlaw.com/constitution/ amendment05/02.html*FindLaw: Double Jeopardy, 2001.

*Oxford Companion to the Supreme Court.*Kermit Hall, ed., Oxford University Press, 1992.

*West's Encyclopedia of American Law.* West Group, 1998.

## Organizations

### American Civil Liberties Union (ACLU)

1400 20th St., NW, Suite 119
Washington, DC 20036 USA

Phone: (202) 457-0800
E-Mail: info@aclu.org
URL: http://www.aclu.org/
Primary Contact: Anthony D. Romero, Executive Director

### Association of Federal Defense Attorneys

8530 Wilshire Blvd., Suite 404
Beverly Hills, CA 90211 USA
Phone: (714) 836-6031
Fax: (310) 397-1001
E-Mail: AFD A2@AOL.com
URL: http://www.afda.org
Primary Contact: Gregory Nicolaysen, Dir.

### National District Attorneys Association (NDAA)

99 Canal Center Plaza
Alexandria, VA 22314 USA
Phone: (703) 549-9222
Fax: (703) 836-3195
URL: http://w ww.ndaa.org
Primary Contact: Thomas J. Charron, Dir.

# CRIMINAL LAW

## DRIVING UNDER THE INFLUENCE

*Sections within this essay:*

- Background
- Elements of the Offense
    - Driving
    - Vehicle
    - Road or Highway
    - Under the Influence
    - Blood Alcohol Content
- Evidence in Drunk Driving Cases
- Sobriety Checkpoints
- Felony Drunk Driving
- Defenses
- Sentences
- License Suspensions
- State Drunk Driving Laws
- Additional Resources

## Background

Drunk driving constitutes the most commonly committed crime in the United States. State laws, most of which define this crime as "driving while intoxicated" (DWI) or "driving under the influence" (DUI), have progressively become more unforgiving over the past 20 years. Several groups, such as Mothers Against Drunk Driving (MADD), have fought with considerable success to modify drunk driving laws.

All states have amended their statutes so that a person is considered under the influence or intoxi-

cated when the person's blood-alcohol concentration (BAC) is above .08 percent. Moreover, sentences for drunk driving have become progressive harsher, as state legislatures have sought to deter the practice of drunk driving. Although sentences and penalties vary among different states and different courts, a person convicted of driving drunk may face any of the following:

- A fine of $1000 or more
- Probation
- Revocation or suspension of the offender's driver's license
- Impoundment of the offender's car or the installation of special locks on the offender's car
- Special classes regarding drunk driving or alcoholism
- Mandatory jail sentence

## Elements of the Offense

Most state laws define crimes of drunk driving as follows: driving a motor vehicle on a road or highway while under the influence of alcohol. Newer statutes also provide for a per se offense, which a person commits when driving a motor vehicle on a road or highway with a blood-alcohol concentration of .08 percent.

## Driving

Several state statutes require that a defendant was driving a vehicle in order to be convicted of a drunk driving offense. Other states use the terms operating a vehicle or being in physical control of the vehicle. These terms are not normally synonymous, and so it is important to determine how an individual state defines the term in the statute.

A number of issues may arise that relate to the "driving" element of a drunk driving offense. For instance, a person may be in a car but has not turned on the ignition. The question in some cases is whether the person was driving or operating a vehicle or whether the person was using the vehicle as a temporary shelter. Courts in various jurisdictions have identified several factors that may be used to determine whether someone has been driving a vehicle. Some of these include the following:

Field evidence may fall into one of five categories, including the following:

- Testimony regarding the defendant's unusual driving

- Testimony regarding the defendant's conduct or physical appearance

- Incriminating statements made by the defendant

- Testimony regarding the defendant's performance during a field sobriety test

- Tapes, film, and/or photographs taken at the scene where the defendant was driving and/or arrested

Police officers will often look at the defendant's physical appearance and symptoms of drunk driving in order to determine whether the defendant is intoxicated. The following are some of the more common symptoms of intoxication:

- The defendant's clothes are disheveled

- The defendant has not shaved or combed his or her hair

- The defendant's eyes appear to be red, glassy, or bloodshot

- The defendant's face appears to be flushed

- The defendant's breath smells like alcohol

- The defendant's speech is thick and slurred

The defendant's BAC level will be determined through one of three methods. The most common of these methods involves an analysis of the defendant's breath. Other tests analyze the blood or urine of the defendant. Refinements in the methods by which a defendant's BAC is determined have strengthened the ability of prosecutors to prove this BAC. However, these tests are not above reproach, and skilled defense attorneys can often successfully attack the methods by which the defendant's BAC was analyzed.

## Field Sobriety Tests and Sobriety Checkpoints

Researchers have developed a variety of tests that are designed to determine whether a person is likely to be intoxicated. A police officer performs these tests on suspects after the officer has stopped a person on suspicion of drunk driving. These tests allow an officer to observe a suspect's balance, physical ability, attention level, or other factors that the officer may use to determine whether the suspect is impaired. Officers often record a suspect's performance of these tests, and this practice generally has been upheld on appeal.

In several states, authorities have set up checkpoints where officers can question drivers in an effort to catch drunk drivers. These checkpoints are often set up during holidays when people are more likely to drink, such as New Year's Eve. Courts in the majority of states have upheld these checkpoints against challenges that these checkpoints are unconstitutional.

## Felony Drunk Driving

Most states have expanded their drunk driving statutes to provide for harsher punishment when drunk driving has resulted in injury to another. Where a person causes injury to another while driving drunk, the person may be charged with a felony, punishable by a term in state prison. In an even more severe expansion of criminal laws, some states now incorporate their murder or manslaughter statutes with their DUI laws where drunk driving results in the death of another. Moreover, in some states, a person may be charged with assault with a deadly weapon for driving a car while intoxicated. In such an instance, the deadly weapon is the car.

All states treat first DUI offenses as misdemeanors. However, in the majority of states, a person's third offense (or third "strike") is treated as a felony.

## Defenses

A person charged with drunk driving usually attacks the arresting officer's observations or opinions. A defendant may also attack witnesses that tested the defendant's BAC, or the defendant may call on someone who can testify that the defendant was sober.

In addition to these strategies, a defendant could rely on one of several defenses. These defenses include the following: (1) necessity, which applies when a person must drive to prevent a greater evil; (2) duress, which applies when the defendant drives in order to avoid serious injury or death; (3) entrapment, which applies when an officer requests that a person drive drunk; (4) mistake of fact, which applies when a person has an honest belief that his or her BAC is below the legal limit; and (5) involuntary intoxication, which applies when the person has ingested alcohol without his or her knowledge.

Individual states take different positions with respect to the availability of these defenses. In general, however, these defenses rely on specific sets of facts and are each very difficult to prove successfully.

## Sentences

A person who is convicted of drunk driving most likely faces some or all of the following in terms of punishment: a fine; time in jail; suspension, restriction, or revocation of the defendant's driver's license; probation; enrollment and completion of a course in drunk driving or alcoholism.

In addition to these, states have also developed other penalties or requirements that drunk drivers must fulfill. One requirement that has become more common throughout the nation involves the use of an ignition-interlock device. Such a device captures a driver's breath and analyzes the BAC of the driver. The device only allows the driver to start the vehicle when the breath analyzer reads below a certain level, such as .02 percent. Another form of punishment is the impoundment of a drunk driver's vehicle for a certain period of time. A more serious form of this punishment is the forfeiture of a vehicle, meaning that a court can order the sale of a person's car after the person has had multiple convictions for drunk driving.

States have also modified their statutes to provide for enhanced sentences under some circumstances. These sentence enhancements may apply when one of the following events occur: (1) the defendant's BAC is very high, such as above .20 percent; (2) the defendant refuses to submit to chemical testing; (3) the defendant greatly exceeds the speed limit or drives recklessly while drunk; (4) a child under the age of 14 is in the car when the defendant is driving drunk; (5) drunk driving is accompanied with an accident or injury to another person.

## State Drunk Driving Laws

Each state has established .08 as the BAC that constitutes a per se drunk driving violation. The states otherwise vary on the specifics of their drunk driving laws. The following summarizes some of these state laws:

ALABAMA: The state does not provide for penalties that include ignition interlocking devices or forfeiture of the defendant's vehicle.

ALASKA: The state provides for penalties that include both ignition interlocking devices and for forfeiture of the defendant's vehicle.

ARIZONA: The state provides for penalties that include both ignition interlocking devices and for forfeiture of the defendant's vehicle. The state provides for enhanced penalties where a defendant's BAC exceeds .15 percent.

ARKANSAS: The state provides for penalties that include both ignition interlocking devices and for forfeiture of the defendant's vehicle. The state provides for enhanced penalties where a defendant's BAC exceeds .15 percent.

CALIFORNIA: The state provides for penalties that include both ignition interlocking devices and for forfeiture of the defendant's vehicle. The state provides for enhanced penalties where a defendant's BAC exceeds .20 percent.

COLORADO: The state provides for ignition interlocking devices but not for the forfeiture of the defendant's vehicle. The state provides for enhanced penalties where a defendant's BAC exceeds .15 percent, with even greater penalties when a defendant's BAC exceeds .20 percent.

CONNECTICUT: The state does not provide for penalties that include ignition interlocking devices or forfeiture of the defendant's vehicle. The state provides for enhanced penalties where a defendant's BAC exceeds .16 percent.

DELAWARE: The state provides for ignition interlocking devices but not for the forfeiture of the defendant's vehicle. The state provides for enhanced penalties where a defendant's BAC exceeds .16 percent, with even greater penalties when a defendant's BAC exceeds .20 percent.

DISTRICT OF COLUMBIA: The state provides for ignition interlocking devices but not for the forfeiture of the defendant's vehicle.

FLORIDA: The state provides for penalties that include both ignition interlocking devices and for forfeiture of the defendant's vehicle. The state provides for enhanced penalties where a defendant's BAC exceeds .20 percent.

GEORGIA: The state provides for penalties that include both ignition interlocking devices and for forfeiture of the defendant's vehicle. The state provides for enhanced penalties where a defendant's BAC exceeds .15 percent.

HAWAII: The state provides for ignition interlocking devices but not for the forfeiture of the defendant's vehicle.

IDAHO: The state provides for ignition interlocking devices but not for the forfeiture of the defendant's vehicle. The state provides for enhanced penalties where a defendant's BAC exceeds .20 percent.

ILLINOIS: The state provides for penalties that include both ignition interlocking devices and for forfeiture of the defendant's vehicle. The state provides for enhanced penalties where a defendant's BAC exceeds .15 percent, with even greater penalties when a defendant's BAC exceeds .20 percent.

INDIANA: The state provides for ignition interlocking devices but not for the forfeiture of the defendant's vehicle. The state provides for enhanced penalties where a defendant's BAC exceeds .15 percent.

IOWA: The state provides for ignition interlocking devices but not for the forfeiture of the defendant's vehicle. The state provides for enhanced penalties where a defendant's BAC exceeds .15 percent.

KANSAS: The state provides for ignition interlocking devices but not for the forfeiture of the defendant's vehicle.

KENTUCKY: The state provides for penalties that include both ignition interlocking devices and for forfeiture of the defendant's vehicle. The state provides for enhanced penalties where a defendant's BAC exceeds .15 percent.

LOUISIANA: The state provides for penalties that include both ignition interlocking devices and for forfeiture of the defendant's vehicle. The state provides for enhanced penalties where a defendant's BAC exceeds .15 percent.

MAINE: The state provides for penalties that include both ignition interlocking devices and for forfeiture of the defendant's vehicle. The state provides for enhanced penalties where a defendant's BAC exceeds .15 percent.

MARYLAND: The state provides for ignition interlocking devices but not for the forfeiture of the defendant's vehicle.

MASSACHUSETTS: The state provides for penalties that include both ignition interlocking devices and for forfeiture of the defendant's vehicle.

MICHIGAN: The state provides for penalties that include both ignition interlocking devices and for forfeiture of the defendant's vehicle.

MINNESOTA: The state provides for penalties that include both ignition interlocking devices and for forfeiture of the defendant's vehicle. The state provides for enhanced penalties where a defendant's BAC exceeds .15 percent.

MISSISSIPPI: The state provides for penalties that include both ignition interlocking devices and for forfeiture of the defendant's vehicle.

MISSOURI: The state provides for penalties that include both ignition interlocking devices and for forfeiture of the defendant's vehicle. The state provides for enhanced penalties where a defendant's BAC exceeds .15 percent.

MONTANA: The state provides for penalties that include both ignition interlocking devices and for forfeiture of the defendant's vehicle. The state provides for enhanced penalties where a defendant's BAC exceeds .18 percent.

NEBRASKA: The state provides for ignition interlocking devices but not for the forfeiture of the defendant's vehicle.

NEVADA: The state provides for ignition interlocking devices but not for the forfeiture of the defendant's vehicle. The state provides for enhanced penalties where a defendant's BAC exceeds .18 percent.

NEW HAMPSHIRE: The state provides for ignition interlocking devices but not for the forfeiture of the defendant's vehicle. The state provides for enhanced penalties where a defendant's BAC exceeds .16 percent.

NEW JERSEY: The state provides for ignition interlocking devices but not for the forfeiture of the defendant's vehicle.

NEW MEXICO: The state provides for ignition interlocking devices but not for the forfeiture of the defendant's vehicle. The state provides for enhanced penalties where a defendant's BAC exceeds .16 percent.

NEW YORK: The state provides for penalties that include both ignition interlocking devices and for forfeiture of the defendant's vehicle.

NORTH CAROLINA: The state provides for penalties that include both ignition interlocking devices and for forfeiture of the defendant's vehicle The state provides for enhanced penalties where a defendant's BAC exceeds .15 percent.

NORTH DAKOTA: The state provides for penalties that include both ignition interlocking devices and for forfeiture of the defendant's vehicle.

OHIO: The state provides for penalties that include both ignition interlocking devices and for forfeiture of the defendant's vehicle. The state provides for enhanced penalties where a defendant's BAC exceeds .17 percent.

OKLAHOMA: The state provides for penalties that include both ignition interlocking devices and for forfeiture of the defendant's vehicle. The state provides for enhanced penalties where a defendant's BAC exceeds .15 percent.

OREGON: The state provides for penalties that include both ignition interlocking devices and for forfeiture of the defendant's vehicle.

PENNSYLVANIA: The state provides for penalties that include both ignition interlocking devices and for forfeiture of the defendant's vehicle.

RHODE ISLAND: The state provides for penalties that include both ignition interlocking devices and for forfeiture of the defendant's vehicle. The state provides for enhanced penalties where a defendant's BAC exceeds .15 percent.

SOUTH CAROLINA: The state provides for penalties that include both ignition interlocking devices and for forfeiture of the defendant's vehicle.

SOUTH DAKOTA: The state does not provide for penalties that include ignition interlocking devices or forfeiture of the defendant's vehicle. The state provides for enhanced penalties where a defendant's BAC exceeds .17 percent.

TENNESSEE: The state provides for penalties that include both ignition interlocking devices and for forfeiture of the defendant's vehicle. The state provides for enhanced penalties where a defendant's BAC exceeds .20 percent.

TEXAS: The state provides for penalties that include both ignition interlocking devices and for forfeiture of the defendant's vehicle.

UTAH: The state provides for ignition interlocking devices but not for the forfeiture of the defendant's vehicle. The state provides for enhanced penalties where a defendant's BAC exceeds .16 percent.

VERMONT: The state provides forfeiture of the defendant's vehicle but not for ignition interlocking devices.

VIRGINIA: The state provides for penalties that include both ignition interlocking devices and for forfeiture of the defendant's vehicle. The state provides for enhanced penalties where a defendant's BAC exceeds .15 percent.

WASHINGTON: The state provides for penalties that include both ignition interlocking devices and for forfeiture of the defendant's vehicle. The state provides for enhanced penalties where a defendant's BAC exceeds .15 percent.

WEST VIRGINIA: The state provides for ignition interlocking devices but not for the forfeiture of the defendant's vehicle.

WISCONSIN: The state provides for penalties that include both ignition interlocking devices and for forfeiture of the defendant's vehicle. The state provides for enhanced penalties where a defendant's BAC exceeds .17 percent, with greater penalties when a defendant's BAC is higher.

WYOMING: The state does not provide for penalties that include ignition interlocking devices or forfeiture of the defendant's vehicle.

## Additional Resources

*Drunk Driving Defense, Fifth Edition.* Taylor, Lawrence, Aspen Law & Business, 2000.

"Still Driving Drunk" Mejeur, Jeanne, *State Legislatures*, December 2003. Available at http://www.ncsl.org/programs/pubs/03SLDec_drunkdrive.pdf

## Organizations

### *Mothers Against Drunk Driving (MADD)*
511 E. John Carpenter Frwy. Suite 700
Irving, TX 75062 USA

Phone: (800) 438-6233
Fax: (972) 869-2206
URL: http://www.madd.org/home

### *National Conference of State Legislatures*
444 North Capitol Street, N.W., Suite 515
Washington, DC 20001 USA
Phone: (202) 624-5400
Fax: (202) 737-1069
URL: http://www.ncsl.org

# CRIMINAL LAW

## EVIDENCE

*Sections within this essay:*

- Background
- Admissibility
- Real Evidence
- Demonstrative Evidence
- Documentary Evidence
- Testimony
- Leading Questions
- The Lay Opinion Rule
- Character
- Hearsay
- Privileges
- Presumptions
- Judicial Notice
- Additional Resources

## Background

The law of **evidence** governs how parties, judges, and juries offer and then evaluate the various forms of proof at trial. In some ways, evidence is an extension of civil and **criminal procedure**. Generally, evidence law establishes a group of limitations that courts enforce against attorneys in an attempt to control the various events that the trial process presents in an adversarial setting. There are many arguments in favor of evidence law; here are five of the most common ones:

1. To ameliorate pervasive mistrust of juries

2. To further legal or social policies relating to a matter being litigated

3. To further substantive policies unrelated to the matter in suit

4. To create conditions to receive the most accurate facts in trials

5. To manage the scope and duration of trials

In the United States, the federal courts must follow the Federal Rules of Evidence (FRE); state courts generally follow their own rules, which are generally imposed by the various state legislatures upon their respective state courts. The FRE is the most influential body of American evidence law. The FRE encompasses the majority of the laws of evidence in 68 brief sections. Its language is accessible, easy to read, and mostly free of technical jargon and complicated cross-referencing. The FRE has been enormously influential in the development of U. S. evidence law. This influence in part is a result of its brevity and simplicity.

Before 1975, U. S. evidence law was mostly a creature of the **common law** tradition. The FRE was drafted and proposed by a distinguished advisory committee composed of practitioners, judges, and law professors appointed by the United States Supreme Court. Just 20 years after the FRE was adopted in the federal system, almost three-quarters of the states had adopted codes that closely resemble the FRE.

The FRE applies in all federal courts in both criminal and civil cases. Understanding some of the basic provisions of the FRE will enable most people to figure out what is going on at trial, even if there are deviations between the FRE and applicable state laws of evidence.

## Admissibility

Evidence comes in four basic forms:

1. Demonstrative evidence
2. **Documentary evidence**
3. **Real evidence**
4. Testimonial evidence

Some rules of evidence apply to all four types and some rules apply to one or two of them. All of these forms of evidence must be **admissible**, though, before they can be considered as probative of an issue in a trial.

Basically, if evidence is to be admitted at court, it must be relevant, material, and competent. To be considered relevant, it must have some reasonable tendency to help prove or disprove some fact. It need not make the fact certain, but at least it must tend to increase or decrease the likelihood of some fact. Once admitted as relevant evidence, the finder of fact (judge or jury) will determine the appropriate weight to give a particular piece of evidence. A given piece of evidence is considered material if it is offered to prove a fact that is in dispute in a case. Competent evidence is that evidence that accords with certain traditional notions of reliability. Courts are gradually diminishing the competency rules of evidence by making them issues related to the **weight of evidence**.

## Real Evidence

Real evidence is a thing. Its existence or characteristics are considered relevant and material to an issue in a trial. It is usually a thing that was directly involved in some event in the case, such as a murder weapon, the personal effects of a victim, or an artifact like a cigarette or lighter belonging to a suspect. Real evidence must be relevant, material, and competent before a judge will permit its use in a trial. The process whereby a lawyer establishes these basic prerequisites (and any additional ones that may apply), is called laying a foundation. In most cases, the relevance and materiality of real evidence are obvious. A lawyer establishes the evidence's competence by showing that it really is what it is supposed to be. Establishing that real or other evidence is what it purports to be is called **authentication**.

## Demonstrative Evidence

Evidence is considered "demonstrative" if it demonstrates or illustrates the **testimony** of a witness. It is admissible when it fairly and accurately reflects the witness's testimony and is otherwise unobjectionable. Maps, diagrams of a crime scene, charts and graphs that illustrate profits and losses are examples of demonstrative evidence.

## Documentary Evidence

Evidence contained in or on documents can be a form of real evidence. For example, a contract offered to prove the terms it contains is both documentary and real evidence. When a party offers a document into evidence, the party must authenticate it the same way as any other real evidence, either by a witness who can identify the document or by witnesses who can establish a chain of **custody** for the document.

When people deal with documentary evidence, it is a good idea to consider these four potential pitfalls:

- Parol evidence
- Best evidence
- Authentication
- **Hearsay**

The parol evidence rule prohibits the admission of certain evidence concerning the terms of a written agreement. Parol evidence is usually considered an issue of substantive law, rather than a pure evidentiary matter.

A party can authenticate documentary evidence in much the same way as it can authenticate other real evidence. Also, some kinds of documents are essentially self-authenticating under the FRE. Some of these are:

- Acknowledged documents to prove the acknowledgment
- Certain **commercial paper** and related documents
- Certificates of the custodians of business records
- Certified copies of public records
- Newspapers
- Official documents

- Periodicals

- Trade inscriptions

The best evidence rule states that when the contents of a written document are offered in evidence, the court will not accept a copy or other proof of the document's content in place of the original document unless an adequate explanation is offered for the absence of the original. The FRE permits the use of mechanically reproduced documents unless one of the parties has raised a genuine question about the accuracy of the copy or can somehow show that its use would be unfair. Also under the FRE, summaries or compilations of lengthy documents may be received into evidence as long as the other parties have made the originals available for **examination**.

## Testimony

Evidence given in the form of testimony is perhaps the most basic type of evidence. Testimonial evidence consists of what a competent witness at the proceeding in question says in court. Generally, witnesses are competent if they meet four broad requirements:

1. The witnesses must take the oath or a substitute and understand the oath,

2. The witnesses must have personal knowledge about the subject of their testimony.

3. The witnesses must recall what was perceived

4. The witnesses must be able to communicate what they perceived

The courts interpret competency quite liberally, which means that testimony based on the competency of a witness is rarely excluded

If at trial witnesses forgets their testimony, the attorney may help to refresh their memory in four ways:

1. First, the attorney can ask the judge for a recess to allow the witnesses time to calm down or otherwise collect themselves.

2. Second, the attorney can ask the witnesses a **leading question** to try to refresh their memory.

3. Third, the attorney can attempt to refresh the witness's recollection through a process known as past recollection refreshed.

The witnesses must first say that they cannot remember the facts the attorney is trying to elicit from them. Then they must say that the refreshing object might help him them to remember. Almost anything that they says might help them can be used to help refresh their memory such as notes, photographs, an item of clothing, a smell, or some other object of some sort.

4. Fourth, the attorney can offer a writing as a past recollection recorded. The witnesses must first claim that they cannot remember the facts the attorney is trying to elicit from her. Next, the attorney presents the writing or other recording the attorney intended to use for the witness. If the attorney can refresh the witness's memory, they will be allowed to answer the question. If the writing does not refresh their memory, they must then identify the writing as one that they made or saw when hey did remember the fact in question and that they knew then that the writing was accurate.

## Leading Questions

A leading question actually suggests an answer or substitutes the words of the questioning attorney for those of the witness. Many leading questions call for answers of either "yes" or "no." But not all questions that call for an answer of "yes" or "no" are leading questions.

Judges have discretion to allow leading questions during the **direct examination** of a witness when the questions have the following traits:

- deal with simple background issues

- will help to elicit the testimony of a witness who, due to age, incapacity, or limited intelligence, is having difficulty communicating her evidence

- are asked of an adverse or hostile witness. Witnesses are considered adverse or hostile when their interests or sympathies may lead them to resist testifying truthfully. In most cases, an adverse party or a witness associated with an adverse party is considered hostile for the purposes of this rule

Questions that call for a narrative answer are more or less the opposite of leading questions. Questions that call for a narrative often produce long speeches that can waste the time of the court and the parties. These kinds of questions are very unpopular with courts and should be avoided.

During **cross-examination**, attorneys may only ask about subjects that were raised upon the direct examination of the witness, including **credibility**. If cross-examiners stray into a new topical area, the judge may permit them to do so in the interest of time or efficiency, but harassment of the witness is not permitted under any circumstances.

## The Lay Opinion Rule

Witnesses must answer questions in the form of statements of what they saw, heard, felt, tasted, or smelled. Usually they are not permitted to express their opinions or draw conclusions. Under the FRE, a court will permit a person who is not testifying as an expert to **testify** in the form of an opinion if the opinion is both rationally based on his perception and helps to explain the witness's testimony. Additionally, a competent layperson may provide opinions on certain subjects that are specifically permitted by rule, **statute**, or **case law**. Some of these are:

- Another person's identity
- Another person's sanity
- Demeanor, mood, or intent
- Identification of handwriting
- Intoxication or sobriety
- Ownership
- The state of health, sickness, or injury
- Speed, distance, and size
- The value of a witness's own property

Opinion testimony is not necessarily objectionable even if such testimony goes to the ultimate issue to be decided in the trial

Extrinsic evidence is evidence other than the answers of the witness whose testimony is being impeached. It may be offered to prove facts relevant to impeaching a witness. In addition to extrinsic evidence, a party may attack the credibility of another witness by attempting to show that the witness is or has:

1. Bias, prejudice, interest in the issue, or corruption

2. Criminal convictions, or other prior bad acts

3. Prior inconsistent statements

4. An untruthful character

There are some limits to questioning a witness about a prior criminal **conviction**. However, according to the FRE, a witness may generally be questioned about criminal convictions when the crime was punishable by a sentence of more than a year or involved **fraud** or a false statement such as **perjury**. Before people attempt to use such evidence in a trial, they need to understand the limits to this kind of evidence.

The FRE allows questions about prior bad acts of a witness to **impeach** that witness's credibility where, in the court's discretion, the questions will help get at the truth. Thus, an attorney may ask questions about prior inconsistent statements if the following apply:

- The questioner has a **good faith** basis for believing that the witness made an inconsistent statement

- The witness needs to be reminded of the time, place, and circumstances of the prior statement

- If the statement is written, a copy of the written statement must be provided to the opposing **counsel** upon request

Another way to impeach the testimony of a witness is to show that the witness has a character of untruthfulness. This departure from the basic rule states a party may not provide evidence of a witness's character to show that the witness acted in conformity with that character trait. The FRE permits evidence to prove a witness has a character of untruthfulness in:

- tTestimony of specific instances of untruthfulness

- The opinion of another witness concerning the honesty of another witness's character

- Testimony about the target witness's reputation for truthfulness in the community

It is important to know that a witness whose testimony is used to impeach the truthfulness of another witness may in turn be impeached

## Character

Character is a general quality usually attributed to a person. Character cannot be used to show that someone acted on a particular occasion in conformity with a particular character trait. On the other hand, habit can be used that way. A habit is a behavior; it is specific, regular, and consistently repeated. Occasionally, some character traits can be linked with a habit, so the distinction between the two can be hard to make at times.

In civil cases, evidence that a person has a character trait generally cannot be used to prove that the person acted in conformity with that character trait on a particular occasion. Evidence of character may be proved where it is an integral issue in a dispute or where a party puts character in issue. Evidence of character is used frequently in criminal trials during the sentencing stage to show that a convicted **defendant** merits a lesser or greater sentence or other **penalty**.

## Hearsay

The rule against hearsay is deceptively simple and full of exceptions. Hearsay is an out of court statement, made in court, to prove the truth of the matter asserted. In other words, hearsay is evidence of a statement that was made other than by a witness while testifying at the **hearing** in question and that is offered to prove the truth of the matter stated. For example, Witness A in a murder trial claimed on the stand: "Witness B (the "declarant") told me that the defendant killed the victim." The definition of hearsay is not too difficult to understand. But the matter can become very confusing when one considers all of the many exceptions to the general rule against hearsay.

Even if a statement meets the requirements for hearsay, the statement may yet be admissible under one of the exceptions to the hearsay rule. The FRE contains nearly thirty of these exceptions. Most of them are generally available, although a few of them are limited to times when the declarant is unavailable.

There are twenty-four exceptions in the federal rules that do not require proof that the person who made the statement is unavailable. These are:

1. Business records, including those of a public agency

2. Certain public records and reports

3. Evidence of a judgment of conviction for certain purposes

4. Evidence of the absence of a business record or entry

5. Excited utterances or spontaneous statements

6. Family records concerning family history

7. Judgments of a court concerning personal history, family history, general history, or **boundaries**, where those matters were essential to the judgment

8. Learned treatises used to question an expert witness

9. Market reports, commercial publications, and the like

10. Marriage, baptismal, and similar certificates

11. Past recollections recorded

12. Recorded documents purporting to affect interests in land

13. Records of religious organizations concerning personal or family history

14. Records of vital statistics

15. Reputation concerning boundaries or general history

16. Reputation concerning family history

17. Reputation of a person's character

18. Statements about the declarant's present sense impressions

19. Statements about the declarant's then existing mental, emotional, or physical condition

20. Statements in authentic ancient documents (at least 20 years old)

21. Statements in other documents purporting to affect interests in land and relevant to the purpose of the document

22. Statements made by the declarant for the purpose of medical diagnosis or treatment

23. Statements of the absence of a public record or entry

24. The "catchall" rule

The last exception, the so-called "catchall" rule, bears some explanation. This rule does not require that the declarant be unavailable to testify. It does say that evidence of a hearsay statement not included in one of the other exceptions may nevertheless be admitted if it meets these following conditions:

- It has sound guarantees of trustworthiness

- It is offered to help prove a material fact

- It is more probative than other equivalent and reasonably obtainable evidence

- Its admission would forward the cause of justice

- The other parties have been notified that it will be offered into evidence

## Privileges

In general terms, privileges are rights held by individuals that permit them to refuse to provide evidence or to prevent certain evidence from being offered against them. Privileges exist only to serve specific interests and relationships; courts give them narrow scope.

Privileges are more or less disfavored by the courts because they run contrary to the principle that all relevant evidence should be admitted in a search for truth. Accordingly, the persons or entities whose confidentiality they are meant to shield or protect can waive their privileges. Individuals who possess a privilege are known as "holders" of the privilege. Often, the nonholder who is a party to a privileged communication must assert the privilege on behalf of the holder.

Congress could not agree on how to make laws regarding privileges, so this area was left up to the courts and to state law to define. Thus, under the FRE, when a party offers evidence on a federal claim the applicable privileges are determined by the federal case law. When a party offers evidence on a state claim, the state's law of privilege applies. The federal law of privilege is still developing, and the federal courts are usually less tolerant of parties' claims to privileges than are state courts.

## Presumptions

Previously, there was a good deal of controversy among legal professionals and scholars over the effect of presumptions, but these have largely ended, at least in the federal system. Presumptions are just that, a presumption that certain evidence is what it is on its face. Sometimes, however, a presumption can be rebutted by other evidence. There are two kinds of rebuttable presumptions: those that affect the burden of producing evidence and those that af-

fect the burden of proof. In most cases, courts interpret presumptions as rebuttable. A list of rebuttable presumptions includes the following:

- that a letter that has been correctly addressed and properly mailed is received by the addressee in the ordinary course of the mail

- that a person who possesses a thing is also the owner of that thing

- that a writing is dated accurately

- that a written obligation that has been surrendered to the **debtor** has been paid by the debtor (and vice versa)

- that some specific ancient documents are authentic

- that statements in the records of a process server are true

- that when a receipt for a payment on an **installment** debt is given, the debtor has paid all previous installment payments

- that the defendant was negligent when the requirements of *res ipsa loquitur* have been proven

- the presumptions that money or property delivered is in fact owed to the recipient

A presumption is not considered evidence. But if an opponent to a presumption puts on no evidence to rebut the presumption, the judge or jury must assume the existence of the presumed fact. On the other hand, if an opponent to a presumption does provide evidence to rebut the presumption, the presumption has no further effect.

## Judicial Notice

Sometimes, the need for evidence on an issue in a case can be satisfied through formal admissions, stipulations, and judicial notice. Likewise, under the FRE, a judge may take judicial notice of facts that are not in issue because they are either generally known (e.g. George Washington was the first president of the United States), or they can be accurately and readily determined (e.g. the exact time of sunrise on a particular day). In addition, state and federal courts can take judicial notice of the laws of the states and of the federal system.

## Additional Resources

*An Introduction to the Law of Evidence* Lilly, Graham C., West Wadsworth, 1996.

*Evidence* 2nd ed., Mueller, Christopher B., and Laird C. Kirkpatrick, Aspen Publishers, Inc., 1999.

*Federal Evidence* 4th ed., Weissenberger, Glen, and James J. Duane. Anderson Publishing Company, 2001.

*"Federal Rules of Evidence."* Legal Information Institute, 2002. Available at http://www.law.cornell.edu/rules/fre/overview.html. Legal Information Institute, 2002.

*Federal Rules of Evidence in a Nutshell, 5th Ed.* 5th ed., Graham, Michael H., West Publishing, 2001.

*The New Wigmore: A Treatise on Evidence: Selected Rules of Limited Admissibility: Regulation of Evidence Tto Promote Extrinsic Policies and Values.*. Leonard, David P., and Richard D. Friedman, editors., Aspen Law & Business, 2002.

*Trial Evidence, Second Edition.* 2nd ed., Mauet, Thomas A., and Warren D. Wolfson. Aspen Law & Business, 2001.

## Organizations

### *Criminal Justice Section of the American Bar Association (ABA)*

740 15th Street, NW, 10th Floor
Washington, DC 20005-1009 USA
Phone: (202) 662-1500
Fax: (202) 662-1501
URL: http://www.abanet.org/crimjust/home.html

### *National Association of Criminal Defense Lawyers (NACDL)*

1025 Connecticut Ave. NW, Ste. 901
Washington, DC 20036 USA
Phone: (202) 872-8600
Fax: (202) 872-8690
E-Mail: assist@n acdl.org
URL: www.nacdl.org

### *National District Attorneys Association*

99 Canal Center Plaza, Suite 510
Alexandria, VA 22314 USA
Phone: (703) 549-9222
Fax: (703) 836-3195
URL: http://www.ndaa.org/index.html

# CRIMINAL LAW

## FIFTH AMENDMENT

*Sections within this essay:*

## Background

Having successfully won their independence from a British monarchy and Parliament that they had accused of being undemocratic and tyrannical, the Framers of the federal Constitution had a strong mistrust of large, centralized governments. The Framers drafted the Bill of Rights, consisting of the Constitution's first ten **amendments**, to serve as a bulwark delineating a range of individual freedoms and thus protecting them from governmental abuse. Laws enacted, implemented, or enforced by governmental officials that infringe on these freedoms are typically invalidated as unconstitutional by the judiciary.

The Fifth Amendment to the U.S. Constitution enumerates five distinct individual freedoms: (1) the right to be indicted by an impartial grand jury before being tried for a federal criminal offense; (2) the right to be free from multiple prosecutions or multiple punishments for a single criminal offense; (3) the right to have individual freedoms protected by **due process of law**; (4) the right to be free from government compelled **self-incrimination**; and (5) the right to receive just compensation when the government takes private property for public use.

### The Text of the Fifth Amendment

The text of the Fifth Amendment reads as follows: "No person shall be held to answer for a capital, or otherwise infamous crime, unless on a presentment or indictment of a Grand Jury, except in cases arising in the land or naval forces, or in the militia, when in actual service in time of War or public danger; nor shall any person be subject for the same offence [sic] to be twice put in jeopardy of life or limb; nor shall be compelled in any criminal case to be a witness against himself, nor be deprived of life, liberty, or property, without due process of law; nor shall private property be taken for public use, without just compensation."

Because the Framers hoped that the Constitution would be an enduring document, they generally avoided using specific language that one might find in a code or a regulation. Instead of specifying particular instances of prohibited governmental conduct in the Bill of Rights, the Framers established broad principles that government officials must take into account before encroaching on individual freedoms.

In this way the Framers required future generations of citizens to determine the Constitution's meaning.

In *Marbury v. Madison*, 5 U.S. (1 Cranch) 137 (1803), the U.S. Supreme Court, per Chief Justice John Marshall, ruled that the ultimate authority for determining the Constitution's meaning lay with the judicial branch of government through the power of judicial review. Pursuant to this power, courts are authorized to review laws enacted by government officials and invalidate those that violate the Constitution.

### Applicability of the Fifth Amendment to the States

As originally ratified it was unclear whether the Fifth Amendment applied only against action taken by the federal government or if it also protected freedoms from state governmental abuse. The Supreme Court in *Barron v. City of Baltimore*, 32 U.S. 243 (1833) ruled that the Fifth Amendment did not apply to the states.

This judgment settled the question until the Fourteenth Amendment was ratified in 1868. It guaranteed the citizens of every state the right to **equal protection** of the laws and the right to due process of law. Following ratification of the Fourteenth Amendment, the Supreme Court began making individual freedoms enumerated in the Bill of Rights applicable to the states via the doctrine of incorporation. Under this doctrine, the Court explained through a series of cases that no state may deny any citizen a fundamental liberty without violating the Fourteenth Amendment's Equal Protection and Due Process clauses. The Court has ruled that these fundamental liberties include every liberty set forth in the Bill of Rights, except the Second Amendment's right to bear arms, the Third Amendment's right against quartering soldiers, the Seventh Amendment's right to trial by jury in civil cases, and the Fifth Amendment's right to **indictment** by grand jury.

### Interpretation and Scope of the Grand Jury Clause

The Fifth Amendment guarantees every person charged with a federal crime the right to be indicted by a grand jury. A grand jury is a group of citizens summoned to criminal court by a law enforcement official to decide whether it is appropriate to indict someone suspected of a crime. Although the right to a grand jury is mandated at the federal level by the U. S. Constitution, about one-third of the state constitutions also require indictment by grand jury for more serious violations of state laws.

Federal grand juries may consist of between 16 and 23 citizens chosen from lists of qualified state residents of legal age, who have not been convicted of a crime, and are not biased against the subject of the investigation. Grand jury proceedings begin with the prosecutor's presenting a bill of indictment, which is a list explaining the case and possible charges. The prosecutor then presents **evidence** to the grand jurors in the form of exhibits, written documents, and oral testimony by witnesses.

Grand jurors are given wide latitude to inquire about the criminal charges and may compel the production of documents and records and **subpoena** witnesses, including the suspect under investigation. They may also question witnesses to satisfy themselves that the evidence is credible and reliable. Unlike at trial, hearsay evidence is admissible before grand juries. But like at trial, witnesses who refuse to answer questions may be held in contempt and incarcerated until they provide answers, unless the question requires disclosure of information that might tend to incriminate the witness. The Fifth Amendment's privilege against self-incrimination may be successfully asserted during grand jury proceedings.

Grand juries are accusatory bodies, and prosecutors have no obligation to present **exculpatory** evidence or testimony that impeaches their witnesses. Nor do suspects enjoy an absolute right to appear before a grand jury to present their case. Suspects may appear before a grand jury with permission of the prosecutor or upon order by subpoena. Despite the prosecutor's partisan role as the government official in charge of obtaining an indictment against the accused, the prosecutor may not compromise the grand jury's function of standing between the accused and a hasty, malicious, oppressive, or corrupt prosecution (see *Wood v. Georgia*, 370 U.S. 375 [1962]). Prosecutors, for example, are prohibited from presenting false information to a grand jury, and convictions stemming from an indictment based on false information are overturned on appeal. Prosecutors are also prohibited from pressuring grand jurors to "rubber stamp" an indictment (see *United States v. Sigma Intern., Inc.*, 244 F.3d 841 [11th Cir. 2001]).

If a majority of grand jury members agree that there is sufficient reason to charge the suspect with a crime, they return an indictment carrying the words, "true bill." But if a majority of grand jurors determine that there is insufficient evidence to go forward with prosecution, they return an indictment carrying the words, "no bill."

### Interpretation and Scope of the Double Jeopardy Clause

The Double Jeopardy Clause of the Fifth Amendment prohibits the government from prosecuting a defendant more than one time for a single offense or imposing more than one punishment for a single offense. Only certain types of legal proceedings invoke double jeopardy protection. If a particular proceeding does not place an individual in "jeopardy," then subsequent proceedings or punishments against that individual for the same conduct are not prohibited by this clause.

The text of the Fifth Amendment suggests that the protection against double jeopardy extends only to proceedings that threaten "life or limb." However, the Supreme Court has extended the right against double jeopardy beyond capital crimes and corporeal punishments to all **felonies**, **misdemeanors**, and juvenile delinquency adjudications, regardless of the punishments they prescribe. At the same time, the Supreme Court has ruled that the right against double jeopardy precludes only subsequent criminal proceedings. It does not preclude a private litigant from initiating a civil proceeding against a defendant who has already been prosecuted for a crime, which explains why O. J. Simpson could be sued in civil court by the surviving family members of Ronald Goldman and Nicole Brown Simpson after he was acquitted in criminal court of murdering them.

A crucial question in any double jeopardy analysis is when jeopardy is said to have "attached." In other words, courts must decide at what point during a criminal prosecution a defendant's right against subsequent prosecution and multiple punishments began. Actions taken by the government before jeopardy attaches, such as dismissing an indictment, will not prevent later proceedings against a person for the same offense. Conversely, once jeopardy has attached, the full panoply of protections against subsequent prosecution and multiple punishments takes hold.

The Supreme Court has ruled that jeopardy attaches during a jury trial when the jury is sworn. In criminal cases tried by a judge without a jury, jeopardy attaches when the first witness is sworn. Jeopardy attaches in juvenile proceedings when the court first hears evidence. If the defendant or juvenile enters a plea agreement, jeopardy does not attach until the plea is accepted.

Determining when jeopardy terminates is no less important. Once jeopardy has terminated, the government cannot hail someone into court for additional criminal proceedings without raising double jeopardy questions. If jeopardy does not terminate at the conclusion of one proceeding, it is deemed to be continuing, and further criminal proceedings are permitted. Jeopardy can terminate in four instances: (1) after an acquittal; (2) after a dismissal of a charge; (3) after a mistrial that was not caused by the defendant; or (4) on appeal after a conviction.

The final question courts must resolve in double jeopardy litigation is whether successive prosecutions or punishments are for the same offense. Jeopardy may have already attached and terminated in a prior criminal proceeding, but the state may bring further criminal action against a person so long as it is not for the same offense. The U.S. Supreme Court has ruled that the government is allowed to prosecute an individual for more than one offense stemming from a single course of conduct only when each offense requires proof of a fact that the other offenses do not (see *Blockburger v. United States*, 284 U.S. 299 [1932]). Depending on the circumstances surrounding the single course of conduct, the Court has adopted various other tests in resolving this question and has allowed lower federal and state courts to do the same.

### Interpretation and Scope of the Due Process Clause

The Fifth Amendment's Due Process Clause has two prongs, one procedural and one substantive. Procedural due process encompasses the process by which legal proceedings are conducted. It requires that all persons who are materially affected by a legal proceeding receive notice of its time, place, and subject matter so that they have an adequate opportunity to prepare. It also requires that legal proceedings be conducted in a fair manner by an impartial judge who will allow the interested parties to fully present their complaints, grievances, and defenses. The procedural prong of the Due Process Clause governs civil, criminal, and administrative proceedings from the pretrial stage through final appeal, and proceedings that produce arbitrary or capricious results will be overturned as unconstitutional.

Substantive due process encompasses the content or substance of particular laws applied during legal proceedings. Before World War II, the U.S. Supreme Court relied on substantive due process to overturn legislation that infringed on a variety of property interests, including the right of employers to determine the wages their employees would be paid and the number of hours they could work. Since World War II, the Supreme Court has relied on substantive due process to protect privacy and autonomy interests of adults, including the right to use contraception and the right to have an abortion.

However, the line separating procedure from substance is not always clear. For example, procedural due process guarantees criminal defendants the right to a fair trial, while substantive due process specifies that twelve jurors must return a unanimous guilty verdict before the death penalty can be imposed. The line is further blurred by judges and lawyers who simply refer to both prongs as "due process," without any express indication as to whether they mean substantive or procedural.

### Interpretation and Scope of the Self-Incrimination Clause

The Fifth Amendment's right against self-incrimination permits individuals to refuse to answer questions or disclose information that could be used against them in a criminal prosecution. The purpose of this right is to inhibit the government from compelling a confession through force, coercion, or deception. Confessions produced by these methods are deemed unreliable because they are often involuntary, unwitting, or the result of the accused's desire to avoid further browbeating rather than being the product of candor or a desire to confess.

The Self-Incrimination Clause applies to every type of legal proceeding, whether it is civil, criminal, or administrative in nature. Traditionally, the privilege against self-incrimination was most frequently asserted during the trial phase of legal proceedings, where individuals are placed under oath and asked questions on the witness stand. However, in the twentieth century application of the privilege was extended to the pretrial stages of legal proceedings as well. In civil cases, for example, the right against self-incrimination may be asserted when potentially incriminating questions are posed in depositions and interrogatories.

In criminal proceedings, the U.S. Supreme Court's decision in *Miranda v. Arizona*, 384 U.S. 436 (1966) established the rules under which the Self-Incrimination Clause applies to proceedings before trial. In *Miranda*, the Court held that any statements made by a defendant while in police custody will be inadmissible during prosecution unless the police first warn the defendants that they have (1) the right to remain silent; (2) the right to consult an attorney

before being questioned by the police; (3) the right to have an attorney present during police questioning; (4) the right to a court appointed attorney if the defendant cannot afford to hire a private attorney; and (5) the right to be informed that any statements they make can and will be used against them at trial.

The *Miranda* case acknowledged that these warnings were not expressly mentioned anywhere in the text of the federal Constitution. However, the Court concluded that the warnings constituted an essential part of a judicially created buffer zone that is necessary to protect rights that throughout the Bill of Rights are expressly afforded to criminal defendants. Thus, if a defendant confesses to a crime or makes an otherwise incriminating statement to the police, that statement will be generally excluded from trial unless the defendant was first read the Miranda warnings.

Because of its lack of textual support in the federal Constitution, legal observers have long predicted the demise of Miranda. Much of this speculation has been fueled by subsequent cases in which the Supreme Court carved out exceptions to Miranda. For example, the Court ruled that when a defendant makes an un-Mirandized incriminating statement followed by a later Mirandized confession, the subsequent confession should not be excluded from trial (see *Oregon v. Elstad*, 470 U.S. 298 [1985]). However, law enforcement officials cannot completely ignore the requirement of Miranda warnings. In 2004, the Court reviewed a case in which officers interrogated a suspect for 30 to 40 minutes without Miranda warnings, eliciting a confession during the process. Once the suspect confessed, the officers gave the Miranda warnings and then led the suspect to give the same account for a second time. In this instance, the Court determined that the confession was involuntary and that this practice violated Miranda. (*Missouri v. Seibert*, 542 U.S. 600 [2004]).

### Interpretation and Scope of the Eminent Domain Clause

When the government takes someone's property for public use, the law calls it a "taking." The Fifth Amendment permits the government to appropriate private property for public use so long as the property owner receives just compensation. The Fifth Amendment allows for governmental appropriation of either real estate or personal property, and the just-compensation provision applies to both kinds of takings. In most eminent domain proceedings, just compensation is normally equated with the fair market value of the property appropriated.

The Supreme Court in 2005 sparked a national debate regarding the use of eminent domain in the decision in *Kelo v. City of New London*, 125 S. Ct. 2655 (2005). In *Kelo*, the City of New London, Connecticut condemned privately-owned properties so that the land could be used as part of a private development plan. Even though the property would be owned by private entities and used for private purposes, the development plan would increase taxes and create new jobs. These and similar reasons led the Court to decide that the city condemnation of the property constituted a "public use," thus permitting the city to take the land.

Many members of the public criticized the decision. Several state legislators responded within a few months by introducing bills that would effectively negate the decision in *Kelo*. The state proposals appeared in several different forms. Some states sought to limit the type of uses of private property could be considered "public uses." Other states considered legislation that would prohibit the use of eminent domain for certain uses, such as private economic development projects.

### State Laws Concerning Rights Enumerated by the Fifth Amendment

The federal constitution and the Supreme Court cases interpreting it establish the minimum amount of protection that a state court must provide when applying a provision of the Bill of Rights to a pending controversy. The same holds true for the four clauses of the Fifth Amendment that have been made applicable to the states through the doctrine of incorporation. However, a state constitution or a state court interpreting the state constitution may provide more protection than is afforded by the federal constitution but not less. Below is a sampling of cases decided in part based on state courts' interpretation of the federal constitution, its own state constitution, or both. Also included are summaries of legislation and constitutional amendments pertaining to eminent domain following the U.S. Supreme Court's decision in *Kelo v. City of New London*.

ALABAMA: In 2005, the state enacted legislation that prohibits use of eminent domain for certain projects, such as commercial development or development for purposes of raising tax revenues.

ARKANSAS: The Due Process Clause in the Arkansas Constitution did not disqualify a trial judge from presiding over a prosecution against the defendant, notwithstanding the defendant's claim of potential judicial bias from judge's service as prosecuting at-

torney in a former case (see *Green v. State*, 729 S.W.2d 17 [Ark. App. 1987]).

ARIZONA: If a mistrial is granted as a result of conduct that the prosecutor knew or should have known would prejudice the defendant and the prejudice cannot be cured short of declaring a mistrial, the double jeopardy clause of state constitution bars retrial (see *Beijer v. Adams ex rel. County of Coconino*, 993 P.2d 1043 [Ariz. App. 1999]).

CALIFORNIA: The California grandparent visitation statute violated the Due Process Clause of both the state and federal constitutions as applied to a mother, who opposed visitation between her child and paternal grandparents, after the trial court failed to apply the statutory presumption that the mother would act in her child's best interests (see *In re Marriage of Harris*, 2001 WL 1113062 [Cal. App. 2001.]).

DELAWARE: The state in 2005 enacted legislation that limits application of eminent domain to recognized public uses.

FLORIDA: For a criminal statute to withstand a void-for-vagueness challenge under both the federal and state Due Process Clauses, the language of the statute must provide adequate notice of the conduct it prohibits when measured by common understanding and practice, and the statute must define the offense in a manner that does not encourage arbitrary and discriminatory enforcement (see *State v. Brake*, 2001 WL 1095088 [Fla. 2001]).

GEORGIA: Routine collection of a suspect's signature on a fingerprint card while booking the suspect into jail, even in the absence of Miranda warnings, does not constitute compelled self-incrimination in violation of the state constitution (see *Thomas v. State*, 549 S.E.2d 359 [Ga. 2001]).

ILLINOIS: The privilege against self-incrimination that is applicable in criminal cases under the Illinois constitution applies to probation revocation proceedings, since a defendant's testimony may subject him to fine or incarceration if probation is revoked (see *People v. McNairy*, 721 N.E.2d 1200 [Ill. App. 1999]).

MASSACHUSETTS: A Due Process violation did not occur under the Massachusetts Constitution based on a prisoner's transfer to another prison, the deprivation of the prisoner's canteen privileges, or the loss of the privilege to attend resident council meetings, since the transfer did not implicate a liberty interest, and the other two claims involved privileges not rights (see *Murphy v. Cruz*, 753 N.E.2d 150 [Mass. App. Ct. 2001]).

MICHIGAN: Convictions for both being a felon in possession of a firearm and possessing a firearm during the commission of a felony did not violate the Double Jeopardy Clause of the Michigan Constitution, since the words of the felony-firearm statute made it clear that the legislature's intent was to provide for an additional felony charge and sentence whenever the person possessing the firearm also committed the felony, and the statutes setting forth those offenses fulfilled distinct purposes that addressed different social norms (see *People v. Dillard*, 631 N.W.2d 755 [Mich. App. 2001]).

MINNESOTA: Taxpayers who were sent three notices concerning their property tax before the property taxes became due and who could have used a variety of statutory means to challenge the taxes received constitutionally sufficient Due Process under both the state and federal constitutions (see *Programmed Land, Inc. v. O'Connor*, 633 N.W.2d 517 [Minn. 2001]).

MISSOURI: A Missouri statute giving any party to a custody or visitation proceeding only one opportunity to disqualify a guardian ad litem (GAL) did not violate the state or federal Due Process rights of the children, since following disqualification the court was required to appoint another GAL if abuse or neglect was alleged (see *Suffian v. Usher*, 19 S.W.3d 130 [Mo. 2000]).

NEW JERSEY: A state statute prohibiting licensing of a check cashing office that is located within 2500 feet of an existing office was rationally related to the health and stability of the industry and to maintaining the statutory fee cap, which itself was a legitimate consumer protection measure, and thus did not violate substantive due process rights of the applicant who sought a license for an office that did not comply with distance restriction (see *Roman Check Cashing, Inc. v. N.J. Dep't of Banking & Ins.*, 777 A.2d 1 [N.J. 2001]).

NEW YORK: The New York City School Construction Authority's proposed condemnation of undeveloped property owned by the city for use as a public school did not violate the federal due process rights of the city's lessee, which had leased the property for urban development purposes, since the lease expressly provided for the exercise of the eminent domain power against the premises and also enabled the city to avoid further liability upon condemnation

(see Westchester Creek Corp. v. N.Y. City Sch. Const. Auth., 730 N.Y.S.2d 95 [N.Y. App. Div. 2001]).

OHIO: The state in 2005 placed a moratorium on the use of eminent domain until December 31, 2006 so that the state could study issues pertaining to eminent domain.

TEXAS: The state approved legislation that prohibits use of eminent domain in certain circumstances, including use of eminent domain to confer a benefit on a private party or for economic development.

## Additional Resources

*American Jurisprudence.* 2d Series. Thomson/West, 2005.

*Criminal Procedure.* 4th Edition. Wayne R. LaFave, Jerold H. Israel, and Nancy J.King, Thomson/West, 2004.

*Oxford Companion to the Supreme Court.* 2d Edition. Hall, Kermit L., James W. Ely, Jr., and Joel B. Grossman eds., Oxford University Press, 2005.

*West's Encyclopedia of American Law.* 2d Edition. Thomson/Gale, 2004.

## Organizations

### *American Civil Liberties Union*
1400 20th Street, NW, Suite 119
Washington, DC 20036 USA
Phone: (202) 457-0800
URL: http://www.aclu.org

### *Association for Federal Defense Attorneys*
8530 Wilshire Blvd., Suite 404
Beverly Hills, CA 90211 USA
Phone: (714) 836-6031
URL: http://www.afda.org

### *Center for Human Rights and Constitutional Law*
256 S. Occidental Blvd.
Los Angeles, CA 90057 USA
Phone: (213) 388-8693
Fax: (213) 386-9484
URL: http://www.centerforhumanrights.org

### *National District Attorneys Association*
99 Canal Center Plaza
Alexandria, VA 22314 USA
Phone: (703) 549-9222
Fax: (703) 836-3195
URL: http://www.ndaa.org

# CRIMINAL LAW

## INSANITY DEFENSE

*Sections within this essay:*

## Background

Although the insanity defense is probably the most controversial of all criminal defense strategies, it is also, somewhat ironically, one of the least used. On many occasions when it has been used, particularly in the much-publicized 1984 acquittal of John W. Hinckley, Jr. for the attempted assassination of President Ronald Reagan, the insanity defense has tended to provoke public debate.

The insanity defense asserts that a criminal defendant should not be found guilty due to the **defendant's** insanity. The theory behind the defense is that a person who is insane lacks the intent required to perform a criminal act because the person either does not know that the act is wrong or cannot control his or her actions even when the person understands that the act is wrong. This theory is controversial because insanity itself is difficult to define, and the circumstances in which insanity can be used to excuse criminal responsibility are difficult to characterize.

The insanity defense has existed since the twelfth century, but initially it was not considered an argument for the defendant to be found not guilty. Instead, it was a way for a defendant to receive a **pardon** or a way to mitigate a sentence. The idea that insanity could bar the conviction of a defendant arose in the early nineteenth century in *The Medical Jurisprudence of Insanity* by an influential scholar named Isaac Ray, as well as in the seminal decision in England called the M'Naghten case.

## The M'Naghten Rule

In 1843, Daniel M'Naghten, an Englishmen who was apparently a paranoid schizophrenic under the delusion that he was being persecuted, shot and killed Edward Drummond, Secretary to British Prime minister Sir Robert Peel. M'Naghten believed that Drummond was Peel. To the surprise of the nation, M'Naghten was found not guilty on the grounds that he was insane at the time of his act. The subsequent public outrage convinced the English House of Lords to establish standards for the defense of insanity, the result subsequently referred to as the M'Naghten Rule.

The M'Naghten Rule provides as follows: "Every man is to be presumed to be sane, and... that to establish a defense on the ground of insanity, it must be clearly proved that, at the time of the committing of the act, the party accused was laboring under such a defect of reason, from disease of mind, and not to know the nature and quality of the act he was doing; or if he did know it, that he did not know he was doing what was wrong."

The test to determine if a defendant can distinguish right from wrong is based on the idea that the defendant must know the difference in order to be convicted of a crime. Determining a defendant's ability to do so may seem straightforward enough, but dilemmas often arise in cases in which the M'Naghten standard is used. For instance, some issues focus on whether a defendant knew that his or her criminal acts were wrong or whether he or she knew that laws exist that prohibit these acts.

Criticism of the M'Naghten test often focuses on the test's concentration on a defendant's cognitive abilities. Questions also crop up about how to treat defendants who know their acts are against the law but who cannot control their impulses to commit them. Similarly, the courts need to determine how to evaluate and assign responsibility for emotional factors and compulsion. Additionally, because of the rule's inflexible cognitive standard, it tends to be difficult for defendants to be found not guilty by reason of insanity. Despite these complications, M'Naghten has survived and is currently the rule in a majority of states with regard to the insanity defense (sometimes combined with the Irresistible Impulse Test, discussed below).

## The Irresistible Impulse Test

In response to criticisms of the M'Naghten Rule, some legal commentators began to suggest expanding the definition of insanity to include more than a cognitive element. Such a test would encompass not only whether defendants know right from wrong but also whether they could control their impulses to commit wrong-doing. The Irresistible Impulse Test was first adopted by the Alabama Supreme Court in the 1887 case of *Parsons v. State*. The Alabama court

stated that even though the defendant could tell right from wrong, he was subject to "the duress of such mental disease [that] he had... lost the power to choose between right and wrong" and that "his free agency was at the time destroyed," and thus, "the alleged crime was so connected with such mental disease, in the relation of cause and effect, as to have been the product of it solely." In so finding, the court assigned responsibility for the crime to the mental illness despite the defendant's ability to distinguish right from wrong.

The Irresistible Impulse Test gained acceptance in various states as an appendage to the M'Naghten Rule, under which right versus wrong was still considered a vital part of any definition of insanity. In some cases, the Irresistible Impulse Test was considered to be a variation on M'Naghten; in others, it was considered to be a separate test. Though the Irresistible Impulse Test was considered to be an important corrective on M'Naghten's cognitive bias, it still came under some criticism of its own. For example, it seemed to make the definition of insanity too broad, failing to take into account the impossibility of determining which acts were uncontrollable rather than merely uncontrolled, and also making it easier to fake insanity. The test was also criticized for being too narrow; like M'Naghten, the test seemed to exclude all but those totally unable to control their actions. Nevertheless, several states currently use this test along with the M'Naghten Rule to determine insanity, and the American Law Institute in its Model Penal Code definition of insanity adopted a modified version of it.

## The Durham Rule

The Durham Rule, a version of which was originally adopted in New Hampshire in 1871, was embraced by the Circuit Court of Appeals for the District of Columbia in the 1954 case of *Durham v. United States*. The Durham Rule, sometimes referred to as the "product test," provides that the defendant is not "criminally responsible if his unlawful act is the product of a mental disease or defect."

The Durham Rule was originally seen as a way of simplifying the M'Naghten Rule and the Irresistible Impulse Test by making insanity and its relation to the crime a matter of objective diagnosis. Nevertheless, such a diagnosis proved to be more difficult to prove in practice than in theory. The test was criticized because the Circuit Court has provided no real definitions of "product," "mental disease," or "defect." Because the Durham Rule proved very difficult to apply, the Circuit Court abandoned it in 1972. Currently, only the state of New Hampshire still uses the Durham Rule as a way to define insanity.

## The American Law Institute's Model Penal Code Test

In response to the criticisms of the various tests for the insanity defense, the American Law Institute (ALI) designed a new test for its Model Penal Code in 1962. Under this test, "a person is not responsible for criminal conduct if at the time of such conduct as a result of mental disease or defect he lacks substantial capacity either to appreciate the criminality of his conduct or to conform his conduct to the requirements of the law."

The Model Penal Code test is much broader than the M'Naghten Rule and the Irresistible Impulse Test. It asks whether defendants have a substantial incapacity to appreciate the criminality of their conduct or to conform their conduct to the law rather than the absolute knowledge required by M'Naghten and the absolute inability to control conduct required by the Irresistible Impulse Test.

The ALI test also requires that the mental disease or defect be a mental diagnosis. In this way, it manages to incorporate elements of all three of its predecessors: the knowledge of right and wrong required by M'Naghten, the prerequisite of lack of control in the Irresistible Impulse Test, and the diagnosis of mental disease and defect required by Durham.

Such a broad based rule received wide acceptance, and by 1982 all federal courts and a majority of state courts had adopted the ALI test. While some states have since dropped the ALI test, and it no longer applies at the federal level, 18 states still use the ALI test in their definitions of insanity.

## The Hinckley Trial

In 1982, John W. Hinckley, who had attempted in 1981 to assassinate President Ronald Reagan, was acquitted of the crime by a District of Columbia court by reason of insanity. The enormous outrage after Hinckley's acquittal led three states to drop the insanity defense entirely (Montana, Utah, and Idaho, joined by a fourth, Kansas, in 1995). Other states reformed their insanity defense statutes, by adopting

the M'Naghten standard over the Model Penal code standard, by shifting the burden of proof from the state to the defense, by changing their commitment and release procedures, or by adopting a "Guilty but Mentally Ill" defense. In addition, the federal courts shifted from the ALI standard to a new law eliminating the Irresistible Impulse Test for insanity defenses in federal crimes.

## Current Application of the Insanity Defense

### Burden of Proof

The question of who has the burden of proof with an insanity defense has been a source of controversy. Before the Hinckley verdict, a majority of states had the burden of proof rest with the state; that is, the prosecutor had to prove that the defendant was not insane. After the Hinckley verdict, the vast majority of states required the defense to prove that the defendant was indeed insane. In states where the burden is on the defense to prove insanity, the defense is required to show either by clear and convincing evidence or by a preponderance of the evidence that the defendant is insane. In states where the burden is still on prosecutors to prove sanity, they are required to prove it **beyond a reasonable doubt**.

### Commitment and Release Procedures

Contrary to uninformed opinion, defendants found not guilty by reason of insanity are not simply released from custody. They are generally committed to mental hospitals where they can be confined for longer than their prison terms would have been. In the case of *Jones v. United States*, the Supreme Court in 1983 backed this proposition, ruling that the sentence that criminal defendants would have received had they been convicted should have no bearing on how long they could be committed to a mental hospital.

After Hinckley, many states changed their commitment policies to ensure that a defendant found not guilty by reason of insanity would be required to stay in a mental hospital for a certain period of time for evaluation following acquittal. Previously, no time was specified. Also, several states changed the burden of proof for release from the state to defendants.

### Distinction Between the Insanity Defense and Competency to Stand Trial

All jurisdictions require that criminal defendants must be competent to stand trial, meaning that defendants understand the nature of the proceedings against them and are able to assist counsel in their defense. A person who is found to be mentally incompetent to stand trial is usually hospitalized for treatment until such time that the person is competent to stand trial. Competency does not address the guilt or innocence of a party, and so competency to stand trial should not be confused with the insanity defense.

### The Federal Insanity Defense Reform Act

The federal Insanity Defense Reform Act of 1984, codified at 18 U.S.C. § 17, provides: "It is an affirmative defense to a prosecution under any Federal statute that, at the time of the commission of the acts constituting the offense, the defendant, as a result of a severe mental disease or defect, was unable to appreciate the nature and quality of the wrongfulness of his acts. Mental disease or defect does not otherwise constitute a defense." This act, a response to the Hinckley verdict, eliminated the Irresistible Impulse Test from the insanity defense under federal law. The act also provided that "the defendant has the burden of proving the defense of insanity by clear and convincing evidence." Previously under federal law, the government had the burden of proving sanity.

### Guilty but Mentally Ill

Finally, the Hinckley verdict accelerated the adoption of "guilty but mentally ill" verdicts by states. The "guilty but mentally ill" verdict allows mentally ill defendants to be found criminally liable and requires them to receive psychiatric treatment while incarcerated, or, alternatively, to be placed in a mental hospital and then, when they are well enough, to be moved to a prison to serve their sentences. Laws allowing pleas and verdicts of guilty but mentally ill were first adopted in Michigan in 1975, and concurrent with or subsequent to the Hinckley trial were adopted by 12 more states.

## Status of the Insanity Defense in Criminal Law

Commentators have noted that the insanity defense is risky for criminal defendants because it virtually eliminates any possibility that prosecutors will agree to a plea bargain. Studies, including an eight-state investigation by the National Institute of Mental Health, have shown that the insanity defense is raised in less than one percent of all felony cases. This defense is successful in only a fraction of those cases.

Nevertheless, when the insanity defense is raised, it continues to spur controversy. For instance, in 2001, Andrea Yates of Texas, who allegedly suffered from a mental illness, drown her five children in less than an hour. At her trial for capital murder, Yates' attorneys pleaded the insanity defense, arguing that she suffered post-partum depression. A jury rejected this argument and found her guilty. She received a life sentence for the murders.

The public showed great interest in the Yates trial. Some members of the public, especially but not limited to women's groups, sympathized with Yates due to her battle with post-partum depression. At her trial, four out of five psychiatrists and one psychologist testified that Yates did not know right from wrong. However, the single mental health expert called by the prosecution testified that Yates indeed knew right from wrong, and the jury eventually rejected her insanity defense. Facts later revealed that the state's expert had presented false testimony regarding Yates, and a Texas appellate court in 2005 reversed her conviction and ordered a new trial. *Yates v. State*, 171 S.W.3d 215 (Tex. App. 2005).

The Yates case demonstrates that in some instances the insanity defense can garner some support. Nevertheless, such a defense is still difficult to prove, and states have not made significant efforts to revise their versions of the insanity defense in recent years.

## The Insanity Defense Among the States

Four states, including Kansas, Montana, Idaho, Utah, do not allow the insanity defense. In other states, the standards for proving this defense vary widely. The following provides the status of the insanity defense in each jurisdiction.

ALABAMA: The state uses the M'Naghten Rule. The burden of proof is on the defendant.

ALASKA: The state uses a modified version of the M'Naghten Rule. The burden of proof is on the defendant. A guilty but mentally ill verdict is allowed.

ARIZONA: The state uses a modified version of the M'Naghten Rule. The burden of proof is on the defendant. A guilty but insane verdict is allowed.

ARKANSAS: The state uses a modified version of the Model Penal Code rule. The burden of proof is on the defendant.

CALIFORNIA: The state uses the M'Naghten Rule. The burden of proof is on the defendant.

COLORADO: The state uses a modified version of the M'Naghten Rule with the Irresistible Impulse Test. The burden of proof is on the state.

CONNECTICUT: The state uses a modified version of the Model Penal Code rule. The burden of proof is on the defendant.

DELAWARE: The state uses a modified version of the Model Penal Code rule. The burden of proof is on the defendant.

DISTRICT OF COLUMBIA: The state uses the Model Penal Code rule. The burden of proof is on the defendant.

FLORIDA: The state uses the M'Naghten Rule. The burden of proof is on the state.

GEORGIA: The state uses a modified version of the M'Naghten Rule. The burden of proof is on the defendant. A guilty but mentally ill verdict is allowed.

HAWAII: The state uses the Model Penal Code rule. The burden of proof is on the defendant.

IDAHO: The state has abolished the insanity defense. The state allows a guilty but insane verdict.

ILLINOIS: The state uses a modified version of the Model Penal Code rule. The burden of proof is on the defendant.

INDIANA: The state uses a modified version of the Model Penal Code rule. The burden of proof is on the defendant.

IOWA: The state uses the M'Naghten Rule. The burden of proof is on the defendant.

KANSAS: The state has abolished the insanity defense.

KENTUCKY: The state uses the Model Penal Code rule. The burden of proof is on the defendant.

LOUISIANA: The state uses the M'Naghten Rule. The burden of proof is on the defendant.

MAINE: The state uses a modified version of the Model Penal Code rule. The burden of proof is on the defendant.

MARYLAND: The state uses the Model Penal Code rule. The burden of proof is on the defendant.

MASSACHUSETTS: The state uses the Model Penal Code rule. The burden of proof is on the state.

MICHIGAN: The state uses the Model Penal Code rule. The burden of proof is on the state.

MINNESOTA: The state uses the M'Naghten Rule. The burden of proof is on the defendant.

MISSISSIPPI: The state uses the M'Naghten Rule. The burden of proof is on the state. An acquitted by reason of insanity verdict is allowed.

MISSOURI: The state uses a modified version of the M'Naghten Rule. The burden of proof is on the defendant.

MONTANA: The state has abolished the insanity defense, although a guilty but insane verdict is allowed.

NEBRASKA: The state uses the M'Naghten Rule. The burden of proof is on the defendant.

NEVADA: The state uses the M'Naghten Rule. The burden of proof is on the defendant.

NEW HAMPSHIRE: The state uses the Durham standard. The burden of proof is on the defendant.

NEW JERSEY: The state uses the M'Naghten Rule. The burden of proof is on the state.

NEW MEXICO: The state uses the M'Naghten Rule with the Irresistible Impulse Test. The burden of proof is on the state.

NEW YORK: The state uses the Model Penal Code rule. The burden of proof is on the defendant.

NORTH CAROLINA: The state uses the M'Naghten Rule. The burden of proof is on the defendant.

NORTH DAKOTA: The state uses the Model Penal Code rule. The burden of proof is on the state.

OHIO: The state uses the M'Naghten Rule. The burden of proof is on the defendant.

OKLAHOMA: The state uses the M'Naghten Rule. The burden of proof is on the state.

OREGON: The state uses the Model Penal Code rule. The burden of proof is on the defendant.

PENNSYLVANIA: The state uses the M'Naghten Rule. The burden of proof is on the defendant.

RHODE ISLAND: The state uses the Model Penal Code rule. The burden of proof is on the defendant.

SOUTH CAROLINA: The state uses the M'Naghten Rule. The burden of proof is on the defendant.

SOUTH DAKOTA: The state uses the M'Naghten Rule. The burden of proof is on the defendant.

TENNESSEE: The state uses the Model Penal Code rule. The burden of proof is on the state.

TEXAS: The state uses the M'Naghten Rule with the Irresistible Impulse Test. The burden of proof is on the defendant.

UTAH: The state has abolished the insanity defense, but guilty but mentally ill verdicts are allowed.

VERMONT: The state uses the Model Penal Code rule. The burden of proof is on the defendant.

VIRGINIA: The state uses the M'Naghten Rule with the Irresistible Impulse Test. The burden of proof is on the defendant.

WASHINGTON: The state uses the M'Naghten Rule. The burden of proof is on the defendant.

WEST VIRGINIA: The state uses the Model Penal Code rule. The burden of proof is on the state.

WISCONSIN: The state uses the Model Penal Code rule. The burden of proof is on the defendant.

WYOMING: The state uses the Model Penal Code rule. The burden of proof is on the defendant.

## Additional Resources

*American Jurisprudence.* 2d Edition. Thomson/West 2005.

*Mental Health and Disability Law in a Nutshell.* Donald H.J. Hermann, West Group, 1997.

*Toward a New Test for the Insanity Defense: Incorporating the Discoveries of Neuroscience into Moral and Legal Theories.* Reider, Laura, UCLA Law Review, Oct. 1998.

## Organizations

### *American Bar Association Criminal Justice Section*

740 15th Street, NW, 10th Floor
Washington, DC 20005-1009 USA
Phone: (202) 662-1500
Fax: (202) 662-1501
URL: http://www.abanet.org/crimjust/contact.html

### *American Psychological Association (APA)*

750 First Street, NE
Washington, DC 20002-4242 USA
Phone: (202) 336-5510
URL: http://www.apa.org/

### *Association of Federal Defense Attorneys*

8530 Wilshire Blvd., Suite 404
Beverly Hills, CA 90211 USA
Phone: (310) 397-1001
URL: http://www.afda.org

# CRIMINAL LAW

## JUVENILES

*Sections within this essay:*

- Background
- Development of the Juvenile Justice System
- Juvenile Case History
- Juveniles and Status Offenses
- Examples of Status Offenses
    - Curfew
    - Truancy
- Juvenile Court Procedure
- Juvenile Waiver
    - Judicial Waiver Offenses
    - Statutory Exclusion
    - Concurrent Jurisdiction
- Juveniles and the Death Penalty
- Additional Resources

## Background

In the eyes of the law, a juvenile or a minor, is any person under the legal adult age. This age varies from state to state, but in most states, the District of Columbia, and in all Federal Districts, any person age 18 or younger is considered a juvenile. In several states, such as New York, Connecticut, and North Carolina, a juvenile is age 16 or less, and in Georgia, Illinois, Louisiana, Massachusetts, Michigan, Missouri, New Hampshire, South Carolina, Texas and Wisconsin, a juvenile is age 17 or less. Wyoming is the only state that has established the age of juveniles to be 19 or younger (Whitehead & Lab, 1999).

As well as having upper age limits, juvenile jurisdictions also have lower age limits. Most states speci-

fy that prior to age six or seven, juveniles lack *mens rea,* or criminal intent. At this young age, juveniles also are thought to lack the ability to tell right from wrong, or *dolci incapax.* Usually, the age of the offender refers to the age of the offender at the time the offense was committed, but in some states, age refers to the offender's age at the time of apprehension. This arrangement allows for the sometimes lengthy periods it takes to clear a case.

One's status as a juvenile or as an adult is pertinent for the court's determination of the **jurisdiction** under which an offender falls—the adult or the juvenile court system. If it is decided that a juvenile will be tried in a juvenile court, most states allow the juvenile to remain under that jurisdiction until the defendant's 21st birthday.

Relying on age as a sole determinant for adulthood has been criticized by many criminologists and policy makers since individuals develop at different rates. Some youth are far more mature at 18 years of age than some adults are. Because of this discrepancy, juvenile court judges have been given broad discretion to waive juveniles to adult court for trial and sentencing (see later section). In rare situations, the courts also have the power to **emancipate** a juvenile in a civil proceeding so that he or she becomes an adult under the law and is granted certain adult privileges. For example, if a 17-year-old loses both parents and has no other living relatives, he or she could be emancipated in order to pursue **custody** of his or her younger siblings.

## Development of the Juvenile Justice System

The legal concept of juvenile status, like the concept of childhood itself, is relatively new. The juvenile court system was established in the United States about two hundred years ago, with the first court appearing in Illinois in 1899. Prior to that time, children and youth were seen as miniature adults and were tried and punished as adults.

During the progressive era, which occurred between 1880 and 1920, social conditions in the United States were characterized by large waves of **immigration** and a dramatic increase in urbanization. As a direct result, hundreds of indigent children wandered the streets, and many became involved in criminal activity. Initially, children who were convicted of crimes were housed with adult criminals. Social activists, law makers, and other officials soon realized that children institutionalized with adults were learning adult criminal behaviors and were exiting those institutions ready for life careers in criminality. Because of this negative influence, separate juvenile court systems and accompanying correctional institutions were developed.

Early juvenile institutions in the United States were based on the English Bridewell institution which emphasized the teaching of life and trade skills. The idea behind teaching skills was that criminality was a result of the social environment and often was a survival mechanism. If youth were taught other skills, they were more likely to make meaningful contributions to society upon their release.

Three other types of juvenile institutions began to appear in the United States during the progressive era: houses of refuge, new reformatories, and separate institutions for juvenile females. Houses of refuge focused on the reeducation of youth and used indeterminate sentencing, religious training, and apprenticeships in various trades. The houses were organized using a military model to promote order and discipline, but the houses were often overcrowded and youth were overworked.

New reformatories, established in the mid to late 1800s, were cottages and foster homes that were often situated on farms. Family-type organization was prevalent, and hard physical labor was stressed. New reformatories suffered from the same types of problems that houses of refuge did. Separate juvenile institutions for girls appeared in the mid 1880s, and these focused on teaching domestic and child-rearing skills to girls.

The first juvenile courts operated under the philosophy of *parens patriae* first articulated in *Prince v. Massachusetts* (1944). This philosophy meant the state could act "as a parent," and gave juvenile courts the power to intervene whenever court officials felt intervention was in the best interests of the child. Any offense committed was secondary to the offender. While *parens patriae* was designed to handle youth committing criminal acts, the discretion of this philosophy became increasingly more broad and was constantly debated in court. A number of pivotal cases ensued which helped the juvenile justice system evolve.

## Juvenile Case History

In 1838, a man by the name of Crouse took the state to court over the **incarceration** of his daughter, Mary Ann. Mary Ann Crouse was being held at a house of refuge against her father's wishes but at the **bequest** of her mother, who felt Mary Ann had become unruly and unmanageable. Mary Ann had not committed any crime. The courts held in *Ex parte Crouse* that the house of refuge was a reformatory rather than a jail, and Mary Ann's behavior could be reformed as long as she remained there. In essence, the court ruled that the judicial system had the right to assist families with troubled youth.

Some thirty years later in *People v. Turner* (1870), Turner protested being held in a house of refuge against the wishes of both his parents. He was incarcerated because the state felt he was in danger of becoming a criminal. His parents actually won this case, and it was decided that the state should only intervene in troubled families given extreme circumstances. However, the verdict was largely ignored by the courts.

In 1905, a juvenile was given a seven-year sentence for a minor crime that would have received a far lesser sentence in an adult court. This dilemma was argued in *Commonwealth v. Fisher*. In this case, the court decided that the long sentence was necessary and in the best interests of the child, thus broadening juvenile court discretion under the *parens patriae* philosophy. It was not until *Kent v. the United States* in 1966, that the courts recognized the discretionary powers of *parens patriae* had gone too far and were perhaps encroaching on the constitutional rights of juveniles. In this case, 16-year-old Morris Kent had been waived to adult court without a **hearing**. Kent's attorney challenged the decision, citing a sixth Amendment violation. This case scrutinized the entire juvenile justice process, and as a result, a more formal set of procedures was established.

In 1967, another juvenile case was argued in the Supreme Court that also addressed the constitutional rights of juveniles. *In re Gault* addressed the separation of adult and juvenile courts, and Fifth and Sixth Amendment privileges for juveniles. Gerald Gault, a 15-year-old juvenile, had been sentenced to a maximum of six years in a state training school for making obscene phone calls to a woman. The case was originally heard in a very informal juvenile court proceeding. The **accused** was not represented by an attorney, and there was no transcript of the hearing. The Supreme Court ruled that the juvenile courts must protect the constitutional rights of juveniles, and rules and regulations must be imposed in the juvenile justice system:

Under our Constitution, the condition of being a boy does not constitute a kangaroo court. The traditional ideas of the juvenile court procedure, indeed, contemplated that time would be available and care would be used to establish precisely what the juvenile did and why he did it. **In re** Gault, 387 U.S. 1 (1967).

The protection of juveniles' rights upheld by *In re Gault* were further reinforced by *In re Winship* (1970), in which the Supreme Court extended the reasonable standard of doubt for guilt to juveniles. However, the following year, the right to trial by a jury of peers for juveniles was denied by the Supreme Court in *McKeiver v. Pennsylvania.* Several reasons were presented for the denial, including the notion that the juvenile system was not meant to be an adversarial one and was instead designed to be less formal and, therefore, more protective of juveniles' privacy. The Supreme Court justices also felt that allowing juvenile trials by jury would be an indication that the juvenile courts had lost their usefulness.

## Juveniles and Status Offenses

With the division of courts into adult and juvenile jurisdictions, there were a number of activities that were deemed offenses for juveniles. As a group, these are called status offenses and are such simply because of the age of the offender. Truancy, possession and consumption of alcohol, incorrigibility, curfew violations, and purchase of cigarettes are examples of status offenses. The theory behind status offenses stems from *parens patriae* in that status offenses are harmful to minors, and the courts need to protect minors from such activities.

During the late 1960s and 1970s, there was a move toward deinstitutionalizing status offenses. The movement was formalized by the 1974 Federal Juvenile Delinquency Act. Deinstitutionalization meant that juveniles who committed status offenses were diverted from the juvenile justice system to agencies outside the juvenile court's jurisdiction. The county or district attorney was given the authority to divert an offender, and this decision was made before a petition was filed (see below section on court procedure). Diversion was implemented because many legislators felt that status offenses were minor in terms of criminal nature, and juveniles were better off having their families or some other agency deal with the matter than being formally processed by the justice system. Formal processing of status offenses was thought to lead to labeling and further delinquent acts, thus negating the whole purpose of rehabilitation. Diversion is till practiced today.

One **status offense**, incorrigibility, received a lot of attention during the 1970s. Juveniles who habitually do not obey their parents are incorrigible. With *parens patriae* still operating, many incarcerated juveniles were serving time for incorrigibility. Critics argued that almost all juveniles disobey their parents at some point, and such behavior may not always **warrant** court action. It seemed that incarceration exposed juveniles to much more severe criminality and sometimes even sexual and physical abuse. In short, juveniles came out of the system less socialized than when they entered it.

After diversion, juveniles who were adjudicated for status offenses were often classified as children in need of supervision (CHINS), persons in need of supervision (PINS), and minors in need of supervision (MINS). Today, status offenses are still illegal in all states, and many juveniles are still confined for such offenses. The Department of Justice estimated that in 1996, juvenile courts around the United States formally disposed of some 162,000 status offenses, 44,800 of which were liquor law violations (OJJDP, 2000).

## Examples of Status Offenses

### *Curfew*

Many cities, such as New Orleans, Atlanta, and Washington, D.C., require individuals under the age of 17 to be off the streets by 11 p.m. Teenagers found violating this curfew are held at a police-designated truancy center until a parent or **guardian** claims them. Parents who are determined to be aiding and abetting curfew violators are subject to fines and community service. Curfew laws have been challenged on the grounds that they violate the First Amendment by prohibiting a juvenile's right to free association. In *Qutb v. Strauss* (1993), the U. S. Court of Appeals held that curfew laws were constitutional because they are designed to protect the community.

### *Truancy*

Most local laws prohibit school-age children from taking unexcused school absences. If caught being truant, juveniles may be processed in juvenile court or processed informally. In some states, such as Virginia and Arizona, parents can also be held accountable for their children's truancy and may be fined or jailed.

## Juvenile Court Procedure

The procedure and organization of the juvenile court system is different from the adult system. After committing an offense, juveniles are detained rather than arrested. Next, a petition is drawn up which outlines the jurisdiction authority of the juvenile court over the offense and detained individuals, gives notice for the reason for the court appearance, serves as notice to the minor's family, and also is the official charging document. Once in court, the juvenile case is adjudicated, and a **disposition** is handed down. Records from juvenile courts are sealed documents, unlike adult records which are accessible by anyone under the **Freedom of Information Act**. Like diversion, this measure is designed to protect the juvenile so that one mistake does not follow the juvenile for life. Juvenile records may also be expunged upon the juvenile's eighteenth birthday provided the juvenile has met certain conditions, such as good behavior. Juvenile court procedure is also far less formal than adult court procedure.

The disposition of a juvenile case is based on the least detrimental alternative, so the legacy of *parens patriae* is still evident. However, one major controversy in juvenile dispositions is the use of indeterminate sentencing, which allows a judge to set a maximum sentence. In such cases, juveniles are monitored during their sentences and are released only when the judge is satisfied that they have been rehabilitated or when the maximum time has been served. Critics argue that this arrangement allows the judge too much discretion and is, therefore, not the least detrimental punishment.

Juvenile courts are typically organized in one of three ways: 1) as a separate entity; 2) as part of a lower court, such as a city court or district court; or 3) as part of a higher court, such as a circuit court or a superior court. The organization model varies state by state, and some states, for example, Alabama, allow each county and city jurisdiction to decide which is the best method of organization. Where the juvenile court sits has profound implications for the juvenile process.

## Juvenile Waiver

One of the more hotly debated subjects with regard to juveniles has to do with the option to **waiver** to adult court. Currently, there are three mechanisms by which a juvenile's case may be waived to an adult court.

### *Judicial Waiver Offenses*

A judicial waiver occurs when a juvenile court judge transfers a case from juvenile to adult court in order to deny the juvenile the protections that juvenile jurisdictions provide. All states except Nebraska, New York, and New Mexico, currently provide for judicial waiver and have set a variety of lower age limits (Snyder, Sickmund & Poe-Yamagata, 2000). In most states, the youngest offender who can be waived to adult court is a 17 or 18-year-old, although in some states, this age is as low as 13 or 14. Usually, the offense allegedly committed must be particularly egregious in order for the case to be waived judicially, or there must be a long history of offenses.

### *Statutory Exclusion*

By 1997, 28 states had **statutory** exclusions, which are provisions in the law to exclude some offenses, such as first-degree murder, from juvenile court jurisdiction. This number is expected to increase.

### *Concurrent Jurisdiction*

Some states also have a legal provision which allows the **prosecutor** to file a juvenile case in both juvenile and adult court because the offense and the age of the accused meet certain criteria. Prosecutorial transfer does not have to meet the due process requirement stipulated by *Kent v. U.S.* Approximately 15 states currently have this provision, although this number is expected to increase in the next few years.

The most important case guiding juvenile waiver is *Breed v. Jones* (1975). This case designates that a juvenile cannot be adjudicated in a juvenile court then be waived and tried in an adult court. To do so is to try the youth twice for the same crime (**double jeopardy**), which violates the Fifth Amendment. However, in reality, this case did not have much impact on the juvenile system since juveniles are now subject to a waiver hearing which appears to be similar to a trial except in outcome.

## Juveniles and the Death Penalty

In a sensitive and controversial case that had repercussions well beyond the bench, a very divided (5-4) U.S. Supreme Court ruled in 2005 that executing a convicted murderer whose capital crime was committed at the age of 17 constituted "cruel and unusual punishment" under the Eighth Amendment. The decision in *Roper v. Simmons*, overruled an earlier Court decision (*Stanford v. Kentucky*). Further, as applicable to the states under the Fourteenth Amendment, the decision rendered several state laws unconstitutional, causing those states (12 in all) to reverse sentences for 72 prisoners on death row who were under 18 at the time of committing capital crimes. As of 2005, at least 20 of 38 states with the death penalty had permitted its application to offenders less than 18 years old.

Prior to this decision, there had been two key court cases that had laid the foundation for juveniles to receive the death penalty.

In *Thompson v. Oklahoma* (1988), the Supreme Court overturned a death sentence for a juvenile who was 15 years old at the time he was involved in a murder. The opinion cited the failure of the state of Oklahoma to stipulate a minimum age for **execution**. This case has also set the minimum age of 16 at which a juvenile can be executed.

In *Stanford v. Kentucky* (1989), the Supreme Court ruled that it was constitutional for a state to execute a juvenile who was between the ages of 16 and 18 at the time of the offense but unconstitutional if the juvenile was under 16.

Although there have been a number of challenges to the minimum age of 16 for juvenile execution set by *Thompson v. Oklahoma,* such as *State v. Stone* (LA, 1988), *Flowers v. State,* (AL, 1991) and *Allen v. State* (FL, 1994), these challenges have only gone as far as the court of appeals.

More than 360 juveniles have been executed over the years, beginning with Thomas Graunger, who was executed in 1642 in Massachusetts. After 1990, the only known countries that execute juveniles are Iran, Pakistan, Yemen, Saudi Arabia, and the United States (www.deathpenaltyinfo.org).

## Additional Resources

*Child Delinquents: Developments, Intervention, and Service Needs.* Ralph Loeber and David P. Farrington, Sage Publications, 2000.

*Juvenile Delinquency: Causes and Controls.* Robert Agnew, Roxbury Publishing, 2001.

*Juvenile Justice: An Introduction (Third Edition).* John T. Whitehead and Steven P. Lab, Anderson Publishing, 1999.

*Juvenile Transfers to Criminal Court in the 1990s: Lessons Learned from Four States.* Howard N. Snyder, Melissa Sickmund, Eileen Poe-Yamagata, Office of Juvenile Justice and Delinquency Prevention, 2000.

## Organizations

### *Juvenile Justice Clearinghouse*
P.O. Box 6000
Rockville, MD 20849-6000 USA
Phone: (800) 638-8769
Fax: (301) 519-5600
E-Mail: tellncjrs@ncjrs.org

### *The American Bar Association Juvenile Justice Center*
740 15th Street NW
Washington, DC 20005 USA
Phone: (202) 662-1506
Fax: (202) 662-1506
URL: http://www.abanet.org/crimjust/juvjust/home.htm

### *The Death Penalty Information Center*
1320 18th Street NW
Washington, DC 20036 USA
Phone: (202) 293-6970
Fax: (202) 822-4787
URL: http://www.deathpenaltyinfo.org

### *The National Center for Juvenile Justice*
710 Fifth Avenue, Suite 3000
Pittsburgh, PA 15219 USA
Phone: (412) 227-6950
Fax: (412) 227-6955
URL: http://brendan.ncjfcj.unr.edu/homepage/ncjj/ncjj2/index.html

**The Office of Juvenile Justice and Delinquency Prevention, U.S. Department of Justice**
Washington, DC USA
URL: http://www.ojjdp.ncjrs.org

# CRIMINAL LAW

## PLEA BARGAINING

*Sections within this essay:*

- Background
- Pros and Cons
- U. S. Supreme Court Cases
- The Alford Plea
- Plea Bargaining in Federal Courts
- Prohibitions and Restrictions
- State Provisions
- Additional Resources

## Background

There is no perfect or simple definition of **plea bargaining**. Black's Law Dictionary defines it as follows:

"[t]he process whereby the **accused** and the **prosecutor** in a criminal case work out a mutually satisfactory **disposition** of the case subject to court approval. It usually involves the defendant's pleading guilty to a lesser offense or to only one or some of the counts of a multi-count **indictment** in return for a lighter sentence than that possible for the graver charge."

In practice, **plea** bargaining often represents not so much "mutual satisfaction" as perhaps "mutual acknowledgement" of the strengths or weaknesses of both the charges and the defenses, against a backdrop of crowded criminal courts and court case dockets. Plea bargaining usually occurs prior to trial

but, in some jurisdictions, may occur any time before a verdict is rendered. It also is often negotiated after a trial that has resulted in a **hung jury**: the parties may negotiate a plea rather than go through another trial.

Plea bargaining actually involves three areas of negotiation:

- Charge Bargaining: This is a common and widely known form of plea. It involves a negotiation of the specific charges (counts) or crimes that the **defendant** will face at trial. Usually, in return for a plea of "guilty" to a lesser charge, a prosecutor will dismiss the higher or other charge(s) or counts. For example, in return for dismissing charges for first-degree murder, a prosecutor may accept a "guilty" plea for **manslaughter** (subject to court approval).

- Sentence Bargaining: Sentence bargaining involves the agreement to a plea of guilty (for the stated charge rather than a reduced charge) in return for a lighter sentence. It saves the prosecution the necessity of going through trial and proving its case. It provides the defendant with an opportunity for a lighter sentence.

- Fact Bargaining: The least used negotiation involves an admission to certain facts ("stipulating "to the truth and existence of provable facts, thereby eliminating the need for the prosecutor to have to prove them) in return for an agreement not to introduce certain other facts into **evidence**.

The validity of a plea bargain is dependent upon three essential components:

- a knowing **waiver** of rights

- a voluntary waiver

- a factual basis to support the charges to which the defendant is pleading guilty

Plea bargaining generally occurs on the telephone or in the prosecutor's office at the courtroom. Judges are not involved except in very rare circumstances. Plea bargains that are accepted by the judge are then placed "on the record" in **open court**. The defendant must be present.

One important point is a prosecuting attorney has no authority to force a court to accept a plea agreement entered into by the parties. Prosecutors may only "recommend" to the court the acceptance of a plea arrangement. The court will usually take proofs to ensure that the above three components are satisfied and will then generally accept the recommendation of the prosecution.

Moreover, plea bargaining is not as simple as it may first appear. In effectively negotiating a criminal plea arrangement, the attorney must have the technical knowledge of every "element" of a crime or charge, an understanding of the actual or potential evidence that exists or could be developed, a technical knowledge of "lesser included offenses" versus separate counts or crimes, and a reasonable understanding of sentencing guidelines.

## Pros and Cons

Although plea bargaining is often criticized, more than 90 percent of criminal convictions come from negotiated pleas. Thus, less than ten percent of criminal cases go to trial. For judges, the key incentive for accepting a plea bargain is to alleviate the need to schedule and hold a trial on an already overcrowded **docket**. Judges are also aware of prison overcrowding and may be receptive to the "processing out" of offenders who are not likely to do much jail time anyway.

For prosecutors, a lightened caseload is equally attractive. But more importantly, plea bargaining assures a **conviction**, even if it is for a lesser charge or crime. No matter how strong the evidence may be, no case is a foregone conclusion. Prosecutors often wage long and expensive trials but lose, as happened in the infamous O. J. Simpson murder trial. Moreover, prosecutors may use plea bargaining to further their case against a co-defendant. They may accept

a plea bargain arrangement from one defendant in return for damaging **testimony** against another. This way, they are assured of at least one conviction (albeit on a lesser charge) plus enhanced chances of winning a conviction against the second defendant. For the defendants, plea bargaining provides the opportunity for a lighter sentence on a less severe charge. If represented by private **counsel**, defendants save the cost for trial and have fewer or less serious offenses listed on their criminal records.

## U. S. Supreme Court Cases

Article III, Section 2[3] of the U. S. Constitution provides that "The trial of all crimes, except in Cases of **Impeachment**, shall be by Jury." However, it has never been judicially determined that engaging in a plea bargaining process to avoid trial subverts the Constitution. To the contrary, there have been numerous court decisions, at the highest levels, that discuss and rule on plea bargains. The U. S. Supreme Court did not address the constitutionality of plea bargaining until well after it had become an integral part of the criminal justice system.

In *United States v. Jackson*, 390 U.S. 570 (1968), the Court questioned the validity of the plea bargaining process if it burdened a defendant's right to a jury trial. At issue in that case was a **statute** that imposed the death penalty only after a jury trial. Accordingly, to avoid the death penalty, defendants were waiving trials and eagerly pleading guilty to lesser charges. Justice Potter Stewart, writing for the majority, noted that the problem with the statute was not that it coerced guilty pleas but that it needlessly encouraged them.

Two years later, the Court actually defended plea bargaining in *Brady v. United States*, 397 U.S. 742 (1970), pointing out that the process actually benefited both sides of the adversary system. The Court noted that its earlier opinion in Jackson merely required that guilty pleas be intelligent and voluntary. The following year, in *Santobello v. New York*, 404 U.S. 260 (1971), the Court further justified the constitutionality of plea bargaining, referring to it as "an essential component of the administration of justice." The Court added that '[as long as it is] properly administered, [plea bargaining] is to be encouraged."

## The Alford Plea

But the most cited and most familiar Supreme Court case on plea bargaining is North Carolina v. Alford, 400 U.S. 25 (1970). In 1970, North Carolina law provided that a penalty of life **imprisonment** would attach to a plea of guilty for a capital offense, but the death penalty would attach following a jury verdict of guilty (unless the jury recommended life imprisonment). Alford faced the death penalty for first-degree murder. Although he claimed innocence on all charges (in the face of strong evidence to the contrary), Alford pleaded guilty to second-degree murder prior to trial. The prosecutor accepted the plea, and he was sentenced to 30 years' imprisonment. Alford then appealed his case, claiming that his plea was involuntary because it was principally motivated by fear of the death penalty. His conviction was reversed on appeal. However, the U. S. Supreme Court held that a guilty plea which represents a voluntary and intelligent choice when considering the alternatives available to a defendant is not "compelled" within the meaning of the Fifth Amendment just because it was entered to avoid the possibility of the death penalty. (Alford had argued that his guilty plea to a lesser charge violated the Fifth Amendment's prohibition that "'No person . . . shall be compelled in any criminal case to be a witness against himself.") The Supreme Court reversed the court of appeals and reinstated Alford's conviction and sentence.

The term "Alford Plea" has come to apply to any case in which the defendant tenders a guilty plea but denies that he or she has in fact committed the crime. The Alford plea is expressly prohibited in some states and limitedly allowed in others. In federal courts, the plea is conservatively permitted for certain defenses and under certain circumstances only.

## Plea Bargaining in Federal Courts

The Federal Rules of **Criminal Procedure** (F.R.Crim.P), and in specific, Rule 11(e), recognizes and codifies the concept of plea agreements. However, because of United States Sentencing Guideline (USSG) provisions, the leeway permitted is very restrictive. Moreover, many federal offenses carry mandatory sentences, with no room for plea bargaining. Finally, statutes codifying many federal offenses expressly prohibit the application of plea arrangements. (See "Sentencing and Sentencing Guidelines.")

Federal criminal practice is governed by Title 18 of the **U.S. Code**, Part II (Criminal Procedure). Chapter 221 of Part II addresses arraignments, pleas, and trial. The U. S. Attorney's Manual (USAM) contains several provisions addressing plea agreements.

For example, Chapter 9-16.300 (Plea Agreements) states that plea agreements should "honestly reflect the totality and seriousness of the defendant's conduct," and any departure must be consistent with Sentencing Guideline provisions. The Justice Department's official policy is to stipulate only to those facts that accurately represent the defendant's conduct. Plea agreements require the approval of the assistant attorney general if counts are being dismissed, if defendant companies are being promised no further prosecution, or it particular sentences are being recommended (USAM 7-5.611).

## Prohibitions and Restrictions

Aside from legal considerations as to the knowing or voluntary nature of a plea, there are other restrictions or prohibitions on the opportunity to plea bargain. In federal practice, U. S. attorneys may not make plea agreements which prejudice civil or tax liability without the express agreement of all affected divisions or agencies (USAM 9-27.630). Moreover, no attorney for the government may seek out, or threaten to seek, the death penalty solely for the purpose of obtaining a more desirable negotiating position for a plea arrangement (USAM 9-10.100). Attorneys are also instructed not to consent to "Alford pleas" except in the most unusual circumstances and only with the recommendation of assistant attorneys general in the subject matter at issue. In any case where a defendant has tendered a plea of guilty but denies that he or she committed the offense, the attorney for the government should make an offer of proof of all facts known to the government to support the conclusion that the defendant is in fact guilty (USAM 9-16.015). Similarly, U. S. attorneys are instructed to require an explicit stipulation of all facts of a defendant's **fraud** against the United States (tax fraud, Medicare/Medicaid fraud, etc.) when agreeing to plea bargain (USAM 9-16.040).

## State Provisions

Plea bargaining is not a creature of law: it is one of legal practice. Therefore, state statutes do not create the right to plea bargain, nor do they prohibit it, with one exception. In 1975, Alaska's attorney general at the time, Avrum Gross, banned plea bargaining in Alaska. Although the ban remains officially "in the books," charge bargaining has become fairly common in most of Alaska's courts. Nonetheless, Alaska has not suffered the unmanageable caseloads or backlogged trials that were predicted when the ban went into effect.

If plea bargaining appears at all in state statutes, it is generally in the context of being prohibited or restricted for certain matters or types of cases. For example, many states have prohibited plea bargaining in drunk driving cases, sex offender cases, or those involving other crimes that place the public at risk for repeat offenses or general harm. Another common provision, found in a majority of states, is a requirement that a prosecutor must inform a victim or the victim's survivors of any plea bargaining in a case. In many states, victims' views and comments regarding both plea bargaining and sentencing are factored into the ultimate decisions or determinations.

At least one state (Alabama) has expressly ruled that once a plea bargain is accepted, or there is detrimental reliance upon the agreement before the plea is entered, it becomes binding and enforceable under constitutional law (substantive due process).*Ex Parte Hon. Orson Johnson,* (Alabama, 1995).

## Additional Resources

"The Core Concerns of Plea Bargaining Critics." Douglas D. Guidorizzi. Available at http://www.law.emory.edu/ELJ/volumes/spg98/guido.html.

*The Court TV Cradle-to-grave Legal Survival Guide* Little, Brown and Company, 1995.

"Criminal Procedure: an Overview." Available athttp://www.law.cornell.edu/topics/civil_procedure.html

"Federal Rules of Criminal Procedure." Available at http://www.law.cornell.edu/topics/civil_procedure.html

"Plea Bargains: Why and When They're Made." Available at http://www.nolo.com/lawcenter/ency/category.

*United States Attorneys Manual.* (USAM. Office of the U. S. Attorney General, Dept. of Justice. Available at http://www.usdoj.gov/usao/eousa/foia_reading_room/usam/title9/16mcrm.htm

*U. S. Code, Title 18: Crimes and Criminal Procedure, Part II: Procedure, Chapter 221: Arraignment, Pleas and Trial..* U. S. House of Representatives. Available at http://caselaw.lp.findlaw.com/casecode/uscodes/18/parts/ii/chapters/221.

# CRIMINAL LAW

## PROBATION AND PAROLE

*Sections within this essay:*

## Background

The use of **probation** and **parole** is governed in part by competing philosophies, classicalism and positivism. In short, classicalists believe that offenders choose their actions and, therefore, in order to prevent (or deter) future criminal acts, such individuals should be punished. Conversely, positivists believe that individuals are forced into the choice of committing crime through no fault of their own and, therefore, the conditions and/or behaviors that caused the action should be remedied, ultimately resulting in rehabilitation of the offender.

Legislative acts and public sentiment further dictate the application of probation and parole. Therefore, universal and consistent definitions and applications of probation and parole are not available as the methods of punishment and governing philosophies have evolved and moved toward the twenty-first century.

While these factors contribute to a lack of consistency when dealing with probation and parole, the primary obstacle to detailing specific state protocols is that the practice of granting probation and/or parole at the state level is dependent on the discretionary powers of select individuals, such as the **prosecutor**, the judicial authority, and the parole board, to name just a few. Information can be obtained regarding state-level agencies governing probation and parole from the American Probation and Parole Association (www.appa-net.org) or federal level parole practices from the U. S. Parole Commission (www.usdoj.gov/uspc/rules_procedures/2-2.pdf).

## Probation

### Definition

Probation is a court-imposed **sanction** that "releases a convicted offender into the community under a conditional suspended sentence." This practice assumes that most offenders are not dangerous and will respond well to treatment. In fact, the average **probationer** is a first time and/or non-violent offender who, it is believed, will be best served by remaining in the community while serving out the sentence.

### History

Historically, probation does not involve **incarceration**, making it a front-end solution to address the overcrowding problem in U. S. prisons and jails. While the immediate goal of any probation program is rehabilitation—in reality, it is more a necessity than an instrument. As a result, other programs have been developed under the umbrella of community corrections that utilize elements of conditional release resulting in the expansion of probation-type programs.

Probation developed as a result of the efforts of philanthropist, John Augustus, to rehabilitate convicted offenders, although references to similar practices exist as early as 437-422 BC. It was favored because it allowed judicial authorities a great deal of discretion when imposing sentences, thereby providing the opportunity to tailor sentences to a particular offender, in theory allowing for the greatest possibility of rehabilitation. While sentences of probation vary widely across and within jurisdictions, the maximum length of time that one can be under supervision is 5 years (60 months).

The functions of probation are difficult to state definitively. It is known that at its inception, John Augustus' goal was behavioral reform. This reflects the sentencing goal of rehabilitation. Fundamentally, it is believed that by allowing the offender to remain in the community, the system is providing a second chance. Further, support and guidance from probation officers may achieve the aim of guiding the offender towards a law-abiding existence.

Given that probation is no longer limited to first-time, non-violent offenders who pose minimal risk to the community, the reality is significantly different. Coupled with low confidence in the effectiveness of rehabilitative success and a burgeoning offender population, actual practices tend to be dictated by conflicting goals on both an individual and administrative level. In an aggressive bid to prevent jail or prison overcrowding, several alternatives to incarceration have developed. Some such programs enable offenders traditionally incarcerated to be released into the community, thereby forcing a shift in focus from rehabilitation to control and supervision.

### Intensive Supervised Probation (ISP)

ISP is a form of release into the community that emphasizes close monitoring of convicted offenders and imposes rigorous conditions on that release, such as the following:

- Multiple weekly contacts w/officer

- Random and unannounced drug testing

- Stringent enforcement of conditions, i.e.,: maintaining employment

- Required participation in treatment, education programs, etc.

Individuals on ISP are those who most likely should NOT be in the community. The restrictions placed on them are often excessive and the level of direct, face-to-face contact required is believed to significantly deter, or at least interfere, with any ongoing criminal activity.

### Shock Probation and Split Sentencing

Shock probation/split sentencing is a sentence for a term of years, but after 30, 60, or 90 days, the offender is removed from jail or prison.

While these terms are used interchangeably, they are actually two different activities. In shock probation, the offender is originally sentenced to jail, then brought before the judge after 30, 60, or 90 days and re-sentenced to probation (Ohio scheme). In split sentencing, probation is part of the original sentence requiring no additional appearance before the judge (California scheme). Nonetheless, the terms refer to the same outcome—some jail, some community.

### Revocation

Since probation is a conditional release, it can be revoked, or taken away, if the conditions governing release are not met (technical violation) or if a new crime is committed during the probationary period (new offense).

Probation revocation is initiated by the probation officer's belief that a violation warranting revocation has occurred. As a result of the 1973 case *Gagnon v. Scarpelli* (411 U.S. 778), the Supreme Court decided that where "liberty interests" are involved, probationers are entitled to retain certain due process rights. Such rights include: (1) written notification of the alleged violations; (2) preliminary (or **probable cause**) **hearing** at which a judicial authority will determine whether sufficient probable cause exists to pursue the case; and (3) if warranted, a revocation hearing.

If a revocation hearing is scheduled, probationers have the right to **testify** in their own behalf, may present witnesses, and may have an attorney present. While the Gagnon court was vague regarding the right to court appointed **counsel** at a revocation hearing, most jurisdictions do provide the right to appointed counsel.

The standard of proof required at a revocation hearing is a "preponderance of the evidence", lower than that required at a criminal trial. Possible outcomes include return to supervision, reprimand with restoration to supervision, or revocation with **imprisonment**.

## Parole

### Definition

Parole is the "conditional early release from prison or jail, under supervision, after a portion of the sentence has been served." This practice assumes that the offender successfully demonstrated conformity to the rules and regulations of the prison environment and shows an ability to conform to society's norms and laws.

### History

The word, parole, derives from the French "parol" meaning "word of honor" and references prisoners of war promising not to take up arms in current conflict if released. How that concept came to apply to the early release of convicted, often violent, offenders is less clear. The first documented official use of early release from prison in the United States is credited to Samuel G. Howe in Boston (1847), but prior to that, other programs using pardons achieved basically the same outcome. In fact, as late as 1938, parole was simply a conditional **pardon** in many states.

Alexander Maconochie (England) ran the Norfolk Island prison. During his tenure, he instituted a system whereby inmates would be punished for the past and trained for the future. He believed that inmates could be rehabilitated so he implemented an open-ended sentencing structure where inmates had to "earn" their release by passing through three stages, each stage increased their liberty and responsibilities. Inmates had an open time frame in which to earn the next level. Compliance advanced them; infractions resulted in a return to the previous stage, thereby lengthening the sentence. The open-ended sentences (today known as indeterminate sentencing) allowed the administration to ensure that when finally released, an offender's behavior had been successfully reformed. Eventually, Maconochie was removed from his position under criticism that his program "coddled" criminals.

At about the same time, Sir Walter Crofton was developing a similar program in Ireland using "tickets of leave". The "Irish System" as it came to be known, employed a similar practice of allowing inmates to earn credits towards early release. However, once the "ticket of leave" was achieved, release from **custody** was conditional. The releasees were supervised in the community by either law enforcement or civilian personnel who were required to secure employment and to conduct home visits. These "supervisors" represented the forerunner to today's parole officer.

In the United States, Zebulon Brockaway (Superintendent) employed elements from both the Irish and Great Britain models in managing the Elmira Reformatory during the 1870s. Brockaway is credited with the passage of the first indeterminate sentencing law in the United States as well as introducing the first good time system to reduce inmates' sentences. However, releasing the offenders was only part of the problem and initially, the greatest challenge was providing adequate supervision once release had been granted.

By 1913, it was clear some independent body was required to supervise inmates in the community and by 1930, Congress formally established a United States Board of Parole. It appeared, at least for awhile, that initiatives and programs were developing that could make parole a viable and useful tool of the criminal justice system. But unfortunate timing contributed ultimately to its downfall.

In 1929, the Great Depression hit the United States. An immediate result was a sharp increase in prison populations. However, the high cost of maintaining prisons as well as a lack of available personnel to staff them made new construction prohibitive and contributed to the popularity of parole. While alleviation of the overcrowding problem is often cited as a secondary (or latent) goal, the reality is that as a back-end solution, parole is vital to the maintenance of the correctional system.

With the onset of the twentieth century, philosophers began to examine the social and psychological aspects of criminal behavior. This heralded a shift from classicalist thinking towards positivism. Under positivism, actions are believed to be caused by forces beyond one's control (such forces could be psychological, biological, or sociological in origin). Therefore, parolees were now viewed as "sick" and the parole department was charged with the responsibility of "fixing" them.

Positivism is consistent with a less punitive approach to sentencing and generally involves an indeterminate sentencing structure allowing for the possibility of early release if the offender demonstrates that they have been successfully rehabilitated. As such, it fit well with the Elmira system and the timing afforded officials the opportunity to use parole as a means to relieve the overcrowded conditions that had developed during the depression.

The fact that parole involves some incarceration suggests that the average parolee has committed a more serious crime than the average probationer and, hence, poses a greater risk to the community. Therefore, primary goals of parole must include crime deterrence and offender control. And given that most offenders will eventually return to the community, a rival goal is reintegration, or the facilitation of an offender's transition from incarceration to freedom.

Unfortunately, it appeared during the 1980s that parole was failing. Street crime rates during this period skyrocketed and in many cases, the crimes were perpetrated by individuals who were released into the community prior to the official expiration of their sentence. This reality led to the development of penal philosophies espousing "tough on crime" approaches and demanding "truth in sentencing". Such philosophies warned criminals, "do the crime, do the time" and resulted in radical changes to sentencing practices across the country that indicated a return to a more punitive sentencing structure.

### Revocation

Since parole is a conditional release, it can be revoked or taken away, if the conditions governing release are not met (technical violation) or if a new crime is committed during the probationary period (new offense). In this manner, it is similar to probation; however, it differs in that probation is governed by judicial decisions whereas parole is governed by administrative procedures. As a result of the administrative nature of parole, the revocation process is so varied among the jurisdictions.

In large part, however, most minor infractions are dealt with by the parole officer and may not necessitate involvement of the parole board. Some jurisdictions empower the parole officer to immediately take a parolee into custody for 24 (New York) to 48 hours (Pennsylvania) for purposes of obtaining an **arrest warrant**. This practice is typically employed when the offender represents an immediate threat to public safety.

With respect to the legal protections afforded to parolees, the first case to explore this issue was *Morrissey v. Brewer* (1972). The Morrissey case explored the extension of due process rights of (1) written no-

tice to parolee prior to general revocation proceeding; (2) identification of the violations being presented and any **evidence** being used to prove that the violation took place; (3) the right of the parolee to confront and cross-examine accusers (subject to exceptions) and (4) a written explanation for the decisions regarding the revocation of the parole and what evidence was employed in making that decision. Perhaps the greatest contribution of the Morrissey case was the creation of a two-stage process wherein first, probable cause that violations had occurred had to exist in order to go to the second stage, which was the actual revocation hearing.

Interestingly, the Supreme Court did not choose to create a bright line rule for the right to court-appointed counsel at a revocation hearing. For the most part, however, most jurisdictions have followed the decision in *Mempa v. Rhay* (1967). While this case specifically dealt with the rights of probationers, it has been applied recently to parolees as well. Basically, the Supreme Court wrote that "any indigent is entitled at every stage of a criminal proceeding to be represented by court-appointed counsel, where substantial rights of a criminal **accused** may be affected." In sum, the Supreme Court considered the liberty interests of the probationers and decided that a probation revocation hearing constituted a "critical stage" which dictated adherence to due process protections. This rationale has consistently been extended to include parole revocation hearings as well.

### Abolishment

As of 2001, 15 states (Arizona, California, Delaware, Illinois, Indiana, Kansas, Maine, Minnesota, Mississippi, Ohio, Oregon, New Mexico, North Carolina, Virginia and Washington) and the Federal government have eliminated parole programs in lieu of a determinate model of sentencing reflective of a more retributive approach to punishment. (New York Gov. George Pataki proposed making New York the sixteenth state)

Such an action may seem warranted given the apparent inability of the system to guarantee the protection of the citizens—but the end result is predictable. Overcrowding still represents the greatest challenge to the correctional industry. In fact, three states (Connecticut, Colorado, and Florida) reinstituted the parole boards after eliminating them due to the unforeseen overcrowding problems. The reality is that removal of parole ultimately leads simply to a shift in power from parole boards to prosecutors, in that the option most often exercised in states without parole, is probation (see above).

## Additional Resources

*History of the Federal Parole System, Part I (1910-1972)* Hoffman, Peter, Federal Probation, Sept. 1997, pp. 23-31.

*History of the Federal Parole System, Part II (1973-1997)* Hoffman, Peter, Federal Probation, Dec. 1997, pp. 49-57.

*Probation and Parole* 7th ed., Abadinsky, Howard, Prentice Hall, 2000.

*Probation and Parole in the United States.* Bureau of Justice Statistics, 2000.

"Probation in the United States: Practices and Challenges" Petersilia, Joan, *National Institute of Justice Journal*, Sept. 1997, pp. 2-8.

*Probation and Parole, 7th edition.* Howard Abadinsky, Prentice Hall, 2000.

*Probation, Parole, and Community Corrections, 3rd Edition.* 3rd ed., Dean J. Champion, Dean J., Prentice Hall, 1999.

*History of the Federal Parole System, Part I (1910-1972).* Peter Hoffman, Federal Probation, Sept. 1997, pp. 23-31.

*History of the Federal Parole System, Part II (1973-1997).* Peter Hoffman, Federal Probation, Dec. 1997, pp. 49-57.

*Probation in the United States: Practices and Challenges.* Joan Petersilia, National Institute of Justice Journal, Sept. 1997, pp. 2-8.

## Organizations

### *American Probation and Parole Association (APPA)*

2760 Research Park Drive
Lexington, KY 40511-8410 USA
Phone: (859) 244-8207
Fax: (859) 244-8001
E-Mail: appa@csg. org

### *U. S. Parole Commission*

5550 Friendship Blvd., Suite 420
Chevy Chase, MD 20815-7286 USA

# CRIMINAL LAW

## RIGHT TO COUNSEL

*Sections within this essay:*

## Background

During the colonial period and the early years of the Republic the practice in the United States was varied with respect to providing **counsel** to suspects in criminal cases. The practice varied from the English method, where no counsel was provided to defendants of **felony** charges, but counsel was made available for defendants of **misdemeanor** charges. Rules in a few states allowed for the appointment of counsel where defendants could not afford to retain a lawyer. The Sixth Amendment to the U.S. Constitution states: "in all criminal prosecutions, the **accused** shall enjoy the right... to have the assistance of counsel for his defense." At the time the Sixth Amendment was ratified, Congress enacted two laws that appeared to indicate an understanding that the

Sixth Amendment guarantee was limited: counsel would not be denied to those who wished for and could afford a lawyer. Much later—in 1930s—the Supreme Court began to expand the clause to its present scope.

Police officers ask questions of victims, witnesses, and suspects. If individuals feel that they are suspects in a criminal investigation or even that they could later be considered a suspect, they should speak with a lawyer before they speak with law enforcement officers. What they say to their lawyer is confidential and cannot be used against them. However, what they say to the police can be used against them, even if there is no recorded or written record of that conversation.

Individuals can always inform the police officer that they wish to speak with a lawyer before they answer any questions. If they are in **custody** (have been arrested or otherwise detained), the police must stop their questioning and they will be given an opportunity to speak with a lawyer. The police may return and begin to ask them questions again after a reasonable amount of time. If they have not yet spoken with a lawyer when the police return to question them, they may continue to refuse to answer any questions until they have obtained legal assistance.

## What the Sixth Amendment Guarantees

The Sixth Amendment guarantees the right to legal counsel at all significant stages of a criminal proceeding. This right is so important that there is an associated right given to people who are unable to pay for legal assistance to have counsel appointed and paid for by the government. The federal criminal justice system and all states have procedures for appointing counsel for indigent defendants. The Sixth Amendment right to counsel has been extended to the following:

- the interrogation phase of a criminal investigation

- the trial itself

- sentencing

- at least an initial appeal of any **conviction**

If individuals are arrested in the United States they have a range of rights that give them certain protections, even if they are not a citizen of the United States. These rights include the following:

- A trial by a jury (in most cases)

- The jury to hear all of the witnesses and see all of the **evidence**

- Presence at the trial and while the jury is **hearing** the case

- The opportunity to see, hear, and confront the witnesses presenting the case against them

- The opportunity to call witnesses and to have the court issue subpoenas to compel the witnesses to appear

- The chance to **testify** themselves should they choose to do so

- The option to refuse to testify

- Access to a criminal defense lawyer. If individuals cannot afford to hire their own criminal defense lawyer, a **public defender** will represent them. This lawyer can act on their behalf before, during, and after the trial

- The right to cross-examine the witnesses giving **testimony** against them

- The right to compel the state to prove its case against them beyond a reasonable doubt.

A judge will appoint an attorney for an indigent **defendant**; this attorney will be compensated at government expense if at the conclusion of the case the defendant could possibly be imprisoned for a period of more than six months. In reality, judges almost always appoint attorneys for indigents in practically every case in which a jail sentence is a possibility—regardless of how long the sentence

may be. Generally, a judge will appoint the attorney for an indigent defendant at the defendant's first court appearance; for most defendants, the first court appearance is an arraignment or a hearing to set **bail**.

## The Miranda Case

In 1966, the United States Supreme Court decision in *Miranda v. Arizona* ushered in a period of court-imposed restraints on the government's ability to interrogate suspects it takes into custody. This famous decision focused on Fifth Amendment protections against **self-incrimination**, but it also spoke to the right to counsel. One of the most important restraints enumerated in the *Miranda* decision is the prohibition against the government's interrogation of suspects or witnesses after the suspect has invoked the right to counsel. Here's what the Miranda warnings generally say:

- You have the right to remain silent.

- Anything you say can be used against you in a court of law.

- You have the right to have an attorney present now and during any future questioning. The right to have counsel present at a custodial interrogation is necessary to protect the Fifth Amendment **privilege against self-incrimination**. A suspect detained for interrogation must be clearly informed that he has the right to consult with a lawyer and to have the lawyer with him during interrogation.

- If you cannot afford an attorney, one will be appointed to you free of charge if you wish. The Supreme Court found it necessary to mandate notice to defendants about their constitutional right to consult with an attorney. They went one step further and declared that if a defendant is poor, the government must appoint a lawyer to represent him.

The Court further instructed the police that if a suspect says he wants a lawyer, the police must cease any interrogation or questioning until an attorney is present. Further, the police must give the suspect an opportunity to confer with his attorney and to have the attorney present during any subsequent questioning.

Individuals need to remember that they can be arrested without being advised of their Miranda Rights.

The Miranda rights do not protect individuals from being arrested, but they help suspects keep from unwittingly incriminating themselves during police questioning.

All the police need to arrest a person is **probable cause** to believe a suspect has committed a crime. Probable cause is merely an adequate reason based on the facts or events. Police are required to read or give suspects their Miranda warnings only before questioning a suspect. Failing to follow the Miranda rules may cause suspects' statements to be **inadmissible** in court; the original arrest may still be perfectly legal and valid.

Police are allowed to ask certain questions without reading the Miranda rights, including the following:

- name
- address
- date of birth
- Social Security number
- Or other questions necessary to establishing a person's identity.

Police can also give alcohol and drug tests without Miranda warnings, but individuals being tested may refuse to answer questions.

## Invoking the Right

Because the invocation of Miranda rights, particularly the right to counsel, has created significant burdens on law enforcement's ability to conduct effective interrogations, several recent court decisions have begun to limit a custodial suspect's ability to invoke that right. Specifically, the Court wants to ensure that a suspect's invocation of rights is not frivolous. To do this, courts require that suspects invoke their right to counsel be made unequivocally, as well as in a timely manner.

If individuals are arrested or questioned, the burden is on them to invoke their right to counsel in a clear and unequivocal manner. They should receive notice that they have the right to an attorney, but law enforcement is not required to ask them whether they want an attorney, nor do they need to ask them clarifying questions if they are unclear in their request for an attorney. Not only must invoking the right to counsel be unequivocal, but courts also have begun to insist that invocations of the Miranda right

to counsel be made in a timely manner. Individuals should not wait to be asked if they want a lawyer, nor should they expect the police to read them Miranda warnings before they ask for counsel.

## Judicial Proceedings Before Trial

Generally, defendants are entitled to counsel from the time of their arraignment until the beginning of their trial. This is because the defendant's need for consultation, investigation, and preparation are critically important for a fair trial. The courts have gradually expanded this idea to the point that there is a legal concept of "a critical stage in a criminal proceeding" that indicates when a defendant must be represented by counsel.

## Custodial Interrogation

Defendants who have been taken into custody and have invoked their Sixth Amendment right to counsel with respect to the offense for which they are being prosecuted may not later waive that right. However, defendants may waive their right under Miranda not to be questioned about unrelated and uncharged offenses.

What happens if the police violate the right to counsel? The remedy for violation of the Sixth Amendment rule is that any statements obtained from defendants under these circumstances will be excluded from the evidence at trial. There is one important exception to the Sixth Amendment **exclusionary rule**: evidence obtained from defendants held in custody that violates the Sixth Amendment may be used for the sole purpose of impeaching the defendants' testimony at trial.

## Lineups and Other Identification Situations

Lineups are considered to be "critical stage" and the prosecution may not admit into evidence in-court identification of defendants based on out-of-court lineups or show-ups if they were obtained without the presence of defendant's counsel. Courts have found that a defendant's counsel is necessary at a **lineup** because the lineup stage is filled with much potential for both intentional and unintentional errors. Without the defendant's attorney present at the lineup, these errors may not be discovered and remedied prior to trial.

This rule does not apply to other methods of obtaining identification and other evidentiary material relating to the defendant, including the following:

- blood samples
- DNA samples
- handwriting samples
- vocal samples

In these cases, there is far less chance that the absence of counsel at the time the evidence is obtained from the defendant might prevent the defendant from getting a fair trial.

The Sixth Amendment does not guarantee the presence of the defendant's counsel at a pretrial proceeding unless the physical presence of the defendant is involved. Furthermore, the defendant's presence must be required at a trial-like confrontation at which the defendant requires the advice and assistance of counsel.

## Post-Conviction Proceedings

In a criminal trial, the law requires a lawyer for defendants to be present at the sentencing stage of the trial. If individuals are convicted of a crime and are placed on **probation**, they still have the right to counsel at a later hearing on the revocation of their probation and imposition of the deferred sentence. Due process and **equal protection** rather than Sixth Amendment rights, however, will apply in the following three post-trial hearings:

1. for granting **parole** or probation
2. for revoking parole when parole was imposed after sentencing
3. for prison disciplinary hearings

## Adequate Representation or Ineffective Assistance of Counsel

Indigent defendants who are represented by appointed lawyers and defendants who can afford to hire their own attorneys are both entitled to adequate representation. But "adequate representation" does not mean perfect representation. However, an incompetent or negligent lawyer can so poorly represent a client that the court is justified in throwing out a guilty verdict based on the attorney's incompetence.

If a defendant's lawyer is ineffective at trial and on direct appeal, the defendant's Sixth Amendment right to a fair trial has been violated. In analyzing claims that a defendant's lawyer was ineffective, the principal goal is to determine whether the lawyer's conduct so undermined the functioning of the judicial process that the trial cannot be relied upon as having produced a just result. Proving this requires two steps:

1. The defendant must show that his own lawyer's job performance was deficient. The defendant must prove that his counsel made errors so serious that the lawyer did not function as the counsel guaranteed the defendant by the Sixth Amendment.

2. The defendant must show that the deficient performance unfairly prejudiced the defense. The defendant must show that his lawyer's errors were so serious as to wholly deprive the defendant of a fair trial.

Unless a defendant proves both steps, the conviction or sentence cannot be said to result from a breakdown in the judicial process such that the result is unreliable. When courts review a lawyer's advocacy of a defendant, they are deferential. Courts are bound by a strong presumption that any given lawyer's conduct falls within the range of reasonable professional assistance.

## Additional Resources

*"Consumer's Guide to Legal Help on the Internet"*. American Bar Association, 2002. Available at http://www.abanet.org/legalservices/public.html

*Gideon's Trumpet* Lewis, Anthony, Vintage Books, 1989.

*Miranda v. Arizona: The Rights of the Accused (Famous Trials)* Hogrogian, John G., Lucent Books, 1999.

*The Right to the Assistance of Counsel: A Reference Guide to the United States* Tomkovicz, James J. Greenwood House, 2002.

*The Sixth Amendment in Modern American Jurisprudence: A Critical Perspective (Contributions in Legal Studies)* Garcia, Alfredo, Greenwood Publishing Group, 1992.

## Organizations

### Federal Defender's Association (FDA)
8530 Wilshire Blvd, Suite 404
Beverly Hills, CA 90211 USA
Fax: (310) 397-1001
E-Mail: defense@afda.org

URL: http://www.afda.org/

### Legal Services Corporation (LSC)

750 First Street NE, Tenth Floor
Washington, DC 20002-4250 USA
Phone: (202) 336-8800
Fax: (202) 336-8959
E-Mail: info@lsc.gov
URL: http://www.lsc.gov/

### National Association of Criminal Defense Lawyers (NACDL)

1025 Connecticut Ave. NW, Suite 901
Washington, DC 20036 USA

Phone: (202) 872-8600
Fax: (202) 872-8690
E-Mail: assist@nacdl.org
URL: www.nacdl.org

### National Legal Aid & Defender Association (NLADA)

1625 K Street NW, Suite 800
Washington, DC 20006-1604 USA
Phone: (202) 452-0620
Fax: (202) 872-103
E-Mail: info@nlada.org
URL: http://www.nlada.org/

# CRIMINAL LAW

## SEARCH AND SEIZURE

*Sections within this essay:*

- Background
- The Text of the Fourth Amendment and Case Law Interpreting It
    - The Text of the Fourth Amendment
    - When the Fourth Amendment Applies
    - How the Fourth Amendment Applies: The Warrant Requirement
    - How the Fourth Amendment Applies: The Reasonableness Requirement
    - How the Fourth Amendment Applies: The Exclusionary Rule
- State Court Decisions Interpreting Constitutional Provisions Governing Search and Seizure
- Additional Resources

## Background

"Search and seizure" refers to the methods used by law enforcement to investigate crimes, track down **evidence**, question witnesses, and arrest suspects. It also refers to the legal rules governing these methods. At the federal level these rules are set forth in the Fourth Amendment to the U.S. Constitution, the Federal Rules of Criminal Procedure, and Title 18 of the United States Code, sections 2231 et seq. The rules and **statutes** refer to each other, and both are designed to provide greater detail for areas left silent by the Constitution. In addition, each state has its own set of applicable statutes, rules of procedure,

and constitutional provisions. But the starting point in understanding any of these rules is the Fourth Amendment, since it sets forth the minimum amount of protection that both the state and federal government must provide against searches and seizures. Under the **Due Process** and **Equal Protection** Clauses of the Fourteenth Amendment, the U.S. Supreme Court has ruled that states may provide their citizens with more protection against searches and seizures but not less.

The American Revolution was fought in part to create a system of government that would operate within the rule of law. The rule of law is represented by the idea that the United States is a nation of laws and not of men and women. Under the rule of law, the actions of government officials are limited by the legal principles, rules, and other norms that make up the U.S. legal system and not by the arbitrary or capricious whim of an individual official. Violating these legal norms in the course of official conduct can transform a law enforcer into a law breaker.

The Framers drafted the Fourth Amendment in response to their colonial experience with British officials whose discretion in collecting revenues for the Crown often went unchecked. Local magistrates were allowed to issue general search warrants to British tax collectors upon mere suspicion that a colonist was not fully complying with the tax code. Magistrates were not authorized to question the source or strength of a tax collector's suspicion, and, once issued, general **warrants** permitted blanket, door-to-door searches of entire neighborhoods without regard to person, place, or time.

The **writ** of assistance was a particularly loathsome form of general warrant. This writ derived its name from the power of British authorities to compel local peace officers and colonial residents to "assist" in executing a particular search. A writ of assistance lasted for the life of the king or queen under whom it was issued and could be enforced by any British law enforcement officer, including customs officials who often relied on them as long-term hunting licenses against suspected smugglers.

Colonial opposition to general warrants was pervasive. In Paxton's case, 1 Quincy 51 (Mass. 1761), James Otis appeared on behalf of the colonists who opposed issuance of another writ, arguing that before a warrant is valid it must be "directed to special officers and to search certain houses" for particular goods and may only be granted "upon oath made" by a government official "that he suspects such goods to be concealed in those very places he desires to search" (quoted in *Illinois v. Krull*, 480 U.S. 340 [1987]). John Adams cited Otis' argument against the writs "as the commencement of the controversy between Great Britain and America."

Ratified by the states in 1791, the Fourth Amendment put an end to writs of assistance by creating a constitutional buffer between U.S. citizens and the often-intimidating power of law enforcement. It has three components: first, the Fourth Amendment establishes a privacy interest by recognizing the right of every citizen to be "secure in their persons, houses, papers, and effects"; second, it protects this privacy interest by prohibiting searches and seizures that are not authorized by a warrant based on "probable cause" or that are otherwise "unreasonable"; and third, for searches requiring a warrant the Fourth Amendment states that the warrant must describe with particularity "the place to be searched, and the persons or things to be seized" and be supported by "oath or affirmation" of the officer requesting its issuance.

## The Text of the Fourth Amendment and Case Law Interpreting It

Although ratification of the Fourth Amendment answered any lingering doubts about the validity of the writs of assistance in the United States, the text of the Fourth Amendment raised questions of its own about the meaning of the terms "unreasonable," "search or seizure," "warrant," "particularity," "oath or affirmation," and "probable cause," not to mention other questions about the scope of such terms as "houses, papers, and effects." The U.S. Supreme Court, lower federal courts, and state courts

have spent more than 200 years grappling with these questions and continue to do so as new cases come before them.

### The Text of the Fourth Amendment

The Fourth Amendment reads as follows: "The right of the people to be secure in their persons, houses, papers, and effects, against unreasonable searches and seizures, shall not be violated, and no Warrants shall issue, but upon probable cause, supported by Oath or affirmation, and particularly describing the place to be searched, and the persons or things to be seized."

### When the Fourth Amendment Applies

Like the rest of the Bill of Rights, the Fourth Amendment originally only applied in federal court. However, in *Wolf v. Colorado*, 338 U.S. 25 (1949), the U.S. Supreme Court ruled that the rights guaranteed by the text of the Fourth Amendment (sans the exclusionary rule to be discussed below) apply equally in state courts via the Fourteenth Amendment, which guarantees to the citizen of every state the right to due process and equal protection of the laws. The process by which the Supreme Court has made certain fundamental liberties protected by the Bill of Rights applicable to the states is known as the doctrine of incorporation.

Not every search and seizure that is scrutinized in state and federal court raises a Fourth Amendment issue. The Fourth Amendment only protects against searches and seizures conducted by the government or pursuant to governmental direction. Surveillance and investigatory actions taken by strictly private persons, such as private investigators, suspicious spouses, or nosey neighbors, are not governed by the Fourth Amendment. However, Fourth Amendment concerns do arise when those same actions are taken by a law enforcement official or a private person working in conjunction with law enforcement.

The Fourth Amendment does not apply even against governmental action unless defendants first establish that they had a reasonable expectation of privacy in the place to be searched or the thing to be seized. The Supreme Court has explained that what "a person knowingly exposes to the public, even in his own home or office, is not a subject of Fourth Amendment protection..." But what he seeks to preserve as private, even in an area accessible to the public, may be constitutionally protected (see *Katz v. United States*, 389 U.S. 347 [1967]).

Applying this principle, the Supreme Court has ruled that individuals generally maintain a reasonable expectation of privacy in their bodies, clothing, and personal belongings. Homeowners possess a privacy interest that extends inside their homes and in the curtilage immediately surrounding the outside of their homes, but not in the "open fields" and "wooded areas" extending beyond the curtilage (see *Hester v. United States*, 265 U.S. 57 [1924]). A business owner's expectation of privacy in commercial property is less than the privacy interest afforded to a private homeowner and is particularly attenuated in commercial property used in "closely regulated" industries (i.e., airports, railroads, restaurants, and liquor establishments), where business premises may be subject to regular administrative searches by state or federal agencies for the purpose of determining compliance with health, safety, or security regulations. Automobile owners have a reasonable expectation of privacy in the cars they own and drive, though the expectation of privacy is less than a homeowner's privacy interest in his or her home.

No expectation of privacy is maintained for property and personal effects held open to the public. Things visible in "plain view" for a person of ordinary and unenhanced vision are entitled to no expectation of privacy and thus no Fourth Amendment protection. Items lying in someone's backseat, growing in someone's outdoor garden, or discarded in someone's curb-side garbage all fall within this category. However, items seen only through enhanced surveillance, such as through high-powered or telescopic lenses, may be subject to the strictures of the Fourth Amendment. Public records, published phone numbers, and other matters readily accessible to the general public enjoy no expectation of privacy. Similarly, the Supreme Court has said that individuals do not possess an expectation of privacy in their personal characteristics (see *United States v. Dionisio*, 410 U.S. 1 [1973]). Thus, the police may require individuals to give handwriting and voice exemplars, as well as hair, blood, DNA, and fingerprint samples, without complying with the Fourth Amendment's requirements.

Finally, to raise a Fourth Amendment objection to a particular search or seizure, a person must have "standing" to do so. Standing in this context means that the rights guaranteed by the Fourth Amendment are personal and may not be asserted on behalf of others. Thus, a passenger may not generally object to a police search of the owner's car and a houseguest may not generally object to a search of the homeowner's premises. These rules can become murky, however, as when a houseguest is actually living with the homeowner or owns things stored on the owner's premises.

### How the Fourth Amendment Applies: The Warrant Requirement

Once the Fourth Amendment applies to a particular search or seizure, the next question is under what circumstances is a warrant required. The Supreme Court has ruled that the Constitution expresses a preference for searches, seizures, and arrests conducted pursuant to a lawfully executed warrant (see *Mincey v. Arizona*, 437 U.S. 385 [1978]). A warrant is a written order signed by a court authorizing a law-enforcement officer to conduct a search, seizure, or arrest. Searches, seizures, and arrests performed without a valid warrant are deemed presumptively invalid, and any evidence seized without a warrant will be suppressed unless a court finds that the search was reasonable under the circumstances.

An application for a warrant must be supported by a sworn, detailed statement made by a law enforcement officer appearing before a neutral judge or magistrate. The Supreme Court has said that probable cause exists when the facts and circumstances within the police officer's knowledge provide a reasonably trustworthy basis for a man of reasonable caution to believe that a criminal offense has been committed or is about to take place (see *Carroll v. United States*, 267 U. S. 132 [1925]). Probable cause can be established by out-of-court statements made by reliable police informants, even though those statements cannot be tested by the magistrate. However, probable cause will not lie where the only evidence of criminal activity is an officer's affirmation of suspicion or belief (see *Aguilar v. Texas*, 378 U.S. 108 [1964]). On the other hand, an officer's subjective reason for making an arrest does not need to be the same criminal offense for which the facts indicate. (*Devenpeck v. Alford*, 543 U.S. 146 [2004]).

Probable cause will not lie unless the facts supporting the warrant are sworn by the officer as true to the best of his or her knowledge. The officer's oath can be written or oral, but the officer must typically swear that no knowing or intentionally false statement has been submitted in support of the warrant and that no statement has been made in reckless disregard of the truth. Inaccuracies due to an officer's negligence or innocent omission do not jeopardize a warrant's validity.

The Fourth Amendment requires not only that warrants be supported by probable cause offered by a sworn police officer, but it also requires that a warrant "particularly" describe the person or place to be searched or seized. Warrants must provide enough detail so that an officer with the warrant can ascertain with reasonable effort the persons and places identified in the warrant. For most residences a street address usually satisfies the particularity requirement, unless the warrant designates an apartment complex, hotel, or other multiple-unit building, in which case the warrant must describe the specific sub-unit to be searched. Warrants must describe individuals with sufficient particularity so that a person of average intelligence can distinguish them from others in the general population.

The magistrate before whom an officer applies for a warrant must be neutral and detached. This qualification means that the magistrate must be impartial and not a member of the "competitive enterprise" of law enforcement (see *California v. Acevedo*, 500 U.S. 565 [1991]). Thus, police officers, prosecutors, and attorney generals are disqualified from becoming a magistrate. States vary as to the requirements that candidates must possess before they will be considered qualified for the job of magistrate. Some states require that magistrates have an attorney's license, while others require only that their magistrates be literate.

### How the Fourth Amendment Applies: The Reasonableness Requirement

Not every search, seizure, or arrest must be made pursuant to a lawfully executed warrant. The Supreme Court has ruled that warrantless police conduct may comply with the Fourth Amendment so long as it is reasonable under the circumstances. The exceptions made to the Fourth Amendment's warrant requirement reflect the Court's reluctance to unduly impede the job of law enforcement officials. The Court has attempted to strike a balance between the practical realities of daily police work and the privacy and freedom interests of the public. Always requiring police officers to take the time to complete a warrant application and locate and appear before a judge could result in the destruction of evidence, the disappearance of suspects and witnesses, or both. The circumstances under which a warrantless search, seizure, or arrest is deemed reasonable generally fall within seven categories.

First, no warrant is required for a felony arrest in a public place, even if the arresting officer had ample time to procure a warrant, so long as the officer possessed probable cause that the suspect committed the crime. Felony arrests in places not open to the public generally do require a warrant, unless the offi-

cer is in "hot pursuit" of a fleeing felon (see *Warden v. Hayden*, 387 U.S. 294 [1967]). The Fourth Amendment also allows warrantless arrests for **misdemeanors** committed in an officer's presence.

Second, no warrant is required for searches incident to lawful arrest. If a police officer has made a lawful arrest, with or without a warrant, the Fourth Amendment permits the officer to conduct a search of the suspect's person, clothing, and all of the areas within the suspect's immediate reach. This kind of warrantless search is justified on grounds that it allows police officers to protect themselves from hidden weapons that might suddenly be wielded against them. Accordingly, officers are only permitted to seize items from the area in the immediate control of the arrestee.

Third, automobiles may be stopped if an officer possesses a reasonable and articulable suspicion that the motorist has violated a traffic law. Once the vehicle has pulled to the side of the road, the Fourth Amendment permits the officer to search the vehicle's interior, including the glove compartment. However, the trunk of a vehicle cannot be searched unless the officer has probable cause to believe that it contains contraband or the instrumentalities of criminal activity. But similar to a search incident to arrest, once a vehicle has been lawfully impounded, its contents may be inventoried without a warrant, including the contents of the trunk.

Fourth, an officer who reasonably believes that criminal activity may be afoot in a public place is authorized to stop any person who is suspected of participating in that criminal activity and conduct a carefully limited search of the suspect's outer clothing for weapons that may be used against the officer (see *Terry v. Ohio*, 392 U.S. 1 [1968]). The officer may also ask for identification, but the suspect is under no obligation to produce it. However, A suspect's refusal to identify himself together with surrounding events may create probable cause to arrest (see *People v. Loudermilk*, 241 Cal. Rptr. 208 (Cal. App. 1987). This kind of warrantless search, called a Terry stop or a Terry frisk, is designed to protect officers from hidden weapons. Accordingly, items that do not feel like weapons, such as a baggie of soft, granular substance tucked inside a jacket pocket, cannot be seized during a Terry frisk, even if it turns out that the item is contraband.

Fifth, warrantless searches, seizures, and arrests may be justified by "exigent" circumstances. To determine whether exigent circumstances justified police conduct, a court must review the totality of the circumstances, including the gravity of the underlying offense and whether the suspect was fleeing or trying to escape. However, the surrounding circumstances must be tantamount to an emergency. Shots fired, screams heard, or fire emanating from inside a building have all been considered sufficiently exigent to dispense with the Fourth Amendment's warrant requirement.

Sixth, the Supreme Court has upheld brief, warrantless seizures at fixed roadside checkpoints aimed at intercepting illegal aliens (see *United States v. Martinez-Fuerte*, 428 U.S. 543 [1976]) and drunk drivers (see *Michigan v. Sitz*, 496 U.S. 444 [1990]). Both checkpoint programs passed constitutional muster because they were tailored to remedying specific problems that law enforcement could not effectively address through more traditional means, namely problems relating to policing the nation's border and ensuring roadway safety. However, when the primary purpose of a checkpoint is simply to detect ordinary criminal activity, the Supreme Court has declared it violative of the Fourth Amendment (see *Indianapolis v. Edmond*, 531 U.S. 32 [2000]).

Seventh, searches, seizures, and arrests made pursuant to a defective warrant may be justified if the officer was proceeding in "good faith." The Supreme Court has said that a search made pursuant to a warrant that is later declared invalid (i.e., it fails to meet the requirements for a valid warrant enumerated above) will still be considered reasonable under the Fourth Amendment so long as the warrant was issued by a magistrate and the defect was not the result of willful police deception (see *United States v. Leon*, 468 U.S. 897 [1984]). This exception to the warrant requirement was created so as not to punish honest police officers who have done nothing wrong while acting in accordance with an ostensibly valid warrant.

### *How the Fourth Amendment Applies: The Exclusionary Rule*

For the more than 100 years after its ratification, the Fourth Amendment was of little value to criminal defendants because evidence seized by law enforcement in violation of the warrant or reasonableness requirements was still admissible during the defendant's prosecution. The Supreme Court dramatically changed Fourth Amendment jurisprudence when it handed down its decision in *Weeks v. United States*, 232 U.S. 383 (1914). *Weeks* involved the appeal of a defendant who had been convicted based on evidence that had been seized by a federal agent with-

out a warrant or other constitutional justification. The Supreme Court reversed the defendant's conviction, thereby creating what is known as the "exclusionary rule." In *Mapp v. Ohio*, 367 U.S. 643 (1961), the Supreme Court made the exclusionary rule applicable to the states.

Designed to deter police misconduct, the exclusionary rule enables courts to exclude incriminating evidence from introduction at trial upon proof that the evidence was procured in contravention of a constitutional provision. The rule allows defendants to challenge the admissibility of evidence by bringing a pre-trial motion to suppress the evidence. If the court allows the evidence to be introduced at trial and the jury votes to convict, the defendant can challenge the propriety of the trial court's decision denying the motion to suppress on appeal. If the defendant succeeds on appeal, however, the Supreme Court has ruled that double jeopardy principles do not bar retrial of the defendant because the trial court's error did not go to the question of guilt or innocence (see *Lockhart v. Nelson*, 488 U.S. 33 [1988]). Nonetheless, obtaining a conviction in the second trial would be significantly more difficult if the evidence suppressed by the exclusionary rule is important to the prosecution.

A companion to the exclusionary rule is the "fruit of the poisonous tree" doctrine. Under this doctrine, a court may exclude from trial not only evidence that itself was seized in violation of the Constitution but also any other evidence that is derived from an illegal search. For example, suppose a defendant is arrested for kidnapping and later confesses to the crime. If a court subsequently declares that the arrest was unconstitutional, the confession will also be deemed tainted and ruled inadmissible at any prosecution of the defendant on the kidnapping charge.

## State Court Decisions Interpreting Constitutional Provisions Governing Search and Seizure

The federal Constitution and the Supreme Court cases interpreting it establish the minimum amount of protection that a state court must provide when it is interpreting a section of the Bill of Rights that has been made applicable to the states via the doctrine of incorporation, including instances when a state court is required to interpret and apply the Fourth Amendment. A state court interpreting the search-and-seizure provisions of its own constitution may provide more protection than is afforded by the federal Constitution but not less. Below is a sampling of cases decided in part based on a state court's interpretation of its own state constitutional provision governing search and seizure.

FLORIDA: Florida courts are constitutionally required to interpret search and seizure issues in conformity with the Fourth Amendment of the United States Constitution as interpreted by the United States Supreme Court (see *State v. Hernandez*, 718 So.2d 833 [Fla. App. 1998]).

GEORGIA: A driver's proceeding through a poorly lit intersection without her headlights on created reasonable suspicion to justify a traffic stop of driver under the state constitution (see *State v. Hammang*, 549 S.E.2d 440 [Ga. App. 2001]).

IDAHO: The term "exigent circumstances" refers to a catalogue of exceptional or compelling circumstances that allow police to enter, search, seize, and arrest without complying with the warrant requirements of the federal or state constitutions, including unannounced entries to search made pursuant to the state and federal "knock and announce" statutes (see *State v. Rauch* 586 P.2d 671 [Idaho 1978]).

ILLINOIS: Officers involved in the surveillance of an arranged drug purchase had sufficient probable cause to make an arrest of both the driver and passenger of an unidentified vehicle that was observed during the surveillance (see *People v. Ortiz*, 823 N.E.2d 1171 [Ill. App. 2005]).

KANSAS: Even though police improperly searched a suspect's pockets and found drugs, these drugs inevitably would have been discovered. Under the inevitable discovery doctrine, the search was permissible. (see *State v. Ingram*, 113 P.3d 228 [Kan. 2005]).

LOUISIANA: Warrantless searches and seizures are unreasonable per se unless justified by one of the specific exceptions to warrant requirement of the federal and state constitutions (see *State v. Manson*, 791 So. 2d 749 [La. App. 2001]).

MICHIGAN: Enhanced search and seizure protection under Michigan's Constitution is available only if the search or seizure occurs inside the curtilage of the house (see Mich. Const. Art. 1, § 11).

MINNESOTA: The purpose of the exclusionary rule based upon the search and seizure provision of the state constitution is to deter police misconduct, and thus there is no compelling reason to apply a more stringent standard when applying the state ex-

clusionary rule than when applying the federal exclusionary rule (see *State v. Martin*, 595 N.W.2d 214 [Minn. App. 1999]).

NEW JERSEY: Racial profiling involves a claim of unlawful search and seizure in violation of the state's constitution (see *State v. Velez*, 763 A.2d 290 [N.J. Super. A.D. 2000]).

NEW MEXICO: The state constitution allows a warrantless arrest only upon a showing of exigent circumstances (see American Civil Liberties Union of New Mexico v. City of Albuquerque, 128 N.M. 315, 992 P.2d 866 (N.M. 1999); NM Const. Art. 2, § 10).

NEW YORK: Liquor retailer had no legitimate expectation of privacy in retail customer sales records maintained by liquor wholesalers with whom the retailer had business dealings, and thus, the retailer lacked standing to challenge, as an unreasonable search and seizure in violation of the New York Constitution, the Department of Taxation and Finance's use of wholesalers' sales records to investigate suspected underreporting of sales tax by liquor retailers (see Roebling Liquors Inc. v. Comm'r of Taxation & Finance, 728 N.Y.S.2d 509 [N.Y. App. Div. 2001]).

NORTH CAROLINA: An informant was sufficiently reliable such that his tip could provide probable cause where the informant had more than 14 years of personal dealings with an officer and had led to more than 100 arrests. (see *State v. Stanley*, 622 S.E.2d 680 [N.C. App. 2005]).

OHIO: An inventory search of a compartment of a lawfully impounded vehicle does not contravene the federal or state constitutions, where the search is administered in good faith and in accordance with reasonable police procedures or established routine (see *State v. Mesa*, 717 N.E.2d 329 [Ohio 1999]).

SOUTH CAROLINA: A court order violated a defendant's Fourth Amendment rights by compelling a blood sample. However, other evidence supported the defendant's conviction for murder and first-degree burglary, and the court determined that the error was harmless (see *State v. Baccus*, 2005 WL 3620398 (S.C. 2006).

WASHINGTON: Without judicial participation, a municipal court clerk may not order the issuance of an arrest warrant in the absence of an authorizing statute, court rule, or ordinance (see *State v. Walker*, 999 P.2d 1296 (Wash. App. 2000).

WISCONSIN: Where police officers act in objectively reasonable reliance upon a facially valid search warrant that has been issued by a detached and neutral magistrate, a good-faith exception to the exclusionary rule applies under the state constitution, provided that the state shows the process used in obtaining the warrant included a significant investigation and review by either a police officer trained and knowledgeable in the requirements of probable cause and reasonable suspicion or a knowledgeable government attorney (see *State v. Eason*, 629 N.W.2d 625 [Wisc. 2001]).

## Additional Resources

*American Jurisprudence*. 2d Series. Thomson/West, 2005.

*Criminal Procedure*. 4th Edition. Wayne R. LaFave, Jerold H. Israel, and Nancy J.King, Thomson/West, 2004.

*Oxford Companion to the Supreme Court*. 2d Edition. Hall, Kermit L., James W. Ely, Jr., and Joel B. Grossman eds., Oxford University Press, 2005.

*West's Encyclopedia of American Law*. 2d Edition. Thomson/Gale, 2004.

## Organizations

### American Civil Liberties Union
1400 20th Street, NW, Suite 119
Washington, DC 20036 USA
Phone: (202) 457-0800
URL: http://www.aclu.org

### Association for Federal Defense Attorneys
8530 Wilshire Blvd., Suite 404
Beverly Hills, CA 90211 USA
Phone: (714) 836-6031
URL: http://www.afda.org

### Center for Human Rights and Constitutional Law
256 S. Occidental Blvd.
Los Angeles, CA 90057 USA
Phone: (213) 388-8693
Fax: (213) 386-9484
URL: http://www.centerforhumanrights.org

### National District Attorneys Association
99 Canal Center Plaza
Alexandria, VA 22314 USA
Phone: (703) 549-9222
Fax: (703) 836-3195
URL: http://www.ndaa.org

# CRIMINAL LAW

## SENTENCING AND SENTENCING GUIDELINES

*Sections within this essay:*

- Background
- Types of Sentences
- Factors Considered in Determining A Sentence
- "Three Strikes" Sentencing Laws
- Uniformity and Consistency
- Alternative Sentences
- Sentencing Commissions
- Selected State Sentencing Provisions
- Additional Resources

## Background

A sentence is a formal judgment pronouncing a specific punishment to be imposed for the **conviction** of a crime. It may involve the payment of a fine, community service, **incarceration**, or, in capital offenses, the death penalty. It also may consist of a term of **probation** or **parole** (although parole has been abolished in many states).

Sentences may be meted out directly following the entry of a verdict or at a "sentencing hearing" scheduled for a later date. In the interim, prosecutors prepare a "sentencing report" which advises the court of the defendant's prior criminal record, aggravating or **mitigating circumstances**, and other information about the **defendant** that may assist the court in deciding an appropriate punishment.

There have been concerted efforts over the years to standardize the approach toward sentencing, particularly in **felony** offenses, and to diminish judicial discretion in sentencing. These efforts reflect a vacillating but recurring perception by lawmakers and the public at large that arbitrary or discriminatory practices may interfere with fair and just sentencing in certain cases or for certain crimes. However, the U.S. Supreme Court severely limited the ability of the federal government and state governments to enacted uniform sentencing guidelines when the Court ruled that these mandatory guidelines were unconstitutional.

## Types of Sentences

Listed below are the types of sentences imposed:

- A concurrent sentence is served at the same time as another sentence imposed earlier or at the same proceeding.

- A consecutive (or cumulative) sentence occurs when a defendant has been convicted of several counts, each one constituting a distinct offense or crime, or when a defendant has been convicted of several crimes at the same time. The sentences for each crime are then "tacked" on to each other, so that each sentence begins immediately upon the expiration of the previous one.

- A deferred sentence occurs when its **execution** is postponed until some later time.

- A determinate sentence is the same as a fixed sentence: It is for a fixed period of time.

- A final sentence puts an end to a criminal case. It is distinguished from an interlocutory or interim sentence.

- An indeterminate sentence, rather than stating a fixed period of time for **imprisonment**, instead declares that the period shall be "not more than" or "not less than" a certain prescribed duration of time. The authority to render indeterminate sentences is usually granted by **statute** in several states.

- A life sentence represents the **disposition** of a serious criminal case, in which the convicted person spends the remainder of his or her life in prison.

- A mandatory sentence is created by state statute and represents the rendering of a punishment for which a judge has/had no room for discretion. Generally it means that the sentence may not be suspended and that no probation may be imposed, leaving the judge with no alternative but the "mandated" sentence.

- A maximum sentence represents the outer limit of a punishment, beyond which a convicted person may not be held in custody.

- A minimum sentence represents the minimum punishment or the minimum time a convicted person must spend in prison before becoming eligible for parole or release.

- A presumptive sentence exists in many states by statute. It specifies an appropriate or "normal" sentence for each offense to be used as a baseline for a judge when meting out a punishment. The **statutory** presumptive sentence is considered along with other relevant factors (aggravating or mitigating circumstances) in determining the actual sentence. Most states have statutory "presumptive guidelines" for major or common offenses.

- A straight or flat sentence is a fixed sentence without a maximum or minimum.

- A **suspended sentence** actually has two different meanings. It may refer to a withholding or postponing of pronouncing a sentence following a conviction or it may refer to the postponing of the execution of a sentence after it has been pronounced.

## Factors Considered in Determining a Sentence

Judges, not juries, determine punishments for a crime (in **capital punishment** cases, the jury usually decides whether to recommend death or life in prison).

The Eighth Amendment to the U. S. Constitution, made applicable to the states by the Fourteenth Amendment, provides that "Excessive **bail** shall not be required, nor excessive fines imposed, nor cruel and unusual punishments inflicted." In addition to the sentencing prohibitions contained in the Constitution, Title 18 of the United States Code, Part II (**Criminal Procedure**), Chapters 227 (Sentences), 228 (Death Sentence), and 232 (Miscellaneous Sentencing Provisions) also govern sentencing in federal courts. Similarly, state court sentencing procedures are governed by state laws and constitutions as discussed below.

Most crimes are specifically enumerated in constitutions or statutes, and the provision that identifies the specific crime will also identify the appropriate punishment. For example, a statute may read, "Violation of this statute constitutes a **misdemeanor**, punishable by a fine not to exceed $500 or imprisonment not to exceed 30 days, or both." Given this range of potential punishment, a judge will then consider certain "aggravating" or "mitigating" circumstances to determine where along the prescribed spectrum a particular criminal's punishment should fall. Common factors considered by judges include:

- whether the offender is a "first-time" or repeat offender

- whether the offender was an **accessory** (helping the main offender) or the main offender

- whether the offender committed the crime under great personal stress or duress

- whether anyone was hurt, and whether the crime was committed in a manner that was unlikely to result in anyone being hurt

- whether the offender was particularly cruel to a victim, or particularly destructive, vindictive, etc.

- (sometimes) whether the offender is genuinely contrite or remorseful

Under Federal Rule of Criminal Procedure 32(a), before imposing a sentence, the court must afford

**counsel** an opportunity to speak on behalf of the defendant. The court will address the defendant personally and ask him if he wishes to make a statement in his own behalf and to present any information in mitigation of punishment. The attorney for the government will have an equivalent opportunity to speak to the court. Similar provisions are contained in most state procedural statutes and rules. In many state courts, a victim or the survivors of a victim may also have the opportunity to address the court and recommend leniency or strictness for the sentence.

## "Three Strikes" Sentencing Laws

Under the Violent Crime Control and Law Enforcement Act of 1994, the "Three Strikes" statute (18 U.S.C. § 3559(c)) provides for mandatory life imprisonment if a convicted felon:

- been convicted in federal court of a "serious violent felony" and

- has two or more previous convictions in federal or state courts, at least one of which is a "serious violent felony." The other offense may be a serious drug offense.

The statute goes on to define a serious violent felony as including murder, **manslaughter**, **sex offenses**, **kidnapping**, robbery, and any offense punishable by 10 years or more which includes an element of the use of force or involves a significant risk of force.

The State of Washington was the first to enact a "Three Strikes" law in 1993. Since then, more than half of the states, in addition to the federal government, have enacted three strikes laws. The primary focus of these laws is the containment of recidivism (repeat offenses by a small number of criminals). California's law is considered the most far-reaching and most often used among the states.

Three strikes laws have been the subject of extensive debate over whether they are effective. Defendants sentenced to long prison terms under these laws have also sought to challenge these laws as unconstitutional. For instance, one defendant was found guilty of stealing $150 worth of video tapes from two California department stores. The defendant had prior convictions, and pursuant to California's three-strikes laws, the judge sentenced the defendant to 50 years in prison for the theft of the video tapes. The defendant challenged his conviction before the U.S. Supreme Court in *Lockyer v. Andrade*

(2003), but the Court upheld the constitutionality of the law.

## Uniformity and Consistency

In addition to "three strikes" laws, other state and all federal criminal statutes include mandatory sentences that require judges to impose identical sentences on all persons convicted of the same offense. Mandatory sentences are a direct result of state legislatures' or Congress' response to the public perception of judicial leniency or inconsistency in sentencing practices.

However, most crimes do not carry mandatory sentences. If sentencing is not mandatory, judges may "fit the punishment to the offender" rather than "fit the punishment to the crime." Competing theories about criminal justice help to fuel the different approaches to sentencing and punishment. These include the severity of punishment meted, and the specific objective sought by the punishment:

- Retribution: Some believe that the primary purpose of punishment should be to punish an offender for the wrong committed, society's vengeance against a criminal. The sentiment is to punish criminals and promote public safety by keeping them "off the streets."

- Rehabilitation: Others believe that the primary purpose of punishment should be to rehabilitate criminals to mend their criminal ways and to encourage the **adoption** of a more socially acceptable lifestyle. Most experts agree that this theory is commendable but not practical in prisons. Many criminals boast of coming out "better criminals" than they were when they entered prison.

- Deterrence: Still others argue that the perceived punishment for a crime should be so undesirable as to result in deterring someone from actually committing a crime for fear of the likely punishment. Again, the theory is commendable, but many crimes are committed on impulse or under the influence of alcohol and other drugs. Fear of punishment is usually not a deterrent under these circumstances. Moreover, repeat offenders do not fear incarceration the way that people who have been free all their lives might.

## Alternative Sentences

Forced to face prison overcrowding and failed attempts at deterrence or rehabilitation, many professionals in the criminal justice system have encouraged "alternative sentencing," which refers to any punishment other than incarceration. Most alternative sentences are really variations of probation, e.g., a fine and community service, along with a set period of probation. Some judges have gotten more creative in their sentencing. In many jurisdictions, convicted persons have been required to do the following:

- install breathalyzer devices in their vehicles ("ignition interlocks") to prevent their operation of the vehicle without blowing into the device to determine whether their breath is free of alcohol

- carry signs which inform the community of their offense

- stay at home under "house arrest"

- complete alcohol or other drug treatment programs

- attend lectures given by crime victims

## Sentencing Commissions

The U. S. Sentencing Commission was created in 1984 as part of the Sentencing Reform Act provisions that were included in the Comprehensive Crime Control Act of 1984 (28 U.S.C. § 994). The Commission's principal purpose has been to establish uniform sentencing guidelines and practices for the federal court system. The guidelines provide 43 levels of offense seriousness that take into account not only the seriousness of the crime, but also the offender's criminal history. They apply to all federal felonies and most serious misdemeanors.

Decisions rendered by the U.S. Supreme Court in 2004 and 2005 altered the use of sentencing guidelines by state and federal courts. First, the Court in *Blakely v. Washington* (2004) ruled that the sentencing guidelines employed by the state of Washington were unconstitutional. The ruling caused many states to evaluate whether their own sentencing guidelines would survive constitutional muster. Moreover, some lower federal courts ruled that the federal sentencing guidelines were also unconstitutional. The Supreme Court resolved the question about whether mandatory provisions in the federal guidelines violated the Constitution. In two related cases, *United States v. Booker* and *United States v. Fanfan*, both decided in 2005, the Court ruled that the federal guidelines were indeed unconstitutional. According to the Court, judges may use their discretion in following the guidelines, but the guidelines may not be mandatory.

Prior to the *Blakely* decision, many states established their own sentencing commissions. The National Association of Sentencing Commissions (NASC), which includes the federal sector as a member, provides a forum, complete with national conferences, to promote the adoption of uniform or similar presumptive sentencing guidelines among jurisdictions. As of 2005, both the U.S. Sentencing Commission and state governments continued to explore possible means by which federal and state sentencing guidelines could be amended to conform to constitutional requirements.

## Selected State Sentencing Provisions

ALABAMA: The Alabama Legislature formed the Alabama Sentencing Commission to study and make recommendations regarding the state's sentencing practices.

ALASKA: Alaska has judicially-created "benchmark" guidelines for felonies, with moderate appellate review. Parole has been abolished for most (two-thirds) felonies. There is no active sentencing commission for the state. The state legislature modified its sentencing scheme following the Supreme Court's decision in *Blakely*.

ARIZONA: Following the Supreme Court's decision in *Blakely*, state courts in Arizona have issued several rulings regarding the constitutionality of sentencing provisions under state law.

ARKANSAS: State courts employ voluntary guidelines for felonies. There is no appellate review. Arkansas has retained its parole system. There are guidelines which incorporate intermediate sanctions, with preliminary discussions for guidelines in juvenile cases. State sentencing commission was established in 1994.

DELAWARE: Delaware utilizes voluntary guidelines for felonies and misdemeanors. Parole has been abolished in the state since 1990. There is moderate appellate review of sentencing decisions. The state's sentencing guidelines incorporate intermediate sanctions.

DISTRICT of COLUMBIA: The district in 2004 created the District of Columbia Sentencing Commission, which reports directly to the city council.

FLORIDA: In Florida, guidelines were repealed in 1997 and replaced with statutory presumptions for minimum sentences for felonies. The state sentencing commission was abolished in 1998 after the adoption of the new statutory presumptive sentences. There is moderate appellate review of sentencing determinations. Parole has been abolished in the system.

IOWA: Iowa has established a legislative commission to study sentencing reform.

KANSAS: Kansas uses presumptive guidelines for felonies, with moderate appellate review. Parole has been abolished in the state. There are no guidelines for intermediate sanctions.

MARLYAND: Maryland's legislature created the Maryland State Commission on Criminal Sentencing Policy in 1998. There are voluntary guidelines for felonies, with no appellate review. Parole has been retained.

MASSACHUSETTS: In Massachusetts, there are presumptive guidelines for felonies and misdemeanors. A proposal is pending in the legislature for appellate review of sentencing determinations. Parole has been retained.

MICHIGAN: Michigan has been a member of the National Association of Sentencing Commissions since 1999. The state employs presumptive guidelines for felonies, with appellate review as authorized by statute. The state also maintains a restricted parole system. Shortly after the Supreme Court's decision in *Blakley*, the Michigan Supreme Court noted that the decision did not affect Michigan sentencing scheme.

MINNESOTA: The state has presumptive guidelines for felonies, with moderate appellate review. Parole has been abolished in the state. There are no guidelines for intermediate sanctions. In 2005, the Minnesota Legislature enacted a statute ensuring that the state's sentencing guidelines passed constitutional muster.

MISSOURI: Missouri uses voluntary guidelines for felonies, with no appellate review. Parole has been retained in the state.

NORTH CAROLINA: In North Carolina, there are presumptive guidelines for felonies and misdemea-

nors, with minimum appellate review. Since 1999, the state has incorporated a special dispositional grid for juvenile cases. Parole has been abolished in the state. In 2005, the North Carolina Legislature passed a statute ensuring that the state's sentencing laws conformed with *Blakely*.

OHIO: Ohio uses presumptive narrative guidelines for felonies. There is limited appellate review. Parole has been abolished and replaced with a judicial release mechanism. The state legislature is also considering structured sentencing for juvenile offenders.

OKLAHOMA: In Oklahoma, presumptive guidelines are in place for felonies. The state has retained a limited parole system. Legislative proposals are pending for appellate review of sentencing determinations.

OREGON: Oregon has presumptive guidelines for felonies, with moderate appellate review. Parole has been abolished. In 2005, the Oregon Legislature approved a statute ensuring that the state sentencing scheme conformed with *Blakely*.

PENNSYLVANIA: Presumptive guidelines are in place for felonies and misdemeanors, with minimum appellate review. Parole has been retained.

SOUTH CAROLINA: The state employs voluntary guidelines for felonies and misdemeanors with potential sentences of one year or more.

TENNESSEE: There are presumptive guidelines for felonies, with moderate appellate review. Parole has been retained. The sentencing commission was abolished in 1995. In 2005, the Tennessee Legislature approved a statute ensuring that the state sentencing scheme conformed with *Blakely*.

UTAH: The state uses voluntary guidelines for felonies and select misdemeanors (sex offenses). There is no appellate review. Parole has been retained in the state. The state also uses voluntary guidelines for its juvenile sentencing.

VIRGINIA: Virginia has voluntary guidelines for felonies, with no appellate review. Parole has been abolished. The state is studying juvenile sentencing guidelines.

WASHINGTON: The state employs presumptive guidelines for felonies, with moderate appellate review. Parole has been abolished in the state. Special guidelines for juvenile sentencing are in effect. In

2005, the Washington Legislature approved a statute ensuring that the state sentencing scheme conformed with *Blakely*.

WISCONSIN: In Wisconsin, the state employs voluntary guidelines for felonies. Legislative proposals are pending, which do not contemplate appellate review. The proposals also contemplate the abolishment of the state's parole system, as well as the creation of a new permanent sentencing commission.

## Additional Resources

*The Law and Policy of Sentencing and Corrections in a Nutshell.* Branham, Lynn S., Thomson/West, 2005.

*Law of Sentencing.* Campbell, Arthur W., Thomson/West, 2004.

"State Sentencing Commissions." National Association of Sentencing Commissions. Available at http://www.ussc.gov/states.htm

## Organizations

### *United States Sentencing Commission*
One Columbus Circle, N.E.
Washington, DC 20002-8002 USA
Phone: (202) 502-4500
URL: http://www.ussc.gov/

# CRIMINAL LAW

## SEX OFFENDERS

*Sections within this essay:*

- Background
- The Impact of Jacob Wetterling
- Megan's Laws: Community Notification Laws
- Residency Restrictions for Sex Offenders
- Other Methods to Deal with Sex Offenders
    - Chemical and Surgical Castration
    - Civil Commitment
    - Amber Alerts
- Additional Resources

## Background

Society and policy makers have long struggled with finding effective ways to protect the public from sex offenders. A sex offender is a person who has been convicted of certain sex offense crimes. Examples of sex offenses include:

- Sexual conduct with a minor
- Sexual assault
- Sexual assault of spouse
- Molestation of a child
- Continuous sexual abuse of a child
- Infamous crimes against nature
- Lewd and lascivious acts
- Indecent exposure and public sexual indecency
- Taking a child for the purpose of prostitution

- Sexual exploitation of a minor
- Incest
- Kidnapping, aggravated assault, murder, unlawful imprisonment, and burglary (when the offense includes evidence of sexual motivation)
- Failure to register as a sex offender
- Violation of Sex Offender Registration statutes

Most offenses involving criminal sexual conduct fall within the jurisdiction of state law, but federal law also includes a number of sexual offenses. The offenses are found in Title 18 of the United States Code. Some of the federal offenses specifically apply to sexual offenses committed within the territorial jurisdiction of the United States or in a federal prison. Other crimes involve offenders who cross state or international borders to commit, or in the commission, of a sexual offense. For example, 18 U.S.C. section 2251 makes it illegal to knowingly print, publish, or cause to be made, "any notice or advertisement seeking or offering to receive, exchange, buy, produce, display, distribute, or reproduce any visual depiction involving the use of a minor engaging in sexually explicit conduct. This statute also applies when such person knows that such notice or advertisement will be, or has been, transported in interstate or foreign commerce by any means, including by computer."

Federal sexual offense include:

- Selling or buying of children (Section 2251A(a)(b))
- Certain activities relating to material involving the sexual exploitation of minors, includ-

ing both distribution and receipt of visual depictions in books, magazines, periodicals, films, and videotapes (Section 2252)

- Certain activities relating to material constituting or containing child pornography (Section 2252A)

- Production of sexually explicit depictions of a minor for importation into the United States (Section 2260)

- Transporting an individual in interstate or foreign commerce with the intent that the individual engage in prostitution or other illegal sexual activity (Section 2421)

- Transportation of minors in interstate or foreign commerce, with intent to engage in criminal sexual activity (Section 2423(a))

- Interstate or foreign travel with intent to engage in a sexual act with a juvenile (Section 2423(b))

- Use of interstate facilities to transmit information about an individual under the age of 16, with "the intent to entice, encourage, offer, or solicit that minor to engage in any sexual activity that can be charged as a criminal offense." (Section 2425)

## The Impact of Jacob Wetterling

On October 22, 1989, eleven-year-old Jacob Wetterling was abducted as he, his brother, and a friend rode their bikes home from a convenience store in St. Joseph, Minnesota. Law enforcement authorities arrived on the scene within minutes. No sign of Wetterling or his abductor has ever been found, despite the involvement of local authorities, the Federal Bureau of Investigation, hundreds of volunteer searchers, and more than 50,000 leads.

Jacob's disappearance spurred his family and supporters to found the Jacob Wetterling Foundation (JWF) in January 1990. The Foundation's mission is to protect children from sexual exploitation and abduction, through prevention education, victims' assistance, and legislation aimed at sex offenders. In 1991 JWF saw its first success with Minnesota's State Sex Offender Registration Act. The law provided law enforcement authorities with a comprehensive list of sex offenders in the state, something authorities lacked when Jacob was abducted.

JWF's agenda has included both state and federal legislative changes. In 1994, Congress passed the

Omnibus Crime Bill. This legislation included the Jacob Wetterling Crimes Against Children and Sex Offender Registration Act. The law mandated that each state create a specific program to register sex offenders.

In 1996, the Wetterling Act was amended by Megan's Law (discussed below), and the Pam Lychner Sex Offender Tracking and Identification Act. The Lychner Act called upon the FBI to establish a national database of names and addresses of sex offenders who are released from prison. It also required lifetime registration for certain offenders. Its purpose is to make it easier for authorities to track the movements of convicted sex offenders throughout all 50 states. The National Sex Offender Registry can be found at http://www.nsor.net.

In 1997 other changes were made to the Wetterling Act. Changes included heightened registration requirements for sexually violent offenders such as members of the U.S. Armed Forces. Additional registration requirements were imposed for sex offenders who live in one state but go to school or work in another state.

## Community Notification Laws

The original impact of the Wetterling Act was to provide law enforcement authorities the means to track and locate convicted sex offenders. Community notification laws have adapted the idea to make information about sex offenders available to the public. Community notification laws, commonly referred to as sex offender registries, are most often associated with the 1994 rape and murder of seven-year-old Megan Kanka. She died just thirty yards from her own front door in Hamilton Township, New Jersey. On July 29, 1994, a neighbor lured the little girl to his house with the promise that she could see his new puppy. The neighbor was a convicted sex offender who had served time in prison for aggravated assault and attempted sexual assault against a child.

The outcry over Megan's death spurred the New Jersey Legislature to quick action. Within three months, the legislature passed the community notification law known as Megan's Law. Less than two years later, on May 17, 1996, President William Jefferson Clinton signed a federal version of the law, amending the Wetterling Act. The amendment required each state to provide public notification and information about sexual offenders living in the area. The law applies to all sex offenders - whether their victims were children or adults.

Sex offender registry requirements vary by state, but share common characteristics. Convicted sexual offenders are required to register with their local law enforcement or corrections agency. This information is forwarded to a central location, such as the state police or state bureau of investigation. Information required for the registry typically includes name, address, date of birth, social security information, physical description, fingerprints, and photographs. Conviction information may also be required, as well as samples for DNA identification.

A court or registering agency informs offenders of their duty to register. Offenders typically must register within days of their release from prison or placement on supervision. Placement on the registry usually lasts ten years. Lifetime registration may be required, particularly if an offender has been denominated a "sexual predator" or where an offender has been convicted of a subsequent sexual offense.

According to the Department of Justice's Bureau of Justice Statistics, in February 2001, approximately 386,000 convicted sex offenders were registered in 49 states and the District of Columbia (excluding Massachusetts). In April 1998, 277,000 offenders were registered. California led the way with more than 88,000 registrants; Texas was next with almost 30,000. Thirty-two states collected DNA information from registrants. The FBI maintains a web site with links to all state sex offender registry web sites. The site is located at http://www.fbi.gov/hq/cid/cac/states.htm.

Every state has a sex offender registry, but states vary greatly in how they release information to the public, and what information is released. Some states require interested citizens to access registry information at their local law enforcement agencies. For example, in South Dakota only a few communities have placed specific offender information online; in most communities interested citizens must request the information from authorities. In the neighboring state of Iowa, anyone can access information online about any person on its sex offender registry in a number of ways. Searches can be conducted by name, geographic location, or gender of the offender or victim. Iowa provides photos, physical descriptions, addresses, and details of convictions.

Law enforcement authorities may also have the obligation to disseminate information about registered sex offenders. Notification may extend to prior victims, neighbors, schools, youth organization, and other relevant individuals or groups. In some cases, community-wide notification may be required. Newspapers, television, radio, and community meetings are some of the methods used to provide community notification.

Critics of sex offender registries claim that they do little to protect the most victims of sexual offenses, because most victims know the perpetrator. According to the Department of Justice, about seven of every ten female rape or sexual assault victims reported that the perpetrator was an intimate, relative, friend, or acquaintance.

The U.S. Supreme Court has addressed the constitutionality of sex offender registries. In *Connecticut Department of Safety v. Doe,* and in *Smith v. Doe,* both decided March 5, 2003, the court found that sex offender registries do not violate sex offenders' constitutional rights.

## Residency Restrictions for Sex Offenders

Residency restriction laws are a fairly new method some jurisdictions are using in an attempt to curb the actions of sex offenders. Alabama passed the first residency restriction law in 1996. The law was part of the states' Community Notification Act. It prohibited child molesters from living within 1,000 feet of a school. By January 2006, approximately 14 states had enacted residency restrictions. Moreover, some local governments have implemented their own residency restrictions.

Critics and supporters of residency restriction laws have watched Iowa's law with interest since its passage in 2002. The Iowa law applies to a "person who has committed a criminal offense against a minor, or an aggravated offense, sexually violent offense, or other relevant offense that involved a minor." According to the law, "A person shall not reside within two thousand feet of the real property comprising a public or nonpublic elementary or secondary school or a child care facility." The law does not apply in certain circumstances, including where the "person has established a residence prior to July 1, 2002, or a school or child care facility is newly located on or after July 1, 2002," or where the person is a minor or a ward under a guardianship. It is an aggravated misdemeanor to reside within 2,000 feet of a school or child care.

The Iowa law took effect on July 1, 2002, but was almost immediately challenged in federal district court. The plaintiffs were three named sex offenders who contended that the law was unconstitutional on its face. The case was certified as a class action, on behalf of other sex offenders to whom the law would apply. At trial, the plaintiffs presented evidence regarding the scope of the law. In many cities, the law would effectively limit sex offenders to small areas of residency. In small towns, a single school or child care center could mean that the entire town was off limits. Expert witnesses on both sides testified to their beliefs in the expected efficacy of the law.

The district court enjoined enforcement of the law, and ruled that it was unconstitutional on several grounds, including:

- The law was unconstitutional because it was an ex post facto law for anyone convicted before July 1, 2002;

- It violated plaintiffs' rights to avoid self-incrimination, because registrants would be required to report their addresses, even when the addresses were not in compliance with the law;

- It violated plaintiffs' procedural due process rights;

- It infringed on fundamental rights to travel and decide how to conduct their family affairs; and

- It was not tailored narrowly enough to serve a compelling state interest.

In a ruling dated April 29, 2005, three judges from the United States Eighth Circuit Court of Appeals unanimously voted to reverse the district court's decision. The appellate court dispensed with each ground relied upon by the district court, and ruled that the law was not unconstitutional on its face. The court ruled that there exists no constitutional right to "live where you want." Therefore, the state only needed to show that the statute rationally advanced some legitimate governmental purpose. Plaintiffs acknowledged that the law was enacted to promote the safety of children, and that this was a legitimate legislative goal. They argued, however, that the law is irrational because there is no scientific evidence to support the conclusion that residency restrictions will enhance the safety of children. The court rejected this argument as well, noting that state policymakers are entitled to employ "common sense" when making a determination that "limiting the frequency of contact between sex offenders and areas where children are located is likely to reduce the risk of an offense."

Two judges agreed that the law did not amount to an ex post facto punishment. They ruled that plaintiffs did not establish by "clearest proof" that the law's punitive effect overrides the legislature's "legitimate intent to enact a nonpunitive, civil regulatory measure that protects health and safety" of the state's citizens.

Municipalities and counties have enacted their own versions of residency restrictions. For example, in Des Moines, Iowa, the state's largest city, officials added parks, libraries, swimming pools, and recreational trails to the list of protected buffer zones.

A report in the *Des Moines Register* on January 22, 2006, reported that since the state's residency law took effect, more sex offenders are eluding tracking by authorities. The paper reported that 298 sex offenders were unaccounted for in January 2006, compared to 142 on June 1, 2005. Critics charge that the law has forced some sex offenders to become homeless; others may lie and say that they are homeless to hide the fact that they are not complying with the law. Iowa has approximately 6,000 registered sex offenders.

## Other Methods to Deal with Sex Offenders

### Chemical and Surgical Castration

A few states, including California and Florida, permit convicted sex offenders to be injected with Depo Provera, an FDA-approved birth control drug. Often called "chemical castration," Depo Provera is meant to quell the sex drive of male sex offenders by lowering their testosterone levels. The drug does not render any permanent physical change to the body. The treatment is believed to be most effective on sex offenders who possess uncontrollable biological urges that take the form of sexual fantasies that are usually only satisfied by acting on the fantasy.

Both the California and Florida statutes provide for mandatory injections for repeat sex offenders, as well as discretionary injections for first-time offenders. Despite the mandatory language in the Florida law, the law has apparently been invoked only a few times since its passage in 1997.

Critics, including the American Civil Liberties Union (ACLU), charge that chemical castration violates sex offenders' constitutional rights. The ACLU contends that chemical castration violates an offender's implied right to privacy under the Fourteenth

Amendment, rights of due process and equal protection, and the Eighth Amendment's ban of cruel and unusual punishment.

Pursuant to a 1997 law, Texas permits surgical castration of offenders. By May 2005, three men had undergone the voluntary procedure. Candidates must be at least 21 years of age, have had at least two sex offense convictions, and have undergone at least 18 months of sex offender treatment, including Depo Provera injections, to understand how their bodies might react with less testosterone.

### Civil Commitment

Some states have used civil commitment proceedings to remove habitual sex offenders from society for extended periods of time. The United States Supreme Court ruled in *Kansas v. Hendricks* (1997) that such laws do not violate the Constitution's double jeopardy or ex post facto clauses.

Minnesota's civil commitment law for habitual sex offenders is fairly typical. Under Minnesota law, a person classified as having a "sexual psychopathic personality" or denominated a "sexually dangerous person" may be committed indefinitely in a secure treatment facility. The commitment is intended to reduce the risk of future dangerous sexual behavior. It is not meant to serve a punishment for past crimes. Civilly committed sex offenders may be held for an indeterminate amount of time. In other words, they may be held as long as warranted to successfully treat them and to satisfy public safety concerns.

According to Minnesota's law, a person with a sexual psychopathic personality is one who:

- Has engaged in a "habitual course" of misconduct in sexual matters

- Suffers from an "utter lack of power to control" sexual impulses

- As a result of this inability to control behavior is "dangerous to other persons"

A sexually dangerous person is defined as someone who has "engaged in a course of harmful sexual conduct." This conduct creates a "substantial likelihood" of serious physical or emotional harm to another. Moreover, the person must be diagnosed with a sexual, personality or mental disorder, and found likely to engage in harmful sexual conduct in the future.

A commitment hearing is held to determine whether civil commitment is warranted. This hearing is usually held shortly before a sex offender is to be released from prison. Commitment proceedings could also be commenced as part of a plea agreement. A petition may also be filed after a person has been released from prison on a conditional or supervised release. It is not necessary that a person have committed any further sexual offenses after the release from imprisonment.

A judge makes commitment determinations in Minnesota. The judge listens to evidence on both sides, which may include evidence of past sexual misconduct that did not result in an arrest or conviction. The state has the burden to prove that commitment is necessary, but its burden of proof is not as high as in a criminal case. If the judge finds by clear and convincing evidence that the individual is a sexual psychopathic personality or a sexually dangerous person, the person will be committed to a secure treatment facility operated by the Minnesota Sex Offender Program.

Officials generally have 60 to 90 days to evaluate the inmate and report back to the court once a person has been committed. The court then holds a second hearing to determine whether an indeterminate commitment is required.

Minnesota mainly relies on group therapy to treat civilly committed sex offenders. The offender progresses through three stages: the evaluation stage, the inpatient treatment stage and the transition stage. The inpatient treatment stage consists of four parts; an offender must pass each before progressing to the next stage. The parts are accountability, insight, integration/behavior change, and preparation for the transition stage.

A review board determines when discharge, transfer, or other change in status is appropriate. Requests for such a hearing may come from the patient, the patient's attorney, or the facility medical director. After a hearing, the review board recommends a course of action to the Commissioner of the Minnesota Department of Human Services. The Commissioner then issues an order denying or granting the petition. The Commissioner's order is subject to appeal, ultimately by the Minnesota Supreme Court.

### Amber Alerts

Although not specifically targeted only at sex offenders, the Amber Alert system is intended to quickly and widely disseminate information about child abductions. AMBER is an acronym for "America's Missing: Broadcast Emergency Response." The system takes its name from nine-year-old Amber Hagerman, who was abducted and murdered in Arlington, Texas, in 1996. It uses various media outlets to inform the general public that a child has been abducted. Alerts go out over radio, television, e-mail, electronic traffic-condition signs, and SMS text messages. Law enforcement typically broadcast the name and a description of the abducted child, and a description of the suspected abductor and the abductor's vehicle, and license plate number, when available.

On April 30, 2003, President George W. Bush signed into law the PROTECT Act, which established the federal government's role in the Amber Alert system. The law appropriated $20 million for the National Amber Alert Network for grants to the states for the development or enhancement of notification systems. Every state has an Amber Alert system. According to the Department of Justice, 71 children were recovered in 2004 due to the Amber Alert system.

## Additional Resources

*Sexual Violence: Opposing Viewpoints*. Helen Cothran, editor, Greenhaven Press, 2003.

*Expert: Castration No Cure for Pedophilia*. Robert Crowe, The Houston Chronicle, Section B, P. 1, May 10, 2005.

*Summary of State Sex Offender Registries, 2001*. Bureau of Justice Statistics, Department of Justice, March 2002, available at http://www.ojp.usdoj.gov/bjs/pub/ascii/sssor01.txt.

*Chemical Procedure for Sex Offender Weighed*. Larry Keller, Palm Beach Post, Page 1B, August 30, 2005.

*Twice as Many Sex Offenders Missing*. Lee Rood, Des Moines Register, Page A1, January 22, 2006.

*Iowa Joins Other States with Tough Molester Laws*. Tim Higgins, Des Moines Register, December 26, 2005, available at http://desmoinesregister.com/apps/pbcs.dll/article?AID=/20051226/NEWS01/512260318.

*Iowa Law has Sex Offenders Packing Bags*. Michael Riley, The Denver Post, January 8, 2006, available at http://www.denverpost.com/nationworld/ci_3382005.

*Sex Offender Civil Commitment Fact Sheet [Minneosota]* Office of the Ombudsman for Mental Health and Mental Retardation, January 2004, available at http://www.ombudmhmr.state.mn.us/cctrc/sexoffenderccfactsheet.htm.

*Reaching Out*. Justine Brown, Government Technology, May 27, 2005, available at http://www.govtech.net/magazine/story.php?id=93808.

*Sex Offender Community Notification Law [Alabama]*. Available at http://www.ago.state.al.us/victim_master.cfm?Action=Offender.

## Organizations

### National Sex Offender Registry (NSOR)
URL: http://www.nsor.net/index.htm

### Jacob Wetterling Foundation (JWF)
2314 University Avenue West, Suite 14
St. Paul, MN 55114 USA
Phone: (800) 325-HOPE
Fax: (651) 714-9098
URL: http://www.jwf.org
Primary Contact: Nancy Sabin, Executive Director

### Office of Justice Programs, U.S. Department of Justice, Amber Alert Program
810 Seventh Street NW
Washington, D.C. 20531 USA
URL: http://www.amberalert.gov
Primary Contact: Regina B. Schofield, Amber Alert Coordinator, Assistant Attorney General

# DISPUTE RESOLUTION ALTERNATIVES

## ARBITRATION

*Sections within this essay:*

- Background
- Contractual vs. Compulsory Arbitration
- Arbitrability
- Who Are the Arbitrators?
- The Arbitration Process
- The Uniform Arbitration Act (UAA)
- Federal Arbitration
- State Arbitrations
- Additional Resources
- Organizations

## Background

**Arbitration** refers to one of several methods, collectively referred to as "alternative dispute resolution" (ADR), for resolving legal disputes other than through a formal court system. Arbitration is very similar to a trial in court, except that the claims and defenses are presented to a privately-retained neutral party ("arbitrator" or "arbiter") rather than a judge or jury. After listening to summary arguments and considering all the **evidence** presented in a dispute, an arbitrator renders a decision tantamount to a court decision or judgment.

Since it is intended to substitute for a trial, formal arbitration is generally as binding as a court **adjudication**. Therefore, like it or not, a decision of an arbitrator may be appealed only under very narrow cir-

cumstances and criteria. (In fact, the arbitration agreement may designate that the decision is final and binding and cannot be appealed.) However, some forms of arbitration may be expressly designated as "non-binding." In those circumstances, one may accept or reject the arbitration decision and continue with **litigation** in the courts.

Arbitration has become a preferred alternative favored by both courts and parties for resolving disputes. All 50 states acknowledge some form of arbitration for the resolution of certain disputes. A majority of states (48 as of 2002, excepting Georgia and Mississippi) have adopted the Uniform Arbitration Act (UAA) and/or its revised version, published in 2000, or substantially similar legislation. Washington, D. C. and Puerto Rico also have adopted versions of the Act.

The use of arbitration has greatly expanded in recent years, because of the fast resolution of disputes, and the relative consistency and near-uniformity in procedural requirements (thanks to the UAA). The arbitration process also affords the parties a degree of privacy for sensitive or personal matters. Health care providers and insurance companies almost universally favor arbitrations because of the opportunity to avoid the publicity of court trials and jury verdicts.

## Contractual versus Compulsory Arbitration

Voluntary arbitration refers to an agreement entered into by two or more parties who choose to arbitrate a matter rather than litigate the matter in court. The agreement is a binding contract, and if a dispute later develops, one cannot choose to ignore the arbitration agreement and file suit instead.

But arbitration is not "compulsory." It simply means that persons have voluntarily agreed in advance to arbitrate any future disputes and cannot back out of that agreement once a dispute arises. Failure to abide with "contractual arbitration" as agreed constitutes a breach of the agreement. If an individual has entered into such an agreement and later decides to file suit instead of arbitrating the dispute, the other person or party may take that individual to court to compel arbitration.

One of the most common circumstances where this situation arises is in the health care and insurance industries. When individuals enter a hospital for treatment or care, or fill out "new patient" forms for a physician, they may be asked to sign a document in which they agree to arbitrate any dispute which may arise. If they later attempt to sue the doctor or hospital for **malpractice** or a billing dispute, the agreement they signed will be presented to the court and their lawsuit will be dismissed and/or the court will order them to arbitrate the matter. The real danger in having their case dismissed is that the time limit for filing a dispute in arbitration may have expired while they were attempting to file a lawsuit in court (in some jurisdictions, a court may "stop the clock" to provide them with enough time to dismiss their court case and file it in arbitration). The lesson to learn is that they should carefully read all documents their health care provider may present to them prior to treatment or care, and they need to be always be certain to retain a copy for their records.

In many states, laws prohibit health care providers from refusing to treat individuals if they will not sign a voluntary arbitration agreement. On the other hand, only in rare circumstances will a court permit them to "set aside" a signed agreement to arbitrate and allow them to file suit instead. Usually, they will have to prove to the court that they did not sign the arbitration agreement "voluntarily." For example, there is some legal precedent for allowing agreements with health care providers to be set aside (making them "voidable") when evidence shows that they were signed while under extreme **duress** or in pain, semi-conscious, etc. In even more rare circumstances, a court may find an agreement to arbitrate "unconscionable" as against **public policy** and determine it to be null and void.

It is common practice for insurance policies (e.g., automobile, home, health, etc.) to contain language that commits an insured to the use of arbitration in the event of a dispute with the insurer. Many in-

sureds do not realize that such language is contained in the lengthy policy language at the time they apply for insurance coverage. It often remains unknown and unrealized until a dispute arises and the insured attempts to sue his or her insurance provider. In most insurance policies, the agreement to arbitrate is not a separate document, but rather a statement contained in the policy, such as, "You agree to arbitrate any dispute relating to . . ." Individuals who sign the application for insurance coverage and have a policy issued to them have agreed to those terms.

On the other hand, "compulsory arbitration" is generally the result of express **statute** or regulation that mandates the arbitration of certain matters. The most common of these is the mandatory arbitration of labor disputes. If individuals are members of a union, the bargaining agreement for their bargaining unit will most likely contain provisions for the arbitration of all disputes.

One of the most compelling reasons for mandating the arbitration of certain matters is that such matters tend to be very complex, specialized, or too time-consuming for a general jury trial. For example, a dispute over a provision in the Internal Revenue Code may be technically complicated. Instead of a jury trial, arbitration will provide the opportunity for appointment of a neutral arbitrator or panel of arbiters who may be knowledgeable and experienced in tax matters and can more readily understand the arguments presented. The "State Provisions" Section below summarizes key areas where states have mandated compulsory arbitration of certain matters.

## Arbitrability

If the subject matter of a particular dispute falls within the scope of subjects that the parties agreed in advance to arbitrate, then the particular dispute is "arbitrable." However, many disputes involve multiple issues, not all of which were contemplated when the arbitration agreement was executed. For example, a claim may state an arbitrable issue of **wrongful discharge** from employment. But the defense may raise an issue of untimely filing of the claim or some other procedural error or **fatal** flaw on the part of the complainant. Who decides that?

Most federal and state **appellate court** decisions have concluded that the only proper inquiry that a court should make, on a motion to compel arbitration, is (1) whether there exists a valid agreement to arbitrate between the parties, and (2) whether the agreement covers the dispute at hand. All other issues, particularly defenses such as untimeliness, **collateral estoppel**, **res** judicata, etc., should properly be decided by the arbitrator.

If such an event should occur (the raising of an issue not related to the subject matter of the dispute at hand), the arbitrator may render one decision covering all or may be forced to render a separate opinion on the "arbitrability" of the separate claim or defense, without ever reaching the main issue of the dispute. Still, sometimes the arbitrability of the main issue is, in itself, the actual dispute, as often occurs in labor contracts.

## Who Are the Arbitrators?

The majority of arbitration agreements contain provisions governing the selection and appointment of an arbitrator or arbitration panel. Private arbitration contracts may designate any person or any method for choosing a person or persons as arbitrators. If an arbitration panel is elected (usually comprised of three persons), each party may nominate or appoint one arbitrator, and both sides will decide on a "neutral" third person. Or, the parties will each select one arbitrator, and the two arbitrators will then select a third "neutral." Alternatively, three "neutrals" may be selected by having each party alternately strike names on one list until only three names remain. In single-arbitrator arbitrations, an external source of available arbitrators is often consulted.

The American Arbitration Association (AAA) is the largest full-service ADR provider in the United States. It maintains a National Roster of Arbitrators and Mediators (containing nearly 17,000 names and resumes as of 2002). The persons named on the Roster have been nominated by leaders in their industry or profession. The AAA has strict criteria for its Roster members, and those selected are generally recognized for their standing and expertise in their fields, their integrity, and their dispute resolution skills. Many are attorneys, but being one is not a requirement. Many arbitration agreements expressly designate the use of AAA as the preferred source for arbitrators.

Under the Federal Arbitration Agreement (FAA) (see below), if an arbitration agreement does not contain a provision for the naming or appointing of an arbitrator, "the court shall designate and appoint an arbitrator . . ." (9 **USC** Section 5).

## The Arbitration Process

The arbitration process generally begins with the filing of a request for arbitration. This action may be performed by direct application to the forum designated in the private arbitration agreement or by court order. Parties who simply wish to arbitrate a matter should contact a local entity that offers arbitration services. Often, a local circuit or district court may have information or services available. There are several national organizations that also offer local arbitrations or supply lists of arbitrators (see listings below).

The chosen forum will most likely furnish the parties with a copy of rules and procedures. Attorneys may or may not represent the parties. Generally, an arbitration **hearing** parallels a court trial, in that there is the taking of **testimony** from witnesses and the introduction of evidence. However, many arbitrations are conducted on the basis of "summary briefs" from each party, which outline the issues and the arguments in document form. Arbitration decisions are always in written form. A decision may or may not be appealable, depending on the forum and the agreement of the parties.

## The Uniform Arbitration Act (UAA)

The Uniform Arbitration Act, promulgated in 1955, has been overwhelmingly adopted by state legislatures and federal district courts for alternate dispute resolution. Its popularity derives from the advantages of uniformity and thoroughness, and in 2000, the National Conference of Commissioners on Uniform State Laws approved and recommended a revised version of the UAA for enactment in all the states. The UAA provides a structured procedure to be followed in all arbitrations, and, most importantly, includes details addressing matters that are often overlooked in privately drafted arbitration agreements. The revised UAA includes provisions not addressed in the original UAA, but deemed important as a result of the increased use of arbitration. Some of the new provisions address matters such as (1) who decides the arbitrability of a dispute and by what criteria; (2) whether arbitrators have the discretion to order **discovery**, issue protective orders, decide motions for **summary judgment**, etc.; and (3) to what extent arbitrators and arbitration organizations are immune from civil lawsuits.

## Federal Arbitration

Amendment VII (1791) provides that "In all suits at **common law**, where the value in controversy shall exceed twenty dollars, the right of trial by jury shall be preserved . . ." This provision guarantees individuals their "day in court" unless they either voluntarily choose an alternative dispute resolution, or the subject matter of their dispute falls under a compulsory arbitration mandate by law. Generally, if arbitration is made compulsory, there is a right of appeal through the courts of an arbitration decision.

Arbitration in the federal courts may be the result of a private contractual agreement to arbitrate, a **statutory** mandate, or a court-ordered arbitration. A majority of federal courts have authorized or established at least one court-wide ADR program, which may include court-ordered **mediation**, arbitration, early neutral evaluation (ENE), etc. These measures are the result of the Civil Justice Reform Act of 1990 (CJRA) (28 USC 471 et seq.). The CJRA has changed the use of ADR from being the initiative of individual judges to being part of court-managed, district wide programs.

The Alternative Dispute Resolution Act of 1998 (ADRA) (28 USC 651 et seq.) further expands upon the CJRA by mandating that courts establish and authorize the use of ADR in all civil actions. The federal government also encourages arbitration and mediation within its own ranks. The Administrative Dispute Resolution Act of 1996 provides a mediation forum for handling disputes within agencies or between citizens and agencies (claims against the government).

Arbitration in the federal court system is governed by the Federal Arbitration Act (FAA), first enacted in 1925 and codified in 1947 under Title 9 of the United States Code. Chapter 1 of Title 9 (General Provisions) contains such directives as the method for naming or appointing an arbitrator (Section 5); for summoning witnesses to **testify** (Section 7); and for remedy and recourse for failing to arbitrate as agreed (Section 4). While the FAA is not in itself a procedural mandate, it provides an authoritative backdrop for arbitrations and commands that arbitration agreements be enforced in accordance with their terms.

Importantly, the FAA "preempts" any state law that conflicts with its pro-arbitration public policy or any state law that renders moot or limits contractual agreements to arbitrate. The rule of preemption applies in both federal and state courts (adjudicating federal claims). However, if the parties clearly express an agreement to conduct their arbitration under state law/rules (under a "choice of law" provision), the FAA will not preempt this.

## State Arbitration

The following states provide for ADR (arbitration or mediation) for certain types of disputes:

ALABAMA: Alabama Code, Ch. 25-7-4 applies to labor disputes.

ALASKA: Alaska Statutes 42.40.840 and 23.40.190 address labor disputes. Family disputes are governed by 25.20.080 and 25.24.080. Disputes involving automobile warranties are governed by 45.45.355.

ARIZONA: Arizona has adopted the UAA under Sections 12-1501 to 12-1518 of the Arizona Statutes. Provisions for arbitration/mediation of family disputes is covered under 25-381.01 to 25-381.24. Automobile warranties are covered under 44-1265.

ARKANSAS: The UAA has been adopted under Arkansas Statutes 16-108-201 to 16-108-224. Sections 11-2-201 to 11-2-206 govern labor disputes.

CALIFORNIA: California's Code contains extensive provisions for the arbitration and/or mediation of many types of disputes. Labor disputes are addressed under Sections 65, 66, and 3518. Family disputes are covered in Sections 5180 to 5183. Education matters are covered by 48260.6, 48263, 48263.5 (truancy), and 56503 (special education). There is a special provision for the arbitration of cable TV franchise disputes under 53066.1(n)(1). Environmental regulatory disputes, including issues involving pesticides, are covered under 13127(c)(1). Water rights disputes are handled under 1219. Community disputes of a business or professional nature are covered under 465 to 471.5.

COLORADO: Colorado's statutes provide ADR for labor disputes under 8-3-113. Family matters are covered by 14-10129.5. Agricultural debts are governed by 6-9-101 to 6-9-106. A special statutory provision exists for ADR of disputes involving mobile homes under 38-12-216. The UAA has been adopted under 13-22-201 to 13-22-223. Dispute resolution in general is covered by 13-22-301 to 13-22-310.

CONNECTICUT: Labor disputes are covered under Connecticut Statutes 31-91 to 31-100, 5-276 and 5-276a. Family disputes are resolved under 46b-59a. Public Act 87-316 Section 8 (1987) is covered under 42-182.

DELAWARE: Delaware's Code covers labor disputes under Title 14 Section 4002 and 4014, Title 19 Section 110 and 113, and Title 19 Section 1614. Automobile warranties are covered under Title 6 Section 5007.

FLORIDA: Florida Statutes Annotated 448.06 and 681.110(4)9d) cover labor disputes. Family disputes are addressed under 44.101, 61.183, 39.42, 39.427 to 39.429, 39.436, 39.44, and 39.442. Automobile **warranty** disputes are provided for under 681.108 and 681.111 Mobile home disputes fall under 723.037 and 723.038. The state maintains "citizen dispute **settlement** centers" for ADR assistance under 44.201.

GEORGIA: Labor disputes are covered under Georgia Code 34-2-6(5), 25-5-1 to 25-5-14, 45-19-32, and 45-19-36. Public employee grievances and "unlawful practices" labor arbitrations are mandated under 45-19-36.

HAWAII: Hawaii Revised Statutes 371-10, 98-11(b)(1)(d), 89-12(a) and (b), 380-8, and 377-3 cover ADR for labor disputes. Automobile warranty disputes are covered under 490-2 and 313-1. Medical **conciliation** is addressed by 671-11 to 671-20. There is a special statutory provision for ADR of geothermal resources disputes under 205-5.1. International disputes are covered by 1988 Haw. Sess. Laws, Ch. 186, Sections 1-9.

IDAHO: Idaho Statutes Title 7, Special Proceedings, Chapter 9 adopts the UAA. Idaho Section 44-106 governs labor disputes.

ILLINOIS: Labor disputes are covered by Illinois Compiled Statutes, Ch. 48, paragraphs 1612, v1706, 1712, 1713(b); and Ch. 10, paragraph 26. Family disputes are covered by Ch. 40, paragraph 602.1 and 607.1. Automobile warranty disputes are covered by Ch.121.5, paragraph 1204(4). Disputes involving **public utilities** fall under Ch. 11, paragraph 702.12a. Illinois operates several nonprofit community dispute resolution centers under the auspices of Ch. 37, paragraph 851.1 to 856.

INDIANA: Labor disputes are covered under Indiana Code 5-14-1.5-6.5(2), 22-1-1-8(d), 22-6-1-7, 20-7.5-1-9 to 20-7.5-1-13. Family disputes are covered under 31-1-24-1 to 31-1-24-9, 31-1-23-5 to 31-1-23-9. Automobile warranties are handled under 24-5-13-19. **Civil Rights** disputes are covered under 22-9-1-6. **Consumer protection** disputes are covered under 4-6-9-4(a)(4). There is a special Code provision for water rights disputes under 13-2-1-6(2).

IOWA: Labor disputes are covered under Iowa Code 20.19 to 20.20 and 679B to 679B.27. Family disputes are covered under 598.16 and 598.41(2). Agricultural debts are handled under 654a1 to 654a14. Civil Rights disputes are covered under 601A.15(3)(c). Informal dispute resolution in general is addressed under 679.1 to 679.14.

KANSAS: Kansas Statutes 5-401 to 5-422 expressly adopt the UAA. Labor disputes are covered under Kansas Statutes 44-817, 44-819(j), 44-820(c), 44-826, 44-828, 72-5413(h), 72-5427, 72-5429, 72-5430(b)(7), 72-5430(c)(7), 75-4322, 75-4323, 75-4332, and 75-4333. The ADR provisions for family disputes are covered under 23-601 to 23-607 and 23-701. Automobile warranties are handled under 50-645(e). Civil Rights disputes are covered under 44-1001 to 44-1005. There is a special ADR provision for barbershop business disputes under 65-1824(4).

KENTUCKY: Kentucky has extensive ADR provisions in its Kentucky Revised Statutes (KRS). The UUAA has been adopted under KRS 417.045 to 417.240. Labor disputes are covered under KRS 337.425, 345.080, 336.010, 336.020, 336.140, and 336.151 to 336.156. Family disputes are covered under KRS 403.140(b) and 403.170. Automobile warranties are handled under KRS 367.860 to 367.880. Civil Rights disputes are covered under KRS 344.190 to 344.290 and 337.425. Education matters are covered under KRS 165A.350 and 360. Disputes involving the production and distribution of agricultural products are covered under KRS 260.020.030(e) and 260.020.040(l) There is a special provision for community agency funding at KRS 273.451.

LOUISIANA: Labor disputes are covered under Louisiana Statutes, Title 23, Section 6. Family disputes are covered under Title 9, Sections 351 to 356. Automobile warranties are handled under Title 23, Section 1944. Housing civil rights matters are addressed under Title 40, Section 597. Barbershop disputes are covered under Title 37, Section 381. There is a special provision for a Medical Review Panel at Title 40, Section 1299-47.

MAINE: Maine's statutes provide ADR for the following areas of dispute: Labor disputes are covered under Title 26, Section 1026, 965, 931 to 936, 979-D, 1281, 1282, and 1285. Family disputes are covered under Title 4, Section 18 (1 to 5), Title 19, Section 214 (1,4), Title 19, Section 518 (1,2, and 4), Title 19, Section 656,665, and Title 19, Section 752(4). Automobile warranties are handled under Title 10, Section 1165. There is a special ADR provision for professional **negligence** claims (malpractice) under Title 24, Sections 2851 to 2859.) Disputes involving the production and distribution of agricultural products are covered under Title 13, Sections 1956 to 1959.

MARYLAND: Labor disputes are covered under Maryland Code Article 6, Section 408(d) and Article 89, Sections 3, 9, and 11. Maryland also has an employment agency dispute ADR provision under Article 56, Section 169. The UAA has been adopted in its original text under gcj, Sections 3-201 to 3-235.

MASSACHUSETTS:. Labor disputes are covered under Chapter 150, Sections 1 to 3 of the General Laws. There is an ADR provision for cable television disputes under Chapter 166A, Section 16. A Community Mediation provision is covered under Chapter 218, Section 43E.

MICHIGAN: ADR provisions for labor disputes are covered under MCL 432.1, 423.9 to 423.9c, 423.25, and 423.207. Family disputes are covered under MCL 552.64, 552.505, 552.513 to 552.527, and 552.531. Automobile warranties (regarding service) are handled under MCL 257.1327. A special ADR provision for general tort actions is contained under MCL 600.4951 to 600.4969. **Medical malpractice** ADR is provided for under 600.4901 to 600.4923, and more generally under 600.4951 to 600.4969. Disputes involving the production and distribution of agricultural products are covered under 290-714. A small claims conciliation statute is contained under MCL 730.147 to 730.155.

MINNESOTA: Minnesota has adopted the UAA under Statute Section 572.08 to 572.30. Labor disputes are covered under Minnesota Statutes 179.01, 179.03, 179.04, 179.06, 179.14, 179.15, and 179.02 to 179.09. Family disputes are covered under 518.167 and 518.619. Automobile warranties are handled under 325F.665. Civil Rights disputes are covered under 63.01 and 63.04 to 63.06. Conciliation Courts are provided for under 487.30. Civil Mediation is outlined under 572.31 to 572.40. Civil litigation ADR is covered separately under 484.74. There is also a statutory ADR provision for community dispute resolution programs under 494.01 to 494.04. A special provision for debtor-creditor mediation is found under 572.41, and worker's compensation disputes under 176.351(2a). Disputes involving the production and distribution of agricultural products are covered under 17.692, 17.695, 17.697 to 17.701. Environmental issues are covered under 40.22, 40.23(3), 40.242, 40.244, 221.035F, 221.036(9), 116.072(1), and 116.072(6) to 116.072(8). Environmental waste management issues are covered separately under 115A.29(2)(a) and 115A.38(2).

MISSISSIPPI: Automobile warranties disputes are handled under Code provisions, 63-17-159 and 63-17-163. Agricultural debt is addressed under 69-2-43 to 69-43-51.

MISSOURI: Labor disputes are covered under Statutes 290.400, 290.420, 290.430, and 295.030 to 290.190, **as is** 105.525. Civil Rights disputes are covered under 213.010(1), 213.020, and 213.075.

MONTANA: Labor disputes are covered under Montana Code 39-31-307. Family disputes are covered under 26-1-81 and 40-3-111 to 40-3-127. Agricultural debt ADR is handled under 80-13-191 and 80-13-201 to 80-13-214. Civil Rights disputes are covered under 49-2-501(1), 49-2-504 to 49-2-506, and 49-2-601. Worker's compensation disputes are covered under 39-71-2401 to 39-71-2411. There is a special Code provision for special education matters under 20-7-462(4). Medical malpractice panels are covered under 27-6-101 to 27-6-704. Disputes involving the production and distribution of agricultural products are covered under 80-1-101 and 80-11-103(9). The UAA has been adopted under MCA 27-5-111 to 27-5-324.

NEBRASKA: The UAA has been expressly adopted under Nebraska Statutes, Sections 25-2601 to 25-2622. Family disputes are covered under 42-801 to 42-823, and 42-360. Agricultural debt is covered under 2-4801 to 2-4816. Civil rights disputes are covered under 20-113.01, 20-114(1)(2).

NEVADA: Nevada has copious provisions for ADR in its statutes. Labor disputes are covered under 288.190, 288.200, 288.205, 288.215, 288.220, 288.270, 614.010, and 614.020. Automobile warranties are handled under 598.761. Civil Rights disputes are covered under 233.020 to 233.210 and 244.161. Consumer credit and civil rights disputes are covered under 598B.150. Educational dispute ADR is found under 394.11, and mobile home disputes are handled under 118B.024, 118B.025, and 118B.260.

NEW HAMPSHIRE: Labor disputes are covered by New Hampshire Statutes 273-A:1, 273-A:12, 273.215, 273.220, 273.270, 614.010 and 614.020. Automobile warranties are handled under 357.0:4.

NEW JERSEY: Labor disputes are covered under 34-13A-4 to 34-13A-16 and 34-13A-15. Civil rights disputes are covered under 52:27E-40, 52:27E-41. A general ADR provision is found at 2A:23A-1 to 2A:23A-19. Disputes involving the developmentally disabled are covered under 52:27E-40 and 41. Home warranties are covered under 46:3 B-9. Radioactive waste issues are handled under 32:31-5.

NEW MEXICO: Family disputes are covered under 40-12-1 to 40-12-6, and 40-4-9.1(B) and (J)(5). Automobile warranties are handled under 57-16A-6. Small claims are handled under 34-8A-10.

NEW YORK: Labor disputes are covered under Sections 205 and 209 for civil service, and Sections 750 to 760 for labor. Family disputes are covered under Sections 911-926. Automobile warranties are handled under Section 198-a (general business) Tax matters fall under Section 170(3a). Community Dispute Resolution Programs are governed by Sections 849-a to 849-g (judicial law).

NORTH CAROLINA: The UAA has been expressly adopted under Statutes Section 1-567.1 to 1-567.20. Labor disputes are covered under Statutes 95-32 to 95-36. Automobile warranties are handled under 20-351.7. Civil Rights disputes are covered under 143-422.3 (unemployment) or 41A-6(6), 41A-7(a), 41A-8 (housing).

NORTH DAKOTA: The UAA is found under Code Sections 32-29.2.01 to 39-29.2.20. Family disputes are covered under Code Sections 14-09.1-01 to 14-09.1-08, and 27-05.1-01 to 27-05.1-18. Automobile warranties are handled under 51-07-18(3). A provision for ADR of agricultural debt can be found at 6.09.10-01 to 10-09. Debtor-creditor disputes are covered under 11-26-01 to 11-26-08.

OHIO: Lengthy provisions under Ohio's Code for labor disputes are covered under 4117.02(A), (E), (H)(7), (N),4117.14(A) and (C). Family disputes are covered under 3117.01 to 08. Automobile warranties are handled under 1345.75 and 77. Civil rights disputes (housing matters) are covered under 1901.331.

OKLAHOMA: The UAA has been adopted in its original text at Title 15, Sections 801 to 818. Automobile warranties are handled under Statute Title 15, Section 901(f). Civil Rights disputes are covered under Title 25, Sections 1505, 1704, and 1705. 22-9-1-6. General dispute resolution programs are covered under Title 12, Sections 1801 to 1813.

OREGON: Oregon's statutes covering labor disputes are found at 662.405 to 455, 662.705(4), 662.715, 662.785, and 243.650 et seq. Family disputes

are covered under 107.510 to 107.615, 107.755 to 107.795, and 107.179(4).

PENNSYLVANIA: Pennsylvania Statutes, Title 42, Part VII, Chapter 73, Subchapters A, B, and C cover statutory arbitration, common law arbitration, and judicial arbitration respectively. Title 43, Section 211.31 to 39, and Title 43, Section 213.13 cover general labor disputes, as well as Title 43, Section 1101..801,.802, and Title 43, Section 217.3. Automobile warranties are handled under Title 73, Section 1959. Civil Rights disputes are covered under Title 43, Section 957(i) (unemployment) or Title 43, Section 959(a) to (c) (employment). Eminent domain issues are covered under Title 52, Section 1406.15.

RHODE ISLAND: Labor disputes are covered under General Law 28-10-1, 28-9.4-10, 28-9.4-17, and 28-7-10. ADR for consumer issues is found at 42-42-5 to 42-42-7.

SOUTH CAROLINA: Codified laws in South Carolina include **adoption** of the UAA under Title 15, Chapter 48. ADR provisions for labor disputes are found under 41-10-70 (wage mediation) and 41-17-10. Civil rights disputes are covered under 1-13-70 and 1-13-90 (employment). Consumer disputes are covered under 37-6-117. Employment grievances are covered under 8-17-360 and 8-17-370.

SOUTH DAKOTA: South Dakota has ADR for labor disputes under 60-10-1 to 60-10-3.

TENNESSEE: The UAA has been adopted under Statutes 29-5-301 to 29-5-320. Bank patrons may resolve their disputes under Tennessee's Code 45-1-301 to 45-1-309.

TEXAS: Labor disputes are covered under Article 5154c-1, Section 9. ADR procedures in general are covered under Article 4590f-1, title 7, 154.001 to 154.073 Section 3.07(d).

UTAH: Family disputes are covered under 30-3-16.2 to 30-3-17.1, 30-3-4.1, and 30-3-4.3. Automobile warranties are handled under 30-20-7. Medical malpractice resolution is provided for under 78-14-1, 78-14-2, and 78-14-12 to 16.

VERMONT: Labor disputes are covered under Vermont Code Title 21, 924 and 925, Title 3, 8.25, and Title 21, 521 to 554. Special education matters are covered by Title 16, Section 2941, 2959.

VIRGINIA: The UAA is found under Code Section 8.01-581.01 to 8.01-581.016. Labor disputes are covered under Virginia's Code, 40.1-70 to 40.1-75. Family disputes are covered under 16.1-69.35 and 16.1-289.1. Automobile warranties are handled under 59.1-207.15. Civil mediation programs are found under 16.1-69.35(d) There is a special Code provision for local government dispute mediation at 15.1-945.1 et seq.

WASHINGTON: Labor disputes are covered under 49.08.010, 41.56.430, 41.56.440, 41.56.450, and 41.59.120. Family disputes are covered under 26.09.015. Automobile warranties are handled under 19.118.150. Civil Rights disputes are covered under 49.60.130. Dispute resolution centers are found at 7.75.010 to 7.75.100

WEST VIRGINIA: West Virginia has an ADR provision for labor disputes at Code Section 21-1A-1. There is also an ADR provision for automobile warranty disputes at 46A-6A-8 and 46A-6A-9.

WISCONSIN: Wisconsin Statutes cover ADR for labor disputes under 101.24, 111.11, 111.39, 111.53-56, 111.70, and 111.77. Family disputes are covered under 753.016 (conciliation), 767.081-82, 767.001(3) and (4), 767.11, and 767.327(1) and (2). Automobile warranties are handled under 218.015(3) to (7). Civil Rights disputes are covered under 118.20 (employment), 230.85 (employment), and 1419 (governor and mediation).

WYOMING: Automobile warranties are handled under Statute 40-17-101(a) and (f). Agricultural debt is covered under 11-41-101 to 110. Environmental issues are handled under 35-11-701(a) to (c).

## Additional Resources

"A Brief Overview of the American Arbitration Association." Available at http://gov.news/press/2001pres/01fsprivacy.html

*Civil Justice Reform Act of 1990.* 28 U.S.C. Section 471 et seq.

"Courts Differ on Arbitrability of Time Limitations." Rivkin, David W. Available at http://www.ilr.cornell.edu/alliance/courts_differ_on_arbitrability_o.htm.

*How and When to Be Your Own Lawyer.* Schachner, Robert W. Avery Publishing Group, Inc.,1995.

*Law for Dummies.* Ventura, John,. IDG Books Worldwide, Inc. 1996.

*Uniform Arbitration Act* National Conference of Commissioners on Uniform State Laws. 2000. Available at http://gov.news/press/2001pres/01fsprivacy.html

*U. S. Code, Title 9, Chapter 1, et seq: The Federal Arbitration Act.* Available at http://www4.law.cornell.edu/uscode/9/.

## Organizations

### *The American Arbitration Association (AAA)*
335 Madison Avenue, Tenth Floor
New York, NY 10017-4605 USA
Phone: (212) 716-5800
Fax: (212) 716-5905
URL: http://www.adr.org

### *The American Bar Association (ADR Section)*
740 15th Street, NW
Washington, DC 20005 USA
Phone: (202) 992-1000

# DISPUTE RESOLUTION ALTERNATIVES

## MEDIATION

*Sections within this essay:*

- Background
- Voluntary versus Mandatory Mediation
- The Mediation Process
- Deciding to Mediate a Dispute
    - Finding an Appropriate Forum and Mediator(s)
    - Checklist
- Uniform Mediation Act
- Federal Mediation
- State Mediation Provisions
- Additional Resources

## Background

**Mediation** refers to one of several methods used to resolve legal disputes other than through formal court trial. Mediation and **arbitration** constitute methods of "alternative dispute resolution" (ADR). Arbitration is used as a substitute for trial, but mediation merely assists the parties in reaching their own resolution of a disputed matter. Instead of a judge or jury rendering a judgment or verdict, or an arbitrator rendering a binding decision, a "mediator" merely facilitates open discussion and tries to assist the parties in resolving their differences on their own. Mediation thus avoids the "win–lose" set-up of a trial or arbitration.

Those who go through formal mediation tend to achieve **settlement** through their own spirit of mu-tual compromise. For that reason, mediation may be particularly helpful or appropriate in situations where parties have an ongoing relationship (neighbors, business associates, divorcing parents of minor children, etc.) and do not want that relationship destroyed by the adversarial process of trial. In addition to being less adversarial than trial or arbitration, mediation tends to be less expensive, faster, and non-binding.

Mediation also may be used as a pre-trial initiative to provide a way for litigating parties to gauge the relative strengths and weaknesses of their claims and defenses before they get to the point of trial. This does not mean that mediation is used as a practice trial; rather, it represents a joint effort in **good faith** to resolve the matter before it gets to trial. In this form of mediation, after parties consider all sides to the dispute, a recommendation for settlement is given to the parties for their consideration. If the parties are unwilling to compromise their respective positions, and no settlement of the dispute results, at least the mediation experience will have given them a better understanding of how the dispute may or may not play out in court.

## Voluntary versus Mandatory Mediation

Mediation of a dispute may occur as a result of voluntary private agreement, community program, or court order (which includes **statutory** mediation of some matters prior to trial). However, the term "mandatory mediation" may be misleading. It merely means that the parties are "forced to the table" to try to resolve their dispute prior to trial. It does not mean that they are required to settle their dispute; it merely requires that they attempt to do so in good faith. The decision to accept the outcome of the mediation and settle the matter remains voluntary. If the attempt at mediation fails to resolve the dispute, the parties may continue to litigate the matter.

A voluntary agreement to mediate a dispute may pre-exist the dispute, as in a private contract provision in which the parties agree to mediate any dispute that may arise in the future. Alternatively, a decision to mediate may come about after a dispute has already occurred and the parties are merely considering a way to resolve the matter without going to court.

Statutory mandatory mediation usually governs disputes concerning certain subject matters, such as labor relations, family matters (e.g., **custody** disputes), or consumer matters. Many states also have mandatory mediation provisions for civil disputes in which the dollar amount in controversy falls within a certain range. In those circumstances, mediation becomes an integral part of "pre-trial procedure," promoting the resolution of the dispute at a stage before the cost of **litigation** has begun to accrue.

## The Mediation Process

Unlike arbitration, mediation is not similar to a trial. In voluntary mediation, there is no "decision," judgment, or verdict rendered. Rather, the neutral mediator acts as a go-between and does not take sides or advocate the cause or defense of any party. The setting is more often informal than not, and the parties may or may not be represented by attorneys (usually, court-ordered mediations are handled by the attorneys representing the parties). Often, the mediation **hearing** takes place in a conference room at a local hotel, court building, or state **bar association**.

The mediation hearing itself differs substantially from a trial, in that there is generally no formal presentation of **evidence**, and generally no witness **testimony**. Rather, each party summarizes its position in written papers filed with the mediator(s) prior to the mediation. In the written summary, each party describes the evidence it intends to produce at trial, if mediation is unsuccessful. The mediation papers may include photographs, affidavits from witnesses who will appear at trial, formal opinions or reports from experts, etc. There is a summarized statement of the issues and the respective positions of the parties, as well as factual/legal arguments identifying the strengths and weaknesses of the opposing posi-

tion(s). The mediator(s) will review the pre-mediation documents in order to become familiar with the issues and arguments, and thus be able to facilitate settlement. It is important that mediations are kept confidential, either by express agreement or by law, so as not to affect trial of the matter if mediation is unsuccessful.

Most often, there is a single, neutral mediator who facilitates and encourages open discussion and negotiation between the parties. However, in court ordered mediation, a panel of mediators may be selected. In many states that utilize mediation panels, the preferred number of mediators is three, one of whom is neutral in role and the other two serve as advocates for the causes of the opposing parties. In such cases, the mediators, after listening to both or all sides of the dispute, render a mediation recommendation (which sometimes is referred to as a mediation "award" or a mediation "decision," but in fact is not binding). The parties will have a set number of days to accept or reject the recommendation of the mediation panel.

In many states that have court-ordered mediation, there are consequences for rejecting mediation recommendations, and/or for failure to negotiate in good faith. For example, if a party rejects a mediator's recommended "award" of a certain dollar amount to settle the case, and instead goes on to trial, that party must succeed at trial and/or improve his/her position with a substantially better verdict than that recommended in mediation. In other words, the rejection of a mediation settlement offer must be premised on a good faith belief that the party has a reasonable chance of substantially improving its position at trial. If the party fails to do better at trial, a monetary **penalty** for rejecting the recommended mediation amount may be imposed. The justification for this rule is that by rejecting mediation, the rejecting party has caused the other party to sustain the cost of trial even though the rejecting party has not ultimately obtained a better result at trial. It follows that the rejecting party should bear the cost of this.

## Deciding to Mediate a Dispute

For individuals who have decided to attempt resolution of their disputes through private mediation, the following may prove helpful.

## Finding an Appropriate Forum and Mediator(s)

The local district court is a good starting source for mediation referral. Some state and local (attorney) bar associations also offer mediation programs. The non-profit National Association for Community Mediation is comprised of member community organizations across the nation that provide local mediators and forums for the resolution of local disputes. Often, the mediators may belong to such entities as the Better Business Bureau or local chambers of commerce, etc. and are quite familiar with the issues presented for resolution.

If the dispute involves more national interests or parties, individuals should consult one of the more established mediation providers, such as the American Arbitration Association (AAA) (which also handles mediations and supplies mediators). Most of these providers will be able to supply individuals with a list of mediators, a set of rules for the mediation, and a date and place for the mediation hearing.

If the forum individuals have chosen does not provide a mediator, but rather requests the parties to select the mediator(s), they should consider, among other factors:

- The appropriate experience
- The appropriate training
- The appropriate site (neutral)
- The fee schedule
- The "neutrality" (absence of **bias** or **conflict of interest** on the part of the mediator).

If the parties cannot agree on a mediator, the general procedure is to alternately strike names from a list (either provided by an outside source or created by the parties) until only a single name remains. Other alternatives (for panel mediation) include each party choosing any person at all (whether or not on a list) and then both parties choosing a neutral third mediator from the formal list.

## Checklist

Once the mediation date, time, place, and mediator(s) have been decided upon, as well as an agreed procedure and/or rules, the following should assist individuals in completing the process:

- People should double check to make sure that confidentiality provisions have been included in their mediation agreement.

- They should make sure that, prior to the mediation, the subject of allocating the costs of mediation has been resolved.

- If the type of mediation allows the appearance of witnesses, individuals should double check to make sure everyone knows when and where to be.

- They should ensure that the person who has authority to settle the matter will be present at the mediation hearing (if different from the actual parties, such as a representative from an insurance company).

- They should make sure that their mediation summary contains a concise statement of issues and positions.

- Try to identify both weaknesses and strengths of opposing positions. They should build on one; diminish the other.

- They should know in advance the least favorable offer they are willing to accept, and be prepared to consider even less than that if surprise testimony or disclosure of previously unknown facts alters their present position.

## Uniform Mediation Act

The Uniform Mediation Act (UMA), drafted and approved for **adoption** in August 2001 by the National Conference of Commissioners on Uniform State Laws, was endorsed by the American Bar Association in early 2002. However, it will take several years for introduction and adoption of the UMA by each state's legislature because legal rules affecting mediation (such as those regarding confidentiality or legal privilege) are spread out in more than 2,500 existing state statutes. Notwithstanding, in a growing global economy that enjoys increased interstate commerce through Internet business, uniformity and standardization of procedure may be a desirable objective.

## Federal Mediation

The Alternative Dispute Resolution Act of 1998 (ADRA) (28 **USC** 651 et seq.) mandates that courts establish and authorize the use of ADR, including mediation and arbitration, in all civil actions. Courts maintain their individual discretion to decide at what stage in the litigation process a court offers mediation or other ADR to the parties. Local rules establish ADR procedure in the federal courts.

In the area of statutory ADR, the Federal Mediation and **Conciliation** Service was created by Congress in 1947 as an independent agency poised to assist and promote sound labor-management relations. It offers ADR services in a variety of formats, including dispute mediation and preventive (issue) mediation.

The U. S. Equal Employment Opportunity Commission's (**EEOC**) mediation program began as a pilot experiment in 1991 in four field offices. By 1999, the EEOC's proposed budget included a $13 million allocation for the expansion of its mediation program. EEOC continues to develop and train internal mediators employed by EEOC s well as external mediators hired on a contract basis, to promote mediation as a possible resolution for some EEOC claims.

The federal government also encourages mediation and arbitration within its own ranks. Federal agencies are free to set up their own procedural ADR programs for the handling of both internal and external disputes. The Administrative Dispute Resolution Act of 1996 provides a mediation forum for handling disputes within agencies, or between citizens and agencies (claims against the government).

## State Mediation Provisions

The following state laws provide for ADR (mediation/arbitration) for certain types of disputes:

ALABAMA: Alabama Code, Ch. 25-7-4 applies to labor disputes.

ALASKA: Alaska Statutes 42.40.840 and 23.40.190 address labor disputes. Family disputes are governed by 25.20.080 and 25.24.080. Disputes involving automobile warranties are governed by 45.45.355.

ARIZONA: Statutory provisions for arbitration/mediation of family disputes is covered under 25-381.01 to 25-381.24. Automobile warranties are covered under 44-1265.

ARKANSAS: Arkansas Statutes 11-2-201 to 11-2-206 governs labor disputes.

CALIFORNIA: California's Code contains extensive provisions for the arbitration and/or mediation of many types of disputes. Labor disputes are addressed under Sections 65, 66, and 3518. Family disputes are covered in Sections 5180 to 5183. Education matters are covered by 48260.6, 48263, 48263.5 (truancy), and 56503 (special education). There is a special pro-

vision for the arbitration of cable TV franchise disputes under 53066.1(n)(1). Environmental regulatory disputes, including issues involving pesticides, are covered under 13127(c)(1). Water rights disputes are handled under 1219. Community disputes of a business or professional nature are covered under 465 to 471.5.

COLORADO: Colorado's statutes provide ADR for labor disputes under 8-3-113. Family matters are covered by 14-10129.5. Agricultural debts are governed by 6-9-101 to 6-9-106. A special statutory provision exists for ADR of disputes involving mobile homes under 38-12-216. Dispute resolution in general is covered by 13-22-301 to 13-22-310.

CONNECTICUT: Labor disputes are covered under Connecticut Statutes 31-91 to 31-100, 5-276 and 5-276a. Family disputes are resolved under 46b-59a. Public Act 87-316 Section 8 (1987) is covered under 42-182.

DELAWARE: Delaware's Code covers labor disputes under Title 14 Section 4002 and 4014, Title 19 Section 110 and 113, and Title 19 Section 1614. Automobile warranties are covered under Title 6 Section 5007.

FLORIDA: Florida Statutes Annotated 448.06 and 681.110(4)9d) cover labor disputes. Family disputes are addressed under 44.101, 61.183, 39.42, 39.427 to 39.429, 39.436, 39.44, and 39.442. Automobile **warranty** disputes are provided for under 681.108 and 681.111 Mobile home disputes fall under 723.037 and 723.038. The state maintains "citizen dispute settlement centers" for ADR assistance under 44.201.

GEORGIA: Labor disputes are covered under Georgia Code 34-2-6(5), 25-5-1 to 25-5-14, 45-19-32, and 45-19-36. Public employee grievances and "unlawful practices" labor arbitrations are mandated under 45-19-36.

HAWAII: Hawaii Revised Statutes 371-10, 98-11(b)(1)(d), 89-12(a) and (b), 380-8, and 377-3 cover ADR for labor disputes. Automobile warranty disputes are covered under 490-2 and 313-1. Medical conciliation is addressed by 671-11 to 671-20. There is a special statutory provision for ADR of geothermal resources disputes under 205-5.1. International disputes are covered by 1988 Haw. Sess. Laws, Ch. 186, Sections 1-9.

IDAHO: Idaho Code Section 44-106 governs labor disputes.

ILLINOIS: Labor disputes are covered by Illinois Compiled Statutes, Ch. 48, paragraphs 1612, v1706, 1712, 1713(b); and Ch. 10, paragraph 26. Family disputes are covered by Ch. 40, paragraph 602.1 and 607.1. Automobile warranty disputes are covered by Ch.121.5, paragraph 1204(4). Disputes involving **public utilities** fall under Ch. 11, paragraph 702.12a. Illinois operates several nonprofit community dispute resolution centers under the auspices of Ch. 37, paragraph 851.1 to 856.

INDIANA: Labor disputes are covered under Indiana Code 5-14-1.5-6.5(2), 22-1-1-8(d), 22-6-1-7, 20-7.5-1-9 to 20-7.5-1-13. Family disputes are covered under 31-1-24-1 to 31-1-24-9, 31-1-23-5 to 31-1-23-9. Automobile warranties are handled under 24-5-13-19. **Civil Rights** disputes are covered under 22-9-1-6. **Consumer protection** disputes are covered under 4-6-9-4(a)(4). There is a special Code provision for water rights disputes under 13-2-1-6(2).

IOWA: Labor disputes are covered under Iowa Code 20.19 to 20.20 and 679B to 679B.27. Family disputes are covered under 598.16 and 598.41(2). Agricultural debts are handled under 654a1 to 654a14. Civil Rights disputes are covered under 601A.15(3)(c). Informal dispute resolution in general is addressed under 679.1 to 679.14.

KANSAS: Labor disputes are covered under Kansas Statutes 44-817, 44-819(j), 44-820(c), 44-826, 44-828, 72-5413(h), 72-5427, 72-5429, 72-5430(b)(7), 72-5430(c)(7), 75-4322, 75-4323, 75-4332, and 75-4333. The ADR provisions for family disputes are covered under 23-601 to 23-607 and 23-701. Automobile warranties are handled under 50-645(e). Civil Rights disputes are covered under 44-1001 to 44-1005. There is a special ADR provision for barbershop business disputes under 65-1824(4).

KENTUCKY: Kentucky has extensive ADR provisions in its Kentucky Revised Statutes (KRS). Labor disputes are covered under KRS 337.425, 345.080, 336.010, 336.020, 336.140, and 336.151 to 336.156. Family disputes are covered under KRS 403.140(b) and 403.170. Automobile warranties are handled under KRS 367.860 to 367.880. Civil Rights disputes are covered under KRS 344.190 to 344.290 and 337.425. Education matters are covered under KRS 165A.350 and 360. Disputes involving the production and distribution of agricultural products are covered under KRS 260.020.030(e) and 260.020.040(l) There is a special provision for community agency funding at KRS 273.451.

LOUISIANA: Labor disputes are covered under Louisiana Statutes, Title 23, Section 6. Family disputes are covered under Title 9, Sections 351 to 356. Automobile warranties are handled under Title 23, Section 1944. Housing civil rights matters are addressed under Title 40, Section 597. Barbershop disputes are covered under Title 37, Section 381. There is a special provision for a Medical Review Panel at Title 40, Section 1299-47.

MAINE: Maine's statutes provide ADR for the following areas of dispute: Labor disputes are covered under Title 26, Section 1026, 965, 931 to 936, 979-D, 1281, 1282, and 1285. Family disputes are covered under Title 4, Section 18 (1 to 5), Title 19, Section 214 (1,4), Title 19, Section 518 (1,2, and 4), Title 19, Section 656,665, and Title 19, Section 752(4). Automobile warranties are handled under Title 10, Section 1165. There is a special ADR provision for professional **negligence** claims (**malpractice**) under Title 24, Sections 2851 to 2859.) Disputes involving the production and distribution of agricultural products are covered under Title 13, Sections 1956 to 1959.

MARYLAND: Labor disputes are covered under Maryland Code Article 6, Section 408(d) and Article 89, Sections 3, 9, and 11. Maryland also has an employment agency dispute ADR provision under Article 56, Section 169.

MASSACHUSETTS:. Labor disputes are covered under Chapter 150, Sections 1 to 3 of the General Laws. There is an ADR provision for cable television disputes under Chapter 166A, Section 16. A Community Mediation provision is at Chapter 218, Section 43E.

MICHIGAN: MCR 2.403 (Michigan Court Rules) covers court-ordered mediations of civil actions involving money damages or division of property. Domestic relations mediation is governed by MCR 3.211. Mediation of health care matters is covered under Michigan statutes, MCL 600.4901 to 600.4923. ADR provisions for labor disputes are covered under MCL 432.1, 423.9 to 423.9c, 423.25, and 423.207. Disputes involving the production and distribution of agricultural products are covered under 290-714. A small claims conciliation **statute** is contained under MCL 730.147 to 730.155.

MINNESOTA: Labor disputes are covered under Minnesota Statutes 179.01, 179.03, 179.04, 179.06, 179.14, 179.15, and 179.02 to 179.09. Family disputes are covered under 518.167 and 518.619. Automobile warranties are handled under 325F.665. Civil Rights disputes are covered under 63.01, and 63.04 to 63.06. Conciliation Courts are provided for under 487.30. Civil Mediation is outlined under 572.31 to 572.40. Civil litigation ADR is covered separately under 484.74. There is also a statutory ADR provision for community dispute resolution programs under 494.01 to 494.04. A special provision for debtor-creditor mediation is found under 572.41, and worker's compensation disputes under 176.351(2a). Disputes involving the production and distribution of agricultural products are covered under 17.692, 17.695, 17.697 to 17.701. Environmental issues are covered under 40.22, 40.23(3), 40.242, 40.244, 221.035F, 221.036(9), 116.072(1), and 116.072(6) to 116.072(8). Environmental waste management issues are covered separately under 115A.29(2)(a) and 115A.38(2).

MISSISSIPPI: Automobile warranties disputes are handled under Code provisions, 63-17-159 and 63-17-163. Agricultural debt is addressed under 69-2-43 to 69-43-51.

MISSOURI: Labor disputes are covered under Statutes 290.400, 290.420, 290.430, and 295.030 to 290.190, **as is** 105.525. Civil Rights disputes are covered under 213.010(1), 213.020, and 213.075.

MONTANA: Labor disputes are covered under Montana Code 39-31-307. Family disputes are covered under 26-1-81 and 40-3-111 to 40-3-127. Agricultural debt ADR is handled under 80-13-191 and 80-13-201 to 80-13-214. Civil Rights disputes are covered under 49-2-501(1), 49-2-504 to 49-2-506, and 49-2-601. Worker's compensation disputes are covered under 39-71-2401 to 39-71-2411. There is a special Code provision for special education matters under 20-7-462(4). **Medical malpractice** panels are covered under 27-6-101 to 27-6-704. Disputes involving the production and distribution of agricultural products are covered under is handled under 80-1-101 and 80-11-103(9).

NEBRASKA: Family disputes are covered under 42-801 to 42-823, and 42-360. Agricultural debt is covered under 2-4801 to 2-4816. Civil rights disputes are covered under 20-113.01, 20-114(1)(2).

NEVADA: Nevada has copious provisions for ADR in its statutes. Labor disputes are covered under 288.190, 288.200, 288.205, 288.215, 288.220, 288.270, 614.010, and 614.020. Automobile warranties are handled under 598.761. Civil Rights disputes are covered under 233.020 to 233.210, and 244.161. Con-

sumer credit and civil rights disputes are covered under 598B.150. Educational dispute ADR is found under 394.11, and mobile home disputes are handled under 118B.024, 118B.025, and 118B.260.

NEW HAMPSHIRE: Labor disputes are covered New Hampshire Statutes 273-A:1, 273-A:12, 273.215, 273.220, 273.270, 614.010 and 614.020. Automobile warranties are handled under 357.0:4.

NEW JERSEY: Labor disputes are covered under 34-13A-4 to 34-13A-16 and 34-13A-15.Civil rights disputes are covered under 52:27E-40, 52:27E-41. A general ADR provision is found at 2A:23A-1 to 2A:23A-19. Disputes involving the developmentally disabled are covered under 52:27E-40 and 41. Home warranties are covered under 46:3 B-9. Radioactive waste issues are handled under 32:31-5.

NEW MEXICO: Family disputes are covered under 40-12-1 to 40-12-6, and 40-4-9.1(B) and (J)(5). Automobile warranties are handled under 57-16A-6. Small claims are handled under 34-8A-10.

NEW YORK: Labor disputes are covered under Sections 205 and 209 for civil service, and Sections 750 to 760 for labor. Family disputes are covered under Sections 911-926. Automobile warranties are handled under Section 198-a (general business) Tax matters fall under Section 170(3a). Community Dispute Resolution Programs are governed by Sections 849-a to 849-g (judicial law).

NORTH CAROLINA: Labor disputes are covered under Statutes 95-32 to 95-36. Automobile warranties are handled under 20-351.7. Civil Rights disputes are covered under 143-422.3 (unemployment) or 41A-6(6), 41A-7(a), 41A-8 (housing).

NORTH DAKOTA: Family disputes are covered under Code Sections 14-09.1-01 to 14-09.1-08, and 27-05.1-01 to 27-05.1-18. Automobile warranties are handled under 51-07-18(3). A provision for ADR of agricultural debt can be found at 6.09.10-01 to 10-09. Debtor-creditor disputes are covered under 11-26-01 to 11-26-08.

OHIO: Lengthy provisions under Ohio's Code for labor disputes are covered under 4117.02(A), (E), (H)(7), (N),4117.14(A) and (C). Family disputes are covered under 3117.01 to 08. Automobile warranties are handled under 1345.75 and 77. Civil rights disputes (housing matters) are covered under 1901.331.

OKLAHOMA: Automobile warranties are handled under Statute Title 15, Section 901(f). Civil Rights disputes are covered under Title 25, Sections 1505, 1704, and 1705. 22-9-1-6. General dispute resolution programs are covered under Title 12, Sections 1801 to 1813.

OREGON: Oregon's statutes covering labor disputes are found at 662.405 to 455, 662.705(4), 662.715, 662.785, and 243.650 et seq. Family disputes are covered under 107.510 to 107.615, 107.755 to 107.795, and 107.179(4).

PENNSYLVANIA: Pennsylvania Statutes, Title 43, Section 211.31 to 39, and Title 43, Section 213.13 cover general labor disputes, as well as Title 43, Section 1101..801,.802, and Title 43, Section 217.3. Automobile warranties are handled under Title 73, Section 1959. Civil Rights disputes are covered under Title 43, Section 957(i) (unemployment) or Title 43, Section 959(a) to (c) (employment. Eminent domain issues are covered under Title 52, Section 1406.15.

RHODE ISLAND: Labor disputes are covered under General Law 28-10-1, 28-9.4-10, 28-9.4-17, and 28-7-10. ADR for consumer issues is found at 42-42-5 to 42-42-7.

SOUTH CAROLINA: Codified laws in South Carolina include ADR provisions for labor disputes under 41-10-70 (wage mediation) and 41-17-10. Civil rights disputes are covered under 1-13-70 and 1-13-90 (employment). Consumer disputes are covered under 37-6-117. Employment grievances are covered under 8-17-360 and 8-17-370.

SOUTH DAKOTA: South Dakota has ADR for labor disputes under 60-10-1 to 60-10-3.

TENNESSEE: Bank patrons may resolve their disputes under Tennessee's Code 45-1-301 to 45-1-309.

TEXAS: Labor disputes are covered under Article 5154c-1, Section 9. ADR procedures in general are covered under Article 4590f-1, title 7, 154.001 to 154.073 Section 3.07(d).

UTAH: Family disputes are covered under 30-3-16.2 to 30-3-17.1, 30-3-4.1, and 30-3-4.3. Automobile warranties are handled under 30-20-7. Medical malpractice resolution is provided for under 78-14-1, 78-14-2, and 78-14-12 to 16.

VERMONT: Labor disputes are covered under Vermont Code Title 21, 924 and 925, Title 3, 8.25, and Title 21, 521 to 554. Special education matters are covered by Title 16, Section 2941, 2959.

VIRGINIA: Labor disputes are covered under Virginia's Code, 40.1-70 to 40.1-75. Family disputes are covered under 16.1-69.35 and 16.1-289.1. Automobile warranties are handled under 59.1-207.15. Civil mediation programs are found under 16.1-69.35(d) There is a special Code provision for local government dispute mediation at 15.1-945.1 et seq.

WASHINGTON: Labor disputes are covered under 49.08.010, 41.56.430, 41.56.440, 41.56.450, and 41.59.120. Family disputes are covered under 26.09.015. Automobile warranties are handled under 19.118.150. Civil Rights disputes are covered under 49.60.130. Dispute resolution centers are found at 7.75.010 to 7.75.100

WEST VIRGINIA: West Virginia has an ADR provision for labor disputes at Code Section 21-1A-1. There is also an ADR provision for automobile warranty disputes at 46A-6A-8 and 46A-6A-9.

WISCONSIN: Wisconsin Statutes cover ADR for labor disputes under 101.24, 111.11, 111.39, 111.53-56, 111.70, and 111.77. Family disputes are covered under 753.016 (conciliation), 767.081-82, 767.001(3) and (4), 767.11, and 767.327(1) and (2). Automobile warranties are handled under 218.015(3) to (7). Civil Rights disputes are covered under 118.20 (employment), 230.85 (employment), and 1419 (governor and mediation).

WYOMING: Automobile warranties are handled under Statute 40-17-101(a) and (f). Agricultural debt is covered under 11-41-101 to 110. Environmental issues are handled under 35-11-701(a) to (c).

## Additional Resources

"A Brief Overview of the American Arbitration Association." Available at http://gov.news/press/2001pres/01fsprivacy.html.

*Administrative Dispute Resolution Act of 1996.* U. S. Congress, 1995. Available at http://gov.news/press/2001pres/01fsprivacy.html.

"Arbitration and Mediation." Consumer Law Center. Available at http://gov.news/press/2001pres/01fsprivacy.html

*Civil Justice Reform Act of 1990.* 28 U.S.C. Section 471 et seq.

"History of EEOC Mediation Program." The U. S. Equal Employment Opportunity Commission. Available at http:// www.eeoc.gov/mediate/history.html.

*How and When to Be Your Own Lawyer.* Robert W. Schachner., Robert W., Avery Publishing Group, Inc.., 1995.

*Law for Dummies.* John Ventura., John, IDG Books Worldwide, Inc., 1996.

*U. S. Code, Title 29, Labor, Subtitle B, Chapter XII, Federal Mediation and Conciliation Service.* Available at http://lula.law.cornell.edu/cfr/.

*Uniform Mediation Act.* National Conference of Commissioners on Uniform State Laws. 2000. Available at http://gov.news/press/2001pres/01fsprivacy.html.

## Organizations

### American Arbitration Association (AAA)
335 Madison Avenue, Tenth Floor
New York, NY 10017-4605 USA
Phone: (212) 716-5800
Fax: (212) 716-5905
URL: http://www.adr.org

### American Bar Association (ADR Section)
740 15th Street NW
Washington, DC 20005 USA

Phone: (202) 992-1000

### Global Arbitration Mediation Association (GAMA)
3660 Druids Drive
Conyers, GA 30013 USA
Phone: (770) 235-7818
URL: http://www.gama.com

### National Association for Community Mediation
1527 New Hampshire Avenue NW
Washington, DC 20036-1206 USA
Phone: (202) 667-9700
URL: http://www.nafcm.org

### National Institute for Dispute Resolution
1726 M Street NW, # 500
Washington, DC 20036 USA
Phone: (202) 466-4764

# DISPUTE RESOLUTION ALTERNATIVES

## MINI-TRIALS

*Sections within this essay:*

- Background
- Mini-trials Distinguished From Other Forms of ADR
- Mini-trials in Federal Courts
- State Provisions
- Additional Resources
- Organizations

## Background

A mini-trial is an alternative method for resolving a legal dispute from a formal court trial. Mini-trials, like mediations and arbitrations, constitute unique forms of "alternative dispute resolution" (ADR) favored by courts and litigants alike. There has been a general increase in all forms of ADR in recent years because of the advantages offered: reduced cost, fast resolution, privacy, and less adversity in effect.

A mini-trial is really not a trial at all. Rather, it is a **settlement** process in which the parties present highly summarized versions of their respective cases to a panel of officials who represent each party (plus a "neutral" official) and who have authority to settle the dispute. The presentation generally takes place outside of the courtroom, in a private forum. After the parties have presented their best case, the panel convenes and tries to settle the matter.

## Mini-Trials Distinguished From Other Forms of ADR

A mini-trial most resembles a **mediation hearing**, in that there is a presentation by each party of a summarized version of his or her case to a panel of persons for the purpose of resolving or settling the dispute. Also like mediation, the parties are generally not bound to an outcome, and may end the process at an impasse.

However, there is one important difference between a mediation and a mini-trial. In mediation, the mediator is a neutral third party who does not take the side of either party, but instead tries to facilitate open communication between the parties themselves in order to achieve compromise and settlement. Even in court-ordered mediations conducted by a panel of mediators, the focus is still on the parties: the mediators merely issue a recommendation to the parties for settlement consideration.

Conversely, in a mini-trial, the mediators themselves are agents and advocates for the parties, and they, rather than the parties, work out a settlement after hearing opposing sides to the controversy (each goes into the mini-trial with advance authorization to settle the matter for a certain dollar amount or under other conditions or criteria).The parties present their cases (usually through their attorneys) but do not take active roles in the settlement negotiations nor generally do their attorneys. The decision-makers in a mini-trial are the actual members of the panel (excepting any neutral member, who may play the role of expert, advisor on substantive law, etc.).

One might ask why the parties themselves do not facilitate the settlement directly in a mini-trial. The answer is two-fold. First, parties involved in a controversy tend to approach and/or perceive the matter subjectively rather than objectively. Parties also tend to inject emotion or **bias** into their negotiations and will seldom compromise unless they have been introduced to damaging information that tends to diminish their claim or defense. Therefore, officials who are one step removed from the controversy, even if they serve as advocates for their respective parties, tend to approach the dispute more objectively. Secondly, the officials at a mini-trial tend to be well-seasoned and experienced in similar matters. For example, they may be representatives of the insurance carrier for the party, or top-level management of a business that is party to a dispute or they may be privately-retained consultants with technical expertise in the subject matter. For these reasons, they may be better equipped to dissect and sort out opposing **evidence** and arguments.

Mini-trials also differ from another ADR technique, the "summary trial" or "summary jury trial." Both mini-trials and summary jury trials involve the presentation of each side's case, usually without live **testimony**, but with opening and closing statements and an outline of evidence they intend to produce at trial. However, summary trials are actually presented before mock juries, who issue advisory "verdicts." Following a jury determination, the parties and their attorneys will attempt settlement.

Finally, a mini-trial differs from other forms of ADR in that it is usually conducted after formal **litigation** has already been undertaken. Parties to a lawsuit generally stipulate to "stay" pending litigation (put a hold on further advancement of the litigation) until the mini-trial is concluded. Thus, mini-trial does not, in and of itself, represent an alternative forum for the resolution of a dispute (such as **arbitration**), but rather it represents a pre-trial alternate attempt to settle the matter before lengthy trial begins. The outcome of the mini-trial is generally confidential and advisory only, and the parties may proceed to trial if settlement negotiations fail.

## Mini-trials in Federal Courts

The Alternative Dispute Resolution Act of 1998 (ADRA) (28 **USC** 651 et seq.) mandates that courts authorize, establish, and promote the use of ADR, including mediation, arbitration, mini-trial and summary jury trial, in all civil actions. Federal district courts maintain their individual discretion to decide at what stage in the litigation process a court may offer ADR

to the parties. Local rules establish ADR procedure in the federal courts.

The federal government also encourages the use of ADR in general within its own ranks. The Administrative Dispute Resolution Act of 1996 provides a forum for handling disputes within agencies or between citizens and agencies (claims against the government). Federal agencies are free to set up their own procedural ADR programs for the handling of both internal and external disputes. For example, the U. S. **Code of Federal Regulations** (CFR) contains several ADR program provisions for federal agencies that contemplate mini-trials (as one of several alternatives); examples include the Federal Aviation Administration (FAA) (14 CFR 17.45), the Department of Energy (10 CFR 1023.8), and the Department of Housing and Urban Development (24 CFR 7.2).

## State Provisions

Generally speaking, state provisions for mini-trials are contained in comprehensive statutes or rules addressing ADR programs in their entirety. It is fair to say that if a court system has a formal ADR program, it will be receptive to the request for a mini-trial. The following state laws provide for ADR of certain types of disputes. Within those provisions, or at the request of the parties, mini-trials may be substituted for other forms of ADR (with the exception of **statutory** mandatory arbitration):

ALABAMA: Alabama Code, Title 6, Chapter 6 covers ADR, including mini-trials.

ALASKA: Family disputes are governed by Alaska Statutes 25.20.080 and 25.24.080. Disputes involving automobile warranties are governed by 45.45.355.

ARIZONA: Statutory provisions for arbitration/mediation of family disputes are covered under 25-381.01 to 25-381.24. Automobile warranties are covered under 44-1265.

ARKANSAS: Title 16, Subtitle 1-17 of the Arkansas Statutes covers ADR, including mini-trials.

CALIFORNIA: California's Code contains extensive provisions for ADR of many types of disputes. Title 2, Division 3, Part 1, Chapter 4.5, Article 5 addresses ADR in general. Family disputes are covered in statutory Sections 5180 to 5183. Education matters are covered by 48260.6, 48263, 48263.5 (truancy), and 56503 (special education). There is a special provision for the arbitration of cable TV franchise disputes under 53066.1(n)(1). Environmental regulatory disputes, including issues involving pesticides, are covered under 13127(c)(1). Water rights disputes are handled under 1219. Community disputes of a business or professional nature are covered under 465 to 471.5.

COLORADO: Colorado's statutes provide ADR for family matters under 14-10129.5. Agricultural debts are governed by 6-9-101 to 6-9-106. A special statutory provision exists for ADR of disputes involving mobile homes under 38-12-216. Dispute resolution in general is covered by 13-22-301 to 13-22-310.

CONNECTICUT: Chapter 909 of the Connecticut Statutes cover ADR in general. Family disputes are resolved under 46b-59a. Public Act 87-316 Section 8 (1987) is codified under 42-182.

DELAWARE: Delaware's Code, Title 10, Chapter 57 addresses ADR in general. Automobile warranties are covered under Title 6 Section 5007.

FLORIDA: Florida Statutes Annotated cover ADR of family disputes under 44.101, 61.183, 39.42, 39.427 to 39.429, 39.436, 39.44, and 39.442. Automobile **warranty** disputes are provided for under 681.108 and 681.111 Mobile home disputes fall under 723.037 and 723.038. The state maintains "citizen dispute settlement centers" for ADR assistance under 44.201.

GEORGIA: Title 15, Chapter 23 under the Georgia Code addresses ADR.

HAWAII: Division 4, Title 32, Chapter 613 covers ADR in general. Automobile warranty disputes are covered under Hawaii Revised Statutes 490-2 and 313-1. Medical **conciliation** is addressed by 671-11 to 671-20. There is a special statutory provision for ADR of geothermal resources disputes under 205-5.1. International disputes are covered by 1988 Haw. Sess. Laws, Ch. 186, Sections 1-9.

IDAHO: Idaho Code Section 44-106 governs labor disputes.

ILLINOIS: Illinois Compiled Statutes address ADR of family disputes in Ch. 40, paragraph 602.1 and 607.1. Automobile warranty disputes are covered by Ch.121.5, paragraph 1204(4). Disputes involving **public utilities** fall under Ch. 11, paragraph 702.12a. Illinois operates several nonprofit community dispute resolution centers under the auspices of Ch. 37, paragraph 851.1 to 856.

INDIANA: Family disputes are covered under Indiana Code 31-1-24-1 to 31-1-24-9, 31-1-23-5 to 31-1-

23-9. Automobile warranties are handled under 24-5-13-19. **Civil Rights** disputes are covered under 22-9-1-6. **Consumer protection** disputes are covered under 4-6-9-4(a)(4). There is a special Code provision for water rights disputes under 13-2-1-6(2).

IOWA: Subtitle 5, Chapter 679 to 679.14 addresses ADR. Family disputes are covered under Iowa Code 598.16 and 598.41(2). Agricultural debts are handled under 654a1 to 654a14. Civil Rights disputes are covered under 601A.15(3)(c).

KANSAS: Kansas Statutes Chapter 60, Article 2 addresses ADR in general. The ADR provisions for family disputes are covered under 23-601 to 23-607 and 23-701. Automobile warranties are handled under 50-645(e). Civil Rights disputes are covered under 44-1001 to 44-1005. There is a special ADR provision for barbershop business disputes under 65-1824(4).

KENTUCKY: Kentucky has extensive ADR provisions in its Kentucky Revised Statutes (KRS). Family disputes are covered under KRS 403.140(b) and 403.170. Automobile warranties are handled under KRS 367.860 to 367.880. Civil Rights disputes are covered under KRS 344.190 to 344.290 and 337.425. Education matters are covered under KRS 165A.350 and 360. Disputes involving the production and distribution of agricultural products are covered under KRS 260.020.030(e) and 260.020.040(l) There is a special provision for community agency funding at KRS 273.451.

LOUISIANA: Family disputes are covered under Louisiana Statutes Title 9, Sections 351 to 356. Automobile warranties are handled under Title 23, Section 1944. Housing civil rights matters are addressed under Title 40, Section 597. Barbershop disputes are covered under Title 37, Section 381. There is a special provision for a Medical Review Panel at Title 40, Section 1299-47.

MAINE: Maine's statutes provide ADR for the following areas of dispute: family disputes are covered under Title 4, Section 18 (1 to 5), Title 19, Section 214 (1,4), Title 19, Section 518 (1,2, and 4), Title 19, Section 656,665, and Title 19, Section 752(4). Automobile warranties are handled under Title 10, Section 1165. There is a special ADR provision for professional **negligence** claims (**malpractice**) under Title 24, Sections 2851 to 2859.) Disputes involving the production and distribution of agricultural products are covered under Title 13, Sections 1956 to 1959.

MARYLAND: Maryland has an employment agency dispute ADR provision under Article 56, Section 169.

MASSACHUSETTS: There is an ADR provision for cable television disputes under Chapter 166A, Section 16. A Community Mediation provision is at Chapter 218, Section 43E.

MICHIGAN: MCR 2.403 (Michigan Court Rules) covers court-ordered ADR (mediations) of civil actions involving money damages or division of property. Domestic relations ADR is governed by MCR 3.211. ADR of health care matters is covered under Michigan statutes, MCL 600.4901 to 600.4923. Disputes involving the production and distribution of agricultural products are covered under 290-714. A small claims conciliation **statute** is contained under MCL 730.147 to 730.155.

MINNESOTA: Chapter 486.76 of the Minnesota Statutes addresses ADR. Family disputes are covered under 518.167 and 518.619. Automobile warranties are handled under 325F.665. Civil Rights disputes are covered under 63.01, and 63.04 to 63.06. Conciliation Courts are provided for under 487.30. Civil Mediation is outlined under 572.31 to 572.40. Civil litigation ADR is covered separately under 484.74. There is also a statutory ADR provision for community dispute resolution programs under 494.01 to 494.04. A special provision for debtor-creditor mediation is found under 572.41, and worker's compensation disputes under 176.351(2a). Disputes involving the production and distribution of agricultural products are covered under 17.692, 17.695, 17.697 to 17.701. Environmental issues are covered under 40.22, 40.23(3), 40.242, 40.244, 221.035F, 221.036(9), 116.072(1), and 116.072(6) to 116.072(8). Environmental waste management issues are covered separately under 115A.29(2)(a) and 115A.38(2).

MISSISSIPPI: Title 11, Chapter 15 of the Mississippi Code addresses ADR in general. Automobile warranties disputes are handled under Code provisions, 63-17-159 and 63-17-163. Agricultural debt is addressed under 69-2-43 to 69-43-51.

MISSOURI: ADR of civil rights disputes is covered under Statutes 213.010(1), 213.020, and 213.075.

MONTANA: Title 25, Chapter 21, Part 5 of the Montana Code addresses ADR generally. Family disputes are covered under 26-1-81 and 40-3-111 to 40-3-127. Agricultural debt ADR is handled under 80-13-191 and 80-13-201 to 80-13-214. Civil Rights disputes are covered under 49-2-501(1), 49-2-504 to 49-2-506,

and 49-2-601. Worker's compensation disputes are covered under 39-71-2401 to 39-71-2411. There is a special Code provision for special education matters under 20-7-462(4). **Medical malpractice** panels are covered under 27-6-101 to 27-6-704. Disputes involving the production and distribution of agricultural products are covered under 80-1-101 and 80-11-103(9).

NEBRASKA: Family disputes are covered under 42-801 to 42-823, and 42-360. Agricultural debt is covered under 2-4801 to 2-4816. Civil rights disputes are covered under 20-113.01, 20-114(1)(2).

NEVADA: Chapter 232.548 covers general ADR provisions in its statutes. Automobile warranties are handled under 598.761. Civil Rights disputes are covered under 233.020 to 233.210, and 244.161. Consumer credit and civil rights disputes are covered under 598B.150. Educational dispute ADR is found under 394.11, and mobile home disputes are handled under 118B.024, 118B.025, and 118B.260.

NEW HAMPSHIRE: New Hampshire Statutes cover ADR of automobile warranties under 357.0:4.

NEW JERSEY: Title 2A, Chapter 23A provides for ADR in general. Civil rights disputes are covered under 52:27E-40, 52:27E-41. A general ADR provision is found at 2A:23A-1 to 2A:23A-19. Disputes involving the developmentally disabled are covered under 52:27E-40 and 41. Home warranties are covered under 46:3 B-9. Radioactive waste issues are handled under 32:31-5.

NEW MEXICO: Chapter 34, Article 6-44 addresses ADR in general. Family disputes are covered under 40-12-1 to 40-12-6, and 40-4-9.1(B) and (J)(5). Automobile warranties are handled under 57-16A-6. Small claims are handled under 34-8A-10.

NEW YORK: Article 75 of the Civil Practice and Law Rules address ADR. Additionally, family disputes are covered under Sections 911-926. Automobile warranties are handled under Section 198-a (general business) Tax matters fall under Section 170(3a). Community Dispute Resolution Programs are governed by Sections 849-a to 849-g (judicial law).

NORTH CAROLINA: Chapter 1, Article 45A covers ADR. Automobile warranties are handled under Statutes 20-351.7. Civil Rights disputes are covered under 143-422.3 (unemployment) or 41A-6(6), 41A-7(a), 41A-8 (housing).

NORTH DAKOTA: Title 32, Chapter 32-42 covers ADR generally. Family disputes are covered under

Code Sections 14-09.1-01 to 14-09.1-08, and 27-05.1-01 to 27-05.1-18. Automobile warranties are handled under 51-07-18(3). A provision for ADR of agricultural debt can be found at 6.09.10-01 to 10-09. Debtor-creditor disputes are covered under 11-26-01 to 11-26-08.

OHIO: Article 2711 of the Ohio Code addresses ADR generally. Family disputes are covered under 3117.01 to 08. Automobile warranties are handled under 1345.75 and 77. Civil rights disputes (housing matters) are covered under 1901.331.

OKLAHOMA: Title 12, Chapter 37, 1809 provides generally for ADR. Automobile warranties are handled under Statute Title 15, Section 901(f). Civil Rights disputes are covered under Title 25, Sections 1505, 1704, and 1705. 22-9-1-6. General dispute resolution programs are covered under Title 12, Sections 1801 to 1813.

OREGON: Most ADR provisions are generally discussed in Oregon's statutes Chapter 36. Family disputes are covered under 107.510 to 107.615, 107.755 to 107.795, and 107.179(4).

PENNSYLVANIA: Pennsylvania Statutes address ADR of disputes involving automobile warranties under Title 73, Section 1959. Civil Rights disputes are covered under Title 43, Section 957(i) (unemployment) or Title 43, Section 959(a) to (c) (employment. Eminent domain issues are covered under Title 52, Section 1406.15.

RHODE ISLAND: ADR for consumer issues is found at 42-42-5 to 42-42-7.

SOUTH CAROLINA: Codified laws in South Carolina include ADR provisions for civil rights disputes under 1-13-70 and 1-13-90 (employment). Consumer disputes are covered under 37-6-117. Employment grievances are covered under 8-17-360 and 8-17-370.

SOUTH DAKOTA: South Dakota has statutory ADR for labor disputes under 60-10-1 to 60-10-3.

TENNESSEE: Title 29, Chapter 5 of the Tennessee Code addresses ADR. Bank patrons may resolve their disputes under Tennessee's Code 45-1-301 to 45-1-309.

TEXAS: Government Code, Title 10, Subtitle A, 2008 provides for ADR in general. ADR procedures are also addressed Texas Code Article 4590f-1, title 7, 154.001 to 154.073 Section 3.07(d).

UTAH: Family disputes are covered under 30-3-16.2 to 30-3-17.1, 30-3-4.1, and 30-3-4.3. Automobile

warranties are handled under 30-20-7. Medical malpractice resolution is provided for under 78-14-1, 78-14-2, and 78-14-12 to 16.

VERMONT: Chapter 192 of the Vermont Code generally addresses ADR. Special education matters are covered by Title 16, Section 2941, 2959.

VIRGINIA: Title 11-71.1 of the Virginia's Code addresses ADR in general. Family disputes are covered under 16.1-69.35 and 16.1-289.1. Automobile warranties are handled under 59.1-207.15. Civil mediation programs are found under 16.1-69.35(d) There is a special Code provision for local government dispute mediation at 15.1-945.1 et seq.

WASHINGTON: Titles 7.04 and 7.75 address ADR. Family disputes are covered under 26.09.015. Automobile warranties are handled under 19.118.150. Civil Rights disputes are covered under 49.60.130. Dispute resolution centers are found at 7.75.010 to 7.75.100

WEST VIRGINIA: Chapter 55, Article 15 of the West Virginia Code addresses ADR generally. There is also an ADR provision for automobile warranty disputes at 46A-6A-8 and 46A-6A-9.

WISCONSIN: Wisconsin Statutes, Chapter 802-12 covers ADR generally. Family disputes are covered under 753.016 (conciliation), 767.081-82, 767.001(3) and (4), 767.11, and 767.327(1) and (2). Automobile warranties are handled under 218.015(3) to (7). Civil Rights disputes are covered under 118.20 (employment), 230.85 (employment), and (esoterically) 1419.

WYOMING: Automobile warranties are handled under Statute 40-17-101(a) and (f). Agricultural debt is covered under 11-41-101 to 110. Environmental issues are handled under 35-11-701(a) to (c).

## Additional Resources

"A Brief Overview of the American Arbitration Association." Available at http://gov.news/press/2001pres/01fsprivacy.html.

*Civil Justice Reform Act of 1990* 28 U.S.C. Section 471 et seq.

*How and When to Be Your Own Lawyer.* Schachner., Robert W., Avery Publishing Group, Inc.,1995.

*Law for Dummies* Ventura., John, IDG Books Worldwide, Inc., 1996.

"Mini-Trials." Available at http://gov.news/press/2001pres/01fsprivacy.html

"Mini-Trials and Summary Jury Trials." Bennett., Nancy J., Available at http://gov.news/press/2001pres/01fsprivacy.html.

"State Statutes by Topic: Alternative Dispute Resolution." Available at http://gov.news/press/2001pres/01fsprivacy.html.

"Title 10-Energy", Chapter X-Department of Energy (General Provisions), Part 1023—Contract Appeals, Section 1023.8(b) *United States Code,* 10 CFR 1023.8.

"Title 14-Aeronautics and Space, Chapter I-Federal Aviation Administration, Part 17-Procedures for Protests and Contracts Disputes, Subpart F-Finality and Review, Section 17.45, Appendix A to Part 17-Alternative Dispute Resolution (ADR),(B)(3). *United States Code,* 14 CFR 17.45.

## Organizations

### *The American Arbitration Association (AAA)*

335 Madison Avenue, Tenth Floor
New York, NY 10017-4605 USA
Phone: (212) 716-5800
Fax: (212) 716-5905
URL: http://www.adr.org

### *The American Bar Association (ADR Section)*

740 15th Street NW
Washington, DC 20005 USA
Phone: (202) 992-1000

# DISPUTE RESOLUTION ALTERNATIVES

## NEGOTIATION

*Sections within this essay:*

## Background

Negotiations consist of written and oral communications undertaken for the purpose of reaching agreement. When undertaken in **good faith**, negotiations include a process of give-and-take, whereby each party to the negotiations presents its position, critiques opposing positions, explores points of common ground, highlights divisive issues, proposes compromises and resolutions, and determines whether a mutually acceptable arrangement can be agreed upon to resolve the matters in dispute. When undertaken in **bad faith**, negotiations often are reduced to rancorous posturing aimed at assigning blame rather than reaching an amicable **settlement**.

Lawyers are constantly negotiating in civil **litigation**. Yet negotiation is not always used often enough, or extensively enough, to avoid litigation. Legal observers have suggested that a factor contributing to the high cost of litigation is the fear that the first side to propose settlement weakens its negotiat-

ing position. Since appearing eager to settle is taken as demonstrating a lack of confidence in one's case, both sides concentrate on **discovery** and preparing for trial so as to strengthen their hands for future negotiation while legal fees continue to mount.

The same fear does not ordinarily impede alternative dispute resolution proceedings, where a negotiated settlement is typically the goal for both parties. Alternative dispute resolution refers to an array of practices, procedures, and techniques that are used to resolve legal disputes by means other than formal civil litigation. Known more commonly as ADR, alternative dispute resolution is usually less costly and more time-efficient than civil litigation. ADR can also be more confidential than civil litigation. Court proceedings, records, and transcripts are generally open to public scrutiny and inspection in most civil litigation and cannot be sealed from the public absent an extraordinary justification. By contrast, parties to ADR proceedings can agree to insulate their dispute and its resolution from the public.

Early Puritan, Quaker, and Dutch settlers were among the first in North America to employ alternative means in resolving legal disputes. These tightly knit communities of settlers preferred even-tempered negotiations to adversarial litigation and treated litigation as a last resort to try only when procedures such as **mediation** and **arbitration** (discussed in detail below) failed to produce an acceptable and effective settlement. However, the term "alternative dispute resolution" was not coined in the United States until sometime during the 1970s, when it drew diverse support from influential members of society, including **Chief Justice** Warren Berger and consumer rights advocate Ralph Nader. Both

Berger and Nader emphasized the perspective of the average citizen, who they said has neither the time nor the money to spend getting bogged down in drawn out court battles. Instead, Berger and Nader argued that average citizens find out-of-court negotiation alternatives to be a more palatable course, at least when done evenhandedly.

Congress helped fuel the ADR movement in the 1980s and 1990s by passing a series of legislative acts. In 1980 it passed the Dispute Resolution Act, which provides financial incentives for state governments and private entities to explore innovative approaches to negotiation and dispute resolution. 28 U.S.C. app. section 1 et seq; Pub. L. No. 96-190, 94 Stat. 17 (1980). In 1990 Congress passed the Administrative Dispute Resolution Act, which encourages federal agencies to use mediation and arbitration for prompt and informal resolution of disputes. 5 U.S.C.A. sections 571 et seq; Pub.L. 101-552, Nov. 15, 1990, 104 Stat. 2738, and renumbered and amended Pub.L. 102-354, Aug. 26, 1992, 106 Stat. 944, 946. Eight years later Congress passed the Alternative Dispute Resolution Act of 1998, which requires all federal district courts to establish an ADR program, making at least one form of ADR available to all federal civil litigants. 28 U.S.C.A. sections 651 et seq; Pub.L. 100-702, Title IX, Nov. 19, 1988, 102 Stat. 4659. By 2001 approximately ninety to ninety-five percent of all legal disputes were being resolved outside of trial by using negotiation through some form of ADR.

## The Role of Negotiations in ADR

A wide variety of processes, practices, and techniques fall within the definition of "alternative dispute resolution." Arbitration and mediation are the best known and most frequently used types of ADR, but not the only ones. Minitrials, early neutral evaluations, and summary jury trials are less well-known forms of ADR. Many of these ADR techniques have little in common except that negotiation plays a prominent role in each. Parties to ADR procedures generally agree that a negotiated settlement is worth pursuing before investing time and money in full-blown civil litigation.

### Arbitration

Arbitration is the process of referring a dispute to an **impartial** intermediary chosen by the parties who agree in advance to abide by the arbitrator's award that is issued after a **hearing** at which all parties have the opportunity to be heard. Arbitration resembles traditional civil litigation in that a neutral intermediary hears the disputants' arguments and imposes a final and binding decision that is enforceable by the courts. One difference is that in arbitration the disputants elect to settle any future disputes by arbitration before a dispute actually arises, whereas with civil litigation the judicial system is generally chosen by a disgruntled party after a dispute has materialized. Another difference is that the disputants to an arbitration select the intermediary who will serve as arbitrator, whereas parties to civil litigation have little to no control over who will preside as the judge in judicial proceedings.

Arbitration also resembles litigation in that many parties use arbitration as a springboard to negotiation. Parties who know that their dispute will wind up in arbitration often fail to commence serious negotiations until shortly before or shortly after the arbitration proceedings have begun. Frequently, negotiations will continue simultaneously with the arbitration proceedings, meaning the parties' representatives will discuss settlement outside the hearing room while the hearing itself is underway inside. Arbitration can even expedite negotiations, since the parties know that once the arbitrator has issued a decision, the decision is typically final and rarely appealable.

There are two different forms of arbitration: private and judicial arbitration. Private arbitration is the most common form of ADR. Sometimes referred to as contractual arbitration, private arbitration is the product of an agreement to arbitrate drafted by the parties who enter a relationship anticipating that disputes will arise, but who mutually desire to keep any such disputes out of the courts. Private arbitration agreements typically identify the person who will serve as arbitrator. The arbitrator need not be a judge or government official. Instead, the arbitrator can be a private person whom the parties feel will have sufficient knowledge, experience, and equanimity to resolve a dispute in a reasonable manner. In some states, legislation prescribes the qualifications one must satisfy to be eligible for appointment as an arbitrator.

A private arbitrator's power is derived completely from the arbitration agreement, which may also limit the issues the arbitrator has authority to resolve. Private arbitration agreements are supported in many states by statutes that provide for judicial enforcement of agreements to arbitrate and arbitrator-rendered awards. However, statutes governing private arbitration often set forth criteria that must be followed before an arbitration agreement will be binding on both parties and enforced by a court. If those criteria are satisfied, a court will normally deem the arbitrator's decision final and enforceable. The losing party may only appeal the decision upon a showing of **fraud**, misrepresentation, arbitrariness, or capriciousness by the arbitrator.

Private arbitration is the primary method of settling labor disputes between unions and employers. For example, unions and employers almost always include an arbitration clause in their formal negotiations, known as **collective bargaining** agreements. By doing so, they agree to arbitrate future employee grievances over wages, hours, working conditions, and job security. Many real estate and insurance contracts also make arbitration the exclusive method of negotiating and resolving certain disputes that can arise between the parties entering those types of relationships.

Judicial arbitration, sometimes called court-annexed arbitration, is a non-binding form of arbitration, which means that any party dissatisfied with the arbitrator's decision may choose to go to trial rather than accept the decision. However, most jurisdictions prescribe a specific time period within which the parties to a judicial arbitration may elect to reject the arbitrator's decision and go to trial. If this time period expires before either party has rejected the arbitrator's decision, the decision becomes final, binding, and just as enforceable as a private arbitrator's decision.

Judicial arbitration is usually mandated by **statute**, court rule, or regulation. Many of these statutes were enacted to govern disputes for amounts that exceed the **jurisdiction** of small claims court but fall short of the amount required for trial in civil court. For example, in New York State claims for over $3,000 and for less than $10,000 must be submitted to non-binding judicial arbitration. NY CPLR Rule section 3405. Ten federal district courts also have mandatory programs for non-binding judicial arbitration that are funded by Congress. For example, rule 30 of the Local Rules of Court for the U. S. District Court for the Western District of Missouri provides that cases designated for compulsory, non-binding arbitration are those in which the damage award could not reasonably be expected to exceed $100,000.

Because judicial arbitration is mandatory but non-binding, it often serves as a means of facilitating negotiation between the parties to a dispute. Civil court calendars are frequently backlogged with hundreds of lawsuits. States hope that by mandating non-binding arbitration for certain disputes the parties will see the value of a negotiated settlement where both parties compromise their positions, since their positions would likely be compromised were their dispute to be resolved in civil court. Seldom do litigants receive everything they ask for in their petitions, complaints, and answers.

Private and judicial arbitration are generally less costly and more time efficient than formal civil litigation. It has been estimated that the average arbitration takes 4 to 5 months while litigation may take several years. The cost of arbitration is minimal compared to civil trials as well, since the American Arbitration Association (AAA) charges only a nominal filing fee and the arbitrator may even work without a fee to broaden his or her professional experience.

### Mediation

Mediation is a rapidly growing ADR technique. It consists of assisted negotiations in which the disputants agree to enlist the help of a neutral intermediary, whose job it is to facilitate a voluntary, mutually acceptable settlement. A mediator's primary function is to identify issues, explore possible bases for agreement, discuss the consequences of reaching impasse, and encourage each party to accommodate the interests of other parties through negotiation. However, unlike arbitrators, mediators lack the power to impose a decision on the parties if they fail to reach an agreement on their own.

Mediation is sometimes referred to as **conciliation**, or conciliated negotiation. However, the terms are not necessarily interchangeable. Conciliation focuses more on the early stages of negotiation, such as opening the channels of communication, bringing the disputants together, and identifying points of mutual agreement. Mediation focuses more on the later stages of negotiation, exploring weaknesses in each party's position, investigating areas where the parties disagree but might be inclined to compromise, and suggesting possible mutually agreeable outcomes. Conciliation and mediation typically work well when the disputants are involved in a long-term relationship, such as husband and wife, wholesaler and retailer, and manufacturer and distributor, to name a few. Mediation and conciliation also work well for "polycentric" problems that are not easily solved by all-or-nothing solutions, as with certain antitrust suits involving a myriad of complex issues.

Although some jurisdictions have enacted statutes that govern mediation, most mediation proceedings are voluntary for both parties. Accordingly, a mediator's influence is limited by the autonomy of the parties and their willingness to negotiate in good faith. Thus, a mediator can go no further than the parties themselves are willing to go. Since agreements reached by mediation bear the parties' own imprint, however, many observers feel that they are more likely to be adhered to than decisions imposed by an arbitrator or court. Disputants who participate in mediation without representation of legal **counsel** are also more likely to adhere to settlements when the alternative is to pursue civil litigation, where attorneys fees consume a significant portion of any monetary award granted to the parties.

### Minitrials

A minitrial is a process by which the attorneys for the parties present a brief version of the case to a panel, often comprised of the clients themselves and a neutral intermediary who chairs the process. Expert witnesses (and less frequently, lay witnesses) may be used in presenting the case. After the presentation, the clients, normally top management representatives who by now are more aware of the strengths and weaknesses of their positions, attempt to negotiate a settlement of the dispute. If a negotiated settlement is not reached, the parties may allow the intermediary to mediate the dispute or render a non-binding advisory opinion regarding the likely outcome of the case were it to be tried in civil court.

Minitrials are increasingly used by businesses to resolve large-scale disputes involving **product liability** questions, antitrust issues, billion dollar construction contracts, and mass tort or disaster litigation. The federal government also makes use of minitrials for disputes involving telecommunications. The **Code of Federal regulations** establishes procedures whereby individuals and entities under investigation by the FCC can request a minitrial prior to commencement of more formal administrative proceedings. 47 CFR section 1.730.

Minitrials are often effective because they usually result in bringing top management officials together to negotiate the legal issues underlying a dispute. Early in the negotiation process, upper management is sometimes pre-occupied by the business side of a dispute. Minitrials tend to shift management's focus to the outstanding legal issues. Minitrials also allow businesses to share information with each other and with their attorneys, providing a forum for initial face-to-face negotiations. Management also generally prefers the time-saving, abbreviated nature of

minitrials over the more time-consuming and costly civil-litigation alternative. Minitrials expedite negotiations as well, by making them more realistic. Once the parties have seen their case play out in court, even in truncated fashion, the parties are less likely to posture over less relevant or meaningless issues.

### Summary Jury Trials

Summary jury trials are an ADR technique used primarily in federal courts, where they provide parties with the opportunity to "try" their cases before an advisory panel of jurors, without having to face the final and possibly adverse decision of a regular jury in civil court. The purpose of the summary jury trial is to facilitate pretrial termination of cases in which a significant impediment to negotiation is disagreement between the attorneys or parties regarding a civil jury's likely findings on liability or damages in the case. Like minitrials, summary jury trials give the parties a chance to reach a preliminary **assessment** of the strengths and weaknesses of their positions and proceed with negotiations from a common starting point, namely the advisory jury's findings. Both summary jury trials and minitrials can ordinarily be scheduled and completed before formal civil cases would normally reach a court's **docket**.

Summary jury trials are presided over by a judge or **magistrate** in federal district court. A ten-member jury venire is presented to counsel for consideration. Counsel are provided with a short character profile of each juror and then given two challenges to arrive at a final six-member jury for the proceeding. Each attorney is given one hour to describe his or her client's case to the jury. After counsel's presentations, the presiding judge or magistrate delivers to the jury a brief statement of the applicable law, and the jury retires to deliberate. Juries are encouraged to return a consensus verdict, but they may return a special report that anonymously lists the view of each juror as to liability and damages. After the verdict or special report has been returned, counsel meet with the presiding judge or magistrate to discuss the verdict and to establish a timetable for settlement negotiations. Evidentiary and procedural rules are few and flexible.

### Early Neutral Evaluation

Early neutral evaluation is an informal process by which a neutral intermediary is appointed to hear the facts and arguments of counsel and the parties. After the hearing, the intermediary provides an evaluation of the strengths and weaknesses of the parties' positions and the parties' potential exposure to liability for money damages. The parties, counsel, and intermediary then engage in discussions designed to assist the parties in identifying the agreed upon facts, isolating the issues in dispute, locating areas in which further investigation would be useful, and devising a plan to streamline the investigative process. Settlement negotiations and mediation may follow, but only if the parties desire. In some jurisdictions, early neutral evaluation is a court-ordered ADR technique. However, even in these jurisdictions the parties are given the option of hiring their own neutral intermediary or having the court appoint one.

The objective of early neutral evaluation is to obtain an early assessment of the parties' dispute by a credible outsider who has no interest in the outcome of the dispute but who has sufficient knowledge and experience to sift through the facts and issues and find the ground shared by the parties and the ground separating them. Much like in the other forms of ADR, the success of early neutral evaluation depends largely on the disputants' faith in the neutral intermediary. It also depends in large part on the disputants' willingness to compromise and settle the dispute. Successful early neutral evaluations can lead directly to meaningful negotiations.

### Conclusion: Negotiation, ADR, and Civil Litigation

The procedures and techniques discussed above are the most commonly employed methods of ADR. Negotiation plays an important role in each method, either primarily or secondarily. However, there are countless other ADR methods, many of which modify or combine the above methods. For example, it is not uncommon for disputants to begin negotiations with early neutral evaluation and then move to nonbinding mediation. If mediation fails, the parties may proceed with binding arbitration. The goal with each type of ADR is for the parties to find the most effective way of resolving their dispute without resorting to litigation. The process has been criticized as a waste of time by some legal observers who believe that the same time could be spent pursuing the claims in civil court, where negotiation also plays a prominent role and litigants are protected by a panoply of formal rights, procedures, and rules. But many participants in unsuccessful ADR proceedings believe it is useful to determine that their disputes are not amenable to a negotiated settlement before commencing a lawsuit.

Despite its success over the past three decades, ADR is not the appropriate choice for all disputants or all legal disputes. Many individuals and entities still resist ADR because it lacks the substantive, procedural, and evidentiary protections available in formal civil litigation. For example, parties to ADR typically waive their rights to object to **evidence** that might be deemed **inadmissible** under the rules of court. **Hearsay** evidence is a common example of evidence that is considered by the parties and intermediaries in ADR forums but that is generally excluded from civil trials. If a disputant believes that he or she would be sacrificing too many rights and protections by waiving the formalities of civil litigation, ADR will not be the appropriate method of dispute resolution.

## Additional Resources

*American Jurisprudence* West Group, 1998.

*http://hg.org/adr.html* Hieros Gamos Guide to Alternative Dispute Resolution.

*"Inside the Minds of America's Family Law Courts: The Psychology of Mediation Versus Litigation in Domestic Disputes"* Ezzell, Bill, 25 *Law and Psychology Review* 119, Spring, 2001.

*West's Encyclopedia of American Law* West Group, 1998.

## Organizations

### The Academy of Experts
2 South Square
LondonEngland WC1R 5HT UK
Phone: +44 (0)20 7637 0333
Fax: (0)207637 1893
URL: http://www.academy-experts.org
Primary Contact: Geoffrey Howe, President

### Coast to Coast Mediation Center
715 Hygeia Ave
Encinitas, CA 92023 USA
Phone: (800) 748-6462
Fax: (760) 634-2628
URL: http://w ww.ctcmediation.com
Primary Contact: Donald D. Mohr and Elizabeth L. Allen, Co-Founders

### National Association For Community Mediation
1527 New Hampshire Avenue
Washington, DC 20036-1206 USA
Phone: (202) 667-9700
Fax: (650) 329-9342
URL: http://www.nafcm.org
Primary Contact: Terry Amsler, Director

# EDUCATION

## ADMINISTERING MEDICINE

*Sections within this essay:*

- Background
- General Policy Overview
- Authority
- Common Provisions
- State Laws
- Additional Resources

## Background

Administering medicine to children and adolescents while on the premises of local schools is an inescapable reality for contemporary educators. The increasing incidence of students needing to take medicine during the course of a school day has forced school systems (and some state legislatures) to enact and implement regulations and policies addressing the matter.

A professional research study published in the November 2000 issue of *Journal of School Health*, based on a random sample of 1000 members of the National Association of School Nurses (with 65 percent responding), reported that during a typical school day, 5.6 percent of children receive medication in school. The most reported medications administered within school settings were (in descending order) ADHD medications (for Attention Deficit Hyperactivity Disorders); nonprescription medications; asthma medications; analgesics, and antiseizure medications. Also common were antibiotics and vitamins.

Seriously ill and/or heavily medicated students are rarely allowed to attend classes, so the issues do not center on them. But for those children who are only marginally ill or disabled, the issue pits educational systems against society at large. Schools must consider safeguarding other children and staff from contagious disease, the prevention of disruption in the classroom by students exhibiting symptoms of illness, the control of cross-medicating (the sharing or selling of medication between classmates); and the potential for self-medication abuse while on school premises. On the other side of the issue, the social realities of the increasing number of households with two working parents (or single working parent households), coupled with employment that does not allow for "sick day" benefits to attend to children's illnesses, often results in sick children being sent to school, with or without medication to take.

Seventy-five percent of reporting nurses in the 2000 study delegated medication administration to unlicensed assistive personnel (UAPs), with secretaries (66 percent) being the most common. Errors in administering medications were reported by nearly 50 percent of the school nurses, the most common error being missed doses (79 percent). Errors were commonly reported to local school and/or state authorities.

Faced with the growing problem of exposure to liability in conjunction with the administration of medicine (and in many circumstances, the administration of controlled substances), schools have mobilized over the years and demanded both guidance and protection from liability by state legislatures. Not all states have addressed the issue at the state level, and persons needing information are best advised to start with their local school districts.

## General Policy Overview

- As of 2001, no national laws or regulations govern school administration of medication. However, national guidelines available for local **adoption** were published at least as early as 1990.

- Guidelines may be found at either state or local levels. Most local policies are developed by school boards, superintendents, individuals, and other school personnel, in collaboration with local physician or medical advisory committees. When individuals searching for applicable policies or regulations, they should always start at the local level and work up.

- According to a 2001 U.S. Congressional Subcommittee report, a total of 37 states and the District of Columbia have statutes, regulations, and/or mandatory policies addressing medication administration at schools.

- Many states have **sovereign immunity** laws that shield public employees, including school personnel and nurses, etc., from liability for **negligence**. Local procedures and policies generally require parents' signatures to release school districts and employees from liability.

- Many state and local policies permit "delegation" of medication administration (usually restricted to licensed nurses) to trained but unlicensed assistive personnel (UAPs) within school settings. They may be school principals, teachers, secretaries, or administrative assistants within the health services office., school principals, or teachers. Certain duties cannot be delegated, such as secured storage of controlled substances.

- Self-administration policies vary greatly from state to state and within school districts. Many require student assessment for age and maturity; others simply require authorizations from prescribers and parents. Almost all include signed releases of liability.

- States may require compulsory medication, in the form of immunizations/vaccinations of school children, as prerequisites to school attendance. As of 2000, 23 states had passed immunization requirements for hepatitis B vaccinations. Many had additional requirements for measles, varicella, tetanus, and diphtheria. Schools may offer free or low-cost immunizations to students in conjunction with these requirements.

## Authority

Federal law mandates that children with health needs receive school health services, e.g., the Education of All Handicapped Children Act of 1975 (P.L. 94-142); Section 504 of the Rehabilitation Act of 1973 (P.L. 93-112). But federal law does not specifically address the administering of medicine at the individual school level. Administering medicine entails physically providing it to the ultimate user, the patient.

Federal laws and regulations that do not expressly address, but, nonetheless impact, the administration of medication within schools deal mostly with controlled substances. They include:

- The Controlled Substances Act, 21 U.S.C. 801

- The Uniform Controlled Substances Act of 1994, 21 U.S.C. 802

- Title 21 (Food and Drugs) of the **Code of Federal Regulations**, Chapter II (Drug Enforcement Administration, Section 1300 (21 CFR 1300.01 et seq.)

The above federal references identify and define those substances included as "controlled substances" (any drug as defined in the five categories of the Acts). They include all opiates and their derivatives, hallucinogenic substances, anabolic steroids, and several psychotropic substances. Within school settings, most drugs used to treat ADHD are controlled substances, **as is** Ritalin. Controlled substances generally fall under the purview of local drug enforcement agencies, which derive their ultimate authority from the Federal Drug Enforcement Administration.

But students who need medications administered to them during the school day already have legal possession (or their parents do) of any controlled substances. The school's role is therefore limited to ensuring safe **custody**, storage, and administering of the medication, once a valid authorization is received from parents/physician.

Most states have enacted statutes that delegate to school systems and school boards the authority to implement local policies addressing the administration of medicine on school premises. But those regulations and policies must comply and coordinate with state laws concerning the "unauthorized practice of medicine" or "unauthorized practice of nursing."

In 1990, the Office of School Health Programs at the University of Colorado Health Science Center published national recommendations for school-based administration of medications to students. The recommendations encouraged local policy development with direct involvement of parents and the public.

In 1993, the American Academy of Pediatrics Committee on School Health published its policy statement, *Guidelines for the Administration of Medication in School* (RE9328) (reaffirmed in June 1997). The purpose of the policy statement was to assist state legislators and local school boards in establishing somewhat uniform approaches to the growing concern. As noted in the statement, "For most students, the use of medication will be a convenient benefit to control acute minor or major illnesses, allowing a timely return to the classroom with minimal interference to the student and to others."

## Common Provisions

Typical state or local policies contain certain key provisions; the two most basic requirements are parental consent and a medication order from the prescribing physician (dentist, physician assistant, nurse practitioner, etc.). Most regulations or policies require that a medication plan be completed by the school nurse or health service employee and that it contains minimum required information such as emergency contacts and telephone numbers, allergies and known side effects, the quantity of the medication delivered to the school, plans for administering medication on school field trips or planned events, and information on self-administration. An individual student log, documenting dates and times of administered medicine, is usually part of the plan on file and ultimately becomes part of the school health record.

Requirements for self-administration of medications evoke more controversy. Students who suffer from asthma and similar respiratory illnesses may suffer undue panic or anxiety attacks when separated from their inhalers. On the other hand, a few asthmatic (and other) students nationwide have been known to sell off their medications to fellow students looking for a "high" or quick thrill. In schools where

students are permitted to keep asthma medication close at hand, there are generally strict instructions as to where the medication may be stored (e.g., locker or backpack) and (sometimes) reserved rights on the part of the school to monitor self-administration. (If schools retain an "overseeing" role in self-medication, they may expose themselves to more liability if they are not protected with **immunity**).

Policies generally should require that all medication brought to school, whether prescriptive or over-the-counter (OTC), remain in original labeled containers. Of key concern is the access to life-sustaining medications administered by injection, such as insulin and epinephrine (to respond to treat emergency allergic reactions). All parenteral medications and drugs controlled by the Drug Enforcement Agency must be appropriately secured by the schools (and many of them require refrigeration, as well). In such circumstances, even those students approved for self-administration must report to a school representative to receive the required medication and any dosage paraphernalia (such as a syringe) if needed. Medication dosages/pills should be counted upon arrival and recounted when tendered to school employees.

## State Laws

ALABAMA: The state has published "recommended guidelines" prepared by an advisory task force comprised of members from Alabama's State Department of Education and the Alabama Department of Public Health. The policy differs from others in that it expressly notes that school nurses may not delegate the administration of medications to unlicensed personnel, pursuant to Alabama's Nurse Practice Act (Title 34-21-1) and the 1993 state guidelines for Delegation of Nursing Functions to Assistive Personnel. The guidelines "are not meant to be regulatory" for local education agencies (LEAs), but intend to offer "best practice" recommendations. The guidelines allow for self-administration of prescription medication by students if permitted by local school board policy. The guidelines are available at http://www.schoolhealth.org/adminmed.html.

ALASKA: No applicable provisions.

ARIZONA: Title 15 of the Arizona Revised Statutes, Chapter 15-344, provides for the administration of prescription, **patent**, or **proprietary** medications by school employees. The law delegates authority to establish policies and procedures to local school district governing boards.

ARKANSAS: No applicable provisions.

CALIFORNIA: The California Education Code 49423, 49423.6 requires the state board of education to adopt regulations regarding the administration of prescription medication in public schools. There is no express delegation of authority.

COLORADO: Colorado Dept. of Reg. Agencies, Chapter XIII, Section 7, and Colorado Board of Health Regulations, Chapter 9, Section 105, address school administration of medications. There is no express delegation of authority.

CONNECTICUT: Connecticut General **Statute** 10-212a, as well as Connecticut State Agencies Regulation 10-212a-2, 5, and 6 authorize school boards of education to adopt written policies. A new Connecticut law passed in 2001 (the first of its kind in the nation) expressly prohibits teachers, counselors, and other school personnel from recommending psychiatric drugs for schoolchildren. The state requires schools to document any skipped dose and the reasons for it.

DELAWARE: The Code of Delaware Regulations 72-000-008, Section 800-9, is applicable to school nurses; there is no express delegation of authority.

DISTRICT OF COLUMBIA: D. C. Code 31-2432 to 2434 requires the D. C. Board of Education and Department of Human Services to issue joint rules and regulations. D.C. schools must obtain authorization from the student's parent or **guardian**, as well as orders/instructions from the licensed physician before administering medication.

FLORIDA: Florida Statutes Annotated 232.46 requires district school boards to adopt local policies and procedures.

GEORGIA: No applicable provisions.

HAWAII: Hawaii Revised Statute 321-242 establishes a statewide school health services program, including statewide requirements for medication administration. Hawaii Administrative Code 11-146-4 is also applicable.

IDAHO: No applicable provisions.

ILLINOIS: 105 Illinois Compiled Statutes Annotated 5/10-20.14b requires school boards to develop local policies for school administration of medication.

INDIANA: Indiana's 511 Indiana Administrative Code 7-21-8 establishes written medication adminis-

tration policies for public schools operating special education programs only.

IOWA: Iowa Administrative Code 41.12(11) requires local education agencies offering special education programs to establish medication administration policies.

KANSAS: No applicable provisions.

KENTUCKY: No applicable provisions.

LOUISIANA: Louisiana Revised Statute 17:436.1 prescribes policies for delegating of administration of medications in schools to unlicensed personnel. Louisiana Administrative Code 28:1.929 requires school boards to establish guidelines consistent with state policy.

MAINE: 20-A Maine Revised Statutes Annotated, Section 254, Subsection 5, requires schools to adopt local written policies and procedures.

MARYLAND: The Annotated Code of Maryland, Education 7-401, in conjunction with Administrative Regulation 13A.05.05.08, and.10 require county boards of education to adopt policies for administration and storage of medication within school systems.

MASSACHUSETTS: Massachusetts was one of the earliest to have a statute in place, dating from the early 1970s. New regulations were promulgated in 1993, and old ones were updated. Four statutes in the Massachusetts General Laws are pertinent. Chapter 71, Section 53, requires registered nurses in all public school districts; Chapter 94C, the Controlled Substance Act, gives the Commissioner of Public Health authority to make certain exceptions for delegation of duties to unlicensed personnel; Chapter 112 (The Nurse Practice Act) has been amended to include regulations governing the delegation of nursing tasks; and Chapter 71, Section 54B contains registration requirements for students receiving medications. 105 Code of Massachusetts Reg. 210.003 to 210.009 requires schools to adopt local policies consistent with the above laws and regulations.

MICHIGAN: MCL 380.1178 (Revised School Code, Act 451 of 1976) was amended in March 2000, to provide immunity from criminal or civil actions for school personnel who administer medication to pupils pursuant to parent/physician authorizations and instructions. The law does not protect **gross negligence** or willful and wanton misconduct. There is no express delegation of authority.

MINNESOTA: Minnesota Statutes Annotated 121A.22 requires local school boards to develop prescription medication administration procedures in conjunction with health care professionals.

MISSISSIPPI: No applicable provisions.

MISSOURI: Chapter 167 of the Missouri Revised Statutes, "Pupils and Special Services," Section 167.627 (August 2001) addresses state requirements of self-administered medications for asthma "or other potentially life-threatening respiratory illnesses." Section 167.181 discusses compulsory immunizations. Section 167.191 expressly prohibits children with contagious diseases from attending school, with penalties of "not less than five nor more than one hundred dollars" for violations.

MONTANA: No applicable provisions.

NEBRASKA: Nebraska Revised Statutes 71-6718 to 6742, in conjunction with Nebraska Administrative Code, Chapters 59 and 95, regulate the administration of medication in schools by unlicensed personnel through competency assessments and procedural requirements.

NEVADA: Nevada Administrative Code 632.226 requires school nurses (rather than local school boards) to develop procedures.

NEW JERSEY: Concerning self-administration of medication by school pupils for asthma, **Public Law** 2001, c.061 (S1372 2R) amends Public Law 1993, c.308, and supplements Chapter 40 of Title 18A of the New Jersey Statutes. In addition, New Jersey Administrative Code 6A:16-2.3 requires district boards of education to adopt written policies.

NEW MEXICO: New Mexico, through its 6 N.M. Administrative Code 4.2.3.1.11.3.2(d) requires the supervisory school nurse to develop and implement written policies and procedures for clinical services, including the administration of medication.

NEW YORK: No applicable provisions.

NORTH CAROLINA: North Carolina General Statute 115C-307(c) authorizes school boards of education to permit school personnel to administer prescriptive medications with parents' written authorizations.

NORTH DAKOTA: No applicable provisions.

OHIO: Ohio Revised Code 3313.713 requires local school boards of education to adopt policies permit-ting school employees to administer medication. In February 2000, Ohio became the 50th state to allow advanced-practice nurses to prescribe medication (under physician supervision). In school settings, they have no independent authority to prescribe.

OKLAHOMA: Under 70 Oklahoma Statutes Annotated 1-116.2, school nurses and other school personnel must administer medications according to **statutory** requirements, which contain no express delegation of authority.

OREGON: Oregon Revised Statutes 339.869 and 339.870, in conjunction with Oregon Administrative Rule 581-021-0037, require local school district boards to adopt policies.

PENNSYLVANIA: Pennsylvania has no statutory authority, but it has a regulation, 22 Pa. Code 7.13 that requires school districts to develop medication administration policies that are consistent with state department of health guidelines. Title 24 (Education) of the Pennsylvania Consolidated Statutes Annotated, PSA 24-13, Article XIV, School Health Services, Sections 13-1413 and 13-1414 address supplemental duties of school physicians and care and treatment of pupils.

RHODE ISLAND: Title 16 (Education), Chapter 16-21 (Health and Safety of Pupils), Section 16-21-22 provides for self-medication by students who have provided schools with medical documentation. The law also provides for immunity from civil damages for those negligently administering epinephrine or prescription inhalers; it does not protect gross negligence or willful/wanton conduct from liability. The Code of R.I. Rules 14-000-011, Section 18 requires schools to develop procedures that include specified minimum requirements.

SOUTH CAROLINA: No applicable provisions, but the Charleston County School District has policies comparable to most states.

SOUTH DAKOTA: Article 46:13 addresses medication administration, including self-administration, through delegation of tasks generally within the purview of licensed registered nurses. There is no express mention of application to schools.

TENNESSEE: Tennessee Code Annotated 49-5-415 requires licensed health care professionals to administer medications, but school boards may authorize unlicensed personnel to assist students with self-administration.

TEXAS: House Bill 1688, signed into law by Governor Perry in June 2001, amends Texas Chapter 38, Education Code, to add provisions regarding self-administration of prescription asthma medicine by public school students while on school property or at school-related events or activities. School-based Health Centers and their services are generally discussed in Chapter 38.011. Texas Education Code 22.052 provides for immunity from civil liability conditioned upon the adoption of compliant school district policies.

UTAH: Utah Code Annotated 53A-11-601 authorizes schools to develop policies.

VERMONT: Vermont has no statutory guidance, but Code of Vermont Rule 22-000-006, Section 4220, requires schools to incorporate specified procedures into their local administration regulations.

VIRGINIA: The Code of Virginia, as amended, Section 22.1-274.2 and Section 22.1-78, address self-administration by students of asthma medication; permissions are granted for each school year and renewed annually. The Code delegates to local school superintendents the authority to establish additional regulations for administration of medicines to students. The Code of Virginia 54.1-3408 authorizes school boards to train employees to administer drugs.

WASHINGTON: The Revised Code of Washington, RCW 28A.210.260, addresses administration of oral medication in public and private schools. It delegates policy-making to public school districts and private schools. RCW 28A.210.270 expressly provides for immunity from liability for school employees.

WEST VIRGINIA: West Virginia Code of State Rules 126-25-1 and 126-27-1 establish standards for administration of oral, topical, and emergency medication in West Virginia public schools by persons not licensed as health care providers. Code 18-5-22a requires school boards of education to develop policies.

WISCONSIN: Wisconsin Statute 118.29 requires school boards to develop policies, including authorizing school employees to administer medications.

WYOMING: The Wyoming Administrative Code, Education, Chapter 6, Section 17(a)(i)(F) requires school districts to establish local programs for handling, storage, and administration of medications.

## Additional Resources

"Appendix VI: State Statutes, Regulations, and Mandatory Policies Addressing the Administration of Medication to Students." U. S. Government Printing Office, GAO Publication-01-1011. Available at http://www.gao.org

"Few Incidents of Diversion or Abuse Identified by Schools." Jones, Paul L., FDCH Government Account Reports, 14 September 2001. Available at http://www.law.cornell.edu/topics/civil_procedure.html

"Guidelines for the Administration of Medication in School (RE9328)." Policy Statement of the American Association of Pediatrics. 1993, 1997. Available at http://www.law.cornell.edu/topics/civil_procedure.html

"Medication Administration Practices of School Nurses." McCarthy, Ann Marie, et al. Journal of School Health, November 2000.

"Who Dispenses Pharmaceuticals to Children?" Esielion, Elaine, and Joanna Persis Hemmat. Journal of School Health, December 1996.

U. S. Code, Title 21: Food and Drugs, Chapter 17:National Drug Enforcement Policy. U. S. House of Representatives. Available at hhtp://uscode.ho,use.gov/title_21.htm

# EDUCATION

## ATHLETICS

*Sections within this essay:*

- Background
- Amateur vs. Professional Athletics
- Collegiate Athletic Associations
- Professional Sports Associations
- Relationship Between Professional Sports Leagues and College Athletics
- Other Legal Issues Affecting Amateur and Professional Athletes
- Title IX and Sex Discrimination in Amateur Athletics
    - Background
    - Parties Subject to Liability
    - Standards for Liability
    - Student-Athletes' Title IX Claims
    - Coaches' Title IX Claims
    - Remedies
    - Criticisms of Title IX
- Additional Resources

## Background

The law governing amateur athletes is an amalgam of statutes, regulations, rules, procedures, and judicial decisions that apply to individual athletes, the academic institutions for which they compete, and most persons employed by those academic institutions. This body of law spans several areas of American jurisprudence, including tort law, tax law, antitrust law, and civil rights law, among others. Thus, the law governing amateur athletics is not a single body of law unto itself.

## Amateur vs. Professional Athletes

The most basic difference between amateur and professional athletes lies in the rewards that each group receives for athletic performances. Generally speaking, amateur athletes are not paid for their athletics performances, though the U.S. Gymnastics Association and the U.S. Figure Skating Association now allow member athletes to sponsor commercial products so long as the money earned is placed into trust. Professional athletes, by contrast, are typically paid annual salaries plus incentives tied to individual and team performance.

Athletic scholarships are the biggest reward offered to amateur athletes. Athletic scholarships pay for some or all of a student-athlete's tuition, including room and board, as long as the student-athlete remains enrolled at the school, continues to participate in the athletic program for which the scholarship was awarded, and maintains academic eligibility. Amateur athletes who are compensated for their performance in any way beyond their athletic scholarships can be stripped of their amateur status by National Collegiate Athletic Association (NCAA) or other college athletic organizations.

## High School Athletic Associations

Each state has established an athletic association that establishes rules and guidelines under which most schools in that state must adhere. These rules and guidelines cover topics such as, for example, the general eligibility of student athletes, including age restrictions; residency requirements; restrictions on supervised practices when a sport is not in session; policies related to broadcasting and sponsorship;

and codes of conduct. These associations also set forth rules for individual sports.

## Collegiate Athletic Associations

Headquartered in Shawnee, Kansas, the NCAA is the governing body that regulates athletic competitions among many colleges and universities. Colleges and universities must elect to join the NCAA, and once they do they relinquish ultimate jurisdiction over their athletic programs, student-athletes, and coaches. To remain a member of the association, colleges and universities have to abide by NCAA rules, regulations, and policies.

Pursuant to its governing authority, the NCAA has established criteria that college athletes must satisfy to stay eligible for NCAA sanctioned athletic competitions. One of these criteria is that student-athletes be in good academic standing and maintain a certain minimum grade-point average. Schools and coaches are subject to NCAA restrictions regulating how high school students may be recruited, while both coaches and athletes are subject to discipline for violating NCAA rules relating to use of illegal or banned substances, gambling, point-shaving, and bribery.

The NCAA conducts its own investigations of alleged rule violations and assesses penalties based on the severity of the violation, after giving the suspected offender an opportunity to be heard during a public proceeding in which most fundamental legal rights may be invoked. Penalties may be assessed against an offending school, coach, or athlete and entail loss of scholarships and loss of post-season awards, including fines, probation, suspensions, forfeiture of games, and forfeiture of tournament and playoff opportunities.

Schools with repeat offenses may receive particularly harsh punishment. For instance, the NCAA cancelled the entire 1987 football season for Southern Methodist University (SMU) after investigators found numerous rules violations related to the football team, including payments to players that amounted to more than $600,000. The so-called "death penalty" that the NCAA administered in the SMU case is the harshest punishment that the NCAA has ever administered, but it is indicative of the level of power that the NCAA holds over athletic programs.

Some schools, particularly smaller colleges, choose not to be members of the NCAA. More than 280 colleges belong to the National Association of In-tercollegiate Athletics (NAIA), which is based in Olathe, Kansas. The NAIA sanctions more than a dozen sports for men and women. Two-year colleges, on the other hand, belong to the National Junior College Athletic Association (NJCAA), based in Colorado Springs, Colorado. Member schools of the NAIA and NJCAA are subject to similar rules as schools that are members of the NCAA.

Most colleges and universities also belong to athletic conferences. These conferences establish additional rules under which their members must operate. Athletic conferences also coordinate efforts to market their sports teams and provide for plans by which revenues from athletics are shared by member schools.

## Professional Sports Associations

Professional sports teams in the National Football League (NFL), Major League Baseball (MLB), the National Hockey League (NHL), and the National Basketball Association (NBA) are also governed by voluntary associations, but their associations are comprised of individual owners who purchase professional sports franchises and agree to abide by the rules, policies, and procedures established by the league. Also known as the constitution and by-laws, these rules, policies and procedures generally govern the circumstances under which franchises may move their team from one city to another; players may be drafted, sign contracts, become free agents, and receive retirement pensions; and owners, coaches, and players may be fined, suspended, banned, or otherwise punished. The league's constitution and by-laws may also be influenced by the terms of any collective bargaining agreement entered into between franchise owners and labor representatives for the players' union and by any applicable antitrust laws (i.e., federal laws that protect trade and commerce from restraints, monopolies, price-fixing, and price discrimination).

## Relationship Between Professional Sports Leagues and College Athletics

Professional sports leagues generally do not have an official relationship with college athletic associations. In some sports, especially baseball and hockey, the best high school players often develop their skills in minor professional leagues rather than colleges. On the other hand, most highly talented football and basketball players traditionally have played in college as amateurs before moving on to play professionally.

Beginning primarily in the 1990s, top high school basketball stars began skipping the college ranks altogether and joining professional teams. With the success and popularity of such individuals as Kevin Garnett, Kobe Bryant, and LeBron James, each of whom were drafted directly out of high school, more NBA teams began selecting high school players in the NBA draft. Football players, however, have not had this option because the NFL forbids players from entering the NFL draft until a minimum of three years has elapsed since the players have graduated from high school.

In 2004, Maurice Clarett, a standout running back with Ohio State University, challenged the NFL's three-year rule on the grounds that it violated federal antitrust laws. A federal district court agreed with Clarett, ruling that the NFL could not prevent him from entering the 2004 draft. After the ruling, Mike Williams, a star receiver for the University of Southern California who had been out of high school for less than three years, announced that he would enter the draft and turn professional as well. The Second Circuit Court of Appeals, however, disagreed with the district court's opinion in the Clarett case, thus requiring Clarett to wait until 2005 to become eligible for the draft. Because Williams had hired an agent, even though it was prior to the Second Circuit's opinion, he was also ineligible to return to play college football. As a result of the Clarett case, the vast majority of football players who eventually turn professional must still first play at the college level.

## Other Legal Issues Confronting Amateur and Professional Athletes

Amateur and professional athletes must comply with state and federal laws that exist independent of the rules established by the athletic association in which they are members. Nonetheless, many professional and amateur athletes are surprised to learn of the extent to which they must understand the intricacies of civil and criminal law if they want to stay out of court. For example, professional athletes are required to pay income tax to every state in which they appear to play a game, and not just to the state in which their teams play home games. Amateur athletes may be taxed on the funds they receive for athletic scholarships when those funds exceed the cost of tuition, room, board, and necessary supplies.

Many amateur and professional athletes are also surprised to learn that they can be held civilly and criminally liable for injuries they inflict on other ath-

letes during competition, even in contact sports such as hockey and football. Contact-sport athletes consent to some contact as part of the game and assume the risk for injuries that are sustained during the normal and ordinary course of an athletic contest. But under the common law, no athlete assumes the risk for injuries that result from the reckless or intentional misconduct of another athlete. Depending on the laws of the state in which an injury is inflicted, the blameworthiness of the misconduct, and the severity of the injury, athletes who recklessly or intentionally injure competitors during an athletic contest may be prosecuted in criminal court or sued in civil court for battery, assault, or other such related unlawful acts. A minority of jurisdictions allow athletes to recover for injuries sustained from the negligent conduct of competitors.

In some cases academic institutions may be held liable for injuries suffered by athletes. As a general rule, coaches, trainers, and referees must exercise reasonable care to prevent foreseeable injuries to athletes, and under no circumstances may a school employee encourage athletes to injure opponents or competitors. If a school employee fails to exercise the degree of care that is reasonable under the circumstances, the school itself may be held vicariously liable under the doctrine of respondent superior, which makes principals liable for the wrongful acts of their agents, when those acts are committed in the ordinary course and scope of the agent's authority.

Because the relationship between the law and amateur and professional athletes can be complicated, many colleges, universities, and pro sports franchises require athletes to attend classes that introduce them to a variety of legal issues. Some of these classes are geared solely toward male athletes. Given the number of highly publicized cases in which male athletes have been accused of sexual assault and violence, these classes are intended to help male athletes avoid situations where they can get themselves into trouble.

## Title IX and Sex Discrimination in Amateur Athletics

Sex discrimination is a hotly debated and litigated issue in amateur athletics. Title IX of the Education Amendments Act of 1972 provides that "[n]o person in the United States may, upon the basis of sex, be excluded from participation in, be denied the benefits of, or be subjected to discrimination under any education program or activity receiving federal finan-

GALE ENCYCLOPEDIA OF EVERYDAY LAW                                                                                    569

cial assistance." 20 U.S.C.A. §§ 1681 *et seq.* The phrase "education program or activity" has been broadly interpreted to include athletic programs. Title IX may be enforced by the federal government in an administrative proceeding or by a private individual in civil court. The law guarantees equal protection at all federally funded academic institutions for both male and female student-athletes and male and female persons employed by school athletic programs.

## Background

Congress enacted Title IX to serve as a catalyst against sex discrimination at federally funded academic institutions, to encourage the development of athletic programs for female student athletes, and to stimulate female participation in school sports. Within eleven years of Title IX's enactment, statistics revealed that progress was being made toward these goals. In 1983, more than 150,000 women were participating in college sports, compared with 32,000 in 1972, while the number of colleges and universities offering athletics scholarships to women increased from 60 in 1974 to 500 in 1981. By 2000, about 151,000 women engaged in athletics in the NCAA and 2.8 million females engaged in high school sports.

The U.S. Department of Education (DOE), acting through the Office of Civil Rights (OCR), is primarily responsible for implementing Title IX. The OCR promulgates regulations to enforce Title IX, initiating administrative proceedings against alleged violators, and terminating federal funding for proven violators. Although neither Title IX nor any of its amendments expressly authorizes an individual to bring a lawsuit against a violator independent of an action brought by the DOE or OCR, the U.S. Supreme Court has ruled that Title IX implies a private cause of action pursuant to which aggrieved individuals may seek redress for sex discrimination in federal court without first having exhausted their administrative remedies. *Cannon v. University of Chicago* (1979).

## Parties Subject to Liability

Title IX conditions the offer of federal funding on each funding recipient's promise not to discriminate on the basis of sex, in what amounts to a contract between the government and the funding recipient. Elementary schools, junior high schools, high schools, and both undergraduate and graduate colleges and universities must comply with Title IX if they receive federal funding and wish to continue receiving it. However, federally funded recipients may be ex-

empted from liability under Title IX if they have had a continuous policy and tradition of admitting students of only one gender. 20 U.S.C.A. § 1681(a)(5). Federally funded recipients are also exempt from Title IX suits that arise from employment discrimination claims over jobs in which sex is a bona fide occupational qualification, as might be the case for persons hired to clean or monitor locker rooms and toilet facilities.

As noted above, athletic departments and athletic programs infrequently receive federal funding directly from the federal government. The same holds true for directors, coaches, trainers, and other individuals employed by school athletic programs. Instead, school boards, school districts, colleges, and universities are the most common recipients of federal funding, and thus they are also the most common targets of Title IX litigation. Since Title IX has been interpreted as abrogating the states' Eleventh Amendment immunity in this area of law, state governments themselves may also be sued in federal court for discrimination that occurs at one of their federally-funded, state-sponsored academic institutions.

## Standards for Liability

Title IX bars sex discrimination in any interscholastic, intercollegiate, intramural, or club athletic program offered by a federally-funded academic institution. This prohibition has two prongs. The first prong prohibits sex discrimination against students participating in or seeking to participate in a school-sponsored sport. The second prong prohibits sex discrimination against persons employed or seeking employment with a school sponsored athletic program, including persons employed or seeking employment as athletic directors, athletic coordinators, coaches, physical therapists, trainers, or any other job within a school's athletic program.

Under both prongs, the law requires federally funded academic institutions to guarantee equal opportunity for student-athletes and employees without regard to gender. Ten specific factors may be considered in determining whether this obligation has been met: (1) the particular sports and levels of competition selected by an institution to accommodate members of both sexes; (2) the quality and quantity of equipment and supplies that are provided to teams of each gender; (3) the scheduling of games and practice time; (4) travel and per diem allowances; (5) the opportunities to receive coaching and academic tutoring; (6) the compensation of coaches and tutors; (7) the provision of locker rooms, as well as practice and competitive facilities; (8) the provision of medical and training facilities and services; (9) the provision of housing and dining facilities and services; and (10) the publicity afforded to each gender's athletic programs. 34 C.F.R. § 106.41.

The circumstances of each case determine how much weight is allotted to a given factor in resolving Title IX disputes. Nonetheless, a significant portion of litigation has focused on the first factor, and courts will normally ask three questions when evaluating whether an academic institution has taken steps to effectively accommodate athletes of both sexes: (1) does the number of athletic opportunities provided for males and females proportionately represent their respective overall enrollments to a substantial degree?; (2) does the academic institution have a history of expanding programs to accommodate female interests and abilities in sports; and, of so, (3) has that institution fully and effectively accommodated those interests and abilities? If a preponderance of the evidence offered during a Title IX proceeding answers these questions in the affirmative, the defendant will normally prevail. Plaintiffs are more likely to prevail when the defendant has a poor or inconsistent record on these issues.

### Student-Athletes' Title IX Claims

A court's analysis will also depend on whether the plaintiff is a disgruntled student-athlete or a disgruntled employee. For disgruntled student-athletes, Title IX does not compel federally funded educational institutions to sponsor one program for each gender in every sport the institution sponsors. However, if a school sponsors only one program for a sport, then that school must allow members of both sexes to try out for the team, unless the sport is a contact sport, in which case the school may limit participation to one gender. Conversely, if a school sponsors only one program for a contact sport and then allows members of both sexes to compete for the team, the school may not exclude an athlete from the team on account of his or her gender. "Contact" sports include boxing, wrestling, rugby, ice hockey, football, and basketball. 45 C.F.R. § 86.41.

Disgruntled students may also allege that they have been victims of sexual harassment in violation of Title IX. Sexual harassment typically consists of receiving unwanted sexually oriented comments, receiving unwanted sexually oriented physical contact, or working in a sexually charged environment. The

threshold of liability is higher for sexual harassment than it is for sex discrimination. To prevail on a Title IX sexual harassment claim, a plaintiff must show that the institution was aware of the harassment, exercised control over both the harassed and the environment in which the harassment occurred, and that harassment was serious enough to have the systemic effect of denying the victim equal access to participate in an athletic program. Mere name-calling or teasing will not give rise to a Title IX harassment claim, even when the offensive comments single out differences in gender.

Courts are more inclined to find that offensive comments give rise to Title IX liability when they are made by a coach or a person acting in an official capacity for the academic institution. Plaintiffs are less likely to prevail when the offensive behavior takes the form of student-on-student or athlete-on-athlete harassment. In such instances, the plaintiff must not only prove that the academic institution was aware of the harassment and had authority to stop the harassment, but also that the harassment was "so severe, pervasive, and objectively offensive" that it amounted to "deliberate indifference" by the institution in failing to stop it. *Davis Next Friend LaShonda D. v. Monroe County Board of Education* (U.S. 1999). Thus, sexual harassment by fans, athletes, or coaches from opposing schools is generally not actionable.

### Coaches' Title IX Claims

The statutory proscription against sex discrimination in education programs and activities encompasses employment discrimination, which means that any person working for an athletic program at a federally funded academic institution is entitled to protection from Title IX. The law protects employees in all aspects of their employment, ranging from hiring and compensation to promotion, demotion, suspension, and termination, regardless of the position held by the employee and regardless of whether the federally funded academic institution is a tiny elementary school or an enormous Division I university.

Since 1990, a large number of Title IX employment discrimination complaints have been filed by college coaches. Frequently, these claims allege that the head coach of a women's college team is being discriminated against because she is being paid less than the head coach of the men's team for the same sport and from the same school. Courts will consider several factors in evaluating these claims, including the following: (1) the differing rates of compensation; (2) the duration of the contracts; (3) provisions relating to contract renewal; (4) the relative training and experience of the two coaches; (5) the nature of the coaching duties performed by each; (6) working conditions; (7) professional standing; (8) other terms and conditions of employment; and (9) other professional qualifications.

### Remedies

A plaintiff instituting a private action to enforce Title IX may not ordinarily recover compensatory damages, unless the plaintiff offers evidence that the discrimination was willful, deliberate, or intentional. Injunctive relief is the remedy most regularly sought in Title IX actions. Injunctions may take the form of an order compelling an academic institution to cease an offending practice or an order compelling the institution to take specific action to level the playing field for the victims of discrimination. Prevailing Title IX plaintiffs may also recover attorney's fees and expert witness fees pursuant to 42 U.S.C.A. § 1988. Additionally, when the Title IX defendant is a state government, plaintiffs may pursue remedies available under the Civil Right Act, which prohibits discrimination by state actors. 42 U.S.C.A. § 1983. Both compensatory and punitive damages are recoverable in section 1983 actions.

Litigants who are unhappy with a federal agency's decision made pursuant to Title IX may generally appeal that decision to a federal district court as provided in 20 U.S.C.A. § 1683. However, if the agency's decision involves terminating or refusing to grant or to continue financial assistance upon a finding of failure to comply with a Title IX requirements, then judicial review may only be pursued as provided in 5 U.S.C.A. § 701 et seq. Title IX does not contain a statute of limitations, so both administrative agencies and judicial bodies rely on the most analogous statute of limitations provided by the law of the state from which the discrimination complaint originated.

### Criticisms of Title IX

Title IX is not without its critics. This is particularly true of those who are involved with low-profile men's sports, such as wrestling or diving. According to some critics, schools have eliminated some smaller men's sports in order to finance women's sports. Supporters of Title IX have countered that the reason why the smaller sports have been sacrificed is because schools refuse to divert money from men's sports that produce the most revenue, particularly football and basketball. In 2003, a 15-member Commission on Opportunities in Athletics studied Title IX in order to make recommendations for strengthening and improving the statute. The report suggested that the Department of Education should reaffirm its commitment to enforcing Title IX and should aggressively enforce its provisions in a uniform way. Nevertheless, the debate about the positive and negative effects of this statute has continued.

## Additional Resources

*American Jurisprudence.* Thomson/West 2005.

*Managing Legal Issues in College Athletics: Proactive Strategies for Administrators.* LRP Publications, 2004.

*A Place on the Team: The Triumph and Tragedy of Title IX* Suggs, Welch, Princeton University Press, 2005.

*West's Encyclopedia of American Law, 2nd Edition,* Thomson/Gale, 2004.

## Organizations

### American Civil Liberties Union (ACLU)
1400 20th Street, NW, Suite 119
Washington, DC 20036 USA
Phone: (202) 457-0800
URL: http://www.aclu.org

### Center for Human Rights and Constitutional Law
256 S. Occidental Blvd.
Los Angeles, CA 90057 USA
Phone: (213) 388-8693
URL: http://www.centerforhumanrights.org

### National Organization of Bar Counsel
515 Fifth Street, NW
Washington, DC 20001 USA
Phone: (202) 638-1501
URL: http://www.nobc.org

# EDUCATION

## BILINGUALISM

*Sections within this essay:*

- Background
    - Types of Bilingual Education
    - Conflicting Philosophies
- Historical Perspective
- Landmark Legislation
    - Setting the Stage
    - Civil Rights Act (1964)
    - Bilingual Education Act (1968)
    - Lau v. Nichols (1974)
- State and Local Initiatives
- Grants and Programs
- Additional Resources

## Background

At the beginning of the twenty-first century there were some three million children in the United States who were classified as Limited English Proficient (LEP). For much of the twentieth century these students would have been placed in so-called "immersion programs," in which they would be taught solely in English until they understood it as well or better than their native tongue. Beginning in the 1960s there was a gradual shift toward bilingual education, in which students can master English while retaining their native-language skills.

### Types of Bilingual Education

There is a difference between bilingual programs and English as a Second Language (ESL) programs, although bilingual programs include an ESL compo-

nent. Bilingual programs are designed to introduce students to English gradually by working with them in both English and their native tongue. The students are able to master English without losing proficiency in the native language. In bilingual or dual language immersion, the class typically includes English speaking students and LEP students who share the same native language. Instruction is given in both English and the native language. In developmental or late-exit programs, all students share the same language; instruction begins in that language but gradually shifts to English as the students become more proficient.

*Transitional or early-exit programs* are similar to developmental programs, except that the goal is mastery of English rather than bilingualism. Students who become proficient in English are transferred to English-only classes.

Bilingualism is not generally a goal in ESL programs. In *sheltered English or structured immersion programs,* LEP students are taught in English (supplemented by gestures and other visual aids). The goal is acquisition of English. *Pull-out ESL programs* include English-only instruction, but LEP participants are "pulled out" of the classroom for part of the day for lessons in their native tongue.

### Conflicting Philosophies

Bilingual education in the United States is a complex cultural issue because of two conflicting philosophies. On the one hand is the idea that the United States welcomes people from all societies, from all walks of life. Immigrants have long seen the States as the "Land of Opportunity," in which individuals can rise to the top through hard work and determination. They can build new identities for themselves, but they can also hold on to their past culture without fear of reprisal. At the same time, the United States is also the great "melting pot" in which immigrants are expected to assimilate if they wish to avail themselves of the many opportunities for freedom and success. Everyone who comes to the States, so they are told, should want to *become* American.

Thus there are people who believe strongly that erasing an immigrant's native tongue is erasing a key cultural element. People are entitled to speak and use their native languages as they please; anything less goes against the freedom for which the United States stands. Besides, having proficiency or fluency in more than one language is a decided advantage in a world that has become more interdependent.

There are other people who believe, equally strongly, that everyone who lives and works in the United States should speak, read, and write in English. Those who oppose bilingual programs for LEP students believe that allowing children to learn in their native tongue puts them at a disadvantage in a country in which English is the common language. A student whose instruction is in another language, they say, may never master English. This closes doors to opportunities including higher education and choice of career.

There is no uniform opinion even among immigrant parents of LEP children. Some parents want their children to be taught in their native tongue as a means of preserving their culture. Others, wishing their children to have the same opportunities as native speakers of English, want their children to be taught in English from the outset.

The one point on which everyone seems to agree is that LEP children deserve the best educational opportunities available, and any language program must be structured enough to give them a good foundation, while it remains flexible enough to meet their varied needs.

## Historical Perspective

Although we tend to think of bilingualism in the United States as a modern issue, in fact it has always been a part of our history. In the early days of exploration and colonization, French, Spanish, Dutch, and German were as common as English. By 1664, the year that the British took control of New York from the Dutch, there were some 18 languages (not including the native American tongues) spoken in lower Manhattan alone. No doubt many of the inhabitants of the colony were conversant in more than two languages.

German and French remained common in colonial North America. Many Germans educated their children in German-language schools. Although many colonial leaders (among them Benjamin Franklin) complained about bilingualism, it was generally accepted. In fact, during and after the American Revolution, such documents as the **Articles of Confederation** were published in both English and German.

During the nineteenth century millions of immigrants came to the United States and brought their languages with them. German remained popular, as did other European tongues. Spanish was introduced when the United States took possession of Texas, Florida, and California from Spain.

The enormous wave of **immigration** that began in the 1880s and lasted until the early 1920s brought a change in sentiment toward bilingual education. The goals of voluntary assimilation were gradually replaced by strident calls for "Americanization." In Puerto Rico, Hawaii, and the Philippines (which the United States had acquired after the Spanish-American War in 1898), English was to be the language of instruction even though most of these new Americans spoke no English at all. In 1906, Congress passed a law, the first language law ever passed, requiring naturalized citizens to be able to speak English. Anti-bilingual sentiment got stronger as more immigrants poured into the United States. Anti-German sentiment, which reached its peak when the United States entered World War I in 1917, caused some communities to ban the use of German in public.

By the end of the war, bilingualism had fallen out of favor even in areas where it had thrived. In 1924 strict immigration quotas sharply reduced the number of new foreigners coming into the United States. For almost the next 40 years, bilingual education in U. S. schools was almost exclusively based on variations of immersion; students were taught in English no matter what their native tongue was, and those who did not master English were required to stay back in the same grade until they became proficient.

# Landmark Legislation

## Setting the Stage

Bilingual education in the United States was pushed back into the spotlight as a direct result of the 1959 revolution in Cuba. After Fidel Castro overthrew the dictatorship and established a Communist government, many middle- and upper-class Cubans fled to the United States. A large number of these refugees settled in Florida. Well-educated but with little in the way of resources, they were assisted quite generously by the federal and state governments.

Among this assistance was ESL instruction, provided by the Dade County (Florida) Public Schools. In addition, the school district launched a "Spanish for Spanish Speakers" program. In 1963, a bilingual education program was introduced at the Coral Way Elementary School in Miami. Directed by both U. S. and Cuban educators, the program began in the first through third grades. U. S. and Cuban students received a half day of English and a half day of Spanish instruction; at lunch time and recess and during music and art classes the groups were mixed together. Within three years the district was able to report benefits for both groups of students, who were now not only bilingual but also bicultural. This was no accident: the goal of the Coral Way initiative was to promote exactly this level of fluency.

## The Civil Rights Act (1964)

The **Civil Rights** Act of 1964 did not address bilingual education directly, but it opened an important door. Title VI of the Act specifically prohibits **discrimination** on the basis of race, color, or national origin in any programs or activities that receive federal financial assistance. What this means, among other aspects, is that school districts that receive federal aid are required to ensure that minority students are getting the same access to programs as non-minorities. This minority group includes language minority (LM) students, defined as students who live in a home in which a language other than English is spoken. (Although some LM students are fluent in English, many are classified as LEP.) Title VI's critical role in bilingualism would be made clear a decade later in the *Lau v. Nichols* case.

## Bilingual Education Act (1968)

The Elementary and Secondary Education Act of 1968 was another important step for bilingual education. In particular, Title VII of that act, known as the Bilingual Education Act, established federal policy for bilingual education. Citing its recognition of "the special educational needs of the large numbers children of limited English-speaking ability in the United States," the Act stipulated that the federal government would provide financial assistance for innovative bilingual programs. Funding would be provided for the development of such programs and for implementation, staffing and staff training, and long-term program maintenance.

Title VII has been amended several times since its establishment, and it was reauthorized in 1994 as part of the Improving America's Schools Act. The basic goal has remained the same: access to bilingual programs for children of limited means.

## Lau v. Nichols

Probably the most important legal event for bilingual education was the *Lau v. Nichols* case, which was brought against the San Francisco Unified School District by the parents of nearly 1,800 Chinese students. It began as a discrimination case in 1970 when a poverty lawyer decided to represent a Chinese student who was failing in school because he could not understand the lessons and was given no special assistance. The school district countered that its policies were not discriminatory because it offered the same instruction to all students regardless of national origin. The lack of English proficiency was not the district's fault.

Lower courts ruled in favor of the San Francisco schools, but in 1974 the U. S. Supreme Court ruled unanimously in favor of the plaintiffs. In his opinion, Justice William O. Douglas stated simply that "there is no equality of treatment merely by providing students with the same facilities, textbooks, teachers, and curriculum; for students who do not understand English are effectively foreclosed from any meaningful education." The Court cited Title VI of the Civil Rights Act, noting that the students in question fall into the protected category established therein.

What *Lau v. Nichols* did not do was establish a specific bilingual policy. Individual school districts were responsible for taking "affirmative steps" toward reaching the goal of providing equal educational opportunities for all students.

# State and Local Initiatives

In the 1960s there were no state bilingual programs; many states actually had English-only instruction laws on their books. After the Civil Rights Act and the Bilingual Education Act, states began to take more initiative. In 1971, Massachusetts became the first state to establish a bilingual mandate. Under this mandate, any school that had 20 or more students of the same language background was required to implement some sort of bilingual program.

A decade later, 11 more states had passed bilingual education laws, and an additional 19 offered some sort of legislative efforts in that direction. Today, bilingual or ESL education is offered in some form by every state. Not surprisingly, those states with the highest concentration of immigrants (New York, California, Texas, Florida) tend to have the most comprehensive programs. In fact, according to the most recent data from the National Clearinghouse for Bilingual Education (NCBE), 18 of the 20 urban school districts with the highest LEP enrollment are in one of these four states. Some states fund all bilingual education programs; others fund only bilingual or only ESL programs.

It should be noted that bilingual needs can differ widely from state to state or district to district. According to the U. S. Department of Education, Spanish-speaking students make up nearly three-quarters of all LEP students in the United States. But in a district in which the predominant foreign language is Chinese, Vietnamese, or Hindi, the needs would of course be geared toward those languages. Local schools can create effective bilingual programs based on their specific needs. At the William Barton Rogers School in Boston, for example, a transitional program for middle-school LEP students who speak Vietnamese has met with success; likewise, a program for elementary school students in the Madawaska School District in Maine has been successful with French-speaking students.

Because each state's needs are different, and because those needs are subject to change, the best way to get comprehensive and up-to-date information on each state's initiatives is to contact individual state education departments (see below).

## Grants and Programs

Obtaining information about bilingual grants, programs, and other initiatives is much easier today than it was in the past thanks to the Internet. Federal, state, and local government agencies offer a surprising variety of information on their web sites. Those who do not own a computer can access these sites at any local public library. Following is a sampling of what is available.

The U. S. Department of Education's Office of Bilingual Education and Minority Language Affairs (OBEMLA) is in charge of awarding Title VII grants to both state and local education agencies. There are 12 types of discretionary grants, which cover training, development, implementation, school reform programs, and foreign language instruction. These grants are awarded only to "education-related organizations." Individuals are not eligible for Title VII grants. Those interested in applying for a Title VII grant can obtain the necessary information by visiting OBEMLA's web site (http://www.ed.gov.offices/OBEMLA)

A good beginning resource for anyone who wishes to find out about programs, grants, and other information on bilingual education and bilingual initiatives is the National Clearinghouse for Bilingual Education (NCBE). Funded by OBEMLA, this organization collects and analyzes information and also provides links to other organizations. The NCBE web site (http://www.ncbe.gwu.edu) is a comprehensive starting point.

Each state's Department of Education provides information on its statewide and local bilingual initiatives; the easiest way to find this information is to visit individual state education department web sites. Also, large cities such as New York, Miami, Houston, Los Angeles, and San Francisco provide information on their web sites about their comprehensive bilingual programs.

## Additional Resources

*Bilingual Education: A Sourcebook.* Alba M. Ambert and Sarah E. Melendez, Garland Publishing, 1985.

*Bilingual Education: History, Politics, Theory, and Practice.* Third Edition. James Crawford, Bilingual Educational Services, Inc., 1995.

*Bilingual Education: Issues and Strategies.* Amado M. Padilla, Halford M. Fairchild, and Concepc.on M. Valadez, editors, Sage Publications, 1990.

*Learning in Two Languages: From Conflict to Consensus in the Reorganization of Schools.* Gary Imhoff, editor, Transaction Publishers, 1990.

## Organizations

### *Center for Applied Linguistics*
4646 40th Street, NW
Washington, DC 20016 USA
Phone: (202) 362-0700

Fax: (202) 362-3740
URL: http://www.cal.org
Primary Contact: Donna Christian, President

### National Association for Bilingual Education (NABE)

1220 L Street, NW, Suite 605
Washington, DC 20005 USA
Phone: (202) 898-1829
Fax: (202) 789-2866
URL: http://www.nabe.org
Primary Contact: Delia Pompa, Executive Director

### National Clearinghouse for Bilingual Education (NCBE)

The George Washington University
Center for the Study of Language and Education
2121 K Street, Suite 260
Washington, DC 20037 USA
Phone: (202) 467-0867
Fax: (800) 531-9347
URL: http://www.ncbe.gwu.edu
Primary Contact: Minerva Gorena, Director

### National Education Association (NEA)

1201 16th Street, NW
Washington, DC 20036 USA
Phone: (202) 833-4000
Fax: (202) 822-7170
URL: http://www.nea.org

Primary Contact: Robert F. Chase, President

### National multicultural Institute (NMCI)

3000 Connecticut Avenue, NW, Suite 438
Washington, DC 20008 USA
Phone: (202) 483-0700
Fax: (202) 483-5233
URL: http://www.nmci,org
Primary Contact: Elizabeth Pathy Salett, President

### Teachers of English to Speakers of Other Languages (TESOL)

700 South Washington Street, Suite 200
Alexandria, VA 22314 USA
Phone: (703) 836-0774
Fax: (703) 836-7864
URL: http://www.tesol.edu
Primary Contact: Charles Amorosino, Executive Director

### U. S. Department of Education

### Office of Bilingual Education and Minority Language Affairs (OBEMLA)

400 Maryland Avenue, SW
Washington, DC 20202 USA
Phone: (202) 205-5463
Fax: (202) 205-8737
URL: http://www.ed.gov.offices/OBEMLA
Primary Contact: Art Love, Acting Director

# EDUCATION

## CODES OF CONDUCT

## Background

Among the many ingredients for successful schools is a student body that is not only eager to learn but also well behaved. Children are taught the difference between good and poor behavior from an early age, and ideally that training goes with them into the classroom. Teachers and school administrators are expected to serve as role models, and they also have an obligation to ensure that students meet certain conduct expectations.

Codes of conduct are designed to serve both the classroom and the individual. They outline students' rights, ensuring that no student will be penalized or singled out based on anything but a violation of established rules. They also outline students' responsibilities, thus letting individual students know that they need to meet certain standards for their own sake and that of the entire class.

"Conduct" covers such a wide variety of behaviors that establishing a formal code within a school system is a complicated matter. A violation of conduct rules can be anything from passing notes in class to carrying a concealed weapon into the building. It is up to the school administration, often working in conjunction with parents and students, to set rules and to enforce them.

A typical school code of conduct begins with an outline of rights and responsibilities for both the students and the faculty. It then lists different infractions (often categorized at different levels of severity) and prescribes appropriate disciplinary measures. It should also explain the student's right to appeal any disciplinary action.

It is important to remember that both the students and the faculty have rights and responsibilities. Students have the right to be informed of the school district's policies and regulations. They also have the right to know the academic requirements of each course and to be advised of their progress. Students have privacy rights as well; their personal possessions are generally off limits. If the school has reason to believe that a student is carrying something illegal, such as a knife, that becomes a different matter. Desks and lockers are school property, and schools can inspect them without student permission.

Teachers, likewise, have the right to be able to do their job without distractions. They also have the right to discipline students in an appropriate manner when necessary. Most codes of conduct are written with enough flexibility to allow teachers some leeway when choosing disciplinary action.

If a student is **accused** of committing a serious offense that results in suspension or expulsion, he or she has the right to appeal the decision under due process rules of law. No student can be singled out for punishment on the basis of race, sex, color, religion, **disability**, or national origin. Moreover, in most cases, school **jurisdiction** applies to the actual school grounds, but codes of conduct are valid when students are attending school-related functions off the actual school property.

## Basic Conduct Issues

The classroom is designed to provide students with a structured environment in which they can learn. In most cases the classroom model works quite well, but it fails to take simple human nature into consideration. Children, even those who are normally well behaved, will try to test the rules for two simple reasons. First, they are away from their parents, which makes them feel independent even though a teacher may be watching them. For this reason, some students habitually come to class late or skip class altogether. Second, as children learn to socialize they seek ways to generate attention, even negative attention for being disruptive, for example, by always talking out of turn or playing the class clown.

In years past, schools offered courses in what was known as "civics." Civics courses often included instruction on the importance of integrity, honesty, and respect for others. Civics courses have fallen out of favor for the most part, although many schools do offer some sort of course work focusing on understanding values. Nonetheless, there are always students who will break the rules.

The point teachers and administrators stress is that even minor infractions can represent more serious behavior problems, and failure to offer discipline and guidance can lead some students to more disruptive or harmful violations.

Among the more innocuous types of behavior that constitute conduct violations are the following:

Repeatedly coming to class without appropriate supplies (books, gym clothes, etc.)

Leaving school property without permission

Defacing school property (vandalizing books, for example)

Wearing inappropriate clothing

Bringing radios or CD players to class

Truancy

Clearly each of these infractions warrants different punishment. Probably the most common punishment is still having the student stay after school. Faculty and administrators have a variety of other options, however. They can give a warning or reprimand, have a student conference, have a parent conference, change the student's class schedule, or impose a suspension. The student who brings a radio to class might benefit most from a reprimand (and from having the radio confiscated for the day). The student who cuts class regularly may require more direct involvement with teachers and parents. Students who drive to school could have their parking privileges revoked if they leave school grounds without permission.

## More Serious Violations

When students commit more serious violations, a good code of conduct should be able to address the problematic behavior and prescribe appropriate punishment. Among those more serious violations are the following:

- Cheating or plagiarizing
- Using profane, obscene, or ethnically offensive language
- Possessing pornographic material
- Theft (from another student or from the school)
- Gambling on school grounds
- Threatening the safety of another student
- Fighting with another student

Students who commit these more serious offenses will face stronger punishment. But no school district wants merely to punish a student and let an incident drop, particularly in light of the heightened sensitivity to school violence. Intervention programs often begin with conferences between the student and his or her parents or guardians and teachers and school administrators. Discipline can be rehabilitative in form. Instead of being suspended from class, for example, a student might be assigned to do a community service project. Someone who vandalizes a school building may have to repair that damage instead of merely paying for it.

## Violence and Other Extreme Behavior

For many years school violence was thought to exist only in poor inner-city schools, with most of that violence directed against specific students (gangs, for example). A series of highly publicized sniper attacks, many in affluent suburban schools, during the 1990s changed the public's perception of school violence. Although the National Center for Education Statistics (NCES) reported that in 1997 only 10 percent of schools reported any instance of serious crime, with 42 percent reporting no crimes at all, many believe that schools have becoming increasingly dangerous. What was particularly chilling about many of the attacks was often the students responsible were regarded as quiet and unassuming.

It is simplistic to say that a code of conduct would have kept some of the most deadly sniper attacks from taking place. That said, a code of conduct does send a clear message to students that certain behavior will not be tolerated, including teasing and bullying. Some of the students who killed their fellow students were said to have been bullied and taunted by their classmates over a period of years.

### Identifying Troubled Students

Truly troubled students who might have tendencies to resort to extreme violence against their peers and teachers cannot be stopped simply by a code of conduct. What a code of conduct can do, however, is help identify behavior patterns in children early on. A youngster who is constantly disrupting class and breaking rules is clearly having trouble adjusting, and the school can work with the youngster and the parents to identify the problem. The class bully needs to be disciplined, but without some sort of additional action (such as counseling) the discipline becomes merely punitive. Not every troubled student will react violently, of course, but that does not mean the school has no obligation to reach out and help when help seems appropriate. Regarding serious crime, students who commit **felony** offenses are removed automatically from most schools; if under age these individuals may be placed in a juvenile detention facility where they can continue their education; if over 16 they can be tried as an adult for their crimes and imprisoned if convicted.

## Conduct and Technology

The Internet has vastly expanded educational resources and opportunities for students and teachers. Students use the Internet both as a research tool and a means of communicating. The question responsible administrators and teachers need to ask is precisely what sort of research and communication the students are doing. There is a big difference between

using the Internet to find biographical material of a local author, for example, and logging onto web sites to find out the latest gossip about a favorite pop music star. More dangerous still, some student use a school e-mail account to join a chat group. Teenagers in particular may feel that they possess enough maturity to make informed choices about what they are doing, but they may inadvertently lead themselves into harm's way. The not uncommon reports of adults being arrested for trying to meet up with minors they met in chat rooms are a red flag for most school districts.

Many districts avoid the issue by not providing students with their own e-mail accounts. They argue, quite convincingly, that student e-mail is difficult to monitor and ties up too many resources that could be used for other activities. A number of educators, however, believe that e-mail has become so essential that students should be trusted with the responsibility until they do something to violate that trust. Software programs that filter e-mail and Internet sites is only a partial solution; a student who wants to view a particular site may be resourceful enough to be able to get past such barriers. Beyond those students who might willfully engage in irresponsible activity online, there are also students who may unwittingly create trouble for themselves or others. A student who is not computer savvy might inadvertently disclose personal information over the Internet, for example.

### Acceptable Use Policies

Districts that do offer e-mail accounts to students have found that establishing an "acceptable-use" policy is essential to maintaining good "netiquette" among students. An acceptable-use policy begins by setting ground rules for when and how students can use the Internet and e-mail. Typically, students are expected to use appropriate language, to avoid off-limit sites and chat rooms, and to refrain from misuse of e-mail, such as spamming (sending unsolicited mass postings to hundreds of e-mail addresses). Students are also prohibited from using Internet information inappropriately (for example, downloading term papers or plagiarizing from web sites). Students are advised that the school has the right to review all electronic correspondence to ensure compliance with the established rules, and anyone violating those rules can be disciplined. For serious or repeat offenses, a student's Internet privileges can be revoked. Both students and parents are usually required to sign the acceptable-use policy.

### Cell Phones and Pagers

The Internet is not the only high-tech tool that students have at their disposal. Cell phones are extremely popular with teenagers; pagers are perhaps less so. Some school districts do allow students to carry pagers for exceptional reasons, such as a medical condition that might require the student to contact help immediately. For general use, however, cell phones and paging devices are as distracting in a school building as they are everywhere else. Most schools have rules against bringing cell phones or pagers onto school property.

## Getting Information

Although codes of conduct follow the same basic pattern, they vary not only from district to district but from school to school. The easiest way to find out about a particular school's code of conduct is to contact the school administration directly. Most likely, the school will have some sort of handbook listing the code, along with guidelines for punishing violations. Individual schools and school districts with web sites may also post their conduct rules online.

Legislatures have taken initiative in formalizing codes of conduct, also. In New York, for example, the Safe Schools and Violence in Education Act (SAVE) was passed by the state legislature in 2000. It required all school districts to create a comprehensive code of conduct by July 2001. Among the key requirements for these codes is a clear definition of teachers' authority to remove disruptive students from the classroom.

## Additional Resources

*Helping Your Child Learn Right from Wrong: A Guide to Values Clarification.* Simon, Sidney B. and Sally Wendkos Olds, Simon and Schuster, 1976.

*Staying Safe at School.* Chaiet, Donna, Rosen Publishing Group, 1995.

*Zero Tolerance: Resisting the Drive for Punishment.* Ayers, Rick, William Ayers, and Bernardine Dohrn, editors, New Press, 2001.

## Organizations

### National Center for Education Statistics (NCES)
1990 K Street, NW, Room 9103
Washington, DC 20006 USA
Phone: (202) 502-7350
Fax: (202) 502-7475
URL: http://www.nces.ed.gov
Primary Contact: Gary W. Phillips, Acting Commissioner

### National Education Association (NEA)
1201 16th Street, NW
Washington, DC 20036 USA
Phone: (202) 833-4000
Fax: (202) 822-7170
URL: http://www.nea.org
Primary Contact: Robert F. Chase, President

### National Governors Association (NGA))
401 North Capitol Street
Washington, DC 20001 USA
Phone: (202) 624-5300
Fax: (202) 624-5313
URL: http://www.nga.org
Primary Contact: John Engler, Chair

### National School Boards Association (NSBA)
1680 Duke Street
Alexandria, VA 22314 USA
Phone: (703) 838-67220
Fax: (703) 683-7590
URL: http://www.nsba.org
Primary Contact: Anne L. Bryant, Executive Director

# EDUCATION

## COMPETENCY TESTING

*Sections within this essay:*

- Background

- "Exit Examinations" for High School Graduates

- Legal Authority for Setting Educational Standards

- Legal Challenges to Educational Testing
    - Due Process Claims
    - Equal Protection Claims

- High School Graduation Exit Options
    - Standard Diploma
    - Individual Education Plan (IEP) Diploma
    - Occupational Diploma

- State Laws

- Additional Resources

## Background

Testing students for academic achievement or competency is not new. As early as the 1970s, some states were making adequate performance on "exit examinations" a prerequisite for high school graduation. This was done in an effort to enhance teacher quality as well as student achievement during an era when many questions were raised by parents, educators, and the public at large about the seeming lack of basic skills in high school graduates.

While varying and inconsistent approaches have been taken to measure student performance at the elementary school level, there is more unison in setting certain minimum criteria for graduation from high school. The vast majority of states require an overall accumulation of "Carnegie units" (reflecting the number of classroom hours spent learning) in addition to passing grades in certain core subjects. But by 2002, nearly half of all states required (or were planning to require within the next two years) "exit exams" in addition to accumulated credit hours in order for students to receive diplomas evidencing high school graduation.

## "Exit Examinations" for High School Graduates

Following years of complaints from both employers and academic institutions of higher learning (that many high school graduates lacked basic educational skills in reading, writing, and math), both legislators and educators agreed to work toward raising educational standards nationwide. This has resulted in renewed focus on learning rather than remediation and more accountability for teachers and school systems.

Educational standards (and correlative exams) for gauging performance have been criticized in the past for being local or parochial in substance, making grades and class standing a "relative" achievement based only upon how well others in the same school system or state performed. The Education Reform Act helped standardize student performance on a national level, but new questions were raised as to whether teachers were actually enhancing learning skills or merely "teaching to the test," (i.e., merely teaching those things they knew students would be tested on, in order to make the school and/or the teacher appear favorably on **assessment** reviews).

However, questions remain as to which system is the best to assess the academic competency of graduating students. By far the most often used tool of assessment is the multiple-choice **examination**, in many cases combined with a writing sample. This, in combination with passing grades in key subjects and a minimum number of credit units, seems to be a growing method of choice for ensuring minimum competency levels of high school graduates in the United States. Because graduation from high school may be dependent upon passing an "exit exam," the process has been dubbed "high stakes testing."

## Legal Authority for Setting Educational Standards

Most education reform since the 1980s has focused on "performance-based standards" which ostensibly indicate a minimum level of academic achievement that all graduating students should have mastered. Some important laws concerning standards-based school reform include:

- The No Child Left Behind Act, signed into law by President George W. Bush in January 2002, refines and makes major amendment to Title I (see below). Among other factors (like substantial flexibility for states in the use of federal funds), the new law requires states to assess reading and math skills in students from grades three to eight on an annual basis.

- The Educate America Act (20 **USC** 5801 et seq.) is only binding upon states that accept its grant funding (nearly all) but sets as its primary goal the development of strategies for setting statewide student performance standards and for assessing achievement of those standards.

- Title I of the Improving America's Schools Act of 1994 (20 USC 6301 et seq.) contains an explicit set of requirements for states to submit plans for challenging content and performance standards and assessing student mastery of the requirements in order to receive Title I funds (the largest federal school aid program).

- The Individuals with Disabilities Education Act (IDEA), (20 USC 1400 et seq.) was sub-

stantially amended in 1997. The Act requires that states which receive grant funds under its auspices must develop IEPs (individual education plans) for students with disabilities or who are deemed in need of special services. The 1997 amendments required states to develop policies and procedures to allow students with disabilities to participate in state and district-wide testing programs, with necessary accommodations.

## Legal Challenges to Educational Testing

Courts have had numerous opportunities over the decades to pass on the validity of education testing in conjunction with high school graduation and promotion (e.g., to the next level grade). Most legal challenges have been grounded in the Due Process Clause and the **Equal Protection** Clause of the Fourteenth Amendment to the U.S. Constitution. Challenges to testing of special education students have invoked IDEA and Section 504 of the Rehabilitation Act of 1973.

### Due Process Claims

The Due Process Clause of the Fourteenth Amendment prohibits a state from depriving "any person of life, liberty or property without due process of law." Over the years, it has been held by several courts that the receipt of a high school diploma was a "property interest" which a state could not deprive an individual of without **due process of law**. Additionally, some courts have found that students have a constitutionally protected "liberty" interest in avoiding the stigma or impaired career advancement that accompanies the failure to achieve high school graduation. (See, e.g., the *Goss* case, 419 U.S. at 574.)

The key to "due process" is the requirement of substantial notice to a person of the manner in which he or she may be denied or deprived of such an interest (graduation from high school) or, alternatively stated, substantial notice of what will be required of the student in order to graduate. With respect to testing, some courts have held that two years' advance notice that graduation was conditioned upon the passing of an exit exam in addition to credit hour completion was adequate; other courts have demanded more time.

Still other courts have held that students had no protected property interest in the expectation that a former, lower standard would continue to be accepted as the threshold for academic promotion to the next grade or graduation. (See, e.g., *Bester v. Tuscaloosa*, 722 F.2d 1514, 11th Circuit).

In determining whether denial of a high school diploma based on a failure to pass a minimum competency exit exam is unconstitutional, courts balance "the private interests of the [students], the risk of an improper deprivation of such interest and the governmental interest involved." (*Mathews v. Eldridge*, 424 U.S. 319) Almost all cases presented on these issues have turned on whether the school system had provided prospective graduates with adequate notice of new diploma requirements.

### Equal Protection Claims

Similarly, the Equal Protection Clause of the Fourteenth Amendment guarantees that no person will be denied the equal protection of the laws in the enjoyment and/or exercise of personal rights as that enjoyed by other persons in like circumstances. In order to ensure equal protection for students, school systems must uniformly apply educational standards and testing procedures across the board (with legal accommodations factored in for learning disabled or special needs students).

Generally, courts are more likely to uphold a testing program if there is a presence of additional factors such as opportunities for retesting, remedial or tutorial programs, and the availability of alternative ways to obtain a diploma.

## High School Graduation Exit Options

While no standardized national test has been implemented for use as a criterion in the granting of a high school diploma, states have developed several ways in which students may meet graduation requirements.

### Standard Diploma

Each state offers a standard diploma to students who have met the regular requirements for graduation. These are commonly the completion of a minimum number of Carnegie Units or credits (with passing grades), an attendance requirement, and (in an increasing number of states) a passing score on an exit exam. "Honors" diplomas are variations of standard diplomas in which student achievers may choose elective courses or independent studies in addition to their core studies. Such diplomas may also indicate accelerated or advanced coursework.

### Individual Education Plan (IEP) Diploma

Students with special needs may be offered an alternative way to earn a high school diploma through completion of individual education plans constructed specifically to the needs of the student. Some states allow modified coursework to count as standard coursework and, therefore, award a standard diploma; others offer "certificates of attainment" or "special certificate of completion" to indicate the student's fulfillment of special criteria for graduation.

### Occupational Diploma

Several states offer work/study diplomas, the most effective of which are those offered in conjunction with exit exams, to ensure that elective coursework directed toward occupational interests does not compromise minimum skill levels in core subject areas.

## State Laws

ALABAMA: Alabama high school graduates must meet minimum credit hour criteria plus pass an exit examination. The state offers exit options of standard diplomas, IEP diplomas, certificates of attendance only, honors diplomas, and occupational diplomas.

ALASKA: Alaska does not require exit exams for high school graduation. The state does offer standard diplomas, IEP diplomas, and certificates of attendance as exit options.

ARIZONA: Graduation from an Arizona high school requires both credit hour completion and an exit exam. Only standard diplomas are granted.

ARKANSAS: Arkansas high school students must meet the credit hour criteria for graduation. The state offers exit options of standard diplomas, IEP diplomas, and certificates of attendance only.

CALIFORNIA: California has state-mandated credit hour requirements that must be met for graduation. Additionally, local education districts have the authority to require passing scores on some form of exit examinations. The state generally offers standard and honors program diplomas.

COLORADO: There are no state-level requirements for high school graduation. Local education associations may establish their own credit hour requirements as well as exit examination criteria. In addition to the standard diploma, a work/study diploma may be granted, as well as IEP diplomas

CONNECTICUT: Connecticut high school students must meet the credit hour criteria for graduation. The state offers exit options of standard diplomas, IEP diplomas, certificates of attendance only, honors diplomas, and GED diplomas.

DELAWARE: Delaware high school students must meet the credit hour criteria for graduation. The state offers exit options of standard diplomas and certificates of attendance only.

DISTRICT OF COLUMBIA: High school students must meet the credit hour criteria only. The state offers exit options of standard diplomas, IEP diplomas, certificates of attendance only.

FLORIDA: Florida high school students must meet the credit hour criteria plus pass an exit examination. The state offers exit options of standard diplomas, IEP diplomas, certificates of attendance, and honors diplomas.

GEORGIA: In Georgia, high school students must meet the credit hour criteria plus pass an exit examination. The state offers exit options of standard diplomas, IEP diplomas, and certificates of attendance.

HAWAII: Hawaii students must meet the credit hour criteria plus pass an exit examination. The state offers exit options of standard diplomas, IEP diplomas, certificates of attendance only, honors diplomas.

IDAHO: Alabama high school students must meet the credit hour criteria. The state offers exit options of standard diplomas only.

ILLINOIS: High school students in Illinois must meet the credit hour criteria for graduation. The state offers exit options of standard diplomas or certificates of attendance only.

INDIANA: Indiana high school students must meet the credit hour criteria plus pass an exit examination. The state offers exit options of standard diplomas, honors diplomas, or GED diplomas. It awards a certificate of achievement for special education students for whom a diploma track is not appropriate.

IOWA: Iowa high school students must meet the credit hour criteria only. However, in addition to state minimum credit requirements, local education boards may establish additional requirements for graduation. The state offers exit options of standard diplomas or IEP diplomas only.

KANSAS: In Kansas, high school students must meet the credit hour criteria to be granted a standard diploma. Kansas law also authorizes local school boards to grant diplomas under separate or special criteria.

KENTUCKY: Kentucky high school students need only meet the credit hour criteria for graduation, but as of 2002, the state was implementing assessment examinations. The state offers exit options of standard diplomas, IEP diplomas, and honors diplomas.

LOUISIANA: High school students in Louisiana must meet the credit hour criteria plus pass an exit examination. The state offers exit options of standard diplomas and certificates of attendance only.

MAINE: Maine high school students must meet the credit hour criteria. The state offers exit options of standard diplomas or IEP diplomas.

MARYLAND: In Maryland, high school students must meet the credit hour criteria plus pass an exit examination. The state offers exit options of standard diplomas, IEP diplomas, certificates of attendance only, or GED diplomas.

MASSACHUSETTS: Massachusetts high school students must meet the credit hour criteria. The state offers standard diplomas only, except that IEP diplomas may be authorized by local school boards. In addition, part of the credit requirements for standard diplomas and the distribution of credits are left to the discretion of local authorities.

MICHIGAN: Michigan high school students must meet locally established criteria for graduation. They receive local high school diplomas with or without state endorsements. If local criteria require exit exams, depending on the performance level on an exit exam, state endorsements will appear on the transcripts. Generally, Michigan schools also offer IEP diplomas and certificates of attendance.

MINNESOTA: In Minnesota, high school students must pass an exit examination and demonstrate mastery of 24 standards. In return, they are granted a state endorsed standard diploma.

MISSISSIPPI: Mississippi high school students must meet the credit hour criteria plus pass an exit examination. The state offers exit options of standard diplomas, or certificates of attendance only.

MISSOURI: Missouri requires that high school students meet the credit hour criteria for receiving a diploma. The state offers exit options of standard diplomas, IEP diplomas, certificates of attendance only, honors diplomas.

MONTANA: In Montana, high school students must meet the credit hour criteria. The state offers exit options of standard diplomas or IEP diplomas.

NEBRASKA: Nebraska high school students must meet the credit hour criteria, but part of the credit requirements and/or the distribution of credits are left to the discretion of local education authorities. The state offers exit options of standard diplomas, certificates of attendance only, or a locally-determined modified diploma for special needs.

NEVADA: High school students in Nevada must meet the credit hour criteria plus pass an exit examination. The state offers exit options of standard diplomas, certificates of attendance only, or adult diplomas.

NEW HAMPSHIRE: In New Hampshire, high school students must meet the credit hour criteria. The state offers exit options of standard diplomas, IEP diplomas, and certificates of attendance only.

NEW JERSEY: New Jersey high school students must meet the credit hour criteria plus pass an exit examination. The state offers standard diplomas only.

NEW MEXICO: New Mexico high school students must meet the credit hour criteria plus pass an exit examination. The state offers exit options of standard diplomas, IEP diplomas, certificates of attendance only, or "career readiness" diplomas.

NEW YORK: In New York, high school students must meet the credit hour criteria plus pass an exit examination. The state offers exit options of standard diplomas, IEP diplomas, certificates of attendance only, honors diplomas, or an annotated local diploma.

NORTH CAROLINA: North Carolina high school students must meet the credit hour criteria plus pass an exit examination. The state offers exit options of standard diplomas, IEP diplomas, certificates of attendance only, and honors diplomas.

NORTH DAKOTA: In North Dakota, high school students must meet the credit hour criteria. The state offers exit options of standard diplomas, IEP diplomas, or certificates of attendance only.

OHIO: Ohio high school students must meet the credit hour criteria plus pass an exit examination. The state offers exit options of standard diplomas, honors diplomas, or a diploma of adult education.

OKLAHOMA: Oklahoma high school students must meet the credit hour criteria. The state offers standard diplomas only.

OREGON: In Oregon, high school students must meet the credit hour criteria. The state offers exit options of standard diplomas or certificates of attendance only.

PENNSYLVANIA: Pennsylvania high school students must meet locally established criteria for graduation. The state offers standard diplomas or GED diplomas only.

RHODE ISLAND: In Rhode Island, high school students must meet the credit hour criteria. The state offers standard diplomas only.

SOUTH CAROLINA: South Carolina high school students must meet the credit hour criteria plus pass an exit examination. The state offers exit options of standard diplomas or certificates of attendance only.

SOUTH DAKOTA: South Dakota high school students must meet the credit hour criteria. The state offers exit options of standard diplomas only.

TENNESSEE: In Tennessee, high school students must meet the credit hour criteria plus pass an exit examination. The state offers exit options of standard diplomas, IEP diplomas, certificates of attendance only, honors diplomas.

TEXAS: Texas high school students must meet the credit hour criteria plus pass an exit examination. The state offers exit options of standard diplomas or certificates of attendance only.

UTAH: Utah high school students must meet the credit hour criteria. The state offers exit options of standard diplomas or certificates of attendance only.

VERMONT: In Vermont high school students must meet the credit hour criteria. The state offers exit options of standard diplomas or certificates of attendance only.

VIRGINIA: Virginia high school students must meet the credit hour criteria plus pass an exit examination. The state offers exit options of standard diplomas, IEP diplomas, certificates of attendance only, honors diplomas, GED diplomas, and special diplomas.

WASHINGTON: In Washington, high school students must meet the credit hour criteria only. The state offers standard diplomas only.

WEST VIRGINIA: West Virginia high school students must meet the credit hour criteria. The state offers exit options of standard diplomas or IEP diplomas only.

WISCONSIN: In Wisconsin, high school students must meet the credit hour criteria. The state offers exit options of standard diplomas or certificates of attendance only.

WYOMING: Wyoming high school students must meet the credit hour criteria. The state offers exit options of standard diplomas or certificates of attendance only.

## Additional Resources

"Analysis: How Standardized Testing Changes Teaching and Learning." Conan, Neal, *Talk of the Nation (NPR)*, March 21, 2002.

*"Fact Sheet: No Child Left Behind Act"* January 2002. Available at http://www.whitehouse.gov/news/releases/2002/01/20020101.html.

"Special Education and High Stakes Testing: An Analysis of Current Law and Policy" O'Neill, Paul T., *Journal of Law & Education*, April 2001.

"State Graduation Requirements for Students With and Without Disabilities" Guy, B., H. Shin, S. Y. Lee, and M. L. Thurlow. University of Minnesota, National Center on Educational Outcomes, 1999. Available (March 30, 2002) at http://education.umn.edu/NCEO/OnlinePUbs.

"Testing." Lawton, Millicent, *Education Week*, April 23, 1997.

# EDUCATION

## COMPULSORY EDUCATION

*Sections within this essay:*

## Background

### *What are Compulsory Attendance Laws?*

Compulsory attendance laws are statutes put into force by state governments that require parents to have their children go to a public or state accredited private or parochial school for a designated period. Each state by law determines when this period starts and ends. Almost all states require a child to begin attending school at an age ranging from five to seven years. The age when a child may stop going to school varies from sixteen to eighteen.

To learn about the age requirements for your state, look in the telephone directory under the listing for state government agencies for either the department or board of education or the office or department of public instruction.

### *History and Development of Compulsory Attendance Laws*

Modern compulsory attendance laws were first enacted in Massachusetts in 1853 followed by New

York in 1854. By 1918, all states had compulsory attendance laws. One reason for the acceptance by the states of these laws was the belief that the public school was the best means to improve the literacy rate of the poor and to help assimilate an immigrant population that grew at a high rate between the mid nineteenth to the early twentieth centuries. Another explanation is that as children were required to attend school for a number of years, factory owners found it more difficult to exploit the cheap and plentiful child labor. This argument is substantiated by Alabama's decision for a period of time to **repeal** its compulsory attendance law due to pressure put upon state authorities by a company opening a large textile mill in that state. This industry was notorious for its use of child labor.

### Penalties for Non-Compliance

Failure to comply is a **misdemeanor** in almost every state. The penalties include fines for the first offense ranging from $20 to $100 and increasing thereafter for subsequent offenses from $250 to $1000 depending upon the **jurisdiction**. Most states also have the option of sentencing parents for as long as 30 days in jail. Some states provide for alternatives such as community service or counseling. In the case of home schooling, although the prosecution is not required to show the parent intended to break the law, it must still prove in some jurisdictions that home education does not provide an adequate alternative.

## Statutory Exemptions from Compulsory Attendance Laws

### Child's Circumstances

Most states will not enforce these laws against parents whose children are physically or mentally disabled, are employed, or have received a designated education level, typically a high school diploma or its equivalent.

### Equivalent Education

Equivalent Education may be obtained in a state accredited private school or a parochial school. According to a ruling by the U. S. Supreme Court in *Pierce v Society of Sisters,* states must recognize these schools as providing an education equivalent to that of the public schools so long as they follow state laws and regulations that bear a reasonable relationship to the interest the state has in educating its citizens and do not burden the religious practices of the parochial schools. These conditions placed upon

non-public schools, including home schools, are permitted under the United States Constitution because the public schools must follow these regulations as well.

All non-public schools must qualify under the laws of that state as schools in order to be considered capable of providing an equivalent education. The criteria used include such factors as whether the school is established, the quality of the teaching, the soundness of the curriculum, how many hours per day are spent for instruction, how many days of the year the school is engaged in teaching, and whether the teachers are certified. A private, parochial, and home schools may have to comply with any combination of the above factors.

## Court Case Exemptions from Compulsory Attendance Laws

Exemptions Accepted by Some Courts

- A threat to the health, safety, or welfare of a student if the parents can show the threat is imminent.

- The child has reached the age of majority.

- The child becomes mentally or physically disabled. However, this ground is now used less frequently because of special services for the disabled mandated by federal law.

- The parent objects to classes because the content violates their religious beliefs or practices.

- Either hazardous conditions are present between the child's home and his designated public school or the distance between the student's home and the school exceeds a distance provided by **statute**.

Exemptions Rejected by Some Courts

- A parent's belief a given teacher is incompetent or otherwise not qualified to teach.

- A parent's belief the school is doing a poor job of educating his or her children.

- Objections to racial integration by the parents on religious grounds.

## Early United States Supreme Court Challenges

### Meyer v. Nebraska (1923)

This decision struck down a state law prohibiting any instructor, either in a public or a private school, from teaching in a language other than English. The Court took this action because of the arbitrary interference from state officials of the right of parents to provide education for their children as they saw fit. The statute was arbitrary because it bore no relationship to a legitimate state purpose and violated the part of the Due Process clause of the 14th Amendment to the Constitution that says no person may be deprived of liberty without **due process of law**. In this case, the right of the parents to employ a teacher to instruct their children in their native language fell under the right to determine how they were to be educated.

### Pierce v. Society of Sisters (1925)

In this case, the Court said an Oregon law was unconstitutional which made it mandatory for parents to send their children to public school. As in *Meyer,* this law was unrelated to the legitimate state goal of educating children because it interfered with the fundamental right of parents to exercise control over how their children were to be taught. Forcing parents to have the educational options for their children limited to public schools infringed upon the above right and was an abuse of the state's police power to insure the health, safety, and morality of all localities in that jurisdiction. This standardization went against the sentiment of the Court often quoted in the part of their opinion that declares a child is not the creature of the state and that the responsibility for educating children should rest with the parents.

This decision is also important because it made clear that state governments had to permit private schools to operate. No challenge has since been made on this point.

### Farrington v. Tokushige (1927)

The Hawaii legislature had passed a law strictly regulating hours, textbooks, and curriculum of schools that taught in the native language of the students. In striking down this law, the Court was indicating that this amount of regulation of private schools was unreasonable and that parents had the right to exercise control over how their children were educated without restrictions that were unrelated to any rational state goal.

## Home Schooling as an Alternative to Public School Education

### Why Parents Home School and its Acceptance by State Governments

Eighty-five percent of the parents surveyed indicated they home schooled out of the religious **conviction** that the authority and power to instruct their children should remain with them and not be given to outside authority. Another reason cited was the declining academic standards of public schools as indicated by decreasing scores on standardized tests beginning in the 1960s. Some parents objected to what was being taught on religious, moral, or philosophical grounds.

### Legislative Requirements for Home Schools

Parents choosing to home school face many of the same hurdles encountered by parochial and private schools. In addition, the question may arise as to whether home instruction in a given state will come under the exemption routinely given to private schools because a home school is not established in the same way as are other non-public schools. In states in which laws remain unclear about what qualifies home instruction to be considered a school, the courts have given the term "school" a broad meaning as a place where instruction of children takes place. This definition eliminates the requirement that a school have its own facilities. So long as the home school meets the standards applied to schools established in the normal sense, the home school comes under the private school exemption.

Once a home school is considered by state statute or **case law** to be a school, it must comply with regulations to insure that students taught at home have an equivalent education. First, many states require parents to notify appropriate authorities, often the local school superintendent, of their intention to instruct their children at home. At this point, some states also make it mandatory for parents to obtain approval from designated local officials of the content of their curriculum and other aspects of how they will teach before they begin instructing their children. Some home school parents have gone to court claiming these officials are not objective in assessing home school programs because public school funding is often determined by the number of students enrolled. The courts have rejected these claims because of the difficulty in proving school officials' **bias** caused their negative decisions and the deference courts give to decisions of administrative officials.

The second requirement home schools face is that they must meet the time or durational requirements as well as at a minimum for their curriculum teach a list of designated subjects. They must do so according to the standards applied to public schools or by those required of home schools.

Third, a number of states require the parent to be certified as a teacher. When parents home school for religious reasons and challenge such laws in court as interfering with their religious practices, the courts have decided to uphold such laws. The courts side with the state officials because they believe the interest of the state in education outweighs the burden on religious practices. The courts contend that if parents do not meet the certification requirements public school teachers are subject to, they are unable to meet the burden of proof of showing they are able to provide an equivalent education as required by state law and regulation.

Fourth, state regulations often require the progress of the students instructed at home to be measured by standardized tests that are widely recognized as valid indicators. The tests must be taken at designated times in the student's studies. In some jurisdictions, the parents must maintain a portfolio of their children's work that is evaluated by state certified teachers.

In addition to these requirements, home schools are subject in some states to visits by state officials to assess the quality of the instruction. This practice is considered permissible by the courts so long as the visits do not hinder parents' efforts to instruct and that these appearances do not occur often. If parents do not wish to consent to these visits, they are given in some jurisdictions the option of going to court to convince a judge an equivalent education is being given.

## Home Schooling Constitutional Defenses

### Due Process Fundamental Rights

In *Meyer v. Pierce* and *Farrington v. Tokushige,* U.S. Supreme Court cases of the 1920s, the fundamental right of parents to direct the education of their children was established. These decisions are still heavily cited today by those claiming the right to home school in federal and state courts. They contend that because these decisions have given parents this right, its denial violates the right of due process. If a right is deemed to be fundamental, it is based on the premise that it is provided for in the U. S. Constitution.

### Due Process Vagueness

Under the Due Process clause, parents of home schooled children have contended the compulsory attendance statutes of their state were so vague and ambiguous, they were unconstitutional because a reasonably intelligent person would not be able to determine when he was violating the law and the person deciding whether such violation had occurred had no clear standards to go by in making his ruling.

Frequently, the **litigation** in this area revolves around the meaning of such terms as "equivalent education" or "private school." The meaning of these terms are important in these cases because it is upon these and other similarly worded phrases that states have granted exemptions from their compulsory attendance laws and their penalties.

### Due Process Arbitrariness

The Due Process clause has also been used to challenge these laws by claims that officials have too much leeway in performing their duty to apply the law. Although court cases involving this issue have not been decided in favor of the parents, the U. S. Supreme Court in a context other than home instruction has said that any decision involving a fundamental right must be made by an **impartial** party. In spite of subsequent U. S. Supreme Court cases which affirmed this principle in home schooling cases, the parents were unsuccessful.

### Free Exercise

By definition, a claim for exemption based on free exercise can only be used, if at all, by those who have home instruction for religious reasons. The only U. S. Supreme Court case that has ever decided any case involving home teaching is *Wisconsin v. Yoder.* Decided in 1972, it involved a group of Amish who challenged the compulsory attendance laws of their state. For three centuries, the members of this religious sect taught their children at home in accordance with their religious belief that education in a public school would violate the tenets of their faith. The Amish pointed out this home education gave their children the skills to function effectively in a society that was isolated from the general public.

Unlike the decisions in *Meyer v. Pierce,* and *Farrington v. Tokshige* the Amish in *Yoder* did not rely upon due process grounds, but on the belief that compulsory attendance laws of Wisconsin violated the Free Exercise clause of the U. S. Constitution prohibiting interference by the government with practices found to be religious and not just personal preferences. The Court balanced the interest of the state in educating children against the right of the Amish to practice their religious beliefs and concluded the state of Wisconsin had failed to show the state interest of educating its citizens in what is clearly the society of the general public outweighed the interest of the Amish in not having governmental interference with their religious practices.

In weighing and balancing the interests of these opposing parties, the Court sharply limited the use of *Yoder* to persons engaged in home schooling for future cases. The Court noted the three-century tradition of home education and that its content did enable Amish children to be able to function as adults in their separate society. Therefore, the state interest present in this case was rendered irrelevant by the Amish isolation from the general society. Through the use of this balancing test and its limited application of the Free Exercise clause to an unusual religious group, the court could affirm the interest of the state in educating its citizens, allowing the compulsory attendance laws to stand. In fact, lower federal court cases subsequent to *Yoder* have decided against other religious groups that instruct their children at home because they lacked the isolation of the Amish from modern life.

With this decision, a principle was established giving in theory greater protection to those who gave home instruction for religious reasons. However, the requirement that the belief of the party claiming Free Exercise protection was religious, and not one of personal preference or philosophy, and that the compulsory attendance law would severely impact such a belief would in practice be difficult to satisfy. The weight of cases subsequent to *Yoder* indicates it is far easier for the state to show the regulation fulfills a compelling or merely legitimate interest.

Only two state supreme court cases decided after *Yoder* involving home schooling parents using the Free Exercise clause resulted in a successful conclusion for them. Those states are Michigan in *Michigan v. DeJonge,* decided in 1993, and North Carolina in *Delconte v. State of North Carolina,* rendered in 1985.

### Free Speech

There have been few successful cases on such claims, but a notable example is *In re Falk,* a New York Family Court case decided in 1981. So far there have been no state or United States Supreme Court cases upholding the use of the right of free speech

under the 1st Amendment as a defense by parents against these laws.

### Right to Privacy

The few cases that have used this defense for prosecution under compulsory attendance laws have not found courts to be receptive to it. The one case decided in favor of the parents was a trial court decision in Massachusetts that is not binding outside the state or to any great extent within that jurisdiction.

### Ninth Amendment

The Ninth Amendment says that the rights of the citizens of each state are not limited by those listed in the Constitution. The contention by parents that a right to home school is implied by this provision has only been agreed with by *Perchemlides v. Frizzle,* the case mentioned under the right of privacy.

## Access of Home Schooling Students to Public School Facilities and Activities

### Home School Parents' View

Parents who choose to home school cope with a number of disadvantages. These include isolation, the lack of opportunity to participate in scholastic sports and other extra curricular activities, and the lack of resources available in public schools, such as a library or instruction in specialized courses. In surveys, a majority of home school parents expressed the desire to have their children enroll in a public school on a part-time basis in order to take special courses that are beyond the parents' ability to teach or to participate in extra-curricular activities including athletics. Most of the litigation on part-time enrollment involves whether these children should be allowed to play on the athletic teams of public schools.

### Oppositions' View

Opposition to access of public schools by those students not enrolled full-time is strong at the local, state, and national levels. Town and city boards of education, state athletic associations, and national trade groups, such as the National School Boards Association, have been against access by outside students because of fairness and administrative reasons. They argue the accessibility by non-enrolled students, including those home schooled, is unfair because since these students have chosen not to enroll, they should not be entitled to benefit from the limited resources of public schools. From an administrative point of view, the public schools would be faced with additional burdens such as providing supervision to a greater number of students participating in a class or activity and having perhaps to transport some students at times different from those of full-time enrolled students.

Furthermore, they argue that the U. S. Constitution does not provide a right for someone not enrolled in a public school to participate in any of its classes or other activities, including athletics. Home school parents have challenged these policies in the courts by using the Free Exercise clause of the First Amendment and the Due Process and **Equal Protection** provisions of the 14th Amendment.

### Constitutional Arguments Raised in Court

Judges have, with few exceptions, been unreceptive to the claims of home school parents. Their unwillingness to grant the parents and their children what they want is based on the general principle cited by school administrators and others that there is no constitutional right to participate in any public school program, including athletics. Instead, whether a student is allowed to join a club or athletic team of a public school is a privilege local school officials can choose to grant or deny at their discretion. Courts agree with them that sports and other extracurricular activities are an integral part of a student's education in a public school, and this legitimate objective would be frustrated if students not enrolled full time were allowed to participate.

In regard to the specific constitutional arguments put forth by home school parents, courts have said that because there is no burden placed on the religious faith and practices of those in home schools, there is no violation of the Free Exercise clause. Fourteenth Amendment claims based on Equal Protection and Due Process have also generally failed. The interest of the public school officials in efficiently carrying out their administrative responsibilities outweighs any concern of the home school students' not being treated equally. Due Process claims also are usually unsuccessful because denial of access to public schools and their programs does not amount to a denial of a fundamental right under the U. S. Constitution. The liberty the parents are entitled to under the U. S. Constitution is inapplicable here because, since participation by home school children in public school activities and programs is a privilege that may be granted or denied, parents only have an expectation their offspring will be allowed to participate. Therefore, no constitutional claim under Due Process is viable.

In addition, courts view the parents' decision to educate their children at home as an exercise of their constitutional rights, and it is inconsistent for the parents to benefit from the public education they have chosen to reject.

### Legislative Action

In recent years, a number of states have chosen to address this problem through their legislatures. Oregon, Idaho, and Florida have enacted laws allowing children educated at home to take part in what is offered by the public schools. Each of these states places conditions on these **statutory** provisions which may require submission to a greater degree of oversight and monitoring than home school students and parents would experience otherwise. For example, a student may have to submit additional documentation to prove to the satisfaction of local school officials that the state home school regulations are being followed. They may also have to obtain a designated minimum score on a standardized test considered credible by that state as well as to satisfy all the district eligibility and other requirements governing the behavior and performance expected of students enrolled full-time in public schools.

What is unique about the Florida statute is that it openly recognizes a state interest in the participation in public school programs and activities of students educated at home. This is significant because the outcome of many court cases involving children educated at home turns on the view of the courts as to whether the rights of these children are outweighed by the interests of the state in public education. Because these statutes have been passed only recently, it is difficult to assess their impact. However, making participation an interest of the state may result in less opposition to the presence of students who are not enrolled full-time.

Other jurisdictions, such as Maine, provide for access to the public school by children educated at home by obtaining approval from the local school superintendent. The decision to allow a home school student to participate will continue to be made on a case-by-case basis. However, the Maine statute and others similar to it require the superintendent not to make these decisions arbitrarily.

## Keeping Current on New Developments in Your State

Compulsory education laws and their impact on home schooling are subject to frequent changes in

EDUCATION—COMPULSORY EDUCATION

any jurisdiction. New laws passed by the legislature, administrative regulations handed down by those state agencies given the responsibility over educational matters, and new court decisions can all affect parents who educate their children at home. Organizations, especially the Home School Legal Defense Association, monitor closely new developments at the state and federal level. In addition, every state now has web sites where you can access recent court decisions as well as the code of laws for that jurisdiction. Many states have also made their code of administrative regulations available to the public. These materials are generally searchable by key words in court decisions, administrative regulations, and the code of laws. The best way to access these kinds of materials for a particular state is to log on to http://www.findlaw.com. A number of links will appear that pertain to different categories of materials. Click on "State Resources" and separate links for each state will appear. A breakdown for each state will direct you to those separate links for the state code of laws, recent court decisions, and administrative regulations.

## Additional Resources

*A Review of Home School Research: Characteristics of Families and Legal Outcomes.* Brian D. Ray, National Home Education Research Institute, 1990.

*Home Centered Learning Annotated Bibliography.* Fourth Edition. Brian D. Ray, National Home Education Research Institute, 1994.

*Home Education Magazine.* Mark and Helen Hegnor, 1983.

*Home Schooling and Research Guide for Fifty States.* Ninth Edition. Steve Deckard, Vision Publishing, 1998.

*Home Schooling on the Threshold: A Survey of Research at the Dawn of the New Millenium.* Brian D. Ray, National Home Education Institute, 1999.

*Home School Digest.* Wisdom's Gate, 1987.

*The Home School Report.* Christopher J. Klinka, Home School Legal Defense Association, 1985.

*Home Schooling in the United States: A Legal Analysis.* Revised Edition. Christopher J. Klinka, Home School Legal Defense Association, 1999.

*Home Schooling: Political, Historical, and Pedagogical Perspectives.* Jane Van Galen and Mary Ann Pitman, Abex Publishing, 1991.

*Home Schooling Today.* S Squared Productions, 1992.

*School Law Reporter.* National Organization on Legal Problems in Education, 1987.

*The Law of Homeschooling.* William M. Gordon and Charles J. Russo, National Organization on Legal Problems in Education, 1994.

*The Right to Home School: A Guide to the Law on Parents' Rights in Education.* Christopher J. Klinka, Carolina Academic Press, 1998.

*The Yearbook on Education Law.* National Organization on Legal Problems in Education, 1988.

## Organizations

### Genesis Institute
740 S. 128 St.
Seattle, WA 98168-2728 USA
Phone: (206) 246-5575
Primary Contact: Rev. Walter Lang, D.D, Director

### Home School Legal Defense Association
P.O. Box 3000
Purcellville, VA 20139-9000 USA
Phone: (540) 338-5600
URL: http://www.hslda.org/
Primary Contact: Charles L. Hurst, Office Mgr.

### National Association for Legal Support of Alternative Schools
P.O. Box 2823
Santa Fe, NM 87504 USA
Phone: (505) 471-6928
Primary Contact: Ed Nagel, Coord.

### National Home Education Research Institute
P.O. Box 13939
Salem, OR 97309 USA
Phone: (503) 364-1490
Primary Contact: Brian Ray, Ph.D., Pres.

### National Homeschool Association
P.O. Box 327
Webster, NY 14580-0327 USA
Phone: (513) 772-9580
Primary Contact: Susan Evans, Office Coordinator.

### National Organization for Legal Problems in Education
300 College Park
Dayton, OH 45469-2280 USA
Phone: (937) 229-3589
Primary Contact: Robert Wagner, Executive Director

### Parents Rights Organization
12571 Northwinds Drive
St. Louis, MO 63146-4503 USA
Phone: (314) 434-4171
Primary Contact: Mae Duggan, President

GALE ENCYCLOPEDIA OF EVERYDAY LAW

**_Rutherford Institute Legal Dept._**
P.O. Box 7482
Charlottesville, VA 22906-7482 USA
Phone: (804) 978-3888
Primary Contact: John W. Whithead, President

# EDUCATION

## CURRICULUM

*Sections within this essay:*

- Background
- Authority over Educational Curricula
    - Federal Authority
    - State Authority
    - Local Authority
    - Parental Authority
- Ideological Content
- Curriculum and Free Speech
- Making Curriculum Decisions
- National Education Goals
- National Standards
- Additional Resources

## Background

According to Black's Law Dictionary, "curriculum" refers to the "set of studies or courses for a particular period, designated by a school or branch of a school." But curriculum also refers to the complete range of activities designed by an educational institution to foster education. Fundamentally, curriculum outlines what students are supposed to learn and how they are to do it. Because there is much room for divergence of personal viewpoints in these issues, a school's curriculum fosters some of the most emotional and contentious debates in education law.

From a legal perspective, curriculum issues focus on two areas:

- The range of courses or instructional programs available to students

- The aggregate of activities, materials, procedures, and instructional aids used in the instructional program

Local school boards and officials typically make the decisions regarding curriculum and instructional materials for their schools, although some state authorities may limit their discretion to some extent.

The subject of curricula touches on federal, state, and local government authority, every course taught in school, and every level of school. The standards and objectives of every state differ with respect to curricula in their schools. All of this makes for a very extensive topic. A focus on the curricula in public schools from kindergarten through grade twelve (primary through secondary grades) touches on the key elements of the topic while reducing the scope of the topic to manageable proportions.

The curricula for primary and secondary schools are designed to integrate across the various grade levels. They are also intended to provide a coherent and comprehensive educational experience for each student who undertakes and completes all grade levels. Curricula are also meant to accommodate the many differences in learning styles and abilities and to account for different interests and aptitudes. Thus, a thoughtful school curriculum offers a broad range of options and tracks. Students either elect or are placed in these options or tracks based on diagnostic counseling, academic performance, and consultation with parents and students. Each state sets curricular policy that applies to schools within its **jurisdiction**, but local and individual variations occur according to the degrees of freedom allowed by the basic policy.

## Authority over Educational Curricula

Some may be surprised to learn that the federal government does not determine what students should know and be able to do in any subject at any level of schooling. Instead, implementing standards for students' performance is left to state and local authorities and to some extent with parents. There are some 16,000 school districts in the United States. Each one is administered and financed by a local community and by one of 50 state departments of education. This extensive local control, one of the defining characteristics of American education, has caused school standards to correlate with the socioeconomic status of the communities in which they are located.

### Federal Authority

As stated above, the federal government has historically played a minor role in education. In fact, the Constitution relegates most of the responsibility for education to the states. Thus, until the 1960s, the federal government largely stayed away from education. While the trend for the federal government to become involved in education issues has continued, even today, the total spending by the federal government accounts for less than 10 percent of the total spent for K-12 education. But because of heavy federal regulation, these federal dollars wield a disproportionate amount of influence.

Federal programs and regulations increased dramatically after 1965. As of 2002, the Department of Education spends over $30 billion per year on K-12 and higher education expenses, and hundreds of education programs are scattered throughout many other federal agencies. Most are designed to help disadvantaged children, though their records of success vary.

Perhaps the most prominent role of the federal government in terms of curricula has been to enforce and enhance rights to educational opportunities and educational equality. This function has involved the enforcement of constitutional rights to education and an adequate curriculum. These federal efforts have generally focused on guaranteeing equality of access to educational content rather than the content or purpose of the instruction itself. Other than these affirmative efforts, the federal government has hesitated to establish or control a school's curriculum. Rather, the government's role has been more to encourage schools to modify and improve curriculum, and currently, these suggestions are being backed up with funding and do not merely rely on persuasion.

### State Authority

The states are the entities primarily responsible for the maintenance and operation of public schools. The states are also heavily involved in the establishment, selection, and regulation of curriculum, teaching methods, and instructional materials in their schools.

Each state's constitution requires it to provide a school system where children may receive an education. Many state constitutions also contain express provisions for creating educational curricula. Some state constitutions even empower state authorities to select textbooks and educational materials. Besides constitutional authority, state governments also have authority to legislate in this area, or they can authorize officials to establish, select, and regulate curriculum.

State legislatures have frequently exercised their authority to mandate specific courses to be taught in public schools. They have also set mandatory requirements for students to graduate. In cases where state rules and regulations for courses do exist, they must be followed. Local school districts may, however, offer courses and activities in the instructional program beyond those required by state **statute**. Other states delegate more of their authority. They usually prescribe a model curriculum framework, allowing local authorities to develop their own curricula based on the general state goals.

In many jurisdictions, state authorities adopt textbooks and instructional materials. Local boards and educators then may select from among the preapproved materials. Generally, local authorities have the authority to declare state-adopted instructional materials unacceptable. States may mandate the use of uniform, adopted textbooks within a school's instructional program, but such exercise of power is rare. Instead, local boards are usually allowed to select materials to supplement the state-selected materials.

### Local Authority

It is well established that local school boards or districts hold a great deal of authority over the curricula in their schools. Their authority is paramount except when there are overriding federal and state concerns. Otherwise, the local school board has complete discretion to determine what courses to offer, continue, or discontinue. Federal and state governments may impose minimum standards with which local boards must conform, but local boards of education are generally permitted to supplement or expand courses or activities and materials.

The history of **litigation** with respect to curricula shows that courts rarely interfere with a local board's authority to select and regulate the curriculum within its jurisdiction. By comparison, there are limits on the relative authority of teachers, students, parents, and the rest of the community. Local school boards have discretion over issues relating to the curriculum that it deems most suitable for students. This extends to the teaching methods that are to be employed and include the books and other educational tools to be used.

### Parental Authority

Parents are free to direct the education of their children, including the choice of a private school. However, states have the power to regulate private schools, with the exception of religious institutions.

Parents are particularly active in issues relating to special education which is available for children with disabilities. A child's **disability** must adversely affect the child's educational performance in order for the child to receive special education assistance. The Individuals with Disabilities Education Act (20 U.S.C. §§ 1400 et seq.) is a federal law that contains a process for evaluating a child's special needs and for prescribing an individualized education program for children with special needs. Most states have enacted their own laws that parallel the Act.

Homeschooling—legal in all fifty states—is an increasingly popular option for some families. It is perhaps the greatest expression of parental control over the curriculum issues that affect their children. Homeschooling requires a large time commitment on the part of the family. There may be additional requirements as well. For example, in some states parents need to register their intent to homeschool with the state's department of education or the parent's local district school board. Furthermore, many states require annual **evidence** of home-schooled children's progress.

## Ideological Content

Schools may decide upon curricula based upon local community views and values as to educational content and methodology. Even so, school boards are limited in their ability to remove materials from the curriculum, especially when a removal is based exclusively on "ideological content." Decisions about the curriculum cannot be used to dictate views on politics, nationalism, religion, or other matters of opinion.

When trying to insure the school board's discretion is being exercised in a constitutionally permissible manner, people need to examine the intent of the board members. Courts are not limited to examining the objective motivation of the board but may consider individual motives and even the mental processes of individual board members.

## Curriculum and Free Speech

Activities in the classroom are supervised by faculty and are designed to teach or convey particular knowledge or skills to students. Consequently, school boards and educators must have broad control over the approval of the materials used. In view of school board responsibilities in this respect, state laws have almost uniformly required the obedience of subordinate employees, including the classroom teacher, to follow the board's curriculum choices and related mandates. Teachers certainly enjoy a degree of academic freedom and First Amendment rights; these rights do not give teachers the authority to disregard the curriculum directives of the board. In sum, the courts have declared that individual teachers may not simply teach what they please.

A school board authority almost always extends to classroom expression. Thus, public schools may limit classroom speech to promote certain educational goals. This also touches on the use of public school facilities by groups that promote a certain agenda or otherwise exercise their right to free speech. Although a school may occasionally open a classroom for other purposes, there is no doubt that during instructional periods the classrooms are reserved for other intended purposes: the teaching of a particular course for credit. In such periods, classroom speech and expression may be reasonably restricted.

As we have seen, a school's curriculum includes actual instruction as well as classroom materials. For example, textbooks, lab equipment, and other routine instructional materials are used to support a school's curriculum. These are subject to the school board's control. Additionally, displays in or around the classroom or the school may be curricular in nature. These materials are therefore subject to broad control by school authorities.

## Making Curriculum Decisions

Decisions about a school's curriculum must be based upon legitimate pedagogical concerns. On occasion, these concerns have included teaching material, classroom expression, or other matter criticized on the grounds of the following issues:

- Advocacy of political or similar matters

- Bias or prejudice

- Conformity or nonconformity to shared or community values

- Distracting from an educational atmosphere

- Inability to teach prescribed curriculum because of disagreements with course content

- Lack of neutrality on religious matters

- Quality or professionalism

- Sexually harassing speech

- Suitability or unsuitability for intended students

- Vulgarity, **profanity**, nudity, sexuality, drug use, violence or other inappropriate themes

The definition of "legitimate pedagogical concerns" may be outlined in state statutes or regulations. State Education Board policies also may be relevant.

An important consideration is the age, maturity, and sophistication of the students to which educational material is to be provided. A school's oversight or authority over curriculum matters is greater where younger students are involved.

Schools need to identify pedagogical concerns before making decisions about a curriculum. Curricular decisions should not be made after a parent or someone else makes a complaint about ideological issues, and when there has been no pedagogical review. Such decisions are as suspect as the self-serving comments that attempt to justify those decisions made after the fact and not based on the previous record.

## National Education Goals

At an education summit held in 1989, President George H. Bush and every state governor agreed upon 6 national education goals for the United States to achieve by the year 2000. Two more goals were added in 1994, and Congress passed legislation known as the National Education Goals. The goals created a framework for improving student achievement and refocusing the objectives of education. At the same time, the goals left specific tactics to state and local governments and to schools. Basically, the goals describe a general set of standards toward which all Americans should strive.

The National Educational Goals to be achieved by the year 2000 are:

1. All children in the United States will start school ready to learn.

2. The high school graduation rate will increase to at least 90 percent.

3. U.S. students will leave grades 4, 8, and 12 having demonstrated competency in challenging subject matters, including English, mathematics, science, foreign languages, civics and government, economics, arts, history, and geography; every school will ensure that all students learn to use their minds well, so they may be prepared for responsible citizenship, further learning, and productive employment in our nation's modern economy.

4. The nation's teaching force will have access to programs for the continued improvement of their professional skills and the opportunity to acquire the knowledge and skills needed to instruct and prepare all students for the next century.

5. U.S. students will be first in the world in mathematics and science achievement.

6. Every adult American will be literate and will possess the knowledge and skills necessary to compete in a global economy and to exercise the rights and responsibilities of citizenship.

7. Every school in the United States will be free of alcohol and other drugs, violence, and the unauthorized presence of firearms and will offer a disciplined environment conducive to learning.

8. Every school will promote partnerships that will increase parental involvement and participation in promoting the social, emotional, and academic growth of children.

The Goals 2000: Educate America Act codified the goals and established federal support for voluntary, state-based systemic reform. These include the development and implementation of high academic standards. The Act calls for state plans to include:

- the development and implementation of content standards in core subjects

- student assessments linked through performance standards

- opportunity-to-learn standards or strategies

The Act also funds states' efforts to support systematic state reform based on state-developed plans. Also as a part of the Act, Congress established the Goals Panel as a new independent federal agency. The 18-member bipartisan panel consists of 8 governors, 4 members of Congress, 4 state legislators, the secretary of U.S. Department of Education, and the assistant to the president for Domestic Policy.

The Goals Panel functions in the following ways:

- monitors and reports progress towards the goals

- builds a national consensus for the reforms necessary to achieve education improvement

- reports on promising or effective actions being taken at the national, state, and local levels to achieve the goals

- identifies actions that federal, state, and local governments should take to enhance progress towards achieving the goals and to provide all students with fair opportunity to learn

- collaborates with the National Education Standards and Improvement Council to review the criteria for voluntary content, performance, and opportunity-to-learn standards

The dialogue about national goals among legislators, educators, and school board members throughout the United States is focused on improving education standards for all students in U.S. schools. This dialogue and the directives and funding embodied in federal legislation have led nearly every state to design and implement curricular frameworks or guidelines. Many states have even developed or are in the process of developing **assessment** instruments to monitor their schools' progress towards higher standards.

## National Standards

In terms of national trends, the consensus has been moving toward establishing a set of national standards for education. So far, there are voluntary national standards for math, science, and history. There are standards being developed for other subjects as well.

Many factors that go into decisions about the development and implementation of curriculum in U.S. schools. Some of these are:

- whether the state and/or district have curriculum guidelines

- whether state and local guidelines conflict with each other

- whether there are a large number of students requiring bilingual education

- whether the state or district requires schools to follow their guidelines or allows them to develop their own curricula

- for schools that retain local autonomy over curricular decisions, whether they may choose to adopt or ignore state or district guidelines

For the latter, the school's choice is likely to be influenced by the school's history of achievement, community standards, financial resources, and how it understands the relationship between these factors and the curriculum guidelines being provided by the state or district.

The issue of standards for learning and teaching has developed in the United States in recent years as policymakers, legislators, educators, parents, and community leaders have all shown an increasing concern with students' achievement levels. The word "standards" has been used in many ways during public discussions. Sometimes the term has been used to represent established levels of achievement; in other cases it refers to commonly shared sets of academic subject content, such as those embodied in state curriculum guidelines.

Curricular guidelines have been used to set standards in many states and have been linked to state-administered achievement tests. But standards in the United States also include more informal means by which schools maintain and promote the desired levels of achievement for their students. These achievement levels for schools and for students have usually been extrapolated from community expectations, and local communities continue to greatly influence curriculum and instructional decisions made at the school level. In the end, standards are partly a result of local decisions, such as those governing the selection of textbooks and those affecting a school's policy on the promotion or retention of students. The guides to standards have developed significantly, and school districts are feeling their influence.

## Additional Resources

*Education and the Law: A Dictionary* Taylor, Bonnie B., ABC-Clio, 1996.

*Educational Policy and the Law, Fourth Edition* Yudof, Mark G., David L. Kirp, Betsy Levin, and Rachel F. Moran, Wadsworth Group, 2002.

*Education Law* Rapp, James A., LexisNexis, 2001.

*"Mid-continent Research for Education and Learning."* http://www.mcrel.org/. McREL, 2002.

"Rethinking Schools Online" Rethinking Schools, 2002. Available at http://www.rethinkingschools.org/.

*"U.S. Department of Education"* U.S. Department of Education, 2002. Available at http://www.ed.gov/.

## Organizations

### The Alliance for Parental Involvement in Education (ALLPIE)
P.O. Box 59
East Chatham, NY 12060 USA
Phone: (518) 392-6900
E-Mail: allpie@taconic.net
URL: http://www.croton.com/allpie/

### American Association of School Administrators (AASA)
1801 N. Moore St.
Arlington, VA 22209-1813 USA
Phone: (703) 528-0700
Fax: (703) 841-1543
E-Mail: Info@aasa.org
URL: http://www.aasa.org/

### Education Law Association (ELA)
300 College Park 0528
Dayton, Ohio 45469 USA
Phone: (937) 229-3589
Fax: (937) 229-3845
E-Mail: ela@udayton.edu
URL: http://www.educationlaw.org/

### National Institute on Student Achievement, Curriculum, and Assessment (NISACA)
555 New Jersey Avenue NW, Room 510
Washington, DC 20208-5573 USA
Phone: (202) 219-2079
Fax: (202) 219-2135
E-Mail: sai@ed.gov
URL: http://www.ed.gov/offices/OERI/SAI/

### National School Boards Foundation (NSBF)
1680 Duke Street
Alexandria, VA 22314-3493 USA
Phone: (703) 838-6722
Fax: (703) 548-5516
E-Mail: info@nsba.org
URL: http://www.nsba.org/index.htm

### U.S. Department of Education (USDE)
400 Maryland Avenue, SW
Washington, DC 20202 USA
Phone: (800) USA-LEARN
Fax: (202) 401-0689
E-Mail: customerservice@inet.ed.gov
URL: http://www.ed.gov

# EDUCATION

## DESEGREGATION/BUSING

*Sections within this essay:*

- Background

- Before Desegregation
  - The Fourteenth Amendment
  - *Plessy v. Ferguson*
  - *Brown v. Board of Education*

- Desegregation in Theory and Practice
  - Busing and "White Flight"
  - The Needs of the Children

- Innovative Approaches
  - Magnet Schools
  - Using Criteria Other than Race

- Additional Resources

## Background

One of the most important rights Americans have is the right to a free public education. No child in the United States, whether native- or foreign-born, can be denied access to a public school for elementary and secondary education. While in theory this means that everyone is entitled to the *same* educational experience, in fact that is not necessarily the case. Public schools can vary dramatically from community to community simply because some districts have more money to spend on education than others.

For years, **segregation** of black and white students was quite common. In some places, it was common because local and state laws mandated segregation in one form or another. In other places it was common because neighborhoods were segregat-

ed (often by choice) and students went to the closest schools. From the late nineteenth century to the mid-twentieth century, segregated schools were protected by the concept of "separate but equal," upheld by the U.S. Supreme Court in 1896. **Separate but equal** was overturned in 1954 in the famous *Brown v. Board of Education* decision, but segregation in the schools continued. In the 1960s and 1970s, efforts were made to desegregate schools across the country. Many of these efforts succeeded, but many failed. A number of desegregation efforts, begun with the best of intentions, turned out to be more divisive than inclusive.

Desegregation is one of the most complex issues educators and parents face. In the 1950s, desegregation was about blacks and whites. When people used the word "minority," they meant blacks. As of 2002, the entire concept of minorities and diversity has shifted. Minorities can include blacks, Central and South Americans, Southeast Asians (Vietnamese, Cambodian, Laotian), Arabs, and a host of others. This sort of multiple ethnicity existed in large cities for decades, but in the 21st century people are more mobile and even small communities can have a dozen or more ethnic minorities. Consequently, communities cannot merely take a "one size fits all" approach. Finding the right approach to desegregation, or rather, to encouraging diversity in the schools, is an ongoing challenge to school districts across the country.

## Before Desegregation

Education was not always the universally accepted right that it is today in the United States. Although some communities did make education a priority, the United States was primarily an agricultural society until the twentieth century. Children might learn to work the land or be apprenticed to a tradesman after having only a few years of formal schooling. Many children had no formal education. Slave children had only as much education as their masters allowed or tolerated; most slave owners did not encourage their slaves even to learn to learn to read or write.

### The Fourteenth Amendment

The Thirteenth Amendment to the U.S. Constitution, ratified shortly after the end of the Civil War prohibited slavery and involuntary servitude. But it did not specifically grant citizenship to freed slaves, and Southern states took advantage of this omission. Congress redressed the balance with the Fourteenth Amendment, which was ratified in 1868. The amendment stated that all citizens, whether by birth or by naturalization, were guaranteed **equal protection** under the law, and called for Federal intervention if states failed to comply. Former Confederate states that wished to rejoin the United States were required to sign the Fourteenth Amendment before being readmitted.

What the Fourteenth Amendment did not do was guarantee equal rights. Southern states used the "separate but equal" argument, which allowed them to keep blacks and whites separate as long as they did not deprive them of basic legal rights. Eventually, this arrangement led to a series of discouraging developments that relegated blacks in the South to inferior status.

### Plessy v. Ferguson

One of the factors affected by while Southern unwillingness to recognize blacks as equals was public transportation. In 1890 the General Assembly of Louisiana passed a law requiring railroads to provide separate cars for whites and blacks, with the stipulation that the separate cars be of equal quality and comfort. The law was immediately attacked by **civil rights** groups, and to force the question of whether it was constitutional, a black man, Adolph Plessy, deliberately broke it by taking a seat in a whites-only car. The law was found constitutional by regional and state courts and went to the U.S. Supreme Court in 1896. The Court ruled seven to one against Plessy and thus established as constitutional the concept of "separate but equal." This concept was a springboard for what was called the "Jim Crow" system. Named for a character in a black minstrel show, the Jim Crow laws made segregation not merely accept-

able but mandatory. Over the next several decades, "separate but equal" became pervasive, particularly in the South. Although there were some civil rights gains for blacks in the ensuing years, a definitive victory against Jim Crow did not come until 1954.

### Brown v. Board of Education

"Separate but equal" may have seemed unconscionable to many, but it was the law in many states. In the 1950s 17 states and the District of Columbia had laws prohibiting **school desegregation**. It was clear to most educators, parents, and children that there could be no such thing as a separate but equal education. Several cases appeared before the U.S. Supreme Court to challenge the constitutionality of segregated schools, and the Court's unanimous ruling on *Oliver Brown et al. v. Board of Education of Topeka, Kansas* on May 17, 1954 turned the doctrine of school segregation on its head. "Separate educational facilities," said the Court, "are inherently unequal."

Although the Brown decision marked the beginning of the end for sanctioned segregation in the schools, segregation's end did not come immediately. In fact, in the late 1950s and early 1960s, several Souther governors, notably Orval Faubus of Arkansas, Ross Barnett of Mississippi, and George Wallace of Alabama, vigorously defended segregation. Not until President Lyndon B. Johnson signed the Civil Rights Act of 1964 was desegregation dealt a definitive blow throughout the United States.

## Desegregation in Theory and Practice

Throughout the 1960s it became evident that desegregation was not a clear-cut issue by any means. As communities struggled with finding the best ways to desegregate, the racial divide seemed to grow rather than diminish.

Southern states, which had borne the brunt of the negative publicity about segregation, began to point out that the Northern states were equally culpable, albeit in a different way. For years the South had *de jure* segregation—in other words, segregation mandated by law. In the North, while there were no segregation laws on the books, most blacks and whites lived in separate enclaves; often the groups did not mix, and their children attended local schools. Thus, in the North there was *de facto* segregation in the schools because neighborhoods were segregated.

### Busing and "White Flight"

Among the methods communities tried to desegregate the schools was the busing of black students to predominantly white schools. Since the black schools tended to be in poorer neighborhoods and had fewer resources, it seemed to make sense to bus black students to white schools until a balance of black and white students was attained. The case in the U.S. Supreme Court that set the ground rules for all future busing decisions in the courts was *Swann v. Charlotte-Mecklenburg Board of Education,* which was decided in 1970. Two years earlier, the Court had ruled in *Green v. County School Board* that the school board had the responsibility to integrate the schools and to do so promptly. The Charlotte-Mecklenburg (Virginia) school board was found to be out of compliance and was assigned a plan known as the Finger Plan (named for the man who devised it). Under the Finger Plan, schools throughout the district were to work to attain more racial balance in the schools by busing children into the schools.

Busing is one illustration of how difficult it is to achieve true desegregation. In the decades after *Swann,* other communities implemented busing. Invariably, busing is not well-received by blacks or whites. Legislating action is one thing, but legislating attitude is quite another. In many large urban cities, whites who could afford to move to the suburbs, where the population (and consequently the schools) were predominantly white, left inner-city schools with dwindling white student populations. In Denver, the school district was found to be practicing "subtle racism" by the U.S. Supreme Court in *Keyes v. School District No. 1.* A busing program was implemented, but the way the system was initially set up many elementary school students spent half a day in a de facto segregated school and half a day in an integrated school.

The 1974 case of *Milliken v. Bradley* addressed the issue of "white flight" to the suburbs by suggesting that one remedy would be to bus suburban children into the inner city schools in which whites were the minority. The U.S. Supreme Court ruled that suburban students could not be used to desegregate inner city schools. White flight continued. Because most of the people left behind were poor or working-class, cities lost a tax base. As cities became poorer, less money was spent on education. Blacks and other minorities who could afford to move did so, and the inner city populations became statistically poorer. By the end of the twentieth century, many of the largest cities in the United States had public schools that were racially imbalanced and sadly in need of funding for maintenance, basic supplies, and more teachers.

### The Needs of the Children

Lost in many of these contentious proceedings was the simple question of what was best for the child. Children are not born with a predisposition to racial prejudice, but they are forced to live with the decisions of adults. In the inner cities, public education has not improved, and in affluent communities, de facto segregation is still common. While some see desegregation efforts such as busing as a positive move, others argue that the money spent on busing programs would be better spent in revitalizing poor neighborhoods and schools so that children could get a good education in their own neighborhood. But that brings back the question of segregated neighborhoods. Many people from all ethnic and racial backgrounds look at desegregation with a mix of cynicism and resignation.

## Innovative Appoaches

Educators, government officials, and parents have all sought approaches to desegregation that are not merely superficial. Thinking up these approaches and implementing them is a challenge, but the fact that people are willing to seek alternatives to court-order remedies that may have inherent weaknesses is a start.

### Magnet Schools

Many communities have created "magnet schools" in which students from across a community attend. These schools often emphasize particular courses of study—science or the arts, for example. Magnet schools, properly funded, can provide educational and social opportunities for children across a wide spectrum of racial and ethnic lines. Magnet schools do not keep people from moving out of the cities, however. In some places school districts have attempted to lure suburban students into inner city magnet schools. In Connecticut, cities such as Hartford and New Haven have created magnet schools that have been well received. One of the goals of these schools is to draw students from the predominantly white suburbs. As part of the state's desegregation efforts, suburban students can take part in a program called Open Choice that allows them to transfer to the inner city schools at no additional cost. Under normal circumstances, a student who goes to a district other than his or her own would have to pay tuition and transportation costs. In Connecticut, those costs are underwritten by the state.

Magnet schools are seen by many as a better way to achieve integration than charter schools, which are often created specifically to serve the needs of local neighborhoods and may not have racial or ethnic diversity as their prevailing goal (although as public entities they are subject to anti-discrimination laws).

### Using Criteria Other than Race

One intriguing idea that some school districts have begun to implement is integrating schools on the basis of *income* rather than race. The idea was first explored in the early 1990s, and as of 2002 several high-profile districts use it, including Wake County, North Carolina (which includes the capital city of Raleigh) and Cambridge, Massachusetts. The idea behind income-based desegregation is that income may play a more critical role in a child's educational experience than race. If parents have enough money to make educational choices for their children, then it matters little what color they are; they can take their children out of the public school system or move to a more affluent community with better public schools. Wealthier schools and school districts will have more and better resources than inner-city schools, and all the students who attend will benefit. In contrast, no student benefits from attending an inner-city school with limited funds and overflowing classrooms.

Cambridge is best known as the home of Harvard University and the Massachusetts Institute of Technology (MIT). Like many college communities, its population is racially and economically mixed. There is no one ethnic majority group. As an article in *Education Week* noted in January 2002, "in a city with enclaves of working-class whites and upper-class African Americans, the lack of diversity in some schools had little to do with skin color or national origin. Instead, students from wealthier families tended to attend the same schools, and needier children were clumped together in other schools who tended to struggle academically." Approximately 40 percent of the 7,300 students qualify for free or reduced-priced school lunches. As of January 2002, the percentages of these students in various schools ranged from 21 percent to 72 percent.

Innovative approaches such as this one may provide a different frame of reference that meets the needs of students and communities better. They will also keep current in the minds of parents and school administrators the need to improve educational facilities across the board. As racial and ethnic groups become less clearly defined, it may become harder to justify any kind of desegregation plan. That said, it will also become harder to justify helping certain schools or school districts thrive at the expense of others.

## Additional Resources

*Beyond Desegregation: The Politics of Quality in African-American Schooling* Mwalimu J. Shujaa, editor, Corwin Press, 1996.

*Politics, Race, and Schools: Racial Integration 1954-1994* Watras, Joseph, Garland Publishing, 1997.

*The Schools We Deserve: Reflections on the Educational Crises of Our Times* Ravitch, Diane, Basic Books, 1985.

*Separate but Not Equal: The Dream and the Struggle* Hasking, James, Scholastic, 1998.

*The Strange Career of Jim Crow* Woodward, C. Vann, Oxford University Press, 1974.

*The Struggle for Equal Education* Lusane, Clarence, Franklin Watts, 1992.

*Swann's Way: The School Busing Case and the Supreme Court* Schwartz, Bernard, Oxford University Press, 1986.

## Organizations

### Center for Education Reform
1001 Connecticut Avenue NW, Suite 204
Washington, DC 20036 USA
Phone: (202) 822-9000
Fax: (202) 822-5077
URL: http://www.edreform.com
Primary Contact: Jeanne Allen, President

### National Association for the Advancement of Colored People (NAACP)
4805 Mt. Hope Drive
Baltimore, MD 21215 USA
Phone: (877) 622-2728
URL: http://www.naacp.org
Primary Contact: Kwesi Mfume, President

### National Center for Education Statistics (NCES)
1990 K Street NW
Washington, DC 20006 USA
Phone: (202) 502-7300
URL: http://www.nces.ed.gov
Primary Contact: Gary W. Phillips, Acting Commissioner

***National Education Association (NEA)***
1201 16th Street NW
Washington, DC 20036 USA
Phone: (202) 833-4000
URL: http://www.nea.org
Primary Contact: Bob Chase, President

***U.S. Department of Education***
400 Maryland Avenue SW
Washington, DC 20202 USA
Phone: (800) 872-5327

URL: http://www.ed.gov
Primary Contact: Rod Paige, Secretary of Education

***U. S. Department of Justice, Educational
Opportunities Section, Civil Rights Division***
950 Pennsylvania Avenue NW, PHB
Washington, DC 20530 USA
Phone: (202) 514-4092
Fax: (202) 514-8337
URL: http://www.usdoj.gov
Primary Contact: Jeremiah Glassman, Chief

# EDUCATION

## DISCIPLINE AND PUNISHMENT

*Sections within this essay:*

## Background

### Current Issues

In the 1990s and 2000s, educators, law enforcement agencies, governments, courts, parents, and the general citizenry in the United States considered new and troubling questions pertaining to student conduct. The late 1990s witnessed a number of spectacular on-campus crimes by juveniles, including acts of murder, suicide, assault, and massive property damage. The seriousness of these events brought attention to the problems public schools face in managing students who act out in life-threatening crimi-

nal ways. Clampdown reaction to enhanced security and student protection competed with legal concerns about student constitutional rights, particularly the right to due process. Other widespread crimes in schools, such as physical conflicts between students and student drug use, weapon possession, and theft, disrupted the academic setting and all too often frustrated the true goals of education: teaching and learning.

### Definition

The word discipline is akin to the word disciple. Discipline in one sense means learning, just as the word disciple refers to one who learns. Additional meanings of discipline suggest the complexity of the subject as it pertains to individuals (in this case specifically minors) and the U.S. public school system. Discipline refers to training and experience that corrects, molds, and strengthens individuals' mental faculties and moral character. It also refers to punishment that intends to correct and that is enforced by those in authority or may be self-imposed.

Discipline likewise refers to the control gained by enforcing obedience, and it pertains to the systematic orderly behavior defined by codes or rules set forth by institutions for their members. Moreover, discipline refers to self-control and to the development of skills that help individuals resist temptation, act positively, and function both independently and cooperatively in ways that enhance personal development and community life. All of these definitions have been central to educators' efforts to find the most effective and useful way to support child development and learning.

### *Origin of Corporal Punishment*

In the colonial era, the Puritan belief that humankind is innately tainted by the Original Sin of Adam and Eve led adults to see children as contaminated by an evil element that needed to be driven out by force. Puritans believed that all disobedience and academic error was the work of Satan, and children's innate proclivity for evil had to be destroyed through pain and humiliation. The idea that suffering can correct unwanted behavior became fundamental to institutional design, whether that design was the stocks in which prisoners were displayed for public abuse or the raised stools and dunce caps intended to correct student misbehavior or ignorance through humiliation. "To spare the rod," it was believed, led inevitably to spoiling the child, so slapping, spanking, and whipping were generally understood as beneficial educational tools. These beliefs persisted. Indeed, as late as 1977, in *Ingraham v. Wright*, the U.S. Supreme Court ruled that spanking did not violate students' rights, noting the widespread use of corporal punishment to maintain discipline in educational settings. Corporal punishment remained legal thereafter in more than 20 states.

### History

The U.S. Constitution does not address the subject of public education. Apparently the founding fathers thought the implementation of schools ought to be the sole responsibility of the states. Initially, education was for the wealthy, and a belief persisted through the eighteenth century that poor individuals were not educable or were not worthy of being educated. In 1852, however, then secretary of state of Massachusetts Horace Mann urged that states be obliged to offer public education to all children. The revolutionary idea behind this plea was that all individuals could and should be educated irrespective of economic class.

During the middle of the nineteenth century, some U.S. educators studied European models, such as the theories of Philipp Emanuel von Fellen-berg (1771-1844), who urged that corporal punishment not be used for academic errors and suggested that learning occurred best with encouragement and kindness. Francis Parker introduced European ideas into the public school system in Quincy, Illinois. What came to be known as the progressive Quincy Movement attached kindergarten to elementary education and extended into the early grades the idea of learning through play. These pedagogical developments examined connections between education and discipline and considered teachers' roles in creating environments conducive to learning.

By 1910 attendance at public school was mandatory; children were thus absent on a daily basis from parental direction and placed under the authority of educators. This transfer extended teachers' roles to parental disciplinarians; teachers functioned *in loco parentis*, meaning in the place of parents. During the first decades of the 1900s, as teachers were stepping further into these parental roles, state legal systems were beginning to evolve ways to handle juvenile offenders which intended to distinguish them from adult perpetrators. One value attached to this development asserted that while adults should be punished for their crimes, children should be rehabilitated for theirs, thus formalizing a beginning to the separation between juvenile misconduct and suffering as its remedy.

At the beginning of the twentieth century, good discipline was evinced as students sitting quietly while they learned by rote. The conventional wisdom saw education as a process of controlling student behavior while information was transferred from teacher to student. This model continues to shape concepts about classroom activities and goals. Challenging this model, however, were the increasingly popular post-World War II theories of Benjamin Spock (1903-1998), who disapproved of rigid child-rearing techniques and urged adults, parents and teachers alike, to be more affectionate and flexible. Some critics of Spock's theories asserted that they contributed to a growing attitude of permissiveness and relativity that blurred children's understanding of right and wrong and encouraged self-defeating traits like selfishness, indolence, or noncompliance.

In the second half of the twentieth century, healthcare professionals and educators became more informed about how student misbehavior may be connected to physiological or psychological problems, like attention deficit disorder, hyperactivity, or emotional disturbance. Changes in the family unit, increase in the Hollywood celebration of violence, and effects of illegal drug use also affected students' ability and willingness to learn in school. Moreover, in the 1990s and 2000s, juveniles committed serious felonies on school property, some of which converted schools temporarily to war zones. Reactions to these events caused many people to advocate for a return to more stringent controls of students, which in some circles acquired to the label, zero tolerance.

# Codes of Conduct

In taking charge of students and teaching them, twentieth-century educators repeatedly faced the challenge of designing codes of conduct. Doing so required attention to multiple and sometimes seemingly conflicting issues: school organizational needs, the goals of education, and the nebulous area of personal rights both for those in charge and for those being controlled. Educators had to identify features conducive for learning and then set forth rules and consequences for misconduct that would allow problem children to be handled constructively while the behaving majority of students continued to learn without disruption. In short, educators had to define ways to support classroom productivity, encourage student academic progress, and bring misbehaving individuals back to positive conduct so that they could resume learning. In this task, educators, administrators, and staff became increasingly conscious of legal issues connected to students' rights, juvenile legal status, and the handling of student crime. All of these issues were addressed independently by different school boards across the nation and handled differently by school boards and courts over time.

## *Creating Codes of Conduct*

The issues involved in the process of developing these codes of conduct constitute an important part of pedagogical debate and ongoing courtroom deliberation. For example, some judicial decisions have attempted to define those school requirements and regulations which a court would deem "reasonable." Under these decisions, a properly written document must meet four criteria in order to carry a legal presumption of validity:

- The rules had to be in writing: Regulations students had to obey without a specific verbal command must be in writing.

- The rules had to be specific: Policies had to clearly stated to students, and without referring to an outside source or document the rules had to explain what was expected and what was prohibited.

- The writing had to be authorized: The writer of the rules had to have the authority to define them.

- The written rules had to be published: The code of conduct had to be printed and distributed, for example in student handbooks, in letters home to parents, in public announcements during class time and assemblies, and in postings on bulletin boards.

Richard Curwin, a professor of Education at San Francisco State University, devised criteria for making codes of conduct more effective. His suggestions were:

- To use positive rather than negative statements

- To be definite about proper and prohibited behavior

- To be brief

- To spell out consequences

Thus, the courts began the process of educating the educators on how to arrange the business of school so that when it responded to misbehavior its rulings would be deemed valid in the legal setting.

## *Content of Codes*

In light of their wisdom, experience, and training, educators have devised codes of conduct to meet their schools' particular goals and challenges. Some school codes employ step programs that distinguish first-time offenders from repeat offenders. These codes hand down mild penalties for first-offense students but then graduate the penalties for the misconduct of repeat offenders. In these cases, students face consequences determined by their records of behavior. Thus, for a repeat offender, a minor infraction might carry the serious penalty of suspension while the same infraction might elicit only a verbal reminder for the first-time offender. Some schools set aside special classrooms for extra training in matters of self-control, conflict resolution, and cooperation. Schools elicit parents' participation and support in encouraging their children back to positive behavior and academic progress.

Discipline policies state clearly that rules benefit everyone in the educational community and are in effect inside school buildings, on school property, inside school-owned vehicles, and at school-sponsored activities on or off campus. Codes include rules about attendance, absence, and tardiness. They outline steps for parents to take in excusing their children from class and instruct teachers how to keep records of student attendance. Patterns of unexcused absence or tardiness are quantified and carry penalties or repercussions that relate to the extent of the patterns of absence. Misbehaving students might be detained in the classroom after other students are free to go on to non-classroom activities, or they might be required to attend a Saturday detention period. During these times, students might be given extra academic work or be required to perform maintenance chores on school property. Repeat offenders are subject to a number of potential penalties, including the following: removal from school; removal from class to a study room; placement in an on-sight suspension area; suspension for a specified time; and expulsion. Although individuals who act out are arguably the ones most in need of education and support, they tend to be separated from others.

When students break the law on school property, police officers must take over for educators. Students who use alcohol or other drugs, who have in their possession or deliver to others controlled substances, who carry weapons, and who assault others, are all subject to the same laws they would face elsewhere in the community. Therefore, these forms of misconduct are not within the school's jurisdiction solely. Students can be charged for crimes committed on school property; they can go to court and face court decisions that place them in juvenile detention centers. Clearly, school codes must address a vast range of conduct, take into consideration innumerable factors that lie in or beyond the education setting. The codes must respond legally, in line with community, state, and federal laws on issues connected to discrimination, harassment, gender, and disability. Academic codes of conduct aim to support educational goals and be in line with criminal and civil laws. Often times the courts have had the task of deciding if the codes achieve this end.

## Students' Constitutional Rights and Selected Cases

Educators have to negotiate the complicated terrain of competing entities, managing difficult students yet remaining mindful of their constitutional rights, such as rights to privacy, just cause, and due process. When criminal acts in schools involve law enforcement, certain subjects, conflicts, and events may come before the courts. Courts elucidate legal issues but not once and for all: these judgments can be subsequently redefined, upheld, or found unconstitutional. Questions recur pertaining to the application of Fourteenth Amendment protections to students as these individuals are subjected to school regulations.

Issues pertaining to a student's right to privacy, to reasonable cause for search and seizure, and to technicalities about *Miranda* rights, all were examined in *New Jersey v. T.L.O.* (1985), a case involving a juvenile (known only by her initials) who was suspected

of smoking and then whose purse was found to contain cigarettes, rolling paper, a bag of hashish, and some file cards containing what appeared to be a list of amounts received for drug sales. The Supreme Court had to evaluate the relative rights of the student's right to privacy against the school's need to enforce an orderly environment. One of its conclusions was that education requires a disciplined environment and that means the authority to educate entails the authority to discipline.

In the 1986 case of *In re William G.*, a California court decided that students as a group have the right to be protected by school officials from dangerous items or substances and to have enforced an environment conducive for learning. In many cases, the courts have to balance competing entities or claims to rights by opposite parties. In *Bethel v. Fraser* (1986) and again in *Veronica v. Acton* (1995), the U.S. Supreme Court decided that students' rights are secondary to students' safety. These and many other cases produce the body of court decisions which evolve social understanding of the law as it applies in ever-changing circumstances.

## Columbine and Its Aftermath: Zero Tolerance

On April 20, 1999 at Columbine High School in Littleton, Colorado, two heavily armed students killed twelve students and one teacher and seriously wounded nearly two dozen others before killing themselves. The following month in Conyers, Georgia, a 15-year-old student wounded six other students. In December, an Oklahoma middle-school student took a semiautomatic handgun to school and wounded five students. Although these incidents were covered heavily in the media, they were by no means unique occurrences. According to one study, 39 students died in school-related acts of violence during the 2004-2005 school year, including 24 deaths by shootings.

These and other murders perpetrated by children against classmates and teachers have caused a furor of reactive security measures, precaution taking, and a new commitment to stringent control. Zero tolerance, which initially referred to students carrying weapons to school, fueled provisions for suspension and expulsion and increased them. In Chicago, in the wake of commitment to zero tolerance, suspensions and expulsions jumped to an average of 90 per week, mostly Latinos and African Americans. Proponents of more stringent codes pointed to the staggering fact that every day in the United States 12 children are killed by gunshot. The fact that one day they were gathered together in their deaths at Columbine brought national consciousness to a new level. Many schools nation-wide, particularly in urban settings, instigated entry-area body and bag searches, stricter dress codes, and random drug testing. Yet critics of this stringent disciplinary action urged educators to return to a positive vision of students and search for punishments that teach rather than using those that increase the drop-out rate.

## State Laws Regarding Corporal Punishment

As of 2005, 28 states outlawed corporal punishment in schools. In the remaining states, more than 300,000 students nationally are subjected to some form of corporal punishment. This number is significantly lower than in previous generations of students. For instance, an estimated 1,408,303 students received paddlings in 1980. This number fell to 613,760 in 1990 and 301,016 in 2003.

The following list indicates those states that have banned corporal punishment.

ALASKA: The state banned corporal punishment in 1989.

CALIFORNIA: The state banned corporal punishment in 1986.

CONNECTICUT: The state banned corporal punishment in 1989.

DELAWARE: The state banned corporal punishment in 2003.

HAWAII: The state banned corporal punishment in 1973.

ILLINOIS: The state banned corporal punishment in 1993.

IOWA: The state banned corporal punishment in 1989.

MAINE: The state banned corporal punishment in 1975.

MARYLAND: The state banned corporal punishment in 1993.

MASSACHUSETTS: The state banned corporal punishment in 1971.

MICHIGAN: The state banned corporal punishment in 1989.

MINNESOTA: The state banned corporal punishment in 1989.

MONTANA: The state banned corporal punishment in 1991.

NEBRASKA: The state banned corporal punishment in 1988.

NEVADA: The state banned corporal punishment in 1993.

NEW HAMPSHIRE: The state banned corporal punishment in 1983.

NEW JERSEY: The state banned corporal punishment in 1867.

NEW YORK: The state banned corporal punishment in 1985.

NORTH DAKOTA: The state banned corporal punishment in 1989.

OREGON: The state banned corporal punishment in 1989.

PENNSYLVANIA: The state banned corporal punishment in 2005.

RHODE ISLAND: The state banned corporal punishment in 1977.

SOUTH DAKOTA: The state banned corporal punishment in

VERMONT: The state banned corporal punishment in 1985.

VIRGINIA: The state banned corporal punishment in 1989.

WASHINGTON: The state banned corporal punishment in 1993.

WEST VIRGINIA: The state banned corporal punishment in 1994.

WISCONSIN: The state banned corporal punishment in 1988.

## Emerging Disciplinary Theories

Many theories about discipline shift attention from external punishment and reward systems to internalization of socialization skills and moral sense. For example, in *Schools Without Failure*, William Glasser explains the short-term value of external punishment and the limitations of trying to control others through fear tactics. Theorists like Abraham Maslow, in *Motivation and Personality*, and W. Edwards Deming, in *Out of the Crisis*, suggest a return to humane education principles and affirmation of human goodness. Many thinkers want educational institutions to find their path into a new way of being that creates the learning moment, which sees misbehavior as an opportunity and instills faith in human nature as it pursues learning and instructs through misconduct. Marvin Marshall, in *Discipline Without Stress, Punishment, or Rewards*, urges people to remember that so long as they are manipulated by outward threats of punishment or hopes of reward, they may be neglecting intrinsic values which in the end are the ones that satisfy, induce self-control, and energize toward self-improvement. These affirmations have to be balanced with the seriousness of turn-of-the-millennium juvenile crimes and the awesome responsibility of educators to keep children safe while they engage in learning.

## Additional Resources

*Discipline without Stress, Punishments, or Rewards: How Teachers and Parents Promote Responsibility and Learning.* Marshall, Marvin. Piper Press, 2001.

*Encyclopedia of American Education.* 2nd ed. Unger, Harlow. G. Facts on File, 2001.

*Safety, Order, and Discipline in American Schools: Defining the Authority of Educators and Law Enforcement Personnel.* Avery, Gary. Law Advisory Group, Inc., 2001.

*Schools Without Failure.* Glasser, William, Harper & Row, 1969.

*U.S.: Statistics on Corporal Punishment by State and Race..* Center for Effective Discipline, 2005. Available at http://www.stophitting.com/disatschool/statesBanning.php.

*Zero Tolerance: Resisting the Drive for Punishment in our Schools.* Eds. Ayers, William, Bernardine Dohrn, Rick Ayers. The New Press, 2001.

## Organizations

### Center for Effective Discipline
155 W. Main Street, Suite 1603
Columbus, OH 43215 USA
Phone: (614) 221-8829
URL: http://www.stophitting.com

### National Association of Elementary School Principals (NAESP)
1615 Duke St.
Alexandria, VA 22314 USA
Phone: (800) 386-2377

### National Education Association (NEA)
1201 16th St., NW
Washington, DC 20036 USA
Phone: (202) 833-4000

# EDUCATION

## DRUG TESTING

*Sections within this essay:*

- Background
- Federal Court Decisions
    - Mandatory Suspicionless Testing of Student Athletes Ruled Constitutional
    - Lower Court Disagreement over Broader Extracurricular Student Testing
- State Court Decisions
- Additional Resources

## Background

Mandatory drug testing in public schools is a relatively new issue for the law. Introduced during the late 1980s and expanding over the next decade, the practice of analyzing student urine for illegal drugs is carried out in a small but growing percentage of schools nationwide. In 2001, the *New York Times* estimated that hundreds out of the nation's 60,000 school districts require some form of testing. Thus students in thousands of individual schools are affected, and more districts have indicated their interest in adopting testing, too. Currently, the practice has been ruled constitutional in one form by the U.S. Supreme Court.

School drug-testing grew out of the so-called war on drugs. Prior to the 1980s, citizens were rarely tested for drugs except by law enforcement officers and primarily when there were grounds for suspicion. Exceptions existed in a few areas, notably in the routine testing of college and pro athletes and prison inmates. But along with other sweeping social changes, the drug war introduced the idea of so-called mandatory suspicionless testing in the workplace. After spreading from the public to the private sector, the trend reached public high schools in limited form—in the testing of student athletes—in the late 1980s.

Legally, mandatory suspicionless drug testing has proved controversial both in the workplace and school. The practice raises questions about how to balance a perceived social need for health and safety with privacy concerns. Not surprisingly, in light of its rulings favorable to workplace testing, the U.S. Supreme Court upheld suspicionless student drug testing in 1995. The Court already viewed the privacy rights of public school students as being lower than those generally enjoyed by adult citizens. Now, the majority saw an important social need for schools to combat drug usage, viewing the loss of student privacy as inconsequential.

However, the legal status of student drug-testing is cloudy. In large part, this is due to dramatic changes following the 1995 decision. School districts correctly saw the Supreme Court's decision as a green light, but some took the practice much further. Not merely student athletes but a range of student activities, such as band and choir, began requiring students to pass drug tests as a condition for eligibility. This trend has brought new lawsuits and divergent verdicts from the federal courts. As a result, the Supreme Court is expected to clarify certain limits on school drug testing in 2002.

Important legal milestones include the following:

- The Supreme Court defined students' reduced Fourth Amendment rights in *New Jersey v. T.L.O.* (1985), where it ruled that schools do not have to follow the customary requirements of having **probable cause** or a **warrant** in order to carry out searches. Instead, school authorities must follow only a simple standard based on "the dictates of reason and common sense."

- In its first landmark drug-testing ruling, the Supreme Court upheld the suspicionless drug-testing of railroad employees who are involved in accidents in *Skinner v. Railway Labor Executives' Ass'n* (1989). The court held that the government has a compelling interest in public safety that overrides Fourth Amendment rights of the employees.

- In a second critical ruling on drug-testing, the Court upheld the suspicionless drug testing of U.S. Customs Service employees in sensitive positions that involve extraordinary safety and national security hazards in *National Treasury Employees Union v. Von Raab* (1989).

- The Supreme Court upheld the constitutionality of mandatory suspicionless drug-testing of student athletes in *Vernonia v. Acton* (1995). Applying its rulings in *Skinner* and *Von Raab*, the Court found that the students' Fourth Amendment rights were outweighed by the government's interest in drug-free schools when it approved a school's policy of random suspicionless testing of student athletes. In the wake of its landmark ruling, hundreds of school districts nationwide adopted similar policies.

- With the expansion of student drug testing beyond athletics, some schools began requiring random drug-testing as a condition for participation in other extracurricular activities. A panel of the Seventh Circuit Court of Appeals upheld the constitutionality of such a school program in *Todd v. Rush County Schools* (1998), and the Supreme Court refused to hear the case, letting the verdict stand.

- In contrast, another circuit court disapproved of broad extracurricular drug testing. A panel of the Tenth Circuit Court of Appeals overturned a school drug policy in *Earls v. Tecumseh* (2001), holding that extracurricular testing went further than what is permitted under *Vernonia*. With the two circuits in obvious disagreement, the Supreme Court accepted the case for review in 2002.

- A federal judge in Texas struck down what had been the nation's first school district policy requiring drug testing of all junior high school students in *Tannahill v. Lockney School District* (2001).

At both the federal and state level, the future of drug-testing policies is in question. In 2001, legal observers began to note a trend in the courts toward rejecting student drug testing as more cases ended in verdicts for plaintiffs who challenged their school policies. Although some viewed this as a shift in public attitudes, it was too early to say definitively what impact the cases would have on this developing area of law.

## Federal Court Decisions

### Mandatory Suspicionless Testing of Student Athletes Ruled Constitutional

The legal foundation for suspicionless student drug testing rests upon *Vernonia v. Acton* (1995). In that landmark decision, the Supreme Court upheld the constitutionality of a school policy requiring student athletes to pass random urinalysis tests as a ground for participation in interscholastic sports. The Court rejected a Fourth Amendment claim asserting that such tests are an unconstitutional invasion of privacy. Closely watched nationwide, the decision effectively opened the door for school districts to institute similar policies of their own.

In the late 1980s, school authorities in the small logging community of Vernonia, Oregon, noticed a sharp increase in illegal drug usage and a doubling in student disciplinary problems. They observed that student athletes were leaders of the drug culture. Officials responded by offering anti-drug classes and presentations, along with conducting drug sweeps with dogs. After these education and interdiction efforts failed, a large segment of the student body was deemed to be in "a state of rebellion," according to findings of the Oregon District Court.

With the support of some parents, school officials next implemented a drug-testing policy for student athletes in fall 1989. It had three goals: prevent athlete drug use, protect student health and safety, and provide drug assistance programs. It imposed strict eligibility requirements: parents of student athletes had to submit a consent form for drug testing of their children, and the student athletes had to submit to tests. Once weekly the school randomly tested 10 percent of all student athletes by taking urine samples that were analyzed for illegal drug usage—a procedure known as urinalysis.

A legal challenge to the policy arose when a student and his parents refused to consent to drug testing and he was denied the chance to play football. Their lawsuit charged that the district violated his Fourth Amendment right to be free from unreasonable searches and seizures as well as his privacy rights under the Oregon state constitution. The District Court rejected their claims, but they won on appeal. The school district then appealed to the U.S. Supreme Court.

In its 6-3 decision, the majority followed earlier precedents. In particular, it looked back on its landmark decision regarding privacy for public school students, *New Jersey v. T.L.O.* (1985). That decision extended the great basis in U.S. law for privacy—Fourth Amendment protections—to public school students. It held that they, too, were protected from "unreasonable" searches and seizures of their persons and property by authorities, since public school authorities are agents of the government. But *T.L.O.* set the standard that Fourth Amendment rights are "different in public schools than elsewhere." In lowering student rights, the Court did so observing that public school authorities have a compelling interest in supervision and maintaining order that outweighs individual student rights.

In *Vernonia*, the majority went further. First, it distinguished the rights of student athletes from the already reduced privacy rights of the public school student body. Justice Antonin Scalia's majority opinion stated that student athletes have an even lower expectation of privacy since they routinely undress in locker rooms, noting that "school sports are not for the bashful." Second, it approved the particulars of the Vernonia school district's policy. The urinalysis was performed under minimally intrusive conditions similar to those in the schools' restrooms. There was no concern that school officials might arbitrarily accuse certain students because every student athlete was subject to being tested. Furthermore, participation was ultimately voluntary, since no one was required to play sports. And finally, the school's goals in reducing a serious drug abuse and disciplinary problem justified the testing.

Three justices dissented. Writing for the dissenters, Sandra Day O'Connor observed that mass suspicionless searches of groups had been found unconstitutional throughout most of the court's history, except in cases where the alternative—searching only those under suspicion—was ineffectual. She concluded that the school's policy was too broad and too imprecise to be constitutional under the Fourth Amendment.

### Lower Court Disagreement over Broader Extracurricular Student Testing

The practical effect of *Vernonia* was to clear the way for student athlete drug-testing in schools nationwide. But the decision did not envision what happened next. By the mid-1990s, schools had begun adopting even broader testing policies that expanded the definition of testable extracurricular activities to include activities such as band and choir and, as in the extreme instance of Lockney, Texas, the entire junior high school student body. This broadening set the stage for the next constitutional challenges, which resulted in conflicting verdicts among federal circuit courts. Given these varying rulings, there is as of 2002 no single standard in federal caselaw for when public schools may require students to pass drug tests.

Initially, one such policy passed constitutional approval. In 1998, a three-judge panel of the Seventh Circuit Court of Appeals upheld a school system's broad drug testing program in *Todd v. Rush County Schools* (1998). At issue was a policy by the Rush County School Board of Indiana, which in 1996 banned a high school student from participation in extracurricular programs unless the student first passed negative for alcohol and other drugs, or tobacco in a random, unannounced urinalysis exam. The policy covered students in activities ranging from the Library Club to the Future Farmers of America Officers, as well as those who merely drove to and from school. Any student failing the urinalysis lost eligibility until such time as he or she successfully passed.

In rejecting a challenge to the policy, the Seventh Circuit found that the policy was consistent with the Supreme Court's ruling in *Vernonia*. Its brief opinion found sufficient similarity between the intent of the Indiana and Vernonia programs: deterring drug use rather than punishing users. The broader scope of the Indiana policy was not a constitutional problem, as the court observed that nonathletic extracurricular activities also "require healthy students." Its own 1988 decision on drug-testing student athletes,

*Schaill v. Tippecanoe County School Corp.*, also supported the broader policy. The Supreme Court declined to review the case. As with the earlier *Vernonia* decision, the New York Times reported that the Seventh Circuit's decision "set off a wave of such policies" nationwide. Ironically, however, the Indiana policy was later struck down on state constitutional grounds.

In 2001, a dramatically different verdict appeared. A panel of the Tenth Circuit Court of Appeals ruled that drug-testing for eligibility for extracurricular activities violated Oklahoma public school students' rights in *Earls v. Tecumseh*. Unlike the Seventh Circuit, the panel followed a very narrow reading of *Vernonia*. It applied that decision's facts and conclusions to the circumstances of the Tecumseh School District in Pottawatomie County, Oklahoma, and found sharp differences. No widespread drug problem existed in the school, unlike the Vernonia district. Moreover, the panel rejected the district's contention that drug testing was justified because extracurricular activities involved safety risks for unsupervised students. Instead, the panel ruled that the tests imposed unreasonable searches upon students in violation of their Fourth Amendment rights.

The Tenth Circuit panel specifically addressed the question of when a school drug testing policy was appropriate. It expressly stated that it did not expect schools to wait until drug abuse problems grew out of control. However, if school officials faced no requirements, they would be free to test students as a condition of attending school—an outcome that the justices did not believe the Supreme Court would uphold.

Significantly, the *Earls* decisions signaled a deep rift between two federal circuits in how to interpret *Vernonia*. Presumably for this reason, the Supreme Court accepted the case for review, with a decision expected some time in 2002. Lingering questions about the permissibility and scope of such policies may also have inspired the Court to return to the question. Indeed, in 2001, legal observers noted a shift in federal opinions away from support for student drug-testing policies. In addition to the *Todd* case, a federal judge struck down the pervasive policy of testing all public school students in grades seven through 12 in *Tannabill v. Lockney School District* (2001), while state courts also ruled against policies.

## State Court Decisions

As a policy matter, student drug testing in public schools is widely determined by school districts. State legislatures have thus far not intruded, leaving these determinations to the discretion of local school boards. As such, policies vary widely nationwide, and even from district to district within given states. Most schools still have no testing policy, but those that have adopted policies tend to fall into two categories: mandatory suspicionless testing is required of students who wish to play intramural athletics, or, more broadly, it is required not only of athletes but also of students wishing to participate in extracurricular clubs and organizations.

Legal direction on school policies has come from the courts. The highest-profile challenges to the policies have been brought in federal court on Fourth Amendment grounds, but some cases have been brought on state constitutional grounds, too. State constitutions often have broader privacy protections than are found under the federal constitution, thus providing powerful legal grounds for plaintiffs who want to challenge overly aggressive school policies.

The first state constitutional challenge against mandatory testing of student athletes came in *Wilson v. Ridgefield Park Board of Education* (1997). The American Civil Liberties Union brought the case against Ridgefield Park, New Jersey school board, arguing that the policy violated state constitutional privacy rights. A state superior court judge agreed, additionally finding that the school had no **evidence** of a severe drug problem among athletes, and temporarily blocked enforcement of the policy pending trial. But before the case could be heard, the school board dropped the policy in a 1998 **settlement**.

State courts in Indiana, Oregon, and Pennsylvania have also found constitutional problems with school policies. Some state courts have addressed themselves to policies resulting from the expansion of student testing to other extracurricular activities. In rejecting one such policy, the Colorado state supreme court applied the U.S. Supreme Court's 1995 standard from *Vernonia v. Acton* when it held that high school marching band members have a higher expectation of privacy than student athletes who undress in locker rooms, in *Trinidad School District No. 1 v. Lopez* (1998). In other state **litigation**, school districts in Maryland and Washington discontinued policies following lawsuits. These cases signal that the legal future of suspicionless student drug testing is far from certain.

## Additional Resources

*Back to School—and a Test You Can't Study For* American Civil Liberties Union. Available at http://www.aclu.org/features/f083000a.html.

*Constitutional Amendments: 1789 to the Present* Palmer, Kris E., ed., Gale Group, 2000.

"Court Rulings Signal a Shift on Random Drug Tests in Schools" Wilgoren, Jodi, *The New York Times*, March 25, 2001.

"Random Drug Testing of Students Proving To Be a Popular Idea" Walsh, Mark. *Education Week*, January 28, 1998. Available at: http://www.edweek.org/ew/vol-17/20drug.h17.

*Vernonia School District 47J v. Wayne Acton* Supreme Court opinion. Available at http://supct.law.cornell.edu/supct/html/94-590.ZO.html.

*West Encyclopedia of American Law* Lippert, Theresa J., ed., West Group, 1998.

## Organizations

### American Civil Liberties Union (ACLU)
125 Broad Street, 18th Floor
New York, NY 10004 USA
Phone: (212) 549-2500
URL: http://www.aclu.org
Primary Contact: Nadine Strossen, Pres.

### Drug-Free Schools Coalition
203 Main St., PMB 327
Flemington, NJ 08822 USA
Phone: (908) 284-5080
Primary Contact: David G. Evans, Exec. Dir.

### National School Boards Association
1680 Duke Street
Alexandria, VA 22314 USA
Phone: (703) 684-7590
URL: www.nsba.org
Primary Contact: Anne L. Bryant, Exec. Dir.

# EDUCATION

## FINANCE/FUNDING

*Sections within this essay:*

## Background

More than half a century ago Adlai Stevenson said, "The most American thing about America is the free common school system." The public school system in the United States is free only in the sense that all students have a right to attend. According to the National Center for Education Statistics (NCES), it cost an average of just over $6,500 per student to keep public elementary and high schools (known in the education community as "el-hi") operating in academic year 1998-99. Overall the revenues raised for that school year totaled over $347 billion.

These revenues came from the federal government, state governments, and local government. (Local government includes individual towns as well as larger municipalities and county governments.) The bulk of that money (nearly half) came from the states. The federal government contributed only 7.1 percent of the revenues. That may seem low, but in fact the federal government has historically contributed only a small portion of public education funds.

Funding for education has always been a contentious issue. Some people believe that education funding should be much higher than it is to ensure that students get the best education they can with the best resources and the most motivated teachers. Others believe that educational expenses should be kept in check so that schools will focus on teaching students instead of adding educational "bells and whistles" that do little to provide real educational value. What constitutes bells and whistles, of course, makes the debate more challenging. In the early and mid 1980s many education experts argued that computers in the classroom were a waste of tax dollars. By the mid 1990s it was clear that computers were in the classroom to stay, a necessary and essential element in the education process.

Still, there are many other issues for people to debate. For example, does increased funding increase student achievement? How long should school equipment last before it is replaced? Do school districts need to fund extracurricular activities, such as athletic teams? The issue of school vouchers (discussed in detail in a separate entry) has raised enormous questions in some communities. The idea of allowing parents to earmark some of their tax dollars for private schooling has generated much controversy. Clearly, taking money away from the public schools puts them at a greater financial disadvantage than they already are. Yet it does children little good to know that the public school they attend is in the first year of a turnaround that may last several more years. Regardless of the many controversies surrounding public education funding, it remains vitally important and guarantees that all children in the United States have access to school.

## What Is Funded?

Educational funding covers a wide variety of expenditures, all of which are necessary to keep school systems running. The U.S. Department of Education defines *current expenditures* as those that take care of a schools' day-to-day operations. Current expenditures include instruction (for example, teacher salaries, textbooks and other equipment), non-instruction (such as cafeteria services and in-school bookstores), and support services (including nurses, libraries, administration, and maintenance). Other expenditures include *facilities equipment and construction*, which covers new school construction including renovation and expansion of older buildings. It also includes the purchase of land on which to build new school structures. *Replacement equipment* includes expenditures for items that are purchased for the long term (furniture, for example). School districts also spend money on programs such as adult education, community colleges, and various other programs that are not actually a part of public el-hi education. School districts often have to borrow money to meet major expenses (such as new school construction) even after they receive government funding. Along with the other expenditures, schools also have to figure in interest expenses as they pay back long-term debt.

## Sources of Funding

Before reading about federal, state, and local funding, it is important to remember that each state has a different breakdown of funds, based on such factors as how much federal funding it gets. The percentages below are average figures for the 50 states and U. S. territories. Using the 1998-99 figures listed above, some states get more in federal funding (in Mississippi the figure was 14 percent), while others got significantly less (in New Jersey the number was 3.7 percent). Likewise, state contributions can vary significantly. In Vermont, 74.4 percent of school funding came from the state, while in New Hampshire only 8.9 percent came from state funding.

Much of these rates are based on the types of programs that exist within each state or the internal tax structure. A state that has more federal education programs for children may end up with a higher percentage of federal funds overall. In general, the breakdowns tend to work. That said, whenever one source cuts back, it has an effect on the other sources. If, for example, the federal government were to decrease its educational contribution across the board by two percent, that would mean states and local communities would have to make up the shortfall. If either of those sources made cutbacks, the remaining source would feel more pressure to contribute more. If the necessary funding was simply not there, the result would either be higher taxes or reduced services.

### Federal Revenues

The federal government contributes money to schools directly and indirectly. Part of this funding comes from the U. S. Department of Education, but other agencies contribute as well. The U. S. Department of Health and Human Services, for example, contributes to education through its Head Start program, while the U. S. Department of Agriculture funds the School Lunch program for students who cannot afford to pay for their own lunches. Even with these added contributions, the federal government accounts for less than 10 percent of school revenues. Using its own words, the Department of Education has long seen its role as "a kind of emergency response system" that fills gaps when state and local sources are inadequate to meet key needs. (For example, the 1944 **GI Bill**, a post-secondary program rather than el-hi program, helps fund college educations for nearly eight million World War II veterans.)

The Education Department's measures are not always merely stop-gap. During and after World War II Congress passed the **Lanham Act** (1941) and the Impact Aid laws (1950) to compensate school districts that housed military and other nontaxable federal installations. Today, the federal government continues to compensate communities that house such institutions. Moreover, Title I of the Elementary and Secondary Education Act of 1965 guaranteed aid to disadvantaged children in poor urban and rural communities. The Higher Education Act, passed the same year, provided financial aid programs to help qualifying students meet college expenses.

### State Funding

The states provide most of the funding that keeps public el-hi schools running in the U.S. For the academic year 1998-99, state sources accounted for 48.7 percent of total school revenues. The states raise this money through a variety of means including various taxes. Some states raise money for education through state-sponsored lottery games. Doing so is somewhat controversial because, while the schools may benefit from the added revenue, some see the lottery as nothing more than state-sponsored gambling, a potentially addictive activity that particularly affects poorer individuals.

Each state has an Education Department that oversees state programs (such as state university systems) as well as individual school districts. In some states a governing body, such as the Board of Regents in New York, plays a significant role. The New York Board of Regents provides a series of examinations for students to establish proficiency in various subjects based on established state standards. Many students in New York receive a Regents diploma as well as their regular school diploma when they graduate high school.

State funding for education can cause huge disagreements among communities with the state. The question state governments face constantly is how to distribute the revenues evenly to ensure that each school district gets its fair share. New York and Pennsylvania offer two examples of how state funds can be fought over. New York City holds nearly half the population of the state, yet it receives proportionally less per student from the state government than other districts in New York. Residents of upstate New York have little desire to see their state tax dollars sent to New York City schools, which they see as too bureaucratic and wasteful. Residents of central Pennsylvania feel the same about education expenditures in Philadelphia and Pittsburgh.

Urban and rural areas have separate needs and challenges. A large city may have an established infrastructure that allows its school officials to approach private companies for assistance. A local computer company may donate computer equipment to the city schools, for example. Yet city schools are often decrepit (many school buildings in New York City are heated by coal furnaces), classes are crowded, and teacher turnover is high. In rural areas, classes are unlikely to be overcrowded, and teachers may stay longer in one place. But having fewer students can also mean having access to fewer resources, and there may not be enough students in a given district to justify the expense of, for example, a special education program for developmentally disabled children.

### Local Funding

Local sources make up nearly as much revenue as state sources. Local sources includes intermediate revenues from county or township governments, but the bulk of local funding comes from individual community school districts. Some of the local revenues come from sources such as revenues from student activities and food services. Most of the money comes from property taxes, which are raised to cover

all community services as well as education. All homeowners pay taxes based on a local **assessment** of their houses. Local school budgets are mapped out by elected officials, including mayors and council members, as well as the local board of education. Residents are able to vote on local school budgets in regularly scheduled elections.

Funding schools with local dollars has benefits and drawbacks. The primary benefit of local funding is accountability. Taxpayers can see exactly how their money is being spent. They can see the new cafeteria at the high school, the new science lab equipment, the new textbooks. The local elected officials who submit school budgets to the voters know that if they fail to keep the promises they make, those same voters will remove them from office in the next election.

Members of the community also have more say in how local dollars are spent. Those who have children in the school system will be particularly interested in how tax dollars are spent. Some of them may become quite active in school affairs by participating in the Parents Teachers Association (PTA) or on the local board of education.

This arrangement can be a drawback to local funding as well as a benefit. Because members of the community know they have a say in the school budgetary process, they may be more likely to examine each expenditure carefully. This scrutiny is not the problem. What creates difficulties is when local residents perceive expenses as unnecessary. Those who no longer have children in the school system may be reluctant to see their property taxes increase for programs that will bring them little if any benefit. Senior citizens likewise may be reluctant to support tax increases (even though in many communities they get a property tax break). People who feel that teacher salaries are already too high or that the old gym is perfectly fine for the students or that new instruments for the marching band are an extravagance, may vote down any school budget increases.

Local elected officials need to be able to show community residents the positive side of spending more money on the schools. Better-equipped schools attract better teachers. Better teachers prepare students better, and more students achieve success. This improvement in turn means more young families, since for young families the quality of the schools is the most important factor when they choose a place to live. As the community becomes more attractive to outsiders, property values will go up; often the rise in value far more than offsets the extra cost incurred by taxes. Of course, higher property values may also mean higher tax assessments, so for the homeowner who has no children and who has no plans to move, the process of increased values may feel like a personal financial burden rather than tax dollars at work. For these and other reasons local funding is more complex than it would appear to be.

## Sources of Information

The federal government offers a number of sources of revenue information through the U. S. Department of Education (which oversees NCES), and other sources. Each state has its own education department, which can provide information about state education funding. Because education is such a critical issue to so many people, elected officials are a good source of statistical information on school revenues. Local government sources and boards of education are useful resources for information about local funding. Most public libraries compile information about local school revenue issues as well.

## Additional Resources

*Funding Sources for K-12 Schools and Adult Basic Education.* Oryx Press, 1998.

*Goals 2000: A Progress Report.* U. S. Department of Education, 1995.

## Organizations

### *National Center for Education Statistics (NCES)*

1990 K Street, NW, Room 9103
Washington, DC 20006 USA
Phone: (202) 502-7350
Fax: (202) 502-7475
URL: http://www.nces.ed.gov
Primary Contact: Gary W. Phillips, Acting Commissioner

### *National Education Association (NEA)*

1201 16th Street, NW
Washington, DC 20036 USA
Phone: (202) 833-4000
Fax: (202) 822-7170
URL: http://www.nea.org
Primary Contact: Robert F. Chase, President

### *National School Boards Association (NSBA)*

1680 Duke Street
Alexandria, VA 22314 USA
Phone: (703) 838-67220
Fax: (703) 683-7590
URL: http://www.nsba.org
Primary Contact: Anne L. Bryant, Executive Director

# EDUCATION

## HOMESCHOOLING

*Sections within this essay:*

- Background
- Homeschooling Laws by State
- Additional Resources

## Background

According to U.S. Department of Education estimates, 1.1 million students were homeschooled in the United States in 2003. These students comprised 2.2 percent of the school-age population in grades Kindergarten through grade 12, compared to approximately 850,000 students (1.7 percent of the school-age population) in 1999. The Home School Legal Defense Association believes the number of students homeschooled is significantly higher; the organization estimates that in 2002-2003, 1.7 to 2.1 million students were homeschooled.

Slightly less than one-third of homeschooling parents surveyed by the Department of Education cited concern for the environment in public schools as their main reason for homeschooling. Nearly an equal percentage decided to homeschool to provide moral or religious instruction. Sixteen percent of parents homeschooled their children because of dissatisfaction with the academic instruction in other available schools.

The United States Supreme Court has not addressed the issue whether states may prohibit homeschooling. Some lower courts have addressed the issue, and concluded that it is constitutionally permissible to ban homeschooling. For example, the New Mexico Court of Appeals ruled in *State v. Eddington* in 1983 that the state's compulsory attendance law did not violate Equal Protection guarantees in the United States and New Mexico Constitutions. The court determined that the compulsory attendance law promotes a legitimate state interest by exposing children to "at least one other set of attitudes, values, morals, lifestyles and intellectual abilities," in addition to those provided by parents, guardians, or other immediate family members.

Prior to 1980, states generally either expressly prohibited homeschooling, or they did not address the issue. Some states still have laws that ban homeschooling. In those states, parents typically are able to homeschool by other means, such as following laws applicable to private schools. However, most states have enacted homeschooling statutes and regulations. In court challenges alleging that it is unconstitutional to treat home schools differently than public schools, courts have typically sided with the state and allowed the differential treatment in part because it is more difficult to asses the quality of home instruction.

Some states specifically permit homeschool students to enroll in public school classes or extracurricular activities. In other states without such statutes, when challenged by homeschooling parents, courts have found that a student does not have a right to participate. Oftentimes, state rules concerning sports or other competitive interscholastic activities preclude participation by students who are not full time. According to U.S. Department of Education figures for 2003, about 80 percent of homeschoolers were homeschooled exclusively.

States vary on how they approach enforcing the statutory restrictions on homeschooling. In some jurisdictions, home instructors bear the burden to show they are complying with the law. In other states, the state bears the burden to show that a home school does not meet legal requirements. Some states have not addressed the issue.

The No Child Left Behind Act of 2001 does not apply to homeschooled students. However, according to the Individuals with Disabilities Education Act, children with disabilities are entitled to a "free, appropriate public education." This entitlement applies to homeschooled children as well, and means that a homeschooled child with a disability is entitled to special education and related services at public expense with public supervision and direction. The services must be provided in conformity with a child's individual education plan.

Homeschool statutes and regulations typically fall into four categories:

- Instructor qualification requirements: A handful of states require home instructors to possess a teaching certification or a bachelor's degree. Some other states have a general requirement that parents be qualified to teach.

- Pupil assessment requirements: More than half the states require homeschooled pupils to be tested or assessed for academic progress. Visitation requirements: Some jurisdictions require that home schools allow visits and observation by state education officials.

- Instruction requirements: Depending upon the jurisdiction, home schools may be required to provide instruction that is "equivalent," "substantially equivalent," or "comparable" to public school programming. Certain subjects may be required.

## Homeschooling Laws by State

ALABAMA: Alabama does not have any laws that specifically address homeschooling. Parents may opt to enroll children under the church school option, which does not require teacher certification. Church schools have little regulation, other than some requirements to report attendance. Under the private tutor option, teachers must be certified. The tutor must teach for at least three hours a day for 140 days each calendar year, and must file with the proper au-

thorities a report describing subjects taught and periods of instruction.

ALASKA: Exempts children from compulsory attendance when they are educated in their home by a parent or legal guardian. There are no prescribed teacher qualifications, nor any requirements to assess or file any information. The state has the burden to show that the child is not receiving proper instruction.

ARIZONA: Within 30 days after homeschooling begins, the parent or guardian is required to file an affidavit of intent to homeschool. The affidavit is filed with the county school superintendent. The state does prescribe any teacher certification requirements for homeschool instructors, nor are there any requirements for assessment or standardized testing. Required subjects are reading, grammar, math, social studies and science.

ARKANSAS: Parents are required to notify the local public school superintendent of the intent to homeschool, and provide information on the curriculum, the schedule, and the qualification of the parent/teacher. There are no subjects specifically required for instruction. Most students are required to take achievement tests selected by the state board of education. Refusing to participate in testing may result in a prosecution for truancy.

CALIFORNIA: The state does not have a specific homeschooling statute. Several options are available. First, the homeschool may qualify as a private school if, among other requirements, the teacher is "capable of teaching" and instruction is in English. As a variation, students may enroll in a private school satellite program and receive independent study from that school. Another option is instruction provided by a certified private tutor. Finally, students may enroll in an independent study program at home, through a public school.

COLORADO: Statute provides that homeschooling programs "shall be subject only to minimum state controls." Instruction must be by a parent, guardian, or adult relative designated by the parents, but teacher certification is not required. Parents must give notice that they are homeschooling, must keep certain records, and submit students for testing or evaluation per state requirements.

CONNECTICUT: Although no statutes address homeschooling, Connecticut State Department of Education regulations permit it when the instruction is "equivalent" to public school instruction. Teacher certification and testing are not required, although a portfolio review with school authorities is used to determine whether instruction in required courses has been provided. Required courses are reading, writing, spelling, English, grammar, geography, arithmetic, United States history, and citizenship. Parents must file a notice of intent to homeschool.

DELAWARE: There are three options provided by statute: single-family homeschool, multiple family homeschool, and single-family homeschool coordinated with the local school district. Attendance and enrollment must be reported. There are no requirements for teacher qualifications or testing.

DISTRICT OF COLUMBIA: Homeschooling falls under laws regarding "private instruction." There are no requirements for teacher certification or student testing. No specific subjects must be taught.

FLORIDA: Florida has a notification requirement in its homeschool law. The state also requires that instructors maintain a portfolio containing specified information. The portfolio must be preserved for two years and be available for inspection, although there is no requirement that authorities actually inspect it. Parents are not required to be certified. However, where the private tutor law is used, instructors must be certified. There is also a statutory provision describing how multiple home schools may operate as a private school. Students must be tested or evaluated annually only where the homeschool is operated by the parent or guardian.

GEORGIA: Parents must file a declaration of intent. Instruction must include, but may not be limited to, reading, language arts, math, social studies, and science. The school day is four and one-half hours. Parents must write an annual progress report, and retain it for three years. The parent must have at least a high school diploma or GED equivalency, and students must submit to a national standardized achievement test every three years, beginning in third grade.

HAWAII: Parents must provide a notice of intent to homeschool and keep a record of planned curriculum. There are no certification requirements. Students must take standardized achievement test of the parent's choice in grades 3, 5, 8, and 10. Parents must submit an annual progress report.

IDAHO: Students are exempt from compulsory attendance if they are "comparably" instructed to those in public schools. There are no teacher certification requirements, nor are assessment tests mandated.

ILLINOIS: A homeschool is considered to be a private school. A statute provides that children in a private school are in compliance with the compulsory attendance law where they are instructed in English and where the instruction corresponds to that given to children of a corresponding age and grade in public school. Teacher qualifications and standardized testing are not prescribed.

INDIANA: Children may attend an alternative form of "equivalent" instruction when it is conducted in English. Teachers need not be certified; testing is not required. Parents must maintain attendance records.

IOWA: Parents must submit an annual private instruction report. For students age eight and older, instruction must be by or under the supervision of a certified teacher, or alternatively, provide instruction which results in "adequate progress" for the student. For students not under the auspices of a certified teacher, yearly assessments are required. Several options are available to satisfy the assessment requirement.

KANSAS: Homeschoolers may register as a non-accredited private school, for which there are no required subjects of instruction. The teacher must be "competent;" there is no testing requirement.

KENTUCKY: Although there is no specific statute on homeschooling, students may be homeschooled by following laws for private, parochial, or church regular day schools. Standardized testing is not required. Teacher certification is not required. Enrollment reports must be made to the local school board.

LOUISIANA: Home school students are exempt from compulsory attendance requirements if a parent applies and receives approval for a program offers a "sustained curriculum of quality at least equal to that offered by public schools." The state also provides for home-based private schools. Standardized tests are required under the first option, but there are no requirements regarding teacher certification.

MAINE: The state has a home school statute, or has an option for non-approved private schools. Under the first option, there are no specified teacher requirements, but students must submit to an annual assessment. Under the private school option, teacher competence is subject to approval, but students do not need to submit to assessment.

MARYLAND: Three options are available to exempt a student from compulsory attendance laws. The "church umbrella option" provides instruction under the supervision of a bona-fide church organization. Students may also be homeschooled under a state approved "non-public school umbrella." The "portfolio option" requires supervision by a public school superintendent. None of the options requires teacher certification or testing.

MASSACHUSETTS: Students are excused from compulsory attendance laws if they are being instructed in a manner that has been approved in advance by the superintendent or the school committee. Required subjects are reading, writing, English language and grammar, geography, arithmetic, drawing, music, history and constitution of United States, citizenship, health, physical education, and good behavior. There are no teacher certification requirements. Students must take standardized tests or submit to an approved, alternative form of assessment.

MICHIGAN: A child may be educated at home by a parent or legal guardian in reading, spelling, mathematics, science, history, civics, literature, writing, and English grammar. Parents are not required to notify the state, and the burden is on the state to show that a child is not receiving an adequate education. The teacher certification requirement was held to be unconstitutional by the Michigan Supreme Court. The state also has a nonpublic school option, which does require certified instructors.

MINNESOTA: Parents may qualify to teach their children in one of six ways, including certification, working under the direct supervision of a qualified instructor, or by holding a baccalaureate degree. Students must take achievement tests, but the results do not need to be submitted to the school district. Required topics are reading, writing, literature, fine arts, math, science, history, geography, government, health, and physical education. Parents must either submit to an on-site visit or provide documentation to show compliance with education laws.

MISSISSIPPI: Parents must file a certificate of enrollment. The child must be enrolled in a "legitimate home instruction program." There are no teacher certification requirements and no provision for mandatory testing or assessment.

MISSOURI: Homeschools must maintain specific records, although there is no requirement to submit them. There are no mandatory testing or teacher certification requirements. Students must have 1,000 hours of instruction, including a minimum 600 hours in reading, math, social studies, language arts, and science. At least 400 hours must be in the home school location.

MONTANA: 720 hours of instruction are required for grades 1-3, and 1,080 for grades 4-12. Home schools must provide the same basic instructional program as public schools. Parents must notify authorities of the intent to home school. There are no mandatory testing or teacher certification requirements.

NORTH CAROLINA: Annual standardized testing is required for English, grammar, reading, spelling, and math. The school must operate for a nine-month period of instruction. Parents must possess a high school diploma or GED. Parents must keep certain records and must provide a notice of intent to homeschool.

NORTH DAKOTA: A certified teacher must administer standardized tests to students in grades 4, 6, 8, and 10. Parents who are not certified teachers may fulfill teacher requirements in other ways, including possession of a baccalaureate degree, and supervision by a certified teacher for those who possess a high school diploma or GED. Parents must file an annual notice of intent to homeschool and must maintain annual reports.

NEBRASKA: Home schools operate under private school laws. Parents must affirm under oath that instruction in language arts, mathematics, science, social studies, and health are being provided to the child. There are no mandatory testing or teacher certification requirements. Elementary students must have 1,032 hours of instruction; high school students must have 1,080 hours.

NEVADA: English, science, math, and social studies are required subjects. Parents must provide evidence that they are providing "equivalent instruction of the kind and amount" as public school students. Parents must provide annual notification of homeschooling status. There are no mandatory testing or teacher certification requirements.

NEW HAMPSHIRE: Parents must provide notification of homeschooling. They must also maintain a portfolio of records and materials used. There are no teacher certification requirements. A number of choices exist to satisfy testing and assessment requirements.

NEW JERSEY: There are no specific statutes addressing homeschooling. Students may be homeschooled under a law that provides for instruction for "equivalent" education elsewhere than a public school. There are no mandatory testing or teacher certification requirements.

NEW MEXICO: The law contains a notification requirement, and parents must possess a high school diploma or a GED. There is no requirement of mandatory testing. Instruction must include reading, language arts, mathematics, social studies, and science.

NEW YORK: The law requires specifies numerous required subjects that vary depending upon grade level. Instruction must be "at least substantially equivalent" to public school instruction. Parents must provide notice of homeschooling, file individualized instruction plans, and file other required reports in a timely manner. Teachers must be "competent." Most students are required to take one of five approved standardized tests at specified intervals. The student must achieve a composite score above the thirty-third percentile.

OHIO: The homeschool law requires instruction in language arts, geography, U.S. and Ohio history, government, math, health, physical education, fine arts, first aid, and science. Parents must provide annual notification of homeschooling, which includes an outline of the intended curriculum. Teacher requirement can be satisfied several ways, including working under the direction of someone with a baccalaureate degree. Parents have three options to satisfy standardized testing requirement. Ohio law also provides for non-chartered schools for parents who object to government-controlled education because of "truly held religious beliefs." Different requirements apply to these schools, including a waiver of the testing requirement.

OKLAHOMA: The state has a constitutional provision which appears to guarantee the right to homeschool, but no specific statutes on the subject. There are no mandatory testing or teacher certification requirements.

OREGON: The parent or legal guardian must provide initial notification to the school district, but need not file annually. Teacher qualifications are not prescribed. Students must be assessed in grades 3, 5, 8, and 10; more testing or oversight over the home school may be required when students perform below specified limits. Children with disabilities will be assessed according to the individualized education plan (IEP).

PENNSYLVANIA: Parents must provide affidavit initially and annually thereafter; affidavit must include information on the courses taught, assurances that instruction will be in English, and certification that none of the adults in the home have been convicted of certain criminal offenses within the last five years. Parents must annually provide a portfolio for review, which includes an annual review by qualified personnel who will determine whether the child's education is appropriate. The program for a special needs child must meet special approval requirements. Parents must have a high school diploma or equivalent, and standardized testing must be done and reported for students in grades 3, 5, and 8. Other statutes provide alternatives, including instruction by a private tutor (who must be certified to teach in the state), and teaching in the home as an extension of a religious day school. The state has mandated an extensive list of required subjects, which vary with grade level.

RHODE ISLAND: Rhode Island requires attendance that is "substantially equal" to public schools. Required subjects include reading, writing, geography, math, U.S. and Rhode Island history and principles of government, English, and physical education. Instruction must be "thorough and efficient." Teacher qualifications are unspecified. There is no statutory requirement of standardized testing.

SOUTH CAROLINA: Statutes in this state delineate three different homeschooling options. First, parents may teach at home with an approved program of instruction. School must run for four and one-half hours per day for 180 days. Parents must have at least a high school diploma or GED, and students must be assessed annually. Second, parents may become members of the South Carolina Association of Independent Home Schools and comply with the association's standards. Finally, parents may join an association of home schools with no fewer than 50 members. Students in the latter two categories are not required to undergo annual testing.

SOUTH DAKOTA: Children are permitted to be homeschooled if the program provides for instruction for an equivalent period of time as the public schools. Required subjects are language arts and mathematics. Parents must apply for permission to home school, and students in grades 2, 4, 8, 11 must take standardized tests. No teacher requirements are prescribed. No person may teach more than 22 students.

TENNESSEE: Three options exist. Parents or legal guardians may homeschool, after they notify the local school district. Instruction must be four hours per day. Other options are to associate with a church-related school, or to operate as a satellite of one. Teacher qualifications and testing requirements vary depending upon the option selected.

TEXAS: The state does not have a specific homeschooling statute, but court decisions have established the right for homeschools to operate under private school rules. Required subjects are reading, spelling, grammar, math and good citizenship. No requirement of standardized testing. State law specifically prohibits Texas colleges from discriminating against homeschooled applicants.

UTAH: Parents must file an annual affidavit with the local school district. Required subjects are language arts, math, science, social studies, arts, health, and computer literacy. The law does not prescribe teacher qualifications or standardized testing. Parents are responsible for evaluation of instruction.

VERMONT: The law requires instruction in reading, writing, math, citizenship, history, United States and Vermont government, physical education, health, English, American and other literature, science and fine arts. Annual notice is required; notice must include a detailed description of the program of study. Teacher requirements are not specified, but students must be evaluated annually. Several options exist to satisfy the evaluation requirement.

VIRGINIA: This state has four statutory options for homeschoolers. First is the typical homeschool statute, which requires notice to the district. Parents must set forth the program of instruction and teach language arts and math. Parents may qualify as teachers in one of four ways. The second option is for students and parents who are conscientiously opposed to attendance at school due to a bona fide religious belief. These students are exempt from the requirements in the homeschool statute. Third, the state has a certified tutor statute. Fourth, groups of homeschooling families may band together to become a private school. These schools are not regulated. Only students under the first option must submit to an annual standardized test or assessment.

WASHINGTON: Students may obtain their education either under the homeschool statute or operate as an extension of a private school. Under the first option, parents must provide equivalent hours of instruction as public schools. Planned and supervised instruction must include occupational education, science, math, language, social studies, history, health, reading, writing, spelling, and art and music appreciation. Teacher qualification requirements can be satisfied in a number of ways. Standardized tests on an annual basis are required, but need not be submitted to the school district. Under the second option, parents must be supervised by a certified teacher who evaluates the student's progress.

WEST VIRGINIA: This state provides for homeschooling either under an ''approval'' or ''notice'' method. The approval method must be approved by the board and is for a term equal to that of the school district. Under the notice option, parents submit evidence that they possess a high school diploma or its equivalent, and provide an outline of the program of instruction. No testing is required under the first option; testing and evaluation under the latter option may be fulfilled in several ways.

WISCONSIN: A homeschool program must include at least 875 hours of instruction. Instruction must provide a ''sequentially progressive curriculum of fundamental instruction'' in reading, language arts, math, social studies, science, and health. Parents must provide information annually to show compliance. Standardized tests are not required, and no teacher qualifications are specified.

WYOMING: Parents must annually submit curriculum plan to the school board. This program must provide a ''sequentially progressive curriculum'' in reading, writing, math, civics, history, literature, and science. The law does not delineate teacher requirements or call for standardized testing.

## Additional Resources

### Organizations

**U.S. Department of Education**
400 Maryland Ave., SW
Washington, DC 20202 USA
Phone: (800) 872-5327
URL: http://www.ed.gov/

**Home School Legal Defense Association**
Purcellville, VA 20134 USA
Phone: (540) 338-5600
URL: http://www.hslda.org/

## *National Home Education Network*

P.O. Box 1652
Hobe Sound, FL 33475-1652 USA
Phone:
Fax: (413) 581-1463
URL: http://www.nhen.org/

# EDUCATION

## NO CHILD LEFT BEHIND ACT OF 2001

*Sections within this essay:*

- Background

- Provisions of No Child Left Behind
  - Title I and Reading First
  - Adequate Yearly Progress
  - Failure to Meet AYP Goals
  - Title II: Teacher Accountability
  - Sex Education and School Prayer
  - School Safety and Drug Use

- Criticism of No Child Left Behind
  - Education as Domain of the States; NCLBA as an Unfunded Federal Mandate
  - Emphasis on Standardized Testing

- The Future of NCLBA

- Additional Resources

## Background

On January 8, 2002, President George W. Bush signed into law the No Child Left Behind Act of 2001 (NCLBA). This legislation reauthorized, and provided major reform, to the Elementary and Secondary Education Act of 1965 (ESEA).

The Cold War and the Soviet Union's successful launch of the Sputnik spacecraft in October 1957 brought calls for improvements to the nation's educational system. In the early 1960s, President John F. Kennedy developed proposals to ensure that American students were competitive with students around the world. His proposals were intended to guarantee that students of every race, religion, and social standing would receive a good education. After Kennedy's assassination, President Lyndon B. Johnson revised Kennedy's proposals, and oversaw their introduction in Congress. Part of Johnson's "War on Poverty," ESEA was the most expansive federal education legislation ever passed. The bill passed with little debate and in only three months' time.

ESEA provided federal funding for 90 percent of the nation's public and parochial schools. Title 1, the law's most important provision, provides guidelines for the education of "educationally disadvantaged" students. It also provides funds: more than 80 percent of the original appropriation under ESEA went to ESEA. In 2005, President Bush's proposed budget for fiscal year 2006 asked for an appropriation of $13.3 billion for Title 1, a $4.6 billion, or 52 percent, increase for Title I since enactment of NCLBA. According to the Department of Education, 12.5 million students in public and private schools are served through Title I.

Part of ESEA's legacy has been controversy. Prior to ESEA, educational policy decisions had been almost exclusively in the hands of state and local governments. Critics have charged that the federal government has become too involved in regulating educational matters better left to local school districts. The federal government now provides approximately seven percent of the total funding for elementary and secondary schools.

Critics of ESEA have also charged that Title 1 has done little to raise student performance, because it did not mandate accountability for academic results. No Child Left Behind was crafted to address that issue. According to Congress, the two goals of

NCLBA are accountability for schools and teachers, and closing the achievement gap for students of lower socioeconomic backgrounds, "so that no child is left behind." No Child Left Behind's lofty and worthy goals brought it broad bipartisan support in Congress, but its implementation has engendered considerable controversy.

## Provisions of No Child Left Behind

No Child Left Behind is comprised of hundreds of pages of text. The law is divided into ten sections, called titles. The titles are:

- Title I: Improving Academic Achievement of the Disadvantaged

- Title II: Preparing, Training, and Recruiting High-Quality Teachers and Principals

- Title III: Language Instruction for Limited English Proficient and Immigrant Students

- Title IV: Twenty-first Century Schools

- Title V: Promoting Parental Choice and Innovative Programs

- Title VI: Flexibility and Accountability

- Title VII: Indian, Native Hawaiian, and Alaska Native Education

- Title VIII: Impact Aid Program

- Title IX: General Provisions

- Title X: Repeals, Redesignations, and Amendments to Other Statutes

### *Title I and Reading First*

Title 1 of NCLBA amends and expands Title I of ESEA and has as its purpose "to ensure that all children have a fair, equal, and significant opportunity to obtain a high-quality education and reach, at a minimum, proficiency on challenging State academic achievement standards and state academic assessments." More specifically, Title I encompasses the following goals and methods:

- Using high-quality academic assessments and other methods to measure progress against common expectations for student academic achievement

- Closing the achievement gap between high- and low-performing children, especially the gaps between minority and nonminority students, and between disadvantaged children and their more advantaged peers

- Meeting the needs of children in need of reading assistance, including minority students, English-language learner students, students with disabilities, and poor students

- Careful distribution and targeting of resources

- Holding schools, local educational agencies, and states accountable for improving the academic achievement of all students

- Improving and strengthening accountability, teaching, and learning by using state assessment systems

According to the Department of Education, prior to enactment of the NCLBA, only 32 percent of the nation's fourth graders were reading at a level deemed "proficient." The huge "Reading First" program in Title I of No Child Left Behind is intended to address the reading deficiency in elementary students. In 2003, more than $990 million was appropriated for the program; the number pushed past the $1 billion level in subsequent years. Money for Reading First is distributed in two ways. First, states receive distributions on the basis of the number of low-income children ages 5-17 who live in the state. Second, districts compete for funds in state-run competitions. Priority goes to districts with high rates of poverty and reading failure.

Reading programs under the Reading First program must be devised from "scientifically based research." This phrase recurs dozens of times in NCLBA, although it is not clearly defined within the act. Essentially, "scientifically based research" means that there is reliable evidence that a program or practice works. With regard to Reading First, students must be explicitly and systematically taught five skills:

- Phonemic awareness (the ability to hear and identify sounds in spoken words)

- Phonics

- Vocabulary

- Comprehension

- Fluency

### *Adequate Yearly Progress*

No Child Left Behind requires that schools demonstrate that each student is on grade level, in key areas such as math and reading, by 2014. Schools that cannot demonstrate this proficiency stand to lose federal funding. States must set goals which will demonstrate schools are making "adequate yearly progress" (AYP) in math and reading on the way to the 2014 deadline. Initially only math and reading/language arts were required to be assessed. However, by the school year 2007-2008, science assessments must be administered at least once during grades 3-5, grades 6-9, and grades 10-12.

States set their own minimum levels of improvement, which must be measurable in terms of student performance. School districts and schools must achieve these minimum levels within NCLBA time frames. States select a "starting point" based on the performance of its lowest-achieving demographic group or of the lowest-achieving schools in the state (the higher of the two). The state then sets a level that schools must reach after two years to show adequate yearly progress. After that, subsequent thresholds are set for at least every three years. As states raise their target goals over time, increasing numbers of students are expected to meet them. After 12 years, all students in the state are expected to attain the proficient level on state reading and math assessments.

School districts are required to make an annual report to the public. This NCLBA report card describes academic achievement for the district at large, for each individual school, and by grade level. The report cards classify student performance as basic, proficient, or advanced. Moreover, the report cards disaggregate the data by student subgroups according to: race, ethnicity, gender, English language proficiency, migrant status, disability status and low-income status. All students must be evaluated, and each subgroup must meet the AYP goals or the school as a whole fails. A district's report card also tells which schools have been identified as needing improvement, corrective action, or restructuring.

NCLBA requires states to provide academic achievement awards to recognize schools that close achievement gaps between groups of students or that exceed academic achievement goals. States may also use Title I money for financial rewards for teachers. Schools that have made the greatest gains in closing the achievement gap or in exceeding achievement goals receive the designation of "distinguished schools."

### Failure to Meet AYP Goals

The consequences of failure to meet AYP, as defined by a state, depend upon how long the school has failed to do so. A Title I school that has not met

state goals for two years is called a "School in Need of Improvement" (SINI). SINI designation means that the school will receive extra help to improve its standing. The school must develop a two-year improvement plan, and local education agencies must provide assistance in development and implementation. Students from low-income families are particularly targeted for assistance when a school is designated as needing improvement. These students may receive free tutoring and other homework help. Students from low-income families are also allowed to transfer to other non-SINI public schools in the district. The district must provide transportation for the student. A school that has failed to make adequate yearly progress for three years, in addition to consequences above, must offer students from low-income families supplemental educational services from a state-approved provider. Supplemental educational services include tutoring and remedial classes.

Drastic changes await schools that do not attain adequate yearly progress in the fourth or fifth years. In the fourth year, in addition to previous remedial actions, a district must implement certain corrective actions to improve the school. Corrective actions include replacing staff and fully implementing a new curriculum. In the fifth year, a school district must implement plans to restructure the school. Options for restructuring include:

- Reopening the school as a charter school

- Replacing all or most of school staff

- Turning over the school operations to the state or to a private company with a demonstrated record of effectiveness

### Title II: Teacher Accountability

Teachers are held to an increased accountability standard under NCLBA. The act prohibits teaching with a temporary, provisional, or emergency teaching certificate. However, under the law, states are encouraged to find ways of alternative certification to allow talented individuals to teach subjects they know.

Teachers in core academic subjects must be "highly qualified." Core subjects are English, reading or language arts, mathematics, science, foreign languages, civics and government, economics, arts, history and geography. Highly qualified means teachers must have full certification, a bachelor's degree and demonstrated competence in subject knowledge and teaching. Title II includes grants intended to strengthen teacher quality, and funding for other teacher quality-related programs. Under Title II, states and individual schools are required to document that they are complying with the highly qualified teacher requirements.

### Sex Education and School Prayer

Under NCLBA, schools must emphasize abstinence, and may not use federal funds for programs to distribute condoms or other contraceptives in the school. School districts must certify each year that their policies do not prevent or deny participation in constitutionally protected prayer in elementary and secondary schools.

### School Safety and Drug Use

NCLBA provides funds to states to award to school districts for drug- and violence-prevention programs. These programs must address specific local needs and involve parents. Under Title IV, states are required to establish a uniform management and reporting system to collect information on school safety and drug use. Reporting must include anonymous student and teacher surveys and incident reports prepared by school officials. Students have the option to change schools under certain circumstances, when school safety is an issue. Students are eligible for school choice when they attend a "persistently dangerous school," as defined by state law. Any child who has been the victim of a violent crime on the grounds of his or her school is also eligible for school choice.

## Criticism of No Child Left Behind

Numerous vocal critics oppose No Child Left Behind. Criticism of NCLBA typically falls into three different categories. First, as with ESEA, critics charge that NCLBA causes the federal government to intrude too much into what has traditionally been the domain of the states. Second, opponents contend that NCLBA has resulted in unfunded federal mandates, which essentially passes financial problems from the federal government to state and local governments. Finally, detractors allege that the law places too much emphasis on standardized testing and stringent teacher qualifications.

Speaking on behalf of its 2.7 million members, the National Education Association (NEA) is an outspoken opponent of the law. The NEA argues that NCLBA requires stringent accountability, but does not provide adequate funding necessary for schools to meet those requirements. The NEA also claims that NCLBA punishes schools rather than providing assistance, and that it promotes privatization of education.

### Education as Domain of the States; NCLBA as an Unfunded Federal Mandate

The United States Constitution strikes a balance between powers reserved for the federal government, and those given to the states. The Tenth Amendment provides, "The powers not delegated to the United States by the Constitution, nor prohibited by it to the States, are reserved to the States respectively, or to the people." The Supreme Court has established in rulings that the Constitution does not implicitly or explicitly delegate education matters to the federal government. In fact, in the landmark Brown v. Board of Education case from 1954, the Supreme Court recognized, "Education is perhaps the most important function of state and local governments." Nevertheless, the federal government has often involved itself in education policies without running afoul of the Constitution.

Congress is able to enact legislation over education because of another constitutional provision, the spending clause in Art. I, sec. 8, clause 1: "The Congress shall have Power To lay and collect Taxes, Duties, Imposts and Excises, to pay the Debts and provide for the common Defence and general Welfare of the United States... ." Under the spending clause, if federal funds are merely an inducement to meet certain conditions, the federal government may intrude on an area normally reserved to the states.

The Supreme Court has held that Congress must meet certain requirements where it relies on the spending clause to enact legislation over which it has no specific authority. Such legislation must:

- Not be prohibited by other constitutional provisions

- Be in pursuit of the "general welfare"

- Be related to the federal interest in particular national projects or programs

- Be unambiguous in describing the conditions for the states' receipt of federal funds, to enable states to knowingly decide to participate or not

Critics of NCLBA charge that the law is unclear in describing what states must do to receive federal funds. Critics support this contention by referring to the Department of Education's massive efforts to clarify the act, as evidenced by regulations, guidance documents, and letters and other communication to various state and local officials.

Virginia politicians called No Child Left Behind "the most sweeping intrusions into state and local control of education in the history of the United States." The Republican-controlled House of Delegates formally asked Congress to exempt it from requirements of the law, because of the way it complicates and conflicts with state education programs to raise standards.

In 2005, Utah approved legislation to allow schools to prioritize the state's standardized testing system ahead of the NCLBA requirements. HB1001 requires school officials to "provide first priority to meeting state goals, objectives, program needs, and accountability systems as they relate to federal programs, and provide second priority to implementing federal goals, objectives, program needs, and accountability systems that do not directly and simultaneously advance state goals, objectives, program needs and accountability systems." Numerous other states have considered or are considering similar measures, including opting-out of NCLBA completely.

Often related to the criticism that the federal government is interfering with the traditional domain of the states, some critics contend that No Child Left Behind has resulted in billions of dollars of unfunded mandates. In other words, the Congress has failed to provide the funding states need to meet mandates in the law. In April 2005, the NEA, on behalf of a number of school districts, sued to exempt the school districts unless program requirements are funded by Congress. A federal judge dismissed the lawsuit in November, but Connecticut filed a similar suit in August. Supporters of the law argue that NCLBA does not present an unfunded mandate, because states are not required to adopt the federal program.

In 2004, Texas was fined $840,000 for exempting too many special education students from standardized testing. Moreover, in 2005 the Department of Education announce it was withholding some Title I funds in Minnesota, because of noncompliance with the law. Some schools have taken matters into their own hands. Consolidated High School, District 230 in Orland Park, Illinois, chose to reject $136,000 in Title I funds to avoid being forced to offer supplemental services and school choice after failing to make their adequate yearly progress goals. Another Illinois school in Palatine returned $238,000 in Title

I money to avoid the cost of sanctions for failure to make AYP.

### Emphasis on Standardized Testing

One recurring criticism of No Child Left Behind is that it forces teachers to "teach to the test" in order to get students to pass standardized tests. These critics say that a consequence of teaching to the test is that teacher creativity and student learning are stifled. Moreover, critics charge that it is unrealistic to expect learning disabled students and non-English speaking students to pass the test.

Another criticism related to testing is that the law often leads to anomalous results. For example, in 2005, Tennessee officials announced that 87 percent of the state's eighth grade students were proficient in math, a number that authorities said was a "cause for celebration." Yet according to the federal standards, only 21 percent of the state's eight graders were proficient in math. Tennessee's experience is by no means unusual, with well over a dozen states showing similar discrepancies. Eighty-nine percent of fourth graders in Mississippi tested at or above proficiency in the state reading assessment, but only 18 percent scored that way on the federal test, as measured by the National Assessment of Educational Progress (NAEP).

## The Future of NCLBA

What lies in the future for NCLBA is unclear, but it is clear that many states and school districts will simultaneously strive to implement its requirements, while challenging certain provisions in court, in legislatures, and by lobbying the Department of Education. Changes to the law will no doubt be made, but Congress appears committed to continued overall support of the program. The law is up for reauthorization in 2007.

There is some evidence that the federal government is moving towards more flexibility in the implementation of No Child Left Behind. This approach coincides with the appointment in late 2004 of Margaret Spellings as Secretary of Education. In January 2005 Spellings replaced Rod Paige; Paige had garnered a fairly hard-nosed reputation in his approach to implementing No Child Left Behind. In April 2005, Spellings said she wanted to take a "common sense" approach to implementing the law. Then the Department of Education announced plans to promote flexibility in parts of NCLBA, including assessment of students with significant cognitive disabilities, assessment of limited English proficient students, determination of when teachers meet the highly qualified definition in NCLBA, and calculation of rates of participation in state assessments to determine is schools and districts have met their AYP goals. In the aftermath of Hurricanes Katrina and Rita, Secretary Spellings gave her approval to allow some schools and districts heavily affected by the storms to create separate subgroups of displaced students for the 2005-2006 year. Students in those subgroups will not be counted in any other subgroup when calculating progress for the year.

In November 2005, Spellings announced a pilot plan to allow ten states to better gauge student progress over the long term, rather than just year to year. The program is intended to allow schools to demonstrate that they are not failing, even when their test scores are not high. Schools will set test-score goals specific to that school. In making the announcement, Secretary Spellings said, "[The] growth model is not a way around accountability standards. It's a way for states that are already raising achievement and following the bright-line principles of the law to strengthen accountability.. .There are many different routes for states to take... but they must all lead to closing the achievement gap and every student reaching grade level by 2014."

## Additional Resources

*No Child Left Behind: A Parents Guide.* U.S. Department of Education, 2003. Available at http://www.ed.gov/parents/academic/involve/nclbguide/parentsguide.html.

*http://www.ed.gov/nclb/landing.jhtml* No Child Left Behind, Department of Education website, 2006.

*Tough Call: Is No Child Left Behind Constitutional?* April 2005. Ann McColl, Phi Delta Kappan, April 2005, available at http://www.pdkintl.org/kappan/k_v86/k0504mcc.htm.

*Many Children Left Behind,* Beacon Press, Boston, 2004. Deborah Meier and George Wood, editors.

*Quick Facts: No Child Left Behind, Legislative Activity 2004-2005,* National Conference of State Legislatures, 2006. Available http://www.ncsl.org/programs/educ/NCLB2005LegActivity.htm#tx2.

A *Progress Report on the No Child Left Behind Act,* Education Week, December 14, 2005.

## Organizations

### U.S. Department of Education
400 Maryland Ave., SW
Washington, DC 20202 USA
Phone: (800) 872-5327
URL: http://www.ed.gov
Primary Contact: Margaret Spellings, Secretary

### National Education Association
1201 16th Street, NW
Washington, DC 20036-3290 USA
Phone: (202) 833-4000
Fax: (202) 822-7974
URL: http://www.nea.org
Primary Contact: Reg Weaver, President

### National School Boards Association
1680 Duke Street
Alexandria, VA 22314 USA
Phone: (703) 838-6722
Fax: (703) 683-7590
E-Mail: goac info@nsba.org

# EDUCATION

## SCHOOL PRAYER/PLEDGE OF ALLEGIANCE

*Sections within this essay:*

- Background
- School Prayer
  - Constitutional Basis for Ban
  - Types of Prayer Banned
  - Permissible Private Prayer and Secular Study of Religion
  - Permissible "Minute of Silence"
  - Congressional Action
- Limits on Pledge of Allegiance
- State and Local Laws
- Additional Resources

## Background

Prayer and the Pledge of Allegiance in public schools remain controversial legal issues. Since the mid-twentieth century, the federal courts have placed limits upon state power to require or even permit these popular cultural practices. Two land-mark Supreme Court decisions in the 1960s banned prayer in public school, and subsequent decisions have mostly strengthened the ban. By comparison, the courts generally have held since the 1940s that the Pledge of Allegiance is permissible, provided that it is voluntary. Nonetheless, some individuals have brought lawsuits in the 2000s, arguing that the Pledge violates the Establishment Clause of the First Amendment to the U.S. Constitution because the Pledge contains the phrase "under God."

Prayer was a common practice in colonial American schools, which were often merely offshoots of a local Protestant church. Along with Bible study, this tradition continued after U. S. independence and flourished well into the nineteenth century. But historical forces changed education. As **immigration** multiplied the ethnic and religious identities of Americans, modernization efforts led by education reformers like Horace Mann gradually minimized religious influences in schools. Although this secular reform swept cities, where diverse populations often disagreed on what religious practice to follow in schools, much of the United States retained school prayer.

As the twentieth century brought legal conflicts, the stage was set for even more far-reaching changes. From 1910 onward, lawsuits challenged mandatory Bible reading in public schools on the ground that students should not be forced to practice a faith other than their own. By the mid-century, social and religious tensions had pushed **litigation** through the federal courts. Subsequently, the Supreme Court ruled repeatedly that school prayer, Bible reading, and related religious practices are violations of the First Amendment. The decisions stand as critical modern mileposts in the contest between federalism and states' rights:

- The Supreme Court first ruled against public school prayer in the 1962 case of *Engle v. Vitale*. The decision struck down a New York State law that required public schools to begin the school day either with Bible reading or recitation of a specially-written, non-denominational prayer.

- One year later, in *District of Abington Township vs. Schempp* (1963), the Supreme Court struck down voluntary Bible readings and recitation of the Lord's Prayer in public schools.

- In 1980, in *Stone v. Graham*, the Supreme Court ruled against a Kentucky law that required the posting of the Ten Commandments in all public school classrooms.

- In 1981, the Supreme Court ruled in *Widmar v. Vincent* that a state university could not prohibit a religious group from using facilities that were made open for use by organizations of all other kinds. Congress responded three years later with the Equal Access Act, guaranteeing religious student groups the same rights of access to school facilities as other student groups.

- In the 1980s and 1990s, some states enacted so-called "moment of silence" or "minute of silence" laws with the intent of allowing students to conduct private prayer or spiritual reflection in the classroom. Although the Supreme Court found an early Alabama law unconstitutional in *Wallace v. Jaffrey* (1985), subsequent laws have generally survived legal challenges.

- In 1992, in *Lee v. Weisman*, the Supreme Court ruled that school officials violated the First Amendment by inviting clergy to give an invocation and a benediction at a public high school graduation.

- In *Santa Fe Independent School District v. Doe* (2000), the Supreme Court ruled against a Texas school district policy of facilitating prayers over the public address system at football games and holding popular elections to choose the student selected to deliver the prayer.

The Pledge of Allegiance is one of the nation's most honored secular symbols, viewed by many in the same light as the National Anthem. Written in 1892 by the socialist Francis Bellamy, the Pledge of Allegiance first appeared in a national family magazine, Youths' Companion, and later was modified by Congress and President Dwight D. Eisenhower in 1954 to include a reference to God. Many public schools featured the pledge as part of the school day throughout the mid-twentieth century.

Legal controversy in public schools grew out of a dispute over religious freedom. In the 1930s, West Virginia mandated compulsory saluting of the flag and recitation of the Pledge. After members of Jeho-

vah's Witnesses objected on religious grounds, students were expelled from school. The Supreme Court first upheld the state law but reversed itself three years later in *West Virginia State Board of Education v. Barnette* (1943). The Court held that schools may not coerce or force students into reciting the Pledge, observing the existence of an individual right of conscience to sit silently while others recited. Most schools responded by making the pledge voluntary.

Contemporary legal challenges to the Pledge have been sporadic, yet they are still passionate and often draw considerable interest from the press. High-profile cases in the late 1990s and 2000s involved lawsuits against schools that instituted mandatory requirements and punished students who did not comply. Interest in the issue intensified again in 2001 following terrorist attacks upon the United States, which prompted states and school districts to revive long-dormant laws requiring students to recite the pledge. The U.S. Supreme Court in 2004 agreed to review a case involving the question of whether the Pledge violates the Constitution, but the Court decided the case on procedural grounds and did not rule on the constitutionality of the Pledge.

## School Prayer

### Constitutional Basis for Ban

Since 1962, the Supreme Court's rejection of school prayer has rested upon its interpretation of the First Amendment. That interpretation has hardly varied, even in the face of public outrage, political opposition, and scholarly criticism. The court's decisions have remained largely consistent across several cases for four decades.

As one of the constitution's most powerful and sweeping guarantees of freedom, the First Amendment is generally thought to contain two contrasting principles with respect to religion. These are announced in the opening words of the amendment, which contains two clauses: "Congress shall make no law respecting an establishment of religion, or prohibiting the free exercise thereof." In constitutional law, the first clause is referred to as the Establishment Clause, and the second as the Free Exercise Clause.

Broadly general in their language, the two clauses say nothing more—and neither does the Constitution itself—about how to apply them. Thus their practical meaning is chiefly known through the ways courts interpret them in individual cases. Under the Establishment Clause, courts have generally held that government is forbidden to enact laws aiding any religion or creating an official religion. Under the Free Exercise Clause, courts have usually held that government is also forbidden to interfere with an individual's free exercise of religion, including the areas of belief, practice, and propagation.

Both principles require a position of government neutrality toward religion but of a different and seemingly contradictory kind. In practice, the two principles easily overlap. Advocates of school prayer have long argued that banning the practice is a violation of religious freedom guaranteed by the Free Exercise Clause. Opponents have argued that the rights to free exercise are outweighed by the prohibition laid out in the Establishment Clause. How the tension between these principles is resolved lies at the heart of the school prayer ban.

In school prayer cases, the Supreme Court has repeatedly given the Establishment Clause precedence. From the earliest case, *Engel v. Vitale*, the Court has held that public school prayer is "wholly inconsistent" with the Establishment Clause. The majority opinion went out of its way to stress that the Court did not oppose religion itself. Instead, the opinion stated that "each separate government in this country should stay out of the business of writing or sanctioning official prayers and leave that purely religious function to the people themselves and to those the people choose to look to for religious guidance."

### Types of Prayer Banned

To date, the Supreme Court has never sanctioned any form of prayer spoken aloud in classrooms under the direction of officials in public schools. In a variety of decisions, it has repeatedly held or affirmed lower court rulings that several types of prayer are unconstitutional:

- Voluntary

- Mandatory

- Sectarian, as in the Lord's Prayer

- Non-sectarian or non-denominational, as in the state-authored prayer at issue in *Engel v. Vitale*

- Teacher or student-led classroom prayer

- Invocations or benedictions

From the start, these decisions have shown no tolerance for attempts to tailor prayers to make them more acceptable to a majority of citizens. In fact, the very first prayer case arose after the State of New York commissioned the writing of an original 22 word prayer that it determined would cover a broad spectrum of religious belief; the prayer was approved by Protestant, Catholic, and Jewish leaders who stated their goal was to avoid causing sectarian disputes. Yet the Supreme Court ruled that the prayer's non-denominational nature gave it no constitutional protection.

On Establishment Clause grounds similar to the prayer ban, the Supreme Court has also struck down related activities and practices involving religious worship in schools:

- Religious invocations at graduation ceremonies

- Prayers read by religious representatives

- Student-led prayers at assemblies and sporting events

- Posting of the Ten Commandments in schools

### Permissible Private Prayer and Secular Study of Religion

Although the prayer ban has proven largely comprehensive, the Supreme Court has not banned religion from schools. Instead, it has held that context is critical in determining what is permissible and impermissible.

The Supreme Court has never banned students from praying voluntarily and privately on their own, provided there is no state intervention. Students simply must do so without the guidance or **coercion** of school authorities. Religious student groups may meet after school like other student clubs, as guaranteed by the federal Equal Access Act, and pray on their own.

Study of religion is also constitutionally permitted. Even in its earliest prayer cases, the Supreme Court noted that schools were free to discuss religion within the context of a secular course of instruction, such as, for instance, a history course.

Between 1971 and 1990 the Supreme Court used a three-part test to determine whether state programs involving religion were permitted under the Establishment Clause. Following the standard first announced in *Lemon v. Kurtzman* (1971), the Court upheld a challenged religious program if it met all three conditions:

- It has a secular purpose

- It has a primary effect that neither advances nor inhibits religion

- It does not excessively entangle government with religion

This test began losing validity in the 1990s as the Supreme Court refused to apply it. Shifts in the court's analytical approach did not signal a reversal on doctrine, however; in fact, in 1992, the majority upheld its original school prayer ruling of 30 years earlier, and subsequent decisions extended the ban to prayers at public school events. By 2001, the test for compliance with the Establishment Clause generally required that a school policy demonstrate a secular purpose that neither advances nor inhibits religion in its principal effect. Courts continued to carefully scrutinize such policies to see that they did not endorse, show favoritism toward, or promote religious ideas.

### Permissible "Minute of Silence"

During the 1980s, school prayer advocates were in search of new approaches that might prove constitutional. The so-called moment of silence has proven the most successful strategy, despite an early setback in which Alabama's requirement that school children be required to observe a moment of silence each day was held unconstitutional by the Supreme Court in *Wallace v. Jaffrey* (1985).

However, states subsequently crafted laws that did survive constitutional review. One example is Virginia's minute of silence law, which requires children to begin the school day with a minute to "meditate, pray or engage in silent activity." In July 2001, a panel of the 4th U. S. Circuit Court of Appeals upheld the constitutionality of the law, noting that it "introduced at most a minor and nonintrusive accommodation of religion" and, because it allowed any type of silent reflection, served both religious and secular interests. The U. S. Supreme Court declined to hear an appeal in the case, thus upholding Virginia's law. Legal observers predicted the law's success would lead to more such legislation in other states; as many as 18 states already permit moments of silence under law.

### Congressional Action

Responding to public demand for school prayer, federal lawmakers have occasionally sought a remedy of their own. Few advocates of school prayer believe legislation can survive **judicial review**. Thus, the chief proposal to enjoy perennial favor is the idea of a **constitutional amendment**.

Following the first 1962 prayer ruling, lawmakers flooded Congress with such proposals but never passed any. Attempts were revived over the decades, with the most serious coming in the late 1990s. But constitutional amendments face difficult legal hurdles. Even before a proposed amendment can be sent for a state-by-state vote on **ratification**, it must pass by a two-thirds majority in the House of Representatives. Historically, lawmakers are significantly reluctant to tamper with the Constitution. Thus in June 1998, House members voted 224 to 203 in favor of a school prayer amendment, but that simple majority fell far short of the two-thirds majority needed for approval.

Another Congressional effort has borne some success for school prayer advocates. In 1984, with strong backing from conservative religious groups, Congress passed and President Ronald Reagan signed the Equal Access Act. The law requires any federally-funded public secondary school to allow all school clubs, including religious organizations, equal access to facilities. As representatives of the state, teachers and officials are instructed not to encourage or solicit participation in these activities.

## Pledge of Allegiance

In *West Virginia State Board of Education v. Barnette* (1943), the Supreme Court ruled that requiring the Pledge of Allegiance in public schools violated the First and Fourteenth Amendments. The case grew out of West Virginia's passage of legislation requiring the pledge and flag-saluting. Lawmakers had intended them to be part of instruction on civics, history, and the Constitution, and they defined noncompliance as insubordination that was punishable by expulsion from school. Parents of expelled students were also subject to fines. After Jehovah's Witnesses students were expelled, their parents brought suit contending that the law infringed upon their religious beliefs, which they said required them not to engage in these secular practices.

The Supreme Court found two constitutional violations. The state law violated the Fourteenth Amendment's requirement of due process and the First Amendment's requirements of religious freedom and free speech upon the state. At heart, said the Court, were the principles of freedom of thought and government by consent. Critically, the majority observed a right of individuals to be free from official pressure to state a particular opinion, including that they honor their government. The opinion declared that "no official, high or petty, can prescribe what shall be orthodox in politics, nationalism, religion, or other matters of opinion or force citizens to confess by word or act their faith therein."

In the 1990s, the American Civil Liberties Union (ACLU) repeatedly defended students in school districts who suffered reprisals for failing to participate in the Pledge of Allegiance. In 1998, for instance, the ACLU filed a federal lawsuit against the Fallbrook Union High School District of San Diego, California, after school officials required a dissenting student to stand silently during the pledge, leave the classroom, or face detention; settling the case out of court, the school district agreed to change its policy.

A decision by a three-judge panel of the Ninth Circuit Court of Appeals in 2002 stirred the debate over whether the Pledge violates the Constitution. Michael A. Newdow, an avowed atheist, challenged a policy of the Elk Grove (California) Unified School District that required students to recite the Pledge. According to Newdow, because the Pledge includes the phrase "under God," the school's required recitation amounted to an unconstitutional endorsement of religion. The panel of the Ninth Circuit agreed with Newdow and held that the school district had violated the Constitution. The full panel of the Ninth Circuit allowed the decision to stand, but the school district appealed to the U.S. Supreme Court. In *Elk Grove Unified School District v. Newdow* (2004), the Court reversed the Ninth Circuit, but only because the Court determined that Newdow did not have standing to bring the case. Accordingly, the Court did not rule on the question of whether the Pledge violates the Establishment Clause.

In 2005, Newdow again challenged the constitutionality of the Pledge by bringing suit in a federal district court in California. The court followed the previous decision of the Ninth Circuit and determined that the Pledge indeed violated the Constitution. Commentators have continued to debate how the Supreme Court will likely rule should the Court agree to hear another appeal.

## State and Local Laws

Despite many Supreme Court rulings against public school prayer, the legal picture in states is far from uniform. In some states and cities, politicians and school officials have simply ignored the Court's prayer decisions. Some school districts continue to allow classroom prayer in the absence of any direct legal challenge. Still others invite litigation, seeing in each lawsuit an opportunity to press the judiciary to reconsider the four-decade-old ban. Thus while federal judicial decisions may say one thing, the practical reality is widely acknowledged to be another: ongoing litigation, for years, has been the norm, with school prayer lawsuits frequently seeing national legal organizations representing both sides in what originate as local disputes.

The situation for the Pledge of Allegiance in public schools is also mixed. Most states, in fact, still have decades-old laws relating to the pledge. The majority of states mention some form of school participation in their laws, while about 20 states require students to recite it. The final resolution of the case brought by Michael Newdow, however, may lead to more challenges.

During the 2000s, several plaintiffs challenged policies involving school prayer or the Pledge of Allegiance. A select listing of these challenges is as follows:

ALABAMA: A student at Parrish high School in Walker County, Alabama claimed that a teacher and the school principal violated the student's constitutional rights by punishing him for raising his fist during a daily recitation of the Pledge. The student also claimed that the teacher violated his rights by conducting a silent moment of prayer prior to class. A federal district court in Alabama dismissed the student's case, but the Eleventh Circuit Court of Appeals in 2004 reversed the district court and remanded the case for further consideration.

ARKANSAS: The Eighth Circuit Court of Appeals in 2004 ruled that the practice of the superintendent of the Devalls Bluff School District of opening teachers' meetings with a prayer violated the Establishment Clause.

DELAWARE: Parents of children enrolled in the Indian River School District challenged a practice by the district's school board of opening meetings with a prayer. A federal district court in Delaware in 2005 held that this practice was constitutional.

FLORIDA: Since the early 1990s, lawsuits have contested the policy of the Jacksonville public school board to allow prayer at graduation ceremonies. In 1998, students and parents in the Duval County Public School District successfully sued to block the practice. The full Eleventh Circuit Court of Appeals, however, declared that student-led prayers at graduation are constitutional. In 2000, the Supreme Court vacated the decision and sent it back to the appeals court for reconsideration. One year later, the Eleventh Circuit again decided that the practice did not violate the Constitution.

LOUISIANA: A student at the Tangipahoa Parish School District in 2005 challenged the practice of the local school board of opening its meetings with an invocation. The U.S. District Court for the Eastern District of Louisiana ruled that the practice violated the Establishment Clause.

NEBRASKA: A student in Madison County, Nebraska sued the local school district after a member of the district's school board recited the Lord's Prayer during a graduation ceremony. The Eighth Circuit Court of Appeals held that the practice did not violate the student's rights under the First Amendment.

PENNSYLVANIA: A Pennsylvania statute enacted in 2002 required students in all public, private, and parochial schools to recite the Pledge of Allegiance. A private school challenged the statute in federal court. The Third Circuit in 2004 ruled that the statute violated the school's right to freedom of expressive association.

TEXAS: A plaintiff sought a declaration in federal court in Texas that the Pledge of Allegiance is unconstitutional. The Fifth Circuit Court of Appeals in 2004 summarily dismissed the case.

VIRGINIA: In 2005, parents of children enrolled in the Loudoun County Public Schools challenged the Virginia Recitation Statute, which required the daily, but voluntary, recitation of the Pledge of Allegiance. The Fourth Circuit Court of Appeals determined that the statute did not violate the Constitution.

## Additional Resources

*A Call for Mandatory Pledge in Schools* Rein, Lisa, The Washington Post, January 25, 2001.

*Constitutional Amendments: 1789 to the Present* Gale Group, Inc., 2000.

*Does God Belong in Public Schools?* Greenawalt, Kent, Princeton University Press, 2005.

*School Prayer: A History of the Debate* Andryszewski, Tricia, Enslow Publishers, 1997.

*West's Encyclopedia of American Law* 2nd Edition, Thomson/Gale, 2004.

## Organizations

### American Civil Liberties Union (ACLU)
125 Broad Street, 18th Floor
New York, NY 10004 USA
Phone: (212) 549-2500
URL: http://www.aclu.org

### American Family Association
P.O. Box 2440
Tupelo, MS 38803 USA
Phone: (662) 844-5036
Fax: (662) 842-7798
URL: http://www.afa.net

### Americans United for Separation of Church and State
518 C Street, NE
Washington, DC 20002 USA
Phone: (202) 466-3234
Fax: (202) 466-2587
URL: http://www.au.org

### Eagle Forum
316 Pennsylvania Avenue, Ste. 203
Washington, DC 20003 USA
Phone: (202) 544-0353
Fax: (202) 547-6996
URL: http://www.eagleforum.org

# EDUCATION

## SPECIAL EDUCATION/DISABILITY ACCESS

*Sections within this essay:*

- Background

- Individuals with Disabilities Education Act
    - Free and Appropriate Public Education
    - State Educational Agencies
    - Local Educational Agencies
    - Individualized Education Programs
    - Parental Involvement

- Additional Legislation Protecting Children with Disabilities
    - Section 504 of the Rehabilitation Act of 1973
    - Americans with Disabilities Act

- Definition of Disability and Eligibility for Special Education Services

- Placement of Children with Disabilities

- Procedures for Alleging Violations of Statutes Protecting Disabled Children

- State Provisions Regarding Special Education and Disability Access

- Additional Resources

## Background

Students with mental and physical disabilities in the United States were historically segregated from other students in most educational systems. While special programs were modified to provide different types of training for disabled children, these children were ordinarily separated from the mainstream students, not only to protect the children in special education but also to avoid disruption among other students without disabilities. The majority of disabled children did not attend school at all.

The move toward the recognition of rights for disabled students began with the famous 1954 case, *Brown v. Board of Education*, which established that "separate but equal" accommodations in education were not, in fact, equal. As other **civil rights** movements gained momentum throughout the 1960s, proponents for rights of disabled individuals also began to assert the rights of these individuals. Two landmark federal district court decisions in 1971 and 1972, *PARC v. Pennsylvania* and *Mills v. Board of Education,* established that denying education to children with disabilities and denying the proper procedures in such cases violated protections under the Fourteenth Amendment to the United States Constitution. A number of other cases since then have further established rights of disabled children.

A number of federal statutes have formed the basis for guaranteeing rights of disabled children since the mid-1970s. The following is a summary of these statutes:

- Rehabilitation Act of 1973: This act established that those who receive federal financial assistance cannot discriminate on the basis of a **disability**.

- Education for All Handicapped Children Act (EAHCA): Passed in 1975, this act provided support to state special education programs to provide free appropriate public education to disabled children.

- Perkins Act: Passed in 1984, this act required that ten percent of federal funding for vocational education must support the education of disabled students.

- Handicapped Children's Protection Act of 1986: This act amended the EAHCA to provide attorney's fees and costs to be awarded to parents who prevailed in an EAHCA case.

- Education to the Handicapped Act Amendments of 1986: These acts added early intervention services for three- to five-year-olds, with incentive programs for younger children with disabilities.

- Individuals with Disabilities Education Act (IDEA): Passed in 1990, this act amended the EAHCA by modifying a number of the provisions in the original **statute**.

- Americans with Disabilities Act (ADA): Passed in 1990, this major piece of legislation set forth broad prohibitions against **discrimination** of disabled individuals by most employers, public agencies, and those who provide public accommodations. Two titles in the Act apply specifically to schools.

## Individuals with Disabilities Education Act

The Individuals with Disabilities Education Act (IDEA) is primarily a funding statute. It requires that each state educational authority develop a policy that ensures free appropriate public education is being provided to all children with disabilities by local agencies. The amount of funding is determined on a state-by-state basis by the number of disabled children between the ages of three and 21 who are receiving special education and/or other related services. At the center of IDEA is a requirement that a local educational agency develop on at least an annual basis an individualize education program for each disabled child. This plan states the current educational status of the child and sets forth goals and objectives for the child to meet. Room for parental consent or involvement is provided at each step in the child's education.

### Free and Appropriate Public Education

IDEA defines free appropriate public education as special education and related services that are provided at public expense, under public supervision and direction. Free appropriate public education

must also meet standards set forth by state educational agencies; must include appropriate education at the preschool, elementary, and secondary levels; and must be provided in conformity with individualized education programs required under IDEA.

### State Educational Agencies

IDEA shifts responsibility for ensuring that educational programs are in compliance with the provisions of IDEA to state education agencies. These agencies are required to promulgate a complaint procedure that provides the following services:

- Receive and resolve complaints against state or local education agencies

- Review appeals from decisions regarding a local education agency complaint

- Conduct independent on-site investigations

- Set forth a 60-day time limit to investigate and resolve complaints

- Allow time extensions only in exceptional circumstances

- Review relevant information and issue written decisions

- Provide an enforcement mechanism

### Local Educational Agencies

As the primary entity required to develop individualized educational programs for each disabled child in a particular locality, local educational agencies are at the center of the provision of IDEA. Residency of each child is the primary consideration for determining which local educational agency has responsibility for developing these educational programs. In some cases, determining the appropriate local agency can become difficult, particularly if the child's parents live in different districts. Many states have included provisions providing that the child's residency is that of the parent.

### Individualized Education Programs

Local educational agencies must include a number of components in each individualized education program for each disabled child in its district. Among these components are the following:

- Descriptions of each child's current educational status, which describes the disabled child's cognitive skills, linguistic ability, emotional behavior, social skills and behavior, and physical ability

- Details of "measurable annual goals, including benchmarks or short-term objectives" related to the specific needs of each child, according to the provisions in IDEA

- Description of the instructional setting or placement of each disabled child

- Details of developmental, corrective, and other services designed to facilitate placement in a regular class or designed to allow disabled children to benefit from special education

- Additional specific statements required by IDEA, which relate to each child's progress, needs, advancement, and goal.

### Parental Involvement

Parents are involved in each stage of the development of a child's individualized education program. Such participation in this process includes the following:

- Parents must approve each stage of the implementation of the individualized education program

- Parents participate in initial meetings and annual meetings reviewing the programs established for their children

- Parents and school districts must sign an individualized education program before each school year begins

- School districts must redevelop a new program for a disabled child at the request of a parent

- Parents are entitled to request a meeting at any time regarding the individualize education program

## Additional Legislation Protecting Children with Disabilities

### Section 504 of the Rehabilitation Act of 1973

Prior to the enactment of the American with Disabilities Act, the statute that provided the most comprehensive rights to disabled children other than IDEA was the Rehabilitation Act of 1973. This act forbids any entity that receives federal financial funding from discriminating on the basis of disability. The act protects all individuals with physical or mental impairments that substantially limit their major life activities and are regarded as having such impairments. Major life activities under this description include an individual's ability to care for himself or herself, per-

formance of manual tasks, walking, seeing, hearing, speaking, breathing, learning and working. If an entity, such as a school, violates the provisions of the Rehabilitation Act, the Department of Education will investigate. The most likely remedy for these violations is termination of federal financial assistance to the entity.

### Americans with Disabilities Act

The American with Disabilities Act (ADA), passed by Congress in 1990, provides many of the same protections for disabled children as the Rehabilitation Act of 1973. However, unlike the Rehabilitation Act, the prohibitions under the ADA are not limited to those that receive federal financial assistance. The ADA is applicable in other areas as well where the provisions of the Rehabilitation Act may not provide protection. This is particularly true with respect to architectural barriers to a building. Part II of the ADA, which is applicable to public schools, requires accessibility for the entire program. Part III, applicable to private schools, contains similar provisions.

### Definition of Disability and Eligibility for Special Education Services

All school districts in the United States are required by law to identify, locate, and evaluate children with disabilities. Once this has occurred, school districts have a duty to evaluate whether the children are eligible for special education and then begin to develop individualized education programs for them. IDEA and the corresponding regulations define "children with disabilities" as those suffering from at least one of the following conditions:

- Mental retardation

- Hearing impairment

- Speech or language impairment

- Visual impairment

- Serious emotional disturbance

- Orthopedic impairment

- Autism

- Traumatic brain injury

- Specific learning disability

- Other health impairments

These disabilities must have adverse effects on disabled children in order for the children to be eligible for special education and services. The definition of disability and the application of this definition is broader under other statutes. The Americans with Disabilities Act, for example, employs a three-part definition of "disability." For the ADA to apply to an individual, the individual's physical or mental impairment must substantially limit the individual's major life activities. This individual must also have a record of such an impairment and be generally regarded as having such an impairment. Physical impairment can include any physiological disorder or condition, cosmetic disfigurement, or anatomical loss affecting one or more of several major body systems, as defined by the statute. Mental impairment may include any mental or psychological disorder, such as mental retardation, organic brain syndrome, emotional or mental illness, and specific learning disabilities. Since the definition is broader under the ADA, a child with a disability may request accommodation under the ADA, but the same child may not be eligible for special education under the provisions of IDEA.

Like the ADA, the provisions of the Rehabilitation Act of 1973 regarding the definition of disability are broader than those of IDEA. For example, a child with Acquired Immune Deficiency Syndrome may not be eligible for special education under IDEA. However, the same child may not be discriminated against on the basis if his or her disease, since AIDS and other diseases are considered disabilities under the Rehabilitation Act.

## Placement of Children with Disabilities

Placement of children with disabilities under IDEA occurs after the development of an individualized education program, described above. Local agencies must take into account a variety of factors, many of which are described in relevant regulations concerning the implementation of IDEA. Such considerations include the child's performance on aptitude and achievement tests; parental input; recommendations from teachers; the physical condition of the child; the social and cultural background of the child; and the adaptive behavior of the child. If the local agency fails to provide appropriate placement, the child's parent(s) may place the child unilaterally and seek reimbursement from the agency.

Several requirements under IDEA apply to the placement of a child. Although placement should be as close to the child's home as possible, there is no absolute requirement that the school selected is the closest to the child's home. If the closest school would not provide what would be considered free appropriate public education, the agency may select a more suitable school, even if it is farther away. The placement must be in the least restrictive environment, which generally restricts the ability of a school to segregate children with special education needs. Only in cases where the disability is so severe that regular classroom attendance would not be appropriate can complete **segregation** occur. This provision is often referred to as a mainstreaming requirement.

The placement of a child must be reviewed annually. If placement is changed, an existing individualized education program must support it, since placement itself is based on the IEP. Parents must be notified under IDEA requirements, and several states require that parental consent must be obtained before a local agency can make a change in placement for a disabled child.

## Procedures for Alleging Violations of Statutes Protecting Disabled Children

Since IDEA is a funding statute, if a local agency fails to provide free appropriate public education to a disabled child, the remedy is that the agency loses its federal funding. Many parents of disabled children, however, seek judicial and other remedies when they feel the education being provided to their child is not sufficient. The initial body required under IDEA and other statutes to hear a complaint is the state education authority, which must hold an **impartial** hearing. Specific procedures that must be followed are set forth in IDEA regulations. Once the state education authority makes its decision, a parent may appeal to another state-level agency. Parents should consult their own state's laws to determine which is the appropriate agency for such an appeal.

Judicial bodies, including either a federal or a state court, may review administrative proceedings. Judicial action may not take place until the parties have exhausted each of their administrative remedies. The most typical remedy sought by parents in cases involving special education is injunctive or declaratory relief, although in some cases, monetary damages may be appropriate.

Complaints for **infringement** of the ADA in schools should be filed with the Department of Education. Once administrative remedies have been exhausted, parties may seek **judicial review**. Like the remedies under IDEA, most parents seek injunctive or declaratory relief, such as a court order requiring that a school provide the requested access.

## State Provisions Regarding Special Education and Disability Access

Special education and disability access have become controlled primarily by federal **statutory** schemes. This is true even though most educational regulation is governed by state statute. Under IDEA, if a state or local agency fails to provide the minimum provisions required by the statute, the state or local entity may lose federal funding. States may, however, provide greater protection than is afforded by the federal statutes.

Parents with disabled children should consult with the state educational agencies, as well as applicable state laws, to determine what rights their children may have in their particular state. The following is a listing of the appropriate agencies in each state.

ALABAMA: The primary state educational agency is the Special Education Services division of the Alabama State Department of Education.

ALASKA: The primary state educational agency is the Alaska Department of Education Special Education Programs.

ARKANSAS: The primary state educational agency is the Special Education Section of the Arkansas Department of Education.

CALIFORNIA: The primary state educational agency is the Special Education Division of the California Department of Education.

COLORADO: The primary state educational agency is the Special Education Services Unit of the Colorado Department of Education.

CONNECTICUT: The primary state educational agency is the Bureau of Special Education and Pupil Services of the Connecticut Department of Education.

DELAWARE: The primary state educational agency is the Exceptional Children Department of the Delaware Department of Education.

FLORIDA: The primary state educational agency is the Education for Exceptional Students Department of the Florida Department of Education.

GEORGIA: The primary state educational agency is the Division of Exceptional Students of the Georgia Department of Education.

HAWAII: The primary state educational agency is the Special Education Section of the Department of Education.

IDAHO: The primary state educational agency is the Bureau of Special Education of the Idaho State Department of Education.

ILLINOIS: The primary state educational agency is the Special Education Department of the Illinois State Board of Education.

INDIANA: The primary state educational agency is the Division of Special Education of the Department of Education.

IOWA: The primary state education agency is the Bureau of Children Family and Community Services of the Department of Education.

KANSAS: The primary state educational agency is the Student Support Services of the Kansas State Department of Education.

KENTUCKY: The primary state educational agency is the Office of Special Instructional Services of the Kentucky Department of Education.

LOUISIANA: The primary state educational agency is the Division of Special Populations of the Louisiana Department of Education.

MAINE: The primary state educational agency is the Special Education Department of the Maine Department of Education.

MARYLAND: The primary state educational agency is the Division of Special Education of the Maryland State Department of Education.

MASSACHUSETTS: The primary state educational agency is the Special Education Programs division of the Massachusetts State Department of Education.

MICHIGAN: The primary state educational agency is the Office of Special Education and Early Intervention Services.

MINNESOTA: The primary state educational agency is the Office of Special Education of the Minnesota Department of Children, Families, and Learning.

MISSISSIPPI: The primary state educational agency is the Office of Special Education of the Mississippi State Department of Education.

MISSOURI: The primary state educational agency is the Division of Special Education of the Missouri State Department of Education.

MONTANA: The primary state educational agency is the Special Education Division of the Montana Office of Public Instruction.

NEBRASKA: The primary state educational agency is the Special Populations Office of the Nebraska Department of Education.

NEVADA: The primary state educational agency is the Division of Special Education of the Nevada Department of Education.

NEW HAMPSHIRE: The primary state educational agency is the Bureau of Special Education of the New Hampshire Department of Education.

NEW JERSEY: The primary state educational agency is the Office of Specialized Populations of the New Jersey State Department of Education.

NEW MEXICO: The primary state educational agency is the Special Education Office of the State of Mexico Department of Education.

NEW YORK: The primary state educational agency is the Vocational and Educational Services for Individuals with Disabilities of the New York State Education Department.

NORTH CAROLINA: The primary state educational agency is the Special Education Division of the North Carolina Department of Public Instruction.

NORTH DAKOTA: The primary state educational agency is the Director of Special Education of the North Dakota Department of Public Instruction.

OHIO: The primary state educational agency is the Special Education Division of the Ohio Department of Education.

OKLAHOMA: The primary state educational agency is the Special Education Services Division of the Oklahoma State Department of Education.

OREGON: The primary state educational agency is the Office of Special Education of the Oregon Department of Education.

PENNSYLVANIA: The primary state educational agency is the Bureau of Special Education of the Pennsylvania Department of Education.

RHODE ISLAND: The primary state educational agency is the Office of Special Needs Services of the Rhode Island Department of Education.

SOUTH CAROLINA: The primary state educational agency is the Office of Special Education of the South Carolina Department of Education.

SOUTH DAKOTA: The primary state educational agency is the Office of Special Education of the Division of Education Resources and Services.

TENNESSEE: The primary state educational agency is the Division of Special Education of the Tennessee Department of Education.

TEXAS: The primary state educational agency is the Office for the Education of Special Populations of the Texas Education Agency.

UTAH: The primary state educational agency is the At Risk and Special Education Services division of the Utah State Office of Education.

VERMONT: The primary state educational agency is the Special Education Division of the Vermont Department of Education.

VIRGINIA: The primary state educational agency is the Division of Special Programs of the Virginia Department of Education.

WASHINGTON: The primary state educational agency is the Special Education Section of the Office of Superintendent of Public Instruction.

WEST VIRGINIA: The primary state educational agency is the Special Education Division of the West Virginia Department of Education.

WISCONSIN: The primary state educational agency is the Division for Learning Support, Equity and Advocacy of the Department of Public Instruction.

WYOMING: The primary state educational agency is the Special Education Programs Division of the Wyoming Department of Education.

## Additional Resources

*The Complete IEP Guide: How to Advocate for Your Special Ed Child* Siegel, Lawrence M., Nolo Press, 1999.

*Education Law* Rapp, James A., Lexis Publishing, 2001.

*Special Education Law* 2nd ed., Guernsey, Thomas F., and Kathe Klare, Carolina Academic Press, 2001.

*Special Education Law* 3rd ed., Rothstein, Laura F., Addison, Wesley, Longman, Inc., 2000.

*U. S. Code, Title 20: Education, Chapter 33, Education of Individuals with Disabilities,* U. S. House of Representatives, 1999. Available at http://uscode.house.gov/title_20.htm.

## Organizations

### *The Council for Exceptional Children (CEC)*
1110 North Glebe Road
Suite 300

Arlington, VA 22201-5704 USA
Phone: (703) 620-3660
Fax: (703) 264-9494

**MAX Foundation**
P.O. Box 22
Rockville Centre, NY 11571 USA
Phone: (516) 763-4787
E-Mail: Kaleipin@aol.com

**United States Department of Education**
Office of Special Education Programs, 330 "C" Street, S.W., Mary Switzer Building
Washington, DC 20202 USA
Phone: (202) 732-1007

**United States Department of Education**
Office for Civil Rights, 330 Independence Avenue, S.W.
Washington, DC 20201 USA
Phone: (202) 732-1213

# EDUCATION

## STUDENT RIGHTS/FREE SPEECH

*Sections within this essay:*

## Background

Sixty years ago, when the U. S. Supreme Court decided its first free speech case involving students and the public schools, the idea that students had any right to free speech would have been considered laughable at best, dangerous at worst. At that time, school was considered a privilege to attend, and rules or regulations the school sought to enforce were untouchable. This generalization was collectively true at the elementary, secondary and college levels of education.

Student rights to free speech did not really become an issue until the Vietnam War, when more

and more students found themselves at opposite ends of the political spectrum from their teachers and school administrators. The Supreme Court's 1969 decision in Tinker v. Des Moines Independent School District opened the floodgates to school free speech **litigation**, and while court decisions have certainly gone back and forth between the right to free speech and the need to impose discipline and respect the feelings of all students, there has never been any attempt to go back to the strict free speech restrictions of the pre-Vietnam War era.

Public school free speech rights for students can be divided into those applying to elementary and secondary students and those dealing with college issues. Since college students are adults, the First Amendment situations dealt with are substantially different. Analyzing student free speech rights in this way can give a cohesive picture of those rights for students today.

## Free Speech Rights in Public Schools

Free speech rights in public elementary and secondary schools have undergone a remarkable transformation in the past 30 years, from nonexistence to a perpetual tension between those rights and the need for schools to control student behavior in order to preserve the sanctity of the learning environment. Today, it would be most accurate to say that public schools students have some First Amendment rights in schools, but certainly not as many as adults do in the real world. Although Tinker v. Des Moines Independent School District was the landmark case that set forth the standards which current student free speech cases are judged, the first case that suggested students had some First Amendment rights was decided much earlier—during World War II, to be exact.

### West Virginia State Board of Education v. Barnette

This 1943 case marked the first time the Supreme Court ever conceded students had First Amendment rights. During World War II, the West Virginia State Board of Education passed a law requiring all students to salute the flag and recite the Pledge of Allegiance. Several students and their parents who were members of the Jehovah's Witnesses challenged the policy, arguing their religion prevented them from swearing allegiance to anyone but God, and so they could not recite the Pledge of Allegiance. The Supreme Court decided the students were in the right, and on First Amendment grounds struck down the West Virginia **ordinance** as violating the right of free expression.

" Educating the young for citizenship is reason for scrupulous protection of constitutional freedoms of the individual," said the Court, "if we are not to strangle the free mind at its source and teach youth to discount important principles of our government as mere platitudes." The Court determined that students had the right not to be coerced by school administrators to doing something that disagreed with their religious beliefs. Free speech in this case meant the right not to say something, in this case, the Pledge of Allegiance.

### Tinker v. Des Moines Independent Community School District

After Barnette, the student First Amendment rights front was quiet in the courts, until the case of *Tinker v. Des Moines Independent Community School District* in 1969 shattered the peace and made sure there would be controversy for a long time to come. The Vietnam War was raging full force when the students at a Des Moines, Iowa, high school decided to wear black armbands to school one day to protest what they saw as an unjust struggle. The school administrators learned of their plan and passed a rule banning black armbands from the school and suspending any student caught wearing one. The students wore the armbands anyway, and as a result were suspended. They sued the school district.

In writing in favor of the students for the majority, Justice Abe Fortas wrote these iconic words: "It can hardly be argued that either students or teachers shed their constitutional rights to **freedom of speech** or expression at the schoolhouse gate...

School officials do not possess absolute authority over their students. Students in school as well as out of school are 'persons' under our Constitution. They are possessed of fundamental rights which the State must respect... In the absence of specific showing of constitutionally valid reasons to regulate their speech, students are entitled to freedom of expression of their views."

But Fortas added an important **caveat**: conduct that "materially disrupts classwork or involves substantial disorder or invasion of the rights of others is, of course, not immunized by the constitutional guarantee of freedom of speech." In other words, not all student conduct is First Amendment protected, only that which does not disturb the classroom environment or invade the rights of others. This standard, also known as the "material and substantial disruption test," has basically remained the standard in which the school's right to prescribe free speech is examined at the secondary rank as well as at public colleges and universities.

After *Tinker,* a host of cases were brought at the lower court level litigating public school free speech issues. Many of these came down on the side of freedom of expression for students. Many lower courts found themselves asking, after Tinker, what student speech can in fact be regulated.

### Bethel School District No. 403 v. Fraser

The Supreme Court finally attempted to set some limits on student First Amendment rights in the 1986 case of *Bethel School District No. 403 v. Fraser.* Matthew Fraser made a speech at an assembly full of obscenities and innuendoes. When school officials attempted to discipline him for his speech, he sued. The Supreme Court sided with the school.

The Court found that Fraser had failed the "substantial disorder" part of the Tinker test. **Chief Justice** Warren Berger, writing for the majority, said that schools have a responsibility to instill students with "habits and manners of civility as values." The effect of Fraser's speech, suggested Berger, was to undermine this responsibility; therefore, he did not receive First Amendment protection for it. Not only can schools take into account whether speech is offensive to other students, said Berger, "the undoubted freedom to advocate unpopular and controversial views in schools and classrooms must be balanced against the society's countervailing interest in teaching students the **boundaries** of socially appropriate behavior." Bethel served notice that the Supreme Court saw limitations on student free speech rights.

The next big school First Amendment case decided by the court served to emphasize that point.

### Hazelwood School District v. Kuhlmeier

The school newspaper at Hazelwood East High School in Missouri was courting controversy when it decided to publish an article on pregnancy among students naming names, as well as an article on students of divorced parents. The principal of the school censored both articles from the school paper. The student editors of the newspaper sued.

In 1988, the Supreme Court handed down its decision: a complete defeat for the students. The majority of the court claimed Tinker did not apply to this case, since the school newspaper was a school-sponsored activity. According to the Court, when an activity is school sponsored, school officials may censor speech as long as such **censorship** is reasonably related to legitimate educational concerns. The Court went on to define these concerns broadly, stating that school officials would have the right to censor material that is "ungrammatical, poorly written, inadequately researched, biased or prejudiced, vulgar or profane, or unsuitable for immature audiences, or inconsistent with shared values of a civilized social order."

Hazelwood did distinguish between school-sponsored publications and other activities, and publications and activities that were not school sponsored, which the Court suggested would be given greater free-speech leeway. Nevertheless, the Hazelwood decision was clearly a defeat for student free speech rights. School officials were now allowed to censor school newspapers, as well as other school sponsored activities such as theatrical productions, in "any reasonable manner."

### Elementary and Secondary Student Rights Since Hazelwood

Since Hazelwood, the Supreme Court has not tackled a non-religious free speech issue involving a public elementary or high school. Lower courts that have dealt with these issues have tended to follow Hazelwood's ruling pretty closely: a if a free speech case involves a school sponsored activity, school officials are given wide latitude. Since all but a few student free speech cases involve a school-sponsored activity, the effect has been that most free speech cases have gone against students, with some minor exceptions.

Lower courts have also determined that school officials have broad discretion at the elementary school

level in controlling student speech, ruling in several cases that Tinker does not apply. However, most legal commentators believe that despite these developments, Tinker still remains in force, at least for high school students. School administrators are still required to show "material and substantial disruption" before limiting student speech in non-school sponsored activities.

## Higher Education Free Speech Issues

Institutions of higher education have generally been held to have less control over student free speech rights than elementary and high school teachers and administrators. In part, this position reflects the fact that college students are adults. However, there have still been areas of controversy in post-secondary student free speech rights, generally having to do with funding issues. The latest area of controversy has been with so-called "hate codes," which ban certain types of speech considered offensive from college campuses.

### Recognizing Student Groups

One way in which colleges and universities have traditionally imposed free speech restrictions on students is by determining which student groups they will recognize. Such recognition traditionally allows these groups to share in mandatory fees and receive space for offices and to hold meetings on college campuses. Generally speaking, colleges are held to have made available a "limited public forum" to such groups, and as such are limited in the restrictions they can impose.

In the 1973 case of Healy v. James, the Supreme Court established that a college or university could not refuse to recognize an organization simply because university officials had an unproven fear of school disruption. Healy applied the material and substantial disruption test of Tinker to the college environment and found that unless the school had a compelling reason to believe that a group, in this case, Students for a Democratic Society, would seriously interfere with learning on the campus environment, it could not deny recognition.

In 1981, the Court went further in the case of Widmar v. Vincent. Involving the decision by the University of Missouri to refuse to recognize and grant access to university property to a religious group, the Court ruled that the University's decision to do so, while allowing access to several secular based groups, violated the First Amendment. The Court's decision in Widmar effectively meant that any decision by a college to deny recognition to a particular group was going to be analyzed with strict scrutiny and most likely struck down.

While none of these cases has reached the Supreme Court, one of the most litigated issues of the past thirty years involving recognition of student groups has involved recognition of homosexual groups. Generally speaking, nearly all attempts by colleges to refuse to recognize gay groups have been held to violate these groups First Amendment rights.

### Mandatory Student Fees

Mandatory student fees constitute another area in which colleges and universities have faced free speech issues. These fees are generally collected by colleges as part of student tuition, and then distributed to a wide variety of groups.

Colleges usually do not impose restrictions in terms of ideology on which groups receive these fees, but they have in the past denied funding to groups promoting a religious viewpoint. However, in 1995 in *Rosenberger v. Rector of the University of Virginia,* the Supreme Court struck down these restrictions at the University of Virginia and ruled the University could not silence the expression of selected viewpoints by denying the groups student fee money. The *Rosenberger* decision stated colleges have to be rigidly neutral in distributing student fee money and cannot discriminate on the basis of content or viewpoint without violating the First Amendment.

A related issue concerning mandatory student fees has been whether it violates a student's First Amendment rights to be forced to pay fees that fund groups with which the student disagrees. In 2000, in the case of Board of Regents v. Southworth, the Supreme Court determined that it does not, as long as the money is distributed in a viewpoint neutral fashion, and does not favor one viewpoint over another.

### Hate Speech Codes

The most recent free-speech issue to hit college campuses involves so-called hate speech codes. These are codes passed by colleges that restrict speech considered offensive to other groups on campus, particularly speech that is believed to be racist or sexist.

While a case involving these hate speech codes has not yet reached the Supreme Court, lower courts have been undecided about allowing them to stand.

For example, in *Doe v. University of Michigan,* in 1993, the United States Court for the Eastern District of Michigan struck down a policy passed by the University of Michigan regulating hate speech. The court found the policy overbroad and unconstitutionally vague. The university could not regulate speech "because it disagreed with the ideas or the messages sought to be conveyed," said the court, "nor because the speech was found to be offensive, even gravely so, by large numbers of people." Added the court: "These principles acquire a special significance in the university setting, where the free and unfettered interplay of competing views is essential to the institution's educational mission." This has been the fate of speech codes that have been litigated, and as of this writing, not one has passed muster at the federal court level.

## Additional Resources

*"The First Amendment and Higher Education Students: Part I: The Religion Cases,"* Zirkel, Perry, West Education Law Reporter, December, 1999.

*"The First Amendment and Higher Education Students: Part II: The Secular Cases,"* Zirkel, Perry, West Education Law Reporter, April 2000.

*"How Free is the Speech of Public School Students?"* Rohr, Marc, Florida Bar Journal, June 2000.

*"Injustice In Our Schools: Students' Free Speech Rights are not Being Vigilantly Protected"* Lloyd, Heather K., Northern Illinois University Law Review, Spring, 2001.

*The Law of Schools, Students and Teachers* Alexander, Kern, M. David Alexander, West Group, 1995.

*"What's Next for Wayne Dick? The Next Phase of the Debate Over College Hate Speech Codes"* Ohio State Law Journal, 2000.

## Organizations

### Coalition For Student And Academic Rights (COSTAR)
Post Office Box 491
Solebury, PA 18963 USA
Phone: (215) 862-9096
Fax: (215) 862-9097
URL: http://www.co-star.org/index.html

### Freedom Forum First Amendment Center
1207 18th Ave. South
Nashville, TN 37212 USA
Phone: (615) 727-1600
Fax: (615) 727-1319

E-Mail: info@fac.org
URL: http://www.freedomforum.org/first/default.asp
Primary Contact: Kenneth Paulson, Executive
Director

**_Student Press Law Center (SPLC)_**
1815 N Fort Myer Drive, Suite 900

Arlington, VA 22209-1817 USA
Phone: (703) 807-1904
URL: http://splc.org/
Primary Contact: Mark Goodman, Executive
Director

# EDUCATION

## TEACHERS' RIGHTS

*Sections within this essay:*

## Background

Teachers in the United States enjoy a number of rights pertaining to their employment, including recognition of certain freedoms, prohibition against certain forms of **discrimination**, and significant protections against **dismissal** from their position. These rights are derived from state and federal constitutional provisions, state and federal statutes, and state and federal regulations.

Constitutional provisions provide protection to teachers at public schools that are generally not available to teachers at private schools. Since public schools are state entities, constitutional restrictions on state action limit some actions that public schools may take with respect to teachers or other employees. Rights that are constitutional in nature include the following:

- Substantive and procedural due process rights, including the right of a teacher to receive notice of termination and a right to a **hearing** in certain circumstances

- Freedom of expression and association provided by the First Amendment of the **Bill of Rights**

- Academic freedom, a limited concept recognized by courts based on principles of the First Amendment

- Protection against unreasonable searches and seizures by school officials of a teacher's **personal property** provided by the Fourth Amendment

Though private school teachers do not generally enjoy as much of the constitutional protection as public school teachers, statutes may provide protection against discrimination. The **Civil Rights** Act of 1964, for example, protects teachers at both public and private schools from racial, sexual, or religious discrimination. Private school teachers may also enjoy rights in their contracts that are similar to due process rights, including the inability of a private school to dismiss the teacher without cause, notice, or a hearing.

## Teacher Certification

### Certification Requirements

Every state requires that teachers complete certain requirements to earn a teacher's certificate in order to teach in that state. Most states extend this requirement to private schools, though some jurisdictions may waive this for certain sectarian or denominational schools. The requirements that must be satisfied and the procedures that must be followed to earn certification vary from state to state. Requirements generally include completion of a certified education program, completion of a student teaching program, acceptable performance on a standardized test or tests, and submission of background information to the appropriate state agency in charge of accreditation. Some states require more extensive physical and mental testing of teachers and a more extensive background check. Some states also require drug testing of applicants prior to certification. An increasing number of states now require teachers to complete a satisfactory number of continuing education credits to maintain certification.

### Denial or Revocation of Teaching Certificate

Courts have held consistently that teaching certificates are not contracts. Thus, requirements to attain or maintain a certificate may be changed and applied to all teachers and prospective teachers. The certification process is administered by state certifying agencies in each state, and most of these agencies have been delegated significant authority with respect to the administration of these rules. Despite this broad delegation, however, the state agencies may not act arbitrarily, nor may these agencies deny or revoke certification on an arbitrary basis. Some state statutes provide that a certificate may be revoked for "just cause." Other common **statutory** grounds include the following:

- Immoral conduct or indecent behavior

- **Incompetency**

- Violations of ethical standards

- Unprofessional conduct

- Misrepresentation or **fraud**

- Willful neglect of duty

## Tenure and Dismissal of Teachers

### Tenure

Most states protect teachers in public schools from arbitrary dismissal through tenure statutes. Under these tenure statutes, once a teacher has attained tenure, his or her contract renews automatically each year. School districts may dismiss tenured teachers only by a showing of cause, after following such procedural requirements as providing notice to the teacher, specifying the charges against the teacher, and providing the teacher with a meaningful hearing. Most tenure statutes require teachers to remain employed during a probationary period for a certain number of years. Once this probationary period has ended, teachers in some states will earn tenure automatically. In other states, the local school board must take some action to grant tenure to the teacher, often at the conclusion of a review of the teacher's performance. Tenure also provides some protection for teachers against demotion, salary reductions, and other discipline. However, tenure does not guarantee that a teacher may retain a particular position, such as a coaching position, nor does it provide indefinite employment.

Prior to attaining tenure, a probationary teacher may be dismissed at the discretion of the school district, subject to contractual and constitutional restrictions. Laws other than those governing tenure will apply to determine whether a discharge of a teacher is wrongful. If a probationary teacher's dismissal does not involve discrimination or does not violate terms of the teacher's contract, the school district most likely does not need to provide notice, summary of charges, or a hearing to the teacher.

In the absence of a state tenure **statute**, a teacher may still attain de facto tenure rights if the customs or circumstances of employment demonstrate that a teacher has a "legitimate claim of entitlement for job tenure." The United States Supreme Court recognized this right in the case of *Perry v. Sindermann*, which also held that where a teacher has attained de facto tenure, the teacher is entitled to due process prior to dismissal by the school district.

State laws do not govern the tenure process at private schools. However, a contract between a private school district and a teacher may provide tenure rights, though enforcement of these rights is related to the contract rights rather than rights granted through the state tenure statute.

### Dismissal for Cause

A school must show cause in order to dismiss a teacher who has attained tenure status. Some state statutes provide a list of circumstances where a school may dismiss a teacher. These circumstances are similar to those in which a state agency may revoke a teacher's certification. Some causes for dismissal include the following:

- Immoral conduct
- Incompetence
- Neglect of duty
- Substantial noncompliance with school laws
- **Conviction** of a crime
- Insubordination
- Fraud or misrepresentation

### Due Process Rights of Teachers

The Due Process Clause of the Fourteenth Amendment, like its counterpart in the Fifth Amendment, provides that no state may "deprive any person of life, liberty, or property, without due process of law." This clause applies to public school districts and provides the minimum procedural requirements that each public school district must satisfy when dismissing a teacher who has attained tenure. Note that in this context, due process does not prescribe the reasons why a teacher may be dismissed, but rather it prescribes the procedures a school must follow to dismiss a teacher. Note also that many state statutory provisions for dismissing a teacher actually exceed the minimum requirements under the Due Process Clause.

The United States Supreme Court case of *Cleveland Board of Education v. Loudermill* is the leading case involving the question of what process is due under the Constitution. This case provides that a tenured teacher must be given oral or written notice of the dismissal and the charges against him or her, an explanation of the **evidence** obtained by the employer, and an opportunity for a fair and meaningful hearing.

## Teacher Contracts

The law of contracts applies to contracts between teachers and school districts. This law includes the concepts of offer, acceptance, mutual **assent**, and consideration. For a teacher to determine whether a contract exists, he or she should consult authority on the general law of contracts. This section focuses on contract laws specific to teaching and education.

### Ratification of Contracts by School Districts

Even if a school official offers a teacher a job and the teacher accepts this offer, many state laws require that the school board ratify the contract before it becomes binding. Thus, even if a principal of a school district informs a prospective teacher that the teacher has been hired, the contract is not final until the school district accepts or ratifies the contract. The same is true if a school district fails to follow proper procedures when determining whether to ratify a contract.

### Teacher's Handbook as a Contract

Some teachers have argued successfully that provisions in a teacher's handbook granted the teacher certain contractual rights. However, this is not common, as many employee handbooks include clauses stating that the handbook is not a contract. For a provision in a handbook to be legally binding, the teacher must demonstrate that the actions of the teacher and the school district were such that the elements for creating a contract were met.

### Breach of Teacher Contract

Either a teacher or a school district can breach a contract. Whether a breach has occurred depends on the facts of the case and the terms of the contract. Breach of contract cases between teachers and school districts arise because a school district has terminated the employment of a teacher, even though the teacher has not violated any of the terms of the employment agreement. In several of these cases, a teacher has taken a leave of absence, which did not violate the employment agreement, and the school district terminated the teacher due to the leave of absence. Similarly, a teacher may breach a contract by resigning from the district before the end of the contract term (usually the end of the school year).

### Remedies for Breach of Contract

The usual remedy for breach of contract between a school district and a teacher is monetary damages. If a school district has breached a contract, the teacher will usually receive the amount the teacher would have received under the contract, less the amount the teacher receives (or could receive) by attaining alternative employment. Other damages, such as the cost to the teacher in finding other employment, may also be available. Non-monetary remedies, such as a court requiring a school district to rehire a teacher or to comply with contract terms, are available in some circumstances, though courts are usually hesitant to order such remedies. If a teacher breaches a contract, damages may be the cost to the school district for finding a replacement. Many contracts contain provisions prescribing the amount of damages a teacher must pay if he or she terminates employment before the end of the contract.

### Collective Bargaining by Teachers

Teachers' contractual rights often arise through **collective bargaining** through teachers' unions. For more information regarding collective bargaining by teachers, see Education: Teacher's Unions/Collective Bargaining.

## Teacher Freedoms and Rights

### Freedom from Discrimination

The **Equal Protection** Clause of the Fourteenth Amendment of the Constitution protects teachers at public schools from discrimination based on race, sex, and national origin. These forms of discrimination are also barred through the enactment of Title VII of the Civil Rights Act of 1964, which was amended in 1972 to include educational institutions. This law provides that it is an unlawful employment practice for any employer to discriminate against an individual based on the race, color, religion, sex, or national origin of the individual. Title IX of the Education Amendments of 1972 provides protection against discrimination based on sex at educational institutions that receive federal financial assistance. Title VII and IX also prohibit **sexual harassment** in the workplace.

A teacher who has been subjected to discrimination has several causes of action, though proof in some of these cases may be difficult. A teacher may bring a cause of action under section 1983 of Title 42 of the United States Code for deprivation of rights under the Equal Protection Clause (or other constitutional provision). However, to succeed under this cause of action, the teacher would need to prove that the school had the deliberate intent to discriminate. Similarly, a teacher bringing a claim under Title VII must demonstrate that the reasons given by a school for an employment decision were false and that the actual reason for the decision was discrimination.

### Academic Freedom

Teachers in public schools have limited freedoms in the classroom to teach without undue restrictions on the content or subjects for discussion. These freedoms are based on rights to freedom of expression under the First Amendment of the Bill of Rights. However, the concept of academic freedom is quite limited. The content taught by a teacher must be relevant to and consistent with the teacher's responsibilities, and a teacher cannot promote a personal or political agenda in the classroom. Factors such as the age, experience, and grade level of students affect the latitude in which a court will recognize the academic freedom of a teacher.

### Freedom of Expression

A leading case in First Amendment **jurisprudence** regarding protected forms of expression is *Pickering v. Board of Education.* This case involved a teacher whose job was terminated when he wrote to a local newspaper an editorial critical of the teacher's employer. The Supreme Court held that the school had unconstitutionally restricted the First Amendment rights of the teacher to speak on issues of public importance. Based on Pickering and similar cases, teachers generally enjoy rights to freedom of expression, though there are some restrictions. Teachers may not materially disrupt the educational interest of the school district, nor may teachers undermine authority or adversely affect working relationships at the school.

### Freedom of Association

Similar to rights to freedom of expression, public school teachers enjoy rights to freedom of association, based on the First Amendment's provision that grants citizens the right to peaceful assembly. These rights generally permit public school teachers to join professional, labor, or similar organizations; run for public office; and similar forms of association. However, teachers may be required to ensure that participation in these activities is completely independent from their responsibilities to the school.

### Freedom of Religion

The First Amendment and Title VII of the Civil Rights Act of 1964 provide protection against religious discrimination by school districts against teachers. Teaches may exercise their religious rights, though there are certain restrictions to such rights. This existence of restrictions is particularly relevant to the public schools, since public schools are restricted from teaching religion through the Establishment Clause of the First Amendment. Thus, for example, a teacher is free to be a practicing Christian, yet the teacher cannot preach Christianity in the classroom.

### Privacy Rights

Teachers enjoy limited rights to personal privacy, though courts will often support disciplinary action taken by a school district when a teacher's private life affects the integrity of the school district or the effectiveness by which a teacher can teach. Thus, for example, a teacher may be terminated from his or her position for such acts as **adultery** or other sexual conduct outside marriage, and courts will be hesitant to overrule the decisions of the school board.

### Age

The Age Discrimination in Employment Act of 1967, with its subsequent amendments, provides protection for teachers over the age of 40 against age discrimination. Under this act, age may not be the sole factor when a school district terminates the employment of a teacher. If a teacher charges a school district with age discrimination, the school district has the burden to show that some factor other than age influenced its decision.

### Pregnancy

The Pregnancy Discrimination Act of 1978 provides protection for teachers who are pregnant. Under this act, a school district may not dismiss or demote a pregnant teacher on the basis of her pregnancy, nor may a district deny a job or deny a promotion to a pregnant teacher on the basis of her pregnancy.

## State and Local Laws Regarding Teachers' Rights

Each state provides laws governing education agencies, hiring and termination of teachers, tenure of teachers, and similar laws. Teachers should consult with statutes and education regulations in their respective states, as well as the education agencies that enforce these rules, for additional information regarding teachers' rights. Moreover, teachers should review their contracts, **collective bargaining agreement**, and/or employee handbook for specific provisions that may have been included in an agreement.

The information below summarizes the grounds on which a state may revoke or suspend a teaching certificate or on which a district may dismiss or suspend a teacher.

ALABAMA: Teacher's certificate may be revoked for immoral conduct, or unbecoming or indecent behavior. Teachers may be dismissed or suspended on similar grounds, except that tenured teachers may not be suspended or terminated on political grounds.

ALASKA: Teacher's certificate may be revoked or suspended for incompetency, immorality, substantial noncompliance with school laws or regulations, violations of ethical or professional standards, or violations of contractual obligations. Teachers may be dismissed or suspended by local school boards on similar grounds.

ARIZONA: Teacher's certificate may be revoked or suspended for immoral or unprofessional conduct, evidence of unfitness to teach, failure to comply with various statutory requirements, failure to comply with student disciplinary procedures, teaching sectarian books or doctrine, or conducting religious exercises. Teachers may be dismissed or suspended on similar grounds. Probationary employees may be dismissed when they are unsuited or not qualified. Permanent employees may be discharged only for cause, and are entitled to due process.

ARKANSAS: Teacher's certificate may be revoked for cause. Teachers may be dismissed for any cause that is not arbitrary, capricious, or discriminatory.

CALIFORNIA: Permanent teachers may be dismissed for immoral or unprofessional conduct, dishonesty, incompetency, evident unfitness for service, a physical or mental condition unfitting for a teacher to instruct or associate with children, persistent violation of school laws or regulations, conviction of a **felony** or crime involving moral turpitude, or alcoholism or drug abuse rendering teacher unfit for service. Teacher's certificate may be revoked or suspended on the same grounds as those for dismissal or suspension.

COLORADO: Teacher's certificate may be annulled, revoked, or suspended if certificate has been obtained through fraud or misrepresentation; teacher is mentally incompetent; teacher violates statutes or regulations regarding unlawful sexual behavior, use of controlled substances, or other violations. Teachers may be dismissed on similar grounds.

CONNECTICUT: Teacher's certificate may be revoked if certificate has been obtained through fraud or misrepresentation; teacher has neglected duties or been convicted of a crime involving moral turpitude; teacher has been neglectful of duties; or other due and sufficient cause exists. Teachers may be dismissed on similar grounds.

DELAWARE: Teacher's certificate may be revoked for immorality, misconduct in office, incompetency, willful neglect of duty, or disloyalty. Teachers may be dismissed or suspended on similar grounds.

FLORIDA: Teacher's certificate may be revoked or suspended for obtaining certificate by fraud, incompetence, gross immorality or an act involving moral turpitude, revocation of a teaching certificate in another state, conviction of a crime other than a minor traffic violation, breach of teaching contract, or delinquency in **child support** obligations. Teachers may be dismissed or suspended on similar grounds.

GEORGIA: Teachers may be dismissed for incompetency, insubordination, willful neglect of duties, immorality, encouraging students to violate the law, failure to secure and maintain necessary educational training, and any other good and sufficient cause.

HAWAII: Teacher's certificate may be revoked for conviction of crime other than traffic offense or if the employer finds that teacher poses a risk to the health, safety, or well being of children. Teacher may be dismissed for inefficiency, immorality, willful violations of policies and regulations, or other good and **just cause**.

IDAHO: Teacher's certificate may be revoked for gross neglect of duty, incompetence, breach of contract, making a false statement on application for certificate, conviction of a crime involving moral turpitude or drugs or a felony offense involving children. Grounds for revocation of a teacher's certificate are also grounds for dismissal.

ILLINOIS: Teacher's certificate may be revoked or suspended for immorality, health condition detrimental to students, incompetence, unprofessional conduct, neglect of duty, willful failure to report **child abuse**, conviction of certain sex or narcotics offenses, or other just cause. Teachers may be dismissed on similar grounds.

INDIANA: Teacher's certificate may be revoked for immorality, misconduct in office, incompetency, willful neglect of duty, or improper cancellation of a contract. Permanent and semi-permanent teachers may be dismissed on similar grounds.

IOWA: Teacher's certificate may be revoked for any cause that would have permitted refusal to grant the certificate. Teachers may be dismissed for just cause.

KANSAS: Teacher's certificate may be revoked for immorality, gross neglect of duty, annulling a written

contract, or any other cause that would have justified refusal to grant the certificate.

KENTUCKY: Teacher's certificate may be revoked for immorality, misconduct in office, incompetency, willful neglect of duty, or submission of false information. Teachers may be dismissed or suspended on similar grounds.

LOUISIANA: Permanent teachers may be dismissed for incompetence, dishonest, willful neglect of duty, or membership or contribution to an unlawful organization.

MAINE: Teacher's certificate may be revoked for evidence of child abuse, gross incompetence, or fraud. Teachers may be dismissed on similar grounds.

MARYLAND: Teachers may be dismissed or suspended for immorality, misconduct in office, insubordination, incompetency, or willful neglect of duty.

MASSACHSETTS: Teacher's certificate may be revoked for cause. Teachers may be dismissed for inefficiency, incapacity, conduct unbecoming of a teacher, insubordination, failure to satisfy teacher performance standards, or other just cause.

MICHIGAN: Teacher's certificate may be revoked or suspended for conviction of **sex offenses** and crimes involving children. Teachers may be dismissed for reasonable and just causes or failure to comply with school law.

MINNESOTA: Teacher's certificate may be revoked or suspended for immoral character or conduct, failure to teach the term of a contract without just cause, gross inefficiency, willful neglect of duty, failure to meet requirements for licensing, or fraud or misrepresentation in obtaining a license. Teachers may be dismissed on similar grounds.

MISSISSIPPI: Teachers may be dismissed or suspended for incompetency, neglect of duty, immoral conduct, intemperance, brutal treatment of a pupil, or other good cause.

MISSOURI: Teacher's certificate may be revoked or suspended for incompetency, cruelty, immorality, **drunkenness**, neglect of duty, annulling a written contract without consent from the local board, or conviction of a crime involving moral turpitude. Teachers may be dismissed on similar grounds.

MONTANA: Teacher's certificate may be revoked or suspended for false statements on an application for the certificate, any reason that would have disqualified the person from receiving a certificate, incompetency, gross neglect of duty, conviction of a crime involving moral turpitude, or nonperformance of an employment contract. Teachers may be dismissed on similar grounds.

NEBRASKA: Teacher's certificate may be revoked for just cause, including incompetence immorality, intemperance, cruelty, certain crimes, neglect of duty, unprofessional conduct, physical or mental incapacity, or breach of contract. Teachers may be dismissed for just cause, as defined by statute.

NEVADA: Teacher's certificate may be revoked for immoral or unprofessional conduct, unfitness for service, physical or mental incapacity, conviction of a crime involving moral turpitude or sex offenses, advocacy of the overthrow of the government, persistent refusal to obey rules, or breach of a teaching contracts. Teachers may be dismissed or suspended on similar grounds.

NEW HAMPSHIRE: Teachers may be dismissed for immorality, incompetence, failure to conform to regulations, or conviction of certain crimes.

NEW JERSEY: Teacher's certificate may be revoked if teacher is a noncitizen; certificate may be suspended if teacher breaches contract. Teachers may be dismissed on similar grounds.

NEW MEXICO: Teacher's certificate may be revoked or suspended for incompetency, immorality, or any other good and just cause. Teachers may be dismissed for good cause.

NEW YORK: Teacher's certificate may be revoked if teacher is unfit to teach due to moral character or if teacher fails to complete a school term without good cause. Teachers may be dismissed on similar grounds.

NORTH CAROLINA: Teachers may be dismissed for inadequate performance, immorality, insubordination, neglect of duty, physical or mental incapacity, **habitual** or excessive use of alcohol or other controlled substances, or conviction of a crime involving moral turpitude.

NORTH DAKOTA: Teacher's certificate may be revoked or suspended for any cause that would permit refusal to issue the certificate, incompetency, immorality, intemperance, cruelty, commission of a crime, refusal to perform duties, violation of professional codes, breach of teacher contract, or wearing reli-

gious garb. Teachers may be dismissed on similar grounds.

OHIO: Teacher's certificate may be revoked for intemperance, immorality, incompetence, **negligence**, or other conduct unbecoming of the position. Teachers may be dismissed on similar grounds, including assisting a student to cheat on an achievement, ability, or proficiency test.

OKLAHOMA: Teachers may be dismissed for immorality, willful neglect of duty, cruelty, incompetency, teaching disloyalty to the U. S. government, moral turpitude, or criminal sexual activity.

OREGON: Teacher's certificate may be revoked or suspended for conviction of certain crimes (including sale or possession of a controlled substance), gross neglect of duty, gross unfitness, or wearing religious dress at school. Teachers may be dismissed or suspended on similar grounds.

PENNSYLVANIA: Teacher's certificate may be revoked for incompetency, cruelty, negligence, immorality, or intemperance. Teachers may be dismissed on similar grounds.

RHODE ISLAND: Teacher's certificate may be revoked, or teacher may be dismissed, for good and just cause.

SOUTH CAROLINA: Teacher's certificate may be revoked for just cause, including incompetence, willful neglect of duty, willful violation of state board rules, unprofessional conduct, drunkenness, cruelty, crime, immorality, conduct involving moral turpitude, dishonesty, evident unfitness, or sale or possession of narcotics. Teachers may be dismissed on similar grounds.

SOUTH DAKOTA: Teacher's certificate may be revoked or suspended for any cause that would have permitted issue of the certificate, violation of teacher's contract, gross immorality, incompetency, flagrant neglect of duty; or conviction of a crime involving moral turpitude. Teachers may be dismissed on similar grounds.

TENNESSEE: Teacher's certificate may be revoked if teacher is guilty of immoral conduct. Teachers may be dismissed or suspended on similar grounds, including incompetence, inefficiency, neglect of duty, unprofessional conduct, and insubordination.

TEXAS: Teacher's certificate may be revoked or suspended if teacher's activities are in violation of the law, the teacher is unworthy to instruct the youth of the state, the teacher abandons his or her contract, or the teacher is convicted of a crime. Teachers may be dismissed or suspended on similar grounds.

UTAH: Teacher's certificate may be revoked or suspended for immoral or incompetent conduct, or evidence of unfitness for teaching. Teachers may be dismissed for cause.

VERMONT: Teacher's certificate may be revoked for cause. Teachers may be dismissed for just and sufficient cause. Teachers may be suspended for incompetence, conduct unbecoming of a teacher, failure to attend to duties, or failure to carry out reasonable orders and directions of superintendent or board.

VIRGINIA: Teachers may be dismissed for incompetency, immorality, noncompliance with school laws or rules, certain **disability**, and convictions of certain crimes. Teachers may be suspended for good and just cause when the safety or welfare of children are threatened.

WASHINGTON: Teacher's certificate may be revoked for immorality, violation of a written contract, intemperance, a crime involving child neglect or abuse, or unprofessional conduct. Teachers may be dismissed for sufficient cause.

WEST VIRGINIA: Teacher's certificate may be revoked for drunkenness; untruthfulness; immorality; unfitness due to physical, mental or moral defect; neglect of duty; using **fraudulent**, unapproved, or insufficient credit; or other cause. Teachers may be dismissed or suspended on similar grounds.

WISCONSIN: Teacher's certificate may be revoked for incompetency, immoral conduct, or conviction of certain felonies. Tenured teachers may be dismissed on similar grounds.

WYOMING: Teacher's certificate may be revoked or suspended for incompetency, immorality, other reprehensible conduct, or gross neglect of duty. Teachers may be dismissed on similar grounds.

## Additional Resources

*Deskbook Encyclopedia of American School Law* Oakstone Legal and Business Publishing, 2001.

*Education Law* Rapp, James A., Lexis Publishing, 2001.

*Education Law, Second Edition* Imber, Michael, and Tyll Van Geel, Lawrence Erlbaum Associates, 2000.

*The Law of Public Education, Fourth Edition* Reutter, E. Edmund, Jr., Foundation Press, 1994.

*Private School Law in America, Twelfth Edition* Oakstone Legal and Business Publishing, 2000.

*School Law and the Public Schools: A Practical Guide for Educational Leaders* Essex, Nathan, Allyn and Bacon, 1999.

*Teachers and the Law* Fischer, Louis, David Schimmel, and Cynthia Kelly, Addison Wesley Longman, 1999.

*U. S. Code, Title 42: Public Health and Welfare, chapter 21: Civil Rights* U.S. House of Representatives, 1999. Available at: http://uscode.house.gov/title_42.htm

## Organizations

*American Association of School Administrators (AASA)*
1801 N. Moore Street
Arlington, VA 22209 USA
Phone: (703) 528-0700
Fax: (703) 841-1543
URL: http://www.aasa.org/
Primary Contact: Paul Houston, Executive Director

*American Federation of Teachers (AFT)*
555 New Jersey Avenue, NW
Washington, DC 20001 USA
Phone: (202) 879-4400
URL: http://www.aft.org/

*Education Law Association (ELA)*
300 College Park
Dayton, OH 45469 USA
Phone: (937) 229-3589
Fax: (937) 229-3845
URL: http://www.educationlaw.org/
Primary Contact: R. Craig Wood, President

*Education Policy Institute (EPI)*
4401-A Connecticut Ave., NW
Washington, DC 20008 USA
Phone: (202) 244-7535
Fax: (202) 244-7584
URL: http://www.educationpolicy.org/
Primary Contact: Charlene K. Haar, President

*National Education Association (NEA)*
1201 16th Street, NW
Washington, DC 20036 USA
Phone: (202) 833-4000
URL: http://www.nea.org/
Primary Contact: Bob Chase, President

# EDUCATION

## TEACHER'S UNIONS/COLLECTIVE BARGAINING

*Sections within this essay:*

- Background

- Constitutional Considerations Regarding Unions

- Forming and Joining a Union to Bargain Collectively
    - Bargaining Units
    - Representation Procedures

- Obligations and Resolution of Conflicts in Collective Bargaining
    - Exclusivity and Good Faith in Bargaining Agreement
    - Terms of the Collective Bargaining Agreement
    - Impasse
    - Strikes

- Collective Bargaining in Higher Education

- State and Local Provisions Governing Collective Bargaining

- Additional Resources

## Background

In 1935 Congress passed the National Labor Relations Act (Wagner Act), which guarantees the right of private employees to form and join unions to bargain collectively. The vast majority of states have extended this right to public employees, including teachers at public school districts. Many states require school districts to bargain collectively with teachers who have formed a union. Other states require districts to meet with teachers' representatives. Some states expressly prohibit **collective bargaining** by public school teachers or other public employees.

A wide range of provisions may be negotiated in collective bargaining between teachers' unions and school districts. Some subjects are mandatory, while others are merely permitted or even prohibited. State law governs the appropriateness of subjects to be bargained. The following are some of the matters that are often the subject of this bargaining:

- Academic freedom

- Curriculum

- Wages and salaries

- Training

- Hours, workload, and teaching responsibilities

- Tenure and probationary period

- Promotion

- Reappointment

- Reclassification and reduction

- Evaluation procedures

- Grievance procedures

- Personnel files

- Student discipline

- Retirement benefits

- Sick leave

- Leaves and sabbaticals

## Constitutional Considerations Regarding Unions

The First Amendment of the **Bill of Rights** provides: "Congress shall make no law . . . prohibiting . . . the right of people peaceably to assemble." This right, as applied to the states through the Fourteenth Amendment of the Constitution, has been interpreted to give teachers and other employees the right to free association, including the right to join a union, such as the National Education Association or the American Federation of Teachers. However, the Constitution does not grant teachers the right to bargain collectively with employers. This right is based on applicable provisions in state constitutions, federal statutes, or state statutes. Similarly, teachers do not have a constitutional right to strike, though other federal law or state law may permit teachers to strike.

## Forming and Joining a Union to Bargain Collectively

Laws governing the representation process are often quite complex. This process prefaces the collective bargaining process and involves numerous considerations, including types of employees that will constitute a "bargaining unit," as well as the selection of an appropriate union to represent teachers. In the public school sector, state law affects both of these determinations. Some states exclude certain employees from a bargaining unit, including supervisors and individuals in management positions.

### Bargaining Units

Teachers seeking to join for collective bargaining must define an appropriate bargaining unit. Under most labor relations statutes, only those individuals who share a "community of interests" may comprise an appropriate bargaining unit. Community of interests generally means that the teachers have substantial mutual interests, including the following:

- Wages or compensation
- Hours of work
- Employment benefits
- Supervision
- Qualifications
- Training and skills
- Job functions
- Contact with other employees
- Integration of work functions with other employees

- History of collective bargaining

Many state statutes prescribe certain requirements or considerations with respect to bargaining units in the public sector. For example, some statutes require labor boards to avoid over-proliferation of bargaining units. Moreover, some statutes also set forth specific bargaining units, such as those for faculty, staff, maintenance, and similar distinctions.

### Representation Procedures

The National Labor Relations Act and most state statutes provide formal processes for designation and recognition of bargaining units. If a dispute arises with respect to union representation, many states direct parties to resolve these dispute with the public employment relations board in that state. After the bargaining units are organized, members may file a petition with the appropriate labor board. The labor board will generally determine that **jurisdiction** over the bargaining unit is appropriate, that the proposed bargaining unit is appropriate, and that a majority of employees approve the bargaining unit through an election. Several procedures are usually in place in the **statute** and rules of the labor board to ensure that the vote is uncoerced and otherwise fair. After this election, the labor board will certify the union as the exclusive representative of the bargaining unit. Once a union is certified, usually for a one-year period, neither employees nor another union may petition for a new election.

## Obligations and Resolution of Conflicts in Collective Bargaining

### Exclusivity and Good Faith in Bargaining Agreement

Once a union has been elected, both public and private school boards are bound to deal exclusively with that union. The elected union must bargain for the collective interests of the members of the bargaining unit. Both the school district and the union representing teachers must bargain in **good faith**. The duty of parties to bargain in good faith is important in the collective bargaining process, since negotiations between school districts and unions can become intense and heated.

Interpretations of the term "good faith" under the National Labor Relations Act typically focus on openness, fairness, mutuality of conduct, and cooperation between parties. Many state statutes define "good faith" similarly, though some states provide more specific guidance regarding what constitutes good faith bargaining. Some states also provide a list of examples that are deemed instances of bargaining in **bad faith**. Refusal to negotiate in good faith constitutes an **unfair labor practice** under the National Labor Relations Act and many state statutes.

### Terms of the Collective Bargaining Agreement

Most state statutes do not require schools to bargain on issues involving the educational policy of the school board. Many states require school boards and unions to bargain on "wages, hours, and terms and conditions of employment." Some states limit bargaining to such mandatory issues as benefits, insurance, or sick leave. When a state statute includes mandatory subjects, these subjects must be bargained over at the request of either the school board or the teachers' union. If either party refuses to negotiate over a mandatory subject, state statutes generally deem this a refusal to negotiate in good faith and, thus, an unfair labor practice.

In the absence of **statutory** language specifying the scope of collective bargaining, teacher unions and school boards must consult relevant **case law** in that state to determine if the courts have set forth parameters. Other limitations to collective bargaining may also be present. A **collective bargaining agreement**, for example, cannot violate or contradict existing statutory law or constitutional provisions. Similarly, the collective bargaining agreement should recognize contract rights that may already exist through other agreements.

### Impasse

Negotiations may fail to lead to a completed agreement between a teachers' union and a school board. When good faith efforts fail to resolve the dispute or disputes between the parties, a legal impasse occurs. At the time impasse occurs, active bargaining between the parties is usually suspended.

Parties usually go through a series of options once an impasse has occurred, though public and private school teachers' options may differ. The first step after an impasse is declared is usually **mediation**. When parties employ a mediator, the mediator acts as a neutral third party to assist the two sides in reaching a compromise. Mediators lack power to make binding decisions, and they are employed only as advisors. Many state statutes require use of mediators in the public sector upon declaration of an impasse. Private sector unions and schools may employ a federal mediator, though federal labor laws do not prescribe further options regarding dispute resolution.

If mediation fails, many state statutes require the parties to employ a fact-finder, who analyzes the facts of the bargaining process and seeks to recognize a potential compromise. The parties are not bound by the recommendations of the fact-finder, though it may influence public opinion regarding the appropriate resolution of the dispute. The recommendations are particularly influential in the public sector, where the school board is a government body consisting of elected officials, and teachers and other staff are public employees. However, this step in the process may not bring resolution to the dispute. In some states, fact-finding is the final stage of impasse resolution, leaving the parties to bargain among themselves.

A third option is **arbitration**, though this is generally only employed in the public education sector. An arbitrator is a third party who performs functions similar to a fact-finder, yet the arbitrator's decision is binding on both parties. In several states, arbitration is permissive, meaning parties may submit their dispute to an arbitrator after fact-finding if they so desire. Some states mandate use of binding arbitration, often as an alternative to the right to strike.

### Strikes

If efforts for impasse resolution fail between a teachers' union and a school district, teachers may choose to strike to persuade or coerce the board to meet the demands of the union. A lockout by an employer is the counterpart to a strike. The right to strike in the private sector is guaranteed under the National Labor Relations Act. However, only about half of the states have extended this right to teachers in the public sector. These states usually limit this right under the respective labor laws. Where teachers do not have the right to strike, state statutes often impose monetary or similar penalties on those who strike illegally.

In states where strikes are permitted in the public sector, teachers often must meet several conditions prior to the strike. For example, a state may require that a bargaining unit has been certified properly, that methods for impasse resolution have been exhausted, that any existing collective bargaining agreement has expired, and that the union has provided sufficient notice to the school board. The purpose of such conditions is to give the parties an opportunity to avoid a strike, which is usually unpopular with both employers and employees.

## Collective Bargaining in Higher Education

Collective bargaining in higher education differs somewhat from bargaining by primary and secondary school teachers. The National Labor Relations Act applies to many private institutions of higher education, which usually have much higher revenues and many more employees than private schools at the primary or secondary level. In many states, the same statutes that govern bargaining at the primary or secondary level govern collective bargaining in higher education. In other states, however, the statutes prescribe different rules with respect to state universities than they do with school districts. Governance of a public university is often much more complex than governance at a primary or secondary school, and the interests of the employees is often much more diverse among university faculty members and other employees than the interests of high school, middle school, or elementary school teachers and employees. Whereas a primary or secondary school may require only a minimal number of bargaining units, a large university may require several bargaining units to represent the various interests of the employees of the university.

## State and Local Provisions Governing Collective Bargaining

The National Labor Relations Act (NLRA) governs labor relations in private schools, subject to some limitations. A teachers' union of a private schools should determine whether the NLRA applies to its school. State labor statutes generally govern labor relations between public school districts and teachers' unions. These provisions are summarized below. Collective bargaining statutes differ considerably from state to state, with some states providing much more guidance and specific rules than others.

ALABAMA: Teachers have a general right to join or refuse to join a labor organization.

ALASKA: Certified employees and school boards must follow specific procedures set forth in the statute. Under the state's Public Employment Relations Act, student representatives must be permitted to attend meetings and have access to documents in negotiations between a postsecondary education institution and a bargaining representative. The statute also permits a strike, with some limitations, by public school employees after mediation if a majority of employees vote by secret ballot to do so.

ARIZONA: Arizona has not enacted a collective bargaining statute governing public schools. Teachers in this state should consult relevant case law to determine when collective bargaining is permitted.

ARKANSAS: Teachers have a general right to organize and bargain collectively.

CALIFORNIA: An extensive statutory scheme is provided for governing collective bargaining between public schools and bargaining representatives, under the Public School Employee Relations Act. The statute limits the scope of representation to matters related to wages, employment hours, and other terms and conditions of employment. Employer and employee representatives are required to "meet and negotiate." If impasse is declared, mediation and, if necessary, fact-finding are required. Arbitration is permitted, but it is not required by statute.

COLORADO: Collective bargaining is permitted by statute. Teachers have a limited right to strike.

CONNECTICUT: A statute permits collective bargaining by members of the teaching profession. However, the state prohibits professional employees from striking and allows courts to enforce this prohibition.

DELAWARE: Public school employees are permitted to bargain collectively. Majority vote is required for union representation from all eligible members of the bargaining unit. The state prohibits strikes by teachers.

FLORIDA: The state constitution guarantees the right to collective bargaining but prohibits strikes by public employees. State statute defines "good faith bargaining," requiring parties to meet at reasonable times and places with the intent to reach a common accord.

HAWAII: Statute permits bargaining by all public employees. Statute defines certain bargaining units, including some supervisory employees. Mediation, fact-finding, and arbitration are provided in the statute. Strikes are permitted, but only in certain narrow circumstances.

IDAHO: Statute prescribes procedures for bargaining between a school board and certificated school employees.

ILLINOIS: Educational employees at all levels permitted to bargain under the Illinois Educational Labor Relations Act. However, several types of employees, including supervisors, managers, confidential employees, short-term employees, and students, are excluded from bargaining by statute. Impasse procedures include mediation and fact-finding. Arbitration is permitted. Strikes are permitted after several conditions set forth in the statute are met.

INDIANA: Certificated educational employees permitted to bargain by statute. Statute prescribes certain subjects that may be bargained and certain subjects that may be discussed. Strikes are prohibited.

IOWA: All public employees permitted to bargain collectively. Mediation and fact-finding required for impasse resolution. The state labor board at the request of the school board or union may order binding arbitration. Strikes are prohibited.

KANSAS: Statute permits bargaining by all public employees. Employer retains a number of rights, including right to direct work of employees. Strikes are prohibited.

LOUISIANA: No collective bargaining statute governs public schools. Teachers in this state should consult relevant case law to determine when collective bargaining is permitted.

MAINE: Statute permits collective bargaining by all public employees. Strikes by all state employees are prohibited.

MARYLAND: Statute permits bargaining by all certified and noncertified public school employees.

MASSACHUSETTES: Statute permits bargaining by all public employees. Strikes by public employees are prohibited.

MICHIGAN: Statute permits bargaining by public employees. Negotiations by teachers limited under some circumstances. Strikes by public employees are prohibited.

MINNESOTA: Statute permits bargaining by all public employees. State permits strikes only under certain circumstances, including completion of impasse resolution.

MISSISSIPPI: Strikes by teaches are illegal by statute.

MISSOURI: Teachers at public schools have the right to bargain collectively. Statute does not grant a right to strike.

MONTANA: Statute permits bargaining by all public employees. Courts have construed state statute to permit the right to strike.

NEBRASKA: Statute permits bargaining by all public employees. State restricts supervisors from joining a bargaining unit but permits some administrators, subject to restrictions, to join such a bargaining unit with teachers. Strikes by teachers are prohibited.

NEVADA: Statute permits bargaining by all public employees. Strikes by public employees are illegal by statute.

NEW HAMPHIRE: Statute permits bargaining by all public employees. Impasse resolution procedures must be implemented within the time period specified by the statute. Strikes by public employees are illegal by statute.

NEW JERSEY: Statute permits bargaining by all public employees but excludes standards of criteria for employee performance from the scope of negotiation.

NEW YORK: Statute permits bargaining by all public employees. The statute limits the scope of negotiations to matters related to wages, employment hours, and other terms and conditions of employment. Arbitration is required by statute when an impasse is declared. Strikes by public employees are prohibited.

NORTH CAROLINA: Statute prohibits collective bargaining by all public employees. Statute also prohibits strikes by public employees.

NORTH DAKOTA: Statute permits bargaining by certificated school employees. Strikes by school employees are prohibited.

OHIO: Statute permits bargaining by public employees. Strikes by public employees are prohibited.

OKLAHOMA: Statute permits bargaining by all public school employees. Strikes by teachers are prohibited.

OREGON: Statute permits bargaining by all public employees. Impasse resolution procedures include mediation and fact-finding. Strikes are permitted after impasse resolution procedures have been implemented.

PENNSYLVANIA: Statute permits bargaining by all public employees under the Public Employee Relations Act. Statute limits which employees may be included in a single bargaining unit. Public school districts are not required to bargain over the "inherent management policy" of the district. Strikes by public employees are permitted after conditions set forth in the statute are met.

RHODE ISLAND: Statute permits bargaining by all certified public school employees. Strikes by public school employees are prohibited.

SOUTH DAKOTA: Statute permits bargaining by all public employees. Strikes by public employees are prohibited.

TENNESSEE: Negotiations by professional educators governed by the Education Professional Negotiations Act. Strikes by education professionals are prohibited.

TEXAS: Statute prohibits public employees from entering into a collective bargaining agreement. Statute also prohibits strikes by public employees.

UTAH: Statute permits union membership by public employees.

VERMONT: Statute permits bargaining by public school teachers, with representation election administered by the American Arbitration Association. Strikes by state employees are prohibited by statute.

VIRGINIA: Strikes by public employees are prohibited by statute.

WASHINGTON: Statute permits bargaining by public employees, including certified educational employees. Strikes by public employees are prohibited by statute.

WEST VIRGINIA: No collective bargaining statute governs public schools. Teachers in this state should consult relevant case law to determine when collective bargaining is permitted.

WISCONSIN: Statute permits bargaining by municipal employees. Impasse resolution procedures include mediation and arbitration. Strikes are permitted after impasse resolution procedures have been exhausted.

WYOMING: Statute permits right to bargain as a matter of **public policy**.

## Additional Resources

*Deskbook Encyclopedia of American School Law* Oakstone Legal and Business Publishing, 2001.

*Education Law* Rapp, James A., Lexis Publishing, 2001.

*Education Law* Imber, Michael, and Tyll Van Geel, Lawrence Erlbaum Associates, 2000.

*The Law of Public Education* Reutter, E. Edmund, Jr., Foundation Press, 1994.

*Private School Law in America* Oakstone Legal and Business Publishing, 2000.

*School Law and the Public Schools: A Practical Guide for Educational Leaders* Essex, Nathan, Allyn and Bacon, 1999.

*Teachers and the Law* Fischer, Louis, David Schimmel, and Cynthia Kelly, Addison Wesley Longman, 1999.

*U. S. Code, Title 29: Public Health and Welfare, Chapter 7: Labor-Management Relations* U. S. House of Representatives, 1999. Available at http://uscode.house.gov/title_29.htm

## Organizations

### American Arbitration Association (AAA)
335 Madison Avenue, Floor 10
New York, NY 10017 USA
Phone: (212) 716-5800
Fax: (212) 716-5905
URL: http://www.adr.org/
Primary Contact: William K. Slate II, President and C.E.O.

### American Association of School Administrators (AASA)
1801 N. Moore St.
Arlington, VA 22209 USA
Phone: (703) 528-0700
Fax: (703) 841-1543
URL: http://www.aasa.org/
Primary Contact: Paul Houston, Executive Director

### American Federation of Teachers (AFT)
555 New Jersey Avenue, NW
Washington, DC 20001 USA
Phone: (202) 879-4400
URL: http://www.aft.org/

### Education Law Association (ELA)
300 College Park
Dayton, OH 45469 USA
Phone: (937) 229-3589
Fax: (937) 229-3845
URL: http://www.educationlaw.org/
Primary Contact: R. Craig Wood, President

### Education Policy Institute (EPI)
4401-A Connecticut Ave., NW

Washington, DC 20008 USA
Phone: (202) 244-7535
Fax: (202) 244-7584
URL: http://www.educationpolicy.org/
Primary Contact: Charlene K. Haar, President

***National Education Association (NEA)***
1201 16th Street, NW
Washington, DC 20036 USA
Phone: (202) 833-4000
URL: http://www.nea.org/
Primary Contact: Bob Chase, President

# EDUCATION

## TRUANCY

*Sections within this essay:*

## Background

Truancy, also called skipping school, is defined by all states as unexcused absences from school without the knowledge of a parent or **guardian**. It has been romanticized through literature and films by characters such as Tom Sawyer and Ferris Bueller as the harmless mischief juveniles do on sunny days. But the fact is juveniles who are school-aged are required by all states to attend school, whether that school be public, private, parochial, or some other educational forum. Truancy is, therefore, a **status offense** as it only applies to people of a certain age. The school age of a juvenile varies from state to state, with most states requiring attendance either from age six to age 17 or from age five to 18. There are a number of exceptions, such as Pennsylvania, which denotes school age as between eight and 17 and Illinois which denotes school age as between seven and 16.

The number of days required in order for a juvenile to be labeled "truant," varies by school, school district, and state. State legislation tends to provide some guidelines for school districts by setting a maximum number of absences allowed. School districts then tighten these guidelines. For example, in Pennsylvania, a truant is a school-aged juvenile who is absent from school more than three times after a notice of truancy has been sent to the juvenile's home. In Louisiana, a juvenile is deemed truant after the fifth unexcused absence from school, provided the absences occur in a single month. Many school districts define truancy as any unexcused absence, where unexcused means the student has left school property without parental or school permission.

## The Rational for Truancy Laws

Compulsory education began about sixty years ago and was strongly influenced by labor unions who were trying to keep children from working. The participation of children in the labor force kept adult wages low. Compulsory attendance in schools also lifted some authority of parents over their children to the state, as parents could no longer force their children to work. The state's authority in school attendance was underscored in *Prince v. Massachusetts* (1944). In this case, the Supreme Court decided that the state had the right to uphold **child labor laws** and parents' authority could not preempt that of the state. Therefore, children had to attend school whether their parents supported education or not.

In recent research conducted by the Office for Juvenile Justice and Delinquency Prevention (OJJDP, 2001), links between truancy and other, more serious forms of delinquency have been delineated. For example, the links between truancy and substance abuse, **vandalism**, auto theft, and gang behavior have all been established in criminology literature (see Loeber & Farrington, 2000 for details). The link between truancy and later, violent offending has been established in studies that examine male criminality (e.g., see Ingersoll & LeBoeuf, 1997). In turn, adults who were truants as juveniles tend to exhibit poorer social skills, have lower paying jobs, are more likely to rely on welfare support, and have an increased likelihood of **incarceration** (Hawkins & Catalano, 1995).

Residents have also put pressure on schools and lawmakers to tighten truancy laws as groups of young people loitering in public during school hours often appear threatening. In Tacoma, Washington, an increase in truancy was associated with an increase in juvenile perpetrated property crimes, such as **burglary** and vandalism. This increase in juvenile daytime crime led to a program targeting the enforcement of truancy laws in this state.

Those school districts with the highest truancy rates also have the lowest academic achievement rates. This link is usually established through truancy policies which deem automatic failure in courses where students are regularly absent. Therefore, students who do not attend school on a regular basis are unlikely to graduate from high school. Between 1992 and 2002 there have been approximately three million young adults each year aged between 16 and 24 who have either failed to complete high school or not enrolled in high school (National Center for Education Statistics, 2001). This number represents about 11 percent of young adults in the United States. Within this group, there are a disproportionate number of minority students; for example, 30 percent of Hispanics are not completing high school (NCES, 2001). This number increases to 44 percent if the students counted were born outside of the United States (NCES, 2001). Thus, the recency of **immigration** seems to have important implications in the study of high school dropout rates. Researchers have linked this correlation to parental attitudes toward education. However, coming from countries where education is not highly valued, parents may not encourage their children to attend school, increasing the truancy rate and also increasing the drop out rate (Alexander et al., 1997).

Failure at high school not only affects the individual, but it also affects society. Affected students cannot attend college, are more likely to have low paying jobs and feel political apathy; they then can constitute a loss in tax revenue, may experience health problems, and place a strain on social services (Rosenfeld, Richman and Bowen, 1998). A recent U.S. Department of Labor study shows that 6.7 percent of adults with no high school diploma are likely to be unemployed, while only 3.5 percent of adults with a high school diploma are likely to be unemployed. With a bachelor's degree, only 1.8 percent of adults are likely to be unemployed (U. S. Dept. of Labor, 1999).

## Extent of the Truancy Problem

Although there are currently no national statistics available on the extent of the truancy, many states and cities do keep their own statistics which are often used to influence policy. A recent national study of school principals revealed that truancy was listed as one of the top five concerns by the majority of respondents (Heaviside, et al., 1998). In Chicago, a study conducted during the 1995-1996 school year indicated that the average 10th grader missed six weeks of instruction (Roderick et. al., 1997). Recent OJJDP research suggests that the number of truants are highest in inner city, public schools, where there are large numbers of students and where a large percentage of the student population participate in the free lunch program (OJJDP, 2001).

In terms of court processing, the number of truancy cases referred to juvenile courts is fairly small; for example, in 1998, about 28 percent of referred status offenses were truancies, which is an 85 percent increase compared with the previous ten years. However, this number is expected to increase dramatically given recent changes to truancy laws. Interestingly, the OJJDP (2001) reports that females are just as likely as males to be adjudicated for truancy.

## Correlates of Truancy

The following factors have been found to have associations with truancy in that the likelihood of truancy is increased given the presence of these variables. First are family factors, such as lack of supervision, physical and psychological abuse, and failure to encourage educational achievement. Second are school factors which can range from inconsistent enforcement of rules to student boredom with curriculum. Economic factors are a third correlate, and these could be factors such as high family mobility or parents with multiple jobs. Last are student characteristics such as drug and alcohol abuse, ignorance of school rules, and lack of interest in education.

## Enforcing Truancy Laws

In all states, the first body responsible for enforcing truancy laws is usually the school. School officials, such as school truancy officers, teachers, and school principals, refer truancy cases to juvenile court **jurisdiction**. However, if truant individuals are found in a public area, they may be detained by police or taken to a detention facility.

Arizona was the first state in the United States to implement and enforce a get-tough approach to truancy laws. Research on truancy in Arizona began in the early 1990s. Pima County had the highest truancy rate in the state during this time period; in fact, truants from this county made up half of all truants in the state. Because of the extent of the problem, Pima County began a program called ACT Now (Abolish Chronic Truancy) which aimed to strictly enforce state and district truancy laws and offer a diversion program to address the root causes of truancy. The program also sought to provide serious sanctions for both juveniles and their parents if truancy persisted or if conditions specified by the diversion program were not met. School districts, school administrators, law enforcement personnel, and community agencies are involved in this program.

Once a student has one unexcused absence from school, a letter is sent home to the student's parents explaining the consequences of truancy. After a third unexcused absence, the juvenile is referred to the Center for Juvenile Alternatives (CJA) which makes a recommendation to the juvenile court. A letter is sent to the juvenile's parents explaining the diversion program or the alternative court imposed sanctions, and the parents decide which course of action they would prefer.

The diversion program consists of counseling, parenting classes, support groups, etc. Very often parents have no idea that their child is missing school, or they do not seem to care. Support groups and classes teach parents about the value of education and also help parents communicate more effectively with their teenagers. In their report, the CJA will identify which type of intervention is best for the family, and the juvenile and his or her parents will be referred accordingly. Both parents and the juvenile must sign an agreement promising to abide by the conditions of the diversion program. Successful completion of the program results in the truancy case being dismissed.

The ACT Now program has been formally evaluated by the American Prosecutors Research Institute

(APRI), and each school district involved in the program has shown a steady decrease in the number of truancies each year. In the district with the highest percentage of truancies, ACT Now helped reduce truancies by 64 percent between 1996 and 1998. This program and versions of it are financially supported by the Department of Justice and have been implemented in many other states.

## Getting Tough on Parents

Many states also hold parents accountable for their children's truancy, and Arizona was the first state to implement such laws. The rationale behind this movement was to coerce parents into taking an active role in their children's education and for all parties to take truancy laws and school attendance seriously. In Virginia, parents can be fined and jailed for failure to adequately supervise school-aged children, which includes making sure they are attending school. In Pennsylvania, parents can also be fined and jailed if they have not taken reasonable steps to ensure their child is attending school. In Texas and many other states, similar laws have recently been passed.

## Truancy and Home Schooling

The popularity of home schooling has increased dramatically between 1997 and 2002, and the Department of Education estimates that between 700,000 and two million children were home schooled during the 1999-2000 academic year. This fact has a large impact on the enforcement of truancy laws, as home schooled children may be out in public during school hours and could be apprehended by police. In many states, the right to home school children is protected by the state's constitution. For example, the constitution of the state of Oklahoma reads:

> The Legislature shall provide for the compulsory attendance at some public or other school, unless other means of education are provided, of all the children in the State who are sound in mind and body, between the ages of eight and 16 years, for at least three months in each year. (Article XIII)

Many states, like Oklahoma, have not yet resolved how home schooling affects the enforcement of truancy laws. For example, in Illinois, there are currently no provisions for home schooled children under the law, and these children would be in violation of the state's truancy laws if those laws were enforced. The only exceptions to the truancy laws, that is, those circumstances in which school-aged individuals are not required to attend a public school in Illinois are: those attending private or parochial schools, those who are physically or mentally unable to attend school, those females who are pregnant or have young children, those who are lawfully employed, and those individuals who are absent for religious holidays.

The regulation of home schooling thus varies greatly by state. Some states have very little regulation and do not require parents to contact the state to inform officials that children will be home schooled. Some of these states are Arkansas, Indiana, Illinois, Oklahoma, Michigan, Missouri, and New Jersey. Other states, such as California, Arizona, New Mexico, Alabama, and Kentucky, have low regulation and require that parents who are home schooling their children report this fact to the state. Other states, such as Virginia, North Carolina, South Carolina, Georgia, Colorado, Oregon, Florida, Tennessee, Arkansas, and Louisiana, have moderate regulation in which parents must report test scores and student evaluations to the state. Some states, such as New York, Pennsylvania, West Virginia, Maine, Rhode Island, Massachusetts, Washington, and Utah, require parents to submit test scores and evaluations of students and also professional evaluations of teachers and curriculum for approval. The level of regulation in each state affects how truancy laws can be enforced. If the state has no record of students being home schooled, it is difficult to enforce truancy laws across the board.

## Examples of Truancy Laws

Although states vary in their responses to truancy, their laws in defining truancy are fairly similar. Below are some examples for various states.

CALIFORNIA: Any school-aged child who is absent from school without valid excuse three full days in one school year or tardy or absent for more than any 30-minute period during one school day on three occasions during the school year or any combination thereof is considered truant and should be reported to the supervisor of the school district.

CONNECTICUT: A truant is a child between the ages of five and 18 who is enrolled in any public or private school and has four unexcused absences in a month or 10 in any school year. A **habitual** truant

is a child of the same age who has 20 unexcused absences from school during a school year.

ILLINOIS: A truant is defined as any child subject to compulsory schooling and who is absent from school unexcused. Absences that are excused are determined by the school board. A chronic or habitual truant is a school-age child who is absent without valid cause for 10 percent out of 180 consecutive days. The truant officer in Illinois is responsible for informing parents of truancy and referring the case to juvenile court.

LOUISIANA: Any student between the ages of seven and seventeen is required to attend school. A student is considered truant when the child has been absent from school for five school days in schools operating on a semester system and for ten days in schools not operating on a semester basis. A student may be referred to juvenile court for habitual absence when all reasonable efforts by school administrators have failed and there have been five unexcused absences in one month. The school principal or truancy officer shall file a report indicating dates of absences, contacts with parents, and other information.

VIRGINIA: Any student between the ages of five and 18 is subject to compulsory school attendance. After a pupil has been absent for five days during the school year without a valid excuse, a notice is sent to parents outlining the consequences of truancy. A conference with school officials and parents is arranged within fifteen school days of the sixth absence. Once a truant has accumulated more than seven absences during the school year, the case will be referred to juvenile and domestic relations court.

## Additional Resources

*Current population survey, March 2000.* U.S. Census Bureau, Government Printing Office, 2001.

*Dropout Rates in the United States: 1999.* National Center for Education Statistics, 2001. Available on-line at http://nces.gov/pubs2001.htm, [Accessed October 28, 2001].

*From First Grade Forward: Early Foundations of High School Dropout.* Alexander, Karl L., Entwisle, Doris R and Horsey, Carrie S. (1997). Sociology of Education, 70, (2), 87-107.

*Habits Hard to Break: A New Look at Truancy in Chicago's Public High Schools.* M. Roderick, J. Chiong, M. Arney, K. DaCosta, M. Stone, L. Villarreal- Sosa and E. Waxman. Research in Brief: University of Chicago, School of Social Service Administration, 1997.

*Manual to Combat Truancy.* U. S. Department of Education and the Department of Justice, 1996. Available online at http://www.ed.gov/pubs/Truancy/index.html [Accessed October 28, 2001].

*Reaching Out to Youth Out of the Education Mainstream.* S. Ingersoll and D. LeBoeuf. Office of Juvenile Justice and Delinquency Prevention, 1997.

*Risk Focused Prevention: Using the Social Development Strategy.* J. D. Hawkins, and R. Catalano. Developmental Research and Programs Inc., 1995.

*Supportive Communication and School Outcomes for Academically At-Risk and Other Low Income Middle School Students.* Lawrence, B. Rosenfeld, Jack, M. Richman, and Gary, L. Bowen (1998). Communication Education, 47, (4), 309- 325.

*Truancy Reduction: Keeping Students in School.* Myriam L. Baker, Jane N. Sigmon and M. Elaine Nugent. Office of Juvenile Justice and Delinquency Prevention, 2001.

*Violence and Discipline Problems in U. S. Public Schools: 1996-1997.* S. Heaviside, C. Rowand, C. Williams and E. Farris. U. S. Department of Education, 1998.

*Young Children who Commit Crime: Epidemiology, Developmental Origins, Risk Factors, Early Interventions, and Policy Implications.* Richard Loeber and David Farrington (2000). Development and Psychopathology, 12 (4), 737- 762.

## Organizations

### Home School Legal Defense Association

P.O. Box 3000
Purcellville, VA 20134-9000 USA
URL: http://www.hslda.org

### Kansas City In School Truancy Prevention Project

1211 McGee Street
Kansas City, MO 64106 USA
Phone: (816) 418-7946
URL: http://www.kcmsd.k12.mo.us/truancy/index.html

### National Home Education Research Institute

P.O. Box 13939
Salem, OR 97309 USA
Phone: (503) 364-1490
Fax: (503) 364-2827

### Project Intercept

1101 South Race Street
Denver, CO 80210 USA
Phone: (303) 777-5870

### The National Center for Juvenile Justice

710 Fifth Avenue, Suite 3000
Pittsburgh, PA 15219 USA
Phone: (412) 227-6950
Fax: (412) 227-6955
URL: http://brendan.ncjfcj.unr.edu/homepage/ncjj/ncjj2/index.html

### The Office of Juvenile Justice and Delinquency Prevention U. S. Department of Justice

Washington, DC USA
URL: http://www.ojjdp.ncjrs.org

### United States Department of Education, OERI At Risk

555 New Jersey Avenue NW, Room 610
Washington, DC 20005 USA
Phone: (202) 208-5521

# EDUCATION

## TYPES OF SCHOOLS

*Sections within this essay:*

- Background
- Public Schools
- Private and Parochial Schools
- Charter Schools
    - Privatization
- Home Schooling
- Vocational Education
- Distance Learning
- Additional Resources

## Background

For parents and students alike, the type of education available within their community is critically important. Many people, in fact, choose the communities in which they live on the basis of the quality of the local schools. Some parents choose to send their children to public school, believing that public education provides a more well-rounded experience for children. Others feel that private education offers students a more varied and creative course of study. Those who wish to instill within their children a sense of their religion may choose religious (often called parochial) schools; these schools provide religious instruction along with the general academic program. In recent years, a growing number of parents have turned to homeschooling, which they feel allows them more control over what and how their children learn.

Each system has its advantages and drawbacks; choosing the best system is determined by a number of considerations. For example, a child who lives in an affluent community with a well- respected public school system will likely want to take advantage of this free education. A child in a poorer community, or one who needs more individualized attention, may fare better in a private school, where classes are smaller and teachers can focus more fully on specific issues. Children in small rural communities, who may have to travel dozens of miles to go to school, may profit more by being home-schooled, or they may be able to hook up to schools via technology (the concept known as distance learning). How a child is educated depends on his or her abilities and needs, the expectations of parents, and the available choices. For parents and children to make informed choices, they need to understand what each type of school offers.

## Public Schools

In an address to educators in 1948, the statesman Adlai Stevenson said, "The most American thing about America is the free common school system." The concept of providing free public education to all children was born in Boston in 1635 with the establishment of a public institution that still exists today as the Boston Latin School. By the time of the American Revolution, free public schools were quite common in the northern colonies; in the South, schooling was done primarily at home until after the Civil War. By the end of the nineteenth century, public education was available to children across the country. Then, as now, the quality of education varied, sometimes dramatically, from region to region. Today, public school curricula are regulated by state and local governments.

According to the National Education Association (NEA), there were 14,568 public school districts in the United States in academic year 1998-99. There are approximately 89,500 public schools in the United States; nearly 63,000 of those schools are elementary (kindergarten through sixth grade). The rest are mostly secondary (middle and high schools), although a small number of schools go from kindergarten to 12th grade (K-12). These schools employ some 2.7 million teachers and serve more than 53 million students.

Public schools are funded primarily by state and local sources; the federal government historically has provided less than 10 percent of public education funding. Each school district has a board of education or similar administrative group to oversee the schools' performance; each state has an education department that sets academic standards for the school districts to follow.

The public school experience varies widely from district to district. A large city such as New York or Los Angeles has to address the education of hundreds of thousands of students with extraordinarily diverse needs. A small rural school district may have only a few hundred students who all come from a similar background. Affluent suburban communities with more local funding may pay higher salaries to attract the best teachers; this makes for strong suburban school districts but leaves poorer areas underserved. State governments do try to **redress** this imbalance (by giving more funds to poorer districts, for example) but often they meet with limited success.

## Private and Parochial Schools

Unlike public schools, private schools do not rely on government funding. They are supported by tuition, by grants from charitable organizations, and in the case of religious schools, by religious institutions. There are approximately 27,500 private schools in the United States, with some 395,000 teachers serving about 6 million students. Private schools include nonsectarian schools and religious schools covering many denominations (the term *parochial* usually denotes Catholic schools but can mean other Christian or Jewish institutions).

Tuition costs for private schools vary. As of 2002, figures available from the National Center for Education Statistics (NCES), indicated that nonsectarian private schools were the most expensive and Catholic schools were the least. Still tuition for school runs into tens of thousands of dollars over the course of a child's school years. Why would parents send their children to private schools when they have the option of sending them to public school for free?

For some, private school represents a stronger curriculum than public education can offer and a more personalized one as well. Public schools are generally much larger than private schools, and class size is also larger. Fewer students per teacher means that the teacher can spend more time one-on-one with each student.

The atmosphere in private and parochial schools is also different, sometimes vastly so, from that of public schools. A private school can focus its attention on a student's particular talents, such as music or science. As for parochial schools, they can provide religious instruction that no public school would be allowed to offer. This religious instruction is included in a curriculum that is generally strong academically.

Not merely the educational experience but also the social experience weighs in the minds of many parents as well. Schools that are unsafe (which could included anything from a building with antiquated electrical and heating systems to a school with a high rate of juvenile crime) make for a difficult atmosphere in which to learn. In general, these problems are more likely to develop in a public school than in a private one.

Teacher salaries tend to be lower in private schools, although some private schools offer teachers perks such as free meals and even free housing on campus. This gives private institutions more of a competitive edge against public systems that can pay quite well. Parents often perceive this as a sign that private school teachers are more committed to teaching than some of their public school counterparts.

## Charter Schools

Charter schools are most simply described as a cross between public and private schools. These schools are often created by teacher and parent groups who are dissatisfied with the bureaucracy that surrounds public education. The rules and regulations that shape a public school district, charter proponents argue, can cripple innovation in the schools. The result may be an uninspired and uninspiring educational program that fails to challenge students or meet their true needs.

The first charter school in the United States opened in St. Paul, Minnesota in 1993. As of the beginning of the school year in September 2001 there were some 2,400 charter schools operating in 34 states and the District of Columbia, serving 576,000 students. (Three additional states, Indiana, New Hampshire, and Wyoming, have charter school laws on the books but had not established charter schools by 2001.)

Typically, a charter school will be proposed by a group consisting of teachers, parents, and community leaders. Local and state organizations provide funding for charter schools, approve their programs, and monitor their quality. Charter schools are "public" in this sense, but unlike traditional public schools they are freed from traditional regulation. In general, the number of students per charter school is lower than in a traditional school, and there are also more teachers per pupil.

Proponents of charter schools claim that the structure not only enhances autonomy from oppressive bureaucracy but also increases accountability. Because they are monitored carefully, they have little room to do poorly. If they fail to accomplish their goal, they are closed. Moreover, because parents actively choose to send their children to charter schools, the school administrators know that if they fail to provide what they promise, parents and students will go elsewhere.

Opponents of charter schools say that they are merely private schools cloaked in a public-school mantle, allowing like-minded individuals to opt out of the public school system at the expense of those schools. This makes it even harder, they maintain, for public schools to excel. proponents counter that charter schools create a healthy competition that forces school districts to offer more and better services to students in their traditional schools.

### Privatization

One of the more controversial ideas in the public school arena is whether to privatize public school districts. This issue gained national attention in 2001 when the state of Pennsylvania initiated plans to take over the Philadelphia city school district and contract with a private firm to administer the city's schools. The move met with widespread opposition despite the fact that Philadelphia public schools had been in decline for some time. The main problem with allowing a private firm to take control of a public school district, say opponents, is that the emphasis will be on cutting costs rather than enhancing education.

For-profit firms claim that they improve schools by streamlining and cutting unnecessary costs. School privatization has been tried in some districts, but the long-term benefits or drawbacks remain to be seen.

## Home Schooling

A growing number of parents are choosing to turn away from public and private schools and instead educate their children in their own homes. In 1999, the most recent year for which NCES has figures, some 850,000 students between the ages of 5 and 17 were being schooled at home. Approximately 697,000 of these children are schooled completely in their homes; the remaining 153,000 are schooled primarily in their homes but also go part-time to a traditional school.

In general, the makeup of a home-schooling family is fairly traditional. Most of these families (80 percent) are two-parent families, and most of them have three or more children. Typically, one parent works while the other assumes the primary role of teacher, although the other parent may also be involved in the education process as well.

The most common reason parents give for home-schooling (a reason voiced by nearly all of them) is that they feel they can provide a better education for their children at home than the schools can. They may feel that the local school's curriculum is inadequate, or that it focuses on the wrong areas. Some parents feel that traditional schools fail to teach values to children; they school their children at home to provide a strong moral education. Or they may school their children at home for religious reasons; they may feel that the public school system is too secular for their tastes. A small number of parents turn to home schooling because they cannot afford to send their children to a private school.

In some cases, parents who home-school their children seek and receive a degree of public school support in the form of supplies, curricular assistance, and allowing home-schoolers to participate in the school's extracurricular programs. Frequently, the parents of home-schoolers do not avail themselves of these resources, preferring to keep the education centered around the home classroom. Home-schooled children are of course required to demonstrate that they are learning at the proper educational level, and parents are expected to provide structured classes, homework, tests, and projects.

## Vocational Education

Before the twentieth century, education for many young people consisted of learning a trade, which usually meant serving as an apprentice to an experienced tradesman. Apprentices learned to be blacksmiths or cabinetmakers or carpenters. In some smaller towns, children were apprenticed to professions such as law. Since the early twentieth century public high schools have offered a version of these apprenticeships in the form of vocational education (also called occupational education). This includes shop and home economics courses, as well as courses geared toward specific occupations such as electrician or automobile mechanic or cosmetologist.

Although the average high school student takes fewer course-hours in occupational education today than in the 1980s (4.68 in 1982; 3.99 in 1998), the more specific programs held steady in the number of course-hours students devoted.

## Distance Learning

Distance learning (the use of telecommunications technologies to broadcast classes from a central location to remote locations) has become quite popular among colleges and universities, particularly with adult or continuing education courses. Since the late 1980s, it has also been used in elementary and high schools. Through a program supported by the Department of Education called the Star Schools Program, some 1.6 million students in all 50 states were receiving long-distance instruction by the beginning of the twenty-first century.

The benefits of distance learning are clear: access to lessons not otherwise available. This arrangement is useful for students living in remote rural areas, but it also proves effective in urban locations. While a distance learning experience is not the same as a person-to-person lesson, it opens up avenues for new experiences. Moreover, many distance learning programs are interactive and thus engage children in a way designed to hold their attention. As technology becomes more efficient and less expensive, it is likely that distance learning will make up a growing element of elementary and secondary education.

## Additional Resources

*Charter Schools: The Parents' Complete Guide.* Birkett, Frederick A., Prima Publishing, 2000.

*Education in a Free Society.* Machan, Tibor R., Hoover Institution Press, 2000.

*How to Pick a Perfect Private School.* Unger, Harlow G., Facts on File Publications, 1999.

*The Manufactured Crisis: Myths, Frauds, and the Attack on America's Public Schools.* Berliner, David C., and Bruce J. Biddle, Addison-Wesley, 1995.

*Parents' Guide to Alternatives in Education.* Koetzsch, Ronald E., Shambhala, 1997.

*The Struggle for Control of Public Education: Market Ideology versus Democratic Values.* Engel, Michael, Temple University Press, 2000.

*Unofficial Guide to Homeschooling.* Ishizuke, Kathy, IDG Books Worldwide, 2000.

## Organizations

### Center for Education Reform
1001 Connecticut Avenue NW, Suite 204
Washington, DC 20036 USA
Phone: (202) 822-9000
Fax: (202) 822-5077
URL: http://www.edreform.com
Primary Contact: Jeanne Allen, President

### National Association of Elementary School Principals (NAESP)
1615 Duke Street
Alexandria, VA 22314 USA
Phone: (703) 684-3345
URL: http://www.naesp.org
Primary Contact: Vincent L. Ferrandino, Executive Director

### National Association of Secondary School Principals (NASSP)
1904 Association Drive
Reston, VA 20191 USA
Phone: (703) 860-0200
URL: http://www.nassp.org
Primary Contact: Gerald N. Tirozzi, Executive Director

### National Education Association (NEA)
1201 16th Street NW
Washington, DC 20036 USA
Phone: (202) 833-4000
URL: http://www.nea.org
Primary Contact: Bob Chase, President

### National Center for Education Statistics (NCES)
1990 K Street NW
Washington, DC 20006 USA

Phone: (202) 502-7300

URL: http://www.nces.ed.gov

Primary Contact: Gary W. Phillips, Acting Commissioner

### U. S. Department of Education

400 Maryland Avenue SW

Washington, DC 20202 USA

Phone: (800) 872-5327

URL: http://www.ed.gov

Primary Contact: Rod Paige, Secretary of Education

# EDUCATION

## VIOLENCE AND WEAPONS

*Sections within this essay:*

- Background
- Weapons at School
  - Ramifications of Possessing Weapons on School Grounds
  - Holding Parents Accountable
  - Holding Teachers Accountable
- Limitations on School Authority
- Constitutional Rights of Students
  - Metal Detectors in Schools
  - Use of Canine Units
  - Drug Testing
  - Vehicle Searches
- Gang Related Violence and Drug Availability at School
- Legislation
- Additional Resources

## Background

Two major issues are central to the school safety debate—Fourth Amendment rights in **search and seizure** and the extent of a school's authority in controlling the school environment and its occupants. Although all states impose minimal guidelines, each school and school district is responsible for its own governing policies. Setting the standard for all states is the 1994 Improving America's Schools Act passed which amended the Elementary and Secondary Education Act of 1965. Title IV of the Improving Schools Act, called Safe and Drug-Free Schools and Commu-

nities, outlines legislation and initiatives to make schools safe. For example, one of the goals of national education was to have drug-free and weapons-free school campuses by the year 2000 and, further, to offer students "a disciplined environment that is conducive to learning."

Violence in school has received much public attention during the past several years because incidents of school violence in which students and/or teachers have died of gunshot wounds have occurred across the United States from Springfield, Oregon to Edinboro, Pennsylvania. However, according to various sources, the number of violent crimes committed on school grounds has been declining for several years, following decreases in other violent crime (see Agnew, 2000; Office of Juvenile Justice and Delinquency Prevention (OJJDP), 1999; U. S. Department of Education (USEd), 1999). In fact, students are three times more likely to be victims of a non-fatal violent crime outside of school than they are at school (Agnew, 2000). The one type of violent crime committed on school grounds that has increased is the number of multiple victim homicides (OJJDP, 1999; USEd, 1999), but the odds of a student being a victim of such a **homicide** are about one in three million (Brezina & Wright, 2000).

The school setting is unique in that it forces large groups of people together for extended periods of time in small areas. Many state legislatures have recognized that certain acts committed under these circumstances have potentially greater harmful effects to the health and safety of people and have implemented legislation accordingly.

# Weapons at School

Violence at school often involves the use of weapons. Traditionally, weapons prohibited on school grounds referred to firearms and explosives, but recently, many states have widened these guidelines. For example, in Kansas, weapons include firearms, explosive devices, bludgeons, metal knuckles, throwing stars, electronic stun guns, specific types of knives (such as switchblades and butterfly knives), and any weapon that "expels a projectile by the action of an explosive" (e.g., gunpowder). Other states have gone much further than these specifications. Georgia defines weapons in its school laws as items complying with these descriptions:

> any pistol, revolver, or any weapon designed or intended to propel a missile of any kind, or any dirk, bowie knife, switchblade knife, ballistic knife, any other knife having a blade of three or more inches, straight-edge razor, razor blade, spring stick, metal knuckles, blackjack, any bat, club, or other bludgeon-type weapon, or any flailing instrument consisting of two or more rigid parts connected in such a manner as to allow them to swing freely, which may be known as a nun chahka, nun chuck, nunchaku, shuriken, or fighting chain, or any disc, of whatever configuration, having at least two points or pointed blades which is designed to be thrown or propelled and which may be known as a throwing star or oriental dart, or any weapon of like kind, and any stun gun or taser (Code 1-33).

The only instances in which all states allow weapons and firearms on school property are when individuals are authorized to do so; for example, school police officers may be armed and teachers having instructional purposes. Many people wonder how many youth have access to weapons. Recent data indicate that about 30 percent of young individuals own a firearm (Brezina & Wright, 2000). Further, a national study conducted by the Center for Disease Control revealed that in 1997 about one-fifth of high school students reported carrying a weapon to school.

## Ramifications of Possessing Weapons on School Grounds

In nearly all states, possession of a firearm on school property is a class C or class D **felony**. In addition to having the right to file criminal charges, all school districts have an automatic expulsion policy for students caught with any type of weapon on school property which action can be appealed on a case-by-case basis. Such policies are mandated by the Gun-Free Schools Act of 1994. Special Education students are protected from automatic expulsion under the Individuals with Disabilities Education Act (IDEA). A special education student who is found to be possessing a weapon on school grounds is subject to removal from the school to an interim setting for a period of up to 45 days. During this time, the incident is studied, and if the possession of the weapon was not due to the student's **disability**, that student can be punished in the same way as a non-special education student.

Some states, for example, Kansas and Florida, have also adopted laws that allow for the revocation of students' driver's licenses if they are found guilty of possessing a firearm or drugs on school property. Kansas goes so far to say that the state can revoke a student's driver's license for any behavior engaged in by a student that was likely to result in serious bodily injury to others at school.

## Holding Parents Accountable

In nearly all states, parents can be held accountable for damages resulting from their child's criminal actions on school property, provided that child is living with the parents. This law means that parents of any student who vandalizes school property or attacks other students or teachers can be held liable. In addition, parents who allow minors access to firearms can be prosecuted on criminal charges, such as contributing to the delinquency of a minor.

## Holding Teachers Accountable

Many states have adopted laws that require teachers to report a crime that they know or have reason to believe was committed on school property or at a school activity. Failure to do so may result in criminal prosecution for a **misdemeanor**. Lacking uniformity on this issue, school districts vary greatly with regard to making criminal charges.

# Limitations on School Authority

Another area that has been debated by the courts is the extent of school authority. Under the Gun Free School Zones Act of 1995, a firearm could not be brought within 1,000 feet of a school. The Supreme Court, in a rare decision that overturned this Congressional Act, decided in *United States v. Lopez* (1995) that it was unconstitutional to declare schools gun-free zones in this manner. Further, the court held that claims of increased school violence could not override Second Amendment constitutional rights.

There have been other challenges to school authority under the Fourteenth Amendment which allows for due process. Students must be given notification of charges against them, in addition to an opportunity to defend themselves, and to be represented when being expelled or suspended. A written school policy on the appeals process is recommended.

## Constitutional Rights of Students

With the advent of increased availability of drugs and weapons for juveniles during the last twenty years, search and seizure laws have been challenged by many students who felt their constitutional rights were violated by unreasonable searches at school. Prior to 1968, the constitutional rights of students took a back seat to the doctrine of **loco parentis**, which meant that the school and its officials took the place of the parent. Under this philosophy, students had few constitutional rights. The first serious challenge to this philosophy came in 1969 when the Supreme Court decided in *Tinker v. De Moines Independent School District* that students should be allowed to wear black arms bands as a symbol of protest against the United States involvement in the Vietnam war. The court held that this was an expression of free speech and therefore was a First Amendment right.

Fourth Amendment protection against search and seizure was argued in the courts for years and was finally resolved in *New Jersey v. T.L.O.* (1985). In this case, a teacher had searched a student's possessions after the student was found smoking a cigarette. Subsequently, the teacher found marijuana and drug paraphernalia. There were two major questions raised by this case. First was whether students who are searched on school property have Fourth Amendment privileges and, second, what determines **probable cause** for a search. In other instances, a **warrant** is required before a search can be conducted.

The courts held that Fourth Amendment Privileges do extent to students, but school authorities can search without a warrant provided the search is reasonable in inception and reasonable in scope. However, in order for law enforcement personnel to conduct a search, a warrant must be procured. This point becomes important in light of the number of schools which have their own police officers. Thus, in order for a search to take place, there must be the following conditions:

> reasonable grounds for suspecting that the search will turn up **evidence** that the student has violated or is violating either the law or the rules of the school. Such a search will be permissible in its scope when the measures adopted are reasonable and related to the objectives of the search and are not excessively intrusive in light of the age and sex of the student and the nature of the **infraction**. (*New Jersey v. T.L.O.* 1985, p. 733)

Whether a search is reasonable in inception has been interpreted as a search based on reasonable suspicion, which is very similar to probable cause. The extent of reasonable suspicion must be much higher for more intrusive searches. For example, a search of a student's locker requires a low level of reasonable suspicion, but in order for a student to be strip searched, there must be a much higher degree of reasonable suspicion. A body cavity search can only be conducted by law enforcement personnel after a warrant has been procured. Further, in order for the search to comply with the law, the search must be in proportion to the suspicion. A student should not be strip searched to find ten dollars that has been stolen.

One example of a situation in which a court determined a search to be reasonable is *Martinez v. School District No. 60* (1992) in which a school dance monitor asked two students to blow on her face after observing them acting in a manner consistent with **drunkenness**. A second example is the *Matter of Gregory M.* (1992/1993) in which a security guard ran his hand along a student's school bag to feel for a gun after the bag had made an unusual noise on contact with the student's locker.

Locker searches are also affected by individual school policies. Some schools maintain that lockers are school property and, therefore, school administrators can conduct random searches of lockers. The courts have held this is permissible provided that students are notified of this policy in writing.

### *Metal Detectors in Schools*
Metal detectors have been installed in schools around the country as a means of decreasing the number of weapons being brought to school. A metal detector is a type of mass search which has been challenged as a violation of Fourth Amendment

privileges. The courts in several states, such as Florida, Louisiana and Tennessee, have held that metal detectors are not violating Fourth Amendment rights and are held to the same legal standards as metal detectors in other facilities, such as airports. Metal detectors are, therefore, considered administrative searches and may provide reasonable suspicion for further individualized searches. Some states have also noted that there is a need to violate privacy to some degree in order for the safety of the greater group. California has stipulated that a written policy detailing policies and the use of metal detectors be given to students and should be based on information about the dangers of students' weapons at school.

### Use of Canine Units

The Supreme Court has not ruled on the constitutional limits of using drug-sniffing dogs in schools at the time of this publication, and the lower courts have had differing opinions on whether such tactics are in violation of the reasonable suspicion test. Some courts have held that a sniffer dog does not constitute a search at all, with the landmark case being *Doe v. Renfrow* (1980). Students who were singled out by dogs in this case were subjected to a strip search, which the Supreme court held was unreasonable. In *Horton v. Goose Creek Independent School District* (1982) courts held that sniffing a person was a search and that such a search was a violation of Fourth Amendment rights unless there was reasonable suspicion as dictated by *T.L.O.*

### Drug Testing

The debate over whether schools can implement mandatory, random drug tests to students using either urine analysis or blood testing has also been widely debated in the courts. In *Jones v. McKenzie* (1986) the courts held that drug tests violate a student's reasonable expectation of privacy. Since this case, the courts have been careful to distinguish between mandatory and voluntary drug testing, since the latter requires consent of the student.

Student athletes have long been subjected to different rules. Many athletic programs are required by their governing bodies to perform random, mandatory drug testing on athletes using urine analysis. In 1998, the U. S. Supreme Court declined to hear a constitutional challenge to a random drug testing policy of students involved in extracurricular activities that was implemented in an Indiana school district (*Todd v. Rush County*). This decision not to hear the case meant that the Supreme Court endorses random drug testing of student athletes and students involved in other extracurricular activities. This decision was in keeping with the courts ruling in *Vernonia School District 47J v. Action* (1995). In this case, the Supreme Court held that urine testing of student athletes was reasonable on the grounds that school order and discipline outweigh individual students' privacy. Further, student athletes should have a reduced expectation of privacy given that their grades and medical history are subject to scrutiny, and they are often placed in a communal setting for dressing and showering.

### Vehicle Searches

Searches of students' vehicles that are parked on school grounds are subject to the *T.L.O.* guidelines. However, like locker searches, it is prudent for school districts to have a written policy regarding vehicle searches and even some type of parking permit system that clearly outlines the school's policy on vehicle searches.

The following is an extract from a Virginia School district statement on policies on search and seizure.

FAIRFAX COUNTY (VIRGINIA): Desks, lockers, and storage spaces are the property of the school and the principal may conduct general inspections of those areas periodically in the presence of a witness. These areas, in addition to vehicles parked on school property may be searched on an individual basis if there is reasonable grounds to believe there may be illegal drugs, weapons, stolen property or other **contraband**. The search must be conducted for maintaining order and discipline at the school rather than for criminal prosecution. Reasonable effort will be made to locate the student prior to the search. Further, students believed to have any contraband on their person may be searched and metal detectors may be used. Personal searches may extend to pockets and the removal of outer garments and also to pocketbooks and backpacks. (Regulation 2601.14P, G)

## Gang Related Violence and Drug Availability at School

The Department of Justice implemented the School Crime Supplements (SCS) to the National Crime Victimization Survey in 1995. Part of the SCS addressed the extent to which gangs and gang violence were present at schools. A little over half of the students interviewed in 1995 who attended school in areas with populations between 50,000 and one million, reported gang activity at their schools (Howell & Lynch, 2000). In terms of victimization at schools where gang activity is prevalent, 54 percent of students reported they had been victimized. The study also demonstrated an association between gangs at school and drug availability, as 69 percent of students said drugs such as marijuana, PCP, LSD, crack cocaine, and Ecstacy were easy to get hold of if there were gang activity present at school. In all states, students caught with drugs on school grounds are subject to criminal prosecution under the laws of the state.

## Legislation

Each state receiving Federal funds under the Elementary and Secondary Education Act of 1965 (ESEA) must comply with the Gun-Free Schools Act of 1994 which prohibits firearms to be brought within 1,000 feet of school property. Although part of this legislation was not upheld by the U. S. Supreme Court in *United States v. Lopez*, the legislation still stands, as various other **gun control** bills have been debated but not passed as of 2002. The following is an extract from the Gun-Free Schools Act of 1994.

SECTION 14601. Gun Free Requirements . . . each State receiving Federal funds under this Act shall have in effect a State law requiring local educational agencies to expel from school for a period of not less than one year a student who is determined to have brought a weapon to a school.

State laws repeat stipulations required by this Act almost verbatim, for example, the following Florida provision:

FLORIDA: a person who exhibits a sword, sword cane, firearm, electric weapon or device, destructive device, or other weapon, including a razor blade, box cutter, or knife... at any school-sponsored event or on the grounds of facilities of any school, school bus, or school bus stop, or within 1,000 feet of the real property that comprises a public or private elementary school, middle school, or secondary school, during school hours or during the time of a sanctioned school activity, commits a felony of the third degree. (790.115)

Laws regarding weapons at school may change in the near future as school safety bills being debated by different states are acted upon. For more information, contact the appropriate state's Department of Education.

## Additional Resources

*1999 Annual Report on school safety.* U. S. Department of Education and U.S. Department of Justice, Government Printing Office, Washington, D.C. 1999.

*Going armed in the school zone.* Brezina, Timothy, & Wright, James D. Forum for Applied Research and Public Policy, 15, (4), 82-87, 2000.

*Juvenile offenders and victims: 1999 National Report.* Office of Juvenile Justice and Delinquency Prevention. Government Printing Office, Washington D.C., 1999.

*School crime: A national crime victimization survey report.* Bureau of Justice Statistics, Washington D.C.: Government Printing Office, 1991.

*Strain theory and school crime.* Robert Agnew. In Of crime and criminality, Sally Simpson (Ed). Pine Forge Press, Thousand Oaks, CA, 2000.

*Youth Gangs in Schools.* James C. Howell and James P. Lynch. Juvenile Justice Bulletin, August 2000.

## Organizations

### *Florida Department of Education*
Turlington Building, 325 West Gaines Street
Tallahassee, FL 32399-0400 USA
URL: http://www.firn.edu/doe/

### *The National Center for Juvenile Justice*
710 Fifth Avenue, Suite 3000
Pittsburgh, PA 15219 USA
Phone: (412) 227-6950
Fax: (412) 227-6955
URL: http://brendan.ncjfcj.unr.edu/homepage/ncjj/ncjj2/index.html

### *The National Drug Strategy Network, Criminal Justice Policy Foundation*
1225 I Street NW, Suite 500
Washington, D.C. 20005-3914 USA
Phone: (202) 312-2015
Fax: (202) 842-2620
URL: http://www.ndsn.org

### *The National Resource Center for Safe Schools*
101 SW Main Street, Suite 500
Portland, OR 97204 USA
Phone: (503) 275-0131
Fax: (503) 275-0444

*The Office of Juvenile Justice and Delinquency Prevention, U. S. Department of Justice*
Washington, DC USA
URL: http://www.ojjdp.ncjrs.org

*Safe Learning*
160 E. Virginia Street #290
San Jose, CA 95112 USA
Phone: (408) 286-8505
Fax: (408) 287-8748

URL: http://www.safe-learning.com

*United States Department of Education*
400 Maryland Ave., SW
Washington, DC 20202-0498 USA
Toll-Free: 800-872-5327
URL: http://www.ed.gov

*Violence Policy Center*
1140 19th Street, NW, Suite 600
Washington, DC 20036
URL: http://www.vpc.org

# ESTATE PLANNING

## ESTATE AND GIFT TAX

*Sections within this essay:*

## Background

Estate and gift taxes are a statutory method of **taxation** that are imposed on large transfers of money and/or property during an individual's lifetime or at death. Gift taxes are imposed on transfers made during an individual's lifetime. Estate taxes are imposed on transfers made as a result of death. Most gifts are not subject to the gift tax and most estates are not subject to the estate tax. According to the Internal Revenue Service, only about 2 percent of all estates are subject to estate taxes. Estate and gift taxes are methods the government uses to limit dynastic or familial wealth. Estate taxes are sometimes called death taxes.

An alternative form of death tax is an **inheritance** tax, which is a tax levied on individuals receiving property from the estate. Federal law does not provide for an inheritance tax, although some states have enacted such laws. A number of individual states also have enacted estate tax laws.

Although the taxation of gifts and estates may seem complex, the calculation of estate and gift taxes is similar to the calculation of personal income taxes. As with the **income tax**, there are exemptions and credits that are applied before the progressive rate schedule is applied. Estate taxes are different in that they are calculated over a lifetime, rather than year by year.

## Gift Tax

According to the Internal Revenue Code, a person gives a gift when he gives property (including money), to another without the expectation of receiving something of approximately equal value in return. A gift may also be the use of or income from property. Selling something at less than its full value, or making an interest-free or reduced interest loan, may also constitute a gift.

Although any gift has the potential to be taxable, there are a number of exceptions. For 2005, the first $11,000 given to any one person during the calendar year is not subject to the gift tax. That amount increases to $12,000 in 2006. Educational and medical expenses paid directly to a medical or educational institution for a person will not trigger gift tax provisions. Moreover, gifts to a spouse, a political organization, or charities are generally also exempt.

### Annual Exclusion

A separate $11,000 annual exclusion ($12,000 beginning in 2006) applies to each person to whom a gift is made. A person may give up to $11,000 each to any number of people each year and none of the gifts will be taxable. Married people can separately give up to $11,000 to the same person each year without making a taxable gift.

### Gift Splitting

If a married couple makes a gift to a third party, the gift can be considered as made one-half by each person. This is known as gift splitting. Both spouses must agree to split the gift. Gift splitting allows a married couple to give up to $22,000 to a person annually ($24,000 in 2006) without making a taxable gift. If a gift is split, the couple should file a gift **tax return** proving the agreement to split the gift existed. This is true even where half of the split gift is less than $11,000 or $12,000 (depending upon the year given).

### Gift Tax Return

A gift tax return is filed with annual income taxes on Form 709. This form is required for gifts of over $11,000 to someone other than a spouse, or where a married couple is splitting a gift. If the gift is something the recipient cannot actually possess, enjoy, or receive income from until sometime in the future, Form 709 must be filed. It must also be filed where a person gives his or her spouse an interest in property that will be ended by some future event.

A gift tax return is not required for gifts to political organizations and gifts made for payment of tuition or medical expenses. A gift tax return is not required for certain charitable gifts, including those made to a qualified conservation **easement**. Under certain circumstances, a charitable gift also need not be reported if the gift is for an entire interest in property.

### Unified Credit

Most gifts above the annual exemption are still not subject to tax because each taxpayer is allowed a lifetime credit against taxable gifts and estate. This credit reduces or eliminates the amount of taxes owed. A unified credit applies to both the gift tax and the estate tax. The unified credit is subtracted from any gift tax owed by the taxpayer. Unified credit used against a gift tax in one year reduces the amount of credit that can be applied against a gift tax in later years. The total amount used against a gift tax reduces the credit available to use against estate tax. In other words, any unified credit not used against gift tax during the taxpayer's lifetime is available to reduce or eliminate an estate tax.

Previously, the law provided the same unified credit amount for both the estate tax and the gift tax. Under current law, however, the unified credit against taxable gifts is $345,800. This credit has the effect of exempting $1 million from tax. This amount will remain the same through 2009. The unified credit amount for estate tax purposes, on the other hand, changes from year to year.

The unified credit for estate tax purposes is $555,800, for a person who dies in either 2004 or 2005. This excludes $1,500,000 from estate tax. In 2006, 2007, and 2008, the unified credit for estate tax purposes is $780,800. This figure translates to an exclusion amount of $2 million from tax. In 2009, the unified credit rises to $1,455,800; the exclusion amount is $3,500,000.

## Estate Tax

A person's taxable estate is defined as the gross estate less allowable deductions. Gross estate means the value of all property in which the decedent had an interest at the time of death. The gross estate includes life insurance proceeds payable to the estate or the heirs, the value of certain annuities payable to the estate or heirs, and the value of certain property transferred three years or less prior to death. Estate taxes are due to the IRS nine months from the date of death. The estate tax return is Form 706.

### Taxable Estate

The taxable estate includes the value of all property and assets owned at the time of death plus any gifts made in the three years prior to death. Allowable deductions from a decedent's taxable estate include funeral expenses, debts the decedent owed at the time of death, costs of administering and settling the estate, and the marital **deduction**. The marital deduction encompasses the value of property that passes from an estate to a surviving spouse.

Any unified credit not used to eliminate gift tax can be used to eliminate or reduce estate tax. The maximum tax rate for the estate of a person who died in 2005 is 47 percent. The rate falls to 46 percent for the estate of someone who dies in 2006, and to 45 percent for someone who dies in 2007, 2008, or 2009.

## Recipients

The recipient of a gift or an estate is not liable for the gift or estate tax. An estate's executor is responsible for payment of any estate tax that is due; the donor is responsible for payment of a gift tax, if one is due. Moreover, gifts and inheritances are not subject to income tax.

## Economic Growth and Tax Relief Reconciliation Act of 2001

The federal estate tax law was enacted in 1916; 1997 amendments to the estate and gift tax laws raised the amount of unified credit over a nine-year period. In 2001 Congress further amended estate and gift tax laws.

The 2001 legislation increased the amount that is exempt from estate tax, while reducing the maximum tax rates on taxable property. Beginning in 2002 and through 2009, the top federal estate and gift tax rates drops from 55% to 50% in 2002, and then by one percentage point annually until reaching 45% for 2007, 2008, and 2009. Gift tax rates will be reduced on the same schedule as the estate tax rate. The law also substantially increased the amount that individuals can pass to their heirs free of federal estate taxes from $1 million in 2002 and gradually to $3.5 million in 2009.

The 2001 law provided that the federal estate tax will be completely eliminated in 2010. However, the law has a "sunset" provision which means that if Congress passes no additional law, the estate tax laws in effect prior to the Tax Relief Act of 2001 would be reinstated in 2011. This means that in 2011, the estate tax exemption will be $1 million and the top tax rate will be 55 percent, if the law is not amended before then.

The future of federal estate tax law is uncertain. President George W. Bush is in favor of a permanent repeal of the tax. In 2002 Congress narrowly rejected legislation that would have permanently repealed the estate tax.

Unlike the estate tax, the gift tax has no sunset provision in 2010, and taxpayers will still be subject to a lifetime gift tax. From 2002 through 2009, the top marginal estate tax and gift tax rates are the same. For 2010, gifts in excess of the $1 million exclusion amount are subject to a gift tax at a rate equal to the top individual income tax rate, 35 percent.

## Generation-skipping Transfer Tax

Generation-skipping **transfer tax** (GST) applies when a person omits their own children as beneficia-

ries and instead leaves the inheritance directly to their grandchildren. The GST tax rates and exemptions were also changed in the 2001 law. The GST exemptions match the estate tax exemptions, and the top tax rate falls accordingly, to a rate of 45 percent in 2009. Mirroring the estate tax, the GST tax also contains a sunset provision for 2010 only.

## Farmers and Small Business Owners

A driving force behind the 1997 and 2001 changes to estate and gift tax laws was to provide some relief to farmers of family-owned farms and other small business owners. Because these two groups often posses a significant amount of business assets, they are more likely than other taxpayers to be subject to estate taxes. Congress responded by enacting provisions for special-use valuation of farmland, a family-business deduction, and installment payment of estate taxes.

A special formula to reduce the value of real estate is employed where heirs continue to use the property as a family farm or business. Moreover, they may not sell it to a non-relative for at least 10 years. This special use valuation serves to reduce the market value of the real estate of most farms by anywhere from 40 to 70 percent.

For estates where farm and business assets amount to more than 35 percent of the gross estate, the estate tax may be paid in installments over a 14-year period. The law provides reduced interest rates, and only interest payments are required for the first five years.

## State Taxes

Federal law previously included a credit for state death taxes, but the 2001 law changes phased out the state tax credit and replaced it with a deduction for state estate taxes paid. This change in the federal law spurred some states to reduce or eliminate their state death taxes.

## Additional Resources

*Options for Reforming the Estate Tax.* Burman, Leonard E., William G. Gale, and Jeffrey Rohaly, Tax Policy Center, April 18, 2005.

*Publication 950.* Internal Revenue Service.

## Organizations

### American College of Trust and Estate Counsel

3415 South Sepulveda Boulevard., Suite 330
Los Angeles, CA 90034 USA
Phone: (310) 398-1888
Fax: (310) 572-7280

### National Academy of Elder Law Attorneys, Inc.

1604 North Country Club Road
Tucson, AZ 85716 USA
Phone: (520) 881-4005
Fax: (520) 325-7925
URL: http://www.naela.com/

# ESTATE PLANNING

## GUARDIANSHIPS AND CONSERVATORSHIPS

*Sections within this essay:*

## Background

If an individual becomes unable to handle his or her own affairs there are two major areas of concern. These are the individual's physical welfare decisions and the management of the individual's finances. A guardianship is the appointment of an individual to provide care and to make personal decisions for a minor or incapacitated person. A **guardian** may be nominated by a Will, by a Trust document, or by any via a petition with the court. The person for whom a guardian is appointed is called a ward. Generally, the ward cannot provide food, clothing, or shelter for himself or herself welfare without assistance. A conservatorship is the appointment of an individual or a corporation with **trustee** powers, to manage the financial affairs of a minor or other person who cannot manage his or her own financial matters. A conservator is not authorized to make decisions regarding the personal care as a guardian does. The person for whom a conservator is appointed is called a protected person. The court may appoint a conservator for a single transaction or indefinitely. A person may need a guardian or a conservator or both and the same person can be appointed in both capacities.

## Guardianship

Guardianship is established by a court order. The court grants the guardian authority and responsibility to act on behalf of another person. The relationship is **fiduciary**, which means that the guardian is obliged to act in the best interests of the ward. The court supervises the guardian to assure proper actions on behalf of the ward. An individual may serve as guardian of a minor or of an incapacitated person. For a minor, the court considers which individual's appointment will be in the best interest of the minor. In some states, a minor ward over fourteen can nominate his or her own choice for guardian. Any competent person may be appointed guardian for an incapacitated person. The appointee might be the spouse, an adult child or parent of the ward, or any responsible adult with whom the ward is residing.

To establish a guardianship, a petition is typically filed in state court where the ward lives. This petition usually names the potential guardian and provides information about the parties' relationship (if any) and usually any pertinent information about the heirs or estate of the ward. If the ward is a minor, information about the minor's parents and whether and where they are living is generally necessary. In the case of an adult ward, if mental incapacity is the reason for the petition, medical documentation should accompany the filing. Notice of the time and place of the **hearing** is given to the potential ward and other persons specified by **statute**.

The documents are served on the interested parties at which point the proposed ward or his or her relatives can object to the guardianship request. A hearing is held. If the court finds sufficient **evidence** to order the guardianship, it may issue subsequent orders, which govern the relationship and the guardian's actions. The court may appoint a guardian if it finds the person is incapacitated and the appointment is necessary to provide continuing care and supervision of the person. Incapacity can result from any number of conditions, including, but not limited to mental illness, mental deficiency, mental disorder, physical illness or **disability**, chronic use of alcohol or other drugs. Essentially, the court must be convinced that the individual lacks sufficient understanding or capacity to make or communicate responsible decisions. The court may terminate a guardianship if a subsequent hearing proves that the need for a guardian no longer exists, or in the case of a minor, when the child reaches the **age of majority**.

A guardianship restricts the individual's right to contract, marry, spend money, make decisions about their own care, or create a new will. The guardian may make personal decisions for the ward such as living arrangements, education, social activities, and authorization or withholding of medical or other professional care, treatment, or advice. A guardian must submit written reports to the court according to the court's orders and the law of the **jurisdiction** in which the guardianship takes place. Generally, a guardian is not charged with managing the income or property of the incapacitated person; however, the guardian may receive funds payable for the support of the ward such as social security as a representative payee.

If a guardianship is contested, the court may appoint a disinterested third party to investigate and make recommendations. Usually called a **guardian ad litem**, this person evaluates both the necessity

for a guardianship, and the appropriateness of the proposed guardian. The ward may also hire separate legal **counsel**. If the proposed ward is indigent, the court sometimes appoints counsel.

## Guardianship of Minors

Guardianship of a minor is typically appropriate when a child is permanently living with someone other than a parent. This might occur if both parents died, or if one parent died and the other is incarcerated or otherwise absent. Guardianships of minors are often established when neither parent is able to provide a safe, secure home for the child because of drug abuse, alcoholism, and other serious personal problems.

The difference between guardianship and **adoption** is that guardianship does not sever the biological parents' rights and responsibilities. Guardianship of a child means that a caregiver is responsible for the care and **custody** of the child. This arrangement allows the guardian to access services on behalf of the child. Unlike adoption, a birth parent can return to court at any time and ask for the guardianship to be terminated.

When a guardian is appointed for a minor child, the court may impose conditions. One common condition is a requirement that the guardian attend parenting classes. Courts sometimes require that grandparent guardians attend grandparent caregiver support groups. Not only are judges aware that parenting techniques have changed in recent years, but if the child's parents are drug addicts, alcoholics, or abusive toward children, is may be appropriate to question why the grandparents will do a better job raising the grandchildren than they did raising their own children. Grandparents seeking guardianship should be prepared to address these issues.

### Guardianship of the Estate

Even if a minor child lives with one or both parents, in some states a guardianship is required if the child inherits property worth more than $20,000. After the court appoints a guardian, an inventory and **appraisal** must be filed, and annual or bi-annual accountings must also be filed with the court until the child reaches age eighteen.

### De Facto Custodian

De Facto Custodian laws give caregivers the same standing as parents in custody cases if they satisfy the definition of de facto custodian. They must be the primary caregiver and must be providing financial support of a child who has lived with the de facto custodian for a certain period of time.

### Standby Guardianship

These laws were originally designed in response to the AIDS crisis and allow a terminally ill parent to designate a standby guardian to take over the day to day care of a child in the event of parental incapacity. There is a Sense of Congress in the Adoption and Safe Families Act (ASFA) that States should pass these laws.

### Permanent Guardianship

Permanent guardianships are for children in state custody. In some states permanent guardianship status may be granted by the juvenile court after it is proven that it is in the best interest of the child that the birth parent should never have physical custody of the child. A birth parent is prohibited from petitioning the court to terminate this permanent guardianship once it is granted.

### Subsidized Guardianship

Some states have programs that provide a monthly subsidy payment to grandparents and other relatives who obtain guardianship of the children they are raising. Subsidized guardianships are designed for those children who have been in state custody, with a relative or non-relative providing the care, for at least six months and in some states up to two years. The subsidy is sometimes less than the foster care payment in that state but usually more than the Temporary Assistance for Needy Families (TANF) child-only grants. Continued eligibility for the subsidy is typically re-determined annually. The subsidy payments usually end when the guardianship terminates or when the child turns 18, although several states continue the subsidy until the child reaches age 21 or 22 provided he or she is attending school. States have some similar programs that do not require the child to be in state custody.

## Conservatorship

Unlike a guardian, a conservator has no power or responsibility over the individual. Only the money and property falls within the conservator's jurisdiction. A conservator has power to invest funds of the estate and to distribute sums reasonably necessary for the support, care, education or benefit of the protected person and any legal dependents of the protected person. Either an individual, or a corporation with general power to serve as a trustee may be ap-

pointed conservator for a protected person. Typically, state laws provide a preferred order of priority for those who may be considered by the court for appointment. A conservator has the powers and responsibilities of a fiduciary and is held to the standard of care applicable to a trustee. The conservator files an inventory of the estate of the protected person with the court and accountings of the administration of the estate.

Conservatorship is established by petitioning the court. The petition can be filed by the person to be protected, or by any person interested in the estate, affairs, or welfare of the protected person. This appointee could be a parent or guardian, or by any individual or entity adversely affected by improper management of the property and affairs of the protected person. In most states, the person to be protected must be represented by an attorney. The court also typically requires an independent physician's report. The court may appoint a conservator if it finds that an individual is unable to manage property and financial affairs effectively for reasons including, but not limited to, mental illness, mental deficiency, mental disorder, physical illness or disability, chronic use of drugs, chronic **intoxication**, confinement, detention by a foreign power, or disappearance.

A conservatorship terminates upon the death of the protected person or upon a court determination that the disability of the protected person has ceased. The protected person, the personal representative of the protected person, the conservator, or any other interested person or entity may petition the court to terminate the conservatorship. Upon termination, title of the assets passes to the former protected person, or if deceased, as provided by the protected person's will.

## Involuntary Commitment

A person who is a danger to self or others can, under certain conditions, be court ordered to a mental hospital. Most states allow commitment to public and private mental hospitals, either as a voluntary patient accepted by the institution or under a court order of involuntary commitment. Legal standards surround the process by which those who are mentally ill can be forced to receive treatment. State laws and rules regarding involuntary commitment are subject to the due process clause of the Fourteenth Amendment, which guarantees the right to be free from governmental restraint and the right not to be confined unnecessarily.

If a guardian or person is not agreeable to a voluntary commitment, state law provisions typically provide a procedure for emergency involuntary hospitalization. In the event of a voluntary hospitalization, a person, or that person's court-ordered guardian, requests admission to the hospital. The hospital can retain the patient indefinitely or discharge the patient provided the staff determines discharge is in the best interest of the patient and the community. In many states, a patient on a voluntary admission who wishes to leave must give the institution three days notice. This gives the hospital the opportunity to apply for involuntary commitment of the patient, if the staff determines that is appropriate. The facility will then typically retain the patient until the court hearing.

## Public Fiduciary

A public fiduciary is a governmental official appointed to serve as guardian, conservator, or personal representative for those individuals or estates with no one else willing or capable of serving. The public fiduciary may file a petition with the court to be named guardian/conservator if the public fiduciary believes such a request is warranted. The court appoints the public fiduciary if the court finds sufficient evidence that a person or estate is in need of the services of the public fiduciary.

## Representative Payee

Sometimes involuntary commitment or even a guardianship or conservatorship is not the best solution. If an elderly person is no longer able to remember to write out checks but can still remember how to eat regularly and take medication appropriately, a representative payeeship may often be an option. A representative payeeship is an arrangement whereby a person's Social Security and/or Supplemental Security Income (SSI) checks, or even his or her private **pension** checks, are issued to another person who is the representative payee. This person can be a family member, friend, social worker, attorney, or accountant. Additionally, many utility companies, if requested, will contact a representative third party prior to the termination of services to an elderly person. Sometimes this is sufficient to assure that an elderly person does not have essential services disconnected.

## Power of Attorney

A **power of attorney** is an authorization for one person to transact business on behalf of another. It can be specific as to one instance, or it can include any conceivable business transaction. Power of attorney documents were once considered void if the maker became mentally incompetent. Most states have now adopted the Uniform Durable Power of Attorney Act which provides that a power of attorney will survive even though its maker has become mentally incompetent.

While a power of attorney is a simple document to draft, it has inherent pitfalls. Power of attorney can be a useful safeguard against potential unknown future incapacity, but it empowers someone else to handle the financial affairs of an incapacitated person. As a result, it may give rise to family disputes and even emergency court filings in a time of family crisis. And, unlike a court appointed guardian or conservator, there is no one charged with overseeing the action of the individual with the power of attorney.

## Joint Ownership

Most common in married couples' financial situations is joint ownership. Individual access to bank accounts can be had by either joint owner, even if the other joint owner is incapacitated. For this reason, elderly people sometimes place an adult child's name on their accounts. This is a simple and effective way of insuring that the child can continue to pay the parent's bills if the parent is unable to do so. It does, however, give the child the legal ability to withdraw everything from the entire account. Placing an adult child's name jointly on an asset can also present problems to the parent if the child incurs debts, is sued, or gets divorced. Since joint ownership means just that, the result can be that the asset which was once solely the parent's can become subject to the adult child's creditors or soon to be ex-spouse.

While joint **tenancy** can transfer assets at death without any type of **probate** proceedings, the legal implications of joint tenancy are governed by state law and will vary from state to state. In some states with **community property** law, property owned by spouses in joint tenancy will not receive the same tax treatment when one spouse dies. The joint tenancy property can lose important benefits otherwise available to the survivor. Finally, because jointly-owned assets transfer directly to the survivor, such property passes outside of a will. A parent can unintentionally leave his or her property to the child who is the joint owner, rather than having the property divided equally among several children.

## Selected State Law Provisions

FLORIDA: A grandparent, adult aunt or uncle or person with power of attorney can consent to medical care or treatment of a minor after a treatment provider has failed in his or her reasonable attempt to contact a parent, legal custodian or legal guardian. Under this law, no writing is necessary to convey consent power.

LOUISIANA: Relatives who become either a child's legal custodian or guardian and have an income less than 150% of the federal poverty guidelines are eligible to receive the monthly subsidy payments.

MISSOURI: Grandparents (or other relatives) who become either the child's legal custodian or guardian and attend foster parent training are eligible to receive the monthly subsidy payments.

NORTH CAROLINA: An adult who is raising a child informally can enroll the child in a school district where the adult is a domiciliary provided an **affidavit** is submitted of the parent, legal guardian or legal custodian or the adult with whom the child lives. If the parent is unable, refuses or is unavailable to submit the affidavit, the adult's affidavit should include a statement that the parent is unable, refuses or is unavailable.

PENNSYLVANIA: A parent, legal guardian or custodian may give an adult, including a relative caregiver, authorization to consent to medical or mental health care for the child. The authorization can be in any written form and must be signed by the parent, legal guardian or custodian and witnessed by two adults, neither of whom is the person to whom authorization is being given. There is no time limit on this authorization, but can be revoked at will. Furthermore, the death of the parent, legal guardian or custodian who executed the authorization will automatically revoke the authorization.

## Additional Resources

*"Bringing Some Sense to Civil Commitment Hearings."* Davoli, Joanmarie I. 2 Catalyst 9 (2000).

## Organizations

### *The Elder Law Project Legal Services for Cape Cod and Islands, Inc.*
460 West Main Street
Hyannis, MA 02601 USA
Phone: (508) 775-7020

### *National Academy of Elder Law Attorneys, Inc.*
1604 North Country Club Road
Tucson, AZ 85716 USA
Phone: (520) 881-4005
Fax: (520) 325-7925
URL: http://www.naela.com/

### *National Alliance for the Mentally Ill*
2107 Wilson Blvd., Suite 300
Arlington, VA 22201 USA
Phone: (703) 524-7600
URL: http://www.nami.org/

# ESTATE PLANNING

## INTESTACY

*Sections within this essay:*

## Background

When a person dies (the decedent), a major concern for those surviving the decedent is how to distribute the decedent's property, or the estate. An age-old problem, this issue has mattered greatly in the past, and it still does. Accordingly, the law has developed to govern not only how the decedent's personal property and real property is distributed to heirs but also how important privileges as well as debts and other responsibilities are passed down to later generations.

Because this issue reaches into ancient times and the consequences of **inheritance** can be so important, there is an enormous body of **statutory** and **case law** relating to "who gets what" when someone dies. There are several key components to these laws. For example, there are laws about wills, trusts, and other methods of leaving property in addition to wills, jurisdiction of **probate** courts, qualifications and duties of executors of wills, and estate and inheritance taxes. Tax consequences for the estate and heirs are important considerations when individuals plan their estates. Whether individuals die with a will or **intestate**, there are tax consequences for estates and potentially for those who would **inherit** property according to the laws of **intestacy**. The negative tax consequences and other potentially unintended consequences that can flow from dying intestate are major reasons that prompt people to create wills.

## Intestacy

When a decedent does not leave a legally binding will, this state is called dying intestate. The estate of a decedent (an estate is the sum of the decedent's property), who dies intestate is distributed according to the intestacy laws where the decedent was domiciled and/or where the decedent owned real property. Federal law leaves the creation of intestacy laws largely up to the states. Consequently, intestacy laws and judicial decisions vary from state to state. Intestacy statutes basically "create" a will for the decedent if the individual died intestate.

The most common way for individuals to influence how their property gets distributed when they die is to create a will. Wills are legal documents that help heirs and courts; local, state and federal governments; and the decedent's creditors know how to distribute that person's property upon death. There is more information about wills in The Gale Encyclopedia of Everyday Law under the topic "Wills."

### Partial Intestacy

If someone dies and has made a will, all state laws strongly favor the decedent's intentions as expressed in his will. However, even if the individual has made a will, it is possible for the person to die partially intestate. This situation occurs when a gift in the will is invalid for some reason, or if the terms of the will simply do not cover all of the property. For example, if the will only disposes of personal property (like jewelry, art, automobiles, and antiques), the **personal property** will be distributed to those named in the will according to the terms of the will. However, if the individual had purchased a parcel of land after the person made the will and failed to later include that land in the will, then the real estate may pass to the heirs under the laws of intestacy. And in some states, if an otherwise valid will is not properly filed with the probate court within a specific time, the entire estate will be distributed according to the state intestacy scheme. Needless to say, these situations may not at all be what the decedent wanted to happen.

### Determining Who Will Receive a Share of an Intestate Estate

If individuals die intestate, their state's intestacy laws will make assumptions about how they would want to leave their property. Some of these assumptions may be correct, and others may result in the distribution of property in a manner far different from their wishes. The law will determine who will inherit the property (heirs) and how the property will be divided among the heirs, but it cannot determine who will receive specific items of property. For example, the law may state that the two children, a daughter and a son, will each take one half of the estate, but it may not say that the daughter should receive the decedent's mother's wedding ring and the decedent's son should receive the decedent's antique desk. Leaving such issues for a judge or other official to determine can cause squabbles among heirs, expense to the estate, and long delays in disposing of the property.

For the most part, states assume that the closer individuals are related to someone, the more likely the decedent would want the property to go to those persons when the decedent dies. In this way, intestate laws generally favor blood relations over other types of relationships. It is also common for state laws to require that heirs survive the decedent by a certain amount of time. This time can be expressed in hours, days, or months, depending on the state. These rules become important when there is an event in which several members of a family are killed at or about the same time. They generally apply whether or not the decedent had a will.

### Intestacy Laws and Surviving Spouses

Of course, there are also many laws that pertain to surviving spouses of decedents who die intestate. Like other aspects of intestacy, these laws vary considerably from state to state. While it seems safe to assume that the spouse will inherit the entire estate if the decedent dies without a will, this is not necessarily the case. It is true that spouses usually inherit the greatest portion of the decedent's estate; however, intestacy laws almost always divide the estate between the decedent's spouse, children, and sometimes even the decedent's parents. If there are no spouse or children, and if the decedent's parents are dead, then the estate usually is distributed among the decedent's siblings or other relatives according to specific rules delineated in the statutes.

It is crucial to keep in mind that state intestacy laws can differ significantly from one state to the next. For example, most states set aside an allowance for a surviving spouse and/or children. This can be true whether or not there is a will. This amount is usually modest, but it is free from any other claims against the estate or debts of the decedent. In these cases, the spouse and/or children take a specific dollar amount of the estate. Their doing so occurs before the creditors, heirs, and other beneficiaries receive their shares of what remains. There are great differences in these allowances among the states. For example, this amount is set at $50,000 in California, but only $2,000 in Delaware. If there is no will, many states also give the surviving spouse a definite financial interest in any real estate owned by the decedent, such as "one-half," or a "life estate."

### Intestacy and Marital Property

The portion of an estate that is distributed to the spouse of a decedent who dies intestate depends to some extent on other laws governing marital property in the decedent's state. For example, in states which employ a **community property** scheme, spouses generally own equal rights to all marital property, regardless of whose name is on the title of the property. But this general rule has some important exceptions. There are currently nine community property states: Arizona, California, Idaho, Louisiana, Nevada, New Mexico, Texas, Washington, and Wisconsin.

In a typical situation involving community property for a decedent who dies intestate, the decedent's share of the community property owned at the time of death will pass automatically to the surviving spouse. Property that the decedent owned individually (e.g. certain property owned prior to the marriage) is usually divided between the surviving spouse and any children. The spouse usually takes one quarter of this individual property and surviving children take the remaining three-quarters of the property. For individuals living in a community property state, the complexity of the intestacy and other probate laws make it is especially important to contact competent legal advice when planning their estates.

## Typical Intestacy Distribution Methods

What happens to their property if individuals die without a will? The answer to this question depends on many factors. Because of the variability of the response, it is perhaps best to explain through illustrations. Here are four examples of some of the most common distribution methods under typical intestacy laws.

- If the Intestate Decedent is Married but has no Children

- If the intestate decedent is married but has no children, most people would probably think that the decedent's surviving spouse would take everything in the estate. However, most states distribute between one-third to one-half of the estate to the surviving spouse. Anything remaining generally goes to the decedent's surviving parent or parents. If both of the decedent's parents are dead, many state intestate statutes **decree** that the remaining portion be distributed among the decedent's surviving brothers and sisters.

- If the Intestate Decedent is Married and has Children

- If the intestate decedent is married and has children, it seems reasonable to assume that the surviving spouse/parent would take all of the deceased spouse's property, especially if

the children are minors at the time of the decedent's death. Yet, most intestacy statutes distribute just one-third to one-half of the decedent's property to the surviving spouse. The remainder is divided among the decedent's surviving children, regardless of their ages.

- If the Intestate Decedent is a Single Person with Children

- If the intestate decedent is a single person with children, state intestacy laws uniformly decree that the entire estate will be distributed equally among the children, regardless of their ages or circumstances. For example, an adult child will receive the same amount as a minor child, and a wealthy child will take the same share as a child in more modest circumstances. The only determining factor is the blood relation to the decedent. Most states also make no distinction between siblings of whole blood and siblings of half blood. Thus, in a case where a decedent has children from two marriages, each child from both marriages will take an equal share of the decedent's estate. Likewise, intestacy laws in all states treat legally adopted children the same as full-blooded relations of the decedent. The laws may differ significantly with respect to the decedent's stepchildren and illegitimate children.

- If the Intestate Decedent is a Single Person with no Children

- If the intestate decedent is a single person with no children, most state intestacy laws favor the decedent's parent(s) in the distribution of his/her property. If both parents predecease the decedent, many states divide the property among the decedent's surviving brothers and sisters.

Intestacy laws that distribute property to surviving children and other relatives use various formulas to divide the property. In a state that employs a "per capita" method, the heirs receive equal shares. For example, if there are eleven heirs of a decedent who dies intestate, each will receive one-eleventh of the decedent's estate. Other states have more complicated schemes that determine the amount of an heir's share according to the degree of relationship to the decedent. For example, let us say that a decedent has two adult children. One of these children is dead, but has two surviving children (the decedent's grandchildren). So in the present case, the decedent's surviving adult child would take one half of the estate and the decedent's two grandchildren would share their deceased parent's half share, each taking one-quarter of the estate. These examples show that the methods of distributing property under intestacy law can range from fairly simple to quite complex.

### *Escheat*

If the intestate decedent has no living spouse, children, parents, or siblings, intestacy laws provide mechanisms to determine other blood relatives qualified to take the estate. Overall, there is a strong statutory preference to distribute the decedent's property to heirs, regardless of how remote they may be to the decedent. Sometimes, the search for heirs can be time-consuming and expensive. The estate bears the expense of a search for heirs. However, in those rare cases where no living **heir** can be located, then the decedent's estate will escheat to the state, that is, the state takes ownership of the decedent's property. Escheat is rare and almost never what the decedent wanted or expected to happen with the estate.

## Estate and Inheritance Tax Considerations

When a person dies the federal and state governments may impose taxes on the transfer of the property. This is true whether the person dies with a will or intestate. These taxes are calculated according to the rules of estate tax law. In some cases, the property received by heirs may also be taxed according to inheritance tax laws. The inheritance tax is usually determined by the amount of property received by the **beneficiary**, as well as by the beneficiary's relationship to the decedent. Basically, it is a tax on the right to receive the property. Every state except Nevada imposes either an estate tax or an inheritance tax; some states employ both. Inheritance taxes are not levied in addition to federal estate taxes because the federal law allows an offset for the payment of state death taxes. The maximum taxes in states with inheritance taxes are:

- Delaware 16%
- Kansas 15%
- Kentucky 16%
- Indiana 15%
- Iowa 15%
- Maryland 10%
- Massachusetts 16%

- Michigan 17%
- Mississippi 16%
- Montana 32%
- Nebraska 18%
- New Hampshire 15%
- New Jersey 16%
- North Carolina 17%
- Ohio 7%
- Oklahoma 15%
- Pennsylvania 15%
- South Dakota 30%
- Tennessee 13%

Currently, the estate of a decedent is liable for a tax if the estate exceeds $650,000. The United States has recently enacted new laws that will increase this amount in certain increments over the next several years. In calculating the value of an estate for tax purposes one starts with the premise that all property owned by the decedent at the time of death is potentially subject to tax. This amount can be modified by several factors:

- The decedent's debts
- Certain transfers to charity
- Certain transfers to the decedent's spouse
- Some **casualty** and theft losses

An intestate estate is the most exposed to estate and inheritance tax liability. The greater the value of the estate, the greater the tax burden on the estate—and potentially on the beneficiaries of the estate. This fact is a powerful inducement for many people to seek estate–planning advice. There are several methods to shield the value of an estate from estate and inheritance tax laws. Along with the creation of a will, some of these methods may include the creation of a trust, purchasing life insurance policies, and making transfers of property prior to your death, known as inter vivos gifts. Attorneys and accountants provide for more specific information about estate and inheritance tax rules.

Individuals who do have wills and believe they would distribute their property differently than their state's intestacy distribution plan should consult their attorneys for advice on estate planning and wills. Likewise, if they believe they are the beneficiaries of an intestate decedent's estate, they should check with their own attorneys for information about the specific laws governing their particular situation and advice about how to proceed to claim their share of the estate. Intestacy laws differ in very significant ways from state to state; understanding their applicability to you may require the advice from an attorney.

## Additional Resources

*The American Bar Association Guide to Wills & Estates.*American Bar Association, Times Books, 1995.

*"Crash Course in Wills and Trusts"* Palermo, Michael T., Attorney at Law, 2001. Available at: http://www.mtpalermo.com.

*"Estate Planning Resources"* EstatePlanningLinks.com, 2001. Available at: http://www.estateplanninglinks.com/ep.html#highlighted

*The Estate Planning Sourcebook.* Berry, Dawn Bradley, Lowell House, 1999.

*"Inheritance and Estate Tax"* Available at: http://www.lawyers.com/lawyers-com/content/aboutlaw/taxation_3.html.lawyers.com, 2001.

*Restatement of the Law, Property Wills and Other Donative Tranfers,* American Law Institute, West Publishing,1999.

*The Wills and Estate Planning Guide: A State and Territorial Summary of Will and Intestacy Statutes.* American Bar Association, The Association, 1995.

*Wills and Trusts in a Nutshell,* Mennell, Robert L., West Publishing, 1994.

*"Wills, Trusts, Estates and Probate"* FindLaw, 2001. Available at: http://www.findlaw.com/01topics/31probate/index.html.

## Organizations

### The American Academy of Estate Planning Attorneys

9360 Towne Centre Drive, Suite 300
San Diego, CA 92121 USA
Phone: (800) 846-1555
Fax: (858) 453-1147
E-Mail: information@aaepa.com
URL: http://www.aaepa.com

### General Practice, Solo and Small Firm Section

### American Bar Association (ABA)

750 N. Lake Shore Drive
Chicago, IL 60611 USA
Phone: (312) 988-5648
Fax: (312) 988-5711
URL: www.abanet.org/genpractice
E-Mail: genpractice@abanet.org

### American Bar Association (ABA), Taxation Section

740 15th Street NW, 10th Floor
Washington, DC 20005-1009 USA
Phone: (202) 662-8670
Fax: (202) 662-8682
E-Mail: taxweb@staff.abanet.org
URL: http://www.abanet.org/tax/home.html

### American College of Trust and Estate Counsel

3415 South Sepulveda Boulevard, Suite 330
Los Angeles, CA 90034 USA
Phone: (310) 398-1888
Fax: (310) 572-7280
E-Mail: info@actec.org
URL: http://www.actec.org

### Americans for Tax Reform (ATR)

1920 L Street NW, Suite 200
Washington, DC 20036 USA
Phone: (202) 785-0266
Fax: (202) 785-0261
URL: www.atr.org

### National Network of Estate Planning Attorneys, Inc.

One Valmont Plaza, Fourth Floor
Omaha, NE 68154-5203 USA
Phone: (800) 638-8681
E-Mail: webmaster@netplanning.com
URL: http://www.netplanning.com

### The National Academy of Elder Law Attorneys

1604 North Country Club Road
Tucson, AZ 85716 USA
Phone: (520) 881-4005
Fax: (520) 325-7925
URL: http://www.naela.com

# ESTATE PLANNING

## LIFE INSURANCE

*Sections within this essay:*

- Background

- Types of Insurance
    - Individual Life Insurance
    - Group Life Insurance
    - Second-To-Die and First-To-Die Insurance
    - Term Life Insurance
    - Cash Value Life Insurance
    - Traditional Whole Life and Universal Life
    - Variable Life and Variable Universal Life

- Insurable Interest

- Examinations

- Claims
    - Denial of Claims
    - Exclusions

- Insurance Regulation

- Rates

- Minors As Beneficiaries

- Additional Resources

## Background

A life insurance policy is simply a contract between an insurance company and the person who buys the policy, the policyholder. In exchange for payment of a specified sum of money, known as a premium, the life insurance company pays a named **beneficiary** a certain amount of money if specific events occur while the policy is in force. In life insurance policies the most common event is the death of the person who is insured, in which case the payment is made to the beneficiary, which may be a person, a trust or other legal entity, or the estate of the owner. Some policies also allow the owner to surrender the policy for its cash value or to take advance payments on the insurance in the event of diagnosis of a terminal condition. The sale of life insurance in the United States has historically been a highly competitive commission sales business with a number of products which combine life insurance and investments.

## Types of Life Insurance

Despite their various names, all life insurance policies fall into either individual or group insurance policies. The difference between Individual and Group Life has become less distinct. Many associations sponsor life insurance plans that are called Group Life coverage but which actually require the same underwriting criteria as for Individual Life.

### Individual Life Insurance

Individual Life insurance generally is underwritten taking into account the actuarial risk of death of the one individual being insured. Life insurance companies' underwriters typically use a combination of factors that statistics indicate equate with the risk of death. These include, but are not limited to applicant's age, applicant's gender (except in states which have uni-sex rate requirements), height and weight, family and applicant health history, marital status, number of children, hazardous occupations, tobacco use, alcohol use, dangerous hobbies, and foreign travel.

### Group Life Insurance

Group Life insurance policies cover the lives of multiple persons within a group. Group Life insurance historically was based on the risk characteristics of the group as a whole. The group might consist of employees of a business, members of a professional organization, members of a **credit union**, or perhaps members of a **labor union**. There are many other possibilities for these groups. The owner of the master group policy is the group itself, such as the employer, the union, the association, or whatever the group may be.

### Second-To-Die and First-To-Die Insurance

Most so–called Second–to–Die policies which pay upon the death of the second of two insured people are still regarded as Individual Life insurance. Similarly the so–called First to Die life insurance, where the lives of a small number of people are covered and the life insurance is payable on the first death is also Individual Life insurance. First to Die is often used to cover partners in a business. The proceeds can be used to buy out the share of the partner who dies first.

### Term Life Insurance

Either Group or Individual polices can be Term Life Insurance. Term Life Insurance is basic insurance in the event of death. The policy owner pays a premium to the insurance company; it can typically be paid monthly, quarterly, or annually. If the insured dies during the time period that the payments are being made, the insurance company pays the face amount of the life insurance to the beneficiary. As the risk of death increases as people get older, the premium generally also increases. At advanced ages, term insurance costs are extremely expensive.

### Cash Value Life Insurance

Cash Value Life Insurance has the same benefits of Term Life Insurance with a savings or investment account. There are several types of Cash Value Life policies.

### Traditional Whole Life and Universal Life

In Traditional Whole Life and Universal Life Insurance policies, money that does not go to pay insurance costs or the sales representative's commission is invested by the insurance company in fixed dollar type investments. Whole-life policies combine life coverage with an investment fund. Cash value builds tax-free each year, and policyholder can usually borrow against the cash accumulation fund without being taxed. Universal life is a whole-life policy that combines term insurance with a money-market-type investment that pays a market rate of return. To get a higher return, these policies generally do not guarantee a certain rate. However, sales of universal policies tend to be higher than those of plain whole life, due to the higher potential yield.

### Variable Life and Variable Universal Life

In Variable Life and Variable Universal Life policies, money that does not go to pay insurance costs or the sales representative's commission is invested by the insurance company in **securities mutual fund** accounts selected by the owner from among the insurer's available choices. Returns are not guaranteed. Variable products are regulated as securities under the Federal Securities Laws and must be sold with a prospectus.

## Insurable Interest

A basic requirement for all types of insurance is the person who buys a policy must have an insurable interest in the subject of the insurance. With respect to life insurance, an insurable interest means a substantial interest engendered by love and affection in the case of persons related by blood and a lawful and substantial economic interest in the continued life of the insured in other business related cases. Everyone has an insurable interest in their own lives and in the lives of their spouses and dependents. Business partners may have an insurable interest in each other, and a corporation may have an insurable interest in its employees' lives. The insurable interest requirement is designed to prevent people from taking out a life insurance policy on some randomly selected persons and then killing them to get the insurance proceeds. The rule also prevents life insurance from becoming a gambling device and prevents someone from taking out insurance policies simply because people are known smokers or known to drink and drive. However, it is not necessary for the beneficiary to have an insurable interest in the life of the insured.

## Examinations

On larger policies, most life insurance companies require the applicant to undergo a physical **examination** by a medical professional. Samples of the applicant's blood and urine typically are taken by a paramedical person contracted by the insurance carrier to conduct such tests. The insurer will typically also request the applicant's medical records from his or her physicians and have them reviewed by the underwriters. The insure usually will also check the applicant's health history with the Medical Information Bureau (MIB).

MIB is a not-for-profit incorporated association of U. S. and Canadian life insurance companies. It is a provider of information and database management services to the financial services industry. Organized in 1902, MIB now consists of over 600 member insurance companies who agree to share information in the form of medical and avocation codes. There are approximately 230 codes, which MIB uses to signify different medical conditions. Some of the codes indicate risks involving hazardous avocations or adverse driving records. While the MIB does not report actual details about the person's medical condition or problem, the codes alert insurance companies to the fact that there was information obtained and reported by a member insurance company on this particular impairment or avocation risk. Individuals can request their own MIB record and can request that the company correct any errors. There is a small processing fee to obtain a report, which is waived if the request is within 60 days of an adverse underwriting decision. All MIB codes are supposed to be purged seven years from the report date.

## Claims

Every life insurance policy specifies certain actions that must take place after a loss has occurred. Typically the beneficiary provides the life insurance company with a **certified copy** of the death certificate. After proof of the death is submitted to the insurance company, the life insurance company should promptly pay the benefits, assuming that the premiums were paid, making the policy in force. Even if premiums on the policy were not currently being paid, the policy may still have been in a paid status, or the company may have failed to send the necessary notices of cancellation, in which case it may be possible to recover on the policy. Usually, once the policy is at least two years old it is beyond the incontestable period and must be paid, except in extraordinary circumstances.

### Denial of Claims

The most common reason life insurance companies use to deny claims is that there was a material misrepresentation in connection with the insurance purchase. The claim regarding material misrepresentation may arise out of the original application for the insurance or from an amendment to the application or in an application for reinstatement. A material misrepresentation sufficient to deny a claim cannot be just any incorrect statement. A material misstatement is almost always one that if it had been disclosed would have meant refusal by the insurer to issue the policy. The most commonly alleged misrepresentations involve an applicant's medical history. Delays in processing claims can sometimes result from legal questions regarding whether the policy was currently in force as of the date of death, or, if the death was a result of foul play, any possibility that the beneficiary may have played a role in the death

### Exclusions

An exclusion is a part of an insurance policy which describes a condition or type of loss that is not covered by the policy. In life insurance, a common exclusion is an exception for accidental deaths caused by acts of war or while in active military service. Certain activities may also fall under the exclusion category. Some policies have an exclusion for deaths that occur while the insured was involved in the commission of a **felony**, or deaths resulting from suicide.

## Insurance Regulation

Because insurance companies handle large amounts of money on behalf of individuals and businesses, the level of **public interest** is sufficient to **warrant** governmental regulation. Historically, the purpose of insurance regulation has been to maintain the insurers' financial **solvency** and soundness and to guarantee the fair treatment of current and prospective policyholders and beneficiaries. There is no central Federal regulatory agency to specifically oversee insurance companies, and as a result, insurance companies in the United States are regulated by the individual states. These regulations include rules about matters such as forms, rates, sales agents, and general insurance business practices.

State laws regulating insurance business also include rules about unfair trade practices and unfair claims practices. It is illegal to refuse to sell insurance to someone because of the person's race, color, sex, religion, national origin, or ancestry. In some states the list of prohibited classifications includes marital status, age, occupation, language, sexual orientation, physical or mental impairment, or the geographic location where a person lives. Insurance underwriting decisions generally must be based on reasons that are related in some way to risk. A person has the right to be informed of any reason for refusal to issue an insurance policy.

## Rates

Insurance companies have a range of payment or premium levels which can be charged for insurance. These are based on such factors as the applicant's age and health condition. Rating factors must be reasonably related to the risk being insured. The rates and rating factors for insurance must be filed with the insurance regulatory agency for each state where the insurance is to be sold. While a policyholder may elect to cancel an insurance policy at any time by giving notice to the insurance company, once a policy is issued, the insurance company cannot simply revoke it at will. The insurance company can only cancel the policy for reasons specifically outlined in the policy. State laws typically put limits on what an insurance company can include in the cancellation section of its policies. Generally, policies will be subject to cancellation only for some type of serious misrepresentation by the policyholder or for failure to pay the required premium on time. State law often requires insurers to allow a **grace period** of as much as 30 days after a payment is late before any insurance coverage can be terminated. Once the grace period expires, however, reinstatement is the sole option of the insurance company.

## Minors as Beneficiaries

While children can lawfully be named as beneficiaries on a life insurance policy, the insurance company will not be permitted to pay benefits to a minor. The funds would likely be dispersed to the legal **guardian** of the minor child. Many divorced parents are shocked to discover that naming their minor children as beneficiaries makes their ex-spouse the direct recipient of any insurance proceeds. This situation can be avoided by creating a trust which can hold the funds until the children are of **legal age**.

## Additional Resources

*Insurance: From Underwriting to Derivatives: Asset Liability Management in Insurance Companies* Briys, Eric, Wiley, John & Sons, Incorporated, 2001.

*True Odds: How Risks Affects Your Life* Walsh, James, Merritt Company, 1995.

## Organizations

### American Council of Life Insurers

1001 Pennsylvania Avenue, N.W.
Washington, DC 20004
Phone: (202) 624-2416
Fax: (202) 624-2319
Primary Contact: Herb Perone Director, Media Relations

### National Association of Independent Life Brokerage Agencies (NAILBA)

8201 Greensboro Drive, Suite 300
McLean, VA 22102
Phone: (703) 610-9020
Fax: (703) 610-9005
URL: http://www.nailba.com

### National Alliance of Life Companies

10600 West Higgins Road, Suite 607
Rosemont, IL 60018
Phone: (847) 699-7008
Fax: (847) 699-7119
URL: http://www.nalc.net
Primary Contact: Scott Cipinko, Executive Director

# ESTATE PLANNING

## POWER OF ATTORNEY

*Sections Within This Essay*

## Background

A **power of attorney** is a legal instrument that individuals create and sign; it gives someone else the authority to make certain decisions and act for the signer. The person who has these powers is called an "agent" or "attorney-in-fact." The signer is the "principal." Merely because the word "attorney" is used does not mean that the agent must be a lawyer.

Even if principals have delegated authority to an agent through a power of attorney, they can still make important decisions for themselves. But, their agents may act for them as well. Their agents must follow directions as long as they are capable of making decisions for themselves. A power of attorney is simply one way to share authority with someone else.

As a principal, if the principal's decisions conflict with those of the agent, the principal's decision will govern, assuming that the agent confers with the principal prior to taking an action. Be aware that if the agent has acted on the principal's behalf and acted within the scope of authority granted by the power of attorney, then the principal may be obligated by the terms and conditions of his actions. If the agent does not respect the principal's wishes, the principal should revoke the power of attorney.

Principals can revoke their agent's authority at any time if they become dissatisfied with the agent's performance. If they do not revoke a power of attorney themselves, it will automatically expires upon their death. The power of attorney is not a substitute for a will. Upon the principal's death, either the will or the state's law of **intestacy** will govern the distribution of the estate.

## Agent

The person designated to be the agent assumes certain responsibilities. First and foremost, the agent is obligated to act in the principal's best interest. The agent must always follow the principal's directions. Agents are "fiduciaries," which means that the agent must act with the highest degree of **good faith** in behalf of their principals.

Although an agent is supposed to make decisions in the principal's best interest and to use the principal's money and other assets only for the principal's benefit, the agent nevertheless has great freedom to act as he or she pleases. Thus, it is crucial that trustworthy individuals are chosen to execute a power of attorney. Before selecting an agent, principals should ask themselves the following questions:

- Do I trust the candidate for agent?

- Will the agent understand my feelings and my point of view?

- Will the agent follow my wishes if I am ever incapacitated?

- Will the agent do the necessary work and spend the time to properly handle my affairs?

- Will the agent be able to visit me or to keep in contact by phone?

- Is this person informed about finances?

- Will the agent need to seek the help of experts?

An agent's relationship with the principal is governed by several basic rules. The agent must:

- keep his money separate from the principal's,

- keep detailed records concerning all transactions he engages in on the principal's behalf,

- not stand to profit by any transaction where the agent represents the principal's interests,

- not make a gift or otherwise transfer any of the principal's money, **personal property**, or real estate to himself unless the power of attorney explicitly states he can do so.

Principals usually grant their agents fairly broad powers to manage their finances and to conduct financial transactions in their behalf. Even so, principals can grant their agents as much or as little authority as they think reasonable. Typical powers include the authority to do the following:

- act for the principal with respect to inheritances or claim property to which the principal is otherwise entitled,

- collect the principal's Social Security, **Medicare** or other governmental benefits,

- conduct real estate transactions (purchase, sell, **mortgage**, etc.),

- conduct transactions with banks and other financial institutions,

- file and pay the principal's state, federal, and local taxes,

- hire a lawyer to represent the principal in court,

- make investment decisions for the principal (purchase and sell stocks, **bonds**, mutual funds, etc.),

- manage the principal's retirement funds,

- purchase or sell insurance policies and annuities for the principal

- run the principal's business, and

- use the principal's money to pay the principal's living expenses.

Whatever powers the principal gives the agent, the agent must act for the principal's best interests, must maintain accurate records, keep the principal's property separate from his or hers and avoid conflicts of interest.

Agents are sometimes paid for their work on the principal's behalf. This depends on the nature of the relationship between the agent and the principal, as well as the nature of the agent's duties. In most situations where the agent's duties are fairly simple, there is no payment for the performance of those duties. If, however, the agent is saddleburdened with substantial responsibilities (such as running a business or managing a complex transaction), payment for the agent's services may be appropriate. If the principal wishes to or expects to pay the agent, the principal should clearly say so and outline the details of payment in the power of attorney. Because of the importance of the agent's duties and the potential for mistake, misunderstanding, or even outright overreaching, the agent will usually be required to maintain separate and accurate records and make them available to the principal or to persons the principal designates.

## Creating a Power of Attorney

When individuals create a power of attorney they are stating what they want their agent to be able to do for them. For the power of attorney to be effective the principal must be competent to give this authority. In other words, the principal must know and understand what types of decisions need to be made. If the principal is mentally competent, but physically unable to sign his name, any mark the principal makes with the full intention that other regard the mark as the principal's signature will be acceptable.

In most cases when individuals create a power of attorney, their signature on the form should be witnessed by a **notary public**. If the power of attorney grants the power to sell, **lease**, or otherwise dispose of the principal's real estate, the principal should also have the power of attorney recorded with the

Registry of Deeds. The Registry of Deeds usually will be located in the county courthouse wherein which the property is located. The principal should give the agent the original power of attorney document to show to any person, business, or organization involved in the transactions. The principal should keep a copy for his records. If the principal intends to delay the agent's ability to conduct business for the principal, he may choose to keep the original document himself until such time as he wants the power of attorney to be used.

In order to create a legally effective power of attorney, the principal must be mentally competent. The principal needs to know and understand what he is doing. A person who is mentally incapacitated cannot meet these requirements. The law does not require the principal to hire a lawyer to draft the power of attorney. However, if the principal intends to grant important powers to the agent, it is a good idea to seek legal advice before the principal signs the document. The principal should make sure that he understands the details built into the power of attorney as well as the potential for legal or financial difficulties it may present.

In most instances, all the principal needs to do to create a legally valid power of attorney is properly complete and sign (before a notary public) a fill-in-the-blanks form that's is a few pages long. Besides the nearly universal requirement for a power of attorney to be witnessed by a notary republic, there are few formalities to executing a power of attorney. Some states require a certain number of competent witnesses to watch the principal sign the document before the notary, and some states recommend certain forms, but none of them are mandatory to create a valid power of attorney. But some powers can be delegated to an agent only if they are specifically mentioned in the power of attorney document. Those requiring explicit language include the power to do the following:

- make gifts of the principal's money or other assets,

- amend the principal's will or **community property** agreement,

- name beneficiaries of the principal's insurance policies.

If the principal is married and are concerned about what would happen if the principal's spouse became ill and needed nursing home care or other long-term care, the principal may want to add some additional specifically authorized powers. It may be helpful for **Medicaid** eligibility to include the power to revoke a community property agreement and to transfer property from the disabled spouse to the principal. It is a good idea to consult with a lawyer about these more complicated issues.

When individuals create a power of attorney, they can name two or more people to serve as agents at the same time. They can also name an alternate agent to assume powers under the power of attorney under certain circumstances, such as the death or incapacity of the first agent. Before principals give authority under their power of attorney to more than one person at the same time, they should consider whether confusion or some other conflict may result. It is wise to discuss the potential advantages and disadvantages with a lawyer before giving powers of attorney to more than one person.

## Types of Powers of Attorney

### General Power of Attorney

A general power of attorney is one that permits the agent to conduct practically every kind of business or financial transaction—with the principal's assets—without any restraints. Because of the great harm to the principal's financial well-being that an incompetent or untrustworthy agent can cause with a general power of attorney, the principal should be extremely careful in choosing an agent. Additionally, the principal should maintain vigilance over the agent's transactions in the principal's behalf.

### Special or Limited Power of Attorney

A special power of attorney, also known as a limited power of attorney, is created to empower an agent to perform a specific act or acts. For example, if the principal is unable to do it himself, he can prepare a special power of attorney so that the agent can complete the purchase or sale of real estate. Most powers of attorney carefully define and enumerate the scope of the agent's authority. Thus, most powers of attorney are limited powers of attorney.

### Springing Power of Attorney

Any power of attorney can be written so that it becomes effective as soon as the principal signs it. But, the principal can also specify that the power of attorney goes into effect only upon the occurrence of some triggering event. In other words, it "springs" into effect at a later date, if ever. The triggering event can be something as simple as the principal's reaching a certain age or when a certain calendar date occurs. It can also be much more specific, such as if and when a doctor certifies that the principal has become incapacitated. These kinds of springing powers of attorney enable individuals to keep control over their affairs unless and until they become incapacitated, when it springs into effect. They are also known as durable powers of attorney.

### Durable Power of Attorney

Unless a power of attorney specifically says otherwise, an agent's authority ends if the principal becomes mentally incapacitated. On the other hand, a power of attorney may state explicitly that it is to remain in effect and not be limited by any future mental incapacity of the principal. A power of attorney with this sort of clause is called a durable power of attorney. The word "durable" means that the principal's agent can continue to conduct business for the principal if the principal becomes incapacitated.

Because of their potential utility to individuals who lack capacity after executing them, durable powers of attorney are arguably the most important form of these versatile legal documents. Durable powers of attorney are intended to address cases wherein which the following applies:

- the principal intends the agent to have authority only if the principal becomes incapacitated.

- the principal intends for the power of attorney to take effect immediately and to REMAIN in effect regardless of the principal's future disability.

The principal must list the specific powers under the durable power of attorney that are given to the agent and when those powers are to take effect. The agent must still act in the principal's best interest, making decisions and using the principal's assets only for the principal's benefit. In North Carolina and South Carolina, a principal must record the power of attorney with the appropriate county authorities for it to be durable.

The alternatives to creating a durable power of attorney may not be what the principal intends. If the principal have not executed a durable power of attorney and subsequently the principal becomes mentally incapacitated, a court may appoint a **guardian** or conservator for the principal. A guardianship or conservatorship must be established by a **probate** court. It is usually easier and much less expensive to manage one's affairs with a power of attorney.

Like all powers of attorney, a durable power of attorney ends or ceases to carry authority upon the death of the principal. It is fruitless to attempt to give the agent authority to handle matters for the principal after the principal's death. Actions such as attempting to pay the principal's debts, making funeral or burial arrangements, or transferring the principal's property to the people who **inherit** it cannot be legally accomplished through a power of attorney executed by a decedent. If the principal wants the agent to have authority to conclude affairs after the principal's death, then prepare a will must be prepared that names the agent as the principal's executor.

In addition to the principal's death, a durable power of attorney will end if any of the following applies:

- The principal revokes it. As long as the principal is mentally competent, he or she can revoke a durable power of attorney any time.

- A court invalidates the power of attorney. This does not happen very often; however, a court will declare a power of attorney invalid if the court finds that the principal lacked mental competency when the power of attorney was executed, or that the principal was the victim of **fraud** or undue influence.

- The principal gets a **divorce**. In Alabama, California, Colorado, Illinois, Indiana, Minnesota, Missouri, Pennsylvania, Texas and Wisconsin, if the principal's spouse is also the agent and the two get a divorce, the authority of principal's former spouse-agent is automatically terminated by **statute**. In any state, however, it is wise to revoke a durable power of attorney after a divorce and make a new one.

- No agent is available to serve. A durable power of attorney will terminate if no one is available to serve as agent. To avoid this dilemma, a principal can name an alternate agent in the power of attorney.

There are two general types of durable powers of attorney: a durable power of attorney for finances, and a durable power of attorney for health care. Depending on the terms of the document, the durable power of attorney for finances allows the agent to serve the interests of the principal in financial matters before, during, or after the agent becomes incapacitated. The durable power of attorney for health care authorizes the agent to make medical decisions for the principal if the principal cannot otherwise make those decisions. An agent's authority over the principal's financial and healthcare decisions can be included in the same power of attorney; however, some durable powers of attorney for finances do not give the agent the legal authority to make medical decisions for the principal. Sometimes financial and healthcare powers are combined in one document to create a durable power of attorney.

A durable power of attorney for health care differs from a **living will**. The durable power of attorney for health care grants a third party—the agent— the authority to make decisions for the principal about the principal's health care. In most states, though, a living will (also called a Healthcare Directive or Directive to Physicians), is a document wherein which the principal informs his doctors of his preferences about certain kinds of medical treatment and life-sustaining procedures in the event the principal cannot communicate his wishes. The living will does not mediate the principal's desires through an agent or other third party. If a living will is prepared properly, a physician is legally bound to respect the wishes in the living will. If for some reason a doctor finds he cannot honor the living will, he is obligated to transfer the principal's care to another doctor who will. Living wills are fairly simple documents, with most states now providing fill-in-the-blanks living will forms.

## Revoking a Power of Attorney

All powers of attorney automatically expire upon the principal's death. Some powers of attorney expire on a particular date set by the principal. It is important to know that all powers of attorney are revocable if the right conditions are met. There are many reasons to revoke a power of attorney, an important one being loss of confidence in the agent; however, the principal does not need a reason to revoke the power of attorney.

Power of attorney can be revoked at any time, as long as the principal is are of sound mind. To revoke a power of attorney, the principal must do so in writing. Typically, the principal merely needs to prepare a simple statement containing the following:

- The principal's name and date.

- The principal's claim to be of sound mind.

- The principal's explicit desire to revoke the durable power of attorney.

- The date the original durable power of attorney was executed.

- The name of the principal's agent or agents.

- The principal's signature.

It is important to distribute copies of this revocation statement to the agent and to any institutions and agencies, such as banks and hospitals, that may have had notice of the principal's power of attorney. If the power of attorney is on file with a county records department, the statement revoking the power of attorney should be filed in the same place. After the durable power of attorney is revoked, the principal can 1) execute a new power of attorney naming someone else as agent to handle the principal's affairs; or 2) handle the affairs independently.

## Additional Resources

*The financial power of attorney workbook.* Irving, Shae, Nolo Press, 1997.

*http://www.eaglelink.com/law-review/poa.htm* "Power of Attorney" EagleLink, 2002.

*http://www.itslegal.com/infonet/powerofattorney/poa-what.asp* "Power of Attorney" Itslegal.com/ Broderbund.com, 2002.

*http://www.oag.state.ny.us/seniors/pwrat.html,* "Power of Attorney" Office of New York State Attorney General Eliot Spitzer, 2002.

*http://www.uslegalforms.com/ftool/patty.htm,* "Power of Attorney Forms" Uslegalforms.com and Forms-Tool.com, 2002.

*http://www.eaglelink.com/law-review/poa.htm,* "Power of Attorney" EagleLink, 2002.

*http://www.itslegal.com/infonet/powerofattorney/poa-what.asp,* "Power of Attorney" Itslegal.com/ Broderbund.com, 2002.

## Organizations

***The American Academy of Estate Planning Attorneys***
9360 Towne Centre Drive, Suite 300
San Diego, CA 92121 USA
Phone: (800) 846-1555
Fax: (858) 453-1147
E-Mail: information@aaepa.com
URL: http://www.aaepa.com

**American College of Trust and Estate Counsel**

3415 South Sepulveda Boulevard, Suite 330
Los Angeles, CA 90034 USA
Phone: (310) 398-1888
Fax: (310) 572-7280
E-Mail: info@actec.org
URL: http://www.actec.org

**National Network of Estate Planning Attorneys, Inc.**

One Valmont Plaza, Fourth Floor
Omaha, Nebraska 68154-5203 USA
Phone: (800) 638-8681
E-Mail: webmaster@netplanning.com
URL: http://www.netplanning.com

**The American Academy of Estate Planning Attorneys**

9360 Towne Centre Drive, Suite 300
San Diego, CA 92121 USA
Phone: (800) 846-1555
Fax: (858) 453-1147
E-Mail: information@aaepa.com
URL: http://www.aaepa.com

**The National Academy of Elder Law Attorneys**

1604 North Country Club Road
Tucson, Arizona 85716 USA
Phone: (520) 881-4005
Fax: (520) 325-7925
URL: http://www.naela.com

**The American Academy of Estate Planning Attorneys**

9360 Towne Centre Drive, Suite 300
San Diego, CA 92121 USA
Phone: (800) 846-1555
Fax: (858) 453-1147
E-Mail: information@aaepa.com
URL: http://www.aaepa.com

**National Network of Estate Planning Attorneys, Inc.**

One Valmont Plaza, Fourth Floor
Omaha, Nebraska 68154-5203 USA
Phone: (800) 638-8681
E-Mail: webmaster@netplanning.com
URL: http://www.netplanning.com/

# ESTATE PLANNING

## PROBATE AND EXECUTORS

*Sections within this essay:*

## Background

**Probate** is a legal proceeding by which a deceased person's property is distributed to the rightful heirs and/or beneficiaries. Probate proceedings are governed by the law of the state where the deceased person resided at the time of death and by the probate laws of any other state where the property was owned. The main purpose of probate is transferring title of the decedent's property to the heirs and/or beneficiaries. If the decedent had no assets, there is typically no need for probate. Probate also allows for collection of taxes due and payment of outstanding debts. The term "probate" refers to a

"proving" of the existence of a valid Will or determining and "proving" who one's legal heirs are if there is no Will.

All property of a decedent may not be subject to the probate process. Life insurance, retirement accounts, real estate held as joint tenants with right of survivorship and other joint **tenancy** property can pass directly to the appropriate **beneficiary** automatically. The involvement of the court to transfer such property is not required. Property held in the trust is not subject to probate. A bank account or motor vehicle title may also specify a death beneficiary and thus be exempt from the probate process.

An Executor or Personal Representative (sometimes referred to as "The PR") is the person or institution named in a will and appointed by a court to carry out the will's instructions and to handle all of the matters of probate. Duties of the Personal Representative include making an inventory and **appraisal** of all property and appropriately distributing the estate.

## Personal Representative

The Personal Representative (also called the "executor" or "executrix" if there is a Will or the "administrator" or "administratix" if there is no Will) is appointed as part of the probate proceeding. The Personal Representative can either be an entity, one individual, or two or more individuals (although this arrangement can become extremely complicated).

### Duties

The Personal Representative has the responsibility for managing the estate in accordance with established probate rules and procedures of the **jurisdiction** where the probate takes place. Responsibilities of a Personal Representative include:

Locating, inventorying, and obtaining an appraisal of the assets of the decedent

Receiving payments owed to the estate, including unpaid salary, vacation pay, or other benefits due the decedent

Opening a checking account for the estate

Determining how property is distributed

Noticing potential creditors

Investigating the validity of claims against the estate

Paying bills, debts, valid claims and expenses of administrating the estate

Discontinuing utilities and credit cards, closing accounts and notifying appropriate private and governmental agencies of the death

Filing and paying income and estate taxes

Closing the probate

### Compensation

Personal Representatives are generally compensated about 2% of the probate estate for their work. This varies moderately from state to state and generally decreases as a percentage as the size of the estate increases. All fees and reimbursed expenses are subject to court approval. Additional fees may be allowed if permitted by the court in certain circumstances. However, if a Personal Representative is incompetent or does not perform as required, the court may deny compensation, and the Personal Representative may be held personally responsible for any damages caused. Liability may arise from improperly managing the assets of the estate, failing to collect claims and moneys due the estate, overpaying claimants, selling an asset without authority or at an inappropriate price, neglecting to file tax returns promptly, or distributing property incorrectly to beneficiaries.

## Probate Court

Probate usually occurs in the local court where the deceased permanently resided at the time of death. If the deceased did not have a Will, each state will have its own pattern for distributing the de-

ceased's real property. Generally it is necessary to go through probate or, in the case of smaller estates, a less formal procedure that is still under the general supervision of the probate court, before the deceased's property can be legally distributed. If a person dies with a Will (which is known as dying "testate"), a court needs an opportunity to allow others to object to the Will. A number of objections, might invalidate a Will, for example, an **allegation** that there is a later Will or that the Will was made at a time the deceased was mentally incompetent. Additional challenges to a Will can include **forgery**, improper **execution** (signature), or a claim that the decedent was subject to undue influence. Dying without a Will is known as dying **intestate**; however, such estates remain subject to the law and rules of the probate code of the decedent's domiciled jurisdiction.

The Personal Representative typically must file a probate petition and notify all those who would have legally been entitled to receive property from the deceased if the deceased died without a Will, plus all those named in the Will, and give anyone who chooses a chance to file a formal objection to the Will.

A **hearing** on the probate petition is typically scheduled several weeks to months after the matter is filed. If no objections are filed the court generally approves the petition and formally appoints the Personal Representative. While it is not required that there be representation by an attorney in probate court, probate is a rather formalistic procedure. The death of a family member is typically a stressful time even when the death is expected, such as with a person of quite advanced age or with someone who is terminally ill. Employing an attorney may be the less expensive alternative in the long run.

### Ancillary Probate

The probate court or division has jurisdiction over all **personal property** the deceased owned, plus all the real property the deceased owned which is located in that same state. If the decedent owned out of state real property, the laws of that jurisdiction will apply, unless there is a Will. If there is no Will, Probate is usually required in each state where the real property is situated, in addition to the home state. Even if there is a Will, after it is admitted to probate in the home state, it usually must be submitted to probate in each other jurisdiction in which the deceased owned real property. A separate probate action for such circumstance is known as **ancillary** probate. Some states require the appointment of a

Personal Representative who is a local resident to administer the in-state property.

### Will Contests

A Will Contest take place where a second, different Will of the decedent is produced or in the event there is an objection to the Will. An individual or entity must have proper standing to contest a Will. This means they must have a claim for some type of interest in the estate based on either another Will or a lawful relationship to the decedent. If the Will is held invalid, the probate court may invalidate all provisions or only the challenged portion. If the entire Will is held invalid, generally the proceeds are distributed under the laws of **intestacy** of the probating state. The fact that the decedent even attempted to create a new Will may invalidate the older one, even if the new Will is found not to be valid. Hiring an attorney is usually necessary to determine whether contesting a Will is even worth the expense.

### Lawsuits

In addition to a Will Contest, estates can be involved in other lawsuits. Estates are legal entities, which can file suit, and be sued. Typically, such suits involve prior acts of the decedent, which gave rise to some claim. There are time limits involving such claims if the estate is to be sued. Potential claimants would be considered potential creditors.

## Creditors

Rules regarding notification of creditors are different for each state. However, in every state, creditors must make a claim for any amounts owed within a fixed period of time. This claim can be made directly to the Personal Representative in some jurisdictions, but in other jurisdictions, it must be made with the court. The PR can pay the claim out of the estate, but if the PR disputes its validity, the **creditor** must seek a court order to receive payment. If there is not enough money to pay all the debts of the estate, state law dictates which creditors are paid first. It is not possible to "inherit" a debt. Beneficiaries and Personal Representatives are not personally liable for the debts of the estate, although the court may order estate property sold to pay certain creditor claims.

## Avoiding Probate

In many estate plans, the Trust is the central tool that is used to control and manage property. A Trust continues despite the incapacity or death of the grantor. It determines how a **Trustee** is to act with respect to the Trust estate. It determines how property is to be distributed after the death of the grantor. A properly drawn Trust is a separate entity that does not die when the creator dies. The successor Trustee can take over management of the Trust estate and pay bills and taxes and promptly distribute the Trust assets to the beneficiaries, without court supervision, if the Trust agreement gives the Trustee that power. Trusts, unlike Wills, are generally private documents. The public would be able to see how much the descendent owned and who the beneficiaries were under a Will, but typically not with a Trust. Like a Will, however, a Trust can be used to provide for minor children, children from a prior marriage, and a second spouse in the same trust, transfer a family-operated or closely-held business, provide for pets, provide for charities, and can remove life insurance benefits from a taxable estate, while still controlling the designation of insurance beneficiaries.

## Taxes

One of the duties of the PR is to pay all taxes due the federal government and the state government, including estate tax, real property tax, and prior to death **income tax**.

### Individual Income Tax

In the United States, even death does not relieve the liability for income tax. Even if the taxpayer is dead on December 31, an income **tax return** has to be filed for the year of death. As always, the income tax return is due by April 15th of the following year. Only the income received and any deductions paid through the date of death will be reported on the return. Income such as dividends and interest received after the date of death will not be reported on the individual income tax return but on the estate income tax return. Any medical deductions on the decedent's part paid within one year of the date of death may be deducted on the final return. All other deductions must have been paid before death to be allowable.

### Estate Income Tax

Income which comes in after the date of death should not be reported on the decedent's personal income tax return. Interest, dividends, or other income paid to the estate, must be reported on the estate income tax return. A separate tax identification number is obtained for the estate. This separate tax return lists the **taxable income** such as dividends, interest, capital gains, and rents, and allows for deductions such as legal and executor's fees. If the estate has been distributed and closed during the tax year, each beneficiary must list his or her proportionate share of the taxable income on his or her personal tax return. If the estate is open, the taxes are paid from the estate.

## State Law

Trusts are often created as an alternative to or in conjunction with a Will. Trusts are today usually considered an estate planning tool. The Uniform Probate Code includes provisions dealing with affairs and estates of the deceased and laws dealing with nontestamentary transfers such as trusts. The theory behind the Code is that wills and trusts are in close relationship and thus in need of unification. Since its creation, over thirty percent of states have adopted most provisions of the Code.

ARIZONA: Without a Will, all property passes to the surviving spouse unless there are children of the decedent. If there are children only the separate property and the one-half of **community property** that belongs to the decedent, passes to the surviving spouse. The remaining goes to the children unless the children are not also children of the surviving spouse in which case one-half of the intestate separate property and all of the community property that belonged to the decedent passes to the children. Creditors have four months to notice the estate regarding claims.

CALIFORNIA: In California Probate **statutory** attorneys and Personal Representatives' fees are usually calculated based on the gross value of the estate. California has a simplified legal process known as a spousal confirmation proceeding in which, if no one objects, the court approves the transfer of all assets to the spouse. This procedure can only be used for married couples.

FLORIDA: Florida implemented a number of major changes in its probate code as of January 2002. Florida **public policy** protects the spouse and, in some circumstances, children from total disinheritance. Absent a **premarital agreement**, a surviving spouse may have **homestead** rights, elective share rights, family allowance rights, and exempt property

rights. In addition, certain surviving children of the decedent may also have homestead rights, pretermitted child rights, family allowance rights, and exempt property rights.

SOUTH CAROLINA: Without a Will, all assets go to the surviving spouse unless there are children in which case one-half goes to the children. Protective provisions of the South Carolina Probate Code grant a spouse who is left out of a Will an election to take a one-third share of the estate. A similar provision grants a share to a child who is left out of a parent's will written before the child's birth.

SOUTH DAKOTA: South Dakota has adopted the Uniform Probate Code.

UTAH: Utah has adopted the Uniform Probate Code.

WEST VIRGINIA: Without a Will, all assets go to the surviving spouse unless there are children in which case one-half goes to the children. If there is a Will, the surviving spouse can also renounce the Will and take the elective share instead. The elective share depends on the length of the marriage. Renouncing the Will requires that papers be filed with a court within certain time frames.

## Additional Resources

*Beyond the Grave: The Right Way and the Wrong Way of Leaving Money to Your Children (and Others)* Condon, Gerald, HarperCollins, 2001.

## Organizations

*The Elder Law Project Legal Services For Cape Cod And Islands, Inc.*
460 West Main Street
Hyannis, MA 02601 USA
Phone: (508) 775-7020

*National Academy of Elder Law Attorneys, Inc.*
1604 North Country Club Road
Tucson, Arizona 85716 USA
Phone: (520) 881-4005
Fax: (520) 325-7925
URL: http://www.naela.com/

# ESTATE PLANNING

## TRUSTS

*Sections within this essay:*

## Background

A trust is a legal entity created for the purpose of holding, managing, and distributing property for the benefit of one or more persons. A trust can hold cash, **personal property**, or real property, or it can be the **beneficiary** of life insurance proceeds. In the most basic sense, a trust is just another form of a con-tract. Centuries ago, English landowners, in order to insure the continued wealth of the family, put their estates in trust to be controlled and managed under the terms of the trust agreement for an indefinite period of time. Once the land was placed in trust, the landowners controlled but technically no longer owned the land. As wealth was primarily measured at that time in history by the amount of land owned, the trust arrangement allowed the landowners **immunity** from creditors and may have absolved them of certain feudal obligations. While feudal concerns no longer exist and wealth is held today in many forms other than land, the concept of placing property in third party hands for the benefit of another while avoiding creditors has survived. A trust remains in many circumstance an effective tool to insure that the trust creator's wishes regarding the trust assets are complied with for many years, even during periods of the creator's mental **incompetency** or after death.

## Types of Trusts

A trust can be created during a person's lifetime and survive the person's death. A trust can also be created by a Will and formed after death. Once assets are put into the trust they belong to the trust itself, not the **trustee**, and remain subject to the rules and instructions of the trust contract. Most basically, a trust is a right in property, which is held in a **fiduciary** relationship by one party for the benefit of another. The trustee is the one who holds title to the trust property, and the beneficiary is the person who receives the benefits of the trust. While there are a number of different types of trusts, the basic types are revocable and irrevocable.

## Revocable Trusts

Revocable Trusts are created during the lifetime of the trustmaker and can be altered, changed, modified or revoked entirely. Often called a **Living Trust**, these are Trusts in which the trustmaker transfers the title of a property to a Trust, serves as the initial Trustee, and has the ability to remove the property from the Trust during his or her lifetime. Revocable Trust are extremely helpful in avoiding **probate**. If ownership of assets is transferred to a revocable trust during the lifetime of the trustmaker so that it is owned by the trust at the time of the trustmaker's death, the assets will not be subject to probate.

Although useful to avoid probate, a revocable trust is not an asset protection technique as assets transferred to the trust during the trustmaker's lifetime will remain available to the trustmaker's creditors. It does make it more somewhat more difficult for creditors to access these assets since the **creditor** must petition a court for an order to enable the creditor to get to the assets held in the trust. Typically, a revocable trust evolves into an irrevocable trust upon the death of the trustmaker.

## Irrevocable Trust

An Irrevocable Trust is one which cannot be altered, changed, modified or revoked after its creation. Once a property is transferred to an Irrevocable Trust, no one, including the trustmaker, can take the property out of the Trust. It is possible to purchase Survivorship Life Insurance, the benefits of which can be held by an Irrevocable Trust. This type of survivorship life insurance can be used for estate tax planning purposes in large estates, however, survivorship life insurance held in an Irrevocable Trust can have serious negative consequences.

## Asset Protection Trust

An Asset Protection Trust is a type of Trust that is designed to protect a person's assets from claims of future creditors. These types of Trusts are often set up in countries outside of the United States, although the assets do not always need to be transferred to the foreign **jurisdiction**. The purpose of an Asset Protection Trust is to insulate assets from creditor attack. These trusts are normally structured so that they are irrevocable for a term of years and so that the trustmaker is not a current beneficiary. An asset protection trust is normally structured so that the undistributed assets of the trust are returned to the trustmaker upon termination of the trust provided there is no current risk of creditor attack, thus permitting the trustmaker to regain complete control over the formerly protected assets.

## Charitable Trust

Charitable Trusts are trusts which benefit a particular charity or the public in general. Typically Charitable Trusts are established as part of an estate plan to lower or avoid imposition of estate and gift tax. A charitable remainder trust (CRT) funded during the grantor's lifetime can be a financial planning tool, providing the trustmaker with valuable lifetime benefits. In addition to the financial benefits, there is the intangible benefit of rewarding the trustmaker's altruism as charities usually immediately honor the donors who have named the charity as the beneficiary of a CRT.

## Constructive Trust

A Constructive Trust is an implied trust. An Implied Trust is established by a court and is determined from certain facts and circumstances. The court may decide that, even though there was never a formal declaration of a Trust, there was an intention on the part of the property owner that the property be used for a particular purpose or go to a particular person. While a person may take legal title to property, equitable considerations sometimes require that the equitable title of such property really belongs to someone else.

## Special Needs Trust

A Special Needs Trust is one which is set up for a person who receives government benefits so as not to disqualify the beneficiary from such government benefits. This is completely legal and permitted under the Social Security rules provided that the disabled beneficiary cannot control the amount or the frequency of trust distributions and cannot revoke the trust. Ordinarily when a person is receiving government benefits, an **inheritance** or receipt of a gift could reduce or eliminate the person's eligibility for such benefits. By establishing a Trust, which provides for luxuries or other benefits which otherwise could not be obtained by the beneficiary, the beneficiary can obtain the benefits from the Trust without defeating his or her eligibility for government benefits. Usually, a Special Needs Trust has a provision which terminates the Trust in the event that it could be used to make the beneficiary ineligible for government benefits.

Special needs has a specific legal definition and is defined as the requisites for maintaining the comfort and happiness of a disabled person, when such requisites are not being provided by any public or private agency. Special needs can include medical and dental expenses, equipment, education, treatment, rehabilitation, eye glasses, transportation (including vehicle purchase), maintenance, insurance (including payment of premiums of insurance on the life of the beneficiary), essential dietary needs, spending money, electronic and computer equipment, vacations, athletic contests, movies, trips, money with which to purchase gifts, payments for a companion, and other items to enhance self-esteem. The list is quite extensive. Parents of a disabled child can establish a Special Needs Trust as part of their general estate plan and not worry that their child will be prevented from receiving benefits when they are not there to care for the child. **Disabled persons** who expect an inheritance or other large sum of money may establish a Special Needs Trust themselves, provided that another person or entity is named as Trustee.

### Spendthrift Trust

A Trust that is established for a beneficiary which does not allow the beneficiary to sell or pledge away interests in the Trust. A Spendthrift Trust is protected from the beneficiaries' creditors, until such time as the Trust property is distributed out of the Trust and given to the beneficiaries.

### Tax By-Pass Trust

A Tax By-Pass Trust is a type of Trust that is created to allow one spouse to leave money to the other, while limiting the amount of Federal Estate tax that would be payable on the death of the second spouse. While assets can pass to a spouse tax-free, when the surviving spouse dies, the remaining assets over and above the exempt limit would be taxable to the children of the couple, potentially at a rate of 55%. A Tax By-Pass Trust avoids this situation and saves the children perhaps hundreds of thousands of dollars in Federal taxes, depending upon the value of the estate.

### Totten Trust

A Totten Trust is one that is created during the lifetime of the grantor by depositing money into an account at a financial institution in his or her name as the Trustee for another. This is a type of revocable Trust in which the gift is not completed until the grantor's death or an unequivocal act reflecting the gift during the grantor's lifetime. An individual or an entity can be named as the beneficiary. Upon death, Totten Trust assets avoid probate. A Totten Trust is used primarily with accounts and **securities** in financial institutions such as savings accounts, bank accounts, and certificates of deposit. A Totten trust cannot be used with real property. A Totten Trust

provides a safer method to pass assets on to family than using joint ownership. To create a Totten Trust, the title on the account should include identifying language, such as "In Trust For", "Payable on Death To", "As Trustee For", or the identifying initials for each, "IFF", "POD", "ATF". If this language is not included, the beneficiary may not be identifiable. A Totten Trust has been called a "poor man's" trust because a written trust document is typically not involved and it often costs the trustmaker nothing to establish.

## Parties to a Trust

There are typically three main parties to a Trust. The Trust Maker, sometimes called the Grantor or Maker, is the person who creates the Trust. The Trustee is the person or entity named to hold the legal title to the Trust estate. There may be one or several Trustees. The Beneficiaries are the persons who the Trust Creator intended to benefit from the Trust estate. The rights of the beneficiaries depend on the terms of the Trust. Beneficiaries have the equitable title to the property held in the Trust. During the lifetime of the Trustmaker, the Trustmaker, Trustee and Beneficiary can all be the same individual. This is most often the case in Revocable Trusts.

### Trustmaker

The Trust Creator, sometimes called the Grantor or Trustmaker, is the person who started out as owner of the property that is to be transferred to and held by the Trust. The trustmaker makes an agreement with the trustee agreeing to convey his or her property into the name of the trustee for the benefit of the beneficiaries.

### Trustee

A Trustee is a person or institution selected to follow the instructions provided by the **declaration of Trust**. A Trustee has a very high "fiduciary duty" to act with the utmost **good faith** in dealing with the Trust estate. Many grantors and their respective spouses act as the initial Trustees of a revocable living Trust. In this way they remain in control until they are incapacitated or die. Then pre-selected successor Trustees are appointed in accordance with the terms of the declaration of Trust. Usually a spouse, family member or trusted friend are selected as successor Trustees. Trustees should be knowledgeable about financial matters, be Trustworthy, know how to manage and invest the Trust estate, care about the beneficiaries of the Trust, and have the financial capacity to reimburse the Trust in the event that they make serious mistakes. If a bank or **Trust company** is selected to serve as a Trustee of a Trust, it will usually charge a fee for this service, which is paid from the Trust estate.

Because the beneficiary, trustmaker, and the trustee can be the same person, the trustmaker and trustee can agree that the trust creator keep complete control over the trust by retaining the right to remove and replace the trustee, sell or transfer the original trust property, **dissolve** or revoke the trust, and change the trust beneficiaries.

### Beneficiaries

The Beneficiaries are the persons whom the Trust Creator intended to benefit from the Trust estate. Beneficiaries are said to have the "equitable title" to the property held in the Trust. The rights of the beneficiaries depend on the terms of the Trust. The trust agreement can provide that the beneficiaries have almost complete control over the manner in which trust assets are held and managed, as well as control over the timing and dollar amounts of distributions. Or the beneficiaries could be given absolutely no control. The decision as to how trust powers are apportioned depends on the trustmaker's objectives, trust, and confidence in the trustee, and tax consequences.

Once the trustmaker of a revocable trust dies and the trust becomes irrevocable, an anti-alienation clause usually protects the assets held in the trust form being used as **collateral** by the beneficiaries. Thus, creditors cannot force a trustee to make a distribution to the trust beneficiaries and the assets held in a trust can remain outside the reach of the beneficiaries' creditors.

## Reasons for Trust Creation

### Asset Control

A trust can be use to maintain control over the trust assets for a designated period of time which may survive death.

### Tax Savings

Tax and asset protection aspects of trusts depend on the financial situation of the creator and the type of trust used. In certain circumstances, a trust can achieve substantial tax savings yet not achieve asset protection from creditors of the trustmaker. Everyone gets a lifetime credit against Federal Estate Taxes that permits a transfer of up to $675,000 Estate Tax free. Individuals and married couples with a total es-

tate value less than $675,000 in 2000 (the amount will gradually increase to the year 2006) do not need a trust to save on Federal Estate or Gift Tax. For those who are married, there is an unlimited marital **deduction**. All estate taxes can be avoided upon the death of the first spouse to die. However, the surviving spouse would have to remarry and give the entire estate to the new spouse in order to get another unlimited marital deduction. Many people would rather their own children benefit from their estate, rather than having a surviving spouse pass it on to a new spouse. A trust can accomplish this. The trustmaker can establish a tax by-pass Trust to hold property for children, while still allowing the trust funds to provide for the surviving spouse. This arrangement enables the trustmaker to place up to $675,000 in a Trust for the benefit of the surviving spouse and children which will not be subject to estate tax upon the death of the surviving spouse. Coupled with the surviving spouse's estate and gift tax credit, the children could then **inherit** up to $1,350,000 free from Federal Estate and Gift Tax. At current Federal Estate Tax rates, this could amount to a significant savings of hundreds of thousands of dollars.

### Asset Protection

Assets may be put in trust because the trust creator has confidence in the prospective trustee's knowledge, experience, or ability to properly manage the type of assets to be transferred into the trusts. The utilization of a trustee in such circumstances may have the additional advantage of relieving the beneficiaries of what may otherwise be a burden.

### Avoiding a Conservatorship

If property is held in a Trust, a successor Trustee can step in and take over management, without the delay and expense of going to court to appoint a conservator to manage the property, if the Trust Creator becomes disabled. This may be particularly important if the trustmaker is self-employed or owns a portion of a business or partnership.

### Avoiding Probate

In many estate plans, the Trust is the central tool that is used to control and manage property. A Trust continues despite the incapacity or death of the grantor. It determines how a Trustee is to act with respect to the Trust estate. It determines how property is to be distributed after the death of the grantor. A properly drawn Trust is a separate entity that does not die when the creator dies. The successor Trustee can take over management of the Trust estate and pay bills and taxes, and promptly distribute the Trust assets to the beneficiaries, without court supervision, if the Trust agreement gives the Trustee that power. Trusts, unlike Wills, are generally private documents. The public would be able to see how much the descendent owned and who the beneficiaries were under a Will, but typically not with a Trust. Like a Will, however, a Trust can be used to provide for minor children, children from a prior marriage and a second spouse in the same trust, transfer a family-operated or closely-held business, provide for pets, provide for charities and can remove life insurance benefits from a taxable estate, while still controlling the designation of insurance beneficiaries.

## State Law

Trusts are often created as an alternative to or in conjunction with a Will. Trusts are today usually considered an estate planning tool. The Uniform Probate Code includes provisions dealing with affairs and estates of the deceased and laws dealing with nontestamentary transfers such as trusts. The theory behind the Code is that wills and trusts are in close relationship and thus in need of unification. Since its cre-ation, over thirty percent of states have adopted most provision of the Code.

## Additional Resources

*Beyond the Grave: The Right Way and the Wrong Way of Leaving Money to Your Children (and Others)* Condon, Gerald, HarperCollins, 2001.

*Make Your Kid a Millionaire: Eleven Easy Ways Anyone Can Secure a Child's Financial Future* McKinley, Kevin, Simon & Schuster, 2002.

## Organizations

### *The Elder Law Project Legal Services For Cape Cod And Islands, Inc.*
460 West Main Street
Hyannis, MA 02601
Phone: (508) 775-7020

### *National Academy of Elder Law Attorneys, Inc.*
1604 North Country Club Road
Tucson, AZ 85716
Phone: (520) 881-4005
Fax: (520) 325-7925
URL: http://www.naela.com

# ESTATE PLANNING

## WILLS

*Sections Within This Essay:*

## Background

A will, sometimes known as a "last will and testament," is a legal document that provides written instructions for the distribution of a decedent's (dead person's) property. Generally, people should consider making a will if they care how their property will be distributed when they die, they want to name the person who will handle financial and legal matters they may leave behind, or they want to name a **guardian** for their minor children.

## What is in a Typical Will?

A will most likely will include the following provisions:

- Your name (the **testator**)
- The name of your spouse and the date of your marriage, if any
- The name of your children (and how you wish any foster and stepchildren to be treated), if any
- A statement revoking any wills you may have previously made
- Your nomination of a personal representative to administer the estate and usually at least one alternate.
- A list of powers that you want your personal representative to have (these are often enumerated in your state's statutes
- A list of any special gifts
- Instructions for distributing the remainder of your estate after your debts, taxes, and ex-

penses incurred in administering your estate have been paid

- A **waiver** of any surety bond requirements

Your will may not cover everything that you consider "your property." The following types of property are examples of assets that may pass directly to a **beneficiary** you have named in a separate document:

- **pension** plan assets
- 401(k) plan assets
- life insurance
- annuities
- property held through a "trust"

These assets would usually pass to beneficiaries you have previously named in documents under the supervision of the manager of the pension plan, the company sponsoring the 401(k), life insurance companies, annuities, and in a trust instrument. However, if you name "my estate" the beneficiary of any of these kinds of assets, then your will would control who receives the property and benefits. Be aware that by doing this your eventual beneficiaries may experience some significant delays and/or some important tax disadvantages.

Your will should be prepared and properly executed (signed by you and a certain number of competent witnesses) while you still have legal capacity. Thus, if you want a will, you should have one prepared and sign it according to the applicable state law while you have full control over your mental functions. If you wait until you suffer an accident or an illness, it could be too late.

## The Personal Representative

When you die, your personal representative (also known as an administrator or executor) will gather and inventory all of your property at the time of your death. Most states require the personal representative to post a surety bond covering his/her actions, although you can explicitly waive this requirement in your will. The personal representative will also determine your outstanding debts, pay your legitimate debts, and distribute the remaining property according to the instructions in your will. Your personal representative will be appointed in a **probate** proceeding. The personal representative must usher your property through the probate process, subject to your state's probate rules and procedures. In many states, the court maintains tight control over the activities of the personal representative. For example, the personal representative must obtain the court's permission to sell, distribute, or otherwise take action with respect to property in your estate.

It is important to choose someone who you think will be competent and trustworthy to serve as your personal representative. The personal representative will have access to all of your property and the authority to conduct certain business on your behalf. To the extent that you can, it is a good idea to choose a person with some business experience, intelligence, and high integrity. Your will should name the person you wish to nominate as your personal representative. You will probably also name one or more alternates to serve in the event that your first choice for personal representative is unwilling or unable to serve. Because you cannot speak in your own behalf, your will acts as your voice to inform the probate court about who you think will be best suited to this job.

## Changing a Will

The most common reasons to change your will after it has been executed include the following:

- You get married or divorced
- Your family increases through the birth or **adoption** of child
- There is a death of a family member or of a beneficiary
- There are changes in the Federal Estate Tax laws or State Tax laws that may effect your estate
- There is a substantial change in the value of your estate
- You change the nature of your property holdings, which impacts your distribution plans.
- A potential guardian, executor, or **Trustee** moves away, dies, or refuses to serve in that capacity.
- Your children reach the **age of majority**, or are old enough to manage financial matters on their own
- You move to a different state
- You need or want to eliminate gifts to certain people

To change your will, there are two basic choices, and professional assistance is in order for both. First, you can prepare and properly execute an entire new will that revokes the previous will. Second, you can prepare and properly execute a **codicil** to the will. A codicil is a separate document that adds to and/or replaces one or more provisions in an existing will. What makes the most sense for you will depend on the facts and circumstances. For example, if there is a new tax provision that favors provisions in existing wills, but not new wills, or there may be a question subsequently raised about your mental competence. In these cases, a codicil would generally be the best choice.

Codicils were used frequently in the past, but lawyers now use computer technologies that can quickly integrate any changes you want to make—even minor ones—into an entirely new will that is up to date. Because of the ease of making the changes, the fees charged to make these modifications are usually modest. Your lawyer may even suggest revisions to your will that take account of new laws, tax rules, and changes in your circumstances that you may have overlooked in your previous will. Regardless of the ease of making these changes, never try to make changes in your will on your own. If you write in the margins, add material, cross out words, lines, or sections of the original will you could possibly create some confusion or ambiguity and thereby invite unpleasant and protracted will contests.

## Competency

Someone trying to have your will accepted for probate generally must establish that you were of sound mind and memory at the time you executed your will. Even if one becomes old, frail, and forgetful, it is difficult to get a court to regard a will as invalid. Generally, those who witnessed the will being signed will almost always say that the deceased was of sound mind, was aware of his surroundings, the day or date, who his family members were, and knew that he was signing a will. The burden then shifts to the person challenging the will to prove it should not be accepted for probate.

Courts maintain a strong presumption that a will is valid. Thus, it can be costly and difficult to prove that someone was mentally incompetent, made a mistake, or was subject to **fraud**, **coercion**, **duress**, or undue influence when making and/or executing the will. Even if the testator suffers weakened mentality after the will was made has no bearing. The va-

lidity of the will is only called into question should an incompetent testator want to change the will at a later date.

## Contesting or Challenging a Will

Will contests challenge the admissibility of wills in probate courts. It is a kind of **litigation** that questions whether a will should be properly admitted by the court as **evidence** of a decedent's wishes regarding the distribution of his estate, appointment of guardians for minor children, or other issues dealing with the decedent's estate. One may not contest the validity of a will merely because that person does not like the will's provisions. A will's validity is not determined by one's sense of "fairness" of the will's contents. Nor is a will's validity determined by how reasonable the will's provisions appear nor on the timing of disbursements.

Despite the feelings of a decedent's family or friends, a will is most likely to be challenged by someone claiming one of the following:

- the will was not properly written, signed or witnessed, or did not meet the state's formal requirements

- the decedent lacked mental capacity at the time the will was executed

- the decedent was a victim of fraud, force, or undue influence

- the will is a forgery

If a will contest is successful, the entire document may be thrown out. Alternatively, the probate court may reject only the part of the will that was challenged. If the entire will is disallowed, the court will distribute the decedent's property as if the person died without a will. If possible, the court may use a previous will, but such action will depend on state law and the facts and circumstances of the case.

If someone files an objection to your will or produces another will, a "will contest" has begun. Will contests are not uncommon, but few people actually win one. They can be very expensive and create lengthy delays in the distribution of an estate's assets. Not just anyone can contest a will. A person must have legal "standing" to object to a will. What constitutes standing is determined by state law, but generally it means someone who either is a party mentioned in a will or perhaps should have been a party to the will based on a legal relationship to the decedent. For example, if a decedent revises his will and the later will is less favorable to someone than an earlier will, that person has standing. Someone may initiate a will contest to have a different person, bank, or **trust company** serve as the personal representative for an estate or serve as a trustee of trusts created by the will. Some of the most common challenges to wills come from potential heirs or beneficiaries who received less than they had anticipated.

## Disinheriting

Can you disinherit your child? The answer is generally yes. To do so, you must explicitly state that you intend to disinherit that child in your will. If your child is a minor, the state laws typically provide some sort of allowance out of the assets of your estate to support your child until he or she reaches the age of majority.

Can you disinherit your spouse? The answer is generally no. But if you and your spouse waived the right to be included in each other's estate in a prenuptial or postnuptial agreement, you may then entirely omit your spouse from taking anything under your will. In the absence of such an agreement, you can limit the amount your spouse will receive to a statutorily defined minimum. All states have laws that shield a surviving spouse from being completely cut off.

Typically, your surviving spouse could choose between the property you left to him or her in your will or a **statutory** share set by state law. Depending on the state law where you reside, this spousal share is usually one-third or one-half of your estate. The rules for calculating the amount of the share differ remarkably from state to state. Additionally, in **community property** states, the surviving spouse already owns half of the community property at the death of the other spouse.

The threat of will contest and the expense and delay they occasion prompts competent lawyers to encourage their clients to avoid completely cutting someone out. Instead, it may be advisable to leave the person a relatively small amount and put in an "in terrorum" clause. These clauses state that if the person contests the will, he will **forfeit** that small amount. The consequences of will contests are another important reason most people should avoid a do-it-yourself will. Lawyers are trained and experienced to prepare wills and will make sure the wording and **execution** is done according to the law. If

it seems possible that someone may later claim that the testator lacked competence, the lawyer can produce qualified medical and other witnesses at the execution ceremony to ameliorate those claims.

## Divorce

The effect of a **divorce** on the legality or sufficiency of a will depends on your state's law. In some states, a divorce **decree** will automatically revoke your entire will. In other states, a divorce will only revoke the provisions that would distribute assets to your former spouse, not the will itself. In either case, should you experience a divorce, you should review the property arrangements in your will. This is also true of other important documents, such as life insurance policies and bank accounts. This is such a fundamental principle that divorce courts frequently require litigants to address these issues as part of divorce decrees.

## Dying Without a Will

If you die without having made a will (also known as dying "intestate"), the probate court will appoint a personal representative for your estate. This representative is frequently known as an "administrator." The administrator will receive creditors' claims against your estate, pay debts, and distribute your remaining property according to the laws of your state. There are many differences between dying **testate** and dying **intestate**. The main difference, however, is that an intestate estate is distributed to beneficiaries according to the distribution plan established by state law; a testate estate is distributed according to the decedent's instructions provided in the decedent's will. For more detailed information about **intestacy**, see the heading "Intestacy" in the *Gale Encyclopedia of Everyday Law*.

## Guardians

A major impetus for making a will is to provide for the care of minor children. If you have a minor child or children you may want to choose a guardian to serve in your place should you die before your children reach the age of majority. There are two basic types of legal guardians: a guardian of the person and a guardian of the estate of minor children, but these functions can be performed by one person. The guardian of the person is responsible for decisions about the health, education, and welfare of the minor child. The guardian of the estate is responsible for the child's property and for managing finances for the minor child.

When one natural parent dies, generally the other natural parent is appointed as the guardian for minor children, whether or not the parents were married at the time. If someone besides a surviving natural parent of a minor child is named as guardian in a will, the surviving natural parent can contest that nomination. The court will then determine whether the appointment of the other parent as the guardian would be detrimental to the best interests of the minor child. Courts strongly prefer that children be placed in the guardianship of their natural parents whenever possible. It is very difficult from a legal standpoint to overcome this presumption. However, if both natural parents are deceased, it is important to name a guardian for minor children, to ensure the children (and their financial assets) will be cared for by someone the parents trust.

## Life Insurance

It is not a good idea to name a beneficiary for your insurance in your will. This adds an unnecessary level of administration and expense as insurance proceeds become caught up in the probate process. Because life insurance proceeds generally pass to your beneficiaries free of the claims of your creditors, passing insurance proceeds through your will may unnecessarily subject your life insurance proceeds to your estate's debts. Currently, you may contact your insurance company to ask for a beneficiary form on which you name your life insurance beneficiaries. If your life insurance is part of your employer's benefit plan, your employer may provide you with insurance beneficiary forms. With the forms from your insurance company or employer, you may name the beneficiaries of your choice and file the new beneficiary designation with the insurance company or with your employer. Do not forget to ask for written confirmation that the form was received and properly filed. In the event of your death, the insurance company would pay the insurance proceeds directly to the beneficiaries you have named without having your beneficiaries going through the delay, expense, and trouble of probate.

## Lost Wills

Sometimes, a family knows that a deceased relative made a will, but the will cannot be found. Miss-

ing wills raise many legal issues. The outcomes of these situations depend on the specific facts and circumstances, as well as on the law of the state in which the deceased resided. If the will is missing because the deceased attempted to revoke it, depending on state law, an earlier will or the state's rules on interstate **succession** would determine how to distribute the deceased's estate. If the will is missing because it was destroyed in an explosion or fire, the probate court may accept a photocopy of the will. The court may also accept the deceased lawyer's draft or computer file. In either of these cases, the court will require evidence that the deceased executed the original will according to state law.

## Moving from State to State

The laws of all states differ with respect to wills. If you move to a different state after you make and execute your will, it may be a good idea to have your will reviewed by a lawyer in your new state. Basically, a will properly drafted and executed in your former state—and that would be valid in your former state—will typically be regarded as valid under the law of your new state.

Do not forget that the laws in your new state may be more favorable than the laws of your previous state. For example, your new state may have different processes to "prove" the will. Or your new state may permit some probate matters to be handled on a less formal and less expensive basis. Sometimes this can be accomplished simply by adding language that refers to certain statutory provisions in your new state's laws.

Sometimes complications will occur because different states maintain different statutory classifications of property. The differences between states without community property schemes and those that have them can create important complications. If your will was executed in a state that does not have a community property scheme and you subsequently move to a community property state (or vice versa), you may want to confer with a lawyer in your new state to determine whether to create a new will to achieve your intended result.

## Revoking a Will

As mentioned above, a change in your marital status may revoke all of your will, or it may revoke the part of your will relating to your former spouse. If you are mentally competent at the time you do it, you can revoke your will by burning it, tearing it up, or otherwise destroying it. Be aware that revoking your will must be properly witnessed and recorded. If not, someone may later claim that your will was simply "lost" and not revoked. Thus, copies of the will you thought you had revoked can be produced and duly probated. Alternatively, someone may claim that you lacked mental competence at the time you "attempted" to revoke your will.

## Probate

Probate is the process by which legal title of your property will be transferred from your estate to your beneficiaries. If you die with a will ("testate"), the probate court determines if your will is valid, hear any objections to your will, orders that your creditors be paid, and supervises the process to assure that property remaining is distributed in accordance with the terms and conditions of your will. The cost of probating your estate is determined either by state law or by practice and custom in your community. The usual cost to probate an estate varies between 3% and 7% of the value of the estate.

## Taxes

As part of his or her duties, your personal representative will file tax returns for your estate to report the assets of your estate. The personal representative will also file an estate income **tax return** to report any income generated by your estate. Federal estate taxes are the highest in the federal tax code. Currently, estate tax is levied on decedents' estates when the estate is valued over $675,000. This exclusion amount will rise in annual increments to $3.5 million in 2009. Federal estate tax rates range between 37% and 50% in 2002. Prior to 2002, the federal estate tax rate was 55%. This tax rate will drop 1% each year until it reaches 45%. The Federal Estate Tax begins in § 2001 of the Internal Revenue Code. (26 U.S.C. 2001). Merely making and executing a will does not reduce federal estate tax. However, through competent legal advice on estate planning, including the careful crafting of your will, you can minimize or avoid these taxes. Such tax benefits would not be available to you and your family if you died without a will.

## Types of Wills

### Do-It-Yourself Wills

So-called do-it-yourself are wills that individuals create themselves, usually with the aid of self-help legal literature. There are numerous guides, form books, websites, and fill-in-the-blank literature in the marketplace geared for non-lawyers. This material purports to help you create a valid will and avoid the costs of hiring an attorney to prepare a will for you. While this may be true in some cases, there is much to be cautious about. Mainly, the consequences of preparing a do-it-yourself will can be potentially devastating. If you die and your will is declared to be invalid, you will not be around to explain what you had intended to accomplish in your will. Instead, a probate court will either interpret your will or distribute your property according to the state intestacy scheme. Keep in mind that your will is an important legal document. If it is not prepared and executed according to state law, your entire will can be set aside by a probate court. Additionally, just about anyone who envisions an alternative distribution of your estate can contest a do-it-yourself will. If it does not meet some very stringent tests mandated by state law, the court can disregard your do-it-yourself will.

### Oral Wills

Oral wills are those whose contents and terms are merely spoken to a witness or witnesses, but not written down. There is great potential for fraud or even simple misunderstanding in oral wills. In most cases an "oral will" is only recognized by a probate court when made by members of the armed services or merchant marine in active service in time of conflict. Oral wills are not uncommon in situations in which a person feels he or she does not have time to prepare a written will and have it properly executed.

### Death-Bed Wills

Deathbed wills are those created and executed when the testator is facing imminent death. These wills may be perfectly valid and binding, but the closer to the testator's death the will is prepared the more likely it is to be challenged. The contest is usually based on a premise that the testator lacked sufficient mental capacity or was subject to undue influence. As previously stated, challenges can lead to costly and protracted will contests.

A deathbed will can potentially lead to errors. Its hasty preparation can be such that the will may not distribute the property in the manner that the testator intended. Hasty preparation can also fail to take advantage of some features that can reduce or eliminate the Federal Estate Tax. It is also more likely that the will would be found invalid because it does not conform to some legal requirement. These are some of the reasons many lawyers urge their clients or potential clients to create and execute their wills while they are still of sound mind and body.

### Holographic Wills

A holographic will is one that you have written yourself. They are generally handwritten, although some states may allow for a holographic will to be created on a typewriter or with word processing software. These kinds of wills are not allowed in some states, but other states permit this kind of informal will. In states that permit them, the laws relating to holographic wills can be very specific or restrictive. For example, California requires that you write all material provisions entirely by hand and that you must sign your holographic will. On occasion, a holographic will is better than no will at all. In cases where the holographic will creates an ambiguity or an unintended result, it may have been better to have no will at all.

### Self-Probating Wills

You can help simplify the probate process by adding to your will the affidavits (sworn statements) of the witnesses who saw you signing your will. When these affidavits are included with a will, it is sometimes called a "self-probating will." In the affidavits, the witnesses state that they saw you execute or sign the will, that you asked them to be witnesses to the will, that you appeared mentally competent at the time, and you acted voluntarily. Without these affidavits, the process is more complicated and lengthy. In those cases, the executor would usually need to contact the original witnesses and have them appear in probate court (if they can). Before the personal representative or executor can even file your will in probate court, the witnesses would usually appear in court (or sometimes provide an **affidavit**) to state the circumstances surrounding the execution of the will. This **testimony** helps to "prove" that the will is genuine.

Probate courts usually permit your will to be filed along with the affidavits, without the need to summon witnesses or obtain new affidavits. The court then gives notice to other heirs at law who are given a specific amount of time to file any objections to the will being admitted to probate. If any of these choose to challenge your will, the probate court is more likely to require your witnesses to come into court (if

they are still available) to **testify** about the circumstances in which your will was signed. In some states, self-authenticating affidavits are not accepted in situations where the testator dies shortly after the will is signed, or the will was not executed with the assistance of a licensed attorney.

### Living Wills

A **Living will** is something of a misnomer. It does not direct how your property is to be disposed of after you die. Rather, it is a document that specifies the general kinds of medical care you would want— or not want—in the event you became unable to communicate with your health care providers. Living wills are sometimes known as "medical directives" or "medical declarations."

## Additional Resources

*The American Bar Association Guide to Wills & Estates: Everything You Need to Know About Wills, Trusts, Estates, and Taxes.* American Bar Association, Times Books, 1995.

*The Estate Planning Sourcebook* Berry, Dawn Bradley, Lowell House, 1999.

*Family Money: Using Wills, Trusts, Life Insurance and Other Financial Planning tools to Leave the Things You Own to People You Love.* Silver Lake Editors, Silver Lake Publishing, 2001.

*http://www.estateplanninglinks.com/ep.html# highlighted.* "Estate Planning Resources." EstatePlanningLinks.com, 2001.

*http://www.findlaw.com/01topics/31probate/index.html.* "Wills, Trusts, Estates and Probate." FindLaw, 2002.

*http://law.freeadvice.com/estate_planning/wills/.* "Wills." FreeAdvice.Com, 2002.

*http://www.nolo.com/lawcenter/index.cfm/catID/ FD1795A9-8049-422 C-9087838F86A2BC2B.* "Wills and Estate Planning." Nolo.Com, 2002.

*http://www.lawyers.com/lawyers-com/content/aboutlaw/ taxation_3.ht ml.* "Inheritance and Estate Tax." lawyers.com, 2001.

*http://www.mtpalermo.com.* "Crash Course in Wills and Trusts." Palermo, Michael T., Attorney at Law, 2002.

*Restatement of the Law, Property-Wills and Other Donative Tranfers, 3d Edition.* American Law Institute, West Publishing, 1999.

*The Wills and Estate Planning Guide: A State and Territorial Summary of Will and Intestacy Statutes.* American Bar Association, The Association, 1995.

*Wills and Trusts in a Nutshell.* Mennell, Robert L., West Publishing, 1994.

## Organizations

### The American Academy of Estate Planning Attorneys

9360 Towne Centre Drive, Suite 300
San Diego, CA 92121 USA
Phone: (800) 846-1555
Fax: (858) 453-1147
E-Mail: infor mation@aaepa.com
URL: http://www.aaepa.com

### American College of Trust and Estate Counsel

3415 South Sepulveda Blvd., Suite 330
Los Angeles, CA 90034 USA
Phone: (310) 398-1888
Fax: (310) 572-7280
E-Mail: info @actec.org
URL: http://www.actec.org

### The National Academy of Elder Law Attorneys

1604 North Country Club Road
Tucson, AZ 85716 USA
Phone: (520) 881-4005
Fax: (520) 325-7925
URL: http://w ww.naela.com

### National Network of Estate Planning Attorneys, Inc.

One Valmont Plaza, Fourth Floor
Omaha, NE 68154-5203 USA
Phone: (800) 638-8681
E-Mail: webmaster@netplanning.com
URL: http://www.netplanning.com/

# FAMILY LAW

## ADOPTION

*Sections within this essay:*

## Background

The decision to adopt a child can be one of the most rewarding that an individual or couple can make. As with any rewarding decision, it can be extraordinarily complex. Those who wish to adopt a child must be willing not merely to welcome a new life into their hearts; they must also be willing to deal with legal and bureaucratic issues that can easily take as long as a typical pregnancy. The key to adopting successfully is to do one's homework: finding reputable attorneys and agencies, knowing the pros and cons of different types of adoptions, and understanding the need to be actively involved at every step without allowing impatience or frustration to take control.

People adopt for a variety of reasons. Many adoptive parents cannot have children. Others want to provide a loving environment for children in need of a home; many parents who adopt have already given birth to children. Some people choose to adopt "special needs" children (children with disabilities, for example). The reasons for **adoption** notwithstanding, the most important requirement for adoptive parents is that they accept adoption as being as irreversible as the birth process.

Beginning in the last decades of the twentieth century, overseas adoptions became increasingly common. More prospective parents turned to Russia, China, and South and Central America for adoption. This trend was spurred on by several factors, the two most important being easier availability and less fear of legal challenges. Domestic adoptions are not subject to widespread legal challenges, but it is not impossible for birth parents or birth relatives to initiate proceedings to revoke an adoption. For these reasons, it is critically important to work with people who are experienced in the adoption process and who understand what makes for a successful adoption.

## Types of Adoption

When people talk about adoption they usually mean "unrelated adoption," the adoption of a child who has no blood or marriage ties to the adoptive parent. Often a grandparent or aunt or uncle will adopt a child whose parents have died or who cannot serve in their role as parents. Step-parents often adopt their step-children as a means of creating a stronger emotional and legal bond within the family. These adoptions are generally much easier and less complicated than a typical unrelated adoption.

When individuals or couples choose to adopt, they have several options.

### Domestic Adoptions

People who wish to adopt a child who is as close to them culturally and physically as possible will often opt for domestic adoptions. A white couple may want to adopt a white baby, a black couple a black baby, and so on. Because there are more minority children available for adoption, prospective parents almost always have a longer wait if they wish to adopt a white child.

### Multiethnic Adoptions

Often a prospective parent is unconcerned about the race or ethnicity of the child. Or the parent may actively seek a child of a different race or ethnic group. Multiethnic adoptions (also called transethnic or transracial adoptions) are generally easier when the parents seek a minority child, again, because there are more minority children available for adoption.

### International Adoptions

Because there are many more children overseas who are waiting to be adopted (in particular, many more who are under one year old), it is often easier for parents to adopt from another country. This action involves extra steps, of course, including dealing with both the U. S. government and the adoptee's government as well. A number of adoption agencies specialize in overseas adoptions.

The costs associated with adoption depend on the type of adoption and the age of the child, among other factors. An agency or other intermediary should be able to give you a detailed breakdown of how much you should expect to pay for the adoption. Agencies are also be able to provide information on sources for funding and possible tax breaks for adoptive parents.

## The Adoption Process

Adoption is a complex process, but it follows a fairly predictable sequence of events. The first step for those who are serious about adopting is to contact someone who can provide assistance. Some people try to handle the adoption process themselves. Because the laws are so complex, doing so is illegal in a number of jurisdictions, and the sheer volume of regulations is often more than the average untrained person can handle.

Most people turn to adoption agencies when they decide to adopt a child. Agencies can be public or state-licenced private groups. Some agencies specialize in specific types of adoption, as mentioned above. Agencies place children whose birth parents have voluntarily surrendered their rights to their offspring or whose birth parents have had their parental rights terminated. Because agencies have considerable experience with adoptions, they can often make the process run more smoothly. A number of people, however, turn to "private placement," in which the biological parent or parents place the child directly with the adoptive parents. Often this action involves a third party (typically a lawyer, doctor, or a member of the clergy) who brings the biological and adoptive parents together and who then acts as an intermediary. Private placement is illegal in Connecticut, Delaware, and Massachusetts, and it is strictly regulated in several other states.

The next step after choosing a third party in the adoption is to arrange for a "home study." This is an evaluation of the prospective parent's fitness to raise a child. Not surprisingly, the process is detailed. A prospective parent is interviewed, often by several people. The parent's home is visited, and letters of reference and recommendation are asked for. The prospective parent needs to provide information about his or her physical and emotional health, financial status, employment history, marital history, and so on. The process is by necessity extremely thorough.

If the child has not yet been born, the prospective parent or the intermediary (whether an agency or an individual) selects a pregnant woman who has decided to give up her baby for adoption. If the child has been born, the prospective parent is offered a chance to meet him or her (for domestic adoptions). Obviously, a prospective parent may not be able to meet a child from overseas right away, but pictures and often videotapes of the child are made available. Some agencies do require that the prospective parent visits the country of the child's birth to meet with the child before the process is finalized. Meeting the child is an important turning point in the adoption process because it is the first chance for the parent and child to bond, if only for a brief time.

At this point the goal is to make sure all the legal requirements have been met. Many forms need to be filled out and filed with different courts and government agencies. For domestic adoptions, the child may be placed with the adoptive family for supervision to ensure that the adjustment is smooth before the adoption is finalized. This step depends on the state laws and the courts. Overseas adoptions by necessity cannot require a supervised adjustment period, so usually when the parent makes a second trip it is to take **custody** of the child. Before this action can be accomplished, however, the child must be granted U. S. citizenship. This step involves more paperwork but usually does not take long. However, adoptive parents should be prepared to wait just in case, since two government bureaucracies are at work instead of one.

Each state has its own regulations regarding the adoption process, so it is important to learn the laws governing your particular state and also to know that the intermediary you choose has a thorough knowledge of your state's laws and requirements.

## Obstacles to the Adoption Process

The adoption process is not thorough simply because bureaucrats like to make people fill out dozens of forms. Adoption is a permanent decision, and each adoption needs to be made ironclad to avoid difficulties later on.

Probably the greatest fear adoptive parents have is that the birth parents will change their minds and petition to get their children back. Although the laws are thorough, sometimes a birth parent will challenge an adoption for any one of a number of reasons. Most states allow birth mothers to revoke or withdraw their consent to give up their children for adoption; in some states this can be done at any time before the adoption has been finalized. By law, birth mothers actually cannot give consent to an adoption until after their babies have been born; Alabama, Hawaii, Washington, and Wisconsin allow prebirth consent in certain circumstances. But there are strict rules regarding consent. A birth parent who has been proved to have deserted the child, for example, has no **legal right** to give or revoke consent.

### Putative Fathers

Many adoptees are the children of single women who may not even know the fathers' identity. Sometimes, birth fathers may wish to exercise their rights to claim their children. Unwed, or "putative" fathers can establish certain rights thanks to changes in state laws since the 1970s. That said, a putative father needs to prove that he has actually earned these rights. Putative fathers have to prove their commitment to their children by having signed the birth certificate, provided support for the child, and communicated with him or her, and by having obtained a court order establishing **paternity**. They should also have submitted their names to a registry of putative fathers in their states. Moreover, in most cases all of these steps need to have been taken *before* a birth mother has made a petition to the court to give up her child for adoption. Court cases involving putative fathers who tried to revoke adoptions after claiming they knew nothing of their children's births have resulted in many states clarifying their laws. Putative fathers may have the law on their side, but again, only if they can prove they are truly concerned for their children's welfare.

### Multiethnic Issues

Within pockets of the adoption community the question of whether to allow children of one race or color to be adopted by parents of another race or color is a source of heated controversy. Some people believe that mixed-race adoptions are a good practice because they break down racial, ethnic, and cultural barriers. Others see mixed-race adoptions as a means of diluting the cultural and ethnic heritage of adopted children.

Multiethnic adoption presents a compelling problem for two reasons. One is that, as noted above, there are many more minority children available for adoption (including mixed-race children). The other is that there are many more whites than minorities who are willing to adopt. Insisting on matching race to race can leave many children without available parents to adopt them. For children of mixed ancestry, matching race to race is hardly possible.

Federal law protects parents and children from this dilemma. The Multi-Ethnic Protection Act (MEPA) of 1994 states that no adoption agencies that receive federal funds can deny or delay a placement based on race or ethnicity. Occasionally there are still some court cases that raise the issue, but parents who work with a reputable agency and knowledgeable attorneys should not have to worry.

MEPA does not cover children of American Indian (Native American) ancestry. The Indian Child Welfare Act of 1978 was passed to protect Indian children from being taken away from their families for adoption without parental or tribal consent. This action was apparently not uncommon in years past, and the protection is thus important. Unfortunately, some have read the law to mean that no child with Indian ancestry can be legally adopted, even with the birth parent's consent, without tribal approval. Complicating the matter is the unclear definition of Indian ancestry; some tribes may consider a person with one drop of Indian blood to be Indian. Clearly there are many layers to this issue, and it requires careful evaluation by the prospective parent with the help of knowledgeable intermediaries.

### Open Adoption

Open adoption allows the birth family to have visitation rights with the child and the adoptive family. The idea is that maintaining contact with the birth family is beneficial for the child. In some cases it may be, but it can also create uncomfortable situations in which the child ends up being forced to make a choice most children should never have to make. An open adoption can take place only if both the adoptive and birth parents sign an agreement and only if that agreement meets the approval of the court. Different states have different rules about open adoption procedures and also different approaches for addressing whether open adoptions are legally enforceable.

Again, this issue requires careful consideration by prospective parents. In some cases agencies encourage open adoption, but if you wish to adopt a child and open adoption makes you uncomfortable, you should make your concerns known early on.

### Searching for Birth Parents

Whether an adopted child may want to know his or her birth parents does not come up at the time of adoption but the question is worth thinking about early on. State laws vary widely on whether adopted children can have access to the names of their biological parents. Often those parents do not want contact with the child. Even if they do, the situation can be problematic for all parties. The issue is not really within the scope of this discussion, but adoption agencies and intermediaries should be able to answer questions about it. Bear in mind that, according to figures form the National Council on Adoption, no more than two percent of adopted adults search for their biological parents.

## Getting Information

Probably the best first step is to conduct some research, either through materials available at the public library or over the Internet. There are a number of adoption-related web sites, but keep in mind that

not all of them offer the same quality of information. The National Adoption Information Clearinghouse, which is run by the U. S. Department of Health and Human Services' Administration on Children and Families, may be a good starting point. Its web address is http://www.calib.com/naic.

Because each state's laws vary so widely, it is critically important to check with state government agencies that regulate adoption to determine your specific rights and responsibilities.

There are numerous adoption agencies, and it makes sense to get information from several before making a decision on which one would be the best option. Once you choose an agency, you will be working with that group for the next several months, so make sure you are comfortable with your choice.

## Additional Resources

*The Adoption Resource Book.* Lois Gilman, HarperPerennial, 1998.

*Family Bonds: Adoption and the Politics of Parenting.* Elizabeth Bartholet, Houghton Mifflin, 1993.

*The Law of Adoption and Surrogate Parenting.* Irving J. Sloan, Oceana Publications, 1988.

*The Unofficial Guide to Adopting a Child.* Andrea Della-Vecchio, IDG Books Worldwide, 2000.

## Organizations

### National Council for Adoption (NCFA)

1930 17th Street NW
Washington, DC 20009 USA
Phone: (202) 328-1200
Fax: (202) 332-0935
URL: http://w ww.ncfa-usa.org
Primary Contact: Patrick Purtill, CEO

### U. S. Department of Health and Human Services, Administration for Children and Families

370 L'Enfant Promenade
Washington, DC 20447 USA
Phone: (202) 401-2337
URL: http://www.acf.dhhs.gov
Primary Contact: Wade F. Horn, Assistant Secretary for Children and Families

# FAMILY LAW

## CHILD ABUSE/CHILD SAFETY/DISCIPLINE

*Sections within this essay:*

- Background
- History
- Defining Child Abuse
- Preventing Child Abuse
- State Laws
- Additional Resources

## Background

**Child abuse** occurs when a parent or caretaker physically, emotionally, or sexually mistreats or neglects a child resulting in the physical, emotional, or sexual harm or exploitation, or imminent risk of harm or exploitation, or in extreme cases the death, of a child. Laws regarding child abuse seek to protect children while at the same time allowing parents the right to raise and discipline their children as they see fit. Controversies over child abuse laws arise when parents or guardians feel that the government is interfering in their private family lives.

## History

Child abuse has a lengthy history. Children have always been subject to abuse by their parents or other adults, and for many centuries laws failed to protect them. Children under English **common law** were considered the property of their fathers until the late 1800s; American colonists in the seventeenth and eighteenth centuries carried this tradition to the early years of the United States.

In the early 1870s, child abuse captured the nation's attention with news that an eight-year-old orphan named Mary Ellen Wilson was suffering daily whippings and beatings at her foster home. With no organization in existence to protect abused children, the orphan's plight fell to attorneys for the American Society for the Prevention of Cruelty to Animals (ASPCA). These attorneys argued that laws protecting animals from abuse should not be greater than laws protecting children. Mary Ellen Wilson's case went before a judge, who convicted the foster mother of **assault and battery** and gave her a one year sentence. More significantly, the orphan's case generated enough outrage over child abuse that in 1874, citizens formed the New York Society for the Prevention of Cruelty to Children.

Child abuse captured the country's attention again in 1962, when an article appearing in the Journal of the American Medical Association described symptoms of child abuse and deemed child abuse to be medically diagnosable. Within ten years, every state had statutes known as mandatory reporting laws. Mandatory reporting laws require certain professionals—doctors and teachers, for example—to report to police suspected child abuse situations. A 1974 federal law further bolstered efforts to eliminate child abuse by funding programs to help individuals identify and report child abuse and to provide shelter and other protective services to victims.

## Defining Child Abuse

Child abuse may involve physical abuse that causes injury. The most obvious types of physical child abuse include children who are beaten, burned, or shaken. Child abuse may involve **sexual**

**abuse**, although sexual abuse need not result in physical injury to the child for it to be illegal. Sexual abuse may include inappropriate touching, fondling, or even sexual intercourse. Finally, child abuse may involve neglect that places a child at risk, such as when a child who is left alone without adult supervision, or a child who is left enclosed and unattended in a car.

## Preventing Child Abuse

In addition to state laws criminalizing child abuse, states have agencies, known as child protective services, that investigate suspected child abuse cases involving the child's parent or **guardian**. When a suspected case of child abuse involves an adult other than the child's parent or guardian, law enforcement agencies such as police departments typically conduct the investigation. An investigation may include a law officer or case worker visiting and interviewing the child. Parents, guardians, and other possible witnesses such as doctors or teachers also may be questioned during an investigation.

Once an investigation is completed, the child protective service or law enforcement agency determines whether the **evidence** substantiates child abuse. If it does, then the agency will intervene. There is a spectrum of intervention modalities. In less severe cases of child abuse— for example, when a parent unwittingly leaves a child in a car while making a quick stop in a grocery store— intervention may be nothing more than requiring the parent to meet with a social worker to learn about the dangers of leaving a child unattended. If it appears to the investigating agency that an abused child is in imminent danger, the agency may take the child from the parents and place the child temporarily in a foster home until the parents demonstrate their willingness to stop the abuse. In extreme cases of child abuse, the investigating agency may seek assistance from a court to terminate the parental rights. When this happens, the child may be placed for permanent **adoption**.

Child protective services, in addition to investigating allegations of child abuse, maintain records regarding child abuse. These records are kept in a central registry, and in some states, parties such as **child care** providers or adoption agencies have access to the central registry. The goal of the central registry is to help child protective services, and sometimes other parties, know whether an individual has a history of abusing children. Although this information

can be invaluable in preventing future child abuse, central registries may contain false or unsubstantiated accounts of child abuse, implicating innocent individuals. For this reason, some groups oppose central registries and argue that child protective services have too much power. One such group, Victims of Child Abuse Laws (VOCAL), seeks a reform in child abuse laws to better protect the rights of parents, who may be falsely **accused** of child abuse or neglect.

VOCAL, and groups like it, maintain that it is too easy for false accusations about child abuse to lead to the removal of children from their parents and their homes. False reports of child abuse can come from children seeking attention or attempting to avoid reasonable forms of discipline. False reports of child abuse also may result from animosity between parents, such as when parents are in the midst of **divorce** and **custody** battles over their children. The evidence of child abuse is sometimes nothing more than a young child's **testimony**. Proponents of child abuse law reform maintain that police and other officials can easily manipulate a young child to support allegations of child abuse. The ramifications of a false report of child abuse can be serious: officials may remove children from their homes and place them in foster care or permanent new adoptive homes, emotionally scarring both children and parents.

Another difficult issue in the arena of child abuse concerns discipline. There are many different views regarding what constitutes discipline and where the line should be drawn between reasonable parental discipline and child abuse. For example, some parents feel that spanking or hitting a child is abusive behavior; other parents rely on spanking, or the threat of a spanking, to teach children to obey and behave. Using physical measures to discipline children is known as corporal punishment. In trying to prevent child abuse, legal and governmental agencies attempt to balance the parents' right to raise their children in the manner they feel is appropriate with the child's right to be safe and unharmed.

Some forms of child abuse are caused not by a parent's willful abuse, but rather, by a parent's **negligence**. One common, and oftentimes tragic, form of neglect occurs when a parent accidentally leaves a sleeping baby in a car on a warm day. In the sun, the interior of a car can heat within minutes to more than 100 degrees, temperatures that a baby cannot survive. Whether to charge parents in these situations with child abuse is a divisive issue. Some people maintain that careless parents should be prosecuted; other people believe that a parent who loses a child due to the parent's mistake suffers enough without being prosecuted.

## State Laws

ALABAMA: **Statute** defines child abuse as harm or threatened harm of physical abuse, neglect, sexual abuse, sexual exploitation, or emotional/mental injury against a child under the age of 18. Statute contains an exemption for religious reasons for a parent's failure to obtain medical help for the child.

ALASKA: Statute defines child abuse as harm or threatened harm of physical abuse, neglect, sexual abuse, sexual exploitation, or emotional/mental injury of a child under the age of 18. Statute contains an exemption for religious reasons for a parent's failure to obtain medical help for the child.

ARIZONA: Statute defines child abuse as inflicting or allowing physical abuse, neglect, sexual abuse, sexual exploitation, emotional/mental injury, or **abandonment** of a child under the age of 18. Statute contains an exemption for Christian Scientists or unavailability of reasonable resources for a parent's failure to obtain medical help for the child.

ARKANSAS: Statute defines child abuse as intentionally, knowingly, or negligently without cause inflicting physical abuse, neglect, sexual abuse, sexual exploitation, abandonment or emotional/mental injury of a child under the age of 18. Statute contains exemptions for poverty or corporal punishment.

CALIFORNIA: Statute defines child abuse as inflicting by non-accidental means physical abuse, neglect, sexual abuse, or sexual exploitation of a child under the age of 18. Statute contains exemptions for religion, reasonable force, and informed medical decision.

COLORADO: Statute prohibits threats to a child's health and welfare due to physical abuse, neglect, sexual abuse, sexual exploitation, emotional/mental injury, or abandonment. Statute contains exemptions for corporal punishment, reasonable force, religious practices, and cultural practices.

CONNECTICUT: Statute prohibits injuries inflicted by non-accidental means involving physical abuse, neglect, sexual abuse, sexual exploitation, emotional/mental injury, or abandonment. Statute contains exemption for Christian Scientists.

DELAWARE: Statute prohibits injuries inflicted by non-accidental means involving physical abuse, neglect, sexual abuse, sexual exploitation, emotional/mental injury, or abandonment. Statute contains exemption for religion.

DISTRICT OF COLUMBIA: Statute prohibits persons from inflicting and requires people to take reasonable care not to inflict injuries involving physical abuse, neglect, sexual abuse, sexual exploitation, or emotional/mental injury. Statute contains exemption for poverty and religion.

FLORIDA: Statute prohibits willful or threatened act that harms or is likely to cause harm of physical abuse, neglect, sexual abuse, sexual exploitation, abandonment, or emotional/mental injury. Statute contains exemptions for religion, poverty, or corporal punishment.

GEORGIA: Statute prohibits injuries inflicted by non-accidental means involving physical abuse, neglect, sexual abuse, or sexual exploitation. Statute contains exemption for religion and corporal punishment.

HAWAII: Statute prohibits acts or omissions resulting in the child being harmed or subject to any reasonably foreseeable, substantial risk of being harmed with physical abuse, neglect, sexual abuse, sexual exploitation, or emotional/mental injury. Statute contains no exemptions.

IDAHO: Statute prohibits conduct or omission resulting in physical abuse, neglect, sexual abuse, sexual exploitation, abandonment, or emotional/mental injury. Statute contains exemption for religion.

ILLINOIS: Statute prohibits persons from inflicting, causing to be inflicted, or allowing to be inflicted, or creating a substantial risk, or committing or allowing to be committed, physical abuse, neglect, sexual abuse, sexual exploitation, or emotional/mental injury. Statute contains exemptions for religion, school attendance, and plan of care.

INDIANA: Statute prohibits act or omission resulting in physical abuse, neglect, sexual abuse, sexual exploitation, abandonment, or emotional/mental injury. Statute contains exemptions for religion, prescription drugs, or corporal punishment.

KENTUCKY: Statute prohibits harm or threat of harm, or infliction or allowance of infliction of physical abuse, neglect, sexual abuse, sexual exploitation, abandonment, or emotional/mental injury. Statute contains exemptions for religion.

MARYLAND: Statute prohibits harm or substantial risk of harm resulting in physical abuse, neglect, sexual abuse, sexual exploitation, or emotional/mental injury. Statute contains no exemptions.

MICHIGAN: Statute prohibits harm or threatened harm of physical abuse, neglect, sexual abuse, sexual exploitation, or emotional/mental injury. Statute contains exemptions for religion.

MISSISSIPPI: Statute prohibits persons from causing or allowing to be caused physical abuse, neglect, sexual abuse, sexual exploitation, or emotional/mental injury. Statute contains exemption for religion and corporal punishment.

NEBRASKA: Statute prohibits knowingly, intentionally, or negligently causing or permitting physical abuse, neglect, sexual abuse, sexual exploitation, or emotional/mental injury. Statute contains no exemptions.

NEW MEXICO: Statute prohibits knowingly, intentionally, or negligently causing or permitting physical abuse, neglect, sexual abuse, sexual exploitation, abandonment, or emotional/mental injury. Statute contains exemption for religion.

NORTH DAKOTA: Statute prohibits serious harm caused by non-accidental means resulting in physical abuse, neglect, sexual abuse, sexual exploitation, abandonment, or emotional/mental injury. Statute contains no exemptions.

OKLAHOMA: Statute prohibits harm or threat of harm resulting in physical abuse, neglect, sexual abuse, sexual exploitation, abandonment, or emotional/mental injury. Statute contains exemptions for religion or corporal punishment.

PENNSYLVANIA: Statute prohibits recent act or failure to act resulting in physical abuse, neglect, sexual abuse, sexual exploitation, or emotional/mental injury. Statute contains exemptions for religion or poverty.

SOUTH DAKOTA: Statute prohibits threat with substantial harm resulting in physical abuse, neglect, sexual abuse, sexual exploitation, abandonment, or emotional/mental injury. Statute contains no exemptions.

TENNESSEE: Statute prohibits persons from committing or allowing to be committed physical abuse, neglect, sexual abuse, sexual exploitation, or emotional/mental injury. Statute contains no exemptions.

UTAH: Statute prohibits harm or threat of harm resulting in physical abuse, neglect, sexual abuse, sexual exploitation, or emotional/mental injury. Statute contains no exemptions.

WASHINGTON: Statute prohibits harm of health, welfare, or safety resulting from physical abuse, neglect, sexual abuse, or sexual exploitation. Statute contains exemptions for Christian Scientists, corporal punishment, or physical **disability**.

## Additional Resources

*National Clearinghouse on Child Abuse and Neglect Information* Available at www.calib.com

*West's Encyclopedia of American Law.* West Group, 1998.

## Organizations

### American Professional Society on the Abuse of Children
940 NE 13th Street
Oklahoma City, OK 73104 USA
Phone: (405) 271-8202
URL: www.apsac.org

### Prevent Child Abuse America
200 South Michigan Avenue, 17th Floor
Chicago, IL 60604-2404 USA
Phone: (312) 663-3520
URL: www.preventchildabuse.org

# FAMILY LAW

## CHILD SUPPORT/CUSTODY

*Sections within this essay:*

## Background

Historically, fathers had sole rights to **custody**. Since custody was connected to **inheritance** and property laws, mothers had no such rights. Beginning in the late nineteenth century courts began to award custody of young boys and of girls of all ages solely to mothers on the presumption that mothers are inherently better caretakers of young children. Most states followed this maternal preference and mothers almost always received custody. Eventually, many state courts found this preference to be unconstitutional, and gender-neutral custody statutes replaced maternal preference standards in forty-five states by 1990. Today, the custody arrangement is typically part of the **divorce decree**. The decree provides specifics as to where the child will live, how visitation will be handled, and who will provide financial support. Courts consider custody and **child support** issues as subject to change until the child involved reaches the **age of majority**. In many divorces physical custody is awarded to the parent with whom the child will live most of the time. Often, the custodial parent shares joint legal custody with the noncustodial parent, meaning that the custodial parent must inform and consult with the noncustodial parent about the child's education, health care, and other concerns. In this situation, courts may order visitation, sometimes called temporary custody, between the child and the noncustodial parent. A clear schedule with dates and times is often incorporated into the decree. Child support is usually paid by the noncustodial parent to the custodial parent. States have formulas to assist judges in determining the appropriate amount of child support.

## Child Custody

### Joint Custody

Some states have a presumption that joint custody is in the best interest of the child, while other states have no provision for it. Advocates of joint custody claim it lessens the feeling of losing a parent that children may experience after a divorce and that it is fair to both parents. However, because of the high degree of cooperation joint custody requires, courts resist ordering it if either of the parents does not want it or if there is **evidence** of past **domestic violence**. Later problems regarding medical or education decisions concerning the child may develop necessitating long and lengthy court proceedings.

### Split Custody

Split custody is an arrangement in which the parents divide custody of their children, with each parent being awarded physical custody of one or more children. In general, courts try to avoid split custody because it separates siblings, which is usually not considered to be in the best interest of the child.

### Custody Disputes

Many states have adopted a standard that places primary emphasis on the best interests of the child when custody is disputed. Today, courts exercise their discretion in awarding custody, considering all relevant factors, including marital misconduct, to determine the children's best interests. The court may consider such matters as the wishes of the child's parents; the wishes of the child; the relationship between each parent and the child, and any other person who interacts with the child (including stepparents); the child's adjustment to home, school, community; the mental and physical health of all individuals involved; which parent will foster a positive parent-child relationship between the child and the other parent; who was the primary caretaker; the nature and extent of **coercion**, if any, by a parent in obtaining an agreement regarding custody; and whether either parent has complied with an order to attend domestic relations education if the state requires it. Domestic violence is considered not to be in the best interest of a child and in many states a parent's **conviction** for any domestic violence can weigh heavily against that parent's bid for custody.

## Child Support

In determining child support obligations, courts generally hold that each parent should contribute in accordance with his or her means. Child support is a mutual duty, although the primary caretaker of pre-school children may not be required to obtain employment. All states have enacted some form of the Reciprocal Enforcement of Support Act. URESA is a uniform law designed to facilitate the interstate enforcement of support obligations. URESA allows an individual who is due **alimony** or child support from someone who lives in a different state to bring action for receipt of the payments in the home state. This measure circumvents such problems as expense and inconvenience inherent in traveling from one state to another in pursuit of support.

In response to federal legislation, state laws regarding child support payments have become more severe. State laws can require employers to withhold child support from the paychecks of parents who are delinquent for one month. Employers are to be held responsible if they do not comply fully. State laws must provide for the imposition of liens against the property of those who owe support. Unpaid support must be deducted from federal and state **income tax** refunds. Expedited hearings are required in support cases.

## Mediation

**Mediation** is a centered resolution process assisted by an **impartial** trained third party to assist the parties in reaching an informed and consensual agreement. Many parents find the process useful in figuring out which custody and visitation arrangement can work best for them and their child. Mediation typically provides a non-adversarial setting in which to resolve the conflicts that arise over financial, parenting, and other issues. It allows the parents to control many aspects of the court process, rather than deferring to a judge. Additionally, parties who are able to reach an agreement in mediation can save significant court costs and attorneys' fees.

## State Laws

State law varies considerably with respect to divorce. States have differing residency requirements, property rules, and spousal support provisions.

ALABAMA: Both parents have an equal right to the custody of their children. Under Alabama law, a court may consider an award of joint custody, whereby the parental rights of both parties remain intact, with one parent as the primary custodian of the children and the other as the secondary custodian. Under this arrangement, both parents remain involved in the decision making responsibilities regarding the children, with each parent having "tie breaking" authority regarding certain issues, such as education, health and dental care, religion, civic and cultural activities, and athletic involvement. Child support is determined under the Alabama Child Support Guidelines, unless the Court finds grounds to deviate from the guidelines. In Alabama, the Department of Human Resources is responsible for enforcing child support obligations. The court retains **jurisdiction** to modify child support, up or down, until the children reach the age of 19.

ALASKA: The court determines custody in accordance with the best interests of the child and may consider all relevant factors. Domestic violence may be considered contrary to the best interest of the child. There is no presumption in favor of sole custody or joint custody. Joint custody may be ordered if both parents agree and submit a written parenting plan and such joint custody is in the child's best interest. Child support is based on Flat Percentage of Income model. Support terminates at age 18, or 19 if child is enrolled in high school or the equivalent and is residing with custodial parent. Court may not require either parent to pay for post-majority college tuition.

ARIZONA: There is no presumption in favor of joint custody. Joint custody may be granted if both parents agree, the parents submit a parenting plan, and the order is in the child's best interests. Evidence of domestic violence must be considered contrary to the best interests of the child. In determining the best interests of the child, the court can consider: the wishes of the child's parents; the wishes of the child; the interaction among the child and relatives; the child's adjustment to school, home, and community; the mental and physical health of the parties; which parent is more likely to involve the child in the life of the other parent; if either parent has been the primary care giver; the nature and extent of coercion used by a parent in obtaining a written agreement regarding custody; whether either parent has complied with an order to attend domestic relations education. The non-custodial parent is entitled to reasonable visitation, which shall not be restricted unless the court finds serious endangerment to the child. Child support guidelines are based on Income Shares Model, and award is calculated on **gross income**. Support terminates at age 18, or when the child graduates from high school. The court may not order the parents to pay for the college education costs of the child.

ARKANSAS: The court shall determine custody in accordance with the best interests of the child. Child Support guidelines adopt Varying Percentage of Income Model, basing noncustodial parent's obligation on a percentage of **net** income, which percentage decreases as income goes higher. Support terminates at age 18 or when child graduates from high school. Parents cannot be compelled to pay for the college education of their children.

CALIFORNIA: There is no presumption in favor of joint or sole custody; custody shall be awarded to both parents jointly or to either parent **as is** in the best interests of the child. However, where the parties agree to joint custody, then joint custody shall be presumed to be in the best interests of the child. In awarding custody, the court shall consider which parent is more likely to foster a positive relationship between the child and the other parent. An explicit

link between custody and child support is made by the provision that a court may order financial compensation to one parent for those periods of time the other parent fails to assume care taking responsibility. There may be additional financial compensation awarded to a parent who has been repeatedly thwarted by the other parent in attempts to exercise custody/visitation. Statewide Uniform Guidelines are an Income Shares model, explicitly taking into consideration the time each parent has custody of the child.

COLORADO: Joint custody, with one parent designated residential custodian, may be awarded when the parties submit a parenting plan. If no plan is submitted, the court shall determine custody in accordance with the best interests of the child. Child Support Guidelines are based on Income Shares model, based on gross income of both parents. Support terminates at age 18 or when child graduates from high school. Parents cannot be compelled to pay for the college education of their children.

CONNECTICUT: If the parents agree to joint custody, then it is presumed that joint custody is in the best interests of the child, and the court must state its reasons for denial of joint custody. The court may award joint legal custody with primary physical custody to one parent. Visitation may be granted to grandparents or any person if it is in the child's best interests. Child Support guidelines are based on the Income Shared Model, taking into consideration the net income of both parents. Child support terminates when the child reaches 18 years of age.

DISTRICT OF COLUMBIA: There is no presumption as to the form of legal custody. The court may order frequent and continuing contact between each party and the child. The court's order shall be based on the best interests of the child. The court can consider the wishes of the parents, the wishes of the child, the interaction and interrelationship among all family members, the mental and physical health of all parties, the capacity of the parties to communicate, the demands of parental employment, the age and number of children, the parents' financial ability to support the custody arrangement and the impact of governmental assistance. Child support guidelines are a hybrid model, sharing aspects of both the income shares and percentage of income model. The award is based on parties' gross incomes, with a self-support reserve for each parent. By **statute**, a child is entitled to support until age 21.

FLORIDA: The court must order that parental responsibility for a minor child be shared by both parents, unless it is detrimental to the child. The court may grant to one party the ultimate responsibility over specific aspects of the child's welfare. The court shall order sole parental responsibility with or without visitation to the other parent when it is in the best interests of the child. The court may order rotating custody. Child Support Guidelines are the Income Shares Model of support, figured on net income. Health insurance, childcare, and education expenses are added to the basic award. Support terminates at age 18, or 19 if the child will graduate from high school by that time.

GEORGIA: The court may award joint custody and may consider agreements of the parties, if they are in the best interests of the child. The court shall award custody as in the best interests of the child. If a child is 14 years old or older, the child shall have the right to select the parent with whom he desires to live, and such selection shall be controlling unless the parent is not fit. The court may consider family violence in making a decision. Visitation shall be ordered unless there is a history of family violence. Child support is **statutory**. It is the flat percentage of income model, calculated on gross income, with most extra expenses being a deviation factor.

HAWAII: Custody is determined according to the best interests of the child. If a child is of sufficient age and capacity to reason, so as to form an intelligent preference, the child's wishes can be considered. Joint custody may be awarded in the discretion of the court. Visitation may be awarded to grandparents or any person interested in the welfare of the child. Guidelines set out in court rule follow the Melson Formula. Support is calculated on net income, with allowances for household members.

ILLINOIS: There is no presumption for or against joint custody. Custody is determined based on the best interests of the child, considering the parents' and the child's wishes. Child support guidelines are statutory, based on a flat percentage of income model based on net income.

INDIANA: Joint custody may be awarded if it is in the child's best interests. The relevant factors for determining custody are the parents' and child's wishes, the interaction and relationship of the child with any person who may significantly affect his or her best interests; the mental and physical health of all individuals involved, and a pattern of domestic violence. Child support guidelines are set out in the Indiana Rules of Court. The guidelines are based on the income shares model, based on gross income. Sup-

port may include sums necessary for a child's education, including post-majority education.

IOWA: If either party requests joint custody, there is a presumption of joint custody. If the court does not grant joint custody, it must clearly state its reasons why joint custody is not in the best interests of the child. Joint custody does not necessarily require joint physical care. Physical care shall be awarded as is in the best interests of the child. Child support guidelines are enacted by the supreme court of Iowa by court rule. The guidelines are based on the income shares model, based on gross income.

KENTUCKY: The court may grant joint custody to the child's parents if it is in the child's best interests. The court may not consider conduct of a custodian that does not affect his or her relationship to the child, nor may it consider **abandonment** of the family residence if it was to avoid physical harm. Child support guidelines set out by statute. The guidelines are based on the income shares model, based on gross income. Support may include sums necessary for a child's education, including post-majority education.

LOUISIANA: The court shall award custody in accordance with the parents' agreement, unless the best interests of the child require otherwise. If there is no agreement or if the agreement is not in the best interests of the child, the court shall award joint custody, unless custody by one parent is shown by clear and convincing evidence to serve the child's best interests. Factors for determining the child's best interests include a stable environment and the primary caretaker preference. The parent not awarded custody is entitled to reasonable visitation. Child support guidelines are statutory. They are based on the Income Shares Model and are based on gross income of the parents.

MARYLAND: The court may award joint custody or sole custody. The court shall deny custody to a party if the court has reasonable grounds to believe that the party abused or neglected the child and that there is a likelihood of further abuse or neglect. Child support guidelines set out by statute. The guidelines are based on the income shares model, based on gross income.

MAINE: When the parties have agreed to shared parental rights and responsibilities, the court shall make such an award absent substantial evidence that it should not be ordered. In making an award of parental rights and responsibilities, the court applies the best interests of the child standard.. The court may not apply a preference for one parent over the other on account of either parent's gender or the child's age and gender. The court may order grandparent or third party visitation. Child support guidelines are statutory. They are based on the Income Shares Model, based on gross income.

MASSACHUSETTS: Each parent must submit to the court a shared custody implementation plan. The court may modify or grant the plan. The court may reject the plan and award sole custody to one parent. Child Support Guidelines are provided in the Massachusetts Court Rules, promulgated by the Supreme Judicial Court. The Massachusetts guidelines are a hybrid form of the Percentage of Income model and Income Shares Model. Support is calculated on the gross income of the non-custodial parent, but then offset by a percentage of income of the custodial parent over a certain floor. Support for education of the child is through age 21.

MICHIGAN: Custody is awarded based on the best interests of the child, based on the following factors: moral character and prudence of the parents; physical, emotional, mental, religious and social needs of the child; capability and desire of each parent to meet the child's emotional, educational, and other needs; preference of the child, if the child is of sufficient age and maturity; the love and affection and other emotional ties existing between the child and each parent; the length of time the child has lived in a stable, satisfactory environment and the desirability of maintaining continuity; the desire and ability of each parent to allow an open and loving frequent relationship between the child and other parent; the child's adjustment to his/her home, school, and community; the mental and physical health of all parties; permanence of the family unit of the proposed custodial home; any evidence of domestic violence; and other factors. There is a joint custody presumption if the parties agree to joint custody. The court may also award joint custody if one party requests joint custody and the court finds it to be in the best interests of the child. In deciding whether to grant joint custody, the court shall consider all of the above factors plus whether the parents will be able to cooperate; whether the parents have agreed to joint custody. Child support payments are made through the Michigan **Friend of the Court** Bureau. Child support guidelines are contained in the Michigan Friend of Court Child Support Manual. The guidelines are based on the Income Shares Model, calculated on each parent's net income.

MINNESOTA: If both parents request joint custody, there is a presumption that such an arrangement is in the best interests of the child, unless there has been spousal abuse. Sole custody can be awarded based on the best interests of the child. Additional visitation may be ordered for wrongful denial or interference with visitation orders. Child support guidelines are based on the Varying Percentage of Income formula, calculated on net income.

MISSISSIPPI: Custody is determined based on the best interests of the child. Joint custody may be awarded if both parents request joint custody, and if they so request joint custody, there is a presumption that joint custody is in the best interests of the child. The court may order any of the following: Joint physical custody to one or both parents, with legal custody to one or both parents; physical custody to both parents, with legal custody to one parent; physical custody to one parent, with legal custody to both parents; custody to a third party if the parents have abandoned the child or are unfit. Child support guidelines are based on the Flat Percentage of Income model, calculated on net income.

MISSOURI: The court determines custody based on the best interests of the child. Custody can be joint legal, joint physical, sole legal, sole physical, or any combination. An award of joint custody is encouraged. Child support guidelines are based on the Income Shares Formula, calculated on gross income.

MONTANA: Each parent is required to submit, either jointly or separately, a proposed "parenting plan." Sole or joint parenting is awarded based on the best interests of the child. Child support guidelines are set out in the Montana Administrative Rules. The support guidelines are based on the Melson Formula, calculated on net income.

NEBRASKA: The court makes a custody determination based on the best interests of the child, which include the relationship of the child to each parent; (b) the desires and wishes of the child; the general health, welfare, and social behavior of the child; credible evidence of any abuse in the household. Joint custody may be awarded when both parents agree to such an arrangement. Child support guidelines were established by court rule and are contained in the Rules of the Supreme Court. The guidelines are based on the Income Shares Formula and are calculated on net income.

NEVADA: Best interests of the child is the standard. The court awards custody in the following order of preference unless in a particular case the best interest of the child requires otherwise: to both parents jointly or to either parent; to a person or persons in whose home the child has been living and where the child has had a wholesome and stable environment; to any person related within the third degree of consanguinity; to any other person or persons whom the court finds suitable and able to provide proper care. In determining the best interests of the child, the court considers: the wishes of the child if the child is of sufficient age and maturity; any nomination by a parent for a **guardian**; whether either parent has engaged in domestic violence. A finding of domestic violence creates a rebuttable presumption that custody would not be appropriate by the **perpetrator**. Child support guidelines are based on the varying percentage of income model. Support is figured by applying a percentage to the obligor's gross income, which percentage gradually decreases as the income rises.

NEW HAMPSHIRE: Joint legal custody is presumed to be in the best interests of the child, unless the child has been abused by one of the parents. Custody is awarded based on preference of the child, education of the child, findings and recommendations of a neutral mediator, and other factors. Child support amounts are set out by statute. The guidelines are based on the Income shares model figured on net income.

NEW MEXICO: Joint custody is presumed to be in the best interests of the child. The court may award joint or sole custody as in the best interests of the child, upon consideration of five enumerated factors. Child support guidelines are based on the Income Shares Model, calculated on gross income.

NEW JERSEY: Sole or joint custody may be awarded based on the needs of the child. There is no preference for either parent and no preference for joint custody. Child support guidelines are contained in New Jersey Court Rules. The guidelines are based on the Income Shares model figured on net income.

NEW YORK: Joint or sole custody is determined according to the best interests of the child. Neither parent is entitled to a preference. Child support guidelines are based on the Income Shares Model, calculated on net income.

NORTH CAROLINA: Joint or sole **child custody** is determined according to the interests and welfare of the child. There is no presumption that either parent is better suited to have custody. The court con-

siders all relevant factors, including acts of domestic violence and the safety of the child. Child support guidelines are based on the Income Shares Model and calculated on gross income.

OHIO: If at least one parent requests shared parenting and files a plan that is in the child's best interests and approved by the court, the court may allocate parental rights and responsibilities of the child to both parents and issue a shared parenting order. Otherwise, the court, consistent with the child's best interests, allocates parental rights and responsibilities primarily to one parent. Child support guidelines are based on the Income Shares Model and is calculated on net income. Termination of child support is at age 18 or graduation from high school, whichever occurs later.

OREGON: The court may order joint custody if the parents agree, but if one parent objects, the court cannot order joint custody. An order for joint custody may specify one home as the primary residence of the child and designate one parent to have sole power to make decisions regarding specific matters while both parents retain equal rights and responsibilities for other matters. When ordering sole custody, the court can consider the conduct, marital status, income, social environment or lifestyle of either party only if it is shown that these factors are causing or may cause damage to the child. Any person who has established emotional ties creating a parent/child relationship with a child may petition for custody, placement, or visitation. The child support guidelines formula is based on the Income Shares Formula, calculated on gross income.

TEXAS: Joint or sole custody is determined according to the best interests of the child. The court considers the best interests of the children deciding upon the terms and conditions of the rights of the parent with visitation. Child support guidelines, by statute, are based on a percentage of income of the noncustodial parent's net income. Support terminates at age 18 or graduation from high school, whichever is later. No statute or **case law** requires support for college.

UTAH: The court considers the best interests of the child along with the past conduct and demonstrated moral standards of the parties. There is a presumption that a spouse who has been abandoned is entitled to custody. State law contains advisory guidelines for visitation schedules, broken down by age of the child. Child support guidelines are based on the income shares model, calculated on gross income. Support terminates at age 18 or when the child graduates from high school. In a divorce action, the court may order support to the age of 21.

WEST VIRGINIA: There is a presumption in favor of the parent who has been the primary caretaker of the child. There is no provision for joint custody. Child support guidelines are based on the income shares model, calculated on **adjusted gross income**. Support terminates at age 20, or up to age 20 if the child is still enrolled in secondary school. The court may award support for college tuition.

## Additional Resources

*Joint Custody with a Jerk: Raising a Child with an Uncooperative EX* Ross, Julie, St. Martin's Press, 1996.

*Why Did You Have to Get a Divorce? and When Can I Get a Hamster?: A Guide to Parenting through Divorce* Wolf, Anthony E., Farrar, Straus & Giroux, 1998.

## Organizations

### *American Bar Association*

750 N. Lake Shore Dr.
Chicago, IL 60611 USA
Phone: (312) 988-5603
Fax: (312) 988-6800
URL: http://www.abanet.org

# FAMILY LAW

## COHABITATION

*Sections within this essay:*

## Background

The law has not traditionally looked favorably upon individuals living together outside marriage. However, the law in this area has changed considerably in the past 40 years, and **cohabitation** has increased dramatically. In 1970, about 530,000 couples reportedly lived together outside marriage. This number increased to 1.6 million in 1980, 2.9 million in 1990, 4.2 million in 1998, and 5.5 million in 2000.

In some respects, unmarried cohabitation can be beneficial from a legal standpoint. Unmarried partners may define the terms of their relationship without being bound by marriage laws that can restrict the marriage relationship. When a relationship ends, unmarried cohabitants need not follow strict procedures to **dissolve** the living arrangement. Moreover, unmarried couples can avoid the so-called "marriage tax" in the Internal Revenue Code that provides a greater tax rate for unmarried couples than it does for two unmarried individuals (notwithstanding efforts to eliminate this **penalty**).

On the other hand, unmarried cohabitants do not enjoy the same rights as married individuals, particularly with respect to property acquired during a relationship. Marital property laws do not apply to unmarried couples, even in long-term relationships. Moreover, laws regarding distribution of property of one spouse to another at death do not apply to unmarried couples. Children of unmarried couples have traditionally not been afforded the same rights as children of married couples, though most of these laws have now been revised to avoid unfairness towards offspring.

A fairly recent trend among both heterosexual and homosexual couples who live together is to enter into contracts that provide rights to both parties that are similar to rights enjoyed by married couples. In fact, many **family law** experts now recommend that unmarried cohabitants enter into such arrangements. Further changes in the laws may also afford greater rights to unmarried partners who live together. However, such arrangements may be invalid in some states, particularly where the contract is based on the sexual relationship of the parties.

## Unmarried Cohabitation Compared with Marriage

Family laws related to marriage simply do not apply to unmarried couples. More specifically, marriage creates a legal status between two individuals that gives rise to certain rights to both parties and to the union generally. Unmarried cohabitants do not enjoy this status and do not enjoy many of the rights afforded to married couples. Thus, if a couple is married for two years, and a spouse dies, the other spouse is most likely entitled to receive property, insurance benefits, death benefits, etc., from the other spouse's estate. If an unmarried couple lives together for 20 years, and one partner dies, the other is not guaranteed any property or benefits.

Though many groups support legal reforms providing protection to unmarried cohabitants that would be analogous to laws governing marriage, very few such laws exist today. Unmarried cohabitants need to know what laws do exist in their state and cities and know what their options are regarding contractual agreements that may provide themselves rights that are analogous to marital rights.

### Criminal Statutes

Laws prohibiting cohabitation and sexual relations outside marriage were very common until about the1970s. Though most of these laws have been repealed or are no longer enforced, they still exist in some state statutes. Eight states still have laws prohibiting cohabitation, which is usually defined as two individuals living together as husband and wife without being legally married. Nine states prohibit fornication, which is usually defined as consensual sexual intercourse outside marriage. More than 15 states prohibit **sodomy**, which includes any "unnatural" sexual activity, such as anal or oral sex. Several of these statutes apply specifically to homosexual activity.

While most of these criminal laws are clearly antiquated, they are sometimes enforced. In the United States Supreme Court case of Bowers v. Hardwick in 1986, the court upheld the enforcement of a criminal **statute** prohibiting sodomy between two homosexual men. Criminal statutes proscribing private sexual activity do not violate the federal constitution under Bowers, though some state courts have held that similar statutes are unconstitutional under the relevant state constitutions.

### Legal Status and Discrimination

A person living as an unmarried cohabitant with another might face some form of **discrimination**.

For example, an employer may expressly forbid employees from living together outside marriage and may terminate the employment of an employee who does cohabit with someone else outside marriage. Such discrimination in employment is not generally forbidden, either under federal law or under the laws of most states. Some state cases have, however, upheld the rights of individuals' cohabiting outside wedlock.

### Acquisition of Property

Marital and **community property** laws govern the ownership of property acquired during a marriage. The characterization of property acquired by unmarried cohabitants is less clear. Some property acquired by unmarried couples may be owned jointly, but it may be difficult to divide such property when the relationship ends. Similarly, if one partner has debt problems, a **creditor** may seek to attach property owned jointly by both partners as if the partner owing the debt solely owned the property. Problems such as these are even more complicated if one partner dies without a will, since the surviving partner has no right to the other partner's property unless the property is devised to the surviving partner.

### Children

Children born out of wedlock have not traditionally enjoyed the same legal protections as children born in wedlock. Such children were historically referred to as "bastards" in a legal context. Though many restrictions on illegitimate children have been repealed, legitimate (or legitimated) children still enjoy some rights that frustrate illegitimate children. This discrepancy is particularly clear with respect to **inheritance**. In most states, a child born in wedlock does not need to establish **paternity** to recover from the father. However, a child born out of wedlock generally must establish paternity before he or she can recover from the father.

### Adoption

State laws have traditionally prevented unmarried couples from adopting children. Though some states have begun permitting unmarried couples to adopt, these couples still face difficulties. Married couples, on the other hand, are permitted to adopt and are usually preferred over unmarried individuals.

### Eligibility for Benefits

Recent changes of policy by insurance companies permit unmarried couples to purchase life insurance policies on the life of the other partner or jointly purchase homeowners' insurance on a house owned by both partners. However, an unmarried couple will often have more trouble jointly obtaining automobile insurance covering an automobile owned by both partners. Similarly, unmarried couples continue to face serious problems with respect to health insurance family coverage paid or co-paid by an employer. A recent trend among some states, municipalities, and private employers is to extend benefits to registered "domestic partners."

## Recognition of Domestic Partners

Several states and municipalities have adopted a system whereby unmarried cohabitants (heterosexual or homosexual) may register as "domestic partners." Other states and municipalities permit domestic partners to recover benefits. These classifications provide some rights that are analogous to marital rights, though these rights are certainly limited. The greatest benefit in registering as domestic partners is that each partner enjoys insurance coverage, family leave, and retirement benefits similar to married couples, though these rights are considerably more restricted than rights afforded to married couples. However, these rights are not generally recognized outside the **jurisdiction** that permits registration of domestic partners.

## Common Law Marriages

A minority of states continues to recognize **common law**, or informal, marriages. Such a marriage requires more than mere cohabitation between a man and a woman. The couple generally must agree to enter into a martial arrangement, must cohabit with one another, and must hold themselves out as husband and wife to others. Parties that enter into such marriages enjoy the same rights as couples married in a formal ceremony, including rights related to insurance and other benefits, property distribution on **dissolution** of the marriage, and distribution of property upon the death of one spouse.

Proof that the marriage exists is often the most difficult aspect of a common law marriage, and this issue often arises after the relationship has ended either in death or **divorce**. For example, the question of whether a common law marriage exists may arise after one of the partners in a relationship dies and the other seeks to prove that the partners were informally married to receive property through the other partner's estate. Similarly, when a relationship ends, a partner may seek to prove that an informal marriage exists in order to seek property distribution under marital or community property laws.

Though a minority of states recognizes common law marriages, all states will recognize the validity of a common law marriage if it is recognized in the state where the parties reside, agreed to be married, and hold themselves out as husband and wife. Common law marriages apply only to partners who are members of the opposite sex.

## Contracts Between Unmarried Cohabitants

### Validity

Unmarried cohabitants can provide rights to one another that are analogous to rights granted to married couples by entering into a contract or contracts with one another. The validity of such agreements was the subject of the well-publicized case of Marvin v. Marvin in the California Supreme Court. In this case, the court held that an express or implied agreement between a couple living together outside wedlock to share income in consideration of companionship could be legally enforceable. The majority of states now recognizes these agreements, though many require that the agreement be in writing. Only a small number of recent cases have held that contracts between unmarried cohabitants are unenforceable.

When an agreement expressly includes consideration of sexual services provided by one of the parties, a court is more likely to find the contract unenforceable. For example, if one partner agrees to share his or her income in return for the other partner's love and companionship, a court may find that the contract implicates meretricious sexual activity and refuses to enforce the contract. Proving an oral agreement or an implied contract between unmarried cohabitants is also difficult, and several courts have refused to recognize such an agreement due to lack of proof.

### Provisions of Written Cohabitation Agreements

Written cohabitation agreements usually involve financial and property arrangements. Parties can provide arrangements analogous to community or marital property laws or can provide other arrangements that are more favorable to the couple. Parties should consult with a lawyer prior to entering into such an agreement to ensure that the provisions are enforceable.

### *Wills and Durable Power of Attorney for Health Care*

Nothing prevents unmarried cohabitants from leaving estate property to the other partner upon death in a will. Alternatively, **intestate succession** laws may not provide that any of the property will pass from one cohabitant to another, since **intestacy** laws are limited to marital and other family relationships. A fellow cohabitant might be able to get a share of the intestate's estate by arguing that the parties entered into a financial or property-sharing arrangement, though such claims are often difficult to prove. A will is generally the best method to ensure that a partner's property is given to the person he or she designates.

Another complicated situation can arise if one cohabitant is disabled and requires a **guardian**. To ensure that one partner is named guardian or is otherwise able to make decisions for the other partner, the parties can prepare a document providing durable **power of attorney** to the other partner. Under this arrangement, the person granted durable power of attorney could make healthcare decisions for the disabled person. Similarly, a party can draft a **living will** (also called a healthcare directive) that dictates the wishes of the party regarding life-prolonging treatments.

## State and Local Provisions Regarding Cohabitation

Sixteen states recognize common law marriages, though several of these states have repealed their laws and only recognize these marriages entered into prior to a certain date. Several states and municipalities now recognize domestic relations rights, providing a registry, extension of benefits, or both. Unmarried cohabitants should check with the state and local laws in their jurisdictions to determine what rights may be available to them.

ALABAMA: The state recognizes common law marriages. Neither the state nor any municipality in the state provides specific rights to domestic partners.

ALASKA: The state does not recognize common law marriages. Neither the state nor any municipality in the state provides specific rights to domestic partners.

ARIZONA: The state does not recognize common law marriages. The cities of Phoenix and Tucson extend benefits to domestic partners.

ARKANSAS: The state does not recognize common law marriages. Neither the state nor any municipality in the state provides specific rights to domestic partners.

CALIFORNIA: The state does not recognize common law marriages. The following cities and counties extend benefits to domestic partners: Alameda County, Berkeley, Laguna Beach, Los Angeles, Los Angeles County, Marin County, Oakland, Petaluma, Sacramento, San Diego, San Francisco, San Francisco County, San Mateo County, Santa Cruz, Santa Cruz County, Ventura County, West Hollywood. The following cities and counties offer domestic partner registries: Arcata, Berkeley, Cathedral City, Davis, Laguna Beach, Long Beach, Los Angeles, Los Angeles County, Oakland, Palo Alto, Sacramento, San Francisco, Santa Barbara County, and West Hollywood.

COLORADO: The state recognizes common law marriages. The city of Denver extends benefits to domestic partners and provides a domestic partner registry.

CONNECTICUT: The state does not recognize common law marriages. The state extends benefits to domestic partners. The city of Hartford extends benefits to domestic partners and provides a domestic partner registry.

DELAWARE: The state does not recognize common law marriages. Neither the state nor any municipality in the state provides specific rights to domestic partners.

FLORIDA: The state does not recognize common law marriages. Broward County extends benefits to domestic partners and provides a domestic partner registry. The city of West Palm Beach extends benefits to domestic partners.

GEORGIA: The state recognizes common law marriages entered into before January 1, 1997. The city of Atlanta extends benefits to domestic partners and provides a domestic partner registry.

HAWAII: The state does not recognize common law marriages. The state extends benefits to domestic partners and provides a domestic partner registry.

IDAHO: The state recognizes common law marriages enter into before January 1, 1996. Neither the state nor any municipality in the state provides specific rights to domestic partners.

ILLINOIS: The state does not recognize common law marriages. The city of Chicago and Cook County extend benefits to domestic partners. The city of Oak Park extends benefits to domestic partners and provides a domestic partner registry.

INDIANA: The state does not recognize common law marriages. The city of Bloomington extends benefits to domestic partners.

IOWA: The state recognizes common law marriages. The city of Iowa City extends benefits to domestic partners and provides a domestic partner registry.

KANSAS: The state recognizes common law marriages. Neither the state nor any municipality in the state provides specific rights to domestic partners.

KENTUCKY: The state does not recognize common law marriages. Neither the state nor any municipality in the state provides specific rights to domestic partners.

LOUISIANA: The state does not recognize common law marriages. The city of New Orleans extends benefits to domestic partners.

MAINE: The state does not recognize common law marriages. The city of Portland extends benefits to domestic partners and provides a domestic partner registry.

MARYLAND: The state does not recognize common law marriages. The cities of Baltimore and Takoma Park and Montgomery County extend benefits to domestic partners.

MASSACHUSETTES: The state does not recognize common law marriages. The following cities extend benefits to domestic partners: Boston, Brewster, Brookline, Nantucket, Provincetown, and Springfield. The following cities provide domestic partner registries: Boston, Brewster, Brookline, Cambridge, Nantucket, and Northampton.

MICHIGAN: The state does not recognize common law marriages. The city of Kalamazoo, Washtenaw County, and Wayne County extend benefits to domestic partners. The cities of Ann Arbor and East Lansing extend benefits to domestic partners and provide a domestic partner registry.

MINNESOTA: The state does not recognize common law marriages. The city of Minneapolis extends benefits to domestic partners and provides a domestic partner registry.

MISSISSIPPI: The state does not recognize common law marriages. Neither the state nor any munici-

pality in the state provides specific rights to domestic partners.

MISSOURI: The state does not recognize common law marriages. The city of St. Louis provides a domestic partner registry.

MONTANA: The state recognizes common law marriages. Neither the state nor any municipality in the state provides specific rights to domestic partners.

NEBRASKA: The state does not recognize common law marriages. Neither the state nor any municipality in the state provides specific rights to domestic partners.

NEVADA: The state does not recognize common law marriages. Neither the state nor any municipality in the state provides specific rights to domestic partners.

NEW HAMPSHIRE: The state recognizes common law marriages but only for inheritance purposes. Neither the state nor any municipality in the state provides specific rights to domestic partners.

NEW JERSEY: The state does not recognize common law marriages. The city of Delaware extends benefits to domestic partners.

NEW MEXICO: The state does not recognize common law marriages. The city of Albuquerque extends benefits to domestic partners.

NEW YORK: The state does not recognize common law marriages. The following cities and counties extend benefits to domestic partners: Brighton, Eastchester, Ithaca, New York City, Rochester, and Westchester County. The following cities provide domestic partner registries: Albany, Ithaca, New York City, and Rochester.

NORTH CAROLINA: The state does not recognize common law marriages. The city of Chapel Hill extends benefits to domestic partners and provides a domestic partner registry. The city of Carrboro also provides a domestic partner registry.

NORTH DAKOTA: The state does not recognize common law marriages. Neither the state nor any municipality in the state provides specific rights to domestic partners.

OHIO: The state recognizes common law marriages entered into prior to October 10, 1991. Neither the state nor any municipality in the state provides specific rights to domestic partners.

OKLAHOMA: The state recognizes common law marriages. Neither the state nor any municipality in the state provides specific rights to domestic partners.

OREGON: The state does not recognize common law marriages. The state extends benefits to domestic partners. The city of Portland and Multnomah County extend benefits to domestic partners. The city of Ashland provides a domestic partner registry.

PENNSYLVANIA: The state recognizes common law marriages. The city of Philadelphia extends benefits to domestic partners.

RHODE ISLAND: The state recognizes common law marriages. Neither the state nor any municipality in the state provides specific rights to domestic partners.

SOUTH CAROLINA: The state recognizes common law marriages. Neither the state nor any municipality in the state provides specific rights to domestic partners.

TENNESSEE: The state does not recognize common law marriages. Neither the state nor any municipality in the state provides specific rights to domestic partners.

TEXAS: The state recognizes common law marriages. Travis County extends benefits to domestic partners.

UTAH: The state recognizes common law marriages. Neither the state nor any municipality in the state provides specific rights to domestic partners.

VERMONT: The state is the first to recognize "civil unions," which extends rights to homosexual partners that are similar to rights granted to married couples. The state also extends benefits to domestic partners. The state does not recognize common law marriages.

VIRGINIA: The state does not recognize common law marriages. Arlington County extends benefits to domestic partners.

WASHINGTON: The state does not recognize common law marriages. The state extends benefits to domestic partners. The cities of Olympia and Tumwater and King County extend benefits to domestic partners. The city of Lacey provides a domestic partner registry. The city of Seattle extends benefits to domestic partners and provides a domestic partner registry.

WEST VIRGINIA: The state does not recognize common law marriages. Neither the state nor any municipality in the state provides specific rights to domestic partners.

WISCONSIN: The state does not recognize common law marriages. The city of Madison extends benefits to domestic partners and provides a domestic partner registry. The city of Sherwood Hills Village and Dane County extend benefits to domestic relations. The city of Milwaukee provides a domestic partner registry.

WYOMING: The state does not recognize common law marriages. Neither the state nor any municipality in the state provides specific rights to domestic partners.

## Additional Resources

*Cohabitation: Law, Practice, and Precedent,* Second Edition. Wood, Helen, Denzil Lush, and David Bishop, 2001.

*Family Law in a Nutshell.* Krause, Harry D., West Publishing, 1995.

*The Living Together Kit: A Legal Guide to Unmarried Couples,* Ninth Edition. Ihara, Toni, Ralph Warner and Frederick Hertz, Nolo Press, 1999.

*Understanding Family Law,* Second Edition. DeWitt, John, Gregory, Peter N. Swisher, and Sheryl L. Wolf, LexisNexis, 2001.

*Unmarried Couples and the Law.* Douthwaite, Graham, Allen Smith Company, 1979.

## Organizations

### Alternatives to Marriage Project
P.O. Box 991010
Boston, MA 02199 USA
Phone: (781) 793-0296
Fax: (781) 394-6625
URL: http://www.unmarried.org/
E-Mail: atmp@unmarried.org

### American Association for Single People (AASP)
415 E. Harvard Street
Suite 204
Glendale, CA 91205 USA
Phone: (818) 242-5100
URL: http://www.singlesrights.com
E-Mail: unmarried@earthlink.net
Primary Contact: Thomas F. Coleman, Executive Director

### Focus on the Family

Colorado Springs, CO 80995 USA
Phone: (719) 531-3328
Fax: (719) 531-3424
URL: http://www.family.org/

### Lambda Legal Defense and Education Fund

120 Wall Street, Suite 1500
New York, NY 10005-3904 USA
Phone: (212) 809-8585
Fax: (212) 809-0055
URL: http://www.lambdalegal.org

# FAMILY LAW

## DIVORCE/SEPARATION/ANNULMENT

*Sections within this essay:*

- Background
- No-fault Divorce
- Legal Separation
- Annulment
- Property Distribution
    - Equitable Distribution
    - Community Property
    - Military Pay
- Spousal Support
- Temporary Orders
- Court Process
- Insurance
- Divorce From Parents (Emancipation)
- State Laws
- Additional Resources

## Background

In primitive civilizations marriage and marriage **dissolution** were considered private matters which did not require involvement of any authority above the individuals in the relationship. The Romans first placed marriage and **divorce** under state regulation during the reign of Augustus. When Christianity spread about 300 A.D., governments came under religious control. The Catholic Church did not permit divorce unless one of the parties had not been converted to Christianity prior to marriage, which then made the marriage null and void.

During the early 1500s, the Protestant Reformation began a slow movement in Europe to separate the laws governing marriage from the precinct of the Roman Catholic Church. Henry VIII wanted the Catholic Church to grant him a divorce from Catherine of Aragon because all the male offspring she bore died shortly after birth, and Henry believed he could secure a male **heir** by marrying another woman. When Pope Clement VII refused, Henry took control of Church properties in England and made himself head of the Anglican Church. This separation from the Vatican made divorce possible in England by an act of Parliament. Still, divorce remained rare; when it occurred it was a costly legislative process and could only be initiated by husbands. The resistance toward and rarity of divorce continued well into the nineteenth century..

Divorce law in the American colonies was somewhat influenced by the British, but more so by the colonists themselves. England did not want its American colonies to enact any type of law, which conflicted with English law. Thus, a colonial divorce was not considered final until the English monarch had approved it. Nevertheless, several colonies adopted their own laws permitting divorce, often under odd circumstances. Under one late seventeenth century Pennsylvania law if a married man committed **sodomy** or bestiality, his punishment was castration, after which the wife was permitted to divorce him. In Connecticut divorce was allowed on the grounds of **adultery**, desertion, and the husband's failure in his **conjugal** duties. In Massachusetts, divorce was permitted if one of the parties committed adultery.

The U.S. Constitution left divorce regulation to the states. State legislatures passed laws that granted divorce based on a showing of fault. If a divorce was contested, the divorcing spouse was required to establish, before a court, specific grounds for the action. If the court felt that the divorcing spouse had not sufficiently proven the grounds alleged, the petition for divorce could be denied and the case dismissed.

The most common traditional grounds for divorce were cruelty, desertion, and adultery. Other grounds included nonsupport or neglect, alcoholism or other drug addiction, insanity, criminal **conviction**, and voluntary separation. In 1933, New Mexico became the first state to allow divorce on the ground of incompatibility. In 1969 California completely revised its divorce laws, providing that a filing party merely show **irreconcilable differences** resulting in an irremediable breakdown of the marriage. California's was the first comprehensive "no-fault" divorce law, and it inspired nationwide divorce law reform. In 1970 the National Conference of Commissioners on Uniform State Laws prepared a Uniform Marriage and Divorce Act, which provides for no-fault divorce if a court finds that the marriage is "irretrievably broken." Many states adopted the act. By 1980, nearly every state legislature had enacted laws allowing no-fault divorces or divorces after a specified period of separation. Some states replaced all traditional grounds with a single no-fault provision. Other states added the ground of irreconcilable differences to existing statutes. In those states a divorce petitioner remains free to file for divorce under traditional grounds.

## No-fault Divorce

By 1987, all fifty states had adopted no-fault divorce laws, exclusively or as an option to traditional fault-grounded divorce. Despite the obvious advantages, no-fault divorce laws sometimes leave parties with no real remedy for harmful acts of a spouse. Most states have laws that prevent one spouse from suing the other. Fault has survived in some aspects of divorce proceedings. Under current theories, marital misconduct is irrelevant to the divorce itself, but it may be relevant to related matters such as **child custody**, **child support**, and child visitation rights, spousal maintenance, and property distribution.

## Legal Separation

Legal separation is similar to a divorce in that papers are filed, there is often a **custody** or **property settlement** ordered by the court, but the parties remain married. There may be benefits to this type of arrangement, but they are few. In most states, it is difficult to convert a legal separation into a divorce, and it requires beginning the process over with the filing of a divorce petition.

## Annulment

**Annulment** is a legal process in which a court essentially determines the parties were never legally married to begin with and the marriage is null and void. Annulments are not often granted, but grounds for doing so include if one party is incapable of consent, due to mental state or **intoxication**, **fraud** about some aspect of the marriage, or a failure to **consummate** the marriage. Annulments are regulated by state law.

## Property Distribution

Property distribution includes issues of real estate, **personal property**, cash savings, stocks, **bonds**, savings plans, and retirement benefits. The statutes that govern property division vary by state, but they can generally be grouped into two types: equitable distribution and **community property**.

### Equitable Distribution

Most states follow the equitable distribution method. Generally, this method provides that courts divide assets in a fair and equitable manner. Some equitable distribution states look to the conduct of the parties and permit findings of marital fault to affect property distribution. In others only fault relating to economic welfare is relevant in property distribution. Yet other states entirely exclude marital misconduct from consideration in **disposition** property. Equitable distribution rules give the court considerable discretion in which to divide property between the parties. The courts consider the joint assets held by the parties and separate assets that the parties either brought with them into the marriage or inherited or received as gifts during the marriage. Generally, if the separate property is kept separate during the marriage and not commingled with joint assets, then the court will recognize that it belongs separately to the individual spouse and will not divide it along with the marital assets.

Equitable distribution states consider contributions (often including homemaker contributions) by each spouse made to the marriage. If one party made a greater contribution, the court may grant that person more of the joint assets. Some states do not consider a professional degree earned by one spouse during the marriage to be a joint asset but do acknowledge any financial support contributed by the other spouse and let that be reflected in the property distribution. Other states do consider a professional degree or license to be a joint marital asset and have devised various ways to distribute it or its benefits.

### Community Property

States that follow community property laws provide that nearly all the property acquired during the marriage belongs to the marital "community," such that the husband and wife each have a one-half interest in it upon death or divorce. It is presumed that all property acquired during the marriage by either spouse, including **earned income**, belongs to the community. Property obtained by gift or through **inheritance** is considered separate, unless it is comingled with community property. Upon divorce each party gets all separate property, as well as one-half of the community property.

### Military Pay

In 1982 Congress passed a law, the Uniformed Services Former Parties' Protection Act, that permits state courts to treat military retired pay as property. In community property states and many other states, a formula is used when the member has already retired. But for an active duty member, there may be no state law that specifies how the award is to be calculated.

## Spousal Support

**Alimony**, or spousal maintenance, is the financial support that one spouse provides to the other after divorce. It is separate from, and in addition to, the division of marital property. It can be either temporary or permanent. Factors relevant to an order of maintenance include the age and marketable skills of the intended recipient, the length of the marriage, and the income of both parties. Maintenance is most often used to provide support to a spouse who was financially dependent on the other during the marriage. Many states allow courts to consider marital fault in determining whether, and how much, maintenance should be granted.

## Temporary Orders

Between the time a dissolution action is filed and the time a judgment of dissolution becomes effec-

tive, the court may use temporary orders to resolve any issue in the case, including temporary support and temporary allocation of assets. Temporary orders address the immediate concerns of the parties, but also frequently form the basis for the permanent orders later in the final **decree**.

## Court Process

**Jurisdiction** over a divorce case is usually determined by residency. That is, a divorcing spouse is required to bring the divorce action in the state where she or he maintains a permanent home. States are obligated to acknowledge a divorce obtained in another state. This rule is from the Full Faith and Credit Clause of the U.S. Constitution, which requires states to recognize the valid laws and court orders of other states. Under the Due Process Clause of the Fourteenth Amendment to the U.S. Constitution, a state must make divorce available to everyone. If a party seeking divorce cannot afford the court expenses, filing fees, and costs attached to the serving or publication of legal papers, the party may file for divorce free of charge. Typically, in a divorce proceeding or dissolution action the parties are referred to as the "petitioner," and the "respondent." The petitioner is the spouse who initiates the dissolution proceeding. The other spouse is the respondent. A dissolution action begins with one spouse filing a document known as a petition or complaint. The other spouse must then be served with these papers and has a specific time frame in which to respond. The ultimate goal of any dissolution action is to obtain a decree or judgment. The decree will resolve every issue in the case, including child support and visitation, division of assets and debts, and spousal support.

There are basically three methods for securing a divorce decree. If the respondent is properly served, but never files a response, the petitioner can request that the court order the divorce by **default**. Also, the couple may agree on all the issues in the case and obtain a decree by **settlement**, stipulation, or agreement. If the parties cannot agree, the case can be decided by a judge after a trial.

## Insurance

Insurance is considered a form of property in a divorce. The owner of the insurance policy controls the policy and has the right to name the beneficiaries. Although some laws prohibit the changing of insurance policies while a divorce is pending, once a divorce is final, insurance can become an important issue. Divorce is a qualifying event for benefits under Consolidated Omnibus Budget Reconciliation Act of 1985 (COBRA). Under this act, any person who would lose employer-based coverage because of divorce can choose to purchase continued coverage for up to 36 months. The act applies to employers with 20 or more employees, but the coverage is not automatic. The spouse seeking coverage must contact the employer within 60 days of the qualifying event and complete the necessary paperwork. Some decrees include a provision for life insurance on the provider, to protect the support order.

## Divorce From Parents (Emancipation)

One method children can use to "divorce" their parents is to become emancipated. The word "emancipation" means to become free from the control or restraint of another. In the context of emancipated minors, **emancipation** is a legal procedure whereby children become legally responsible for themselves and their parents are no longer responsible. Emancipated children are freed from parental custody and control and are adults for most legal purposes. Parents of a child have not only responsibility for the child but also legal control over any money the child may earn. Many famous child performers and athletes have sued their parents, often claiming that money earning by the child star was mismanaged, seeking to have the courts declare the child an adult. In fact, it is possible for a child or a teenager to seek legal emancipation and be declared an adult before age 18, although the process can be difficult. In order to become emancipated, a minor must convince a judge he or she has a place to live and sufficient money and income to be self-supporting. But since minors are not permitted to sign legally binding contracts such as rental agreements, proving such self-sufficiency can be difficult. Emancipation does not require any proof of abuse or neglect by the parents. It can be granted for educational purposes, if a teenager is starting college early and wants to rent an apartment. Many young actors and musicians who are not fighting with their parents over money seek emancipation in order to avoid strict **child labor laws**. Emancipation laws vary from state to state. Some states have no age restrictions, while others set the age from 14 to 17. Some states also require parental consent or **acquiescence**, which may be demonstrated by **circumstantial evidence**. Emancipation is typically automatic when a teenager marries or joins the military; however, emancipation

does not override age restrictions for getting married. Some states require the emancipated teen to undergo counseling with an appointed advisor.

An emancipated minor is entitled to make almost all medical, dental, and psychiatric care decisions, enter into a contract, sue and be sued, make a will, buy or sell property, and apply for a work permit without parental consent. The emancipated minor is obligated to self-support but must also follow state laws regarding such requirements as compulsory school attendance. Federal age rules relating to actions such as selective service registration, and voting rights do not change simply because a minor is emancipated.

## State Laws

State law varies considerably with respect to divorce. States have various residency requirements, property rules, and spousal support provisions. In the United States, each state regulates its own domestic relations. Most courts ignore marital fault in determining whether to grant a divorce, but many still consider fault in setting future obligations between the parties. To determine the rights and obligations of the parties in a dissolution proceeding, one must consult the divorce laws for the state in which the divorce was filed.

ALABAMA: The party filing for divorce must have resided in the State for at least six months before filing for divorce. At a minimum, Alabama law has a 30-day waiting period before a divorce can be granted.

ALASKA: No period of residence is required. After filing of complaint, however, 30 days must elapse before divorce action may be heard. A divorce may be granted for any of the following grounds: failure to consummate the marriage at the time of the marriage and continuing at the commencement of the action; adultery; conviction of a **felony**; willful desertion for a period of one year; cruel and inhuman treatment calculated to impair health or endanger life; personal indignities rendering life burdensome; incompatibility of temperament; **habitual** gross **drunkenness** contracted since marriage and continuing for one year prior to the commencement of the action; incurable mental illness when the spouse has been confined to an institution for a period of at least 18 months immediately preceding the commencement of the action; addiction of either party, subsequent to the marriage, to the habitual use of opium, morphine, cocaine, or a similar drug. Parties may jointly petition for dissolution of marriage on ground of incompatibility of temperament causing an irremediable breakdown of the marriage, so long as they have agreed to property distribution, support, custody, and visitation. Alaska's equitable distribution **statute** establishes a three-tier version of the dual classification model. Property acquired during the marriage, except for gifts and inheritance, is classified as marital property, and it is divided equitably upon divorce. Property acquired before the marriage is not marital property but can be divided upon divorce if "the balancing of the equities between the parties requires it." The court may allow an amount of money for spousal support, for either a limited time or an indefinite time, in gross or in installments, without regard to fault.

ARIZONA: One party must be domiciled in the state for 90 days prior to the filing of the action. Arizona requires only that the filing party **allege** irretrievable breakdown of the marriage. Arizona is a community property state. Property held in common must be divided equitably without regard to marital conduct. The court may consider excessive or abnormal expenditures, destruction, concealment, or **fraudulent** disposition of community, joint **tenancy**, and other property held in common in dividing the property. Spousal support may be granted to either spouse if the spouse seeking such spousal is unable, through appropriate employment, to provide self-support or is the custodian of a child at home. Support can also be awarded if a spouse contributed to the educational opportunities of the other spouse or had a long marriage and is of an age that may preclude employment. If spousal support is awarded it is without regard to marital fault. Factors the court will consider include: the couple's standard of living during marriage; the duration of the marriage; the age, employment history, earning ability, physical and emotional condition of the recipient spouse; financial resources and earning abilities of parties; any reduced income or career opportunities; and excessive or abnormal expenditures, destruction, concealment or fraudulent disposition of community assets.

ARKANSAS: Presence is required in the state by one party for 60 days before commencement of the action, plus another 30 days before the final decree may be entered. Grounds for divorce in Arkansas include voluntary separation without **cohabitation** for 18 months; impotency; felony conviction; habitual drunkenness for one year; cruel and barbarous treatment; indignities to the person; adultery; three year separation by reason of confinement for incur-

able insanity; willful nonsupport. Marital property is divided equally between the parties unless the court finds that equal division is inequitable. The only usual aspect of Arkansas equitable distribution law is its treatment of property held as tenants by the entireties, which is divided by legal title. Spousal support may be awarded to either party in fixed installments for a specific period of time.

CALIFORNIA: Either party must be a resident of the state for six months, and a resident of the county for three months. A filing party need only allege irreconcilable differences or incurable insanity. California is a community property state. Community property is property acquired by either party during the marriage in any type of joint form. Unless the parties otherwise agree, the court divides the community property estate equally. The court may award spousal support in an amount, and for a period of time, that the court determines is just and reasonable, based upon the standard of living established during the marriage. In awarding spousal support, there is a goal that the supported spouse be self-supporting within a reasonable period of time. The court retains jurisdiction to modify spousal support in all cases of marriages over ten years unless the parties otherwise agree. There is a presumption for spousal support decreases on the recipient's cohabitation.

COLORADO: Either party must be domiciled in the state for 90 days before commencement of the proceeding. A filing party need only allege irretrievable breakdown of the marriage. Colorado adopts the traditional dual classification of property under Uniform Marriage and Divorce Act. Separate property, defined as property owned before the marriage and property acquired by gift, inheritance, is retained by the owning party. Marital property includes property that is not separate property, property acquired during the marriage, including the increase in value of separate property. The court divides the marital property as it deems just, without regard to marital fault, considering the contributions of each spouse to the acquisition of the marital property, the value of each party's separate property, the economic circumstances of the parties, depletion of separate property for marital purposes. The court may order spousal support if a spouse lacks sufficient property to provide for his/her reasonable needs, is unable to support him/herself through appropriate employment, or is the custodian of a child whose age or condition makes it inappropriate for the spouse to seek employment outside the home.

CONNECTICUT: There is no residence requirement for filing; however, the Decree of Divorce can only be entered after one party has been a resident for a year. The party filing may allege irretrievable breakdown of the marriage or that the parties have lived apart for 18 months due to incompatibility, with no reasonable prospect of reconciliation. Adultery, fraudulent contract, desertion for one year, seven years' absence, habitual intemperance, intolerable cruelty, or sentencing to **imprisonment** for life or the commission of any infamous crime involving a violation of conjugal duty and punishable by imprisonment for over one year are also valid grounds. The court values and distributes all property and awards spousal support by considering the causes of the dissolution, the length of the marriage, the age, health, station, occupation, amount and sources of income, vocational skills, employability, estate, liabilities, needs of each party, opportunity for future acquisition of capital assets and income, contribution of each party to the marital and separate estates.

DISTRICT OF COLUMBIA: The party filing must live in the jurisdiction for six months. The parties must have mutually and voluntarily lived separate and apart without cohabitation for a period of six months, or the parties have lived separate and apart for one year. Factors for equitable division of property include length of the marriage, and the age, health, and occupation of parties. The court takes into consideration the value of homemaker services. The court may grant spousal support and may decree that a party retains dower rights in the other's estate.

FLORIDA: One party must live in the state for six months prior to the commencement of the action. The filing party need only allege irretrievable breakdown of the marriage or spousal mental incapacity for three years. If there are minor children, or if a claim of irretrievable breakdown is denied the court may order counseling, continue the proceedings for three months, or take such other action as may be in the best interests of the parties and children of the marriage. Florida follows an equitable distribution of property policy, based on dual classification of property into separate and marital estates. In distributing the marital estate, the court presumes a 50/50 division, but that may be altered by factors including the contribution to the marriage by each spouse, including homemaker services, the economic circumstances of the parties, the duration of the marriage, any interruption in career or educational opportunities, the contribution of each spouse to the acquisition, enhancement, and production of income or

marital assets, and any action during the pending divorce proceedings which depletes marital assets. The court may grant spousal support to either party, which may be permanent or rehabilitative in nature. The court may order periodic payments or payments in lump sum, or both. The court may consider the adultery of each spouse. The court considers the standard of living established during the marriage, the duration of the marriage, the age and health of the parties, the financial resources of the parties, the time necessary to become fully employed, and the contribution of the parties to the marriage.

GEORGIA: One spouse must have resided in Georgia for six months prior to filing. Grounds include irretrievable breakdown; mental incapacity or impotency at the time of the marriage; fraud in obtaining the marriage; adultery; desertion for one year; conviction of an offense involving moral turpitude and imprisonment for two or more years; habitual intoxication or other drug addiction; cruel treatment; incurable mental illness. A dual classification system was adopted, with separate property comprising property acquired before marriage, property acquired by gift, and property acquired by inheritance. Temporary or permanent spousal support may be granted, except in cases of adultery and desertion. The court may consider the conduct of the parties toward one another, in addition to needs and ability to pay, in deciding whether to award spousal support. If spousal support is to be awarded, the court considers, in deciding the amount, the standard of living established during the marriage, duration of the marriage, age and physical and emotional condition of the parties; contributions to the marriage, and financial condition of the parties.

HAWAII: The filing party must have lived in Hawaii for six months prior to filing. The filing party need only allege irretrievable breakdown or the marriage or that the parties have lived separate and apart for more than two years. Hawaii law provides for equitable distribution of all property, whether community, joint, or separate. The court considers the condition in which each party will be left by the divorce, the burdens imposed upon either party for the benefit of the children of the parties, and all other circumstances of the case. The court may award indefinite or rehabilitative periodic spousal support. The court considers the respective merits of the parties, the usual occupation of the parties during the marriage, and the vocational skills and employability of the party seeking support and spousal support.

ILLINOIS: The filing party must have lived in the state for 90 days prior to filing. The filing party need only allege irreconcilable differences causing the irretrievable breakdown of the marriage. Fault grounds are impotency, **bigamy**, adultery, desertion for one year, habitual drunkenness or other drug addiction for two years, an attempt to take the life of the other, physical or mental cruelty, conviction of a felony or other infamous crime, or infecting the other with a sexually transmitted disease. Illinois law provides for equitable distribution of marital property upon divorce, without regard to marital misconduct, based on dual classification of property. Marital property is all property acquired during the marriage, except property acquired by gift, **bequest**, devise, or descent, and property acquired before the marriage. The court may award rehabilitative, periodic, or permanent spousal support, without regard to marital misconduct. Spousal support terminates on cohabitation.

INDIANA: The party filing must live in the state for six months and for three months in the county where the petition is filed. The party filing need only allege irretrievable breakdown of the marriage. Fault grounds include conviction of a felony, impotency existing at the time of the marriage, and incurable insanity for three years. Division of property carries a presumption that equal division is just and reasonable. The presumption may be overcome by sufficient proof. Rehabilitative spousal support may be granted for a maximum of three years. The court may order permanent periodic spousal support if a spouse is physically or mentally incapacitated or where a spouse lacks sufficient property and is the custodial parent of a child whose incapacity requires the **guardian** to forego employment.

IOWA: The complainant must live in the jurisdiction one year. Divorce may be granted upon breakdown of the marriage relationship to the extent that the legitimate objects of matrimony have been destroyed and there remains no reasonable likelihood that the marriage can be saved. Marital property is property acquired during the marriage except that acquired by gift or bequest. The court may grant limited or indefinite spousal support.

KENTUCKY: The filing party must reside in the state for 180 days prior to filing. The filing party need only allege irretrievable breakdown of marriage. The decree cannot be entered until the parties have lived separate and apart for at least 60 days. Kentucky follows an equitable division of property theory, based

on dual classification of property found in the Uniform Marriage and Divorce Act. Property is divided without regard to marital misconduct. Spousal support may be rehabilitative, periodic, or lump sum. The court may order spousal support only if it finds that the spouse seeking spousal support lacks sufficient property, is unable to be self supporting, or is the custodian or a child whose age or condition makes it appropriate that the custodian not seek employment outside the home.

LOUISIANA: Six months residence is required of the filing party. Except in the case of a covenant marriage, divorce shall be granted upon motion of either spouse upon proof of 180 days' lapse since service or petition and separation of 180 days before filing of motion. Louisiana is a community property state. Community assets and liabilities are divided so that each spouse receives property of equal value. The court may award final periodic support, up to 1/3 of the obligor's **net** income, to a party free from fault based on the needs of that party and the ability of the other to pay.

MARYLAND: Maryland requires residence or one year residence if the cause of action for divorce occurred outside the state. Marital property is defined as property acquired during the marriage. This includes pensions and profit sharing plans. In dividing the marital property, the court considers: contributions, monetary and non-monetary, of each party to the well-being of the family; the value of the property interest of each party; the economic circumstances of the parties at the time the award is made; the circumstances that contributed to the estrangement of the parties; the duration of the marriage; the age of each party; the physical and mental condition of each party; how and when specific marital property or interest in a **pension**, retirement, profit sharing, or deferred compensation plan was acquired; contribution of non-marital property to entireties property; any spousal support award; any other factor deemed necessary. The court may award rehabilitative or indefinite spousal support, periodic or lump sum. Indefinite spousal support, however is awardable only if the requesting spouse cannot reasonably be expected to make substantial progress toward becoming self-sufficient or the parties' respective standards of living would be unconscionably disparate.

MAINE: The filing party must live in the jurisdiction for six months prior to filing. Marital property is defined as all property acquired by either spouse during the marriage, except property acquired by gift, bequest, devise or descent; property acquired in exchange for pre-marital property or in exchange for property acquired by gift, bequest, devise or descent; property acquired after decree of legal separation; property excluded by valid agreement of the parties; increase in value of property acquired prior to the marriage. The court divides the marital property after considering the contribution of reach spouse to the acquisition of marital property, including homemaker efforts; the value of each spouse's separate property; the economic circumstances of each spouse. The court may award periodic or lump sum spousal support. The court may also award non-modifiable spousal support.

MASSACHUSETTS: Either party can be a resident if the cause of action occurred within the state. Otherwise, there is a one-year residency requirement. Fault grounds include: adultery; impotency; desertion for one year; confirmed habits of intoxication cause by the use of alcohol or other drugs; cruel and abusive treatment; refusal to provide suitable spousal support. The parties also have the option of filing affidavits that the marriage is irretrievably broken, and can then, within 90 days, file a separation agreement. Parties may also file a complaint alleging irretrievable breakdown without a separation agreement, and the court may order the divorce after six months have elapsed. The court may assign to either the husband or the wife part of the estate of the other. The court may award periodic or lump sum spousal support. Factors in awarding spousal support include: homemaker's contributions; the employability of each party; the needs of each party; the opportunity for the future acquisition of capital assets and income.

MICHIGAN: Immediately prior to filing for divorce, one of the parties must have been a resident for 180 days and a resident of the county where the divorce is filed for 10 days. The filing party need only allege breakdown of the marriage relationship to the extent that the objects of matrimony have been destroyed and there remains no reasonable likelihood that the marriage can be preserved. The court can award one spouse any property owned by the other party if it appears from the **evidence** in the case that the party contributed to the acquisition, improvement, or accumulation of the property. Either spouse may be ordered to pay spousal support "in gross" or otherwise. Factors to be considered include the ability of either spouse to pay and the respective circumstances of the parties.

MINNESOTA: One of the parties must have been a resident for 180 days immediately before the petition for divorce is filed. The petition may be filed in a county where either spouse resides. The filing party need allege irrevocable breakdown of the marriage relationship demonstrated by living separate and apart for 180 days or serious marital discord adversely affecting the attitude of one or both parties. In dividing marital property, the court considers the contribution of each spouse to the acquisition of the property, including homemaker contributions; the economic circumstances of the parties; the length of the marriage; the age and health of the parties; the occupation of the parties; the amount and sources of income of the parties; the vocational skills of the parties; the employability of each spouse; the liabilities and needs of the parties, and the opportunity for further acquisition of capital assets; any prior marriage of each spouse; any other factor necessary to achieve equity and justice between the parties. The court may order temporary or permanent spousal support, without regard to marital fault, after the consideration of eleven factors, including need, the ability to become employed, the standard of living during the marriage, the duration of the marriage, loss of earnings, age and condition of both parties.

MISSISSIPPI: One of the parties must have been a resident for at least six months prior to filing and not have secured residency solely for the purpose of procuring a divorce. Special venue provisions based on whether the divorce is no-fault or fault-based. Irreconcilable differences are sufficient for divorce. Other grounds include: impotence; adultery; imprisonment; alcoholism and/or other drug addiction; confinement for incurable insanity for at least three years before the divorce is filed; the wife was pregnant by another man at the time of the marriage without husband's knowledge; willful desertion for at least one year; cruel and inhumane treatment; spouse lacked mental capacity at time of marriage; **incest**; bigamous marriage. Mississippi is an equitable distribution dual classification state. Either spouse may be awarded spousal support if it is equitable.

MISSOURI: One of the parties must be a resident of Missouri for 90 days before filing. The dissolution petition must be filed in the county where the plaintiff resides. There is a 30-day waiting period after filing before the dissolution will be granted. Irretrievable breakdown of marriage is sufficient for divorce. Missouri adopted the Uniform Marriage and Divorce Act. The court may award rehabilitative, periodic, or lump sum spousal support. The spousal support shall be in such amounts and for such periods of time as the court deems just.

MONTANA: One of the parties must be a resident of Montana for 90 days immediately prior to filing. The dissolution of marriage petition must be filed in the county where the petitioner has been a resident for the previous 90 days. The party must allege irretrievable breakdown of marriage, supported by evidence that the parties have lived separate and apart for 180 days. Montana adopted the all-property provisions of the Uniform Marriage and Divorce Act. The court may divide, without regard to marital misconduct, the property of the parties and assets belonging to either or both. Either spouse may be awarded spousal support. The award is made without regard to marital fault.

NEBRASKA: One of the parties must have been a resident for at least one year, or the marriage must have been performed in Nebraska and one of the parties lived in Nebraska for the entire marriage. The dissolution may be filed in a county where either spouse lives. There is a 30-day waiting period after service of the petition before the court can decide the case. Irretrievable breakdown of marriage or lack of mental capacity at time of marriage is sufficient to obtain a divorce. The parties keep any separate property acquired before the marriage. All marital property, which includes gifts and inheritances acquired during the marriage, may be divided. Either spouse may be ordered to pay reasonable spousal support, without regard to marital fault.

NEVADA: One of the parties must have lived in Nevada for at least six weeks prior to filing to divorce. The filing party need only allege. Nevada is a community property state. The court can make an unequal disposition of community property if the court finds a compelling reason to do so. The court may award such spousal support to the husband or the wife in specified principal sum or a specified period of payments.

NEW HAMPSHIRE: Both parties must be residents of the state when the divorce is filed, or the spouse filing for divorce must have been a resident of New Hampshire for one year immediately prior to the filing of the divorce and the other spouse was personally served with process in New Hampshire, or the cause of divorce must have arisen in New Hampshire and one of the parties must be living in New Hampshire when the divorce is filed for. Irreconcilable differences, which have caused irremediable break-

down of the marriage, are sufficient grounds for divorce. The court may award spousal support to either party in need, either temporary or permanent, for a definite or indefinite period of time.

NEW MEXICO: One of the parties must have been a resident of New Mexico for at least six months immediately preceding the filing and have a home in New Mexico. Incompatibility because of discord and conflicts of personalities such that the legitimate ends of the marriage relationship have been destroyed, preventing any reasonable expectation of reconciliation is **just cause**. New Mexico is a community property state. Each spouse retains his/her separate property acquired before the marriage. Separate property comprises property designated as such by written agreement, gifts, or inheritances. Community property shall be divided equally between the parties. "Quasi-community property," defined as property acquired outside New Mexico, which would be community property if acquired in New Mexico, is also be divided equally. Either spouse may be awarded a just and proper amount of spousal support, without regard to marital fault. Factors considered include: duration of the marriage, parties' current and future earning capacities, **good faith** efforts to maintain employment or become self-supporting, needs and obligations of each spouse, age and health of each spouse, amount of property each spouse owns, standard of living during the marriage, medical and life insurance maintained during the marriage, assets of the parties, each spouse's liabilities, and any marital settlement agreements.

NEW JERSEY: One party must be a resident of New Jersey for at least one year prior to the filing for divorce, unless the cause of divorce is adultery and took place in New Jersey, in which case one of the spouses must be a resident at the time of filing. Living separate and apart for 18 months and no reasonable prospect of reconciliation is sufficient to obtain a no-fault divorce in New Jersey. Marital property is property legally and beneficially acquired during the marriage, except for property acquired by gift, devise, interstate **succession**, except that gifts between spouses are considered marital property. Either party may be awarded spousal support without regard to marital fault. Spousal support may be permanent or rehabilitative.

NEW YORK: If both spouses resided in New York at the time of the filing of the divorce and the grounds for divorce arose in New York, there is no residency requirement. No-fault divorce is obtainable by living separate and apart. Fault grounds include: adultery; **abandonment** for one year; imprisonment for three or more consecutive years; and cruel and inhuman treatment. Separate property comprises property acquired before the marriage, gifts, inheritances, increase in value of separate property, and property acquired in exchange for separate property. Marital property is property acquired during the marriage and not separate property. Marital property is divided based on factors including custodial provisions, dissipation, and contributions as spouse, parent, wage earner, and homemaker. Either spouse may be awarded maintenance without regard to marital fault.

NORTH CAROLINA: Either spouse must have been a resident of North Carolina for at least six months prior to filing for divorce. Living separate and apart without cohabitation for one year is sufficient grounds to obtain a no-fault divorce. Separate property comprises any property acquired before the marriage, gifts and inheritances, property acquired in exchange for separate property, increase in value of separate property, expectation of a non-vested pension, retirement, or other deferred compensation rights. Marital property is property acquired during the marriage. Either spouse may be awarded spousal support. The amount, duration, and manner of payment is in the court's discretion; however, an award of spousal support is barred by "illicit sexual behavior."

OHIO: The spouse filing the divorce must have been a resident of Ohio for at least six months and a resident of the county for at least 90 days immediately prior to filing incompatibility is sufficient to obtain a divorce. Divorce may be obtained by filing a separation agreement, according to specific procedures. Each party retains separate property, defined as gifts, inheritances, property acquired prior to the marriage, income or **appreciation** of separate property, individual proceeds from **personal injury** awards. Marital fault and spousal support are not to be considered in the division of property. Either spouse may be awarded reasonable spousal support, in real property or personal property, or both, or by decreeing a sum of money, payable either in gross or by installments, from future income or otherwise. Marital fault is not a consideration.

OKLAHOMA: Either party must have been a resident of Oklahoma for six months immediately prior to filing for divorce. Incompatibility is sufficient to obtain a divorce. Each spouse keeps separate prop-

erty, defined as property owned prior to the marriage, gifts, and inheritances. All property held or acquired jointly during the marriage is divided between the spouses in a just and equitable manner. Marital fault is not a factor. Spousal support may be awarded to either spouse, in money or property, in lump sum or installments, having regard for the value of the property at the time of the award. Marital fault is not a consideration.

OREGON: If the marriage was not performed in Oregon, one spouse must have been a resident for six months immediately prior to filing. If the marriage was performed in Oregon and either spouse is a resident of Oregon, there is no residency requirement. Irreconcilable differences between the spouses that have caused the irretrievable breakdown of the marriage is the only grounds on which to obtain a divorce. Fault is abolished completely. Regardless of whether the property is held jointly or individually, there is a presumption that the spouses contributed equally to the acquisition of the property, unless proven otherwise. Either spouse may be required to make allowances for support of the other for his or her life or for a shorter period, having regard to the circumstances of the parties respectively.

PENNSYLVANIA: Either spouse must have been a resident for at least six months before filing. Pennsylvania's no-fault provisions require **allegation** of an irretrievable breakdown of the marriage with the spouses living separate and apart without cohabitation for two years. The couple can also file alleging irretrievable breakdown of the marriage with affidavits from both spouses that they consent to the divorce. The divorce can then be granted after 90 days. Separate and apart is defined as no cohabitation but is not precluded by living in the same residence. The parties retain their separate property, defined as property acquired before marriage, acquired in exchange for separate property, gifts and inheritances, and property designated separate by valid agreement. All other property is marital and is divided by the court equitably between the parties. A court may allow alimony to either party only if it finds that alimony is necessary. Pennsylvania has statewide spousal support guidelines that are presumed to be correct unless there is a showing that the amount would be unjust or inappropriate under the circumstances of the case.

RHODE ISLAND: Either spouse must have been a resident for one year prior to filing. Irreconcilable differences, which have caused the irremediable breakdown of the marriage, are sufficient grounds to obtain a divorce. Each spouse shall keep separate property, defined as property owned prior to the marriage, gifts, and inheritances. All property held or acquired jointly during the marriage is be divided in an equitable manner. Marital fault is not a factor. Spousal support may be awarded to either spouse, in money or property, in lump sum or installments. Marital fault is not an issue.

SOUTH CAROLINA: If both spouses are residents, the spouse filing for divorce must have been a resident for three months. If one of the spouses is not a resident, then the other spouse must have been a resident for one year. No-fault grounds are sufficiently established by the couple living separate and apart without cohabitation for one year. Fault grounds include: adultery; alcoholism or other drug addiction; physical abuse or reasonable apprehension of physical abuse; and willful desertion. During the marriage, a spouse acquires a vested special equity and ownership right in marital property. Each party retains separate property, defined as property acquired before the marriage, by gift or inheritance, in exchange for separate property, or from an increase in value of separate property. All other property is marital, subject to division on divorce. Fault is a factor. Either spouse may be awarded spousal support; however, no alimony may be awarded to a spouse who commits adultery.

SOUTH DAKOTA: The spouse filing the divorce must be a resident of South Dakota or a member of the Armed Forces stationed in South Dakota at the time of filing and must remain a resident until the divorce is final. Irreconcilable differences, which have caused the irretrievable breakdown of the marriage, are sufficient to obtain a divorce. Marital fault is not to be considered in apportioning the property. Either spouse may be awarded permanent or time-limited maintenance, based on the needs of the spouses.

TENNESSEE: No residency requirement if the party filing was a resident of Tennessee when the grounds for divorce arose. If the cause for divorce arose outside of Tennessee, then either spouse must have been a resident of Tennessee for six months. Irreconcilable differences are sufficient to obtain a divorce if there is no denial of this ground or if the spouses submit an executed marital dissolution agreement. Fault grounds include: impotence; adultery; conviction of a felony and imprisonment; alcoholism and/or other drug addiction; wife is pregnant

by another man at the time of the marriage without husband's knowledge; and refusing the move to Tennessee with a spouse and willfully absenting oneself from a new residence for two years. Each spouse keeps separate property, defined as property owned prior to the marriage, gifts and inheritances, property acquired in exchange for separate property, income and appreciation of separate property. All property held or acquired jointly during the marriage shall be divided between the couple. Marital fault is not a factor. Spousal support may be lump sum, periodic, or rehabilitative, based on sixteen factors. Rehabilitative support is favored.

TEXAS: One of the parties must have resided in Texas for six months and must have resided for 90 days in the county prior to the filing of the petition There is a 60-day waiting period between filing for and granting of divorce. That the marriage has become unsupportable because of discord or conflict that has destroyed the legitimate ends of marriage is sufficient grounds to obtain a no-fault divorce. Texas is a community property state. Property acquired by either spouse during the marriage is presumed to be community property, and such property shall be divided equally. The court may also divide property acquired by either party during the marriage while residing outside the state of Texas which would have been community property had the parties been residing in Texas. The court may award maintenance for a spouse in limited circumstances. Spousal support may be ordered if the spouse from whom maintenance is sought has been convicted of **domestic violence** within 2 years before the suit for dissolution. Spousal support may also be ordered if the duration of the marriage is over 10 years and the spouse seeking maintenance lacks sufficient property to provide for his/her reasonable minimum needs or is unable to support him/herself through employment because of an incapacitating physical or mental **disability** or is the custodial of a child who requires substantial care and supervision on account of a physical or mental disability or clearly lacks earning ability in the labor market to provide for minimum reasonable needs. A maintenance award may not last longer than three years unless there is a compelling impediment to the recipient spouse obtaining gainful employment.

UTAH: Either spouse must have been a resident of Utah or a member of the armed forces stationed in Utah and a resident of the county where the divorce is filed for more than three months immediately prior to the filing. There is a 90-day waiting period after filing before a divorce may be granted. Irreconcilable differences are sufficient grounds for a divorce to be granted. All of the couple's property, including gifts, inheritances, and any property acquired prior to or during the marriage, is divided by the court. Either spouse may be ordered to pay an equitable amount of spousal support, based on fault and the equity of equalizing the parties' incomes. Typically the court will not order spousal support for a period longer than the marriage existed.

VIRGINIA: One of the spouses must have been a resident of Virginia for at least six months prior to filing for divorce. Living separate and apart without cohabitation is sufficient grounds for a no-fault divorce. Marital property comprises property acquired during the marriage, excluding gifts from third parties and inheritances. Separate property is property acquired before the marriage, gifts from third parties and inheritances, any increase in value of separate property, property acquired in exchange for separate property The court cannot order the conveyance of separate or marital property not titled in the names of both parties, but it can award a monetary payment. Either spouse may be awarded maintenance, to be paid either in a lump sum, periodic payments, or both.

WASHINGTON: The spouse filing for dissolution must be a resident of Washington or a member of the armed forces stationed in Washington. The court will not act on the petition for divorce until 90 days after the filing of the complaint and service of the **summons**. Irretrievable break-down of marriage is sufficient grounds for the court to order a divorce. Washington is a community property state. The court divides community property in a just and equitable manner, without regard to marital conduct. Property acquired in another state is "quasi-community property" and is divided as community property. The court may award rehabilitative, periodic, or lump-sum alimony to either spouse without regard to marital fault.

WEST VIRGINIA: One party must have been a resident for one year immediately prior to the filing. If the marriage was performed in West Virginia and one spouse is a resident at the time of filing, there is no residency requirement. Irreconcilable differences are sufficient grounds for a no-fault divorce. The court divides the marital property equally. Marital property is property acquired during the marriage, the increases in value of separate property that is the result

of the use of marital funds or work performed by either party during the marriage. Either spouse may be ordered to provide the other spouse with spousal support; however, spousal support will not be ordered for a party who committed adultery, was convicted of a felony during the marriage, or deserted or abandoned the other spouse for six months.

WISCONSIN: One of the spouses must have been a resident of Wisconsin for six months and a resident of the county where the divorce is filed for thirty days immediately prior to filing. Irretrievable breakdown of marriage is sufficient grounds for divorce. Wisconsin is a community property state. The court may also divide any spouse's separate property in order to prevent a hardship for a spouse or for the children of the marriage. The court may award rehabilitative, limited, or indefinite, maintenance, without regard to marital misconduct. Additionally, the court may combine spousal and child support payments into a single family support payment.

WYOMING: The spouse filing for divorce must have been a resident of Wyoming for 60 days immediately prior to filing, or if the marriage was performed in Wyoming, then the spouse filing must have resided in Wyoming from the time of the marriage until the time of the filing. Irreconcilable differences are sufficient to obtain a divorce. The state follows a plan of equitable distribution of all property of both spouses, including gifts and inheritances. Either spouse may be awarded spousal support.

## Additional Resources

*What Every Woman Should Know About Divorce and Custody: Judges, Lawyers, and Therapists Share Winning Strategies On How to Keep the Kids, the Cash, and Your Sanity* Rosenwald, Gayle, Berkley Publishing Group, 1998.

*Your Divorce Advisor: A Lawyer and a Psychologist Guide You through the Legal and Emotional Landscape of Divorce* Mercer, Diana, Diane and Pruett, Marsha Kline. Simon & Schuster, 2001.

## Organizations

### *American Bar Association*

750 N. Lake Shore Dr.
Chicago, IL 60611 USA
Phone: (312) 988-5603
Fax: (312) 988-6800
URL: http://www.abanet.org

# FAMILY LAW

## DOMESTIC VIOLENCE

*Sections within this essay:*

## Background

**Domestic violence** consists of acts committed in the context of an adult intimate relationship. It is a **continuance** of aggressive and controlling behaviors, including physical, sexual, and psychological attacks, that one adult intimate does to another. Domestic violence is purposeful and instrumental behavior directed at achieving compliance from, or control over, the abused party. It is one of the most under-reported crimes in the United States, and the Department of Justice in 1998 estimated that there are between 960,000 and four million domestic incidents each year. In 1994, the Bureau of Justice Statistics estimated that about 92 percent of domestic violence cases involve female victims.

Legal definitions of domestic violence are usually delineated by the relationship between the parties and by the nature of the perpetrator's abusive behaviors. For example, the relationship may be a current spouse, a former spouse, a family member, a child, parents of a child in common, unmarried persons of different genders living as spouses, intimate partners of the same gender, dating relationships, and persons offering refuge. Such definitions recognize that victims may not be exclusively women, and domestic assaults may not just occur between heterosexual couples. The types of behavior frequently encountered in domestic violence are physical attacks, sexual attacks, psychological abuse, and the destruction of property or pets.

## History of Police Responses to Domestic Violence

Police responses to domestic violence have historically been clouded by notions, for example, the idea that a wife is the "property" of a husband and he has the right to carry out whatever behavior is necessary to "keep her in line." This idea and others like it reflect attitudes held by the greater society. Further aggravating the situation was the perception that domestic violence is not "real police work," and such disputes are private matters that should be kept within the household. Prior to 1980, when domestic situations were brought to the attention of police, calls were often diverted by dispatchers, given a lower priority, or officers responded to the scene and departed again as quickly as possible without achieving any type of meaningful intervention. Laws such as the "rule of thumb" (whereby it was legal for a husband to beat his wife with a stick not wider than his thumb) were still on the books until very recent times.

Prior to the 1980s, the practice of police agencies was to use mediation in domestic incidents. But ironically, much of this so-called mediation was done only when only one spouse was present. Several prominent court cases helped change legislation. In 1972, Ruth Bunnell was killed as a result of police non-intervention. The case of **wrongful death** against the City of San Jose was dismissed in the California Court of Appeals but received much publicity. In 1985, a jury verdict awarded $2.3 million in favor of plaintiff Tracy Thurman who sued the Torrington, CT, police department after they repeatedly failed to arrest her abusive husband (*Thurman v. City of Torrington,* 1985). Her husband eventually caused her serious bodily injury.

Another landmark case is currently being heard in the California courts system. In 1996, Maria Macias was killed by her estranged husband after an order of protection was not enforced by the Sonoma County Sheriff's Department. The victim had requested help from the department on 22 occasions. The lower courts held that women have a constitutional right to safety and **equal protection**, and the Sonoma County Sheriff's Department provided inadequate police protection based on the victim's status as a woman and a victim of domestic violence. The case is due to be heard in April, 2002 in the Appeals Court of California (99-15662).

Beginning in the late 1980s, there were many attempts to change the way police departments intervened in domestic violence situations. Inspired by Sherman's Minneapolis experiment, many police agencies adopted preferred or mandatory arrest policies. Arrest both acknowledges that society views domestic violence as a criminal offense and also provides immediate safety for the victim. Accompanying these new arrest policies were civil proceedings (discussed below).

## Recent Federal Legislation

The 1994 Violence Against Women Act (VAWA), with additions passed in 1996, outlined grant programs to prevent violence against women and established a national domestic violence hotline. In addition, new protections were given to victims of domestic abuse, such as confidentiality of new address and changes to **immigration** laws that allow a battered spouse to apply for permanent residency.

According to the VAWA Act, a domestic violence **misdemeanor** is one in which someone is convicted for a crime "committed by an intimate partner, parent, or **guardian** of the victim that required the use or attempted use of physical force or the threatened use of a deadly weapon" (Section 922 (g)[9]). Under these guidelines, an intimate partner is a spouse, a former spouse, a person who shares a child in common with the victim, or a person who cohabits or has cohabited with the victim.

Another area this act addresses is interstate traveling for the purposes of committing an act of domestic violence or violating an order of protection. A convicted abuser may not follow the victim into another state, nor may a convicted abuser force a victim to move to another state. Previously, orders of protection issued in one **jurisdiction** were not always recognized in another jurisdiction. The VAWA specifies full faith and credit to all orders of protection issued in any civil or criminal proceeding, or by any Indian tribe, meaning that those orders can be fully enforced in another jurisdiction. Forty-seven states have now passed legislation that recognizes orders of protection issued in other jurisdictions. Three states, Alaska, Montana, and Pennsylvania, require that an out of state order be filed with an in state jurisdiction before the order can be enforced.

There are several landmark cases that have been decided under these new interstate provisions. For example, in the *United States v. Rita Gluzman* (NY), the **defendant** traveled from New Jersey to New York with the intention of killing her estranged husband. The weapons she took with her were used in the murder. Gluzman was convicted for this crime. In the **United States v. Mark A. Sterkel** (1997), the defendant was convicted of interstate **stalking** after traveling from Utah to Arizona to threaten his former boss.

The VAWA also allows victims of domestic abuse to sue for damages in civil court. However, this part of the VAWA was recently overturned by the U. S. Supreme Court in *Brzonkala v. Morrison* (2000) in which the court held that Congress did not have the authority to implement such a law.

Another goal of the VAWA was to influence state legislators, particularly in regard to arrest policy for domestic situations. In order to receive Federal funding, states must adopt certain responses. The Act reads: VAWA 1994: (1) To implement mandatory arrest or pro-arrest programs and policies in police departments, including mandatory arrest programs and policies for protection order violations (Part U, **SEC**. 2101).This act has had a profound effect on state laws governing domestic abuse.

## State Legislation

Until about ten years ago, many states still had laws that required an officer to witness an **assault** before making an arrest. Today, officers in all states can arrest someone they suspect has committed a domestic assault without having witnessed the event. The majority of states have adopted preferred arrest policies which require police to either arrest one or both parties at the scene, or write a report justifying why an arrest is not made. Arrest policies do differ by jurisdiction even in the same state. Some states, such as New York, Wisconsin, and Minnesota, have adopted mandatory arrest policies which dictate that an officer must make an arrest at a domestic situation. Such policies were adopted after it was realized how serious domestic situations could be for the victims and their children. An arrest is usually made after the following conditions have been satisfied:

- There is **probable cause** of a crime;

- The suspect and the victim fit the definition of having a domestic relationship;

- The suspect's alleged act fits the definitions of domestic assault;

- There is reason to believe that the domestic abuse will continue if the suspect is not arrested and/or there **evidence** of injury;

- The incident was reported within 28 days of occurrence.

Usually, if any of these conditions is not satisfied, the officer may use his or her discretion in deciding whether to make an arrest. Although different states have variations on definitions of domestic violence, most are similar to the following example.

MINNESOTA: 1) domestic abuse means physical harm, bodily injury, or assault; 2) the infliction of fear of imminent physical harm, bodily injury, or assault or; 3) terrorist threats or criminal sexual conduct (518B.01).

## Civil and Other Proceedings

There are several available civil options that can provide for the safety of victims of domestic assaults

and their families, such as an order of protection or a judicial ex parte order. All 51 states have allowances for orders of protection. An order of protection can prohibit the abuser from contacting, attacking, striking, telephoning, or disturbing the peace of the victim; force the abuser to move from a residence shared with the victim; order the abuser to stay at least 100 yards away from the victim, his or her place of residence, and place of employment; order the abuser to attend counseling; and prohibit the abuser from purchasing a firearm. Orders of protection may also include a provision for the safety of children and others living in the home.

An ex parte order requires the abusive cohabitant to temporarily vacate the premises. Issued only after the battered spouse seeks it, this order is sometimes referred to as a temporary **restraining order**. In most states, a cohabitant refers to a person who has a sexual relationship with the victim and has lived with the victim for at least 90 days during the year prior to the order being filed. A victim who is threatened with imminent harm or has already been harmed by the abuser and/or already has an order of protection against the abuser has no other legal remedy than to seek a restraining order. In most states, an attorney is needed to get a restraining order.

Violation of an order of protection is the equivalent of **contempt** of a court order. In many states, police policy is to arrest violators automatically. A violator can also be fined and jailed and may be charged with a misdemeanor or a **felony**.

## Domestic Violence and the Workplace

Domestic violence can reach beyond the home and into the workplace. Although a victim may leave the home and go to a shelter or change her or his address, the abuser usually knows where the victim works. Not only do abusers harass their partners at work, domestic violence can lead to missed days of work because of injuries or court appearances. Federal and state legislation has recently been amended so that victims of domestic violence are not penalized by employers for missed work.

At the Federal level, **Labor Law** Section 593 (1) states that when a victim of domestic violence voluntarily terminates his or her job, he or she is eligible for unemployment benefits. The Penal Law, Section 215.14, passed in 1996, makes it a crime to penalize an employee who has been a victim or a witness to a criminal offense and who must attend court. Further, both state and federal guidelines mandate that employers maintain a safe work environment.

## Domestic Violence and Firearms

Under the 1994 VAWA Act, it is illegal for individuals who have been convicted of a domestic-violence related incident or who have an order of protection against them, to possess a firearm. Specifically, federal law prohibits the shipping, transporting, possessing, or receiving firearms or ammunition. Military and law enforcement personnel are not exempt from this law, even if they carry weapons when they are on duty. Questions about this policy should be directed to local branches of the Alcohol, Tobacco and Firearms (ATF) Office.

It is illegal for a person to possess a firearm while subject to a court order restraining such a person from harassing, stalking or threatening an intimate partner or the child of an intimate partner (18 U.S.C. 922 (g) [8]). It is also illegal to transfer a firearm to a person subject to a court order that restrains such a person from harassing, stalking, or threatening an intimate partner or the child of an intimate partner (18 U.S.C. 922 (d) [8]).

As of September 30, 1996, it is illegal to possess a firearm after **conviction** of a misdemeanor crime of domestic violence. This prohibition applies to persons convicted of such misdemeanors at any time, even if the conviction occurred prior to the new law's effective date (18 U.S.C. 922, (g) [9]).

Further, The **Gun Control** Act of 1994, which was amended in 1996, also makes it illegal to possess a firearm and/or ammunition if the individual is subject to an order of protection or if the individual has been convicted of a misdemeanor domestic assault.

## Stalking

Domestic situations may also involve stalking of the victim by the estranged partner. Stalking usually involves repeated threatening or harassing behaviors, such as phone calls, following or shadowing a person, appearing at a person's home or place of employment, vandalizing property, and any other activity that makes a person fear for his or her safety. Stalking laws vary greatly from state to state, with some requiring a minimum of two acts or other proof that the event was not an isolated occurrence, and others specifying that the threat of harm must be imminent.

Some states also include activities such as lying-in-wait, surveillance, and non-consensual communication.

In its 1998 research on state codes and stalking, the National Institute of Justice defined stalking as "a course of conduct directed at a specific person that involves repeated visual or physical proximity, non-consensual communication, or verbal, written, or implied threats, or a combination thereof, that would cause a reasonable person fear," with repeated meaning on two or more occasions. There are three types of stalking: erotomania, which is often committed by a female and is a delusional obsession with a **public figure** or someone out of the stalker's reach; love obsessional, which involves individuals' stalking someone with whom they think they are in love; and simple obsessional, which is stalking by someone the victim knows. Domestic violence stalking fits into this last category and is usually perpetrated by an ex-spouse or lover, employer or co-worker.

The following examples of state legislation on stalking illustrate differences in definitions of and punishment for stalking.

DISTRICT OF COLUMBIA: Stalking refers to more than one incident of willfully, maliciously, and repeatedly following or harassing or without a legal purpose, willfully, maliciously, and repeatedly following or harassing another person with the intent of causing emotional distress or creating reasonable fear of death or bodily injury. Harassment refers to engaging in a course of conduct either in person, by telephone, or in writing, directed at a specific person, which seriously alarms, annoys, frightens, or torments the victim or engaging in a course of conduct either in person, by telephone, or in writing, which would cause a reasonable person to be seriously alarmed, annoyed, frightened, or tormented. Such an offense can be punishable by a fine of not more than $500 or **imprisonment** of up to 12 months or both (Title 22, Section 504). A second offense occurring within two years can result in a fine of up to $750 and/or imprisonment for up to one and a half years. A third offense is punishable by a fine of not more than $1500 and/or imprisonment for up to three years.

TENNESSEE: (a)(1) A person commits the offense of stalking who intentionally and repeatedly follows or harasses another person in such a manner as would cause that person to be in reasonable fear of being assaulted or suffering bodily injury or death.

(A) "Follows" means maintaining a visual or physical proximity over a period of time to a specific person in such a manner as would cause a reasonable person to have a fear of an assault, bodily injury, or death;

(B) "Harasses" means a course of conduct directed at a specific person, which would cause a reasonable person to fear a sexual offense, bodily injury, or death, including, but not limited to, verbal threats, written threats, **vandalism**, or physical contact that was non-consensual;

(C) "Repeatedly" means on two (2) or more occasions.

(b) (1) Stalking is a Class A misdemeanor.

In Tennessee, if there is a subsequent violation of this law within a seven-year period, the offense becomes a class E felony. A subsequent violation denotes a class C felony.

## Battered Women's Syndrome

A phenomenon which has received much attention in the realm of domestic violence and particularly with women who kill is battered women's syndrome (BWS), which is a subcategory of post-traumatic stress disorder (PTSD). According to Walker, battered women's syndrome is:

A group of usually transient psychological symptoms that are frequently observed in a particular recognizable pattern in women who report having been physically, sexually, and/or seriously psychologically abused by their male domestic partners.

BWS develops as a battering relationship unfolds. This is typically a three-stage process that includes: 1) small incidents of verbal and minor physical abuse that begin infrequently but increase in frequency; 2) actual acute battering that often causes serious injury needing medical attention; and 3) a cycle where the abuser is contrite to the abused and ultimately teaches the abused to be submissive and passive toward further abuse.

A woman displaying symptoms of BWS may be apathetic toward subjects or activities for which she used to be enthusiastic, she may become involved in drug or alcohol abuse, and she may also experience completely different attitudes and emotions toward her spouse than she did before the abuse began. The

importance in knowing about BWS lies in recognizing predictable, psychological effects caused by domestic violence. BWS is now recognized in legislation by many states and is considered when defending battered wives who kill their spouses. BWS is not used as a defense but more as an indication of the defendant's state of mind or as a mitigating circumstance. A reasonable fear of imminent danger (especially used in **self-defense**) can be proven using BWS.

## Identifying Signs of Domestic Violence

Montgomery County (MD) Sheriff's Department suggests that the following behaviors may indicate domestic violence to a police officer or dispatcher:

- the victim is very fearful of the partner;
- the victim states that the partner is extremely jealous;
- the victim describes the relationship as full of conflict;
- the victim makes references to being forced to have sexual relations with the partner;
- the victim states police have often been called to the home;
- the victim states that the partner controls everything the victim does.

Police and attorneys should recommend the victim apply for an order of protection if the victim has been abused or threatened, and if either of the following is present:

- the victim fears further abuse;
- the victim needs the abuser out of the home in order to protect herself and/or her family;
- the abuser has threatened to take the children;
- the victim cannot or does not wish to file criminal charges;
- the victim wants the abuser to attend a counseling program;
- the victim wants a period of separation from the abuser but is unsure whether to file for **divorce** or **custody** yet;
- criminal charges are pending and the victim fears for her safety;
- the victim's children have been abused.

## Additional Resources

*Police Responses to Wife Beating: Neglect of a Crime of Violence.* Stephen E. Brown, Journal of Criminal Justice (1984) 277-288.

*Stalking and Domestic Violence: The Third Annual Report to Congress under the Violence Against Women Act.* Office of Justice Programs, U. S. Department of Justice, 1998. Available on- line at: http://www.ojp.usdoj.gov/vawo/grants/stalk98/welcome.html.

*The Battered Woman Syndrome.* Leonore E.Walker, Springer, 1984.

*The Federal Domestic Violence Laws and the Enforcement of These Laws.* Margaret S. Groban, Violence Against Women On Line Resources, 2001. http://www.umn.edu/FFC/chapter5.htm

*The Impact of Arrest on Domestic Violence.* Eva S. Buzawa and Carl G. Buzawa, American Behavioral Scientist, 1993, 558-574.

*The Scientific Evidence Is Not Conclusive: Arrest Is No Panacea.* Eva S. Buzawa and Carl G. Buzawa. Chapter 21. Issues in Social Intervention. Sage Publications, 1993.

*Victimology and the Psychological Perspectives of Battered Women.* Lenore E. Walker, Victimology: An International Journal, 8 (1/2), 82-104.

*Violence Against Women.* Bureau of Justice Statistics, U. S. Department of Justice, January 1994.

*Violence Against Women Act of 1994.* Available on-line at http://www.ojp.usdoj.gov/vawo/laws/vawa/vawa.htm.

*Violence by Intimates: Analysis of Data on Crimes by Current or Former Spouses, Boyfriends, and Girlfriends.* U. S. Department of Justice, March 1998.

## Organizations

### American Bar Association Commission on Domestic Violence
740 15th Street NW
Washington, DC 20005-1022 USA
URL: http://www.abanet.org
Primary Contact:

### Family Violence Department of the National Council of Juvenile and Family Court Judges
P.O. Box 89507
Reno, NV 89507 USA
Toll-Free: 800-527-3223
URL: http://www.natioanlcouncilfvd.org
Primary Contact:

### Family Violence Prevention Fund
383 Rhode Island Street, Suite 304
San Francisco, CA 94103-5133 USA
Phone: (415) 252-8900
Fax: (415) 252-8991
URL: http://e ndabuse.org
Primary Contact:

### Immigrant Women Program of NOW Legal Defense Fund
1522 K St., NW
Washington, DC 20005 USA
Phone: (202) 326-0004
Primary Contact:

### National Coalition Against Domestic Violence
1532 16th St., NW
Washington, DC 20036
Phone: (202) 745-1211
Fax: (202) 745-0088
URL: http://w ww.ncadv.org
Primary Contact:

### National Domestic Violence Hotline
P.O. Box 161810
Austin, TX 78716 USA
Toll-Free: 800-799-SAFE
Toll-Free: 800-787-3224
Primary Contact:

### Safe Work Coalition
395 Hudson Street
New York, NY 10014 USA
Phone: (212) 925-6635
Fax: (212) 226-1066
URL: http://w ww.safeatworkcoalition.org
Primary Contact:

# FAMILY LAW

## EMANCIPATION

*Sections within this essay:*

- Background
- Age
- Automatic Emancipation
- Petition to Courts
- Criteria for Emancipation
- Rights, Privileges, and Duties Inherent in Emancipation
- Examination of Certain State Provisions on Emancipation
- Additional Resources

## Background

Historically, parents are responsible for their children. They are also required to feed, clothe, educate, and act in their children's best interest until they reach the "age of majority" or the age in which, for most purposes, the children are considered to be adults. State law can allow a minor to ask a state court to determine that the minor is able to assume adult responsibilities before reaching the **age of majority**. The term, **emancipation** refers to the point at which a minor becomes self-supporting, assumes adult responsibility for his or her welfare, and is no longer under the care of his or her parents. Upon achieving emancipation, the minor thereby assumes the rights, privileges, and duties of adulthood before actually reaching the "age of majority" (adulthood). At that point, the minor's parents are no longer responsible for that child and, also, have no claim to

the minor's earnings. During the court proceedings and before granting emancipation, the court considers, primarily, the best interests and level of maturity of the minor and confirms that the minor is able to financially support him or herself.

However, even when minors achieve emancipation, they cannot take part in any activity such as purchasing and/or drinking alcohol, voting, or getting married which, by **statute**, may require that the participant have attained an older age.

Close to half of the states, including New York and Pennsylvania, provide no separate **statutory** provisions for emancipation. Instead, these states rely on the fact that emancipation is automatically achieved upon a minor getting married, joining the armed forces, or reaching the age of majority which is now lower (usually eighteen years of age) than what was once commonly mandated as twenty-one years of age.

## Age

Generally, the statutory age in which a minor can petition a court for emancipation is at least sixteen years or older but below the age of majority (which among the vast majority of states is eighteen years of age). California allows a minor of the age of fourteen to petition its courts for emancipation.

## Automatic Emancipation

Even though minors may be under the age of majority, certain actions on their part will cause them to be emancipated from their parents' care and control even without seeking a court order. These actions are usually limited to the following:

- Joining the armed forces

- Getting married

- Reaching the actual age of majority (which is usually eighteen years of age)

The state of Michigan also allows for a temporary automatic emancipation when minors are in police **custody** and emergency medical care is required. The minors are considered emancipated and allowed to consent to such care. This emancipation ends when the medical care or treatment is completed.

## Petition to Courts

Minors petitioning their state courts for emancipation from their parents' care and control are normally required to prove their age and that they are residents of the state where the petition is being filed. They must tell the court why they seek emancipation. Parents must be given notice of the proceeding. Also, the minors must show the court that they are of sufficient maturity to care for themselves. This means that they are able to support themselves financially, provide for their own shelter, and make decisions on their own behalf. Some states require that the minors already support themselves and live totally or partially on their own. Most statutes exclude state financial support or "general assistance" when determining minors' ability to support themselves.

The court then looks at all the **evidence** in order to determine whether emancipation is in the minor's best interest. Also, since an order for emancipation must be in the minor's best interest, if the minor's situation changes, such an order may be rescinded by the court and the minor declared to be returned to the parents' care and control. The state of Illinois allows for court decrees of "partial" emancipation, where the court clearly states the limits of emancipation, if such an order is in the best interests of the minor.

States with no statutory provision or procedures for minors to apply for emancipation may still determine or confirm that minors have been emancipated. Minors file a petition with the court and provide the information necessary (such as proof of financial independence, adequate housing arrangements, and sufficient maturity) for the court to determine that such a confirmation of emancipation from parental care and control is in the best interests of the minor.

## Criteria for Emancipation

Criteria for determining whether a **decree** declaring emancipation is in the minor's best interest vary among the states. However, certain criteria can commonly be found:

- The minors' ability to support themselves financially, either currently or in the future

- The minors are currently living apart from their parents or have made adequate arrangements for future housing

- The minors can adequately make decisions for themselves

- The minors are attending school or have already received a diploma

- The minors exhibit sufficient maturity to function as adults

## Rights, Privileges, and Duties Inherent in Emancipation

Once declared to be emancipated, minors have the same rights, privileges, and duties in society as adults. Although the specific aspects vary among the states, generally, emancipated minors can do the following:

- Enter into contracts and leases

- Be a party to a law suit, either as a plaintiff or a **defendant**, in their own name

- Buy or sell real estate or other property

- Write a valid will

- Inherit property

- Enroll in school

- Get married

- Agree to various types of medical treatments

Emancipated minors can also vote and obtain a driver's license but only if they are of sufficient age to do so.

## Examination of Certain State Provisions on Emancipation

Of the states with specific emancipation provisions, some of the more significant state requirements include the following:

ALABAMA: In Alabama, the age of majority is nineteen. The Alabama code describing the emancipation procedure is designed to expand the rights of minors over the age of 18 but under the age of majority. Parents can file an emancipation petition with the court or the minor seeking emancipation can file the petition if that minor has no parents or if a living parent is insane or has abandoned the minor. The court will then decide if a decree of emancipation is in the "interest of such minor."

CALIFORNIA: In California, the age of majority is eighteen. Minors are considered emancipated without court intervention if they are married, are a member of the armed forces, or have previously been declared emancipated by a California court. Otherwise, in order to seek court mandated emancipation, the minors must be no younger than fourteen years old, be already living apart from their parents, be able to demonstrate the ability to take adequate care of themselves financially, and not receive any income from illegal or criminal activity.

If the court grants the order of emancipation, the minor then has the privilege and right to: sign contracts; approve medical care; buy, **lease**, and sell real property; be the plaintiff or defendant in a law suit; write a will; live in their own home; go to school and get a work permit. If the minor's situation changes, the court has the ability to end the emancipation and advise the minor's parents that they are once again responsible for the minor.

FLORIDA: The age of majority in Florida is eighteen. In order to seek a court mandated emancipation, minors must submit a statement of "character, habits, income, and mental capacity for business, and an explanation of how the needs of the minor with respect to food, shelter, clothing, medical care, and other necessities will be met." In addition, minors must state whether they are party to any court action taking place in Florida or another state. Minors must also submit a statement explaining why they seek an order of emancipation. Parents must be notified of any such proceeding.

The court then asks for any additional evidence to determine if the decree of emancipation is in the minors' best interest. If the order of emancipation is granted, the minor will have all of the rights, responsibilities, and privileges of anyone who has reached the age of majority (eighteen years of age).

ILLINOIS: The age of majority in Illinois is eighteen. The Illinois statute allows the court to give an order of emancipation to a "mature minor who has demonstrated the ability and capacity to manage his

(or her) own affairs and to live wholly or partially independent of his (or her) parents." The Illinois statute also seeks to tailor the content of the emancipation order to fit the needs of the minor seeking the order.

The statute states that for an order of emancipation from the court to be valid, neither the parents nor the minor can offer any objections. Also, the court will examine the situation and determine whether a full or partial order of emancipation will be given. Also, once the emancipation order is entered, the court will determine what adult privileges and rights, in addition to the right to enter into contracts, will be given the minor. Only those rights listed in the order will be in effect for that minor.

In order to seek a court mandated emancipation order, the minor must be at least sixteen years old but under eighteen years old. The minor must confirm that he or she lives in Illinois, explain why he or she wants a complete or partial order or emancipation, demonstrate that he or she is a "mature minor," and show that he or she has lived on their own.

MICHIGAN: The age of majority in Michigan is eighteen. The Michigan statute defines emancipation as the "termination of the rights of the parents to the custody, control, services and earnings of a minor." Absent an order of emancipation, the statute confirms that parents are responsible for supporting their minor children. In fact, one or both parents can object to the emancipation proceedings. In that case, the court may decide to dismiss the proceedings.

The Michigan statute states the four ways that a minor can be emancipated without a court order as being by marriage, reaching the age of majority (eighteen years of age), joining the armed forces, and temporarily while in police custody in order to consent to needed medical treatment.

The statute requires the petition to the court to be brought by the minor. The minors must submit information showing that they can take care of themselves financially, without seeking assistance from the state of Michigan. Minors must also show the court that they can take care of their other personal needs as well. The petition to the court must include a statement from an adult sufficiently familiar with the minor that the individual can offer information that explains to the court why emancipation is "in the best interest of the minor."

At this point, the court may seek additional information and may ask someone from the court staff to investigate the situation further and report back to the court. The court then determines if an order of emancipation is in the minor's best interests.

If the minor is emancipated, the adult rights and responsibilities applicable to the minor do not include those limited by age and by law such as using and purchasing alcohol and voting. However, they do include signing contracts, being a plaintiff or defendant to a law suit, keeping whatever money the minor earns, living away from the parents, approving health care and medical procedures, getting married, writing a will, and enrolling in school.

If the minor's circumstances change, the emancipation order can be rescinded by the court. If that happens, the parents "are not liable for any debts incurred by the minor during the period of emancipation."

NORTH CAROLINA: The age of majority in North Carolina is eighteen. A minor must be at least sixteen years of age in order to seek an order of emancipation from the court. The court will consider several factors—including the parents' need for the minor's earnings as well as the minor's ability to accept adult responsibilities—in determining the best interests of the minor.

If the emancipation is granted, the minor will have the adult rights to sign contracts, take part in law suits, and conduct other adult-related business. The parents' duties of support to the minor are thereby ended.

OREGON: The age of majority in Oregon is eighteen. A minor must be sixteen years of age to seek an order of emancipation from the court. The minor must show that they can support him or herself and otherwise assume adult responsibilities. If the court determines that an order of emancipation is in the best interests of the minor, then the minor "has all of the rights and is subject to all liabilities of a citizen of full age."

### Vermont

A minor must be at least sixteen years old in order to seek an order of emancipation from the court. Minors are considered to be emancipated without a court order if they are married or have entered the armed forces. In order for the court to consider making an order of emancipation, the minors must have already lived separately from their parents, successfully taken care of their own finances, shown that they can take care of other personal business, either have received a high school diploma or are working toward one, and not be a ward of the social services or corrections department.

WEST VIRGINIA: A minor must be at lease sixteen years old in order to seek an order of emancipation from the court. Minors must also show the court that they can provide for themselves and their "physical and financial well-being and has the ability to make decisions" for themselves. If an emancipation order is entered, minors have the rights and privileges of adults.

## Additional Resources

*http://www.law.cornell.edu/topics/Table_ Emancipation.htm.* "Laws of the Fifty States, District of Columbia and Puerto Rico Governing the Emancipation of Minors," Legal Information Institute, January 9, 2002. Available at: http://www.law.cornell.edu/topics/Table_ Emancipation.htm

*West's Encyclopedia of American Law.* West Group, 1998.

## Organizations

### Focus Adolescent Services
113 Woodland Road, Suite 1000
Salisbury, MD 21801 USA
Phone: (877) 362-8727
URL: http://www.focusac.com
Primary Contact: Linda Lebelle, Director

### Legal Information Institute
Myron Taylor Hall
Ithaca, NY 14853 USA
E-Mail: lii@lii.law.cornell.edu
URL: http://www.law.cornell.edu/topics/Table_ Emancipation.htm

### Northwest Justice Project (NJP)
401 Second Avenue South, Ste. 407
Seattle, WA 98104 USA
Phone: (888) 201-9737
URL: http://www.nwjustice.org/
Primary Contact: Scott E. Collins, Board of Directors

# FAMILY LAW

## FAMILY PLANNING/ABORTION/BIRTH CONTROL

*Sections within this essay:*

## Background

Family planning involves decisions made by women and men concerning their reproductive lives and whether, when, and under what circumstances they have children. Family planning most often involves the decisions of whether to engage in sexual activity that could lead to pregnancy, whether to use **birth control**, and whether to terminate a pregnancy. Individuals faced with these decisions often rely on moral or religious beliefs. Because moral and religious beliefs vary widely in the United States, family planning laws are frequently controversial.

## History

During the nineteenth century in the United States, birth rates began to decline, in part due to an increase in scientific information about conception and contraception, or birth control. The average white woman in 1800 gave birth seven times; by 1900, that number dropped to an average of three-and-a-half. At the beginning of the nineteenth century, early stage abortions generally were legal. The use of birth control and **abortion**, however, declined as growing public opinion considered information about birth control methods to be obscene and abortion to be unsafe.

## Birth Control

Birth control is any method used to protect a woman from getting pregnant. Beginning in the 1800s, laws in the United States prohibited birth control, when temperance and anti-vice groups advocated outlawing birth control devices and information about birth control devices. These groups considered birth control information to be obscene, a belief that was popular enough that in 1873, Congress passed the Comstock Act outlawing the dissemination of birth control devices or information through the mail. Most states followed suit by passing their own laws outlawing the advertising, sale, and distribution, of contraception.

The turn of the century brought increasing attention to issues involving women's rights. Margaret Sanger, a strong advocate of birth control, opened the country's first birth control clinic in New York City in 1916 and was prosecuted for violating New York's version of the Comstock Act. She served a 30-day sentence in a workhouse but later established the National Committee for Federal Legislation for Birth Control. Sanger proposed a federal bill that outlined the health and death risks to women who underwent illegal abortions or who completed unwanted pregnancies. The bill sought to reverse the federal position prohibiting birth control, but under pressure from religious groups such as the Catholic Church, Congress did not pass Sanger's bill.

Sanger then sought to challenge the Comstock Act by sending contraception through the mail to a doctor. Her actions were prosecuted, but she achieved her goal when a federal district court deemed that the Comstock Act did not prohibit the mailing of contraceptives when such an act could save a life or promote the health of a doctor's patients. Sanger continued to lead a growing national movement advocating more information and access to birth control, and in 1921 she founded the American Birth Control League.

In 1942, the American Birth Control League became the Planned Parenthood Federation of America, still in existence today. Planned Parenthood advocates for a range of safe, legal, and accessible birth control options. In the 1950s, Sanger and Planned Parenthood supported the research efforts of Dr. Gregory Pincus that led to the development of the birth control pill. The birth control pill revolutionized family planning, and by the 1960s popular opinion was shifting in favor of making contraception and information about contraception readily available.

By the 1950s and 1960s, most states had legalized birth control, but many state laws still prohibited the dissemination of information about contraception, and some states still prohibited the possession of contraception. A 1965 landmark Supreme Court decision further eroded these laws sanctioning birth control. In Griswold v. Connecticut, the Court addressed the prosecution of a Planned Parenthood executive director charged with violating a Connecticut state law that prohibited the distribution of contraceptives, information about contraceptives, and prohibited the possession of contraceptives. The Court found that although the U. S. Constitution does not explicitly offer a right to privacy, that right can be inferred from the language in various sections of the **Bill of Rights**. The Constitution therefore does contain what the Court called a "zone of privacy." Connecticut's **statute** violated that zone of privacy in the realm of marriage because it permitted police officers to search the bedroom of a married couple for **evidence** of contraception. The Court deemed this action to be overly intrusive and an unconstitutional violation of the right to marital privacy, and it threw out the Connecticut law insofar as it applied to married couples.

In 1966, the federal government, with an endorsement by U.S. President Lyndon B. Johnson, began public funding of contraception services for low-income families. President Richard M. Nixon in 1970 signed into law an act promoting research of population and family planning issues. Finally, in 1971, Congress repealed the key elements of the Comstock Act.

Some states, however, kept birth control laws despite the **repeal** of the federal Comstock Act. In 1972, the Supreme Court found unconstitutional a Massachusetts law that only permitted married couples to receive contraception. The Court found this law to violate the **equal protection** rights of single persons. In 1977, the Court addressed a New York state law that permitted only physicians to distribute contraceptives to minors under the age of sixteen, and only physicians or pharmacists to distribute contraceptives to adults. The Court struck down this law as well. It became clear that the Supreme Court viewed as constitutionally protected the right of an individual, married or unmarried, to make personal decisions regarding whether to have children.

## Abortion

Abortion occurs when an embryo or fetus is expelled from a woman's body. Abortions can be spontaneous or induced. In the legal context, discussions about abortions usually involve induced, or intentional, abortions.

Before the United States became a country, the **common law** of England permitted abortions before the fetus "quickened." Quickening was the term used to describe the mother's first feeling of the fetus moving in her uterus. Typically, quickening occurs between the sixteenth and eighteenth weeks of pregnancy.

After the founding of the United States, laws regarding abortions did not exist until the 1800s. Women at that time were not allowed to vote and were not allowed to be doctors or members of the American Medical Association, which, along with religious leaders, advocated the passage of laws outlawing abortion. Abortions in the nineteenth century were generally unsafe, and women who survived abortions frequently were left sterile. By the 1880s, all states had laws criminalizing abortions. These laws stayed on the books until the 1960s and 1970s.

Beginning in the mid-twentieth century, women's groups, along with doctors and lawyers, organized a movement to reform abortion laws. Reformers cited inequalities between men and women that were exacerbated by women's inability to adequately control their reproductive lives. The post World War II population explosion also increased awareness about the environment and the need to limit family size. In other countries, abortions were legal and generally safe, but in the United States, women continued to undergo illegal abortions and risk permanent injury or death. In the 1960s, the anti-nausea drug thalidomide and an outbreak of German measles caused a rash of birth defects in babies born during that decade. The increase in birth defects brought further attention to the issue since women wishing to avoid the birth of a seriously deformed child could not seek legal abortions.

Women's rights organizations, including the National Organization for Women (NOW), lobbied for abortion law reform and filed lawsuits when **lobbying** efforts failed. States responded, reforming their laws about abortion, but women's rights groups continued to fight for unfettered access to abortion services for women. Anti-abortion groups fought back, arguing that a woman's right to reproductive freedom is no greater than the right of an unborn child to be born. The battle ultimately went before the U. S. Supreme Court, which in 1973 decided the landmark abortion case of *Roe v. Wade*.

### *Roe v. Wade*

Jane Roe was a pseudonym for Norma McCorvey, an unmarried pregnant Texas woman who sought an abortion but was denied under Texas law. Roe, with the help of attorneys, filed a federal lawsuit seeking to have the Texas law thrown out as unconstitutional. She argued that a law prohibiting her from obtaining an abortion violated her constitutional right to privacy. The Supreme Court, voting 7-2, agreed with Roe that the law criminalizing abortion violated her right to privacy. But the Court held that states do have an interest in ensuring the safety and well-being of pregnant women as well as the potential of human life. Acknowledging that the rights of pregnant women may conflict with the rights of the state to protect potential human life, the Court defined the rights of each party by dividing the pregnancy into three 12-week trimesters. During a pregnant woman's first trimester, the Court held, a state cannot regulate abortion beyond requiring that the procedure be performed by a licensed doctor in medically safe conditions. During the second trimester,

the Court held, a state may regulate abortion if the regulations are reasonably related to the health of the pregnant woman. During the third trimester of pregnancy, the state's interest in protecting the potential human life outweighs the woman's right to privacy, and the state may prohibit abortions unless abortion is necessary to save the life or health of the mother. The Court further held that a fetus is not a person protected by the constitution.

### After *Roe v. Wade*

*Roe v. Wade* established the limited right of a woman to have an abortion. Recognizing that fact, states liberalized their abortion laws following the Supreme Court's decision, but abortion soon became an even more divisive issue in the United States. Groups opposed to abortion, including the Catholic Church, became organized and politically powerful. The issue of abortion became a platform issue for all candidates for federal office, including the office of the U. S. president. During the 1980s, President Ronald Reagan, an opponent of abortion, used his presidency to argue for a reversal of *Roe v. Wade*. He appointed C. Everett Koop, another abortion opponent, to the position of surgeon general and referred to abortion as a "silent holocaust." Reagan believed that abortion caused pain to the fetus and that the rights of the fetus were not outweighed by the rights of the pregnant woman.

Groups opposed to abortion, known as pro-life groups, have worked in various ways to reduce or eliminate entirely abortions in the United States. These groups have sponsored legislation limiting access to abortion and have attempted unsuccessfully to reverse *Roe v. Wade* by way of a **constitutional amendment**. Some groups opposed to abortion attempt to persuade patients not to undergo abortions by demonstrating outside of abortion clinics. In some extreme cases, individuals and groups opposed to abortion have bombed abortion clinics, injuring and killing patients and staff members, or have murdered doctors who provide abortions. Because of these extreme actions, many doctors are unwilling to perform abortions and many abortion clinics have shut down, making access to abortion difficult in some regions.

Other attempts to reduce the number of abortions have involved eliminating public funding of abortions and even prohibiting health care clinics that receive public funding from counseling women about the option of abortion. Soon after taking office in 1993, President Bill Clinton effectively reversed federal regulations that prohibited staff members at health care clinics that receive public funding from dispersing information about abortions or referring women to abortion providers. Once this so-called "gag rule" was lifted, these clinics once again were able to give women information about abortion.

Also complicating the issue of abortion rights are rules requiring a woman to get **informed consent** or parental consent. Informed consent involves a requirement that before undergoing an abortion, the abortion provider must give the woman information about the risks of abortion, alternatives to abortion, the age of the fetus, and the availability of government assistance for carrying the pregnancy to term. Parental consent involves a requirement that a minor wishing to undergo an abortion first obtain consent from her parent or **guardian**. The Supreme Court generally has upheld parental consent laws provided the laws allow a minor the ability to obtain permission to have an abortion from a judge rather than a parent and provided that the judge's decision take into account the minor's best interests, maturity, and ability to make decisions. The Supreme Court generally has upheld laws requiring the notification, as opposed to consent, of parents of minors seeking to undergo an abortion. The Supreme Court generally has upheld informed consent laws so long as the laws do not create an undue burden on the woman seeking an abortion. The Supreme Court has not upheld laws requiring a woman to obtain her spouse's permission before undergoing an abortion.

Laws regarding the right to undergo an abortion continue to evolve. The pro-choice movement and the anti-abortion movement battle aggressively to protect their causes, and the issue remains deeply mired in differing opinions about ethics, religion, and medical science. There is little question that abortion will remain a divisive and powerful political issue in decades to come.

## Additional Resources

*Reproductive Health Online* Johns Hopkins University, 2001. Available at: www.reproline.jhu.edu.

*West's Encyclopedia of American Law*. West Group, 1998.

## Organizations

### Planned Parenthood Federation of America

810 Seventh Avenue
New York, NY 10019 USA
Phone: (212) 541-7800
URL: www.plannedparenthood.org

### National Abortion and Reproductive Rights Action League (NARAL)

1156 15th Street Suite 700
Washington, DC 20005 USA
Phone: (202) 973-3000
URL: www.naral.org

### National Right to Life Committee

512 10th Street, NW
Washington, DC 20004 USA
Phone: (202) 626-8800
URL: www.nrlc.org

### Feminists for Life

733 15th Street, NW
Washington, DC 20005 USA
Phone: (202) 737-FFLA
URL: www.feministsforlife.org

# FAMILY LAW

## FOSTER CARE

*Sections within this essay:*

- Background
- Federal Child Welfare Programs Today
- Foster Care Funding
- Medical Issues
- Children With Disabilities
- Aging Out of Foster Care
- Child Abuse
- Foster Parent Requirements
- Group Homes
- Kinship Care
- The Adoption and Safe Families Act
- The Indian Child Welfare Act
- Adoption of Foster Children
- Additional Resources

## Background

Children in foster homes is a concept which goes as far back as the Old **Testament**, which refers to caring for dependent children as a duty under law. Early Christian church records indicate orphaned children lived with widows who were paid by the church. English Poor Laws in the 1500s allowed the placement of poor children into indentured service until they became adults. This practice was imported to the United States and was the beginning of placing children into foster homes. Even though indentured

service permitted exploitation, it was an improvement over almshouses where children did not learn and were exposed to unsanitary conditions and abusive caretakers.

In 1853, Charles Loring Brace, a minister, founded the Children's Aid Society. Brace saw many immigrant children sleeping in the streets. He located families in the West willing to provide free homes for these children. These children were sent by train to these families and were often required to work long hours. Nevertheless, Brace's system became the foundation for today's foster care movement.

In the 1900s, social agencies began to pay and supervise foster parents. The government began state inspections of foster homes. Services were provided to natural families to enable the child to return home and foster parents were now seen as part of a team effort to provide for dependent children.

## Federal Child Welfare Programs Today

The Social Security Act contains the primary sources of Federal funds available to States for child welfare, foster care, and **adoption** activities. These funds include both nonentitlement authorizations (for which the amount of funding available is determined through the annual appropriations process) and authorized entitlements (under which the Federal Government has a binding obligation to make payments to any person or unit of government that meets the eligibility criteria established by law). Family preservation services are intended for children and families, including extended and adoptive families, that are at risk or in crisis. Services include: programs to help reunite children with their biological families, if appropriate, or to place them for adoption or another permanent arrangement; programs to prevent placement of children in foster care, including intensive family preservation services; programs to provide follow-up services to families after a child has been returned from foster care; respite care to provide temporary relief for parents and other care givers (including foster parents); and services to improve parenting skills. The Foster Care Program is a permanently authorized entitlement that provides open-ended matching payments to States for the costs of maintaining certain children in foster care, and associated administrative, child placement, and training costs.

## Foster Care Funding

The Federal government provides funds to States to administer child welfare programs. State grant programs have their own matching requirements and allocations, and all require that funds go to and be administered by State child welfare agencies, or in some programs, Indian Tribes or Tribal organizations. In most states foster children are eligible for **Medicaid** cards which cover medical, dental, and counseling services. Foster parents receive reimbursement for the child's food and clothing. Some states provide a clothing **voucher** at the time of the child's first placement. Others provide clothing vouchers at the beginning of each school year. Foster children have the same minimum health benefits as children in the Aid to Families with Dependent Children (AFDC) program. Most Federal funds for AFDC and foster children's health care come through Federal Medicaid (Title XIX of the Social Security Act).

## Medical Issues

As wards of the state, foster care children are dependent on government-funded health services. As a group, children in foster care suffer high rates of serious physical or psychological problems. Nearly half of these children suffer from chronic conditions such as asthma, cognitive abnormalities, visual and auditory problems, dental decay and malnutrition, as well as birth defects, developmental delays or emotional and behavioral problems. Over half require ongoing medical treatment. Studies indicate that well over half have moderate to severe mental health problems. These conditions stem from exposure to alcohol and drugs, lack of medical care, poor parenting, **domestic violence**, neglect, and unstable living conditions prior to family removal. The trauma of family separation, frequent moves, and the stress and disruptions brought about by impermanent placements in the foster care system aggravate the situation. Children in foster care typically suffer serious health, emotional, and developmental problems.

## Children With Disabilities

Children with disabilities sometimes enter foster care because their parents have not received the type or level of support to meet their needs. In many cases, parents must work and responsible after-school childcare is not available. Sometimes the parents become overwhelmed with the needs of the disabled child and the demands of other children in the family. Children with disabilities are abused at a high rate. Their parents are often frustrated with their children's disabilities or with their own inability to help them. Disabled girls are more often sexually abused that other girls. Children with developmental disabilities have a hard time explaining what happened to the social worker or police. In foster homes, the foster parents are trained to care for these children and given support within the dependency system.

## Aging Out of Foster Care

Children age-out of foster care at age 18 or when they graduate from high school, whichever happens first. This event is referred to as **emancipation**. Some maintain a continuing relationship with their foster families while others do not. Many face a difficult future when state and federal funding ends, and housing, food, and medical care stops.

The John H. Chafee Foster Care Independence Program (CFCIP), Title I of the Foster Care Independence Act of 1999, provides funds to states to assist youth and young adults (up to age 21) in the foster care component of the child welfare system make a smoother, more successful transition to adulthood. This recent program replaces and expands the Social Security Act and allows states to use these funds for a broader array of services to youth "aging out" of the foster care system, including room and board. Most importantly, the Chafee program enables states to expand the scope and improve the quality of educational, vocational, practical, and emotional supports in their programs for adolescents in foster care and for young adults who have recently left foster care.

## Child Abuse

Many children become participants in the Foster Care system due to neglect or abuse by their primary caretakers. Investigations by child protective services (CPS) agencies in all States determine that close to a million children are victims of child maltreatment every year. More than half of all reports alleging maltreatment came from professionals, including educators, law enforcement and justice officials, medical and mental health professionals, social service professionals, and **child care** providers. Federal agencies have no authority to intervene in individual **child abuse** and neglect cases. Each State has **jurisdiction** over these matters and has specific laws and procedures for reporting and investigating. Individual States have a Child Protective Services agency set up to investigate complaints and allegations. In some States, all citizens are mandated reporters by State law and must report any suspicion of child abuse or neglect.

More children suffer neglect than any other form of maltreatment. Investigations determined that about half of children victimized suffered neglect, 22 percent physical abuse, 12 percent **sexual abuse**, 6 percent emotional maltreatment, 2 percent medical neglect, and 25 percent other forms of maltreatment. Some children suffer more than one type of abuse. Unfortunately, maltreatment is rarely the only issue of families who enter into the child welfare system. Substance abuse and other addictions, serious physical or mental illness, domestic violence, and HIV/AIDS are often critical factors. Poverty is pervasive, and inadequate or unsafe housing are significant problems. These serious difficulties can result in extremely complex family situations that need multiple and coordinated services.

## Foster Parent Requirements

Generally, foster parents must be over 21, have a regular source of income, have no record of **felony** convictions, submit to a home **assessment** of all family members, and agree to attend parent training sessions. Foster parents can usually work outside the home, however, if the foster child requires day care, the foster parent is typically responsible for that expense. Foster parents need no make a certain minimum income, nor even own a large home. Foster children can usually share a bedroom with another child of the same sex. Both single persons and married couples are generally accepted as foster parents, however, some states do not certify homes in which

unmarried adults are living together unless they are relatives.

The length of time a child may remain in foster care varies. The Adoption and Safe Families Act of 1997 requires states to seek a permanent placement for the child as quickly as possible, be it reunification with the birth parents, kinship care, or adoption.

## Group Homes

Group homes have a history of being problematic in the Foster Care system. Initially, there was a shortage of experienced operators, the industry was unregulated, and a few took advantage of it. While many were run by competent social workers or those in religious communities who, though without formal training, were instrumental in having a positive impact on these children. Unfortunately, in others, children were abused, forced to participate in the beliefs of their caretakers. Sometimes untrained workers tried behavior modification techniques that were cruel and inhumane. With little monitoring by the government, it was possible to cut back on food, clothing, education and program to make a profit for the operators.

Group homes are now subject to a number of federal regulations. Any care facility that houses six or more children is considered a group home. Most group homes are small and try to integrate the children into the community. The residents attend local schools, are closely supervised, have a structured life, with a counselor on duty around the clock in most cases, and a schedule of counseling, tutoring, and other services.

## Kinship Care

Kinship care is the full time care of children by relatives, godparents, stepparents, or any adult who has a kinship bond with a child. The expansion of kinship foster care is, perhaps, the most dramatic shift to occur in child welfare practice over the past two decades. Informal kinship care is when a family decides that the child will live with relatives or other kin. In this informal kinship care arrangement, a social worker may be involved in helping family members plan for the child, but a child welfare agency does not assume legal **custody** of or responsibility for the child. Because the parents still have custody of the child, relatives need not be approved, licensed, or supervised by the state.

Formal kinship care involves the parenting of children by relatives as a result of a determination by the court and the child protective service agency. The courts rule that the child must be separated from his or her parents because of abuse, neglect, dependency, **abandonment** or special medical circumstances. The child is placed in the legal custody of the child welfare agency, and the relatives provide full time care. Formal kinship care is linked to state and federal child welfare laws. Federal legislation impacting kinship care includes The Adoption Assistance and Child Welfare Act of 1980, Title IV of the Social Security Act, and The Indian Child Welfare Act. Thus, kinship caregivers may be able to access Social Security Funds for the child, Temporary Assistance for Needy Families (TANF) funds for the child, and medical assistance for the child.

## The Adoption and Safe Families Act

The Adoption and Safe Families Act of 1997 established time lines and conditions for filing termination of parental rights. The Act provides a new legislative framework that sets the direction and parameters for the operation of state and local child welfare agencies and courts. States must file a petition to terminate parental rights and concurrently, identify, recruit, process and approve a qualified adoptive family on behalf of any child, regardless of age, if the child has been in foster care for 15 out of the most recent 22 months. Exceptions can be made to these requirements if a relative is caring for a child. The Act requires notice of court reviews and an opportunity to be heard is sent to relatives, foster parents, and pre-adoptive parents. A relative, foster parent or pre-adoptive parent caring for a child must be given notice of an opportunity to be heard in any review or **hearing** involving the child. This provision does not require that any relative, foster, or pre-adoptive parent be made a party to such a review or hearing. The Act also mandates that the Federal Department of Health and Human Services (HHS) complete a study on kinship care.

## The Indian Child Welfare Act

The Indian Child Welfare Act (ICWA) of 1973 described the role that Native American families and tribal governments must play in decisions about the protection and placement of their children. It strengthened the role of tribal governments in determining the custody of Native American children and specified that preference should be given first to placements with extended family, then to Native American foster homes. The law mandated that state courts act to preserve the integrity and unity of Native American families.

## Adoption of Foster Children

If a child has been in placement with a foster care family for a significant period of time and the parental rights of the natural parents have been terminated, the foster parents may seek an adoption under the state law. See Adoption.

## Additional Resources

*Grandparents Raising Grandchildren: A Guide to Finding Help and Hope* Takas, Marianne, The Brookdale Foundation, 1995.

*Relatives Raising Children: An Overview of Kinship Care* Crumbley, Joseph & Robert L. Little, Child Welfare League of America, 1997.

*The Strengths of African American Families* Hill, Robert B., R & B Publishers, 1997.

## Organizations

### *Child Welfare League of America*
50 F Street, NW, 6th Floor
Washington, DC 20001-2085 USA
Phone: (202) 638-2952
Fax: (202) 638-4004

### *National Association of Child Advocates*
1522 K Street, NW, Suite 600
Washington, DC 20005-1202 USA

# FAMILY LAW

## GAY COUPLES

*Sections within this essay:*

- Background
- Pre-1993
- Baehr v. Lewin
- The Reaction
  - The Defense of Marriage Act (DOMA)
  - The Call for a Constitutional Amendment
- Massachusetts and San Francisco
- Civil Unions in Vermont
- Recent Court Rulings against Same-sex Marriage
- State Laws
- Municipalities and Corporations
- Additional Resources

## Background

Within the already controversial realm of gay rights, no area is more controversial than gay marriage. For some, the idea that homosexual couples should have the same matrimonial benefits as heterosexual couples is purely a question of civil rights. According to this argument, the constitutional concepts of equal protection and due process require that same-sex couples be treated no differently than heterosexual married couples. Others see homosexual marriage as a moral question, and conclude that such unions violate traditional ethical values found in the Judeo-Christian moral tradition. Another argument is that it undermines family values: heterosexual marriage is founded upon the need to procreate, but that is something homosexual couples cannot do. To counter this argument, those in favor of same-sex marriages note that elderly, disabled, and infertile people are free to marry without thought to procreation, and that advances in fertility technology have opened many paths to parenthood.

The debate over gay marriage is not confined to the marriage ceremony itself, although being allowed to participate legally in that rite drives much of the emotionalism of the debate. It also has a more pragmatic side, including issues such as whether same-sex couples should receive the same tax and estate advantages, the same rights to surviving children, the same **community property** rights, and the same health care benefits as heterosexual couples.

Although same-sex marriages have occurred privately for years, only recently has the issue been litigated. Only since 1993, with the Hawaii Supreme Court decision in *Baehr v. Lewin*, have gay rights supporters seen any measurable progress in state laws concerning homosexual marriage. Since that decision, both sides in the battle over same-sex marriage have experienced some victories and some setbacks.

## Pre-1993

Unions between two members of the same sex in some sort of ceremony, religious or otherwise, existed for many years before the anyone sought to gain legal recognition of them. Generally, these unions were kept private, with knowledge limited to immediate friends and family members. Then, in 1971 the first lawsuit seeking to legalize a same-sex marriage was filed. *Baker v. Nelson* was inspired by the 1967 U. S. Supreme Court decision in *Loving v. Virginia*. In *Loving*, the Supreme Court invalidated a state **statute** that prohibited interracial marriage. The court ruled that to deny marriage on the basis of race was a violation of the constitutional principles of **equal protection** and **due process of law**, because the law had "no legitimate purpose independent of invidious racial discrimination."

The Minnesota Supreme Court was not swayed by the reasoning in *Loving*. It struck down Jack Baker's attempt to gain legal status for his marriage to Mike McConnell. The court ruled that marriage was by definition between a man and a woman, and thus, unlike in *Loving*, there was no fundamental right to marry. Moreover, in a 1974 case, the Washington Supreme Court determined that the state's **Equal Rights Amendment** could not be held to allow homosexuals the right to marry. The law provided protection only on the basis of sex, not sexual orientation.

Following these cases, all attempts failed to get a state or federal court to recognize the right of homosexuals to marry. There were decisions allowing unmarried partners to sue for enforcement of promises of support or financial sharing (so-called "palimony" cases), beginning with the landmark *Marvin v. Marvin* case involving actor Lee Marvin in California in 1976. Gays also attempted to form legal relationships by having one partner "adopt" the other. Some municipalities, beginning with Berkeley in 1984, adopted domestic partnership laws that extended some recognition and benefits of marriage to registered same-sex couples. But gay activists considered that these gains fell far short of their ultimate goal: granting marriage recognition to gay unions.

## Baehr v. Lewin

Activists scored their first major victory in 1993, in the Hawaii case of *Baehr v. Lewin*. Nina Baehr sued the state of Hawaii; she alleged that the state's refusal to issue her and her same-sex partner a marriage license amounted to illegal **discrimination**. In a **plurality** decision, the Hawaii Supreme Court said her case had merit. The Court ruled the state's prohibition of same-sex marriages amounted to discrimination on the basis of sex. Under the state's Equal Rights Amendment, the state would have to establish

a compelling state interest supporting such a ban, a fairly strict standard. Although the court did not directly rule that the state's prohibition of same-sex marriages was illegal, it left little doubt of its skepticism regarding the proposition. The court remanded the case to a lower court to determine whether the state could prove this compelling state interest in prohibiting same-sex marriage.

For the first time, a state Supreme Court had ruled that gay couples might have the right to marry. Although its immediate impact was only in Hawaii, the decision heartened gay rights supporters and discouraged opponents throughout the country. One reason for these responses was the Full Faith and Credit Clause, found in Article IV, Section 1, of the United States Constitution: "Full Faith and Credit shall be given in each state to the public Acts, Records and judicial Proceedings of every other state." The Clause requires states to grant full weight to legal actions in other states, including marriages, divorces, and other family-related situations. Both opponents and proponents of gay marriage realized that the Full Faith and Credit Clause of the Constitution might mean that if same-sex marriages were legal in Hawaii, the marriages would be entitled to legal recognition in other states as well.

## The Reaction

The *Baehr* decision mobilized opponents of same-sex marriages, who feared that gay marriage would soon be legal in Hawaii. Yet some disagreed over whether Hawaii's potential legalization of gay marriage would necessarily overrule other states' anti-gay marriage laws. Nevertheless, anti-gay marriage legislation was passed on both the state and federal level. Voters in Hawaii adopted a **constitutional amendment** allowing legislators to ban same-sex marriages, thus making the state's Equal Rights Amendment no longer applicable. In late 1999, the Hawaiian Supreme Court determined that this new ban was effective and refused to recognize same-sex marriages in the state.

### The Defense of Marriage Act

In 1996, in response to the *Baehr* decision, the U. S. Congress passed the Defense of Marriage Act (DOMA). President Clinton signed DOMA into law. The act was designed to prevent the Full Faith and Credit Clause from being applied to states' refusal to recognize same sex marriages. DOMA states in part that "No state, territory or possession of the United States . . . shall be required to give effect to any public act, record, or judicial proceeding of any other State, territory, possession or tribe respecting a relationship between persons of the same sex that is treated as a marriage under the laws of such other State, territory, possession, or tribe, or a right or claim arising from such a relationship."

DOMA does not ban same-sex marriages in itself. Neither does it require any state to ban them. DOMA defines marriage as a union between a man and a woman only. The act also specifically denies federal benefits to same-sex couples. The act states that any federal law that applies to married couples does not apply to same-sex couple: **statutory** and administrative use of terms such as "marriage" and "spouse" under federal law only apply to heterosexual couples. In addition to the federal law, many states passed their own defense of marriage laws.

### *The Call for a Constitutional Amendment*

In February 2004, President George W. Bush called for a constitutional amendment to protect marriage. The president said that DOMA was vulnerable to attack under the Full Faith and Credit clause, a sentiment echoed by numerous commentators. He stated only way to ensure that DOMA would not be struck down by "activist courts" is through an amendment that would" fully protect marriage, while leaving the state legislatures free to make their own choices in defining legal arrangements other than marriage." Proposed amendments have been introduced in Congress, but no vote has yet taken place.

Bush threw his support behind a federal marriage amendment after events in Massachusetts and San Francisco. In late 2003 and early 2004, officials in both places seemingly authorized same-sex marriages.

## Massachusetts and San Francisco

On November 18, 2003, the Supreme Judicial Court of Massachusetts ruled in *Goodridge v. Department of Public Health* that the state could not deny civil marriage to two members of the same sex who wished to marry. The court stayed its ruling for 180 days, so that the state legislature could address the issue. The legislature moved quickly to prohibit same-sex marriages, but voted to allow "civil unions," a category that was intended to be separate but legally equivalent to marriage. In February 2004, the Supreme Judicial Court issued an advisory opinion that concluded the proposed legislation was un-

constitutional. This opinion paved the way for city and town clerks to issue marriage licenses to same-sex couples beginning in May 2004. Massachusetts is currently the only state in the U.S. where same-sex couples may legally marry.

At the same time the marriage debate raged in Massachusetts, the issue was heating up in San Francisco as well. In February 2004, the county clerk, acting on orders of San Francisco mayor Gavin Newsom, began to issue marriage licenses to same-sex couples. Couples from all around the U.S. flocked to the city to get married. Issuance of licenses was halted when the California Supreme Court issued a temporary stay on March 11, 2004. By that time, however, more than four thousand same-sex marriages had been performed.

In early September 2005, the California legislature approved a bill to permit homosexual marriage. Governor Arnold Schwarzenegger vetoed the bill on September 29, 2005.

## Civil Unions in Vermont

In 1999, the same year the Hawaiian Supreme Court refused to recognize same-sex marriages, the Vermont Supreme Court handed down its decision in *Baker v. State*. In that decision, the court said that same-sex couples must be granted the same benefits and protections that heterosexual couples received under state law. The court instructed the state legislature to determine how to grant homosexual couples those benefits and protections. It did not require the state to allow same-sex couples to be legally married but told the state legislature it had to find some way to treat those couples the same as if they were legally married.

The next year, the state passed a bill allowing same-sex couples to enter into "civil unions." Town clerks were authorized to give licenses to same-sex couples for these unions in the same way they would give out marriage licenses. They could be married by anyone authorized to perform marriages under state law and would have to **divorce** under state law in the same way heterosexual couples would.

Same-sex couples in civil unions in Vermont are entitled to all the benefits available under state law to married couples, including medical decisions, estate **inheritance**, overseeing burials, transferring properties, and certain tax breaks. Employers are required to treat civil union couples in the same way they treated other married couples, in matters including health benefits, marital status discrimination law, **workers' compensation** benefits, **taxation**, family leave benefits and **wage assignment** laws. The Vermont civil union bill was a landmark in the fight over gay marriages. For the first time, a state allowed gay couples to have all the same benefits as married couples under state law. Because Vermont refused to label these unions as marriages, it is less likely that they will conflict with other states nonrecognition laws, although some commentators have suggested the Full Faith And Credit Clause might still apply.

According to the Vermont Secretary of State, in the first five years since the passage of the civil union law, 1,142 Vermont couples have been joined in civil unions. Moreover, 6,424 couples from other states and nations have also been joined in civil union in Vermont.

## Recent Court Rulings against Same-sex Marriage

In 2003 in *Standhardt v. Superior Court,* the Arizona Court of appeals upheld a statute that prohibited same-sex couples from marrying. The court ruled that the statute was constitutional based on due process, equal protection, and rights of privacy provided in the Arizona constitution. The Indiana Court of Appeals made a similar ruling in January 2005 in *Morrison v. Sadler.* Numerous other states have right-to-marry cases winding their way through the court system.

## State Laws

State DOMA laws are widespread; about half the states have enacted statutes that provide that marriage is confined to one man and one woman. About a third of the states have constitutional provisions that define marriage as only permitted between a man and a woman.

Massachusetts is currently the only state to allow same-sex marriages. Connecticut and Vermont permit civil unions. Vermont defines civil union as follows: "Parties to a civil union shall have all the same benefits, protections and responsibilities under Vermont law, whether they derive from statute, policy, administrative or court rule, common law or any other source of civil law, as are granted to spouses in a marriage."

Although most states prohibit same-sex marriages and civil unions, many provide some rights for same-sex couples that are available to married persons. The amount of protection provided varies greatly from just one or two rights in some states, to dozens of rights in other states. Following are some examples of rights that states have conferred to same-sex couples:

- hospital visitation
- the right to make healthcare decisions
- eligibility for certain tort claims
- family leave
- workers' compensation
- inheritance under intestacy laws
- state tax deductions or exemptions
- eligibility for family health insurance for state employees

## Municipalities and Corporations

Municipalities have been generally more likely than states to grant same-sex couples the benefits of marriage than states. Since Berkeley passed the first domestic partnership law in 1984, dozens of cities and municipalities have enacted domestic partnership policies, including New York City and San Francisco. Although these policies do not legalize same-sex marriages (only the states can do that), they provide that same-sex couples will be treated the same as heterosexual couples under city ordinances and for such employment related purposes as health and **disability** benefits.

Many **corporations**, including companies such as Disney, Microsoft and IBM, also provide same-sex couples with the same benefits as married couples. This trend appears to be growing. According to the American Bar Association, as of March 2005, more than 7,600 private sector companies offered domestic partnership health benefits, and slightly less than half of all Fortune 500 companies did so as well.

## Additional Resources

*"A Matter of Full Faith"* ABA Journal, July,1996.

*An Analysis of the Law Regarding Same-sex Marriages, Civil Unions, and Domestic Partnerships,* American Bar Association, 2005.

*The Case for Same-Sex Marriage: From Sexual Liberty to Civilized Commitment,* Eskridge, William N., Jr., Free Press, 1996.

*From This Day Forward: Commitment, Marriage, and Family in Lesbian and Gay Relationships* Stiers, Gretchen A., St. Martin's Griffin, 2000.

*Gaylaw: Challenging the Apartheid of the Closet* Eskridge, William N., Jr., Harvard University Press, 1999.

*"More Battles Ahead Over Gay Marriage"* ABA Journal, February, 1997.

## Organizations

### *Lambda Legal Defense and Education Fund*

120 Wall Street, Suite 1500

New York, NY 10005-3904 USA

Phone: (212) 809-8585

Fax: (212) 809-0055

URL: www.lamdalegal.org

Primary Contact: Kevin Cathcart, Executive Director

# FAMILY LAW

## GRANDPARENTS' RIGHTS

*Sections within this essay:*

## Background

Grandparents in every state in the United States have rights, in some circumstances, to be awarded **custody** of their grandchildren or to be awarded court-mandated visitation with their grandchildren. Grandparents' rights are not constitutional in nature, nor did they exist at **common law**. Recognition of grandparents' rights by state legislatures is a fairly recent trend, and most of the statutes have been in effect for less than 40 years.

Federal legislation may affect grandparents' rights, though these rights are based primarily on state law. Congress passed the Parental **Kidnapping** Prevention Act in 1980, which requires that each state give full faith and credit to **child custody** decrees from other states. Federal legislation passed in 1998 also requires that courts in each state recognize and enforce grandparental visitation orders from courts in other states. All states have adopted a version of the Uniform Child Custody **Jurisdiction** and Enforcement Act (UCCJEA, previously the Uniform Child Custody Jurisdiction Act), which requires courts in the state where a child resides to recognize and enforce valid child custody orders from another state. Though the UCCJEA is not a federal **statute**, the provisions of this uniform law as adopted in each state are similar.

Some courts have determined that state statutes providing visitation to grandparents are unconstitutional. The United States Supreme Court in the case of *Troxel v. Granville* (2000) determined that the Washington visitation statute violated the due process rights of parents to raise their children. This case and similar decisions by state courts caused several state legislatures to consider bills that would modify or completely revise the visitation rights in those states. Most state laws related to grandparent rights, however, have survived intact. Nevertheless, grandparents who seek to attain visitation rights should check the current status of state legislation in their respective states.

## Factors Considered for Custody or Visitation

Courts grant visitation or custody to grandparents only when certain conditions provided in state statutes are met. Conditions for a grandparent to attain custody differ from those conditions required for visitation rights. A grandparent should be familiar with the conditions for either custody or visitation before determining whether to file a petition to request either from a court of law.

### Best Interests of the Child

Courts in every jurisdiction must consider the "best interest of the child" when granting custody or visitation rights to a grandparent. In some states, the relevant statute provides a list of factors the court should considered when determining a child's best interests. Other states do not provide factors in the statute, but courts in those states typically identify factors in custody and visitation cases interpreting the state statutes.

The following factors in determining the best interest of the child are among those included in state statutes and **case law**:

- The needs of the child, including considerations of physical and emotional health of the child, the safety of the child, and the welfare of the child

- The capability of the parents and/or grandparents to meet the needs of the child

- The wishes of the parent(s) and the grandparent(s)

- The wishes of the child, if the child is capable of making decisions for himself or herself

- The strength of the relationship between the grandparent(s) and grandchild

- The length of the relationship between the grandparent(s) and grandchild

- **Evidence** of abuse or neglect by the parent(s) or grandparent(s)

- Evidence of substance abuse by the parent(s) or grandparent(s)

- The child's adjustment to the home, school, or community

- The ability of the parent(s) or grandparent(s) to provide love, affection, and contact with the child

- The distance between the child and the parent(s) or grandparent(s)

### Requirements for Awarding Custody to Grandparents

**Statutory** provisions for child custody (termed "conservatorship" in a few states) are usually less specific than the statutes regarding grandparent visitation. Courts must first consider the relationship of the parent or parents with the child before considering whether granting custody to grandparent(s) is appropriate. Several states specifically include consideration of grandparents as custodians if both parents are deceased. If either or both parents are alive, courts in most states will presume that the parent of the child should retain custody. Grandparents must generally prove the parent(s) unfit in order to overcome the judicial presumption in favor of the parent. Even if the relationship between the grandparent and grandchild is strong, it is very difficult for a grandparent to attain custody of a grandchild against the wishes of the parent or parents.

### Requirements for Awarding Visitation to Grandparents

State statutes providing visitation to grandparents generally require that a number of conditions occur before visitation rights can be granted. The marital status of the parents must be considered in a majority of states before a court will evaluate the relevant factors to determine if visitation is appropriate. In some of these states, the parents' marital status is considered only if the grandparent or grandparents have been denied visitation by the parents. In other states, marital status is considered only if the grandchild resided with the grandparents for a certain length of time.

A minority of states require that at least one parent is deceased before a court can award visitation to the parent of the deceased parent of the child. For example, a maternal grandparent in one of these states may be awarded visitation only if the mother of the child is deceased.

State statutes vary in their treatment of cases in which a grandchild has been adopted. In several states, **adoption** by anyone, including a stepparent or another grandparent, terminates the visitation rights of the grandparent. In some states, adoption by a stepparent or another grandparent does not terminate visitation rights, but adoption by anyone else does terminate these rights. In other states, adoption has no effect on the visitation rights of grandparents, so long as other statutory requirements are met.

Once the statutory conditions for visitation are met, grandparents must establish the factors that courts may or must consider to grant visitation rights. In every state, grandparents must prove that granting visitation to the grandchild is in the best interest of the child. Several states also require that the court consider the prior relationship between the grandparent and the grandchild, the effect grandparental visitation will have on the relationship between the parent and child, and/or a showing of harm to the grandchild if visitation is not allowed.

## Courts' Jurisdiction over Custody and Visitation Cases

### Parties Residing in the Same State

Each state provides the appropriate venue which can make custody and visitation determinations in a case where all of the parties reside in the same state. Where a **divorce** is pending, the appropriate venue for making a custody or visitation decision involving the grandparents and grandchildren is almost always the court **hearing** the divorce proceedings. Some states require visitation petitions to be filed with another domestic relations suit. Some states also permit visitation requests after a domestic relations order has been rendered or as an original proceeding.

### Parties Residing in Different States

If a child's parents and/or grandparents live in different states, one of several laws will determine the appropriate court to hear a custody or visitation case. If a valid custody or visitation **decree** has been entered in one state, the Parental Kidnapping Prevention Act requires that another state must enforce and must not modify the decree. Another state may modify the decree only if the original state no longer has jurisdiction over the case or has declined jurisdiction to modify the custody or visitation decree. Congress amended this statute in 1998 to include a grandparent in the definition of "contestant."

If no state has made a valid custody determination, the provisions of the Uniform Child Custody Jurisdiction and Enforcement Act, as adopted by each state, will apply. A court in a particular state has power to hear a custody case if that state is the child's "home state" or has been the home state of the child within six months of the date the legal action was brought and at least one parent continues to reside in the state. Other situations include those in which a state with jurisdiction over a custody case declines jurisdiction or no other state may assert jurisdiction over the child.

## State Provisions for Custody and Visitation

Grandparents should check a number of provisions in the statutes in their respective states to determine the conditions for visitation, the factors a court must consider to order visitation, and the proper venue to file a request for visitation. Though many state statutes are similar, state courts may apply statutory provisions differently. Every statute requires courts to consider the best interest of the child before awarding custody or visitation to grandparents.

As noted above, courts in a few states have ruled that statutes providing for grandparent visitation violate either the federal or the respective state constitutions. Several states have revised the statutory visitation provisions, but the constitutionality of these statutes may still be in question.

ALABAMA: Alabama courts struck down portions of the grandparent visitation statute as unconstitutional. The Alabama Legislature in 2003 amended the statute to comport with constitutional requirements. Under the revised statute, a court may grant visitation to a grandparent if visitation is in the child's best interest and one of five events has occurred: (1) one or both parents of the child are deceased; (2) the marriage of the parents of the child has been dissolved; (3) a parent of the child has abandoned the child; (4) the child was born out of wedlock; or (5) the child lives with both biological parents, but one or both of the parents has prevented a grandparent from visiting the child. The state's custody statute requires courts to consider the moral character of the parents and the age and sex of the child to determine the best interests of the child.

ALASKA: Determination of grandparent visitation rights must be made in an action for divorce, legal separation, or child placement action, or when both parents have died. Adoption cuts off the visitation rights of grandparents unless the adoption decree provides for visitation between the child and the natural relatives.

ARIZONA: A court may award visitation rights if the child's parents' marriage has been dissolved for at least three months, or the child is born out of wedlock. Adoption cuts off the visitation rights of the grandparents unless the adoption is granted to a stepparent.

ARKANSAS: The custody statute requires that court grant custody "without regard to the sex of the parent but solely in accordance with the welfare and best interest of the children." Conditions for grandparent visitation rights include several circumstances where the grandchild has resided with the grandparent, the child's parents are divorced, the child is in the custody of someone other than a parent, or the child has been born out of wedlock. Adoption cuts off all visitation rights of the natural grandparents.

CALIFORNIA: Conditions for grandparent visitation rights include a determination of whether a parent is deceased, the child's parents are divorced or separated, the whereabouts of one parent is unknown, or the child is not residing with either parent. In addition to determining that visitation is in the child's best interests, the court must find that the grandparents had a preexisting relationship with the grandchild. The court must also balance visitation with the parents' rights. If both parents agree that the court should not grant visitation to the grandchild, the court will presume that visitation is not in the child's best interests. Adoption does not automatically cut off the visitation rights of grandparents.

COLORADO: A court may award visitation rights if the child's parents' marriage has been terminated, legal custody of the child has been given to a third party, the child has been placed outside the home of either of the child's parents, or the grandparent is the parent of a deceased parent of the child. Adoption cuts off the visitation rights of the grandparents unless the adoption is granted to a stepparent.

CONNECTICUT: A court may award visitation rights if visitation is in the child's best interest. Adoption does not automatically cut off the visitation rights of grandparents.

DELAWARE: A court may award visitation rights if visitation is in the child's best interest. Adoption cuts off all visitation rights of grandparents.

FLORIDA: The Florida Supreme Court has on more than one occasions ruled that the application some provisions of the Florida statute providing grandparental visitation is unconstitutional. Under the current statute, Florida courts may award visitation to a grandparent when visitation is in the child's best interest and (1) the marriage of the child's parents has been dissolved; (2) a parent has deserted a child; or (3) the child was born out of wedlock.

GEORGIA: The custody statute does not list specific factors for the court to consider for determining the best interest of the child. A court may award visi-

tation rights if an action is pending where there is an issue involving the custody of a minor child, divorce of the child's parents, termination of a parent's rights, or visitation rights. Adoption cuts off the visitation rights of the grandparents unless the adoption is granted to a stepparent or a natural relative of the child.

HAWAII: The custody statute requires courts to consider the child's wishes, if the child is old enough and has the capacity to reason, and evidence of any **domestic violence**, when determining the best interest of the child. A court may award visitation rights if Hawaii is the home state of the child at the time visitation is requested, and visitation is in the best interest of the child. Adoption cuts off all visitation rights of grandparents.

IDAHO: A court may award visitation rights if visitation is in the child's best interest. Adoption cuts off all visitation rights of grandparents.

ILLINOIS: In 2002, the Illinois Supreme Court determined that the Illinois Grandparent Visitation Act violated the Illinois Constitution. A new visitation statute became effective on January 1, 2005. Under the new statute, a court can grant visitation to a grandparent if visitation is in the best interest of the child and the grandparent has been unreasonably denied visitation to the child. A court may not grant visitation to a grandparent where both parents object to such visitation.

INDIANA: A court may award visitation rights if either of the child's parents is deceased, the child's parents' marriage has been terminated, or the child was born out of wedlock. In addition to considering whether visitation is in the child's best interest, a grandparent must show that he or she has had, or attempted to have, meaningful contact with the grandchild. Adoption cuts off the visitation rights of the grandparents unless the adoption is granted to a stepparent or a natural grandparent, sibling, aunt, uncle, niece, or nephew of the child.

IOWA: The custody statute requires courts to consider the best interest of the child that will provide the "maximum continuing physical and emotional contact with both parents." The Iowa Supreme Court has ruled on more than one occasion that the Iowa statute providing grandparental visitation is unconstitutional, and the Iowa Legislature has not adopted an alternative statute.

KANSAS: A court may award visitation rights in a custody order. Adoption cuts off the visitation rights of the grandparents unless the grandparent is the parent of a deceased parent and the surviving parent's spouse adopts the child.

KENTUCKY: A court may award visitation rights if visitation would be in the child's best interest. A court may award a grandparent the same visitation rights as a parent without custody if the grandparent's child is deceased and the grandparent has provided **child support** to the grandchild. Adoption cuts off the visitation rights of grandparents unless the adoption is granted to a stepparent, and the grandparent's child has not had his or her parental rights terminated.

LOUISIANA: A court may award visitation rights if the child's parent is deceased or declared legally incompetent, a grandparent is the parent of the deceased or incompetent parent to the grandchild, and visitation is in the child's best interest. Adoption cuts off the visitation rights of grandparents except in circumstances where the grandparents are the parents of a deceased party to the marriage or the parents of a party who has forfeited his or her rights to object to the child's adoption.

MAINE: A court may award visitation right if at least one of the child's parents is deceased, visitation is in the child's best interest, and visitation will not interfere significantly with the relationship between the parent and the child. Adoption cuts off all visitation rights of grandparents.

MARYLAND: The custody statute does not provide a list of factors for determining the best interest of the child. A court may award visitation rights if visitation is in the child's best interest. The factors for determining the child's best interest have been set forth in case law. Adoption cuts off all visitation rights of grandparents.

MASSACHUSETTS: The custody statute does not provide a list of factors for determining the best interest of the child. A court may award visitation rights if the child's parents' marriage is terminated, the parents are separated, one of the parents is deceased, or the child was born out of wedlock and paternity has been established. Adoption cuts off the visitation rights of grandparents unless the adoption is granted to a stepparent.

MICHIGAN: A court may award visitation rights if the child's parents' marriage is terminated, the parents separate, or custody of the child is given to a third party other than the child's parents. Adoption

cuts off the visitation rights of grandparents unless the adoption is granted to a stepparent.

MINNESOTA: A court may award visitation rights if a child's parent is deceased and the grandparents are the parents of the deceased parent. Visitation may also be granted during or after divorce, custody, separation, **annulment**, or paternity proceedings. Adoption cuts off the visitation rights of grandparents unless the adoption is granted to a stepparent or another grandparent.

MISSISSIPPI: The custody statute does not provide a list of factors for determining the best interest of the child. If the child is at least 12 years old, he or she may choose who takes custody. Conditions for grandparent visitation rights include determination of whether one of the child's parents is deceased, or a parent has had his or her parental rights terminated. The court must also consider the relationship between the grandparent and grandchild. Adoption cuts off the visitation rights of grandparents unless the adoption is granted to a stepparent or a blood relative.

MISSOURI: A court may award visitation rights if the child's parents have filed for divorce, one parent is deceased and the other parent has unreasonably denied visitation to the grandparent, or when a parent or parents unreasonably deny visitation to a grandparent for more than 90 days. Adoption cuts off the visitation rights of grandparents unless adoption is granted to a stepparent, another grandparent, or a blood relative.

MONTANA: A court may award visitation rights if the court finds that visitation is in the child's best interest. Adoption cuts off the visitation rights of grandparents unless adoption is granted to a stepparent or another grandparent.

NEBRASKA: A court may award visitation rights if at least one parent is deceased, the parents' marriage has been dissolved or a petition for **dissolution** has been filed, or the child is born out of wedlock and paternity has been established. Grandparents must demonstrate that a beneficial relationship exists between themselves and the grandchild and that visitation is in the child's best interest. Visitation cannot interfere with the parent-child relationship. Adoption cuts off all visitation rights of grandparents.

NEVADA: A court may award visitation rights if the child's parents are deceased, the child's parents are divorced or separated, or one of the child's parents have had his or her parental rights terminated. The child's parent or parents must have unreasonably restricted visitation between the grandparent and grandchild before a court may award visitation to a grandparent. If a child's parent or parents has denied or unreasonably restricted access to a grandparent, a court will presume that visitation is not in the child's best interest. Adoption cuts off all rights of grandparents unless grandparents request visitation before the termination of the parental rights of the child's parent or parents.

NEW HAMPSHIRE: A court may award visitation rights if the child's parents are divorced or have filed for divorce, one of the parents is deceased, one of the parents has had his or her parental rights terminated, or the child has been born out of wedlock, if the child has been legitimated. Adoption cuts off all rights of grandparents.

NEW JERSEY: A court may grant visitation rights if visitation is in the child's best interest. Adoption cuts off the rights of grandparents, unless adoption is granted to a stepparent.

NEW MEXICO: A court may grant visitation rights if the child's parents are divorced, separated, or deceased. Visitation rights may also be granted if the child is over six years old, lived with the grandparent for more than six months, and was subsequently removed from the grandparent's home (if the child is under six, the residence requirement is reduced to three months). Adoption cuts off the rights of grandparents unless adoption is granted to a stepparent, a relative of the child, a caretaker designated in a deceased parent's will, or a person who sponsored the child at a baptism or confirmation.

NEW YORK: The custody statute does not provide statutory factors for determining the best interest of the child. A court may grant visitation rights if at least one of the child's parents is deceased or if the court finds that equity demands intervention based on the circumstances of the case. Adoption does not automatically cut off the visitation rights of grandparents.

NORTH CAROLINA: The custody statute does not provide statutory factors for determining the best interest of the child. A court may grant visitation rights as part of an order determining custody of the child. Adoption cuts off the visitation rights of grandparents unless adoption is granted to a stepparent or a relative of the child, where the grandparent proves that a substantial relationship exists between the grandparent and grandchild.

NORTH DAKOTA: A court must grant visitation rights unless the court determines that visitation would not be in the child's best interest. The amount of contact between the child, the grandparent, and the parent are factors to be considered when determining the child's best interest. Adoption cuts off the rights of grandparents, unless visitation was granted prior to the adoption.

OHIO: A court may grant visitation rights if the child's parents are deceased, divorced, separated, were parties to a suit for annulment or child support, or were never married to one another. Grandparents must show they have an interest in the child's welfare. Adoption cuts off the visitation rights of grandparents unless adoption is granted to a stepparent.

OKLAHOMA: A court may grant visitation rights if visitation is in the child's best interest. The statute provides special rules when the child is born out of wedlock. Adoption cuts off the visitation rights of grandparents unless the grandparents can show a previous relationship existed between them and the grandchild, and visitation is in the child's best interest.

OREGON: Determination of grandparent visitation rights include consideration of the relationship between the grandparent and grandchild, as well as the relationship between the parent and child. Adoption cuts off all visitation rights of grandparents.

PENNSYLVANIA: A court may grant visitation if at least one of the child's parents is deceased, the parents are divorced or separated for more than six months, or the child has lived with the grandparent for more than 12 months. Determination of grandparent visitation must include consideration of the best interest of the child, potential interference with the parent-child relationship, and the contact between the grandparent and grandchild. Adoption cuts off visitation rights of grandparents unless adoption is granted to a stepparent or grandparent.

RHODE ISLAND: The custody statute does not provide statutory factors for determining the best interest of the child. Determination of grandparent visitation must include consideration of the relationship of the grandparent and grandchild, including the best interest of the child. Courts may also grant visitation if the child's parents are divorced or the parent who is the child of the grandparent is deceased. Adoption cuts off all visitation rights.

SOUTH CAROLINA: A court may grant visitation if one parent is deceased, or the parents are divorced or separated. The court must consider the relationship between the grandparent and the child, as well as the parent and the child. Adoption cuts off all visitation rights of grandparents.

SOUTH DAKOTA: The custody statute does not provide statutory factors for a court to determine proper custody. A court may grant visitation if one parent is deceased, or the parents are divorced or separated. Adoption cuts off the visitation rights of grandparents unless adoption is granted to a stepparent or grandparent of the child.

TENNESSEE: Tennessee courts held that the previous version of the grandparent visitation statute was unconstitutional. The Tennessee Legislature amended the statute to comport with the state constitution. Under the revised statute, a court may grant visitation rights to a grandparent only in one of the following situations: (1) the mother or father of the child is deceased; (2) the child's parents are divorced or were never married to one another; (3) the child's mother or father has been missing for the preceding six months; (4) a court in another state has ordered grandparent visitation; (5) the child previously lived with the grandparent for 12 months or more; (6) the child and grandparent(s) maintained a significant relationship for 12 months. If one of these events occurs, the court may award visitation right if the child is in danger of substantial harm should the court deny visitation and visitation is in the best interests of the child.

TEXAS: The custody statute does not provide statutory factors for a court to determine proper custody. Conditions for grandparent visitation rights include a determination that one of the child's parents is deceased, incompetent, incarcerated, or has had his or her parental rights terminated. Visitation may also be awarded if the parents are divorced, the child has been abused or neglected, the child has been adjudicated a delinquent or in need of supervision, or the child has lived with the grandparent for at least six months within 24 months of the filing of the petition for visitation. Adoption cuts off the visitation rights of the grandparent unless the adoption is granted to a stepparent.

UTAH: Conditions for grandparent visitation rights include whether a parent is deceased, or whether the parents are divorced or separated. Adoption cuts off all visitation rights of grandparents.

VERMONT: Conditions for grandparent visitation rights include consideration of whether a parent is deceased, incompetent, or whether the child has been abandoned. Adoption cuts off all visitation rights of grandparents unless the adoption is granted to a stepparent or a relative of the child.

VIRGINIA: Determination of grandparent visitation is made during a suit for dissolution of the marriage of the child's parents. Adoption cuts off all visitation rights of grandparents.

WASHINGTON: The United States Supreme Court case of Troxel v. Granville ruled the Washington grandparent visitation statute was unconstitutional. Although the Washington legislature subsequently amended the statute, the Washington Supreme Court in 2005 struck don

WEST VIRGINIA: The custody statute does not provide statutory factors for a court to determine proper custody. Conditions for grandparent visitation rights include consideration of whether a parent is deceased, the child has resided with the grandparent and subsequently was removed by a parent, or the grandparent in several circumstances has been denied visitation by a parent. Adoption cuts off all visitation rights of grandparents.

WISCONSIN: Conditions for grandparent visitation rights include consideration of the relationship between the grandparent and grandchild. Visitation may also be permitted if one of the child's parents is deceased. Adoption cuts off the visitation rights of grandparents unless adoption is granted to a stepparent.

WYOMING: The custody statute does not provide statutory factors for a court to determine proper custody. Conditions for grandparent visitation rights include consideration of the child's best interest and the impairment of the rights of the parents.

## Additional Resources

*Grandparents: An Annotated Bibliography on Roles, Rights, and Relationships.* Carol Ann Strauss, Scarecrow Press, 1996.

*Grandparents' Rights, 3rd Edition.* Tracy Truly, Sourcebooks, Inc. 2001.

*Grandparents' Visitation Rights: A Legal Research Guide.* M. Kristine Taylor Warren, W. S. Hein, 2001.

*Uniform Child Custody Jurisdiction and Enforcement Act.* National Conference of Commissioners on Uniform State Laws, 1997. Available at http://www.law.upenn.edu/bll/ulc/uccjea/chldcus2.htm.

*U. S. Code, Title 28: Judiciary and Judicial Procedure, Part V: Procedure, Chapter 115: Evidence; Documen-*

*tary.* U. S. House of Representatives, 2000. Available at http://uscode.house.gov/title_28.htm.

## Organizations

### *American Association of Retired Persons (AARP)*

601 E. St., NW
Washington, DC 20049 USA
Toll-Free: 800-424-3410
URL: http://www.aarp.org
Primary Contact:

### *Association for Conflict Resolution (ACR)*

1527 New Hampshire Avenue NW
Washington, DC 20036 USA
Phone: (202) 667-9700
Fax: (202) 265-1968
URL: http://acresolution.org
Primary Contact:

### *Grandparent Rights Organization (GRO*

100 West Long Lake Rd., Ste. 250
Bloomfield Hills, MI 48304 USA
Phone: (248) 646-7177
Fax: (248) 646-9722
URL: http://www.grandparentsrights.org

# FAMILY LAW

## GUARDIANSHIP

*Sections within this essay:*

- Background
- Guardianship of Minors
- Testamentary Guardianship
- Temporary Guardianship
- Guardianship of Persons who are Mentally or Physically Incapacitated
- Removal of Guardian
- Examination of Certain State Provisions on Guardianship
- Additional Resources

## Background

A **guardian** is someone who is chosen, either by a court or by being named in a will, to make decisions for someone else when that person—generally referred to as the ward—cannot do the same for him or herself. These types of decisions include: giving consent to medical care or treatment; purchasing or arranging for purchase of such necessities as food, clothes, cars, household items, and other personal items; arranging for education; and managing finances and bank accounts.

A guardianship requires that someone act on behalf of and protect the ward during the period of time when the ward is incapable of doing so. When asking the court appoints a guardian in a particular situation, the court must be sure that the potential ward is incapacitated and cannot make decisions for

him or herself because of a mental or physical **disability**, disease, or addiction to alcohol or other drugs. The fact that potential wards are minors who lack someone to make certain decisions on their behalf until they reach the **age of majority** is also sufficient reason to ask the court to appoint a guardian.

The selection of a guardian is an extremely important task. Certain people, with ties to the ward, are preferred by courts as possible guardians. These include the person designated by the ward, before the period of incapacity occurred, by legal document or otherwise to handle his or her affairs; the spouse; parents; or another relative; or a state employee or private person familiar with the ward and the incapacity at issue. Whoever is chosen by the court must be willing and able to perform the duties at hand and to represent the best interests of the ward. In selecting the guardian, the court considers the prospective guardian's character, history, physical capacity, and other relevant attributes. A potential guardian's limited education or financial resources are not disqualifying conditions in and of themselves.

The guardianship statutes of each state detail the specific duties, responsibilities, and powers of the guardian. They should be examined in order to determine the regulations that apply to each situation.

## Guardianship of Minors

The guardianship of a minor can be over the actual minor (or what is commonly referred to as the minor's person), the property (or estate) of the minor, or both. Preferred guardians for a minor are parents and then other relatives. However, the primary consideration in selecting a guardian is the best interests of the minor. If the parents are still alive, before a nonparent is chosen as a guardian, the parents must be determined to be unable or unfit to look after the best interests of the minor. When minors are removed from the care and supervision of their parents, and **adoption** is either not forthcoming or not a viable option, guardianship is considered a reasonable alternative.

Even after a guardian is chosen for a minor, most state statutes allow that at age fourteen (or other reasonable age), the minor may select or at least voice a preference, concerning who will be selected to serve a guardian.

The guardian of a minor looks after the direct physical well-being of the minor and the assets of the minor's estate. A guardian is also necessary to provide a **legal residence** in order for the ward to attend a public school; to apply for public assistance benefits for a minor if needed; to apply for public housing on behalf of a minor where necessary; and to bring a lawsuit on behalf of the minor. The guardian also receives and maintains any money due the minor for his or her care or support. The guardian is required to maintain, account for, and preserve any excess funds beyond what is necessary to support the minor. The guardian has a duty to look after the minor's **personal property** and assure the proper education of the ward. The guardian is also required to authorize any necessary medical or other care for the well-being and health of the ward. Generally, the guardian provides whatever care would be given to a child by its parents.

When a guardianship of a minor is instituted because of the age of the ward, the guardianship may be terminated when the minor reaches the age of majority. The guardianship may be reinstated by the court after the ward reaches the age of majority where it can be shown that the ward still requires supervision. Guardianship may be terminated if the ward marries. Guardianship is automatically terminated at the death of the ward. In addition, the guardianship may be terminated, and a new guardian appointed, when it can be shown that the guardian did not adequately perform his or her duties to the ward.

## Testamentary Guardianship

Generally, parents may, in a properly drafted will, appoint or indicate their preference for a guardian for a minor child or an adult child with a disability who requires supervision over his or her person or estate. Courts will then make a determination as to the availability or appropriateness of the parents' selection.

## Temporary Guardianship

Some state statutes provide for temporary or limited guardianships. These guardianships are generally granted by the courts to achieve a specific purpose for a certain amount of time. Once the purpose is accomplished, the guardianship is terminated.

Also, emergency guardianships have been granted. In these situations, an emergency situation exists and someone is needed to give approval in order for the person to receive emergency services. A temporary guardian is appointed by the court to serve during the existence of the emergency situation. Generally, the person being served by the temporary guardian is disabled or incapacitated in some way. The court must determine that the person being served by the guardian is unable to make the emergency decision because of mental disability, addiction, debilitating disease, or some other similar limitation. The court must also determine that if a guardian is not appointed, the person is at risk of serious harm or even death. Finally, the court must determine that there is no other person available who can make the emergency determination for the incapacitated person.

The order for emergency guardianship is generally granted for a short period of time which is sufficient to allow the situation to be handled properly. After the emergency situation has ended or subsided, the temporary guardian must file a report with the court detailing the nature of the services rendered by the guardian and describing the outcome of the situation.

## Guardianship of Persons who are Mentally or Physically Incapacitated or Disabled

State statutes define mental and physical disability. However, generally, such disability or incapacity involves severe and long-term conditions that impose great limitations upon individuals' ability to take care of themselves, express themselves verbally, earn a living, and live independently of the care of others. Such a disability also reflects the necessity for a combination of treatments and services.

Guardianships for physically or mentally disabled or incapacitated persons have, in recent decades, been understood to facilitate the independence and self-reliance of the ward. They are limited as much **as is** reasonable in order to allow wards to exercise as much control over their lives as possible while maintaining as much dignity and self-reliance as possible. The desires of the wards are given primary consideration. Also, wards are allowed to do as much of their own care giving as is physically and mentally possible.

The guardian will be granted only those powers necessary to accomplish for the ward what the ward cannot accomplish independently. These powers may include assuring the availability and maintenance of care for the ward, making sure that educational and medical services are maintained and adequate, and submitting updates to the court of the ward's condition. These court updates describe the ward's living situation, status of mental and physical health based upon medical examinations and official records, provide a list of services being received by the ward, describe services rendered by the guardian, account for the ward's monetary assets, and any other information necessary to submit to the court in order for it to assess the status of the ward and the guardian's duties.

## Removal of Guardian

A guardian may be removed if a court determines that the ward no longer needs the services of the guardian. Also, a guardian may be removed when he or she has not provided adequate care for the ward or when it is determined that the guardian is guilty of neglect. Neglect can include using the ward's money or property for the guardian's own benefit and not obeying court orders. Upon court order, the guardian will be removed and a new guardian (or temporary guardian) will be substituted in place of the original guardian.

## Examination of Certain State Provisions on Guardianship

FLORIDA: The **statute** on guardianships for incapacitated persons requires that the court find the "least restrictive form of guardianship to assist persons who are only partially incapable of caring for their needs." The statute also confirms the legislative intent that incapacitated persons function and live as independently as possible, managing their finances

and developing their potential for self-sufficiency. To that end, they will be encouraged to develop their living skills to the extent that they may, for example, be able to marry, vote, travel, sign contracts, complete their educational objectives, and apply for a driver's license.

MASSACHUSETTS: Regarding the guardian of a minor, the statute states that the court will choose the guardian for any minor under the age of fourteen. A minor over the age of fourteen may suggest his or her own guardian and the court will try to honor that request. If the court does not find the guardian desired by the minor to be appropriate, then the court will appoint another guardian. Regarding the care of a mentally ill person by a guardian, the statute declares that a guardian will not have the authority to commit the ward to a mental institution or agree to the administering of "antipsychotic medication" unless the court first finds that such an action is in the "best interests" of the ward and then authorizes such a commitment or treatment. Regarding testamentary guardians, the statute allows parents to appoint such a guardian on behalf of a minor child, even if the child is not born at the time the testamentary instrument is drafted. Such a testamentary guardian will have the same powers and duties as one appointed by the court.

NEW HAMPSHIRE: Regarding the duties of a guardian for a minor, the guardian will "protect and preserve" the personal and real property assets of the minor and any income the comes from rents, income, or the sale of such property. The guardian is also given the authority, with the courts approval, to open a trust to which the minor's assets can be transferred. This trust would end no later than the ward's twenty-fifth birthday.

SOUTH CAROLINA: Regarding persons with disabilities, the spouse (if the incapacitated person is married) or parents of an incapacitated person may make a testamentary appointment of a guardian for the incapacitated person in their will. Such an appointment by a spouse or parent becomes effective if, after the incapacitated person and the person giving him or her care or the "nearest adult relative" has received twenty days written notice and "the guardian files acceptance of appointment in the court." When both a spouse and a parent appoint guardians in their wills, the appointment of the spouse has priority.

## Additional Resources

*Corpus Juris Secundum* Volume 39, West Publishing, 1976.

*Guardianship Manual* (Chapter Five) The Maryland Institute for Continuing Professional Education of Lawyers, Inc., 1999.

*Michigan Guardianship and Conservatorship Handbook* Institute of Continuing Legal Education, 2000.

*"Permanency Outcomes in Legal Guardianships of Abused/Neglected Children."* Henry, Jim "Families in Society: The Journal of Contemporary Human Services" 80 (1999): 561.

*Representing the Child Client.* New York: Lexis Publishing, 2001.

## Organizations

### California Coalition for Youth (CCY)
1220 H Street, Ste, 103
Sacramento, CA 95814 USA
Phone: (916) 340-0505
URL: http://www.ccyfc.org/
Primary Contact: Cheryl Zando, Board Chair (Youth)

### Citizens for Better Care (CBC)
4750 Woodward Aveneu, Ste,. 410
Detroit, MI 48201 USA
Phone: (800) 833-9548
Fax: (313) 832-7407
URL: http://www.cbcmi.org
Primary Contact: Nida Donar, Executive Director

### National Guardianship Association (NGA)
1604 North Country Club Road
Tucson, AZ 85716 USA
Phone: (520) 881-6561
Fax: (520) 325-7925
URL: http://www.guardianship.org/
Primary Contact: Terry W. Hammond, Board Member

# FAMILY LAW

## MARRIAGE/MARRIAGE AGE

*Sections within this essay:*

- Background
- Consent
- Age
- Capacity
- Marriage Between Close Relatives
- Common Law Marriage
- Interracial Marriage
- Polygamy
- Same Sex/Gay Marriage
- Change of Last Name
- State by State Summary (age of consent, etc.)
- Additional Resources

## Background

Marriage has generally been defined as a contract between a man and a woman who have consented to become husband and wife. More specifically, the U.S. Congress, in the Defense of Marriage Act (DOMA), **Public Law** 104-199, passed in 1996, defines marriage as "a legal union between one man and one woman as husband and wife." The status of DOMA has been challenged by proponents of same-sex marriage, who believe among other things that only legal marriage can guarantee full spousal rights such as inheritance, health care decisions, and parental rights. In 2004, Massachusetts passed legisla-

tion recognizing same-sex marriage; several states have varying degrees of spousal rights for same-sex couples.

Marriage requirements are defined by the laws of each state. Yet, there are certain aspects of a valid marriage that are required of any couple desiring to become husband and wife. These additional considerations include the capacity of the parties to enter into the marriage, the consent of the parties, and the age of each person. Regarding age, if individuals are minors, they must obtain the consent of either one or both of their parents, depending upon the laws of the state.

The fact that the states can regulate marriage has given rise to laws that control other aspects of the ability of a couple to wed including the race of the each party in the couple, the sex of each party, and whether either party is already married. Although the states have the authority to regulate the institution of marriage and establish the laws that do so, some laws, such as those forbidding people of different races to marry, have been struck down by the Supreme Court of the United States as unconstitutional. The Congress of the United States has also enacted limitations to the marital union, the most recent being the enactment of DOMA, which not only defines marriage but also gives individual states the right not to recognize "a relationship between persons of the same sex that is treated as a marriage under the laws of such other State." In other words, such laws from one state do not have to be recognized by another state.

Because the laws regarding marriage vary considerably from state to state, couples desiring more specific information should contact their state government.

## Consent

Before a marital union is recognized by a state, there must, foremost, be consent—or agreement—between the parties of the union to be married. For consent to exist, both parties must agree to the marriage and there must be no mistake as to the nature of the union. In addition, no force must be used upon either party to enter into the union. Once consent is determined to exist, the laws of the individual states determine the status of the couple as husband and wife.

## Age

Age is an additional aspect of consent to marry. All states prescribe the age which must be reached by both parties to the marriage for the couple to be able to legally agree to become husband and wife without parental permission. For all but two states this "age of consent" is eighteen (in Mississippi the age is twenty-one and in Nebraska the age is nineteen).

The states vary in determining the minimum age at which a couple can marry with parental consent. However, for the majority of states, this age is sixteen though in a very few states, this age is as low as fourteen.

## Capacity

Capacity generally refers to the mental ability of one or both of the parties to the marriage to agree to become husband and wife. Both parties must be of "sound" mind and capable of agreeing to the marriage. Not all forms of mental illness and insanity serve to render someone incapable of entering into a marriage. A common test of capacity is the ability of individuals to understand the nature of marriage and what their responsibilities are to their partners once they enter into the union. Physical incapacity, and in particular the physical inability to have sexual intercourse, does not in and of itself render one incapable of marrying and does not on its face void a marriage that has already occurred.

## Between Close Relatives

The laws of each state strictly regulate the marriage between relatives (also known as consanguini-

ty). According to the "rules of consanguinity," no state allows marriage to a child, grandchild, parent, grandparent, uncle, aunt, niece, or nephew. However, for all other familial relationships, the states vary widely and the particular laws of the state of marriage must be consulted.

## Common Law Marriage

Though laws regarding marriage are well regulated by the states, at one point, most state laws allowed for the institution of **common law** marriage. Common law marriages were based not just on the desire of the couple to live together or by their actually living or having lived together. For a common law marriage to achieve validity as a marriage, the couple must have lived together for a certain amount of time, had sexual relations, and represented themselves as husband and wife in all affairs and to all people. Though no marriage ceremony had taken place, their children are viewed as legitimate and surviving families are entitled to state sanctioned **inheritance**.

Currently, the majority of states do not recognize common law marriage. Three states that do not recognize common law marriages (Georgia, Idaho, and Indiana) recognize unions that were entered into before certain dates (for Georgia and Idaho the year is 1997, for Indiana the year is 1958).

## Interracial Marriage

There are no prohibitions to interracial unions in the United States. At one time, many states had enacted statutes forbidding marriages between people of different races. Such a mixed-race union is also known as "miscegenation." These antimiscegenation statutes were found across the United States and particularly in Southern states. Though most states had repealed such laws by the time of the case of *Loving v. Virginia*, in 1967 the U. S. Supreme Court, in deciding that case, decreed all such laws to be unconstitutional because they violated the **Equal Protection** Clause of the U. S. Constitution.

## Polygamy

**Polygamy** occurs when a spouse is married to more than one person at the same time. Polygamous marriages have been illegal in the United States since 1878 when the U. S. Supreme Court ruled that one of the basic tenets of Western civilization was the marriage of one man to one woman. Therefore, anyone who marries for the second time without ending a first marriage could be charged with polygamy.

## Same Sex/Gay Marriage

Traditionally in the United States, the marital union has been confined to a relationship between a man and a woman. That notion has been challenged in several states, culminating in Massachusetts becoming the first state to allow same-sex marriage. In response to these and other challenges, at least twenty-five states have passed marriage laws prohibiting same sex marriages. In almost as many states, bills prohibiting same sex/gay marriage have been defeated. In 1996, the Congress of the United States passed the Defense of Marriage Act (DOMA). This act defines the word marriage as a "legal union between one man and one woman as husband and wife." In addition, in response to the possibility that some states would recognize a same sex relationship as a marriage while others would not, DOMA determines that other states do not have to "give effect to" or recognize "a right or claim arising from" such unions which may be legal in other states.

On July 1, 2000, the state of Vermont enacted a law, the first in the country, permitting same sex couples to be parties to a "civil union." These unions, though not technically marriages, give same sex couples all the "benefits, protections, and responsibilities under Vermont law . . . as are granted to spouses in a marriage." This law also allows parties who reside outside Vermont to enter the state to achieve a civil union. However, in accordance with DOMA, other states are not required to recognize these unions.

Vermont spurred activists in other states to champion not just civil unions but same-sex marriage, in defiance of DOMA. In 2003 and 2004, several municipalities including San Francisco, Sandoval County (New Mexico), Muntnomah County (Oregon), and New Paltz, New York, issued marriage licences to same-sex couples. State courts later nullified many of these marriages, but on May 17, 2004, Massachusetts became the first state in the nation to grant same-sex marriage licenses statewide. In 2005, Connecticut became the second state to recognize civil unions. Other states that passed legislation to offer some spousal rights (such as the right to inherit property from each other in the absence of a will) include California, Hawaii, Maine, and New Jersey. The District

of Columbia also has domestic partnership legislation. Proponents of same-sex marriage have argued that only legal marriage can ensure full spousal rights (including federal rights such as the survivor's right to Social Security benefits).

## Change of Last Name

A woman is not legally required to change her last name to that of her husband upon her marriage.

## State by State Summary (age of consent, etc.)

The following is a state by state summary of the "age of consent" for marriage and other pertinent marriage information for the fifty states, the District of Columbia, and Puerto Rico

ALABAMA: The **age of consent** is eighteen. With parental consent, parties can marry at age fourteen. However, this parental consent is not required if the minor has already been married. (Other **statutory** laws apply.) Common law marriage is recognized.

ALASKA: The age of consent is eighteen. With parental consent, parties can marry at the age sixteen. Parties can marry at a younger age, also with parental consent. Common law marriage is not recognized.

ARIZONA: The age of consent is eighteen. With parental consent, parties can marry at the age of sixteen. Parties can marry at a younger age, but with both parental and judicial consent.

ARKANSAS: The age of consent is eighteen. With parental consent, males can marry at the age of seventeen and under the age of seventeen can marry with parental consent and can receive a license by reason of pregnancy or the birth of a child. With parental consent, females can marry at age sixteen and under the age of sixteen can marry with parental consent and can receive a license by reason of pregnancy or the birth of a child.

CALIFORNIA: The age of consent is eighteen. With parental consent, there are no age limits regarding the minimum age for a couple to marry. (Other statutory laws apply.) California offers some spousal rights for registered same-sex domestic partners.

COLORADO: The age of consent is eighteen. Parties can marry at a younger age, also with parental consent. Common law marriage is recognized.

CONNECTICUT: The age of consent is eighteen. With parental consent, parties can marry at the age of sixteen. Parties can marry at a younger age, but with both parental and judicial consent. Like Vermont (see below), Connecticut permits same sex couples to be parties to a "civil union."

DELAWARE: The age of consent is eighteen. Males can marry under the age of eighteen with parental consent and under the age of seventeen can receive a license by reason of pregnancy or the birth of a child. With parental consent, females can marry at age sixteen and under the age of sixteen can apply for and receive a license by reason of pregnancy or the birth of a child. Common law marriage is not recognized.

FLORIDA: The age of consent is eighteen. With parental consent, parties can marry at age sixteen and parties under the age of sixteen can receive a license by reason of pregnancy or the birth of a child. However, this parental consent is not required if the minor has already been married. Common law marriage is not recognized.

GEORGIA: The age of consent is eighteen. With parental consent and/or the consent of a judge, parties can marry at age sixteen and under the age of sixteen can apply for and receive a license by reason of pregnancy or the birth of a child. Common law marriages are not recognized except for those that were entered into before 1997.

HAWAII: The age of consent is eighteen. With parental consent and/or the consent of a judge, parties can marry at age fifteen. Hawaii offers some spousal rights for registered same-sex domestic partners. Common law marriage is not recognized.

IDAHO: The age of consent is eighteen. With parental consent, parties can marry at age sixteen. Common law marriages are not recognized except for those that were entered into before 1997.

ILLINOIS: The age of consent is eighteen. With parental consent, parties can marry at age sixteen. If parents refuse to consent, judicial consent may be obtained on behalf of the parties. Common law marriage is not recognized.

INDIANA: The age of consent is eighteen. With parental consent, parties can marry at age seventeen and under the age of seventeen can receive a license by reason of pregnancy or the birth of a child. Common law marriages are not recognized except for those that were entered into before 1958.

IOWA: The age of consent is eighteen. With parental consent and/or the consent of a judge, parties

can marry at age sixteen. Common law marriage is recognized.

KANSAS: The age of consent is eighteen. With parental consent and/or the consent of a judge, males can marry at age fourteen and females at age twelve. Common law marriage is recognized.

KENTUCKY: The age of consent is eighteen. With parental consent and/or the consent of a judge, parties can marry under eighteen years of age. Common law marriage is not recognized.

LOUISIANA: The age of consent is eighteen. Parties under eighteen years of age can marry with parental consent. Common law marriage is not recognized.

MAINE: The age of consent is eighteen. With parental consent, parties can marry at age sixteen. With parental consent, parties can marry at age sixteen. Maine offers some spousal rights to registered same-sex domestic partners. Common law marriage is not recognized.

MARYLAND: The age of consent is eighteen. With parental consent, parties can marry at age sixteen and younger parties may receive a license by reason of pregnancy or the birth of a child. Parties giving consent must appear in person to give consent and provide proof of age if the parties seeking marriage are at least sixteen years old. Also, if one of the parents giving consent is ill both an **affidavit** by the ill parent and from a physician is required to submit. Common law marriage is recognized.

MASSACHUSETTS: The age of consent is eighteen. With parental consent and/or the consent of a judge, males can marry at fourteen years of age and females can marry at the age of twelve. On May 17, 2004, Massachusetts became the first state to recognize same-sex marriage. Common law marriage is not recognized.

MICHIGAN: The age of consent is eighteen. With parental consent, parties can marry at age sixteen. Common law marriage is not recognized.

MINNESOTA: The age of consent is eighteen. With parental consent and/or the consent of the judge, parties can marry at age sixteen. Common law marriage is not recognized.

MISSISSIPPI: The age of consent is twenty-one. With parental consent and/or the consent of the judge, males can marry at age seventeen and females can marry at age fifteen. Common law marriage is not recognized.

MISSOURI: The age of consent is eighteen. With parental consent, parties can marry at age fifteen and younger parties may receive a license by reason of special circumstances. Common law marriage is not recognized.

MONTANA: The age of consent is eighteen. With parental consent and/or consent of a judge, parties can marry at age sixteen and younger parties may receive a license by reason of special circumstances. Common law marriage is recognized.

NEBRASKA: The age of consent is nineteen. With parental consent, parties can marry at age seventeen. Common law marriage is not recognized.

NEVADA: The age of consent is eighteen. With parental consent, parties can marry at age sixteen and younger. Common law marriage is not recognized.

NEW HAMPSHIRE: The age of consent is eighteen. With parental consent and the consent of the judge, males can marry at age fourteen and females can marry at age thirteen. Common law marriage is not recognized.

NEW JERSEY: The age of consent is eighteen. With parental consent, parties can marry at age sixteen or younger. Also, younger parties may receive a license by reason of pregnancy or the birth of a child or other special circumstances. New Jersey offers some spousal rights to registered same-sex domestic partners. Common law marriage is not recognized.

NEW MEXICO: The age of consent is eighteen. With parental consent, parties can marry at age sixteen and younger parties may receive a license by reason of pregnancy or the birth of a child or other special circumstances. Common law marriage is not recognized.

NEW YORK: The age of consent is eighteen. With parental and judicial consent, parties can marry at age sixteen. Common law marriage is not recognized.

NORTH CAROLINA: The age of consent is eighteen. With parental consent, parties can marry at age sixteen and younger parties may receive a license by reason of pregnancy or the birth of a child. Common law marriage is not recognized.

NORTH DAKOTA: The age of consent is eighteen. With parental consent, parties can marry at age sixteen. Common law marriage is not recognized.

OHIO: The age of consent is eighteen. With parental consent, males under the age of 18 can marry and females at age sixteen can marry and younger parties may receive a license by reason of pregnancy or the birth of a child. Common law marriage is not recognized.

OKLAHOMA: The age of consent is eighteen. With parental consent, parties can marry at age sixteen (and younger) and, in addition, younger parties may receive a license by reason of pregnancy or the birth of a child. Common law marriage is recognized.

OREGON: The age of consent is eighteen. With parental consent, parties can marry at age seventeen with the exception that if one party does not have a parent who resides in the state and one party has been a resident in Oregon for at least six months, then no permission is necessary. Common law marriage is not recognized.

PENNSYLVANIA: The age of consent is eighteen. With parental consent, parties can marry at age sixteen and younger parties may receive a license by reason of special circumstances. Common law marriage is recognized.

RHODE ISLAND: The age of consent is eighteen. With parental consent, males can marry under age eighteen and females at sixteen and younger parties may receive a license under special circumstances. Common law marriage is recognized.

SOUTH CAROLINA: The age of consent is eighteen. With parental consent, males can marry at age sixteen and females at age fourteen and younger parties may receive a license by reason of pregnancy or the birth of a child. Common law marriage is recognized.

SOUTH DAKOTA: The age of consent is eighteen. With parental consent, parties can marry at age sixteen and younger parties may receive a license by reason of pregnancy or the birth of a child. Common law marriage is not recognized.

TENNESSEE: The age of consent is eighteen. With parental consent, parties can marry at age sixteen. Under special circumstances, younger minors can receive a license to marry. Common law marriage is not recognized.

TEXAS: The age of consent is eighteen. With parental and judicial consent, parties can marry but not below the age of fourteen for males and thirteen for females. Common law marriage is recognized.

UTAH: The age of consent is eighteen. With parental consent, parties can marry at age fourteen.

However, this parental consent is not required if the minor has already been married. In addition, each county is authorized to provide premarital counseling before issuing a marriage license to applicants under the age of eighteen and those who are divorced. Common law marriage is recognized.

VERMONT: The age of consent is eighteen. With parental or judicial consent, parties can marry at age sixteen. Common law marriage is not recognized. In addition, a Vermont law, the first in the country, permits same-sex couples to be parties to a "civil union."

VIRGINIA: The age of consent is eighteen. With parental consent, parties can marry at age sixteen and under the age of sixteen may receive a license by reason of pregnancy or the birth of a child. Common law marriage is not recognized.

WASHINGTON: The age of consent is eighteen. With parental consent, parties can marry at age seventeen and at a younger age under special circumstances. Common law marriage is not recognized.

WEST VIRGINIA: The age of consent is eighteen. With parental consent, parties under the age of eighteen may receive a license at a younger age by reason of pregnancy or the birth of a child. Common law marriage is not recognized.

WISCONSIN: The age of consent is eighteen. With parental consent, parties can marry at age sixteen. Common law marriage is not recognized.

WYOMING: The age of consent is eighteen. With parental consent, parties can marry at age sixteen. They may obtain a license and marry at a younger age under special circumstances. Common law marriage is not recognized.

DISTRICT OF COLUMBIA: The age of consent is eighteen. With parental consent, parties can marry at age sixteen. However, this parental consent is not required if the minor has already been married. The District of Columbia offers some rights to registered same-sex domestic partners. Common law marriage is recognized.

PUERTO RICO: The age of consent is twenty-one for males. The age of consent is also twenty-one for females who may apply for and receive a license at a younger age by reason of pregnancy or the birth of a child. Male applicants eighteen years of age and female applicants sixteen years of age may marry with parental consent. Younger males and females can marry with parental consent and receive a license by reason of pregnancy, the birth of a child, or other special circumstances. Common law marriage is not recognized.

## Additional Resources

*The American Bar Association Guide to Family Law.* Times Books, 1996.

*Corpus Juris Secundum.* Volume 55, West Publishing Co., 1948.

*The Defense of Marriage Act. 28 U. S. Code 1738C.* One Hundred Fourth Congress of the United States of America, 1996. Available at http://www.indiana.edu/~glbtpol/dome.html.

*http://ameasite.org/loving.asp.* Association of MultiEthnic Americans, Inc. (Loving Decision) 2002.

*http://www.aclu.org/issues/gay/gaymar.html.* "Statewide Anti-Gay Marriage Laws," American Civil Liberties Union, 1998.

*http://www.law.cornell.edu/topics/Table_Marriage.htm.* "Marriage Laws of the Fifty States, District of Columbia, and Puerto Rico," Legal Information Institute, 1999.

*http://www.sec.state.vt.us/pubs/civilunions.htm#faq1.* "The Vermont Guide to Civil Unions," Office of the Secretary of State, 2002.

*West's Encyclopedia of American Law.* West Group, 1998.

## Organizations

### Family Life
P O Box 7111
Little Rock, AR 72223 USA
Phone: (800) 358-6329
URL: http://www.familylife.com/
Primary Contact: Dennis Rainey, President

### Human Rights Campaign
1640 Rhode Island Avenue NW
Washington, DC 20036-3278 USA
Phone: (202) 628-4160
Phone: (800) 777-4723
Fax: (202) 347-5323
URL: http://www.hrc.org/
Primary Contact: Joe Solmonese, President

### Institute for Equality in Marriage
250 West 57th Street, Suite 2404
New York, NY 10107 USA
Phone: (212) 489-5590
Fax: (212) 489-5332
URL: http://www.equalityinmarriage.org

Primary Contact: Ellen Sabin, Executive Director

### Marriage Ministries International (MMI)
8565 South Poplar Way
Highlands Ranch, CO 80130 USA
Phone: (303) 933-3331
Fax: (303) 933-2153
URL: http://www.marriage.org
Primary Contact: Mike and Marilyn Phillipps,
Founding Directors

### Marriage Savers
9311 Harrington Drive
Potomac, MD 20854 USA
Phone: (301) 469-5873
URL: http://www.marriagesavers.org
Primary Contact: Mike and Harriet McManus,
Founders and Co-Chairs

### The National Marriage Project
54 Joyce Kilmer Ave., Lucy Stone Hall, B217
Piscataway, NJ 08854 USA
Phone: (732) 445-7922
Fax: (732) 445-6110
E-Mail: marriage@rci.rutgers.edu
URL: http://marriage.rutgers.edu
Primary Contact: David Popenoe, Ph.D., and
Barbara Dafoe Whitehead, Ph.D., Co-Directors

# FAMILY LAW

## PARENT LIABILITY CHILD'S ACT

*Sections within this essay:*

## Background

Parental liability is the term used to refer to a parent's obligation to pay for damage done by negligent, intentional, or criminal acts of that parent's child. In most states, parents are responsible for all malicious or willful property damage done by their children. Parental liability usually ends when the child reaches the **age of majority** and does not begin until the child reaches an age of between eight and ten. Laws vary from state to state regarding the monetary thresholds on damages collected, the age limit of the child, and the inclusion of **personal injury** in the tort claim. Hawaii enacted, more than a century before statehood, such legislation in 1846, and its law remains one of the most broadly applied in that it does not limit the financial bounds of recovery and imposes liability for both negligent and intentional torts by underage persons. Laws making parents criminally responsible for the delinquent acts of their children followed civil liability statutes. In 1903, Colorado became the first state to establish the crime of contributing to the delinquency of a minor. Today, most states have laws relating to parental liability in various applications. Children's offenses can be civil and/or criminal in nature. Civil cases are lawsuits for money damages. The government brings criminal cases for violations of criminal law. Many acts can trigger both civil and criminal legal repercussions.

## Minors

A minor is a person under the age of majority. The age of majority is the age at which a minor, in the eyes of the law, becomes an adult. This age is 18 in most states. In a few other states, the age of majority is 19 or 21. A minor is considered to be a resident of the same state as the minor's custodial parent or **guardian**.

## Civil Responsibility

Each state has its own law regarding parents' financial responsibility for the acts of their children. Parents are responsible for their children's harmful actions much the same way that employers are responsible for the harmful actions of their employees. This legal concept is known a vicarious liability. The parent is vicariously liable, despite not being directly responsible for the injury. A number of states hold parents financially responsible for damages caused by their children. Some of these states, however, place limits on the amount of liability. The laws vary from state to state, but many cover such acts as **vandalism** to government or school property; defacement or destruction of the national and state flags, cemetery headstones, public monuments/historical markers; also, property destroyed in hate crimes, based on race or religion, such as ransacking a synagogue. Personal injury in connection with any of these may also be included.

### Teenage Parents

Each year thousands of teenage girls, some as young as 12, enter into the Aid to Families with Dependent Children (AFDC) system because they become pregnant. These girls are eligible to receive welfare benefits for their children because the fathers are almost always noncustodial. Many of the fathers are also teenagers still attending high school and are frequently unable to pay **child support** because of their lack of income. These cases, commonly called "minor-mother" cases, are automatically referred to the state child support enforcement agency by the welfare department. When the agency receives a minor-mother referral, it begins **legal proceedings** against three parties: the father of the minor-mother, the mother of the minor-mother, and the father of the minor-mother's child. Because the parents of minor-mothers are legally responsible to support their daughters until **emancipation**, they must pay child support for their minor-mother daughters. The Welfare Reform Act has enacted important changes for teenage parents and minor-mothers. In order for a minor-mother to be eligible to receive AFDC benefits, she must enroll in high school or a state-approved GED program and live under adult supervision. The Welfare Reform Act has thus eliminated the enticement of physical and financial independence from one's parents. Another significant change implemented by the Welfare Reform Act is that parents of a noncustodial teenage father (the grandparents of the minor-mother's child) are liable to pay child support until their teenage son emancipates, if the minor-mother receives welfare. Prior to enactment of the Welfare Reform Act, grandparents were never liable to pay child support for their grandchildren, and the government could not collect child support from a minor-father until he became employed.

Additionally, the parents of a minor teenage noncustodial parent may face **paternity** action requests for child support from them, rather than the father of the newborn. When a minor child gives birth, that minor child is responsible for her baby, and the minor's parents remain responsible for her. However, if the young person under the age of 18 continues to live at home, the grandparents' income will be "deemed available" to the grandchild to determine eligibility for Temporary Assistance to Needy Families (TANF), and the mother may seek through the court to have the paternal grandparent's income "deemed available" for child support purposes.

An important issue facing the U.S. Supreme Court in its 2005-2006 session was a 2003 New Hampshire state law requiring pregnant minors to advise a parent or legal guardian at least 48 hours in advance of having an abortion. The subject law allowed a single exception if the procedure was necessary to prevent the minor's death. (*Ayotte v. Planned Parenthood*, No. 04-1144)

### Negligent Supervision

A parent is liable for a child's negligent acts if the parent knows or has reason to know that it is necessary to control the child and the parent fails to take reasonable actions to do so. This legal theory is known as negligent supervision. Liability for negligent supervision is not limited to parents. Grandparents, guardians, and others with **custody** and control of a child may also be liable under these circumstances. There is usually no dollar limit on this type of liability. An umbrella or homeowner's insurance policy may offer the adult some protection in a lawsuit.

### Family Car Doctrine

The family car doctrine holds the owner of a family car legally responsible for any damage caused by a family member when driving if the owner knew of and consented to the family member's use of the car. This doctrine is applied by about half of the states. Thus, even if a parent does not have a minor household member listed on the auto insurance policy, under the family car doctrine, the adult remains liable. Most insurance policies have special provisions for members of the household under eighteen. Typically, minor drivers must be included on the policy. The car owner would not be able to invoke the uninsured motorist provision for a minor child driver residing in the insured's household, driving the insured's vehicle.

## Criminal Responsibility

Although some states impose criminal liability on parents of delinquent youth, many more have enacted less stringent types of parental responsibility laws. Kansas, Michigan, and Texas require parents to attend the hearings of children adjudicated delinquent or face **contempt** charges. Legislation in Alabama, Kansas, Kentucky, and West Virginia requires parents to pay the court costs associated with these proceedings. Other states impose financial responsibility on parents for the costs incurred by the state when youth are processed through the juvenile justice system. Florida, Idaho, Indiana, North Carolina, and Virginia require parents to reimburse the state for the costs associated with the care, support, detention, or treatment of their children while under the supervision of state agencies. Idaho, Maryland, Missouri, and Oklahoma require parents to undertake **restitution** payments.

### Child Access Protection Laws

Some states have laws which hold parents liable when children gain access to a firearms. At least nine states hold adults criminally responsible for storing a loaded firearm in such a way as to allow a minor to gain access. Some of these provisions include an enhanced **penalty** if the minor causes injury or death and create exceptions for parental liability when the minor gains access to a weapon by unlawful entry into the home or place of storage or if the firearm is used in **self-defense**. In addition, several states have provisions that create criminal liability when a custodial adult or parent is aware that his or her child possesses a firearm unlawfully and does not take it away. A number of jurisdictions have enacted laws making it a crime to leave a loaded firearm where it is accessible by children. Typically, these laws apply, and parents can be charged, only if the minor gains access to the gun. There are usually exceptions if the firearm is stored in a locked box, secured with a trigger lock, or obtained by a minor through unlawful entry. In most states, the penalty for unlawful access is a **misdemeanor** unless the minor injures someone else, in which case the parent can be charged with a **felony**.

### Computer Hacking and Internet Crimes

Another kind of illegal access by minors is that which involves computer and Internet activities. In 2003, The Recording Industry Association sued 261 persons for downloading protected music onto their personal computers and infringing copyrights. Among the defendants were several surprised parents who had no knowledge of their minor child's downloading activities. In *Thrifty-Tel v. Bezenek,* the California Court of Appeals upheld a verdict against the parents of juvenile computer hackers who ac-

cessed the phone company's network in order to make long-distance calls without cost. And with the appearance of camera cell-phones and computer video cameras in the early 2000s, the opportunity for minors to sell pornographic images of themselves or otherwise engage in illegal Internet activities has increased dramatically. In such matters, federal law (e.g. Section 301 of the Copyright Act) may preempt state laws and provide a more uniform guidance for resolution. However, these examples point to the need for a more comprehensive approach to parental liability across state lines.

### Juvenile Delinquents

In addition to Access Protection Laws, some states hold parents responsible for paying restitution as well as criminal fines where crimes are committed by minors. Once a minor becomes involved in the juvenile justice system, parents may find themselves reimbursing the state for costs associated with their child's prosecution and rehabilitation. Minors who run away from home, exhibit chronic truancy, or refuse to obey their parents are classified by many states as incorrigible. Incorrigible minors are often referred to as status offenders because they would not be in court but for their status as minors. When a minor commits a criminal act that would still be a crime if committed by an adult, most states will classify the minor as a juvenile delinquent.

## Insurance Coverage

Since homeowners insurance includes both property and liability coverage, wrongful acts of children or negligent supervision claims may be covered even if the act took place away from a policyholder's residence. Homeowner's policies typically cover legal liability in the event that anyone suffers an injury while on the insured property, even if the injury was committed by another household member or the result of **negligence** on the part of the policyholder.

## Selected State Laws

ARIZONA: Parents are liable for intentional acts of their children that injure others or damage their property. Parents can be held automatically liable for up to $10,000 in damage. Although not automatic, under some circumstances, this legal responsibility may extend to the full value of the victim's damages.

CALIFORNIA: Parents are responsible if the parent has knowledge of the child's potential for misconduct and fails to take reasonable steps to prevent such misconduct; if the parent has signed the child's driver's license application or the child drives the parent's car with the parent's knowledge and permission; if the child is guilty of willful misconduct; or if the child is given ready access to a firearm.

COLORADO: The governor signed Senate Bill 253 in 2003, which validates certain parental liability waivers, signed for their minor children who engage is various sports or recreational activities.

ILLINOIS: It is illegal for a person to store or leave any loaded firearm in a way that allows a minor to gain access to the firearm without permission from a parent or guardian and use it to injure or kill. A firearm is properly stored if it is secured by a trigger lock, placed in a securely locked box, or placed in some other location that a reasonable person would believe to be secured from a minor.

INDIANA: If the juvenile is adjudicated a delinquent, the parents or custodians of the juvenile may be required to participate in programs of care, treatment, or rehabilitation for the juvenile and will be held financially responsible for any services provided. These costs may include the costs incurred by the County on behalf of the juvenile for attorneys, institutional or foster care placement, detention, inpatient/outpatient treatment, or counseling. It may also include the costs of returning the child from another **jurisdiction** and court costs associated with the juvenile proceedings. If the parent or guardian defaults in reimbursing the county or fails to pay any fee required, the Juvenile Court may find him/her in contempt and may enter judgment for the amount due. A parent is liable to another person for up to $5,000.00 in actual damages arising from harm to person or property caused by a child in their custody and may be fully liable for all actual damages resulting from gang activity.

MASSACHUSETTS: It is unlawful to store or keep any firearm, rifle, or shotgun including, but not limited to, large capacity weapons or machine guns in any place unless such weapon is secured in a locked container or equipped with a tamper-resistant mechanical lock or other safety device, properly engaged so as to render such weapon inoperable by any person other than the owner or other lawfully authorized user. Dealers must conspicuously post at each purchase counter the following warning in bold type not less than one inch in height: "IT IS UNLAWFUL TO STORE OR KEEP A FIREARM, RIFLE, SHOTGUN OR MACHINE GUN IN ANY PLACE UNLESS THAT WEAP-

ON IS EQUIPPED WITH A TAMPER-RESISTANT SAFETY DEVICE OR IS STORED OR KEPT IN A SECURELY LOCKED CONTAINER." Each dealer must provide the warning, in writing, to the purchaser or transferee of any firearm, rifle, shotgun, or machine gun in bold type not less than one-quarter inch in height.

MISSOURI: Parents may be liable in an amount up to $2,000 under the parental liability **statute**. Parents may be liable for greater amounts if the court determines that the child's actions were a result of parental negligence. The child must act purposely before the parent is liable.

NEW YORK: Parents are liable when their children "willfully, maliciously, or unlawfully" damage property. There is a cap of $5,000 per incident. Damages may be mitigated by a limiting financial status of the parents, or by showing diligent supervision.

TEXAS: It is a misdemeanor offense when a child gains access to a firearm because an adult fails to secure a readily dischargeable firearm or left the firearm in a place to which the person knew or should have known that a child could gain access. It also requires firearms dealers to post a sign with this warning: "It is unlawful to store, transport, or abandon an unsecured firearm in a place where children are likely to be and can obtain access to the firearm."

VIRGINIA: It is a misdemeanor to recklessly leave a loaded firearm so as to endanger the **life or limb** of any child under the age of fifteen.

WISCONSIN: The Grandparents Liability Law holds grandparents (parents of minor children) financially responsible for the support of any grandchildren born to their minor teen sons or daughters (under 18).

## Additional Resources

*Jack and Jill, Why They Kill* Shaw, James, Onjinjinkta Publishing, 2000.

*Juvenile Crime* Ojeda, Auriana, Gale Group, 2001.

*Parental Liability - The Basics.* Available at http://consumeraffairs.com/parenting/blaming_mom_and_dad_02.htm. 2000.

Tomaszewsk, Amy L. "From Columbine to Kazaa: Parental Liability in a New World." *University of Illinois Law Review,* 2005, pp.573-600.

## Organizations

### American Bar Association
750 N. Lake Shore Dr.
Chicago, IL 60611 USA
Phone: (312) 988-5603
Fax: (312) 988-6800
URL: htt p://www.abanet.org

### Child Welfare League of America
50 F Street NW, 6th Floor
Washington, DC 20001-2085 USA

Phone: (202) 638-2952
Fax: (202) 638-4004

### Families Worldwide
5278 Pinemont Dr., Suite A-180
Salt Lake City, UT 84123 USA
Phone: (801) 262-6878
Fax: (801) 262-7107

### National Association of Child Advocates
1522 K Street, NW, Suite 600
Washington, DC 20005-1202 USA

# FAMILY LAW

## PATERNITY

*Sections within this essay:*

- Background

- Significance

- Voluntary Paternity Determinations
  - Voluntary Petitions
  - Voluntary Testing

- Formal Paternity Proceedings
  - Legal Standing
  - Complaint for Paternity

- Challenging Paternity

- The Uniform Parentage Act

- State Laws

- Additional Resources

## Background

Consider the early days of courtroom drama: where a resistant father would be wrestled into court and a jury would compare the physical features of the alleged father and the fatherless child in question to render their verdict. In later years, blood grouping tests were performed, but this only served to rule out a certain class of blood types (such as men with type A, B, or O blood types). Cases were often dismissed if witnesses could show that the mother had sexual relations with other men during the same time as the alleged father.

Today, the use of DNA testing for positive identification in paternity litigation has rendered most of the previous legal practice and procedure obsolete.

The alleged father need only submit a painless DNA sample (usually in the form of a saliva swab) to prove or disprove his parentage. DNA matching has replaced the Human Leukocyte Antigen (HLA) Test, which was used to match not only blood type, but also tissue type and other genetic factoring. Experts had asserted that the HLA was at least 98 percent accurate. But presumptive fathers (based upon HLA results) could rebut those presumptions by proving they were out of the state, impotent (in pre-Viagra years), or sterile at the time the child was conceived. Conversely, DNA testing has a more conclusive accuracy (close to 100 percent) that becomes almost impossible to defeat.

## Significance

A child born to a married couple is considered legitimate in the eyes of the law. However, the fact that a person's name appears on a birth certificate is not conclusive proof of paternity. Since there is no requirement that a father sign a birth certificate, a mother may list anyone whom she believes is, or wants to be, the father.

The significance of a paternity determination is multifold. For a father who resists parentage, it means that he will now be held accountable for his share of support and responsibility. For a father who wishes to establish that he is the biological parent, he can do so with relative ease of procedure. Importantly, if the child is born out of wedlock, consent from the biological father is needed before the mother can give the child up for adoption.

For a mother, paternity determinations secure financial support as well as custody and visitation rights. For a child, at stake is the right to shelter and aid, as well as the emotional and psychological relief in knowing whom his or her father is. Paternity also secures the right to inherit, the right to access personal information about the known health risks and profiles of the paternal family, and the right to sue for harm or death of the father, resulting in loss to the child. Likewise, a child for whom parentage has been established may also be eligible to receive workers' compensation benefits resulting from the father's death, or other dependent-based governmental assistance.

## Voluntary Paternity Determinations

The establishment of paternity need not always conjure up images of court battles and adversity. A father may be very willing to support a child, but simply wants to ensure that he is indeed the biological parent. He may want a judicial determination before he commits to making child support payments or playing an emotionally-committed supportive role in the child's life.

Other fathers believe they have been unjustly denied knowledge of, or access to, children they may have fathered. This may occur following a contentious parting of ways between parents, and the mother wants no further involvement or contact with the father, and does not want the father involved in the child's life.

Finally, some men fear that they may not learn until years later (and perhaps at an inopportune time) that they have fathered a child. To ensure against this, men may wish to voluntarily submit to DNA testing and (in limited circumstances) compel women with whom they have had prior sexual contact to undergo a pregnancy test. (Generally, only a man alleging that he is the father of an expected child has legal standing to initiate a paternity action.) This brings closure to the relationship, and men know their future lives will not be unexpectedly jolted by news of having fathered children unknown to them.

### Voluntary Petitions

Most states will permit a father to execute an affidavit acknowledging paternity, which eliminates the need for a court action. The affidavit must also be signed by both mother and father, notarized, and filed with the court. Once a paternity affidavit is filed and signed by a judge (if required by state law), the father cannot later attempt to rescind or void the affi-davit. If the father's name does not already appear on the child's birth certificate, a corrected one will be reissued, showing the names of both parents.

Paternity affidavits are often encouraged to remove the stigma sometimes attaching to children who may grow up believing they were unwanted because a parent denied or avoided parentage. Attendant to a voluntary petition for a paternity determination are other determinations that the court may rule on at the same time, mostly addressing the support, involvement, and active role in a child's life that the father will assume.

### Voluntary Testing

Likewise, voluntary submission of a DNA sample produces the same result as voluntary affidavits, without an adversarial court proceeding. Generally, testing involves a saliva sample, taken from the mouth with a cotton swab. Costs usually range from $200 to $600, and some health or medical insurance companies will cover the cost of the test. Laboratories that may perform such voluntary tests are generally listed in telephone directories under "Genetic Screening."

## Formal Paternity Proceedings

In most states, a paternity action takes the form of a civil lawsuit, and is clearly not a criminal matter. Importantly, in most instances, paternity actions must be filed prior to the alleged father's death, to provide for a fair and just defense. In posthumous actions, the alleged father must have affirmatively done something to acknowledge the child prior to death (e.g., putting his name on the child's birth certificate or identifying himself as the father in some other legal or formal action).

### Standing

Only certain persons or parties have legal **standing** to bring a paternity action:

- the mother of the child

- the mother of an expected child

- a man alleging that he is the biological father of a child

- a man alleging that he is the biological father of an expected child

- the child

- a personal representative of the child

- the mother and father of a child (a voluntary action filed together)

- the mother and father of an expected child (a voluntary action filed together)
- a state social service agency, interceding in cases of child neglect or need
- a prosecutor's office, interceding in cases of child neglect or need

### Complaint for Paternity

The complaining party has the legal burden of establishing requisite facts in a paternity action. A petition filed with the court should contain the following basic statements:

- a citation of the state paternity statute under which the action is being brought (the legal authority)
- a statement of residency for the complaining party (for establishing the court's jurisdiction over the parties)
- a statement of residency for the responding party (for establishing the court's jurisdiction over the parties)
- the child's full name and date of birth
- a statement of relationship between the complaining party and the child or unborn child
- a statement of relationship between the responding party and the child or unborn child
- a statement that the child was or was not born while the mother was married to someone else
- a statement addressing the status of any pending custody or visitation actions related to the child
- a statement of any facts tending to support a finding of paternity

Similar to other civil suits, the party who files the action will be responsible for providing supporting documents, paying the filing fee with the court, and serving the responding party with a summons and copy of the complaint. There is usually a requirement that other necessary parties be notified. For example, if the action is filed by a guardian of the child or a social services office, the mother or anyone having legal custody of the child must be served along with the alleged father.

A court will not automatically order paternity tests simply because a paternity action has been filed. It will review the petition to determine if there is sufficient information contained therein to warrant or justify the compelling of such a test. If the court orders a paternity test, the mother, child, and alleged father will all be tested at a court-designated facility. If the man did not initiate the paternity action, and test results determine that he is not the father, the cost of the testing will be charged to the party who filed the paternity action.

A court determination of paternity is final, and a copy of the court's order will be needed to establish the child's rights, both present and future. Parties should seek court-certified "true copies" of original orders.

## Challenging Paternity

Even with the proven accuracy of DNA testing, it is possible, though improbable, that the results are incorrect. Some of the grounds for challenging a paternity determination include:

- Tainted lab results (e.g., evidence of prior errors in lab results and routinely substandard work)
- Fraudulent lab results (e.g., evidence that the opposing party sent someone else to take the lab test on his behalf)
- Proof of infertility/sterility
- Proof that test results were tampered with

## The Uniform Parentage Act

The Uniform Parentage Act has been adopted in at least a third of the states. One of its most significant provisions is an expansion of persons with standing to bring a paternity action before a court. Under the Act, any interested party may file a paternity suit on behalf of a child.

## State Laws

The following state provisions address proper designation of parties in an action for paternity, custody, child support, and termination of parental rights. All of these issues may be ruled upon in conjunction with a paternity action:

- AL: (C.A. 30-2-1) Plaintiff v. Defendant. Custody Factors: moral character, age and gender of child. Child Support: until age 19, either party may be ordered to pay, "as may seem right and proper," based on moral character and prudence, age and gender of child. Termination of Parental Rights: abandonment; emotional illness or mental illness or deficiency; excessive substance abuse; physical injury resulting from neglect; felony conviction.

- AK: (A.S. 25.24.010) Plaintiff v. Respondent. Custody Factors: best interests of the child, various criteria. Child Support: until age 18. Termination of Parental Rights: non-custodial parent withholds consent to adoption, child conceived as a result of sexual abuse of a minor.

- AZ: (A.R.S. 25-311) Petitioner v. Respondent. Custody Factors: best interests of the child, various criteria. Child Support: until age 18, either party may be ordered to pay, "as may seem right and proper," based on moral character and prudence, age and gender of child. Termination of Parental Rights: abandonment; neglect or willful abuse; emotional illness or mental illness or deficiency; felony conviction; potential father failed to file paternity action within 30 days as prescribed by law; formal relinquishment of rights.

- AR: (A.C.A. 9-12-301) Plaintiff v. Defendant. Custody Factors: best interest of child, without regard to gender of parent. Child Support: until age 18, Termination of Parental Rights: abandonment; neglect or abuse; non-custodial parent withholds consent to adoption.

- CA: (Several Code provisions)Petitioner v. Respondent. Irrebutable presumption of paternity for husband for all children born during marriage. Custody Factors: best interests of child; nature and contact with each parent; any other relevant factor. Child Support: until age 18. Termination of Parental Rights: abandonment; neglect or abuse; emotional illness or mental illness or deficiency; substance abuse.

- CO: (C.R.S.A. 14-10-106) Petitioner v. Respondent. Custody Factors: best interests of child, including wishes of all parties. Child Support: until age 21. Termination of Parental Rights: physical or sexual abuse; emotional illness or mental illness or deficiency; substance abuse; violent conduct.

- CT: (C.G.S.A. 46b-40) Plaintiff v. Defendant. Custody Factors: best interests of the child, law favors joint custody. Child Support: until age 18, either party may be ordered to pay, various criteria. Termination of Parental Rights: abandonment or neglect.

- DE: (D.C.A. 13-1502)) Petitioner v. Respondent. Custody Factors: best interests of child. Child Support: until age 18. Termination of Parental Rights: abandonment or neglect; emotional illness or mental illness or deficiency; felony conviction in which child was a victim.

- DC: (D.C.C. 16-901-916) Plaintiff v. Defendant. Custody Factors: best interest of child. Child Support: until age 18. Termination of Parental Rights: physical, emotional or mental illness or deficiency; substance abuse.

- FL: (F.S. 61.001) Petitioner v. Respondent. Custody Factors: Joint is preferred, but best interests of child to establish primary residence. Child Support: until age 18. Termination of Parental Rights: abandonment; egregious conduct which threatens life or wellbeing of child; incarceration.

- GA: (C.G.A. 19-5-1) Petitioner v. Respondent. Custody Factors: non-specific, but children over 14 can choose which parent to live with. moral character, age and gender of child. Child Support: until age 18.Termination of Parental Rights: abandonment; emotional illness or mental illness or deficiency; excessive substance abuse; physical or emotional neglect; felony conviction.

- HI: (H.R.S. 580-41) Plaintiff v. Defendant. Custody Factors: best interests of child, child's wishes. Child Support: until age 18, Termination of Parental Rights: abandonment; emotional illness or mental illness or deficiency; neglect.

- IL: (750 ILCS 5/101) Petitioner v. Respondent. Custody Factors: wishes of the parties and child, and additional criteria Child Support: until age 18 (750 ILCS 5/505). Termination of Parental Rights: abuse.

- IN: (A.I.C. 31-1-11.5) Petitioner v. Respondent. Custody Factors: wishes of the parties and child, and additional criteria Child Support: until age 18. Termination of Parental Rights: abandonment; emotional illness or mental illness or deficiency; best interest of the child.

- IA: (I.C.A. 598.1) Petitioner v. Respondent. Custody Factors: best interests of child, various factors. Child Support: until age 18. Termination of Parental Rights: abandonment; abuse or neglect;emotional illness or mental illness or deficiency; excessive substance abuse.

- KS: (K.S.A. 60-1601) Petitioner v Respondent. Custody Factors: moral character, age and gender of child. Child Support: until age 19, either party may be ordered to pay, "as may seem right and proper," based on moral character and prudence, age and gender of child. Termination of Parental Rights: emotional illness or mental illness or deficiency; abuse or neglect; substance abuse; physical injury resulting from neglect; felony conviction.

- KY: (K.R.S. 403.010) Petitioner v Respondent. Custody Factors: best interest of the child, considering various factors. Child Support: until age 18. Termination of Parental Rights: abandonment; abuse or neglect.

- LA: (LSA C.C. Art. 102) Plaintiff v. Defendant. Custody Factors: Joint custody is preferred; best interest of child using various factors.moral character, age and gender of child. Child Support: until age 18 (LSA Rev. St. 9:315) Termination of Parental Rights: abandonment; extreme abuse, all forms; misconduct of parent toward child.

- MN: (19 M.R.S.A. 661) Plaintiff v. Defendant. Custody Factors: best interest of child, various factors. Child Support: until age 18. Termination of Parental Rights: abandonment; misconduct toward child; felony conviction where child was the victim.

- MD: (A.C.M Family Law 7-101) Plaintiff v. Defendant. Custody Factors: none. Child Support: until age 18. Termination of Parental Rights: child has been out of the custody of natural parents for over one year; abuse conviction; crime of violence conviction.

- MA: (A.L.M. C208-1) Plaintiff v. Defendant. Custody Factors: none in statute. Child Support: until age 18. Termination of Parental Rights: abandonment; all forms of neglect or abuse; felony conviction.

- MI: (M.C.L.A. 552.1/M.S.A. 25.96) Complainant v. Defendant. Custody Factors: best interest of child, with various factors. Child Support: until age 18 or beyond if still completing high school. Termination of Parental Rights: abandonment; all forms of abuse; parental long-term imprisonment; chronic neglect.

- MN: (M.S.A. 518.002) Petitioner v Respondent. Custody Factors: the parties' wishes and child's preference, if of sufficient age, various factors. Child Support: until age 18 (M.S.A. 518.551). Termination of Parental Rights: abandonment; unfit parent; chemical dependency of parent; parent palpably unfit; abuse or neglect; child experienced severe harm while in parent's care.

- MS: (M.C. 93-5-1)Complainant v. Defendant. Custody Factors: none by statute, but child of 12 may choose. Child Support: until age 21. Termination of Parental Rights: abandonment; emotional illness or mental illness or deficiency; abusive incidents; substance abuse.

- MO: (A.M.S. 452.300) Petitioner v Respondent. Custody Factors: best interest of child, various factors. Child Support: until age 18. Termination of Parental Rights: abandonment; abuse or neglect; child was conceived as a result of rape; substance abuse; felony conviction in which child was victim.

- MT: (M.C.A.40-4-101) Petitioner v Respondent. Custody Factors: parties' wishes, various factors. Child Support: until age 18, various factors. Termination of Parental Rights: unfit parent; absence of child-parent relationship; irrevocable waiver.

- NE: (R.S.N. 42-301) Petitioner v Respondent. Custody Factors: best interest of child, considering various factors. Termination of Parental Rights: abandonment; emotional illness or mental illness or deficiency; excessive substance abuse; physical injury resulting from neglect; felony conviction. Plaintiff v. Defendant.

- NV: (N.R.S.A. 125.010) Plaintiff v. Defendant. Custody Factors: best interest of child, various factors. Child Support: until age 18. several factors. Termination of Parental Rights: abandonment; neglect; parental unfitness;

risk of physical, mental, or emotional harm to child.

- NH: (N.H.R.S.A. 458:4) Petitioner v Respondent. Custody Factors: joint custody presumed in the child's best interest. Child Support: until age 18, both parties responsible. Termination of Parental Rights: abandonment; emotional illness or mental illness or deficiency; all forms of abuse or neglect; felony conviction.

- NJ: (NJSA 2A:34-2) Plaintiff v. Defendant. Custody Factors: best interest of child, various factors. Child Support: until age 18. Termination of Parental Rights: abandonment; or potential for harm to child.

- NM: (N.M.S.A. 40-4-1) Petitioner v Respondent. Custody Factors: best interest of child, various factors. Child Support: until age 18. Termination of Parental Rights: abandonment; neglect or abuse; child placed in the permanent care of others.

- NY: (C.L.N.Y, D.R.I 170) Plaintiff v. Defendant. Custody Factors: best interest of child. Child Support: until age 18, needs are determined as a percentage of parents' combined income. Termination of Parental Rights: abandonment; emotional illness or mental illness or deficiency; surrender of child to authorities.

- NC: (G.S.N.C. 50-1) Plaintiff v. Defendant. Custody Factors: best interest of child. Child Support: until age 18, various factors. Termination of Parental Rights: neglect or abuse; leaving child in foster care for more than 12 months; abandonment.

- ND: (N.D.C.C. 14-05-01) Plaintiff v. Defendant. Custody Factors: several factors. Child Support: until age 18. Termination of Parental Rights: neglect or misconduct, faults or habits of parent; physical illness or mental illness or deficiency; child suffers from mental, moral, or emotional harm.

- OH: (O.R.C. 3105.01) Plaintiff v. Defendant. Custody Factors: best interest of child, with various factors. Child Support: until age 18, medical insurance payment must be made to enforcement agency. Termination of Parental Rights: abandonment; abuse or neglect.

- OK: (43 O.S.A. 101) Plaintiff v. Defendant. Custody Factors: best interest of child and

child preference. Child Support: until age 18. Termination of Parental Rights: abandonment; conviction for child abuse or neglect; all forms of abuse; emotional illness or mental illness or deficiency.

- OR: (O.R.S. 107.015) Petitioner v Respondent. Custody Factors: joint custody only awarded of both parties agree. Child Support: until age 18. Termination of Parental Rights: physical or sexual abuse or neglect; emotional illness or mental illness or deficiency; substance abuse.

- PA: (Pa.C.S.A. 3101) Plaintiff v. Defendant. Custody Factors: best interest of child, various factors. Child Support: until age 21. Termination of Parental Rights: abandonment; abuse or neglect; child removed from parents by court; child conceived as a result of rape or incest.

- RI: (G.L.R.I. 15-5-1) Plaintiff v. Defendant. Custody Factors: best interest of child. Child Support: until age 18. Termination of Parental Rights: abandonment; emotional illness or mental illness or deficiency; parental unfitness.

- SC: (C.L.S.C. 20-3-10) Plaintiff v. Defendant. Custody Factors: various factors in interest of child. Child Support: until age 18. Termination of Parental Rights: best interest of child; abuse or neglect; abandonment; substance abuse; mental of physical deficiency of parent.

- SD: (S.D.C.L. 25-4-1) Plaintiff v. Defendant. Custody Factors: "as may seem necessary and proper." Child Support: until age 18. Termination of Parental Rights: abandonment.

- TN: (T.C.A. 36-4-101) Petitioner v Respondent. Custody Factors: Best interest of child, various factors. Child Support: until age 18. Termination of Parental Rights: abandonment; child removed by court order; severe child abuse; incarceration sentence of 10 years; incompetency.

- TX: (T.C.A., F.C. 3.01) Petitioner v Respondent Custody Factors: referred to as "managing conservatorship," various factors. moral character, age and gender of child. Child Support: until age 19, either party may be ordered to pay, "as may seem right and proper," based on moral character and prudence, age and gender of child. Termination of Parental Rights: abandonment; abuse or neglect; sexual abuse of other child by parent.

- UT: (U.C. 30-3-1) Plaintiff v. Defendant. Custody Factors: best interest of child, various factors. Child Support: until age 18 (U.C. 78-45-7). Termination of Parental Rights: abandonment; neglect or abuse; parental unfitness.

- VT: (15 V.S.A. 551) Plaintiff v. Defendant. Custody Factors: best interest of child, various factors. Child Support: until age 18. Termination of Parental Rights: failure to support child or exercise parental responsibility; conviction of crime of violence; risk of harm to child.

- VA: (C.V. 20-91) Plaintiff v. Defendant. Custody Factors: best interest of child, various factors. Child Support: until age 18. Termination of Parental Rights: emotional illness or mental illness or deficiency; neglect or abuse; habitual substance abuse.

- WA: (R.C.W.A. 26.09.010) Petitioner v Respondent. Custody Factors: each parties relative fitness and agreement between parties, other criteria. Child Support: until age 18. Termination of Parental Rights: habitual substance abuse; emotional illness or mental illness or deficiency.

- WV: (W.V.C. 48-2-1) Plaintiff v. Defendant. Custody Factors: none, but presumption in favor of primary caretaker. Child Support:

until age 18. Termination of Parental Rights: abandonment; abuse or neglect.

- WI: (W.S.A. 767.001) Petitioner v Respondent. Custody Factors: "legal custody and physical placement." Best interest of child. Child Support: until age 18. Termination of Parental Rights: abandonment; continuing need for protective services; abuse; failure to assume parental responsibility; incestuous parenthood; intentional killing of other parent.

- WY: (W.S.A. 20-2-104) Plaintiff v. Defendant. Custody Factors: best interest of child. Child Support: until age 18. Termination of Parental Rights: abandonment; neglect or abuse; parental incarceration or unfitness.

Stanley, Jacqueline D. *Unmarried Parents' Rights.* 2nd Edition, 2003. Naperville, IL: Sphinx Publishing

## Organizations

### American Coalition for Fathers and Children
1718 Main Street NW, Suite 187
Washington, DC 20036 USA
Phone: (800) 978-DADS
URL: www.acfc.org

### Parents Anonymous
675 West Foothill Drive, Suite 220
Claremont, CA 91711-3475 USA
Phone: (909) 621-6184
URL: www.parentsananymous.org

# FAMILY LAW

## PHYSICIAN-ASSISTED SUICIDE

*Sections within this essay:*

- Background

- Supreme Court Rulings

- Oregon's Death With Dignity Act
    - The DWDA and the Controlled Substances Act of 1970

## Background

Physician-assisted suicide involves the hastening of death through the administration of lethal drugs, upon request of the patient. Physician-assisted suicide is sometimes known as active euthanasia. It differs from withholding or discontinuing medical treatment in circumstances that will result in death. Withholding or discontinuing medical treatment is sometimes called passive euthanasia. Passive euthanasia is generally accepted, although not without controversy, in the United States as an individual's right to refuse medical treatment. Examples of passive euthanasia include turning off respirators, stopping medication, discontinuing food and water, or failing to resuscitate.

The Hippocratic Oath has been used by physicians as a code of ethics for more than two thousand years. Attributed to Hippocrates, (ca. 460-370 BCE), the oath provides in part: "I will follow that method of treatment, which, according to my ability and judgment, I consider for the benefit of my patients, and abstain from whatever is deleterious and mischievous. I will give no deadly medicine to anyone if asked, nor suggest any such counsel."

The American Medical Association takes this stance: "It is understandable, though tragic, that some patients in extreme duress-such as those suffering from a terminal, painful, debilitating illness-may come to decide that death is preferable to life. However, allowing physicians to participate in assisted suicide would cause more harm than good. Physician-assisted suicide is fundamentally incompatible with the physician's role as healer, would be difficult or impossible to control, and would pose serious societal risks."

Dr. Jack Kevorkian, self-styled "Dr. Death," has garnered much publicity for his role in physician-assisted suicides. Kevorkian escaped conviction on murder charges several times during the 1990s as he assisted in numerous suicides. Kevorkian operated on his own set of rules to determine whom he would assist; he supposedly assisted more than 130 patients. When he began, Michigan did not have a law that specifically prohibited assisted suicide. As his notoriety grew, the Michigan legislature passed a law prohibiting assisted suicide. The Michigan Supreme Court upheld the statute in 1994, ruling that no constitutional right to suicide exists, including assisted suicide. Kevorkian's second-degree murder conviction was upheld.

The Supreme Court has determined that no right exists for physician-assisted suicide. However, states are free to enact laws to permit it. Oregon is the only state that currently permits physician-assisted suicide. Technically, however, a death under Oregon's Death With Dignity Act is not considered suicide, assisted suicide, or homicide. Oregon's law has survived numerous legal challenges since its enactment in 1994. In January 2006, the United States Supreme

Court the law against former Attorney General John Ashcroft's attempt to render the statute illegal under federal law.

In 1997 President William Jefferson Clinton signed the Assisted Suicide Funding Restriction Act of 1997. The law's intent was "to clarify Federal law with respect to restricting the use of Federal funds in support of assisted suicide," euthanasia, or mercy killing. The act banned the funding of assisted suicide through Medicaid, Medicare, military and federal employee health plans, veterans' health care systems and other federally funded programs. It also prohibited the use of taxpayer funds to subsidize legal assistance or other advocacy in support of legal protection for assisted suicide.

## Supreme Court Rulings

In two cases from 1997, the U.S. Supreme Court ruled that physician-assisted suicide is not a protected liberty interest under the Constitution. However, the rulings in Vacco v. Quill and Washington v. Glucksberg left the door open for states to permit physician-assisted suicide. Washington v. Glucksberg dealt with the constitutionality of a Washington statute that made it felony for a person to assist in the suicide of another. According to the statute, "A person is guilty of promoting a suicide attempt when he knowingly causes or aids another person to attempt suicide." Maximum punishment for conviction was five years' imprisonment and a $10,000 fine. Another statute in Washington, the Natural Death Act, provided, "Withholding or withdrawal of life-sustaining treatment" at a patient's direction "shall not, for any purpose, constitute a suicide." A number of physicians and their terminally ill patients brought suit to challenge the constitutionality of the assisted suicide law. These plaintiffs claimed "the existence of a liberty interest protected by the Fourteenth Amendment which extends to a personal choice by a mentally competent, terminally ill adult to commit physician-assisted suicide."

The district court agreed with the doctors and patients. The court ruled that the law placed an undue burden on the exercise of a constitutionally protected liberty interest. The state appealed the case to the Ninth Circuit Court of Appeals. A three-judge panel reversed the district court. According to that opinion, this country has never recognized a "constitutional right to aid in killing." However, a subsequent en band hearing before all the judges of the Ninth Circuit resulted in victory for the doctors. According to the **en banc decision**, "the Constitution encompasses a due process liberty interest in controlling the time and manner of one's death—that there is, in short, a constitutionally-recognized 'right to die.'" Furthermore, Washington's law was unconstitutional, "as applied to terminally ill competent adults who wish to hasten their deaths with medication prescribed by their physicians."

The state appealed, and the Supreme Court reversed. The opinion, written by Chief Justice William Rehnquist, traced the history of assisted suicide. The court noted that few exceptions to the rules against assisted suicide exist anywhere in Western democracies and states. Moreover, the punishment or disapproval of suicide or assisted suicide reaches back more than 700 years. The earliest statute to outlaw assisted suicide came in 1828, but long before that, **common law** recognized it as a crime. The court noted that advances in medicine and technology have caused many states to reexamine their stances on assisted suicide. For the most part, states have reaffirmed deeply-rooted bans on assisted suicide. To rule in favor of the doctors, the court noted, it would have to "reverse centuries of legal doctrine and practice, and strike down the considered policy choice of almost every State." Quoting another case, the court recognized that if something has been practiced for two hundred years by common consent, it will "need a strong case for the Fourteenth Amendment to affect it." The court also noted the danger of allowing policy preferences of the members of the court to subtly transform constitutional law.

Based on the history of assisted suicide laws in this country, the Supreme Court ruled that there is no fundamental liberty interest in a right to assisted suicide that is protected by the due process clause. Moreover, the ban on assisted suicide, as set forth in Washington's law, was rationally related to legitimate government interests. Those government interests include:

- To preserve life

- To prevent suicide

- To avoid the involvement of third parties and the use of arbitrary, unfair, or undue influence

- To protect the integrity of the medical profession

- To avoid future movement toward euthanasia and other abuses

The Supreme Court did not, however, ban assisted suicide. The opinion recognized the right of states to engage "in serious, thoughtful examinations of physician-assisted suicide."

## Oregon's Death With Dignity Act

Only in Oregon is physician-assisted suicide legal. Voters in Oregon passed the Death With Dignity Act (DWDA) in 1994 by a narrow margin. The measure legalized physician-assisted suicide under certain circumstances. Physicians may not be forced to participate in the DWDA. A person who sought to employ the law needed to show:

- Patient must be at least 18 years of age

- Suffering from a terminal illness

- With a life expectancy of six months or less

- The patient must make two oral requests for assistance in dying

- The patient must make one written request for assistance

- Two physicians must be convinced that the patient is sincere, not acting on a whim, and that the decision is voluntary

- The patient must not be influenced by depression

- The patient must be informed of "feasible alternatives" such as hospice care and pain control

- The patient must wait 15 days between the verbal requests

Almost immediately after passage, court challenges succeeded in suspending the law. After the Supreme Court rulings in *Glucksberg and Vacco v. Quill* in 1997, the Ninth Circuit Court of Appeals lifted an injunction on DWDA. The law took effect on October 27, 1997. Voters in Oregon were asked to vote whether to retain the law in 1997. This time, 60 percent of voters approved of it.

In 2004, according to figures supplied in an annual report by the Oregon Department of Human Services, forty physicians wrote prescriptions for the lethal dosages. The total number of prescriptions written was 60, which represented the first decline since the law took effect. The high was 68, in 2003. Thirty-seven Oregonians "ingested medications prescribed under provisions of the Act;" compared to 42 patients in 2003. This number reflects that about one in 800 deaths in Oregon is attributed to DWDA. By December 31, 2004, 25 people who had been given the medication had not ingested them. Thirteen of the people had died from their illnesses, while the rest were still alive. (The numbers do not add up to 60 because of prescriptions issued in 2003, but not used before December 31, 2003.)

The median age of a patient receiving a prescription under DWDA in 2004 was 64. Just over one-half had at least a baccalaureate degree. Males and females were equally likely to avail themselves of the law. Malignant tumors accounted for 78 percent of the illnesses. According to the report, the three most frequently cited reasons for requesting assisted suicide were: a decreasing ability to participate in activities that made life enjoyable, loss of autonomy, and a loss of dignity. Death came anywhere from five minutes to 31 hours after ingestion of either pentobarbital or secobarbital.

### *The DWDA and the Controlled Substances Act of 1970*

The stated purpose of the Controlled Substances Act is to "to provide increased research into, and prevention of, drug abuse and drug dependence... and to strengthen existing law enforcement authority in the field of drug abuse." A regulation promulgated under the act provided, "A prescription for a controlled substance to be effective must be issued for a legitimate medical purpose by an individual practitioner acting in the usual course of his professional practice."

In 1984 the act was amended to give the U.S. Attorney General the authority to revoke a physician's prescription privileges upon a determination that the physician has "committed such acts as would render his registration... inconsistent with the public interest."

On November 6, 2001, U.S. Attorney General John Ashcroft issued an interpretation of the Controlled Substances Act. Ashcroft's interpretation made it illegal for doctors to prescribe controlled substances under Oregon's Death With Dignity law. According to Ashcroft's determination, prescribing such drugs was a violation of the Controlled Substances Act because physician-assisted suicide was not a "legitimate medical purpose." A doctor who made such prescriptions could have his or her registration to distribute controlled substances under the act revoked or could be criminally prosecuted.

Ashcroft's determination reflected a reversal of administration policy from Clinton's presidency to that of George W. Bush. Janet Reno, attorney general under President Clinton, had determined that the pertinent section in the Controlled Substances Act would not apply in states where physician-assisted suicide was legal. Ashcroft's decision on the subject has come to be known as the "Ashcroft Directive."

The state, along with a doctor, a pharmacist, and a group of terminally ill patients, filed a lawsuit to challenge Ashcroft's interpretation of the Controlled Substances Act. On November 20, 2001, a federal judge issued a restraining order from implementation of the Ashcroft Directive. In April 2002 U.S. District Court Judge Robert Jones upheld the DWDA in light of the Controlled Substances Act. The U.S. appealed; the Ninth Circuit Court of Appeals upheld the federal district court decision. The appellate decision opined that the Ashcroft Directive violated the plain language of the Controlled Substances Act: "Contrary to the Attorney General's characterization, physician-assisted suicide is not a form of 'drug abuse' that Congress intended the CSA to cover." Moreover, the Ashcroft Directive undermined Congressional intent, and overstepped the bounds of the attorney general's authority.

Judge Richard Tallman's decision also noted that the federal government was interfering in an area delegated to the states. "The principle that state governments bear the primary responsibility for evaluating physician assisted suicide follows from our concept of federalism, which requires that state lawmakers, not the federal government are the 'primary regulators of professional [medical] conduct,'" Tallman wrote. He concluded, "The Attorney General's unilateral attempt to regulate general medical practices historically entrusted to state lawmakers interferes with the democratic debate about physician assisted suicide and far exceeds the scope of his authority under federal law." Moreover, "To be perfectly clear, we take no position on the merits or morality of physician assisted suicide. We express no opinion on whether the practice is inconsistent with the public interest or constitutes illegitimate medical care. This case is simply about who gets to decide."

On January 17, 2006, in a 6-3 decision, the Supreme Court upheld Oregon's statute. Writing for the majority, Justice Anthony Kennedy found that the "authority claimed by the attorney general is both beyond his expertise and incongruous with the statutory purposes and design." Although the Oregon law may stand under the decision, the case did not resolve the controversy surrounding physician-assisted suicide. Congress could amend the Controlled Substances Act to allow the Attorney General to determine whether Oregon's law is permissible under the statute, and this amendment would effectively negate the Court's decision.

## Additional Resources

*State of Oregon, Physician-assisted Suicide Home page*, http://egov.oregon.gov/DHS/ph/pas/index.shtml (January 3, 2006).

*Death and Dying: Who Decides?* Sandra Alters. Thomson Gale, 2005.

*Death and Dying: Opposing Viewpoints,* James Haley, editor. Greenhaven Press, 2003.

*Terminal Illness: Opposing Viewpoints,* Andrea C. Nakaya, editor. Greenhaven Press, 2005.

## Organizations

### American Medical Association (AMA)
515 North State Street
Chicago, IL 60610 USA
Phone: (800) 621-8335
URL: http://www.ama-assn.org/

# FAMILY LAW

## PRENUPTIAL AGREEMENTS

*Sections within this essay:*

- Background
- Requirements for Prenuptial Agreements
- Provisons of a Prenuptial Agreement
    - Inventory
    - Character of Property
    - Spousal Support
    - Escalator Clause
- Contested Agreements
- Child Custody and Child Support
- Postmarital Agreements
- Living Together Agreements
- Engagement Rings
- Probate Concerns
- Additional Resources

## Background

A prenuptial agreement is a contract between two persons who are planning to marry. Prenuptial agreements are often called premarital agreements, and, if entered into subsequent to the marriage, postmarital or antenuptial agreements. These types of contracts typically set forth the rights that each party has to the other's property. Couples can enter into prenuptial agreements prior to a first marriage or prior to a subsequent marriage after death or **divorce** of a prior spouse. Premarital agreements become operative in the event of divorce or the death of one spouse.

Prenuptial agreements can avoid uncertainty about how a judge would divide property and decide spousal support if the marriage ends in divorce. Either party may be seeking to avoid a major loss of assets, income, investments, or a business in the event of a divorce. People marrying for a second or third time often want to make their children the beneficiaries of all of their assets, rather than have the property pass to a second spouse and that spouse's offspring from a prior marriage. A valid prenuptial agreement will generally supersede whatever state law exists regarding **probate** or divorce issues.

## Requirements for Prenuptial Agreements

In general, as with any contract, in order to be valid, a prenuptial agreement must be in writing and signed by the parties. In most states, the parties must fully disclose all income and assets to the other party. In a few states, it may be possible to waive a full disclosure of income and assets, but the spouse waiving that right must do so knowingly. If it is difficult to determine the exact validity of all of the assets, for example in a small family-owned business, the agreement should acknowledge some type of approximate value.

Additionally, the terms of the agreement must be reasonable. An agreement cannot be unusually harsh and unfair or the court will likely decline to uphold it. Blatantly unfair agreements are termed unconscionable agreements. Usually this means no reasonable person would enter into agreement with such terms. If a court finds an agreement to be unconscionable, the agreement will not be enforced.

Finally, both parties must have a fair opportunity to review the proposed agreement and to have independent legal **counsel**. While an agreement where both parties did not hire counsel is not necessarily invalid, hiring attorneys is another step that can demonstrate to the court that the agreement is fairly drafted and that both parties are making informed decisions. This is particularly true if two attorneys negotiate the agreement drafting and redrafting various provisions to the satisfaction of the parties.

## Provisons of a Prenuptial Agreement

Although each couple will have different circumstances, prenuptial agreements generally address a number of different aspects of the couple's agreement. These usually include the following:

### Inventory

The agreement should have an inventory, often attached as an exhibit to the agreement of each party's property, assets and debts which will be brought into the marriage.

### Character of Property

The agreement should specify the character of certain types of property, whether they will be owned as marital or separate property, or a combination thereof. This would include investment earnings from property previously owned, the earnings of each spouse, and any subsequent **inheritance**. The agreement should also set forth how property will be distributed in the event of death of either spouse or in the event of divorce.

### Spousal Support

The agreement should also specify the level (if any) of spousal support in the event of divorce. State laws do not set a specific amount of support that must be provided for premarital agreements. Many courts will apply broader notions of fairness and require support at a level higher than subsistence, so the level of support must be reasonable given the party's circumstances.

### Escalator Clause

An escalator clause increases the amount of assets or support given to one spouse based on the length of the marriage or sometimes on a significant increase in one spouse's assets or income. If one spouse is concerned that assets or income could devalue in the future, that spouse could include a provision that the amount of property given to the other spouse would never exceed a certain percentage of the entire value of all the assets.

## Contested Agreements

A prenuptial agreement can be contested, not simply during a divorce of the parties, but by the children or parents of a deceased spouse. The party contesting the agreement is usually seeking to have it declared void so that the existing probate or divorce laws will apply. Claims may be made that a spouse did not fully understand the agreement or that one spouse forced the other, physically or mentally do sign the agreement. A challenge of this type is often termed **duress**. To avoid this sort of challenge, the couple should enter into the agreement well before the wedding. While most jurisdictions do not specify a particular time frame, the more time the couple has to review and consider the provisions of the agreement, the more chance a court would find it voluntary. While an agreement proposed and signed a day or two before the wedding is not **per se** invalid, it may be a factor, which the court considers in deciding whether to uphold the agreement at a later date.

Other grounds for contesting an agreement may be that some misrepresentations took place which induced one spouse to sign the agreement. One spouse may have made misrepresentations about the agreement itself, perhaps that it was non-binding, only for tax purposes, or temporary. The agreement may also face a serious challenge if all assets were not fully disclosed. Although this is another form of misrepresentation, a challenge of this sort is typically termed **fraud**. An agreement may well be invalid on this basis if one spouse intentionally misrepresents certain aspects of income or assets.

Another theory used to contest prenuptial agreements is that one spouse lacked capacity. If a party was ill, taking medication, which affected mental capacity, or was intoxicated by alcohol or influenced by other drugs, the agreement may not be valid under the rules of basic contract law.

## Child Custody and Child Support

A prenuptial agreement may contain provisions regarding **child custody**, visitation, and **child support**; however, a divorce court would not be bound by such provisions. Courts have the power to decide on child **custody**, visitation rights, and child support. The court would look with particular disfavor on these provisions for children of both parties who were not even born at the time of the prenuptial agreement.

## Postmarital Agreements

Postmarital or antenuptial agreements are drafted after the marriage has taken place but before either party separates, divorces, leaves, or dies. These contracts contain provisions similar to those in premarital contracts. Courts look carefully at these types of agreements since once the marriage has taken place it is sometimes the case that one of the parties is unwilling to enter into the agreement. A postmarital agreement may alter the rules for the division of property between the spouses in the event of divorce or death. A married couple may seek to enter into a postmarital agreement after a significant financial change or after a reunification subsequent to a separation. A Marital **Settlement** Agreement is a particular form of postmarital agreement that specifies the distribution of property and responsibility for debt between the respective spouses as part of a divorce.

## Living Together Agreements

The same concerns and considerations by couples who do plan to marry and who draw up a premarital contract apply to couples who plan never to marry. There is nothing illegal about an unmarried couple living together. Any governmental interference with a couple's right to live together would be considered a violation of the couple's right to free association under the First Amendment to the United States Constitution. An unmarried couple living together can enter into an agreement to share expenses or acquire property, including real estate. An unmarried couple can also enter into a trust, which would allow for a more specific distribution of certain assets and would protect the couple in the event of **disability** or incapacity of one of the partners.

## Engagement Rings

There are two legal theories with respect to engagement rings. One theory is that an engagement ring is a gift and belongs to the person receiving it. The other theory is that an engagement ring is a conditional gift, a gift given in anticipation of marriage. Under this theory, if the marriage will not take place, the condition upon which the gift was given has been removed, and the ring belongs to the giver. A number of court cases have actually addressed this issue. In some states, if the person who gave the ring broke off the engagement, the person who received the ring is entitled to keep it. Since property which

is a gift is generally considered separate property, once the marriage takes place, the ring then belongs to the wearer even if the marriage ends in divorce.

## Probate Concerns

When a couple enters into a prenuptial agreement, the parties may also sign other documents relating to probate concerns and plans. The couple may contract to make a will or a trust with particular terms once they are married. (Signing new wills at the same time as a prenuptial agreement is an option; however, once the marriage takes place, the wills would need to be redrafted to reflect the marriage in order for the terms to remain valid.) The couple may choose to create a trust to manage certain aspects of estate planning. A trust created in connection with a **premarital agreement** might be used as a tool to manage and protect the assets of each spouse, as well as to establish a fund for the benefit of the less wealthy spouse. The prenuptial agreement might provide that in the event of divorce or death, the less wealthy spouse's entitlement to assets might be limited to the money or property in the trust.

In many estate plans, the Trust is the central tool that is used to control and manage property. A Trust continues despite the incapacity or death of the grantor. It determines how a **Trustee** is to act with respect to the Trust estate. It determines how property is to be distributed after the death of the grantor. A properly drawn Trust is a separate entity that does not die when the creator dies. The successor Trustee can take over management of the Trust estate and pay bills and taxes and promptly distribute the Trust assets to the beneficiaries, without court supervision, if the Trust agreement gives the Trustee that power. Trusts, unlike Wills, are generally private documents. The public would be able to see how much the descendent owned and who the beneficiaries were under a Will, but typically not with a Trust. Like a Will, however, a Trust can be used to provide for minor children, children from a prior marriage and a second spouse in the same trust, transfer a family-operated or closely-held business, provide for pets, provide for charities and can remove life insurance benefits from a taxable estate, while still controlling the designation of insurance beneficiaries.

## Additional Resources

*Complete Premarital Contracting: Loving Communication for Today's Couples* Rickard, Jacqueline, Evans, 1993.

*Cupid, Couples, & Contracts: A Guide to Living Together, Prenuptial Agreements, and Divorce* Wallman, Lester, Master Media, 1994.

## Organizations

### American Bar Association
750 N. Lake Shore Dr.
Chicago, IL 60611 USA
Phone: (312) 988-5603
Fax: (312) 988-6800
URL: http://www.abanet.org

### The Elder Law Project Legal Services For Cape Cod And Islands, Inc.
460 West Main Street
Hyannis, MA 02601 USA
Phone: (508) 775-7020

### National Academy of Elder Law Attorneys, Inc.
1604 North Country Club Road
Tucson, AZ 85716 USA
Phone: (520) 881-4005
Fax: (520) 325-7925
URL: http://www.naela.com/

### American Bar Association
750 N. Lake Shore Dr.
Chicago, IL 60611 USA
Phone: (312) 988-5603
Fax: (312) 988-6800
URL: http://www.abanet.org

# FAMILY LAW

## UNMARRIED PARENTS

*Sections within this essay:*

- Background
- Unmarried Parents Living Together
- Paternity Actions
- Paternity Tests
    - Blood Tests
    - DNA Tests
- Custody and Visitation
- Artificial Conception
    - Artificial Insemination
    - Invitro Fertilization
    - Surrogate Mothers
- Welfare
- Names
- Taxes
- Additional Resources

## Background

Children born out of wedlock are entitled to the same rights and protections as children born in wedlock. Unmarried fathers have rights and duties similar to those of married fathers. One of the most important legal responsibilities of parents is supporting their children. Parents are legally obligated to provide their children with all the necessities of life. The failure of parents to marry does not affect their responsibility to support their children. If parents are unmarried and cannot agree upon how much each should contribute toward the support of their chil-

dren, the courts may decide. A court can order one parent to make specified payments to the other for **child support**.

State laws provide that biological parents make all the decisions involving their children, including education, health care, and religious upbringing. Parents are not required to secure the **legal right** to make these decisions if they are married and are listed on the child's birth certificate. However, if there is disagreement about who has the right to make these decisions courts can decide.

## Unmarried Parents Living Together

Couples who are living together but are not married should take steps to ensure that both are recognized as the legal parents. Both parents can be listed on the birth certificate. A parent who is not listed can be added after the birth of a child if the parent contacts the state Bureau of Vital Statistics in which the birth took place. Most states require unmarried fathers to sign an **affidavit** or acknowledgment of **paternity**.

## Paternity Actions

A paternity action is a legal proceeding that allows unmarried parents to resolve issues about **child custody** and visitation similar to those dealt with in a **divorce** proceeding. Establishing paternity means establishing the identity of the child's father. A father can acknowledge paternity by signing a written admission or voluntary acknowledgment of paternity. All States have programs under which birthing hospitals give unmarried parents of a newborn the opportunity to acknowledge the father's paternity of the child. States must also help parents acknowledge paternity up to the child's eighteenth birthday through vital records offices or other entities designated by the State. Parents are not required to apply for child support enforcement services when acknowledging paternity.

Paternity cases do not have to involve a dispute between the parties about who the father is. Sometimes the parties will stipulate that they are the parents of the child. If however, parentage is an issue in the case, then it must be handled prior to addressing other matters such as support and visitation. Paternity establishment can provide basic emotional, social, and economic ties between a father and his child. Once paternity is established, a child gains legal rights and privileges. Among these may be rights to **inheritance**, rights to the father's medical and life insurance benefits, and to social security and possibly veterans' benefits. The child also has a chance to develop a relationship with the father and to develop both a sense of identity and connection. It may be important for the health of the child for doctors to have knowledge of the father's medical history.

## Paternity Tests

Paternity can be determined by highly accurate tests conducted on blood or tissue samples of the father, or alleged father, mother and child. These tests have an accuracy range of between 90 and 99 percent. They can exclude a man who is not the biological father and can also show the likelihood of paternity if he is not excluded. Each party in a contested paternity case must submit to genetic tests at the request of either party. If the father could be one of several men, each may be required to take a genetic test. It is almost always possible to determine who fathered a baby and to rule out anyone who did not. There are several different ways to establish whether an alleged father is the natural and legal father of the minor child.

### Blood Tests

Paternity blood testing was first performed in the middle half of the twentieth century by comparing blood types of tested parties. This involved isolation of blood sera from antigen-challenged individuals that did not possess certain red blood cell antigens. These antigens are protein molecules that may be combined with sugar molecules and reside in the red blood cell membrane. These sera cause coagulation of red blood cells in individuals that possess that par-

ticular red blood cell antigen. In the ABO blood typing system, humans can possess the A antigen (A blood type), the B antigen (B blood type), both the A and B antigen (AB blood type), or neither of these antigens (O blood type). Red blood cell antigen systems of this sort can be used for paternity testing because there are genes that code for the antigens and these are inherited genes. A mother who has Type B blood and a father who has Type O blood could not have a child who has type AB blood. The true father of the child must have the gene for the A antigen. Using RBC antigen systems for paternity testing did not provide for a very powerful test because the frequencies of the genes that coded for the antigens are not very low.

In the 1970s a more powerful test using white blood cell antigens or Human Leukocyte Antigens (HLA) was developed. This produced a test that was able to exclude about 95 percent of falsely **accused** fathers. Several milliliters of blood are required to perform the test. Blood types can not be used to determine who the father is; however, blood types can be used to determine the biological possibility of fatherhood.

### DNA Tests

DNA (Deoxyribonucleic Acid) is the genetic material present in every cell of the human body. Except in the case of identical multiple births, each individual's DNA is unique. A child receives half of his or her genetic material (DNA) from the biological mother and half from the biological father. During DNA testing, the genetic characteristics of the child are compared to those of the mother. Characteristics that cannot be found in the mother must have been inherited from the father. DNA paternity testing is the most accurate form of paternity testing possible. If DNA patterns between the child and the alleged father do not match on two or more DNA probes, then the alleged father can be totally ruled out. If the DNA patterns between mother, child, and the alleged father match on every DNA probe, the likelihood of paternity is 99.9 percent. Either a blood test known as Restriction Fragment Length Polymorphism (RFLP) or a procedure called a Buccal scrap is used for DNA testing. A swab is rubbed vigorously against the inside of the subject's cheek. This provides a DNA sample for testing. Children can be tested at any age. Paternity testing can even be done on an umbilical cord blood specimen at birth. DNA testing is one of the easiest medical procedures for children. Since DNA is the same in every cell of the human body, the accuracy of testing performed on cheek cells utilizing the Buccal Swab is the same as an actual blood sample.

## Custody and Visitation

In most states, when a child born to an unmarried mother, if there is no **adjudication** or registration of paternity, the mother has **custody**. Once paternity has been established, a father has the right to seek custody of or visitation with his child. Even after paternity has been adjudicated or registered, as long as there is no court order on custody, many states presume that the mother has custody of the child. A custody agreement between the parents or a court order can clarify custody and visitation issues. Unmarried parents without custody are entitled to the same visitation rights as divorced parents, absence extraordinary factors such as abuse or **domestic violence**.

## Artificial Conception

Modern medicine and science have allowed opportunities for conceiving children through **artificial insemination**, in vitro fertilization, and embryo transplantation. Combined with these techniques is the practice of **surrogate motherhood**. These new techniques have also created legal questions and disputes regarding the child's status and the rights and designation of the parents.

### Artificial Insemination

When a married woman, with the consent of her husband, conceives a child by artificial insemination from a **donor** other than her husband, the law generally recognizes the child as the husband's legitimate child. Most states have presumption laws which presume a child born to a married woman is the child of her husband, and the designation of the husband as father in a case involving artificial insemination derives from those laws.

### Invitro Fertilization

Invitro fertilization and egg transplantation involves the fertilization of the egg outside the womb. Where the egg is donated by another woman, the birth mother will be treated in law as the legitimate mother of the child.

### Surrogate Mothers

Undoubtably a legally complex area is that of surrogate motherhood. In the most common arrangement, a married couple in which the husband is fer-

tile but the wife is unable to carry a pregnancy, enter into a privately arranged contract with a fertile woman. This fertile woman (the surrogate mother) agrees to be artificially inseminated with the sperm of the fertile husband. Alternatively, the surrogate mother may be impregnated with an embryo produced by the wife's ovum. In either case, the surrogate mother carries the pregnancy until delivery, and then, per the contract, assumes no parental rights or responsibilities and relinquishes the infant to the couple initiating the contract. These reproductive arrangements enable one woman to bear a child for another, thus separating genetic, gestational, and rearing parentage. Surrogate motherhood raises medical, psychological, ethical, and legal questions involving procreative privacy and the nature of parenting and family life.

The desire to have a child who is genetically related to at least one parent may make surrogacy a more attractive option than **adoption** for some couples. When women take on the role of surrogate mother to assist members of their own family, few legal complications arise. In some cases where women have agreed to the procedure for financial compensation, major legal issues have arisen. About half the states have laws which address surrogacy. In some states, surrogate mother contracts are illegal and entering into them can result in criminal charges. Other states rule that such contracts are invalid.

In an artificial insemination case, in which the husband is the donor to the surrogate, a court order can be obtained prior to the birth of the child that the husband is the father of the child. After the child is born, the surrogate mother signs consent forms which either terminate her parental rights, leaving the man with sole custody of the child or which allow the wife of the couple to adopt. In a case involving egg fertilization outside the womb and an embryo transplant to the womb of the surrogate, a pre-birth court order can be obtained indicating that the couple is the child's biological parents. In this case, no adoption is necessary.

## Welfare

Federal welfare law requires minor custodial parents receiving cash assistance to attend school and live with their parents or in an adult-supervised setting. Congress established these requirements as part of the Personal Responsibility and Work Opportunity Reconciliation Act (PRWORA), which created the program for Temporary Assistance for Needy

Families (TANF) and abolished the Aid to Families with Dependent Children (AFDC) program. A number of States have also established similar requirements.

Welfare policies that apply specifically to teenage parents pose a special challenge, because many young parents do not head their own cash assistance case. When an assistance case includes an older adult, an adolescent, and a very young child, it is often unclear whether the adolescent or the older adult is the parent of the young child, at least for assistance purposes. States are not supposed to use TANF block grant funds to provide financial assistance to unmarried minor custodial parents who do not have a high school diploma or its equivalent unless they are attending school. To meet this requirement, state welfare agencies must define school attendance requirements, obtain attendance information, and follow up with teenager parents who fail to attend school.

## Names

The parents (as recognized by law) of a child are allowed to name the child whatever they choose. This is true for the first, middle and last names. A child is not required to have the last name of the father, or of either parent. Unmarried parents may give the child the last name of the father on the theory that a name is something inherited and passed down through paternal lineage. Unmarried parents may give the child the last name of the mother on the theory that if men were the ones spending numerous hours in labor, they would hardly be naming their children after women. The parents may select a hyphenated name or an entirely unrelated name.

## Taxes

If a couple is unmarried, only one person can claim the child as a dependent for income **tax return** purposes in any given year. An unmarried couple can alternate years or decide that the person with the higher income takes the tax **deduction**. While both parents may be entitled to claim a child, only one person can legally take the exemption each year.

## Additional Resources

*Cupid, Couples, & Contracts: A Guide to Living Together, Prenuptial Agreements, and Divorce* Wallman, Lester, Master Media, 1994.

*Joint Custody with a Jerk: Raising a Child with an Uncooperative EX* Ross, Julie, St. Martin's Press, 1996.

## Organizations

### Child Welfare League of America
50 F Street NW, 6th Floor
Washington, DC 20001-2085 USA
Phone: (202) 638-2952
Fax: (202) 638-4004

### American Bar Association
750 N. Lake Shore Dr.
Chicago, IL 60611 USA
Phone: (312) 988-5603
Fax: (312) 988-6800
URL: http://www.abanet.org

### National Association of Child Advocates
1522 K Street, NW, Suite 600
Washington, DC 20005-1202 USA